Structure and Organization of This Text

Parts I-IV: Concepts and Techniques for Crafting and Executing Strategy

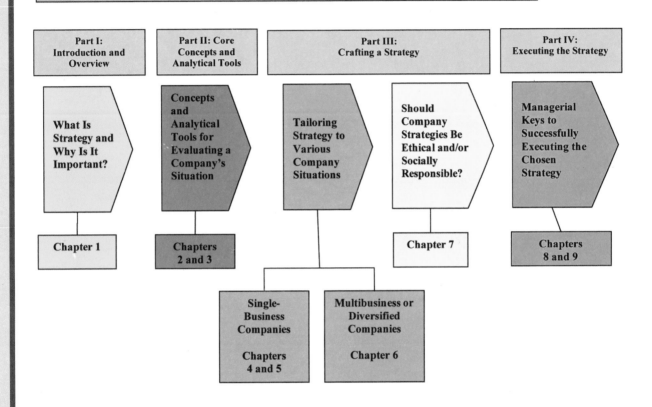

| Part I: Introduction and Overview | Part II: Core Concepts and Analytical Tools | Part III: Crafting a Strategy | Part IV: Executing the Strategy |

What Is Strategy and Why Is It Important?

Concepts and Analytical Tools for Evaluating a Company's Situation

Tailoring Strategy to Various Company Situations

Should Company Strategies Be Ethical and/or Socially Responsible?

Managerial Keys to Successfully Executing the Chosen Strategy

Chapter 1

Chapters 2 and 3

Chapter 7

Chapters 8 and 9

Single-Business Companies

Chapters 4 and 5

Multibusiness or Diversified Companies

Chapter 6

Part V: Cases in Crafting and Executing Strategy
Section A: Crafting Strategy in Single-Business Companies (21 cases)
Section B: Crafting Strategy in Diversified Companies (2 cases)
Section C: Implementing and Executing Strategy (7 cases)
Section D: Strategy, Ethics, and Social Responsibility (2 cases)

IMPORTANT

HERE IS YOUR REGISTRATION CODE TO ACCESS MCGRAW-HILL
PREMIUM CONTENT AND MCGRAW-HILL ONLINE RESOURCES

For key premium online resources you need THIS CODE to
gain access. Once the code is entered, you will be able to
use the web resources for the length of your course.

Access is provided only if you have purchased a new book.

If the registration code is missing from this book, the registration screen on our
website, and within your WebCT or Blackboard course will tell you how to obtain
your new code. Your registration code can be used only once to establish
access. It is not transferable

To gain access to these online resources

1. USE your web browser to go to: **http://www.mhhe.com/thompson2e**

2. CLICK on "First Time User"

3. ENTER the Registration Code printed on the tear-off bookmark on the right

4. After you have entered your registration code, click on "Register"

5. FOLLOW the instructions to setup your personal UserID and Password

6. WRITE your UserID and Password down for future reference. Keep it in a safe place.

If your course is using WebCT or Blackboard, you'll be able to use this code to
access the McGraw-Hill content within your instructor's online course.

To gain access to the McGraw-Hill content in your instructor's WebCT or
Blackboard course simply log into the course with the user ID and Password
provided by your instructor. Enter the registration code exactly as it appears to
the right when prompted by the system. You will only need to use this code the
first time you click on McGraw-Hill content.

These instructions are specifically for student access. Instructors are not required
to register via the above instructions.

The McGraw-Hill Companies

Thank you, and welcome to your
McGraw-Hill/Irwin Online Resources.

Thompson/Gamble/Strickland
Strategy: Winning in the Marketplace, 2/e
0-07-320104-9

ZXFD-FS47-8AYM-K0WP-6UF8

REGISTRATION CODE
REGISTRATION CODE

McGraw-Hill
Irwin

The McGraw-Hill Companies

STRATEGY

STRATEGY
Winning in the Marketplace

Core Concepts, Analytical Tools, Cases

Second Edition

Arthur A. Thompson, Jr.
University of Alabama

John E. Gamble
University of South Alabama

A. J. Strickland III
University of Alabama

McGraw-Hill
Irwin

Boston   Burr Ridge, IL   Dubuque, IA   Madison, WI   New York   San Francisco   St. Louis
Bangkok   Bogotá   Caracas   Kuala Lumpur   Lisbon   London   Madrid   Mexico City
Milan   Montreal   New Delhi   Santiago   Seoul   Singapore   Sydney   Taipei   Toronto

McGraw-Hill
Irwin

STRATEGY, WINNING IN THE MARKETPLACE:
CORE CONCEPTS, ANALYTICAL TOOLS, CASES

Published by McGraw-Hill/Irwin, a business unit of The McGraw-Hill Companies, Inc., 1221
Avenue of the Americas, New York, NY, 10020. Copyright © 2006, 2004 by The McGraw-Hill
Companies, Inc. All rights reserved. No part of this publication may be reproduced or distributed
in any form or by any means, or stored in a database or retrieval system, without the prior written
consent of The McGraw-Hill Companies, Inc., including, but not limited to, in any network or
other electronic storage or transmission, or broadcast for distance learning.

Some ancillaries, including electronic and print components, may not be available to customers outside
the United States.

This book is printed on acid-free paper.

1 2 3 4 5 6 7 8 9 0 DOW/DOW 0 9 8 7 6 5

ISBN 0-07-298990-4

Editorial director: *John E. Biernat*
Executive editor: *John Weimeister*
Managing developmental editor: *Laura Hurst Spell*
Senior marketing manager: *Lisa Nicks*
Media producer: *Benjamin Curless*
Project manager: *Harvey Yep*
Senior production supervisor: *Rose Hepburn*
Lead designer: *Matthew Baldwin*
Photo research coordinator: *Lori Kramer*
Media project manager: *Joyce J. Chappetto*
Supplement producer: *Gina F. DiMartino*
Developer, Media technology: *Brian Nacik*
Cover design: *Kiera Pohl*
Interior design: *Kiera Pohl*
Typeface: *10.5/12 Times New Roman*
Compositor: *Cenveo*
Printer: *R. R. Donnelley*

Library of Congress Cataloging-in-Publication Data
Thompson, Arthur A., 1940–
     Strategy: winning in the marketplace: core concepts, analytical tools, cases / Arthur A.
     Thompson, John E. Gamble, A.J. Strickland.—2nd ed.
         p. cm.
     Includes index.
     ISBN 0-07-298990-4 (alk. paper)
     1. Strategic planning. 2. Industrial management. 3. Conglomerate
corporations—Management. 4. Strategic planning—Case studies. I. Gamble, John (John E.)
II. Strickland, A. J. (Alonzo J.) III. Title
HD30.28.T543 2006
658.4'012—dc22   2005041626

www.mhhe.com

To our families and especially our wives:
Hasseline, Debra, and Kitty

About the Authors

Arthur A. Thompson, Jr., earned his BS and PhD degrees in economics from the University of Tennessee in 1961 and 1965, respectively; spent three years on the economics faculty at Virginia Tech; and served on the faculty of the University of Alabama's College of Commerce and Business Administration for 24 years. In 1974 and again in 1982, Dr. Thompson spent semester-long sabbaticals as a visiting scholar at the Harvard Business School.

His areas of specialization are business strategy, competition and market analysis, and the economics of business enterprises. He has published over 30 articles in some 25 different professional and trade publications and has authored or coauthored five textbooks and four computer-based simulation exercises.

Dr. Thompson is a frequent speaker and consultant on the strategic issues confronting the electric utility industry, particularly as concerns the challenges posed by industry restructuring, reregulation, competition, and customers' freedom of choice. He spends much of his off-campus time giving presentations to electric utility groups and conducting management development programs for electric utility executives all over the world.

Dr. Thompson and his wife of 44 years have two daughters, two grandchildren, and a Yorkshire terrier.

John E. Gamble is currently Associate Dean and Professor of Management in the Mitchell College of Business at The University of South Alabama. His teaching specialty at USA is strategic management and he also conducts a course in strategic management in Germany through a collaborative MBA program sponsored by the University of Applied Sciences in Ludwigshafen/Worms, the State of Rhineland Westphalia, and the University of South Alabama.

Dr. Gamble's research interests center on strategic issues in entrepreneurial, health care, and manufacturing settings. His work has been published in such scholarly journals as *Journal of Business Venturing, Journal of Labor Research, Health Care Management Review,* and *Journal of Occupational and Organizational Psychology.* He is the author or co-author of more than 30 case studies published in various strategic management and strategic marketing texts. He has done consulting on industry and market analysis and strategy formulation and implementation issues with clients in public utilities, technology, non-profit, and entrepreneurial businesses.

Professor Gamble received his Ph.D. in management from the University of Alabama in 1995. Dr. Gamble also has a Bachelor of Science degree and a Master of Arts degree from The University of Alabama.

Dr. A. J. (Lonnie) Strickland, a native of North Georgia, attended the University of Georgia, where he received a bachelor of science degree in math and physics in 1965. Afterward he entered the Georgia Institute of Technology, where he received a master of science in industrial management. He earned a PhD in business administration from Georgia State University in 1969. He currently holds the title of Professor of Strategic Management in the Graduate School of Business at the University of Alabama.

Dr. Strickland's experience in consulting and executive development is in the strategic management area, with a concentration in industry and competitive analysis. He has developed strategic planning systems for such firms as the Southern Company, BellSouth, South Center Bell, American Telephone and Telegraph, Gulf States Paper, Carraway Methodist Medical Center, Delco Remy, Mark IV Industries, Amoco Oil Company, USA Group, General Motors, and Kimberly Clark Corporation (Medical Products). He is a very popular speaker on the subject of implementing strategic change and serves on several corporate boards.

He has served as director of marketing for BellSouth, where he had responsibility for $1 billion in revenues and $300 million in profits.

In the international arena, Dr. Strickland has done extensive work in Europe, the Middle East, Central America, Malaysia, Australia, and Africa. In France he developed a management simulation of corporate decision making that enables management to test various strategic alternatives.

In the area of research, he is the author of 15 books and texts. His management simulations, Tempomatic IV and Micromatic, were pioneering innovations that enjoyed prominent market success for two decades.

Recent awards for Dr. Strickland include the Outstanding Professor Award from the Graduate School of Business and the Outstanding Commitment to Teaching Award from the University of Alabama, in which he takes particular pride. He is a member of various honor leadership societies: Mortar Board, Order of Omega, Beta Gamma Sigma, Omicron Delta Kappa, and Jasons. He is a past national president of Pi Kappa Phi social fraternity.

Preface

Strategy: Winning in the Marketplace is intended for core courses in strategic management. It has two very distinctive features: (1) a crisp, substantive treatment of the principles of crafting and executing strategy and (2) an unusually appealing lineup of 32 freshly written cases that are tightly linked to both the chapter content and the strategy-making, strategy-executing challenges in today's companies. We have covered the main elements of strategic thinking and strategic analysis in nine manageable chapters (348 pages), striving for a presentation that is appropriately rigorous but that also can be readily digested by students and comfortably covered in a single term. Skirting the temptation to incorporate too many topics and include too much detail (in a 12- to 16-chapter presentation) results, we think, in three very positive benefits for adopters and students: (1) It creates more leeway for case assignments. (2) It opens up time to utilize a substantive, stimulating simulation exercise—which not only is a pedagogically powerful way for students to learn about strategy but also introduces a welcome degree of added excitement and variety into the course. (3) It helps make the course workload less intimidating or overwhelming for students.

Like most authors of second editions, we are confident that the content of this edition represents a solid improvement over the first edition. It includes an all-new and very timely chapter entitled "Strategy, Ethics, and Social Responsibility," a more streamlined two-chapter treatment of strategy execution (down from three chapters), and a raft of improvements and updates of all the chapter presentations. Although the book is shorter than most leading texts, you'll find that the nine chapters cover the principles of crafting and executing strategy with plenty of depth and substance. There's a straightforward, integrated flow from one chapter to the next. The writing style aims squarely at making the discipline of business strategy relevant and professionally interesting to students. And the lineup of cases in this second edition is virtually all-new, with 27 freshly written cases and 4 holdover cases that have been updated and revised. The cases, which range from 2 to 30 pages in length, will push students to apply the concepts and analytical tools covered in the chapters and do some first-rate strategic thinking.

A Text with On-Target Content

In our view, for a senior-level/MBA strategy text to qualify as having on-target content, it must:

- Explain core concepts in language that students can grasp and provide examples of their relevance and use by actual companies.
- Take care to thoroughly describe the tools of strategic analysis, how they are used, and where they fit in the managerial process of crafting and executing strategy.

- Be up to date and comprehensive, presenting solid coverage of the landmark changes in competitive markets and company strategies that are being driven by globalization and Internet technology.

- Focus squarely on what every student needs to know about crafting, implementing, and executing business strategies in today's market environments.

- Contain freshly researched, value-adding cases that feature interesting products and companies, illustrate the important kinds of strategic challenges managers face, tie closely to the chapter content, contain valuable teaching points, and ignite lively class discussions.

We believe this second edition measures up on all five of these criteria. Chapter discussions cut straight to the chase about what students really need to know. Our explanations of core concepts and analytical tools are covered in enough depth to make them understandable and usable, the rationale being that a shallow explanation carries little punch and has almost no instructional value. All the chapters are flush with convincing examples of strategy in action; we made a point of choosing current examples that students can easily relate to. We have striven to incorporate all relevant state-of-the-art research pertinent to a first course in strategy. And, thanks to the excellent case research and case writing being done by colleagues in strategic management, this edition includes a truly fine collection of timely, interesting, and relevant cases to drive home valuable lessons in the whys and hows of successfully crafting and executing strategy. You'll find this case collection up to the tasks of sparking student interest and giving class members a solid workout in applying the concepts and analytical tools covered in the text chapters.

Organization, Content, and Features of the Text Chapters

The inclusion of the all-new chapter on strategy, ethics, and social responsibility and the combining of the former three-chapter presentation on the managerial aspects of executing strategy into two chapters give this edition a different texture and feel. We think the new chapter will (1) better alert students to the role and importance of incorporating business ethics and social responsibility into decision making and (2) address the accreditation requirements of the AACSB, which mandate that business ethics be visibly and thoroughly embedded in the core curriculum. In addition to making these two highly visible changes, we have thoroughly overhauled the opening chapter, which introduces the concept of strategy and the managerial process of crafting and executing strategy; added a host of current examples and new Company Spotlights; and embellished and refined the presentation of numerous topics and concepts throughout the chapters.

No other text comes close to matching our coverage of the resource-based theory of the firm and business ethics. The resource-based view of the firm is *prominently* and *comprehensively* integrated into our coverage of crafting both single-business and multibusiness strategies. Chapters 2, 3, 4, 5, and 6 emphasize that a company's strategy must be matched both to its external market circumstances and to its internal resources and competitive capabilities. Moreover, Chapters 8 and 9 have a strong resource-based perspective that makes it unequivocally clear how and why the tasks of assembling intellectual capital and building core competencies and competitive capabilities are absolutely critical to successful strategy execution and operating excellence. The all-new, 34-page Chapter 7 contains a very meaty and comprehensive treatment of business ethics and socially responsible behavior as it applies to crafting and executing company strategies.

As always, we have endeavored to highlight the latest developments in the theory and practice of strategic management and to keep the chapter presentations solidly in the mainstream of contemporary strategic thinking. You'll find up-to-date coverage of the continuing march of industries and companies to wider globalization, the growing scope and strategic importance of collaborative alliances, the spread of high-velocity change to more industries and company environments, and the way implementation of Internet technology applications in countries all across the world is driving fundamental changes in both strategy and internal operations.

The following rundown summarizes the noteworthy chapter features and topical emphasis in this edition:

■   Chapter 1 continues to focus squarely on the central questions of "what is strategy and why is it important?" It introduces and defines a host of core concepts—strategy, business model, strategic visions and business missions, strategic versus financial objectives, strategic plans, strategic intent, strategy crafting, and strategy execution. Clear distinction is made between a company's strategy and its business model. A section on strategic visions and mission statements hammers home the importance of clear direction setting and a motivating strategic vision; there's an accompanying discussion of how core values and ethics tie in to a company's vision and business purpose. Emphasis is placed on why companies have to rapidly adapt strategy to newly unfolding market conditions and why strategy life cycles are often short.

Following Henry Mintzberg's pioneering research, we stress how and why a company's strategy emerges from (1) the deliberate and purposeful actions of management and (2) as-needed reactions to unanticipated developments and fresh competitive pressures. There's a section underscoring that a company's strategic plan is a collection of strategies devised by different managers at different levels in the organizational hierarchy. We've taken pains to explain why *all managers are on a company's strategy-making, strategy-implementing team,* why every manager is well advised to make the concepts and techniques of strategic management a basic part of his or her toolkit, and why the best companies want their personnel to be true "students of the business." The chapter concludes with a substantially expanded section on corporate governance and a discussion of why *good strategy making + good strategy execution = good management.*

The role of this first chapter is to give readers a solid grasp of what the term *strategy* means, pique their interest, and convince them that the ins and outs of crafting and executing a winning strategy are things every business student should know. We intend this chapter to be a perfect accompaniment for the instructor's first one or two lectures on what the course is all about and why it matters.

■   Chapter 2 sets forth the now-familiar analytical tools and concepts of industry and competitive analysis and demonstrates the importance of tailoring strategy to fit the circumstances of a company's industry and competitive environment. The standout feature of this chapter is a presentation of Michael E. Porter's "five forces model of competition" that we think is the clearest, most straightforward discussion of this model in any text in the field. Globalization and Internet technology are treated as potent driving forces capable of reshaping industry competition—their roles as change agents have become factors that most companies in most industries must reckon with in forging winning strategies.

■ Chapter 3 establishes the importance of doing solid company situation analysis as a basis for matching strategy to organizational resources, competencies, and competitive capabilities. The roles of core competencies and organizational resources and capabilities in creating customer value and helping build competitive advantage are *center stage* in the discussions of company resource strengths and weaknesses. SWOT analysis is cast as a simple, easy-to-use way to assess a company's resources and overall situation. There is solid coverage of the now-standard tools of value chain analysis, benchmarking, and competitive strength assessments—all of which, we believe, provide insight into a company's relative cost position and market standing vis-à-vis rivals. There's solid coverage of how company implementation of Internet technology applications is altering company and industry value chains and the performance of specific value chain activities.

■ Chapter 4 deals with a company's quest for competitive advantage—the options for crafting a strategy that simultaneously holds good prospects for competitive advantage while also being well suited both to industry and competitive conditions and to its own resources and competitive circumstances. While the chapter is framed around the five generic competitive strategies—low-cost leadership, differentiation, best-cost provider, focused differentiation, and focused low cost—you'll also find important sections on what use to make of strategic alliances and collaborative partnerships, what use to make of mergers and acquisitions in strengthening the company's competitiveness, when to integrate backward or forward into more stages of the industry value chain, the merits of outsourcing certain value chain activities to outside specialists, whether and when to employ offensive and defensive moves, and the different types of Web site strategies that companies can employ to position themselves in the marketplace.

■ Chapter 5 explores a company's strategy options for expanding beyond its domestic boundary and competing in the markets of either a few or a great many countries—options ranging from an export strategy to licensing and franchising to multicountry strategies to global strategies to heavy reliance on strategic alliances and joint ventures. Four strategic issues unique to competing multinationally are given special attention: (1) whether to customize the company's offerings in each different country market to match the tastes and preferences of local buyers or whether to offer a mostly standardized product worldwide; (2) whether to employ essentially the same basic competitive strategy in the markets of all countries where the company operates or whether to modify the company's competitive approach country by country as may be needed to fit the specific market conditions and competitive circumstances it encounters; (3) locating production facilities, distribution centers, and customer service operations to maximum competitive advantage; and (4) efficient cross-border transfer of a company's resource strengths and capabilities to build competitive advantage. There's also coverage of the concepts of profit sanctuaries and cross-market subsidization, the special problems associated with entry into the markets of emerging countries, and strategies that local companies in such emerging countries as India, China, Brazil, and Mexico can use to defend against the invasion of opportunity-seeking, resource-rich global giants.

■ Our rather meaty treatment of diversification strategies for multibusiness enterprises in Chapter 6 begins by laying out the various paths for becoming diversified, explains how a company can use diversification to create or compound competitive advantage for its business units, and examines the strategic options an already-diversified company has to improve its overall performance. In the middle part of the chapter, the analytical spotlight is on the techniques and procedures for assessing the strategic attractiveness of a diversified company's business portfolio—the relative attractiveness of the various businesses the company has diversified into, a multiindustry company's competitive strength in each of its lines of business, and the *strategic fits* and *resource fits* among a diversified company's different businesses. The chapter concludes with a brief survey of a company's four main postdiversification strategy alternatives: (1) broadening the diversification base, (2) divesting some businesses and retrenching to a narrower diversification base, (3) restructuring the makeup of the company's business lineup, and (4) engaging in multinational diversification.

■ Our all-new Chapter 7, "Strategy, Ethics, and Social Responsibility," zeroes in on whether and why a company's strategy should pass the test of moral scrutiny. Students usually acknowledge that a company and its personnel have a legal duty to obey the law and play by the rules of fair competition. But today's students seem to be much less clear on (1) whether a company has a *duty* to operate according to ethical standards and (2) whether a company has a *duty* or *obligation* to contribute to the betterment of society independent of the needs and preferences of the customers it serves. Is it in the best interests of shareholders for a company to operate ethically and/or to operate in a socially responsible manner? There is substantive discussion of what linkage, if any, there should be between a company's efforts to craft and execute a winning strategy and its duties to (1) conduct its activities in an ethical manner and (2) demonstrate socially responsible behavior by being a committed corporate citizen and attending to the needs of nonowner stakeholders—employees, the communities in which it operates, the disadvantaged, and society as a whole. The chapter reflects the very latest in the literature. The opening section of the chapter addresses whether ethical standards are universal (as maintained by the school of ethical universalism) or dependent on local norms and situational circumstances (as maintained by the school of ethical relativism) or a combination of both (as maintained by integrative social contracts theory). Following this is a section on the three categories of managerial morality (moral, immoral, and amoral), a section on the drivers of unethical strategies and shady business behavior, a section on the approaches to managing a company's ethical conduct, a section on linking a company's strategy to its ethical principles and core values, a section on the concept of a "social responsibility strategy," and sections that explore the business case for ethical and socially responsible behavior. The chapter gives students some serious ideas to chew on and, hopefully, will make them far more ethically conscious. It has been written as a stand-alone chapter that can be assigned in the early, middle, or late part of the course.

■ The two-chapter module on executing strategy (Chapters 8 and 9) is anchored around a solid, compelling conceptual framework: (1) building the resource strengths and organizational capabilities needed to execute the strategy in competent fashion; (2) allocating ample resources to strategy-critical activities; (3) ensuring that policies and procedures facilitate rather than impede strategy execution; (4) instituting best practices and pushing for continuous improvement in how value chain activities are performed; (5) installing information and operating systems that enable company personnel to better carry out their strategic roles proficiently; (6) tying rewards and incentives directly to the achievement of performance targets and good strategy execution; (7) shaping the work environment and corporate culture to fit the strategy; and (8) exerting the internal leadership needed to drive execution forward. The recurring theme of these two chapters is that implementing and executing strategy entails figuring out the specific actions, behaviors, and conditions that are needed for a smooth strategy-supportive operation and then following through to get things done and deliver results—the goal here is to ensure that students understand that the strategy-implementing/strategy-executing phase is a make-things-happen and make-them-happen-right kind of managerial exercise.

Our top priority has been to ensure that the nine chapters of text hit the bull's-eye with respect to content and represent the best thinking of both academics and practitioners. But, at the same time, we've gone the extra mile to stay on message with clear, crisp explanations laced with enough relevant examples and Company Spotlights to make the presentation convincing, pertinent, and worthwhile to readers preparing for careers in management and business. We have gone all out to create chapter discussions and compile a case lineup capable of persuading students that the discipline of strategy merits their rapt attention.

The Case Collection

The 36 cases included in this edition are the very latest and best that we could find. The lineup is flush with examples of strategy in action and valuable lessons for students in the art and science of crafting and executing strategy. And there's a good blend of cases from a length perspective—close to one-fourth are under 15 pages, yet offer plenty for students to chew on; about one-fourth are medium-length cases; and the remainder are longer, detail-rich cases that call for more sweeping and detailed analysis.

At least 26 of the 32 cases involve high-profile companies, products, or people that students will have heard of, know about from personal experience, or can easily identify with. There are four dot-com company cases, plus several others that will provide students with insight into the special demands of competing in industry environments where technological developments are an everyday event, product life cycles are short, and competitive maneuvering among rivals comes fast and furious. Close to two-thirds of the cases involve situations where company resources and competitive capabilities play as large a role in the strategy-making, strategy-executing scheme of things as industry and competitive conditions do. Scattered throughout the lineup are 13 cases concerning non-U.S. companies, globally competitive industries, and/or cross-cultural situations; these cases, in conjunction with the globalized content of the text chapters, provide ample material for linking the study of strategic management tightly to the ongoing globalization of the world economy. You'll also find 5 cases dealing with the strategic problems of family-owned or relatively small entrepreneurial businesses and 28 cases involving public companies about which students can do further research on the Internet. Nine of the cases (Starbucks, Competition in the Digital Music Industry, Competition in the Bottled Water Industry, eBay, Google, Harley-Davidson, Atkins Nutritionals, Wal-Mart, and Merck and the Recall of Vioxx) have accompanying videotape segments. We believe instructors will find the collection of 36 cases quite appealing, eminently teachable, and very suitable for drilling students on the use of the concepts and analytical treatments in Chapters 1 through 9. With this case lineup, instructors should have no difficulty whatsoever choosing a set of cases to assign that will capture the interest of students from start to finish.

In addition, the publisher is making nine other recent cases from prior editions available to students who purchase the text and to adopters—these cases are posted at the *Strategy: Winning in the Marketplace* Web site (www.mhhe.com/thompson2e). This extends the number of cases available in the total package to 41.

Two Accompanying Online, Fully Automated Simulation Exercises: *GLO-BUS and The Business Strategy Game*

GLO-BUS: Developing Winning Competitive Strategies and *The Business Strategy Game* (the online eighth edition)—two strategy-related simulations that are available online and that feature automatic processing of student decisions—are being marketed by the publisher as companion supplements for use with this and other texts in the field. *The Business Strategy Game* is the world's leading strategy simulation, having been played by well over 350,000 students at universities throughout the world. *GLO-BUS,* a somewhat less complicated online simulation that was introduced in fall 2003, has been played by over 10,000 students at more than 100 universities worldwide and is equally suitable for courses in business strategy. All activity for *GLO-BUS* occurs at www.glo-bus.com and all activity for *The Business Strategy Game* takes place at www.bsg-online.com. Table 1 provides a comparison of the industry and competitive features of *GLO-BUS* and the online edition of *The Business Strategy Game.*

Both simulations have attractive operating and administrative characteristics that make them a breeze to utilize in giving students valuable practice in thinking strategically and applying basic strategy concepts and analytical tools:

■ *Time requirements for instructors to administer the simulations are minimal.* Instructors must go through Industry Set-up and specify a decision schedule and desired scoring weights (which can be altered later). Setting up the simulation for the course is done online and takes about 10 to 15 minutes. Once set-up is completed, no other administrative actions are required beyond moving participants to a different team (should the need arise) and monitoring the progress of the simulation (to whatever extent desired). Instructors who wish to do so can track happenings in the simulation by printing copies of the Industry and Company reports (done online), change selected costs and rates to introduce different operating conditions (players are automatically notified of any changes if instructors so choose), and serve as a consultant to troubled companies.

■ *There's no software for students or administrators to download and no disks to fool with.* When participants log on to the Web site, the needed programming and company data are automatically transferred into Excel on the user's PC for the duration of the session and then automatically saved and uploaded back to the server on exit. All work must be done online, and the speed for participants using dial-up modems is quite satisfactory.

■ *Participant's guides for both simulations are available at the Web site*—students can read either guide on their monitors or print out a copy, as they prefer. The Participant's Guide for *GLO-BUS* is 25 pages, and the Participant's Guide for *The Business Strategy Game* is 33 pages.

■ *There are extensive built-in help screens* explaining (1) each decision entry, (2) the information on each page of the Industry Reports, and (3) the numbers presented in the Company Reports. The help screens allow company comanagers to figure things out for themselves, thereby curbing the need for students to always run to the instructor with questions about how things work.

■ *The results of each decision are processed automatically* on the simulation's server and are available to all participants *within one hour after the decision deadline*

Table 1   A COMPARISON OF *GLO-BUS* AND *THE BUSINESS STRATEGY GAME*

	GLO-BUS	The Business Strategy Game
Industry setting	Digital camera industry	Athletic footwear industry
Market scope	Worldwide. Production occurs at a single plant in Taiwan and sales are made to retailers in 4 regions: North America, Latin America, Europe-Africa, and Asia Pacific.	Worldwide. Both production and sales activities can be pursued in North America, Latin America, Europe-Africa, and Asia Pacific.
Number of market segments	A total of 8—4 geographic segments for entry-level cameras and 4 geographic segments for multifeatured cameras.	A total of 12—4 geographic segments each for branded footwear sales to retailers, for online footwear sales direct to consumers, and for private-label sales to multistore retailers.
Number of decision variables	■ Character and performance of the camera line (10 decisions) ■ Production operations and worker compensation (15 decisions) ■ Pricing and marketing (15 decisions in 4 geographic regions) ■ Financing of company operations (4 decisions)	■ Production operations and worker compensation (16 decisions each plant, with a maximum of 4 plants) ■ Shipping (up to 8 decisions each plant) ■ Pricing and marketing (13 decisions in 4 geographic regions) ■ Financing of company operations (5 decisions)
Competitive variables used to determine market share (All sales and market share differences are the result of differing competitive efforts among rival companies.)	■ Price ■ Performance/quality rating ■ Number of quarterly sales promotions ■ Length of promotions in weeks ■ Promotional discounts ■ Advertising ■ Number of camera models ■ Size of dealer network ■ Warranty period ■ Technical support	■ Price ■ Number of models/styles ■ Styling/quality rating ■ Advertising ■ Size of retailer network ■ Celebrity endorsements ■ Delivery time ■ Retailer support ■ Mail-in rebates ■ Shipping charges (Internet sales only)
Time frame of decisions	One year, with an option to update as many as 8 of the 44 decisions quarterly.	One year.
Strategy options (Which options deliver the best performance hinges on the interaction and competitive strength of the strategies employed by rival companies—not on "silver bullet" decision combinations that players are challenged to discover.)	Companies can pursue competitive advantage based on (1) low-cost or differentiation, (2) competing globally or in select segments, and (3) using largely the same strategy across all regions or strategies that are tailored to conditions in each market segment.	Companies have the widest possible strategy-making latitude—striving for competitive advantage based on (1) low-cost or differentiation, (2) competing globally or in select segments, and (3) using largely the same strategy across all regions or strategies that are tailored to conditions in each market segment.

Table 1 (CONCLUDED)

	GLO-BUS	The Business Strategy Game
Degree of complexity	■ *GLO-BUS* Basic (easy to moderate) ■ *GLO-BUS* Plus (easy to moderate) ■ *GLO-BUS* Total (medium) Less complex than BSG because all production is in a single plant, there are no finished-goods inventories (newly assembled cameras are built to order and shipped directly to retailers), and sales forecasting is simpler.	More complex than *GLO-BUS* because companies can operate up to 4 plants, there are 12 market segments (as compared to 8 in *GLO-BUS*), finished-goods inventories have to be managed at 4 distribution centers, and players have to develop a sales forecast based on their competitive strategy and the expected competitive efforts of rivals.
Time required to make a complete decision	About 1.5 hours per decision (once players gain familiarity with software and reports). *GLO-BUS* Plus requires about 10 minutes more than *GLO-BUS* Basic per decision, and *GLO-BUS* Total can entail up to 30 minutes additional time per decision.	1.75 to 2.25 hours per decision (once players gain familiarity with software and reports).

specified by the instructor or game administrator—typically the results are available 15 to 20 minutes after the decision deadline. The servers dedicated to hosting the two simulations have appropriate backup capability and are maintained by a prominent Web-hosting service that guarantees 99.9 percent reliability on a 24/7 basis.

■ *Participants and instructors are notified via e-mail when the results are ready;* the e-mail contains highlights of the results.

■ *Decision schedules are determined by the instructor* (done online and automatically communicated to all players). Decisions can be made once per week, twice per week, or even twice daily, depending on how instructors want to conduct the exercise. One popular decision schedule involves 1 or 2 practice decisions, 6 to 10 regular decisions, and decisions made once a week across the whole term. A second popular schedule is 1 or 2 practice decisions, 6 to 8 regular decisions, and biweekly decisions, all made during the last four or five weeks of the course (when it can be assumed that students have pretty much digested the contents of Chapters 1 to 5, gotten somewhat comfortable with what is involved in crafting strategy for a single-business company situation, and have prepared several assigned cases).

■ *Instructors have the flexibility to prescribe 0, 1, or 2 practice decisions and from 3 to 10 regular decisions.*

■ *Company teams can be composed of 1 to 5 players each, and the number of teams in a single industry can range from 4 to 12.* If your class size is too large for a single industry, then it is a simple matter to create two or more industries for a single class section. You'll find that having more than one industry per class presents no significant change in administrative requirements, because everything is processed automatically and all company and individual performances are automatically recorded in your online grade book. Thus it turns out not to be an extra administrative burden to divide a large class into two or more industries.

■ *Following each decision, participants are provided with a complete set of reports*—a six-page Industry Report, a one-page Competitive Intelligence report for each geographic region that includes strategic group maps and bulleted lists of competitive strengths and weaknesses, and a set of Company Reports (income statement, balance sheet, cash flow statement, and assorted production, marketing, and cost statistics).

- *Two open-book multiple-choice tests of 20 questions* (optional, but strongly recommended) *are included as part of each of the two simulations.* The quizzes are taken online and automatically graded, with scores reported instantaneously to participants and automatically recorded in the instructor's electronic grade book. Quiz 1 has a time limit of 45 minutes and covers contents of the Participant's Guide. Quiz 2 has a time limit of 75 minutes and checks whether players understand what the numbers in the company reports mean and how they are calculated. Students are automatically provided with three sample questions for each test.

- At the end of the simulation exercises, *there are peer evaluations that instructors can have students complete.* The peer evaluations are optional but strongly recommended; they are completed online and automatically recorded in the instructor's electronic grade book. Results can be reviewed by clicking on each comanager's peer scores in the grade book.

Simulations now have a track record as a proven and very effective vehicle for giving students valuable practice in being active strategic thinkers, reading the signs of industry change, reacting to the moves of competitors, evaluating strengths and weaknesses in their company's competitive position, and deciding what to do to improve a company's financial performance.

Why Simulations Are Widely Used in Capstone Strategy Courses

All three coauthors of this book are avid, longtime simulation users. Our own experiences over the years, together with numerous discussions with colleagues around the world, have convinced us that competition-based simulation games are *the single most powerful pedagogical device for hammering home the core concepts and analytical techniques that constitute the discipline of business and competitive strategy.* We see three big reasons why simulations are rapidly growing in popularity and have earned a place in so many of today's strategy courses:

- Both *GLO-BUS* and *The Business Strategy Game* have been carefully designed to connect directly to the chapter material and give students the experience of putting what they read in the chapters into play. Company comanagers have to wrestle with charting a long-term direction for their company, setting strategic and financial objectives, and crafting strategies that produce good results and perhaps lead to competitive advantage. In crafting and executing a strategy, they can choose from a wide array of the strategic options discussed in the text chapters and they can practice using the tools of strategic analysis. In both *GLO-BUS* and *The Business Strategy Game*, students are provided with strategic group maps and lists of competitive strengths and weaknesses, as well as an assortment of cost benchmarks and comparative financial statistics, allowing them to diagnose their company's market standing vis-à-vis rivals and decide on a course of action to improve it. Moreover, simulations provide instructors with opportunity after opportunity to draw upon the industry and company circumstances in the simulation for examples to use in lectures on the text chapters—examples that all students in the class can relate to because of their personal experience in running their companies.

- The market and competitive dynamics of an industry simulation—which make the simulation a "live case" in which class members are active managerial participants—give students valuable practice in thinking strategically and in making responsible, results-oriented decisions. Company comanagers can pursue a competitive advantage keyed to low cost/low price or to top-notch features and styling or to more value for the money. They can try to gain an edge over rivals with more advertising or wider product selection. They can focus on one or two geographic regions or strive for geographic balance. They can pursue essentially the same strategy worldwide or craft slightly or very different strategies for the Europe-Africa, Asia-Pacific, Latin America, and North America markets. Almost any well-conceived, well-executed competitive approach is capable of succeeding *provided it is not overpowered by the strategies of competitors or defeated by the presence of too many copycat strategies that dilute its effectiveness.* In other words, which company strategies end up delivering the best performance hinges on the interaction and competitive strength of the strategies employed by rival companies—not on "silver bullet" decision combinations that players are challenged to discover. Since, in a simulation, students have to live with all the decisions they make and the results they produce, they experience firsthand what is involved in crafting and executing a strategy that delivers good results—*it is this understanding that is the essence of a course in business strategy.*

- Based on the classroom experiences of hundreds of instructors and the mushrooming use of simulations in strategy courses worldwide, incorporating a simulation as a centerpiece turns strategy courses into a livelier, richer, more powerful learning experience. A realistic, substantive, "learn by doing" simulation like *GLO-BUS* or *The Business Strategy Game* sparks a highly desirable degree of student excitement about the subject matter of crafting and executing strategy. More and more professors who teach strategy courses are finding that simulations are every bit as pedagogically effective as case analysis as the prime vehicle for showing students how to make use of core concepts and analytical techniques.

There are two other reasons why a simulation is a good exercise to include as an integral and featured part of the course:

- A well-conceived simulation adds an enormous amount of student interest and excitement—a head-to-head competitive battle for market share and industry leadership is certain to stir students' competitive juices and emotionally involve them in the subject matter. Most students will enjoy the exercise, recognize its practical value, and learn a lot—all of which tends to result in higher instructor evaluations at the end of the course.

- Students will almost certainly learn more about the ins and outs of crafting and executing strategy from playing a simulation than they will learn from preparing two or three extra cases or doing a second or third written case analysis. Since use of *GLO-BUS* or *The Business Strategy Game* can add net time to the course requirements from a student perspective, instructors can compensate by trimming the total number of assigned cases or using a simulation as a substitute for a written case, an hour exam, or both. Happily, a simulation lightens the grading burden for instructors as compared to written cases or essay exams.

In sum, the value that a first-rate simulation adds to a strategy course boils down to two things:

1. The "WOW! This is great, plus I am learning a lot" reaction of students.

2. The contribution a good simulation exercise makes to better preparing students for a career in business and management—*a simulation makes courses in strategy much more of a true capstone experience* and puts students under the gun of competition to improve their business acumen and managerial judgment.

To learn more about *GLO-BUS* or *The Business Strategy Game*, please visit www.glo-bus.com or www.bsg-online.com and browse the wealth of information that is at your fingertips. There is a Guided Tour link on each of the Web sites that provides a quick bird's-eye view and takes about five minutes—enough to determine whether there's sufficient interest on your part to explore further. There are also instructor's guides and PowerPoint presentation slides that you can skim to preview the two simulations. If you call the senior author of this text at 205-348-8923, the simulation authors will be glad to provide you with a personal tour of either or both Web sites (while you are at your PC) and walk you through the many features that are built into the simulations. We think you'll be quite impressed with the capabilities that have been programmed into *The Business Strategy Game* and *GLO-BUS,* the simplicity with which both simulations can be administered, and their exceptionally tight connection to the text chapters, core concepts, and standard analytical tools.

Adopters of the text who want to incorporate use of either of the two simulation supplements should instruct their bookstores to order the "book-simulation package"—the publisher has a special ISBN number for this package that entails a discounted price; shrink-wrapped with each text is a special card that provides students with a prepaid access code for participating in either simulation.

Student Support Materials

Key Points Summaries

At the end of each chapter is a synopsis of the core concepts, analytical tools, and other key points discussed in the chapter. These chapter-end synopses, along with the margin notes scattered throughout each chapter, help students focus on basic strategy principles, digest the messages of each chapter, and prepare for tests.

Chapter-End Exercises

Each chapter contains a select number of exercises, most related to research on the Internet, that reinforce key concepts and topics covered in the chapters.

A Value-Added Web Site

The student section of www.mhhe.com/thompson2e contains a number of helpful aids:

- Twenty-question self-scoring chapter tests that students can take to measure their grasp of the material presented in each of the nine chapters.
- A "Guide to Case Analysis" containing sections on what a case is, why cases are a standard part of courses on strategy, preparing a case for class discussion, doing a written case analysis, doing an oral presentation, and using financial ratio analysis to assess a company's financial condition.

- A table containing formulas and brief explanations of all the various financial ratios that are commonly used in evaluating a company's financial statements and financial strengths.
- A select number of PowerPoint slides for each chapter.

PowerWeb

With each new copy of this text, students gain access to the publisher's PowerWeb site offering current news, articles from 6,300 premium sources, a Web research guide, current readings from annual editions, and links to related sites.

Case-TUTOR Software

Accompanying the 32 cases in the text is a downloadable software package containing assignment questions for all 32 cases, plus analytically structured exercises for 10 of the cases that coach students in doing the strategic thinking needed to arrive at solid answers to the assignment questions for those cases. Conscientious completion of the case preparation exercises helps students gain quicker command of the concepts and analytical techniques and points them toward doing good strategic analysis. The 10 cases that have case preparation exercises are indicated by the Case-TUTOR logo in the case listing section of the Table of Contents (the Case-TUTOR logo also appears on the first page of every case for which there is an exercise). Students can download the Case-TUTOR software at the publisher's Web site.

Instructor Support Materials

Instructor's Manual

The accompanying instructor's manual contains a section on suggestions for organizing and structuring your course, sample syllabi and course outlines, a copy of the test bank, and comprehensive teaching notes for each of the 32 cases.

Test Bank

The test bank, prepared by the coauthors, contains about 800 multiple-choice questions and 200 short-answer and essay questions.

Computest

A computerized version of the test bank allows you to generate tests quite conveniently and to add your own questions.

PowerPoint Slides

To facilitate preparation of your lectures and to serve as chapter outlines, approximately 500 colorful and professional-looking slides are available. You'll have access to slides displaying core concepts, analytical procedures, key points, and all the figures in the text chapters. The slides are the creation of Professor Jana Kuzmicki of Troy State University.

Accompanying Case Videos

Nine of the cases (Starbucks, Competition in the Digital Music Industry, Competition in the Bottled Water Industry, eBay, Google, Harley-Davidson, Atkins Nutritionals, Wal-Mart, and Merck and the Recall of Vioxx) have accompanying videotape segments that you can show during the course of the case discussions. Suggestions for using each video are contained in the teaching note for the case.

Presentation CD-ROM

The instructor's manual, all of the PowerPoint slides, the video clips, teaching notes for the 32 cases in the text, and the 9 supplemental e-cases and teaching notes available with *Strategy: Winning in the Marketplace; Core Concepts, Analytical Tools, Cases* have been installed on a CD that is available to all adopters. The CD is a useful aid for compiling a syllabus and daily course schedule, preparing customized lectures, and developing tests on the text chapters.

The Business Strategy Game and *GLO-BUS* Online Simulations

Using one of the two companion simulations is a powerful and constructive way of emotionally connecting students to the subject matter of the course. We know of no more effective and interesting way to stimulate the competitive energy of students and prepare them for the rigors of real-world business decision making than to have them match strategic wits with classmates as they run a company in head-to-head competition for global market leadership.

With this second edition, we've done our level best to provide you with a comprehensive teaching/learning package that squarely targets what every business student needs to know about crafting and executing business strategies, that works magic in the classroom, and that wins the applause of students. Our goal has been to raise the bar for what a text package in the discipline of strategy ought to deliver. We tried to equip you with a smorgasbord of teaching/learning opportunities and keep the nature of student assignments varied and interesting. We've pursued every avenue we know to provide you with all the resources and materials you'll need to design and deliver a course that is on the cutting edge and is pedagogically effective.

Acknowledgments

We heartily acknowledge the contributions of the case researchers whose case-writing efforts appear herein and the companies whose cooperation made the cases possible. To each one goes a very special thank-you. We cannot overstate the importance of timely, carefully researched cases in contributing to a substantive study of strategic management issues and practices. From a research standpoint, strategy-related cases are invaluable in exposing the generic kinds of strategic issues that companies face, in forming hypotheses about strategic behavior, and in drawing experience-based generalizations about the practice of strategic management. From an instructional standpoint, strategy cases give students essential practice in diagnosing and evaluating the strategic situations of companies and organizations, in applying the concepts and tools of strategic analysis, in weighing strategic options and crafting strategies, and in tackling the challenges of successful strategy execution. Without a continuing stream of fresh, well-researched, and well-conceived cases, the discipline of strategic management would lose its close ties to the very institutions whose strategic actions and behavior it is aimed at explaining. There's no question, therefore, that first-class case research constitutes a valuable scholarly contribution to the theory and practice of strategic management.

In addition, a great number of colleagues and students at various universities, business acquaintances, and people at McGraw-Hill provided inspiration, encouragement, and counsel during the course of this project. Like all text authors in the strategy field, we are intellectually indebted to the many academics whose research and writing have blazed new trails and advanced the discipline of strategic management. We are most grateful to the reviewers who made valuable suggestions that guided our preparation of the first edition: Seyda Deligonul, David Flanagan, Esmeralda Garbi, Mohsin Habib, Kim Hester, Jeffrey E. McGee, and Diana Wong. The following reviewers provided seasoned advice and suggestions for improving the chapters in this second edition:

Donald P. Austin, *Saint Michael's College of Vermont*

R. Ivan Blanco, *Emporia State University*

Debbie Gilliard, *Metropolitan State College–Denver*

Dale Henderson, *Radford University*

Matthew Howard, *Park University*

Tammy G. Hunt, *University of North Carolina at Wilmington*

Dennis M. Kripp, *Roosevelt University*

Thomas C. Leach, *University of New England*

Paul D. Maxell, *St. Thomas University*

Raza Mir, *William Paterson University*

Gordon Riggle, *University of Colorado*

Daniel A. Sauers, *Winona State University*

Srivatsa Seshadri, *University of Nebraska at Kearney*

As always, we value your recommendations and thoughts about the book. Your comments regarding coverage and contents will be taken to heart, and we always are grateful for the time you take to call our attention to printing errors, deficiencies, and other shortcomings. Please e-mail us at athompso@cba.ua.edu, jgamble@usouthal.edu, or astrickl@cba.ua.edu; fax us at 205-348-6695; or write us at PO Box 870225, Department of Management and Marketing, The University of Alabama, Tuscaloosa, AL 35487-0225.

Arthur A. Thompson
John E. Gamble
A. J. Strickland

Guided Tour

Chapter Structure and Organization

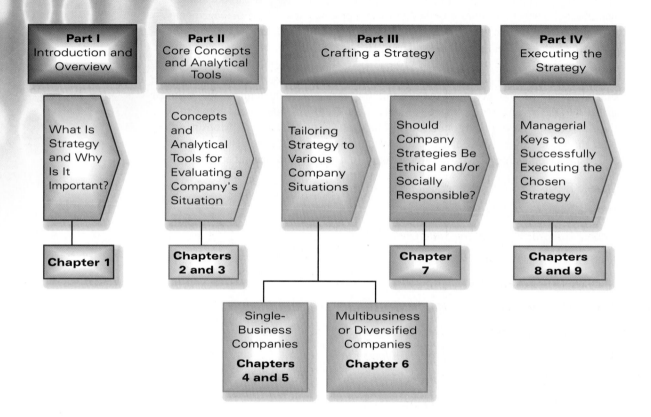

Part I
Introduction and Overview

What Is Strategy and Why Is It Important?

Chapter 1

Part II
Core Concepts and Analytical Tools

Concepts and Analytical Tools for Evaluating a Company's Situation

Chapters 2 and 3

Part III
Crafting a Strategy

Tailoring Strategy to Various Company Situations

Should Company Strategies Be Ethical and/or Socially Responsible?

Chapter 7

Single-Business Companies

Chapters 4 and 5

Multibusiness or Diversified Companies

Chapter 6

Part IV
Executing the Strategy

Managerial Keys to Successfully Executing the Chosen Strategy

Chapters 8 and 9

Each chapter begins with a series of pertinent quotes and an introductory preview of its contents.

CHAPTER 1

What Is Strategy and Why Is It Important?

A strategy is a commitment to undertake one set of actions rather than another.
—*Sharon Oster, professor, Yale University*

Without a strategy the organization is like a ship without a rudder.
—*Joel Ross and Michael Kami*

Unless we change our direction we are likely to end up where we are headed.
—*Ancient Chinese proverb*

If you don't know where you are going, any road will take you there.
—*The Koran*

Management's job is not to see the company as it is . . . but as it can become.
—*John W. Teets, former CEO, Greyhound Corp.*

COMPANY SPOTLIGHT 1.1
Comcast's Strategy to Revolutionize the Cable Industry

In 2004 cable TV giant Comcast was putting the finishing touches on a bold strategy to change the way people watched television and to grow its business by introducing Internet phone service. With revenues of $18 billion and almost 22 million of the 74 million U.S. cable subscribers, Comcast became the industry leader in the U.S. market in 2002 when it acquired AT&T Broadband and its 13 million cable subscribers for about $50 billion. Comcast's strategy in 2004 had the following elements:

- *Roll out a new video-on-demand service that would allow customers to watch TV programs whenever they wanted to watch them.* The service allowed customers to use their remotes to choose from a menu of thousands of programs, stored on Comcast's servers as they were first broadcast, and included network shows, news, sports, and movies; viewers had the ability to pause, stop, restart, and save programs, without having to remember to record them when they were broadcast. After only 18 months, Comcast had signed up close to 5 million of its subscribers for the service and it was introducing the service in additional geographic markets at a brisk pace.

service with many snazzy features, including call forwarding, caller ID, and conferencing.

- *Use the video-on-demand and VOIP service offerings to differentiate Comcast's service offering and combat mounting competition from direct-to-home satellite TV providers.* Cable's two-way communications connection to homes enabled viewers to call up the programs they wanted with a few clicks of the remote; satellite TV had no such capability, nor did satellite providers yet have the capability to offer reliable high-speed Internet access. Satellite TV had been stealing customers away from cable TV because of its lower monthly fees—in the first six months of 2004, Direct TV and Echostar together added about 1.7 million new subscribers, whereas Comcast had lost 61,000 subscribers.

- *Employ a sales force (currently numbering about 3,200 people) to sell advertising to businesses that were shifting some of their advertising dollars from sponsoring network programs to sponsoring cable programs.* Ad sales generated revenues of $1.3 billion, and Comcast had cable operations in 21 of the 25 largest markets in the United States.

In-depth examples—**Company Spotlights** and **Global Spotlights**—appear in boxes throughout each chapter to illustrate important chapter topics, connect the text presentation to real-world companies, and convincingly demonstrate strategy in action.

GLOBAL SPOTLIGHT 5.1
Multicountry Strategies at Electronic Arts and Coca-Cola

Electronic Arts' Multicountry Strategy in Video Games

Electronic Arts (EA), the world's largest independent developer and marketer of video games, designs games that are suited to the differing tastes of game players in different countries and also designs games in multiple languages. EA has two major design studios—one in Vancouver, British Columbia, and one in Los Angeles—and smaller design studios in San Francisco, Orlando, London, and Tokyo. This dispersion of design studios helps EA to design games that are specific to different cultures—for example, the London studio took the lead in designing the popular FIFA Soccer game to suit European tastes and to replicate the stadiums, signage, and team rosters; a U.S. studio took the lead in designing games involving NFL football, NBA basketball, and NASCAR racing. No other game software company had EA's ability to localize games or to launch games on multiple platforms in multiple countries in multi-

ple languages. EA's *Harry Potter and the Chamber of Secrets* was released simultaneously in 75 countries, in 31 languages, and on 7 platforms.

Coca-Cola's Multicountry Strategy in Beverages

Coca-Cola strives to meet the demands of local tastes and cultures, offering 300 brands in some 200 countries. Its network of bottlers and distributors is distinctly local, and the company's products and brands are formulated to cater to local tastes. The ways in which Coca-Cola's local operating units bring products to market, the packaging that is used, and the advertising messages that are employed are all intended to match the local culture and fit in with local business practices. Many of the ingredients and supplies for Coca-Cola's products are sourced locally.

Source: www.ea.com and www.cocacola.com, accessed September 2004.

Strategy and Ethics: Passing the Test of Moral Scrutiny

In choosing among strategic alternatives, company managers are well advised to embrace actions that are aboveboard and can pass the test of moral scrutiny. Just keeping a company's strategic actions within the bounds of what is legal does not make them ethical. Ethical and moral standards are not governed by what is legal. Rather, they involve issues of "right" versus "wrong" and *duty*—what one *should* do. A strategy is ethical only if it does not entail actions and behaviors that cross the line from "should do" to "should not do" (because such actions are "unsavory" or unconscionable, injurious to other people, or unnecessarily harmful to the environment).

Admittedly, it is not always easy to categorize a given strategic behavior as definitely ethical or definitely unethical; many strategic actions fall in a gray zone in between. Whether they are deemed ethical or unethical hinges on how high one sets the bar. For example, is it ethical for advertisers of alcoholic products to place ads in media having an audience of as much as 50 percent underage viewers? (In 2003, growing concerns about underage drinking prompted some beer and distilled-spirits companies to agree to place ads in media with an audience at least 70 percent adult, up from a standard of 50 percent adult.) Is it ethical for an apparel retailer attempting to keep prices attractively low to source clothing from foreign manufacturers that pay substandard wages, utilize child labor, or engage in unsavory sweatshop practices? Many people would say no, but some might argue that a company is not unethical simply because it does not police the business practices of its suppliers. Is it ethical for pharmaceutical manufacturers to charge higher prices for life-saving drugs in some countries than they charge in others? (This is a fairly common practice that has recently come under scrutiny because it raises the costs of health care for consumers who are charged higher prices.) Is it ethical for a pharmaceutical company to downplay issues about the

Core Concept

A strategy cannot be considered ethical just because it involves actions that are legal. To meet the standard of being ethical, a strategy must entail actions that can pass moral scrutiny and that are aboveboard in the sense of not being shady or unconscionable, injurious to others, or unnecessarily harmful to the environment.

Margin notes define core concepts and call attention to important ideas and principles.

Figure 2.5   Factors Affecting the Threat of Entry

Entry threats are weaker when:
- The pool of entry candidates is small.
- Entry barriers are high.
- Existing competitors are struggling to earn healthy profits.
- The industry's outlook is risky or uncertain.
- Buyer demand is growing slowly or is stagnant.
- Industry members will strongly contest the efforts of new entrants to gain a market foothold.

Rivalry among Competing Sellers

How strong are the competitive pressures associated with the entry threat from new rivals?

Potential New Entrants

Entry threats are stronger when:
- The pool of entry candidates is large and some of the candidates have resources that would make them formidable market contenders.
- Entry barriers are low or can be readily hurdled by the likely entry candidates.
- Existing industry members are looking to expand their market reach by entering product segments or geographic areas where they currently do not have a presence.
- Newcomers can expect to earn attractive profits.
- Buyer demand is growing rapidly.
- Industry members are unable (or unwilling) to strongly contest the entry of newcomers.

Figures scattered throughout the chapters provide conceptual and analytical frameworks.

---

being performed in actual companies and in making analysis-based recommendations for improvement. At the very least, we hope to convince you that capabilities in crafting and executing strategy are basic to managing successfully and have a prominent place in a manager's toolkit.

As you tackle the following pages, ponder an observation made by Ralph Waldo Emerson: "Commerce is a game of skill which many people play, but which few play well." If the content of this book helps you become a more savvy player and better equips you to succeed in business, then your journey through the following pages will indeed be time well spent.

Key Points

The tasks of crafting and executing company strategies are the heart and soul of managing a business enterprise and winning in the marketplace. A company's strategy consists of the competitive moves and business approaches that management is using to grow the business, stake out a market position, attract and please customers, compete successfully, conduct operations, and achieve organizational objectives. The central thrust of a company's strategy is undertaking moves to build and strengthen the company's long-term competitive position and financial performance and, ideally, gain a competitive advantage over rivals that then becomes a company's ticket to above-average profitability. A company's strategy typically evolves and re-forms over time, emerging from a blend of (1) proactive and purposeful actions on the part of company managers and (2) as-needed reactions to unanticipated developments and fresh market conditions.

Closely related to the concept of strategy is the concept of a company's business model. A company's business model is management's story line for how and why the company's product offerings and competitive approaches will generate a revenue stream and have an associated cost structure that produces attractive earnings and return on investment; in effect, a company's business model sets forth the economic logic for answering the question "How do we intend to make money in this business, given our current strategy?"

The managerial process of crafting and executing a company's strategy consists of five interrelated and integrated phases:

1. *Developing a strategic vision* of where the company needs to head and what its future product-customer-market-technology focus should be. This managerial step provides long term direction, infuses the organization with a sense of purposeful action, and communicates to stakeholders what management's aspirations for the company are.

2. *Setting objectives* and using the targeted results and outcomes as yardsticks for measuring the company's performance and progress. Objectives need to spell out *how much* of *what kind* of performance *by when*, and they need to require a significant amount of organizational stretch. A balanced-scorecard approach for measuring company performance entails setting both *financial objectives* and *strategic objectives*.

3. *Crafting a strategy to achieve the objectives* and move the company along the strategic course that management has charted. Crafting strategy is concerned principally with forming responses to changes under way in the external environment,

The Key Points section at the end of each chapter provides a handy summary of essential ideas and things to remember.

Several short, mostly Internet-research-related exercises at the end of each chapter provide a supplement to assigned cases and a further way to reinforce core concepts.

Boards of directors have a duty to shareholders to play a vigilant oversight role in a company's strategy-making, strategy-executing process. They are obligated to (1) critically appraise and ultimately approve strategic action plans, (2) evaluate the strategic leadership skills of the CEO and others in line to succeed the incumbent CEO, (3) institute a compensation plan for top executives that rewards them for actions and results that serve stakeholder interests, most especially those of shareholders, and (4) ensure that the company issues accurate financial reports and has adequate financial controls.

Exercises

1. Go to www.redhat.com and check the company's latest financial reports to determine how well the company's business model is working. Is the company profitable? Is its revenue stream from selling technical support services growing or declining as a percentage of total revenues? Does your review of the company's financial performance suggest that its business model and strategy are changing?

2. Go to www.levistrauss.com/about/vision and read what Levi Strauss & Company says about how its corporate values of originality, empathy, integrity, and courage are connected to its vision of clothing the world. Do you buy what the company says, or are its statements just a bunch of nice pontifications that represent the personal values of the CEO (and make for good public relations)? Explain.

3. Go to the investors' section of www.heinz.com and read the letter to the shareholders in the company's fiscal 2003 annual report. Is the vision for Heinz that is articulated by Chairman and CEO William R. Johnson sufficiently clear and well defined? Why or why not? If you were a shareholder, would you be satisfied with what Johnson has told you about the company's direction, performance targets, and strategy? Now read Johnson's letter to the shareholders in Heinz's 2004 annual report. Do the results he cites change your mind about Johnson's vision for Heinz and the caliber of his strategy?

CASE 1

Whole Foods Market:
Mission, Core Values, and Strategy

Arthur A. Thompson
The University of Alabama

Founded in 1980 as a local supermarket for natural and health foods in Austin, Texas, Whole Foods Market had by 2005 evolved into the world's largest retail chain of natural and organic foods supermarkets. The company had 163 stores in the United States, Canada, and Great Britain and 2004 sales of $3.9 billion; revenues had grown at a compound annual rate of 20 percent since 1998. John Mackey, the company's cofounder and CEO, believed that Whole Foods' rapid growth and market success had much to do with its having "remained a uniquely mission-driven company—highly selective about what we sell, dedicated to our core values and stringent quality standards and committed to sustainable agriculture." The company's stated mission was to promote vitality and well-being for all individuals by offering "the highest qual... preserved foods." But as the company... Planet" implied, its core mission exten...

John Mackey's vision was for Wh... synonymous with natural and organic f... munity it served. In pursuit of this visio... ing its retail operations to offer the high... more customers and promoting organic... tainability of the entire ecosystem. Dur... been a leader in the natural and organic... ing the industry gain acceptance among... long-term objectives were to have 400...

The Natural and O...

The combined sales of natural and or... sented 5.5 percent of the roughly $775... *foods* are defined as foods that are min... artificial ingredients, preservatives, an... as near to their whole, natural state as... Food and Safety Inspection Service d... artificial ingredient or added color an...

CASE 3

Netflix in 2004
What Strategic Moves to Make Next?

Braxton Maddox
The University of Alabama

Netflix had a wild ride in 2004. Since... ing online DVD rental compan... numbers of subscribers and proved to skeptics that i... rentals could be very profitable. But the company's... downside—the online rental market was proving to... cess and growing reputation had induced both retail... leader Blockbuster Video to enter the DVD rental m... nanza. Amazon.com was expected to enter the DVD...

Reed Hastings, founder and CEO of Netflix, s... pany's six-month plummeting stock performance, s... analysts about the next strategic moves that Netfli... challenges of being a pioneer in a growing industry... Mart and Blockbuster had entered the competitive a... the single dominant player in the business. Hastin... pany was to survive competitive attack from Wal-Ma... to the short list of dot-com wonder businesses that n... With large competitors holding enough resources t... against Netflix, and with the ever-changing aspects c... dustry, Hastings was faced with the challenge of ho... determine the best ways to protect its industry-leadin... petition from strong rivals.

CASE 21

Globalizing Volkswagen
Creating Excellence on All Fronts

Z. Jan Kubes
International Institute for Management Development

George Rädler
International Institute for Management Development

Is there room for Volkswagen? As its market shrinks, Europe seems to have one car-maker too many. Could it be troubled Volkswagen? (...) The biggest danger is that with its problems at home and abroad, VW will have to abandon any notion of becoming a global car maker.

—*The Economist*, August 28, 1993: 59

No doubt about it: Volkswagen CEO Ferdinand Piëch engineered one of Europe's greatest turnarounds ever. The grandson of auto pioneer Ferdinand Porsche inherited a loss of more than $1 billion and declining market share in 1993. With a battery of new models, Piëch seized European market share from Ford Motor Company and General Motors Corp. Including its Audi, Skoda and Seat brands, VW now has almost 19 percent of Western European car sales, up from a low of 15 percent in 1994. Profits last year topped $1.2 billion on sales of $71.4 billion.

—*Business Week*, November 22, 1999: 20

When Dr. Ferdinand Piëch took over as CEO of the Volkswagen Group (VW) in early 1993, things did not look good: Customers complained about high prices, the main factory in Wolfsburg, Germany was only breaking even at utilization rates above 100 percent, and Japanese competitors enjoyed a cost advantage of up to €2,500 per car in their newly built plants in the UK. 1992 ended with profits down 85 percent.

The 32 cases detail the strategic circumstances of actual companies and provide practice in applying the concepts and tools of strategic analysis.

Case Organization
Part V: Cases in Crafting and Executing Strategy
Section A: Crafting Strategy in Single-Business Companies (21 cases)
Section B: Crafting Strategy in Diversified Companies (2 cases)
Section C: Implementing and Executing Strategy (7 cases)
Section D: Strategy, Ethics, and Social Responsibility (2 cases)

Student Support Materials

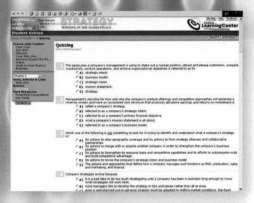

Web Site: www.mhhe.com/ thompson2E

The student portion of the Web site features the "Guide to Case Analysis," with special sections on what a case is, why cases are a standard part of courses in strategy, preparing a case for class discussion, doing a written case analysis, doing an oral presentation, and using financial ratio analysis to assess a company's financial condition. In addition, there are 20-question self-scoring chapter tests and a select number of PowerPoint slides for each chapter.

Case-TUTOR Software

Accompanying the 32 cases in the text is a software package containing assignment questions for all 32 cases, plus analytically structured exercises for 10 of the cases that coach students in doing the strategic thinking needed to arrive at solid answers to the assignment questions for those cases. Conscientious completion of the exercises helps students gain quicker command of the concepts and analytical techniques and points them toward doing good strategic analysis.

The *GLO-BUS* Online Simulation and the Online Edition of *The Business Strategy Game*

Either of these course supplements emotionally connects you to the subject matter of the course by having teams of students manage companies in a head-to-head contest for global market leadership. A simulation puts you in a situation where you and your co-managers have to make decisions relating to production operations, workforce compensation, pricing and marketing, and finance. It is your job to craft and execute a strategy for your company that is powerful enough to deliver good bottom-line performance despite the efforts of rival companies to take away your company's sales and market share. Each company competes in North America, Latin America, Europe-Africa, and Asia.

PowerWeb

With each new copy of this text, students gain access to the publisher's PowerWeb site offering current news, articles from 6,300 premium sources, a Web research guide, current readings from annual editions, and links to related sites.

Contents in Brief

Contents

5 Competing in Foreign Markets 158

6 Diversification: Strategies for Managing a Group of Businesses 190

7 Strategy, Ethics, and Social Responsibility 238

What Do We Mean by Business Ethics? 239

Where Do Ethical Standards Come From—Are They Universal or Dependent on Local Norms and Situational Circumstances? 239

The School of Ethical Universalism 240

The School of Ethical Relativism 240

Ethics and Integrative Social Contracts Theory 244

The Three Categories of Management Morality 246

Do Company Strategies Need to Be Ethical? 247

What Are the Drivers of Unethical Strategies and Business Behavior? 249

Part Four Executing the Strategy

8 Executing the Strategy: Building a Capable Organization and Instilling a Culture 272

9 Managing Internal Operations in Ways That Promote Good Strategy Execution 316

Part Five Cases in Crafting and Executing Strategy

STRATEGY

CHAPTER 1

What Is Strategy and Why Is It Important?

A strategy is a commitment to undertake one set of actions rather than another.

—*Sharon Oster, professor, Yale University*

Without a strategy the organization is like a ship without a rudder.

—*Joel Ross and Michael Kami*

Unless we change our direction we are likely to end up where we are headed.

—*Ancient Chinese proverb*

If you don't know where you are going, any road will take you there.

—*The Koran*

Management's job is not to see the company as it is . . . but as it can become.

—*John W. Teets, former CEO, Greyhound Corp.*

Managers

Managers at all companies must address and have timely answers to three central questions: What's the company's present situation? Where does the company need to go from here? How should it get there? The question *"What's the company's present situation?"* pushes managers to evaluate industry conditions and competitive pressures, the company's current performance and market standing, its resource strengths and capabilities, and its competitive weaknesses. The question *"Where does the company need to go from here?"* forces management to think strategically about the direction the company should be headed in order to grow the business and strengthen the company's market standing and financial performance. The question *"How should it get there?"* challenges managers to craft and execute a strategy to move the company down the chosen strategic path and achieve the targeted outcomes.

What Is Strategy?

A company's **strategy** is management's game plan for growing the business, staking out a market position, attracting and pleasing customers, competing successfully, conducting operations, and achieving targeted objectives. In crafting a strategy, management is in effect saying, "Among all the strategic paths we could have chosen and all the strategic actions we could have taken, we have decided to focus on these markets and customer needs, compete in this fashion, allocate our resources and energies in these ways, and use these particular approaches to doing business." A company's strategy thus indicates the choices its managers have made about the specific actions it is taking and plans to take in order to move the company in the intended direction and achieve the targeted outcomes. It is partly the result of trial-and-error organizational learning about what worked in the past and what didn't and partly the product of managerial analysis and strategic thinking about what actions need to be taken in light of all the circumstances surrounding the company's situation.

> **Core Concept**
>
> A company's **strategy** consists of the competitive moves and business approaches that managers employ to grow the business, stake out a market position, attract and please customers, compete successfully, conduct operations, and achieve targeted objectives.

In most industries companies have considerable strategic freedom in choosing the hows of strategy.[1] Thus some rivals strive to improve their performance and market standing by driving down costs, while others pursue product superiority or personalized customer service or development of competencies and capabilities that rivals cannot match. Some target the high end of the market, while others go after the middle or low end; some opt for wide product lines, while others concentrate their energies on a narrow product lineup. Some competitors position themselves in only one part of the industry's chain of production/distribution activities (preferring to be just in manufacturing or wholesale distribution or retailing), while others are partially or fully integrated, with operations ranging from components production to manufacturing and assembly to wholesale distribution or retailing. Some rivals deliberately confine their operations to local or regional markets; others opt to compete nationally, internationally (several countries), or globally (as many countries as possible). Some companies decide to operate in only one industry, while others diversify broadly or narrowly, into related or unrelated industries, via acquisitions, joint ventures, strategic alliances, or internal start-ups.

At companies intent on gaining sales and market share at the expense of competitors, managers lean toward mostly offensive strategies, frequently launching fresh initiatives of one kind or another to make the company's product offering more distinctive and appealing to buyers. Conservative, risk-avoiding companies prefer a sound defense to an aggressive offense; their strategies emphasize making gradual gains in the marketplace, fortifying the company's market position, and defending against the latest maneuvering of rivals and other developments that threaten the company's well-being.

There is no shortage of opportunity to fashion a strategy that tightly fits a company's own particular situation and that is discernibly different from the strategies of rivals. Carbon-copy strategies among companies in the same industry are the exception rather than the rule.

For a concrete example of the actions and approaches that comprise strategy, see Company Spotlight 1.1, describing Comcast's strategy to revolutionize the cable TV business.

Strategy and the Quest for Competitive Advantage

> **Core Concept**
>
> A company achieves sustainable competitive advantage when an attractive number of buyers prefer its products or services over the offerings of competitors and when the basis for this preference is durable.

Typically, the central thrust of a company's strategy involves crafting moves to strengthen the company's long-term competitive position and financial performance. Indeed, what separates a powerful strategy from an ordinary or weak one is management's ability to forge a series of moves, both in the marketplace and internally, that makes the company *distinctive*, tilts the playing field in the company's favor by giving buyers reason to prefer its products or services, and produces a *sustainable competitive advantage* over rivals. With a durable competitive advantage, a company has good prospects for winning in the marketplace and realizing above-average profitability. Without competitive advantage, a company risks being outcompeted by stronger rivals and/or locked into mediocre financial performance.

Four of the most frequently used strategic approaches to setting a company apart from rivals and achieving a sustainable competitive advantage are:

1. *Striving to be the industry's low-cost provider, thereby aiming for a cost-based competitive advantage over rivals.* Wal-Mart and Southwest Airlines have earned strong market positions because of the low-cost advantages they have achieved over their rivals and their consequent ability to underprice their competitors.

2. *Outcompeting rivals on the basis of such differentiating features as higher quality, wider product selection, added performance, better service, more attractive styling, technological superiority, or unusually good value for the money.* Successful adopters of differentiation strategies include Johnson & Johnson in baby products (product reliability), Harley-Davidson (bad-boy image and king-of-the-road styling), Chanel and Rolex (top-of-the-line prestige), Mercedes and BMW (engineering design and performance), L.L. Bean (good value), and Amazon.com (wide selection and convenience).

3. *Focusing on a narrow market niche and winning a competitive edge by doing a better job than rivals of serving the special needs and tastes of buyers constituting the niche.* Prominent companies that enjoy competitive success in a specialized market niche include eBay in online auctions, Jiffy Lube International in quick oil

COMPANY SPOTLIGHT 1.1

Comcast's Strategy to Revolutionize the Cable Industry

In 2004 cable TV giant Comcast was putting the finishing touches on a bold strategy to change the way people watched television and to grow its business by introducing Internet phone service. With revenues of $18 billion and almost 22 million of the 74 million U.S. cable subscribers, Comcast became the industry leader in the U.S. market in 2002 when it acquired AT&T Broadband and its 13 million cable subscribers for about $50 billion. Comcast's strategy in 2004 had the following elements:

- *Roll out a new video-on-demand service that would allow customers to watch TV programs whenever they wanted to watch them.* The service allowed customers to use their remotes to choose from a menu of thousands of programs, stored on Comcast's servers as they were first broadcast, and included network shows, news, sports, and movies; viewers had the ability to pause, stop, restart, and save programs, without having to remember to record them when they were broadcast. After only 18 months, Comcast had signed up close to 5 million of its subscribers for the service and it was introducing the service in additional geographic markets at a brisk pace.

- *Partner with Sony, MGM, and others to expand Comcast's library of movie offerings.* In 2004, Comcast agreed to develop new cable channels using MGM and Sony libraries, which had a combined 7,500 movies and 42,000 TV shows—it took about 300 movies to feed a 24-hour channel for a month.

- *Continue to roll out high-speed Internet or broadband service to customers via cable modems.* Comcast was already America's number-one provider of broadband service with about 6 million customers that generated revenues of $3 billion annually.

- *Use "voice-over-Internet-protocol" (VOIP) technology to offer subscribers Internet-based phone service at a fraction of the cost charged by other providers.* VOIP is an appealing low-cost technology that is widely seen as the most significant new communication technology since the invention of the telephone, with the capability to alter the world's $750 billion voice communications industry. Comcast was planning on a VOIP service with many snazzy features, including call forwarding, caller ID, and conferencing.

- *Use the video-on-demand and VOIP service offerings to differentiate Comcast's service offering and combat mounting competition from direct-to-home satellite TV providers.* Cable's two-way communications connection to homes enabled viewers to call up the programs they wanted with a few clicks of the remote; satellite TV had no such capability, nor did satellite providers yet have the capability to offer reliable high-speed Internet access. Satellite TV had been stealing customers away from cable TV because of its lower monthly fees—in the first six months of 2004, Direct TV and Echostar together added about 1.7 million new subscribers, whereas Comcast had lost 61,000 subscribers.

- *Employ a sales force (currently numbering about 3,200 people) to sell advertising to businesses that were shifting some of their advertising dollars from sponsoring network programs to sponsoring cable programs.* Ad sales generated revenues of $1.3 billion, and Comcast had cable operations in 21 of the 25 largest markets in the United States.

- *Significantly improve Comcast's customer service.* Almost all cable subscribers were dissatisfied with the caliber of customer service offered by their local cable companies. Comcast management believed that service would be a big issue given the need to support video on demand, cable modems, high-definition TV, phone service, Internet access, and the array of customer inquiries and problems such services entailed. In 2004, Comcast employed about 12,500 people to answer an expected volume of 200 million phone calls. Newly hired customer service personnel were given five weeks of classroom training, followed by three weeks of taking calls while a supervisor listened in—it cost Comcast about $7 to handle each call. The company's goal was to answer 90 percent of calls within 30 seconds.

Sources: Marc Gunter, "Comcast Wants to Change the World, but Can It Learn to Answer the Phone?" *Fortune*, October 16, 2004, pp. 140–156, and Stephanie N. Mehta, "The Future Is on the Line," *Fortune*, July 26, 2004, pp. 121–130. ©2004 TIME INC. Reprinted by permission.

changes, McAfee in virus protection software, Starbucks in premium coffees and coffee drinks, Whole Foods Market in natural and organic foods, and Krispy Kreme in doughnuts.

4. *Developing expertise and resource strengths that give the company competitive capabilities that rivals can't easily imitate or trump with capabilities of their own.* FedEx has superior capabilities in next-day delivery of small packages, Walt Disney has hard-to-beat capabilities in theme park management and family entertainment, and IBM has wide-ranging capabilities in helping corporate customers develop information systems and effectively utilize information technology.

In established industries, most companies recognize that winning a durable competitive edge over rivals hinges more on building competitively valuable expertise and capabilities than it does on having a distinctive product. Rivals can nearly always copy the attributes of a popular or innovative product, but for rivals to match experience, know-how, and specialized competitive capabilities that a company has developed and perfected over a long period of time is substantially harder to do and takes much longer—despite years of trying, discounters like Kmart and Target have struck out trying to match Wal-Mart's sophisticated distribution systems and its finely honed merchandising expertise. Company initiatives to build competencies and capabilities that rivals don't have and cannot readily match can relate to greater product innovation capabilities than rivals (3M Corporation), better mastery of a complex technological process (Michelin in making radial tires), expertise in defect-free manufacturing (Toyota and Honda), specialized marketing and merchandising know-how (Coca-Cola), global sales and distribution capability (Black & Decker in power tools), superior e-commerce capabilities (Dell Computer), unique ability to deliver personalized customer service (Ritz Carlton and Four Seasons hotels), or anything else that constitutes a competitively valuable strength in creating, producing, distributing, or marketing the company's product or service.

But there's also another way to achieve a dramatic and durable competitive advantage: by abandoning efforts to beat out competitors in existing markets and, instead, inventing a new industry or distinctive market segment that makes existing competitors largely irrelevant and allows a company to create and capture altogether new demand.[2] To understand this approach a bit better, think of the business universe as consisting of two distinct types of market space. In one, industry boundaries are defined and accepted, the competitive rules of the game are well understood by all industry members, and companies try to outperform rivals by capturing a bigger share of existing demand; in such markets, lively competition constrains a company's prospects for rapid growth and superior profitability since rivals move quickly to either imitate or counter the successes of competitors. In the other type of market space, the industry does not really exist yet, is untainted by competition, and offers wide-open opportunity for profitable and rapid growth if a company can come up with a product offering and strategy that allows it to create new demand rather than fight over existing demand. A terrific example of the latter is eBay's creation and domination of the online auction industry. Another example is Cirque du Soleil, which has increased its revenues by 22 times during the 1993–2003 period in the circus business, an industry that has been in long-term decline for 20 years. How did Cirque du Soleil pull this off against long-time industry leader Ringling Bros. and Barnum & Bailey? By "reinventing the circus," creating a distinctively different market space for its performances (Las Vegas nightclubs and theater-type settings), and pulling in a whole new group of customers—adults and corporate clients—who were noncustomers of traditional circuses and were willing to pay several times more than the price of a conventional circus ticket to have an "entertainment experience" featuring sophisticated clowns and star-quality acrobatic acts in a comfortable, tentlike atmosphere—Cirque studiously avoided the use of animals because of costs and concerns over the treatment of circus animals; Cirque's market research led management to conclude that the lasting allure of the traditional circus came down to just three factors: the clowns, classic acrobatic acts, and a tentlike stage. As of 2004, Cirque du Soleil had nine different touring shows (each with its own theme and story line) running on three continents, was performing before audiences of about 7 million people annually, and had performed 250 engagements in 90 cities before 40 million spectators since its formation in 1984. Other examples of companies that have achieved competitive advantages by creating new market spaces include AMC via its pioneering of megaplex movie theaters, IBM with its invention of the business computer industry in the 1950s, CNN and The Weather Channel in cable TV, Home Depot in "big-box" retailing of hardware and building supplies, and FedEx in overnight package delivery. Companies that create new market spaces can usually sustain their initially won competitive advantage without encountering major competitive challenge for 10 to 15 years because of barriers to imitation and the strong brand-name awareness that their strategies produce.

Identifying a Company's Strategy

A company's strategy is reflected in its actions in the marketplace and the statements of senior managers about the company's current business approaches, future plans, and efforts to strengthen its competitiveness and performance. Figure 1.1 shows what to look for in identifying the substance of a company's overall strategy.

Once it is clear what to look for, the task of identifying a company's strategy is mainly one of researching information about the company's actions in the marketplace and its business approaches. In the case of publicly owned enterprises, the strategy is often openly discussed by senior executives in the company's annual report and 10-K report, in press releases and company news (posted on the company's Web site), and in the information provided to investors at the company's Web site. To maintain the confidence of investors and Wall Street, most public companies have to be fairly open about their strategies. Company executives typically lay out key elements of their strategies in presentations to securities analysts (such presentations are usually posted in the investor relations section of the company's Web site). Hence, except for some about-to-be-launched moves and changes that remain under wraps and in the planning stage, there's usually nothing secret or undiscoverable about what a company's present strategy is.

Strategy Is Partly Proactive and Partly Reactive

A company's strategy is typically a blend of (1) proactive actions on the part of managers to improve the company's market position and financial performance and (2) as-needed reactions to unanticipated developments and fresh market conditions—see Figure 1.2.[3] The biggest portion of a company's current strategy flows from previously initiated actions and business approaches that are working well enough to merit continuation and newly launched managerial initiatives to strengthen the company's overall position and performance. This part of management's game plan is deliberate and proactive, standing as the product of management's analysis and strategic thinking

Figure 1.1   Identifying a Company's Strategy—What to Look For

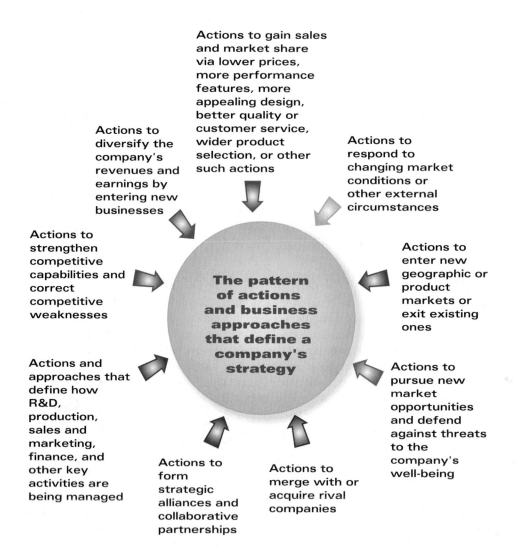

Actions to gain sales and market share via lower prices, more performance features, more appealing design, better quality or customer service, wider product selection, or other such actions

Actions to diversify the company's revenues and earnings by entering new businesses

Actions to respond to changing market conditions or other external circumstances

Actions to strengthen competitive capabilities and correct competitive weaknesses

Actions to enter new geographic or product markets or exit existing ones

The pattern of actions and business approaches that define a company's strategy

Actions and approaches that define how R&D, production, sales and marketing, finance, and other key activities are being managed

Actions to pursue new market opportunities and defend against threats to the company's well-being

Actions to form strategic alliances and collaborative partnerships

Actions to merge with or acquire rival companies

about the company's situation and its conclusions about how to position the company in the marketplace and compete for buyer patronage.

But not every strategic move is the result of proactive plotting and deliberate management design. Things happen that cannot be fully anticipated or planned for. When market and competitive conditions take an unexpected turn or certain aspects of a company's strategy hit a stone wall, some kind of strategic reaction or adjustment is required. Hence, a portion of a company's strategy is always developed on the fly, coming as a reasoned response to fresh strategic maneuvers on the part of rival firms, shifting customer requirements and expectations, new technologies and market opportunities, a changing political or economic climate, or other unanticipated happenings in the surrounding environment. But apart from adapting strategy to changing conditions, there is also a need to adapt strategy as new learning emerges about which pieces

Figure 1.2   A Company's Actual Strategy Is Partly Proactive and Partly Reactive

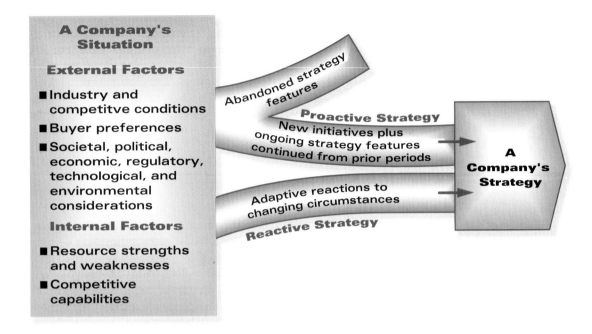

of the strategy are working well and which aren't and as management hits upon new ideas for improving the strategy. Crafting a strategy thus involves stitching together a *proactive/intended strategy* and then adapting first one piece and then another as circumstances surrounding the company's situation change or better options emerge—which results in same portion of the overall strategy being *reactive/adaptive*. In short, a company's actual strategy is something managers shape and reshape as circumstances dictate and as managers learn from experience what has worked well enough to continue and what needs to be changed.

A Company's Strategy Evolves over Time   A company's strategy should always be viewed as a work in progress. Most of the time a company's strategy evolves incrementally from management's ongoing efforts to fine-tune this or that piece of the strategy and to adjust certain strategy elements in response to unfolding events. On occasion, fine-tuning the existing strategy is not enough and major strategy shifts are called for, such as when a strategy is clearly failing and the company faces a financial crisis, when market conditions or buyer preferences change significantly and new opportunities arise, when competitors do something unexpected, or when important technological breakthroughs occur. Some industries are more volatile than others. Industry environments characterized by *high-velocity change* require companies to rapidly adapt their strategies.[4] For example, in high-technology industries and industries where buyer demand moves up and down very quickly, companies find it essential to revise demand forecasts, adjust key elements of their strategies, and update their financial projections every few months.

> **Core Concept**
>
> Changing circumstances and ongoing management efforts to improve the strategy cause a company's strategy to evolve over time—a condition that makes the task of crafting a strategy a work in progress, not a one-time event.

Regardless of whether a company's strategy changes gradually or swiftly, the important point is that a company's present strategy is always temporary and on trial, pending new ideas for improvement from management, changes in industry conditions, and any other new developments that management believes warrant strategic adjustments. Thus, a company's strategy at any given point is fluid, representing the temporary outcome of an ongoing process that, on the one hand, involves reasoned and intuitive management efforts to craft an effective strategy and, on the other hand, involves ongoing responses to market change and constant experimentation and tinkering. Adapting to new conditions and constantly learning what is working well enough to continue and what needs to be improved is consequently a normal part of the strategy-making process and results in an evolving strategy.

> A company's strategy is shaped partly by management analysis and choice and partly by the necessity of adapting and learning by doing.

Strategy and Ethics: Passing the Test of Moral Scrutiny

In choosing among strategic alternatives, company managers are well advised to embrace actions that are aboveboard and can pass the test of moral scrutiny. Just keeping a company's strategic actions within the bounds of what is legal does not make them ethical. Ethical and moral standards are not governed by what is legal. Rather, they involve issues of "right" versus "wrong" and *duty*—what one *should* do. A strategy is ethical only if it does not entail actions and behaviors that cross the line from "should do" to "should not do" (because such actions are "unsavory" or unconscionable, injurious to other people, or unnecessarily harmful to the environment).

Core Concept

> A strategy cannot be considered ethical just because it involves actions that are legal. To meet the standard of being ethical, a strategy must entail actions that can pass moral scrutiny and that are aboveboard in the sense of not being shady or unconscionable, injurious to others, or unnecessarily harmful to the environment.

Admittedly, it is not always easy to categorize a given strategic behavior as definitely ethical or definitely unethical; many strategic actions fall in a gray zone in between. Whether they are deemed ethical or unethical hinges on how high one sets the bar. For example, is it ethical for advertisers of alcoholic products to place ads in media having an audience of as much as 50 percent underage viewers? (In 2003, growing concerns about underage drinking prompted some beer and distilled-spirits companies to agree to place ads in media with an audience at least 70 percent adult, up from a standard of 50 percent adult.) Is it ethical for an apparel retailer attempting to keep prices attractively low to source clothing from foreign manufacturers that pay substandard wages, utilize child labor, or engage in unsavory sweatshop practices? Many people would say no, but some might argue that a company is not unethical simply because it does not police the business practices of its suppliers. Is it ethical for pharmaceutical manufacturers to charge higher prices for life-saving drugs in some countries than they charge in others? (This is a fairly common practice that has recently come under scrutiny because it raises the costs of health care for consumers who are charged higher prices.) Is it ethical for a pharmaceutical company to downplay issues about the safety of a best-selling drug until more conclusive studies are done (which is apparently what Merck did before it decided to recall Vioxx, which had been taken by some 80 million people)? Is it ethical for a company to turn a blind eye to the damage its operations do to the environment even though they are in compliance with current environmental regulations—especially if it has the know-how and the means to prevent such damage by utilizing different technologies or operating practices?

Senior executives with strong ethical convictions are generally proactive in linking strategic action and ethics; they forbid the pursuit of ethically questionable business opportunities and insist that all aspects of company strategy reflect high ethical standards.[5] They make it clear that all company personnel are expected to act with integrity, and they put organizational checks and balances into place to monitor behavior, enforce ethical codes of conduct, and provide guidance to employees regarding any gray areas. Their commitment to conducting the company's business in an ethical manner is genuine, not hypocritical lip service.

Recent instances of corporate malfeasance, ethical lapses, and fraudulent accounting practices at Enron, WorldCom, Tyco, Adelphia, HealthSouth, and other companies leave no room to doubt the damage to a company's reputation and business that can result from ethical misconduct, corporate misdeeds, and even criminal behavior on the part of company personnel. Aside from just the embarrassment and black marks that accompany headline exposure of a company's unethical practices, the hard fact is that many customers and many suppliers are wary of doing business with a company that engages in sleazy practices or that turns a blind eye to illegal or unethical behavior on the part of employees. They are turned off by unethical strategies or behavior, and rather than become victims or get burned themselves, wary customers will quickly take their business elsewhere and wary suppliers will tread carefully. Moreover, employees with character and integrity do not want to work for a company whose strategies are shady or whose executives lack character and integrity. There's little lasting benefit to unethical strategies and behavior, and the downside risks can be substantial. Besides, such actions are plain wrong.

The Relationship between a Company's Strategy and Its Business Model

Closely related to the concept of strategy is the concept of a company's **business model.** While the word *model* conjures up images of ivory-tower ideas that may be loosely connected to the real world, such images do not apply here. A company's business model sets forth the economic logic of how an enterprise's strategy can deliver value to customers at a price and cost that yields acceptable profitability.[6]

> **Core Concept**
>
> A company's **business model** deals with how and why the revenues and costs flowing from its strategy will result in attractive profits and return on investment. Without the ability to deliver profitability, the strategy is not viable and the survival of the business is in doubt.

A company's business model thus is management's story line for how and why the company's product offerings and competitive approaches will generate a revenue stream and have an associated cost structure that produces attractive earnings and return on investment. The nitty-gritty issue surrounding a company's business model is whether the chosen strategy makes good business sense from a money-making perspective. The concept of a company's business model is, consequently, more narrowly focused than the concept of a company's business strategy. A company's strategy *relates broadly to its competitive initiatives and business approaches (irrespective of the financial outcomes it produces),* while a company's business model *deals with how and why the revenues and costs flowing from the strategy will result in attractive profits and return on investment*—without the ability to deliver good profits, the strategy and the business are not viable. Companies that have been in business for a while and are making acceptable profits have a "proven" business model—because there is hard evidence that their strategies are capable of profitability and that they are viable business enterprises. Companies that are in a start-up mode or that are losing money have a "questionable" business model; their current strategies have yet to produce good bottom-line results, putting their story line about how they intend to make money and their viability as business enterprises in doubt. Company Spotlight 1.2 discusses the contrasting business models of Microsoft and Red Hat Linux.

What Makes a Strategy a Winner?

Core Concept

A winning strategy must fit the enterprise's external and internal situations, build sustainable competitive advantage, and improve company performance.

Three questions can be used to test the merits of one strategy versus another and distinguish a winning strategy from a losing or mediocre strategy:

1. *How well does the strategy fit the company's situation?* To qualify as a winner, a strategy has to be well matched to industry and competitive conditions, a company's best market opportunities, and other aspects of the enterprise's external environment. At the same time, it has to be tailored to the company's resource strengths and weaknesses, competencies, and competitive capabilities. Unless a strategy exhibits tight fit with both the external and the internal aspects of a company's overall situation, it is likely to produce less than the best possible business results.

2. *Is the strategy helping the company achieve a sustainable competitive advantage?* Winning strategies enable a company to achieve a competitive advantage that is durable. The bigger and more durable the competitive edge that a strategy helps build, the more powerful and appealing the strategy is.

3. *Is the strategy resulting in better company performance?* A winning strategy boosts company performance. Two kinds of performance improvements tell the most about the caliber of a company's strategy: (1) gains in profitability and financial strength and (2) gains in the company's competitive strength and market standing.

speech), and, in some cases, because they are anti-Microsoft and want to have a part in undoing what they see as a Microsoft monopoly.

- Collect and test enhancements and new applications submitted by the open-source community of volunteer programmers. Linux's originator, Linus Torvalds, and a team of more than 300 Red Hat engineers and software developers evaluate which incoming submissions merit inclusion in new releases of Red Hat Linux—the evaluation and integration of new submissions are Red Hat's only up-front product development costs.

- Market the upgraded and tested family of Red Hat Linux products to large enterprises and charge them a subscription fee that includes a limited number of days of service, support, and patches. Provide subscribers with updated versions of Red Hat Linux every 12 to 18 months.

- Make the source code open and available to all users, allowing them to create a customized version of Linux.

- Capitalize on the specialized expertise required to use Linux in multiserver, multiprocessor applications by providing fee-based training, consulting, support, engineering, and content management

services to Red Hat Linux users. Red Hat offers Linux certification training programs at all skill levels at more than 60 global locations—Red Hat certification in the use of Linux is considered the best in the world.

Microsoft's business model—sell proprietary code software and give service away free—is a proven moneymaker that generates billions in profits annually. On the other hand, the jury is still out on Red Hat's business model of selling subscriptions to open-source software to large corporations and depending heavily on sales of technical support services, training, and consulting to generate revenues sufficient to cover costs and yield a profit. Red Hat posted losses of $140 million on revenues of $79 million in fiscal year 2002 and losses of $6.6 million on revenues of $91 million in fiscal year 2003, but it earned $14 million on revenues of $126 million in fiscal 2004. And the profits came from a shift in Red Hat's business model that involved putting considerably more emphasis on selling subscriptions to the latest Red Hat Linux updates to large enterprises.

Source: Company documents and information posted on their Web sites.

Once a company commits to a particular strategy and enough time elapses to assess how well it fits the situation and whether it is actually delivering competitive advantage and better performance, the company can determine what grade to assign its strategy. Strategies that come up short on one or more of the above questions are plainly less appealing than strategies passing all three test questions with flying colors. Managers can use the same questions to pick and choose among alternative strategic actions. A company determining which of several strategic options to employ can evaluate how well each option measures up against each of the three questions. The strategic option with the highest prospective passing scores on all three questions can be regarded as the best or most attractive strategic alternative.

Other criteria for judging the merits of a particular strategy include internal consistency and unity among all the pieces of the strategy, the degree of risk the strategy poses as compared to alternative strategies, and the degree to which it is flexible and adaptable to changing circumstances. These criteria are relevant and merit consideration, but they seldom override the importance of the three test questions posed above.

What Does the Strategy-Making, Strategy-Executing Process Entail?

The managerial process of crafting and executing a company's strategy consists of five interrelated and integrated phases:

1. *Developing a strategic vision* of where the company needs to head and what its future product-customer-market-technology focus should be.

Figure 1.3   The Strategy-Making, Strategy-Executing Process

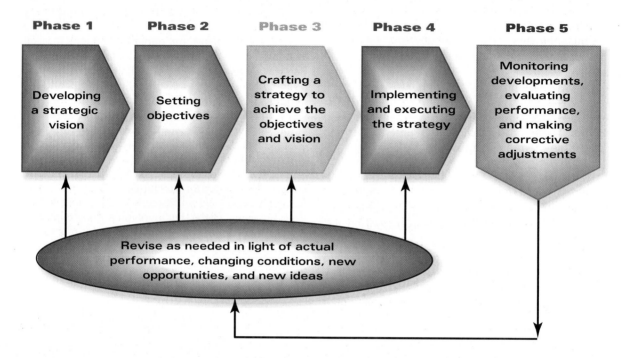

2. *Setting objectives* and using them as yardsticks for measuring the company's performance and progress.

3. *Crafting a strategy to achieve the objectives* and move the company along the strategic course that management has charted.

4. *Implementing and executing the chosen strategy efficiently and effectively.*

5. *Evaluating performance and initiating corrective adjustments* in the company's long-term direction, objectives, strategy, or execution in light of actual experience, changing conditions, new ideas, and new opportunities.

Figure 1.3 displays this five-task process. Let's examine each task in enough detail to set the stage for the forthcoming chapters and give you a bird's-eye view of what this book is about.

Developing a Strategic Vision: Phase 1 of the Strategy-Making, Strategy-Executing Process

Very early in the strategy-making process, a company's senior managers must wrestle with the issue of what directional path the company should take and what changes in the company's product-market-customer-technology focus would improve its current market position and future prospects. Deciding to commit the company to one path versus another pushes managers to draw some carefully reasoned conclusions about how to try to modify the company's business makeup and the market position it should

Table 1.1   FACTORS TO CONSIDER IN DECIDING TO COMMIT THE COMPANY TO ONE DIRECTIONAL PATH VERSUS ANOTHER

External Considerations	Internal Considerations
▪ Is the outlook for the company promising if it simply maintains its present product-market-customer-technology focus—does sticking with the company's present strategic course present attractive growth opportunities?	▪ What are our ambitions for the company—what industry standing do we want the company to have?
▪ Are changes that are under way in the market and competitive landscape acting to enhance or weaken the outlook for the company's present business?	▪ Will our present business generate sufficient growth and profitability in the years ahead to please shareholders?
▪ What, if any, new customer groups and/or geographic markets should the company get in position to serve?	▪ What organizational strengths ought we be trying to leverage in terms of adding new products/services and/or getting into new businesses?
▪ Which emerging market opportunities should the company pursue, and which ones should not be pursued?	▪ Is the company stretching its resources too thinly by trying to compete in too many markets or segments, some of which are unprofitable?
▪ Should we plan to abandon any of the markets, market segments, or customer groups we are currently serving?	▪ Is the company's technological focus too broad or too narrow? Are any changes needed?

stake out. A number of direction-shaping factors need to be considered in deciding where to head and why such a direction makes good business sense—see Table 1.1.

Top management's views and conclusions about the company's direction and future product-customer-market-technology focus constitute a **strategic vision** for the company. A strategic vision delineates management's aspirations for the business, providing a panoramic view of "where we are going" and a convincing rationale for why this makes good business sense for the company. A strategic vision thus points an organization in a particular direction, charts a strategic path for it to follow in preparing for the future, and molds organizational identity. A clearly articulated strategic vision communicates management's aspirations to stakeholders and helps steer the energies of company personnel in a common direction. For instance, Henry Ford's vision of a car in every garage had power because it captured the imagination of others, aided internal efforts to mobilize the Ford Motor Company's resources, and served as a reference point for gauging the merits of the company's strategic actions.

> **Core Concept**
>
> A **strategic vision** describes the route a company intends to take in developing and strengthening its business. It paints a picture of a company's destination and provides a rationale for going there.

Well-conceived visions are distinctive and specific to a particular organization; they avoid generic, feel-good statements like "We will become a global leader and the first choice of customers in every market we choose to serve"—which could apply to any of hundreds of organizations.[7] And they are not the product of a committee charged with coming up with an innocuous but well-meaning one-sentence vision that wins consensus approval from various stakeholders. Nicely worded vision statements with no specifics about the company's product-market-customer-technology focus are suspect. A strategic vision proclaiming management's quest "to be the market leader" or "to be the first choice of customers" or "to be the most innovative" or "to be recognized as the best company in the industry" offers scant guidance about a company's direction and what management intends to do to get there.

For a strategic vision to function as a valuable managerial tool, it must provide understanding of what management wants the company's business to look like and provide managers with a reference point in making strategic decisions and preparing the company for the future. It must say something definitive about how the company's leaders

Table 1.2   CHARACTERISTICS OF AN EFFECTIVELY-WORDED VISION STATEMENT

Graphic: Paints a picture of the kind of company that management is trying to create and the market position the company is striving to stake out.

Directional: Says something about the company's journey or destination and signals the kinds of business and strategic changes that will be forthcoming.

Focused: Is specific enough to provide managers with guidance in making decisions and allocating resources.

Flexible: Is not a once and for all time statement—visions about a company's future state and directional path may need to change as events unfold and circumstances change.

Feasible: Is within the realm of what the company can reasonably expect to achieve in due time.

Desirable: Appeals to the long-term interests of stakeholders—particularly shareowners, employees, and customers.

Easy to communicate: Is explainable in 5 to 10 minutes and, ideally, can be reduced to a simple, memorable "slogan" (like Henry Ford's famous vision of "a car in every garage").

Source: Based partly on John P. Kotter, *Leading Change* (Boston: Harvard Business School Press, 1996), p. 72, and Hugh Davidson, *The Committed Enterprise* (Oxford: Butterworth Heinemann, 2002), Chapters 1 and 2.

Table 1.3   COMMON SHORTCOMINGS IN COMPANY VISION STATEMENTS

1. Vague or incomplete—short on specifics about where the company is headed, what kind of company management is trying to create, and whether or how management intends to alter the company's current product-market-customer-technology focus.
2. Bland or lacking in motivational power.
3. Not distinctive—could apply to almost any company (or at least several others in the same industry).
4. Too reliant on such superlatives as *best, most successful, recognized leader, global* or *worldwide leader,* or *first choice of customers.*
5. Fails to identify what business or industry the vision applies to—the vision is so generic that it could apply to companies in any of several industries.
6. So broad that it doesn't rule out almost any opportunity that management might opt to pursue.

Source: Adapted from Hugh Davidson, *The Committed Enterprise* (Oxford: Butterworth Heinemann, 2002), Chapter 2, and Michel Robert, *Strategy Pure and Simple II* (New York: McGraw-Hill, 1998), Chapters 2, 3, and 6.

intend to position the company beyond where it is today. A good vision always needs to be a bit beyond a company's reach, but progress toward the vision is what unifies the efforts of company personnel. Table 1.2 lists some characteristics of an effective vision statement.

A sampling of vision statements currently in use shows a range from strong and clear to overly general and generic. A surprising number of the vision statements found on company Web sites and in annual reports are vague and unrevealing—some are nice-sounding but say little, others read like something written by a committee and worded to win the support of different stakeholders, and some are so generic and short on specifics as to apply to almost any company in any industry. Many read like a public relations statement—high-sounding words that someone came up with because it is fashionable for companies to have an official vision statement.[8] Table 1.3 provides a list of the most common shortcomings in company vision statements. The one- or two-sentence vision statements most companies make available to the public, of course, provide only a glimpse of what company executives are really thinking and the strategic course they have charted—company personnel nearly always have a much better understanding of the ins and outs of where the company is headed and why than is revealed in the official vision statement. But the real purpose of a vision statement is to serve as a management tool for giving the organization a sense of direction. Like any tool, it can be used properly or improperly, either clearly conveying a company's strategic course or not doing so.

Company Spotlight 1.3 provides examples of strategic visions of several prominent companies and nonprofit organizations. See if you can tell which ones are mostly meaningless or nice-sounding and which ones are managerially useful in communicating "where we are headed and the kind of company we are trying to become."

A Strategic Vision Is Different from a Mission Statement

Whereas the chief concern of a strategic vision is "where we are going and why," a company mission statement usually deals with a company's *present* business scope and purpose—"who we are, what we do, and why we are here." *A company's mission is defined by the buyer needs it seeks to satisfy, the customer groups and market segments it is endeavoring to serve, and the resources and technologies it is deploying in trying to please its customers.* (Many companies prefer the term *business purpose* to *mission statement,* but the two phrases are essentially conceptually identical and are used interchangeably.) A typical example is the mission statement of Trader Joe's (a unique grocery chain):

> The mission of Trader Joe's is to give our customers the best food and beverage values that they can find anywhere and to provide them with the information required for informed buying decisions. We provide these with a dedication to the highest quality of customer satisfaction delivered with a sense of warmth, friendliness, fun, individual pride, and company spirit.

> The distinction between a strategic vision and a mission statement is fairly clear-cut: A *strategic vision* portrays a company's future business scope ("where we are going") whereas a company's *mission* typically describes its present business scope and purpose ("who we are, what we do, and why we are here").

The mission statements that one finds in company annual reports or on company Web sites typically provide a brief overview of the company's present business purpose and raison d'être and sometimes its geographic coverage or standing as a market leader. They may or may not single out the company's present products/services, the buyer needs it is seeking to satisfy, the customer groups it serves, or its technological and business capabilities. But rarely do company mission statements say anything about where the company is headed, the anticipated changes in its business, or its aspirations; hence they lack the essential quality of a strategic vision in defining a company's future product-customer-market-technology focus.

Occasionally, companies couch their mission in terms of making a profit. This is misguided. Profit is more correctly an *objective* and a *result* of what a company does. Moreover, earning a profit is the obvious intent of every commercial enterprise. Such companies as BMW, Google, Caterpillar, Nintendo, and Nokia are each striving to earn a profit for shareholders; but plainly the fundamentals of their business are substantially different when it comes to "who we are and what we do." It is management's answer to "make a profit doing what and for whom?" that reveals a company's true substance and business purpose. A well-conceived mission statement distinguishes a company's business makeup from that of other profit-seeking enterprises in language specific enough to give the company its own identity.

Communicating the Strategic Vision

Effectively communicating the strategic vision down the line to lower-level managers and employees is as important as the strategic soundness of the long-term direction top management has chosen. People have a need to believe that senior management knows where it's trying to take the company and is planning for what changes lie ahead both externally and internally. Unless frontline employees understand why the strategic course that management has charted is reasonable and beneficial, they are unlikely to unite behind managerial efforts to get the organization moving in the intended direction.

> **Core Concept**
> An effectively communicated vision is a valuable management tool for enlisting the commitment of company personnel to actions that get the company moving in the intended direction.

Winning the support of organization members for the vision nearly always means putting "where we are going and why" in writing, distributing the statement organizationwide, and having executives personally explain the vision and its rationale to as many people as feasible. Ideally, executives should present their vision for the company in a manner that reaches out and grabs people. An engaging and convincing strategic vision has enormous motivational value—for the same reason that a stonemason is more inspired by building a great cathedral for the ages than by simply laying stones to create floors and walls. When managers articulate a vivid and compelling case for where the company is headed, organization members begin to say, "This is interesting and has a lot of merit. I want to be involved and do my part to help make it happen." The more that a vision evokes positive support and excitement, the greater its impact in terms of arousing a committed organizational effort and getting people to move in a common direction.[9] Thus executive ability to paint a convincing and inspiring picture of a company journey and destination is an important element of effective strategic leadership.

Expressing the Essence of the Vision in a Slogan   The task of effectively conveying the vision to company personnel is assisted when management can capture the vision of where to head in a catchy or easily remembered slogan. A number of organizations have summed up their vision in a brief phrase:

- *Levi Strauss & Company:* "We will clothe the world by marketing the most appealing and widely worn casual clothing in the world."
- *Nike:* "To bring innovation and inspiration to every athlete in the world."
- *Mayo Clinic:* "The best care to every patient every day."
- *Scotland Yard:* "To make London the safest major city in the world."
- *Greenpeace:* "To halt environmental abuse and promote environmental solutions."
- *Charles Schwab:* "To provide customers with the most useful and ethical financial services in the world."

> Strategic visions become real only when the vision statement is imprinted in the minds of organization members and then translated into hard objectives and strategies.

Creating a short slogan to illuminate an organization's direction and purpose and then using it repeatedly as a reminder of "where we are headed and why" helps rally organization members to hurdle whatever obstacles lie in the company's path and to maintain their focus.

Linking the Vision with Company Values

In the course of deciding "who we are and where we are going," many companies also come up with a statement of values to guide the company's pursuit of its vision. By *values,* we mean the beliefs, business principles, and ways of doing things that govern company operations and the behavior of organization members. Values, good and bad, exist in every organization. They relate to such things as fairness, integrity, ethics, innovativeness, teamwork, quality, customer service, social responsibility, and community citizenship. Company value statements tend to contain between four and eight values, which, ideally, are tightly connected to and reinforce the company's vision, strategy, and operating practices. Home Depot embraces eight values (entrepreneurial spirit, excellent customer service, giving back to the community, respect for all people, doing the

> **Core Concept**
>
> A company's *values* are the beliefs, business principles, and practices that guide the conduct of its business, the pursuit of its strategic vision, and the behavior of company personnel.

right thing, taking care of people, building strong relationships, and creating shareholder value) in its quest to become the world's largest home improvement retailer by operating warehouse stores filled with a wide assortment of products at the lowest prices and staffed with trained associates giving absolutely the best customer service in the industry. Du Pont stresses four values—safety, ethics, respect for people, and environmental stewardship; the first three have been in place since the company was founded 200 years ago by the Du Pont family. Loblaw, a major grocery chain in

Canada, focuses on just two main values in operating its stores—competence and honesty; it expects employees to display both, and top management strives to promote only those employees who are smart and honest. At Johnson & Johnson, the two core values are teamwork and manufacturing the highest-quality products.

Company managers connect values to the strategic vision in one of two ways. In companies with long-standing and deeply entrenched values, managers go to great lengths to explain how the vision matches the company's values, sometimes reinterpreting the meaning of existing values to indicate their relevance to the strategic vision. In new companies or companies having weak or incomplete sets of values, top management considers what values, beliefs, and operating principles will help drive the vision forward. Then new values that fit the vision are drafted and circulated among managers and employees for discussion and possible modification. A final value statement that connects to the vision and that reflects the beliefs and principles the company wants to uphold is then officially adopted. Some companies combine their vision and values into a single statement or document provided to all organization members and often posted on the company's Web site.

Of course, a wide gap sometimes opens between a company's stated values and its business practices. Enron, for example, touted its four corporate values—respect, integrity, communication, and excellence—but some top officials did not behave in accordance with those values and the $100 billion high-profile company imploded in late 2000 when executive failure to "walk the talk" was exposed. Once one of the world's Big Five public accounting firms, Arthur Andersen was renowned for its commitment to the highest standards of audit integrity, but its audit failures at Enron, WorldCom, and other companies led to Andersen's rapid demise.

Setting Objectives: Phase 2 of the Strategy-Making, Strategy-Executing Process

The managerial purpose of setting **objectives** is to convert the strategic vision into specific performance targets—results and outcomes the company's management wants to achieve—and then use these objectives as yardsticks for tracking the company's progress and performance. Well-stated objectives are *quantifiable,* or *measurable,* and contain a *deadline for achievement.* As Bill Hewlett, cofounder of Hewlett-Packard, shrewdly observed, "You cannot manage what you cannot measure. . . . And what gets measured gets done."[10] The experiences of countless companies and managers teach that precisely spelling out *how much* of *what kind* of performance *by when* and then pressing forward with actions and incentives calculated to help achieve the targeted outcomes greatly improve a company's actual performance. It definitely beats setting vague targets like "maximize profits," "reduce costs," "become more efficient," or "increase sales," which specify neither how much nor when, or exhorting company personnel to try hard to do the best they can and then living with whatever results they deliver.

Ideally, managers ought to use the objective-setting exercise as a tool for *stretching an organization to reach its full potential.* Challenging company personnel to go all out and deliver big gains in performance pushes an enterprise to be more inventive, to

Core Concept

Objectives are an organization's performance targets—the results and outcomes management wants to achieve. They function as yardsticks for measuring how well the organization is doing.

exhibit some urgency in improving both its financial performance and its business position, and to be more intentional and focused in its actions. *Stretch objectives* spur exceptional performance and help build a firewall against contentment with slow, incremental improvements in organizational performance. As Mitchell Leibovitz, former CEO of the auto parts and service retailer Pep Boys, once said, "If you want to have ho-hum results, have ho-hum objectives."

What Kinds of Objectives to Set— The Need for a Balanced Scorecard

> **Core Concept**
>
> *Financial objectives* relate to the financial performance targets management has established for the organization to achieve. *Strategic objectives* relate to target outcomes that indicate a company is strengthening its market standing, competitive vitality, and future business prospects.

Two very distinct types of performance yardsticks are required: those relating to *financial performance* (outcomes relating to profitability, creditworthiness, and shareholder well-being) and those relating to *strategic performance* (outcomes that indicate a company is strengthening its marketing standing, competitive vitality, and future business prospects). Examples of commonly used financial and strategic objectives include the following:

Financial Objectives

- An *x* percent increase in annual revenues
- Annual increases in after-tax profits of *x* percent
- Annual increases in earnings per share of *x* percent
- Annual dividend increases
- Larger profit margins
- An *x* percent return on capital employed (ROCE) or shareholder investment (ROE)
- Increased shareholder value—in the form of an upward-trending stock price and annual dividend increases
- Strong bond and credit ratings
- Sufficient internal cash flows to fund new capital investment
- Stable earnings during periods of recession

Strategic Objectives

- Winning an *x* percent market share
- Achieving lower overall costs than rivals
- Overtaking key competitors on product performance or quality or customer service
- Deriving *x* percent of revenues from the sale of new products introduced within the past five years
- Achieving technological leadership
- Having better product selection than rivals
- Strengthening the company's brand-name appeal
- Having stronger national or global sales and distribution capabilities than rivals
- Consistently getting new or improved products to market ahead of rivals

Achieving acceptable financial results is a must. Without adequate profitability and financial strength, a company's pursuit of its strategic vision, as well as its long-term health and ultimate survival, is jeopardized. Further, subpar earnings and a weak balance sheet alarm shareholders and creditors and put the jobs of senior executives at risk. But good financial performance, by itself, is not enough. Of equal or greater importance is a company's strategic performance—outcomes that indicate whether a company's market position and competitiveness are deteriorating, holding steady, or improving.

The Case for a Balanced Scorecard: Improved Strategic Performance Fosters Better Financial Performance

A company's financial performance measures are really *lagging indicators* that reflect the results of past decisions and organizational activities. But a company's past or current financial performance is not a reliable indicator of its future prospects—poor financial performers often turn things around and do better, while good financial performers can fall upon hard times. The best and most reliable *leading indicators* of a company's future financial performance and business prospects are strategic outcomes that indicate whether the company's competitiveness and market position are stronger or weaker. For instance, if a company has set aggressive strategic objectives and is achieving them—such that its competitive strength and market position are on the rise—then there's reason to expect that its *future* financial performance will be better than its current or past performance. If a company is losing ground to competitors and its market position is slipping—outcomes that reflect weak strategic performance (and, very likely, failure to achieve its strategic objectives)—then its ability to maintain its present profitability is highly suspect. Hence the degree to which a company's managers set, pursue, and achieve stretch strategic objectives tends to be a reliable leading indicator of its ability to generate higher profits from business operations.

> **Core Concept**
>
> A company that pursues and achieves strategic outcomes that boost its competitiveness and strength in the marketplace is in a much better position to improve its future financial performance.

Thus, a balanced scorecard for measuring company performance—one that includes both financial objectives and strategic objectives—is essential. Just setting financial objectives overlooks the fact that what ultimately enables a company to deliver better financial results from its operations is the achievement of strategic objectives that improve its competitiveness and market strength. Indeed, *the surest path to boosting company profitability quarter after quarter and year after year is to relentlessly pursue strategic outcomes that strengthen the company's market position and produce a growing competitive advantage over rivals.*

Company Spotlight 1.4 shows selected objectives of several prominent companies.

Both Short-Term and Long-Term Objectives Are Needed

As a rule, a company's set of financial and strategic objectives ought to include both near-term and longer-term performance targets. Having quarterly or annual objectives focuses attention on delivering immediate performance improvements. Targets to be achieved within three to five years prompt considerations of what to do *now* to put the company in position to perform better later. If trade-offs have to be made between achieving long-run objectives and achieving short-run objectives, the long-run objectives should generally take precedence. A company rarely prospers from repeated management actions that put better short-term performance ahead of better long-run performance.

The Concept of Strategic Intent

A company's objectives sometimes play another role: Very ambitious or aggressive objectives often signal **strategic intent** to stake out a particular business position and be a winner in the marketplace, often against long odds.[11] A company's strategic intent can entail becoming the recognized industry leader, unseating the existing industry leader, delivering the best customer service of any company in the industry (or the world), or turning a new technology into products capable of changing the way people work and live. Nike's strategic intent during the 1960s was to overtake Adidas (which connected nicely with Nike's core purpose "to experience the emotion of competition, winning, and crushing competitors"). Canon's strategic intent in

> **Core Concept**
>
> A company exhibits **strategic intent** when it relentlessly pursues an ambitious strategic objective, concentrating the full force of its resources and competitive actions on achieving that objective.

COMPANY SPOTLIGHT 1.4
Examples of Company Objectives

Nissan
(Strategic and Financial Objectives)

Increase sales to 4.2 million cars and trucks by 2008 (up from 3 million in 2003); cut purchasing costs 20 percent and halve the number of suppliers; have zero net debt; maintain a return on invested capital of 20 percent; maintain a 10 percent or better operating margin.

The Kroger Company
(Strategic and Financial Objectives)

Narrow the retail price gap with major discounters (like Wal-Mart) and widen the price advantage over traditional supermarket competitors. Use one-third of the company's cash flow for debt reduction and two-thirds for stock repurchase and dividend payments. Reduce operating and administrative costs by $500 million; leverage Kroger's $51 billion size to achieve greater economies of scale; and grow earnings per share by 13 to 15 percent annually starting in 2004.

DuPont
(Financial and Strategic Objectives)

To achieve annual revenue growth of 5 to 6 percent and annual earnings-per-share growth averaging 10 percent. Grow per-share profits faster than revenues by (a) increasing productivity, (b) selling enough new products each year that average prices and average margins rise, and (c) using surplus cash to buy back shares. Sell the company's low-margin textiles and interiors division (with sales of $6.6 billion and operating profits of only $114 million); this division makes Lycra and other synthetic fibers for carpets and clothes.

Heinz
(Financial and Strategic Objectives)

Achieve earnings per share in the range of $2.15 to $2.25 in 2004; increase operating cash flow by 45 percent to $750 million; reduce net debt by $1.3 billion in 2003 and further strengthen the company's balance sheet in 2004; continue to introduce new and improved food products; remove the clutter in company product offerings by reducing the number of SKUs (stock-keeping units); increase spending on trade promotion and advertising by $200 million to strengthen the recognition and market shares of the company's core brands; and divest noncore underperforming product lines.

Seagate Technology
(Strategic Objectives)

Solidify the company's number-one position in the overall market for hard-disk drives; get more Seagate drives into popular consumer electronics products (i.e., video recorders); take share away from Western Digital in providing disk drives for Microsoft's Xbox; and capture a 10 percent share of the market for 2.5-inch hard drives for notebook computers by 2004.

3M Corporation
(Financial and Strategic Objectives)

To achieve long-term sales growth of 5 to 8 percent organic plus 2 to 4 percent from acquisitions; annual growth in earnings per share of 10 percent or better, on average; a return on stockholders' equity of 20 to 25 percent; a return on capital employed of 27 percent or better; to double the number of qualified new 3M product ideas and triple the value of products that win in the marketplace; to have at least 30 percent of sales come from products introduced in the past four years; and to build the best sales and marketing organization in the world.

Source: Company documents; *Business Week,* July 28, 2003, p. 106; *Business Week,* September 8, 2003, p. 108.

copying equipment was to "beat Xerox." For some years, Toyota has been driving to overtake General Motors as the world's largest motor vehicle producer (and it surpassed Ford Motor Company in total vehicles sold in 2003, to move into second place); Toyota has expressed its strategic intent in the form of a global market share objective of 15 percent by 2010, up from 5 percent in 1980 and 10 percent in 2003. Starbucks strategic intent is to make the Starbucks brand the world's most recognized and respected brand. Ambitious companies almost invariably begin with strategic intents that are out of proportion to their immediate capabilities and market positions. But they set aggressive stretch objectives and pursue them relentlessly, sometimes even obsessively. Capably managed, up-and-coming enterprises with strategic intents exceeding their present reach and resources often prove to be more formidable competitors over time than larger, cash-rich rivals with modest market ambitions.

The Need for Objectives at All Organizational Levels Objective setting should not stop with top management's establishing of companywide performance targets. Company objectives need to be broken down into performance targets for each of the organization's separate businesses, product lines, functional departments, and individual work units. Company performance can't reach full potential unless each area of the organization does its part and contributes directly to the desired companywide outcomes and results. This means setting performance targets for each organizational unit that support—rather than conflict with or negate—the achievement of companywide strategic and financial objectives.

The ideal situation is a team effort in which each organizational unit strives to produce results in its area of responsibility that contribute to the achievement of the company's performance targets and strategic vision. Such consistency signals that organizational units know their strategic role and are on board in helping the company move down the chosen strategic path and produce the desired results.

Crafting a Strategy: Phase 3 of the Strategy-Making, Strategy-Executing Process

The task of stitching a strategy together entails addressing a series of hows: *how* to grow the business, *how* to please customers, *how* to outcompete rivals, *how* to respond to changing market conditions, *how* to manage each functional piece of the business and develop needed organizational capabilities, *how* to achieve strategic and financial objectives. It also means exercising astute entrepreneurship—proactively searching for opportunities to do new things or to do existing things in new or better ways.[12] The faster a company's business environment is changing, the more critical the need for its managers to be good entrepreneurs in diagnosing the direction and force of the changes under way and in responding with timely adjustments in strategy. Strategy makers have to pay attention to early warnings of future change and be willing to experiment with dare-to-be-different ways to establish a market position in that future. When obstacles unexpectedly appear in a company's path, it is up to management to adapt rapidly and innovatively. *Masterful strategies come partly (maybe mostly) by doing things differently from competitors where it counts—outinnovating them, being more efficient, being more imaginative, adapting faster—rather than running with the herd.* Good strategy making is therefore inseparable from good business entrepreneurship. One cannot exist without the other.

Who Participates in Crafting a Company's Strategy?

A company's senior executives obviously have important strategy-making roles. The chief executive officer (CEO), as captain of the ship, carries the mantles of chief direction setter, chief objective setter, chief strategy maker, and chief strategy implementer for the total enterprise. Ultimate responsibility for *leading* the strategy-making, strategy-executing process rests with the CEO. In some enterprises the CEO or owner functions as strategic visionary and chief architect of strategy, personally deciding which of several strategic options to pursue, although others may well assist with data gathering and analysis and the CEO may seek the advice of other senior managers and key employees on which way to go. Such an approach to strategy development is characteristic of small owner-managed companies and sometimes large corporations that have been founded by the present CEO or that have strong CEOs—Meg Whitman at eBay, Andrea Jung at Avon, Jeffrey Immelt at General Electric, and Howard Schultz at Starbucks are prominent examples of corporate CEOs who maintain a heavy hand in shaping their company's strategy.

In most companies, however, the heads of business divisions and major product lines, the chief financial officer, and vice presidents for production, marketing, human resources, and other functional departments have influential strategy-making roles. Normally, a company's chief financial officer is in charge of devising and implementing an appropriate financial strategy; the production vice president takes the lead in developing and executing the company's production strategy; the marketing vice president orchestrates sales and marketing strategy; a brand manager is in charge of the strategy for a particular brand in the company's product lineup; and so on.

But it is a mistake to view strategy making as exclusively a top-management function, the province of owner-entrepreneurs, CEOs, and other senior executives. The more wide-ranging a company's operations are, the more that strategy making is a collaborative team effort involving managers (and sometimes key employees) down through the whole organizational hierarchy. Take a company like Toshiba—a $43 billion corporation with 300 subsidiaries, thousands of products, and operations extending across the world. It would be a far-fetched error to assume that a few senior executives in Toshiba headquarters have either the expertise or a sufficiently detailed understanding of all the relevant factors to wisely craft all the strategic initiatives taken in Toshiba's numerous and diverse organizational units. Rather, it takes involvement on the part of Toshiba's whole management team to craft and execute the thousands of strategic initiatives that constitute the whole of Toshiba's strategy.

> **Core Concept**
>
> Every company manager has a role in the strategy-making, strategy-executing process; it is flawed thinking to view crafting and executing strategy as something only high-level managers do.

Major organizational units in a company—business divisions, product groups, functional departments, plants, geographic offices, distribution centers—normally have a leading or supporting role in the company's strategic game plan. Because senior executives in the corporate office seldom know enough about the situation in every geographic area and operating unit to direct every strategic move made in the field, it is common practice for top-level managers to delegate strategy-making authority to middle- and lower-echelon managers who head the organizational subunits where specific strategic results must be achieved. The more that a company's operations cut across different products, industries, and geographic areas, the more that headquarters executives are prone to delegate considerable strategy-making authority to on-the-scene personnel who have firsthand knowledge of customer requirements, can better evaluate market opportunities, and are better able to keep the strategy responsive to changing market and competitive conditions. While managers further down in the managerial hierarchy obviously have a narrower, more specific strategy-making, strategy-executing role than managers closer to the top, the important understanding here is that in most of today's companies *every company manager typically has a strategy-making, strategy-executing role—ranging from minor to major—for the area he or she heads.* Hence any notion that an organization's strategists are at the top of the management hierarchy and that mid-level and frontline personnel merely carry out the strategic directives of senior managers needs to be cast aside.

With decentralized decision making becoming common at companies of all stripes, it is now typical for key pieces of a company's strategy to originate in a company's middle and lower ranks.[13] In some companies, top management makes a regular practice of encouraging individuals and teams to develop and champion proposals for new product lines and new business ventures. The idea is to unleash the talents and energies of promising "corporate intrapreneurs," letting them try out untested business ideas and giving them the room to pursue new strategic initiatives. Executives judge which proposals merit support, give the chosen intrapreneurs the organizational and budgetary support they need, and let them run with the ball. Thus important pieces of company strategy can originate with those intrapreneurial individuals and teams who succeed in championing a proposal through the approval stage and then end up being charged with the lead role in launching new products, overseeing the company's entry into new geographic markets, or heading up new business ventures. W. L. Gore and Associates, a privately owned company famous for its Gore-Tex waterproofing film, is an avid and highly successful practitioner of the corporate intrapreneur approach to strategy making. Gore expects all employees to initiate improvements and to display innovativeness. Each employee's intrapreneurial contributions are prime considerations in determining raises, stock option bonuses, and promotions. W. L. Gore's commitment to intrapreneurship has produced a stream of product innovations and new strategic initiatives that has kept the company vibrant and growing for nearly two decades.

A Company's Strategy-Making Hierarchy

It thus follows that *a company's overall strategy is a collection of strategic initiatives and actions* devised by managers and key employees up and down the whole organizational hierarchy. The larger and more diverse the operations of an enterprise, the more points of strategic initiative it has and the more managers and employees at more levels of management there are who have a relevant strategy-making role. Figure 1.4 shows who is generally responsible for devising what pieces of a company's overall strategy.

In diversified, multibusiness companies where the strategies of several different businesses have to be managed, the strategy-making task involves four distinct types or levels of strategy, each of which involves different facets of the company's overall strategy:

1. *Corporate strategy* consists of the kinds of initiatives the company uses to establish business positions in different industries, the approaches corporate executives pursue to boost the combined performance of the set of businesses the company has diversified into, and the means of capturing cross-business synergies and turning them into competitive advantage. Senior corporate executives normally have lead responsibility for devising corporate strategy and for choosing among whatever recommended actions bubble up from the organization below. Key business-unit heads may also be influential, especially in strategic decisions affecting the businesses they head. Major strategic decisions are usually reviewed and approved by the company's board of directors. We will look deeper into the strategy-making process at diversified companies when we get to Chapter 6.

Figure 1.4   A Company's Strategy-Making Hierarchy

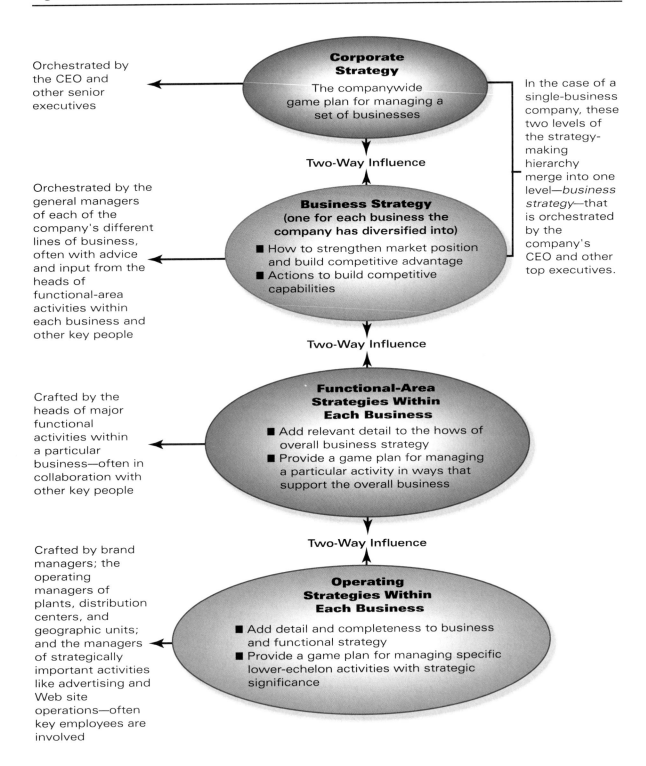

2. *Business strategy* concerns the actions and the approaches crafted to produce successful performance in one specific line of business. The key focus is crafting responses to changing market circumstances and initiating actions to strengthen market position, build competitive advantage, and develop strong competitive capabilities. Orchestrating the development of business-level strategy is the responsibility of the manager in charge of the business. The business head has at least two other strategy-related roles: (1) seeing that lower-level strategies are well conceived, consistent, and adequately matched to the overall business strategy, and (2) getting major business-level strategic moves approved by corporate-level officers (and sometimes the board of directors) and keeping them informed of emerging strategic issues. In diversified companies, business-unit heads may have the additional obligation of making sure business-level objectives and strategy conform to corporate-level objectives and strategy themes.

3. *Functional-area strategies* concern the actions, approaches, and practices to be employed in managing particular functions or business processes or key activities within a business. A company's marketing strategy, for example, represents the managerial game plan for running the sales and marketing part of the business. A company's product development strategy represents the managerial game plan for keeping the company's product lineup fresh and in tune with what buyers are looking for. Functional strategies add specifics to the hows of business-level strategy. Plus, they aim at establishing or strengthening a business unit's competencies and capabilities in performing strategy-critical activities so as to enhance the business's market position and standing with customers. The primary role of a functional strategy is to *support* the company's overall business strategy and competitive approach.

   Lead responsibility for functional strategies within a business is normally delegated to the heads of the respective functions, with the general manager of the business having final approval and perhaps even exerting a strong influence over the content of particular pieces of the strategies. To some extent, functional managers have to collaborate and coordinate their strategy-making efforts to avoid uncoordinated or conflicting strategies. For the overall business strategy to have maximum impact, a business's marketing strategy, production strategy, finance strategy, customer service strategy, product development strategy, and human resources strategy should be compatible and mutually reinforcing rather than each serving its own narrower purposes. If inconsistent functional-area strategies are sent up the line for final approval, the business head is responsible for spotting the conflicts and getting them resolved.

4. *Operating strategies* concern the relatively narrow strategic initiatives and approaches for managing key operating units (plants, distribution centers, geographic units) and specific operating activities with strategic significance (advertising campaigns, the management of specific brands, supply chain–related activities, and Web site sales and operations). A plant manager needs a strategy for accomplishing the plant's objectives, carrying out the plant's part of the company's overall manufacturing game plan, and dealing with any strategy-related problems that exist at the plant. A company's advertising manager needs a strategy for getting maximum audience exposure and sales impact from the ad budget. Operating strategies, while of limited scope, add further detail and completeness to functional strategies and to the overall business strategy. Lead responsibility for

operating strategies is usually delegated to frontline managers, subject to review and approval by higher-ranking managers.

Even though operating strategy is at the bottom of the strategy-making hierarchy, its importance should not be downplayed. A major plant that fails in its strategy to achieve production volume, unit cost, and quality targets can undercut the achievement of company sales and profit objectives and wreak havoc with strategic efforts to build a quality image with customers. Frontline managers are thus an important part of an organization's strategy-making team because many operating units have strategy-critical performance targets and need to have strategic action plans in place to achieve them. One cannot reliably judge the strategic importance of a given action simply by the strategy level or location within the managerial hierarchy where it is initiated.

In single-business enterprises, the corporate and business levels of strategy making merge into one level—business strategy—because the strategy for the whole company involves only one distinct line of business. Thus a single-business enterprise has three levels of strategy: business strategy for the company as a whole, functional-area strategies for each main area within the business, and operating strategies undertaken by lower-echelon managers to flesh out strategically significant aspects for the company's business and functional-area strategies. Proprietorships, partnerships, and owner-managed enterprises may have only one or two strategy-making levels since their strategy-making, strategy-executing process can be handled by just a few key people.

Uniting the Strategy-Making Effort   Ideally, the pieces of a company's strategy should fit together like a jigsaw puzzle. To achieve such unity, the strategizing process must generally proceed from the corporate level to the business level and then from the business level to the functional and operating levels. *Mid-level and frontline managers cannot do good strategy making without understanding the company's long-term direction and higher-level strategies.* The strategic disarray that occurs in an organization when senior managers don't exercise strong top-down direction setting and set forth a clearly articulated companywide strategy is akin

> **Core Concept**
> A company's strategy is at full power only when its many pieces are united.

to what would happen to a football team's offensive performance if the quarterback decided not to call a play for the team but instead let each player pick whatever play he thought would work best at his respective position. In business, as in sports, all the strategy makers in a company are on the same team, and the many different pieces of the overall strategy crafted at various organizational levels need to be in sync and united. Anything less than a unified collection of strategies weakens company performance.

Achieving unity is partly a function of communicating the company's basic strategy themes effectively across the organization and establishing clear strategic principles and guidelines for lower-level strategy making. Cohesive strategy making becomes easier to achieve when company strategy is distilled into pithy, easy-to-grasp terminology that can be used to drive consistent strategic action down through the hierarchy.[14] The greater the numbers of company personnel who know, understand, and buy into the company's basic direction and strategy, the smaller the risk that people and organization units will go off in conflicting strategic directions when decision making is pushed down to frontline levels and many people are given strategy-making, strategy-executing roles. Good communication of long-term direction and higher-level strategic themes thus serves a valuable strategy-unifying purpose.

Merging the Strategic Vision, Objectives, and Strategy into a Strategic Plan

Developing a strategic vision and mission, setting objectives, and crafting a strategy are basic direction-setting tasks. They map out where a company is headed, its short-range and long-range performance targets, and the competitive moves and internal action approaches to be used in achieving the targeted business results. Together, they constitute a **strategic plan** for coping with industry and competitive conditions, the expected actions of the industry's key players, and the challenges and issues that stand as obstacles to the company's success.[15]

> **Core Concept**
>
> A company's **strategic plan** lays out its future direction, performance targets, and strategy.

In companies committed to regular strategy reviews and the development of explicit strategic plans, the strategic plan may take the form of a written document that is circulated to most managers and perhaps selected employees. In small, privately owned companies, strategic plans usually take the form of oral understandings and commitments among managers and key employees about where to head, what to accomplish, and how to proceed. Near-term performance targets are the part of the strategic plan most often spelled out explicitly and communicated to managers and employees. A number of companies summarize key elements of their strategic plans in the company's annual report to shareholders, in postings on their Web site, or in statements provided to the business media, whereas others, perhaps for reasons of competitive sensitivity, make only vague, general statements about their strategic plans.

Implementing and Executing the Strategy: Phase 4 of the Strategy-Making, Strategy-Executing Process

Managing the implementation and execution of strategy is an operations-oriented, make-things-happen activity aimed at shaping the performance of core business activities in a strategy-supportive manner. It is easily the most demanding and time-consuming part of the strategy management process. Converting strategic plans into actions and results tests a manager's ability to direct organizational change, motivate people, build and strengthen company competencies and competitive capabilities, create a strategy-supportive work climate, and meet or beat performance targets. Initiatives have to be launched and managed on many organizational fronts.

Management's action agenda for implementing and executing the chosen strategy emerges from assessing what the company will have to do differently or better, given its particular operating practices and organizational circumstances, to execute the strategy proficiently and achieve the targeted performance. Each company manager has to think through the answer to "What has to be done in my area to execute my piece of the strategic plan, and what actions should I take to get the process under way?" How much internal change is needed depends on how much of the strategy is new, how far internal practices and competencies deviate from what the strategy requires, and how well the present work climate/culture supports good strategy execution. Depending on the amount of internal change involved, full implementation and proficient execution of company strategy (or important new pieces thereof) can take several months to several years.

In most situations, managing the strategy execution process includes the following principal aspects:

- Staffing the organization with the needed skills and expertise, consciously building and strengthening strategy-supportive competencies and competitive capabilities, and organizing the work effort.

- Creating a company culture and work climate conducive to successful strategy implementation and execution.

- Developing budgets that steer ample resources into those activities critical to strategic success.

- Ensuring that policies and operating procedures facilitate rather than impede effective execution.

- Using the best-known practices to perform core business activities and pushing for continuous improvement. Organizational units have to periodically reassess how things are being done and diligently pursue useful changes and improvements.

- Installing information and operating systems that enable company personnel to better carry out their strategic roles day in and day out.

- Motivating people to pursue the target objectives energetically and, if need be, modifying their duties and job behavior to better fit the requirements of successful strategy execution.

- Tying rewards and incentives directly to the achievement of performance objectives and good strategy execution.

- Exerting the internal leadership needed to drive implementation forward and keep improving on how the strategy is being executed. When stumbling blocks or weaknesses are encountered, management has to see that they are addressed and rectified on a timely basis.

Good strategy execution requires creating strong fits between strategy and organizational capabilities, between strategy and the organization's work climate and culture, between strategy and the reward structure, and between strategy and internal operating systems. The stronger these fits—that is, the more that the company's capabilities, culture, reward structure, and internal operating systems facilitate and promote proficient strategy execution—the better the execution and the higher the company's odds of achieving its performance targets. Furthermore, deliberately shaping the performance of core business activities around the strategy helps unite the organization.

Evaluating Performance and Initiating Corrective Adjustments: Phase 5 of the Strategy-Making, Strategy-Executing Process

The fifth phase of the strategy management process—evaluating the company's progress, assessing the impact of new external developments, and making corrective adjustments—is the trigger point for deciding whether to continue or change the company's vision, objectives, strategy, and/or strategy execution methods. As long as the company's direction and strategy seem well matched to industry and competitive conditions and performance targets are being met, company executives may well decide to stay the course. Simply fine-tuning the strategic plan and continuing with efforts to improve strategy execution are sufficient.

But whenever a company encounters disruptive changes in its environment, questions need to be raised about the appropriateness of its direction and strategy. If a company experiences a downturn in its market position or shortfalls in performance, then company managers are obligated to ferret out the causes—do they relate to poor strategy, poor strategy execution, or both?—and take timely corrective action. A company's direction, objectives, and strategy have to be revisited anytime external or internal conditions warrant. It is to be expected that a company will modify its strategic vision, direction, objectives, and strategy over time.

> **Core Concept**
>
> A company's vision, objectives, strategy, and approach to strategy execution are never final; managing strategy is an ongoing process, not an every-now-and-then task.

Likewise, it is not unusual for a company to find that one or more aspects of its strategy implementation and execution are not going as well as intended. Proficient strategy execution is always the product of much organizational learning. It is achieved unevenly—coming quickly in some areas and proving nettlesome in others. It is both normal and desirable to periodically assess strategy execution to determine which aspects are working well and which need improving. Successful strategy execution entails vigilantly searching for ways to improve and then making corrective adjustments whenever and wherever it is useful to do so.

Corporate Governance: The Role of the Board of Directors in the Strategy-Making, Strategy-Executing Process

Although senior managers have *lead responsibility* for crafting and executing a company's strategy, it is the duty of the board of directors to exercise strong oversight and see that the five tasks of strategic management are done in a manner that benefits shareholders (in the case of investor-owned enterprises) or stakeholders (in the case of not-for-profit organizations). In watching over management's strategy-making, strategy-executing actions and making sure that executive actions are not only proper but also aligned with the interests of stakeholders, the members of a company's board of directors have four important obligations to fulfill:

1. *Be inquiring critics and oversee the company's direction, strategy, and business approaches.* Board members must ask probing questions and draw on their business acumen to make independent judgments about whether strategy proposals have been adequately analyzed and whether proposed strategic actions appear to have greater promise than alternatives. If executive management is bringing well-supported and reasoned strategy proposals to the board, there's little reason for board members to aggressively challenge and try to pick apart everything put before them. Asking incisive questions is usually sufficient to test whether the case for management's proposals is compelling and to exercise vigilant oversight. However, when the company's strategy is failing or is plagued with faulty execution, and certainly when there is a precipitous collapse in profitability, board members have a duty to be proactive, expressing their concerns about the validity of the strategy and/or operating methods, initiating debate about the company's strategic path, having one-on-one discussions with key executives and other board

members, and perhaps directly intervening as a group to alter the company's executive leadership and, ultimately, its strategy and business approaches.

2. *Evaluate the caliber of senior executives' strategy-making and strategy-executing skills.* The board is always responsible for determining whether the current CEO is doing a good job of strategic leadership (as a basis for awarding salary increases and bonuses and deciding on retention or removal). Boards must also exercise due diligence in evaluating the strategic leadership skills of other senior executives in line to succeed the CEO. When the incumbent CEO steps down or leaves for a position elsewhere, the board must elect a successor, either going with an insider or deciding that an outsider is needed to perhaps radically change the company's strategic course.

3. *Institute a compensation plan for top executives that rewards them for actions and results that serve stakeholder interests, most especially those of shareholders.* A basic principle of corporate governance is that the owners of a corporation delegate operating authority and managerial control to top management in return for compensation. In their role as *agents* of shareholders, top executives have a clear and unequivocal duty to make decisions and operate the company in accord with shareholder interests (but this does not mean disregarding the interests of other stakeholders, particularly those of employees, with whom they also have an agency relationship). Most boards of directors have a compensation committee, composed entirely of outside directors, to develop a salary and incentive compensation plan that motivates executives to operate the business in a manner that benefits the owners; the compensation committee's recommendations are presented to the full board for approval. But in addition to creating compensation plans intended to align executive actions with owner interests, it is incumbent on the board of directors to put a halt to self-serving executive perks and privileges that simply enrich the personal welfare of executives. Numerous media reports have recounted instances in which boards of directors have gone along with opportunistic executive efforts to secure excessive, if not downright obscene, compensation of one kind or another (multimillion-dollar interest-free loans, personal use of corporate aircraft, excessive severance and retirement packages, outsized stock incentive awards, and so on).

4. *Oversee the company's financial accounting and financial reporting practices.* While top management, particularly the company's CEO and CFO (chief financial officer), is primarily responsible for seeing that the company's financial statements fairly and accurately report the results of the company's operations, it is well established that board members have a fiduciary duty to protect shareholders by exercising oversight of the company's financial practices, ensuring that generally accepted accounting principles are properly used in preparing the company's financial statements, and determining whether proper financial controls are in place to prevent fraud and misuse of funds. Virtually all boards of directors monitor the financial reporting activities by appointing an audit committee, always composed entirely of outside directors. The members of the audit committee have lead responsibility for overseeing the company's financial officers and consulting with both internal and external auditors to ensure accurate financial reporting and adequate financial controls.

Every corporation should have a strong, independent board of directors that (1) is well-informed about the company's performance, (2) guides and judges the CEO and other top executives, (3) has the courage to curb management actions it believes are inappropriate or unduly risky, (4) certifies to shareholders that the CEO is doing what the board expects, (5) provides insight and advice to management, and (6) is intensely involved in debating the pros and cons of key decisions and actions.[16] Boards of directors that lack the backbone to challenge a strong-willed or "imperial" CEO or that rubber-stamp almost anything the CEO recommends without probing inquiry and debate (perhaps because the board is stacked with the CEO's cronies) abdicate their duty to represent and protect shareholder interests. The whole fabric of effective corporate governance is undermined when boards of directors shirk their responsibility to maintain ultimate control over the company's strategic direction, the major elements of its strategy, the business approaches management is using to implement and execute the strategy, executive compensation, and the financial reporting process. Boards of directors thus have a very important oversight role in the strategy-making, strategy-executing process even though *lead responsibility* for crafting and executing strategy falls to top executives.

The number of prominent companies that have fallen on hard times because of the actions of scurrilous or out-of-control CEOs and CFOs, the growing propensity of disgruntled stockholders to file lawsuits alleging director negligence, and the escalating costs of liability insurance for directors all underscore the responsibility that a board of directors has for overseeing a company's strategy-making, strategy-executing process and ensuring that management actions are proper and responsible. Moreover, holders of large blocks of shares (mutual funds and pension funds), regulatory authorities, and the financial press consistently urge that board members, especially outside directors, be active and diligent in their oversight of company strategy and maintain a tight rein on executive actions.

Why Crafting and Executing Strategy Are Important Tasks

Crafting and executing strategy are top-priority managerial tasks for two very big reasons. First, there is a compelling need for managers to *proactively shape*, or *craft*, how the company's business will be conducted. A clear and reasoned strategy is management's prescription for doing business, its road map to competitive advantage, its game plan for pleasing customers and achieving performance targets. Winning in the marketplace requires implementing a well-conceived, opportunistic strategy, usually one characterized by strategic offensives to outinnovate and outmaneuver rivals and secure sustainable competitive advantage, and then using this market edge to achieve superior financial performance. A powerful strategy that delivers a home run in the marketplace can propel a firm from a trailing position into one of leadership, often making the firm's products/services the industry standard. High-achieving enterprises are nearly always the product of shrewd strategy making—companies don't get to the top of the industry rankings or stay there with strategies built around timid efforts to do better. And only a handful of companies can boast of strategies that hit home runs in the marketplace due to lucky breaks or the good fortune of having stumbled into the right market at the right time with the right product. So there can be little argument that the caliber of a company's strategy matters—and matters a lot.

Second, a *strategy-focused organization* is more likely to be a strong bottom-line performer than an organization that views strategy as secondary and puts its priorities elsewhere. The quality of managerial strategy making and strategy execution has a highly positive impact on earnings, cash flow, and return on investment. A company that lacks clear-cut direction, has vague or undemanding performance targets, has a muddled or flawed strategy, or can't seem to execute its strategy competently is a company whose financial performance is probably suffering, whose business is at long-term risk, and whose management is sorely lacking. On the other hand, when the five phases of the strategy-making, strategy-executing process drive management's whole approach to managing the company, the odds are much greater that the initiatives and activities of different divisions, departments, managers, and work groups will be unified into a *coordinated, cohesive effort*. Mobilizing the full complement of company resources in a total team effort behind good execution of the chosen strategy and achievement of the targeted performance allows a company to operate at full power. The chief executive officer of one successful company put it well when he said:

> In the main, our competitors are acquainted with the same fundamental concepts and techniques and approaches that we follow, and they are as free to pursue them as we are. More often than not, the difference between their level of success and ours lies in the relative thoroughness and self-discipline with which we and they develop and execute our strategies for the future.

Good Strategy + Good Strategy Execution = Good Management

Crafting and executing strategy are thus core management functions. Among all the things managers do, nothing affects a company's ultimate success or failure more fundamentally than how well its management team charts the company's direction, develops competitively effective strategic moves and business approaches, and pursues what needs to be done internally to produce good day-in, day-out strategy execution. Indeed, *good strategy and good strategy execution are the most trustworthy signs of good management.* Managers don't deserve a gold star for designing a potentially brilliant strategy but failing to put the organizational means in place to carry it out in high-caliber fashion—weak implementation and execution undermine the strategy's potential and pave the way for shortfalls in customer satisfaction and company performance. Competent execution of a mediocre strategy scarcely merits enthusiastic applause for management's efforts either. The rationale for using the twin standards of good strategy making and good strategy execution to determine whether a company is well managed is therefore compelling: *The better conceived a company's strategy and the more competently it is executed, the more likely that the company will be a standout performer in the marketplace.*

Core Concept

Excellent execution of an excellent strategy is the best test of managerial excellence—and the most reliable recipe for turning companies into standout performers.

Throughout the text chapters to come and the accompanying case collection, the spotlight is trained on the foremost question in running a business enterprise: What must managers do, and do well, to make a company a winner in the marketplace? The answer that emerges, and that becomes the message of this book, is that doing a good job of managing inherently requires good strategic thinking and good management of the strategy-making, strategy-executing process.

The mission of this book is to explore what "good strategic thinking" entails, to present the core concepts and tools of strategic analysis, to describe the ins and outs of crafting and executing strategy, and, through the cases that are included, to help you build your skills both in diagnosing how well the five aspects of managing strategy are being performed in actual companies and in making analysis-based recommendations for improvement. At the very least, we hope to convince you that capabilities in crafting and executing strategy are basic to managing successfully and have a prominent place in a manager's toolkit.

As you tackle the following pages, ponder an observation made by Ralph Waldo Emerson: "Commerce is a game of skill which many people play, but which few play well." If the content of this book helps you become a more savvy player and better equips you to succeed in business, then your journey through the following pages will indeed be time well spent.

Key Points

The tasks of crafting and executing company strategies are the heart and soul of managing a business enterprise and winning in the marketplace. A company's strategy consists of the competitive moves and business approaches that management is using to grow the business, stake out a market position, attract and please customers, compete successfully, conduct operations, and achieve organizational objectives. The central thrust of a company's strategy is undertaking moves to build and strengthen the company's long-term competitive position and financial performance and, ideally, gain a competitive advantage over rivals that then becomes a company's ticket to above-average profitability. A company's strategy typically evolves and re-forms over time, emerging from a blend of (1) proactive and purposeful actions on the part of company managers and (2) as-needed reactions to unanticipated developments and fresh market conditions.

Closely related to the concept of strategy is the concept of a company's business model. A company's business model is management's story line for how and why the company's product offerings and competitive approaches will generate a revenue stream and have an associated cost structure that produces attractive earnings and return on investment; in effect, a company's business model sets forth the economic logic for answering the question "How do we intend to make money in this business, given our current strategy?"

The managerial process of crafting and executing a company's strategy consists of five interrelated and integrated phases:

1. *Developing a strategic vision* of where the company needs to head and what its future product-customer-market-technology focus should be. This managerial step provides long term direction, infuses the organization with a sense of purposeful action, and communicates to stakeholders what management's aspirations for the company are.

2. *Setting objectives* and using the targeted results and outcomes as yardsticks for measuring the company's performance and progress. Objectives need to spell out *how much* of *what kind* of performance *by when,* and they need to require a significant amount of organizational stretch. A balanced-scorecard approach for measuring company performance entails setting both *financial objectives* and *strategic objectives.*

3. *Crafting a strategy to achieve the objectives* and move the company along the strategic course that management has charted. Crafting strategy is concerned principally with forming responses to changes under way in the external environment,

devising competitive moves and market approaches aimed at producing sustainable competitive advantage, building competitively valuable competencies and capabilities, and uniting the strategic actions initiated in various parts of the company.

4. *Implementing and executing the chosen strategy efficiently and effectively.* Managing the implementation and execution of strategy is an operations-oriented, make-things-happen activity aimed at shaping the performance of core business activities in a strategy-supportive manner.

5. *Evaluating performance and initiating corrective adjustments in vision, long-term direction, objectives, strategy, or execution* in light of actual experience, changing conditions, new ideas, and new opportunities. This phase of the strategy management process is the trigger point for deciding whether to continue or change the company's vision, objectives, strategy, and/or strategy execution methods.

Developing a strategic vision and mission, setting objectives, and crafting a strategy are the basic direction-setting tasks that together constitute a *strategic plan* for coping with industry and competitive conditions, the actions of rivals, and the challenges and issues that stand as obstacles to the company's success.

Boards of directors have a duty to shareholders to play a vigilant supervisory role in a company's strategy-making, strategy-executing process. They are obligated to (1) critically appraise and ultimately approve strategic action plans, (2) evaluate the strategic leadership skills of the CEO and others in line to succeed the incumbent CEO, (3) institute a compensation plan for top executives that rewards them for actions and results that serve stakeholder interests, most especially those of shareholders, and (4) ensure that the company issues accurate financial reports and has adequate financial controls.

Exercises

1. Go to www.redhat.com and check the company's latest financial reports to determine how well the company's business model is working. Is the company profitable? Is its revenue stream from selling technical support services growing or declining as a percentage of total revenues? Does your review of the company's financial performance suggest that its business model and strategy are changing?

2. Go to www.levistrauss.com/about/vision and read what Levi Strauss & Company says about how its corporate values of originality, empathy, integrity, and courage are connected to its vision of clothing the world. Do you buy what the company says, or are its statements just a bunch of nice pontifications that represent the personal values of the CEO (and make for good public relations)? Explain.

3. Go to the investors' section of www.heinz.com and read the letter to the shareholders in the company's fiscal 2003 annual report. Is the vision for Heinz that is articulated by Chairman and CEO William R. Johnson sufficiently clear and well defined? Why or why not? If you were a shareholder, would you be satisfied with what Johnson has told you about the company's direction, performance targets, and strategy? Now read Johnson's letter to the shareholders in Heinz's 2004 annual report. Do the results he cites change your mind about Johnson's vision for Heinz and the caliber of his strategy?

CHAPTER 2

Analyzing a Company's External Environment

Analysis is the critical starting point of strategic thinking.

—Kenichi Ohmae, consultant and author

Things are always different—the art is figuring out which differences matter.

—Laszlo Birinyi, investments manager

Competitive battles should be seen not as one-shot skirmishes but as a dynamic multiround game of moves and countermoves.

—Anil K. Gupta, professor

Managers

are not prepared to act wisely in steering a company in a different direction or altering its strategy until they have a deep understanding of the company's situation. Two facets of the company's situation are particularly pertinent: (1) the industry and competitive environment in which the company operates and the forces acting to reshape this environment and (2) the company's own market position and competitiveness—its resources and capabilities, its strengths and weaknesses vis-à-vis rivals, and its windows of opportunity.

A probing, analysis-based diagnosis of a company's external and internal environments is a prerequisite for managers to succeed in crafting a strategy that is an excellent fit with the company's situation, is capable of building competitive advantage, and holds good prospect for boosting company performance—the three criteria of a winning strategy. Developing a strategy begins with an appraisal of the company's external and internal situation (to form a strategic vision of where the company needs to head), then moves toward an evaluation of the most promising alternative strategies and business models, and finally culminates in choosing a specific strategy (see Figure 2.1).

This chapter presents the concepts and analytical tools for assessing a single-business company's external environment. Attention centers on the competitive arena in which a company operates, together with the technological, societal, regulatory, or demographic influences in the larger macroenvironment that are acting to reshape the company's future market arena. In Chapter 3 we explore the methods of evaluating a company's internal circumstances and competitiveness.

Figure 2.1   From Thinking Strategically to Choosing a Strategy

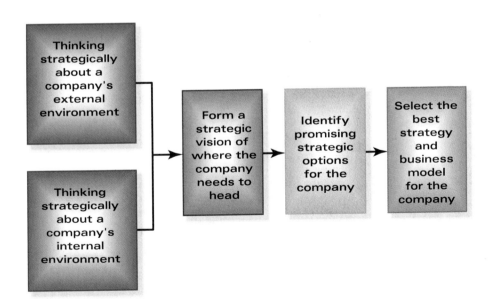

The Strategically Relevant Components of a Company's External Environment

All companies operate in a "macroenvironment" shaped by influences emanating from the economy at large; population demographics; societal values and lifestyles; governmental legislation and regulation; technological factors; and, closer to home, the industry and competitive arena in which the company operates (see Figure 2.2). Strictly speaking, a company's macroenvironment includes *all relevant factors and influences* outside the company's boundaries; by *relevant*, we mean important enough to have a

Figure 2.2   The Components of a Company's Macroenvironment

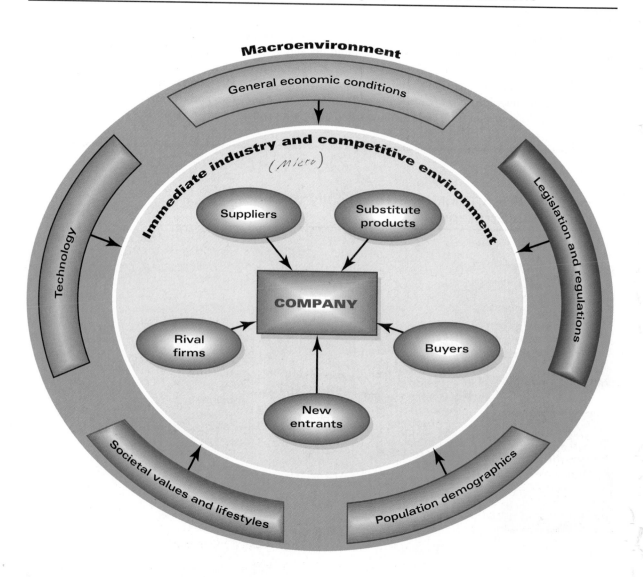

bearing on the decisions the company ultimately makes about its direction, objectives, strategy, and business model. For the most part, influences coming from the outer ring of the macroenvironment have a low impact on a company's business situation and shape only the edges of the company's direction and strategy. (There are notable exceptions, though. The strategic opportunities of cigarette producers to grow their business are greatly reduced by antismoking ordinances and the growing cultural stigma attached to smoking; the market growth potential for health care and prescription drug companies is quite favorably affected by the demographics of an aging population and longer life expectancies; and companies in almost all industries have to craft strategies that are responsive to environmental regulations, ups and downs in the level of economic activity, changing interest rates, and energy prices.) But while the strategy-shaping impact of outer-ring influences is normally low, there are enough strategically relevant trends and developments in the outer ring of the macroenvironment to justify a watchful eye. As company managers scan the external environment, they must be alert for potentially important outer-ring forces, assess their impact and influence, and adapt the company's direction and strategy as needed.

The factors and forces in a company's macroenvironment having the biggest strategy-shaping impact almost always pertain to the company's immediate industry and competitive environment. Consequently, it is on these factors that we concentrate our attention in this chapter.

Thinking Strategically about a Company's Industry and Competitive Environment

To gain a deep understanding of a company's industry and competitive environment, managers do not need to gather all the information they can find and spend lots of time digesting it. Rather, the task is much more focused. Thinking strategically about a company's industry and competitive environment entails using some well-defined concepts and analytical tools to get clear answers to seven questions:

1. What are the industry's strategy-shaping economic features?
2. What kinds of competitive forces are industry members facing, and how strong is each force?
3. What forces are driving changes in the industry, and what impact will these changes have on competitive intensity and industry profitability?
4. What market positions do industry rivals occupy—who is strongly positioned and who is not?
5. What strategic moves are rivals likely to make next?
6. What are the key factors for future competitive success?
7. Does the outlook for the industry present the company with sufficiently attractive prospects for profitability?

Analysis-based answers to these questions provide managers with a solid diagnosis of the industry and competitive environment. The remainder of this chapter is devoted to describing the methods of analyzing a company's industry and competitive environment.

Identifying Strategically Relevant Industry Features

Because industries differ so significantly in their basic character and structure, analyzing a company's industry and competitive environment begins with an overview of the industry's dominant economic features. The following economic features and corresponding questions need to be considered:

Economic Feature	Strategically Relevant Issues and Considerations
■ Market size and growth rate	■ How big is the industry, and how fast is it growing? ■ What does the industry's position in the growth cycle (early development, rapid growth and takeoff, early maturity, maturity, saturation and stagnation, decline) indicate about the industry's growth prospects?
■ Number of buyers	■ Is the number of buyers of the industry's product large enough that no one buyer accounts for a significant fraction of overall market demand, or do a fairly small number of buyers account for a big fraction of total sales?
■ Buyer needs and requirements	■ Are buyer needs or requirements changing, and, if so, what is driving such changes? ■ What are buyers looking for—what attributes prompt buyers to choose one brand over another?
■ Number of rivals	■ Is the industry fragmented into many small companies or concentrated and dominated by a few large companies? ■ Is the industry going through a period of consolidation to a smaller number of competitors? ■ Is the industry big enough or growing fast enough to attract the attention of opportunity-seeking new entrants?
■ Scope of competitive rivalry	■ Is the geographic area over which most companies compete local, regional, national, multinational, or global? ■ Is having a presence in the foreign-country markets becoming more important to a company's long-term competitive success?
■ Degree of product differentiation	■ Are the products of rival sellers strongly differentiated, weakly differentiated, or mostly identical? ■ Are the products of rivals becoming more differentiated or less differentiated? ■ Are increasingly "look-alike" products of rivals causing heightened price competition?

■ Product innovation	■ Is the industry characterized by rapid product innovation and short product life cycles?
	■ How important are R&D and product innovation?
	■ Are there opportunities to overtake key rivals by being first to market with next-generation products?
■ Production capacity	■ Is a surplus of capacity pushing prices and profit margins down?
	■ Is the industry overcrowded with too many competitors?
■ Pace of technological change	■ What role does advancing technology play in this industry?
	■ Are ongoing upgrades of facilities/equipment essential because of rapidly advancing production process technologies?
	■ Do most industry members have or need strong technological capabilities? Why?
■ Vertical integration	■ Do most industry members operate in only one stage of the industry (parts and components production, manufacturing and assembly, wholesale distribution, retailing), or are some or many partially or fully integrated?
	■ Does being fully integrated, partially integrated, or nonintegrated appear to result in a competitive advantage or disadvantage?
■ Economies of scale	■ Is the industry characterized by important economies of scale in purchasing, manufacturing, advertising, shipping, or other activities?
■ Learning- and experience-curve effects	■ Are certain industry activities characterized by strong learning and experience effects ("learning by doing") such that unit costs decline as a company's experience in performing the activity builds?[1]

Identifying an industry's economic features not only sets the stage for the analysis to come but also promotes understanding of the kinds of strategic moves that industry members are likely to employ. For example, in an industry characterized by important scale economies and/or learning- and experience-curve effects, industry members are strongly motivated to go after increased sales volumes and capture the cost-saving economies of larger-scale operations; small-scale firms are under considerable pressure to grow sales in order to become more cost-competitive with large-volume rivals. In industries characterized by one product advance after another, companies must invest in R&D and develop strong product innovation capabilities; a strategy of continuous product innovation becomes a condition of survival. An industry that has recently passed through the rapid-growth stage and is looking at single-digit percentage increases in buyer demand is likely to be experiencing a competitive shakeout and much stronger strategic emphasis on cost reduction and improved customer service.

Analyzing the Nature and Strength of Competitive Forces

The character, mix, and subtleties of the competitive forces operating in a company's industry are never the same from one industry to another. Far and away the most powerful and widely used tool for systematically diagnosing the principal competitive pressures in a market and assessing the strength and importance of each is the *five-forces model of competition.*[2] This model, depicted in Figure 2.3, holds that the state of competition in an industry is a composite of competitive pressures operating in five areas of the overall market:

1. Competitive pressures associated with the market maneuvering and jockeying for buyer patronage that goes on among *rival sellers* in the industry.

2. Competitive pressures associated with the threat of *new entrants* into the market.

3. Competitive pressures coming from the attempts of companies in other industries to win buyers over to their own *substitute products.*

4. Competitive pressures stemming from *supplier* bargaining power and supplier-seller collaboration.

5. Competitive pressures stemming from *buyer* bargaining power and seller-buyer collaboration.

The way one uses the five-forces model to determine what competition is like in a given industry is to build the picture of competition in three steps or stages. Step 1 is to identify the specific competitive pressures associated with each of the five forces. Step 2 is to evaluate how strong the pressures composing each of the five forces are (fierce, strong, moderate to normal, or weak). Step 3 is to determine whether the collective strength of the five competitive forces is conducive to earning attractive profits.

The Rivalry among Competing Sellers

The strongest of the five competitive forces is nearly always the market maneuvering and jockeying for buyer patronage that goes on among rival sellers of a product or service. In effect, *a market is a competitive battlefield* where it is customary for rival sellers to employ whatever weapons they have in their business arsenal to improve their market positions and performance. The strategy-making challenge of managers is to craft a competitive strategy that, at the very least, allows their company to hold its own against rivals and that, ideally, strengthens the company's standing with buyers, delivers good profitability, and *produces a competitive edge over rivals.* But when one firm makes a strategic move that produces good results, its rivals often react and respond with offensive or defensive counter-moves, shifting their strategic emphasis from one combination of product attributes, marketing tactics, and capabilities to another. This pattern of action and reaction, move and countermove, adjust and readjust is what makes competitive rivalry a combative, ever-changing contest. Market battles for buyer patronage involve a continually evolving competitive landscape as industry rivals initiate new rounds of market maneuvers, with one or more rivals gaining or losing momentum in the marketplace according to whether their adjustments succeed or fail.

Core Concept

Competitive jockeying among industry rivals is ever-changing, as rivals initiate fresh offensive and defensive moves and emphasize first one mix of competitive weapons and then another in efforts to improve their market positions.

Figure 2.3   **The Five-Forces Model of Competition:**
A Key Tool for Diagnosing the Competitive Environment

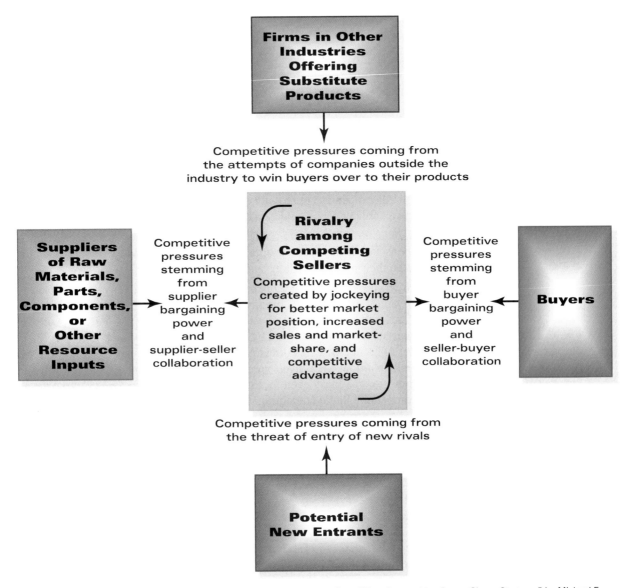

Figure 2.4 shows a sampling of competitive weapons that firms can deploy in battling rivals and indicates the factors that influence the intensity of their rivalry. A brief discussion of some of the factors that influence the tempo of rivalry among industry competitors is in order:[3]

- *Rivalry among competing sellers intensifies the more frequently and more aggressively that industry members undertake fresh actions to boost their market standing and performance—perhaps at the expense of rivals.* Rivalry tends to be fairly intense whenever sellers actively compete on price—lively price competition pressures rival companies to aggressively pursue ways to drive costs out of the business; high-cost companies are hard-pressed to survive. Other indicators of the intensity of rivalry among industry members include:

- Whether industry members are racing to offer better performance features, higher quality, improved customer service, or a wider product selection.

- How frequently rivals resort to such marketing tactics as special sales promotions, heavy advertising, rebates, or low-interest-rate financing to drum up additional sales.

- How actively industry members are pursuing efforts to build stronger dealer networks, establish positions in foreign markets, or otherwise expand their distribution capabilities and market presence.

- How frequently rivals introduce new and improved products (and thus are competing on the basis of their product innovation capabilities).

- How hard companies are striving to gain a market edge over rivals by developing valuable expertise and capabilities.

Normally, industry members are proactive in drawing on their arsenal of competitive weapons and deploying their organizational resources in a manner calculated to strengthen their market positions and performance.

■ *Rivalry intensifies as the number of competitors increases and as competitors become more equal in size and capability.* Competition is not as strong in PC operating systems, where Linux is one of the few challengers to Microsoft, as it is in fast-food restaurants, where buyers have many choices. Up to a point, the greater the number of competitors, the greater the probability of fresh, creative strategic initiatives. In addition, when rivals are nearly equal in size and capability, they can usually compete on a fairly even footing, making it harder for one or two firms to win the competitive battle and dominate the market.

■ *Rivalry is usually weaker when there are fewer than five competitors or else so many rivals that the impact of any one company's actions is spread thinly across all industry members.* When an industry contains only a few rival sellers, each company tends to recognize that its actions can have an immediate and significant impact on the others and, if aggressive, may provoke direct retaliation. Although occasional warfare can break out, competition among the few tends to produce a live-and-let-live approach to competing and thus a restrained use of competitive weaponry. Rivalry also tends to be weak when an industry is fragmented with so many competitors that successful moves by one have little discernible adverse impact on the others and thus may provoke no immediate response or countermove on the part of its rivals.

■ *Rivalry is usually stronger in slow-growing markets and weaker in fast-growing markets.* Rapidly expanding buyer demand produces enough new business for all industry members to grow. Indeed, in a fast-growing market, a company may find itself stretched just to keep abreast of incoming orders, let alone devote resources to stealing customers away from rivals. But in markets where growth is sluggish or where buyer demand drops off unexpectedly, expansion-minded firms and/or firms with excess capacity often are quick to cut prices and initiate other sales-increasing tactics, thereby igniting a battle for market share that can result in a shakeout of weak, inefficient firms.

Figure 2.4   Weapons for Competing and Factors Affecting the Strength of Rivalry

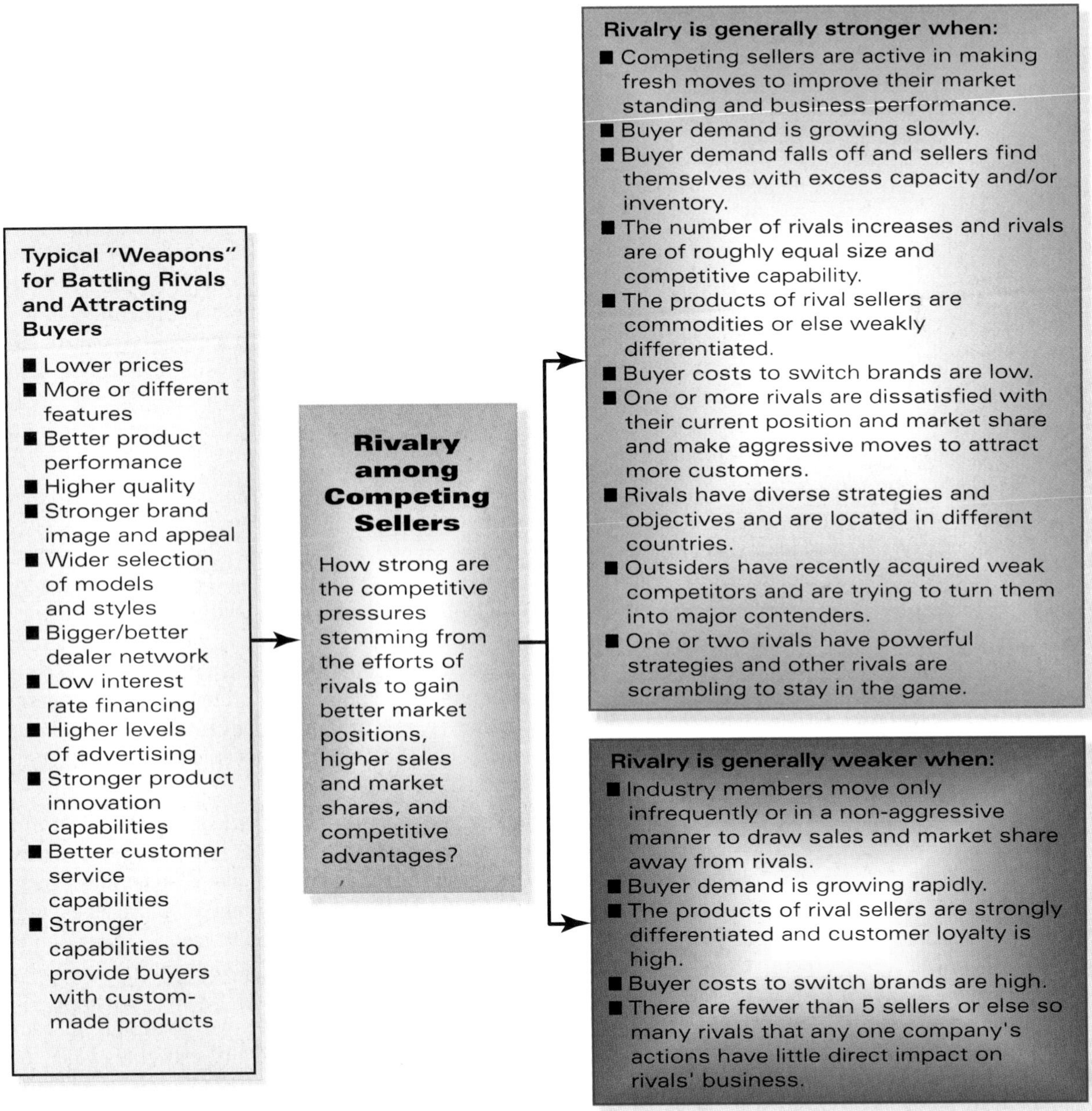

Typical "Weapons" for Battling Rivals and Attracting Buyers

- Lower prices
- More or different features
- Better product performance
- Higher quality
- Stronger brand image and appeal
- Wider selection of models and styles
- Bigger/better dealer network
- Low interest rate financing
- Higher levels of advertising
- Stronger product innovation capabilities
- Better customer service capabilities
- Stronger capabilities to provide buyers with custom-made products

Rivalry among Competing Sellers

How strong are the competitive pressures stemming from the efforts of rivals to gain better market positions, higher sales and market shares, and competitive advantages?

Rivalry is generally stronger when:

- Competing sellers are active in making fresh moves to improve their market standing and business performance.
- Buyer demand is growing slowly.
- Buyer demand falls off and sellers find themselves with excess capacity and/or inventory.
- The number of rivals increases and rivals are of roughly equal size and competitive capability.
- The products of rival sellers are commodities or else weakly differentiated.
- Buyer costs to switch brands are low.
- One or more rivals are dissatisfied with their current position and market share and make aggressive moves to attract more customers.
- Rivals have diverse strategies and objectives and are located in different countries.
- Outsiders have recently acquired weak competitors and are trying to turn them into major contenders.
- One or two rivals have powerful strategies and other rivals are scrambling to stay in the game.

Rivalry is generally weaker when:

- Industry members move only infrequently or in a non-aggressive manner to draw sales and market share away from rivals.
- Buyer demand is growing rapidly.
- The products of rival sellers are strongly differentiated and customer loyalty is high.
- Buyer costs to switch brands are high.
- There are fewer than 5 sellers or else so many rivals that any one company's actions have little direct impact on rivals' business.

- *Rivalry increases as the products of rival sellers become more standardized and/or when buyer costs to switch from one brand to another are low.* When the offerings of rivals are quite similar, it is usually easy and inexpensive for buyers to switch their purchases from one seller to another. Strongly differentiated products raise the probability that buyers will find it costly to switch brands.

- *Rivalry is more intense when industry conditions tempt competitors to use price cuts or other competitive weapons to boost unit volume.* When a product is perishable, seasonal, or costly to hold in inventory, or when demand slacks off, competitive pressures build quickly anytime one or more firms decide to cut prices and dump excess supplies on the market. Likewise, whenever fixed costs account for a large fraction of total cost and thus unit costs tend to be lowest at or near full capacity, then firms come under significant pressure to cut prices or otherwise try to boost sales. Unused capacity imposes a significant cost-increasing penalty because there are fewer units over which to spread fixed costs. The pressure of high fixed costs can push rival firms into price concessions, special discounts, rebates, low-interest-rate financing, and other volume-boosting tactics.

- *Rivalry increases when one or more competitors become dissatisfied with their market position and launch moves to bolster their standing at the expense of rivals.* Firms that are losing ground or in financial trouble often react aggressively by acquiring smaller rivals, introducing new products, boosting advertising, discounting prices, and so on. Such actions heighten rivalry and can trigger a hotly contested battle for market share. The market maneuvering among rivals usually heats up when a competitor makes new offensive moves—because it sees an opportunity to better please customers or is under pressure to improve its market share or profitability.

- *Rivalry increases in proportion to the size of the payoff from a successful strategic move.* The greater the benefits of going after a new opportunity, the more likely it is that one or more rivals will initiate moves to capture it. Competitive pressures nearly always intensify when several rivals start pursuing the same opportunity. For example, competition in online music sales heated up with the entries of Amazon.com, Barnesandnoble.com, and Buy.com. Furthermore, the size of the strategic payoff can vary with the speed of retaliation. When competitors respond slowly (or not at all), the initiator of a fresh competitive strategy can reap benefits in the intervening period and perhaps gain a first-mover advantage that is not easily surmounted. The greater the benefits of moving first, the more likely some competitor will accept the risk and try it.

- *Rivalry becomes more volatile and unpredictable as the diversity of competitors increases in terms of visions, strategic intents, objectives, strategies, resources, and countries of origin.* A diverse group of sellers often contains one or more mavericks willing to try novel or high-risk or rule-breaking market approaches, thus generating a livelier and less predictable competitive environment. Globally competitive markets often contain rivals with different views about where the industry is headed and a willingness to employ perhaps radically different competitive approaches. Attempts by cross-border rivals to gain stronger footholds in each other's domestic markets usually boost the intensity of rivalry, especially when the aggressors have lower costs or products with more attractive features.

- *Rivalry increases when strong companies outside the industry acquire weak firms in the industry and launch aggressive, well-funded moves to transform their newly acquired competitors into major market contenders.* A concerted effort to turn a weak rival into a market leader nearly always entails launching well-financed strategic initiatives to dramatically improve the competitor's product offering, excite buyer interest, and win a much bigger market share—actions that, if successful, put added pressure on rivals to counter with fresh strategic moves of their own.

■ *A powerful, successful competitive strategy employed by one company greatly intensifies the competitive pressures on its rivals to develop effective strategic responses or be relegated to also-ran status.*

Rivalry can be characterized as *cutthroat* or *brutal* when competitors engage in protracted price wars or habitually employ other aggressive tactics that are mutually destructive to profitability. Rivalry can be considered *fierce* to *strong* when the battle for market share is so vigorous that the profit margins of most industry members are squeezed to bare-bones levels. Rivalry can be characterized as *moderate* or *normal* when the maneuvering among industry members, while lively and healthy, still allows most industry members to earn acceptable profits. Rivalry is *weak* when most companies in the industry are relatively well satisfied with their sales growth and market shares, rarely undertake offensives to steal customers away from one another, and have comparatively attractive earnings and returns on investment.

The Potential Entry of New Competitors

Several factors affect the strength of the competitive threat of potential entry in a particular industry (see Figure 2.5). One factor relates to the size of the pool of likely entry candidates and the resources at their command. As a rule, competitive pressures intensify the bigger the pool of entry candidates. This is especially true when some of the likely entry candidates have ample resources and the potential to become formidable contenders for market leadership. Frequently, the strongest competitive pressures associated with potential entry come not from outsiders but from current industry participants looking for growth opportunities. *Existing industry members are often strong candidates to enter market segments or geographic areas where they currently do not have a market presence.* Companies already well established in certain product categories or geographic areas often possess the resources, competencies, and competitive capabilities to hurdle the barriers of entering a different market segment or new geographic area.

A second factor concerns whether the likely entry candidates face high or low entry barriers. The most widely encountered barriers that entry candidates must hurdle include:[4]

■ *The presence of sizable economies of scale in production or other areas of operation:* When incumbent companies enjoy cost advantages associated with large-scale operation, outsiders must either enter on a large scale (a costly and perhaps risky move) or accept a cost disadvantage and consequently lower profitability. Trying to overcome the disadvantages of small size by entering on a large scale at the outset can result in long-term overcapacity problems for the new entrant (until sales volume builds up), and it can so threaten the market shares of existing firms that they launch strong defensive maneuvers (price cuts, increased advertising and sales promotion, and similar blocking actions) to maintain their positions and make things hard on a newcomer.

■ *Cost and resource disadvantages not related to size:* Existing firms may have low unit costs as a result of experience or learning-curve effects, key patents, partnerships with the best and cheapest suppliers of raw materials and components, proprietary technology know-how not readily available to newcomers, favorable locations, and low fixed costs (because they have older plants that have been mostly depreciated).

Figure 2.5   Factors Affecting the Threat of Entry

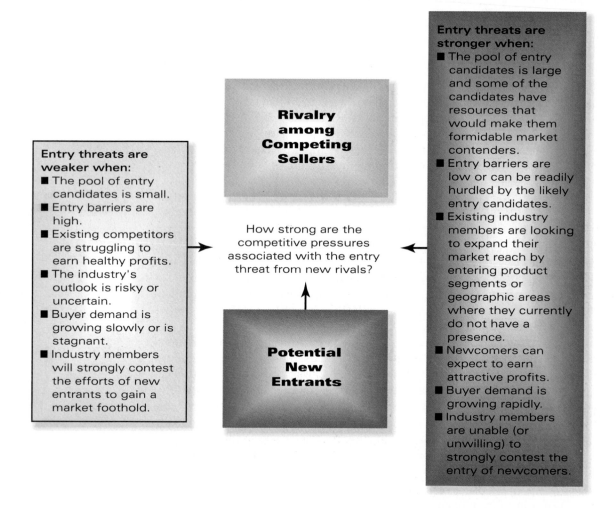

Entry threats are weaker when:
- The pool of entry candidates is small.
- Entry barriers are high.
- Existing competitors are struggling to earn healthy profits.
- The industry's outlook is risky or uncertain.
- Buyer demand is growing slowly or is stagnant.
- Industry members will strongly contest the efforts of new entrants to gain a market foothold.

Rivalry among Competing Sellers

How strong are the competitive pressures associated with the entry threat from new rivals?

Potential New Entrants

Entry threats are stronger when:
- The pool of entry candidates is large and some of the candidates have resources that would make them formidable market contenders.
- Entry barriers are low or can be readily hurdled by the likely entry candidates.
- Existing industry members are looking to expand their market reach by entering product segments or geographic areas where they currently do not have a presence.
- Newcomers can expect to earn attractive profits.
- Buyer demand is growing rapidly.
- Industry members are unable (or unwilling) to strongly contest the entry of newcomers.

■ *Brand preferences and customer loyalty:* In some industries, buyers are strongly attached to established brands. Japanese consumers, for example, are fiercely loyal to Japanese brands of motor vehicles, electronics products, cameras, and film. European consumers have traditionally been loyal to European brands of major household appliances. High brand loyalty means that a potential entrant must commit to spending enough money on advertising and sales promotion to overcome customer loyalties and build its own clientele. Establishing brand recognition and building customer loyalty can be a slow and costly process. In addition, if it is difficult or costly for a customer to switch to a new brand, a new entrant must persuade buyers that its brand is worth the switching costs. To overcome switching-cost barriers, new entrants may have to offer buyers a discounted price or an extra margin of quality or service. All this can mean lower expected profit margins for new entrants, which increases the risk to start-up companies dependent on sizable early profits to support their new investments.

- *Capital requirements:* The larger the total dollar investment needed to enter the market successfully, the more limited the pool of potential entrants. The most obvious capital requirements for new entrants are those associated with investing in the necessary manufacturing facilities and equipment, being able to finance the introductory advertising and sales promotion campaigns to build brand awareness and establish a clientele, securing the working capital to finance inventories and customer credit, and having sufficient cash reserves to cover start-up losses.

- *Access to distribution channels:* In consumer goods industries, a potential entrant may face the barrier of gaining adequate access to consumers. Wholesale distributors may be reluctant to take on a product that lacks buyer recognition. A network of retail dealers may have to be set up from scratch. Retailers have to be convinced to give a new brand ample display space and an adequate trial period. Entry is tough when existing producers have strong, well-functioning distributor-dealer networks and a newcomer must struggle to squeeze its way into existing distribution channels. To overcome the barrier of gaining adequate access to consumers, potential entrants may have to "buy" their way into wholesale or retail channels by cutting their prices to provide dealers and distributors with higher markups and profit margins or by giving them big advertising and promotional allowances. As a consequence, a potential entrant's own profits may be squeezed unless and until its product gains enough consumer acceptance that distributors and retailers want to carry it.

- *Regulatory policies:* Government agencies can limit or even bar entry by requiring licenses and permits. Regulated industries like cable TV, telecommunications, electric and gas utilities, radio and television broadcasting, liquor retailing, and railroads entail government-controlled entry. In international markets, host governments commonly limit foreign entry and must approve all foreign investment applications. Stringent government-mandated safety regulations and environmental pollution standards are entry barriers because they raise entry costs.

- *Tariffs and international trade restrictions:* National governments commonly use tariffs and trade restrictions (antidumping rules, local content requirements, quotas, etc.) to raise entry barriers for foreign firms and protect domestic producers from outside competition.

Whether an industry's entry barriers ought to be considered high or low and how hard it is for new entrants to compete on a level playing field depend on the resources and competencies possessed by the pool of potential entrants. Entry barriers can be formidable for newly formed enterprises that have to find some way to gain a market foothold and then over time make inroads against well-established companies. But opportunity-seeking companies in other industries, if they have suitable resources, competencies, and brand-name recognition, may be able to hurdle an industry's entry barriers rather easily. In evaluating the potential threat of entry, company managers must look at (1) how formidable the entry barriers are for each type of potential entrant—start-up enterprises, specific candidate companies in other industries, and current industry participants looking to expand their market reach—and (2) how attractive the growth and profit prospects are for new entrants. *Rapidly growing market demand and high potential profits act as magnets, motivating potential entrants to commit the resources needed to hurdle entry barriers.*[5]

However, even if a potential entrant has or can acquire the needed competencies and resources to attempt entry, it still faces the issue of how existing firms will react.[6] Will incumbent firms offer only passive resistance, or will they aggressively defend their market positions using price cuts, increased advertising, product improvements, and whatever else they can think of to give a new entrant (as well as other rivals) a hard time? A potential entrant can have second thoughts when financially strong incumbent firms send clear signals that they will stoutly defend their market positions against newcomers. A potential entrant may also turn away when incumbent firms can leverage distributors and customers to retain their business.

> The threat of entry is stronger when entry barriers are low, when there's a sizable pool of entry candidates, when industry growth is rapid and profit potentials are high, and when incumbent firms are unable or unwilling to vigorously contest a newcomer's entry.

The best test of whether potential entry is a strong or weak competitive force in the marketplace is to ask if the industry's growth and profit prospects are strongly attractive to potential entry candidates. When the answer is no, potential entry is a weak competitive force. When the answer is yes and there are actively interested entry candidates with sufficient expertise and resources, then potential entry adds significantly to competitive pressures in the marketplace. The stronger the threat of entry, the more that incumbent firms are driven to seek ways to fortify their positions against newcomers, pursuing strategic moves not only to protect their market shares but also to make entry more costly or difficult.

One additional point: *The threat of entry changes as the industry's prospects grow brighter or dimmer and as entry barriers rise or fall.* For example, in the pharmaceutical industry the expiration of a key patent on a widely prescribed drug virtually guarantees that one or more drug makers will enter with generic offerings of their own. Use of the Internet for shopping is making it much easier for e-tailers to enter into competition against some of the best-known retail chains. In international markets, entry barriers for foreign-based firms fall as tariffs are lowered, as host governments open up their domestic markets to outsiders, as domestic wholesalers and dealers seek out lower-cost foreign-made goods, and as domestic buyers become more willing to purchase foreign brands.

Competitive Pressures from the Sellers of Substitute Products

Companies in one industry come under competitive pressure from the actions of companies in a closely adjoining industry whenever buyers view the products of the two industries as good substitutes. For instance, the producers of sugar experience competitive pressures from the sales and marketing efforts of the makers of artificial sweeteners. Similarly, the producers of eyeglasses and contact lenses are currently facing mounting competitive pressures from growing consumer interest in corrective laser surgery. Newspapers are feeling the competitive force of the general public's turning to cable news channels for late-breaking news and using Internet sources to get information about sports results, stock quotes, and job opportunities.

Just how strong the competitive pressures are from the sellers of substitute products depends on three factors: (1) whether substitutes are readily available and attractively priced; (2) whether buyers view the substitutes as being comparable or better in terms of quality, performance, and other relevant attributes; and (3) how much it costs end users to switch to substitutes. Figure 2.6 lists factors affecting the strength of competitive pressures from substitute products and lists signs that indicate substitutes are a strong competitive force.

The presence of readily available and attractively priced substitutes creates competitive pressure by placing a ceiling on the prices industry members can charge without giving customers an incentive to switch to substitutes and risking sales erosion.[7]

Figure 2.6   Factors Affecting Competition from Substitute Products

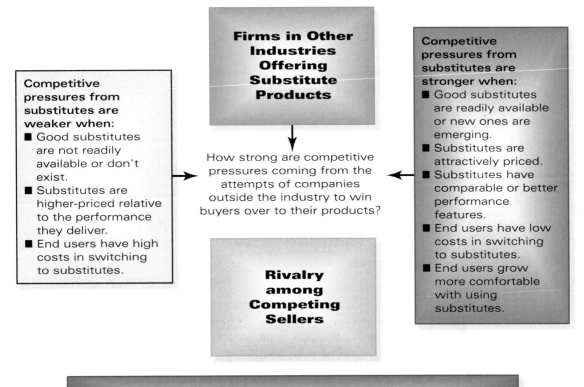

Competitive pressures from substitutes are weaker when:
- Good substitutes are not readily available or don't exist.
- Substitutes are higher-priced relative to the performance they deliver.
- End users have high costs in switching to substitutes.

Firms in Other Industries Offering Substitute Products

How strong are competitive pressures coming from the attempts of companies outside the industry to win buyers over to their products?

Rivalry among Competing Sellers

Competitive pressures from substitutes are stronger when:
- Good substitutes are readily available or new ones are emerging.
- Substitutes are attractively priced.
- Substitutes have comparable or better performance features.
- End users have low costs in switching to substitutes.
- End users grow more comfortable with using substitutes.

Signs That Competition from Substitutes Is Strong
- Sales of substitutes are growing faster than sales of the industry being analyzed (an indication that the sellers of substitutes are drawing customers away from the industry in question).
- Producers of substitutes are moving to add new capacity.
- Profits of the producers of substitutes are on the rise.

This price ceiling, at the same time, puts a lid on the profits that industry members can earn unless they find ways to cut costs. When substitutes are cheaper than an industry's product, industry members come under heavy competitive pressure to reduce their prices and find ways to absorb the price cuts with cost reductions.

The availability of substitutes inevitably invites customers to compare performance, features, ease of use, and other attributes as well as price. For example, ski boat manufacturers are experiencing strong competition from personal water-ski craft because water sports enthusiasts are finding that personal water skis are fun to ride and less expensive. The users of paper cartons constantly weigh the performance trade-offs of plastic containers and metal cans. Competition from good-performing substitute products pushes industry participants to incorporate new performance features and heighten efforts to convince customers their product has attributes that are superior to those of substitutes.

The strength of competition from substitutes is significantly influenced by how difficult or costly it is for the industry's customers to switch to a substitute.[8] Typical switching costs include the time and inconvenience that may be involved, the costs of additional equipment, the time and cost spent on testing the quality and reliability of the substitute, the psychological costs of severing old supplier relationships and establishing new ones, payments for technical help in making the changeover, and employee retraining costs. When buyers incur high costs in switching to substitutes, the competitive pressures that industry members experience from substitutes are usually lessened unless the sellers of substitutes begin offering price discounts or major performance benefits that entice the industry's customers away. When switching costs are low, it's much easier for sellers of substitutes to convince buyers to change to their products.

As a rule, then, the lower the price of substitutes, the higher their quality and performance, and the lower the user's switching costs, the more intense the competitive pressures posed by substitute products. Good indicators of the competitive strength of substitute products are the rate at which their sales and profits are growing, the market inroads they are making, and their plans for expanding production capacity.

Competitive Pressures Stemming from Supplier Bargaining Power and Seller-Supplier Collaboration

Whether supplier-seller relationships represent a weak or strong competitive force depends on (1) whether the major suppliers can exercise sufficient bargaining power to influence the terms and conditions of supply in their favor and (2) the nature and extent of supplier-seller collaboration in the industry.

How Supplier Bargaining Power Can Create Competitive Pressures   Whenever the major suppliers to an industry have considerable leverage in determining the terms and conditions of the item they are supplying, then they are in a position to exert competitive pressure on one or more rival sellers. For instance, Microsoft and Intel, both of whom supply PC makers with products that most PC users consider essential, are known for using their dominant market status not only to charge PC makers premium prices but also to leverage PC makers in other ways. Microsoft pressures PC makers to load only Microsoft products on the PCs they ship and to position the icons for Microsoft software prominently on the screens of new computers that come with factory-loaded software. Intel pushes greater use of Intel microprocessors in PCs by granting PC makers sizable advertising allowances on PC models equipped with "Intel Inside" stickers; it also tends to give PC makers who use the biggest percentages of Intel chips in their PC models top priority in filling orders for newly introduced Intel chips. Being on Intel's list of preferred customers helps a PC maker get an allocation of the first production runs of Intel's latest and greatest chips and thus get new PC models equipped with these chips to market ahead of rivals who are heavier users of chips made by Intel's rivals. The ability of Microsoft and Intel to pressure PC makers for preferential treatment of one kind or another in turn affects competition among rival PC makers.

Several other instances of supplier bargaining power are worth citing. Small-scale retailers must often contend with the power of manufacturers whose products enjoy prestigious and well-respected brand names; when a manufacturer knows that a retailer needs to stock the manufacturer's product because consumers expect to find the product on the shelves of retail stores where they shop, the manufacturer usually has some degree of pricing power and can also push hard for favorable shelf displays. Motor vehicle manufacturers typically exert considerable power over the terms and conditions with which they supply new vehicles to their independent automobile dealerships. The operators of franchised units of such chains as Krispy Kreme Doughnuts, Burger King, Pizza Hut, and Hampton Inns must frequently agree not only to source some of their supplies from the franchisor at prices and terms favorable to that franchisor but also to operate their facilities in a manner largely dictated by the franchisor. Strong supplier bargaining power is a competitive factor in industries where unions have been able to organize the workforces of some industry members but not others; those industry members that must negotiate wages, fringe benefits, and working conditions with powerful unions (which control the supply of labor) often find themselves with higher labor costs than their competitors with nonunion labor forces. The bigger the gap between union and nonunion labor costs in an industry, the more that unionized industry members must scramble to find ways to relieve the competitive pressure associated with their disadvantage on labor costs. High labor costs are proving a huge competitive liability to unionized supermarket chains like Kroger and Safeway in trying to combat the market share gains being made by Wal-Mart in supermarket retailing—Wal-Mart has a nonunion workforce and the prices for supermarket items at its supercenters tend to run 5 to 20 percent lower than those at unionized supermarket chains.

The factors that determine whether any of the suppliers to an industry are in a position to exert substantial bargaining power or leverage are fairly clear-cut:[9]

- *Whether the item being supplied is a commodity that is readily available from many suppliers at the going market price.* Suppliers have little or no bargaining power or leverage whenever industry members have the ability to source their requirements at competitive prices from any of several alternative and eager suppliers, perhaps dividing their purchases among two or more suppliers to promote lively competition for orders. The suppliers of commoditylike items have market power only when supplies become quite tight and industry members are so eager to secure what they need that they agree to terms more favorable to suppliers.

- *Whether a few large suppliers are the primary sources of a particular item.* The leading suppliers may well have pricing leverage unless they are plagued with excess capacity and are scrambling to secure additional orders for their products. Major suppliers with good reputations and strong demand for the items they supply are harder to wring concessions from than struggling suppliers striving to broaden their customer base or more fully utilize their production capacity.

- *Whether it is difficult or costly for industry members to switch their purchases from one supplier to another or to switch to attractive substitute inputs.* High switching costs signal strong bargaining power on the part of suppliers, whereas low switching costs and ready availability of good substitute inputs signal weak bargaining power. Soft-drink bottlers, for example, can counter the bargaining power of aluminum-can suppliers by shifting or threatening to shift to greater use of plastic containers and introducing more attractive plastic-container designs.

- *Whether certain needed inputs are in short supply.* Suppliers of items in short supply have some degree of pricing power, whereas a surge in the availability of particular items greatly weakens supplier pricing power and bargaining leverage.

- *Whether certain suppliers provide a differentiated input that enhances the performance or quality of the industry's product.* The more valuable a particular input is in terms of enhancing the performance or quality of the products of industry members or of improving the efficiency of their production processes, the more bargaining leverage its suppliers are likely to possess.

■ *Whether certain suppliers provide equipment or services that deliver valuable cost-saving efficiencies to industry members in operating their production processes.* Suppliers that provide cost-saving equipment or other valuable or necessary production-related services are likely to possess bargaining leverage. Industry members that do not source from such suppliers may find themselves at a cost disadvantage and thus under competitive pressure to do so (on terms that are favorable to the suppliers).

■ *Whether suppliers provide an item that accounts for a sizable fraction of the costs of the industry's product.* The bigger the cost of a particular part or component, the more opportunity for the pattern of competition in the marketplace to be affected by the actions of suppliers to raise or lower their prices.

■ *Whether industry members are major customers of suppliers.* As a rule, suppliers have less bargaining leverage when their sales to members of one industry constitute a big percentage of their total sales. In such cases, the well-being of suppliers is closely tied to the well-being of their major customers. Suppliers then have a big incentive to protect and enhance their customers' competitiveness via reasonable prices, exceptional quality, and ongoing advances in the technology of the items supplied.

■ *Whether it makes good economic sense for industry members to integrate backward and self-manufacture items they have been buying from suppliers.* The make-or-buy issue generally boils down to whether suppliers that specialize in the production of a particular part or component and make it in volume for many different customers have the expertise and scale economies to supply an as-good or better component at a lower cost than industry members could achieve via self-manufacture. Frequently, it is difficult for industry members to self-manufacture parts and components more economically than they can obtain them from suppliers that specialize in making such items. For instance, most producers of outdoor power equipment (lawn mowers, rotary tillers, leaf blowers, etc.) find it cheaper to source the small engines they need from outside manufacturers that specialize in small-engine manufacture than to make their own engines because the quantity of engines they need is too small to justify the investment in manufacturing facilities, master the production process, and capture scale economies. Specialists in small-engine manufacture, by supplying many kinds of engines to the whole power equipment industry, can obtain a big-enough sales volume to fully realize scale economies, become proficient in all the manufacturing techniques, and keep costs low. As a rule, suppliers are safe from the threat of self-manufacture by their customers *until* the volume of parts a customer needs becomes large enough for the customer to justify backward integration into self-manufacture of the component. Suppliers also gain bargaining power when they have the resources and profit incentive to integrate forward into the business of the customers they are supplying and thus become a strong rival.

Figure 2.7 summarizes the conditions that tend to make supplier bargaining power strong or weak.

How Seller-Supplier Collaboration Can Create Competitive Pressures   In more and more industries, sellers are forging strategic partnerships with select suppliers in efforts to (1) reduce inventory and logistics costs (e.g., through just-in-time deliveries), (2) speed the availability of next-generation components, (3) enhance the quality of the parts and components being supplied and reduce defect

Figure 2.7   Factors Affecting the Bargaining Power of Suppliers

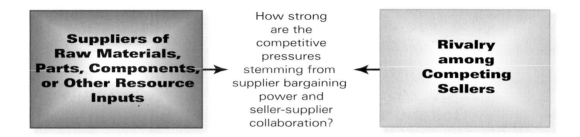

Supplier bargaining power is stronger when:
- Industry members incurs high costs in switching their purchases to alternative suppliers.
- Needed inputs are in short supply (which gives suppliers more leverage in setting prices).
- A supplier has a differentiated input that enhances the quality or performance of sellers' products or is a valuable or critical part of sellers' production processes.
- There are only a few suppliers of a particular input.
- Some suppliers threaten to integrate forward into the business of industry members and perhaps become a powerful rival.

Supplier bargaining power is weaker when:
- The item being supplied is a commodity that is readily available from many suppliers at the going market price.
- Seller switching costs to alternative suppliers are low.
- Good substitute inputs exist or new ones emerge.
- There is a surge in the availability of supplies (thus greatly weakening supplier pricing power).
- Industry members account for a big fraction of suppliers' total sales and continued high volume purchases are important to the well-being of suppliers.
- Industry members are a threat to integrate backward into the business of suppliers and to self-manufacture their own requirements.
- Seller collaboration or partnering with selected suppliers provides attractive win-win opportunities.

rates, and (4) squeeze out important cost savings for both themselves and their suppliers. Numerous Internet technology applications are now available that permit real-time data sharing, eliminate paperwork, and produce cost savings all along the supply chain. The many benefits of effective seller-supplier collaboration can translate into competitive advantage for industry members who do the best job of managing supply chain relationships.

Dell Computer has used strategic partnering with key suppliers as a major element in its strategy to be the world's lowest-cost supplier of branded PCs, servers, and workstations. Because Dell has managed its supply chain relationships in ways that contribute to a low-cost, high-quality competitive edge in components supply, it has put enormous pressure on its PC rivals to try to imitate its supply chain management practices. Effective partnerships with suppliers on the part of one or more industry members can thus become a major source of competitive pressure for rival firms.

The more opportunities that exist for win-win efforts between a company and its suppliers, the less their relationship is characterized by who has the upper hand in bargaining with the other. As long as the relationship is producing valuable benefits for both parties, it will last; only if a supply partner is falling behind alternative suppliers is a company likely to switch suppliers and incur the costs and trouble of building close working ties with a different supplier.

Competitive Pressures Stemming from Buyer Bargaining Power and Seller–Buyer Collaboration

Whether seller-buyer relationships represent a weak or strong competitive force depends on (1) whether some or many buyers have sufficient bargaining leverage to obtain price concessions and other favorable terms and conditions of sale and (2) the extent and competitive importance of seller-buyer strategic partnerships in the industry.

How Buyer Bargaining Power Can Create Competitive Pressures
As with suppliers, the leverage that certain types of buyers have in negotiating favorable terms can range from weak to strong. Individual consumers, for example, rarely have much bargaining power in negotiating price concessions or other favorable terms with sellers; the primary exceptions involve situations in which price haggling is customary, such as the purchase of new and used motor vehicles, homes, and certain big-ticket items like luxury watches, jewelry, and pleasure boats. For most consumer goods and services, individual buyers have no bargaining leverage—their option is to pay the seller's posted price or take their business elsewhere.

In contrast, large retail chains like Wal-Mart, Circuit City, Target, and Home Depot typically have considerable negotiating leverage in purchasing products from manufacturers because of manufacturers' need for broad retail exposure and the most appealing shelf locations. Retailers may stock two or three competing brands of a product but rarely all competing brands, so competition among rival manufacturers for visibility on the shelves of popular multistore retailers gives such retailers significant bargaining strength. Major supermarket chains like Kroger, Safeway, and Royal Ahold, which provide access to millions of grocery shoppers, have sufficient bargaining power to demand promotional allowances and lump-sum payments (called *slotting fees*) from food products manufacturers in return for stocking certain brands or putting them in the best shelf locations. Motor vehicle manufacturers have strong bargaining power in negotiating to buy original-equipment tires from Goodyear, Michelin, Bridgestone/Firestone, Continental, and Pirelli not only because they buy in large quantities but also because tire makers believe they gain an advantage in supplying replacement tires to vehicle owners if their tire brand is original equipment on the vehicle. "Prestige" buyers have a degree of clout in negotiating with sellers because a seller's reputation is enhanced by having prestige buyers on its customer list.

Even if buyers do not purchase in large quantities or offer a seller important market exposure or prestige, they gain a degree of bargaining leverage in the following circumstances:[10]

- *If buyers' costs of switching to competing brands or substitutes are relatively low.* Buyers who can readily switch brands or source from several sellers have more negotiating leverage than buyers who have high switching costs. When the products of rival sellers are virtually identical, it is relatively easy for buyers to switch from seller to seller at little or no cost and anxious sellers may be willing to make concessions to win or retain a buyer's business.

■ *If the number of buyers is small or if a customer is particularly important to a seller.* The smaller the number of buyers, the less easy it is for sellers to find alternative buyers when a customer is lost to a competitor. The prospect of losing a customer not easily replaced often makes a seller more willing to grant concessions of one kind or another.

■ *If buyer demand is weak and sellers are scrambling to secure additional sales of their products.* Weak or declining demand creates a "buyers' market"; conversely, strong or rapidly growing demand creates a "sellers' market" and shifts bargaining power to sellers.

■ *If buyers are well-informed about sellers' products, prices, and costs.* The more information buyers have, the better bargaining position they are in. The mushrooming availability of product information on the Internet is giving added bargaining power to individuals. Buyers can easily use the Internet to compare prices and features of vacation packages, shop for the best interest rates on mortgages and loans, and find the best prices on big-ticket items such as digital cameras. Bargain-hunting individuals can shop around for the best deal on the Internet and use that information to negotiate a better deal from local retailers; this method is becoming commonplace in buying new and used motor vehicles. Further, the Internet has created opportunities for manufacturers, wholesalers, retailers, and sometimes individuals to join online buying groups to pool their purchasing power and approach vendors for better terms than could be gotten individually. A multinational manufacturer's geographically scattered purchasing groups can use Internet technology to pool their orders with parts and components suppliers and bargain for volume discounts. Purchasing agents at some companies are banding together at third-party Web sites to pool corporate purchases to get better deals or special treatment.

■ *If buyers pose a credible threat of integrating backward into the business of sellers.* Companies like Anheuser-Busch, Coors, and Heinz have integrated backward into metal-can manufacturing to gain bargaining power in obtaining the balance of their can requirements from otherwise powerful metal-can manufacturers. Retailers gain bargaining power by stocking and promoting their own private-label brands alongside manufacturers' name brands. Wal-Mart, for example, competes against Procter & Gamble, its biggest supplier, with its own brand of laundry detergent, called Sam's Choice, which is priced 25 to 30 percent lower than P&G's Tide. Wal-Mart also markets over 2,000 other grocery items under its Sam's Choice and Great Value private labels—its growing strategic emphasis on private-label products adds to its bargaining power with name-brand manufacturers.

■ *If buyers have discretion in whether and when they purchase the product.* Many consumers, if they are unhappy with the present deals offered on major appliances or hot tubs or home entertainment centers, may be in a position to delay purchase until prices and financing terms improve. If business customers are not happy with the prices or security features of bill-payment software systems, they can either delay purchase until next-generation products become available or attempt to develop their own software in-house. If college students believe that the prices of new textbooks are too high, they can purchase used copies.

Figure 2.8 summarizes the circumstances that make for strong or weak bargaining power on the part of buyers.

Figure 2.8   Factors Affecting the Bargaining Power of Buyers

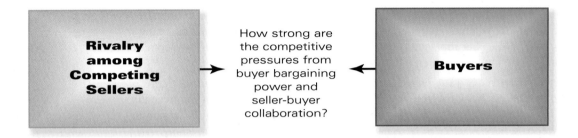

Buyer bargaining power is stronger when:
■ Buyer switching costs to competing brands or substitute products are low.
■ Buyers are large and can demand concessions when purchasing large quantities.
■ Large-volume purchases by buyers are important to sellers.
■ Buyer demand is weak or declining.
■ There are only a few buyers—so each one's business is important to sellers.
■ Identity of buyer adds prestige to the seller's list of customers.
■ Quantity and quality of information available to buyers improve.
■ Buyers have the ability to postpone purchases until later if they do not like the present deals being offered by sellers.
■ Some buyers are a threat to integrate backward into the business of sellers and become an important competitor.

Buyer bargaining power is weaker when:
■ Buyers purchase the item infrequently or in small quantities.
■ Buyer switching costs to competing brands are high.
■ There is a surge in buyer demand that creates a "sellers' market."
■ A seller's brand reputation is important to a buyer.
■ A particular seller's product delivers quality or performance that is very important to buyer and that is not matched in other brands.
■ Buyer collaboration or partnering with selected sellers provides attractive win-win opportunities.

A final point to keep in mind is that *not all buyers of an industry's product have equal degrees of bargaining power with sellers*, and some may be less sensitive than others to price, quality, or service differences. For example, independent tire retailers have less bargaining power in purchasing tires than do Honda, Ford, and Daimler-Chrysler (which buy in much larger quantities), and they are also less sensitive to quality. Motor vehicle manufacturers are very particular about tire quality and tire performance because of the effects on vehicle performance, and they drive a hard bargain with tire manufacturers on both price and quality. Apparel manufacturers confront significant bargaining power when selling to retail chains like JCPenney, Sears, or Macy's, but they can command much better prices selling to small owner-managed apparel boutiques.

How Seller-Buyer Collaboration Can Create Competitive Pressures   Partnerships between sellers and buyers are an increasingly important element of the competitive picture in *business-to-business relationships* (as opposed to business-to-consumer relationships). Many sellers that provide items to business customers have found it in their mutual interest to collaborate closely on such matters as just-in-time deliveries, order processing, electronic invoice payments, and data sharing. Wal-Mart, for example, provides the manufacturers with which it does business (like Procter & Gamble) with daily sales data from each of its stores so that the manufacturers can maintain sufficient inventories at Wal-Mart's distribution centers to keep the shelves at each Wal-Mart store amply stocked. Dell Computer has partnered with its largest customers to create online systems for over 50,000 corporate customers, providing their employees with information on approved product configurations, global pricing, paperless purchase orders, real-time order tracking, invoicing, purchasing history, and other efficiency tools. Dell also loads a customer's software at the factory and installs asset tags so that customer setup time is minimal; it also helps customers upgrade their PC systems to next-generation hardware and software. Dell's partnerships with its corporate customers have put significant competitive pressure on other PC makers.

Determining Whether the Collective Strength of the Five Competitive Forces Is Conducive to Good Profitability

Scrutinizing each of the five competitive forces one by one provides a powerful diagnosis of what competition is like in a given market. Once the strategist has gained an understanding of the specific competitive pressures composing each force and determined whether these pressures constitute a strong or weak competitive force, the next step is to evaluate the collective strength of the five forces and determine whether the state of competition is conducive to good profitability. Is the collective impact of the five competitive forces stronger than "normal"? Are some of the competitive forces sufficiently strong to undermine industry profitability? Can companies in this industry reasonably expect to earn decent profits in light of the prevailing competitive forces?

Are Competitive Pressures Conducive to Good Profitability?

As a rule, the stronger the collective impact of the five competitive forces, the lower the combined profitability of industry participants. The most extreme case of a "competitively unattractive" industry is one in which all five forces are producing strong competitive pressures: rivalry among sellers is vigorous, low entry barriers allow new rivals to gain a market foothold, competition from substitutes is intense, and both suppliers and customers are able to exercise considerable bargaining leverage. Fierce to strong competitive pressures coming from all five directions nearly always drive industry profitability to unacceptably low levels, frequently producing losses for many industry members and forcing some out of business. But an industry can be competitively unattractive without all five competitive forces being strong. Intense competitive pressures from just two or three of the five forces may suffice to destroy the conditions for good profitability and prompt some companies to exit the business. The manufacture of disk drives, for example, is brutally competitive; IBM recently announced the sale of its disk drive business to Hitachi, taking a loss of over $2 billion on its exit from the business. Especially intense competitive conditions seem to be the norm in tire manufacturing and apparel, two industries where profit margins have historically been thin.

> **Core Concept**
>
> The stronger the forces of competition, the harder it becomes for industry members to earn attractive profits.

In contrast, when the collective impact of the five competitive forces is moderate to weak, an industry is competitively attractive in the sense that industry members can reasonably expect to earn good profits and a nice return on investment. The ideal competitive environment for earning superior profits is one in which both suppliers and customers are in weak bargaining positions, there are no good substitutes, high barriers block further entry, and rivalry among present sellers generates only moderate competitive pressures. Weak competition is the best of all possible worlds for also-ran companies because even they can usually eke out a decent profit—if a company can't make a decent profit when competition is weak, then its business outlook is indeed grim.

In most industries, the collective strength of the five competitive forces is somewhere near the middle of the two extremes of very intense and very weak, typically ranging from slightly stronger than normal to slightly weaker than normal and typically allowing well-managed companies with sound strategies to earn attractive profits.

> A company's strategy is increasingly effective the more it provides some insulation from competitive pressures and shifts the competitive battle in the company's favor.

Matching Company Strategy to Competitive Conditions   Working through the five-forces model step by step not only aids strategy makers in assessing whether the intensity of competition allows good profitability but also promotes sound strategic thinking about how to better match company strategy to the specific competitive character of the marketplace. Effectively matching a company's strategy to the particular competitive pressures and competitive conditions that exist has two aspects:

1. Pursuing actions to shield the firm from the prevailing competitive pressures as much as possible.

2. Initiating actions calculated to produce sustainable competitive advantage, thereby shifting the competitive battle in the company's favor, putting added competitive pressure on rivals, and perhaps even defining the business model for the industry.

But making headway on these two fronts first requires identifying competitive pressures, gauging the relative strength of each, and gaining a deep enough understanding of the state of competition in the industry to know which strategy buttons to push.

The Drivers of Industry Change: What Impacts Will They Have?

An industry's present conditions don't necessarily reveal much about the strategically relevant ways in which the industry environment is changing. All industries are characterized by trends and new developments that gradually or speedily produce changes important enough to require a strategic response from participating firms. The popular hypothesis that industries go through a life cycle of takeoff, rapid growth, early maturity, market saturation, and stagnation or decline helps explain industry change—but it is far from complete.[11] There are more causes of industry change than an industry's normal progression through the life cycle.

The Concept of Driving Forces

Although it is important to judge what growth stage an industry is in, there's more analytical value in identifying the specific factors causing fundamental industry and competitive adjustments. Industry and competitive conditions change because forces are enticing or pressuring certain industry participants (competitors, customers, suppliers) to alter their actions in important ways.[12] **Driving forces** are those that have the biggest influence on the changes under way in the industry's structure and competitive environment. Some driving forces originate in the outer ring of the company's macroenvironment (see Figure 2.2), but most usually originate in the company's more immediate industry and competitive environment. Driving-forces analysis has two steps: (1) identifying what the driving forces are and (2) assessing the impact they will have on the industry.

> **Core Con**
>
> Industry con…
> cause important forces a… industry participants to alter their actions; the **driving forces** in an industry are the *major underlying causes* of changing industry and competitive conditions—some driving forces originate in the macroenvironment and some originate within a company's immediate industry and competitive environment.

Identifying the Industry's Driving Forces

Many events can affect an industry powerfully enough to qualify as driving forces—as shown in Table 2.1. Some are unique and specific to a particular industry situation, but most drivers of change fall into one of the following categories:[13]

- *Growing use of the Internet and adoption of emerging new Internet technology applications:* Over the past 10 years, the Internet and the adoption of Internet technology applications have been major drivers of change in industry after industry. As cases in point, consider how downloading music from the Internet is reshaping the music industry and the business of traditional brick-and-mortar retailers and how the use of e-mail is affecting the business of providing fax services and the revenues of governmental postal services worldwide. The Internet has proved to be an important new distribution channel in a growing number of industries, enabling manufacturers to access customers directly rather than distribute exclusively through traditional wholesale and retail channels, and also allowing companies of all types to extend their geographic reach and vie for sales in areas where they formerly did not have a presence. The ability of companies to reach

Table 2.1   THE MOST COMMON DRIVING FORCES

1. Growing use of the Internet and emerging new Internet technology applications.
2. Increasing globalization of the industry.
3. Changes in the industry's long-term growth rate.
4. Changes in who buys the product and how they use it.
5. Product innovation.
6. Technological change and manufacturing process innovation.
7. Marketing innovation.
8. Entry or exit of major firms.
9. Diffusion of technical know-how across more companies and more countries.
10. Changes in cost and efficiency.
11. Growing buyer preferences for differentiated products instead of standardized commodity products (or for a more standardized product instead of strongly differentiated products).
12. Reductions in uncertainty and business risk.
13. Regulatory influences and government policy changes.
14. Changing societal concerns, attitudes, and lifestyles.

consumers via the Internet increases the number of rivals a company faces and often escalates rivalry by pitting pure online sellers against combination brick-and-click sellers against pure brick-and-mortar sellers. The Web sites of rival sellers are only a few clicks apart and are open for business 24 hours a day every day of the year, giving buyers unprecedented ability to research the product offerings of competitors and shop the market for the best value. Companies are increasingly using online technology to (1) collaborate closely with suppliers and streamline their supply chains and (2) revamp internal operations and squeeze out cost savings. Internet technology has so many business applications that companies across the world are pursuing its operational benefits and making online systems a normal part of everyday operations. But the impacts vary from industry to industry and company to company, and the industry and competitive implications are continuously evolving. The challenges here are to assess precisely how the Internet and Internet technology applications are altering a particular industry's landscape and to factor these impacts into the strategy-making equation.

■ *Increasing globalization:* Competition begins to shift from primarily a regional or national focus to an international or global focus when industry members begin seeking customers in foreign markets or when production activities begin to migrate to countries where costs are lowest. Globalization of competition really starts to take hold when one or more ambitious companies precipitate a race for worldwide market leadership by launching initiatives to expand into more and more country markets. Globalization can also be precipitated by the blossoming of consumer demand in more and more countries and by the actions of government officials in many countries to reduce trade barriers or open up once-closed markets to foreign competitors, as is occurring in many parts of Europe, Latin America, and Asia. Significant differences in labor costs among countries give manufacturers a strong incentive to locate plants for labor-intensive products in low-wage countries and use these plants to supply market demand across the world. Wages in China, India, Singapore, Mexico, and Brazil, for example, are about one-fourth those in the United States, Germany, and Japan. The forces of globalization are sometimes such a strong driver that companies find it highly advantageous, if not necessary, to spread their operating reach into more and more country markets. Globalization is very much a driver of industry change in such industries as credit cards, mobile phones, motor vehicles, steel, refined petroleum products, public accounting, and textbook publishing.

■ *Changes in the long-term industry growth rate:* Shifts in industry growth up or down are a driving force for industry change, affecting the balance between industry supply and buyer demand, entry and exit, and the character and strength of competition. An upsurge in buyer demand triggers a race among established firms and newcomers to capture the new sales opportunities; ambitious companies with trailing market shares may see the upturn in demand as a golden opportunity to broaden their customer base and move up several notches in the industry standings to secure a place among the market leaders. A slowdown in the rate at which demand is growing nearly always portends mounting rivalry and increased efforts by some firms to maintain their high rates of growth by taking sales and market share away from rivals. If industry sales suddenly turn flat or begin to shrink after years of rising steadily, competition is certain to intensify as industry members scramble for the available business and as mergers and acquisitions result in industry consolidation to a smaller number of competitively stronger participants. Dimming sales prospects usually prompt both competitively weak and growth-oriented companies to sell their business operations to those industry members that elect to stick it out; as demand for the industry's product continues to shrink, the remaining industry members may be forced to close inefficient plants and retrench to a smaller production base—all of which results in a much-changed competitive landscape.

■ *Changes in who buys the product and how they use it:* Shifts in buyer demographics and new ways of using the product can alter the state of competition by opening the way to market an industry's product through a different mix of dealers and retail outlets, prompting producers to broaden or narrow their product lines, bringing different sales and promotion approaches into play, and forcing adjustments in customer service offerings (credit, technical assistance, maintenance and repair). The mushrooming popularity of downloading music from the Internet, storing music files on PC hard drives, and burning custom discs has forced recording companies to reexamine their distribution strategies and raised questions about the future of traditional retail music stores; at the same time, it has stimulated sales of disc burners and blank discs. Longer life expectancies and growing percentages of relatively well-to-do retirees are driving changes in such industries as health care, prescription drugs, recreational living, and vacation travel. The growing percentage of households with PCs and Internet access is opening opportunities for banks to expand their electronic bill-payment services and for retailers to move more of their customer services online.

■ *Product innovation:* Competition in an industry is always affected by rivals racing to be first to introduce one new product or product enhancement after another. An ongoing stream of product innovations tends to alter the pattern of competition in an industry by attracting more first-time buyers, rejuvenating industry growth, and/or creating wider or narrower product differentiation among rival sellers. Successful new product introductions strengthen the market positions of the innovating companies, usually at the expense of companies that stick with their old products or are slow to follow with their own versions of the new product. Product innovation has been a key driving force in such industries as digital cameras, golf clubs, video games, toys, and prescription drugs.

■ *Technological change and manufacturing process innovation:* Advances in technology can dramatically alter an industry's landscape, making it possible to produce new and better products at lower cost and opening up whole new industry frontiers. For instance, growing use of Voice Over Internet Protocol technology (VOIP) has given rise to an Internet-based phone network and is rapidly eroding the business of AT&T and other long-distance providers worldwide. Flat-screen technology for PC monitors is killing the demand for conventional CRT monitors. LCD and plasma-screen technology and high-definition technology are precipitating a revolution in the television industry. MP3 technology is altering the shape of the music industry. Digital technology is driving huge changes in the camera and film industries. Technological developments can also produce competitively significant changes in capital requirements, minimum efficient plant sizes, distribution channels and logistics, and experience or learning-curve effects. In the steel industry, ongoing advances in electric-arc minimill technology (which involve recycling scrap steel to make new products) have allowed steelmakers with state-of-the-art minimills to gradually expand into the production of more and more steel products, steadily taking sales and market share from higher-cost integrated producers (which make steel from scratch using iron ore, coke, and traditional blast furnace technology). Nucor, the leader of the minimill technology revolution in the United States, began operations in 1970 and has ridden the wave of technological advances in minimill technology to become the biggest U.S. steel producer (as of 2004) and rank among the lowest-cost producers in the world. In a space of 30 years, advances in minimill technology have changed the face of the steel industry worldwide.

- *Marketing innovation:* When firms are successful in introducing new ways to market their products, they can spark a burst of buyer interest, widen industry demand, increase product differentiation, and lower unit costs—any or all of which can alter the competitive positions of rival firms and force strategy revisions. In today's world, Internet marketing is shaking up competition in such industries as electronics retailing, stock brokerage (where online brokers have taken significant business away from traditional brokers), and office supplies (where Office Depot, Staples, and Office Max are using their Web sites to market office supplies to corporations, small businesses, schools and universities, and government agencies). Increasing numbers of music artists are marketing their recordings at their own Web sites rather than entering into contracts with recording studios that distribute through music retailers and online music stores.

- *Entry or exit of major firms:* The entry of one or more foreign companies into a geographic market once dominated by domestic firms nearly always shakes up competitive conditions. Likewise, when an established domestic firm from another industry attempts entry either by acquisition or by launching its own start-up venture, it usually applies its skills and resources in some innovative fashion that pushes competition in new directions. Entry by a major firm thus often produces a new ball game, not only with new key players but also with new rules for competing. Similarly, exit of a major firm changes the competitive structure by reducing the number of market leaders (perhaps increasing the dominance of the leaders that remain) and causing a rush to capture the exiting firm's customers.

- *Diffusion of technical know-how across more companies and more countries:* As knowledge about how to perform a particular activity or execute a particular manufacturing technology spreads, the competitive advantage held by firms originally possessing this know-how erodes. Knowledge diffusion can occur through scientific journals, trade publications, on-site plant tours, word of mouth among suppliers and customers, employee migration, and Internet sources. It can also occur when those possessing technological know-how license others to use it for a royalty fee or team up with a company interested in turning the technology into a new business venture. Quite often, technological know-how can be acquired by simply buying a company that has the wanted skills, patents, or manufacturing capabilities. In recent years, *rapid technology transfer across national boundaries has been a prime factor in causing industries to become more globally competitive.* As companies worldwide gain access to valuable technical know-how, they upgrade their manufacturing capabilities in a long-term effort to compete head-on with established companies. Cross-border technology transfer has made the once domestic industries of automobiles, tires, consumer electronics, telecommunications, computers, and others increasingly global.

- *Changes in cost and efficiency:* Widening or shrinking differences in the costs among key competitors tend to dramatically alter the state of competition. The low cost of e-mail and fax transmission has put mounting competitive pressure on the relatively inefficient and high-cost operations of the U.S. Postal Service—sending a one-page fax is cheaper and far quicker than sending a first-class letter; sending e-mail is faster and cheaper still. In the electric power industry, sharply lower costs to generate electricity at newly constructed combined-cycle generating plants during 1998–2001 forced older coal-fired and gas-fired plants to lower their production costs to remain competitive. Shrinking cost differences in producing multifeatured mobile phones is turning the mobile phone market into a commodity business and causing more buyers to base their purchase decisions on price.

■ *Growing buyer preferences for differentiated products instead of a commodity product (or for a more standardized product instead of strongly differentiated products):* When buyer tastes and preferences start to diverge, sellers can win a loyal following with product offerings that stand apart from those of rival sellers. In recent years, beer drinkers have grown less loyal to a single brand and have begun to drink a variety of domestic and foreign beers; as a consequence, beer manufacturers have introduced a host of new brands and malt beverages with different tastes and flavors. Buyer preferences for motor vehicles are becoming increasingly diverse, with few models generating sales of more than 250,000 units annually. When a shift from standardized to differentiated products occurs, the driver of change is the contest among rivals to cleverly differentiate themselves.

However, buyers sometimes decide that a standardized, budget-priced product suits their requirements as well as or better than a premium-priced product with lots of snappy features and personalized services. Online brokers, for example, have used the lure of cheap commissions to attract many investors willing to place their own buy-sell orders via the Internet; growing acceptance of online trading has put significant competitive pressures on full-service brokers whose business model has always revolved around convincing clients of the value of asking for personalized advice from professional brokers and paying their high commission fees to make trades. Pronounced shifts toward greater product standardization usually spawn lively price competition and force rival sellers to drive down their costs to maintain profitability. The lesson here is that competition is driven partly by whether the market forces in motion are acting to increase or decrease product differentiation.

■ *Reductions in uncertainty and business risk:* An emerging industry is typically characterized by much uncertainty over potential market size, how much time and money will be needed to surmount technological problems, and what distribution channels and buyer segments to emphasize. Emerging industries tend to attract only risk-taking entrepreneurial companies. Over time, however, if the business model of industry pioneers proves profitable and market demand for the product appears durable, more conservative firms are usually enticed to enter the market. Often, these later entrants are large, financially strong firms looking to invest in attractive growth industries.

Lower business risks and less industry uncertainty also affect competition in international markets. In the early stages of a company's entry into foreign markets, conservatism prevails and firms limit their downside exposure by using less risky strategies like exporting, licensing, joint marketing agreements, or joint ventures with local companies to accomplish entry. Then, as experience accumulates and perceived risk levels decline, companies move more boldly and more independently, making acquisitions, constructing their own plants, putting in their own sales and marketing capabilities to build strong competitive positions in each country market, and beginning to link the strategies in each country to create a more globalized strategy.

- *Regulatory influences and government policy changes:* Government regulatory actions can often force significant changes in industry practices and strategic approaches. Deregulation has proved to be a potent procompetitive force in the airline, banking, natural gas, telecommunications, and electric utility industries. Government efforts to reform Medicare and health insurance have become potent driving forces in the health care industry. In international markets, host governments can drive competitive changes by opening their domestic markets to foreign participation or closing them to protect domestic companies. Note that this driving force is spawned by forces in a company's macroenvironment.

- *Changing societal concerns, attitudes, and lifestyles:* Emerging social issues and changing attitudes and lifestyles can be powerful instigators of industry change. Growing antismoking sentiment has emerged as a major driver of change in the tobacco industry; concerns about terrorism are having a big impact on the travel industry. Consumer concerns about salt, sugar, chemical additives, saturated fat, cholesterol, carbohydrates, and nutritional value have forced food producers to revamp food-processing techniques, redirect R&D efforts into the use of healthier ingredients, and compete in developing nutritious, good-tasting products. Safety concerns have driven product design changes in the automobile, toy, and outdoor power equipment industries, to mention a few. Increased interest in physical fitness has spawned new industries in exercise equipment, biking, outdoor apparel, sports gyms and recreation centers, vitamin and nutrition supplements, and medically supervised diet programs. Social concerns about air and water pollution have forced industries to incorporate expenditures for controlling pollution into their cost structures. Shifting societal concerns, attitudes, and lifestyles alter the pattern of competition, usually favoring those players that respond quickly and creatively with products targeted to the new trends and conditions. As with the preceding driving force, this driving force springs from factors at work in a company's macroenvironment.

That there are so many different *potential driving forces* explains why it is too simplistic to view industry change only in terms of moving through the different stages in an industry's life cycle and why a full understanding of the *causes* underlying the emergence of new competitive conditions is a fundamental part of industry analysis. However, while many forces of change may be at work in a given industry, no more than three or four are likely to be true driving forces powerful enough to qualify as the *major determinants* of why and how the industry is changing. Thus company strategists must resist the temptation to label every change they see as a driving force; the analytical task is to evaluate the forces of industry and competitive change carefully enough to separate major factors from minor ones.

Assessing the Impact of the Driving Forces

The second phase of driving-forces analysis is to determine whether the driving forces are, on the whole, acting to make the industry environment more or less attractive. Answers to three questions are needed here:

1. Are the driving forces causing demand for the industry's product to increase or decrease?
2. Are the driving forces acting to make competition more or less intense?
3. Will the driving forces lead to higher or lower industry profitability?

Getting a handle on the collective impact of the driving forces usually requires looking at the likely effects of each force separately, since the driving forces may not all be pushing change in the same direction. For example, two driving forces may be acting to spur demand for the industry's product while one driving force may be working to curtail demand. Whether the net effect on industry demand is up or down hinges on which driving forces are the more powerful. The analyst's objective here is to get a good grip on what external factors are shaping industry change and what difference these factors will make.[14]

The Link between Driving Forces and Strategy

Sound analysis of an industry's driving forces is a prerequisite to sound strategy making. Without understanding the forces driving industry change and the impacts these forces will have on the character of the industry environment and on the company's business over the next one to three years, managers are ill-prepared to craft a strategy tightly matched to emerging conditions. Similarly, if managers are uncertain about the implications of each driving force, or if their views are incomplete or off-base, it's difficult for them to craft a strategy that is responsive to the drivers of industry change. So driving-forces analysis is not something to take lightly; it has practical value and is basic to the task of thinking strategically about where the industry is headed and how to prepare for the changes.

Diagnosing the Market Positions of Industry Rivals: Who Is Strongly Positioned and Who Is Not?

Since competing companies commonly sell in different price/quality ranges, emphasize different distribution channels, incorporate product features that appeal to different types of buyers, have different geographic coverage, and so on, it stands to reason that some companies enjoy stronger or more attractive market positions than other companies. Understanding which companies are strongly positioned and which are weakly positioned is an integral part of analyzing an industry's competitive structure. The best-technique for revealing the market positions of industry competitors is **strategic group mapping**.[15] This analytical tool is useful for comparing the market positions of each firm separately or for grouping them into like positions when an industry has so many competitors that it is not practical to examine each one in depth.

> **Core Concept**
>
> **Strategic group mapping** is a technique for displaying the different market or competitive positions that rival firms occupy in the industry.

Using Strategic Group Maps to Assess the Market Positions of Key Competitors

A **strategic group** consists of those industry members with similar competitive approaches and positions in the market.[16] Companies in the same strategic group can resemble one another in any of several ways: they may have comparable product-line breadth, sell in the same price/quality range, emphasize the same distribution channels,

> **Core Concept**
>
> A **strategic group** is a cluster of industry rivals that have similar competitive approaches and market positions.

use essentially the same product attributes to appeal to similar types of buyers, depend on identical technological approaches, or offer buyers similar services and technical assistance.[17] An industry contains only one strategic group when all sellers pursue essentially identical strategies and have comparable market positions. At the other extreme, an industry may contain as many strategic groups as there are competitors when each rival pursues a distinctively different competitive approach and occupies a substantially different market position.

The procedure for constructing a *strategic group map* is straightforward:

- Identify the competitive characteristics that differentiate firms in the industry; typical variables are price/quality range (high, medium, low), geographic coverage (local, regional, national, global), degree of vertical integration (none, partial, full), product-line breadth (wide, narrow), use of distribution channels (one, some, all), and degree of service offered (no-frills, limited, full).

- Plot the firms on a two-variable map using pairs of these differentiating characteristics.

- Assign firms that fall in about the same strategy space to the same strategic group.

- Draw circles around each strategic group, making the circles proportional to the size of the group's share of total industry sales revenues.

This produces a two-dimensional diagram like the one for the retailing industry in Company Spotlight 2.1.

Several guidelines need to be observed in mapping the positions of strategic groups in the industry's overall strategy space.[18] First, the two variables selected as axes for the map should *not* be highly correlated; if they are, the circles on the map will fall along a diagonal and strategy makers will learn nothing more about the relative positions of competitors than they would by considering just one of the variables. For instance, if companies with broad product lines use multiple distribution channels while companies with narrow lines use a single distribution channel, then looking at broad versus narrow product lines reveals just as much about who is positioned where as looking at single versus multiple distribution channels; that is, one of the variables is redundant. Second, the variables chosen as axes for the map should expose big differences in how rivals position themselves to compete in the marketplace. This, of course, means analysts must identify the characteristics that differentiate rival firms and use these differences as variables for the axes and as the basis for deciding which firm belongs in which strategic group. Third, the variables used as axes don't have to be either quantitative or continuous; rather, they can be discrete variables or defined in terms of distinct classes and combinations. Fourth, drawing the sizes of the circles on the map proportional to the combined sales of the firms in each strategic group allows the map to reflect the relative sizes of each strategic group. Fifth, if more than two good competitive variables can be used as axes for the map, several maps can be drawn to give different exposures to the competitive positioning relationships present in the industry's structure. Because there is not necessarily one best map for portraying how competing firms are positioned in the market, it is advisable to experiment with different pairs of competitive variables.

What Can Be Learned from Strategic Group Maps?

One thing to look for is to what extent *industry driving forces and competitive pressures favor some strategic groups and hurt others.*[19] Firms in adversely affected strategic

COMPANY SPOTLIGHT 2.1

Comparative Market Positions of Selected Retail Chains: A Strategic Group Map Application

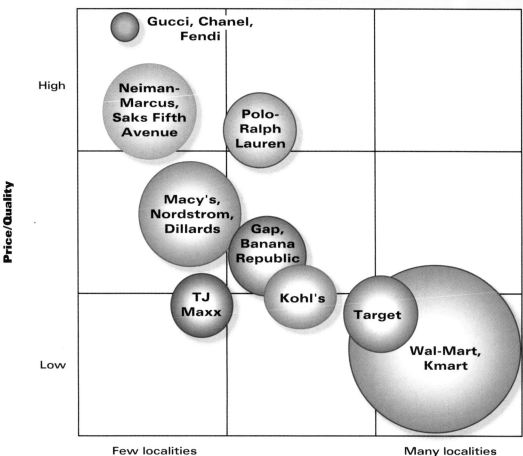

Note: Circles are drawn roughly proportional to the sizes of the chains, based on revenues.

groups may try to shift to a more favorably situated group; how hard such a move proves to be depends on whether entry barriers for the target strategic group are high or low. Attempts by rival firms to enter a new strategic group nearly always increase competitive pressures. If certain firms are known to be trying to change their competitive positions on the map, then attaching arrows to the circles showing the targeted direction helps clarify the picture of competitive maneuvering among rivals.

Another consideration is to what extent *the profit potential of different strategic groups varies due to the strengths and weaknesses in each group's market position.* Differences in profitability can occur because of differing degrees of bargaining leverage or collaboration with suppliers and/or customers, differing degrees of exposure to

> Driving forces and competitive pressures do not affect all strategic groups evenly. Profit prospects vary from group to group based on the relative attractiveness of their market positions.

competition from substitute products outside the industry, differing degrees of competitive rivalry within strategic groups, and differing growth rates for the principal buyer segments served by each group.

Generally speaking, *the closer strategic groups are to each other on the map, the stronger the cross-group competitive rivalry tends to be.* Although firms in the same strategic group are the closest rivals, the next closest rivals are in the immediately adjacent groups.[20] Often, firms in strategic groups that are far apart on the map hardly compete at all. For instance, Tiffany & Co. and Wal-Mart both sell gold and silver jewelry, but their clientele and the prices and quality of their products are much too different to justify calling them competitors. For the same reason, Timex is not a meaningful competitive rival of Rolex, and Subaru is not a close competitor of Lincoln or Mercedes-Benz.

Predicting the Next Strategic Moves Rivals Are Likely to Make

Unless a company pays attention to what competitors are doing and knows their strengths and weaknesses, it ends up flying blind into competitive battle. As in sports, scouting the opposition is essential. **Competitive intelligence** about rivals' strategies, their latest actions and announcements, their resource strengths and weaknesses, the efforts being made to improve their situation, and the thinking and leadership styles of their executives is valuable for predicting or anticipating the strategic moves competitors are likely to make next in the marketplace. Having good information to predict the strategic direction and likely moves of key competitors allows a company to prepare defensive countermoves, to craft its own strategic moves with some confidence about what market maneuvers to expect from rivals, and to exploit any openings that arise from competitors' missteps or strategy flaws.

> Good scouting reports on rivals provide a valuable assist in anticipating what moves rivals are likely to make next and outmaneuvering them in the marketplace.

Identifying Competitors' Strategies and Resource Strengths and Weaknesses

Keeping close tabs on a competitor's strategy entails monitoring what the rival is doing in the marketplace, what its management is saying in company press releases, information posted on the company's Web site (especially press releases and the presentations management has recently made to securities analysts), and such public documents as annual reports and 10-K filings, articles in the business media, and reports of securities analysts. (Figure 1.1 in Chapter 1 indicates what to look for in identifying a company's strategy.) Company personnel may be able to pick up useful information from a rival's exhibits at trade shows and from conversations with a rival's customers, suppliers, and former employees.[21] Many companies have a competitive intelligence unit that sifts through the available information to construct up-to-date strategic profiles of rivals—their current strategies, their resource strengths and competitive capabilities, their competitive shortcomings, and the latest pronouncements and leadership styles of their executives. Such profiles are typically updated regularly and made available to managers and other key personnel.

Those who gather competitive intelligence on rivals, however, can sometimes cross the fine line between honest inquiry and unethical or even illegal behavior. For example, calling rivals to get information about prices, the dates of new product introductions, or wage and salary levels is legal, but misrepresenting one's company affiliation during such calls is unethical. Pumping rivals' representatives at trade shows is ethical only if one wears a name tag with accurate company affiliation indicated. Avon Products at one point secured information about its biggest rival, Mary Kay Cosmetics (MKC), by having its personnel search through the garbage bins outside MKC's headquarters.[22] When MKC officials learned of the action and sued, Avon claimed it did nothing illegal, since a 1988 Supreme Court case had ruled that trash left on public property (in this case, a sidewalk) was anyone's for the taking. Avon even produced a videotape of its removal of the trash at the MKC site. Avon won the lawsuit—but Avon's action, while legal, scarcely qualifies as ethical.

In sizing up the strategies and the competitive strengths and weaknesses of competitors, it makes sense for company strategists to make three assessments:

1. Which competitor has the best strategy? Which competitors appear to have flawed or weak strategies?

2. Which competitors are poised to gain market share, and which ones seem destined to lose ground?

3. Which competitors are likely to rank among the industry leaders five years from now? Do one or more up-and-coming competitors have powerful strategies and sufficient resource capabilities to overtake the current industry leader?

The industry's *current* major players are generally easy to identify, but some of the leaders may be plagued with weaknesses that are causing them to lose ground; others may lack the resources and capabilities to remain strong contenders given the superior strategies and capabilities of up-and-coming companies. In evaluating which competitors are favorably or unfavorably positioned to gain market ground, company strategists need to focus on why there is potential for some rivals to do better or worse than other rivals. Usually, a competitor's prospects are a function of its vulnerability to driving forces and competitive pressures, whether its strategy has resulted in competitive advantage or disadvantage, and whether its resources and capabilities are well suited for competing on the road ahead.

Predicting Competitors' Next Moves

Predicting the next strategic moves of competitors is the hardest yet most useful part of competitor analysis. Good clues about what actions a specific company is likely to undertake can often be gleaned from how well it is faring in the marketplace, the problems or weaknesses it needs to address, and how much pressure it is under to improve its financial performance. Content rivals are likely to continue their present strategy with only minor fine-tuning. Ailing rivals can be performing so poorly that fresh strategic moves are virtually certain. Ambitious rivals looking to move up in the industry ranks are strong candidates for launching new strategic offensives to pursue emerging market opportunities and exploit the vulnerabilities of weaker rivals.

Since the moves a competitor is likely to make are generally predicated on the views their executives have about the industry's future and their beliefs about their firm's situation, it makes sense to closely scrutinize the public pronouncements of rival company executives about where the industry is headed and what it will take to be successful, what they are saying about their firm's situation, information from the grapevine about what they are doing, and their past actions and leadership styles. Other considerations in trying to predict what strategic moves rivals are likely to make next include the following:

- Which rivals badly need to increase their unit sales and market share? What strategic options are they most likely to pursue: lowering prices, adding new models and styles, expanding their dealer networks, entering additional geographic markets, boosting advertising to build better brand-name awareness, acquiring a weaker competitor, or placing more emphasis on direct sales via their Web site?

- Which rivals have a strong incentive, along with the resources, to make major strategic changes, perhaps moving to a different position on the strategic group map? Which rivals are probably locked in to pursuing the same basic strategy with only minor adjustments?

- Which rivals are good candidates to be acquired? Which rivals may be looking to make an acquisition and are financially able to do so?

- Which rivals are likely to enter new geographic markets?

- Which rivals are strong candidates to expand their product offerings and enter new product segments where they do not currently have a presence?

> Managers who fail to study competitors closely risk being caught napping by the new strategic moves of rivals.

To succeed in predicting a competitor's next moves, company strategists need to have a good feel for each rival's situation, how its managers think, and what its best options are. Doing the necessary detective work can be tedious and time-consuming, but scouting competitors well enough to anticipate their next moves allows managers to prepare effective countermoves (perhaps even beat a rival to the punch) and to take rivals' probable actions into account in crafting their own best course of action.

Pinpointing the Key Factors for Future Competitive Success

An industry's **key success factors (KSFs)** are those competitive factors that most affect industry members' ability to prosper in the marketplace—the particular strategy elements, product attributes, resources, competencies, competitive capabilities, and market achievements that spell the difference between being a strong competitor and a weak competitor and sometimes between profit and loss. KSFs by their very nature are so important to future competitive success that *all firms* in the industry must pay close attention to them or risk becoming an industry also-ran. To indicate the significance of KSFs another way, how well a company's product offering, resources, and capabilities measure up against an industry's KSFs determines just how financially and competitively successful that company will be. Identifying KSFs, in light of the prevailing and anticipated industry and competitive conditions, is therefore always a top-priority analytical and strategy-making consideration. Company strategists

Core Concept

Key success factors are the product attributes, competencies, competitive capabilities, and market achievements with the greatest impact on future competitive success in the marketplace.

need to understand the industry landscape well enough to separate the factors most important to competitive success from those that are less important.

In the beer industry, the KSFs are full utilization of brewing capacity (to keep manufacturing costs low), a strong network of wholesale distributors (to get the company's brand stocked and favorably displayed in retail outlets where beer is sold), and clever advertising (to induce beer drinkers to buy the company's brand and thereby pull beer sales through the established wholesale/retail channels). In apparel manufacturing, the KSFs are appealing designs and color combinations (to create buyer interest) and low-cost manufacturing efficiency (to permit attractive retail pricing and ample profit margins). In tin and aluminum cans, because the cost of shipping empty cans is substantial, one of the keys is having can-manufacturing facilities located close to end-use customers. Key success factors thus vary from industry to industry, and even from time to time within the same industry, as driving forces and competitive conditions change. Table 2.2 lists the most common types of key success factors.

An industry's key success factors can usually be deduced from what was learned from the previously described analysis of the industry and competitive environment. The factors that are most important to future competitive success flow directly from the industry's dominant characteristics, the nature of the competition, the impacts of the driving forces, the comparative market positions of industry members, and the likely next moves of key rivals. In addition, the answers to three questions help identify an industry's key success factors:

1. On what basis do buyers of the industry's product choose between the competing brands of sellers? That is, what product attributes are crucial?

2. Given the nature of competitive rivalry and the competitive forces prevailing in the marketplace, what resources and competitive capabilities does a company need to have to be competitively successful?

3. What shortcomings are almost certain to put a company at a significant competitive disadvantage?

Only rarely are there more than five or six key factors for future competitive success. And even among these, two or three usually outrank the others in importance. Managers should therefore bear in mind the purpose of identifying key success factors—to determine which factors are most important to future competitive success—and resist the temptation to label a factor that has only minor importance a KSF. To compile a list of every factor that matters even a little bit defeats the purpose of concentrating management attention on the factors truly critical to long-term competitive success.

Correctly diagnosing an industry's KSFs raises a company's chances of crafting a sound strategy. The goal of company strategists should be to design a strategy aimed at stacking up well on all of the industry's future KSFs and trying to be *distinctively better* than rivals on one (or possibly two) of the KSFs. Indeed, companies that stand out or excel on a particular KSF are likely to enjoy a stronger market position—*being distinctively better than rivals on one or two key success factors tends to translate into competitive advantage*. Hence, using the industry's KSFs as *cornerstones* for the company's strategy and trying to gain sustainable competitive advantage by excelling at one particular KSF is a fruitful competitive strategy approach.[23]

> **Core Concept**
>
> A sound strategy incorporates the intent to stack up well on all of the industry's key success factors and to excel on one or two KSFs.

Table 2.2   COMMON TYPES OF INDUSTRY KEY SUCCESS FACTORS

Technology-related KSFs	■ Expertise in a particular technology or in scientific research (important in pharmaceuticals, Internet applications, mobile communications, and most "high-tech" industries) ■ Proven ability to improve production processes (important in industries where advancing technology opens the way for higher manufacturing efficiency and lower production costs)
Manufacturing-related KSFs	■ Ability to achieve scale economies and/or capture experience-curve effects (important to achieving low production costs) ■ Quality control know-how (important in industries where customers insist on product reliability) ■ High utilization of fixed assets (important in capital-intensive/high-fixed-cost industries) ■ Access to attractive supplies of skilled labor ■ High labor productivity (important for items with high labor content) ■ Low-cost product design and engineering (reduces manufacturing costs) ■ Ability to manufacture or assemble products that are customized to buyer specifications
Distribution-related KSFs	■ A strong network of wholesale distributors/dealers ■ Strong direct-sales capabilities via the Internet and/or company-owned retail outlets ■ Ability to secure favorable display space on retailer shelves
Marketing-related KSFs	■ Breadth of product line and product selection ■ A well-known and well-respected brand name ■ Fast, accurate technical assistance ■ Courteous, personalized customer service ■ Accurate filling of buyer orders (few back orders or mistakes) ■ Customer guarantees and warranties (important in mail-order and online retailing, big-ticket purchases, new product introductions) ■ Clever advertising
Skills- and capability-related KSFs	■ A talented workforce (superior talent is important in professional services like accounting and investment banking) ■ National or global distribution capabilities ■ Product innovation capabilities (important in industries where rivals are racing to be first to market with new product attributes or performance features) ■ Design expertise (important in fashion and apparel industries) ■ Short delivery time capability ■ Supply chain management capabilities ■ Strong e-commerce capabilities—a user-friendly Web site and/or skills in using Internet technology applications to streamline internal operations
Other types of KSFs	■ Overall low costs (not just in manufacturing) so as to be able to meet low-price expectations of customers ■ Convenient locations (important in many retailing businesses) ■ Ability to provide fast, convenient after-the-sale repairs and service ■ A strong balance sheet and access to financial capital (important in newly emerging industries with high degrees of business risk and in capital-intensive industries) ■ Patent protection

Deciding Whether the Industry Presents an Attractive Opportunity

The final step in evaluating the industry and competitive environment is to use the preceding analysis to decide whether the outlook for the industry presents the company with a sufficiently attractive business opportunity. The important factors on which to base such a conclusion include:

- The industry's growth potential.

- Whether powerful competitive forces are squeezing industry profitability to subpar levels and whether competition appears destined to grow stronger or weaker.

- Whether industry profitability will be favorably or unfavorably affected by the prevailing driving forces.

- The degrees of risk and uncertainty in the industry's future.

- Whether the industry as a whole confronts severe problems—regulatory or environmental issues, stagnating buyer demand, industry overcapacity, mounting competition, and so on.

- The company's competitive position in the industry vis-à-vis rivals. (Being a well-entrenched leader or strongly positioned contender in a lackluster industry may present adequate opportunity for good profitability; however, having to fight a steep uphill battle against much stronger rivals may hold little promise of eventual market success or good return on shareholder investment, even though the industry environment is attractive.)

- The company's potential to capitalize on the vulnerabilities of weaker rivals (perhaps converting a relatively unattractive *industry* situation into a potentially rewarding *company* opportunity).

- Whether the company has sufficient competitive strength to defend against or counteract the factors that make the industry unattractive.

- Whether continued participation in this industry adds importantly to the firm's ability to be successful in other industries in which it may have business interests.

As a general proposition, *if an industry's overall profit prospects are above average, the industry environment is basically attractive; if industry profit prospects are below average, conditions are unattractive.* However, it is a mistake to think of a particular industry as being equally attractive or unattractive to all industry participants and all potential entrants. Attractiveness is relative, not absolute, and conclusions one way or the other have to be drawn from the perspective of a particular company. Industries attractive to insiders may be unattractive to outsiders. Companies on the outside may look at an industry's environment and conclude that it is an unattractive business for them to get into, given the prevailing entry barriers, the difficulty of challenging current market leaders with their particular resources and competencies, and the opportunities they have elsewhere. Industry environments unattractive to weak competitors may be attractive to strong competitors. A favorably positioned company may survey a business environment and see a host of opportunities that weak competitors cannot capture.

> **Core Concept**
>
> The degree to which an industry is attractive or unattractive is not the same for all industry participants and all potential entrants; the attractiveness of the opportunities an industry presents depends heavily on whether a company has the resource strengths and competitive capabilities to capture them.

When a company decides an industry is fundamentally attractive and presents good opportunities, a strong case can be made that it should invest aggressively to capture the opportunities it sees and to improve its long-term competitive position in the business. When a strong competitor concludes an industry is relatively unattractive and lacking in opportunity, it may elect to simply protect its present position, investing cautiously, if at all, and looking for opportunities in other industries. A competitively weak company in an unattractive industry may see its best option as finding a buyer, perhaps a rival, to acquire its business.

Key Points

Thinking strategically about a company's external situation involves probing for answers to the following seven questions:

1. *What are the industry's strategy-shaping economic features?* Industries differ significantly on such factors as market size and growth rate, the geographic scope of competitive rivalry, the number and relative sizes of both buyers and sellers, the ease of entry and exit, the extent of vertical integration, how fast basic technology is changing, the extent of scale economies and learning-curve effects, the degree of product standardization or differentiation, and overall profitability. In addition to setting the stage for the analysis to come, identifying an industry's economic features also promotes understanding of the kinds of strategic moves that industry members are likely to employ.

2. *What kinds of competitive forces are industry members facing, and how strong is each force?* The strength of competition is a composite of five forces: the rivalry among competing sellers, the presence of attractive substitutes, the potential for new entry, the competitive pressures stemming from supplier bargaining power and supplier-seller collaboration, and the competitive pressures stemming from buyer bargaining power and seller-buyer collaboration. These five forces have to be examined one by one to identify the specific competitive pressures they each comprise and to decide whether these pressures constitute a strong or weak competitive force. The next step in competition analysis is to evaluate the collective strength of the five forces and determine whether the state of competition is conducive to good profitability. Working through the five-forces model step by step not only aids strategy makers in assessing whether the intensity of competition allows good profitability but also promotes sound strategic thinking about how to better match company strategy to the specific competitive character of the marketplace. Effectively matching a company's strategy to the particular competitive pressures and competitive conditions that exist has two aspects: (a) pursuing avenues that shield the firm from as many of the prevailing competitive pressures as possible, and (b) initiating actions calculated to produce sustainable competitive advantage, thereby shifting competition in the company's favor, putting added competitive pressure on rivals, and perhaps even defining the business model for the industry.

3. *What forces are driving changes in the industry, and what impact will these changes have on competitive intensity and industry profitability?* Industry and competitive conditions change because forces are in motion that create incentives or pressures for change. The first phase is to identify the forces that are driving change in the industry; the most common driving forces include the Internet and

Internet technology applications, globalization of competition in the industry, changes in the long-term industry growth rate, changes in buyer composition, product innovation, entry or exit of major firms, changes in cost and efficiency, changing buyer preferences for standardized versus differentiated products or services, regulatory influences and government policy changes, changing societal and lifestyle factors, and reductions in uncertainty and business risk. The second phase of driving-forces analysis is to determine whether the driving forces, taken together, are acting to make the industry environment more or less attractive. Are the driving forces causing demand for the industry's product to increase or decrease? Are the driving forces acting to make competition more or less intense? Will the driving forces lead to higher or lower industry profitability?

4. *What market positions do industry rivals occupy—who is strongly positioned and who is not?* Strategic group mapping is a valuable tool for understanding the similarities, differences, strengths, and weaknesses inherent in the market positions of rival companies. Rivals in the same or nearby strategic groups are close competitors, whereas companies in distant strategic groups usually pose little or no immediate threat. The lesson of strategic group mapping is that some positions on the map are more favorable than others. The profit potential of different strategic groups varies due to strengths and weaknesses in each group's market position. Often, industry driving forces and competitive pressures favor some strategic groups and hurt others.

5. *What strategic moves are rivals likely to make next?* This analytical step involves identifying competitors' strategies, deciding which rivals are likely to be strong contenders and which are likely to be weak, evaluating rivals' competitive options, and predicting their next moves. Scouting competitors well enough to anticipate their actions can help a company prepare effective countermoves (perhaps even beating a rival to the punch) and allows managers to take rivals' probable actions into account in designing their own company's best course of action. Managers who fail to study competitors risk being caught unprepared by the strategic moves of rivals.

6. *What are the key factors for competitive success?* An industry's key success factors (KSFs) are the particular strategy elements, product attributes, competitive capabilities, and business outcomes that spell the difference between being a strong competitor and being a weak competitor—and sometimes between profit and loss. KSFs by their very nature are so important to competitive success that *all firms* in the industry must pay close attention to them or risk becoming an industry also-ran. Correctly diagnosing an industry's KSFs raises a company's chances of crafting a sound strategy. The goal of company strategists should be to design a strategy aimed at stacking up well on all of the industry KSFs and trying to be *distinctively better* than rivals on one (or possibly two) of the KSFs. Indeed, using the industry's KSFs as *cornerstones* for the company's strategy and trying to gain sustainable competitive advantage by excelling at one particular KSF is a fruitful competitive strategy approach.

7. *Does the outlook for the industry present the company with sufficiently attractive prospects for profitability?* The answer to this question is a major driver of company strategy. An assessment that the industry and competitive environment is fundamentally attractive typically suggests employing a strategy calculated to build a stronger competitive position in the business, expanding sales efforts, and

investing in additional facilities and equipment as needed. If the industry is relatively unattractive, outsiders considering entry may decide against it and look elsewhere for opportunities, weak companies in the industry may merge with or be acquired by a rival, and strong companies may restrict further investments and employ cost-reduction strategies or product innovation strategies to boost long-term competitiveness and protect their profitability. On occasion, an industry that is unattractive overall is still very attractive to a favorably situated company with the skills and resources to take business away from weaker rivals.

A competently conducted industry and competitive analysis generally tells a clear, easily understood story about the company's external environment. Different analysts can have different judgments about competitive intensity, the impacts of driving forces, how industry conditions will evolve, how good the outlook is for industry profitability, and the degree to which the industry environment offers the company an attractive business opportunity. However, while no method can guarantee a single conclusive diagnosis about the state of industry and competitive conditions and an industry's future outlook, this doesn't justify shortcutting hard-nosed strategic analysis and relying instead on opinion and casual observation. Managers become better strategists when they know what questions to pose and what tools to use. This is why this chapter has concentrated on suggesting the right questions to ask, explaining concepts and analytical approaches, and indicating the kinds of things to look for. There's no substitute for staying on the cutting edge of what's happening in the industry—anything less weakens managers' ability to craft strategies that are well matched to the industry and competitive situation.

Exercises

1. As the owner of a new fast-food enterprise seeking a loan from a bank to finance the construction and operation of three new store locations, you have been asked to provide the loan officer with a brief analysis of the competitive environment in fast food. Draw a five-forces diagram for the fast-food industry, and briefly discuss the nature and strength of each of the five competitive forces in fast food.

2. Based on the strategic group map in Company Spotlight 2.1, (a) who are Wal-Mart's two closest competitors? (b) between which two strategic groups is competition the weakest? and (c) which strategic group faces the weakest competition from the members of other strategic groups?

3. Based on your knowledge of the ice-cream industry, which of the following factors might qualify as possible driving forces capable of causing fundamental change in the industry's structure and competitive environment?

   a) Increasing sales of frozen yogurt and frozen sorbets.

   b) The potential for additional makers of ice cream to enter the market.

   c) Growing consumer interest in low-calorie/low-fat/low-carb/sugar-free dessert alternatives.

d) A slowdown in consumer purchases of ice-cream products.

e) Rising prices for milk, sugar, and other ice-cream ingredients.

f) A decision by Häagen-Dazs to increase its prices by 10 percent.

g) A decision by Ben & Jerry's to add five new flavors to its product line.

h) A trend on the part of several prominent ice-cream manufacturers to introduce low-fat, low-carb, sugar-free ice-cream products in response to consumer interest in healthier ice-cream alternatives.

CHAPTER 3

Analyzing a Company's Resources and Competitive Position

Before executives can chart a new strategy, they must reach common understanding of the company's current position.

—*W. Chan Kim and Rene Mauborgne*

The real question isn't how well you're doing today against your own history, but how you're doing against your competitors.

—*Donald Kress*

Organizations succeed in a competitive marketplace over the long run because they can do certain things their customers value better than can their competitors.

—*Robert Hayes, Gary Pisano, and David Upton*

Only firms who are able to continually build new strategic assets faster and cheaper than their competitors will earn superior returns over the long term.

—*C. C. Markides and P. J. Williamson*

In Chapter 2 we described how to use the tools of industry and competitive analysis to assess a company's external environment and lay the groundwork for matching a company's strategy to its external situation. In this chapter we discuss the techniques of evaluating a company's internal circumstances and competitiveness—its resource capabilities, relative cost position, and competitive strength versus rivals. The analytical spotlight will be trained on five questions:

1. How well is the company's present strategy working?
2. What are the company's resource strengths and weaknesses and its external opportunities and threats?
3. Are the company's prices and costs competitive?
4. Is the company competitively stronger or weaker than key rivals?
5. What strategic issues and problems merit front-burner managerial attention?

In probing for answers to these questions, four analytical tools—SWOT analysis, value chain analysis, benchmarking, and competitive strength assessment—will be used. All four are valuable techniques for revealing a company's competitiveness and for helping company managers match their strategy to the company's own particular circumstances.

Evaluating How Well a Company's Present Strategy Is Working

In determining how well a company's present strategy is working, a manager has to start with what the strategy is. Figure 3.1 shows the key components of a single-business company's strategy. The first thing to pin down is the company's competitive approach. Is the company striving to be a low-cost leader *or* stressing ways to differentiate its product offering from rivals? Is it concentrating its efforts on serving a broad spectrum of customers *or* a narrow market niche? Another strategy-defining consideration is the firm's competitive scope within the industry—what its geographic market coverage is and whether it operates in just a single stage of the industry's production/distribution chain or is vertically integrated across several stages. Another good indication of the company's strategy is whether the company has made moves recently to improve its competitive position and performance—for instance, by cutting prices, improving design, stepping up advertising, entering a new geographic market (domestic or foreign), or merging with a competitor. The company's functional strategies in R&D, production, marketing, finance, human resources, information technology, and so on, further characterize company strategy.

While there's merit in evaluating the strategy from a *qualitative* standpoint (its completeness, internal consistency, rationale, and relevance), the best *quantitative* evidence of how well a company's strategy is working comes from its results. The two best empirical indicators are (1) whether the company is achieving its stated financial and strategic objectives and (2) whether the company is an above-average industry performer. Persistent shortfalls in meeting company performance targets and weak performance relative to rivals are reliable warning signs that the company suffers from

Figure 3.1   Identifying the Components of a Single-Business Company's Strategy

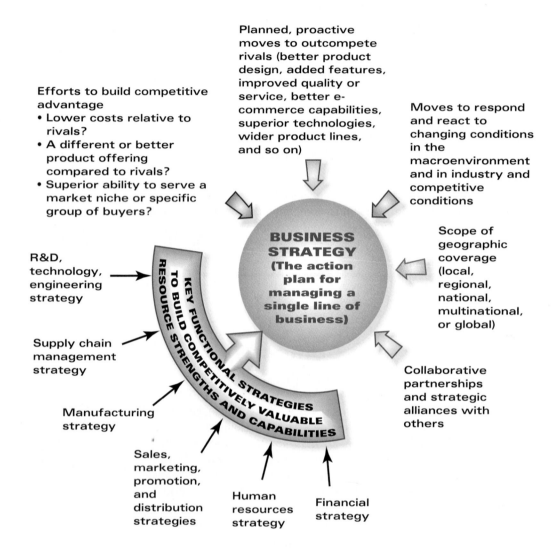

poor strategy making, less-than-competent strategy execution, or both. Other indicators of how well a company's strategy is working include:

- Whether the firm's sales are growing faster than, slower than, or about the same pace as the market as a whole, thus resulting in a rising, eroding, or stable market share.

- Whether the company is acquiring new customers at an attractive rate as well as retaining existing customers.

- Whether the firm's profit margins are increasing or decreasing and how well its margins compare to rival firms' margins.

- Trends in the firm's net profits and return on investment and how these compare to the same trends for other companies in the industry.

- Whether the company's overall financial strength and credit rating are improving or declining.

- Whether the company can demonstrate continuous improvement in such internal performance measures as days of inventory, employee productivity, unit cost, defect rate, scrap rate, misfilled orders, delivery times, warranty costs, and so on.

- How shareholders view the company based on trends in the company's stock price and shareholder value (relative to the stock price trends at other companies in the industry).

- The firm's image and reputation with its customers.

- How well the company stacks up against rivals on technology, product innovation, customer service, product quality, delivery time, price, speed in getting newly developed products to market, and other relevant factors on which buyers base their choice of brands.

The stronger a company's current overall performance, the less likely the need for radical changes in strategy. The weaker a company's financial performance and market standing, the more its current strategy must be questioned. Weak performance is almost always a sign of weak strategy, weak execution, or both.

> The stronger a company's financial performance and market position, the more likely it has a well-conceived, well-executed strategy.

Sizing Up a Company's Resource Strengths and Weaknesses and Its External Opportunities and Threats

Appraising a company's resource *strengths* and *weaknesses* and its external *opportunities* and *threats*, commonly known as **SWOT analysis**, provides a good overview of whether its overall situation is fundamentally healthy or unhealthy. Just as important, a first-rate SWOT analysis provides the basis for crafting a strategy that capitalizes on the company's resources, aims squarely at capturing the company's best opportunities, and defends against the threats to its well-being.

> **SWOT analysis** is a simple but powerful tool for sizing up a company's resource capabilities and deficiencies, its market opportunities, and the external threats to its future well-being.

Identifying Company Resource Strengths and Competitive Capabilities

A *strength* is something a company is good at doing or an attribute that enhances its competitiveness. A strength can take any of several forms:

- *A skill or important expertise*—low-cost manufacturing capabilities, technological know-how, strong e-commerce expertise, skills in improving production processes, a proven track record in defect-free manufacture, expertise in providing consistently good customer service, excellent mass-merchandising skills, or unique advertising and promotional talents.

- *Valuable physical assets*—state-of-the-art plants and equipment, attractive real estate locations, worldwide distribution facilities, or ownership of valuable natural resource deposits.

■ *Valuable human assets*—an experienced and capable workforce, talented employees in key areas, cutting-edge knowledge and intellectual capital, collective learning embedded in the organization and built up over time, or proven managerial know-how.[1]

■ *Valuable organizational assets*—proven quality control systems, proprietary technology, key patents, mineral rights, a cadre of highly trained customer service representatives, sizable amounts of cash and marketable securities, a strong balance sheet and credit rating (thus giving the company access to additional financial capital), or a comprehensive list of customers' e-mail addresses.

■ *Valuable intangible assets*—a powerful or well-known brand name, a reputation for technological leadership, or strong buyer loyalty and goodwill.

■ *Competitive capabilities*—product innovation capabilities, short development times in bringing new products to market, a strong dealer network, cutting-edge supply chain management capabilities, quickness in responding to shifting market conditions and emerging opportunities, or state-of-the-art systems for doing business via the Internet.

■ *An achievement or attribute that puts the company in a position of market advantage*—low overall costs relative to competitors, market share leadership, a superior product, a wider product line than rivals, wide geographic coverage, a well-known brand name, superior e-commerce capabilities, or exceptional customer service.

■ *Competitively valuable alliances or cooperative ventures*—fruitful partnerships with suppliers that reduce costs and/or enhance product quality and performance; alliances or joint ventures that provide access to valuable technologies, competencies, or geographic markets.

> **Core Concept**
>
> A company is better positioned to succeed if it has a competitively valuable complement of resources at its command.

Taken together, a company's strengths determine the complement of competitively valuable *resources* with which it competes—a company's resource strengths represent *competitive assets*. The caliber of a firm's resource strengths and competitive capabilities, along with its ability to mobilize them in the pursuit of competitive advantage, is a big determinant of how well a company will perform in the marketplace.[2]

Company Competencies and Competitive Capabilities   Sometimes a company's resource strengths relate to fairly specific skills and expertise (like just-in-time inventory control), and sometimes they flow from pooling the knowledge and expertise of different organizational groups to create a company competence or competitive capability. Competence or capability in continuous product innovation, for example, comes from teaming the efforts of people and groups with expertise in market research, new product R&D, design and engineering, cost-effective manufacturing, and market testing. Company competencies can range from merely a competence in performing an activity to a core competence to a distinctive competence:

> **Core Concept**
>
> A **competence** is an activity that a company has learned to perform well.

1. A **competence** is something an organization is good at doing. It is nearly always the product of experience, representing an accumulation of learning and the buildup of proficiency in performing an internal activity. Usually a company competence originates with deliberate efforts to develop the organizational ability to do something, however imperfectly or inefficiently. Such efforts involve

selecting people with the requisite knowledge and skills, upgrading or expanding individual abilities as needed, and then molding the efforts and work products of individuals into a cooperative group effort to create organizational ability. Then, as experience builds, such that the company gains proficiency in performing the activity consistently well and at an acceptable cost, the ability evolves into a true competence and company capability. Examples of competencies include proficiency in merchandising and product display, the capability to create attractive and easy-to-use Web sites, expertise in a specific technology, proven capabilities in selecting good locations for retail outlets, and a proficiency in working with customers on new applications and uses of the product.

2. A **core competence** is a proficiently performed internal activity that is *central* to a company's strategy and competitiveness. A core competence is a more valuable resource strength than a competence because of the well-performed activity's core role in the company's strategy and the contribution it makes to the company's success in the marketplace. A core competence can relate to any of several aspects of a company's business: expertise in integrating multiple technologies to create families of new products, know-how in creating and operating systems for cost-efficient supply chain management, the capability to speed new or next-generation products to market, good after-sale service capabilities, skills in manufacturing a high-quality product at a low cost, or the capability to fill customer orders accurately and swiftly. A company may have more than one core competence in its resource portfolio, but rare is the company that can legitimately claim more than two or three core competencies. Most often, *a core competence is knowledge-based, residing in people and in a company's intellectual capital and not in its assets on the balance sheet.* Moreover, a core competence is more likely to be grounded in cross-department combinations of knowledge and expertise than to be the product of a single department or work group.

> **Core Concept**
> A **core competence** is a *competitively important* activity that a company performs better than other internal activities.

3. A **distinctive competence** is a competitively valuable activity that a company *performs better than its rivals.* A distinctive competence thus represents a *competitively superior resource strength.* A company may perform one competitively important activity well enough to claim that activity as a core competence, but what a company does best internally doesn't translate into a distinctive competence unless the company enjoys *competitive superiority in performing that activity.* For instance, most retailers believe they have core competencies in product selection and in-store merchandising, but many retailers run into trouble in the marketplace because they encounter rivals whose core competencies in product selection and in-store merchandising are better than theirs. Consequently, *a core competence becomes a basis for competitive advantage only when it rises to the level of a distinctive competence.* The distinctive competencies of Toyota and Honda in low-cost, high-quality manufacturing and in short design-to-market cycles for new models have proved to be considerable competitive advantages in the global market for motor vehicles. Toyota's production system is far superior to that of any other automaker's, and the company is pushing the boundaries of its production advantage with a new type of assembly line—the "Global Body line"—that costs 50 percent less to install and can be changed to accommodate a new model for 70 percent less

> **Core Concept**
> A **distinctive competence** is a competitively important activity that a company performs better than its rivals—it thus represents *a competitively superior resource strength.*

than its previous production system.[3] Intel's distinctive competence in rapidly developing new generations of ever-more-powerful semiconductor chips for PCs and network servers has helped give the company a dominating presence in the semiconductor industry. Starbucks' distinctive competence in store ambience and innovative coffee drinks has made it the leading coffee drink retailer.

The conceptual differences between a competence, a core competence, and a distinctive competence draw attention to the fact that competitive capabilities are not all equal.[4] Some competencies and competitive capabilities merely enable market survival because most rivals have them—indeed, not having a competence or capability that rivals have can result in competitive disadvantage. Core competencies are *competitively* more important than competencies because they add power to the company's strategy and have a bigger positive impact on its market position and profitability. A distinctive competence is even more important because it represents a *uniquely strong* competitive capability that holds the potential for yielding competitive advantage. It is always easier to build competitive advantage when a firm has a distinctive competence in performing an activity important to market success, when rival companies do not have offsetting competencies, and when it is costly and time-consuming for rivals to imitate the competence. A distinctive competence can thus be the mainspring of a company's success—unless it is trumped by more powerful resources of rivals.

> **Core Concept**
>
> The importance of a distinctive competence to strategy making rests with (1) the competitively valuable capability it gives a company, (2) its value as a cornerstone of strategy, and (3) the competitive edge it can produce in the marketplace.

What Is the Competitive Power of a Resource Strength?   It is not enough to simply compile a list of a company's resource strengths and competitive capabilities. What is most telling about a company's strengths, individually and collectively, is how powerful they are in the marketplace. The competitive power of a company strength is measured by how many of the following four tests it can pass:[5]

1. *Is the resource strength hard to copy?* The more difficult and more expensive it is to imitate a company's resource strength, the greater its potential competitive value. Resources tend to be difficult to copy when they are unique (a fantastic real estate location, patent protection), when they must be built over time in ways that are difficult to imitate (a brand name, mastery of a technology), and when they carry big capital requirements (a cost-effective plant to manufacture cutting-edge microprocessors). Wal-Mart's competitors have failed miserably in their attempts over the past two decades to match Wal-Mart's superefficient state-of-the-art distribution capabilities. Hard-to-copy strengths and capabilities are valuable competitive assets, adding to a company's market strength and contributing to sustained profitability.

2. *Is the resource strength durable—does it have staying power?* The longer the competitive value of a resource lasts, the greater the value of the resource. Some resources lose their clout in the marketplace quickly because of the rapid speeds at which technologies or industry conditions are moving. The value of Eastman Kodak's resources in film and film processing is rapidly being undercut by the growing popularity of digital cameras. The investments that commercial banks have made in branch offices are a rapidly depreciating asset because of growing use of direct deposits, automated teller machines, and telephone and Internet banking options.

3. *Is the resource really competitively superior?* Companies have to guard against pridefully believing that their core competences are distinctive competences or that their brand name is more powerful than the brand names of rivals. Who can really say whether Coca-Cola's consumer marketing prowess is better than PepsiCo's or whether the Mercedes-Benz brand name is more powerful than that of BMW or Lexus?

4. *Can the resource strength be trumped by the different resource strengths and competitive capabilities of rivals?* Many commercial airlines (American Airlines, Delta Airlines, Continental Airlines, Singapore Airlines) have attracted large numbers of passengers because of their resources and capabilities in offering safe, convenient, reliable air transportation services and in providing an array of amenities to passengers. However, Southwest Airlines has consistently been a more profitable air carrier because it provides safe, reliable, basic services at radically lower fares. The prestigious brand names of Cadillac and Lincoln have faded in the market for luxury cars because Mercedes, BMW, Audi, and Lexus have introduced the most appealing luxury vehicles in recent years. Amazon.com is putting a big dent in the business prospects of brick-and-mortar bookstores; likewise, Wal-Mart (with its lower prices) is putting major competitive pressure on Toys "R" Us, at one time the leading toy retailer in the United States.

The vast majority of companies are not well endowed with competitively valuable resources, much less with competitively superior resources capable of passing all four tests with high marks. Most firms have a mixed bag of resources—one or two quite valuable, some good, many satisfactory to mediocre. Only a few companies, usually the strongest industry leaders or up-and-coming challengers, possess a distinctive competence or competitively superior resource.

Even if a company doesn't possess a competitively superior resource, it can still marshal potential for winning in the marketplace if it has an assortment of good-to-adequate resources that *collectively* have competitive power in the marketplace. Toshiba's laptop computers were the market share leader throughout most of the 1990s—an indicator that Toshiba had competitively valuable resource strengths. Yet Toshiba's laptops were not demonstrably faster than rivals' laptops; nor did they have bigger screens, more memory, longer battery power, a better pointing device, or other superior performance features; nor did Toshiba provide clearly superior technical support services to buyers of its laptops. Further, Toshiba laptops were definitely not cheaper, model for model, than the comparable models of its rivals, and they seldom ranked first in the overall performance ratings done by various organizations. Rather, Toshiba's market share leadership stemmed from a *combination* of *good* resource strengths and capabilities—its strategic partnerships with suppliers of laptop components, efficient assembly capability, design expertise, skills in choosing quality components, a wide selection of models, the attractive mix of built-in performance features found in each model when balanced against price, the better-than-average reliability of its models (based on buyer ratings), and very good technical support services (based on buyer ratings). The verdict from the marketplace was that PC buyers perceived Toshiba laptops as better, all things considered, than competing brands. (Shortly after 2000, however, Dell Computer overtook Toshiba as the global market leader in laptop PCs.)

> Winning in the marketplace becomes more likely when a company has appropriate and ample resources with which to compete, and especially when it has strengths and capabilities with competitive advantage potential.

Identifying Company Resource Weaknesses and Competitive Deficiencies

A *weakness, or competitive deficiency,* is something a company lacks or does poorly (in comparison to others) or a condition that puts it at a disadvantage in the marketplace. A company's weaknesses can relate to (1) inferior or unproven skills, expertise, or intellectual capital in competitively important areas of the business; (2) deficiencies in competitively important physical, organizational, or intangible assets; or (3) missing or competitively inferior capabilities in key areas. *Internal weaknesses are thus shortcomings in a company's complement of resources and represent competitive liabilities.* Nearly all companies have competitive liabilities of one kind or another. Whether a company's resource weaknesses make it competitively vulnerable depends on how much they matter in the marketplace and whether they are offset by the company's resource strengths.

> **Core Concept**
>
> A company's resource strengths represent competitive assets; its resource weaknesses represent competitive liabilities.

Table 3.1 lists the kinds of factors to consider in compiling a company's resource strengths and weaknesses. Sizing up a company's complement of resource capabilities and deficiencies is akin to constructing a *strategic balance sheet,* on which resource strengths represent *competitive assets* and resource weaknesses represent *competitive liabilities.* Obviously, the ideal condition is for the company's competitive assets to outweigh its competitive liabilities by an ample margin—a 50-50 balance is definitely not the desired condition!

Identifying a Company's Market Opportunities

Market opportunity is a big factor in shaping a company's strategy. Indeed, managers can't properly tailor strategy to the company's situation without first identifying its opportunities and appraising the growth and profit potential each one holds. Depending on the prevailing circumstances, a company's opportunities can be plentiful or scarce and can range from wildly attractive (an absolute "must" to pursue) to marginally interesting (because the growth and profit potential are questionable) to unsuitable (because there's not a good match with the company's strengths and capabilities). A checklist of potential market opportunities is included in Table 3.1.

In evaluating a company's market opportunities and ranking their attractiveness, managers have to guard against viewing every *industry* opportunity as a *company* opportunity. Not every company is equipped with the resources to successfully pursue each opportunity that exists in its industry. Some companies are more capable of going after particular opportunities than others, and a few companies may be hopelessly outclassed. *The market opportunities most relevant to a company are those that match up well with the company's financial and organizational resource capabilities, offer the best growth and profitability, and present the most potential for competitive advantage.*

> A company is well advised to pass on a particular market opportunity unless it has or can acquire the resources to capture it.

Identifying the Threats to a Company's Future Profitability

Often, certain factors in a company's external environment pose *threats* to its profitability and competitive well-being. Threats can stem from the emergence of cheaper or better technologies, rivals' introduction of new or improved products, the entry of

Table 3.1 WHAT TO LOOK FOR IN IDENTIFYING A COMPANY'S STRENGTHS, WEAKNESSES, OPPORTUNITIES, AND THREATS

Potential Resource Strengths and Competitive Capabilities	Potential Resource Weaknesses and Competitive Deficiencies
■ A powerful strategy	■ No clear strategic direction
■ Core competencies in _____.	■ Resources that are not well matched to industry key success factors
■ A distinctive competence in _____.	■ No well-developed or proven core competencies
■ A product that is strongly differentiated from those of rivals	■ A weak balance sheet; burdensome debt
■ Competencies and capabilities that are well matched to industry key success factors	■ Higher overall unit costs relative to key competitors
■ A strong financial condition; ample financial resources to grow the business	■ Weak or unproven product innovation capabilities
■ Strong brand-name image and/or company reputation	■ A product/service with ho-hum attributes or features inferior to those of rivals
■ An attractive customer base	■ Too narrow a product line relative to rivals
■ Economy of scale and/or learning and experience-curve advantages over rivals	■ Weak brand image or reputation
■ Proprietary technology, superior technological skills, important patents	■ Weaker dealer network than key rivals and/or lack of adequate global distribution capability
■ Superior intellectual capital relative to key rivals	■ Behind on product quality, R&D, and/or technological know-how
■ Cost advantages over rivals	■ In the wrong strategic group
■ Strong advertising and promotion	■ Losing market share because _____.
■ Product innovation capabilities	■ Lack of management depth
■ Proven capabilities in improving production processes	■ Inferior intellectual capital relative to leading rivals
■ Good supply chain management capabilities	■ Subpar profitability because _____.
■ Good customer service capabilities	■ Plagued with internal operating problems or obsolete facilities
■ Better product quality relative to rivals	■ Behind rivals in e-commerce capabilities
■ Wide geographic coverage and/or strong global distribution capability	■ Short on financial resources to grow the business and pursue promising initiatives
■ Alliances or joint ventures with other firms that provide access to valuable technology, competencies, and/or attractive geographic markets	■ Too much underutilized plant capacity

Potential Market Opportunities	Potential External Threats to a Company's Future Profitability
■ Openings to win market share from rivals	■ Increasing intensity of competition among industry rivals—may squeeze profit margins
■ Sharply rising buyer demand for the industry's product	■ Slowdowns in market growth
■ Serving additional customer groups or market segments	■ Likely entry of potent new competitors
■ Expanding into new geographic markets	■ Loss of sales to substitute products
■ Expanding the company's product line to meet a broader range of customer needs	■ Growing bargaining power of customers or suppliers
■ Utilizing existing company skills or technological know-how to enter new product lines or new businesses	■ A shift in buyer needs and tastes away from the industry's product
■ Online sales via the Internet	■ Adverse demographic changes that threaten to curtail demand for the industry's product
■ Integrating forward or backward	■ Vulnerability to industry driving forces
■ Falling trade barriers in attractive foreign markets	■ The introduction of restrictive trade policies in countries where the company does business
■ Acquiring rival firms or companies with attractive technological expertise or capabilities	■ Costly new regulatory requirements
■ Entering into alliances or joint ventures to expand the firm's market coverage or boost its competitive capability	■ The emergence of cheaper or better technologies
■ Openings to exploit emerging new technologies	■ Key rivals introduce innovative new products
	■ Adverse changes in foreign exchange rates, interest rates, or energy prices

lower-cost foreign competitors into a company's market stronghold, new regulations that are more burdensome to a company than to its competitors, vulnerability to a rise in interest rates, the potential of a hostile takeover, unfavorable demographic shifts, adverse changes in foreign exchange rates, political upheaval in a foreign country where the company has facilities, and the like. External threats may pose no more than a moderate degree of adversity (all companies confront some threatening elements in the course of doing business), or they may be so imposing as to make a company's situation and outlook quite tenuous. It is management's job to identify the threats to the company's future well-being and to evaluate what strategic actions can be taken to neutralize or lessen their impact.

A list of potential threats to a company's future profitability and market position is included in Table 3.1.

What Do the SWOT Listings Reveal?

> Simply making lists of a company's strengths, weaknesses, opportunities, and threats is not enough; the payoff from SWOT analysis comes from the conclusions about a company's situation and the implications for strategy improvement that flow from the four lists.

SWOT analysis involves more than making four lists. The two most important parts of SWOT analysis are *drawing conclusions* from the SWOT listings about the company's overall situation and *acting on those conclusions* to better match the company's strategy to its resource strengths and market opportunities, to correct the important weaknesses, and to defend against external threats. Figure 3.2 shows the three steps of SWOT analysis.

What story the SWOT listings tell about the company's overall situation is often revealed in the answers to the following sets of questions:

- Does the company have an attractive set of resource strengths? Does it have any strong core competencies or a distinctive competence? Are the company's strengths and capabilities well matched to the industry key success factors? Do they add adequate power to the company's strategy, or are more or different strengths needed? Will the company's current strengths and capabilities matter in the future?

- How serious are the company's weaknesses and competitive deficiencies? Are they mostly inconsequential and readily correctable, or could one or more prove fatal if not remedied soon? Are some of the company's weaknesses in areas that relate to the industry's key success factors? Are there any weaknesses that, if uncorrected, would keep the company from pursuing an otherwise attractive opportunity? Does the company have important resource gaps that need to be filled for it to move up in the industry rankings and/or boost its profitability?

- Do the company's resource strengths and competitive capabilities (its competitive assets) outweigh its resource weaknesses and competitive deficiencies (its competitive liabilities) by an attractive margin?

- Does the company have attractive market opportunities that are well suited to its resource strengths and competitive capabilities? Does the company lack the resources and capabilities to pursue any of the most attractive opportunities?

- Are the threats alarming, or are they something the company appears able to deal with and defend against?

- All things considered, how strong is the company's overall situation? Where on a scale of 1 to 10 (where 1 is alarmingly weak and 10 is exceptionally strong) should the firm's position and overall situation be ranked? What aspects of the company's situation are particularly attractive? What aspects are of the most concern?

Figure 3.2   **The Three Steps of SWOT Analysis:** Identify, Draw Conclusions, Translate into Strategic Action

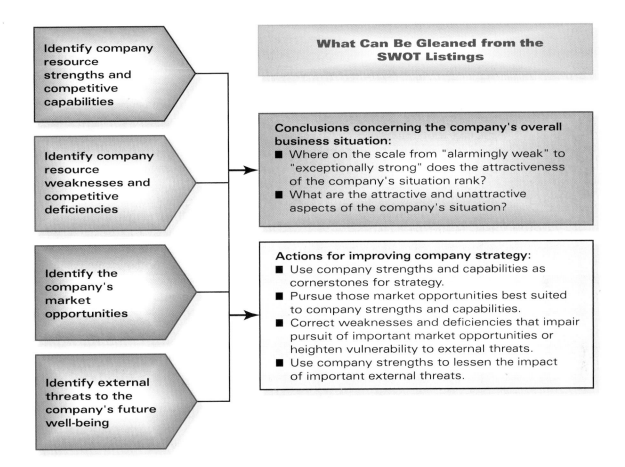

The final piece of SWOT analysis is to translate the diagnosis of the company's situation into actions for improving the company's strategy and business prospects. The following questions point to implications the SWOT listings have for strategic action:

- Which competitive capabilities need to be strengthened immediately (so as to add greater power to the company's strategy and boost sales and profitability)? Do new types of competitive capabilities need to be put in place to help the company better respond to emerging industry and competitive conditions? Which resources and capabilities need to be given greater emphasis, and which merit less emphasis? Should the company emphasize leveraging its existing resource strengths and capabilities, or does it need to create new resource strengths and capabilities?

- What actions should be taken to reduce the company's competitive liabilities? Which weaknesses or competitive deficiencies are in urgent need of correction?

- Which market opportunities should be top priority in future strategic initiatives (because they are good fits with the company's resource strengths and competitive capabilities, present attractive growth and profit prospects, and/or offer the best potential for securing competitive advantage)? Which opportunities should be ignored, at least for the time being (because they offer less growth potential or are not suited to the company's resources and capabilities)?

■ What should the company be doing to guard against the threats to its well-being?

A company's resource strengths should generally form the cornerstones of strategy because they represent the company's best chance for market success.[6] As a rule, strategies that place heavy demands on areas where the company is weakest or has unproven ability are suspect and should be avoided. If a company doesn't have the resources and competitive capabilities around which to craft an attractive strategy, managers need to take decisive remedial action either to upgrade existing organizational resources and capabilities and add others as needed or to acquire them through partnerships or strategic alliances with firms possessing the needed expertise. Plainly, managers have to look toward correcting competitive weaknesses that make the company vulnerable, hold down profitability, or disqualify it from pursuing an attractive opportunity.

At the same time, sound strategy making requires sifting through the available market opportunities and aiming strategy at capturing those that are most attractive and suited to the company's circumstances. Rarely does a company have the resource depth to pursue all available market opportunities simultaneously without spreading itself too thin. How much attention to devote to defending against external threats to the company's market position and future performance hinges on how vulnerable the company is, whether there are attractive defensive moves that can be taken to lessen their impact, and whether the costs of undertaking such moves represent the best use of company resources.

Analyzing Whether a Company's Prices and Costs Are Competitive

Company managers are often stunned when a competitor cuts its price to "unbelievably low" levels or when a new market entrant comes on strong with a very low price.

> The higher a company's costs are above those of close rivals, the more competitively vulnerable it becomes.

The competitor may not, however, be "dumping" (an economic term for selling at prices that are below cost), buying market share, or waging a desperate move to gain sales; it may simply have substantially lower costs. One of the most telling signs of whether a company's business position is strong or precarious is whether its prices and costs are competitive with industry rivals. Price-cost comparisons are especially critical in a commodity-product industry where the value provided to buyers is the same from seller to seller, price competition is typically the ruling market force, and lower-cost companies have the upper hand. But even in industries where products are differentiated and competition centers on the different attributes of competing brands as much as on price, rival companies have to keep their costs *in line* and make sure that any added costs they incur, and any price premiums they charge, create ample buyer value.

For a company to compete successfully, its costs must be *in line* with those of close rivals. While some cost disparity is justified as long as the products or services of closely competing companies are sufficiently differentiated, a high-cost firm's market position becomes increasingly vulnerable the more its costs exceed those of close rivals.

Two analytical tools are particularly useful in determining whether a company's prices and costs are competitive and thus conducive to winning in the marketplace: value chain analysis and benchmarking.

The Concept of a Company Value Chain

Every company's business consists of a collection of activities undertaken in the course of designing, producing, marketing, delivering, and supporting its product or service. A company's **value chain** consists of the linked set of value-creating activities the company performs internally. As shown in Figure 3.3, the value chain consists of two broad categories of activities: the *primary activities* that are foremost in creating value for customers and the requisite *support activities* that facilitate and enhance the performance of the primary activities.[7] The value chain includes a profit margin because a markup over the cost of performing the firm's value-creating activities is customarily part of the price (or total cost) borne by buyers—a fundamental objective of every enterprise is to create and deliver a value to buyers whose margin over cost yields an attractive profit.

> **Core Concept**
>
> A company's **value chain** identifies the primary activities that create customer value and the related support activities.

Disaggregating a company's operations into primary and secondary activities exposes the major elements of the company's cost structure. Each activity in the value chain gives rise to costs and ties up assets; assigning the company's operating costs and assets to each individual activity in the chain provides cost estimates and capital requirements. Quite often, there are links between activities such that the manner in which one activity is done can affect the costs of performing other activities. For instance, how a product is designed has a huge impact on the number and manufacturing costs of different parts and components and on the time and costs required to assemble it.

The combined costs of all the various activities in a company's value chain define the company's internal cost structure. Further, the cost of each activity contributes to whether the company's overall cost position relative to rivals is favorable or unfavorable. The tasks of value chain analysis and benchmarking are to develop the data for comparing a company's costs activity by activity against the costs of key rivals and to learn which internal activities are a source of cost advantage or disadvantage. A company's relative cost position is a function of how the overall costs of the activities it performs in conducting business compare to the overall costs of the activities performed by rivals.

Why the Value Chains of Rival Companies Often Differ

A company's value chain and the manner in which it performs each activity reflect the evolution of its own particular business and internal operations, its strategy, the approaches it is using to execute its strategy, and the underlying economics of the activities themselves.[8] Because these factors differ from company to company, the value chains of rival companies sometimes differ substantially—a condition that complicates the task of assessing rivals' relative cost positions. For instance, competing companies may differ in their degrees of vertical integration. Comparing the value chains of a fully integrated rival and a partially integrated rival requires adjusting for differences in the scope of activities performed. Clearly the internal costs for a manufacturer that *makes* all of its own parts and components will be greater than the internal costs of a producer that *buys* the needed parts and components from outside suppliers and performs only assembly operations.

Likewise, there is legitimate reason to expect value chain and cost differences between a company that is pursuing a low-cost/low-price strategy and a rival that is positioned on the high end of the market. The costs of certain activities along the low-cost company's value chain should indeed be relatively low, whereas the high-end firm may

Figure 3.3   A Representative Company Value Chain

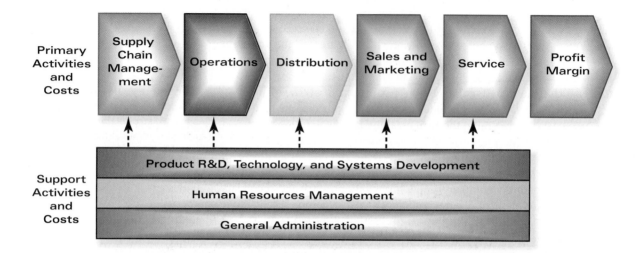

PRIMARY ACTIVITIES

- **Supply Chain Management**—activities, costs, and assets associated with purchasing fuel, energy, raw materials, parts, and components, merchandise, and consumable items from vendors; receiving, storing, and disseminating inputs from suppliers; inspection; and inventory management.
- **Operations**—activities, costs, and assets associated with converting inputs into final product form (production, assembly, packaging, equipment maintenance, facilities, operations, quality assurance, environmental protection).
- **Distribution**—activities, costs, and assets dealing with physically distributing the product to buyers (finished-goods warehousing, order processing, order picking and packing, shipping, delivery vehicle operations, establishing and maintaining a network of dealers and distributors).
- **Sales and Marketing**—activities, costs, and assets related to sales force efforts, advertising and promotion, market research and planning, and dealer/distributor support.
- **Service**—activities, costs, and assets associated with providing assistance to buyers, such as installation, spare parts delivery, maintenance and repair, technical assistance, buyer inquiries, and complaints.

SUPPORT ACTIVITIES

- **Product R&D, Technology, and Systems Development**—activities, costs, and assets relating to product R&D, process R&D, process design improvement, equipment design, computer software development, telecommunications systems, computer-assisted design and engineering, database capabilities, and development of computerized support systems.
- **Human Resources Management**—activities, costs, and assets associated with the recruitment, hiring, training, development, and compensation of all types of personnel; labor relations activities; and development of knowledge-based skills and core competencies.
- **General Administration**—activities, costs, and assets relating to general management, accounting and finance, legal and regulatory affairs, safety and security, management information systems, forming strategic alliances and collaborating with strategic partners, and other "overhead" functions.

understandably be spending relatively more to perform those activities that create the added quality and extra features of its products.

Moreover, cost and price differences among rival companies can have their origins in activities performed by suppliers or by distribution channel allies involved in getting the product to end users. Suppliers or wholesale/retail dealers may have excessively high cost structures or profit margins that jeopardize a company's cost-competitiveness even though its costs for internally performed activities are competitive. For example, when determining Michelin's cost-competitiveness vis-à-vis Goodyear and Bridgestone in supplying replacement tires to vehicle owners, we have to look at more than whether Michelin's tire manufacturing costs are above or below Goodyear's and Bridgestone's. Let's say that a buyer has to pay $400 for a set of Michelin tires and only $350 for a comparable set of Goodyear or Bridgestone tires; Michelin's $50 price disadvantage can stem not only from higher manufacturing costs (reflecting, perhaps, the added costs of Michelin's strategic efforts to build a better-quality tire with more performance features) but also from (1) differences in what the three tire makers pay their suppliers for materials and tire-making components and (2) differences in the operating efficiencies, costs, and markups of Michelin's wholesale-retail dealer outlets versus those of Goodyear and Bridgestone. Company value chains can also be different when different distribution channels are used to reach customers. In the music industry, music retailers like Blockbuster and Musicland that purchase CDs from recording studios and wholesale distributors have different value chains than online music stores like Apple's iTunes and Musicmatch that sell downloadable files. Thus, determining whether a company's prices and costs are competitive from an end user's standpoint requires looking at the activities and costs of competitively relevant suppliers and forward allies, as well as the costs of internally performed activities.

The Value Chain System for an Entire Industry

As the tire industry example makes clear, a company's value chain is embedded in a larger system of activities that includes the value chains of its suppliers and the value chains of whatever distribution channel allies it utilizes in getting its product or service to end users.[9] *Accurately assessing a company's competitiveness in end-use markets thus requires that company managers understand the entire value chain system for delivering a product or service to end users, not just the company's own value chain.* At the very least, this means considering the value chains of suppliers and forward channel allies (if any), as shown in Figure 3.4.

Suppliers' value chains are relevant because suppliers perform activities and incur costs in creating and delivering the purchased inputs used in a company's own value chain. The costs, performance features, and quality of these inputs influence a company's own costs and product differentiation capabilities. Anything a company can do to help its suppliers' take costs out of their value chain activities or improve the quality and performance of the items being supplied can enhance its own competitiveness—a powerful reason for working collaboratively with suppliers in managing supply chain activities.[10]

Forward channel and customer value chains are relevant because (1) the costs and margins of a company's distribution allies are part of the price the end user pays and (2) the activities that distribution allies perform affect the end user's satisfaction. For these reasons, companies normally work closely with their forward channel allies (who are their direct customers) to perform value chain activities in mutually

> A company's cost-competitiveness depends not only on the costs of internally performed activities (its own value chain) but also on costs in the value chains of its suppliers and forward channel allies.

Figure 3.4   A Representative Value Chain for an Entire Industry

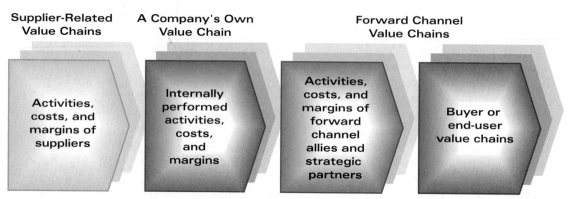

beneficial ways. For instance, some aluminum-can producers have constructed plants next to beer breweries and deliver cans on overhead conveyors directly to the breweries' can-filling lines; this has resulted in significant savings in production scheduling, shipping, and inventory costs for both container producers and breweries.[11] Many automotive parts suppliers have built plants near the auto assembly plants they supply to facilitate just-in-time deliveries, reduce warehousing and shipping costs, and promote close collaboration on parts design and production scheduling. Irrigation equipment companies, suppliers of grape-harvesting and winemaking equipment, and firms making barrels, wine bottles, caps, corks, and labels all have facilities in the California wine country to be close to the nearly 700 winemakers they supply.[12] The lesson here is that a company's value chain activities are often closely linked to the value chains of its suppliers and the forward allies or customers to whom it sells.

Although the value chains in Figures 3.3 and 3.4 are representative, actual value chains vary by industry and by company. The primary value chain activities in the pulp and paper industry (timber farming, logging, pulp mills, and papermaking) differ from the primary value chain activities in the home appliance industry (parts and components manufacture, assembly, wholesale distribution, retail sales). The value chain for the soft-drink industry (processing of basic ingredients and syrup manufacture, bottling and can filling, wholesale distribution, advertising, and retail merchandising) differs from that for the computer software industry (programming, disk loading, marketing, distribution). A producer of bathroom and kitchen faucets depends heavily on the activities of wholesale distributors and building supply retailers in winning sales to homebuilders and do-it-yourselfers; a producer of small gasoline engines internalizes its distribution activities by selling directly to the makers of lawn and garden equipment. A wholesaler's most important activities and costs deal with purchased goods, inbound logistics, and outbound logistics. A hotel's most important activities and costs are in operations—check-in and checkout, maintenance and housekeeping, dining and room service, conventions and meetings, and accounting. Outbound logistics is a crucial activity at Domino's Pizza but comparatively insignificant at Blockbuster. Advertising and promotion are dominant activities at Anheuser-Busch but only minor

Table 3.2   **THE DIFFERENCE BETWEEN TRADITIONAL AND ACTIVITY-BASED COST ACCOUNTING: A PURCHASING DEPARTMENT EXAMPLE**

Traditional Cost Accounting Categories in Purchasing Department Budget		Cost of Performing Specific Purchasing Department Activities Using Activity-Based Cost Accounting	
Wages and salaries	$340,000	Evaluate supplier capabilities	$100,300
Employee benefits	95,000	Process purchase orders	82,100
Supplies	21,500	Collaborate with suppliers on just-in-time deliveries	140,200
Travel	12,400		
Depreciation	19,000	Share data with suppliers	59,550
Other fixed charges (office space, utilities)	112,000	Check quality of items purchased	94,100
Miscellaneous operating expenses	40,250	Check incoming deliveries against purchase orders	48,450
	$640,150	Resolve disputes	15,250
		Conduct internal administration	100,200
			$640,150

Source: Adapted from information in Terence P. Par, "A New Tool for Managing Costs," *Fortune,* June 14, 1993, pp. 124–129.

activities at interstate gas-pipeline companies. Consequently, generic value chains like those in Figures 3.3 and 3.4 are illustrative, not absolute, and have to be drawn to fit the activities of a particular company or industry.

Developing the Data to Measure a Company's Cost-Competitiveness

Once the major value chain activities are identified, the next step in evaluating a company's cost-competitiveness involves breaking down departmental cost accounting data into the costs of performing specific activities.[13] The appropriate degree of disaggregation depends on the economics of the activities and how valuable it is to develop cross-company cost comparisons for narrowly defined activities as opposed to broadly defined activities. A good guideline is to develop separate cost estimates for activities having different economics and for activities representing a significant or growing proportion of cost.[14]

Traditional accounting identifies costs according to broad categories of expenses—wages and salaries, employee benefits, supplies, maintenance, utilities, travel, depreciation, R&D, interest, general administration, and so on. A newer method, *activity-based costing,* entails defining expense categories according to the specific activities being performed and then assigning costs to the activity responsible for creating the cost. An illustrative example is shown in Table 3.2.[15] Perhaps 25 percent of the companies that have explored the feasibility of activity-based costing have adopted this accounting approach. To fully understand the costs of activities all along the industry value chain, cost estimates for activities performed in the competitively relevant portions of suppliers' and customers' value chains also have to be developed—an advanced art in competitive intelligence. But despite the tediousness of developing cost estimates activity by activity and the imprecision of some of the estimates, the payoff in exposing the costs of particular activities makes activity-based

COMPANY SPOTLIGHT 3.1
Estimated Value Chain Costs for Recording and Distributing Music CDs through Traditional Music Retailers

The table below presents the representative costs and markups associated with producing and distributing a music CD retailing for $15 in music stores (as opposed to Internet sources).

Value Chain Activities and Costs in Producing and Distributing a CD		
1. Record company direct production costs:		$ 2.40
Artists and repertoire	$0.75	
Pressing of CD and packaging	1.65	
2. Royalties		.99
3. Record company marketing expenses		1.50
4. Record company overhead		1.50
5. Total record company costs		6.39
6. Record company's operating profit		1.86
7. Record company's selling price to distributor/wholesaler		8.25
8. Average wholesale distributor markup to cover distribution activities and profit margins		1.50
9. Average wholesale price charged to retailer		9.75
10. Average retail markup over wholesale cost		5.25
11. Average price to consumer at retail		$15.00

Source: Developed from information in "Fight the Power," a case study prepared by Adrian Aleyne, Babson College, 1999.

costing a valuable analytical tool.[16] Company Spotlight 3.1 shows representative costs for various activities performed by the producers and marketers of music CDs.

    The most important application of value chain analysis is to expose how a particular firm's cost position compares with the cost positions of its rivals. What is needed are competitor-versus-competitor cost estimates for supplying a product or service to a well-defined customer group or market segment. The size of a company's cost advantage or disadvantage can vary from item to item in the product line, from customer group to customer group (if different distribution channels are used), and from geographic market to geographic market (if cost factors vary across geographic regions).

Benchmarking the Costs of Key Value Chain Activities

Many companies today are **benchmarking** their costs of performing a given activity against competitors' costs (and/or against the costs of a noncompetitor that efficiently and effectively performs much the same activity in another industry). Benchmarking is a tool that allows a company to determine whether the manner in which it performs particular functions and activities represents industry "best practices" when both cost and effectiveness are taken into account.

    Benchmarking entails comparing how different companies perform various value chain activities—how materials are purchased, how suppliers are paid, how inventories are managed, how products are assembled, how fast the company can get new products to market, how the quality control function is performed, how customer orders are filled and shipped, how employees are trained, how payrolls are processed, and how maintenance is performed—and then making cross-company comparisons of the costs of these activities.[17] The objectives of benchmarking are to identify the best practices in performing an activity, to learn how other companies have actually achieved lower costs or better results in performing benchmarked activities, and to take action to improve a company's competitiveness whenever benchmarking reveals that its costs and results of performing an activity do not match those of other companies (either competitors or noncompetitors).

> **Core Concept**
>
> **Benchmarking** has proved to be a potent tool for learning which companies are best at performing particular activities and then using their techniques (or "best practices") to improve the cost and effectiveness of a company's own internal activities.

In 1979, Xerox became an early pioneer in the use of benchmarking when Japanese manufacturers began selling midsize copiers in the United States for $9,600 each—less than Xerox's production costs.[18] Although Xerox management suspected its Japanese competitors were dumping, it sent a team of line managers to Japan, including the head of manufacturing, to study competitors' business processes and costs. Fortunately, Xerox's joint-venture partner in Japan, Fuji-Xerox, knew the competitors well. The team found that Xerox's costs were excessive due to gross inefficiencies in the company's manufacturing processes and business practices; the study proved instrumental in Xerox's efforts to become cost-competitive and prompted Xerox to embark on a long-term program to benchmark 67 of its key work processes against companies identified as having the best practices in performing these processes. Xerox quickly decided not to restrict its benchmarking efforts to its office equipment rivals but to extend them to any company regarded as "world class" in performing *any activity* relevant to Xerox's business.

Thus, benchmarking has quickly come to be a tool for comparing a company against rivals not only on cost but on almost any relevant activity or competitively important measure. Toyota managers got their idea for just-in-time inventory deliveries by studying how U.S. supermarkets replenished their shelves. Southwest Airlines reduced the turnaround time of its aircraft at each scheduled stop by studying pit crews on the auto racing circuit. Over 80 percent of Fortune 500 companies reportedly engage in some form of benchmarking.

The tough part of benchmarking is not whether to do it but rather how to gain access to information about other companies' practices and costs. Sometimes benchmarking can be accomplished by collecting information from published reports, trade groups, and industry research firms and by talking to knowledgeable industry analysts, customers, and suppliers. On occasion, customers, suppliers, and joint-venture partners often make willing benchmarking allies. Usually, though, benchmarking requires field trips to the facilities of competing or non-

> Benchmarking the costs of company activities against rivals provides hard evidence of whether a company is cost competitive.

competing companies to observe how things are done, ask questions, compare practices and processes, and perhaps exchange data on productivity, staffing levels, time requirements, and other cost components. The problem is that because benchmarking involves competitively sensitive cost information, close rivals can't be expected to be completely open, even if they agree to host facilities tours and answer questions. Making reliable cost comparisons is complicated by the fact that participants often use different cost accounting systems.

However, the explosive interest of companies in benchmarking costs and identifying best practices has prompted consulting organizations (e.g., Accenture, A. T. Kearney,

Benchnet—The Benchmarking Exchange, Towers Perrin, and Best Practices) and several councils and associations (the International Benchmarking Clearinghouse, the Strategic Planning Institute's Council on Benchmarking) to gather benchmarking data, do benchmarking studies, and distribute information about best practices without identifying the sources. Having an independent group gather the information and report it in a manner that disguises the names of individual companies permits companies to avoid having to disclose competitively sensitive data to rivals and lessens the potential for unethical behavior on the part of company personnel in gathering their own data about competitors.

Strategic Options for Remedying a Cost Disadvantage

Value chain analysis and benchmarking can reveal a great deal about a firm's cost competitiveness. Examining the costs of a company's own value chain activities and comparing them to rivals' indicates who has how much of a cost advantage or disadvantage and which cost components are responsible. Such information is vital in strategic actions to eliminate a cost disadvantage or create a cost advantage. One of the fundamental insights of value chain analysis and benchmarking is that a company's competitiveness on cost depends on how efficiently it manages its value chain activities relative to how well competitors manage theirs.[19] There are three main areas in a company's overall value chain where important differences in the costs of competing firms can occur: a company's own activity segments, suppliers' part of the industry value chain, and the forward channel portion of the industry chain.

When the source of a firm's cost disadvantage is internal, managers can use any of the following nine strategic approaches to restore cost parity:[20]

1. Implement the use of best practices throughout the company, particularly for high-cost activities.

2. Try to eliminate some cost-producing activities altogether by revamping the value chain. Examples include cutting out low-value-added activities or bypassing the value chains and associated costs of distribution allies and marketing directly to end users (the approach used by Dell in PCs).

3. Relocate high-cost activities (such as R&D or manufacturing) to geographic areas where they can be performed more cheaply.

4. Attempt to squeeze out cost savings by greatly improving the company's supply chain.[21]

5. Search for activities that can be outsourced from vendors or performed by contractors more cheaply than they can be done internally.

6. Invest in productivity-enhancing, cost-saving technological improvements (robotics, flexible manufacturing techniques, state-of-the-art electronic networking).

7. Innovate around the troublesome cost components—computer chip makers regularly design around the patents held by others to avoid paying royalties; automakers have substituted lower-cost plastic and rubber for metal at many exterior body locations.

8. Simplify the product design so that it can be manufactured or assembled quickly and more economically.

9. Try to make up the internal cost disadvantage by achieving savings in the other two parts of the value chain system—usually a last resort.

Table 3.3 OPTIONS FOR ATTACKING COST DISADVANTAGES ASSOCIATED WITH SUPPLY CHAIN ACTIVITIES OR FORWARD CHANNEL ALLIES

Options for Attacking the High Costs of Items Purchased from Suppliers	Options for Attacking the High Costs of Forward Channel Allies
■ Negotiate more favorable prices with suppliers. ■ Work with suppliers on the design and specifications for what is being supplied to identify cost savings that will allow them to lower their prices. ■ Switch to lower-priced substitute inputs. ■ Collaborate closely with suppliers to identify mutual cost-saving opportunities. For example, just-in-time deliveries from suppliers can lower a company's inventory and internal logistics costs and may also allow its suppliers to economize on their warehousing, shipping, and production scheduling costs—a win-win outcome for both. ■ Integrate backward into the business of high-cost suppliers to gain control over the costs of purchased items—seldom an attractive option. ■ Try to make up the difference by cutting costs elsewhere in the chain—usually a last resort.	■ Push distributors and other forward channel allies to reduce their markups. ■ Work closely with forward channel allies to identify win-win opportunities to reduce costs. A chocolate manufacturer learned that by shipping its bulk chocolate in liquid form in tank cars instead of 10-pound molded bars, it could not only save its candy-bar manufacturing customers the costs associated with unpacking and melting but also eliminate its own costs of molding bars and packing them. ■ Change to a more economical distribution strategy, including switching to cheaper distribution channels (perhaps direct sales via the Internet) or perhaps integrating forward into company-owned retail outlets. ■ Try to make up the difference by cutting costs earlier in the cost chain—usually a last resort.

If a firm finds that it has a cost disadvantage stemming from costs in the supplier or forward channel portions of the industry value chain, then the task of reducing its costs to levels more in line with competitors usually has to extend beyond the firm's own in-house operations. Table 3.3 presents the strategy options for attacking high costs associated with supply chain activities or forward channel allies.

Translating Proficient Performance of Value Chain Activities into Competitive Advantage

A company that does a first-rate job of managing its value chain activities relative to competitors stands a good chance of leveraging its competitively valuable competencies and capabilities into sustainable competitive advantage. With rare exceptions, company attempts to achieve competitive advantage with unique attributes and performance features seldom result in a durable competitive advantage. It is too easy for resourceful competitors to clone, improve on, or find an effective substitute for any unique features of a product or service.[22] A more fruitful approach to achieving and sustaining a competitive edge over rivals is for a company to develop competencies and capabilities that please buyers and that rivals don't have or can't quite match.

The process of translating proficient company performance of value chain activities into competitive advantage is shown in Figure 3.5. The road to competitive advantage begins with management efforts to build more organizational expertise in performing certain competitively important value chain activities, deliberately striving to develop competencies and capabilities that add power to its strategy and competitiveness. If management begins to make one or two of these competencies and capabilities cornerstones of its strategy and continues to invest resources in building greater and greater proficiency in performing them, then over time one (or maybe

> Performing value chain activities in ways that give a company the capabilities to outmatch rivals is a source of competitive advantage.

Figure 3.5   Translating Company Performance of Value Chain Activities into Competitive Advantage

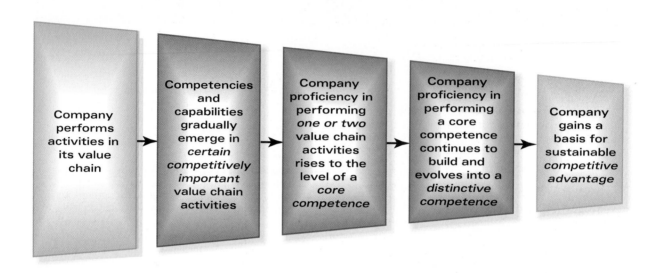

both) of the targeted competencies/capabilities may rise to the level of a core competence. Later, following additional organizational learning and investments in gaining still greater proficiency, the core competence could evolve into a distinctive competence, giving the company superiority over rivals. Such superiority, if it gives the company significant competitive clout in the marketplace, could produce an attractive competitive edge over rivals and, more important, prove difficult for rivals to match or offset with competencies and capabilities of their own making. As a general rule, it is substantially harder for rivals to achieve "best in industry" proficiency in performing a key value chain activity than it is for them to clone the features and attributes of a hot-selling product or service. This is especially true when a company with a distinctive competence avoids becoming complacent and works diligently to maintain its industry-leading expertise and capability.

There are numerous examples of companies that have gained a competitive edge by building competencies and capabilities that outmatch those of rivals. Merck and Glaxo, two of the world's most competitively capable pharmaceutical companies, built their business positions around expert performance of a few competitively crucial activities: extensive R&D to achieve first discovery of new drugs, a carefully constructed approach to patenting, skill in gaining rapid and thorough clinical clearance through regulatory bodies, and unusually strong distribution and sales force capabilities.[23] Federal Express has linked and integrated the performance of its aircraft fleet, truck fleet, support systems, and personnel so tightly and smoothly across the company's different value chain activities that it has created the capability to provide customers with guaranteed overnight delivery services. McDonald's can turn out identical-quality fast-food items at some 25,000-plus outlets around the world—an impressive demonstration of its capability to replicate its operating systems at many locations via an omnibus manual of detailed rules and procedures for each activity and intensive training of franchise operators and outlet managers.

Assessing a Company's Competitive Strength

Using value chain analysis and benchmarking to determine a company's competitiveness on price and cost is necessary but not sufficient. A more comprehensive assessment needs to be made of the company's overall competitive strength. The answers to two questions are of particular interest: First, how does the company rank relative to competitors on each of the important factors that determine market success? Second, all things considered, does the company have a net competitive advantage or disadvantage versus major competitors?

An easy-to-use method for answering the two questions posed above involves developing quantitative strength ratings for the company and its key competitors on each industry key success factor and each competitively decisive resource capability. Much of the information needed for doing a competitive strength assessment comes from previous analyses. Industry and competitive analysis reveals the key success factors and competitive capabilities that separate industry winners from losers. Benchmarking data and scouting key competitors provide a basis for judging the competitive strength of rivals on such factors as cost, key product attributes, customer service, image and reputation, financial strength, technological skills, distribution capability, and other competitively important resources and capabilities. SWOT analysis reveals how the company in question stacks up on these same strength measures.

Step 1 in doing a competitive strength assessment is to make a list of the industry's key success factors and most telling measures of competitive strength or weakness (6 to 10 measures usually suffice). Step 2 is to rate the firm and its rivals on each factor. Numerical rating scales (e.g., from 1 to 10) are best to use, although ratings of stronger (1), weaker (2), and about equal (5) may be appropriate when information is scanty and assigning numerical scores conveys false precision. Step 3 is to sum the strength ratings on each factor to get an overall measure of competitive strength for each company being rated. Step 4 is to use the overall strength ratings to draw conclusions about the size and extent of the company's net competitive advantage or disadvantage and to take specific note of areas of strength and weakness.

Table 3.4 provides two examples of competitive strength assessment, using the hypothetical ABC Company against four rivals. The first example employs an *unweighted rating system*. With unweighted ratings, each key success factor and competitive strength measure is assumed to be equally important (a rather dubious assumption). Whichever company has the highest strength rating on a given measure has an implied competitive edge on that factor; the size of its edge is mirrored in the margin of difference between its rating and the ratings assigned to rivals—a rating of 9 for one company versus ratings of 5, 4, and 3, respectively, for three other companies indicates a bigger advantage than a rating of 9 versus ratings of 8, 7, and 6. Summing a company's ratings on all the measures produces an overall strength rating. The higher a company's overall strength rating, the stronger its overall competitiveness versus rivals. The bigger the difference between a company's overall rating and the scores of *lower-rated* rivals, the greater its implied *net competitive advantage*. Conversely, the bigger the difference between a company's overall rating and the scores of *higher-rated* rivals, the greater its implied *net competitive disadvantage*. Thus, ABC's total score of 61 (see the top half of Table 3.4) signals a much greater net competitive advantage over rival 4 (with a score of 32) than over rival 1 (with a score of 58) but indicates a moderate net competitive disadvantage against rival 2 (with an overall score of 71).

Table 3.4   ILLUSTRATIONS OF UNWEIGHTED AND WEIGHTED COMPETITIVE STRENGTH ASSESSMENTS

A. Sample of an Unweighted Competitive Strength Assessment
(Rating scale: 1 = very weak; 10 = very strong)

Key Success Factor/ Strength Measure	ABC Co.	Rival 1	Rival 2	Rival 3	Rival 4
Quality/product performance	8	5	10	1	6
Reputation/image	8	7	10	1	6
Manufacturing capability	2	10	4	5	1
Technological skills	10	1	7	3	8
Dealer network/distribution capability	9	4	10	5	1
New product innovation capability	9	4	10	5	1
Financial resources	5	10	7	3	1
Relative cost position	5	10	3	1	4
Customer service capabilities	5	7	10	1	4
Unweighted overall strength rating	61	58	71	25	32

B. Sample of a Weighted Competitive Strength Assessment
(Rating scale: 1 = very weak; 10 = very strong)

Key Success Factor/ Strength Measure	Importance Weight	Rating/Score				
		ABC Co.	Rival 1	Rival 2	Rival 3	Rival 4
Quality/product performance	0.10	8 0.80	5 0.50	10 1.00	1 0.10	6 0.60
Reputation/image	0.10	8 0.80	7 0.70	10 1.00	1 0.10	6 0.60
Manufacturing capability	0.10	2 0.20	10 1.00	4 0.40	5 0.50	1 0.10
Technological skills	0.05	10 0.50	1 0.05	7 0.35	3 0.15	8 0.40
Dealer network/ distribution capability	0.05	9 0.45	4 0.20	10 0.50	5 0.25	1 0.05
New product innovation capability	0.05	9 0.45	4 0.20	10 0.50	5 0.25	1 0.05
Financial resources	0.10	5 0.50	10 1.00	7 0.70	3 0.30	1 0.10
Relative cost position	0.30	5 1.50	10 3.00	3 0.95	1 0.30	4 1.20
Customer service capabilities	0.15	5 0.75	7 1.05	10 1.50	1 0.15	4 0.60
Sum of importance weights	1.00					
Weighted overall strength rating		5.95	7.70	6.85	2.10	3.70

> A weighted competitive strength analysis is conceptually stronger than an unweighted analysis because of the inherent weakness in assuming that all the strength measures are equally important.

However, a better method is a *weighted rating system* (shown in the bottom half of Table 3.4) because the different measures of competitive strength are unlikely to be equally important. In an industry where the products/services of rivals are virtually identical, for instance, having low unit costs relative to rivals is nearly always the most important determinant of competitive strength. In an industry with strong product differentiation, the most significant measures of competitive strength may be brand awareness, amount of advertising, product attractiveness, and distribution capability. In a weighted rating system each measure of competitive strength is assigned a weight based on its perceived importance in

shaping competitive success. A weight could be as high as 0.75 (maybe even higher) in situations where one particular competitive variable is overwhelmingly decisive, or a weight could be as low as 0.20 when two or three strength measures are more important than the rest. Lesser competitive strength indicators can carry weights of 0.05 or 0.10. Whether the differences between the importance weights are big or little, *the sum of the weights must add up to 1.0.*

Weighted strength ratings are calculated by rating each competitor on each strength measure (using the 1 to 10 rating scale) and multiplying the assigned rating by the assigned weight (a rating of 4 times a weight of 0.20 gives a weighted rating, or score, of 0.80). Again, the company with the highest rating on a given measure has an implied competitive edge on that measure, with the size of its edge reflected in the difference between its rating and rivals' ratings. The weight attached to the measure indicates how important the edge is. Summing a company's weighted strength ratings for all the measures yields an overall strength rating. Comparisons of the weighted overall strength scores indicate which competitors are in the strongest and weakest competitive positions and who has how big a net competitive advantage over whom.

Note in Table 3.4 that the unweighted and weighted rating schemes produce different orderings of the companies. In the weighted system, ABC Company drops from second to third in strength, and rival 1 jumps from third to first because of its high strength ratings on the two most important factors. Weighting the importance of the strength measures can thus make a significant difference in the outcome of the assessment.

Competitive strength assessments provide useful conclusions about a company's competitive situation. The ratings show how a company compares against rivals, factor by factor or capability by capability, thus revealing where it is strongest and weakest, and against whom. Moreover, the overall competitive strength scores indicate how all the different factors add up—whether the company is at a net competitive advantage or disadvantage against each rival. The firm with the largest overall competitive strength rating enjoys the strongest competitive position, with the size of its net competitive advantage reflected by how much its score exceeds the scores of rivals.

Knowing where a company is competitively strong and where it is weak in comparison to specific rivals is valuable in deciding on specific actions to strengthen its ability to compete. As a general rule, a company should try to leverage its competitive strengths (areas where it scores higher than rivals) into sustainable competitive advantage. Furthermore, it makes sense for the company to initiate actions to remedy its important competitive weaknesses (areas where its scores are below those of rivals); at the very least, it should try to narrow the gap against companies with higher strength ratings—when the leader is at 10, improving from a rating of 3 to a rating of 7 can be significant.

> High competitive strength ratings signal a strong competitive position and possession of competitive advantage; low ratings signal a weak position and competitive disadvantage.

In addition, the competitive strength ratings point to which rival companies may be vulnerable to competitive attack and the areas where they are weakest. When a company has important competitive strengths in areas where one or more rivals are weak, it makes sense to consider offensive moves to exploit rivals' competitive weaknesses.

Identifying the Strategic Issues That Merit Managerial Attention

The final and most important analytical step is to zero in on exactly what strategic issues company managers need to address—and resolve—for the company to be more

> Zeroing in on the strategic issues a company faces and compiling a "worry list" of problems and roadblocks creates a strategic agenda of problems that merit prompt managerial attention.

financially and competitively successful in the years ahead. This step involves drawing on the results of both industry and competitive analysis and the evaluations of the company's own competitiveness. The task here is to get a clear fix on exactly what strategic and competitive challenges confront the company, which of the company's competitive shortcomings need fixing, what obstacles stand in the way of improving the company's competitive position in the marketplace, and what specific problems merit front-burner attention by company managers. *Pinpointing the precise things that management needs to worry about sets the agenda for deciding what actions to take next to improve the company's performance and business outlook.*

The "worry list" of issues and problems that have to be wrestled with can include such things as *how* to stave off market challenges from new foreign competitors, *how* to combat the price discounting of rivals, *how* to reduce the company's high costs and pave the way for price reductions, *how* to sustain the company's present rate of growth in light of slowing buyer demand, *whether* to expand the company's product line, *whether* to correct the company's competitive deficiencies by acquiring a rival company with the missing strengths, *whether* to expand into foreign markets rapidly or cautiously, *whether* to reposition the company and move to a different strategic group, *what to do* about growing buyer interest in substitute products, and *what to do* about the aging demographics of the company's customer base.

> A good strategy must contain ways to deal with all the strategic issues and obstacles that stand in the way of the company's financial and competitive success in the years ahead.

If the worry list is relatively minor, thus suggesting the company's strategy is mostly on track and reasonably well matched to the company's overall situation, company managers seldom need to go much beyond fine-tuning of the present strategy. If, however, the issues and problems confronting the company are serious and indicate the present strategy is not well suited for the road ahead, the task of crafting a better strategy has got to go to the top of management's action agenda.

Key Points

There are five key questions to consider in analyzing a company's particular competitive circumstances and its competitive position vis-à-vis key rivals:

1. *How well is the present strategy working?* This involves evaluating the strategy from a qualitative standpoint (completeness, internal consistency, rationale, and suitability to the situation) and also from a quantitative standpoint (the strategic and financial results the strategy is producing). The stronger a company's current overall performance, the less likely the need for radical strategy changes. The weaker a company's performance and/or the faster the changes in its external situation (which can be gleaned from industry and competitive analysis), the more its current strategy must be questioned.

2. *What are the company's resource strengths and weaknesses and its external opportunities and threats?* A SWOT analysis provides an overview of a firm's situation and is an essential component of crafting a strategy tightly matched to the company's situation. The two most important parts of SWOT analysis are (1) drawing conclusions about what story the compilation of strengths, weaknesses, opportunities, and threats tells about the company's overall situation and (2) acting on those conclusions to better match the company's strategy to its resource

strengths and market opportunities to correct the important weaknesses and defend against external threats. A company's resource strengths, competencies, and competitive capabilities are strategically relevant because they are the most logical and appealing building blocks for strategy; resource weaknesses are important because they may represent vulnerabilities that need correction. External opportunities and threats come into play because a good strategy necessarily aims at capturing a company's most attractive opportunities and at defending against threats to its well-being.

3. *Are the company's prices and costs competitive?* One telling sign of whether a company's situation is strong or precarious is whether its prices and costs are competitive with those of industry rivals. Value chain analysis and benchmarking are essential tools in determining whether the company is performing particular functions and activities cost-effectively, learning whether its costs are in line with competitors, and deciding which internal activities and business processes need to be scrutinized for improvement. Value chain analysis teaches that how competently a company manages its value chain activities relative to rivals is a key to building valuable competencies and competitive capabilities and then leveraging them into sustainable competitive advantage.

4. *Is the company competitively stronger or weaker than key rivals?* The key appraisals here involve how the company matches up against key rivals on industry key success factors and other chief determinants of competitive success and whether and why the company has a competitive advantage or disadvantage. Quantitative competitive strength assessments, using the method presented in Table 3.4, indicate where a company is competitively strong and weak and provide insight into the company's ability to defend or enhance its market position. As a rule a company's competitive strategy should be built around its competitive strengths and should aim at shoring up areas where it is competitively vulnerable. Also, the areas where company strengths match up against competitor weaknesses represent the best potential for new offensive initiatives.

5. *What strategic issues and problems merit front-burner managerial attention?* This analytical step zeros in on the strategic issues and problems that stand in the way of the company's success. It involves using the results of both industry and competitive analysis and company situation analysis to identify a "worry list" of issues to be resolved for the company to be financially and competitively successful in the years ahead.

Good company situation analysis, like good industry and competitive analysis, is a valuable precondition for good strategy making. A competently done evaluation of a company's resource capabilities and competitive strengths exposes strong and weak points in the present strategy and how attractive or unattractive the company's competitive position is and why. Managers need such understanding to craft a strategy that is well suited to the company's competitive circumstances.

Exercises

Review the information in Company Spotlight 3.1 concerning the costs of the different value chain activities associated with recording and distributing music CDs through traditional brick-and-mortar retail outlets. Then answer the following questions:

1. Does the growing popularity of downloading music from the Internet give rise to a new music industry value chain that differs considerably from the traditional value chain? Explain why or why not.

2. What costs would be cut out of the traditional value chain or bypassed in the event that recording studios sell downloadable files of artists' recordings direct to online buyers and buyers make their own custom CDs, load them onto their MP3 players, or play music directly from their PCs?

3. What costs would be cut out of the traditional value chain or bypassed in the event that online music retailers (Apple, Sony, Microsoft, Musicmatch, Napster, Cdigix, and others) sell direct to online buyers and buyers load the music files directly onto their MP3 players, make their own custom CDs, or play music directly from their PCs? (Note: In 2004, online music stores were selling download-only titles for $0.79 to $0.99 per song and $9.99 for most albums.)

4. What will happen to the traditional value chain if more and more music lovers use peer-to-peer file-sharing software to download music from the Internet to play music on their PCs or MP3 players or make their own CDs? (Note: It was estimated in 2004 that about 1 billion songs were available for online trading and file sharing via such programs as Kazaa, Grokster, Shareaza, BitTorrent, and eDonkey, despite the fact that some 4,000 people had been sued by the Recording Industry Association of America for pirating copyrighted music via peer-to-peer file sharing.)

CHAPTER 4

Crafting a Strategy
The Quest for Competitive Advantage

The process of developing superior strategies is part planning, part trial and error, until you hit upon something that works.

—*Costas Markides, professor, London Business School*

Successful business strategy is about actively shaping the game you play, not just playing the game you find.

—*Adam M. Brandenburger and Barry J. Nalebuff*

The essence of strategy lies in creating tomorrow's competitive advantages faster than competitors mimic the ones you possess today.

—*Gary Hamel and C. K. Prahalad*

Competitive strategy is about being different. It means deliberately choosing to perform activities differently or to perform different activities than rivals to deliver a unique mix of value.

—*Michael E. Porter*

Winners in business play rough and don't apologize for it. The nicest part of playing hardball is watching your competitors squirm.

—*George Stalk, Jr., and Rob Lachenauer*

$\textsf{This}$ chapter focuses on the primary options a company has in crafting a strategy to compete successfully in a particular industry and secure an attractive market position. The strategy-making challenge is to stitch together a winning strategy—one that fits industry and competitive conditions, capitalizes on the company's resources and competitive capabilities, builds a sustainable competitive advantage, and boosts company performance. We begin our survey of a company's menu of strategic options by describing the five *generic competitive strategy options*—what basic competitive approach to employ is a company's first and foremost choice in crafting an overall strategy. Next on a company's menu of strategic choices are the various *strategic actions* it can take to complement its choice of a basic competitive strategy:

- What use to make of strategic alliances and collaborative partnerships.
- What use to make of mergers and acquisitions.
- Whether to integrate backward or forward into more stages of the industry value chain.
- Whether to outsource certain value chain activities or perform them in-house.
- Whether and when to employ offensive and defensive moves.
- What Web site strategy to employ.

This chapter contains sections discussing the pros and cons of each of the above complementary strategic options. The next-to-last section in the chapter discusses the need for strategic choices in each functional area of a company's business (R&D, production, sales and marketing, finance, and so on) to support its basic competitive approach and complementary strategic moves. The chapter concludes with a brief look at the competitive importance of timing strategic moves—when it is advantageous to be a first-mover and when it is better to be a fast-follower or late-mover.

Figure 4.1 shows the menu of options a company has in crafting a strategy and the order in which the choices should generally be made. It also illustrates the structure of the chapter and the topics that will be covered.

The Five Generic Competitive Strategies

A company's **competitive strategy** deals exclusively with its plans for competing successfully—its specific efforts to please customers, its offensive and defensive moves to counter the maneuvers of rivals, its responses to whatever market conditions prevail at the moment, and its initiatives to strengthen its market position. Companies the world over are imaginative in conceiving competitive strategies to win customer favor. At most companies the aim, quite simply, is to gain a competitive advantage by doing a significantly better job than rivals of providing buyers with the best overall value. There are many routes to competitive advantage, but they all involve giving buyers what they perceive as superior value compared to the offerings of rival sellers. Superior value can mean a good product at a lower price, a superior product that is worth paying more for, or a best-value offering that represents an attractive combination of price, features, quality, service, and other appealing attributes. Delivering superior value—whatever form it

> **Core Concept**
>
> The objective of **competitive strategy** is to knock the socks off rival companies by doing a better job of providing a product offering that best satisfies buyer needs and preferences.

Figure 4.1   A Company's Menu of Strategy Options

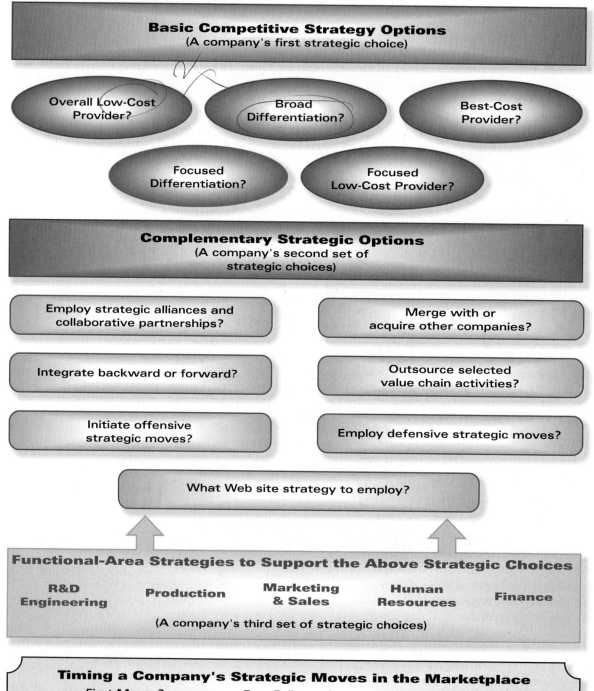

takes—nearly always requires performing value chain activities differently than rivals and building competencies and resource capabilities that are not readily matched.

There are countless variations in the competitive strategies that companies employ, mainly because each company's strategic approach entails custom-designed actions to fit its own circumstances and industry environment. The custom-tailored nature of each company's strategy makes the chances remote that any two companies—even companies in the same industry—will employ strategies that are exactly alike in every detail. Managers at different companies always have a slightly different spin on what future market conditions will be like and how to best align their company's strategy with these conditions; moreover, they have different notions of how they intend to outmaneuver rivals and what strategic options make the most sense for their particular company. However, when one strips away the details to get at the real substance, the biggest and most important differences among competitive strategies boil down to (1) whether a company's market target is broad or narrow and (2) whether the company is pursuing a competitive advantage linked to low costs or product differentiation. Five distinct competitive strategy approaches stand out:[1]

1. *A low-cost provider strategy*—striving to achieve lower overall costs than rivals and appealing to a broad spectrum of customers, usually by underpricing rivals.

2. *A broad differentiation strategy*—seeking to differentiate the company's product offering from rivals' in ways that will appeal to a broad spectrum of buyers.

3. *A best-cost provider strategy*—giving customers more value for the money by incorporating good-to-excellent product attributes at a lower cost than rivals; the target is to have the lowest (best) costs and prices compared to rivals offering products with comparable attributes.

4. *A focused (or market niche) strategy based on low costs*—concentrating on a narrow buyer segment and outcompeting rivals by having lower costs than rivals and thus being able to serve niche members at a lower price.

5. *A focused (or market niche) strategy based on differentiation*—concentrating on a narrow buyer segment and outcompeting rivals by offering niche members customized attributes that meet their tastes and requirements better than rivals' products.

Each of these five generic competitive approaches stakes out a different market position, as shown in Figure 4.2.

Low-Cost Provider Strategies

A company achieves low-cost leadership when it becomes the industry's lowest-cost provider rather than just being one of perhaps several competitors with comparatively low costs. A low-cost provider's strategic target is meaningfully lower costs than rivals—but not necessarily the absolutely lowest possible cost. In striving for a cost advantage over rivals, managers must take care to include features and services that buyers consider essential—*a product offering that is too frills-free sabotages the attractiveness of the company's product and can turn buyers off even if it is cheaper than competing products.* For maximum effectiveness, companies employing a low-cost provider strategy need to achieve their cost advantage in ways difficult for

> **Core Concept**
>
> A low-cost leader's basis for competitive advantage is lower overall costs than competitors. Successful low-cost leaders are exceptionally good at finding ways to drive costs out of their businesses.

Figure 4.2   The Five Generic Competitive Strategies:
Each Stakes Out a Different Market Position

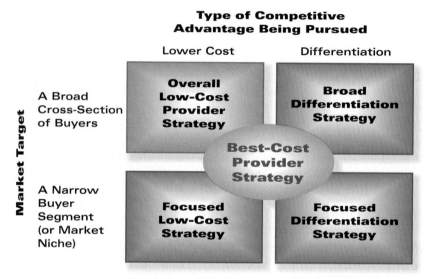

rivals to copy or match. If rivals find it relatively easy or inexpensive to imitate the leader's low-cost methods, then the leader's advantage will be too short-lived to yield a valuable edge in the marketplace.

A company has two options for translating a low-cost advantage over rivals into attractive profit performance. Option 1 is to use the lower-cost edge to underprice competitors and attract price-sensitive buyers in great-enough numbers to increase total profits. The trick to profitably underpricing rivals is either to keep the size of the price cut smaller than the size of the firm's cost advantage (thus reaping the benefits of both a bigger profit margin per unit sold and the added profits on incremental sales) or to generate enough added volume to increase total profits despite thinner profit margins (larger volume can make up for smaller margins provided the underpricing of rivals brings in enough extra sales). Option 2 is to maintain the present price, be content with the present market share, and use the lower-cost edge to earn a higher profit margin on each unit sold, thereby raising the firm's total profits and overall return on investment.

Company Spotlight 4.1 describes Nucor Corporation's strategy for gaining low-cost leadership in manufacturing a variety of steel products.

The Two Major Avenues for Achieving a Cost Advantage   To achieve a cost advantage, a firm's cumulative costs across its overall value chain must be lower than competitors' cumulative costs. There are two ways to accomplish this:[2]

1. Outmanage rivals in the efficiently performing value chain activities and in controlling the factors that drive the costs of value chain activities.

2. Revamp the firm's overall value chain to eliminate or bypass some cost-producing activities.

COMPANY SPOTLIGHT 4.1
Nucor Corporation's Low-Cost Provider Strategy

Nucor Corporation is the world's leading minimill producer of such steel products as carbon and alloy steel bars, beams, sheet, and plate; steel joists and joist girders; steel deck; cold finished steel; steel fasteners; metal building systems; and light-gauge steel framing. In 2004 it had close to $10 billion in sales, 9,000 employees, and annual production capacity of nearly 22 million tons, making it the largest steel producer in the United States. The company has pursued a strategy that has made it among the lowest-cost producers of steel in the world and has allowed it to consistently outperform its rivals in terms of financial and market performance.

Nucor's low-cost strategy aims to give the company a cost and pricing advantage in the commoditylike steel industry and leaves no part of the company's value chain neglected. The key elements of the strategy include the following:

- Using electric-arc furnaces where scrap steel and directly reduced iron ore are melted and then sent to a continuous caster and rolling mill to be shaped into steel products, thereby eliminating an assortment of production processes from the value chain used by traditional integrated steel mills. Nucor's minimill value chain makes the use of coal, coke, and iron ore unnecessary, cuts investment in facilities and equipment (eliminating coke ovens, blast furnaces, basic oxygen furnaces, and ingot casters), and requires fewer employees than integrated mills.

- Striving hard for continuous improvement in the efficiency of its plants and frequently investing in state-of-the-art equipment to reduce unit costs. Nucor is known for its technological leadership and its aggressive pursuit of production process innovation.

- Carefully selecting plant sites to minimize inbound and outbound shipping costs and to take advantage of low rates for electricity (electric-arc furnaces are heavy users of electricity). Nucor tends to avoid locating new plants in geographic areas where labor unions are a strong influence.

- Hiring a nonunion workforce that uses team-based incentive compensation systems (often opposed by unions). Operating and maintenance employees and supervisors are paid weekly bonuses based on the productivity of their work group. The size of the bonus is based on the capabilities of the equipment employed and ranges from 80 to 150 percent of an employee's base pay; no bonus is paid if the equipment is not operating. Nucor's compensation program has boosted the company's labor productivity to levels nearly double the industry average while rewarding productive employees with annual compensation packages that exceed what their union counterparts earn by as much as 20 percent. Nucor has been able to attract and retain highly talented, productive, and dedicated employees. In addition, the company's healthy culture and results-oriented self-managed work teams allow Nucor to employ fewer supervisors than would be needed with an hourly union workforce.

- Heavily emphasizing consistent product quality and rigorous quality systems.

- Minimizing general and administrative expenses by maintaining a lean staff at corporate headquarters (fewer than 125 employees) and allowing only four levels of management between the CEO and production workers. Headquarters offices are modestly furnished and located in an inexpensive building. The company minimizes reports, paperwork, and meetings to keep managers focused on value-adding activities. Nucor is noted not only for its streamlined organizational structure but also for its frugality in travel and entertainment expenses—the company's top managers set the example by flying coach class, avoiding pricey hotels, and refraining from taking customers out for expensive dinners.

In 2001–2003, when many U.S. producers of steel products were in dire economic straits because of weak demand for steel and deep price discounting by foreign rivals, Nucor began acquiring state-of-the-art steelmaking facilities from bankrupt or nearly bankrupt rivals at bargain-basement prices, often at 20 to 25 percent of what it cost to construct the facilities. This has given Nucor much lower depreciation costs than rivals having comparable plants.

Nucor management's outstanding execution of its low-cost strategy and its commitment to driving down costs throughout its value chain has allowed it to compete aggressively on price, earn higher profit margins than rivals, and grow its business at a considerably faster rate than its integrated steel mill rivals.

Source: Company annual reports, news releases, and Web site.

Let's look at both of the approaches to securing a cost advantage.

Controlling the Cost Drivers   There are nine major cost drivers that come into play in determining a company's costs in each activity segment of the value chain:[3]

1. *Economies or diseconomies of scale:* The costs of a particular value chain activity are often subject to economies or diseconomies of scale. Economies of scale arise whenever activities can be performed more cheaply at larger volumes than at smaller volumes and whenever certain costs like R&D and advertising can be spread out over a greater sales volume. Astute management of activities subject to scale economies or diseconomies can be a major source of cost savings. For example, manufacturing economies can usually be achieved by simplifying the product line, scheduling longer production runs for fewer models, and using common parts and components in different models. In global industries, making separate products for each country market instead of selling a mostly standard product worldwide tends to boost unit costs because of lost time in model changeover, shorter production runs, and the inability to reach the most economic scale of production for each country model.

2. *Experience- and learning-curve effects:* The cost of performing an activity can decline over time as the learning and experience of company personnel build. Learning/experience economies can stem from debugging and mastering newly introduced technologies, finding ways to improve plant layout and work flows, making product design modifications that streamline the assembly process, and capitalizing on the added speed and knowledge that accrues from repeatedly siting and building new plants, retail outlets, or distribution centers. Aggressively managed low-cost providers pay diligent attention to capturing the benefits of learning and experience and to keeping the benefits proprietary to whatever extent possible.

3. *The cost of key resource inputs:* The cost of performing value chain activities depends in part on what a firm has to pay for key resource inputs. Competitors do not all incur the same costs for items purchased from suppliers or for other resources. How well a company manages the costs of acquiring key resource inputs is often a big driver of costs. Input costs are a function of four factors:

   a) *Union versus nonunion labor:* Avoiding the use of union labor is often a key to keeping labor input costs low, not just because unions demand high wages but also because union work rules can stifle productivity. Such highly regarded low-cost manufacturers as Nucor and Cooper Tire are noted for their incentive compensation systems that promote very high levels of labor productivity—at both companies, nonunion workers earn more than their unionized counterparts at rival companies but their high productivity results in lower labor costs per unit produced.

   b) *Bargaining power vis-à-vis suppliers:* Many large enterprises (e.g., Wal-Mart, Home Depot, the world's major motor vehicle producers) have used their bargaining clout in purchasing large volumes to wrangle good prices on their purchases from suppliers. Having greater buying power than rivals can be an important source of cost advantage.

   c) *Location variables:* Locations differ in their prevailing wage levels, tax rates, energy costs, inbound and outbound shipping and freight costs, and so on. Opportunities may exist for reducing costs by relocating plants, field offices, warehousing, or headquarters operations.

d) *Supply chain management expertise:* Some companies have more efficient supply chain expertise than others and are able to squeeze out cost savings via partnerships with suppliers that lower the costs of purchased materials and components, e-procurement systems, and inbound logistics.

4. *Links with other activities in the company or industry value chain:* When the cost of one activity is affected by how other activities are performed, costs can be managed downward by making sure that linked activities are performed in cooperative and coordinated fashion. For example, when a company's materials inventory costs or warranty costs are linked to the activities of suppliers, cost savings can be achieved by working cooperatively with key suppliers on the design of parts and components, quality-assurance procedures, just-in-time delivery, and integrated materials supply. The costs of new product development can often be managed downward by having cross-functional task forces (perhaps including representatives of suppliers and key customers) jointly work on R&D, product design, manufacturing plans, and market launch. Links with forward channels tend to center on location of warehouses, materials handling, outbound shipping, and packaging. Nail manufacturers, for example, learned that delivering nails in prepackaged 1-, 5-, and 10-pound assortments instead of 100-pound bulk cartons could reduce a hardware dealer's labor costs in filling individual customer orders. The lesson here is that effective coordination of linked activities anywhere in the value chain holds potential for cost reduction.

5. *Sharing opportunities with other organizational or business units within the enterprise:* Different product lines or business units within an enterprise can often share the same order processing and customer billing systems, utilize a common sales force to call on customers, share the same warehouse and distribution facilities, or rely on a common customer service and technical support team. Such combining of like activities and sharing of resources across sister units can create significant cost savings. Furthermore, there are times when the know-how gained in one division or geographic unit can be used to help lower costs in another; sharing know-how across organizational lines has significant cost-saving potential when cross-unit value chain activities are similar and know-how is readily transferred from one unit to another.

6. *The benefits of vertical integration versus outsourcing:* Partially or fully integrating into the activities of either suppliers or distribution channel allies can allow an enterprise to detour suppliers or buyers with considerable bargaining power. Vertical integration forward or backward also has potential if there are significant cost savings from having a single firm perform adjacent activities in the industry value chain. But more often it is cheaper to outsource certain functions and activities to outside specialists, who by virtue of their expertise and volume can perform the activity/function more cheaply.

7. *Timing considerations associated with first-mover advantages and disadvantages:* Sometimes the first major brand in the market is able to establish and maintain its brand name at a lower cost than later brand arrivals. Competitors looking to go head-to-head against such first-movers as eBay, Yahoo!, and Amazon.com have to spend heavily to come close to achieving the same brand awareness and name recognition. On other occasions, such as when technology is developing fast, late purchasers can benefit from waiting to install second- or third-generation equipment that is both cheaper and more efficient; first-generation users often incur

added costs associated with debugging and learning how to use an immature and unperfected technology. Likewise, companies that follow, rather than lead, new product development efforts sometimes avoid many of the costs that pioneers incur in performing pathbreaking R&D and opening up new markets.

8. *The percentage of capacity utilization:* Capacity utilization is a big cost driver for those value chain activities associated with substantial fixed costs. Higher rates of capacity utilization allow depreciation and other fixed costs to be spread over a larger unit volume, thereby lowering fixed costs per unit. The more capital intensive the business, or the higher the percentage of fixed costs as a percentage of total costs, the more important this cost driver becomes because there's such a stiff unit-cost penalty for underutilizing existing capacity. In such cases, finding ways to operate close to full capacity year-round can be an important source of cost advantage.

9. *Strategic choices and operating decisions:* A company's costs can be driven up or down by a fairly wide assortment of managerial decisions:

   a) Adding/cutting the services provided to buyers.

   b) Incorporating more/fewer performance and quality features into the product.

   c) Increasing/decreasing the number of different channels utilized in distributing the firm's product.

   d) Lengthening/shortening delivery times to customers.

   e) Putting more/less emphasis than rivals on the use of incentive compensation, wage increases, and fringe benefits to motivate employees and boost worker productivity.

   f) Raising/lowering the specifications for purchased materials.

> Outperforming rivals in controlling the factors that drive costs is a very demanding managerial exercise.

For a company to outmanage rivals in performing value chain activities cost-effectively, its managers must possess a sophisticated understanding of the factors that drive the costs of each activity. And then they must not only use their knowledge about the cost drivers to squeeze out cost savings all along the value chain but also be so much more ingenious and committed than rivals in achieving cost-saving efficiencies that the company ends up with a sustainable cost advantage.

Revamping the Value Chain   Dramatic cost advantages can emerge from finding innovative ways to eliminate or bypass cost-producing value chain activities. The primary ways companies can achieve a cost advantage by reconfiguring their value chains include:

■ *Making greater use of Internet technology applications:* In recent years the Internet and Internet technology applications have become powerful and pervasive tools for reengineering company and industry value chains. For instance, Internet technology has revolutionized supply chain management. Using software packages from any of several vendors, company procurement personnel can—with only a few mouse clicks within one seamless system—check materials inventories against incoming customer orders, check suppliers' stocks, check the latest prices for parts and components at auction and e-sourcing Web sites, and check Federal Express delivery schedules. Electronic data interchange software permits the relevant details of incoming customer orders to be instantly shared with the suppliers of needed parts and components. All this lays the foundation for just-in-time deliveries of parts and components, and for the production of parts and components, to be matched closely to assembly plant requirements and production schedules—

and such coordination produces savings for both suppliers and manufacturers. Via the Internet, manufacturers can collaborate closely with parts and components suppliers in designing new products and reducing the time it takes to get them into production. Warranty claims and product performance problems involving supplier components can be made available instantly to the relevant suppliers so that corrections can be expedited. Various e-procurement software packages streamline the purchasing process by eliminating much of the manual handling of data and by substituting electronic communication for paper documents such as requests for quotations, purchase orders, order acceptances, and shipping notices.

Manufacturers are using Internet applications to link customer orders to production at their plants and to deliveries of components from suppliers. Real-time sharing of customer orders with suppliers facilitates just-in-time deliveries of parts and slices parts inventory costs. It also allows both manufacturers and their suppliers to gear production to match demand for both components and finished goods. Online systems that monitor actual sales permit more accurate demand forecasting, thereby helping both manufacturers and their suppliers adjust their production schedules as swings in buyer demand are detected. Data sharing, starting with customer orders and going all the way back to components production, coupled with the use of enterprise resource planning (ERP) and manufacturing execution system (MES) software, can make custom manufacturing just as cheap as mass production—and sometimes cheaper. It can also greatly reduce production times and labor costs. Lexmark used ERP and MES software to cut its production time for inkjet printers from 4 hours to 24 minutes.

The instant communications features of the Internet, combined with all the real-time data sharing and information availability, have the further effect of breaking down corporate bureaucracies and reducing overhead costs. The whole "back-office" data management process (order processing, invoicing, customer accounting, and other kinds of transaction costs) can be handled quickly, accurately, and efficiently, with less paperwork and fewer personnel. The time savings and transaction cost reductions associated with doing business online has allowed companies in many industries to streamline their supply chains and has resulted in significant cost savings in the back-office activities of stock brokerages and banks.

■ *Using direct-to-end-user sales and marketing approaches:* Costs in the wholesale/retail portions of the value chain frequently represent 35 to 50 percent of the price final consumers pay. Software developers are increasingly using the Internet to market and deliver their products directly to buyers; allowing customers to download software directly from the Internet eliminates the costs of producing and packaging CDs and cuts out the host of activities, costs, and markups associated with shipping and distributing software through wholesale and retail channels. By cutting all these costs and activities out of the value chain, software developers have the pricing room to boost their profit margins and still sell their products below levels that retailers would have to charge. The major airlines now sell most of their tickets directly to passengers via their Web sites, ticket counter agents, and telephone reservation systems, allowing them to save hundreds of millions of dollars in commissions once paid to travel agents.

■ *Simplifying product design:* Using computer-assisted design techniques, reducing the number of parts, standardizing parts and components across models and styles, and shifting to an easy-to-manufacture product design can all simplify the value chain.

- *Stripping away the extras:* Offering only basic products or services can help a company cut costs associated with multiple features and options. Stripping extras is a favorite technique of the no-frills airlines like Southwest Airlines.

- *Shifting to a simpler, less capital-intensive, or more streamlined or flexible technological process:* Computer-assisted design and manufacture, or other flexible manufacturing systems, can accommodate both low-cost efficiency and product customization.

- *Bypassing the use of high-cost raw materials or component parts:* High-cost raw materials and parts can be designed out of the product.

- *Relocating facilities:* Moving plants closer to suppliers, customers, or both can help curtail inbound and outbound logistics costs.

- *Dropping the "something for everyone" approach:* Pruning slow-selling items from the product lineup and being content to meet the needs of most buyers, rather than all buyers, can eliminate activities and costs associated with numerous product versions.

Company Spotlight 4.2 describes how Wal-Mart has managed its value chain in the retail grocery portion of its business to achieve a dramatic cost advantage over rival supermarket chains and become the world's biggest grocery retailer.

> Success in achieving a low-cost edge over rivals comes from exploring all the avenues for cost reduction and pressing for continuous cost reductions across all aspects of the company's value chain year after year.

The Keys to Success in Achieving Low-Cost Leadership   To succeed with a low-cost provider strategy, company managers have to scrutinize each cost-creating activity and determine what drives its cost. Then they have to use this knowledge about the cost drivers to manage the costs of each activity downward, exhaustively pursuing cost savings throughout the value chain. They have to be proactive in restructuring the value chain to eliminate nonessential work steps and low-value activities. Normally, low-cost producers work diligently to create cost-conscious corporate cultures that feature broad employee participation in continuous cost improvement efforts and limited perks and frills for executives. They strive to operate with exceptionally small corporate staffs to keep administrative costs to a minimum.

But while low-cost providers are champions of frugality, they are usually aggressive in investing in resources and capabilities that promise to drive costs out of the business. Wal-Mart, one of the foremost practitioners of low-cost leadership, employs state-of-the-art technology throughout its operations—its distribution facilities are an automated showcase, it uses online systems to order goods from suppliers and manage inventories, it equips its stores with cutting-edge sales-tracking and checkout systems, and it operates a private satellite communications system that daily sends point-of-sale data to 4,000 vendors. Wal-Mart's information and communications systems and capabilities are more sophisticated than those of virtually any other retail chain in the world.

Other companies noted for their successful use of low-cost provider strategies include Lincoln Electric in arc welding equipment, Briggs & Stratton in small gasoline engines, Bic in ballpoint pens, Black & Decker in power tools, Stride Rite in footwear, Beaird-Poulan in chain saws, and General Electric and Whirlpool in major home appliances.

When a Low-Cost Provider Strategy Works Best   A competitive strategy predicated on low-cost leadership is particularly powerful when:

How Wal-Mart Managed Its Value Chain to Achieve a Huge Low-Cost Advantage over Rival Supermarket Chains

Wal-Mart has achieved a very substantial cost and pricing advantage over rival supermarket chains both by revamping portions of the grocery retailing value chain and by outmanaging its rivals in efficiently performing various value chain activities. Its cost advantage stems from a series of initiatives and practices:

- Instituting extensive information sharing with vendors via online systems that relay sales at its checkout counters directly to suppliers of the items, thereby providing suppliers with real-time information on customer demand and preferences (creating an estimated 6 percent cost advantage). It is standard practice at Wal-Mart to collaborate extensively with vendors on all aspects of the purchasing and store delivery process to squeeze out mutually beneficial cost savings. Procter & Gamble, Wal-Mart's biggest supplier, went so far as to integrate its enterprise resource planning (ERP) system with Wal-Mart's.

- Pursuing global procurement of some items and centralizing most purchasing activities so as to leverage the company's buying power (creating an estimated 2.5 percent cost advantage).

- Investing in state-of-the-art automation at its distribution centers, efficiently operating a truck fleet that makes daily deliveries to Wal-Mart stores, and putting various other cost-saving practices into place at its headquarters, distribution centers, and stores (resulting in an estimated 4 percent cost advantage).

- Striving to optimize the product mix and achieve greater sales turnover (resulting in about a 2 percent cost advantage).

- Installing security systems and store operating procedures that lower shrinkage rates (producing a cost advantage of about 0.5 percent).

- Negotiating preferred real estate rental and leasing rates with real estate developers and owners of its store sites (yielding a cost advantage of 2 percent).

- Managing and compensating its workforce in a manner that produces lower labor costs (yielding an estimated 5 percent cost advantage).

Altogether, these value chain initiatives give Wal-Mart an approximately 22 percent cost advantage over Kroger, Safeway, and other leading supermarket chains. With such a sizable cost advantage, Wal-Mart has been able to underprice its rivals and become the world's leading supermarket retailer in little more than a decade.

Source: Reprinted by permission of *Harvard Business Review,* an excerpt from "Strategy as Ecology," by Marco Iansiti and Roy Levien, March 2004, Copyright ©2004 by the President and Fellows of Harvard College, all rights reserved.

1. *Price competition among rival sellers is especially vigorous.* Low-cost providers are in the best position to compete offensively on the basis of price, to use the appeal of lower price to grab sales (and market share) from rivals, to remain profitable in the face of strong price competition, and to survive price wars.

2. *The products of rival sellers are essentially identical, and supplies are readily available from any of several eager sellers.* Commoditylike products and/or ample supplies set the stage for lively price competition; in such markets, it is the less efficient, higher-cost companies whose profits get squeezed the most.

3. *There are few ways to achieve product differentiation that have value to buyers.* When the differences between brands do not matter much to buyers, buyers are nearly always very sensitive to price differences and shop the market for the best price.

4. *Most buyers use the product in the same way.* With common user requirements, a standardized product can satisfy the needs of buyers, in which case low selling price, not features or quality, becomes the dominant factor in causing buyers to choose one seller's product over another's.

5. *Buyers incur low costs in switching their purchases from one seller to another.* Low switching costs give buyers the flexibility to shift purchases to lower-priced

sellers having equally good products or to attractively priced substitute products. A low-cost leader is well positioned to use low price to induce its customers not to switch to rival brands or substitutes.

6. *Buyers are large and have significant power to bargain down prices.* Low-cost providers have partial profit-margin protection in bargaining with high-volume buyers, since powerful buyers are rarely able to bargain price down past the survival level of the next most cost-efficient seller.

7. *Industry newcomers use introductory low prices to attract buyers and build a customer base.* The low-cost leader can use price cuts of its own to make it harder for a new rival to win customers; the pricing power of the low-cost provider acts as a barrier for new entrants.

> A low-cost provider is in the best position to win the business of price-sensitive buyers, set the floor on market price, and still earn a profit.

As a rule, the more price sensitive buyers are, the more appealing a low-cost strategy becomes. A low-cost company's ability to set the industry's price floor and still earn a profit erects protective barriers around its market position.

The Pitfalls of a Low-Cost Provider Strategy   Perhaps the biggest pitfall of a low-cost provider strategy is getting carried away with overly aggressive price cutting and ending up with lower, rather than higher, profitability. A low-cost/low-price advantage results in superior profitability only if (1) prices are cut by less than the size of the cost advantage or (2) the added gains in unit sales are large enough to bring in a bigger total profit despite lower margins per unit sold. A company with a 5 percent cost advantage cannot cut prices 20 percent, end up with a volume gain of only 10 percent, and still expect to earn higher profits!

A second big pitfall is not emphasizing avenues of cost advantage that can be kept proprietary or that relegate rivals to playing catch-up. The value of a cost advantage depends on its sustainability. Sustainability, in turn, hinges on whether the company achieves its cost advantage in ways difficult for rivals to copy or match.

> A low-cost provider's product offering must always contain enough attributes to be attractive to prospective buyers—low price, by itself, is not always appealing to buyers.

A third pitfall is becoming too fixated on cost reduction. Low cost cannot be pursued so zealously that a firm's offering ends up being too features-poor to generate buyer appeal. Furthermore, a company driving hard to push its costs down has to guard against misreading or ignoring increased buyer interest in added features or service, declining buyer sensitivity to price, or new developments that start to alter how buyers use the product. A low-cost zealot risks losing market ground if buyers start opting for more upscale or features-rich products.

Even if these mistakes are avoided, a low-cost competitive approach still carries risk. Cost-saving technological breakthroughs or the emergence of still-lower-cost value chain models can nullify a low-cost leader's hard-won position. The current leader may have difficulty in shifting quickly to the new technologies or value chain approaches because heavy investments lock it in (at least temporarily) to its present value chain approach.

Differentiation Strategies

> **Core Concept**
> The essence of a broad differentiation strategy is to be unique in ways that are valuable to a wide range of customers.

Differentiation strategies are attractive whenever buyers' needs and preferences are too diverse to be fully satisfied by a standardized product or by sellers with identical capabilities. A company attempting to succeed through differentiation must study buyers' needs and behavior carefully to learn what buyers consider important, what they think has value, and what they are willing to pay for. Then the company has to incorporate buyer-desired attributes into its product or service offering that will clearly set it apart from rivals. Competitive advantage results once a sufficient number of buyers become strongly attached to the differentiated attributes.

Successful differentiation allows a firm to:

- Command a premium price for its product, and/or

- Increase unit sales (because additional buyers are won over by the differentiating features), and/or

- Gain buyer loyalty to its brand (because some buyers are strongly attracted to the differentiating features and bond with the company and its products).

Differentiation enhances profitability whenever the extra price the product commands outweighs the added costs of achieving the differentiation. Company differentiation strategies fail when buyers don't value the brand's uniqueness and/or when a company's approach to differentiation is easily copied or matched by its rivals.

Types of Differentiation Themes   Companies can pursue differentiation from many angles: a unique taste (Dr Pepper, Listerine); multiple features (Microsoft Windows, Microsoft Office); wide selection and one-stop shopping (Home Depot, Amazon.com); superior service (FedEx); spare parts availability (Caterpillar guarantees 48-hour spare parts delivery to any customer anywhere in the world or else the part is furnished free); engineering design and performance (Mercedes, BMW); prestige and distinctiveness (Rolex); product reliability (Johnson & Johnson in baby products); quality manufacture (Karastan in carpets, Michelin in tires, Honda in automobiles); technological leadership (3M Corporation in bonding and coating products); a full range of services (Charles Schwab in stock brokerage); a complete line of products (Campbell's soups); and top-of-the-line image and reputation (Ralph Lauren and Starbucks).

The most appealing approaches to differentiation are those that are hard or expensive for rivals to duplicate. Indeed, resourceful competitors can, in time, clone almost any product or feature or attribute. If Coca-Cola introduces a vanilla-flavored soft drink, so can PepsiCo; if Ford offers a 50,000-mile bumper-to-bumper warranty on its new vehicles, so can Volkswagen and Nissan. As a rule, differentiation yields a longer-lasting and more profitable competitive edge when it is based on product innovation, technical superiority, product quality and reliability, comprehensive customer service, and unique competitive capabilities. Such differentiating attributes tend to be tough for rivals to copy or offset profitably, and buyers widely perceive them as having value.

> Easy-to-copy differentiating features cannot produce sustainable competitive advantage.

Where along the Value Chain to Create the Differentiating Attributes   Differentiation is not something hatched in marketing and advertising departments, nor is it limited to the catchalls of quality and service. Differentiation opportunities can exist in activities all along an industry's value chain; possibilities include the following:

- *Supply chain activities* that ultimately spill over to affect the performance or quality of the company's end product. Starbucks gets high ratings on its coffees partly because it has very strict specifications on the coffee beans purchased from suppliers.

- *Product R&D activities* that aim at improved product designs and performance features, expanded end uses and applications, more frequent first-on-the-market victories, wider product variety and selection, added user safety, greater recycling capability, or enhanced environmental protection.

- *Production R&D and technology-related activities* that permit custom-order manufacture at an efficient cost, make production methods safer for the environment, or improve product quality, reliability, and appearance. Many manufacturers have developed flexible manufacturing systems that allow different models to be made or different options to be added on the same assembly line. Being able to provide buyers with made-to-order products can be a potent differentiating capability.

- *Manufacturing activities* that reduce product defects, prevent premature product failure, extend product life, allow better warranty coverages, improve economy of use, result in more end-user convenience, or enhance product appearance. The quality edge enjoyed by Japanese automakers stems partly from their distinctive competence in performing assembly-line activities.

- *Outbound logistics and distribution activities* that allow for faster delivery, more accurate order filling, lower shipping costs, and fewer warehouse and on-the-shelf stockouts.

- *Marketing, sales, and customer service activities* that result in superior technical assistance to buyers, faster maintenance and repair services, more and better product information for customers, more and better training materials for end users, better credit terms, quicker order processing, or greater customer convenience.

Managers need keen understanding of the sources of differentiation and the activities that drive uniqueness to devise a sound differentiation strategy and evaluate various differentiation approaches.

Achieving a Differentiation-Based Competitive Advantage

While it is easy enough to grasp that a successful differentiation strategy must entail creating buyer value in ways unmatched by rivals, the big question is which of four basic differentiating approaches to take in delivering unique buyer value. One approach is to *incorporate product attributes and user features that lower the buyer's overall costs of using the company's product.* Making a company's product more economical for a buyer to use can be done by reducing the buyer's raw materials waste (providing cut-to-size components), reducing a buyer's inventory requirements (providing just-in-time deliveries), increasing maintenance intervals and product reliability so as to lower a buyer's repair and maintenance costs, using online systems to reduce a buyer's procurement and order processing costs, and providing free technical support.

A second approach is to *incorporate features that raise product performance.*[4] This can be accomplished with attributes that provide buyers greater reliability, durability, convenience, or ease of use. Other performance-enhancing options include making the company's product or service cleaner, safer, quieter, or more maintenance-free than rival brands. A third approach is to *incorporate features that enhance buyer satisfaction in noneconomic or intangible ways.* Goodyear's Aquatread tire design appeals to safety-conscious motorists wary of slick roads. BMW, Ralph Lauren, and Rolex have differentiation-based competitive advantages linked to buyer desires for status, image, prestige, upscale fashion, superior craftsmanship, and the finer things in life. L.L. Bean makes its mail-order customers feel secure in their purchases by providing an unconditional guarantee with no time limit: "All of our products are guaranteed to give 100 percent satisfaction in every way. Return anything purchased from us

Core Concept

A differentiator's basis for competitive advantage is either a product/service offering whose attributes differ significantly from the offerings of rivals or competitive capabilities and resource strengths that set it apart from rivals.

at any time if it proves otherwise. We will replace it, refund your purchase price, or credit your credit card, as you wish."

A fourth approach is to differentiate on the basis of capabilities—*to deliver value to customers via competitive capabilities that rivals don't have or can't afford to match.*[5] Japanese automakers can bring new models to market faster than American and European automakers, thereby allowing the Japanese companies to satisfy changing consumer preferences for one vehicle style versus another. CNN has the capability to cover breaking news stories faster and more completely than the major networks. Microsoft has stronger capabilities to design, create, distribute, and advertise an array of software products for PC applications than any of its rivals.

Keeping the Cost of Differentiation in Line   Company efforts to achieve differentiation usually raise costs. The trick to profitable differentiation is either to keep the costs of achieving differentiation below the price premium the differentiating attributes can command in the marketplace (thus increasing the profit margin per unit sold) or to offset thinner profit margins with enough added volume to increase total profits. It usually makes sense to incorporate differentiating features that are not costly but that add to buyer satisfaction. Federal Express (FedEx) installed systems that allowed customers to track packages in transit by connecting to FedEx's Web site and entering the airbill number; some hotels and motels provide free continental breakfasts, exercise facilities, and in-room coffee-making amenities; publishers are using their Web sites to deliver complementary educational materials to the buyers of their textbooks.

When a Differentiation Strategy Works Best   Differentiation strategies tend to work best in market circumstances where:

- *There are many ways to differentiate the product or service, and many buyers perceive these differences as having value.* Unless buyers have strong preferences about certain features, profitable differentiation opportunities are very restricted.

- *Buyer needs and uses are diverse.* The more diverse buyer preferences are, the more room firms have to pursue different approaches to differentiation.

> **Core Concept**
> Any differentiating feature that works well tends to draw imitators.

- *Few rival firms are following a similar differentiation approach.* There is less head-to-head rivalry when differentiating rivals go separate ways in pursuing uniqueness and try to appeal to buyers on different combinations of attributes.

- *Technological change is fast-paced, and competition revolves around rapidly evolving product features.* Rapid product innovation and frequent introductions of next-version products help maintain buyer interest and provide space for companies to pursue separate differentiating paths.

The Pitfalls of a Differentiation Strategy   There are, of course, no guarantees that differentiation will produce a meaningful competitive advantage. If buyers see little value in the unique attributes or capabilities of a product, then the company's differentiation strategy will get a ho-hum market reception. In addition, attempts at differentiation are doomed to fail if competitors can quickly copy most or all of the appealing product attributes a company comes up with. Rapid imitation means that no rival achieves differentiation, since whenever one firm introduces some aspect of uniqueness that strikes the fancy of buyers, fast-following copycats quickly reestablish similarity. Thus, to build competitive advantage through differentiation, a firm must rely on sources of uniqueness that are time-consuming or burdensome for rivals to match. Other common pitfalls and mistakes in pursuing differentiation include:[6]

- Trying to differentiate on the basis of something that does not lower a buyer's cost or enhance a buyer's well-being, as perceived by the buyer.
- Overdifferentiating, so that the features and attributes incorporated end up exceeding buyers' needs.
- Trying to charge too high a price premium. (The bigger the price differential, the harder it is to keep buyers from switching to lower-priced competitors.)

A low-cost provider strategy can defeat a differentiation strategy when buyers are satisfied with a basic product and don't think "extra" attributes are worth a higher price.

Best-Cost Provider Strategies

Best-cost provider strategies aim at giving customers *more value for the money.* The objective is to deliver superior value to buyers by satisfying their expectations on key quality/service/features/performance attributes and beating their expectations on price (given what rivals are charging for much the same attributes). A company achieves best-cost status from an ability to incorporate attractive attributes at a lower cost than rivals. To become a best-cost provider, a company must have the resources and capabilities to achieve good-to-excellent quality, incorporate appealing features, match product performance, and provide good-to-excellent customer service—all at a lower cost than rivals.

As Figure 4.1 indicates, best-cost provider strategies stake out a middle ground between pursuing a low-cost advantage and pursuing a differentiation advantage and between appealing to the broad market as a whole and appealing to a narrow market niche. From a competitive positioning standpoint, best-cost strategies are a *hybrid,* balancing a strategic emphasis on low cost against a strategic emphasis on differentiation (superior value). *The target market is value-conscious buyers,* perhaps a very sizable part of the overall market. *The competitive advantage of a best-cost provider is lower costs than rivals* in incorporating good-to-excellent attributes, putting the company in a position to underprice rivals whose products have similar appealing attributes.

A best-cost provider strategy is very appealing in markets where buyer diversity makes product differentiation the norm *and* where many buyers are sensitive to price, product quality, and product performance. This is because a best-cost provider can position itself near the middle of the market with either a medium-quality product at a below-average price or a high-quality product at an average price. Often, substantial numbers of buyers prefer midrange products rather than the cheap, basic products of low-cost providers or the expensive products of top-of-the-line differentiators. But unless a company has the resources, know-how, and capabilities to incorporate upscale product or service attributes at a lower cost than rivals, this strategy is ill-advised.

Company Spotlight 4.3 describes how Toyota has used a best-cost approach with its Lexus models.

The Big Risk of a Best-Cost Provider Strategy   The danger of a best-cost provider strategy is that a company using it will get squeezed between the strategies of firms using low-cost and differentiation strategies. Low-cost leaders may be able to siphon customers away with the appeal of a lower price. High-end differentiators may be able to steal customers away with the appeal of better product attributes. Thus, to be successful, a best-cost provider must offer buyers *significantly* better product attributes in order to justify a price above what low-cost leaders are charging. Likewise, it

Toyota's Best-Cost Producer Strategy for Its Lexus Line

Toyota Motor Company is widely regarded as a low-cost producer among the world's motor vehicle manufacturers. Despite its emphasis on product quality, Toyota has achieved low-cost leadership because it has developed considerable skills in efficient supply chain management and low-cost assembly capabilities and because its models are positioned in the low-to-medium end of the price spectrum, where high production volumes are conducive to low unit costs. But when Toyota decided to introduce its new Lexus models to compete in the luxury-car market, it employed a classic best-cost provider strategy. Toyota took the following four steps in crafting and implementing its Lexus strategy:

- Designing an array of high-performance characteristics and upscale features into the Lexus models so as to make them comparable in performance and luxury to other high-end models and attractive to Mercedes, BMW, Audi, Jaguar, Cadillac, and Lincoln buyers.

- Transferring its capabilities in making high-quality Toyota models at low cost to making premium-quality Lexus models at costs below other luxury-car makers. Toyota's supply chain capabilities and low-cost assembly know-how allowed it to incorporate high-tech performance features and upscale quality into Lexus models at substantially less cost than Mercedes and BMW.

- Using its relatively lower manufacturing costs to underprice comparable Mercedes and BMW models. Toyota believed that with its cost advantage it could price attractively equipped Lexus cars low enough to draw price-conscious buyers away from Mercedes and BMW and perhaps induce dissatisfied Lincoln and Cadillac owners to move up to a Lexus.

- Establishing a new network of Lexus dealers, separate from Toyota dealers, dedicated to providing a level of personalized, attentive customer service unmatched in the industry.

Lexus models have consistently ranked first in the widely watched J. D. Power & Associates quality survey, and the prices of Lexus models are typically several thousand dollars below those of comparable Mercedes and BMW models—clear signals that Toyota has succeeded in becoming a best-cost producer with its Lexus brand.

---

has to achieve significantly lower costs in providing upscale features so that it can outcompete high-end differentiators on the basis of an attractively lower price.

Focused (or Market Niche) Strategies

What sets focused strategies apart from low-cost leadership or broad differentiation strategies is concentrated attention on a narrow piece of the total market. The target segment, or niche, can be defined by geographic uniqueness, by specialized requirements in using the product, or by special product attributes that appeal only to niche members. Examples of firms that concentrate on a well-defined market niche include eBay (in online auctions); Porsche (in sports cars); Cannondale (in top-of-the-line mountain bikes); Jiffy Lube International (a specialist in quick oil changes and simple maintenance for motor vehicles); Enterprise Rent-a-Car (specializing in providing rental cars to repair-garage customers); Pottery Barn Kids (a retail chain featuring children's furniture and accessories); E-Loan (in online consumer lending); and Bandag (a specialist in truck-tire recapping that promotes its recaps aggressively at over 1,000 truck stops). Microbreweries, local bakeries, bed-and-breakfast inns, and local owner-managed retail boutiques are all good examples of enterprises that have scaled their operations to serve narrow or local customer segments.

> Even though a focuser may be small, it still may have substantial competitive strength because of the attractiveness of its product offering and its strong expertise and capabilities in meeting the needs and expectations of niche members.

COMPANY SPOTLIGHT 4.4
Motel 6's Focused Low-Cost Strategy

Motel 6 caters to price-conscious travelers who want a clean, no-frills place to spend the night. To be a low-cost provider of overnight lodging, the company (1) selects relatively inexpensive sites on which to construct its units (usually near interstate exits and high-traffic locations but far enough away to avoid paying prime-site prices); (2) builds only basic facilities (no restaurant or bar and only rarely a swimming pool); (3) relies on standard architectural designs that incorporate inexpensive materials and low-cost construction techniques; and (4) provides simple room furnishings and decorations. These approaches lower both investment costs and operating costs. Without restaurants, bars, and all kinds of guest services, a Motel 6 unit can be operated with just front-desk personnel, room cleanup crews, and skeleton building-and-grounds maintenance.

To promote the Motel 6 concept with travelers who have simple overnight requirements, the chain uses unique, recognizable radio ads done by nationally syndicated radio personality Tom Bodett; the ads describe Motel 6's clean rooms, no-frills facilities, friendly atmosphere, and dependably low rates (usually under $40 a night).

Motel 6's basis for competitive advantage is lower costs than competitors in providing basic, economical overnight accommodations to price-constrained travelers.

A Focused Low-Cost Strategy A focused strategy based on low cost aims at securing a competitive advantage by serving buyers in the target market niche at a lower cost and lower price than do rival competitors. This strategy has considerable attraction when a firm can lower costs significantly by limiting its customer base to a well-defined buyer segment. The avenues to achieving a cost advantage over rivals also serving the target market niche are the same as those for low-cost leadership— outmanage rivals in controlling the factors that drive costs and reconfigure the firm's value chain in ways that yield a cost edge over rivals.

Focused low-cost strategies are fairly common. Producers of private-label goods are able to achieve low costs in product development, marketing, distribution, and advertising by concentrating on making generic items imitative of name-brand merchandise and selling directly to retail chains wanting a basic house brand to sell to price-sensitive shoppers. Several small printer-supply manufacturers have begun making low-cost clones of the premium-priced replacement ink and toner cartridges sold by Hewlett-Packard, Lexmark, Canon, and Epson; the clone manufacturers dissect the cartridges of the name-brand companies and then reengineer a similar version that won't violate patents. The components for remanufactured replacement cartridges are acquired from various outside sources, and the clones are then marketed at prices as much as 50 percent below the name-brand cartridges. Cartridge remanufacturers have been lured to focus on this market because replacement cartridges constitute a multi-billion-dollar business with considerable profit potential given their low costs and the premium pricing of the name-brand companies. Company Spotlight 4.4 describes how Motel 6 has kept its costs low in catering to budget-conscious travelers.

A Focused Differentiation Strategy A focused strategy based on differentiation aims at securing a competitive advantage by offering niche members a product they perceive as unusually well suited to their own unique tastes and preferences. Successful use of a focused differentiation strategy depends on the existence of a buyer segment that is looking for special product attributes or seller capabilities and on a firm's ability to stand apart from rivals competing in the same target market niche.

Companies like Godiva Chocolates, Chanel, Rolls-Royce, Häagen-Dazs, and W. L. Gore (the maker of Gore-Tex) employ successful differentiation-based focused

COMPANY SPOTLIGHT 4.5

Progressive Insurance's Focused Differentiation Strategy in Auto Insurance

Progressive Insurance has fashioned a strategy in auto insurance focused on people with a record of traffic violations who drive high-performance cars, drivers with accident histories, motorcyclists, teenagers, and other so-called high-risk categories of drivers that most auto insurance companies steer away from. Progressive discovered that some of these high-risk drivers are affluent and pressed for time, making them less sensitive to paying premium rates for their car insurance. Management learned that it could charge such drivers high-enough premiums to cover the added risks, plus it differentiated Progressive from other insurers by expediting the process of obtaining insurance and decreasing the annoyance that such drivers face in obtaining insurance coverage.

In further differentiating and promoting Progressive policies, management created teams of roving claims adjusters who arrive at accident scenes to assess claims and issue checks for repairs on the spot. Progressive also studied the market segments for insurance carefully enough to discover that some motorcycle owners are not especially risky (middle-aged suburbanites who sometimes commute to work or use their motorcycles mainly for recreational trips with their friends). Progressive's strategy allowed it to become a leader in the market for luxury-car insurance for customers who appreciate Progressive's streamlined approach to doing business.

Source: Reprinted by permission of *Harvard Business Review,* an excerpt from "Global Gamesmanship," by Ian C. McMillan, Alexander van Putten, and Rita Gunther McGrath, May 2003. Copyright ©2003 by the President and Fellows of Harvard College, all rights reserved.

strategies targeted at upscale buyers wanting products and services with world-class attributes. Indeed, most markets contain a buyer segment willing to pay a big price premium for the very finest items available, thus opening the strategic window for some competitors to pursue differentiation-based focused strategies aimed at the very top of the market pyramid. Another successful focused differentiator is a "fashion food retailer" called Trader Joe's, a 150-store East and West Coast chain that is a combination gourmet deli and food warehouse.[7] Customers shop Trader Joe's as much for entertainment as for conventional grocery items—the store stocks out-of-the-ordinary culinary treats like raspberry salsa, salmon burgers, and jasmine fried rice, as well as the standard goods normally found in supermarkets. What sets Trader Joe's apart is not just its unique combination of food novelties and competitively priced grocery items but also its capability to turn an otherwise mundane grocery excursion into a whimsical treasure hunt that is just plain fun. Company Spotlight 4.5 describes Progressive Insurance's focused differentiation strategy.

When Focusing Is Attractive A focused strategy aimed at securing a competitive edge based either on low cost or differentiation becomes increasingly attractive as more of the following conditions are met:

1. The target market niche is big enough to be profitable and offers good growth potential.

2. Industry leaders do not see that having a presence in the niche is crucial to their own success—in which case focusers can often escape battling head-to-head against some of the industry's biggest and strongest competitors.

3. It is costly or difficult for multisegment competitors to put capabilities in place to meet the specialized needs of the target market niche and at the same time satisfy the expectations of their mainstream customers.

4. The industry has many different niches and segments, thereby allowing a focuser to pick a competitively attractive niche suited to its resource strengths and capabilities.

Also, with more niches there is more room for focusers to avoid each other in competing for the same customers.

5. Few, if any, other rivals are attempting to specialize in the same target segment—a condition that reduces the risk of segment overcrowding.

6. The focuser can compete effectively against challengers by relying on its capabilities and resources to serve the targeted niche and the customer goodwill it may have built up.

The Risks of a Focused Strategy   Focusing carries several risks. One is the chance that competitors will find effective ways to match the focused firm's capabilities in serving the target niche—perhaps by coming up with more appealing product offerings or by developing expertise and capabilities that offset the focuser's strengths. A second is the potential for the preferences and needs of niche members to shift over time toward the product attributes desired by the majority of buyers. An erosion of the differences across buyer segments lowers entry barriers into a focuser's market niche and provides an open invitation for rivals in adjacent segments to begin competing for the focuser's customers. A third risk is that the segment may become so attractive it is soon inundated with competitors, intensifying rivalry and splintering segment profits.

The Five Generic Competitive Strategies Entail Different Operating Approaches

Deciding which generic competitive strategy should serve as the framework for the rest of the company's strategy is not a trivial matter. Each of the five generic competitive strategies positions the company differently in its market and competitive environment. Each establishes a central theme for how the company will endeavor to defeat rivals. Each creates some boundaries or guidelines for maneuvering as market circumstances unfold and as ideas for improving the strategy are debated. Each points to different ways of experimenting and tinkering with the basic strategy—for example, employing a low-cost leadership strategy means experimenting with ways that costs can be cut and value chain activities can be streamlined, whereas a broad differentiation strategy means exploring ways to add new differentiating features or to perform value chain activities differently if the result is to add value for customers in ways they are willing to pay for. Each entails differences in terms of product line, production emphasis, marketing emphasis, and means of sustaining the strategy. Thus a choice of which generic strategy to employ spills over to affect several aspects of the way the business will be operated and the manner in which value chain activities must be managed. Deciding which generic strategy to employ is perhaps the most important strategic commitment a company makes—it tends to drive the rest of the strategic actions a company decides to undertake.

One of the big dangers here is that managers, torn between the pros and cons of the various generic strategies, will opt for *"stuck in the middle" strategies* that represent compromises between lower costs and greater differentiation and between broad and narrow market appeal. Compromise or middle-ground strategies rarely produce sustainable competitive advantage or a distinctive competitive position—well-executed best-cost-producer strategies are the only exception where a compromise between low cost and differentiation succeeds. Usually, companies with compromise strategies end up with a middle-of-the-pack industry ranking—they have average costs, some but not a lot of product differentiation relative to rivals, an average image and reputation, and little prospect of industry leadership. Having a competitive edge over rivals is the single most dependable contributor to above-average company profitability. Hence, only if a company makes a strong and unwavering commitment to one of the five generic competitive strategies does it stand much chance of achieving the sustainable competitive advantage that such strategies can deliver if properly executed.

Collaborative Strategies: Strategic Alliances and Partnerships

During the past decade, companies in all types of industries and in all parts of the world have elected to form strategic alliances and partnerships to complement their own strategic initiatives and strengthen their competitiveness in domestic and international markets. This is an about-face from times past, when the vast majority of companies were content to go it alone, confident that they already had or could independently develop whatever resources and know-how were needed to be successful in their markets. But globalization of the world economy, revolutionary advances in technology across a broad front, and untapped opportunities in national markets in Asia, Latin America, and Europe that are opening up, deregulating, and/or undergoing privatization have made strategic partnerships of one kind or another integral to competing on a broad geographic scale.

Many companies now find themselves thrust into two very demanding competitive races: (1) *the global race to build a market presence in many different national markets* and join the ranks of companies recognized as global market leaders and (2) *the race to seize opportunities on the frontiers of advancing technology* and build the resource strengths and business capabilities to compete successfully in the industries and product markets of the future.[8] Even the largest and most financially sound companies have concluded that simultaneously running the races for global market leadership and for a stake in the industries of the future requires more diverse and expansive skills, resources, technological expertise, and competitive capabilities than they can assemble and manage alone. Such companies, along with others that are missing the resources and competitive capabilities needed to pursue promising opportunities, have determined that the fastest way to fill the gap is often to form alliances with enterprises having the desired strengths. Consequently, these companies form **strategic alliances** or collaborative partnerships in which two or more companies join forces to achieve mutually beneficial strategic outcomes. Typically, alliances are formed for such purposes as joint marketing, joint sales or distribution, joint production, design collaboration, joint research and development, and technology licensing. Strategic alliances may entail formal agreements to work together, but they usually stop short of full partnership with formal ownership ties; some strategic alliances, however, do involve arrangements whereby one or more allies have minority ownership in certain of the other alliance members. Five factors make an alliance "strategic," as opposed to just a convenient business arrangement:[9]

> **Core Concept**
>
> **Strategic alliances** are collaborative arrangements where two or more companies join forces to achieve mutually beneficial strategic outcomes.

1. It is critical to the company's achievement of an important objective.
2. It helps build, sustain, or enhance a core competence or competitive advantage.
3. It helps block a competitive threat.
4. It helps open up important new market opportunities.
5. It mitigates a significant risk to a company's business.

The Pervasive Use of Alliances   Companies in many different industries all across the world have made strategic alliances a core part of their overall strategy; U.S. companies alone announced nearly 68,000 alliances from 1996 through 2003.[10] In the personal computer industry, alliances are pervasive because the different components of PCs and the software to run them are supplied by so many different companies—one set of companies provides the microprocessors, another group makes the motherboards, another the monitors, another the disk drives, another the memory chips, and so on. Moreover, their facilities are scattered across the United States, Japan, Taiwan, Singapore, Malaysia, and parts of Europe. Strategic alliances among companies in the various parts of the PC industry facilitate the close cross-company collaboration required on next-generation product development, logistics, production, and the timing of new product releases.

Toyota has forged long-term strategic partnerships with many of its suppliers of automotive parts and components, both to achieve lower costs and to improve the quality and reliability of its vehicles. Microsoft collaborates very closely with independent software developers to ensure that their programs will run on the next-generation versions of Windows. Genentech, a leader in biotechnology and human genetics, has a partnering strategy to increase its access to novel biotherapeutic products and technologies and has formed alliances with over 30 companies to strengthen its research and development pipeline. During the 1998–2004 period, Samsung Electronics, a South Korean corporation with $54 billion in sales, entered into over 50 major strategic alliances involving such companies as Sony, Yahoo, Hewlett-Packard, Nokia, Motorola, Intel, Microsoft, Dell, Mitsubishi, Disney, IBM, Maytag, and Rockwell Automation; the alliances involved joint investments, technology transfer arrangements, joint R&D projects, and agreements to supply parts and components—all of which facilitated Samsung's strategic efforts to transform itself into a global enterprise and establish itself as a leader in the worldwide electronics industry.

Studies indicate that large corporations are commonly involved in 30 to 50 alliances and that a number have hundreds of alliances. One recent study estimated that about 35 percent of corporate revenues in 2003 came from activities involving strategic alliances, up from 15 percent in 1995.[11]

Why and How Strategic Alliances Are Advantageous

> The best alliances are highly selective, focusing on particular value chain activities and on a particular competitive benefit. They tend to enable a firm to build on its strengths and to learn.

The most common reasons why companies enter into strategic alliances are to expedite the development of promising new technologies or products, to overcome deficits in their own technical and manufacturing expertise, to bring together the personnel and expertise needed to create desirable new skill sets and capabilities, to improve supply chain efficiency, to gain economies of scale in production and/or marketing, and to acquire or improve market access through joint marketing agreements.[12] A company that is racing for *global market leadership* needs alliances to:

- *Get into critical country markets quickly* and accelerate the process of building a potent global market presence.

- *Gain inside knowledge about unfamiliar markets and cultures through alliances with local partners.* For example, U.S., European, and Japanese companies wanting to build market footholds in the fast-growing Chinese market have pursued partnership arrangements with Chinese companies to help in dealing with government regulations, to supply knowledge of local markets, to provide guidance on adapting their products to better match the buying preferences of Chinese consumers, to set up local manufacturing capabilities, and to assist in distribution, marketing, and promotional activities. The policy of the Chinese government has long been to limit foreign companies to a 50 percent ownership in local companies, making alliances with local Chinese companies a virtual necessity to gain market access.

■   *Access valuable skills and competencies* that are concentrated in particular geographic locations (such as software design competencies in the United States, fashion design skills in Italy, and efficient manufacturing skills in Japan and China).

A company that is racing to *stake out a strong position in an industry of the future* needs alliances to:

■   *Establish a stronger beachhead* for participating in the target industry.

■   *Master new technologies and build new expertise and competencies* faster than would be possible through internal efforts.

■   *Open up broader opportunities* in the target industry by melding the firm's own capabilities with the expertise and resources of partners.

Allies can learn much from one another in performing joint research, sharing technological know-how, and collaborating on complementary new technologies and products—sometimes enough to enable them to pursue other new opportunities on their own. Manufacturers typically pursue alliances with parts and components suppliers to gain the efficiencies of better supply chain management and to speed new products to market. By joining forces in components production and/or final assembly, companies may be able to realize cost savings not achievable with their own small volumes—Volvo, Renault, and Peugeot formed an alliance to join forces in making engines for their large car models because none of the three needed enough such engines to operate its own engine plant economically. Information systems consultant Accenture has developed strategic alliances with such leading technology providers as SAP, PeopleSoft, Oracle, Siebel, Microsoft, BEA, and Hewlett-Packard to give it greater capabilities in designing and integrating information systems for its corporate clients. Dell Computer entered into an alliance with IBM that involved Dell's purchasing $16 billion in parts and components from IBM for use in Dell's PCs, servers, and workstations over a three-year period; Dell determined that IBM's growing expertise and capabilities in PC components justified using IBM as a major supplier even though Dell and IBM competed in supplying laptop computers and servers to corporate customers. Johnson & Johnson and Merck entered into an alliance to market Pepcid AC; Merck developed the stomach distress remedy and Johnson & Johnson functioned as marketer—the alliance made Pepcid products the best-selling remedies for acid indigestion and heartburn. United Airlines, American Airlines, Continental, Delta, and Northwest created an alliance to form Orbitz, an Internet travel site designed to compete with Expedia and Travelocity to provide consumers with low-cost airfares, rental cars, lodging, cruises, and vacation packages.

Strategic cooperation is a much-favored, indeed necessary, approach in industries where new technological developments are occurring at a furious pace along many different paths and where advances in one technology spill over to affect others (often

> The competitive attraction of alliances is in allowing companies to bundle competencies and resources that are more valuable in a joint effort than when kept separate.

blurring industry boundaries). Whenever industries are experiencing high-velocity technological change in many areas simultaneously, firms find it virtually essential to have cooperative relationships with other enterprises to stay on the leading edge of technology and product performance even in their own area of specialization.

Why Many Alliances Are Unstable or Break Apart   The stability of an alliance depends on how well the partners work together, their success in responding and adapting to changing internal and external conditions, and their willingness to renegotiate the bargain if circumstances so warrant. A successful alliance requires real in-the-trenches collaboration, not merely an arm's-length exchange of ideas. Unless partners place a high value on the skills, resources, and contributions each brings to the alliance and the cooperative arrangement results in valuable win-win outcomes, it is doomed. A surprisingly large number of alliances never live up to expectations. A 1999 study by Accenture, a global business consulting organization, revealed that 61 percent of alliances were either outright failures or "limping along." In 2004, McKinsey & Co. estimated that the overall success rate of alliances was around 50 percent, based on whether the alliance achieved the stated objectives. Many alliances are dissolved after a few years. The high "divorce rate" among strategic allies has several causes—diverging objectives and priorities, an inability to work well together (the alliance between Disney and Pixar is a classic example of an alliance coming apart because of clashes between key managers), changing conditions that render the purpose of the alliance obsolete, the emergence of more attractive technological paths, and marketplace rivalry between one or more allies.[13] Experience indicates that alliances stand a reasonable chance of helping a company reduce competitive disadvantage but very rarely have they proved a durable device for achieving a competitive edge over rivals.

The Strategic Dangers of Relying Heavily on Alliances and Cooperative Partnerships   The Achilles heel of alliances and cooperative strategies is becoming dependent on other companies for *essential* expertise and capabilities. To be a market leader (and perhaps even a serious market contender), a company must ultimately develop its own capabilities in areas where internal strategic control is pivotal to protecting its competitiveness and building competitive advantage. Moreover, some alliances hold only limited potential because the partner guards its most valuable skills and expertise; in such instances, acquiring or merging with a company possessing the desired resources is a better solution.

Merger and Acquisition Strategies

Combining the operations of two companies, via merger or acquisition, is an attractive strategic option for achieving operating economies, strengthening the resulting company's competencies and competitiveness, and opening up avenues of new market opportunity.

Mergers and acquisitions are much-used strategic options—for example, from 1996 through 2003 U.S. companies alone made 90,000 acquisitions.[14] Mergers and acquisitions are especially suited for situations in which alliances and partnerships do not go far enough in providing a company with access to needed resources and capabilities.[15] Ownership ties are more permanent than partnership ties, allowing the operations of the merger/acquisition participants to be tightly integrated and creating more in-house control and autonomy. A *merger* is a pooling of equals, with the newly created company often taking on a new name. An *acquisition* is a combination in which one company, the acquirer, purchases and absorbs the operations of another, the acquired. The difference between a merger and an acquisition relates more to the details of ownership, management control, and financial arrangements than to strategy and competitive advantage. The resources, competencies, and competitive capabilities of the newly created enterprise end up much the same whether the combination is the result of acquisition or merger.

Many mergers and acquisitions are driven by strategies to achieve one of five strategic objectives:[16]

1. *To pave the way for the acquiring company to gain more market share and, further, create a more efficient operation out of the combined companies by closing high-cost plants and eliminating surplus capacity industrywide:* The merger that formed DaimlerChrysler was motivated in large part by the fact that the motor vehicle industry had far more production capacity worldwide than was needed; management at both Daimler Benz and Chrysler believed that the efficiency of the two companies could be significantly improved by shutting some plants and laying off workers, realigning which models were produced at which plants, and squeezing out efficiencies by combining supply chain activities, product design, and administration. Quite a number of acquisitions are undertaken with the objective of transforming two or more otherwise high-cost companies into one lean competitor with average or below-average costs.

2. *To expand a company's geographic coverage:* Many industries exist for a long time in a fragmented state, with local companies dominating local markets and no company having a significantly visible regional or national presence. Eventually, though, expansion-minded companies will launch strategies to acquire local companies in adjacent territories. Over time, companies with successful growth via acquisition strategies emerge as regional market leaders and later perhaps as companies with national coverage. Often the acquiring company follows up on its acquisitions with efforts to lower the operating costs and improve the customer service capabilities of the local businesses it acquires.

3. *To extend the company's business into new product categories or international markets:* PepsiCo acquired Quaker Oats chiefly to bring Gatorade into the Pepsi family of beverages, and PepsiCo's Frito-Lay division has made a series of acquisitions of foreign-based snack-food companies to begin to establish a stronger presence in international markets. Companies like Nestlé, Kraft, Unilever, and Procter & Gamble—all racing for global market leadership—have made acquisitions an integral part of their strategies to widen their geographic reach and broaden the number of product categories in which they compete.

4. *To gain quick access to new technologies and avoid the need for a time-consuming R&D effort* (which might not succeed): This type of acquisition strategy is a favorite of companies racing to establish attractive positions in emerging markets. Such companies need to fill in technological gaps, extend their technological capabilities along some promising new paths, and position themselves to launch next-wave products and services. Cisco Systems purchased over 75 technology companies to give it more technological reach and product breadth, thereby buttressing its standing as the world's biggest supplier of systems for building the infrastructure of the Internet. Intel has made over 300 acquisitions in the past five or so years to broaden its technological base, put it in a stronger position to be a major supplier of Internet technology, and make it less dependent on supplying microprocessors for PCs. This type of acquisition strategy enables a company to

build a market position in attractive technologies quickly and serves as a substitute for extensive in-house R&D programs.

5. *To try to invent a new industry and lead the convergence of industries whose boundaries are being blurred by changing technologies and new market opportunities:* Such acquisitions are the result of a company's management betting that a new industry is on the verge of being born and deciding to establish an early position in this industry by bringing together the resources and products of several different companies. Examples include the merger of AOL and media giant Time Warner and Viacom's purchase of Paramount Pictures, CBS, and Blockbuster—both of which reflected bold strategic moves predicated on beliefs that all entertainment content will ultimately converge into a single industry and be distributed over the Internet.

In addition to the above objectives, there are instances when acquisitions are motivated by a company's desire to fill resource gaps, thus allowing the new company to do things it could not do before. Global Spotlight 4.1 describes how Clear Channel Worldwide has used mergers and acquisitions to build a leading global position in outdoor advertising and radio and TV broadcasting.

All too frequently, mergers and acquisitions do not produce the hoped-for outcomes.[17] Combining the operations of two companies, especially large and complex ones, often entails formidable resistance from rank-and-file organization members, hard-to-resolve conflicts in management styles and corporate cultures, and tough problems of integration. Cost savings, expertise sharing, and enhanced competitive capabilities may take substantially longer than expected or, worse, may never materialize at all. Integrating the operations of two fairly large or culturally diverse companies is hard to pull off—only a few companies that use merger and acquisition strategies have proved they can consistently make good decisions about what to leave alone and what to meld into their own operations and systems. In the case of mergers between companies of roughly equal size, the management groups of the two companies frequently battle over which one is going to end up in control.

A number of previously applauded mergers/acquisitions have yet to live up to expectations—the merger of AOL and Time Warner, the merger of Daimler Benz and Chrysler, Hewlett-Packard's acquisition of Compaq Computer, and Ford's acquisition of Jaguar. The AOL–Time Warner merger has proved to be mostly a disaster, partly because AOL's rapid growth has evaporated, partly because of a huge clash of corporate cultures, and partly because most of the expected benefits have yet to materialize. Ford paid a handsome price to acquire Jaguar but has yet to make the Jaguar brand a major factor in the luxury-car segment in competition against Mercedes, BMW, and Lexus. Novell acquired WordPerfect for $1.7 billion in stock in 1994, but the combination never generated enough punch to compete against Microsoft Word and Microsoft Office—Novell sold WordPerfect to Corel for $124 million in cash and stock less than two years later. In 2001 electronics retailer Best Buy paid $685 million to acquire Musicland, a struggling 1,300-store music retailer that included stores operating under the Musicland, Sam Goody, Suncoast, Media Play, and On Cue names. But Musicland's sales, already declining, dropped even further. In June 2003 Best Buy "sold" Musicland to a Florida investment firm. No cash changed hands, and the "buyer" received shares of stock in Best Buy in return for assuming Musicland's liabilities.

Clear Channel Communications—Using Mergers and Acquisitions to Become a Global Market Leader

In 2004, Clear Channel Worldwide was the world's fourth-largest media company, behind Disney, Time Warner, and Viacom/CBS. The company, founded in 1972 by Lowry Mays and Billy Joe McCombs, got its start by acquiring an unprofitable country-music radio station in San Antonio, Texas. Over the next 10 years, Mays learned the radio business and slowly bought other radio stations in a variety of states. Going public in 1984 helped the company raise the equity capital needed to continue acquiring radio stations in additional geographic markets.

When the Federal Communications Commission loosened the rules regarding the ability of one company to own both radio and TV stations in the late 1980s, Clear Channel broadened its strategy and began acquiring small, struggling TV stations. By 1998, Clear Channel had used acquisitions to build a leading position in radio and television stations. Domestically, it owned, programmed, or sold airtime for 69 AM radio stations, 135 FM stations, and 18 TV stations in 48 local markets in 24 states. Clear Channel began expanding internationally, purchasing an ownership interest in a domestic Spanish-language radio broadcaster, two radio stations and a cable audio channel in Denmark, and ownership interests in radio stations in Australia, Mexico, New Zealand, and the Czech Republic.

In 1997, Clear Channel used acquisitions to establish a major position in outdoor advertising. Its first acquisition was Phoenix-based Eller Media Company, an outdoor advertising company with over 100,000 billboard facings. This was quickly followed by additional acquisitions of outdoor advertising companies, the most important of which were ABC Outdoor in Milwaukee, Wisconsin; Paxton Communications (with operations in Tampa and Orlando, Florida); Universal Outdoor; and the More Group, with outdoor operations and 90,000 displays in 24 countries.

Then, in October 1999, Clear Channel merged with AM-FM, Inc. The new company, named Clear Channel Communications, had operations in 32 countries, including 830 radio stations, 19 TV stations, and more than 425,000 outdoor displays.

Additional acquisitions were completed during the 2000–2003 period. The emphasis was on buying radio, TV, and outdoor advertising properties with operations in many of the same local markets, which made it feasible to (1) cut costs by sharing facilities and staffs, (2) improve programming, and (3) sell advertising to customers in packages for all three media simultaneously. Packaging ads for two or three media not only helped Clear Channel's advertising clients distribute their messages more effectively but also allowed the company to combine its sales activities and have a common sales force for all three media, achieving significant cost savings and boosting profit margins.

Going into 2004, Clear Channel Worldwide (the company's latest name) owned radio and television stations, outdoor displays, and entertainment venues in 66 countries around the world. It operated 1,182 radio and 39 television stations in the United States and had equity interests in over 240 radio stations internationally. It also operated a U.S. radio network of syndicated talk shows with about 180 million weekly listeners. In addition, the company owned or operated close to 800,000 outdoor advertising displays, including billboards, street furniture, and transit panels around the world. The company's Clear Channel Entertainment division was a leading promoter, producer, and marketer of about 32,000 live entertainment events annually and also owned leading athlete management and sports marketing companies. In 2003, the company earned $1.1 billion on revenues of $8.9 billion.

Source: www.clearchannel.com, September 2004, and *Business Week,* October 19, 1999, p. 56.

Vertical Integration Strategies: Operating across More Stages of the Industry Value Chain

Vertical integration extends a firm's competitive and operating scope within the same industry. It involves expanding the firm's range of activities backward into sources of supply and/or forward toward end users. Thus, if a manufacturer invests in facilities to produce certain component parts that it formerly purchased from outside suppliers, it remains in essentially the same industry as before. The only change is that it has operations in two stages of the industry value chain. Similarly, if a paint manufacturer, Sherwin-Williams for example, elects to integrate forward by opening 100 retail stores to market its paint products directly to consumers, it remains in the paint business even though its competitive scope extends from manufacturing to retailing.

Vertical integration strategies can aim at *full integration* (participating in all stages of the industry value chain) or *partial integration* (building positions in selected stages of the industry's total value chain). A firm can pursue vertical integration by starting its own operations in other stages in the industry's activity chain or by acquiring a company already performing the activities it wants to bring in-house.

The Advantages of a Vertical Integration Strategy

> **Core Concept**
>
> A vertical integration strategy has appeal *only* if it significantly strengthens a firm's competitive position.

The two best reasons for investing company resources in vertical integration are to strengthen the firm's competitive position and/or boost its profitability.[18] Vertical integration has no real payoff unless it produces sufficient cost savings and/or profit increases to justify the extra investment, adds materially to a company's technological and competitive strengths, and/or helps differentiate the company's product offering.

Integrating Backward to Achieve Greater Competitiveness Integrating backward generates cost savings only when the volume needed is big enough to capture the same scale economies suppliers have and when suppliers' production efficiency can be matched or exceeded with no drop-off in quality. The best potential for being able to reduce costs via backward integration exists in situations where suppliers have sizable profit margins, where the item being supplied is a major cost component, and where the needed technological skills are easily mastered or can be gained by acquiring a supplier with the desired technological know-how. Integrating backward can sometimes significantly enhance a company's technological capabilities and give it expertise needed to stake out positions in the industries and products of the future. Intel, Cisco, and many other Silicon Valley companies have been active in acquiring companies that will help them speed the advance of Internet technology and pave the way for next-generation families of products and services.

Backward vertical integration can produce a differentiation-based competitive advantage when a company, by performing in-house activities that were previously outsourced, ends up with a better-quality product/service offering, improves the caliber of its customer service, or in other ways enhances the performance of its final product. On occasion, integrating into more stages along the industry value chain can add to a company's differentiation capabilities by allowing it to build or strengthen its core competencies, better master key skills or strategy-critical technologies, or add features that deliver greater customer value. Other potential advantages of backward integration include sparing a company the uncertainty of being dependent on suppliers for crucial components or support services and lessening a company's vulnerability to powerful suppliers inclined to raise prices at every opportunity.

Integrating Forward to Enhance Competitiveness The strategic impetus for forward integration is to gain better access to end users and better market visibility. In many industries, independent sales agents, wholesalers, and retailers handle competing brands of the same product; having no allegiance to any one company's brand, they tend to push whatever sells and earns them the biggest profits. Half-hearted commitments by distributors and retailers can frustrate a company's attempt to boost sales and market share, give rise to costly inventory pileups and frequent under-utilization of capacity, and disrupt the economies of steady, near-capacity production. In such cases, it can be advantageous for a manufacturer to integrate forward into wholesaling or retailing via company-owned distributorships or a chain of retail stores. But often a company's product line is not broad enough to justify stand-alone distributorships or retail outlets. This leaves the option of integrating forward into the activity of selling directly to end users—perhaps via the Internet. Bypassing regular wholesale/retail channels in favor of direct sales and Internet retailing can have appeal if it lowers distribution costs, produces a relative cost advantage over certain rivals, and results in lower selling prices to end users.

The Disadvantages of a Vertical Integration Strategy

Vertical integration has some substantial drawbacks, however.[19] First, it boosts a firm's capital investment in the industry, increasing business risk (what if industry growth and profitability go sour?) and perhaps denying financial resources to more worthwhile pursuits. A vertically integrated firm has vested interests in protecting its technology and production facilities. Because of the high costs of abandoning such investments before they are worn out, fully integrated firms tend to adopt new technologies slower than partially integrated or nonintegrated firms. Second, integrating forward or backward locks a firm into relying on its own in-house activities and sources of supply (which later may prove more costly than outsourcing) and potentially results in less flexibility in accommodating buyer demand for greater product variety. In today's world of close working relationships with suppliers and efficient supply chain management systems, very few businesses can make a case for integrating backward into the business of suppliers to ensure a reliable supply of materials and components or to reduce production costs.

Third, vertical integration poses all kinds of capacity-matching problems. In motor vehicle manufacturing, for example, the most efficient scale of operation for making axles is different from the most economic volume for radiators, and different yet again for both engines and transmissions. Building the capacity to produce just the right number of axles, radiators, engines, and transmissions in-house—and doing so at the lowest unit costs for each—is much easier said than done. If internal capacity for making transmissions is deficient, the difference has to be bought externally. Where internal capacity for radiators proves excessive, customers need to be found for the surplus. And if by-products are generated—as occurs in the processing of many chemical products—they require arrangements for disposal.

Fourth, integration forward or backward often calls for radical changes in skills and business capabilities. Parts and components manufacturing, assembly operations, wholesale distribution and retailing, and direct sales via the Internet are different businesses with different key success factors. Managers of a manufacturing company should consider carefully whether it makes good business sense to invest time and money in developing the expertise and merchandising skills to integrate forward into wholesaling and retailing. Many manufacturers learn the hard way that company-owned wholesale/retail networks present many headaches, fit poorly with what they do best, and don't always add the kind of value to their core business they thought they would. Selling to customers via the Internet poses still another set of problems—it is usually easier to use the Internet to sell to business customers than to consumers.

Integrating backward into parts and components manufacture isn't as simple or profitable as it sounds either. Producing some or all of the parts and components needed for final assembly can reduce a company's flexibility to make desirable changes in using certain parts and components—it is one thing to design out a component made by a supplier and another to design out a component being made in-house. Companies that alter designs and models frequently in response to shifting buyer preferences often find outsourcing the needed parts and components cheaper and less complicated than making them in-house. Most of the world's automakers, despite their expertise in automotive technology and manufacturing, have concluded that purchasing many of their key parts and components from manufacturing specialists results in higher quality, lower costs, and greater design flexibility than does the vertical integration option.

Weighing the Pros and Cons of Vertical Integration

All in all, therefore, a strategy of vertical integration can have both important strengths and weaknesses. The tip of the scales depends on (1) whether vertical integration can enhance the performance of strategy-critical activities in ways that lower cost, build expertise, or increase differentiation; (2) the impact of vertical integration on investment costs, flexibility and response times, and the administrative costs of coordinating operations across more value chain activities; and (3) whether the integration substantially enhances a company's competitiveness. Vertical integration strategies have merit according to which capabilities and value chain activities truly need to be performed in-house and which can be performed better or cheaper by outsiders. Without solid benefits, integrating forward or backward is not likely to be an attractive competitive strategy option. In a growing number of instances, companies are proving that deintegrating (i.e., focusing on a narrower portion of the industry value chain) is a cheaper and more flexible competitive strategy.

Outsourcing Strategies

Core Concept

Outsourcing involves farming out certain value chain activities to outside vendors.

Over the past decade, **outsourcing** the performance of more value chain activities to outside suppliers and vendors has become increasingly popular. The two big drivers behind outsourcing are that (1) outsiders can often perform certain activities better or cheaper and (2) outsourcing allows a firm to focus its entire energies on those activities that are at the center of its expertise (its core competencies) and that are the most critical to its competitive and financial success. Outsourcing strategies thus involve a conscious decision to abandon or forgo attempts to perform certain value chain activities *internally* and, instead, to farm them out to outside specialists and strategic allies.

The outsourcing trend represents a big departure from the way that most companies used to deal with their suppliers and vendors. In years past, it was common for companies to maintain arm's-length relationships with suppliers and outside vendors, insisting on items being made to precise specifications and negotiating long and hard over price.[20] Although a company might place orders with the same supplier repeatedly, there was no expectation that this would be the case; price usually determined which supplier was awarded an order, and companies used the threat of switching suppliers to get the lowest possible prices. To enhance their bargaining power and to make the threat of switching credible, it was standard practice for companies to source key parts and components from several suppliers as opposed to dealing with only a single supplier. But today, most companies are abandoning such approaches in favor of forging alliances and strategic partnerships with a small number of highly capable suppliers. Collaborative relationships are replacing contractual, purely price-oriented relationships because companies have discovered that many of the advantages of performing value chain activities in-house can be captured and many of the disadvantages avoided by forging close, long-term cooperative partnerships with able suppliers and vendors and tapping into the expertise and capabilities that they have painstakingly developed.

Benefits of Outsourcing

Outsourcing pieces of the value chain to narrow the boundaries of a firm's business makes strategic sense whenever:

- *An activity can be performed better or more cheaply by outside specialists.* Many PC makers, for example, have shifted from assembling units in-house to using contract assemblers because of the sizable scale economies associated with purchasing PC components in large volumes and assembling PCs. By outsourcing the distribution of shoes made in its two plants in Germany to UPS, German shoemaker Birkenstock has cut the time for delivering orders to U.S. footwear retailers from seven weeks to three weeks.[21]

- *The activity is not crucial to the firm's ability to achieve sustainable competitive advantage and won't hollow out its core competencies, capabilities, or technical know-how.* Outsourcing of maintenance services, data processing and data storage, fringe benefit management, Web site operations, and similar administrative support activities to specialists has become commonplace. American Express, for instance, recently entered into a seven-year, $4 billion deal whereby IBM's Services division will host American Express's Web site, network servers, data storage, and help-desk support; American Express indicated that it would save several hundred million dollars by paying only for the services it needed when it needed them (as opposed to funding its own full-time staff). A number of companies have begun outsourcing their call center operations to foreign-based contractors that have access to lower-cost labor supplies and can employ lower-paid call center personnel to respond to customer inquiries or requests for technical support.

- *It reduces the company's risk exposure* to changing technology and/or changing buyer preferences. When a company outsources certain parts, components, and services, its suppliers must bear the burden of incorporating state-of-the-art technologies and/or undertaking redesigns and upgrades to accommodate a company's plans to introduce next-generation products. If what a supplier provides falls out of favor with buyers or is designed out of next-generation products, it is the supplier's business that suffers rather than a company's own internal operations.

- *It improves a company's ability to innovate.* Collaborative partnerships with world-class suppliers that have cutting-edge intellectual capital and are early adopters of the latest technology give a company access to ever better parts and components—such supplier-driven innovations, when incorporated into a company's own product offering, fuel a company's ability to introduce its own new and improved products.

- *It streamlines company operations* in ways that improve organizational flexibility and cut cycle time. Outsourcing gives a company the flexibility to switch suppliers in the event that its present supplier falls behind competing suppliers. To the extent that its suppliers can speedily get next-generation parts and components into production, then a company can get its own next-generation product offerings into the marketplace quicker. Moreover, seeking out new suppliers with the needed capabilities already in place is frequently quicker, easier, less risky, and cheaper than hurriedly retooling internal operations to replace obsolete capabilities or try to install and master new technologies.

- *It allows a company to assemble diverse kinds of expertise speedily and efficiently.* A company can nearly always gain quicker access to first-rate capabilities and expertise by partnering with suppliers that already have them in place than it can by trying to build them from scratch with its own company personnel.

- *It allows a company to concentrate on its core business and do what it does best.* A company is better able to build and develop its own competitively valuable competencies and capabilities when it concentrates its full resources and energies on performing those activities internally that it can perform better than outsiders and/or that it needs to have under its direct control. Cisco Systems, for example, devotes its energy to designing new generations of switches, routers, and other Internet-related equipment, opting to outsource the more mundane activities of producing and assembling its routers and switching equipment to contract manufacturers that together operate 37 factories, all closely monitored and overseen by Cisco personnel via online systems.

Dell Computer's partnerships with the suppliers of PC components have allowed it to operate with fewer than four days of inventory, to realize substantial savings in inventory costs, and to get PCs that are equipped with next-generation components into the marketplace in less than a week after the newly upgraded components start shipping. Cisco's contract suppliers work so closely with Cisco that they can ship Cisco products to Cisco customers without a Cisco employee ever touching the gear. This system of alliances saves $500 million to $800 million annually.[22] Hewlett-Packard, IBM, Silicon Graphics (now SGI), and others have sold plants to suppliers and then contracted to purchase the output. Starbucks finds purchasing coffee beans from independent growers far more advantageous than trying to integrate backward into the coffee-growing business.

When Outsourcing Can Be Disadvantageous

The biggest danger of outsourcing is that a company will farm out too many or the wrong types of activities and thereby hollow out its own capabilities.[23] In such cases, a company loses touch with the very activities and expertise that over the long run determine its success. Cisco Systems guards against loss of control and protects its manufacturing expertise by designing the production methods that its contract manufacturers must use. Cisco keeps the source code for its design proprietary and is thus the source of all improvements and innovations. Further, Cisco uses the Internet to monitor the factory operations of contract manufacturers around the clock and can therefore know immediately when problems arise and whether to get involved.

Offensive Strategies—Improving Market Position and Building Competitive Advantage

Almost every company must at times go on the offensive to improve its market position and try to build a competitive advantage or widen an existing one. Companies like Dell, Wal-Mart, and Toyota play hardball, aggressively pursuing competitive advantage and trying to reap the benefits its offers—a leading market share, excellent profit margins and rapid growth (as compared to rivals), and all the intangibles of being known as a company on the move and one that plays to win.[24] Offensive strategies are also important when a company has no choice but to try to whittle away at a strong rival's competitive advantage and when it is possible to gain profitable market share at the expense of rivals despite whatever resource strengths and capabilities they have. How long it takes for an offensive to yield good results varies with the competitive circumstances.[25] It can be short if buyers respond immediately (as can occur with a dramatic price cut, an imaginative ad campaign, or an especially appealing new product). Securing a competitive edge can take much longer if winning consumer acceptance of an innovative product will take some time or if the firm may need several years to debug a new technology, put new production capacity in place, or develop and perfect new competitive capabilities. Ideally, an offensive move will improve a company's market standing or result in a competitive edge fairly quickly; the longer it takes, the more likely it is that rivals will spot the move, see its potential, and begin a counterresponse.

> **Core Concept**
>
> It takes successful offensive strategies to build competitive advantage—good defensive strategies can help protect competitive advantage but rarely are the basis for creating it.

Several types of strategic offensives merit consideration:

1. *Offering an equally good or better product at a lower price:* This is the classic offensive for improving a company's market position vis-à-vis rivals. Advanced Micro Devices (AMD), wanting to grow its sales of microprocessors for PCs, has on several occasions elected to attack Intel head-on, offering a faster alternative to Intel's Pentium chips at a lower price. Believing that the company's survival depends on eliminating the performance gap between AMD chips and Intel chips, AMD management has been willing to risk that a head-on offensive might prompt Intel to counter with lower prices of its own and accelerated development of faster Pentium chips. Lower prices can produce market share gains if competitors don't respond with price cuts of their own and if the challenger convinces buyers that its product is just as good or better. However, such a strategy increases total profits only if the gains in additional unit sales are enough to offset the impact of lower prices and thinner margins per unit sold. General Motors, for instance, repeatedly attacked rival carmakers with aggressive rebates and 0 percent financing (at a cost of about $3,100 per vehicle sold) in 2001–2003, but it failed to gain more than 1 percent additional market share and such deals definitely cut into GM's profitability. Price-cutting offensives generally work best when a company *first achieves a cost advantage and then hits competitors with a lower price.*[26]

2. *Leapfrogging competitors by being the first adopter of next-generation technologies or being first to market with next-generation products:* In 2004–2005, Microsoft waged an offensive to get its next-generation Xbox to market four to six months ahead of Sony's PlayStation 3, anticipating that such a lead time would

help it convince video gamers to switch to the Xbox rather than wait for the new PlayStation to hit the market.

3. *Adopting and improving on the good ideas of other companies (rivals or otherwise):*[27] The idea of warehouse-type hardware and home improvement centers did not originate with Home Depot founders Arthur Blank and Bernie Marcus; they got the "big box" concept from their former employer Handy Dan Home Improvement. But they were quick to improve on Handy Dan's business model and strategy and take Home Depot to the next plateau in terms of product line breadth and customer service. Casket-maker Hillenbrand greatly improved its market position by adapting Toyota's production methods to casket making. Ryanair has succeeded as a low-cost airline in Europe by imitating many of Southwest Airlines' operating practices and applying them in a different geographic market.

4. *Deliberately attacking those market segments where a key rival makes big profits:*[28] Dell Computer's recent entry into printers and printer cartridges—the market arena where number-two PC maker Hewlett-Packard enjoys hefty profit margins and makes the majority of its profits—while mainly motivated by Dell's desire to broaden its product line and save its customers money (because of Dell's lower prices), nonetheless represented a hardball offensive calculated to weaken HP's market position in printers. To the extent that Dell might be able to use lower prices to woo away some of HP's printer customers, it would have the effect of eroding HP's "profit sanctuary," distracting HP's attention away from PCs, and reducing the financial resources HP has available for battling Dell in the global market for PCs.

5. *Attacking the competitive weaknesses of rivals:* Such offensives can include going after the customers of rivals whose products lag on quality, features, or product performance; making special sales pitches to the customers of rivals who provide subpar customer service; trying to win customers away from rivals with weak brand recognition (an attractive option if the aggressor has strong marketing skills and a recognized brand name); emphasizing sales to buyers in geographic regions where a rival has a weak market share or is exerting less competitive effort; and paying special attention to buyer segments that a rival is neglecting or is weakly equipped to serve.

6. *Maneuvering around competitors and concentrating on capturing unoccupied or less contested market territory:* Examples include launching initiatives to build strong positions in geographic areas where close rivals have little or no market presence and trying to create new market segments by introducing products with different attributes and performance features to better meet the needs of selected buyers.[29]

7. *Using hit-and-run tactics to grab sales and market share from complacent or distracted rivals:* Such "guerrilla offensives" include occasionally low-balling on price (to win a big order or steal a key account from a rival); surprising key rivals with sporadic but intense bursts of promotional activity (offering a 20 percent discount for one week to draw customers away from rival brands); or undertaking special campaigns to attract buyers away from rivals plagued with a strike or problems in meeting buyer demand.[30] Guerrilla offensives are particularly well suited to small challengers who have neither the resources nor the market visibility to mount a full-fledged attack on industry leaders.

8. *Launching a preemptive strike to secure an advantageous position that rivals are prevented or discouraged from duplicating:*[31] What makes a move preemptive is its one-of-a-kind nature—whoever strikes first stands to acquire competitive assets that rivals can't readily match. Examples of preemptive moves include (1) securing the best distributors in a particular geographic region or country; (2) moving to obtain the most favorable site along a heavily traveled thoroughfare, at a new interchange or intersection, in a new shopping mall, in a natural beauty spot, close to cheap transportation or raw material supplies or market outlets, and so on; (3) tying up the most reliable, high-quality suppliers via exclusive partnership, long-term contracts, or even acquisition; and (4) moving swiftly to acquire the assets of distressed rivals at bargain prices. To be successful, a preemptive move doesn't have to totally block rivals from following or copying; it merely needs to give a firm a prime position that is not easily circumvented.

Other offensives that may be attractive in the right circumstances include trying to trump the products of rivals by introducing new/improved products with features calculated to win customers away from rivals, running comparison ads, constructing major new plant capacity in a rival's backyard, expanding the product line to match one or more rivals model for model, and developing customer service capabilities that rivals don't have.

As a rule, challenging rivals on competitive grounds where they are strong is an uphill struggle.[32] Offensive initiatives that exploit competitor weaknesses stand a better chance of succeeding than do those that challenge competitor strengths, especially if the weaknesses represent important vulnerabilities and weak rivals can be caught by surprise with no ready defense. Strategic offensives should, as a general rule, be grounded in a company's competitive assets and strong points—its core competencies, competitive capabilities, and such resource strengths as a well-known brand name, a cost advantage in manufacturing or distribution, and a new or much-improved product. Otherwise, its prospects for success are dim unless its resources and competitive strengths amount to a competitive advantage over the targeted rivals.

Defensive Strategies—Protecting Market Position and Competitive Advantage

In a competitive market, all firms are subject to offensive challenges from rivals. The purposes of defensive strategies are to lower the risk of being attacked, weaken the impact of any attack that occurs, and influence challengers to aim their efforts at other rivals. While defensive strategies usually don't enhance a firm's competitive advantage, they can definitely help fortify its competitive position, protect its most valuable resources and capabilities from imitation, and defend whatever competitive advantage it might have. Defensive strategies can take either of two forms: actions to block challengers and signals to indicate the likelihood of strong retaliation.

> It is just as important to discern when to fortify a company's present market position with defensive actions as it is to seize the initiative and launch strategic offensives.

Blocking the Avenues Open to Challengers

The most frequently employed approach to defending a company's present position involves actions that restrict a challenger's options for initiating competitive attack.

There are many ways to throw obstacles in the path of challengers.

There are any number of obstacles that can be put in the path of would-be challengers.[33] A defender can participate in alternative technologies as a hedge against rivals attacking with a new or better technology. A defender can introduce new features, add new models, or broaden its product line to close off gaps and vacant niches to opportunity-seeking challengers. It can thwart the efforts of rivals to attack with a lower price by maintaining economy-priced options of its own. It can try to discourage buyers from trying competitors' brands by lengthening warranties, offering free training and support services, developing the capability to deliver spare parts to users faster than rivals can, providing coupons and sample giveaways to buyers most prone to experiment, and making early announcements about impending new products or price changes to induce potential buyers to postpone switching. It can challenge the quality or safety of rivals' products. Finally, a defender can grant volume discounts or better financing terms to dealers and distributors to discourage them from experimenting with other suppliers, or it can convince them to handle its product line *exclusively* and force competitors to use other distribution outlets.

Signaling Challengers That Retaliation Is Likely

The goal of signaling challengers that strong retaliation is likely in the event of an attack is either to dissuade challengers from attacking at all or to divert them to less threatening options. Either goal can be achieved by letting challengers know the battle will cost more than it is worth. Would-be challengers can be signaled by:[34]

- Publicly announcing management's commitment to maintain the firm's present market share.

- Publicly committing the company to a policy of matching competitors' terms or prices.

- Maintaining a war chest of cash and marketable securities.

- Making an occasional strong counterresponse to the moves of weak competitors to enhance the firm's image as a tough defender.

Web Site Strategies: Which One to Employ?

Companies today must wrestle with the strategic issue of how to use their Web sites in positioning themselves in the marketplace—whether to use their Web sites just to disseminate product information or whether to operate an e-store to sell direct to online shoppers.

Companies across the world are deep into the process of implementing a variety of Internet technology applications—the chief question companies face at this point is what additional Internet technology applications to incorporate into day-to-day operations. But the larger and much tougher *strategic* issue is just what role the company's Web site should play in a company's competitive strategy. In particular, to what degree should a company use the Internet as a distribution channel for accessing buyers? Should a company use its Web site *only as a means of disseminating product information* (with traditional distribution channel partners making all sales to end users), as a *secondary or minor channel for selling direct to buyers* of its product, as *one of several important distribution channels* for accessing customers, as *the primary distribution channel* for accessing customers, or as *the exclusive channel* for transacting sales with customers?[35] Let's look at each of these strategic options in turn.

Product-Information-Only Strategies— Avoiding Channel Conflict

Operating a Web site that contains extensive product information but that relies on click-throughs to the Web sites of distribution channel partners for sales transactions (or that informs site users where nearby retail stores are located) is an attractive market positioning option for manufacturers and/or wholesalers that have invested heavily in building and cultivating retail dealer networks and that face nettlesome channel conflict issues if they try to sell online in direct competition with their dealers. A manufacturer or wholesaler that aggressively pursues online sales to end users is signaling both a weak strategic commitment to its dealers and a willingness to cannibalize dealers' sales and growth potential. To the extent that strong partnerships with wholesale and/or retail dealers are critical to accessing end users, selling direct to end users via the company's Web site is a very tricky road to negotiate. A manufacturer's effort to use its Web site to sell around its dealers is certain to anger its wholesale distributors and retail dealers, who may respond by putting more effort into marketing the brands of rival manufacturers that don't sell online. As a consequence, the manufacturer may stand to lose more sales by offending its dealers than it gains from its own online sales effort. Moreover, dealers may be in a better position to employ a brick-and-click strategy than a manufacturer is because dealers have a local presence to complement their online sales approach (which consumers may find appealing). Consequently, in industries where the strong support and goodwill of dealer networks is essential, manufacturers may conclude that their Web sites should be designed to partner with dealers rather than compete with them—just as the auto manufacturers are doing with their franchised dealers.

Web Site E-Stores as a Minor Distribution Channel

A second strategic option is to use online sales as a relatively minor distribution channel for achieving incremental sales, gaining online sales experience, and doing marketing research. If channel conflict poses a big obstacle to online sales, or if only a small fraction of buyers can be attracted to make online purchases, then companies are well advised to pursue online sales with the strategic intent of gaining experience, learning more about buyer tastes and preferences, testing reaction to new products, creating added market buzz about their products, and boosting overall sales volume a few percentage points. Sony and Nike, for example, sell almost all of their products at their Web sites without provoking resistance from their retail dealers since most buyers of their products prefer to do their buying at retail stores rather than buying online. They use their Web sites not so much to make sales as to glean valuable marketing research data from tracking the browsing patterns of Web site visitors. The behavior and actions of Web surfers are a veritable gold mine of information for companies seeking to keep their finger on the market pulse and respond more precisely to buyer preferences and interests.

Despite the channel conflict that exists when a manufacturer sells directly to end users at its Web site in head-to-head competition with its distribution channel allies, manufacturers might still opt to pursue online sales at their Web sites and try to establish online sales as an important distribution channel because (1) their profit margins from online sales are bigger than those earned from selling to their wholesale/retail customers; (2) encouraging buyers to visit the company's Web site helps educate them to the ease and convenience of purchasing online and, over time, prompts more and more buyers to purchase online (where company profit margins are greater)—which makes incurring channel conflict in the short term and competing against traditional distribution allies potentially worthwhile; and (3) selling directly to end users allows a manufacturer to make greater use of build-to-order manufacturing and assembly, which, if met with growing buyer acceptance and satisfaction, would increase the rate at which sales migrate from distribution allies to the company's Web site—such migration could lead to streamlining the company's value chain and boosting its profit margins.

Brick-and-Click Strategies

Brick-and-click strategies have two big strategic appeals for wholesale and retail enterprises: they are an economic means of expanding a company's geographic reach, and they give both existing and potential customers an additional way of how to communicate with the company, shop for product information, make purchases, or resolve customer service problems. Software developers, for example, have come to rely on the Internet as a highly effective distribution channel to complement sales through brick-and-mortar wholesalers and retailers. Selling online directly to end users has the advantage of eliminating the costs of producing and packaging CDs and cutting out the costs and margins of software wholesalers and retailers (often 35 to 50 percent of the retail price). However, software developers are still strongly motivated to continue to distribute their products through wholesalers and retailers (to maintain broad access to existing and potential users who, for whatever reason, may be reluctant to buy online). Chain retailers like Wal-Mart and Circuit City operate online stores for their products primarily as a convenience to customers who want to buy online rather than making a shopping trip to nearby stores.

Many brick-and-mortar companies can enter online retailing at relatively low cost—all they need is a Web store and systems for filling and delivering individual customer orders. Brick-and-mortar distributors and retailers (as well as manufacturers with company-owned retail stores) can employ brick-and-click strategies by using their current distribution centers and/or retail stores for picking orders from on-hand inventories and making deliveries. Blockbuster, the largest chain of video and DVD rental stores, utilizes the inventories at its stores to fill orders for its online subscribers who pay a monthly fee for unlimited DVDs delivered by mail carrier; using local stores to fill orders typically allows delivery in 24 hours versus 48 hours for shipments made from a regional shipping center. Walgreen's, a leading drugstore chain, allows customers to order a prescription online and then pick it up at the drive-through window or inside counter of a local store. In banking, a brick-and-click strategy allows customers to use local branches and ATMs for depositing checks and getting cash while using online systems to pay bills, check account balances, and transfer funds. Many industrial distributors are finding it efficient for customers to place their orders over the Web rather than phoning them in or waiting for salespeople to call in person.

Strategies for Online Enterprises

A company that elects to use the Internet as its exclusive channel for accessing buyers is essentially an online business from the perspective of the customer. The Internet becomes the vehicle for transacting sales and delivering customer services; except for advertising, the Internet is the sole point of all buyer-seller contact. Many so-called pure dot-com enterprises have chosen this strategic approach—prominent examples include eBay, Amazon.com, Yahoo, Buy.com, and Priceline.com. For a company to succeed in using the Internet as its exclusive distribution channel, its product or service must be one for which buying online holds strong appeal.

A company that decides to use online sales as its exclusive method for sales transactions must address several strategic issues:

- *How it will deliver unique value to buyers:* Online businesses must usually attract buyers on the basis of low price, convenience, superior product information, build-to-order systems, or attentive online service.

- *Whether it will pursue competitive advantage based on lower costs, differentiation, or better value for the money:* For an online-only sales strategy to succeed in head-to-head competition with brick-and-mortar and brick-and-click rivals, an online seller's value chain approach must hold potential for low-cost leadership, competitively valuable differentiating attributes, or a best-cost provider advantage. If an online firm's strategy is to attract customers by selling at cut-rate prices, then it must possess cost advantages in those activities it performs, and it must outsource the remaining activities to low-cost specialists. If an online seller is going to differentiate itself on the basis of a superior buying experience and top-notch customer service, then it needs to concentrate on having an easy-to-navigate Web site, an array of functions and conveniences for customers, "Web reps" who can answer questions online, and logistical capabilities to deliver products quickly and accommodate returned merchandise. If it is going to deliver more value for the money, then it must manage value chain activities so as to deliver upscale products and services at lower costs than rivals.

- *Whether it will have a broad or a narrow product offering:* A one-stop shopping strategy like that employed by Amazon.com (which offers over 30 million items for sale at its Web sites in the United States, Britain, France, Germany, Denmark, and Japan) has the appealing economics of helping spread fixed operating costs over a wide number of items and a large customer base. Other e-tailers, such as E-Loan and Hotel.com, have adopted classic focus strategies and cater to a sharply defined target audience shopping for a particular product or product category.

- *Whether to perform order fulfillment activities internally or to outsource them:* Building central warehouses, stocking them with adequate inventories, and developing systems to pick, pack, and ship individual orders all require substantial start-up capital but may result in lower overall unit costs than would paying the fees of order fulfillment specialists who make a business of providing warehouse space, stocking inventories, and shipping orders for e-tailers. However, outsourcing order fulfillment activities is likely to be more economical unless an e-tailer has high unit volume and the capital to invest in its own order fulfillment capabilities. Buy.com, an online superstore consisting of some 30,000 items, obtains products from name-brand manufacturers and uses outsiders to stock and ship those products; thus, its focus is not on manufacturing or order fulfillment but, rather, on selling.

- *How it will draw traffic to its Web site:* Web sites have to be cleverly marketed. Unless Web surfers hear about the site, like what they see on their first visit, and are intrigued enough to return again and again, the site is unlikely to generate adequate revenues. Marketing campaigns that result only in heavy site traffic and lots of page views are seldom sufficient; the best test of effective marketing is the ratio at which page views are converted into revenues (the "look-to-buy" ratio). For example, in 2001 Yahoo's site traffic averaged 1.2 *billion* page views daily but generated only about $2 million in daily revenues; in contrast, the traffic at the Web site of brokerage firm Charles Schwab averaged only 40 *million* page views per day but resulted in an average of $5 million daily in online commission revenues.

Choosing Appropriate Functional-Area Strategies

A company's strategy is not complete until company managers have made strategic choices about how the various functional parts of the business—R&D, production, human resources, sales and marketing, finance, and so on—will be managed in support of its basic competitive strategy approach and the other important competitive moves being taken. Normally, functional-area strategy choices rank third on the menu of choosing among the various strategy options, as shown in Figure 4.1 (see page 114). But whether commitments to particular functional strategies are made before or after the choices of complementary strategic options shown in Figure 4.1 is beside the point—what's really important is what the functional strategies are and how they mesh to enhance the success of the company's higher-level strategic thrusts.

In many respects, the nature of functional strategies is dictated by the choice of competitive strategy. For example, a manufacturer employing a low-cost provider strategy needs an R&D and product design strategy that emphasizes cheap-to-incorporate features and facilitates economical assembly, a production strategy that stresses capture of scale economies and actions to achieve low-cost manufacture (such as high labor productivity, efficient supply chain management, and automated production processes), and a low-budget marketing strategy. A business pursuing a high-end differentiation strategy needs a production strategy geared to top-notch quality and a marketing strategy aimed at touting differentiating features and using advertising and a trusted brand name to "pull" sales through the chosen distribution channels. A company using a focused differentiation strategy (like Krispy Kreme) needs a marketing strategy that stresses growing the niche (getting more people hooked on Krispy Kreme doughnuts), keeping buyer interest at a high level, and protecting the niche against invasion by outsiders.

Beyond very general prescriptions, it is difficult to say just what the content of the different functional-area strategies should be without first knowing what higher-level strategic choices a company has made, the industry environment in which it operates, the resource strengths that can be leveraged, and so on. Suffice it to say here that company personnel—both managers and employees charged with strategy-making responsibility down through the organizational hierarchy—must be clear about which higher-level strategies top management has chosen and then must tailor the company's functional-area strategies accordingly.

First-Mover Advantages and Disadvantages

When to make a strategic move is often as crucial as *what* move to make. Timing is especially important when *first-mover advantages* or *disadvantages* exist.[36] Being first to initiate a strategic move can have a high payoff when (1) pioneering helps build a firm's image and reputation with buyers; (2) early commitments to new technologies, new-style components, new or emerging distribution channels, and so on, can produce an absolute cost advantage over rivals; (3) first-time customers remain strongly loyal to pioneering firms in making repeat purchases; and (4) moving first constitutes a preemptive strike, making imitation extra hard or unlikely. The bigger the first-mover advantages, the more attractive making the first move becomes.[37] In e-commerce, companies like America Online, Amazon.com, Yahoo, eBay, and Priceline.com that were first with a new technology, network solution, or business model enjoyed lasting first-mover advantages in gaining the visibility and reputation needed to remain market leaders. But just being a first-mover by itself is seldom enough to win a sustainable competitive advantage. A first-mover also needs to be a fast learner and continue to move aggressively to capitalize on any initial pioneering advantage, and it helps immensely if the first-mover has deep financial pockets, important competencies and competitive capabilities, and high-quality management. What makes being a first-mover strategically important is not being the first company to do something but, rather, being the first competitor to put together the precise combination of features, customer value, and sound revenue/ cost/profit economics that gives it an edge over rivals in the battle for market leadership.[38]

However, being a fast-follower or even a wait-and-see late-mover doesn't always carry a significant or lasting competitive penalty. There are times when a first-mover's skills, know-how, and actions are easily copied or even surpassed, allowing late-movers to catch or overtake the first-mover in a relatively short period. And there are times when there are actually *advantages* to being an adept follower rather than a first-mover. Late-mover advantages (or *first-mover disadvantages*) arise when (1) pioneering leadership is more costly than imitating followership and only negligible experience or learning-curve benefits accrue to the leader—a condition that allows a follower to end up with lower costs than the first-mover; (2) the products of an innovator are somewhat primitive and do not live up to buyer expectations, thus allowing a clever follower to win disenchanted buyers away from the leader with better-performing products; and (3) technology is advancing rapidly, giving fast-followers the opening to leapfrog a first-mover's products with more attractive and full-featured second- and third-generation products.

In weighing the pros and cons of being a first-mover versus a fast-follower versus a slow-mover, it matters whether the race to market leadership in a particular industry is a marathon or a sprint. In marathons, a slow-mover is not unduly penalized—first-mover advantages can be fleeting, and there's ample time for fast-followers and sometimes even late-movers to play catch-up.[39] For instance, it took 18 months for 10 million users to sign up for Hotmail, 5.5 years for worldwide mobile phone use to grow from 10 million to 100 million, 7 years for videocassette recorders to find their way into 1 million U.S. homes, and close to 10 years for the number of at-home broadband subscribers to grow to 100 million worldwide. The lesson here is that there is a market-penetration curve for every emerging opportunity; typically, the curve has an inflection point at which all the pieces of the business model fall into place, buyer demand explodes, and the market takes off. The inflection point can come early on a fast-rising curve (like use of e-mail) or later on a slow-rising curve (like use of broadband). Any company that seeks competitive advantage by being a first-mover thus needs to ask some hard questions: Does market takeoff depend on the development of complementary products or services that currently are not available? Is new infrastructure

> **Core Concept**
> Because of first-mover advantages and disadvantages, competitive advantage can spring from *when* a move is made as well as from *what* move is made.

COMPANY SPOTLIGHT 4.6
The Battle in Consumer Broadband: First-Movers versus Late-Movers

In 1988 an engineer at the Bell companies' research labs figured out how to rush signals along ordinary copper wire at high speed using digital technology, thus creating the digital subscriber line (DSL). But the regional Bells, which dominated the local telephone market in the United States, showed little interest over the next 10 years, believing it was more lucrative to rent T-1 lines to businesses that needed fast data transmission capability and rent second phone lines to households wanting an Internet connection that didn't disrupt their regular telephone service. Furthermore, telephone executives were skeptical about DSL technology—there were a host of technical snarls to overcome, and early users encountered annoying glitches. Many executives doubted that it made good sense to invest billions of dollars in the infrastructure needed to roll out DSL to residential and small business customers, given the success they were having with T-1 and second-line rentals. As a consequence, the Bells didn't seriously begin to market DSL until the late 1990s, two years after the cable TV companies began their push to market cable broadband.

Cable companies were more than happy to be the first-movers in marketing broadband service via their copper cable wires, chiefly because their business was threatened by satellite TV technology and they saw broadband as an innovative service they could provide that the satellite companies could not. (Delivering broadband service via satellite has yet to become a factor in the marketplace, winning only a 1 percent share in 2003.) Cable companies were able to deploy broadband on their copper wire economically because during the 1980s and early 1990s most cable operators had spent about $60 billion to upgrade their systems with fiber-optic technology in order to handle two-way traffic rather than just one-way TV signals and thereby make good on their promises to local governments to develop "interactive" cable systems if they were awarded franchises. Although the early interactive services were duds, technicians discovered in the mid-1990s that the

required before buyer demand can surge? Will buyers need to learn new skills or adopt new behaviors? Will buyers encounter high switching costs? Are there influential competitors in a position to delay or derail the efforts of a first-mover? When the answers to any of these questions are yes, then a company must be careful not to pour too many resources into getting ahead of the market opportunity—the race is likely going to be more of a 10-year marathon than a 2-year sprint. But being first out of the starting block is competitively important if it produces clear and substantial benefits to buyers and competitors will be compelled to follow.

While being an adept fast-follower has the advantages of being less risky and skirting the costs of pioneering, rarely does a company have much to gain from being a slow-follower and concentrating on avoiding the "mistakes" of first-movers. Habitual late-movers, while often able to survive, are usually fighting to retain their customers and scrambling to keep pace with more progressive and innovative rivals. For a habitual late-mover to catch up, it must count on first-movers to be slow learners and complacent in letting their lead dwindle. Plus it has to hope that buyers will be slow to gravitate to the products of first-movers, again giving it time to catch up. And it has to have competencies and capabilities that are sufficiently strong to allow it to close the gap fairly quickly once it makes its move. Counting on all first-movers to stumble or otherwise be easily overtaken is usually a bad bet that puts a late-mover's competitive position at risk.

Company Spotlight 4.6 describes the challenges that late-moving telephone companies have in winning the battle to supply at-home high-speed Internet access and overcoming the first-mover advantages of cable companies.

two-way systems enabled high-speed Internet hookups.

With Internet excitement surging in the late 1990s, cable executives saw high-speed Internet service as a no-brainer and began rolling it out to customers in 1998, securing about 362,000 customers by year-end versus only about 41,000 for DSL. Part of the early success of cable broadband was due to a cost advantage in modems—cable executives, seeing the potential of cable broadband several years earlier, had asked CableLabs to standardize the technology for cable modems, a move that lowered costs and made cable modems marketable in consumer electronics stores. DSL modems were substantially more complicated, and it took longer to drive the costs down from several hundred dollars each to under $100—in 2004, both cable and phone companies paid about $50 for modems, but cable modems got there much sooner.

As cable broadband began to attract more and more attention in the 1998–2002 period, the regional Bells continued to move slowly on DSL. The technical problems lingered, and early users were disgruntled by a host of annoying and sometimes horrendous installation difficulties and service glitches. Not only did providing users with convenient and reliable service prove to be a formidable challenge, but some regulatory issues stood in the way as well. Even in 2003 phone company executives found it hard to justify multibillion-dollar investments to install the necessary equipment and support systems to offer, market, manage, and maintain DSL service on the vast scale of a regional Bell company. SBC Communications figured it would cost at least $6 billion to roll out DSL to its customers. Verizon estimated that it would take 3.5 to 4 million customers to make DSL economics work, a number it would probably not reach until the end of 2005.

In 2003–2004, high-speed consumer access to the Internet was a surging business with a bright outlook—the number of U.S. Internet users upgrading to high-speed service was growing by close to 500,000 monthly. In the U.S., cable broadband was the preferred choice—70 percent of the market was opting for cable modems supplied by cable TV companies, and cable modem subscribers outnumbered DSL subscribers 40 million to 10.6 million. DSL's late start made it questionable whether DSL would be able to catch cable broadband in the U.S. marketplace. In the rest of the world, however, DSL was the broadband connection of choice.

Source: Wall Street Journal. Eastern Edition [staff produced copy only] by Shawn Young and Peter Grant. Copyright 2003 by Dow Jones & Co Inc. Reproduced with permission of Dow Jones & Co Inc in the format textbook via Copyright Clearance Center.

Key Points

A company competing in a particular industry or market has a varied menu of strategy options for seeking and securing a competitive advantage (see Figure 4.1). The first and foremost strategic choice is which of the five basic competitive strategies to employ—overall low-cost, broad differentiation, best-cost, focused low-cost, or focused differentiation.

Once a company has decided which of the five basic competitive strategies to employ in its quest for competitive advantage, then it must decide whether to supplement its choice of a basic competitive strategy approach with strategic actions relating to alliances and collaborative partnerships, mergers and acquisitions, integration forward or backward, outsourcing of certain value chain activities, offensive and defensive moves, and the use of the Internet in selling directly to end users, as shown in Figure 4.1.

Once all the higher-level strategic choices have been made, company managers can turn to the task of crafting functional and operating-level strategies to flesh out the details of the company's overall business and competitive strategy.

The timing of strategic moves also has relevance in the quest for competitive advantage. Because of the competitive importance that is sometimes associated with when a strategic move is made, company managers are obligated to carefully consider the advantages or disadvantages that attach to being a first-mover versus a fast-follower versus a wait-and-see late-mover. At the end of the day, though, the proper objective of a first-mover is that of being the first competitor to put together the precise combination of features, customer value, and sound revenue/cost/profit economics that puts it ahead of the pack in capturing an attractive market opportunity. Sometimes the company that first unlocks a profitable market opportunity is the first-mover and sometimes it is not—but the company that comes up with the key is surely the smart mover.

Exercises

1. Go to www.google.com and do a search for "low-cost producer." See if you can identify five companies that are pursuing a low-cost strategy in their respective industries.

2. Using the advanced search engine function at www.google.com, enter "best-cost producer" in the exact-phrase box and see if you can locate three companies that indicate they are employing a best-cost producer strategy.

3. Go to www.google.com and do a search on "strategic alliances." Identify at least two companies in different industries that are making a significant use of strategic alliances as a core part of their strategies. In addition, identify who their alliances are with and describe the purpose of the alliances.

4. Go to www.google.com and do a search on "acquisition strategy." Identify at least two companies in different industries that are using acquisitions to strengthen their market positions. Identify some of the companies that have been acquired, and research the purpose behind the acquisitions.

CHAPTER 5

Competing in Foreign Markets

You have no choice but to operate in a world shaped by globalization and the information revolution. There are two options: Adapt or die.

—Andrew S. Grove, chairman, Intel Corporation

You do not choose to become global. The market chooses for you; it forces your hand.

—Alain Gomez, CEO, Thomson, S.A.

Industries actually vary a great deal in the pressures they put on a company to sell internationally.

—Niraj Dawar and Tony Frost, professors, Richard Ivey School of Business

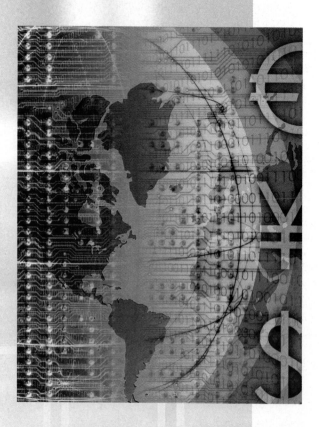

Any company that aspires to industry leadership in the 21st century must think in terms of global, not domestic, market leadership. The world economy is globalizing at an accelerating pace as countries previously closed to foreign companies open up their markets, as the Internet shrinks the importance of geographic distance, and as ambitious growth-minded companies race to build stronger competitive positions in the markets of more and more countries. Companies in industries that are already globally competitive or are in the process of becoming so are under the gun to come up with a strategy for competing successfully in foreign markets.

This chapter focuses on strategy options for expanding beyond domestic boundaries and competing in the markets of either a few or a great many countries. The spotlight will be on four strategic issues unique to competing multinationally:

1. Whether to customize the company's offerings in each different country market to match the tastes and preferences of local buyers or to offer a mostly standardized product worldwide.

2. Whether to employ essentially the same basic competitive strategy in all countries or modify the strategy country by country.

3. Where to locate the company's production facilities, distribution centers, and customer service operations so as to realize the greatest location advantages.

4. How to efficiently transfer the company's resource strengths and capabilities from one country to another in an effort to secure competitive advantage.

In the process of exploring these issues, we will introduce a number of core concepts—multicountry competition, global competition, profit sanctuaries, and cross-market subsidization. The chapter includes sections on cross-country differences in cultural, demographic, and market conditions; strategy options for entering and competing in foreign markets; the growing role of alliances with foreign partners; the importance of locating operations in the most advantageous countries; and the special circumstances of competing in such emerging markets as China, India, and Brazil.

Why Companies Expand into Foreign Markets

A company may opt to expand outside its domestic market for any of four major reasons:

1. *To gain access to new customers:* Expanding into foreign markets offers potential for increased revenues, profits, and long-term growth and becomes an especially attractive option when a company's home markets are mature. Firms like Cisco Systems, Dell, Sony, Nokia, Avon, and Toyota, which are racing for global leadership in their respective industries, are moving rapidly and aggressively to extend their market reach into all corners of the world.

2. *To achieve lower costs and enhance the firm's competitiveness:* Many companies are driven to sell in more than one country because domestic sales volume is not large enough to fully capture manufacturing economies of scale or learning-curve effects and thereby substantially improve the firm's cost-competitiveness. The relatively small size of country markets in Europe explains why companies like

Michelin, BMW, and Nestlé long ago began selling their products all across Europe and then moved into markets in North America and Latin America.

3. *To capitalize on its core competencies:* A company may be able to leverage its competencies and capabilities into a position of competitive advantage in foreign markets as well as domestic markets. Nokia's competencies and capabilities in mobile phones have propelled it to global market leadership in the wireless telecommunications business.

4. *To spread its business risk across a wider market base:* A company spreads business risk by operating in a number of different foreign countries rather than depending entirely on operations in its domestic market. Thus, if the economies of certain Asian countries turn down for a period of time, a company with operations across much of the world may be sustained by buoyant sales in Latin America or Europe.

In a few cases, companies in industries based on natural resources (e.g., oil and gas, minerals, rubber, and lumber) often find it necessary to operate in the international arena because attractive raw material supplies are located in foreign countries.

The Difference between Competing Internationally and Competing Globally

Typically, a company will start to compete internationally by entering just one or maybe a select few foreign markets. Competing on a truly global scale comes later, after the company has established operations on several continents and is racing against rivals for global market leadership. Thus, there is a meaningful distinction between the competitive scope of a company that operates in a few foreign countries (with perhaps modest ambitions to enter several more country markets) and a company that markets its products in 50 to 100 countries and is expanding its operations into additional country markets annually. The former is most accurately termed an *international competitor,* while the latter qualifies as a *global competitor.* In the discussion that follows, we'll continue to make a distinction between strategies for competing internationally and strategies for competing globally.

Cross-Country Differences in Cultural, Demographic, and Market Conditions

Regardless of a company's motivation for expanding outside its domestic markets, the strategies it uses to compete in foreign markets must be situation-driven. Cultural, demographic, and market conditions vary significantly among the countries of the world. Cultures and lifestyles are the most obvious areas in which countries differ; market demographics are close behind. Consumers in Spain do not have the same tastes, preferences, and buying habits as consumers in Norway; buyers differ yet again in Greece, Chile, New Zealand, and Taiwan. Less than 10 percent of the populations of Brazil, India, and China have annual purchasing power equivalent to $20,000. Middle-class consumers represent a much smaller portion of the population in these and other emerging countries than in North America, Japan, and much of Western Europe.[1] Sometimes, product designs suitable in one country are inappropriate in another—for example, in the United States electrical devices run on 110-volt electric systems, but in some European countries the standard is a 240-volt electric system, necessitating the use of different electric designs and components. In France consumers prefer top-loading washing machines, while in most other European countries consumers prefer front-loading machines. Northern Europeans want large refrigerators because they tend to shop once a week in supermarkets; southern Europeans can get by on small refrigerators because they shop daily. In parts of Asia refrigerators are a status symbol and may be placed in the living room, leading to preferences for stylish designs and colors—in India bright blue and red are popular colors. In other Asian countries household space is constrained and many refrigerators are only 4 feet high so that the top can be used for storage. In Hong Kong the preference is for compact European-style appliances, but in Taiwan large American-style appliances are more popular. In Italy, most people use automatic washing machines, but there is a strongly entrenched tradition and cultural preference for hanging the clothes out to dry on a clothesline and ironing them rather than using clothes dryers—the widespread belief that sun-dried clothes are fresher virtually shuts down any opportunities for appliance makers to market clothes dryers in Italy. In China, many parents are reluctant to purchase PCs even when they can afford them because of concerns that their children will be distracted from their schoolwork by surfing the Web, playing PC-based video games, and downloading and listening to pop music.

Similarly, market growth varies from country to country. In emerging markets like India, China, Brazil, and Malaysia, market growth potential is far higher than in the more mature economies of Britain, Denmark, Canada, and Japan. In automobiles, for example, the potential for market growth is explosive in China, where sales amount to only 1 million vehicles annually in a country with 1.3 billion people. In India there are efficient, well-developed national channels for distributing trucks, scooters, farm equipment, groceries, personal care items, and other packaged products to the country's 3 million retailers, whereas in China distribution is primarily local and there is no national network for distributing most products. The marketplace is intensely competitive in some countries and only moderately contested in others. Industry driving forces may be one thing in Spain, quite another in Canada, and different yet again in Turkey or Argentina or South Korea.

One of the biggest concerns of companies competing in foreign markets is whether to customize their offerings in each different country market to match the tastes and preferences of local buyers or whether to offer a mostly standardized product worldwide. While the products of a company that is responsive to local tastes will appeal to local buyers, customizing a company's products country by country may have the effect of raising production and distribution costs due to the greater variety of designs and components, shorter production runs, and the complications of added inventory handling and distribution logistics. Greater standardization of a global company's product offering, on the other hand, can lead to scale economies and learning-curve effects, thus contributing to the achievement of a low-cost advantage. The tension between the market pressures to customize and the competitive pressures to lower costs is one of the big strategic issues that participants in foreign markets have to resolve.

Aside from the basic cultural and market differences among countries, a company also has to pay special attention to location advantages that stem from country-to-country variations in manufacturing and distribution costs, the risks of shifting exchange rates, and the economic and political demands of host governments.

Gaining Competitive Advantage Based on Where Activities Are Located

Differences in wage rates, worker productivity, inflation rates, energy costs, tax rates, government regulations, and the like, create sizable variations in manufacturing costs from country to country. Plants in some countries have major manufacturing cost advantages because of lower input costs (especially labor), relaxed government regulations, the proximity of suppliers, or unique natural resources. In such cases, the low-cost countries become principal production sites, with most of the output being exported to markets in other parts of the world. Companies that build production facilities in low-cost countries (or that source their products from contract manufacturers in these countries) have a competitive advantage over rivals with plants in countries where costs are higher. The competitive role of low manufacturing costs is most evident in low-wage countries like China, India, Pakistan, Cambodia, Vietnam, Mexico, Brazil, Guatemala, the Philippines, and several countries in Africa that have become production havens for manufactured goods with high labor content (especially textiles and apparel). China is fast becoming the manufacturing capital of the world—virtually all of the world's major manufacturing companies now have facilities in China, and China attracted more foreign direct investment in 2002 and 2003 than any other country in the world. Likewise, concerns about short delivery times and low shipping costs make some countries better locations than others for establishing distribution centers.

The quality of a country's business environment also offers locational advantages—the governments of some countries are anxious to attract foreign investments and go all-out to create a business climate that outsiders will view as favorable. A good example is Ireland, which has one of the world's most pro-business environments. Ireland offers companies very low corporate tax rates, has a government that is responsive to the needs of industry, and aggressively recruits high-tech manufacturing facilities and multinational companies. Such policies were a significant force in making Ireland the most dynamic, fastest-growing nation in Europe during the 1990s. Ireland's policies were a major factor in Intel's decision to locate a $2.5 billion chip manufacturing plant in Ireland that employs over 4,000 people. Another locational advantage is the clustering of suppliers of components and capital equipment, infrastructure suppliers (universities, vocational training providers, research enterprises), trade associations, and makers of complementary products in a single geographic area—such clustering can be an important source of cost savings in addition to facilitating close collaboration with key suppliers.

The Risks of Adverse Exchange Rate Shifts

The volatility of exchange rates greatly complicates the issue of geographic cost advantages. Currency exchange rates often move up or down 20 to 40 percent annually. Changes of this magnitude can either totally wipe out a country's low-cost advantage or transform a former high-cost location into a competitive-cost location. For instance, in the mid-1980s, when the dollar was strong relative to the Japanese yen (meaning that $1 would purchase, say, 125 yen as opposed to only 100 yen), Japanese heavy-equipment maker Komatsu was able to undercut U.S.-based Caterpillar's prices by as much as 25 percent, causing Caterpillar to lose sales and market share. But starting in 1985, when exchange rates began to shift and the dollar grew steadily weaker against the yen (meaning that $1 was worth fewer and fewer yen), Komatsu had to raise its prices six times over two years as its yen-based costs in terms of dollars soared. With its competitiveness against Komatsu restored, Caterpillar regained sales and market share. The lesson of fluctuating exchange rates is that companies that export goods to foreign countries always gain in competitiveness when the currency of the country in which the goods are manufactured is weak. Exporters are disadvantaged when the currency of the country where goods are being manufactured grows stronger. Sizable long-term shifts in exchange rates thus shuffle the global cards of which rivals have the upper hand in the marketplace and which countries represent the low-cost manufacturing location.

As a further illustration of the risks associated with fluctuating exchange rates, consider the case of a U.S. company that has located manufacturing facilities in Brazil (where the currency is *reals*—pronounced "ray-alls") and that exports most of the Brazilian-made goods to markets in the European Union (where the currency is *euros*). To keep the numbers simple, assume that the exchange rate is 4 Brazilian reals for 1 euro and that the product being made in Brazil has a manufacturing cost of 4 Brazilian reals (or 1 euro). Now suppose that for some reason the exchange rate shifts from 4 reals per euro to 5 reals per euro (meaning that the real has declined in value and that the euro is stronger). Making the product in Brazil is now more cost-competitive because a Brazilian good costing 4 reals to produce has fallen to only 0.8 euro at the new exchange rate. If, in contrast, the value of the Brazilian real grows stronger in relation to the euro—resulting in an exchange rate of 3 reals to 1 euro—the same good costing 4 reals to produce now has a cost of 1.33 euros. Clearly, the attraction of manufacturing a good in Brazil and selling it in Europe is far greater when the euro is strong (an exchange rate of 1 euro for 5 Brazilian reals) than when the euro is weak and exchanges for only 3 Brazilian reals.

> **Core Concept**
>
> Companies with manufacturing facilities in a particular country are more cost-competitive in exporting goods to world markets when the local currency is weak (or declines in value relative to other currencies); their competitiveness erodes when the local currency grows stronger relative to the currencies of the countries to which the locally made goods are being exported.

Insofar as U.S.-based manufacturers are concerned, declines in the value of the U.S. dollar against foreign currencies reduce or eliminate whatever cost advantage foreign manufacturers might have over U.S. manufacturers and can even prompt foreign companies to establish production plants in the United States. Likewise, a weak euro enhances the cost-competitiveness of companies manufacturing goods in Europe for export to foreign markets; a strong euro versus other currencies weakens the cost-competitiveness of European plants that manufacture goods for export.

In 2002, when the Brazilian real declined in value by about 25 percent against the dollar, the euro, and several other currencies, the ability of companies with manufacturing plants in Brazil to compete in world markets was greatly enhanced—of course, in future years this windfall gain in cost advantage might well be eroded by sustained rises in the value of the Brazilian real against these same currencies. Herein lies the risk: Currency exchange rates are rather unpredictable, swinging first one way and then another way, so the competitiveness of any company's facilities in any country is partly dependent on whether exchange rate changes over time have a favorable or unfavorable cost impact. Companies making goods in one country for export to foreign countries always gain in competitiveness as the currency of that country grows weaker. Exporters are disadvantaged when the currency of the country where goods are being manufactured grows stronger. On the other hand, domestic companies that are under

> **Core Concept**
>
> Fluctuating exchange rates pose significant risks to a company's competitiveness in foreign markets. Exporters win when the currency of the country where goods are being manufactured grows weaker, and they lose when the currency grows stronger. Domestic companies under pressure from lower-cost imports are benefited when their government's currency grows weaker in relation to the countries where the imported goods are being made.

pressure from lower-cost imported goods gain in competitiveness when their currency grows weaker in relation to the currencies of the countries where the imported goods are made.

Host-Government Policies

National governments enact all kinds of measures affecting business conditions and the operation of foreign companies in their markets. Host governments may set local content requirements on goods made inside their borders by foreign-based companies, put restrictions on exports to ensure adequate local supplies, regulate the prices of imported and locally produced goods, and impose tariffs or quotas on the imports of certain goods. Until 2002, when it joined the World Trade Organization, China imposed a 100 percent tariff on motor vehicle imports. Governments may or may not have burdensome tax structures, stringent environmental regulations, or strictly enforced worker safety standards. Sometimes outsiders face a web of regulations regarding technical standards, product certification, prior approval of capital spending projects, withdrawal of funds from the country, and required minority (sometimes majority) ownership of foreign company operations by local citizens. A few governments may be hostile to or suspicious of foreign companies operating within their borders. Some governments provide subsidies and low-interest loans to domestic companies to help them compete against foreign-based companies. Other governments, anxious to obtain new plants and jobs, offer foreign companies a helping hand in the form of subsidies, privileged market access, and technical assistance. All of these possibilities explain why the managers of companies opting to compete in foreign markets have to take a close look at a country's politics and policies toward business in general, and foreign companies in particular, in deciding which country markets to participate in and which ones to avoid.

The Concepts of Multicountry Competition and Global Competition

There are important differences in the patterns of international competition from industry to industry.[2] At one extreme is **multicountry competition,** in which there's so much cross-country variation in market conditions and in the companies contending for leadership that the market contest among rivals in one country is not closely connected to the market contests in other countries. The standout features of multicountry competition are that (1) buyers in different countries are attracted to different product attributes, (2) sellers vary from country to country, and (3) industry conditions and competitive forces in each national market differ in important respects. Take the banking industry in Italy, Brazil, and Japan as an example— the requirements and expectations of banking customers vary among the three countries, the lead banking competitors in Italy differ from those in Brazil or in Japan, and the competitive battle going on among the leading banks in Italy is unrelated to the rivalry taking place in Brazil or Japan. Thus, with multicountry competition, rival firms battle for national championships and winning in one country does not necessarily signal the ability to fare well in other countries. In multicountry competition, the power of a company's strategy and resource capabilities in one country may not enhance its competitiveness

> **Core Concept**
>
> **Multicountry competition** exists when competition in one national market is not closely connected to competition in another national market—there is no global or world market, just a collection of self-contained country markets.

to the same degree in other countries where it operates. Moreover, any competitive advantage a company secures in one country is largely confined to that country; the spillover effects to other countries are minimal to nonexistent. Industries characterized by multicountry competition include radio and TV broadcasting, consumer banking, life insurance, apparel, metals fabrication, many types of food products (coffee, cereals, breads, canned goods, frozen foods), and retailing.

At the other extreme is **global competition,** in which prices and competitive conditions across country markets are strongly linked and the term *global* or *world market* has true meaning. In a globally competitive industry, much the same group of rival companies competes in many different countries, but especially so in countries where sales volumes are large and where having a competitive presence is strategically important to building a strong global position in the industry. Thus, a company's competitive position in one country both affects and is affected by its position in other countries. In global competition, a firm's overall competitive advantage grows out of its entire world-

wide operations; the competitive advantage it creates at its home base is supplemented by advantages growing out of its operations in other countries (having plants in low-wage countries, being able to transfer expertise from country to country, having the capability to serve customers who also have multinational operations, and having brand-name recognition in many parts of the world). Rival firms in globally competitive industries vie for worldwide leadership. Global competition exists in motor vehicles, television sets, tires, mobile phones, personal computers, copiers, watches, digital cameras, bicycles, and commercial aircraft.

An industry can have segments that are globally competitive and segments in which competition is country by country.[3] In the hotel/motel industry, for example, the low- and medium-priced segments are characterized by multicountry competition—competitors mainly serve travelers within the same country. In the business and luxury segments, however, competition is more globalized. Companies like Nikki, Marriott, Sheraton, and Hilton have hotels at many international locations, use worldwide reservation systems, and establish common quality and service standards to gain marketing advantages in serving businesspeople and other travelers who make frequent international trips. In lubricants, the marine-engine segment is globally competitive—ships move from port to port and require the same oil everywhere they stop. Brand reputations in marine lubricants have a global scope, and successful marine-engine lubricant producers (ExxonMobil, BP Amoco, and Shell) operate globally. In automotive motor oil, however, multicountry competition dominates—countries have different weather conditions and driving patterns, production of motor oil is subject to limited scale economies, shipping costs are high, and retail distribution channels differ markedly from country to country. Thus, domestic firms—like Quaker State and Pennzoil in the United States and Castrol in Great Britain—can be leaders in their home markets without competing globally.

It is also important to recognize that an industry can be in transition from multicountry competition to global competition. In a number of today's industries—beer and major home appliances are prime examples—leading domestic competitors have begun expanding into more and more foreign markets, often acquiring local companies or brands and integrating them into their operations. As some industry members start to build global brands and a global presence, other industry members find themselves pressured to follow the same strategic path—especially if establishing multinational operations results in important scale economies and a powerhouse brand name. As the industry consolidates to fewer players, such that many of the same companies find themselves in head-to-head competition in more and more country markets, global competition begins to replace multicountry competition.

At the same time, consumer tastes in a number of important product categories are converging across the world. Less diversity of tastes and preferences opens the way for companies to create global brands and sell essentially the same products in almost all countries of the world. Even in industries where consumer tastes remain fairly diverse, companies are learning to use "custom mass production" to economically create different versions of a product and thereby satisfy the tastes of people in different countries.

In addition to taking the obvious cultural and political differences between countries into account, a company has to shape its strategic approach to competing in foreign markets according to whether its industry is characterized by multicountry competition, global competition, or a transition from one to the other.

Strategy Options for Entering and Competing in Foreign Markets

There are a host of generic strategic options for a company that decides to expand outside its domestic market and compete internationally or globally:

1. *Maintain a national (one-country) production base and export goods to foreign markets,* using either company-owned or foreign-controlled forward distribution channels.

2. *License foreign firms to use the company's technology or to produce and distribute the company's products.*

3. *Employ a franchising strategy.*

4. *Follow a multicountry strategy,* varying the company's strategic approach (perhaps a little, perhaps a lot) from country to country in accordance with local conditions and differing buyer tastes and preferences.

5. *Follow a global strategy,* using essentially the same competitive strategy approach in all country markets where the company has a presence.

6. *Use strategic alliances or joint ventures with foreign companies as the primary vehicle for entering foreign markets,* and perhaps also use them as ongoing strategic arrangements aimed at maintaining or strengthening the company's competitiveness.

The following sections discuss the first five options in more detail; the sixth option is discussed in a separate section later in the chapter.

Export Strategies

Using domestic plants as a production base for exporting goods to foreign markets is an excellent initial strategy for pursuing international sales. It is a conservative way to test the international waters. The amount of capital needed to begin exporting is often quite minimal; existing production capacity may well be sufficient to make goods for export. With an export strategy, a manufacturer can limit its involvement in foreign markets by contracting with foreign wholesalers experienced in importing to handle the entire distribution and marketing function in their countries or regions of the world. If it is more advantageous to maintain control over these functions, however, a manufacturer can establish its own distribution and sales organizations in some or all of the target foreign markets. Either way, a home-based production and export strategy helps the firm minimize its direct investments in foreign countries. Such strategies are commonly favored by Chinese, Korean, and Italian companies—products are designed and manufactured at home and then distributed through local channels in the importing countries; the primary functions performed abroad relate chiefly to establishing a network of distributors and perhaps conducting sales promotion and brand awareness activities.

Whether an export strategy can be pursued successfully over the long run hinges on the relative cost-competitiveness of the home-country production base. In some industries, firms gain additional scale economies and learning-curve benefits from centralizing production in one or several giant plants whose output capability exceeds demand in any one country market; obviously, a company must export to capture such economies. However, an export strategy is vulnerable when (1) manufacturing costs in the home country are substantially higher than in foreign countries where rivals have plants, (2) the costs of shipping the product to distant foreign markets are relatively high, or (3) adverse shifts occur in currency exchange rates. Unless an exporter can both keep its production and shipping costs competitive with rivals and successfully hedge against unfavorable changes in currency exchange rates, its success will be limited.

Licensing Strategies

Licensing makes sense when a firm with valuable technical know-how or a unique patented product has neither the internal organizational capability nor the resources to enter foreign markets. Licensing also has the advantage of avoiding the risks of committing resources to country markets that are unfamiliar, politically volatile, economically unstable, or otherwise risky. By licensing the technology or the production rights to foreign-based firms, the firm does not have to bear the costs and risks of entering foreign markets on its own, yet it is able to generate income from royalties. The big disadvantage of licensing is the risk of providing valuable technological know-how to foreign companies and thereby losing some degree of control over its use; monitoring licensees and safeguarding the company's proprietary know-how can prove quite difficult in some circumstances. But if the royalty potential is considerable and the companies to whom the licenses are being granted are both trustworthy and reputable, then licensing can be a very attractive option. Many software and pharmaceutical companies use licensing strategies.

Franchising Strategies

While licensing works well for manufacturers and owners of proprietary technology, franchising is often better suited to the global expansion efforts of service and retailing enterprises. McDonald's, Yum! Brands (the parent of Pizza Hut, KFC, and Taco Bell), the UPS Store, Jani-King International (the world's largest commercial cleaning franchisor), Roto-Rooter, 7-Eleven, and Hilton Hotels have all used franchising to build a presence in foreign markets. Franchising has much the same advantages as licensing. The franchisee bears most of the costs and risks of establishing foreign locations; a franchisor has to expend only the resources to recruit, train, support, and monitor franchisees. The big problem a franchisor faces is maintaining quality control; foreign franchisees do not always exhibit strong commitment to consistency and standardization, especially when the local culture does not stress the same kinds of quality concerns. Another problem that can arise is whether to allow foreign franchisees to make modifications in the franchisor's product offering so as to better satisfy the tastes and expectations of local buyers. Should McDonald's allow its franchised units in Japan to modify Big Macs slightly to suit Japanese tastes? Should the franchised KFC units in China be permitted to substitute spices that appeal to Chinese consumers? Or should the same menu offerings be rigorously and unvaryingly required of all franchisees worldwide?

Localized Multicountry Strategies or a Global Strategy?

The issue of whether to vary the company's competitive approach to fit specific market conditions and buyer preferences in each host country or whether to employ essentially the same strategy in all countries is perhaps the foremost strategic issue that companies must address when they operate in two or more foreign markets. Figure 5.1 shows a company's options for resolving this issue.

Think-Local, Act-Local Approaches to Strategy Making   The bigger the differences in buyer tastes, cultural traditions, and market conditions in different countries, the stronger the case for a "think-local, act-local" approach to strategy making, in which a company tailors its product offerings and perhaps its basic competitive strategy to fit buyer tastes and market conditions in each country where it opts to compete. The strength of employing a set of *localized* or *multicountry strategies* is that the company's actions and business approaches are deliberately crafted to accommodate the differing tastes and expectations of buyers in each country and to stake out the most attractive market positions vis-à-vis local competitors. A think-local, act-local approach means giving local managers considerable strategy-making latitude. It means having plants produce different product versions for different local markets and adapting marketing and distribution to fit local customs and cultures. The bigger the country-to-country variations, the more that a company's overall strategy is a collection of its localized country strategies rather than a common or "global" strategy.

> **Core Concept**
>
> A *localized* or *multicountry strategy* is one where a company varies its product offering and competitive approach from country to country in an effort to be responsive to differing buyer preferences and market conditions.

A think-local, act-local approach to strategy making is essential when there are significant country-to-country differences in customer preferences and buying habits, when there are significant cross-country differences in distribution channels and marketing methods, when host governments enact regulations requiring that products sold locally meet strict manufacturing specifications or performance standards, and when the trade restrictions of host governments are so diverse and complicated that they preclude a uniform, coordinated worldwide market approach. With localized strategies, a company often has different product versions for different countries and sometimes sells them under different brand names. Sony markets a different Walkman in Norway than in Sweden to better meet the somewhat different preferences and habits of the users in each market. Castrol, a specialist in oil lubricants, has over 3,000 different formulas of lubricants, many of which have been tailored for different climates, vehicle types and uses, and equipment applications that characterize different country markets. In the food products industry, it is common for companies to vary the ingredients in their products and sell the localized versions under local brand names in order to cater to country-specific tastes and eating preferences. Motor vehicle manufacturers routinely produce smaller, more fuel-efficient vehicles for markets in Europe, where roads are often narrower and gasoline prices two to three times higher, than they produce for the North American market; the models they manufacture for the Asian market are different yet again. DaimlerChrysler, for example, equips all of the Jeep Grand Cherokees and many of its Mercedes cars sold in Europe with fuel-efficient diesel engines. The

Figure 5.1   A Company's Strategic Options for Dealing with Cross-Country Variations in Buyer Preferences and Market Conditions

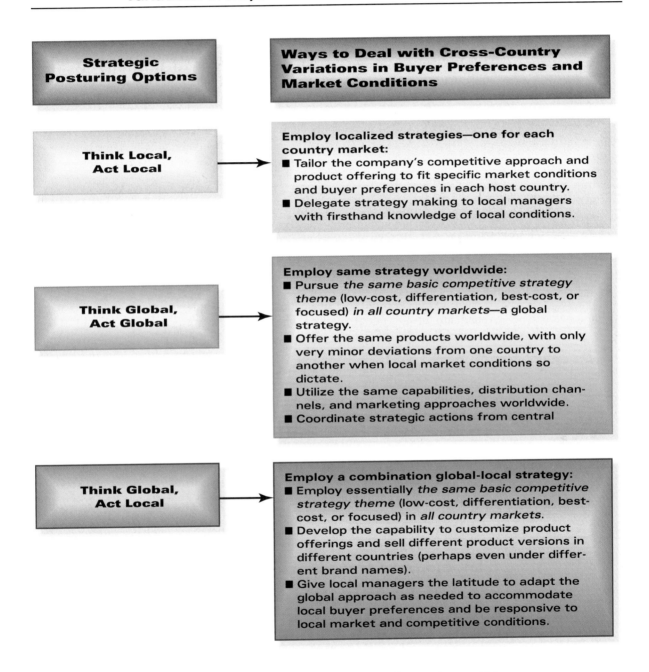

Buicks that General Motors sells in China are small compacts, whereas those sold in the United States are large family sedans and SUVs.

However, think-local, act-local strategies have two big drawbacks: they hinder transfer of a company's competencies and resources across country boundaries (since different competencies and capabilities may be used in different host countries), and they do not promote building a single, unified competitive advantage—especially one based on low cost. Companies employing highly localized or multicountry strategies face big hurdles in achieving low-cost leadership *unless* they find ways to customize their products and *still* be in a position to capture scale economies and learning-curve effects. Companies like Dell Computer and Toyota, because they have mass-customization production capabilities, can cost-effectively adapt their product offerings to local buyer tastes.

Think-Global, Act-Global Approaches to Strategy Making

While multicountry or localized strategies are best suited for industries where multicountry competition dominates and a fairly high degree of local responsiveness is competitively imperative, global strategies are best suited for globally competitive industries. A *global strategy* is one in which the company's approach is predominantly the same in all countries—it sells the same products under the same brand names everywhere, utilizes much the same types of distribution channels in all countries, and competes on the basis of the same capabilities and marketing approaches worldwide. Although the company's strategy or product offering may be adapted in very minor ways to accommodate specific situations in a few host countries, the company's fundamental competitive approach (low-cost, differentiation, best-cost, or focused) remains very much intact worldwide and local managers stick close to the global strategy. A "think-global, act-global" strategic theme prompts company managers to integrate and coordinate the company's strategic moves worldwide and to expand into most, if not all, nations where there is significant buyer demand. It puts considerable strategic emphasis on building a *global* brand name and aggressively pursuing opportunities to transfer ideas, new products, and capabilities from one country to another.[4] Indeed, with a think-global, act-global approach to strategy making, a company's operations in each country can be viewed as experiments that result in learning and in capabilities that may merit transfer to other country markets.

> **Core Concept**
>
> A *global strategy* is one in which a company employs the same basic competitive approach in all countries where it operates, sells much the same products everywhere, strives to build global brands, and coordinates its actions worldwide.

Whenever country-to-country differences are small enough to be accommodated within the framework of a global strategy, a global strategy is preferable to localized strategies because a company can more readily unify its operations and focus on establishing a brand image and reputation that is uniform from country to country. Moreover, with a global strategy a company is better able to focus its full resources on building the resource strengths and capabilities to secure a sustainable low-cost or differentiation-based competitive advantage over both domestic rivals and global rivals racing for world market leadership. Figure 5.2 summarizes the basic differences between a localized or multicountry strategy and a global strategy.

Think-Global, Act-Local Approaches to Strategy Making

Often, a company can accommodate cross-country variations in buyer tastes, local customs, and market conditions with a "think-global, act-local" approach to developing strategy. This middle-ground approach entails utilizing the same basic competitive theme (low-cost, differentiation, best-cost, or focused) in each country but allowing local managers the latitude to (1) incorporate whatever country-specific variations in product attributes are needed to best satisfy local buyers and (2) make whatever adjustments in production, distribution, and marketing are needed to be responsive to local market conditions and compete successfully against local rivals. Slightly different product versions sold under the same brand name may suffice to satisfy local tastes, and it may be feasible to accommodate these versions rather economically in the course of designing and manufacturing the company's product offerings. The build-to-order component of Dell Computer's strategy, for example, makes it simple for Dell to

Figure 5.2   How a Localized or Multicountry Strategy Differs from a Global Strategy

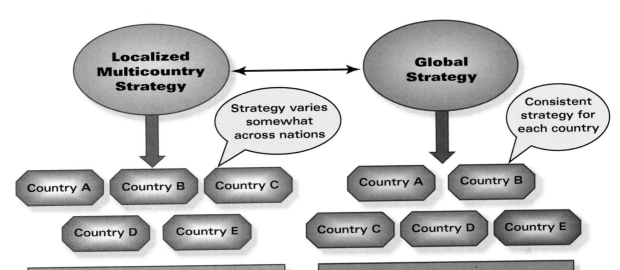

- Customize the company's competitive approach as needed to fit market and business circumstances in each host country—strong responsiveness to local conditions.
- Sell different product versions in different countries under different brand names—adapt product attributes to fit buyer tastes and preferences country by country.
- Scatter plants across many host countries, each producing product versions for local markets.
- Preferably use local suppliers (some local sources may be required by host government).
- Adapt marketing and distribution to local customs and culture of each country.
- Transfer competencies and capabilities from country to country where feasible.
- Give country managers fairly wide strategy-making latitude and autonomy over local operations.

- Pursue same basic competitive strategy worldwide (low-cost, differentiation, best-cost, focused low-cost, focused differentiation)-minimal responsiveness to local conditions.
- Sell same products under same brand name worldwide; focus efforts on building global brands as opposed to strengthening local/regional brands sold in local/regional markets.
- Locate plants on basis of maximum locational advantage, usually in countries where production costs are lowest but plants may be scattered if shipping costs are high or other locational advantages dominate.
- Use best suppliers from anywhere in world.
- Coordinate marketing and distribution worldwide; make minor adaptation to local countries where needed.
- Compete on basis of same technologies, competencies, and capabilities worldwide; stress rapid transfer of new ideas, products, and capabilities to other countries.
- Coordinate major strategic decisions worldwide; expect local managers to stick close to global strategy.

be responsive to how buyers in different parts of the world want their PCs equipped. However, Dell has not wavered in its strategy to sell direct to customers rather than through local retailers even though the majority of buyers in countries such as China are concerned about ordering online and prefer to personally inspect PCs at stores before making a purchase.

As a rule, most companies that operate multinationally endeavor to employ as global a strategy as customer needs and market conditions permit. Philips Electronics, the Netherlands-based electronics and consumer products company, operated successfully with localized strategies for many years but has recently begun moving more toward a unified strategy within the European Union and within North America.[5] Whirlpool has been globalizing its low-cost leadership strategy in home appliances for over 15 years, striving to standardize parts and components and move toward worldwide designs for as many of its appliance products as possible. But it has found it necessary to continue producing significantly different versions of refrigerators, washing machines, and cooking appliances for consumers in different regions of the world because the needs and tastes of local buyers for appliances of different sizes and designs have not converged sufficiently to permit standardization of Whirlpool's product offerings worldwide. General Motors began an initiative in 2004 to insist that its worldwide units share basic parts and work together to design vehicles that can be sold, with modest variations, anywhere in the world; by reducing the types of radios used in its cars and trucks from 270 to 50, it expected to save 40 percent in radio costs.

Global Spotlight 5.1 describes how two companies localize their strategies for competing in country markets across the world.

The Quest for Competitive Advantage in Foreign Markets

There are three important ways in which a firm can gain competitive advantage (or offset domestic disadvantages) by expanding outside its domestic market.[6] One, it can use location to lower costs or achieve greater product differentiation. Two, it can transfer competitively valuable competencies and capabilities from its domestic markets to foreign markets. And three, it can use cross-border coordination in ways that a domestic-only competitor cannot.

Using Location to Build Competitive Advantage

To use location to build competitive advantage, a company must consider two issues: (1) whether to concentrate each activity it performs in a few select countries or to disperse performance of the activity to many nations and (2) in which countries to locate particular activities.[7]

> Companies that compete multinationally can pursue competitive advantage in world markets by locating their value chain activities in whatever nations prove most advantageous.

When to Concentrate Activities in a Few Locations   Companies tend to concentrate their activities in a limited number of locations in the following circumstances:

- *When the costs of manufacturing or other activities are significantly lower in some geographic locations than in others:* For example, much of the world's athletic footwear is manufactured in Asia (China and Korea) because of low labor costs; much of the production of motherboards for PCs is located in Taiwan because of both low costs and the high-caliber technical skills of the Taiwanese labor force.

- *When there are significant scale economies:* The presence of significant economies of scale in components production or final assembly means that a company can gain major cost savings from operating a few superefficient plants as opposed to a host of small plants scattered across the world. Important marketing and distribution economies associated with multinational operations can also yield low-cost leadership. In situations where some competitors are intent on global dominance, being the worldwide low-cost provider is a powerful competitive advantage. Achieving low-cost provider status often requires a company to have the largest worldwide manufacturing share, with production centralized in one or a few world-scale plants in low-cost locations. Some companies even use such plants to manufacture units sold under the brand names of rivals. Manufacturing share (as distinct from brand share or market share) is significant because it provides more certain access to production-related scale economies. Japanese makers of VCRs, microwave ovens, TVs, and DVD players have used their large manufacturing share to establish a low-cost advantage.[8]

- *When there is a steep learning curve associated with performing an activity in a single location:* In some industries learning-curve effects in parts manufacture or assembly are so great that a company establishes one or two large plants from which it serves the world market. The key to riding down the learning curve is to concentrate production in a few locations to increase the accumulated volume at a plant (and thus the experience of the plant's workforce) as rapidly as possible.

■ *When certain locations have superior resources, allow better coordination of related activities, or offer other valuable advantages:* A research unit or a sophisticated production facility may be situated in a particular nation because of its pool of technically trained personnel. Samsung became a leader in memory chip technology by establishing a major R&D facility in Silicon Valley and transferring the know-how it gained back to headquarters and its plants in South Korea. Where just-in-time inventory practices yield big cost savings and/or where an assembly firm has long-term partnering arrangements with its key suppliers, parts manufacturing plants may be clustered around final assembly plants. An assembly plant may be located in a country in return for the host government's allowing freer import of components from large-scale, centralized parts plants located elsewhere. A customer service center or sales office may be opened in a particular country to help cultivate strong relationships with pivotal customers located nearby.

When to Disperse Activities across Many Locations   There are several instances when dispersing activities is more advantageous than concentrating them. Buyer-related activities—such as distribution to dealers, sales and advertising, and after-sale service—usually must take place close to buyers. This means physically locating the capability to perform such activities in every country market where a global firm has major customers (unless buyers in several adjoining countries can be served quickly from a nearby central location). For example, firms that make mining and oil-drilling equipment maintain operations in many international locations to support customers' needs for speedy equipment repair and technical assistance. The four biggest public accounting firms have numerous international offices to service the foreign operations of their multinational corporate clients. A global competitor that effectively disperses its buyer-related activities can gain a service-based competitive edge in world markets over rivals whose buyer-related activities are more concentrated—this is one reason the Big Four public accounting firms (PricewaterhouseCoopers, KPMG, Deloitte & Touche, and Ernst & Young) have been so successful relative to regional and national firms. Dispersing activities to many locations is also competitively advantageous when high transportation costs, diseconomies of large size, and trade barriers make it too expensive to operate from a central location. Many companies distribute their products from multiple locations to shorten delivery times to customers. In addition, it is strategically advantageous to disperse activities to hedge against the risks of fluctuating exchange rates; supply interruptions (due to strikes, mechanical failures, and transportation delays); and adverse political developments. Such risks are greater when activities are concentrated in a single location.

The classic reason for locating an activity in a particular country is low cost.[9] Even though multinational and global firms have strong reason to disperse buyer-related activities to many international locations, such activities as materials procurement, parts manufacture, finished-goods assembly, technology research, and new product development can frequently be decoupled from buyer locations and performed wherever advantage lies. Components can be made in Mexico; technology research done in Frankfurt; new products developed and tested in Phoenix; and assembly plants located in Spain, Brazil, Taiwan, or South Carolina. Capital can be raised in whatever country is available on the best terms.

Using Cross-Border Transfers of Competencies and Capabilities to Build Competitive Advantage

Expanding beyond domestic borders is a way for companies to leverage their core competencies and resource strengths, using them as a basis for competing successfully in additional country markets and growing sales and profits in the process. Transferring competencies, capabilities, and resource strengths from country to country contributes to the development of broader or deeper competencies and capabilities—ideally helping a company achieve dominating depth in some competitively valuable area. Dominating depth in a competitively valuable capability, resource, or value chain activity is a strong basis for sustainable competitive advantage over other multinational or global competitors and especially so over domestic-only competitors. A one-country customer base is often too small to support the resource buildup needed to achieve such depth; this is particularly true when the market is just emerging and sophisticated resources have not been required.

Whirlpool, the leading global manufacturer of home appliances, with plants in 14 countries and sales in 170 countries, has used the Internet to create a global information technology platform that allows the company to transfer key product innovations and production processes across regions and brands quickly and effectively. Wal-Mart is slowly but forcefully expanding its operations with a strategy that involves transferring its considerable domestic expertise in distribution and discount retailing to other countries. Its status as the largest, most resource-deep, and most sophisticated user of distribution-retailing know-how has served it well in building its foreign sales and profitability. But Wal-Mart is not racing madly to position itself in many foreign markets; rather, it is establishing a strong presence in select country markets and learning how to be successful in these before tackling entry into other major markets.

However, cross-border resource transfers are not a guaranteed recipe for success. Philips Electronics sells more color TVs and DVD recorders in Europe than any other company does; its biggest technological breakthrough was the compact disc, which it invented in 1982. Philips has worldwide sales of about 32 billion euros, but as of 2002 Philips had lost money for 15 consecutive years in its U.S. consumer electronics business. In the United States, the company's color TVs and DVD recorders (sold under the Magnavox and Philips brands) are slow sellers. Philips is notoriously slow in introducing new products into the U.S. market and has been struggling to develop an able sales force that can make inroads with U.S. electronics retailers and change its image as a clunky brand.

Using Cross-Border Coordination to Build Competitive Advantage

Coordinating company activities across different countries contributes to sustainable competitive advantage in several different ways.[10] Multinational and global competitors can choose where and how to challenge rivals. They may decide to retaliate against an aggressive rival in the country market where the rival has its biggest sales volume or its best profit margins in order to reduce the rival's financial resources for competing in other country markets. They may also decide to wage a price-cutting offensive against weak rivals in their home markets, capturing greater market share and subsidizing any short-term losses with profits earned in other country markets.

If a firm learns how to assemble its product more efficiently at, say, its Brazilian plant, the accumulated expertise can be quickly communicated via the Internet to assembly plants in other world locations. Knowledge gained in marketing a company's product in Great Britain can readily be exchanged with company personnel in New Zealand or Australia. A global or multinational manufacturer can shift production from a plant in one country to a plant in another to take advantage of exchange rate fluctuations, to enhance its leverage with host-country governments, and to respond to changing wage rates, components shortages, energy costs, or changes in tariffs and quotas. Production schedules can be coordinated worldwide; shipments can be diverted from one distribution center to another if sales rise unexpectedly in one place and fall in another.

Using Internet technology applications, companies can collect ideas for new and improved products from customers and sales and marketing personnel all over the world, permitting informed decisions about what can be standardized and what should be customized. Likewise, Internet technology can be used to involve the company's best design and engineering personnel (wherever they are located) in collectively coming up with next-generation products—it is becoming increasingly easy for company personnel in one location to use the Internet to collaborate closely with personnel in other locations in performing strategically relevant activities. Efficiencies can also be achieved by shifting workloads from locations where they are unusually heavy to locations where personnel are underutilized.

A company can enhance its brand reputation by consistently incorporating the same differentiating attributes in its products worldwide. The reputation for quality that Honda established worldwide first in motorcycles and then in automobiles gave it competitive advantage in positioning Honda lawn mowers at the upper end of the U.S. outdoor power equipment market—the Honda name gave the company instant credibility with U.S. buyers. Whirlpool's efforts to link its product R&D and manufacturing operations in North America, Latin America, Europe, and Asia allowed it to accelerate the discovery of innovative appliance features, coordinate the introduction of these features in the appliance products marketed in different countries, and create a cost-efficient worldwide supply chain. Whirlpool's conscious efforts to integrate and coordinate its various operations around the world have helped it become a low-cost producer and also speed product innovations to market, both of which have helped give Whirlpool advantages over rivals in designing and rapidly introducing innovative and attractively priced appliances worldwide.

Profit Sanctuaries, Cross-Market Subsidization, and Global Strategic Offensives

Core Concept

Companies with large, protected **profit sanctuaries** have competitive advantage over companies that don't have a protected sanctuary. Companies with multiple profit sanctuaries have a competitive advantage over companies with a single sanctuary.

Profit sanctuaries are country markets in which a company derives substantial profits because of its strong or protected market position. Japan, for example, is a profit sanctuary for most Japanese companies because trade barriers erected by the Japanese government effectively block foreign companies from competing for a large share of Japanese sales. Protected from the threat of foreign competition in their home market, Japanese companies can safely charge somewhat higher prices to their Japanese customers and thus earn attractively large profits on sales made in Japan. In most cases, a company's biggest and most

Figure 5.3 **Profit Sanctuary Potential of Domestic-Only, International, and Global Competitors** (profit sanctuary = 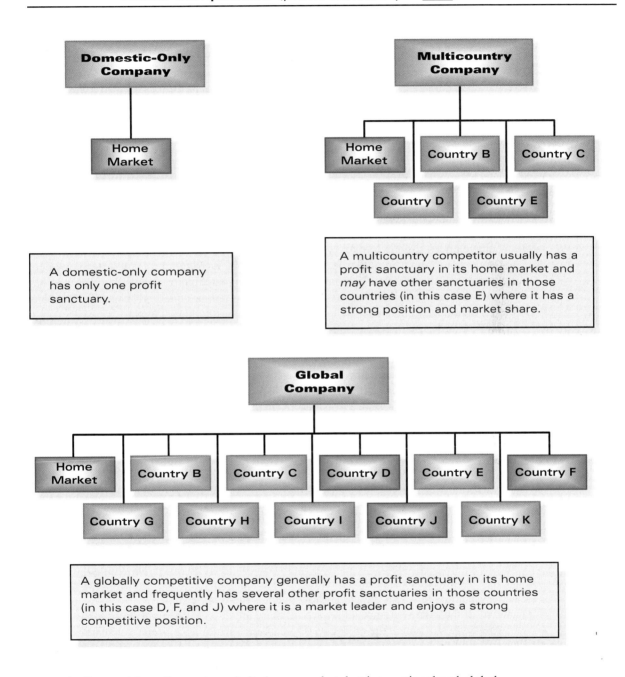)

Domestic-Only Company

Home Market

A domestic-only company has only one profit sanctuary.

Multicountry Company

Home Market | Country B | Country C

Country D | Country E

A multicountry competitor usually has a profit sanctuary in its home market and *may* have other sanctuaries in those countries (in this case E) where it has a strong position and market share.

Global Company

Home Market | Country B | Country C | Country D | Country E | Country F

Country G | Country H | Country I | Country J | Country K

A globally competitive company generally has a profit sanctuary in its home market and frequently has several other profit sanctuaries in those countries (in this case D, F, and J) where it is a market leader and enjoys a strong competitive position.

strategically crucial profit sanctuary is its home market, but international and global companies may also enjoy profit sanctuary status in other nations where they have a strong competitive position, big sales volume, and attractive profit margins. Companies that compete globally are likely to have more profit sanctuaries than companies that compete in just a few country markets; a domestic-only competitor, of course, can have only one profit sanctuary (see Figure 5.3).

Using Cross-Market Subsidization to Wage a Strategic Offensive

Profit sanctuaries are valuable competitive assets, providing the financial strength to support strategic offensives in selected country markets and aid a company's race for global market leadership. The added financial capability afforded by multiple profit sanctuaries gives a global or multicountry competitor the financial strength to wage a market offensive against a domestic competitor whose only profit sanctuary is its home market. Consider the case of a purely domestic company in competition with a company that has multiple profit sanctuaries and that is racing for global market leadership. The global company has the flexibility of lowballing its prices in the domestic company's home market and grabbing market share at the domestic company's expense, subsidizing razor-thin margins or even losses with the healthy profits earned in its profit sanctuaries—a practice called **cross-market subsidization.** The global company can adjust the depth of its price cutting to move in and capture market share quickly, or it can shave prices slightly to make gradual market inroads (perhaps over a decade or more) so as not to threaten domestic firms precipitously or trigger protectionist government actions. If the domestic company retaliates with matching price cuts, it exposes its entire revenue and profit base to erosion; its profits can be squeezed substantially and its competitive strength sapped, even if it is the domestic market leader.

> ### Core Concept
>
> **Cross-market subsidization**—supporting competitive offensives in one market with resources and profits diverted from operations in other markets—is a powerful competitive weapon.

Global Strategic Offensives

One of the most frequently used offensives is dumping goods at unreasonably low prices in the markets of foreign rivals. Such a strategy, if used repeatedly in the same country, can put domestic firms in dire financial straits or drive them out of business. Many governments have antidumping laws aimed at protecting domestic firms from unfair pricing by foreign rivals. In 2002, for example, the U.S. government imposed tariffs of up to 30 percent on selected steel products that Asian and European steel manufacturers were said to be selling at ultralow prices in the U.S. market.

But more usually the offensive strategies of companies that compete in multiple country markets with multiple products (several brands of cigarettes or different brands of food products) are more sophisticated. In deciding how to attack a multinational rival, a company needs to be alert to a competitor's incentive to react strongly and forcefully (often indicated by the size of the rival's market share or the growth potential of the market) and the rival's ability to defend its position (who has more clout in this arena—the attacker or the defender?).[11] The company also has to decide just how important it is to defeat the rival—how much is there to be gained?

If the offensive appears attractive, there are at least three options. One is a *direct onslaught,* in which the objective is to capture a major slice of market share and force the rival to retreat. Such onslaughts nearly always involve (1) price cutting (often without regard to immediate profits), (2) heavy expenditures on marketing, advertising, and promotion, and (3) attempts to gain the upper hand in one or more distribution channels. Direct onslaughts require a massive commitment of resources and make sense only if the market arena is highly attractive to the attacker.

A second type of offensive is the *contest,* which is more subtle and more focused than an onslaught. A contest offensive zeros in on a particular market segment that is unsuited to the capabilities and strengths of the defender and in which the attacker has a new next-generation or breakthrough product. Warner Brothers recently slashed the prices of its DVDs to such low levels that rivals were loath to follow suit; the move put enormous pressure on movie rental companies like Blockbuster. Warner Brothers' motive was to get people accustomed to buying DVDs instead of renting them. Such offensives often become a contest of whose strategy and business model will prevail.

A third offensive is the *feint*, a move designed to divert the defender's attention away from the attacker's main target. A good example of a feint offensive is Philip Morris's move in 1993 to reduce the U.S. price of its best-selling Marlboro cigarettes by 20 percent. Its rival R. J. Reynolds, which at the time was strapped for resources, was forced to institute matching price cuts on its Camel and Winston brands and scramble to defend its already eroding market share. But while Reynolds was busily engaged protecting its turf in the U.S. market, Philip Morris launched a major offensive into Russia and Eastern Europe (where cigarette sales were on the rise) and spent $800 million to get its brands established there. Philip Morris won the battle for market share in Eastern Europe hands down over Reynolds.

Strategic Alliances and Joint Ventures with Foreign Partners

Strategic alliances, joint ventures, and other cooperative agreements with foreign companies are a favorite and potentially fruitful means for entering a foreign market or strengthening a firm's competitiveness in world markets. Historically, export-minded firms in industrialized nations sought alliances with firms in less developed countries to import and market their products locally—such arrangements were often necessary to win approval for entry from the host country's government. More recently, companies from different parts of the world have formed strategic alliances and partnership arrangements to strengthen their mutual ability to serve whole continents and move toward more global market participation. Both Japanese and American companies are actively forming alliances with European companies to strengthen their ability to compete in the 25-nation European Union and to capitalize on the opening up of Eastern European markets. Many U.S. and European companies are allying with Asian companies in their efforts to enter markets in China, India, and other Asian countries.

Cooperative arrangements between domestic and foreign companies have strategic appeal for reasons besides gaining wider access to attractive country markets.[12] One is to capture economies of scale in production and/or marketing—cost reduction can be the difference that allows a company to be cost-competitive. By joining forces in producing components, assembling models, and marketing their products, companies can realize cost savings not achievable with their own small volumes. A second reason is to fill gaps in technical expertise and/or knowledge of local markets (buying habits and product preferences of consumers, local customs, and so on). Allies learn much from one another in performing joint research, sharing technological know-how, studying one another's manufacturing methods, and understanding how to tailor sales and marketing approaches to fit local cultures and traditions. A third reason is to share distribution facilities and dealer networks, thus mutually strengthening their access to buyers. Fourth, allied companies can direct their competitive energies more toward mutual rivals and less toward one another; teaming up may help them close the gap on leading companies. Fifth, companies opt to form

> Strategic alliances can help companies in globally competitive industries strengthen their competitive positions while still preserving their independence.

alliances with local companies (even where not legally required) because of the partner's local market knowledge and working relationships with key officials in the host-country government.[13] And, finally, alliances can be a particularly useful way to gain agreement on important technical standards—they have been used to arrive at standards for DVD players, assorted PC devices, Internet-related technologies, high-definition televisions, and mobile phones.

The Risks of Strategic Alliances with Foreign Partners

Alliances and joint ventures have their pitfalls, however. Achieving effective collaboration between independent companies, each with different motives and perhaps conflicting objectives, is not easy.[14] It requires many meetings of many people working in good faith over a period of time to iron out what is to be shared, what is to remain proprietary, and how the cooperative arrangements will work. Cross-border allies typically have to overcome language and cultural barriers; the communication, trust-building, and coordination costs are high in terms of management time. Often, once the bloom is off the rose, partners discover they have conflicting objectives and strategies and/or deep differences of opinion about how to proceed. Tensions build up, working relationships cool, and the hoped-for benefits never materialize.[15] Even if the alliance proves fruitful, there is the danger of becoming overly dependent on foreign partners for essential expertise and competitive capabilities. If a company is aiming for global market leadership and needs to develop capabilities of its own, then at some juncture cross-border merger or acquisition may have to be substituted for cross-border alliances and joint ventures.

Another major problem is getting alliance partners to make decisions fast enough to respond to rapidly advancing technological developments. Large telecommunications companies striving to achieve "global connectivity" have made extensive use of alliances and joint ventures with foreign counterparts, but they are encountering serious difficulty in reaching agreements on which of several technological approaches to employ and how to adapt to the swift pace at which all of the alternatives are advancing. AT&T and British Telecom, which formed a $10 billion joint venture to build an Internet-based global network linking 100 major cities, took eight months to find a CEO to head the project and even longer to come up with a name; the joint venture was abandoned in 2002.

Allies often find it difficult to collaborate effectively in competitively sensitive areas, thus raising questions about mutual trust and forthright exchanges of information and expertise. There can also be clashes of egos and company cultures. The key people on whom success or failure depends may have little personal chemistry, be unable to work closely together or form a partnership, or be unable to come to consensus. For example, an alliance between Northwest Airlines and KLM Royal Dutch Airlines linking their hubs in Detroit and Amsterdam resulted in a bitter feud among both companies' top officials (who, according to some reports, refused to speak to each other) and precipitated a battle for control of Northwest engineered by KLM. The dispute was rooted in a clash of business philosophies (the American way versus the European way), basic cultural differences, and an executive power struggle.[16]

> Strategic alliances are more effective in helping establish a beachhead of new opportunity in world markets than in achieving and sustaining global leadership.

Global Spotlight 5.2 relates the experiences of various companies with cross-border strategic alliances.

GLOBAL SPOTLIGHT 5.2

Cross-Border Strategic Alliances and Joint Ventures: Five High-Profile Examples

Of late, the number of strategic alliances and cooperative agreements of one kind or another among companies from different parts of the world has exploded. Five high-profile alliances are highlighted below:

- Two auto firms, Renault of France and Nissan of Japan, formed a broad-ranging global partnership in 1999 and then strengthened and expanded the alliance in 2002. The initial objective was to gain sales for new Nissan vehicles introduced in the European market, but the alliance now extends to full cooperation in all major areas, including the use of common platforms, joint development and use of engines and transmissions, fuel cell research, purchasing and use of common suppliers, and exchange of best practices. When the alliance was formed in 1999, Renault acquired a 36.8 percent ownership stake in Nissan; this was extended to 44.4 percent in 2002 when the alliance was expanded. Also, in 2002, the partners formed a jointly and equally owned strategic management company, named Renault-Nissan, to coordinate cooperative efforts.

- Verizon Wireless, one of the two largest cellphone carriers in the United States, is a joint venture between Verizon Communications and Vodafone AirTouch PLC (a leader in wireless communications in Europe). In February 2004, the alliance came close to unraveling when Vodafone made a $38 billion bid to acquire AT&T Wireless. The bid failed when Cingular Wireless (a joint venture between BellSouth Corp. and SBC Communications) bid $41 billion. But Vodafone's bid showed a desire to strike out on its own, control its destiny in the pivotal North American market, and further establish itself as a truly global cell-phone company.

- Microsoft and Fujitsu entered into an alliance in 2004 to collaborate on (1) the development of Fujitsu servers based on Intel's Itanium processors and (2) Microsoft's Windows Server 2003 and next-generation operating system (codenamed "Longhorn"); the objective was to improve interoperability between their respective software applications.

- Toyota and First Automotive Works, China's biggest automaker, entered into an alliance in 2002 to make luxury sedans, sport-utility vehicles, and minivehicles for the Chinese market. The intent was to make as many as 400,000 vehicles annually by 2010, an amount equal to the number that Volkswagen, the company with the largest share of the Chinese market, was making as of 2002. The alliance envisioned a joint investment of about $1.2 billion. At the time of the announced alliance, Toyota was lagging behind Honda, General Motors, and Volkswagen in setting up production facilities in China. Capturing a bigger share of the Chinese market was seen as crucial to Toyota's success in achieving its strategic objective of having a 15 percent share of the world's automotive market by 2010.

- General Electric (GE) and SNECMA, a French maker of jet engines, have had a long-standing 50-50 partnership in two ventures, one called CFM International, which makes jet engines to power aircraft made by Boeing and Airbus Industrie, and a second called CFAN, which functions as the exclusive supply source for wide-chord blades for commercial jet engines made by GE. The GE/SNECMA alliance has enjoyed great success since the 1970s. SNECMA was an attractive alliance partner from GE's perspective because it gave GE a France-based connection to help market the alliance's products to Airbus Industrie; likewise, SNECMA found the alliance attractive because it could serve as an entrée for marketing the alliance's products to Boeing. CFM International has sold over 15,000 jet engines since the early 1980s, winning market shares for large commercial aircraft of about 35 percent through the 1980s and market shares approaching 50 percent since 1995. As of mid-2004, CFM had delivered some 14,200 jet engines for aircraft deployed by 390 customers.

Source: Company Web sites and press releases; and Yves L. Doz and Gary Hamel, *Alliance Advantage: The Art of Creating Value through Partnering* (Boston: Harvard Business School Press, 1998).

Making the Most of Strategic Alliances with Foreign Partners

Whether or not a company realizes the potential of alliances and collaborative partnerships with foreign enterprises seems to be a function of six factors:[17]

1. *Picking a good partner:* A good partner not only has the desired expertise and capabilities but also shares the company's vision about the purpose of the alliance. Experience indicates that it is generally wise to avoid a partnership in which there is strong potential of direct competition because of overlapping product lines or other conflicting interests—agreements to jointly market each other's products hold much potential for conflict unless the products are complements rather than substitutes and unless there is good chemistry among key personnel.

2. *Being sensitive to cultural differences:* Unless the outsider exhibits respect for the local culture and local business practices, productive working relationships are unlikely to emerge.

3. *Recognizing that the alliance must benefit both sides:* Information must be shared as well as gained, and the relationship must remain forthright and trustful. Many alliances fail because one or both partners grow unhappy with what they are learning. Also, if either partner plays games with information or tries to take advantage of the other, the resulting friction can quickly erode the value of further collaboration.

4. *Ensuring that both parties live up to their commitments:* Both parties have to deliver on their commitments for the alliance to produce the intended benefits. The division of work has to be perceived as fairly apportioned, and the caliber of the benefits received on both sides has to be perceived as adequate.

5. *Structuring the decision-making process so that actions can be taken swiftly when needed:* In many instances, the fast pace of technological and competitive changes dictates an equally fast decision-making process. If the parties get bogged down in discussion or in gaining internal approval from higher-ups, the alliance can turn into an anchor of delay and inaction.

6. *Managing the learning process and then adjusting the alliance agreement over time to fit new circumstances:* In today's fast-moving markets, few alliances can succeed by holding only to initial plans. One of the keys to long-lasting success is learning to adapt to change; the terms and objectives of the alliance must be adjusted as needed.

Most alliances with foreign companies that aim at technology sharing or providing market access turn out to be temporary, fulfilling their purpose after a few years because the benefits of mutual learning have occurred and because the businesses of both partners have developed to the point where they are ready to go their own ways. In such cases, it is important for the company to learn thoroughly and rapidly about a partner's technology, business practices, and organizational capabilities and then transfer valuable ideas and practices into its own operations promptly. Although long-term alliances sometimes prove mutually beneficial, most partners don't hesitate to terminate the alliance and go it alone when the payoffs run out.

Alliances are more likely to be long-lasting when (1) they involve collaboration with suppliers or distribution allies and each party's contribution involves activities in different portions of the industry value chain or (2) both parties conclude that continued collaboration is in their mutual interest, perhaps because new opportunities for learning are emerging or perhaps because further collaboration will allow each partner to extend its market reach beyond what it could accomplish on its own.

In 2004, Coca-Cola developed a strategy to dramatically boost its market penetration in such emerging countries as China and India, where annual growth had recently dropped from about 30 percent in 1994–1998 to 10 to 12 percent in 2001–2003. Prior to 2003 Coca-Cola had focused its marketing efforts in China and India on making its drinks attractive to status-seeking young people in urbanized areas (cities with populations of 500,000 or more), but as annual sales growth steadily declined in these areas during the 1998–2003 period, Coca-Cola management decided a new, bolder strategy aimed at more rural areas of these countries was needed. It began promoting the sales of small 6.5-ounce returnable glass bottles of Coke in smaller cities and outlying towns with populations in the 50,000 to 250,000 range. Returnable bottles (which could be reused about 20 times) were much cheaper than plastic bottles or aluminum cans, and the savings in packaging costs were enough to slash the price of single-serve bottles to 1 yuan in China and about 5 rupees in India, the equivalent in both cases of about 12 cents. Initial results were promising. Despite the fact that annual disposable incomes in these rural areas were often less than $1,000 annually, the 1-yuan and 5-rupee prices proved attractive. Sales of the small bottles of Coke for one local Coca-Cola distributor in Anning, China, soon accounted for two-thirds of the distributor's total sales; a local distributor in India boosted sales from 9,000 cases in 2002 to 27,000 cases in 2003 and was expecting sales of 45,000 cases in 2004. Coca-Cola management expected that greater emphasis on rural sales would boost Coca-Cola's growth rate in Asia to close to 20 percent and help boost worldwide volume growth to the 3 to 5 percent range as opposed to the paltry 1 percent rate experienced in 2003.

However, PepsiCo, which had a market share of about 27 percent in China, versus Coca-Cola's 55 percent, was skeptical of Coca-Cola's rural strategy and continued with its all-urban strategy of marketing to consumers in China's 165 cities with populations greater than 1 million people.

Source: Wall Street Journal. Eastern Edition [staff produced copy only] by Gabriel Kahn and Eric Bellman. Copyright 2004 by Dow Jones & Co. Inc. Reproduced with permission of Dow Jones & Co. Inc. in the format textbook via Copyright Clearance Center.

Competing in Emerging Foreign Markets

Companies racing for global leadership have to consider competing in emerging markets like China, India, Brazil, Indonesia, and Mexico—countries where the business risks are considerable but where the opportunities for growth are huge, especially as their economies develop and living standards climb toward levels in the industrialized world.[18] With the world now comprising more than 6 billion people—fully one-third of whom are in India and China, and hundreds of millions more in other less developed countries of Asia and Latin America—a company that aspires to world market leadership (or to sustained rapid growth) cannot ignore the market opportunities or the base of technical and managerial talent such countries offer. For example, in 2003 China's population of 1.3 billion people consumed nearly 33 percent of the world's annual cotton production, 51 percent of the world's pork, 35 percent of all the cigarettes, 31 percent of worldwide coal production, 27 percent of the world's steel production, 19 percent of the aluminum, 23 percent of the TVs, 20 percent of the cell phones, and 18 percent of the washing machines.[19] China is the world's largest consumer of copper, aluminum, and cement and the second-largest importer of oil; it is the world's biggest market for mobile phones and the second biggest for PCs, plus it is on track to become the second-largest market for motor vehicles by 2010. No company that aspires to global market leadership can thus afford to ignore the strategic importance of establishing a competitive market position in China, India, other parts of the Asian Pacific, Latin America, and Eastern Europe. Global Spotlight 5.3 describes Coca-Cola's strategy to boost its sales and market share in China.

Tailoring products for big emerging markets, however, often involves more than making minor product changes and becoming more familiar with local cultures.[20] Ford's attempt to sell a Ford Escort in India at a price of $21,000—a luxury-car price, given that India's best-selling Maruti-Suzuki model sold at the time for $10,000 or less and that fewer than 10 percent of Indian households have annual purchasing power greater than $20,000—met with a less-than-enthusiastic market response. McDonald's has had to offer vegetable burgers in parts of Asia and to rethink its prices, which are often high by local standards and affordable only by the well-to-do. Kellogg has struggled to introduce its cereals successfully because consumers in many less developed countries do not eat cereal for breakfast—changing habits is difficult and expensive. Coca-Cola has found that advertising its world image does not strike a chord with the local populace in a number of emerging country markets. Single-serving packages of detergents, shampoos, pickles, cough syrup, and cooking oils are very popular in India because they allow buyers to conserve cash by purchasing only what they need immediately.

Strategy Implications

Consumers in emerging markets are highly focused on price, in many cases giving local low-cost competitors the edge. Companies wishing to succeed in these markets have to attract buyers with bargain prices as well as better products—an approach that can entail a radical departure from the strategy used in other parts of the world. If building a market for the company's products is likely to be a long-term process and involve reeducation of consumers, a company must not only be patient with regard to sizable revenues and profits but also be prepared in the interim to invest sizable sums to alter buying habits and tastes. Also, specially designed or packaged products may be needed to accommodate local market circumstances. For example, when Unilever entered the market for laundry detergents in India, it realized that 80 percent of the population could not afford the brands it was selling to affluent consumers there (as well as in wealthier countries). To compete against a very low-priced detergent made by a local company, Unilever came up with a low-cost formula that was not harsh to the skin, constructed new low-cost production facilities, packaged the detergent (named Wheel) in single-use amounts so that it could be sold very cheaply, distributed the product to local merchants by handcarts, and crafted an economical marketing campaign that included painted signs on buildings and demonstrations near stores—the new brand quickly captured $100 million in sales and was the number-one detergent brand in India in 2004 based on dollar sales. Unilever later replicated the strategy with low-priced packets of shampoos and deodorants in India and in South America with a detergent brand named Ala.

> Profitability in emerging markets rarely comes quickly or easily—new entrants have to be very sensitive to local conditions, be willing to invest in developing the market for their products over the long term, and be patient in earning a profit.

Because managing a new venture in an emerging market requires a blend of global knowledge and local sensitivity to the culture and business practices, the management team must usually consist of a mix of expatriate and local managers. Expatriate managers are needed to transfer technology, business practices, and the corporate culture and to serve as conduits for the flow of information between the corporate office and local operations; local managers bring needed understanding of the area's nuances and deep commitment to its market.

Defending against Global Giants: Strategies for Local Companies in Emerging Markets

If large, opportunity-seeking, resource-rich companies are looking to enter emerging markets, what strategy options can local companies use to survive? As it turns out, the prospects for local companies facing global giants are by no means grim. Their optimal strategic approach hinges on (1) whether their competitive assets are suitable only for the home market or can be transferred abroad and (2) whether industry pressures to move toward global competition are strong or weak. The four generic options are shown in Figure 5.4.

Using Home-Field Advantages

When the pressures for global competition are low and a local firm has competitive strengths well suited to the local market, a good strategy option is to concentrate on the advantages enjoyed in the home market, cater to customers who prefer a local touch, and accept the loss of customers attracted to global brands.[21] A local company may be able to astutely exploit its local orientation—its familiarity with local preferences, its expertise in traditional products, its long-standing customer relationships. In many cases, a local company enjoys a significant cost advantage over global rivals (perhaps because of simpler product design or lower operating and overhead costs), allowing it

Figure 5.4   Strategy Options for Local Companies in Competing against Global Companies

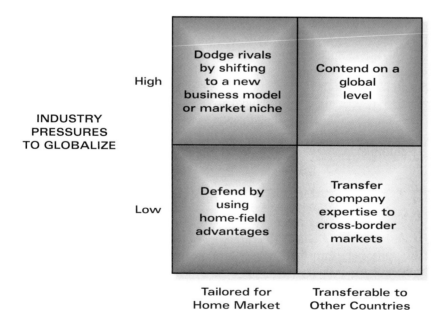

to compete on the basis of price. Its global competitors often aim their products at upper- and middle-income urban buyers, who tend to be more fashion-conscious, more willing to experiment with new products, and more attracted to global brands.

Another competitive approach is to cater to the local market in ways that pose difficulties for global rivals. A small Middle Eastern cell-phone manufacturer competes successfully against industry giants Nokia, Samsung, and Motorola by selling a model designed especially for Muslims—it is loaded with the Koran, alerts people at prayer times, and is equipped with a compass that points them toward Mecca. Two Chinese PC makers, Lenovo and Founder Electronics, have been able to retain their market share lead in China over global leader Dell because Chinese PC buyers strongly prefer to personally inspect PCs before making a purchase; thus Dell with its build-to-order, sell-direct business model is at a competitive disadvantage against Lenovo and Founder, both of which have vast retail dealer networks across China that allow prospective buyers to check out their offerings in nearby stores. Bajaj Auto, India's largest producer of scooters, has defended its turf against Honda (which entered the Indian market with local joint-venture partner Hero Group to sell scooters, motorcycles, and other vehicles on the basis of its superior technology, quality, and brand appeal) by focusing on buyers who want low-cost, durable scooters and easy access to maintenance in the countryside. Bajaj designed a rugged, cheap-to-build scooter for India's rough roads, increased its investments in R&D to improve reliability and quality, and created an extensive network of distributors and roadside-mechanic stalls, a strategic approach that allowed it to remain the market leader with a 70 to 75 percent market share through 2004 despite growing unit sales of Hero Honda motorcycles and scooters.

Transferring the Company's Expertise to Cross-Border Markets

When a company has resource strengths and capabilities suitable for competing in other country markets, launching initiatives to transfer its expertise to cross-border markets becomes a viable strategic option.[22] Televisa, Mexico's largest media company, used its expertise in Spanish culture and linguistics to become the world's most prolific producer of Spanish-language soap operas. Jollibee Foods, a family-owned company with 56 percent of the fast-food business in the Philippines, combated McDonald's entry first by upgrading service and delivery standards and then by using its expertise in seasoning hamburgers with garlic and soy sauce and making noodle and rice meals with fish to open outlets catering to Asian residents in Hong Kong, the Middle East, and California.

Shifting to a New Business Model or Market Niche

When industry pressures to globalize are high, any of the following three options makes the most sense: (1) shift the business to a piece of the industry value chain where the firm's expertise and resources provide competitive advantage, (2) enter into a joint venture with a globally competitive partner, or (3) sell out to (be acquired by) a global entrant into the home market that concludes the company would be a good entry vehicle.[23] When Microsoft entered China, local software developers shifted from cloning Windows products to developing Windows application software customized to the Chinese market. When the Russian PC market opened to IBM, Compaq, and

Hewlett-Packard, local Russian PC maker Vist focused on assembling very low-cost models, marketing them through exclusive distribution agreements with selected local retailers, and opening company-owned full-service centers in dozens of Russian cities. Vist focused on providing low-cost PCs, giving lengthy warranties, and catering to buyers who felt the need for local service and support. Vist's strategy allowed it to remain the market leader, with a 20 percent share. An India-based electronics company has been able to carve out a market niche for itself by developing an all-in-one business machine designed especially for India's 1.2 million small shopkeepers that tolerates heat, dust, and power outages and that sells for a modest $180 for the smallest of its three models.[24]

Contending on a Global Level

If a local company in an emerging market has transferable resources and capabilities, it can sometimes launch successful initiatives to meet the pressures for globalization head-on and start to compete on a global level itself.[25] When General Motors (GM) decided to outsource the production of radiator caps for all of its North American vehicles, Sundaram Fasteners of India pursued the opportunity; it purchased one of GM's radiator cap production lines, moved it to India, and became GM's sole supplier of radiator caps in North America—at 5 million units a year. As a participant in GM's supplier network, Sundaram learned about emerging technical standards, built its capabilities, and became one of the first Indian companies to achieve QS 9000 certification, a quality standard that GM now requires for all suppliers. Sundaram's acquired expertise in quality standards enabled it then to pursue opportunities to supply automotive parts in Japan and Europe. Chinese communications equipment maker Huawei has captured a 16 percent share in the global market for Internet routers because its prices are up to 50 percent lower than industry leaders like Cisco Systems; Huawei's success in low-priced Internet networking gear has allowed it to expand aggressively outside China, including such country markets as Russia and Brazil, and achieve the number-two worldwide market share in broadband networking gear.[26]

Key Points

Most issues in competitive strategy that apply to domestic companies apply also to companies that compete internationally. But there are four strategic issues unique to competing across national boundaries:

1. Whether to customize the company's offerings in each different country market to match the tastes and preferences of local buyers or offer a mostly standardized product worldwide.

2. Whether to employ essentially the same basic competitive strategy in all countries or modify the strategy country by country to fit the specific market conditions and competitive circumstances the company encounters.

3. Where to locate the company's production facilities, distribution centers, and customer service operations so as to realize the greatest locational advantages.

4. Whether and how to efficiently transfer the company's resource strengths and capabilities from one country to another in an effort to secure competitive advantage.

Multicountry competition exists when competition in one national market is independent of competition in another national market—there is no "international market," just a collection of self-contained country markets. Global competition exists when competitive conditions across national markets are linked strongly enough to form a true world market and when leading competitors compete head-to-head in many different countries.

In posturing to compete in foreign markets, a company has three basic options: (1) a think-local, act-local approach to crafting a strategy, (2) a think-global, act-global approach to crafting a strategy, and (3) a combination think-global, act-local approach. A think-local, act-local, or multicountry, strategy is appropriate for industries where multicountry competition dominates; a localized approach to strategy making calls for a company to vary its product offering and competitive approach from country to country in order to accommodate differing buyer preferences and market conditions. A think-global, act-global approach (or global strategy) works best in markets that are globally competitive or beginning to globalize; global strategies involve employing the same basic competitive approach (low-cost, differentiation, best-cost, focused) in all country markets and marketing essentially the same products under the same brand names in all countries where the company operates. A think-global, act-local approach can be used when it is feasible for a company to employ essentially the same basic competitive strategy in all markets but still customize its product offering and some aspect of its operations to fit local market circumstances.

Other strategy options for competing in world markets include maintaining a national (one-country) production base and exporting goods to foreign markets, licensing foreign firms to use the company's technology or produce and distribute the company's products, employing a franchising strategy, and using strategic alliances or other collaborative partnerships to enter a foreign market or strengthen a firm's competitiveness in world markets.

There are three ways in which a firm can gain competitive advantage (or offset domestic disadvantages) in global markets. One way involves locating various value chain activities among nations in a manner that lowers costs or achieves greater product differentiation. A second way involves efficient and effective transfer of competitively valuable competencies and capabilities from its domestic markets to foreign markets. A third way draws on a multinational or global competitor's ability to deepen or broaden its resource strengths and capabilities and to coordinate its dispersed activities in ways that a domestic-only competitor cannot.

Profit sanctuaries are country markets in which a company derives substantial profits because of its strong or protected market position. They are valuable competitive assets, providing the financial strength to support competitive offensives in one market with resources and profits diverted from operations in other markets, and aid a company's race for global market leadership. Companies with large, protected profit sanctuaries have a competitive advantage over companies that don't have a protected sanctuary. Companies with multiple profit sanctuaries have a competitive advantage over companies with a single sanctuary. The cross-market subsidization capabilities provided by multiple profit sanctuaries gives a global or international competitor a powerful offensive weapon.

The outlook for local companies in emerging markets wishing to survive against the entry of global giants is by no means grim. The optimal strategic approach hinges on whether a firm's competitive assets are suitable only for the home market or can be transferred abroad and on whether industry pressures to move toward global competition are strong or weak. Local companies can compete against global newcomers by

(1) defending on the basis of home-field advantages, (2) transferring their expertise to cross-border markets, (3) dodging large rivals by shifting to a new business model or market niche, or (4) launching initiatives to compete on a global level themselves.

Exercises

1. Log on to www.caterpillar.com and search for information about Caterpillar's strategy in foreign markets. Is the company pursuing a global strategy or a localized multicountry strategy? Support your answer.

2. Assume you are in charge of developing the strategy for a multinational company selling products in some 50 different countries around the world. One of the issues you face is whether to employ a multicountry strategy or a global strategy.

   a) If your company's product is personal computers, do you think it would make better strategic sense to employ a multicountry strategy or a global strategy? Why?

   b) If your company's product is dry soup mixes and canned soups, would a multicountry strategy seem to be more advisable than a global strategy? Why?

   c) If your company's product is washing machines, would it seem to make more sense to pursue a multicountry strategy or a global strategy? Why?

   d) If your company's product is basic work tools (hammers, screwdrivers, pliers, wrenches, saws), would a multicountry strategy or a global strategy seem to have more appeal? Why?

CHAPTER 6

Diversification

Strategies for Managing a Group of Businesses

To acquire or not to acquire: that is the question.

—*Robert J. Terry*

Fit between a parent and its businesses is a two-edged sword: a good fit can create value; a bad one can destroy it.

—*Andrew Campbell, Michael Goold, and Marcus Alexander*

Achieving superior performance through diversification is largely based on relatedness.

—*Philippe Very*

Make winners out of every business in your company. Don't carry losers.

—*Jack Welch, former CEO, General Electric*

We measure each of our businesses against strict criteria: growth, margin, and return-on-capital hurdle rate, and does it have the ability to become number one or two in its industry? We are quite pragmatic. If a business does not contribute to our overall vision, it has to go.

—*Richard Wambold, CEO, Pactiv*

In this chapter, we move up one level in the strategy-making hierarchy, from strategy making in a single-business enterprise to strategy making in a diversified enterprise. Because a diversified company is a collection of individual businesses, the strategy-making task is more complicated. In a one-business company, managers have to come up with a plan for competing successfully in only a single industry environment—the result is what we labeled in Chapter 1 as *business strategy* (or *business-level strategy*). But in a diversified company, the strategy-making challenge involves assessing multiple industry environments and developing a *set* of business strategies, one for each industry arena in which the diversified company operates. And top executives at a diversified company must still go one step further and devise a companywide or *corporate strategy* for improving the attractiveness and performance of the company's overall business lineup and for making a rational business whole out of its collection of individual businesses.

In most diversified companies, corporate-level executives delegate considerable strategy-making authority to the heads of each business, usually giving them the latitude to craft a business strategy suited to their particular industry and competitive circumstances and holding them accountable for producing good results. But the task of crafting a diversified company's overall or corporate strategy falls squarely in the lap of top-level executives and involves four distinct facets:

1. *Picking new industries to enter and deciding on the means of entry:* The first concerns in diversifying are what new industries to get into and whether to enter by starting a new business from the ground up, acquiring a company already in the target industry, or forming a joint venture or strategic alliance with another company. A company can diversify narrowly into a few industries or broadly into many industries. The choice of whether to enter an industry via a start-up operation, a joint venture, or the acquisition of an established leader, an up-and-coming company, or a troubled company with turnaround potential shapes what position the company will initially stake out for itself.

2. *Initiating actions to boost the combined performance of the businesses the firm has entered:* As positions are created in the chosen industries, corporate strategists typically zero in on ways to strengthen the long-term competitive positions and profits of the businesses the firm has invested in. Corporate parents can help their business subsidiaries by providing financial resources, by supplying missing skills or technological know-how or managerial expertise to better perform key value chain activities, and by providing new avenues for cost reduction. They can also acquire another company in the same industry and merge the two operations into a stronger business or acquire new businesses that strongly complement existing businesses. Typically, a company will pursue rapid-growth strategies in its most promising businesses, initiate turnaround efforts in weak-performing businesses with potential, and divest businesses that are no longer attractive or that don't fit into management's long-range plans.

3. *Pursuing opportunities to leverage cross-business value chain relationships and strategic fits into competitive advantage:* A company that diversifies into businesses with competitively important value chain matchups (pertaining to technology, supply chain logistics, production, overlapping distribution channels, or common customers) gains competitive advantage potential not open to a company that diversifies into businesses whose value chains are totally unrelated. Capturing this competitive advantage potential requires that corporate strategists spend considerable time trying to capitalize on such cross-business opportunities

as transferring skills or technology from one business to another, reducing costs via sharing use of common facilities and resources, and utilizing the company's well-known brand names and distribution muscle to grow the sales of newly acquired products.

4. *Establishing investment priorities and steering corporate resources into the most attractive business units:* A diversified company's different businesses are usually not equally attractive from the standpoint of investing additional funds. It is incumbent on corporate management to (a) decide on the priorities for investing capital in the company's different businesses, (b) channel resources into areas where earnings potentials are higher and away from areas where they are lower, and (c) divest business units that are chronically poor performers or are in an increasingly unattractive industry. Divesting poor performers and businesses in unattractive industries frees up unproductive investments either for redeployment to promising business units or for financing attractive new acquisitions.

The demanding and time-consuming nature of these four tasks explains why corporate executives generally refrain from becoming immersed in the details of crafting and implementing business-level strategies, preferring instead to delegate lead responsibility for business strategy to the heads of each business unit.

In the first portion of this chapter we describe the various paths through which a company can become diversified, and we explain how a company can use diversification to create or compound competitive advantage for its business units. The second part of the chapter surveys techniques and procedures for assessing the attractiveness of a diversified company's business lineup, evaluating its diversification strategy, and coming up with its next set of strategic moves. In the chapter's concluding section, we survey the strategic options open to already diversified companies.

When to Diversify

As long as a company has its hands full trying to capitalize on profitable growth opportunities in its present industry, there is no urgency to pursue diversification. The big risk of a single-business company, of course, is having all of the firm's eggs in one industry basket. If demand for the industry's product is eroded by the appearance of alternative technologies, substitute products, or fast-shifting buyer preferences, or if the industry becomes competitively unattractive and unprofitable, then a company's prospects can quickly dim. Consider, for example, what digital cameras are doing to companies dependent on making camera film and doing film processing, what CD and DVD technology have done to producers of cassette tapes and 3.5-inch disks, and what mobile phones are doing to AT&T's long-distance business and the need for ground-line telephones in homes.

Thus, diversifying into new industries always merits strong consideration whenever a single-business company encounters diminishing market opportunities and stagnating sales in its principal business. But there are four other instances in which a company becomes a prime candidate for diversifying:[1]

1. When it spots opportunities for expanding into industries whose technologies and products complement its present business.

2. When it can leverage existing competencies and capabilities by expanding into businesses where these same resource strengths are key success factors and valuable competitive assets.

3. When diversifying into closely related businesses opens new avenues for reducing costs.

4. When it has a powerful and well-known brand name that can be transferred to the products of other businesses and thereby used as a lever for driving up the sales and profits of such businesses.

The decision to diversify presents wide-open possibilities. A company can diversify into closely related businesses or into totally unrelated businesses. It can diversify its present revenue and earning base to a small extent (such that new businesses account for less than 15 percent of companywide revenues and profits) or to a major extent (such that new businesses produce 30 or more percent of revenues and profits). It can move into one or two large new businesses or a greater number of small ones. It can achieve multibusiness/multiindustry status by acquiring an existing company already in a business/industry it wants to enter, starting up a new business subsidiary from scratch, or entering into a joint venture.

Building Shareholder Value: The Ultimate Justification for Diversifying

Diversification must do more for a company than simply spread its business risk across various industries. In principle, diversification cannot be considered a success unless it results in *added shareholder value*—value that shareholders cannot capture on their own by purchasing stock in companies in different industries or investing in mutual funds so as to spread their investments across several industries.

For there to be reasonable expectations that a company's diversification efforts can produce added value, a move to diversify into a new business must pass three tests:[2]

1. *The industry attractiveness test:* The industry to be entered must be attractive enough to yield consistently good returns on investment. Whether an industry is attractive depends chiefly on the presence of industry and competitive conditions that are conducive to earning as-good or better profits and return on investment than the company is earning in its present business(es). It is hard to justify diversifying into an industry where profit expectations are *lower* than those in the company's present businesses.

2. *The cost-of-entry test:* The cost to enter the target industry must not be so high as to erode the potential for good profitability. A catch-22 can prevail here, however. The more attractive an industry's prospects are for growth and good long-term profitability, the more expensive it can be to get into. Entry barriers for start-up companies are likely to be high in attractive industries; were barriers low, a rush of new entrants would soon erode the potential for high profitability. And buying a well-positioned company in an appealing industry often entails a high acquisition cost that makes passing the cost-of-entry test less likely. For instance, suppose that the price to purchase a company is $3 million and that the company is earning after-tax profits of $200,000 on an equity investment of $1 million (a 20 percent annual return). Simple arithmetic requires that the profits be tripled if the purchaser (paying $3 million) is to earn the same 20 percent return. Building the acquired

firm's earnings from \$200,000 to \$600,000 annually could take several years—and require additional investment on which the purchaser would also have to earn a 20 percent return. Since the owners of a successful and growing company usually demand a price that reflects their business's profit prospects, it's easy for such an acquisition to fail the cost-of-entry test.

3. *The better-off test:* Diversifying into a new business must offer potential for the company's existing businesses and the new business to perform better together under a single corporate umbrella than they would perform operating as independent, stand-alone businesses. For example, let's say that company A diversifies by purchasing company B in another industry. If A and B's consolidated profits in the years to come prove no greater than what each could have earned on its own, then A's diversification won't provide its shareholders with added value. Company A's shareholders could have achieved the same 1 + 1 = 2 result by merely purchasing stock in company B. Shareholder value is not created by diversification unless it produces a 1 + 1 = 3 effect, where the businesses perform better together as part of the same firm than they could have performed as independent companies.

> **Core Concept**
>
> Creating added value for shareholders via diversification requires building a multibusiness company where the whole is greater than the sum of its parts.

Diversification moves that satisfy all three tests have the greatest potential to grow shareholder value over the long term. Diversification moves that can pass only one or two tests are suspect.

Strategies for Entering New Businesses

Entry into new businesses can take any of three forms: acquisition, internal start-up, or joint ventures or strategic partnerships.

Acquisition of an Existing Business

Acquisition is the most popular means of diversifying into another industry. Not only is it quicker than trying to launch a brand-new operation, but it also offers an effective way to hurdle such entry barriers as acquiring technological know-how, establishing supplier relationships, becoming big enough to match rivals' efficiency and unit costs, having to spend large sums on introductory advertising and promotions, and securing adequate distribution. Buying an ongoing operation allows the acquirer to move directly to the task of building a strong market position in the target industry, rather than getting bogged down in going the internal start-up route and trying to develop the knowledge, resources, scale of operation, and market reputation necessary to become an effective competitor within a few years.

The big dilemma an acquisition-minded firm faces is whether to pay a premium price for a successful company or to buy a struggling company at a bargain price.[3] If the buying firm has little knowledge of the industry but ample capital, it is often better off purchasing a capable, strongly positioned firm—unless the price of such an acquisition is prohibitive and flunks the cost-of-entry test. However, when the acquirer sees promising ways to transform a weak firm into a strong one and has the resources, the know-how, and the patience to do so, a struggling company can be the better long-term investment.

Internal Start-Up

Achieving diversification through *internal start-up* involves building a new business subsidiary from scratch. This entry option takes longer than the acquisition option and poses some hurdles. A newly formed business unit not only has to overcome entry barriers but also has to invest in new production capacity, develop sources of supply, hire and train employees, build channels of distribution, grow a customer base, and so on. Generally, forming a start-up subsidiary to enter a new business has appeal only when (1) the parent company already has in-house most or all of the skills and resources it needs to piece together a new business and compete effectively; (2) there is ample time to launch the business; (3) internal entry has lower costs than entry via acquisition; (4) the targeted industry is populated with many relatively small firms such that the new start-up does not have to compete head-to-head against larger, more powerful rivals; (5) adding new production capacity will not adversely impact the supply-demand balance in the industry; and (6) incumbent firms are likely to be slow or ineffective in responding to a new entrant's efforts to crack the market.[4]

> The biggest drawbacks to entering an industry by forming an internal start-up are the costs of overcoming entry barriers and the extra time it takes to build a strong and profitable competitive position.

Joint Ventures and Strategic Partnerships

Joint ventures typically entail forming a new corporate entity owned by the partners, whereas strategic partnerships represent a collaborative arrangement that usually can be terminated whenever one of the partners so chooses. A strategic partnership or joint venture can be useful in at least three types of situations.[5] First, a strategic alliance or joint venture is a good way to pursue an opportunity that is too complex, uneconomical, or risky for a single organization to pursue alone. Second, strategic alliances and joint ventures make sense when the opportunities in a new industry require a broader range of competencies and know-how than any one organization can marshal. Many of the opportunities in satellite-based telecommunications, biotechnology, and network-based systems that blend hardware, software, and services call for the coordinated development of complementary innovations and the integration of a host of financial, technical, political, and regulatory factors. In such cases, pooling the resources and competencies of two or more independent organizations is essential to generate the capabilities needed for success.

Third, joint ventures are sometimes the only way to gain entry into a desirable foreign market, especially when the foreign government requires companies wishing to enter the market to secure a local partner. Alliances with local partners have become a favorite mechanism for global companies wanting to establish footholds in desirable foreign-country markets; local partners offer outside companies the benefits of local knowledge about market conditions, customs and cultural factors, and customer buying habits. They can also be a source of managerial and marketing personnel and provide access to distribution outlets. The foreign partner's role is usually to provide specialized skills, technological know-how, and other resources needed to crack the local market and serve it efficiently.

However, as discussed in Chapters 4 and 5, partnering with another company—in the form of either an alliance or a joint venture—has significant drawbacks due to the potential for conflicting objectives, disagreements over how to best operate the venture, and so on. Joint ventures are generally the least durable of the entry options, usually lasting only until the partners decide to go their own ways.

Figure 6.1   **Strategy Alternatives for a Company Looking to Diversify**

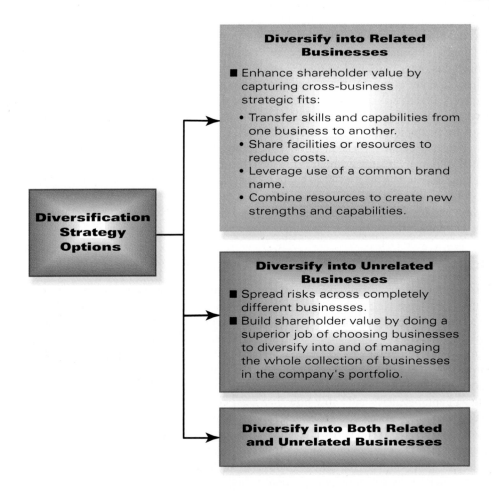

Choosing the Diversification Path: Related versus Unrelated Businesses

Once a company decides to diversify, its first big strategy decision is whether to diversify into **related businesses, unrelated businesses,** or some mix of both (see Figure 6.1). *Businesses are said to be related when their value chains possess competitively valuable cross-business relationships that present opportunities for the businesses to perform better under the same corporate umbrella than they could by operating as stand-alone entities.* The big appeal of related diversification is to build shareholder value by leveraging these cross-business relationships into competitive advantage, thus allowing the company as a whole to perform better than just the sum of its individual businesses. *Businesses are said to be unrelated when the activities constituting their respective*

Figure 6.2   **Related Businesses Possess Related Value Chain Activities and Competitively Valuable Strategic Fits**

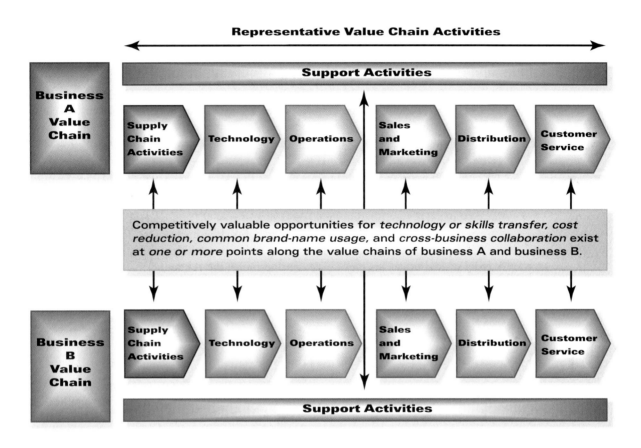

value chains are so dissimilar that no competitively valuable cross-business relationships are present.

The next two sections explore the ins and outs of related and unrelated diversification.

The Case for Diversifying into Related Businesses

A related diversification strategy involves building the company around businesses whose value chains possess competitively valuable strategic fits, as shown in Figure 6.2. **Strategic fit** exists whenever one or more activities constituting the value chains of different businesses are sufficiently similar as to present opportunities for:[6]

■ Transferring competitively valuable expertise, technological know-how, or other capabilities from one business to another.

■ Combining the related value chain activities of separate businesses into a single operation to achieve lower costs. For instance,

> **Core Concept**
>
> **Strategic fit** exists when the value chains of different businesses present opportunities for cross-business resource transfer, lower costs through combining the performance of related value chain activities, cross-business use of a potent brand name, and cross-business collaboration to build new or stronger competitive capabilities.

it is often feasible to manufacture the products of different businesses in a single plant or use the same warehouses for shipping and distribution or have a single sales force for the products of different businesses (because they are marketed to the same types of customers).

- Exploiting common use of a well-known and potent brand name. For example, Honda's name in motorcycles and automobiles gave it instant credibility and recognition in entering the lawn-mower business, allowing it to achieve a significant market share without spending large sums on advertising to establish a brand identity for its lawn mowers. Canon's reputation in photographic equipment was a competitive asset that facilitated the company's diversification into copying equipment. Sony's name in consumer electronics made it easier and cheaper for Sony to enter the market for video games with its PlayStation console and lineup of PlayStation video games.

- Collaborating across businesses to create competitively valuable resource strengths and capabilities.

Related diversification thus has strategic appeal from several angles. It allows a firm to reap the competitive advantage benefits of skills transfer, lower costs, a powerful brand name, and/or stronger competitive capabilities and still spread investor risks over a broad business base. Furthermore, the relatedness among the different businesses provides sharper focus for managing diversification and a useful degree of strategic unity across the company's various business activities.

Identifying Cross-Business Strategic Fits along the Value Chain

Cross-business strategic fits can exist anywhere along the value chain—in R&D and technology activities, in supply chain activities and relationships with suppliers, in manufacturing, in sales and marketing, in distribution activities, or in administrative support activities.[7]

Strategic Fits in R&D and Technology Activities   Diversifying into businesses where there is potential for sharing common technology, exploiting the full range of business opportunities associated with a particular technology and its derivatives, or transferring technological know-how from one business to another has considerable appeal. Businesses with technology-sharing benefits can perform better together than apart because of potential cost savings in R&D and potentially shorter times in getting new products to market; also, technological advances in one business can lead to increased sales for both. Technological innovations have been the driver behind the efforts of cable TV companies to diversify into high-speed Internet access (via the use of cable modems) and, further, to explore providing local and long-distance telephone service to residential and commercial customers in a single wire.

Strategic Fits in Supply Chain Activities   Businesses that have supply chain strategic fits can perform better together because of the potential for skills transfer in procuring materials, greater bargaining power in negotiating with common suppliers, the benefits of added collaboration with common supply chain partners, and/or added leverage with shippers in securing volume discounts on incoming parts and components. Dell Computer's strategic partnerships with leading suppliers of microprocessors, motherboards, disk drives, memory chips, monitors, modems, flat-panel displays, long-life batteries, and other PC-related components have been an important element of the company's strategy to diversify into servers, data storage devices, MP3 players, and LCD TVs—products that include many components common to PCs and that can be sourced from the same strategic partners that provide Dell with PC components.

Manufacturing-Related Strategic Fits   Cross-business strategic fits in manufacturing-related activities can represent an important source of competitive advantage in situations where a diversifier's expertise in quality manufacture and cost-efficient production methods can be transferred to another business. When Emerson Electric diversified into the chain-saw business, it transferred its expertise in low-cost manufacture to its newly acquired Beaird-Poulan business division; the transfer drove Beaird-Poulan's new strategy—to be the low-cost provider of chain-saw products—and fundamentally changed the way Beaird-Poulan chain saws were designed and manufactured. Another benefit of production-related value chain matchups is the ability to consolidate production into a smaller number of plants and significantly reduce overall production costs. When snowmobile maker Bombardier diversified into motorcycles, it was able to set up motorcycle assembly lines in the same manufacturing facility where it was assembling snowmobiles. When Smucker's acquired Procter & Gamble's Jif peanut butter business, it was able to combine the manufacture of its own Smucker's peanut butter products with those of Jif, plus it gained greater leverage with vendors in purchasing its peanut supplies.

Distribution-Related Strategic Fits   Businesses with closely related distribution activities can perform better together than apart because of potential cost savings in sharing the same distribution facilities or using many of the same wholesale distributors and retail dealers to access customers. When Sunbeam acquired Mr. Coffee, it was able to consolidate its own distribution centers for small household appliances with those of Mr. Coffee, thereby generating considerable cost savings. Likewise, since Sunbeam products were sold to many of the same retailers as Mr. Coffee products (Wal-Mart, Kmart, Target, department stores, home centers, hardware chains, supermarket chains, and drugstore chains), Sunbeam was able to convince many of the retailers carrying Sunbeam appliances to also take on the Mr. Coffee line and vice versa.

Strategic Fits in Sales and Marketing Activities   Various cost-saving opportunities spring from diversifying into businesses with closely related sales and marketing activities. The same distribution centers can be utilized for warehousing and shipping the products of different businesses. When the products are sold directly to the same customers, sales costs can often be reduced by using a single sales force and avoiding having two different salespeople call on the same customer. The products of related businesses can be promoted at the same Web site and included in the same media ads and sales brochures. After-sale service and repair organizations for the products of closely related businesses can often be consolidated into a single operation. There may be opportunities to reduce costs by consolidating order processing and billing and using common promotional tie-ins (cents-off couponing, free samples and trial offers, seasonal specials, and the like). When global power-tool maker Black & Decker acquired General Electric's domestic small household appliance business, it was able to use its own global sales force and distribution facilities to sell and distribute the newly acquired GE line of toasters, irons, mixers, and coffeemakers because the types of customers that carried its power tools (discounters like Wal-Mart and Target, home centers, and hardware stores) also stocked small appliances. The economies Black & Decker achieved for both product lines were substantial.

A second category of benefits arises when different businesses use similar sales and marketing approaches; in such cases, there may be competitively valuable opportunities to transfer selling, merchandising, advertising, and product differentiation skills from one business to another. Procter & Gamble's product lineup includes Folgers coffee, Tide laundry detergent, Crest toothpaste, Ivory soap, Charmin toilet tissue, and Head & Shoulders shampoo. All of these have different competitors and different supply chain and production requirements, but they all move through the same wholesale distribution systems, are sold in common retail settings to the same shoppers, are advertised and promoted in much the same ways, and require the same marketing and merchandising skills.

Strategic Fits in Managerial and Administrative Support Activities   Often, different businesses require comparable types of managerial know-how, thereby allowing the know-how in one line of business to be transferred to another. At General Electric (GE), managers who were involved in GE's expansion into Russia were able to expedite entry because of information gained from GE managers involved in expansions into other emerging markets. The lessons GE managers learned in China were passed along to GE managers in Russia, allowing them to anticipate that the Russian government would demand that GE build production capacity in the country rather than enter the market through exporting or licensing. In addition, GE's managers in Russia were better able to develop realistic performance expectations and make tough up-front decisions since experience in China and elsewhere warned them (1) that there would likely be increased short-term costs during the early years of start-up and (2) that if GE committed to the Russian market for the long term and aided the country's economic development, it could eventually expect to be given the freedom to pursue profitable penetration of the Russian market.[8]

Likewise, different businesses can often use the same administrative and customer service infrastructure. For instance, an electric utility that diversifies into natural gas, water, appliance sales and repair services, and home security services can use the same customer data network, the same customer call centers and local offices, the same billing and customer accounting systems, and the same customer service infrastructure to support all of its products and services.

Company Spotlight 6.1 lists the businesses of five companies that have pursued a strategy of related diversification.

Strategic Fit, Economies of Scope, and Competitive Advantage

What makes related diversification an attractive strategy is the opportunity to convert cross-business strategic fits into a competitive advantage over business rivals whose operations do not offer comparable strategic-fit benefits. The greater the relatedness among a diversified company's businesses, the bigger a company's window for converting strategic fits into competitive advantage via (1) skills transfer, (2) combining related value chain activities to achieve lower costs, (3) leveraging use of a well-respected brand name, and/or (4) cross-business collaboration to create new resource strengths and capabilities.

Core Concept

Economies of scope are cost reductions that flow from operating in multiple businesses; such economies stem directly from strategic-fit efficiencies along the value chains of related businesses.

Economies of Scope: A Path to Competitive Advantage   One of the most important competitive advantages that a related diversification strategy can produce is lower costs than competitors. Related businesses often present opportunities to eliminate or reduce the costs of performing certain value chain activities; such cost savings are termed **economies of scope**—a concept distinct

COMPANY SPOTLIGHT 6.1

Related Diversification at Gillette, Darden Restaurants, L'Oréal, Johnson & Johnson, and PepsiCo

See if you can identify the value chain relationships which make the businesses of the following companies related in competitively relevant ways.

Gillette

- Blades and razors
- Toiletries (Right Guard, Foamy, Dry Idea, Soft & Dry, White Rain)
- Oral-B toothbrushes
- Braun shavers, coffeemakers, alarm clocks, mixers, hair dryers, and electric toothbrushes
- Duracell batteries

Darden Restaurants

- Olive Garden restaurant chain (Italian-themed)
- Red Lobster restaurant chain (seafood-themed)
- Bahama Breeze restaurant chain (Caribbean-themed)

L'Oréal

- Maybelline, Lancôme, Helena Rubenstein, Kiehl's, Garner, and Shu Uemura cosmetics
- L'Oréal and Soft Sheen/Carson hair care products
- Redken, Matrix, L'Oréal Professional, and Kerastase Paris professional hair care and skin care products
- Ralph Lauren and Giorgio Armani fragrances
- Biotherm skin care products
- La Roche-Posay and Vichy Laboratories dermo-cosmetics

Johnson & Johnson

- Baby products (powder, shampoo, oil, lotion)
- Band-Aids and other first-aid products
- Women's health and personal care products (Stayfree, Carefree, Sure & Natural)
- Neutrogena and Aveeno skin care products
- Nonprescription drugs (Tylenol, Motrin, Pepcid AC, Mylanta, Monistat)
- Prescription drugs
- Prosthetic and other medical devices
- Surgical and hospital products
- Accuvue contact lenses

PepsiCo, Inc.

- Soft drinks (Pepsi, Diet Pepsi, Pepsi One, Mountain Dew, Mug, Slice)
- Fruit juices (Tropicana and Dole)
- Sports drinks (Gatorade)
- Other beverages (Aquafina bottled water, SoBe, Lipton ready-to-drink tea, Frappucino—in partnership with Starbucks, international sales of 7UP)
- Snack foods (Fritos, Lay's, Ruffles, Doritos, Tostitos, Santitas, Smart Food, Rold Gold pretzels, Chee-tos, Grandma's cookies, Sun Chips, Cracker Jack, Frito-Lay dips and salsas)
- Cereals, rice, and breakfast products (Quaker oatmeal, Cap'n Crunch, Life, Rice-A-Roni, Quaker rice cakes, Aunt Jemima mixes and syrups, Quaker grits)

Source: Company annual reports.

---

from *economies of scale.* Economies of *scale* are cost savings that accrue directly from a larger-size operation; for example, unit costs may be lower in a large plant than in a small plant, lower in a large distribution center than in a small one, lower for large-volume purchases of components than for small-volume purchases. Economies of *scope,* however, stem directly from cost-saving strategic fits along the value chains of related businesses. Such economies are open only to a multibusiness enterprise and are the result of a related diversification strategy that allows sister businesses to share technology, perform R&D together, use common manufacturing or distribution facilities, share a common sales force or distributor/dealer network, use the same established brand name, and/or share the same administrative infrastructure. *The greater the cross-business economies associated with cost-saving strategic fits, the greater the potential for a related diversification strategy to yield a competitive advantage based on lower costs than rivals.*

From Competitive Advantage to Added Profitability and Gains in Shareholder Value The competitive advantage potential that flows from economies of scope and the capture of other strategic-fit benefits is what enables a company pursuing related diversification to achieve $1 + 1 = 3$ financial performance and the hoped-for gains in shareholder value. The strategic and business logic is compelling: capturing strategic fits along the value chains of its related businesses gives a diversified company a clear path to achieving competitive advantage over undiversified competitors and competitors whose own diversification efforts don't offer equivalent strategic-fit benefits.[9] Such competitive advantage potential provides a company with a dependable basis for earning profits and a return on investment that exceed what the company's businesses could earn as stand-alone enterprises. Converting the competitive advantage potential into greater profitability is what fuels $1 + 1 = 3$ gains in shareholder value—the necessary outcome for satisfying the better-off test and proving the business merit of a company's diversification effort.

> **Core Concept**
>
> Diversifying into related businesses where competitively valuable strategic-fit benefits can be captured puts sister businesses in position to perform better financially as part of the same company than they could have performed as independent enterprises, thus providing a clear avenue for boosting shareholder value.

There are two things to bear in mind here. One, capturing cross-business strategic fits via a strategy of related diversification builds shareholder value in ways that shareholders cannot undertake by simply owning a portfolio of stocks of companies in different industries. Two, the capture of cross-business strategic-fit benefits is possible only via a strategy of related diversification.

The Case for Diversifying into Unrelated Businesses

An unrelated diversification strategy discounts the merits of pursuing cross-business strategic fits and, instead, focuses squarely on entering and operating businesses in industries that allow the company as a whole to grow its revenues and earnings. Companies that pursue a strategy of unrelated diversification generally exhibit a willingness to diversify into *any industry* where senior managers see *opportunity* to realize consistently good financial results—*the basic premise of unrelated diversification is that any company or business that can be acquired on good financial terms and that has satisfactory growth and earnings potential represents a good acquisition and a good business opportunity.* With a strategy of unrelated diversification, the emphasis is on satisfying the attractiveness and cost-of-entry tests and each business's prospects for good financial performance. As indicated in Figure 6.3, there's no deliberate effort to satisfy the better-off test in the sense of diversifying only into businesses having strategic fits with the firm's other businesses.

Thus, with an unrelated diversification strategy, company managers spend much time and effort screening acquisition candidates and evaluating the pros and cons of keeping or divesting existing businesses, using such criteria as:

- Whether the business can meet corporate targets for profitability and return on investment.

Figure 6.3 **Unrelated Businesses Have Unrelated Value Chains and No Strategic Fits**

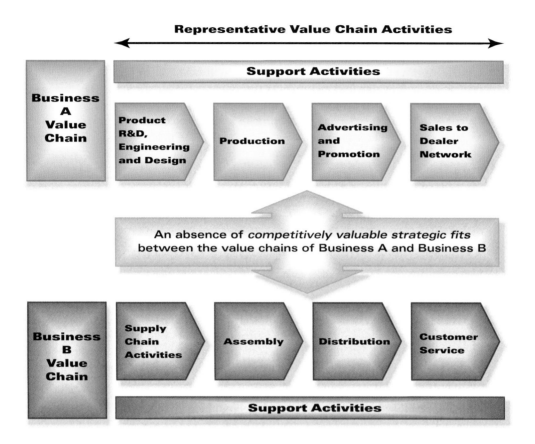

- Whether the business is in an industry with attractive growth potential.
- Whether the business is big enough to contribute *significantly* to the parent firm's bottom line.
- Whether the business has burdensome capital requirements (associated with replacing out-of-date plants and equipment, growing the business, and/or providing working capital).
- Whether the business is plagued with chronic union difficulties and labor problems.
- Whether there is industry vulnerability to recession, inflation, high interest rates, tough government regulations concerning product safety or the environment, and other potentially negative factors.

Companies that pursue unrelated diversification nearly always enter new businesses by acquiring an established company rather than by forming a start-up subsidiary within their own corporate structures. The premise of acquisition-minded corporations is that growth by acquisition can deliver enhanced shareholder value through upward-trending corporate revenues and earnings and a stock price that *on average* rises enough year after year to amply reward and please shareholders. Three types of acquisition candidates are usually of particular interest: (1) businesses that have bright growth prospects but are short on investment capital—cash-poor, opportunity-rich businesses are highly coveted acquisition targets for cash-rich companies scouting for good market opportunities; (2) undervalued companies that can be acquired at a bargain price; and (3) struggling companies whose operations can be turned around with the aid of the parent company's financial resources and managerial know-how.

A key issue in unrelated diversification is how wide a net to cast in building a portfolio of unrelated businesses. In other words, should a company pursuing unrelated diversification seek to have few or many unrelated businesses? How much business diversity can corporate executives successfully manage? A reasonable way to resolve the issue of how much diversification to pursue comes from answering two questions: "What is the least diversification it will take to achieve acceptable growth and profitability?" and "What is the most diversification that can be managed, given the complexity it adds?"[10] The optimal amount of diversification usually lies between these two extremes.

Company Spotlight 6.2 lists the businesses of three companies that have pursued unrelated diversification. Such companies are frequently labeled *conglomerates* because their business interests range broadly across diverse industries.

The Merits of an Unrelated Diversification Strategy

A strategy of unrelated diversification has appeal from several angles:

1. Business risk is scattered over a set of truly *diverse* industries. In comparison to related diversification, unrelated diversification more closely approximates *pure* diversification of financial and business risk because the company's investments are spread over businesses whose technologies and value chain activities bear no close relationship and whose markets are largely disconnected.[11]

2. The company's financial resources can be employed to maximum advantage by (a) investing in *whatever industries* offer the best profit prospects (as opposed to considering opportunities only in industries with related value chain activities) and (b) diverting cash flows from company businesses with lower growth and profit prospects to acquiring and expanding businesses with higher growth and profit potentials.

3. To the extent that corporate managers are exceptionally astute at spotting bargain-priced companies with big upside profit potential, shareholder wealth can be enhanced by buying distressed businesses at a low price, turning their operations around fairly quickly with infusions of cash and managerial know-how supplied by the parent company, and then riding the crest of the profit increases generated by the newly acquired businesses.

4. Company profitability may prove somewhat more stable over the course of economic upswings and downswings because market conditions in all industries don't move upward or downward simultaneously—in a broadly diversified company, there's a chance that market downtrends in some of the company's businesses will be partially offset by cyclical upswings in its other businesses, thus producing somewhat less earnings volatility. (In actual practice, however, there's no convincing evidence that the consolidated profits of firms with unrelated diversification strategies are more stable or less subject to reversal in periods of recession and economic stress than the profits of firms with related diversification strategies.)

COMPANY SPOTLIGHT 6.2

Unrelated Diversification at General Electric, United Technologies, and Lancaster Colony

There are few competitively valuable cross-business relationships in the value chains of the businesses that make up General Electric, United Technologies, and Lancaster Colony. Peruse the business listings of each company below and see if you can confirm why it is fair to say that these three companies are pursuing unrelated diversification.

General Electric

- Advanced materials (engineering thermoplastics, silicon-based products and technology platforms, and fused quartz and ceramics)—revenues of $8.3 billion in 2004.

- Commercial and consumer finance (loans, operating leases, financing programs, and financial services provided to corporations, retailers, and consumers in 38 countries)—revenues of $39.2 billion in 2004.

- Major appliances, lighting, and integrated industrial equipment, systems, and services—revenues of $13.8 billion in 2004.

- Commercial insurance and reinsurance products and services for insurance companies, Fortune 1000 companies, self-insurers, health care providers, and other groups—revenues of $23.1 billion in 2004.

- Jet engines for military and civil aircraft, freight and passenger locomotives, motorized systems for mining trucks and drills, and gas turbines for marine and industrial applications—revenues of $15.6 billion in 2004.

- Electric power generation equipment, power transformers, high-voltage breakers, distribution transformers and breakers, capacitors, relays, regulators, substation equipment, metering products—revenues of $17.3 billion in 2004.

- Medical imaging and information technologies, medical diagnostics, patient monitoring systems, disease research, drug discovery and biopharmaceuticals—revenues of $13.5 billion in 2004.

- NBC Universal—owns and operates the NBC television network, a Spanish-language network (Telemundo), several news and entertainment networks (CNBC, MSNBC, Bravo, Sci-Fi Channel, USA Network), Universal Studios, various television production operations, a group of television stations, and theme parks—revenues of $12.9 billion in 2004).

- Chemical treatment programs for water and industrial process systems, precision sensors, security and safety systems for intrusion and fire detection, access and building control, video surveillance, explosives and drug detection, and real estate services—revenues of $3.4 billion in 2004.

- Equipment Services—Penske truck leasing; operating leases, loans, sales, and asset management services for owners of computer networks, trucks, trailers, railcars, construction equipment, and shipping containers—revenues of $8.5 billion in 2004.

United Technologies, Corp.

- Pratt & Whitney aircraft engines—2004 revenues of $8.3 billion.

- Carrier heating and air-conditioning equipment—2004 revenues of $10.6 billion.

- Otis elevators and escalators—2004 revenues of $9.0 billion.

- Sikorsky helicopters and Hamilton Sunstrand aerospace systems—2004 revenues of $6.4 billion.

- Chubb fire detection and security systems—2004 revenues of $2.9 billion.

Lancaster Colony Corp.

- Cardini, Marzetti, Girard's, and Pfeiffer salad dressings; Chatham Village croutons; New York Brand, Sister Schubert, and Mamma Bella frozen breads and rolls; Reames frozen noodles and pastas; Mountain Top frozen pies; and Romanoff caviar—fiscal 2004 revenues of $639 million.

- Candle-lite candles, Indiana Glass drinkware and tabletop items, Colony giftware, and Brody floral containers—fiscal 2004 revenues of $231 million.

- Automotive floor mats, Dee Zee aluminum accessories for light trucks, Koneta truck and trailer splash guards, Protecta truck bed mats, and Rubber Queen plastic accessories—fiscal 2004 revenues of $227 million.

Source: Company press releases.

Unrelated diversification certainly merits consideration when a firm is trapped in or overly dependent on an endangered or unattractive industry, especially when it has no competitively valuable resources or capabilities it can transfer to an adjacent industry. A case can also be made for unrelated diversification when a company has a strong preference for spreading business risks widely and not restricting itself to investing in a family of closely related businesses.

Building Shareholder Value via Unrelated Diversification
Given the absence of cross-business strategic fits with which to capture added competitive advantage, the task of building shareholder value via unrelated diversification ultimately hinges on the business acumen of corporate executives. To succeed in using a strategy of unrelated diversification to produce companywide financial results above and beyond what the businesses could generate operating as stand-alone entities, corporate executives must:

- Do a superior job of diversifying into new businesses that can produce consistently good earnings and returns on investment (thereby satisfying the attractiveness test).

- Do an excellent job of negotiating favorable acquisition prices (thereby satisfying the cost-of-entry test).

- Do such a good job of overseeing the firm's business subsidiaries and contributing to how they are managed—by providing expert problem-solving skills, creative strategy suggestions, and high-caliber decision-making guidance to the heads of the various business subsidiaries—that the subsidiaries perform at a higher level than they would otherwise be able to do through the efforts of the business-unit heads alone (a possible way to satisfy the better-off test).

- Be shrewd in identifying when to shift resources out of businesses with dim profit prospects and into businesses with above-average prospects for growth and profitability.

- Be good at discerning when a business needs to be sold (because it is on the verge of confronting adverse industry and competitive conditions and probable declines in long-term profitability) and also at finding buyers who will pay a price higher than the company's net investment in the business (so that the sale of divested businesses will result in capital gains for shareholders rather than capital losses).

To the extent that corporate executives are able to craft and execute a strategy of unrelated diversification that produces enough of the above outcomes to result in a stream of dividends and capital gains for stockholders greater than a $1 + 1 = 2$ outcome, a case can be made that shareholder value has truly been enhanced.

The Drawbacks of Unrelated Diversification

Unrelated diversification strategies have two important negatives that undercut the pluses: very demanding managerial requirements and limited competitive advantage potential.

Demanding Managerial Requirements　Successfully managing a set of fundamentally different businesses operating in fundamentally different industry and competitive environments is a very challenging and exceptionally difficult proposition for corporate-level managers. It is difficult because key executives at the corporate level, while perhaps having personally worked in one or two of the company's businesses, rarely have the time and expertise to be sufficiently familiar with all the circumstances surrounding each of the company's businesses to be able to give high-caliber guidance to business-level managers. Indeed, the greater the number of businesses a company is in and the more diverse they are, the harder it is for corporate managers to (1) stay abreast of what's happening in each industry and each subsidiary and thus judge whether a particular business has bright prospects or is headed for trouble, (2) know enough about the issues and problems facing each subsidiary to pick business-unit heads having the requisite combination of managerial skills and know-how, (3) be able to tell the difference between those strategic proposals of business-unit managers that are prudent and those that are risky or unlikely to succeed, and (4) know what to do if a business unit stumbles and its results suddenly head downhill.[12]

> **Core Concept**
>
> The two biggest drawbacks to unrelated diversification are the difficulties of competently managing many different businesses and being without the added source of competitive advantage that cross-business strategic fit provides.

In a company like General Electric (see Company Spotlight 6.2) or Tyco International (which acquired over 1,000 companies during the 1990–2001 period), corporate executives are constantly scrambling to stay on top of fresh industry developments and the strategic progress and plans of each subsidiary, often depending on briefings by business-level managers for many of the details. As a rule, the more unrelated businesses that a company has diversified into, the more that corporate executives are dependent on briefings from business-unit heads and "managing by the numbers"—that is, keeping a close track on the financial and operating results of each subsidiary and assuming that the heads of the various subsidiaries have most everything under control so long as the latest key financial and operating measures look good. Managing by the numbers works okay if the heads of the various business units are quite capable and consistently meet their numbers. But the problem comes when things start to go awry in a business despite the best efforts of business-unit managers and corporate management has to get deeply involved in turning around a business it does not know all that much about. As the former chairman of a Fortune 500 company advised, "Never acquire a business you don't know how to run." Because every business tends to encounter rough sledding, a good way to gauge the merits of acquiring a company in an unrelated industry is to ask, "If the business gets into trouble, is corporate management likely to know how to bail it out?" When the answer is no (or even a qualified yes or maybe), growth via acquisition into unrelated businesses is a chancy strategy.[13] Just one or two unforeseen declines or big strategic mistakes (misjudging the importance of certain competitive forces or the impact of driving forces or key success factors, encountering unexpected problems in a newly acquired business, or being too optimistic about turning around a struggling subsidiary) can cause a precipitous drop in corporate earnings and crash the parent company's stock price.

Hence, competently overseeing a set of widely diverse businesses can turn out to be much harder than it sounds. In practice, comparatively few companies have proved that they have top-management capabilities that are up to the task. There are far more companies whose corporate executives have failed at delivering consistently good financial results with an unrelated diversification strategy than there are companies with corporate executives who have been successful.[14] It is simply more difficult than it might seem for corporate executives to achieve $1 + 1 = 3$ gains in shareholder value based on their expertise in (1) picking which industries to diversify into and which companies in these industries to acquire, (2) shifting resources from low-performing businesses into high-performing businesses, and (3) giving high-caliber decision-making guidance to the general managers of their business subsidiaries. The odds are that the result of unrelated diversification will be $1 + 1 = 2$ or less.

> Relying solely on the expertise of corporate executives to wisely manage a set of unrelated businesses is *a much weaker foundation for enhancing shareholder value* than is a strategy of related diversification where corporate performance can be boosted by competitively valuable cross-business strategic fits.

Limited Competitive Advantage Potential   The second big negative is that *unrelated diversification offers no potential for competitive advantage beyond what each individual business can generate on its own.* Unlike a related diversification strategy, there are no cross-business strategic fits to draw on for reducing costs, beneficially transferring skills and technology, leveraging use of a powerful brand name, or collaborating to build mutually beneficial competitive capabilities and thereby *adding to any competitive advantage possessed by individual businesses.* Yes, a cash-rich corporate parent pursuing unrelated diversification can provide its subsidiaries with much-needed capital and maybe even the managerial know-how to help resolve problems in particular business units, but otherwise it has little to offer in the way of enhancing the competitive strength of its individual business units. *Without the competitive advantage potential of strategic fits, consolidated performance of an unrelated group of businesses stands to be little or no better than the sum of what the individual business units could achieve if they were independent.*

Combination Related-Unrelated Diversification Strategies

There's nothing to preclude a company from diversifying into both related and unrelated businesses. Indeed, in actual practice the business makeup of diversified companies varies considerably. Some diversified companies are really *dominant-business enterprises*—one major "core" business accounts for 50 to 80 percent of total revenues, and a collection of small related or unrelated businesses accounts for the remainder. Some diversified companies are *narrowly diversified* around a few (two to five) related or unrelated businesses. Others are *broadly diversified* around a wide-ranging collection of related businesses, unrelated businesses, or a mixture of both. And a number of multibusiness enterprises have diversified into unrelated areas but have a collection of related businesses within each area—thus giving them a business portfolio consisting of *several unrelated groups of related businesses.* There's ample room for companies to customize their diversification strategies to incorporate elements of both related and unrelated diversification, as may suit their own risk preferences and strategic vision.

Figure 6.4 indicates what to look for in identifying the main elements of a company's diversification strategy. Having a clear fix on the company's current corporate strategy sets the stage for evaluating how good the strategy is and proposing strategic moves to boost the company's performance.

Evaluating the Strategy of a Diversified Company

Strategic analysis of diversified companies builds on the concepts and methods used for single-business companies. But there are some additional aspects to consider and a couple of new analytical tools to master. The procedure for evaluating the pluses and minuses of a diversified company's strategy and deciding what actions to take to improve the company's performance involves six steps:

1. Assessing the attractiveness of the industries the company has diversified into, both individually and as a group.

2. Assessing the competitive strength of the company's business units and determining how many are strong contenders in their respective industries.

3. Checking the competitive advantage potential of cross-business strategic fits among the company's various business units.

4. Checking whether the firm's resources fit the requirements of its present business lineup.

5. Ranking the performance prospects of the businesses from best to worst and determining what the corporate parent's priority should be in allocating resources to its various businesses.

6. Crafting new strategic moves to improve overall corporate performance.

The core concepts and analytical techniques underlying each of these steps merit further discussion.

Figure 6.4   Identifying a Diversified Company's Strategy

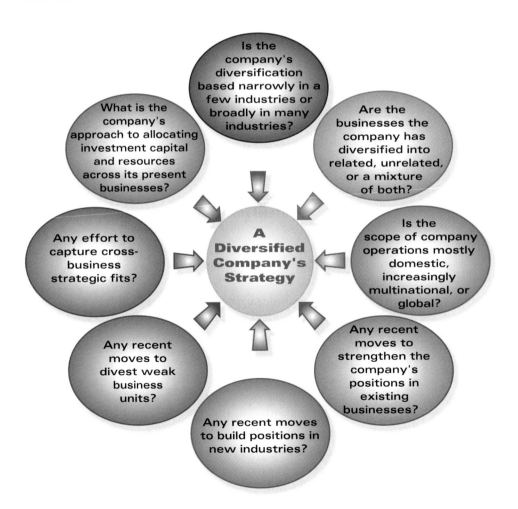

Step 1: Evaluating Industry Attractiveness

A principal consideration in evaluating a diversified company's business makeup and the caliber of its strategy is the attractiveness of the industries in which it has business operations. Answers to several questions are required:

1. *Does each industry the company has diversified into represent a good business for the company to be in?* Ideally, each industry in which the firm operates will pass the attractiveness test.

2. *Which of the company's industries are most attractive, and which are least attractive?* Comparing the attractiveness of the industries and ranking them from most to least attractive is a prerequisite to wise allocation of corporate resources across the various businesses.

3. *How appealing is the whole group of industries in which the company has invested?* The answer to this question points to whether the group of industries holds promise for attractive growth and profitability. A company whose revenues and profits come chiefly from businesses in relatively unattractive industries probably needs to look at divesting businesses in unattractive industries and entering industries that qualify as highly attractive.

The more attractive the industries (both individually and as a group) a diversified company is in, the better its prospects for good long-term performance.

Calculating Industry Attractiveness Scores for Each Industry into Which the Company Has Diversified   A simple and reliable analytical tool involves calculating quantitative industry attractiveness scores, which can then be used to gauge each industry's attractiveness, rank the industries from most to least attractive, and make judgments about the attractiveness of all the industries as a group.

The following measures are typically used to gauge an industry's attractiveness:

- *Market size and projected growth rate:* Big industries are more attractive than small industries, and fast-growing industries tend to be more attractive than slow-growing industries, other things being equal.

- *The intensity of competition:* Industries where competitive pressures are relatively weak are more attractive than industries where competitive pressures are strong.

- *Emerging opportunities and threats:* Industries with promising opportunities and minimal threats on the near horizon are more attractive than industries with modest opportunities and imposing threats.

- *The presence of cross-industry strategic fits:* The more the industry's value chain and resource requirements match up well with the value chain activities of other industries in which the company has operations, the more attractive the industry is to a firm pursuing related diversification. However, cross-industry strategic fits may be of no consequence to a company committed to a strategy of unrelated diversification.

- *Resource requirements:* Industries having resource requirements within the company's reach are more attractive than industries where capital and other resource requirements could strain corporate financial resources and organizational capabilities.

- *Seasonal and cyclical factors:* Industries where buyer demand is relatively steady year-round and not unduly vulnerable to economic ups and downs tend to be more attractive than industries where there are wide swings in buyer demand within or across years. However, seasonality may be a plus for a company that is in several seasonal industries, if the seasonal highs in one industry correspond to the lows in another industry, thus helping even out monthly sales levels. Likewise, cyclical market demand in one industry can be attractive if its up-cycle runs counter to the market down-cycles in another industry where the company operates, thus helping reduce revenue and earnings volatility.

■ *Social, political, regulatory, and environmental factors:* Industries that have significant problems in such areas as consumer health, safety, or environmental pollution or that are subject to intense regulation are less attractive than industries where such problems are not burning issues.

■ *Industry profitability:* Industries with healthy profit margins and high rates of return on investment are generally more attractive than industries where profits have historically been low or unstable.

■ *Industry uncertainty and business risk:* Industries with less uncertainty on the horizon and lower overall business risk are more attractive than industries whose prospects, for one reason or another, are quite uncertain, especially when the industry has formidable resource requirements.

After settling on a set of attractiveness measures that suit a diversified company's circumstances, each attractiveness measure is assigned a weight reflecting its relative importance in determining an industry's attractiveness—it is weak methodology to assume that the various attractiveness measures are equally important. The intensity of competition in an industry should nearly always carry a high weight (say, 0.20 to 0.30). Strategic-fit considerations should be assigned a high weight in the case of companies with related diversification strategies; for companies with unrelated diversification strategies, strategic fits with other industries may be given a low weight or even dropped from the list of attractiveness measures altogether. Seasonal and cyclical factors generally are assigned a low weight (or maybe even eliminated from the analysis) unless a company has diversified into industries strongly characterized by seasonal demand and/or heavy vulnerability to cyclical upswings and downswings. The importance weights must add up to 1.

Next, each industry is rated on each of the chosen industry attractiveness measures, using a rating scale of 1 to 10 (where a *high* rating signifies *high* attractiveness and a *low* rating signifies *low* attractiveness). Keep in mind here that the more intensely competitive an industry is, the *lower* the attractiveness rating for that industry. Likewise, the higher the capital and resource requirements associated with being in a particular industry, the lower the attractiveness rating. And an industry that is subject to stringent pollution control regulations or that causes societal problems (like cigarettes or alcoholic beverages) should be given a low attractiveness rating. Weighted attractiveness scores are then calculated by multiplying the industry's rating on each measure by the corresponding weight. For example, a rating of 8 times a weight of 0.25 gives a weighted attractiveness score of 2.00. The sum of the weighted scores for all the attractiveness measures provides an overall industry attractiveness score. This procedure is illustrated in Table 6.1.

Interpreting the Industry Attractiveness Scores   Industries with a score much below 5 probably do not pass the attractiveness test. If a company's industry attractiveness scores are all above 5, it is probably fair to conclude that the group of industries the company operates in is attractive as a whole. But the group of

Table 6.1   CALCULATING WEIGHTED INDUSTRY ATTRACTIVENESS SCORES

(Rating scale: 1 = very unattractive to company; 10 = very attractive to company.)

Industry Attractiveness Measure	Importance Weight	Rating/Score			
		Industry A	Industry B	Industry C	Industry D
Market size and projected growth rate	0.10	8/0.80	5/0.50	7/0.70	3/0.30
Intensity of competition	0.25	8/2.00	7/1.75	3/0.75	2/0.50
Emerging opportunities and threats	0.10	2/0.20	9/0.90	4/0.40	5/0.50
Cross-industry strategic fits	0.20	8/1.60	4/0.80	8/1.60	2/0.40
Resource requirements	0.10	9/0.90	7/0.70	10/1.00	5/0.50
Seasonal and cyclical influences	0.05	9/0.45	8/0.40	10/0.50	5/0.25
Societal, political, regulatory, and environmental factors	0.05	10/1.00	7/0.70	7/0.70	3/0.30
Industry profitability	0.10	5/0.50	10/1.00	3/0.30	3/0.30
Industry uncertainty and business risk	0.05	5/0.25	7/0.35	10/0.50	1/0.05
Sum of the assigned weights	1.00				
Overall industry attractiveness scores		**7.70**	**7.10**	**5.45**	**3.10**

industries takes on a decidedly lower degree of attractiveness as the number of industries with scores below 5 increases, especially if industries with low scores account for a sizable fraction of the company's revenues.

For a diversified company to be a strong performer, a substantial portion of its revenues and profits must come from business units with relatively high attractiveness scores. It is particularly important that a diversified company's principal businesses be in industries with a good outlook for growth and above-average profitability. Having a big fraction of the company's revenues and profits come from industries with slow growth, low profitability, or intense competition tends to drag overall company performance down. Business units in the least attractive industries are potential candidates for divestiture, unless they are positioned strongly enough to overcome the unattractive aspects of their industry environments or they are a strategically important component of the company's business makeup.

The Difficulties of Calculating Industry Attractiveness Scores   There are two hurdles to using this method of evaluating industry attractiveness. One is deciding on appropriate weights for the industry attractiveness measures. Not only may different analysts have different views about which weights are appropriate for the different attractiveness measures, but also different weightings may be appropriate for different companies—based on their strategies, performance targets, and financial circumstances. For instance, placing a low weight on industry resource requirements may be justifiable for a cash-rich company, whereas a high weight may be more appropriate for a financially strapped company. The second hurdle is gaining sufficient command of the industry to assign accurate and objective ratings. Generally, a company can come up with the statistical data needed to compare its industries on such factors as market size, growth rate, seasonal and cyclical influences, and industry profitability. Cross-industry fits and resource requirements are also fairly easy to judge. But the attractiveness measure where judgment weighs most heavily is that of intensity of competition. It is not always easy to conclude whether competition is stronger or weaker in one industry than in another industry because of the different types of competitive influences that prevail and the differences in their relative importance. In the event that the available information is too skimpy to confidently assign a rating value to an industry on a particular attractiveness measure, then it is usually best to use a score of 5, which avoids biasing the overall attractiveness score either up or down.

Despite the hurdles, calculating industry attractiveness scores is a systematic and reasonably reliable method for ranking a diversified company's industries from most to least attractive—numbers like those shown for the four industries in Table 6.1 help pin down the basis for judging which industries are more attractive and to what degree.

Step 2: Evaluating Business-Unit Competitive Strength

The second step in evaluating a diversified company is to appraise how strongly positioned each of its business units are in their respective industry. Doing an appraisal of each business unit's strength and competitive position in its industry not only reveals its chances for industry success but also provides a basis for ranking the units from competitively strongest to competitively weakest and sizing up the competitive strength of all the business units as a group.

Calculating Competitive Strength Scores for Each Business Unit
Quantitative measures of each business unit's competitive strength can be calculated using a procedure similar to that for measuring industry attractiveness. The following factors are used in quantifying the competitive strengths of a diversified company's business subsidiaries:

- *Relative market share:* A business unit's *relative market share* is defined as the ratio of its market share to the market share held by the largest rival firm in the industry, with market share measured in unit volume, not dollars. For instance, if business A has a market-leading share of 40 percent and its largest rival has 30 percent, A's relative market share is 1.33. (Note that only business units that are market share leaders in their respective industries can have relative market shares greater then 1.) If business B has a 15 percent market share and B's largest rival has 30 percent, B's relative market share is 0.5. The further below 1 a business unit's relative market share is, the weaker its competitive strength and market position vis-à-vis rivals. A 10 percent market share, for example, does not signal much competitive strength if the leader's share is 50 percent (a 0.20 relative market share), but a 10 percent share is actually quite strong if the leader's share is only 12 percent (a 0.83 relative market share)—this is why a company's relative market share is a better measure of competitive strength than a company's market share based on either dollars or unit volume.

> Using relative market share to measure competitive strength is analytically superior to using straight-percentage market share.

- *Costs relative to competitors' costs*: Business units that have low costs relative to key competitors' costs tend to be more strongly positioned in their industries than business units struggling to maintain cost parity with major rivals. Assuming that the prices charged by industry rivals are about the same, there's reason to expect that business units with higher relative market shares have lower unit costs than competitors with lower relative market shares because their greater unit sales volumes offer the possibility of economies from larger-scale operations and the benefits of any experience- or learning-curve effects. Another indicator of low cost can be a business unit's supply chain management capabilities. The only time when a business unit's competitive strength may not be undermined by having higher costs than rivals is when it has incurred the higher costs to strongly differentiate its product offering and its customers are willing to pay premium prices for the differentiating features.

- *Ability to match or beat rivals on key product attributes*: A company's competitiveness depends in part on being able to satisfy buyer expectations with regard to features, product performance, reliability, service, and other important attributes.

- *Ability to benefit from strategic fits with sister businesses*: Strategic fits with other businesses within the company enhance a business unit's competitive strength and may provide a competitive edge.

- *Ability to exercise bargaining leverage with key suppliers or customers*: Having bargaining leverage signals competitive strength and can be a source of competitive advantage.

- *Caliber of alliances and collaborative partnerships with suppliers and/or buyers*: Well-functioning alliances and partnerships may signal a potential competitive advantage vis-à-vis rivals and thus add to a business's competitive strength. Alliances with key suppliers are often the basis for competitive strength in supply chain management.

- *Brand image and reputation*: A strong brand name is a valuable competitive asset in most industries.

- *Competitively valuable capabilities*: Business units recognized for their technological leadership, product innovation, or marketing prowess are usually strong competitors in their industry. Skills in supply chain management can generate valuable cost or product differentiation advantages. So can unique production capabilities. Sometimes a company's business units gain competitive strength because of their knowledge of customers and markets and/or their proven managerial capabilities. *An important thing to look for here is how well a business unit's competitive assets match industry key success factors.* The more a business unit's resource strengths and competitive capabilities match the industry's key success factors, the stronger its competitive position tends to be.

- *Profitability relative to competitors*: Business units that consistently earn above-average returns on investment and have bigger profit margins than their rivals usually have stronger competitive positions. Moreover, above-average profitability signals competitive advantage, while below-average profitability usually denotes competitive disadvantage.

After settling on a set of competitive strength measures that are well matched to the circumstances of the various business units, weights indicating each measure's importance need to be assigned. A case can be made for using different weights for different business units whenever the importance of the strength measures differs significantly from business to business, but otherwise it is simpler just to go with a single set of weights and avoid the added complication of multiple weights. As before, the importance weights must add up to 1. Each business unit is then rated on each of the chosen strength measures, using a rating scale of 1 to 10 (where a *high* rating signifies competitive *strength* and a *low* rating signifies competitive *weakness*). In the event that the available information is too skimpy to confidently assign a rating value to a business unit on a particular strength measure, then it is usually best to use a score of 5, which avoids biasing the overall score either up or down. Weighted strength ratings are

Table 6.2   CALCULATING WEIGHTED COMPETITIVE STRENGTH SCORES FOR A DIVERSIFIED COMPANY'S BUSINESS UNITS

(Rating scale: 1 = very weak; 10 = very strong.)

Competitive Strength Measure	Importance Weight	Rating/Score			
		Business A in Industry A	Business B in Industry B	Business C in Industry C	Business D in Industry D
Relative market share	0.15	10/1.50	1/0.15	6/0.90	2/0.30
Costs relative to competitors' costs	0.20	7/1.40	2/0.40	5/1.00	3/0.60
Ability to match or beat rivals on key product attributes	0.05	9/0.45	4/0.20	8/0.40	4/0.20
Ability to benefit from strategic fits with company's other businesses	0.20	8/1.60	4/0.80	8/0.80	2/0.60
Bargaining leverage with suppliers/buyers; caliber of alliances	0.05	9/0.90	3/0.30	6/0.30	2/0.10
Brand image and reputation	0.10	9/0.90	2/0.20	7/0.70	5/0.50
Competitively valuable capabilities	0.15	7/1.05	2/0.20	5/0.75	3/0.45
Profitability relative to competitors	0.10	5/0.50	1/0.10	4/0.40	4/0.40
Sum of the assigned weights	1.00				
Overall industry attractiveness scores		8.30	2.35	5.25	3.15

calculated by multiplying the business unit's rating on each strength measure by the assigned weight. For example, a strength score of 6 times a weight of 0.15 gives a weighted strength rating of 0.90. The sum of weighted ratings across all the strength measures provides a quantitative measure of a business unit's overall market strength and competitive standing. Table 6.2 provides sample calculations of competitive strength ratings for four businesses.

Interpreting the Competitive Strength Scores   Business units with competitive strength ratings above 6.7 (on a scale of 1 to 10) are strong market contenders in their industries. Businesses with ratings in the 3.3 to 6.7 range have moderate competitive strength vis-à-vis rivals. Businesses with ratings below 3.3 are in competitively weak market positions. If a diversified company's business units all have competitive strength scores above 5, it is fair to conclude that its business units are all fairly strong market contenders in their respective industries. But as the number of business units with scores below 5 increases, there's reason to question whether the company can perform well with so many businesses in relatively weak competitive positions. This concern takes on even more importance when business units with low scores account for a sizable fraction of the company's revenues.

Using a Nine-Cell Matrix to Simultaneously Portray Industry Attractiveness and Competitive Strength   The industry attractiveness and business strength scores can be used to portray the strategic positions of each business in a diversified company. Industry attractiveness is plotted on the vertical axis, and competitive strength on the horizontal axis. A nine-cell grid emerges from dividing the vertical axis into three regions (high, medium, and low attractiveness) and the horizontal axis into three regions (strong, average, and weak competitive strength). As shown in Figure 6.5, high attractiveness is associated with scores of 6.7 or greater

**Figure 6.5   A Nine-Cell Industry Attractiveness–Competitive
Strength Matrix**

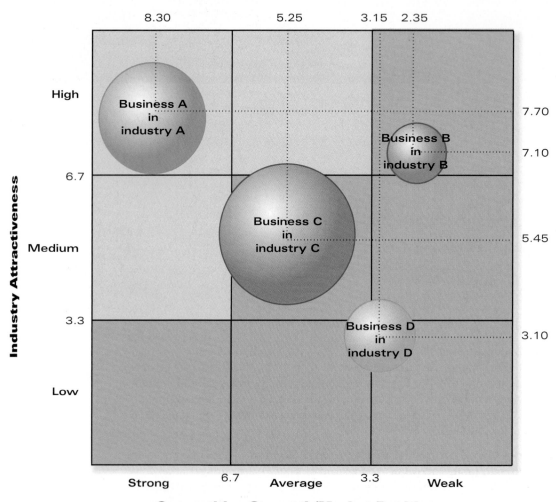

High priority for resource allocation
Medium priority for resource allocation
Low priority for resource allocation

Note: Circle sizes are scaled to reflect the
percentage of companywide revenues
generated by the business unit.

on a rating scale of 1 to 10; medium attractiveness, to scores of 3.3 to 6.7; and low attractiveness, to scores below 3.3. Likewise, high competitive strength is defined as
scores greater than 6.7; average strength, as scores of 3.3 to 6.7; and low strength, as
scores below 3.3. *Each business unit is plotted on the nine-cell matrix according to its
overall attractiveness score and strength score and then shown as a "bubble."* The
size of each bubble is scaled to what percentage of revenues the business generates relative to total corporate revenues. The bubbles in Figure 6.5 were located on the grid using the four industry attractiveness scores from Table 6.1 and the strength scores for
the four business units in Table 6.2.

The locations of the business units on the attractiveness-strength matrix provide valuable guidance in deploying corporate resources to the various business units. In general, *a diversified company's prospects for good overall performance are enhanced by concentrating corporate resources and strategic attention on those business units having the greatest competitive strength and positioned in highly attractive industries*—specifically, businesses in the three cells in the upper left portion of the attractiveness-strength matrix, where industry attractiveness and competitive strength/market position are both favorable. The general strategic prescription for businesses falling into these three cells (for instance, business A in Figure 6.5) is "grow and build," with businesses in the high-strong cell standing first in line for resource allocations by the corporate parent.

Next in priority come businesses positioned in the three diagonal cells stretching from the lower left to the upper right (businesses B and C in Figure 6.5). Such businesses usually merit medium or intermediate priority in the parent's resource allocation ranking. However, some businesses in the medium-priority diagonal cells may have brighter or dimmer prospects than others. For example, a small business in the upper right cell of the matrix (like business B), despite being in a highly attractive industry, may occupy too weak a competitive position in its industry to justify the investment and resources needed to turn it into a strong market contender and shift its position leftward in the matrix over time. If, however, a business in the upper right cell has attractive opportunities for rapid growth and a good potential for winning a much stronger market position over time, it may merit a high claim on the corporate parent's resource allocation ranking and be given the capital it needs to pursue a grow-and-build strategy—the strategic objective here would be to move the business leftward in the attractiveness-strength matrix over time.

Businesses in the three cells in the lower right corner of the matrix (like business D in Figure 6.5) typically are weak performers and have the lowest claim on corporate resources. Most such businesses are good candidates for being divested (sold to other companies) or else managed in a manner calculated to squeeze out the maximum cash flows from operations—the cash flows from low-performing/low-potential businesses can then be diverted to financing expansion of business units with greater market opportunities. In exceptional cases where a business located in the three lower right cells is nonetheless fairly profitable (which it might be if it is in the low-average cell) or has the potential for good earnings and return on investment, the business merits retention and the allocation of sufficient resources to achieve better performance.

The nine-cell attractiveness-strength matrix provides clear, strong logic for why a diversified company needs to consider both industry attractiveness and business strength in allocating resources and investment capital to its different businesses. A good case can be made for concentrating resources in those businesses that enjoy higher degrees of attractiveness and competitive strength, being very selective in making investments in businesses with intermediate positions on the grid, and withdrawing resources from businesses that are lower in attractiveness and strength unless they offer exceptional profit or cash flow potential.

Step 3: Checking the Competitive Advantage Potential of Cross-Business Strategic Fits

While this step can be bypassed for diversified companies whose businesses are all unrelated (since, by design, no strategic fits are present), a high potential for converting strategic fits into competitive advantage is central to concluding just how good a

Core Concept

A company's related diversification strategy derives its power in large part from the presence of competitively valuable strategic fits among its businesses.

company's related diversification strategy is. Checking the competitive advantage potential of cross-business strategic fits involves searching for and evaluating how much benefit a diversified company can gain from value chain matchups that present (1) opportunities to combine the performance of certain activities, thereby reducing costs and capturing economies of scope, (2) opportunities to transfer skills, technology, or intellectual capital from one business to another, thereby leveraging use of existing resources, (3) opportunities to share use of a well-respected brand name, and (4) opportunities for the company's other businesses to collaborate in creating valuable new competitive capabilities (such as enhanced supply chain management capabilities, quicker first-to-market capabilities, or greater product innovation capabilities).

Figure 6.6 illustrates the process of comparing the value chains of a company's businesses and identifying competitively valuable cross-business strategic fits. *But more than just strategic-fit identification is needed. The real test is what competitive value can be generated from these fits.* To what extent can cost savings be realized? How much competitive value will come from cross-business transfer of skills, technology, or

Figure 6.6   Identifying the Competitive Advantage Potential of Cross-Business Strategic Fits

Value Chain Activities

	Purchases from suppliers	Technology	Operations	Sales and marketing	Distribution	Service
Business A	▨	▬	⠿	☐	☐	☐
Business B	☐	☐	☐	⊠	⊠	⊠
Business C	☐	☐	⠿	⊠	⊠	⊠
Business D	▨	☐	⠿	⊠	⊠	⊠
Business E	☐	▬	⠿	☐	☐	☐

▨ Opportunity to combine purchasing activities and gain more leverage with suppliers and realize supply chain economies

▬ Opportunity to share technology, transfer technical skills, combine R&D

⊠ Opportunity to combine sales and marketing activities, use common distribution channels, leverage use of a common brand name, and/or combine after-sale service activities

⠿ Collaboration to create new competitive capabilities

☐ No strategic-fit opportunities

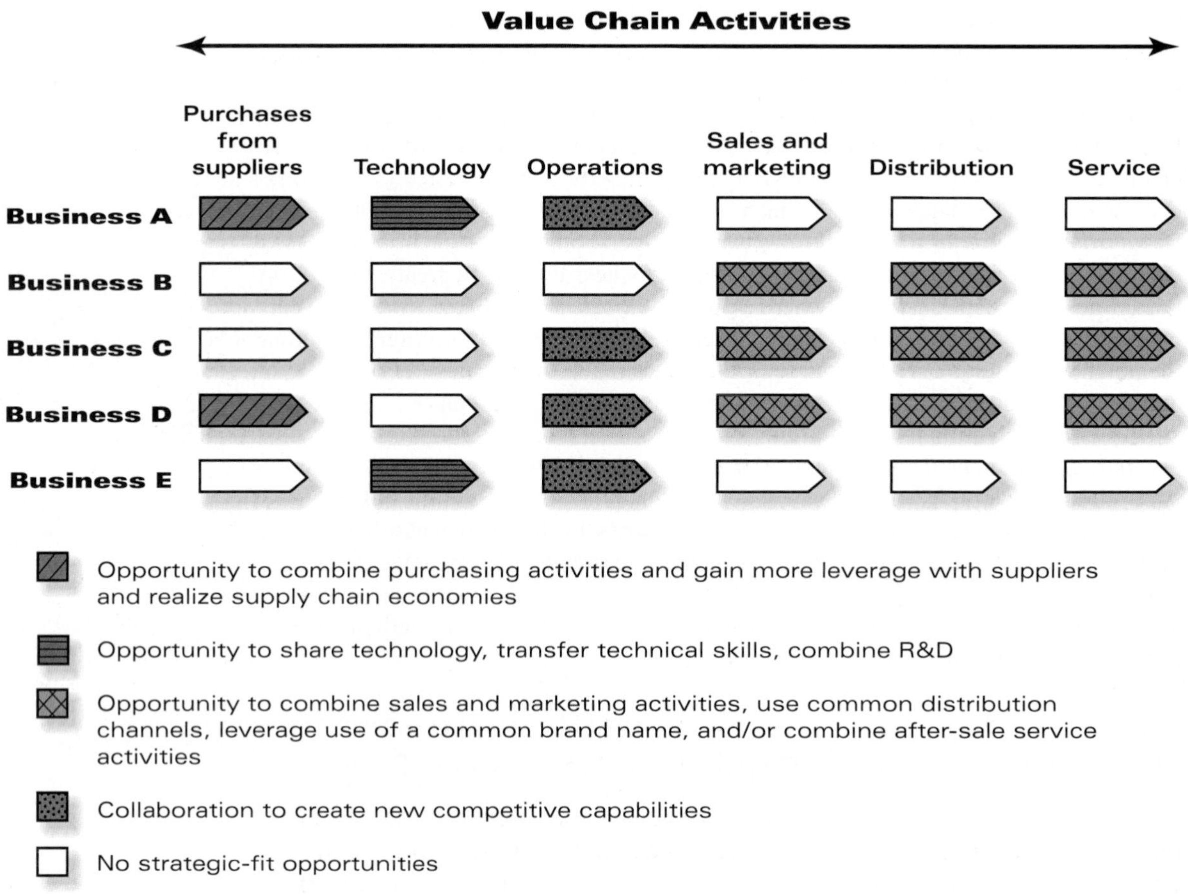

intellectual capital? Will transferring a potent brand name to the products of sister businesses grow sales significantly? Will cross-business collaboration to create or strengthen competitive capabilities lead to significant gains in the marketplace or in financial performance? Without significant strategic fits and dedicated company efforts to capture the benefits, one has to be skeptical about the potential for a diversified company's businesses to perform better together than apart.

Step 4: Checking for Resource Fit

The businesses in a diversified company's lineup need to exhibit good **resource fit.** Resource fit exists when (1) the businesses add to a company's overall resource strengths and (2) a company has the resources to adequately support its businesses as a group without spreading itself too thin. One important dimension of resource fit concerns whether a diversified company can generate the internal cash flows sufficient to fund the capital requirements of its businesses, pay its dividends, meet its debt obligations, and otherwise remain financially healthy.

> **Core Concept**
>
> A company's businesses exhibit **resource fit** when the various businesses, individually and collectively, add to the company's overall resource strengths and when the company's complement of resources is adequate to support the requirements of its business units.

Financial Resource Fits: Cash Cows versus Cash Hogs   Different businesses have different cash flow and investment characteristics. For example, business units in rapidly growing industries are often **cash hogs**—so labeled because the cash flows they are able to generate from internal operations aren't big enough to fund their expansion. To keep pace with rising buyer demand, rapid-growth businesses frequently need sizable annual capital investments—for new facilities and equipment, for new product development or technology improvements, and for additional working capital to support inventory expansion and a larger base of operations. A business in a fast-growing industry becomes an even bigger cash hog when it has a relatively low market share and is pursuing a strategy to become an industry leader. Because a cash hog's financial resources must be provided by the corporate parent, corporate managers have to decide whether it makes good financial and strategic sense to keep pouring additional money into a business that continually needs cash infusions.

> **Core Concept**
>
> A **cash hog** is a business whose internal cash flows are inadequate to fully fund its needs for working capital and new capital investment.

In contrast, business units with leading market positions in mature industries may, however, be **cash cows**—businesses that generate substantial cash surpluses over what is needed to adequately fund their operations. Market leaders in slow-growth industries often generate sizable positive cash flows *over and above what is needed for growth and reinvestment* because their industry-leading positions tend to give them the sales volumes and reputation to earn attractive profits and because the slow-growth nature of their industries often entails relatively modest annual investment requirements. Cash cows, though not always attractive from a growth standpoint, are valuable businesses from a financial resource perspective. The surplus cash flows they generate can be used to pay corporate dividends, finance acquisitions, and provide funds for investing in the company's promising cash hogs. It makes good financial and strategic sense for diversified companies to keep cash cows in healthy condition, fortifying and defending their market position so as to preserve their cash-generating capability over the long term and thereby have an ongoing source of financial resources to deploy elsewhere. The cigarette business is one of the world's biggest cash-cow businesses. General Electric, whose business lineup is

> **Core Concept**
>
> A **cash cow** is a business that generates cash flows over and above its internal requirements, thus providing a corporate parent with funds for investing in cash hog businesses, financing new acquisitions, or paying dividends.

shown in Company Spotlight 6.2 on page 205, considers that its advanced materials, equipment services, and appliance and lighting businesses are cash cow businesses.

Viewing a diversified group of businesses as a collection of cash flows and cash requirements (present and future) is a major step forward in understanding what the financial ramifications of diversification are and why having businesses with good financial resource fit is so important. For instance, *a diversified company's businesses exhibit good financial resource fit when the excess cash generated by its cash-cow businesses is sufficient to fund the investment requirements of promising cash-hog businesses.* Ideally, investing in promising cash-hog businesses over time results in growing the hogs into self-supporting *star businesses* that have strong or market-leading competitive positions in attractive, high-growth markets and have high levels of profitability. Star businesses are often the cash cows of the future—when the markets of star businesses begin to mature and their growth slows, their competitive strength should produce self-generated cash flows more than sufficient to cover their investment needs. The "success sequence" is thus cash hog to young star (but perhaps still a cash hog) to self-supporting star to cash cow.

If, however, a cash hog has questionable promise (either because of low industry attractiveness or a weak competitive position), then it becomes a logical candidate for divestiture. Pursuing an aggressive invest-and-expand strategy for a cash hog with an uncertain future seldom makes sense because it requires the corporate parent to keep pumping more capital into the business with only a dim hope of eventually turning the cash hog into a future star and realizing a good return on its investments. Such businesses are a financial drain and fail the resource-fit test because they strain the corporate parent's ability to adequately fund its other businesses. Divesting a less attractive cash-hog business is usually the best alternative unless (1) it has valuable strategic fits with other business units or (2) the capital infusions needed from the corporate parent are modest relative to the funds available and there's a decent chance of growing the business into a solid bottom-line contributor yielding a good return on invested capital.

Other Tests of Resource Fit   Aside from cash flow considerations, there are two other factors to consider in determining whether the businesses constituting a diversified company's portfolio exhibit good resource fit from a financial perspective:

- *Does the business adequately contribute to achieving companywide performance targets?* A business has good financial fit when it contributes to the achievement of corporate performance objectives (growth in earnings per share, above-average return on investment, recognition as an industry leader, etc.) and when it materially enhances shareholder value via helping drive increases in the company's stock price. A business exhibits poor financial fit if it soaks up a disproportionate share of the company's financial resources, makes subpar or inconsistent bottom-line contributions, is unduly risky and its failure would jeopardize the entire enterprise, or remains too small to make a material earnings contribution even though it performs well.

- *Does the company have adequate financial strength to fund its different businesses and still maintain a healthy credit rating?* A diversified company's strategy fails the resource-fit test when its financial resources are stretched across so many businesses that its credit rating is impaired. Severe financial strain sometimes occurs when a company borrows so heavily to finance new acquisitions that it has to trim way back on capital expenditures for existing businesses and use the big majority of its financial resources to meet interest obligations and to pay down debt. Time Warner, Royal Ahold, and AT&T, for example, have found themselves so financially overextended that they have had to sell off some of their business units to raise the money to pay down burdensome debt obligations and continue to fund essential capital expenditures for the remaining businesses.

■ *Does the company have or can it develop the specific resource strengths and competitive capabilities needed to be successful in each of its businesses?*[15] Sometimes the resource strengths a company has accumulated in its core or mainstay business prove to be a poor match with the key success factors and competitive capabilities needed to succeed in one or more businesses it has diversified into. For instance, BTR, a multibusiness company in Great Britain, discovered that its resources and managerial skills were quite well suited for parenting industrial manufacturing businesses but not for parenting its distribution businesses (National Tyre Services and Texas-based Summers Group); as a consequence, BTR decided to divest its distribution businesses and focus exclusively on diversifying around small industrial manufacturing.[16] One company with businesses in restaurants and retailing decided that its resource capabilities in site selection, control of operating costs, management selection and training, and supply chain logistics would enable it to succeed in the hotel business and in property management; but what management missed was that these businesses had some significantly different key success factors—namely, skills in controlling property development costs, maintaining low overheads, branding products (hotels), and recruiting a sufficient volume of business to maintain high levels of facility utilization.[17] Thus, a mismatch between the company's resource strengths and the key success factors in a particular business can be serious enough to warrant divesting an existing business or not acquiring a new business. In contrast, when a company's resources and capabilities are a good match with the key success factors of industries it is not presently in, it makes sense to take a hard look at acquiring companies in these industries and expanding the company's business lineup.

■ *Are recently acquired businesses acting to strengthen a company's resource base and competitive capabilities, or are they causing its competitive and managerial resources to be stretched too thinly?* A diversified company has to guard against overtaxing its resource strengths, a condition that can arise when (1) it goes on an acquisition spree and management is called upon to assimilate and oversee many new businesses very quickly or (2) it lacks sufficient resource depth to do a creditable job of transferring skills and competencies from one of its businesses to another (especially, a large acquisition or several lesser ones). The broader the diversification, the greater the concern about whether the company has sufficient managerial depth to cope with the diverse range of operating problems its wide business lineup presents. And the more a company's diversification strategy is tied to transferring its existing know-how or technologies to new businesses, the more it has to develop a big-enough and deep-enough resource pool to supply these businesses with sufficient capability to create competitive advantage.[18] Otherwise, its strengths end up being thinly spread across many businesses, and the opportunity for competitive advantage slips through the cracks.

A Cautionary Note about Transferring Resources from One Business to Another   Just because a company has hit a home run in one business doesn't mean it can easily enter a new business with similar resource requirements and hit a second home run.[19] Noted British retailer Marks & Spencer, despite possessing a range of impressive resource capabilities (ability to choose excellent store locations, having a supply chain that gives it both low costs and high merchandise quality, loyal employees, an excellent reputation with consumers, and strong management expertise) that have made it one of Britain's premier retailers for 100 years, has failed repeatedly in its efforts to diversify into department store retailing in the United States. Even though Philip Morris (now named Altria) had built powerful consumer marketing capabilities in its cigarette and beer businesses, it floundered in soft drinks and ended up divesting its acquisition of 7UP after several frustrating years of competing against strongly entrenched and resource-capable rivals like Coca-Cola and PepsiCo. Then in 2002 it decided to divest its Miller Brewing business—despite its long-standing marketing successes in cigarettes and in its Kraft Foods subsidiary—because it was unable to grow Miller's market share in head-to-head competition against the considerable marketing prowess of Anheuser-Busch.

Step 5: Ranking the Performance Prospects of Business Units and Assigning a Priority for Resource Allocation

Once a diversified company's strategy has been evaluated from the perspective of industry attractiveness, competitive strength, strategic fit, and resource fit, the next step is to rank the performance prospects of the businesses from best to worst and determine which businesses merit top priority for resource support and new capital investments by the corporate parent.

The most important considerations in judging business-unit performance are sales growth, profit growth, contribution to company earnings, and return on capital invested in the business. Sometimes, cash flow is a big consideration. Information on each business's past performance can be gleaned from a company's financial records. While past performance is not necessarily a good predictor of future performance, it does signal whether a business already has good-to-excellent performance or has problems to overcome.

Furthermore, the industry attractiveness/business strength evaluations provide a solid basis for judging a business's prospects. Normally, strong business units in attractive industries have significantly better prospects than weak businesses in unattractive industries. And, normally, the revenue and earnings outlook for businesses in fast-growing industries is better than for businesses in slow-growing industries—one important exception occurs when a business in a slow-growing industry has the competitive strength to draw sales and market share away from its rivals and thus achieve much faster growth than the industry as a whole. As a rule, the prior analyses, taken together, signal which business units are likely to be strong performers on the road ahead and which are likely to be laggards. And it is a short step from ranking the prospects of business units to drawing conclusions about whether the company as a whole is capable of strong, mediocre, or weak performance in upcoming years.

The rankings of future performance generally determine what priority the corporate parent should give to each business in terms of resource allocation. The task here is to decide which business units should have top priority for corporate resource support and new capital investment and which should carry the lowest priority. *Business subsidiaries with the brightest profit and growth prospects and solid strategic and resource fits generally should head the list for corporate resource support.* More specifically, corporate executives need to consider whether and how corporate resources can be used to enhance the competitiveness of particular business units. And they must be diligent in steering resources out of low-opportunity areas into high-opportunity areas. Divesting marginal businesses is one of the best ways of freeing unproductive assets for redeployment. Surplus funds from cash cows also add to the corporate treasury.

Figure 6.7   **The Chief Strategic and Financial Options for Allocating a Diversified Company's Financial Resources**

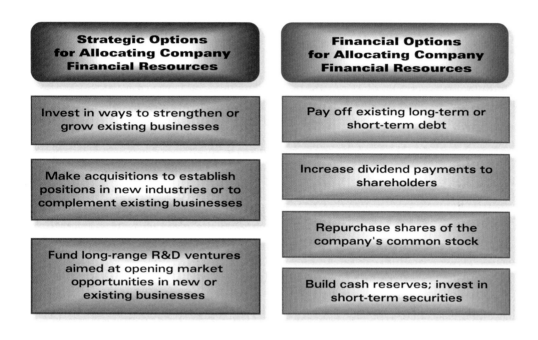

Figure 6.7 shows the chief strategic and financial options for allocating a diversified company's financial resources. Ideally, a company will have enough funds to do what is needed, both strategically and financially. If not, strategic uses of corporate resources should usually take precedence unless there is a compelling reason to strengthen the firm's balance sheet or divert financial resources to pacify shareholders.

Step 6: Crafting New Strategic Moves to Improve Overall Corporate Performance

The diagnosis and conclusions flowing from the five preceding analytical steps set the agenda for crafting strategic moves to improve a diversified company's overall performance. The strategic options boil down to five broad categories of actions:

1. Sticking closely with the existing business lineup and pursuing the opportunities these businesses present.
2. Broadening the company's business scope by making new acquisitions in new industries.
3. Divesting certain businesses and retrenching to a narrower base of business operations.
4. Restructuring the company's business lineup and putting a whole new face on the company's business makeup.
5. Pursuing multinational diversification and striving to globalize the operations of several of the company's business units.

The option of sticking with the current business lineup makes sense when the company's present businesses offer attractive growth opportunities and can be counted on to generate good earnings and cash flows. As long as the company's set of existing businesses puts it in good position for the future and these businesses have good strategic and/or resource fits, then rocking the boat with major changes in the company's business mix is usually unnecessary. Corporate executives can concentrate their attention on getting the best performance from each of its businesses, steering corporate resources into those areas of greatest potential and profitability. The specifics of "what to do" to wring better performance from the present business lineup have to be dictated by each business's circumstances and the preceding analysis of the corporate parent's diversification strategy.

However, in the event that corporate executives are not entirely satisfied with the opportunities they see in the company's present set of businesses and conclude that changes in the company's direction and business makeup are in order, they can opt for any of the four other strategic alternatives listed above. These options are discussed in the following section.

After a Company Diversifies: The Four Main Strategy Alternatives

Diversifying is by no means the final chapter in the evolution of a company's strategy. Once a company has diversified into a collection of related or unrelated businesses and concludes that some overhaul is needed in the company's present lineup and diversification strategy, there are four main strategic paths it can pursue (see Figure 6.8). To more fully understand the strategic issues corporate managers face in the ongoing process of managing a diversified group of businesses, we need to take a brief look at the central thrust of each of the four postdiversification strategy alternatives.

Strategies to Broaden a Diversified Company's Business Base

Diversified companies sometimes find it desirable to build positions in new industries, whether related or unrelated. There are several motivating factors. One is sluggish growth that makes the potential revenue and profit boost of a newly acquired business look attractive. A second is vulnerability to seasonal or recessionary influences or to threats from emerging new technologies. A third is the potential for transferring resources and capabilities to other related or complementary businesses. A fourth is rapidly changing conditions in one or more of a company's core businesses brought on by technological, legislative, or new product innovations that alter buyer requirements and preferences. For instance, the passage of legislation in the United States allowing banks, insurance companies, and stock brokerages to enter each other's businesses spurred a raft of acquisitions and mergers to create full-service financial enterprises capable of meeting the multiple financial needs of customers. Citigroup, already the largest U.S. bank with a global banking franchise, acquired Salomon Smith Barney to position itself in the investment banking and brokerage business and acquired insurance giant Travelers Group to enable it to offer customers insurance products.

A fifth, and often very important, motivating factor for adding new businesses is to complement and strengthen the market position and competitive capabilities of one or more of its present businesses. Viacom's acquisition of CBS strengthened and extended Viacom's reach into various media businesses—it was the parent of Paramount Pictures,

Figure 6.8   A Company's Four Main Strategic Alternatives after
It Diversifies

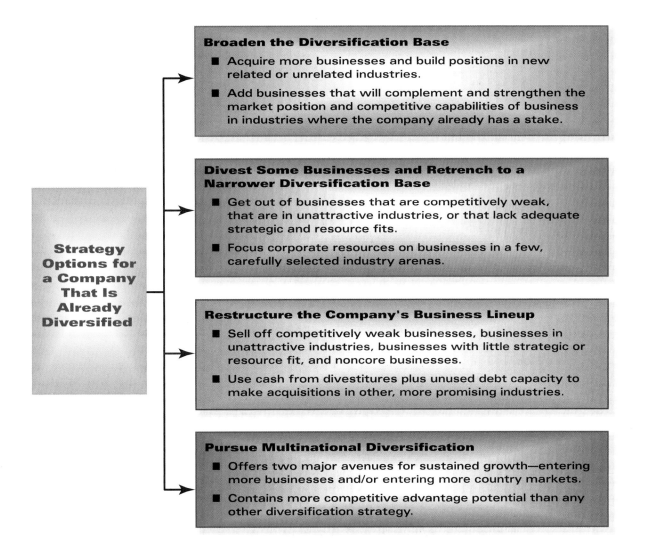

an assortment of cable TV networks (UPN, MTV, Nickelodeon, VH1, Showtime, The Movie Channel, Comedy Central), Blockbuster video stores, 2 movie theater chains, and 19 local TV stations. Unilever, a leading maker of food and personal care products, expanded its business lineup by acquiring SlimFast, Ben & Jerry's Homemade Ice Cream, and Bestfoods (whose brands included Knorr's soups, Hellman's mayonnaise, Skippy peanut butter, and Mazola cooking oils). Unilever saw these businesses as giving it more clout in competing against such other diversified food and household products companies as Nestlé, Kraft, Procter & Gamble, Campbell Soup, and General Mills.

Usually, expansion into new businesses is undertaken by acquiring companies already in the target industry. Some companies depend on new acquisitions to drive a major portion of their growth in revenues and earnings, and thus are always on the acquisition trail. Cisco Systems built itself into a worldwide leader in networking

COMPANY SPOTLIGHT 6.3
Managing Diversification at Johnson & Johnson— The Benefits of Cross-Business Strategic Fits

Johnson & Johnson (J&J), once a consumer products company known for its Band-Aid line and its baby care products, has evolved into a $47 billion diversified enterprise consisting of some 200-plus operating companies organized into three divisions: drugs, medical devices and diagnostics, and consumer products. Over the past decade J&J has acquired 54 businesses at a cost of about $30 billion; about 10 to 15 percent of J&J's annual growth in revenues has come from acquisitions. Much of the company's recent growth has been in the pharmaceutical division, which in 2004 accounted for 47 percent of J&J's revenues and 57 percent of its operating profits.

While each of J&J's business units sets its own strategies and operates with its own finance and human resources departments, corporate management strongly encourages cross-business cooperation and collaboration, believing that many of the advances in 21st-century medicine will come from applying advances in one discipline to another. J&J had 9,300 scientists working in 40 research labs in 2003, and the frequency of cross-disciplinary collaboration was increasing. One of J&J's new drug-coated stents grew out of a discussion between a drug researcher and a researcher in the company's stent business. (When stents are inserted to prop open arteries following angioplasty, the drug coating helps prevent infection.) A gene technology database compiled by the company's gene research lab was shared with personnel from the diagnostics division, who developed a test that the drug R&D people could use to predict which patients would most benefit from an experimental cancer therapy. J&J experts in various diseases have been meeting quarterly for the past five years to share information, and top management is setting up cross-disciplinary groups to focus on new treatments for particular diseases. J&J's new liquid Band-Aid product (a liquid coating applied to hard-to-cover places like fingers and knuckles) is based on a material used in a wound-closing product sold by the company's hospital products company.

J&J's corporate management maintains that close collaboration among people in its diagnostics, medical devices, and pharmaceutical businesses— where numerous cross-business strategic fits exist— gives J&J an edge on competitors, most of whom cannot match the company's breadth and depth of expertise.

Source: Amy Barrett, "Staying on Top," *BusinessWeek,* May 5, 2003, pp. 60–68, and www.jnj.com, accessed October 28, 2004 and January 25, 2005.

---

systems for the Internet by making 87 technology-based acquisitions during 1993–2004 to extend its market reach from routing and switching into voice and video over Internet protocol, optical networking, wireless, storage networking, security, broadband, and content networking. Tyco International, now recovering from charges of looting on the part of several top executives, transformed itself from an obscure company in the early 1990s into a $36 billion global manufacturing enterprise with operations in over 100 countries as of 2004 by making over 1,000 acquisitions; the company's far-flung diversification includes businesses in electronics, electrical components, fire and security systems, health care products, valves, undersea telecommunications systems, plastics, and adhesives. Tyco made over 700 acquisitions of small companies in the 1999–2001 period alone.

Company Spotlight 6.3 describes how Johnson & Johnson has used acquisitions to diversify far beyond its well-known Band-Aid and baby care businesses and become a major player in pharmaceuticals, medical devices, and medical diagnostics.

Divestiture Strategies Aimed at Retrenching to a Narrower Diversification Base

A number of diversified firms have had difficulty managing a diverse group of businesses and have elected to get out of some of them. Retrenching to a narrower diversification base is usually undertaken when top management concludes that its diversification strategy has ranged too far afield and that the company can improve long-term performance by concentrating on building stronger positions in a smaller number of core businesses and industries. Hewlett-Packard spun off its testing and measurement businesses into a stand-alone company called Agilent Technologies so that it could better concentrate on its PC, workstation, server, printer and peripherals, and electronics businesses. PepsiCo divested its cash-hog group of restaurant businesses, consisting of Kentucky Fried Chicken, Pizza Hut, Taco Bell, and California Pizza Kitchens, to provide more resources for strengthening its soft-drink business (which was losing market share to Coca-Cola) and growing its more profitable Frito-Lay snack foods business. Kmart divested OfficeMax, Sports Authority, and Borders Bookstores in order to refocus management attention and all of the company's resources on restoring luster to its distressed discount retailing business, which was (and still is) being totally outclassed in the marketplace by Wal-Mart and Target. In 2003–2004, Tyco International began a program to divest itself of some 50 businesses, including its entire undersea fiber-optics telecommunications network and an assortment of businesses in its fire and security division; the initiative also involved consolidating 219 manufacturing, sales, distribution, and other facilities and reducing its workforce of some 260,000 people by 7,200. Lucent Technology's retrenchment strategy is described in Company Spotlight 6.4.

> Focusing corporate resources on a few core and mostly related businesses avoids the mistake of diversifying so broadly that resources and management attention are stretched too thin.

But there are other important reasons for divesting one or more of a company's present businesses. Sometimes divesting a business has to be considered because market conditions in a once attractive industry have badly deteriorated. A business can become a prime candidate for divestiture because it lacks adequate strategic or resource fit, because it is a cash hog with questionable long-term potential, or because it is weakly positioned in its industry with little prospect that the corporate parent can realize a decent return on its investment in the business. Sometimes a company acquires businesses that, down the road, just do not work out as expected even though management has tried all it can think of to make them profitable—mistakes cannot be completely avoided because it is hard to foresee how getting into a new line of business will actually work out. Subpar performance by some business units is bound to occur, thereby raising questions of whether to divest them or keep them and attempt a turnaround. Other business units, despite adequate financial performance, may not mesh as well with the rest of the firm as was originally thought.

On occasion, a diversification move that seems sensible from a strategic-fit standpoint turns out to be a poor *cultural fit.*[20] Several pharmaceutical companies had just this experience. When they diversified into cosmetics and perfume, they discovered their personnel had little respect for the "frivolous" nature of such products compared to the far nobler task of developing miracle drugs to cure the ill. The absence of shared values and cultural compatibility between the medical research and chemical-compounding expertise of the pharmaceutical companies and the fashion/marketing orientation of the cosmetics business was the undoing of what otherwise was diversification into businesses with technology-sharing potential, product development fit, and some overlap in distribution channels.

Recent research indicates that pruning businesses and narrowing a firm's diversification base improve corporate performance.[21] Corporate parents often end up selling off businesses too late and at too low a price, sacrificing shareholder value.[22] A useful guide to determine whether or when to divest a business subsidiary is to ask, "If we were not in this business today, would we want to get into it now?"[23] When the answer

At the height of the telecommunication boom in 1999–2000, Lucent Technology was a company with $38.3 billion in revenues and 157,000 employees; it was the biggest maker of telecommunications equipment in the United States and a recognized leader worldwide. The company's strategy was to build positions in a number of blossoming technologies and industry arenas and achieve 20 percent annual revenue growth in each of 11 different business groups. But when customers' orders for new equipment began to evaporate in 2000–2001, Lucent's profits vanished and the once-growing company found itself battling to overcome bloated costs, deep price discounting, and customer defaults on the $7.5 billion in loans Lucent had made to finance their purchases. As it became clear that equipment sales and prices would never return to former levels, Lucent executives concluded that the company had overextended itself trying to do too many things and needed to pare its lineup of businesses.

Alongside efforts to curtail lavish spending at the company's fabled Bell Labs research unit, make deep workforce cutbacks, streamline order-taking and billing systems, shore up the balance sheet, and conserve cash by ending dividend payments, management launched a series of retrenchment initiatives:

- In 2000, Lucent spun off the business which made gear for sending business calls through data networks as an independent company named Avaya, Inc.

- In 2002, still under intense financial pressure, Lucent exited the chip-making business by spinning the operation off as a company named Agere Systems.

- Lucent ceased all manufacturing operations, opting to outsource everything.

- It stopped making gear for wireless phone networks based on a technology known as GSM (the dominant technology used in Europe and much of the world) in order to focus more fully on wireless gear using CMDA technology (a technology prevalent in the United States and some developing nations). As of 2004 Lucent had an estimated 45 percent share in the CMDA market, and the CMDA gear division was the company's chief revenue and profit producer.

- Of the 40 businesses Lucent acquired since 1996, 27 were sold, closed, or spun off.

These strategic moves to retrench stemmed a string of 13 straight money-losing quarters. Going into 2005, Lucent was a company with sales of about $9 billion and a workforce of 32,000. The company's stock price, which reached a high of $62 in 1999 before crashing to below $1 in 2002, was trading in the $3 to $4 range. In May 2004, Lucent announced its first acquisition in four years, buying a maker of Internet transmission technology for $300 million; the acquisition was intended to help Lucent become a leader in Internet telephone technology and grow the company's overall revenues.

Sources: Shawn Young, "Less May Be More," *The Wall Street Journal*, October 23, 2004, p. R10, and www.lucent.com, accessed October 28, 2004.

---

is no or probably not, divestiture should be considered. Another signal that a business should become a divestiture candidate is whether it is worth more to another company than to the present parent; in such cases, shareholders would be well served if the company sells the business and collects a premium price from the buyer for whom the business is a valuable fit.[24]

The Two Options for Divesting a Business: Selling It or Spinning It Off as an Independent Company   Selling a business outright to another company is far and away the most frequently used option for divesting a business. But sometimes a business selected for divestiture has ample resource strengths to compete successfully on its own. In such cases, a corporate parent may elect to spin the unwanted business off as a financially and managerially independent company, either by selling shares to the investing public via an initial public offering or by distributing shares in the new company to existing shareholders of the corporate parent. When a corporate parent decides to spin off one of its businesses as a separate company, there's the issue of whether or not to retain partial ownership. Retaining partial ownership makes sense when the business to be divested has a hot product or technological capabilities that give it good profit prospects. When 3Com elected to divest its PalmPilot business, which investors then saw as having very promising profit potential, it elected to retain a substantial ownership interest so as to provide 3Com shareholders a way of participating in whatever future market success PalmPilot (now Palm, Inc.) might have on its own. In 2001, when Philip Morris became concerned that its popular Kraft Foods subsidiary was suffering because of its affiliation with PM's cigarette business (antismoking groups were leading a national boycott of Kraft Macaroni & Cheese and a Harris poll revealed that about 16 percent of people familiar with Philip Morris had boycotted its products), Philip Morris executives opted to spin Kraft Foods off as an independent public company but retained a controlling ownership interest. R.J. Reynolds Tobacco was also spun off from Nabisco Foods in 1999 in an effort to distance the tobacco operations part of the company from the food operations part (Nabisco was then acquired by Philip Morris in 2000 and integrated into Kraft Foods).

Selling a business outright requires finding a buyer. This can prove hard or easy, depending on the business. As a rule, a company selling a troubled business should not ask, "How can we pawn this business off on someone, and what is the most we can get for it?"[25] Instead, it is wiser to ask, "For what sort of company would this business be a good fit, and under what conditions would it be viewed as a good deal?" Enterprises for which the business is a good fit are likely to pay the highest price. Of course, if a buyer willing to pay an acceptable price cannot be found, then a company must decide whether to keep the business until a buyer appears; spin it off as a separate company; or, in the case of a crisis-ridden business that is losing substantial sums, simply close it down and liquidate the remaining assets. Liquidation is obviously a last resort.

Strategies to Restructure a Company's Business Lineup

Restructuring strategies involve divesting some businesses and acquiring others so as to put a whole new face on the company's business lineup. Performing radical surgery on a company's group of businesses is an appealing strategy alternative when its financial performance is being squeezed or eroded by:

> **Core Concept**
>
> **Restructuring** involves divesting some businesses and acquiring others so as to put a whole new face on the company's business lineup.

- Too many businesses in slow-growth, declining, low-margin, or otherwise unattractive industries (a condition indicated by the number and size of businesses with industry attractiveness ratings below 5 and located on the bottom half of the attractiveness-strength matrix—see Figure 6.5).

- Too many competitively weak businesses (a condition indicated by the number and size of businesses with competitive strength ratings below 5 and located on the right half of the attractiveness-strength matrix).

- Ongoing declines in the market shares of one or more major business units that are falling prey to more market-savvy competitors.

- An excessive debt burden with interest costs that eat deeply into profitability.

- Ill-chosen acquisitions that haven't lived up to expectations.

Restructuring can also be mandated by the emergence of new technologies that threaten the survival of one or more of a diversified company's important businesses or by the appointment of a new CEO who decides to redirect the company. On occasion, restructuring can be prompted by special circumstances—like when a firm has a unique opportunity to make an acquisition so big and important that it has to sell several existing business units to finance the new acquisition or when a company needs to sell off some businesses in order to raise the cash for entering a potentially big industry with wave-of-the-future technologies or products.

Candidates for divestiture in a corporate restructuring effort typically include not only weak or up-and-down performers or those in unattractive industries but also business units that lack strategic fit with the businesses to be retained, businesses that are cash hogs or that lack other types of resource fit, and businesses incompatible with the company's revised diversification strategy (even though they may be profitable or in an attractive industry). As businesses are divested, corporate restructuring generally involves aligning the remaining business units into groups with the best strategic fits and then redeploying the cash flows from the divested business to either pay down debt or make new acquisitions to strengthen the parent company's business position in the industries it has chosen to emphasize.[26]

Over the past decade, corporate restructuring has become a popular strategy at many diversified companies, especially those that had diversified broadly into many different industries and lines of business. For instance, one struggling diversified company over a two-year period divested 4 business units, closed down the operations of 4 others, and added 25 new lines of business to its portfolio (16 through acquisition and 9 through internal start-up). PerkinElmer used a series of divestitures and new acquisitions to transform itself from a supplier of low-margin services sold to the government agencies into an innovative high-tech company with operations in over 125 countries and businesses in four industry groups—life sciences (drug research and clinical screening), optoelectronics, instruments, and fluid control and containment (for customers in aerospace, power generation, and semiconductors). Before beginning a restructuring effort in 1995, British-based Hanson PLC owned companies with more than $20 billion in revenues in industries as diverse as beer, exercise equipment, tools, construction cranes, tobacco, cement, chemicals, coal mining, electricity, hot tubs and whirlpools, cookware, rock and gravel, bricks, and asphalt. By early 1997, Hanson had restructured itself into a $3.8 billion enterprise focused more narrowly on gravel, crushed rock, cement, asphalt, bricks, and construction cranes; the remaining businesses were divided into four groups and divested.

During Jack Welch's first four years as CEO of General Electric (GE), the company divested 117 business units, accounting for about 20 percent of GE's assets; these divestitures, coupled with several important acquisitions, provided GE with 14 major business divisions and led to Welch's challenge to the managers of GE's divisions to become number one or number two in their industry. Ten years after Welch became CEO, GE was a different company, having divested operations worth $9 billion, made new acquisitions totaling $24 billion, and cut its workforce by 100,000 people. Then, during the 1990–2001 period, GE continued to reshuffle its business lineup, acquiring over 600 new companies, including 108 in 1998 and 64 during a 90-day period in 1999. Most of the new acquisitions were in Europe, Asia, and Latin America and were aimed at transforming GE into a truly global enterprise. In 2003, GE's new CEO, Jeffrey Immelt, began a further restructuring of GE's business lineup with three initiatives: (1) spending $10 billion to acquire British-based Amersham and extend GE's Medical Systems business into diagnostic pharmaceuticals and biosciences, thereby creating a $15 billion business designated as GE Healthcare; (2) acquiring the entertainment assets of debt-ridden French media conglomerate Vivendi Universal Entertainment (Universal Studios, five Universal theme parks, USA Network, Sci-Fi Channel, the Trio cable channel, and Spanish-language broadcaster Telemundo) and integrating its operations into GE's NBC division (the owner of NBC, 29 television stations, and cable networks CNBC, MSNBC, and Bravo), thereby creating a broad-based $13 billion media business positioned to compete against Walt Disney, Time Warner, Fox, and Viacom; and (3) beginning a withdrawal from the insurance business by divesting several companies in its insurance division and preparing to spin off its remaining life and mortgage insurance businesses through an IPO for a new company called Genworth Financial.

In a study of the performance of the 200 largest U.S. corporations from 1990 to 2000, McKinsey & Company found that those companies that actively managed their business portfolios through acquisitions and divestitures created substantially more shareholder value than those that kept a fixed lineup of businesses.[27]

Multinational Diversification Strategies

The distinguishing characteristics of a multinational diversification strategy are a *diversity of businesses* and a *diversity of national markets*.[28] Such diversity makes multinational diversification a particularly challenging and complex strategy to conceive and execute. Managers have to develop business strategies for each industry (with as many multinational variations as conditions in each country market dictate). Then, they have to pursue and manage opportunities for cross-business and cross-country collaboration and strategic coordination in ways calculated to result in competitive advantage and enhanced profitability.

Moreover, the geographic operating scope of individual businesses within a diversified multinational company (DMNC) can range from only one country to several countries to many countries to global. Thus, each business unit within a DMNC often competes in a somewhat different combination of geographic markets than the other businesses do—adding another element of strategic complexity and perhaps an element of opportunity.

Global Spotlight 6.1 shows the scope of four prominent DMNCs.

The Appeal of Multinational Diversification: More Opportunities for Sustained Growth and Maximum Competitive Advantage Potential Despite their complexity, multinational diversification strategies have great appeal. They contain *two major avenues* for growing revenues and profits: one is to grow by entering additional businesses, and the other is to grow by extending the operations of existing businesses into additional country markets. Moreover, a strategy of multinational diversification also contains six attractive paths to competitive advantage, *all of which can be pursued simultaneously*:

1. *Full capture of economies of scale and experience- and learning-curve effects:* In some businesses, the volume of sales needed to realize full economies of scale and/or benefit fully from experience- and learning-curve effects is rather sizable, often exceeding the volume that can be achieved operating within the boundaries of a single-country market, especially a small one. *The ability to drive down unit costs by expanding sales to additional country markets is one reason why a diversified multinational may seek to acquire a business and then rapidly expand its operations into more and more foreign markets.*

Company	Global Scope	Businesses into Which the Company Has Diversified
Sony	Operations in more than 100 countries and sales offices in more than 200 countries	■ Televisions, VCRs, DVD players, radios, digital cameras and video equipment, Vaio PCs, Trinitron computer monitors; PlayStation game consoles and video game software; Columbia, Epic, and Sony Classical prerecorded music; Columbia TriStar motion pictures; syndicated television programs; entertainment complexes; and insurance.
Nestlé	Operations in 70 countries and sales offices in more than 200 countries	■ Beverages (Nescafé and Taster's Choice coffees; Nestea, Perrier, Arrowhead, and Calistoga mineral and bottled waters); milk products (Carnation, Gloria, Neslac, Coffee Mate, Nestlé ice cream and yogurt); pet foods (Friskies, Alpo, Fancy Feast, Mighty Dog); Contadina, Libby's, and Stouffer's food products and prepared dishes; chocolate and confectionery products (Nestlé Crunch, Smarties, Baby Ruth, Butterfinger, KitKat); and pharmaceuticals (Alcon opthalmic products, Galderma dermatological products).
Siemens	Operations in 160 countries and sales offices in more than 190 countries	■ Electrical power generation, transmission, and distribution equipment and products; manufacturing automation systems; industrial motors, machinery, and tools; plant construction and maintenance; corporate communication networks; telephones; PCs, mainframes, computer network products, consulting services; mass-transit and light-rail systems, rail cars, locomotives; lighting products (bulbs, lamps, theater and television lighting systems); semiconductors; home appliances; vacuum cleaners; and financial, procurement, and logistics services.
Samsung	Operations in more than 60 countries and sales in more than 200 countries	■ Notebook computers, hard-disk drives, CD/DVD-ROM drives, monitors, printers, and fax machines; televisions (big-screen TVs, plasma-screen TVs, and LCD-screen TVs); DVD and MP3 players; cell phones and various other telecommunications products; compressors; home appliances; DRAM chips, flash memory chips, and graphics memory chip; and optical fibers, fiber-optics cables, and fiber-optics connectors.

Source: Company annual reports and Web sites.

2. *Opportunities to capitalize on cross-business economies of scope:* Diversifying into related businesses offering economies of scope can drive the development of a low-cost advantage over less diversified rivals. For example, a DMNC that uses mostly the same distributors and retail dealers worldwide can diversify into new businesses using these same worldwide distribution channels at relatively little incremental expense. The cost savings of piggybacking distribution activities can be substantial. Moreover, with more businesses selling more products in more countries, a DMNC acquires more bargaining leverage in its purchases from suppliers and more bargaining leverage with retailers in securing attractive display space for its products. Consider, for example, the competitive power that Sony derived from these very sorts of economies of scope when it decided to diversify into the video game business with its PlayStation product line. Sony had in-place capability to go after video game sales in all country markets where it presently did business in other electronics product categories (TVs, computers, DVD players, VCRs, radios, CD players, and camcorders). And it had the marketing clout and brand-name credibility to persuade retailers to give Sony's PlayStation products prime shelf space and visibility. These strategic-fit benefits helped Sony quickly overtake longtime industry leaders Nintendo and Sega and defend its market leadership against Microsoft's new Xbox.

3. *Opportunities to transfer competitively valuable resources both from one business to another and from one country to another:* A company pursuing related diversification can gain a competitive edge over less diversified rivals by transferring competitively valuable resources from one business to another; a multinational company can gain competitive advantage over rivals with narrower geographic coverage by transferring competitively valuable resources from one country to another. But a strategy of multinational diversification enables simultaneous pursuit of both sources of competitive advantage.

4. *Ability to leverage use of a well-known and competitively powerful brand name:* Diversified multinational companies whose businesses have brand names that are well known and respected across the world possess a valuable strategic asset with competitive advantage potential. For example, Sony's well-established global brand-name recognition gives it an important marketing and advertising advantage over rivals with lesser-known brands. When Sony goes into a new marketplace with the stamp of the Sony brand on its product families, it can command prominent display space with retailers. It can expect to win sales and market share simply on the confidence that buyers place in products carrying the Sony name. While Sony may spend money to make consumers aware of the availability of its new products, it does not have to spend nearly as much on achieving brand recognition and market acceptance as would a lesser-known competitor looking at the marketing and advertising costs of entering the same new product/business/country markets and trying to go head-to-head against Sony. Further, if Sony moves into a new country market for the first time and does well selling Sony PlayStations and video games, it is easier to sell consumers in that country Sony TVs, digital cameras, PCs, MP3 players, and so on—plus, the related advertising costs are likely to be less than they would be without having already established the Sony brand strongly in the minds of buyers.

5. *Ability to capitalize on opportunities for cross-business and cross-country collaboration and strategic coordination:*[29] A multinational diversification strategy allows competitively valuable cross-business and cross-country coordination of certain value chain activities. For instance, by channeling corporate resources directly into a combined R&D/technology effort for all related businesses, as opposed to letting each business unit fund and direct its own R&D effort however it sees fit, a DMNC can merge its expertise and efforts *worldwide* to advance core technologies, expedite cross-business and cross-country product improvements, speed the development of new products that complement existing products, and pursue promising technological avenues to create altogether new businesses—all significant contributors to competitive advantage and better corporate performance.[30] Honda has been very successful in building R&D expertise in gasoline engines and transferring the resulting technological advances to its businesses in automobiles, motorcycles, outboard engines, snow blowers, lawn mowers, garden tillers, and portable power generators. Further, a DMNC can reduce costs through cross-business and cross-country coordination of purchasing and procurement from suppliers, from collaborative introduction and shared use of e-commerce technologies and online sales efforts, and from coordinated product introductions and promotional campaigns. Firms that are less diversified and less global in scope have less such cross-business and cross-country collaborative opportunities.

6. *Opportunities to use cross-business or cross-country subsidization to outcompete rivals:* A financially successful DMNC has potentially valuable organizational

resources and multiple profit sanctuaries in both certain country markets and certain business that it can draw on to wage a market offensive. In comparison, a one-business domestic company has only one profit sanctuary—its home market. A diversified one-country competitor may have profit sanctuaries in several businesses, but all are in the same country market. A one-business multinational company may have profit sanctuaries in several country markets, but all are in the same business. All three are vulnerable to an offensive in their more limited profit sanctuaries by an aggressive DMNC willing to lowball its prices and/or spend extravagantly on advertising to win market share at their expense. A DMNC's ability to keep hammering away at competitors with low prices year after year may reflect either a cost advantage growing out of its related diversification strategy or a willingness to accept low profits or even losses in the market being attacked because it has ample earnings from its other profit sanctuaries. For example, Sony's global-scale diversification strategy gives it unique competitive strengths in out-competing Nintendo and Sega, neither of which are diversified. If need be, Sony can maintain low prices on its PlayStations or fund high-profile promotions for its latest video game products, using earnings from its other business lines to fund its offensive to wrest market share away from Nintendo and Sega in video games. At the same time, Sony can draw on its considerable resources in R&D, its ability to transfer electronics technology from one electronics product family to another, and its expertise in product innovation to introduce better and better video game players, perhaps players that are multifunctional and do more than just play video games. Such competitive actions not only enhance Sony's own brand image but also make it very tough for Nintendo and Sega to match Sony's prices, advertising, and product development efforts and still earn acceptable profits.

The Combined Effects of These Advantages Is Potent

A strategy of diversifying into *related* industries and then competing *globally* in each of these industries thus has great potential for being a winner in the marketplace because of the long-term growth opportunities it offers and the multiple corporate-level competitive advantage opportunities it contains. Indeed, *a strategy of multinational diversification contains more competitive advantage potential* (above and beyond what is achievable through a particular business's own competitive strategy) *than any other diversification strategy.* The strategic key to maximum competitive advantage is for a DMNC to concentrate its diversification efforts in those industries where there are resource-sharing and resource-transfer opportunities and where there are important economies of scope and brand-name benefits. The more a company's diversification strategy yields these kinds of strategic-fit benefits, the more powerful a competitor it becomes and the better its profit and growth performance is likely to be.

> **Core Concept**
>
> A strategy of multinational diversification has more built-in potential for competitive advantage than any other diversification strategy.

However, it is important to recognize that while a DMNC's cross-subsidization capabilities are a potent competitive weapon in theory, in actual practice cross-subsidization can be used only sparingly. It is one thing to *occasionally* divert a portion of the profits and cash flows from existing businesses to help fund entry into a new business or country market or wage a competitive offensive against select rivals. It is quite another thing to *regularly* use cross-subsidization tactics and thereby weaken overall company performance. A DMNC is under the same pressures as any other company to demonstrate consistently acceptable profitability across its whole operation.[31] At some juncture, every business and every country market needs to make a profit contribution or become a candidate for abandonment. As a general rule, *cross-subsidization tactics are justified only when there is a good prospect that the short-term impairment to corporate profitability will be offset by stronger competitiveness and better overall profitability over the long term.*

Key Points

The purpose of diversification is to build shareholder value. Diversification builds shareholder value when a diversified group of businesses can perform better under the auspices of a single corporate parent than they would as independent, stand-alone businesses—the goal is to achieve not just a $1 + 1 = 2$ result but to realize important $1 + 1 = 3$ performance benefits. Whether getting into a new business has potential to enhance shareholder value hinges on whether a company's entry into that business can pass the attractiveness test, the cost-of-entry test, and the better-off test.

There are two fundamental approaches to diversification—into related businesses and into unrelated businesses. The rationale for *related* diversification is *strategic:* diversify into businesses with strategic fits along their respective value chains, capitalize on strategic-fit relationships to gain competitive advantage, and then use competitive advantage to achieve the desired $1 + 1 = 3$ impact on shareholder value.

The basic premise of unrelated diversification is that any business that has good profit prospects and can be acquired on good financial terms is a good business to diversify into. Unrelated diversification strategies surrender the competitive advantage potential of strategic fit in return for such advantages as (1) spreading business risk over a variety of industries and (2) providing opportunities for financial gain (if candidate acquisitions have undervalued assets, are bargain-priced and have good upside potential given the right management, or need the backing of a financially strong parent to capitalize on attractive opportunities).

Analyzing how good a company's diversification strategy involves a six-step process:

Step 1: *Evaluate the long-term attractiveness of the industries into which the firm has diversified.* Industry attractiveness needs to be evaluated from three angles: the attractiveness of each industry on its own, the attractiveness of each industry relative to the others, and the attractiveness of all the industries as a group.

Step 2: *Evaluate the relative competitive strength of each of the company's business units.* The purpose of rating the competitive strength of each business is to gain clear understanding of which businesses are strong contenders in their industries, which are weak contenders, and the underlying reasons for their strength or weakness. The conclusions about industry attractiveness can be joined with the conclusions about competitive strength by drawing an industry attractiveness–competitive strength matrix displaying the positions of each business on a nine-cell grid.

Step 3: *Check for cross-business strategic fits.* A business is more attractive strategically when it has value chain relationships with sister business units that present opportunities to transfer skills or technology, reduce overall costs, share facilities, or share a common brand name—any of which can represent a significant avenue for producing competitive advantage beyond what any one business can achieve on its own.

Step 4: *Check whether the firm's resource strengths fit the resource requirements of its present business lineup.* Resource fit exists when (1) businesses add to a company's resource strengths, either financially or strategically; (2) a company has the resources to adequately support the resource requirements of its businesses as a group without spreading itself too thin; and (3) there are close matches between a company's resources and industry key success factors.

Step 5: *Rank the performance prospects of the businesses from best to worst and determine what the corporate parent's priority should be in allocating resources to its various businesses.* The most important considerations in judging business-unit performance are sales growth, profit growth, contribution to company earnings, and the return on capital invested in the business. Sometimes, cash flow generation is a big consideration. Normally, strong business units in attractive industries have significantly better performance prospects than weak businesses or businesses in unattractive industries. Business subsidiaries with the brightest profit and growth prospects and solid strategic and resource fits generally should head the list for corporate resource support.

Step 6: *Craft new strategic moves to improve overall corporate performance.* This step entails using the results of the preceding analysis as the basis for devising actions to strengthen existing businesses, make new acquisitions, divest weak-performing and unattractive businesses, restructure the company's business lineup, expand the scope of the company's geographic reach multinationally or globally, and otherwise steer corporate resources into the areas of greatest opportunity.

Once a company has diversified, corporate management's task is to manage the collection of businesses for maximum long-term performance. There are four different strategic paths for improving a diversified company's performance: (1) broadening the firm's business base by diversifying into additional businesses, (2) retrenching to a narrower diversification base by divesting some of its present businesses, (3) corporate restructuring, and (4) multinational diversification.

Exercises

1. What do you see as the strategic fits that exist among the value chains of the diversified companies listed in Company Spotlight 6.1?

2. Consider the business lineup of General Electric shown in Company Spotlight 6.2. What problems do you think the top executives at GE encounter in trying to stay on top of all the businesses the company is in? How might they decide the merits of adding new businesses or divesting poorly performing businesses? What types of advice might they be in a position to give to the general managers of each of GE's business units?

3. Go to Johnson & Johnson's Web site at www.jnj.com, click on the "Our Company" link, and review all the different businesses that J&J is in and the variety of products that it produces and markets. Would you characterize the company strategy as one of related or unrelated diversification? What opportunities do you see for cross-business collaboration to capture strategic-fit benefits? Based on the discussion presented in Company Spotlight 6.3, do you see good reason for shareholders to be optimistic about the extent to which cross-business strategic fits might really produce a competitive edge for J&J and lead to added shareholder value?

4. The Walt Disney Company is in the following businesses: theme parks, Disney Cruise Line, resort properties, movie, video, and theatrical productions (for both children and adults), television broadcasting (ABC, Disney Channel, Toon Disney, Classic Sports Network, ESPN and ESPN2, E!, Lifetime, and A&E networks), radio broadcasting (Disney Radio), musical recordings and sales of animation art, Anaheim Mighty Ducks NHL franchise, Anaheim Angels major league baseball franchise (25 percent ownership), books and magazine publishing, interactive software and Internet sites, and The Disney Store retail shops.

Based on the above listing, would you say that Walt Disney's business lineup reflects a strategy of related or unrelated diversification? Be prepared to justify and explain your answer in terms of the extent to which the value chains of Disney's different businesses seem to have competitively valuable cross-business relationships.

CHAPTER 7

Strategy, Ethics, and Social Responsibility

When morality comes up against profit, it is seldom profit that loses.

—Shirley Chisholm, former congresswoman

But I'd shut my eyes in the sentry box so I didn't see nothing wrong.

—Rudyard Kipling, author

Leaders must be more than individuals of high character. They must "lead" others to behave ethically.

—Linda K. Treviño and Michael E. Brown, professors

There is one and only one social responsibility of business—to use its resources and engage in activities designed to increase its profits so long as it stays within the rules of the game, which is to say engages in free and open competition, without deception or fraud.

—Milton Friedman, Nobel Prize–winning economist

Corporations are economic entities, to be sure, but they are also social institutions that must justify their existence by their overall contribution to society.

—Henry Mintzberg, Robert Simons, and Kunal Basu, professors

Knowing all the moral theory in the world does not equip a person to specify in advance the moral norms of business ethics.

—Thomas Donaldson and Thomas W. Dunfee, professors

Clearly, a company has a responsibility to make a profit and grow the business—in capitalistic or market economies, management's fiduciary duty to create value for shareholders is not a matter for serious debate. Just as clearly, a company and its personnel also have a duty to obey the law and play by the rules of fair competition. But does a company have a duty to operate according to the ethical norms of the societies in which it operates—should it be held to some standard of ethical conduct? And does it have a duty or obligation to contribute to the betterment of society independent of the needs and preferences of the customers it serves? Should a company display a social conscience and devote a portion of its resources to bettering society?

The focus of this chapter is to examine what link, if any, there should be between a company's efforts to craft and execute a winning strategy and its duties to (1) conduct its activities in an ethical manner and (2) demonstrate socially responsible behavior by being a committed corporate citizen and directing corporate resources to the betterment of employees, the communities in which it operates, and society as a whole.

What Do We Mean by Business Ethics?

Business ethics is the application of ethical principles and standards to business behavior.[1] Business ethics does not really involve a special set of ethical standards applicable only to business situations. Ethical principles in business are not materially different from ethical principles in general. Why? Because business actions have to be judged in the context of society's ethical standards, not by a special set of rules that businesspeople decide to apply to their own conduct. If dishonesty is considered to be unethical and immoral, then dishonest behavior in business—whether it relates to customers, suppliers, employees, or shareholders—qualifies as equally unethical and immoral. If being ethical entails not deliberately harming others, then recalling a defective or unsafe product is ethically necessary and failing to undertake such a recall or correct the problem in future shipments of the product is unethical. If society deems bribery to be unethical, then it is unethical for company personnel to make payoffs to government officials to facilitate business transactions or bestow gifts and other favors on prospective customers to win or retain their business.

> **Core Concept**
>
> **Business ethics** concerns the application of general ethical principles and standards to the actions and decisions of companies and the conduct of company personnel.

Ethical Standards—Universal or Dependent on Local Norms and Circumstances?

Notions of right and wrong, fair and unfair, moral and immoral, ethical and unethical are present in all societies, organizations, and individuals. But there are three schools of thought about the extent to which the ethical standards travel across cultures and whether multinational companies can apply the same set of ethical standards in any and all of the locations where they operate.

The School of Ethical Universalism

Core Concept

According to the school of **ethical universalism,** the same standards of what's ethical and what's unethical resonate with peoples of most societies regardless of local traditions and cultural norms; hence, common ethical standards can be used to judge the conduct of personnel at companies operating in a variety of country markets and cultural circumstances.

According to the school of **ethical universalism,** some concepts of what is right and what is wrong are *universal* and transcend almost all cultures, societies, and religions. For instance, being truthful (or not lying or not being deliberately deceitful) strikes a chord of what's right in the peoples of all nations. Likewise, demonstrating integrity of character, not cheating, and treating people with dignity and respect are concepts that resonate with people of most cultures and religions. In most societies, people believe that companies should not pillage or degrade the environment in the course of conducting their operations. In most societies, people would concur that it is unethical to knowingly expose workers to toxic chemicals and hazardous materials or to sell products known to be unsafe or harmful to the users. *To the extent there is common moral agreement about right and wrong actions and behaviors across multiple cultures and countries, there exists a set of universal ethical standards to which all societies, all companies, and all individuals can be held accountable.* These universal ethical principles or norms put limits on which actions and behaviors fall inside the boundaries of what is right and which ones fall outside. They set forth the traits and behaviors that are considered virtuous and that a good person is supposed to believe in and to display.

Many ethicists believe that the most important moral standards travel well across countries and cultures and thus are universal—universal norms include being honest or trustworthy, respecting the rights of others, practicing the Golden Rule, avoiding unnecessary harm to workers or to the users of the company's product or service, and respecting the environment.[2] In all such instances where there is cross-cultural agreement as to what actions and behaviors are inside and outside ethical and moral boundaries, adherents of the school of ethical universalism maintain that the conduct of personnel at companies operating in a variety of country markets and cultural circumstances can be judged against the resulting set of common ethical standards.

The strength of ethical universalism is that it draws upon the collective views of multiple societies and cultures to put some clear boundaries on what constitutes ethical business behavior and what constitutes unethical business behavior no matter what country market or culture a company or its personnel are operating in. This means that in those instances where basic moral standards really do not vary significantly according to local cultural beliefs, traditions, religious convictions, or time and circumstance, a multinational company can develop a code of ethics that it applies more or less evenly across its worldwide operations.[3] It can avoid the slippery slope that comes from having different ethical standards for different company personnel depending on where in the world they are working.

The School of Ethical Relativism

But apart from select universal basics—honesty, trustworthiness, fairness, a regard for worker safety, and respect for the environment—there are meaningful variations in what societies generally agree is right and wrong in the conduct of business activities. Divergent religious beliefs, historic traditions, social customs, and prevailing political and economic doctrines (whether a country leans more toward a capitalistic market economy or one heavily dominated by socialistic or communistic principles) frequently produce ethical norms that vary from one country to another. The school of

ethical relativism holds that when there are cross-country or cross-cultural differences in what is deemed fair or unfair, what constitutes proper regard for human rights, and what is considered ethical or unethical in business situations, it is appropriate for local moral standards to take precedence over what the ethical standards may be elsewhere—for instance, in a company's home market. The thesis is that whatever a culture thinks is right or wrong really *is* right or wrong for that culture.[4] Hence, the school of ethical relativism contends that there are important occasions when cultural norms and the circumstances of the situation determine whether certain actions or behaviors are right or wrong. Consider the following examples.

> **Core Concept**
>
> According to the school of **ethical relativism** different societal cultures and customs have divergent values and standards of right and wrong—thus what is ethical or unethical must be judged in the light of local customs and social mores and can vary from one culture or nation to another.

The Use of Underage Labor   In industrialized nations, the use of "underage" workers is considered taboo; social activists are adamant that child labor is unethical and that companies should neither employ children under the age of 18 as full-time employees nor source any products from foreign suppliers that employ underage workers. However, in India, Bangladesh, Botswana, Sri Lanka, Ghana, Somalia, Turkey, and more than 100 other countries, it is customary to view children as potential, even necessary, workers.[5] Many poverty-stricken families cannot subsist without the income earned by young family members, and sending their children to school instead of having them participate in the workforce is not a realistic option. In 2000, the International Labor Organization estimated that 211 million children ages 5 to 14 were working around the world.[6] If such children are not permitted to work—due to pressures imposed by activist groups in industrialized nations—they may be forced to seek work in lower-wage jobs in "hidden" parts of the economy of their countries, be out on the street begging, or even be reduced to trafficking in drugs or engaging in prostitution.[7] So if all businesses succumb to the protests of activist groups and government organizations that, based on their values and beliefs, loudly proclaim that underage labor is unethical, then have either businesses or the protesting groups really done something good on behalf of society in general?

The Payment of Bribes and Kickbacks   A particularly thorny area facing multinational companies is the degree of cross-country variability in paying bribes. In many countries in Eastern Europe, Africa, Latin America, and Asia, it is customary to pay bribes to government officials in order to win a government contract or to facilitate a business transaction. In some developing nations, it is difficult for any company, foreign or domestic, to move goods through customs without paying off low-level officials.[8] Likewise, in many countries it is normal to make payments to prospective customers in order to win or retain their business. According to a 1999 *Wall Street Journal* report, 30 to 60 percent of all business transactions in Eastern Europe involved paying bribes, and the costs of bribe payments averaged 2 to 8 percent of revenues.[9] The 2004 Global Corruption Report, sponsored by Berlin-based Transparency International, found that corruption among public officials and in business transactions is widespread across the world.[10]

Companies that forbid the payment of bribes and kickbacks in their codes of ethical conduct and that are serious about enforcing this prohibition face a formidable challenge in those countries where bribery and kickback payments have been entrenched as a local custom for decades and are not considered unethical by the local population. The same goes for multinational companies that do business in countries where bribery is illegal and also in countries where bribery and kickbacks are tolerated or customary. Some people say that bribing government officials to get goods through customs or giving kickbacks to customers to retain their business or win an order is simply a payment for services rendered, in the same way that people tip for service at restaurants.

U.S. companies are prohibited by the Foreign Corrupt Practices Act (FCPA) from paying bribes to government officials, political parties, political candidates, or others in all countries where they do business; the FCPA requires U.S. companies with foreign operations to adopt accounting practices that ensure full disclosure of a company's transactions so that illegal payments can be detected. The 35 member countries of the Organization for Economic Cooperation and Development (OECD) in 1997 adopted a convention to combat bribery in international business transactions; the Anti-Bribery Convention obligated the countries to criminalize the bribery of foreign public officials, including payments made to political parties and party officials. However, so far there has been only token enforcement of the OECD convention, and the payment of bribes in global business transactions remains a common practice in many countries.

At the level most managers confront it, the custom of paying bribes and kickbacks in certain country markets is a particularly vexing ethical issue and has no satisfactory solution.[11] Refusing to pay bribes or kickbacks is very often tantamount to losing business. Frequently, the sales and profits are lost to more unscrupulous companies, with the result that both ethical companies and ethical individuals are penalized.

> Varying ethical norms across countries and conflicting interpretations of what exactly constitutes honesty, respect for human rights, respect for the environment, and so on, indicate that there are few absolutes when it comes to business ethics and thus few ethical absolutes for consistently judging a company's conduct in various countries and markets.

Other Examples of Varying Ethical Standards   In Japan, China, and other Asian societies, for instance, there's a strong ethic of loyalty to work groups and corporations; such fidelity stems from Confucianism and centuries-long traditions that hold that one's primary obligation is not to oneself but rather to family, clan, government, and employer.[12] In Japan, such beliefs translate into high cultural expectations that company personnel will exhibit strong loyalty to superiors and to their employer. Japanese employees, believing in the importance of loyalty to their employer, are therefore unlikely to blow the whistle when they see their company engage in wrongdoing. Moreover, some Japanese corporations will fire an employee for breach of loyalty if the employee simply interviews for a job with another firm. In China, there's greater societal toleration of child labor, dangerous working conditions, and fake or inferior products than in some other parts of the world. In addition, some Chinese ethicists even contend that traditional concepts of morality are irrelevant insofar as behavior in a market economy is concerned because the manner in which competitive markets operate is inherently amoral.[13]

In Italy, people are relatively carefree; they live for the moment and are generally willing to take chances about what the future will bring. As a consequence, an Italian manager may be disinclined to keep a promise or fulfill long-term contractual obligations; further, there are often low levels of trust between parties in business deals, and honest communications are frequently lacking.[14] In the former Soviet Union, decades of authoritarian government rule and socialistic traditions created a system where Communist party officials issued a blizzard of rules and orders about how industries were to operate in the planned economy. Bribes and favors were frequently used to get government officials to act favorably. Because Soviet managers found it onerous and sometimes impossible to comply with all the various dictates, many of which were conflicting or inefficient, they routinely broke rules, manipulated production data, fabricated accounts, and traded favors in the course of conducting operations. Since the collapse of communist rule and the breakup of the Soviet Union in the late 1980s, many Russian people, long accustomed to the communist idea that people are supposed to work for the collective good of society, have exhibited considerable mistrust of how business is conducted in Russia. Such views are particularly understandable given that the actions of some Russian businesspeople have proved wildly corrupt based on ethical standards in the United States and Western Europe, with unethical practices being more the norm than the exception.

There are also cross-country variations in the *degree* to which certain behaviors are considered unethical. One study revealed that managers in Hong Kong rank taking credit for another's work and accomplishments at the top of a list of unethical behaviors and, in contrast to managers in Western cultures, considered it more unethical than bribery or illicitly obtaining information about competitors.[15] In Mexico, nepotism (favoritism based on family or social ties) is more acceptable than in the United States or many other countries. Ethical standards for gift giving and entertainment commonly vary from one country to another. In the United States, for instance, it is ethically permissible for a company to provide customers with such small favors as tickets to sporting events or take them on golfing or hunting trips (are these not small "bribes" that are calculated to win favor?), but it is considered both unethical and unlawful to give them cash or "large" gifts in return for steering an order to the company.

Ethical Relativism Equates to Multiple Sets of Ethical Standards   The existence of varying ethical norms such as those cited above causes advocates of ethical relativism to maintain that there are comparatively few absolutes when it comes to business ethics and thus comparatively few ethical absolutes for consistently judging a company's conduct in various countries and markets. Indeed, the thesis of ethical relativists is that while there are some general moral prescriptions that apply in almost every society and business circumstance, there are plenty of situations where ethical norms must be contoured to fit the local customs, traditions, and notions of fairness shared by the parties involved. A "one-size-fits-all" template for judging the ethical appropriateness of business actions and the behaviors of company personnel simply does not exist—in other words, ethical problems in business cannot be fully resolved without appealing to the shared convictions of the parties in question.[16] European and American managers may want to impose standards of business conduct that give heavy weight to such core human rights as personal freedom, individual security, political participation, the ownership of property, and the right to subsistence, as well as the obligation to respect the dignity of each human person, uphold adequate health and safety standards for all employees, and respect the environment. Japanese managers may prefer ethical standards that show respect for the collective good of society. Muslim managers may wish to apply ethical standards compatible with the teachings of Mohammed. Individual companies may want to give explicit recognition to the importance of company personnel's living up to the company's own espoused values and business principles. Clearly, there is merit in the school of ethical relativism's view that what is deemed right or wrong, fair or unfair, moral or immoral, ethical or unethical in business situations has to be viewed in the context of each country's local customs, religious traditions, and societal norms. Businesses need some room to tailor their ethical standards to fit local situations. A company has to be very cautious about exporting its home-country values and ethics to foreign countries where it operates—"photocopying" ethics is disrespectful of other cultures and neglects the important role of moral free space.

> Under ethical relativism, there can be no one-size-fits-all set of authentic ethical norms against which to gauge the conduct of company personnel.

Pushed to Extreme, Ethical Relativism Breaks Down   While the ethical relativism rule of "when in Rome, do as the Romans do" appears reasonable, it nonetheless presents a big problem—when the envelope starts to be pushed, as will inevitably be the case, *it is tantamount to rudderless ethical standards.* Consider, for instance, the following example: In 1992, the owners of the SS *United States,* an aging luxury ocean liner constructed with asbestos in the 1940s, had the liner towed to Turkey, where a contractor had agreed to remove the asbestos for $2 million (versus a far higher cost in the United States, where asbestos removal safety standards were much more stringent).[17] When Turkish officials blocked the asbestos removal because of the dangers to workers of contracting cancer, the owners had the liner towed to the Black Sea port of Sevastopol, in the Crimean Republic, where the asbestos-removal standards were quite lax and where a contractor had agreed to remove more than 500,000 square feet of carcinogenic asbestos for less than $2 million. There are no moral grounds for arguing that exposing workers to carcinogenic asbestos is ethically correct, irrespective of what a country's law allows or the value the country places on worker safety.

A company that adopts the principle of ethical relativism and holds company personnel to local ethical standards necessarily assumes that what prevails as local morality is an adequate guide to ethical behavior. This can be ethically dangerous—it leads to the conclusion that if a country's culture is accepting of bribery or environmental degradation or dangerous working conditions (toxic chemicals or bodily harm), then so much the worse for honest people and protection of the environment and safe working conditions. Such a position is morally unacceptable.

> Managers in multinational enterprises have to figure out how to navigate the gray zone that arises when operating in two cultures with two sets of ethics.

Moreover, from a global markets perspective, ethical relativism results in a maze of conflicting ethical standards for multinational companies wanting to address the very real issue of what ethical standards to enforce companywide. On the one hand, multinational companies need to educate and motivate their employees worldwide to respect the customs and traditions of other nations; on the other hand, they must enforce compliance with the company's own particular code of ethical behavior. It is a slippery slope indeed to resolve such ethical diversity without any kind of higher-order moral compass.

Ethics and Integrative Social Contracts Theory

> **Core Concept**
>
> According to **integrated social contracts theory,** universal ethical principles or norms based on the collective views of multiple cultures and societies combine to form a "social contract" that all individuals in all situations have a duty to observe. Within the boundaries of this social contract, local cultures can specify other impermissible actions; however, universal ethical norms always take precedence over local ethical norms.

Social contracts theory provides yet a middle position between the opposing views of universalism (that the same set of ethical standards should apply everywhere) and relativism (that ethical standards vary according to local custom).[18] According to **integrative social contracts theory,** the ethical standards a company should try to uphold are governed by both (1) a limited number of universal ethical principles that are widely recognized as putting legitimate ethical boundaries on actions and behavior in all situations and (2) the circumstances of local cultures, traditions, and shared values that further prescribe what constitutes ethically permissible behavior and what does not. In other words, universal ethical principles apply when almost all societies—endowed with rationality and moral knowledge—have common moral agreement on what is wrong and thereby put limits on which actions and behaviors fall inside the boundaries of what is right and which ones fall outside. *Universal ethical principles or norms thus establish "moral free space" based on the collective views of multiple societies and cultures; these commonly held views about morality and ethical principles combine to form a "social contract" or contract with society.* This, however, leaves room for societies and national or religious cultures (as well as companies) to make specific interpretations of what other actions may or may not be permissible within the free space defined by universal ethical principles. Where firms, industries, professional associations, and other business-relevant groups have developed ethical codes and norms, then the standards they call for provide appropriate guidance. In all other instances, however, social contracts theory holds that *universal ethical norms take precedence over local ethical norms.*

The strength of integrated social contracts theory is that it accommodates the best parts of ethical universalism and ethical relativism. It is indisputable that cultural differences abound in global business activities and that these cultural differences sometimes give rise to different ethical norms. But it is just as indisputable that some ethical norms are more authentic or universally applicable than others, meaning that in many instances of cross-country differences one side may be more "ethically correct" or "more right" than another. In such instances, resolving cross-cultural differences in what is ethically permissible versus what is not entails applying universal or "first-order" ethical norms and overriding the local or "second-order" ethical norms. A good example is the payment of bribes and kickbacks. Yes, bribes and kickbacks seem to be common in some countries, but does this justify paying them? Just because bribery flourishes in a country does not mean that it is an authentic or legitimate ethical norm. Virtually all of the world's major religions (Buddhism, Christianity, Confucianism, Hinduism, Islam, Judaism, Sikhism, and Taoism) and all moral schools of thought condemn bribery and corruption.[19] Bribery is commonplace in India, but when interviewed, Indian CEOs whose companies constantly engaged in payoffs indicated disgust for the practice and expressed no illusions about its impropriety.[20] Therefore, a multinational company might reasonably conclude that the right ethical standard is one of refusing to condone bribery and kickbacks on the part of company personnel no matter what the local custom is and no matter what the sales consequences are.

Granting an automatic preference to local-country ethical norms presents vexing problems to multinational company managers when the ethical standards followed in a foreign country are lower than those in its home country or in the company's code of ethics. Sometimes there can be no compromise on what is ethically permissible and what is not. *This is precisely what integrated social contracts theory maintains—adherence to universal or first-order ethical norms should always take precedence over local or second-order norms.* Integrated social contracts theory offers managers in multinational companies clear guidance in resolving cross-country ethical differences: those parts of the company's code of ethics that involve universal ethical norms must be enforced worldwide, but within these boundaries there is room for ethical diversity and opportunity for host-country cultures to exert *some* influence in setting their own moral and ethical standards. Such an approach detours the somewhat scary case of a self-righteous multinational company trying to operate as the standard-bearer of moral truth and imposing its interpretation of its code of ethics worldwide no matter what. And it avoids the equally scary case of a company's ethical conduct being no higher than local ethical norms in situations where such norms permit practices that are generally considered immoral or when local norms clearly conflict with a company's code of ethical conduct. But even with the guidance provided by integrated social contracts theory, there are many instances where cross-country differences in ethical norms create all kinds of "gray areas" where it is tough to draw a line in the sand between right and wrong decisions, actions, and business practices.

The Three Categories of Management Morality

Three categories of managers stand out with regard to ethical and moral principles in business affairs:[21]

- *The moral manager:* Moral managers are dedicated to high standards of ethical behavior, both in their own actions and in their expectations of how the company's business is to be conducted. They see themselves as stewards of ethical behavior and believe it is important to exercise ethical leadership. Moral managers may well be ambitious and have a powerful urge to succeed, but they pursue success in business within the confines of both the letter and the spirit of what is ethical and legal—they typically regard the law as an ethical minimum and have a habit of operating well above what the law requires.

- *The immoral manager:* Immoral managers have no regard for so-called ethical standards in business and pay no attention to ethical principles in making decisions and conducting the company's business. Their philosophy is that good business-people cannot spend time watching out for the interests of others and agonizing over "the right thing to do" from an ethical perspective. In the minds of immoral managers, nice guys come in second and the competitive nature of business requires that you either trample on others or get trampled yourself. They believe what really matters is single-minded pursuit of their own best interests—they are living examples of capitalistic greed, caring only about their own or their organization's gains and successes. Immoral managers may even be willing to short-circuit legal and regulatory requirements if they think they can escape detection. And they are always on the lookout for legal loopholes and creative ways to get around rules and regulations that block or constrain actions they deem in their own or their company's self-interest. Immoral managers are thus the bad guys—they have few scruples, have little or no integrity, and are willing to do almost anything they believe they can get away with. It doesn't bother them much to be seen by others as wearing the black hats.

- *The amoral manager:* Amoral managers appear in two forms: the intentionally amoral manager and the unintentionally amoral manager. *Intentionally amoral managers* are of the strong opinion that business and ethics are not to be mixed. They are not troubled by failing to factor ethical considerations into their decisions and actions because it is perfectly legitimate for businesses to do anything they wish as long as they stay within legal and regulatory bounds—in other words, if particular actions and behaviors are legal and comply with existing regulations, then they qualify as permissible and should not be seen as unethical. Intentionally amoral managers view the observance of high ethical standards (doing more than what is required by law) as too Sunday-schoolish for the tough competitive world of business, even though observing some higher ethical considerations may be appropriate in life outside business. Their concept of right and wrong tends to be lawyer-driven—how much can we get by with and can we go ahead even if it is borderline? Thus intentionally amoral managers hold firmly to the view that anything goes, as long as actions and behaviors are not clearly ruled out by prevailing legal and regulatory requirements.

Unintentionally amoral managers do not pay much attention to the concept of business ethics either, but for different reasons. They are simply casual about, careless about, or inattentive to the fact that certain kinds of business decisions or company activities are unsavory or may have deleterious effects on others—in short, they go about their jobs as best they can without giving serious thought to the ethical dimension of decisions and business actions. They are ethically unconscious when it comes to business matters, partly or mainly because they have never stopped to consider whether and to what extent business decisions or company actions sometimes spill over to create adverse impacts on others. Uninten-

> **Core Concept**
>
> Amoral managers believe that businesses ought to be able to do whatever current laws and regulations allow them to do without being shackled by ethical considerations—they think that what is permissible and what is not is governed entirely by prevailing laws and regulations, not by societal concepts of right and wrong.

tionally amoral managers may even see themselves as people of integrity and as personally ethical. But, like intentionally amoral managers, they are of the firm view that businesses ought to be able to do whatever the current legal and regulatory framework allows them to do without being shackled by ethical considerations.

By some accounts, the population of managers is said to be distributed among all three types in a bell-shaped curve, with immoral managers and moral managers occupying the two tails of the curve, and amoral managers (especially intentionally amoral managers) occupying the broad middle ground.[22] Furthermore, within the population of managers, there is experiential evidence to support that while the average manager may be amoral most of the time, he or she may slip into a moral or immoral mode on occasion, based on a variety of impinging factors and circumstances.

A landscape that is apparently so cluttered with amoral and immoral managers does not bode well for the frequency with which company managers ground their strategies on exemplary ethical principles or for the vigor with which they try to ingrain ethical behavior into company personnel. And, as many business school professors have noted, there are considerable numbers of amoral business students in our classrooms. So efforts to root out shady and corrupt business practices and implant high ethical principles into the managerial process of crafting and executing strategy are unlikely to produce an ethically strong global business climate anytime in the near future, barring major effort to address and correct the ethical amorality and immorality of company managers.

Do Company Strategies Need to Be Ethical?

Company managers may formulate strategies that are ethical in all respects, or they may decide to employ strategies that, for one reason or another, have unethical or at least gray-area components. While most company managers are usually careful to ensure that a company's strategy is within the bounds of what is legal, they are not always so careful to ensure that all elements of their strategies are within the bounds of what is generally deemed ethical. Senior executives with strong ethical convictions are proactive in insisting that all aspects of company strategy fall within ethical boundaries. But at other companies, namely those whose senior executives are either immoral or amoral, shady strategies and unethical or borderline business practices may well be utilized, especially if their managers are clever at devising schemes to keep ethically questionable actions hidden from view.

In October 2004, *Wall Street Journal* headlines trumpeted that a cartel among insurance brokers had been busted. Among the ringleaders was worldwide industry leader Marsh & McLennan Cos., Inc., with 2003 revenues of $11.5 billion and a U.S. market share of close to 20 percent. The gist of the cartel was to cheat corporate clients by rigging the bids brokers solicited for insurance policies and thereby collecting big fees (called "contingent commissions") from major insurance companies for steering business their way. Two family members of Marsh & McLennan CEO Jeffrey Greenberg were CEOs of major insurance companies to which Marsh sometimes steered business. Greenberg's father was CEO of insurance giant AIG (which had total revenues of $81 billion and insurance premium revenues of $28 billion in 2003), and Greenberg's younger brother was CEO of ACE, Ltd., the 24th-biggest property-casualty insurer in the United States, with 2003 revenues of $10.7 billion and insurance premium revenues of more than $5 billion worldwide. Prior to joining ACE, Greenberg's younger brother had been president and COO of AIG, headed by his father.

Several months prior to the cartel bust, a Marsh subsidiary, Putnam Investments, had paid a $110 million fine for securities fraud and another Marsh subsidiary, Mercer Consulting, was placed under SEC investigation for engaging in "pay to play" practices that forced investment managers to pay fees to get Mercer's endorsement of them to pension funds.

The cartel scheme arose from the practice of large corporations of hiring the services of such brokers as Marsh & McLennan, Aon Corp., A.J. Gallaher & Co., Wells Fargo, or BB&T Insurance Services to manage their risks and take out appropriate property and casualty insurance on their behalf. The broker's job was to solicit bids from several insurers and obtain the best policies at the lowest prices for the client.

Marsh's insurance brokerage strategy was to solicit artificially high business from some insurance companies so it could guarantee that the bid of a preferred insurer on a given deal would win the business. The scheme involved Marsh brokers' calling underwriters at various insurers, often including AIG and ACE, and asking for "B" quotes—bids that were deliberately high. Insurers that were asked for B quotes knew that Marsh wanted another insurer to win the business, but were willing to participate because Marsh could on other policy solicitations end up steering the business to them via Marsh's B-quote strategy. Sometimes Marsh even asked underwriters that were providing B quotes to attend a meeting with Marsh's client and make a presentation regarding the insurer's policy to help bolster the credibility of the firm's inflated bid.

During the past five years, there has been an ongoing series of revelations where managers at such companies as Enron, Tyco International, HealthSouth, Rite Aid, Citicorp, Bristol-Myers, Adelphia, Royal Dutch/Shell, Parmalat (an Italy-based food products company), Mexican oil giant Pemex, Marsh & McLennan and other insurance brokers, several leading brokerage houses and investment banking firms, and a host of mutual fund companies have ignored ethical standards, deliberately stepped out of bounds, and been called to account by the media, regulators, and the legal system. The consequences of crafting strategies that cannot pass the test of moral scrutiny are manifested in the sharp drops in the stock prices of the guilty companies that have cost shareholders billions of dollars, the frequently devastating public relations hits that the accused companies have taken, the sizes of the fines that have been levied (often amounting to several hundred million dollars), the growing legion of criminal indictments and convictions of company executives, and the numbers of executives who have been dismissed from their jobs, shoved into early retirement, and/or suffered immense public embarrassment. The fallout from all these scandals has resulted in heightened management attention to legal and ethical considerations in crafting strategy. Company Spotlight 7.1 details the ethically flawed strategy at the world's leading insurance broker and the resulting consequences to those concerned.

Since it was widespread practice among insurers to pay brokers contingent commissions based on the volume or profitability of the business the broker directed to them, Marsh's B-quote solicitation strategy allowed it to steer business to those insurers' paying the largest contingent commissions—these commissions were in addition to the fees the broker earned from the corporate client for services rendered in conducting the bidding process for the client. A substantial fraction of the policies that Marsh steered went to two Bermuda-based insurance companies that it helped start up and in which it had ownership interests (some Marsh executives also indirectly owned shares of stock in one of the companies); indeed, these two insurance companies received 30 to 40 percent of their total business from policies that were steered to them by Marsh.

At Marsh, steering business to insurers paying the highest contingent commission was a key component of the company's overall strategy. Marsh's contingent commissions generated revenues of close to $1.5 billion over the 2001–2003 period, including $845 million in 2003 (without these commission revenues, Marsh's $1.5 billion in net profits would have been close to 40 percent lower in 2003).

Within days of headlines about the cartel bust, Marsh's stock price had fallen by 48 percent (costing shareholders about $11.5 billion in market value), and the company was looking down the barrel of a criminal indictment. To stave off the indictment (something no company had ever survived), board members forced Jeffrey Greenberg to resign as CEO. Another top executive was suspended. Criminal charges against several Marsh executives for their roles in the bid-rigging scheme were filed several weeks thereafter.

In an attempt to lead industry reform, Greenberg's successor quickly announced a new business model for Marsh that included not accepting any contingent commissions from insurers. Marsh's new strategy and business model involved charging fees only to its corporate clients for soliciting bids, placing their insurance, and otherwise managing clients' risks and crises. This eliminated the conflict of interest Marsh had in earning fees from both sides of the transactions it made on behalf of its corporate clients. Marsh also committed to provide up-front disclosure to clients of the fees it would earn on their business (in the past such fees had been murky and incomplete). Even so, several lawsuits, some involving class action, were filed against the company.

Meanwhile, all major commercial property-casualty insurers were scrambling to determine whether their payment of contingent commissions was ethical, since such arrangements clearly gave insurance brokers a financial incentive to place insurance with companies paying the biggest contingent commissions, not those with the best prices or terms. Prosecutors of the cartel had referred to the contingent commissions as kickbacks.

Sources: Monica Langley and Theo Francis, "Insurers Reel from Bust of a 'Cartel,'" *The Wall Street Journal*, October 18, 2004, pp. A1, A14; Monica Langley and Ian McDonald, "Marsh Averts Criminal Case with New CEO," *The Wall Street Journal*, October 26, 2004, pp. A1, A10; Christopher Oster and Theo Francis, "Marsh and Aon Have Holdings in Two Insurers," *The Wall Street Journal*, November 1, 2004, p. C1; and Marcia Vickers, "The Secret World of Marsh Mac," *BusinessWeek*, November 1, 2004, pp. 78–89.

What Are the Drivers of Unethical Strategies and Business Behavior?

The apparent pervasiveness of immoral and amoral businesspeople is one obvious reason why ethical principles are an ineffective moral compass in business dealings and why companies may resort to unethical strategic behavior. But apart from "the business of business is business, not ethics" kind of thinking, three other main drivers of unethical business behavior also stand out:[23]

- Faulty oversight such that overzealous or obsessive pursuit of personal gain, wealth, and other selfish interests is overlooked by or escapes the attention of higher-ups (most usually the board of directors).

- Heavy pressures on company managers to meet or beat performance targets.

- A company culture that puts profitability and good business performance ahead of ethical behavior.

Overzealous Pursuit of Personal Gain, Wealth, and Selfish Interests People who are obsessed with wealth accumulation, greed, power, status, and other selfish interests often push ethical principles aside in their quest for self-gain. Driven by their ambitions, they exhibit few qualms in skirting the rules or doing whatever is necessary to achieve their goals. The first and only priority of such corporate "bad apples" is to look out for their own best interests, and if climbing the ladder of success means having few scruples and ignoring the welfare of others, so be it. A general disregard for business ethics can prompt all kinds of unethical strategic maneuvers and behaviors at companies. Top executives, directors, and majority shareholders at cable TV company Adelphia Communications ripped off the company for amounts totaling well over $1 billion, diverting hundreds of millions of dollars to fund their Buffalo Sabres hockey team, build a private golf course, and buy timber rights—among other things—and driving the company into bankruptcy. Their actions, which represent one of the biggest instances of corporate looting and self-dealing in American business, took place despite the company's public pontifications about the principles it would observe in trying to care for customers, employees, stockholders, and the local communities where it operated. Andrew Fastow, Enron's chief financial officer (CFO), set himself up as the manager of one of Enron's off-the-books partnerships and as the part-owner of another, allegedly earning extra compensation of $30 million for his owner-manager roles in the two partnerships; Enron's board of directors agreed to suspend the company's conflict-of-interest rules designed to protect the company from this kind of executive self-dealing.

According to a civil complaint filed by the Securities and Exchange Commission, the chief executive officer (CEO) of Tyco International, a well-known $35.6 billion manufacturing and services company, conspired with the company's CFO to steal more than $170 million, including a company-paid $2 million birthday party for the CEO's wife held on Sardinia, an island off the coast of Italy; a $7 million Park Avenue apartment for his wife; and secret low-interest and interest-free loans to fund private businesses and investments and purchase lavish artwork, yachts, estate jewelry, and vacation homes in New Hampshire, Connecticut, Nantucket, and Park City, Utah. The CEO allegedly lived rent-free in a $31 million Fifth Avenue apartment that Tyco purchased in his name, directed millions of dollars of charitable contributions in his own name using Tyco funds, diverted company funds to finance his personal businesses and investments, and sold millions of dollars of Tyco stock back to Tyco itself through Tyco subsidiaries located in offshore bank-secrecy jurisdictions. Tyco's CEO and CFO were further charged with conspiring to reap more than $430 million from sales of stock, using questionable accounting to hide their actions, and engaging in deceptive accounting practices to distort the company's financial condition from 1995 to 2002. At the trial on the charges filed by the SEC, the prosecutor told the jury in his opening statement, "This case is about lying, cheating and stealing. These people didn't win the jackpot—they stole it." Defense lawyers countered that "every single transaction…was set down in detail in Tyco's books and records" and that the authorized and disclosed multimillion-dollar compensation packages were merited by the company's financial performance and stock price gains.

Prudential Securities paid a total of about $2 billion in the 1990s to settle misconduct charges relating to practices that misled investors on the risks and rewards of limited-partnership investments. Providian Financial Corporation, despite an otherwise glowing record of social responsibility and corporate citizenship, paid $150 million in 2001 to settle claims that its strategy included systematic attempts to cheat credit card holders. Ten prominent Wall Street securities firms in 2003 paid $1.4 billion to settle charges that they knowingly issued misleading stock research to investors in an effort to prop up the stock prices of client corporations. A host of mutual fund firms made under-the-table arrangements to regularly buy and sell stock for their accounts at special after-hours trading prices that disadvantaged long-term investors, and they had to pay nearly $2 billion in fines and restitution when their unethical practices were discovered by authorities during 2002–2003. Salomon Smith Barney, Goldman Sachs, Credit Suisse First Boston, and several other financial firms were assessed close to $2 billion in fines and restitution for the unethical manner in which they contributed to the scandals at Enron and WorldCom (now MCI) and for the shady practice of allocating shares of hot IPO stocks to a select list of corporate executives who either steered or were in a position to steer investment banking business their way.

Heavy Pressures on Company Managers to Meet or Beat Earnings Targets When companies find themselves scrambling to achieve ambitious earnings growth and meet the quarterly and annual performance expectations of Wall Street analysts and investors, managers often feel enormous pressure to do whatever it takes to sustain the company's reputation for delivering good financial performance. Executives at high-performing companies know that investors will see the slightest sign of a slowdown in earnings growth as a red flag and unload some of their shares, thus driving down the company's stock price. The company's credit rating could be downgraded if it has used lots of debt to finance its growth. The pressure to watch the scoreboard and "never miss a quarter"—in meeting or beating earnings targets—so as not to upset the expectations of Wall Street analysts and fickle stock market investors—prompts managers to cut costs wherever savings show up immediately, squeeze extra sales out of early deliveries, and engage in other short-term maneuvers to meet earnings expectations. As the pressure builds to keep performance numbers looking good, company personnel start stretching the rules further and further, until the limits of ethical conduct are overlooked.[24] Once ethical boundaries are crossed in efforts to "meet or beat the numbers," the threshold for making more extreme ethical compromises becomes lower.

Several top executives at WorldCom (now MCI), a company built with scores of acquisitions in exchange for WorldCom stock, allegedly concocted a fraudulent $11 billion accounting scheme to hide costs and inflate revenues and profit over several years; the scheme was said to have helped the company keep its stock price propped up high enough to make additional acquisitions, support its nearly $30 billion debt load, and allow executives to cash in on their lucrative stock options. At Qwest Communications, a company created by the merger of a go-go telecom start-up and U.S. West (one of the regional Bell companies), management was charged with scheming to improperly book $2.4 billion in revenues from a variety of sources and deals, thereby inflating the company's profits and thus making it appear that the company's strategy to create a telecommunications company of the future was on track when, in fact, it was faltering badly behind the scenes. Top-level Qwest executives were dismissed and in 2004 new management agreed to $250 million in fines for all the misdeeds.

At Bristol-Myers Squibb, the world's fifth-largest drug maker, management apparently engaged in a series of numbers-game maneuvers to meet earnings targets, including such actions as:

- Offering special end-of-quarter discounts to induce distributors and local pharmacies to stock up on certain prescription drugs—a practice known as "channel stuffing."

- Issuing last-minute price increase alerts to spur purchases and beef up operating profits.

- Setting up excessive reserves for restructuring charges and then reversing some of the charges as needed to bolster operating profits.

- Making repeated asset sales small enough that the gains could be reported as additions to operating profit rather than being flagged as one-time gains. (Some accountants have long used a rule of thumb that says a transaction that alters quarterly profits by less than 5 percent is "immaterial" and need not be disclosed in the company's financial reports.)

Such numbers games were said to be a common "earnings management" practice at Bristol-Myers and, according to one former executive, "sent a huge message across the organization that you make your numbers at all costs."[25]

Company executives often feel pressured to hit financial performance targets because their compensation depends heavily on the company's performance. During the late 1990s, it became fashionable for boards of directors to grant lavish bonuses, stock option awards, and other compensation benefits to executives for meeting specified performance targets. So outlandishly large were these rewards that executives had strong personal incentives to bend the rules and engage in behaviors that allowed the targets to be met. Much of the accounting hocus-pocus at the root of recent corporate scandals has entailed situations in which executives benefited enormously from misleading accounting or other shady activities that allowed them to hit the numbers and receive incentive awards ranging from $10 million to $100 million. At Bristol-Myers Squibb, for example, the pay-for-performance link spawned strong rules-bending incentives. About 94 percent of one top executive's $18.5 million in total compensation in 2001 came from stock option grants, a bonus, and long-term incentive payments linked to corporate performance; about 92 percent of a second executive's $12.9 million of compensation was incentive-based.[26] Company Spotlight 7.2 describes elements of the strategies that three of the world's most prominent investment banking firms employed to gain new business and help meet performance targets—judge for yourself whether their strategies were ethical or shady.

The fundamental problem with a "make the numbers and move on" syndrome is that a company doesn't really serve its customers or its shareholders by putting top priority on the bottom line. In the final analysis, shareholder interests are best served by doing a really good job of serving customers (observing the rule that customers are "king") and by improving the company's competitiveness in the marketplace. Cutting ethical corners or stooping to downright illegal actions in the name of profits first is convoluted and misguided—when the spotlight is shined on such scurrilous behavior, the resulting fallout actually depreciates shareholder value rather than enhancing it.

Company Cultures That Put the Bottom Line Ahead of Ethical Behavior   When a company's culture spawns an ethically corrupt or amoral work climate, people have a company-approved license to ignore "what's right" and engage in almost any behavior or employ almost any strategy they think they can get away with. Such cultural norms as "No one expects strict adherence to ethical standards," "Everyone else does it," and "It is politic to bend the rules to get the job done" permeate the work environment.[27] At such companies, ethically immoral or amoral people are certain to play down observance of ethical strategic actions and business conduct. Moreover, the pressures to conform to cultural norms can prompt otherwise honorable people to make ethical mistakes and succumb to the many opportunities around them to engage in unethical practices.

COMPANY SPOTLIGHT 7.2
Strategies to Gain New Business at Wall Street Investment Banking Firms: Ethical or Unethical?

At Salomon Smith Barney (a subsidiary of Citigroup), Credit Suisse First Boston (CSFB), and Goldman Sachs—three of the world's most prominent investment banking companies—part of the strategy for securing the investment banking business of large corporate clients (to handle the sale of new stock issues or new bond issues or advise on mergers and acquisitions) involved (1) hyping the stocks of companies that were actual or prospective customers of their investment banking services and (2) allocating hard-to-get shares of hot initial public offerings (IPOs) to select executives and directors of existing and potential client companies, who then made millions of dollars in profits when the stocks went up once public trading began. Former WorldCom CEO Bernie Ebbers reportedly made more than $11 million in trading profits over a four-year period on shares of IPOs received from Salomon Smith Barney; Salomon served as WorldCom's investment banker on a variety of deals during this period. Jack Grubman, Salomon's top-paid research analyst at the time, enthusiastically touted WorldCom stock and was regarded as the company's biggest cheerleader on Wall Street.

To help draw in business from new or existing corporate clients, CSFB established brokerage accounts for corporate executives who steered their company's investment banking business to CSFB. Apparently, CSFB's strategy for acquiring more business involved promising the CEOs and/or CFOs of companies about to go public for the first time or to issue new long-term bonds that if CSFB was chosen to handle the public offering or bond issue, then it would ensure that they would be allocated shares at the initial offering price of all subsequent IPOs in which CSFB was a participant. During 1999–2000, it was common for the stock of a hot IPO to rise 100 to 500 percent above the initial offering price in the first few days or weeks of public trading; the shares allocated to these executives were then sold for a tidy profit over the initial offering price. According to investigative sources, CSFB increased the number of companies whose executives were allowed to partic-

ipate in its IPO offerings from 26 companies in January 1999 to 160 companies in early 2000; executives received anywhere from 200 to 1,000 shares each of every IPO in which CSFB was a participant in 2000. CSFB's accounts for these executives reportedly generated profits of about $80 million for the participants. Apparently, it was CSFB's practice to curtail access to IPOs for some executives if their companies didn't come through with additional securities business for CSFB or if CSFB concluded that other securities offerings by these companies would be unlikely.

Goldman Sachs also used an IPO-allocation scheme to attract investment banking business, giving shares to executives at 21 companies—among the participants were the CEOs of eBay, Yahoo, and Ford Motor Company. The CEO of eBay was a participant in over 100 IPOs managed by Goldman during the 1996–2000 period and was on Goldman's board of directors part of this time; eBay paid Goldman Sachs $8 million in fees for services during the 1996–2001 period.

Questions to Consider

1. If you were a top executive at Salomon Smith Barney, CSFB, or Goldman Sachs, would you be proud to defend your company's actions?

2. Would you want to step forward and take credit for having been a part of the group who designed or approved of the strategy for gaining new business at any of these three firms?

3. Is it accurate to characterize the allocations of IPO shares to "favored" corporate executives as bribes or kickbacks?

Sources: Charles Gasparino, "Salomon Probe Includes Senior Executives," *The Wall Street Journal*, September 3, 2002, p. C1; Randall Smith and Susan Pulliam, "How a Star Banker Pressed for IPOs," *The Wall Street Journal*, September 4, 2002, pp. C1, C14; Randall Smith and Susan Pulliam, "How a Technology-Banking Star Doled Out Shares of Hot IPOs," *The Wall Street Journal*, September 23, 2002, pp. A1, A10; and Randall Smith, "Goldman Sachs Faces Scrutiny for IPO-Allocation Practices," *The Wall Street Journal*, October 3, 2002, pp. A1, A6.

A perfect example of a company culture gone awry on ethics is Enron.[28] Enron's leaders encouraged company personnel to focus on the current bottom line and to be innovative and aggressive in figuring out what could be done to grow current revenues and earnings. Employees were expected to pursue opportunities to the utmost in the electric utility industry, which at the time was undergoing looser regulation. Enron executives viewed the company as a laboratory for innovation; the company hired the best and brightest people and pushed them to be creative, look at problems and opportunities in new ways, and exhibit a sense of urgency in making things happen. Employees were encouraged to make a difference and do their part in creating an entrepreneurial environment where creativity flourished, people could achieve their full potential, and everyone had a stake in the outcome. Enron employees got the message—pushing the limits and meeting one's numbers were viewed as survival skills. Enron's annual "rank and yank" formal evaluation process, where the 15 to 20 percent lowest-ranking employees were let go or encouraged to seek other employment, made it abundantly clear that achieving bottom-line results and being the "mover and shaker" in the marketplace were what counted. The name of the game at Enron became devising clever ways to boost revenues and earnings, even if doing so sometimes meant operating outside established policies and without the knowledge of superiors. In fact, outside-the-lines behavior was celebrated if it generated profitable new business. Enron's energy contracts and its trading and hedging activities grew increasingly more complex and diverse as employees pursued first this avenue and then another to help keep Enron's financial performance looking good.

As a consequence of Enron's well-publicized successes in creating new products and businesses and leveraging the company's trading and hedging expertise into new market arenas, Enron came to be regarded as an exceptionally innovative company. It was ranked by its corporate peers as the most innovative U.S. company for three consecutive years in *Fortune* magazine's annual surveys of the most admired companies. A high-performance–high-rewards climate came to pervade the Enron culture, as the best workers (determined by who produced the best bottom-line results) received impressively large incentives and bonuses (amounting to as much as $1 million for traders and even more for senior executives). On Car Day at Enron, an array of luxury sports cars arrived for presentation to the most successful employees. Understandably, employees wanted to be seen as part of Enron's star team and partake in the benefits that being one of Enron's best and smartest employees entailed. The high monetary rewards, the ambitious and hard-driving people that the company hired and promoted, and the competitive, results-oriented culture combined to give Enron a reputation not only for trampling competitors at every opportunity but also for internal ruthlessness. The company's super-aggressiveness and win-at-all-costs mind-set nurtured a culture that gradually and then more rapidly fostered the erosion of ethical standards, eventually making a mockery of the company's stated values of integrity and respect. When it became evident in the fall of 2001 that Enron was a house of cards propped up by deceitful accounting and a myriad of unsavory practices, the company imploded in a matter of weeks—the biggest bankruptcy of all time cost investors $64 billion in losses (between August 2000, when the stock price was at its five-year high, and November 2001), and Enron employees lost their retirement assets, which were almost totally invested in Enron stock.

More recently, a team investigating an ethical scandal at oil giant Royal Dutch/Shell Group that resulted in the payment of $150 million in fines found that an ethically flawed culture was a major contributor to why managers made rosy forecasts that they couldn't meet and why top executives engaged in maneuvers to mislead investors by overstating Shell's oil and gas reserves by 25 percent (equal to 4.5 billion barrels of oil). The investigation revealed that top Shell executives knew that a variety of internal practices, together with unrealistic and unsupportable estimates submitted by overzealous and bonus-conscious managers in Shell's exploration and production group, were being used to overstate reserves. An e-mail written by Shell's top executive for exploration and production (who was caught up in the ethical misdeeds and later forced to resign) said, "I am becoming sick and tired about lying about the extent of our reserves issues and the downward revisions that need to be done because of our far too aggressive/optimistic bookings."[29]

Approaches to Managing a Company's Ethical Conduct

The stance a company takes in dealing with or managing ethical conduct at any given point can take any of four basic forms:[30]

- The unconcerned or nonissue approach.
- The damage control approach.
- The compliance approach.
- The ethical culture approach.

The differences in these four approaches are discussed briefly below and summarized in Table 7.1.

The Unconcerned or Nonissue Approach   The unconcerned approach is prevalent at companies whose executives are immoral and unintentionally amoral. Senior executives at companies using this approach ascribe to the view that notions of right and wrong in matters of business are defined entirely by government via the prevailing laws and regulations. They maintain that trying to enforce ethical standards above and beyond what is legally required is a nonissue because businesses are entitled to conduct their affairs in whatever manner they wish as long as they comply with the letter of what is legally required. Hence, there is no need to spend valuable management time trying to prescribe and enforce standards of conduct that go above and beyond legal and regulatory requirements. In companies where senior managers are immoral, the prevailing view may well be that under-the-table dealing can be good business if it can be kept hidden or if it can be justified on grounds that others are doing it too. Companies in this mode usually engage in almost any business practices they believe they can get away with, and the strategies they employ may well embrace elements that are either borderline from a legal perspective or ethically shady and unsavory.

The Damage Control Approach   Damage control is favored at companies whose managers are intentionally amoral but who are wary of scandal and adverse public relations fallout that could cost them their jobs or tarnish their careers. Companies using this approach, not wanting to risk tarnishing the reputations of key personnel or the company, usually make some concession to window-dressing ethics, going so far as to adopt a code of ethics—so that their executives can point to it as evidence of good-faith efforts to prevent unethical strategy making or unethical conduct on the part of company personnel. But the code of ethics exists mainly as nice words on paper, and company

> The main objective of the damage control approach is to protect against adverse publicity and any damaging consequences brought on by headlines in the media, outside investigation, threats of litigation, punitive government action, or angry or vocal stakeholders.

Table 7.1   FOUR APPROACHES TO MANAGING BUSINESS ETHICS

	Unconcerned or Nonissue Approach	Damage Control Approach	Compliance Approach	Ethical Culture Approach
Underlying beliefs	■ The business of business is business, not ethics ■ Ethics has no place in the conduct of business ■ Companies should not be morally accountable for their actions	■ Need to make a token gesture in the direction of ethical standards (a code of ethics)	■ Company must be committed to ethical standards and monitoring ethics performance ■ Unethical behavior must be prevented and punished if discovered ■ Important to have a reputation for high ethical standards	■ Ethics is basic to the culture ■ Behaving ethically must be a deeply held corporate value and become a "way of life" ■ Everyone is expected to walk the talk
Ethics management approaches	■ There's no need to make decisions concerning business ethics—if it's legal, it is okay ■ No intervention regarding the ethical component of decisions is needed	■ Act to protect against the dangers of unethical strategies and behavior ■ Ignore unethical behavior or allow it to go unpunished unless the situation is extreme and requires action	■ Establish a clear, comprehensive code of ethics ■ Prevent unethical behavior ■ Provide ethics training for all personnel ■ Have formal ethics compliance procedures, an ethics compliance office, and a chief ethics officer	■ Ethical behavior is ingrained and reinforced as part of the culture ■ Much reliance on coworker peer pressure—"that's not how we do things here" ■ Everyone is an ethics watchdog—whistle-blowing is required ■ Ethics heroes are celebrated; ethics stories are told
Challenges	■ Financial consequences can become unaffordable ■ Some stakeholders are alienated	■ Credibility problems with stakeholders can arise ■ The company is susceptible to ethical scandal ■ The company has a subpar ethical reputation—executives and company personnel don't walk the talk	■ Organization members come to rely on the existing rules for moral guidance—fosters a mentality of what is not forbidden is allowed ■ Rules and guidelines proliferate ■ The locus of moral control resides in the code and in the ethics compliance system rather than in an individual's own moral responsibility for ethical behavior	■ New employees must go through strong ethics induction program ■ Formal ethics management systems can be underutilized ■ Relying on peer pressures and cultural norms to enforce ethical standards can result in eliminating some or many of the compliance trappings and, over time, induce moral laxness

Source: Adapted from Gedeon J. Rossouw and Leon J. van Vuuren, "Modes of Managing Morality: A Descriptive Model of Strategies for Managing Ethics," *Journal of Business Ethics* 46, no. 4 (September 2003), pp. 392–393.

personnel do not operate within a strong ethical context—there's a notable gap between talking ethics and walking ethics. Employees quickly get the message that rule bending is tolerated and may even be rewarded if the company benefits from their actions.

Company executives who practice the damage control approach are prone to look the other way when shady or borderline behavior occurs—adopting a kind of "see no evil, hear no evil, speak no evil" stance (except when exposure of the company's actions puts executives under great pressure to redress any wrongs that have been done). They may even condone questionable actions that help the company reach earnings targets or bolster its market standing—such as pressuring customers to stock up on the company's product (channel stuffing), making under-the-table payments to win new business, stonewalling the recall of products claimed to be unsafe, bad-mouthing the products of rivals, or trying to keep prices low by sourcing goods from disreputable suppliers in low-wage countries that run sweatshop operations or use child labor. But they are usually careful to do such things in a manner that lessens the risks of exposure or damaging consequences. This generally includes making token gestures to police compliance with codes of ethics and relying heavily on all sorts of "spin" to help extricate the company or themselves from claims that the company's strategy has unethical components or that company personnel have engaged in unethical practices.

The Compliance Approach   Anywhere from light to forceful compliance is favored at companies whose managers (1) lean toward being somewhat amoral but are highly concerned about having ethically upstanding reputations or (2) are moral and see strong compliance methods as the best way to impose and enforce ethical rules and high ethical standards. Companies that adopt a compliance mode usually do some or all of the following to display their commitment to ethical conduct: make the code of ethics a visible and regular part of communications with employees, implement ethics training programs, appoint a chief ethics officer or ethics ombudsperson, have ethics committees to give guidance on ethics matters, institute formal procedures for investigating alleged ethics violations, conduct ethics audits to measure and document compliance, give ethics awards to employees for outstanding efforts to create an ethical climate and improve ethical performance, and/or try to deter violations by setting up ethics hotlines for anonymous callers to use in reporting possible violations.

Emphasis here is usually on securing broad compliance and measuring the degree to which ethical standards are upheld and observed. However, violators are disciplined and sometimes subjected to public reprimand and punishment (including dismissal), thereby sending a clear signal to company personnel that complying with ethical standards needs to be taken seriously. The driving force behind the company's commitment to eradicate unethical behavior normally stems from a desire to avoid the cost and damage associated with unethical conduct or from a quest to gain favor with stakeholders (especially ethically conscious customers, employees, and investors) for having a highly regarded reputation for ethical behavior. One of the weaknesses of the compliance approach is that moral control resides in the company's code of ethics and in the ethics compliance system rather than in (1) the strong peer pressures for ethical behavior that come from ingraining a highly ethical corporate culture and (2) an individual's own moral responsibility for ethical behavior.[31]

The Ethical Culture Approach   At some companies, top executives believe that high ethical principles must be deeply ingrained in the corporate culture and function as guides for "how we do things around here." A company using the ethical culture approach seeks to gain employee buy-in to the company's ethical standards, business principles, and corporate values. The ethical principles embraced in the company's code of ethics and/or in its statement of corporate values are seen as integral to the company's identity and ways of operating—they are at the core of the company's soul and are promoted as part of "business as usual." The integrity of the ethical culture approach depends heavily on the ethical integrity of the executives who create and nurture the culture—it is incumbent on them to determine how high the bar is to be set and to exemplify ethical standards in their own decisions and behavior. Further, it is essential that the strategy be ethical in all respects and that ethical behavior be ingrained in the means that company personnel employ to execute the strategy. Such insistence on observing ethical standards is what creates an ethical work climate and a workplace where displaying integrity is the norm.

Many of the trappings used in the compliance approach are also manifest in the ethical culture mode, but one other is added—strong peer pressure from coworkers to observe ethical norms. Thus, responsibility for ethics compliance is widely dispersed throughout all levels of management and the rank and file. Stories of former and current moral heroes are kept in circulation, and the deeds of company personnel who display ethical values and are dedicated to "walking the talk" are celebrated at internal company events. The message that ethics matters—and matters a lot—resounds loudly and clearly throughout the organization and in its strategy and decisions. However, one of the challenges to overcome in the ethical culture approach is relying too heavily on peer pressures and cultural norms to enforce ethics compliance rather than on an individual's own moral responsibility for ethical behavior—in the absence of unrelenting peer pressure or strong internal compliance systems, there is a danger that over time company personnel may become lax about ethical standards. Compliance procedures need to be an integral part of the ethical culture approach to help send the message that management takes the observance of ethical norms seriously and that behavior that falls outside ethical boundaries will have negative consequences.

Why a Company Can Change Its Ethics Management Approach   Regardless of the approach they have used to manage ethical conduct, a company's executives may sense that they have exhausted a particular mode's potential for managing ethics and that they need to become more forceful in their approach to ethics management. Such changes typically occur when the company's ethical failures have made the headlines and created an embarrassing situation for company officials or when the business climate changes. For example, the recent raft of corporate scandals, coupled with aggressive enforcement of anticorruption legislation such as the Sarbanes-Oxley Act of 2002 (which addresses corporate governance and accounting practices), has prompted numerous executives and boards of directors to clean up their acts in accounting and financial reporting, review their ethical standards, and tighten up ethics compliance procedures. Intentionally amoral managers using the unconcerned or nonissue approach to ethics management may see less risk in shifting to the damage control approach (or, for appearance's sake, maybe a "light" compliance mode). Senior managers who have employed the damage control mode may be motivated by bad experiences to mend their ways and shift to a compliance mode. In the wake of so many corporate scandals, companies in the compliance mode may move closer to the ethical culture approach.

Why Should Company Strategies Be Ethical?

There are two reasons why a company's strategy should be ethical: (1) because a strategy that is unethical in whole or in part is morally wrong and reflects badly on the character of the company personnel involved and (2) because an ethical strategy is good business and is in the self-interest of shareholders.

Managers do not dispassionately assess what strategic course to steer. Ethical strategy making generally begins with managers who themselves have strong character (i.e., who are honest, have integrity, are ethical, and truly care about how they conduct the company's business). Managers with high ethical principles and standards are usually advocates of a corporate code of ethics and strong ethics compliance, and they are typically genuinely committed to certain corporate values and business principles. They walk the talk in displaying the company's stated values and living up to its business principles and ethical standards. They understand there's a big difference between adopting values statements and codes of ethics that serve merely as window dressing and adopting those that truly paint the white lines for a company's actual strategy and business conduct. As a consequence, ethically strong managers consciously opt for strategic actions that can pass moral scrutiny—they display no tolerance for strategies with ethically controversial components.

But there are solid business reasons to adopt ethical strategies even if most company managers are not of strong moral character and personally committed to high ethical standards. Pursuing unethical strategies not only damages a company's reputation but can also have costly consequences that are wide-ranging. Some of the costs are readily visible; others are hidden and difficult to track down—as shown in Figure 7.1. The costs of fines and penalties and any declines in the stock price are easy enough to calculate. The administrative "cleanup" (or level 2) costs are usually buried in the general costs of doing business and can be difficult to ascribe to any one ethical misdeed. Level 3 costs can be quite difficult to quantify but can sometimes be the most devastating—the aftermath of the Enron debacle left Arthur Andersen's reputation in shreds and led to the once-revered accounting firm's almost immediate demise. It remains to be seen whether Marsh & McLennan can overcome the problems described in Company Spotlight 7.1 or whether Merck, once one of the world's most respected pharmaceutical firms, can survive the revelation that senior management deliberately concealed that its Vioxx painkiller, which the company pulled off the market in September 2004, was tied to much greater risk of heart attack and strokes—some 20 million people in the United States had taken Vioxx over the years and Merck executives had reason to suspect as early as 2000 (and perhaps earlier) that Vioxx had dangerous side effects.[32]

Rehabilitating a company's shattered reputation is time-consuming and costly. Customers shun companies known for their shady behavior. Companies with reputations for unethical conduct have considerable difficulty in recruiting and retaining talented employees. Most hardworking, ethically upstanding people are repulsed by a work environment where unethical behavior is condoned; they don't want to get entrapped in a compromising situation, nor do they want their personal reputations tarnished by the actions of an unsavory employer. A 1997 survey revealed that 42 percent of the respondents took into account a company's ethics when deciding whether to accept a job.[33] Creditors are usually unnerved by the unethical actions of a borrower because of the potential business fallout and subsequent risk of default on any loans. To some significant degree, therefore, companies recognize that ethical

> Conducting business in an ethical fashion is in a company's enlightened self-interest.

Figure 7.1   **The Business Costs of Ethical Failures**

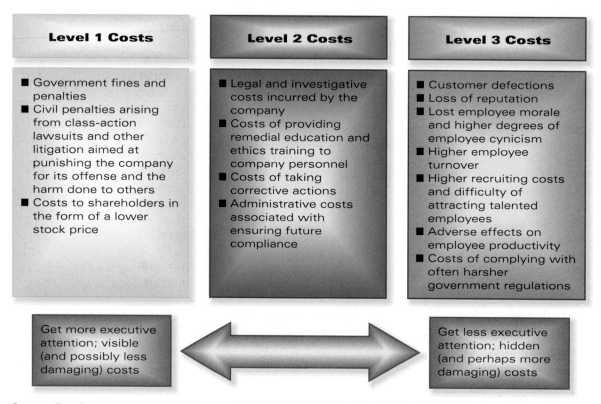

Source: Terry Thomas, John R. Schermerhorn, and John W. Dienhart, "Strategic Leadership of Ethical Behavior," *Academy of Management Executive* 18, no. 2 (May 2004), p. 58.

strategies and ethical conduct are good business. Most companies have strategies that pass the test of being ethical, and most companies are aware that both their reputations and their long-term well-being are tied to conducting their business in a manner that wins the approval of suppliers, employees, investors, and society at large.

Strategy and Social Responsibility

The idea that businesses have an obligation to foster social betterment, a much-debated topic in the past 40 years, took root in the 19th century when progressive companies in the aftermath of the industrial revolution began to provide workers with housing and other amenities. The notion that corporate executives should balance the interests of all stakeholders—shareholders, employees, customers, suppliers, the communities in which they operated, and society at large—began to blossom in the 1960s. A group of chief executives of America's 200 largest corporations, calling themselves the Business Roundtable, promoted the concept of corporate social responsibility. In 1981, the Roundtable's "Statement on Corporate Responsibility" said:

Balancing the shareholder's expectations of maximum return against other priorities is one of the fundamental problems confronting corporate management. The shareholder must receive a good return but the legitimate concerns of other constituencies (customers, employees, communities, suppliers and society at large) also must have the appropriate attention. . . . [Leading managers] believe that by giving enlightened consideration to balancing the legitimate claims of all its constituents, a corporation will best serve the interest of its shareholders.[34]

Today, corporate social responsibility is a concept that resonates in Western Europe, the United States, Canada, and such developing nations as Brazil and India.

What Do We Mean by Social Responsibility?

The essence of **social responsibility** as applied to business behavior is that a company should balance strategic actions to benefit shareholders against the *duty* to be a good corporate citizen. Company managers must display a *social conscience* in operating the business and specifically take into account how management decisions and company actions affect the well-being of employees, local communities, the environment, and society at large. Acting in a socially responsible manner thus encompasses more than just participating in community service projects and donating monies to charities and other worthy social causes. Demonstrating social responsibility also entails undertaking actions that earn trust and respect from all stakeholders—operating in an honorable and ethical manner, striving to make the company a great place to work, demonstrating genuine respect for the environment, and trying to make a difference in bettering society. As depicted in Figure 7.2, the menu for demonstrating a social conscience and choosing specific ways to exercise social responsibility includes:

> **Core Concept**
>
> The notion of **social responsibility** as it applies to businesses concerns a company's *duty* to operate in an honorable manner, provide good working conditions for employees, be a good steward of the environment, and actively work to better the quality of life in the local communities where it operates and in society at large.

- *Efforts to employ an ethical strategy and observe ethical principles in operating the business:* A sincere commitment to observing ethical principles is necessary here simply because unethical strategies and conduct are incompatible with the concept of good corporate citizenship and socially responsible business behavior.

- *Making charitable contributions, donating money and the time of company personnel to community service endeavors, supporting various worthy organizational causes, and reaching out to make a difference in the lives of the disadvantaged:* Some companies fulfill their corporate citizenship and community outreach obligations by spreading their efforts over a multitude of charitable and community activities; for instance, Microsoft and Johnson & Johnson support a broad variety of community art, social welfare, and environmental programs. Others prefer to focus their energies more narrowly. McDonald's, for example, concentrates on sponsoring the Ronald McDonald House program (which provides a home away from home for the families of seriously ill children receiving treatment at nearby hospitals), preventing child abuse and neglect, and participating in local community service activities; in 2004, there were 240 Ronald McDonald Houses in 25 countries and more than 6,000 bedrooms available nightly. British Telecom gives 1 percent of its profits directly to communities, largely for education—teacher training, in-school workshops, and digital technology. Leading prescription drug maker GlaxoSmithKline and other pharmaceutical companies either donate or heavily discount medicines for distribution in the least developed nations. Numerous

Figure 7.2   Demonstrating a Social Conscience—The Five Components of Socially Responsible Business Behavior

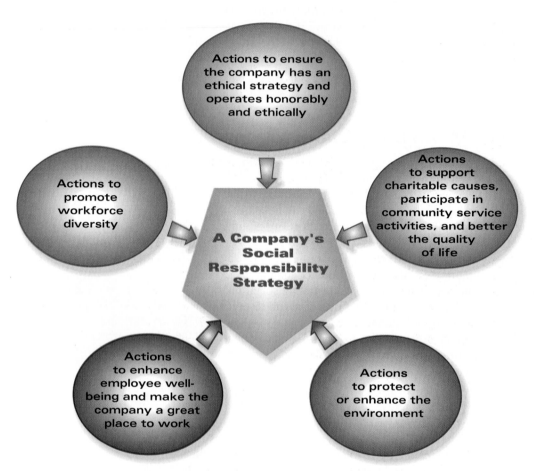

Source: Adapted from material in Ronald Paul Hill, Debra Stephens, and Iain Smith, "Corporate Social Responsibility: An Examination of Individual Firm Behavior," *Business and Society Review* 108, no. 3 (September 2003), p. 348.

health-related businesses take a leading role in community activities that promote effective health care. Many companies work closely with community officials to minimize the impact of hiring large numbers of new employees (which could put a strain on local schools and utility services) and to provide outplacement services for laid-off workers. Companies frequently reinforce their philanthropic efforts by encouraging employees to support charitable causes and participate in community affairs, often through programs to match employee contributions.

■ *Actions to protect or enhance the environment and, in particular, to minimize or eliminate any adverse impact on the environment stemming from the company's own business activities:* Social responsibility as it applies to environmental protection means doing more than what is legally required. From a social responsibility perspective, companies have an obligation to be stewards of the environment. This means using the best available science and technology to achieve higher-than-required environmental standards. Even more ideally, it means putting time and money into improving the environment in ways that extend past a company's own industry boundaries—such as participating in recycling projects, adopting energy conservation practices, and supporting efforts to clean up local water supplies. Retailers such as Home Depot in the United States and B&Q in the United Kingdom have pressured their suppliers to adopt stronger environmental protection practices.[35]

> Business leaders who want their companies to be regarded as exemplary corporate citizens not only must see that their companies operate ethically but must personally display a social conscience in making decisions that affect employees, the environment, the communities in which they operate, and society at large.

- *Actions to create a work environment that enhances the quality of life for employees and makes the company a great place to work:* Numerous companies go beyond providing the ordinary kinds of compensation and exert extra efforts to enhance the quality of life for their employees, both at work and at home. This can include varied and engaging job assignments, career development programs and mentoring, rapid career advancement, appealing compensation incentives, ongoing training to ensure future employability, added decision-making authority, onsite day care, flexible work schedules for single parents, workplace exercise facilities, special leaves to care for sick family members, work-at-home opportunities, gender pay equity, showcase plants and offices, special safety programs, and the like.

- *Actions to build a workforce that is diverse with respect to gender, race, national origin, and perhaps other aspects that different people bring to the workplace:* Most large companies in the United States have established workforce diversity programs, and some go the extra mile to ensure that their workplaces are attractive to ethnic minorities and inclusive of all groups and perspectives. The pursuit of workforce diversity can be good business—Johnson & Johnson, Pfizer, and Coca-Cola believe that a reputation for workforce diversity makes recruiting employees easier (talented employees from diverse backgrounds often seek out such companies). And at Coca-Cola, where strategic success depends on getting people all over the world to become loyal consumers of the company's beverages, efforts to build a public persona of inclusiveness for people of all races, religions, nationalities, interests, and talents have considerable strategic value. Multinational companies are particularly inclined to make workforce diversity a visible strategic component; they recognize that respecting individual differences and promoting inclusiveness resonate well with people all around the world. At a few companies the diversity initiative extends to suppliers—sourcing items from small businesses owned by women or ethnic minorities.

Crafting a Social Responsibility Strategy— The Starting Point for Demonstrating a Social Conscience

While striving to be socially responsible entails choosing from the menu outlined in the preceding section, there's plenty of room for every company to make its own statement about what charitable contributions to make, what kinds of community service projects to emphasize, what environmental actions to support, how to make the company a good place to work, where and how workforce diversity fits into the picture, and what else the company will do to support worthy causes and projects that benefit society. *The particular combination of socially responsible endeavors a company elects to pursue defines its* **social responsibility strategy.** However, unless a company's social responsibility initiatives become part of the way it operates its business

> ### Core Concept
>
> A company's **social responsibility strategy** is defined by the specific combination of socially beneficial activities it opts to support with its contributions of time, money, and other resources.

every day, the initiatives are unlikely to catch fire and be fully effective. As an executive at Royal Dutch/Shell put it, corporate social responsibility "is not a cosmetic; it must be rooted in our values. It must make a difference to the way we do business."[36] Thus some companies are integrating social responsibility objectives into their missions and overall performance targets—they see social performance and environmental metrics as an essential component of judging the company's overall future performance. Some 2,500 companies around the world are not only articulating their social responsibility strategies and commitments but also issuing annual social responsibility reports (much like an annual report) that set forth their commitments and the progress they are making for all the world to see and evaluate.[37]

At Green Mountain Coffee Roasters, social responsibility includes fair dealing with suppliers and trying to do something about the poverty of small coffee growers; in its dealings with suppliers at small farmer cooperatives in Peru, Mexico, and Sumatra, Green Mountain pays "fair-trade" prices for coffee beans (in 2002, the fair-trade prices were a minimum of $1.26 per pound for conventional coffee and $1.41 for organically grown versus market prices of 24 to 50 cents per pound). Green Mountain also purchases about 25 percent of its coffee direct from farmers so as to cut out intermediaries and see that farmers realize a higher price for their efforts—coffee is the world's second most heavily traded commodity after oil, requiring the labor of some 20 million people, most of whom live at the poverty level.[38] At General Mills the social responsibility focus is on serving the community and bettering the employment opportunities for minorities and women. Stonyfield Farm, a producer of yogurt and ice-cream products, employs a social responsibility strategy focused on wellness, good nutrition, and "earth-friendly" actions (10 percent of profits are donated to help protect and restore the earth, and yogurt lids are used as minibillboards to help educate people about environmental issues); in addition, it is stressing the development of an environmentally friendly supply chain, sourcing from farmers that grow organic products and refrain from using artificial hormones in milk production. Chick-Fil-A, an Atlanta-based fast-food chain with 1,125 outlets, has a charitable foundation, supports 14 foster homes and a summer camp (for some 1,600 campers from 22 states and several foreign countries), funds two scholarship programs (including one for employees that has awarded more than $18 million in scholarships), and has a closed-on-Sunday policy to ensure that every Chick-Fil-A employee and restaurant operator has an opportunity to worship, spend time with family and friends, or just plain rest from the workweek.[39]

> Many companies tailor their strategic efforts to operate in a socially responsible manner to fit their core values and business mission, thereby making their own statement about "how we do business and how we intend to fulfill our duties to all stakeholders and society at large."

It is common for companies engaged in natural resource extraction, electric power production, forestry and paper products, motor vehicles, and chemicals production to place more emphasis on addressing environmental concerns than, say, software and electronics firms or apparel manufacturers. Companies whose business success is heavily dependent on maintaining high employee morale or attracting and retaining the best and brightest employees are somewhat more prone to stress the well-being of their employees and foster a positive, high-energy workplace environment that elicits the dedication and enthusiastic commitment of employees, thus putting real meaning behind the claim "Our people are our greatest asset." Ernst & Young, one of the four largest global accounting firms, stresses its "People First" workforce diversity strategy, which is all about respecting differences, fostering individuality, and promoting inclusiveness, so that its 105,000 employees in 140 countries can feel valued, engaged, and empowered in developing creative ways to serve the firm's clients.

Thus, while the strategies and actions of all socially responsible companies have a sameness in the sense of drawing on the five categories of socially responsible behavior shown in Figure 7.2, each company's version of being socially responsible is unique.

The Moral Case for Corporate Social Responsibility

The moral case for why businesses should actively promote the betterment of society and act in a manner that benefits all of the company's stakeholders—not just the interests of shareholders—boils down to "it's the right thing to do." Ordinary decency, civic-mindedness, and contributions to the well-being of society should be expected of any business. In today's social and political climate most business leaders can be expected to acknowledge that socially responsible actions are important and that businesses have a duty to be good corporate citizens. But there is a complementary school of thought that business operates on the basis of an implied social contract with the members of society. According to this contract, society grants a business the right to conduct its business affairs and agrees not to unreasonably restrain its pursuit of a fair profit for the goods or services it sells; in return for this "license to operate," a business is obligated to act as a responsible citizen and do its fair share to promote the general welfare. Such a view clearly puts a moral burden on a company to take corporate citizenship into consideration and to do what's best for shareholders within the confines of discharging its duties to operate honorably, provide good working conditions to employees, be a good environmental steward, and display good corporate citizenship.

> Every action a company takes can be interpreted as a statement of what it stands for.

The Business Case for Socially Responsible Behavior

Whatever the merits of the moral case for socially responsible business behavior, it has long been recognized that it is in the enlightened self-interest of companies to be good citizens and devote some of their energies and resources to the betterment of employees, the communities in which they operate, and society in general. In short, there are several reasons why the exercise of social responsibility is good business:

■ *It generates internal benefits (particularly as concerns employee recruiting, workforce retention, and training costs).* Companies with deservedly good reputations for contributing time and money to the betterment of society are better able to attract and retain employees compared to companies with tarnished reputations. Some employees just feel better about working for a company committed to improving society.[40] This can contribute to lower turnover and better worker productivity. Other direct and indirect economic benefits include lower costs for staff recruitment and training. For example, Starbucks is said to enjoy much lower rates of employee turnover because of its full benefits package for both full-time and part-time employees, management efforts to make Starbucks a great place to work, and the company's socially responsible practices. When a U.S. manufacturer of recycled paper, taking eco-efficiency to heart, discovered how to increase its fiber recovery rate, it saved the equivalent of 20,000 tons of waste paper—a factor that helped the company become the industry's lowest-cost producer.[41] Various bench-marking and measurement mechanisms have shown that workforce diversity initiatives promote the success of companies that stay behind them. Making a company a great place to work pays dividends in the recruiting of talented workers, more creativity and energy on the part of workers, higher worker productivity, and greater employee commitment to the company's business mission/vision and success in the marketplace.

- *It reduces the risk of reputation-damaging incidents and can lead to increased buyer patronage.* Firms may well be penalized by employees, consumers, and shareholders for actions that are not considered socially responsible. When a major oil company suffered damage to its reputation on environmental and social grounds, the CEO repeatedly said that the most negative impact the company suffered—and the one that made him fear for the future of the company—was that bright young graduates were no longer attracted to work for the company.[42] Consumer, environmental, and human rights activist groups are quick to criticize businesses whose behavior they consider to be out of line, and they are adept at getting their message into the media and onto the Internet. Pressure groups can generate widespread adverse publicity, promote boycotts, and influence like-minded or sympathetic buyers to avoid an offender's products. Research has shown that product boycott announcements are associated with a decline in a company's stock price.[43] Outspoken criticism of Royal Dutch/Shell by environmental and human rights groups and associated boycotts were said to be major factors in the company's decision to tune in to its social responsibilities. For many years, Nike received stinging criticism for not policing sweatshop conditions in the Asian factories of its contractors, causing Nike CEO Phil Knight to observe that "Nike has become synonymous with slave wages, forced overtime, and arbitrary abuse."[44] In 1997, Nike began an extensive effort to monitor conditions in the 800 overseas factories to which it outsourced its shoes; Knight said, "Good shoes come from good factories and good factories have good labor relations." Nonetheless, Nike has continually been plagued by complaints from human rights activists that its monitoring procedures are flawed and that it is not doing enough to correct the plight of factory workers. In contrast, to the extent that a company's socially responsible behavior wins applause from consumers and fortifies its reputation, the company may win additional patron-age; Ben & Jerry's, Whole Foods Market, Stonyfield Farm, and the Body Shop have definitely expanded their customer bases because of their visible and well-publicized activities as socially conscious companies. More and more companies are recognizing the strategic value of social responsibility strategies that reach out to people of all cultures and demographics—in the United States, women are said to have buying power of $3.7 trillion; retired and disabled people, close to $4.1 trillion; Hispanics, nearly $600 billion; African-Americans, some $500 billion; and Asian-Americans, about $255 billion.[45] So reaching out in ways that appeal to such groups can pay off at the cash register. Some observers and executives are convinced that a strong, visible social responsibility strategy gives a company an edge in differentiating itself from rivals and in appealing to those consumers who prefer to do business with companies that are solid corporate citizens. Yet there is only limited evidence that consumers

> The higher the public profile of a company or brand, the greater the scrutiny of its activities and the higher the potential for it to become a target for pressure-group action.

go out of their way to patronize socially responsible companies if doing so means paying a higher price or purchasing an inferior product.[46]

■ *It is in the best interest of shareholders.* Well-conceived social responsibility strategies work to the advantage of shareholders in several ways. Socially responsible business behavior helps avoid or preempt legal and regulatory actions that could prove costly and otherwise burdensome. Increasing numbers of mutual fund and pension benefit managers are restricting their stock purchases to companies that meet social responsibility criteria. According to one survey, one out of every eight dollars under professional management in the United States involved socially responsible investing.[47] Moreover, the growth in socially responsible investing and in identifying socially responsible companies has led to a substantial increase in the number of companies that publish formal reports on their social and environmental activities.[48] The stock prices of companies that rate high on social and environmental performance criteria have been found to perform 35 to 45 percent better than the average of the 2,500 companies constituting the Dow Jones Global Index.[49] A two-year study of leading companies found that improving environmental compliance and developing environmentally friendly products can enhance earnings per share, profitability, and the likelihood of winning contracts.[50] Nearly 100 studies have examined the relationship between corporate citizenship and corporate financial performance over the past 30 years; the majority point to a positive relationship. Of the 80 studies that examined whether a company's social performance is a good predictor of its financial performance, 42 concluded yes, 4 concluded no, and the remainder reported mixed or inconclusive findings.[51] To the extent that socially responsible behavior is good business, then, a social responsibility strategy that packs some punch and is more than rhetorical flourish turns out to be in the best interest of shareholders.

> There's little hard evidence indicating shareholders are disadvantaged in any meaningful way by a company's actions to be socially responsible.

In sum, companies that take social responsibility seriously can improve their business reputations and operational efficiency while also reducing their risk exposure and encouraging loyalty and innovation. Overall, companies that take special pains to protect the environment (beyond what is required by law), are active in community affairs, and are generous supporters of charitable causes and projects that benefit society are more likely to be seen as good investments and as good companies to work for or do business with. Shareholders are likely to view the business case for social responsibility as a strong one, even though they certainly have a right to be concerned about whether the time and money their company spends to carry out its social responsibility strategy outweighs the benefits and reduces the bottom line by an unjustified amount.

Companies are, of course, sometimes rewarded for bad behavior—a company that is able to shift environmental and other social costs associated with its activities onto society as a whole can reap large short-term profits. The major cigarette producers for many years were able to earn greatly inflated profits by shifting the health-related costs of smoking onto others and escaping any responsibility for the harm their products caused to consumers and the general public. But the profitability of shifting costs onto society is a risky practice because it attracts scrutiny from pressure groups, raises the threat of regulation and/or legislation to correct the inequity, and prompts socially conscious buyers to take their business elsewhere.

How Much Attention to Social Responsibility Is Enough?

What is an appropriate balance between the imperative to create value for shareholders and the obligation to proactively contribute to the larger social good? What fraction of a company's resources ought to be aimed at addressing social concerns and bettering the well-being of society and the environment? A few companies have a policy of setting aside a specified percentage of their profits (typically 5 percent or maybe 10 percent) to fund their social responsibility strategy; they view such percentages as a fair amount to return to the community as a kind of thank-you or a tithe to the betterment of society. Other companies shy away from a specified percentage of profits or revenues because it entails upping the commitment in good times and cutting back on social responsibility initiatives in hard times (even cutting out social responsibility initiatives entirely if profits temporarily turn into losses). If social responsibility is an ongoing commitment rooted in the corporate culture and enlists broad participation on the part of company personnel, then a sizable portion of the funding for the company's social responsibility strategy has to be viewed as simply a regular and ongoing cost of doing business.

But judging how far a particular company should go in pursuing particular social causes is a tough issue. Consider, for example, Nike's commitment to monitoring the workplace conditions of its contract suppliers.[52] The scale of this monitoring task is significant: Nike has over 800 contract suppliers employing over 600,000 people in 50 countries. How frequently should sites be monitored? How should it respond to the use of underage labor? If children only above a set age are to be employed by suppliers, should suppliers still be required to provide schooling opportunities? At last count, Nike had some 80 people engaged in site monitoring. Should Nike's monitoring budget be $2 million, $5 million, $10 million, or whatever it takes?

Consider another example: If pharmaceutical manufacturers donate or discount their drugs for distribution to low-income people in less developed nations, what safeguards should they put in place to see that the drugs reach the intended recipients and are not diverted by corrupt local officials for reexport to markets in other countries? Should drug manufacturers also assist in drug distribution and administration in these less developed countries? How much should a drug company invest in R&D to develop medicines for tropical diseases commonly occurring in less developed countries when it is unlikely to recover its costs in the foreseeable future?

And how much should a company allocate to charitable contributions? Is it falling short of its responsibilities if its donations are less than 1 percent of profits? Is a company going too far if it allocates 5 percent or even 10 percent of its profits to worthy causes of one kind or another? The point here is that there is no simple or widely accepted standard for judging when a company has or has not gone far enough in fulfilling its citizenship responsibilities.

Linking Social Performance Targets to Executive Compensation

Perhaps the most surefire way to enlist a genuine commitment to corporate social responsibility initiatives is to link the achievement of social performance targets to executive compensation. If a company's board of directors is serious about corporate citizenship, then it will incorporate measures of the company's social and environmental performance into its evaluation of top executives, especially the CEO. And if the CEO uses compensation incentives to further enlist the support of down-the-line company personnel in effectively crafting and executing a social responsibility strategy, the company will over time build a culture rooted in socially responsible and ethical behavior. According to one study, 80 percent of surveyed CEOs believe that environmental and social performance metrics are a valid part of measuring a company's overall performance. At Verizon Communications, 10 percent of the annual bonus of the company's top 2,500 managers is tied directly to the achievement of social responsibility targets; for the rest of the staff, there are corporate recognition awards in the form of cash for employees who have made big contributions toward social causes. The corporate social responsibility reports being issued annually by 2,500 companies across the world that detail social responsibility initiatives and the results achieved are a good basis for compensating executives and judging the effectiveness of their commitment to social responsibility.

Key Points

Ethics involves concepts of right and wrong, fair and unfair, moral and immoral. Beliefs about what is ethical serve as a moral compass in guiding the actions and behaviors of individuals and organizations. Ethical principles in business are not materially different from ethical principles in general.

There are three schools of thought about ethical standards:

- According to the *school of ethical universalism,* the same standards of what's ethical and what's unethical resonate with peoples of most societies regardless of local traditions and cultural norms; hence, common ethical standards can be used to judge the conduct of personnel at companies operating in a variety of country markets and cultural circumstances.

- According to the *school of ethical relativism,* different societal cultures and customs have divergent values and standards of right and wrong—thus what is ethical or unethical must be judged in the light of local customs and social mores and can vary from one culture or nation to another.

- According to *integrated social contracts theory,* universal ethical principles or norms based on the collective views of multiple cultures and societies combine to form a "social contract" that all individuals in all situations have a duty to observe. Within the boundaries of this social contract, local cultures can specify other impermissible actions; however, universal ethical norms always take precedence over local ethical norms.

Three categories of managers stand out in terms of their prevailing beliefs in and commitments to ethical and moral principles in business affairs: the moral manager, the immoral manager, and the amoral manager. By some accounts, the population of managers is said to be distributed among all three types in a bell-shaped curve, with immoral managers and moral managers occupying the two tails of the curve and the amoral managers, especially the intentionally amoral managers, occupying the broad middle ground.

The stance a company takes in dealing with or managing ethical conduct at any given time can take any of four basic forms:

- The unconcerned or nonissue approach.
- The damage control approach.
- The compliance approach.
- The ethical culture approach.

There are two reasons why a company's strategy should be ethical: (1) because a strategy that is unethical in whole or in part is morally wrong and reflects badly on the character of the company personnel involved and (2) because an ethical strategy is good business and in the self-interest of shareholders.

The term *corporate social responsibility* concerns a company's duty to operate in an honorable manner, provide good working conditions for employees, be a good steward of the environment, and actively work to better the quality of life in the local communities where it operates and in society at large. The menu of actions and behavior for demonstrating social responsibility includes:

- Employing an ethical strategy and observing ethical principles in operating the business.

- Making charitable contributions, donating money and the time of company personnel to community service endeavors, supporting various worthy organizational causes, and making a difference in the lives of the disadvantaged. Corporate commitments are further reinforced by encouraging employees to support charitable and community activities.

- Protecting or enhancing the environment and, in particular, striving to minimize or eliminate any adverse impact on the environment stemming from the company's own business activities.

- Creating a work environment that makes the company a great place to work.

- Employing a workforce that is diverse with respect to gender, race, national origin, and perhaps other aspects that different people bring to the workplace.

There's ample room for every company to tailor its social responsibility strategy to fit its core values and business mission, thereby making its own statement about "how we do business and how we intend to fulfill our duties to all stakeholders and society at large."

The moral case for social responsibility boils down to a simple concept: it's the right thing to do. The business case for social responsibility holds that it is in the enlightened self-interest of companies to be good citizens and devote some of their energies and resources to the betterment of such stakeholders as employees, the communities in which they operate, and society in general.

The case for ethical and socially responsible behavior is about attracting and retaining talented staff, about managing risk, and about ensuring a company's reputation with customers, suppliers, local communities, and society.

Exercises

1. Based on the description of Marsh & McLennan's strategy presented in Company Spotlight 7.1, would it be fair to characterize the payment of contingent commissions by property-casualty insurers as nothing more than thinly disguised kickbacks? Why or why not? If you were the manager of a company that hired Marsh & McLennan to provide risk management services, would you see that Marsh had a conflict of interest in steering your company's insurance policies to insurers in which it has an ownership interest? Given Marsh's unethical and illegal foray into rigging the bids on insurance policies for its corporate clients, what sort of fines and penalties would you impose on the company for its misdeeds (assuming you were asked to recommend appropriate penalties by the prosecuting authorities). Using

Internet research tools, determine what Marsh & McLennan ended up paying in fines and restitution for its unethical and illegal strategic behavior and assess the extent to which the conduct of company personnel damaged shareholders.

2. Log on to www.business-ethics.com. Review the companies listed as the "100 Best Corporate Citizens" in the most recent year and the criteria for earning a spot on this list. Do the criteria seem reasonable? Is there ample reason to believe that the 100 companies on this list pursue strategies that are ethical? Or do the criteria used to determine the 100 Best Corporate Citizens point more to companies that have some standout socially responsible practices?

3. Assume you are a manager of a chain of fast-food restaurants in Russia, in partnership with a Russian company. One day you discover that a senior officer of your Russian joint-venture partner has been "borrowing" equipment from the joint-venture company and utilizing it in another of his business ventures. When you confront him, the Russian officer defends his actions, arguing that as an owner of both companies he is entitled to share use of the equipment. What would you say?

CHAPTER 8

Executing the Strategy
Building a Capable Organization and Instilling a Culture

The best game plan in the world never blocked or tackled anybody.

—*Vince Lombardi, NFL Hall of Fame football coach*

Strategies most often fail because they aren't executed well.

—*Larry Bossidy, CEO, Honeywell International, and Ram Charan, author and consultant*

Organizing is what you do before you do something, so that when you do it, it is not all mixed up.

—*A. A. Milne, author*

An organization's capacity to execute its strategy depends on its "hard" infrastructure—its organizational structure and systems—and on its "soft" infrastructure—its culture and norms.

—*Amar Bhide, professor*

The biggest levers you've got to change a company are strategy, structure, and culture. If I could pick two, I'd pick strategy and culture.

—*Wayne Leonard, CEO, Entergy*

Values can't just be words on a page. To be effective, they must shape action.

—*Jeffrey R. Immelt, CEO, General Electric*

Once managers have decided on a strategy, the emphasis turns to converting it into actions and good results. Putting the strategy into place and getting the organization to execute it well call for different sets of managerial skills. Whereas crafting strategy is largely a market-driven activity, executing strategy is primarily an operations-driven activity revolving around the management of people and business processes. Whereas successful strategy making depends on business vision, solid industry and competitive analysis, and shrewd market positioning, successful strategy execution depends on doing a good job of building and strengthening organizational capabilities, motivating and rewarding people in a strategy-supportive manner, and instilling a discipline of getting things done. Executing strategy is an action-oriented, make-things-happen task that tests a manager's ability to direct organizational change, achieve continuous improvement in operations and business processes, create and nurture a strategy-supportive culture, and consistently meet or beat performance targets.

Experienced managers are emphatic in declaring that it is a whole lot easier to develop a sound strategic plan than it is to execute the plan and achieve the desired outcomes. According to one executive, "It's been rather easy for us to decide where we wanted to go. The hard part is to get the organization to act on the new priorities."[1] What makes executing strategy a tougher, more time-consuming management challenge than crafting strategy is the wide array of managerial activities that have to be attended to, the many ways managers can proceed, the demanding people-management skills required, the perseverance necessary to get a variety of initiatives launched and moving, the number of bedeviling issues that must be worked out, the resistance to change that must be overcome, and the difficulties of integrating the efforts of many different work groups into a smoothly functioning whole.

Just because senior managers announce a new strategy doesn't mean that organization members will agree with it or enthusiastically move forward in implementing it. Senior executives cannot simply tell their immediate subordinates to implement new strategic initiatives and expect that the wheels will quickly start grinding and smoothly deliver the intended results. Skeptical managers and employees may see the strategy as contrary to the organization's best interests, unlikely to succeed, or threatening to their departments or careers. Moreover, individual employees may have different ideas about what internal changes are needed to execute the strategy. Long-standing attitudes, vested interests, inertia, and ingrained organizational practices don't melt away when managers decide on a new strategy and begin efforts to implement it—especially when only comparatively few people have been involved in crafting the strategy and when the rationale for strategic change has to be sold to enough organization members to root out the status quo. It takes adept managerial leadership to convincingly communicate the new strategy and the reasons for it, overcome pockets of doubt and disagreement, secure the commitment and enthusiasm of concerned parties, identify and build consensus on all the hows of implementation and execution, and get all the pieces into place and working well. Depending on how much consensus building, motivating, and organizational change is involved, the process of implementing strategy changes can take several months to several years.

Like crafting strategy, executing strategy is a job for the whole management team, not just a few senior managers. While an organization's chief executive officer and the heads of major units (business divisions, functional departments, and key operating units) are ultimately responsible for seeing that strategy is executed successfully, the process typically affects every part of the firm, from the biggest operating unit to the smallest frontline work group. Top-level managers have to rely on the

Core Concept

Implementing and executing a company's strategy is a job for the entire management team, not just a few senior managers.

active support and cooperation of middle and lower managers to push strategy changes into functional areas and operating units and to see that the organization actually operates in accordance with the strategy on a daily basis. Middle and lower-level managers not only are responsible for initiating and supervising the execution process in their areas of authority but also are instrumental in getting subordinates to continuously improve on how strategy-critical value chain activities are being performed and in producing the operating results that allow company performance targets to be met—their role on the company's strategy execution team is by no means minimal. *Strategy execution thus requires every manager to think through the answer to "What does my area have to do to implement its part of the strategic plan, and what should I do to get these things accomplished efficiently and effectively?"* Indeed, the bigger the organization or the more geographically scattered its operating units, the more that *successful strategy execution depends on the cooperation and implementing skills of operating managers who can push needed changes at the lowest organizational levels and consistently deliver good results.* Only in small organizations can top-level managers get around the need for a team effort on the part of management and personally orchestrate the action steps and implementation sequence.

A Framework for Executing Strategy

The first step in implementing strategic changes is for management to communicate the case for organizational change so clearly and persuasively to organization members that a determined commitment takes hold throughout the ranks to find ways to put the strategy into place, make it work, and meet performance targets. The ideal condition is for managers to arouse enough enthusiasm for the strategy to turn the implementation process into a companywide crusade. Then top executives can move to figuring out all the hows—the specific techniques, actions, and behaviors that are needed for a smooth strategy-supportive operation—and then following through to get things done and deliver results.

The Principal Managerial Components of the Strategy Execution Process

While a company's strategy-executing approaches always have to be tailored to the particulars of a company's situation, certain managerial bases have to be covered no matter what the circumstances. Eight managerial tasks crop up repeatedly in company efforts to execute strategy (see Figure 8.1):

1. Building an organization with the competencies, capabilities, and resource strengths to execute strategy successfully.

2. Shaping the work environment and corporate culture to fit the strategy.

3. Allocating ample resources to strategy-critical activities.

4. Ensuring that policies and procedures facilitate rather than impede strategy execution.

Figure 8.1   The Eight Components of the Strategy Execution Process

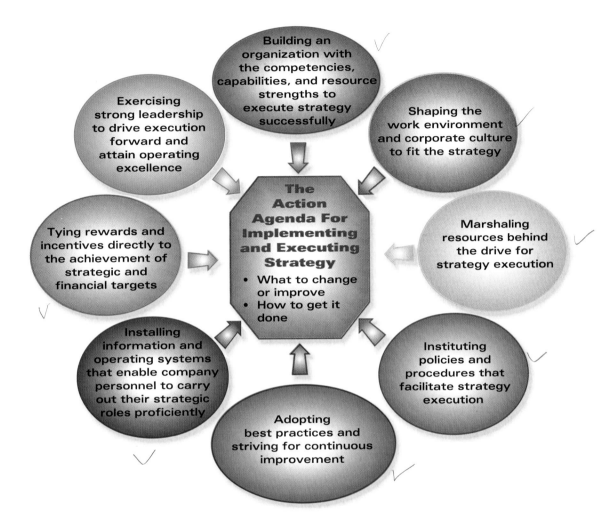

5. Instituting best practices and pushing for continuous improvement in how value chain activities are performed.

6. Installing information and operating systems that enable company personnel to carry out their strategic roles proficiently.

7. Tying rewards directly to the achievement of strategic and financial targets and to good strategy execution.

8. Exercising strong leadership to drive implementation forward, keep improving on how the strategy is being executed, and attain operating excellence.

How well managers perform these eight tasks has a decisive impact on whether the outcome is a spectacular success, a colossal failure, or something in between.

The specific hows of executing a strategy—the exact items that need to be placed on management's action agenda—always have to be customized to fit the particulars of a company's situation. The place for managers to start is with *a probing assessment of what the organization must do differently and better to carry out the strategy successfully.* They should then consider *precisely how to make the necessary internal changes* as rapidly as possible. Successful strategy implementers have a knack for diagnosing what their organizations need to do to execute the chosen strategy well and figuring out how to get things done—they are masters in promoting results-oriented behaviors on the part of company personnel and following through on making the right things happen in a timely fashion.[2] *Management's handling of the strategy implementation process can be considered successful if things go smoothly enough that the company meets or beats its performance targets and shows good progress in achieving its strategic vision.*

> When strategies fail, it is often because of poor execution—things that were supposed to get done slip through the cracks.

Making minor changes in an existing strategy differs from implementing radical strategy changes. The hot buttons for successfully executing a low-cost provider strategy are different from those for executing a high-end differentiation strategy. Implementing and executing a new strategy for a struggling company in the midst of a financial crisis is a different job than improving strategy execution in a company where the execution is already pretty good. Moreover, some managers are more adept than others at using this or that approach to achieving the desired kinds of organizational changes. Hence, there's no definitive recipe for successfully undertaking the eight managerial tasks shown in Figure 8.1.

What's Covered in Chapters 8 and 9   In the remainder of this chapter and the next chapter, we will discuss what is involved in performing the eight key managerial tasks that shape the process of implementing and executing strategy. This chapter explores building a capable organization and instilling a strategy-supportive corporate culture. Chapter 9 looks at the remaining six tasks: marshaling resources, establishing strategy-facilitating policies and procedures, instituting best practices, installing strategy-supportive operating systems, tying rewards to achievement, and exercising strong strategic leadership.

Building an Organization Capable of Proficient Strategy Execution

Proficient strategy execution depends heavily on competent personnel, better-than-adequate competencies and competitive capabilities, and effective internal organization. Building a capable organization is thus always a top priority in strategy execution. As shown in Figure 8.2, three types of organization-building actions are paramount:

1. *Staffing the organization*—putting together a strong management team, and recruiting and retaining employees with the needed experience, technical skills, and intellectual capital.

2. *Building core competencies and competitive capabilities*—developing the skills and expertise that will enable good strategy execution and updating all this know-how as strategy and external conditions change.

3. *Structuring the organization and work effort*—organizing value chain activities and business processes and deciding how much decision-making authority to push down to lower-level managers and frontline employees.

Figure 8.2   **The Three Components of Building an Organization Capable of Proficient Strategy Execution**

Staffing the Organization
- Putting together a strong management team
- Recruiting and retaining talented employees

Building Core Competencies and Competitive Capabilities
- Developing a set of competencies and capabilities suited to the current strategy
- Updating and revising this set as external conditions and strategy change
- Training and retraining employees as needed to maintain skills-based competencies

Matching the Organization Structure to Strategy
- Instituting organizational arrangements that will facilitate strategy execution
- Deciding how much decision-making authority to push down to lower-level managers and frontline employees

A Company with the Organizational Capability Needed for Proficient Strategy Execution

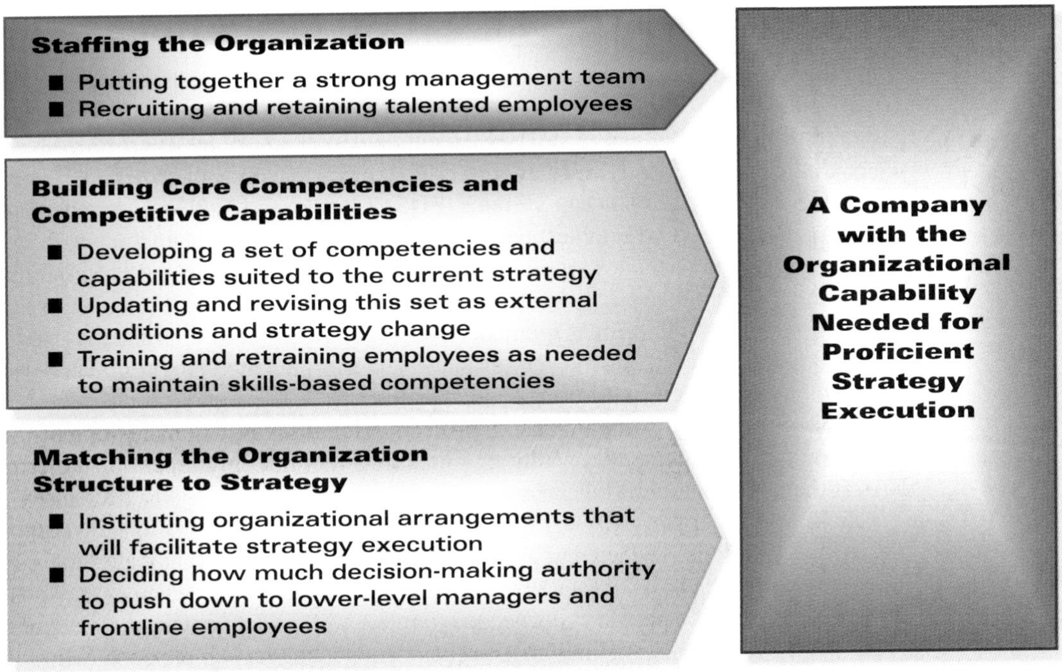

Staffing the Organization

No company can hope to perform the activities required for successful strategy execution without attracting and retaining talented managers and employees who give it suitable skills and *intellectual capital.*

Putting Together a Strong Management Team

Assembling a capable management team is a cornerstone of the organization-building task.[3] Different strategies and company circumstances call for different mixes of managerial backgrounds, experiences, know-how, values, beliefs, management styles, and personalities. The personal chemistry among the members of the management team needs to be right, and the talent base needs to be appropriate for the chosen strategy. But the most important condition is to fill key managerial slots with people who are good at diagnosing what needs to be done and who can be counted on to deliver good results; otherwise, the implementation-execution process can't proceed at full speed.[4] Sometimes the existing management team is suitable; at other times it may need to be strengthened or expanded by promoting qualified people from within or by bringing in outsiders whose experience, skills, and leadership styles better suit the situation. In turnaround and rapid-growth

> **Core Concept**
>
> Putting together a talented management team with the right mix of skills and experiences is one of the first strategy-implementing steps.

situations, and in instances when a company doesn't have insiders with the requisite experience or know-how, filling key management slots from the outside is a fairly standard organization-building approach.

Recruiting and Retaining Capable Employees

Assembling a capable management team is not enough. Staffing the organization with the right kinds of people must go much deeper than managerial jobs in order to build an organization capable of effective strategy execution. Companies like Microsoft, McKinsey & Company, Southwest Airlines, Cisco Systems, Amazon.com, Procter & Gamble, PepsiCo, Nike, Electronic Data Systems (EDS), Google, and Intel make a concerted effort to recruit the best and brightest people they can find and then retain them with excellent compensation packages, opportunities for rapid advancement and professional growth, and challenging and interesting assignments. Having a pool of "A players" with strong skill sets and budding management potential is essential to their business. Microsoft makes a point of hiring the very brightest and most talented programmers it can find and motivating them with both good monetary incentives and the challenge of working on cutting-edge software design projects. McKinsey & Company, one of the world's premier management consulting companies, recruits only cream-of-the-crop MBAs at the nation's top-10 business schools; such talent is essential to McKinsey's

> **Core Concept**
>
> In many industries adding to a company's talent base and building intellectual capital are more important to good strategy execution than additional investments in plants, equipment, and capital projects.

strategy of performing high-level consulting for the world's top corporations. The leading global accounting firms screen candidates not only on the basis of their accounting expertise but also on whether they possess the people skills needed to relate well with clients and colleagues. Southwest Airlines goes to considerable lengths to hire people who can have fun and be fun on the job; it uses special interviewing and screening methods to gauge whether applicants for customer-contact jobs have outgoing personality traits that match its strategy of creating a high-spirited, fun-loving, in-flight atmosphere for passengers, and it is so selective that only about 3 percent of the people who apply are offered jobs.

In high-tech companies, the challenge is to staff work groups with gifted, imaginative, and energetic people who can bring life to new ideas quickly and inject into the organization what one Dell Computer executive calls "hum."[5] The saying "People are our most important asset" may seem hollow, but it fits high-technology companies dead-on. Besides checking closely for functional and technical skills, Dell Computer tests applicants for their tolerance of ambiguity and change, their capacity to work in teams, and their ability to learn on the fly. Companies like Amazon.com and Cisco Systems have broken new ground in recruiting, hiring, cultivating, developing, and retaining talented employees—most all of whom are in their 20s and 30s. Cisco goes after the top 10 percent, raiding other companies and endeavoring to retain key people at the companies it acquires so as to maintain a cadre of star engineers, programmers, managers, salespeople, and support personnel in executing its strategy to remain the world's leading provider of Internet infrastructure products and technology.

Where intellectual capital is crucial to good strategy execution, companies have instituted a number of practices in staffing their organizations and developing a strong knowledge base:

1. Spending considerable effort in screening and evaluating job applicants, selecting only those with suitable skill sets, energy, initiative, judgment, and aptitudes for learning and adaptability to the company's work environment and culture.

2. Putting employees through training programs that continue throughout their careers.

3. Providing promising employees with challenging, interesting, and skill-stretching assignments.

4. Rotating people through jobs that not only have great content but also span functional and geographic boundaries. Providing people with opportunities to gain experience in a variety of international settings is increasingly considered an essential part of career development in multinational or global companies.

5. Encouraging employees to be creative and innovative, to challenge existing ways of doing things and offer better ways, and to submit ideas for new products or businesses. Progressive companies work hard at creating an environment in which ideas and suggestions bubble up from below rather than proceed from the top down. Employees are made to feel that their opinions count.

6. Fostering a stimulating and engaging work environment such that employees will consider the company a great place to work.

7. Exerting efforts to retain high-potential, high-performing employees with salary increases, performance bonuses, stock options and equity ownership, and other long-term incentives.

8. Coaching average performers to improve their skills and capabilities, while weeding out underperformers and benchwarmers.

Building Core Competencies and Competitive Capabilities

High among the organization-building priorities in the strategy-implementing/-executing process is the need to build and strengthen competitively valuable core competencies and organizational capabilities. Whereas managers identify the desired competencies and capabilities in the course of crafting strategy, good strategy execution requires putting the desired competencies and capabilities in place, upgrading them as needed, and then modifying them as market conditions evolve. Sometimes a company already has the needed competencies and capabilities, in which case managers can concentrate on nurturing them to promote better strategy execution. Usually, however, company managers have to add new competencies and capabilities to implement strategic initiatives and promote proficient strategy execution.

A number of prominent companies have succeeded in establishing core competencies and capabilities that have been instrumental in making them winners in the marketplace. Honda's core competence is its depth of expertise in gasoline-engine technology and small-engine design. Intel's is in the design of complex chips for personal computers. Procter & Gamble's core competencies reside in its superb marketing/distribution skills and its R&D capabilities in five core technologies—fats, oils, skin chemistry, surfactants, and emulsifiers. Ciba Specialty Chemicals has technology-based competencies that allow it to quickly manufacture products for customers wanting customized products relating to coloration, brightening and whitening, water treatment and paper processing, freshness, and cleaning. General Electric has a core competence in developing professional managers with broad problem-solving skills and proven ability to grow global businesses.

Disney has core competencies in theme park operation and family entertainment. Sony's core competencies are its expertise in electronic technology and its ability to translate that expertise into innovative products (cutting-edge video game hardware, miniaturized radios and video cameras, TVs and DVDs with unique features, attractively designed PCs). Dell Computer has the capabilities to deliver state-of-the-art products to its customers within days of next-generation components' coming available—and to do so at attractively low costs (it has leveraged its collection of competencies and capabilities into being the global low-cost leader in PCs).

The Three-Stage Process of Developing and Strengthening Competencies and Capabilities

Building core competencies and competitive capabilities is a time-consuming, managerially challenging exercise. While some organization-building assist can be gotten from discovering how best-in-industry or best-in-world companies perform a particular activity, trying to replicate and then improve on the competencies and capabilities of others is much easier said than done—for the same reasons that one is unlikely to ever become a good golfer simply by studying what Tiger Woods does. Putting a new capability in place is more complicated than just forming a new team or department and charging it with becoming highly competent in performing the desired activity, using whatever it can learn from other companies having similar competencies or capabilities. Rather, it takes a series of deliberate and well-orchestrated organizational steps to achieve mounting proficiency in performing an activity. The capability-building process has three stages:

> Building competencies and capabilities is a multi-stage process that occurs over a period of months and years, not something that can be done overnight.

Stage 1: First, the organization must develop the *ability* to do something, however imperfectly or inefficiently. This entails selecting people with the requisite skills and experience, upgrading or expanding individual abilities as needed, and then molding the efforts and work products of individuals into a collaborative effort to create organizational ability.

Stage 2: As experience grows and company personnel learn how to perform the activity *consistently well and at an acceptable cost,* the ability evolves into a tried-and-true *competence* or *capability.*

Stage 3: Should the organization continue to polish and refine its know-how and otherwise sharpen its performance such that it becomes *better than rivals* at performing the activity, the core competence rises to the rank of a *distinctive competence* (or the capability becomes a competitively superior capability), thus providing a path to competitive advantage.

Many companies manage to get through stages 1 and 2 in performing a strategy-critical activity, but comparatively few achieve sufficient proficiency in performing strategy-critical activities to qualify for the third stage.

Managing the Process   Four traits concerning core competencies and competitive capabilities are important in successfully managing the organization-building process:[6]

1. *Core competencies and competitive capabilities are bundles of skills and know-how that most often grow out of the combined efforts of cross-functional work groups and departments performing complementary activities at different locations in the firm's value chain.* Rarely does a core competence or capability consist of narrow skills attached to the work efforts of a single department. For

instance, a core competence in speeding new products to market involves the collaborative efforts of personnel in R&D, engineering and design, purchasing, production, marketing, and distribution. Similarly, the capability to provide superior customer service is a team effort among people in customer call centers (where orders are taken and inquiries are answered), shipping and delivery, billing and accounts receivable, and after-sale support. Complex activities (like designing and manufacturing a sports-utility vehicle or creating the capability for secure credit card transactions over the Internet) usually involve a number of component skills, technological disciplines, competencies, and capabilities—some performed in-house and some provided by suppliers/allies. An important part of the organization-building function is to think about which activities of which groups need to be linked and made mutually reinforcing and then to forge the necessary collaboration both within the company and with outside resource providers.

2. *Normally, a core competence or capability emerges incrementally* out of company efforts either to bolster skills that contributed to earlier successes or to respond to customer problems, new technological and market opportunities, the competitive maneuverings of rivals. Migrating from the one-time ability to do something up the ladder to a core competence or competitively valuable capability is usually an organization-building process that takes months and often years to accomplish—it is definitely not an overnight event.

3. The key to leveraging a core competence into a distinctive competence (or a capability into a competitively superior capability) is *concentrating more effort and more talent than rivals on deepening and strengthening the competence or capability, so as to achieve the dominance needed for competitive advantage.* This does not necessarily mean spending more money on such activities than competitors, but it does mean consciously focusing more talent on them and striving for best-in-industry, if not best-in-world, status. To achieve dominance on lean financial resources, companies like Cray in large computers and Honda in gasoline engines have leveraged the expertise of their talent pool by frequently re-forming high-intensity teams and reusing key people on special projects. The experiences of these and other companies indicate that the usual keys to successfully building core competencies and valuable capabilities are superior employee selection, thorough training and retraining, powerful cultural influences, effective cross-functional collaboration, empowerment, motivating incentives, short deadlines, and good databases—not big operating budgets.

4. Evolving changes in customers' needs and competitive conditions often require *tweaking and adjusting a company's portfolio of competencies and intellectual capital to keep its capabilities freshly honed and on the cutting edge.* This is particularly important in high-tech industries and fast-paced markets where important developments occur weekly. As a consequence, wise company managers work at anticipating changes in customer-market requirements and staying ahead of the curve in proactively building a package of competencies and capabilities that can win out over rivals.

Managerial actions to develop core competencies and competitive capabilities generally take one of two forms: either strengthening the company's base of skills, knowledge, and intellect or coordinating and networking the efforts of the various work groups and departments. Actions of the first sort can be undertaken at all managerial levels, but actions of the second sort are best orchestrated by senior managers who not only appreciate the strategy-executing significance of strong competencies/ capabilities but also have the clout to enforce the necessary networking and coopera- tion among individuals, groups, departments, and external allies.

One organization-building question is whether to develop the desired competen- cies and capabilities internally or to outsource them by partnering with key suppliers or forming strategic alliances. The answer depends on what can be safely delegated to outside suppliers or allies versus what internal capabilities are key to the company's long-term success. Either way, though, calls for action. Outsourcing means launching initiatives to identify the most attractive providers and to establish collaborative rela- tionships. Developing the capabilities in-house means marshaling personnel with rele- vant skills and experience, collaboratively networking the individual skills and related cross-functional activities to form organizational capability, and building the desired levels of proficiency through repetition (practice makes perfect).[7]

Sometimes the tediousness of internal organization building can be shortcut by buying a company that has the requisite capability and integrating its competencies into the firm's value chain. Indeed, a pressing need to acquire certain capabilities quickly is one reason to acquire another company—an acquisition aimed at building greater capability can be every bit as competitively valuable as an acquisition aimed at adding new products or services to the company's business lineup. Capabilities- motivated acquisitions are essential (1) when a market opportunity can slip by faster than a needed capability can be created internally and (2) when industry conditions, technology, or competitors are moving at such a rapid clip that time is of the essence. But usually there's no good substitute for ongoing internal efforts to build and strengthen the company's competencies and capabilities in performing strategy- critical value chain activities.

Updating and Reshaping Competencies and Capabilities as External Conditions and Company Strategy Change   Even after core competencies and competitive capabilities are in place and functioning, company managers can't relax. Competencies and capabilities that grow stale can impair com- petitiveness unless they are refreshed, modified, or even phased out and replaced in re- sponse to ongoing market changes and shifts in company strategy. Indeed, the buildup of knowledge and experience over time, coupled with the imperatives of keeping ca- pabilities in step with ongoing strategy and market changes, makes it appropriate to view a company as *a bundle of evolving competencies and capabilities.* Management's organization-building challenge is one of deciding when and how to recalibrate exist- ing competencies and capabilities and when and how to develop new ones. Although the task is formidable, ideally it produces a dynamic organization with "hum" and mo- mentum as well as a distinctive competence.

From Competencies and Capabilities to Competitive Advantage

Core Concept

Building competencies and capabilities has a huge payoff— improved strategy execution and a potential for competitive advantage.

While strong core competencies and competitive capabilities are a ma- jor assist in executing strategy, they are an equally important avenue for securing a competitive edge over rivals in situations where it is rel- atively easy for rivals to copy smart strategies. Any time rivals can readily duplicate successful strategy features, making it difficult or impossible to beat rivals in the marketplace with a superior strategy, the chief way to achieve lasting competitive advantage is to beat them by performing certain value chain activities in superior fashion. Building core competencies, resource strengths, and organizational capabilities that rivals can't match is thus one of the best and most reliable ways to beat them. Moreover, cutting-edge core competencies and organizational capabilities are not easily duplicated by rival firms; thus, any competitive edge they produce is likely to be sustainable, paving the way for above-average organizational performance.

The Strategic Role of Employee Training

Training and retraining are important when a company shifts to a strategy requiring different skills, competitive capabilities, managerial approaches, and operating methods. Training is also strategically important in organizational efforts to build skills-based competencies. And it is a key activity in businesses where technical know-how is changing so rapidly that a company loses its ability to compete unless its skilled people have cutting-edge knowledge and expertise. Successful strategy implementers see to it that the training function is both adequately funded and effective. If the chosen strategy calls for new skills, deeper technological capability, or new capabilities, training should be placed near the top of the action agenda.

The strategic importance of training has not gone unnoticed. Over 600 companies have established internal "universities" to lead the training effort, facilitate continuous organizational learning, and help upgrade company competencies and capabilities. Many companies conduct orientation sessions for new employees, fund an assortment of competence-building training programs, and reimburse employees for tuition and other expenses associated with obtaining additional college education, attending professional development courses, and earning professional certification of one kind or another. A number of companies offer online, just-in-time training courses to employees around the clock. Increasingly, employees at all levels are expected to take an active role in their own professional development, assuming responsibility for keeping their skills and expertise up to date and in sync with the company's needs.

Execution-Related Aspects of Organizing the Work Effort

There are few hard-and-fast rules for organizing the work effort to support good strategy execution. Every firm's organization chart is partly a product of its particular situation, reflecting prior organizational patterns, varying internal circumstances, executive judgments about reporting relationships, and the politics of who gets which assignments. Moreover, every strategy is grounded in its own set of key success factors and value chain activities. But some organizational considerations are common to all companies. These are summarized in Figure 8.3 and discussed in turn in the following sections.

Deciding Which Value Chain Activities to Perform Internally and Which to Outsource

The advantages of a company's having an outsourcing component in its strategy were discussed in Chapter 4 (pages 142–144), but there is also a need to consider the role of outsourcing in executing the strategy. Aside from the fact that an outsider, because of

Figure 8.3   Structuring the Work Effort to Promote Successful Strategy Execution

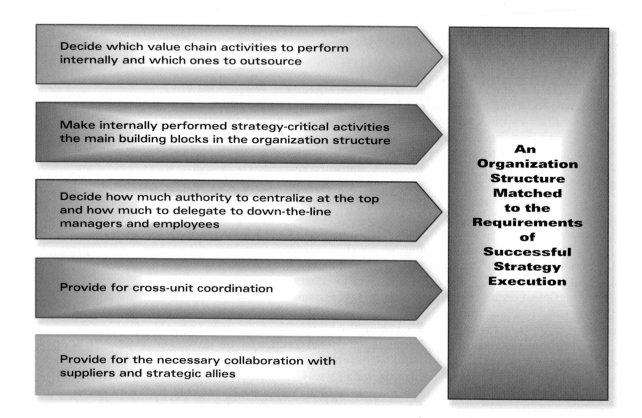

its expertise and specialized know-how, may be able to perform certain value chain activities better or cheaper than a company can perform them internally, outsourcing can have several organization-related benefits. Managers too often spend inordinate amounts of time, mental energy, and resources haggling with functional support groups and other internal bureaucracies over needed services, leaving less time for them to devote to performing strategy-critical activities in the most proficient manner. One way to reduce such distractions is to outsource the performance of assorted administrative support functions and perhaps even selected core or primary value chain activities to outside vendors, thereby enabling the company to *heighten its strategic focus and concentrate its full energies and resources on even more competently performing those value chain activities that are at the core of its strategy and for which it can create unique value.* For example, E. & J. Gallo Winery outsources 95 percent of its grape production, letting farmers take on the weather and other grape-growing risks while it concentrates its full energies on wine production and sales.[8] A number of PC makers outsource the mundane and highly specialized task of PC assembly, concentrating their energies instead on product design, sales and marketing, and distribution.

When a company uses outsourcing to zero in on ever better performance of those truly strategy-critical activities where its expertise is most needed, then it may be able to realize three very positive benefits:

1. *The company improves its chances for outclassing rivals in the performance of these activities and turning a core competence into a distinctive competence.* At the very least, the heightened focus on performing a select few value chain activities should meaningfully strengthen the company's existing core competencies and promote more innovative performance of those activities—either of which could lower costs or materially improve competitive capabilities. Eastman Kodak, Ford, ExxonMobil, Merrill Lynch, and Chevron have outsourced their data processing activities to computer service firms, believing that outside specialists can perform the needed services at lower costs and equal or better quality. A relatively large number of companies outsource the operation of their Web sites to Web design and hosting enterprises. Many businesses that get a lot of inquiries from customers or that have to provide 24/7 technical support to users of their products across the world have found that it is considerably less expensive to outsource these functions to specialists (often located in foreign countries where skilled personnel are readily available and worker compensation costs are much lower) than to operate their own call centers.

2. *The streamlining of internal operations that flows from outsourcing often acts to decrease internal bureaucracies, flatten the organizational structure, speed internal decision making, and shorten the time it takes to respond to changing market conditions.*[9] In consumer electronics, where advancing technology drives new product innovation, organizing the work effort in a manner that expedites getting next-generation products to market ahead of rivals is a critical competitive capability. The world's motor vehicle manufacturers have found that they can shorten the cycle time for new models, improve the quality and performance of those models, and lower overall production costs by outsourcing the big majority of their parts and components from independent suppliers and then working closely with their vendors to advance the design and functioning of the items being supplied, to swiftly incorporate new technology, and to better integrate individual parts and components to form engine cooling systems, transmission systems, and electrical systems.

3. *Partnerships can add to a company's arsenal of capabilities and contribute to better strategy execution.* By building, continually improving, and then leveraging partnerships, a company enhances its overall organizational capabilities and builds resource strengths—strengths that deliver value to customers and consequently pave the way for competitive success. Soft-drink and beer manufacturers all cultivate their relationships with their bottlers and distributors to strengthen access to local markets and build loyalty, support, and commitment for corporate marketing programs, without which their own sales and growth are weakened. Similarly, fast-food enterprises like McDonald's and Taco Bell find it essential to work hand-in-hand with franchisees on outlet cleanliness, consistency of product quality, in-store ambience, courtesy and friendliness of store personnel, and other aspects of store operations. Unless franchisees continuously deliver sufficient customer satisfaction to attract repeat business, a fast-food chain's sales and competitive standing will suffer quickly. Companies like Boeing, Aerospatiale, Verizon Communications, and Dell Computer have learned that their central R&D groups cannot begin to match the innovative capabilities of a well-managed network of supply chain partners having the ability to advance the technology, lead the development of next-generation parts and components, and supply them at a relatively low price.[10]

> **Core Concept**
>
> Wisely choosing which activities to perform internally and which to outsource can lead to several strategy-executing advantages—lower costs, heightened strategic focus, less internal bureaucracy, speedier decision making, and a better arsenal of competencies and capabilities.

As a general rule, companies refrain from outsourcing those value chain activities over which they need direct strategic and operating control in order to build core competencies, achieve competitive advantage, and effectively manage key customer-supplier-distributor relationships. It is the strategically less important activities—like handling customer inquiries and providing technical support, doing the payroll, administering employee benefit programs, providing corporate security, managing stockholder relations, maintaining fleet vehicles, operating the company's Web site, conducting employee training, and managing an assortment of information and data processing functions—for which outsourcing is most used.

However, a number of companies have found ways to successfully rely on outside vendors to perform strategically significant value chain activities.[11] For years Polaroid Corporation bought its film from Eastman Kodak, its electronics from Texas Instruments, and its cameras from Timex and others, while it concentrated on producing its unique self-developing film packets and designing its next-generation cameras and films. Nike concentrates on design, marketing, and distribution to retailers, while outsourcing virtually all production of its shoes and sporting apparel. Cisco Systems outsources virtually all manufacturing of its routers, switches, and other Internet gear; yet it protects its market position by retaining tight internal control over product design, and it closely monitors the daily operations of its manufacturing vendors. So while performing core value chain activities in-house normally makes good sense, there can be times when outsourcing some of them works to good advantage.

The Dangers of Excessive Outsourcing   Critics contend that a company can go overboard on outsourcing and so hollow out its knowledge base and capabilities as to leave itself at the mercy of outside suppliers and short of the resource strengths needed to be master of its own destiny.[12] The point is well taken. Outsourcing strategy-critical activities must be done judiciously and with safeguards against losing control over the performance of key value chain activities and becoming overly dependent on outsiders. Thus, many companies refuse to source key components from a single supplier, opting to use two or three suppliers as a way to avoid becoming overly dependent on any one supplier and giving any one supplier too much bargaining power. Moreover, they regularly evaluate their suppliers, looking not only at the supplier's overall performance but also at whether they should switch to another supplier or even bring the activity back in-house. To avoid loss of control, companies typically work closely with key suppliers, endeavoring to make sure that suppliers' activities are closely integrated with their own requirements and expectations. Most companies appear alert to the primary danger of taking outsourcing to an extreme and finding themselves without the internal capabilities needed to be a master of their own destiny and protect their well-being in the marketplace.

Making Strategy-Critical Activities the Main Building Blocks of the Organizational Structure

In any business, some activities in the value chain are always more critical to strategic success and competitive advantage than others. For instance, hotel/motel enterprises have to be good at fast check-in/checkout, housekeeping and facilities maintenance, food service, and creating a pleasant ambience. For a manufacturer of chocolate bars, buying quality cocoa beans at low prices is vital and reducing production costs by a fraction of a cent per bar can mean a seven-figure improvement in the bottom line. In discount stock brokerage, the strategy-critical activities are fast access to information, accurate order execution, efficient record keeping and transactions processing, and good customer service. In specialty chemicals, the critical activities are R&D, product innovation, getting new products onto the market quickly, effective marketing, and expertise in assisting customers. Where such is the case, it is important for management to build its organizational structure around proficient performance of these activities, making them the centerpieces or main building blocks on the organization chart.

The rationale for making strategy-critical activities the main building blocks in structuring a business is compelling: if activities crucial to strategic success are to have the resources, decision-making influence, and organizational impact they need, they have to be centerpieces in the organizational scheme. Plainly, implementing a new or changed strategy is likely to entail new or different key activities, competencies, or capabilities and therefore to require new or different organizational arrangements. If workable organizational adjustments are not forthcoming, the resulting mismatch between strategy and structure can open the door to execution and performance problems.[13] Hence, attempting to carry out a new strategy with an old organizational structure is usually unwise.

The primary organizational building blocks within a business are usually *traditional functional departments* (R&D, engineering and design, production and operations, sales and marketing, information technology, finance and accounting, and human resources) and *process-complete departments* (supply chain management, customer order fulfillment, customer service, quality control, direct sales via the company's Web site). For instance, a technical instruments manufacturer may be organized around research and development, engineering, supply chain management, assembly, quality control, marketing, technical services, and corporate administration. A hotel may have a functional organization based on front-desk operations, housekeeping, building maintenance, food service, convention services and special events, guest services, personnel and training, and accounting. A discount retailer may organize around such functional units as purchasing, warehousing and distribution, store operations, advertising, merchandising and promotion, customer service, and corporate administrative services.

In enterprises with operations in various countries around the world (or with geographically scattered organizational units within a country), the basic building blocks may also include *geographic organizational units*, each of which has profit/loss responsibility for its assigned geographic area. In vertically integrated firms, the major building blocks are *divisional units performing one or more of the major processing steps along the value chain* (raw materials production, components manufacture, assembly, wholesale distribution, retail store operations); each division in the value chain may operate as a profit center for performance measurement purposes. The typical building blocks of a diversified company are its *individual businesses*, with each business unit usually operating as an independent profit center and with corporate headquarters performing assorted support functions for all of its business units.

Determining the Degree of Authority and Independence to Give Each Unit and Each Employee

In executing the strategy and conducting daily operations, companies must decide how much authority to delegate to the managers of each organizational unit—especially the

Table 8.1   ADVANTAGES AND DISADVANTAGES OF CENTRALIZED VERSUS DECENTRALIZED DECISION MAKING

Centralized Organizational Structures	Decentralized Organizational Structures
Basic Tenets ■ Decisions on most matters of importance should be pushed to managers up the line who have the experience, expertise, and judgment to decide what is the wisest or best course of action. ■ Frontline supervisors and rank-and-file employees can't be relied upon to make the right decisions—because they seldom know what is best for the organization and they do not have the time or the inclination to properly manage the tasks they are performing (letting them decide "what to do" is thus risky). **Chief Advantage** ■ Tight control from the top fixes accountability. **Primary Disadvantages** ■ Lengthens response times because management bureaucracy must decide on a course of action. ■ Does not encourage responsibility among lower-level managers and rank-and-file employees. ■ Discourages lower-level managers and rank-and-file employees from exercising any initiative—they are expected to wait to be told what to do.	**Basic Tenets** ■ Decision-making authority should be put in the hands of the people closest to and most familiar with the situation, and these people should be trained to exercise good judgment. ■ A company that draws on the combined intellectual capital of all its employees can outperform a command-and-control company. **Chief Advantages** ■ Encourages lower-level managers and rank-and-file employees to exercise initiative and act responsibly. ■ Promotes greater motivation and involvement in the business on the part of more company personnel. ■ Spurs new ideas and creative thinking. ■ Allows fast response times. ■ Entails fewer layers of management. **Primary Disadvantages** ■ Puts the organization at risk if many "bad" decisions are made at lower levels—top management lacks "full control." ■ Impedes cross-unit coordination and capture of strategic fits.

heads of business subsidiaries, functional and process departments, plants, sales offices, distribution centers, and other operating units—and how much decision-making latitude to give individual employees in performing their jobs. The two extremes are to *centralize decision making* at the top (the CEO and a few close lieutenants) or to *decentralize decision making* by giving managers and employees considerable decision-making latitude in their areas of responsibility. As shown in Table 8.1, the two approaches are based on sharply different underlying principles and beliefs, with each having its pros and cons.

Centralized Decision Making: Pros and Cons   *In a highly centralized organizational structure, top executives retain authority for most strategic and operating decisions and keep a tight rein on business-unit heads, department heads, and the managers of key operating units; comparatively little discretionary authority is granted to frontline supervisors and rank-and-file employees.* The command-and-control paradigm of centralized structures is based on the underlying assumption that frontline personnel have neither the time nor the inclination to direct and properly control the work they are performing and that they lack the knowledge and judgment to make wise decisions about how best to do it—hence the need for managerially prescribed policies and procedures, close supervision, and tight control. The thesis underlying authoritarian structures is that strict enforcement of detailed procedures backed by rigorous managerial oversight is the most reliable way to keep the daily execution of strategy on track.

> There are disadvantages to having a small number of top-level managers micromanage the business either by personally making decisions or by requiring lower-level subordinates to gain approval before taking action.

The big advantage of an authoritarian structure is tight control by the manager in charge—it is easy to know who is accountable when things do not go well. But there are some serious disadvantages. Hierarchical command-and-control structures make an organization sluggish in responding to changing conditions because of the time it takes for the review/approval process to run up all the layers of the management bureaucracy. Furthermore, to work well, centralized decision making requires top-level managers to gather and process whatever information is relevant to the decision. When the relevant knowledge resides at lower organizational levels (or is technical, detailed, or hard to express in words), it is difficult and time-consuming to get all of the facts and nuances in front of a high-level executive located far from the scene of the action—full understanding of the situation cannot be readily copied from one mind to another. Hence, centralized decision making is often impractical—the larger the company and the more scattered its operations, the more that decision-making authority has to be delegated to managers closer to the scene of the action.

Decentralized Decision Making: Pros and Cons

In a highly decentralized organization, decision-making authority is pushed down to the lowest organizational level capable of making timely, informed, competent decisions. The objective is to put adequate decision-making authority in the hands of the people closest to and most familiar with the situation and train them to weigh all the factors and exercise good judgment. Decentralized decision making means that the managers of each organizational unit are delegated lead responsibility for deciding how best to execute it (as well as some role in shaping the strategy for the units they head). Decentralization thus requires selecting strong managers to head each organizational unit and holding them accountable for crafting and executing appropriate strategies for their units. Managers who consistently produce unsatisfactory results have to be weeded out.

The case for empowering down-the-line managers and employees to make decisions related to daily operations and execution of the strategy is based on the belief that a company that draws on the combined intellectual capital of all its employees can outperform a command-and-control company.[14] Decentralized decision making means, for example, that in a diversified company the various business-unit heads have broad authority to execute the agreed-on business strategy with comparatively little interference from corporate headquarters; moreover, the business-unit heads delegate considerable decision-making latitude to functional and process department heads and the heads of the various operating units (plants, distribution centers, sales offices) in implementing and executing their pieces of the strategy. In turn, work teams may be empowered to manage and improve their assigned value chain activities, and employees with customer contact may be empowered to do what it takes to please customers. At Starbucks, for example, employees are encouraged to exercise initiative in promoting customer satisfaction—there's the story of a store employee who, when the computerized cash register system went offline, enthusiastically offered free coffee to waiting customers.[15] *With decentralized decision making, top management maintains control by limiting empowered managers' and employees' discretionary authority and holding people accountable for the decisions they make.*

> The ultimate goal of decentralized decision making is to put decision-making authority in the hands of those persons or teams closest to and most knowledgeable about the situation.

Decentralized organizational structures have much to recommend them. Delegating greater authority to subordinate managers and employees creates a more horizontal organizational structure with fewer management layers. Whereas in a centralized vertical structure managers and workers have to go up the ladder of authority for an answer, in a decentralized horizontal structure they develop their own answers and action plans—making decisions in their areas of responsibility and being accountable for results is an integral part of their job. Pushing decision-making authority down to middle and lower-level managers and then further on to work teams and individual employees shortens organizational response times and spurs new ideas, creative thinking, innovation, and greater involvement on the part of subordinate managers and employees. In worker-empowered structures, jobs can be defined more broadly, several tasks can be integrated into a single job, and people can direct their own work. Fewer managers are needed because deciding how to do things becomes part of each person's or team's job. Further, today's electronic communication systems make it easy and relatively inexpensive for people at all organizational levels to have direct access to data, other employees, managers, suppliers, and customers. They can access information quickly (via the Internet or company intranet), readily check with superiors or whomever else as needed, and take responsible action. Typically, there are genuine gains in morale and productivity when people are provided with the tools and information they need to operate in a self-directed way. Decentralized decision making can not only shorten organizational response times but also spur new ideas, creative thinking, innovation, and greater involvement on the part of subordinate managers and employees.

The past decade has seen a growing shift from authoritarian, multilayered hierarchical structures to flatter, more decentralized structures that stress employee empowerment. There's strong and growing consensus that authoritarian, hierarchical organizational structures are not well suited to implementing and executing strategies in an era when extensive information and instant communication are the norm and when a big fraction of the organization's most valuable assets consists of intellectual capital and resides in the knowledge and capabilities of its employees. Many companies have therefore begun empowering lower-level managers and employees throughout their organizations, giving them greater discretionary authority to make strategic adjustments in their areas of responsibility and to decide what needs to be done to put new strategic initiatives into place and execute them proficiently.

Maintaining Control in a Decentralized Organizational Structure   Pushing decision-making authority deep down into the organizational structure and empowering employees presents its own organizing challenge: *how to exercise adequate control over the actions of empowered employees so that the business is not put at risk at the same time that the benefits of empowerment are realized.*[16] Maintaining adequate organizational control over empowered employees is generally accomplished by placing limits on the authority that empowered personnel can exercise, holding people accountable for their decisions, instituting compensation incentives that reward people for doing their jobs in a manner that contributes to good company performance, and creating a corporate culture where there's strong peer pressure on individuals to act responsibly.

Capturing Strategic Fits in a Decentralized Structure   Diversified companies striving to capture cross-business strategic fits have to beware of giving business heads full rein to operate independently when cross-business collaboration is essential in order to gain strategic-fit benefits. Cross-business strategic fits typically have to be captured either by enforcing close cross-business collaboration or by centralizing performance of functions having strategic fits at the corporate level.[17] For example, if businesses with overlapping process and product technologies have their own independent R&D departments—each pursuing its own priorities, projects, and strategic agenda—it's hard for the corporate parent to prevent duplication of effort, capture either economies of scale or economies of scope, or broaden the company's R&D efforts to embrace new technological paths, product families, end-use applications, and customer groups. Where cross-business R&D fits exist, the best solution is usually to centralize the R&D function and have a coordinated corporate R&D effort that serves the interests of both individual businesses and the company as a whole. Likewise, centralizing the related activities of separate businesses makes sense when there are opportunities to share a common sales force, use common distribution channels, rely on a common field service organization to handle customer requests for technical assistance or provide maintenance and repair services, use common e-commerce systems and approaches, and so on.

The point here is that efforts to decentralize decision making and give organizational units leeway in conducting operations have to be tempered with the need to maintain adequate control and cross-unit coordination—decentralization doesn't mean delegating authority in ways that allow organizational units and individuals to do their own thing. There are numerous instances when decision-making authority must be retained at high levels in the organization and ample cross-unit coordination strictly enforced.

Providing for Internal Cross-Unit Coordination

The classic way to coordinate the activities of organizational units is to position them in the hierarchy so that the most closely related ones report to a single person (a functional department head, a process manager, a geographic area head, a senior executive). Managers higher up in the ranks generally have the clout to coordinate, integrate, and arrange for the cooperation of units under their supervision. In such structures, the chief executive officer, chief operating officer, and business-level managers end up as central points of coordination because of their positions of authority over the whole unit. When a firm is pursuing a related diversification strategy, coordinating the related activities of independent business units often requires the centralizing authority of a single corporate-level officer. Also, diversified companies commonly centralize such staff support functions as public relations, finance and accounting, employee benefits, and information technology at the corporate level both to contain the costs of support activities and to facilitate uniform and coordinated performance of such functions within each business unit.

But, as explained earlier, close cross-unit collaboration is usually needed to build core competencies and competitive capabilities in such strategically important activities as speeding new products to market and providing superior customer service. To achieve the desired degree of cross-unit cooperation and collaboration, most companies supplement their functional organizational structures. Sometimes this takes the form of creating process departments to bring together the pieces of strategically important activities previously performed in separate functional units. And sometimes the coordinating mechanisms involve the use of cross-functional task forces, dual reporting relationships, informal organizational networking, voluntary cooperation, incentive compensation tied to group performance measures, and strong executive-level insistence on teamwork and cross-department cooperation (including removal of recalcitrant managers who stonewall collaborative efforts). At one European-based company, a top executive promptly replaced the managers of several plants who were not fully committed to collaborating closely on eliminating duplication in product development and production efforts among plants in several different countries. Earlier, the executive, noting that negotiations among the managers had stalled on which labs and plants to close, had met with all the managers, asked them to cooperate to find a solution, discussed with them which options were unacceptable, and given them a deadline to find a solution. When the asked-for teamwork wasn't forthcoming, several managers were replaced.

Providing for Collaboration with Outside Suppliers and Strategic Allies

Someone or some group must be authorized to collaborate as needed with each major outside constituency involved in strategy execution. Forming alliances and cooperative relationships presents immediate opportunities and opens the door to future possibilities, but nothing valuable is realized until the relationship grows, develops, and blossoms. Unless top management sees that constructive organizational bridge building with strategic partners occurs and that productive working relationships emerge, the value of alliances is lost and the company's power to execute its strategy is weakened. If close working relationships with suppliers are crucial, then supply chain management must be given formal status on the company's organization chart and a significant position in the pecking order. If distributor/dealer/franchisee relationships are important, someone must be assigned the task of nurturing the relationships with forward channel allies. If working in parallel with providers of complementary products and services contributes to enhanced organizational capability, then cooperative organizational arrangements have to be put in place and managed to good effect.

Building organizational bridges with external allies can be accomplished by appointing "relationship managers" with responsibility for making particular strategic partnerships or alliances generate the intended benefits. Relationship managers have many roles and functions: getting the right people together, promoting good rapport, seeing that plans for specific activities are developed and carried out, helping adjust internal organizational procedures and communication systems, ironing out operating dissimilarities, and nurturing interpersonal cooperation. Multiple cross-organization ties have to be established and kept open to ensure proper communication and coordination.[18] There has to be enough information sharing to make the relationship work and periodic frank discussions of conflicts, trouble spots, and changing situations.[19]

Instilling a Corporate Culture That Promotes Good Strategy Execution

Every company has its own unique culture. The character of a company's culture or work climate is a product of the core values and business principles that executives espouse, the standards of what is ethically acceptable and what is not, the operating practices and behaviors that define "how we do things around here," the company's approach to people management, the "chemistry" and the "personality" that permeate its work environment, and the stories that get told over and over to illustrate and reinforce the company's values, business practices, and traditions. The meshing together of stated beliefs, business principles, style of operating, ingrained behaviors and attitudes, and work climate define a company's **corporate culture.**

Corporate cultures vary widely. For instance, the bedrock of Wal-Mart's culture is dedication to customer satisfaction, zealous pursuit of low costs and frugal operating practices, a strong work ethic, ritualistic Saturday-morning headquarters meetings to exchange ideas and review problems, and company executives' commitment to visiting stores, listening to customers, and soliciting suggestions from employees. At Nordstrom, the corporate culture is centered on delivering exceptional service to customers; the company's motto is "Respond to unreasonable customer requests"—each out-of-the-ordinary request is seen as an opportunity for a "heroic" act by an employee that can further the company's reputation for a customer-pleasing shopping environment. Nordstrom makes a point of promoting employees noted for their heroic acts and dedication to outstanding service; the company motivates its salespeople with a commission-based compensation system that enables Nordstrom's best salespeople to earn more than double what other department stores pay. General Electric's culture is founded on a hard-driving, results-oriented atmosphere (where all of the company's business divisions are held to a standard of being number one or two in their industries as well as achieving good business results); extensive cross-business sharing of ideas, best practices, and learning; reliance on "workout sessions" to identify, debate, and resolve burning issues; a commitment to Six Sigma quality; and globalization of the company. At Microsoft, there are stories of the long hours programmers put in, the emotional peaks and valleys in encountering and overcoming coding problems, the exhilaration of completing a complex program on schedule, the satisfaction of working on cutting-edge projects, the rewards of being part of a team responsible for a popular new software program, and the tradition of competing aggressively. Enron's collapse in 2001 was partly the product of a flawed corporate culture—one based on the positives of product innovation, aggressive risk taking, and a driving ambition to lead global change in the energy business but also on the negatives of arrogance, ego, greed, deliberately obscure accounting practices, and an "ends-justify-the-means" mentality in pursuing stretch revenue and profitability targets. In the end, Enron came unglued because a few top executives chose unethical and illegal paths to pursue corporate revenue and profitability targets—in a company that publicly preached integrity and other notable corporate values but was lax in making sure that key executives walked the talk.

Company Spotlight 8.1 presents Alberto-Culver's description of its corporate culture.

What to Look For in Identifying a Company's Corporate Culture

The taproot of corporate culture is the organization's values, beliefs, and business principles that set forth how its affairs ought to be conducted—the reasons why it does things the way it does. A company's culture is manifested in the values and business principles that management preaches and practices, in official policies and procedures, in its revered traditions and oft-repeated stories, in the attitudes and behaviors of employees, in the peer pressures that exist to do things in particular ways, in the organization's politics, in its approaches to people management and problem solving, in its relationships with external stakeholders (particularly vendors and local communities where it has operations), and in the "chemistry" and the "personality" that permeates its work environment. Some of these sociological forces are readily apparent, and others operate quite subtly.

The values, beliefs, and practices that undergird a company's culture can come from anywhere in the organization hierarchy, sometimes representing the philosophy of an influential executive and sometimes resulting from exemplary actions on the part of company personnel or a particular organizational unit.[20] Most often, key elements of the culture originated with a founder or certain strong leaders who articulated them as a set of business principles, company policies, or ways of dealing with employees, customers, vendors, shareholders, and the communities in which it operated. Over time, these cultural underpinnings take root, become embedded in how the company conducts its business, come to be accepted and shared by company managers and employees, and then persist as new employees are encouraged to adopt and follow the professed values and practices.

The Role of Stories Frequently, a significant part of a company's culture is captured in the stories that get told over and over again to illustrate to newcomers the importance of certain values and the depth of commitment that various company personnel have displayed. One of the folktales at FedEx, world renowned for the reliability of its next-day package delivery guarantee, is about a deliveryman who had been given the wrong key to a FedEx drop box. Rather than leave the packages in the drop box until the next day when the right key was available, the deliveryman unbolted the drop box from its base, loaded it into the truck, and took it back to the station. There, the box was pried open and the contents removed and sped on their way to their destination the next day. Nordstrom keeps a scrapbook commemorating the heroic acts of its employees and uses it as a regular reminder of the above-and-beyond-the-call-of-duty behaviors that employees are encouraged to display. At Frito-Lay, there are dozens of stories about truck drivers who went to extraordinary lengths in overcoming adverse weather conditions in order to make scheduled deliveries to retail customers and keep store shelves stocked with Frito-Lay products. Such stories serve the valuable purpose of illustrating the kinds of behavior the company encourages and reveres. Moreover, each retelling of a legendary story puts a bit more peer pressure on company personnel to display core values and do their part in keeping the company's traditions alive.

Perpetuating the Culture   Once established, company cultures are perpetuated in six important ways: (1) by screening and selecting new employees who will mesh well with the culture, (2) by systematic indoctrination of new members in the culture's fundamentals, (3) by the efforts of senior group members to reiterate core values in daily conversations and pronouncements, (4) by the telling and retelling of company legends, (5) by regular ceremonies honoring members who display desired cultural behaviors, and (6) by visibly rewarding those who display cultural norms and penalizing those who don't.[21] The more new employees a company is hiring, the more important it becomes to screen job applicants every bit as much for how well their values, beliefs, and personalities match up with the culture as for their technical skills and experience. For example, a company that stresses operating with integrity and fairness has to hire people who themselves have integrity and place a high value on fair play. A company whose culture revolves around creativity, product innovation, and leading change has to screen new hires for their ability to think outside the box, generate new ideas, and thrive in a climate of rapid change and ambiguity. Southwest Airlines, whose two core values—"LUV" and fun—permeate the work environment and whose objective is to ensure that passengers have a positive and enjoyable flying experience, goes to considerable lengths to hire flight attendants and gate personnel who are witty, cheery, and outgoing and who display "whistle while you work" attitudes. Fast-growing companies risk creating a culture by chance rather than by design if they rush to hire employees mainly for their talents and credentials and neglect to screen out candidates whose values, philosophies, and personalities aren't a good fit with the organizational character, vision, and strategy being articulated by the company's senior executives.

As a rule, companies are attentive to the task of hiring people who will fit in and who will embrace the prevailing culture. And, usually, job seekers lean toward accepting jobs at companies where they feel comfortable with the atmosphere and the people they will be working with. Employees who don't hit it off at a company tend to leave quickly, while employees who thrive and are pleased with the work environment stay on, eventually moving up the ranks to positions of greater responsibility. The longer people stay at an organization, the more that they come to embrace and mirror the corporate culture—their values and beliefs tend to be molded by mentors, coworkers, company training programs, and the reward structure. Normally, employees who have worked at a company for a long time play a major role in indoctrinating new employees into the culture.

Forces That Cause a Company's Culture to Evolve   However, even stable cultures aren't static—just like strategy and organizational structure, they evolve. New challenges in the marketplace, revolutionary technologies, and shifting internal conditions—especially eroding business prospects, an internal crisis, or top-executive turnover—tend to breed new ways of doing things and, in turn, cultural evolution. An incoming CEO who decides to shake up the existing business and take it in new directions often triggers a cultural shift, perhaps one of major proportions. Likewise, diversification into new businesses, expansion into foreign countries, rapid growth, an influx of new employees, and merger with or acquisition of another company can all precipitate cultural changes of one kind or another.

Company Subcultures: The Problems Posed by New Acquisitions and Multinational Operations   Although it is common to speak about corporate culture in the singular, companies typically have multiple cultures (or subcultures).[22] Values, beliefs, and practices within a company sometimes vary significantly by department, geographic location, division, or business unit. A company's subcultures can clash, or at least not mesh well, if they embrace conflicting business philosophies or operating approaches, if key executives employ different approaches to people management, or if important differences between a company's culture and those of recently acquired companies have not yet been ironed out. *Global and multinational companies tend to be at least partly multicultural* because cross-country organization units have different operating histories and work climates, as well as members who have grown up under different social customs and traditions and who have different sets of values and beliefs. The human resources manager of a global pharmaceutical company who took on an assignment in the Far East discovered, to his surprise, that one of his biggest challenges was to persuade his company's managers in China, Korea, Malaysia, and Taiwan to accept promotions—their cultural values were such that they did not believe in competing with their peers for career rewards or personal gain, nor did they relish breaking ties with their local communities to assume cross-national responsibilities.[23] Many companies that have merged with or acquired foreign companies have to deal with language- and custom-based cultural differences.

Nonetheless, the existence of subcultures does not preclude important areas of commonality and compatibility. For example, General Electric's cultural traits of boundarylessness, workout, and Six Sigma quality can be implanted and practiced successfully in different countries. AES, a global power company with operations in over 20 countries, has found that the four core values of integrity, fairness, fun, and social responsibility underlying its culture are readily embraced by people in most countries. Moreover, AES tries to define and practice its cultural values the same way in all of its locations while still being sensitive to differences that exist among various people groups across the world; top managers at AES express the views that people across the world are more similar than different and that the company's culture is as meaningful in Buenos Aires or Kazakhstan as in Virginia.

In today's globalizing world, multinational companies are learning how to make strategy-critical cultural traits travel across country boundaries and create a workably uniform culture worldwide. Likewise, company managements are quite alert to the importance of cultural compatibility in making acquisitions and the need to address how to merge and integrate the cultures of newly acquired companies—cultural due diligence is often as important as financial due diligence in deciding whether to go forward on an acquisition or merger. On a number of occasions, companies have decided to forgo acquiring particular companies because of culture conflicts that they believed would be hard to resolve.

Culture: Ally or Obstacle to Strategy Execution?

A company's present culture and work climate may or may not be compatible with what is needed for effective implementation and execution of the chosen strategy. *When a company's present work climate promotes attitudes and behaviors that are well suited to first-rate strategy execution, its culture functions as a valuable ally in the strategy execution process.* When the culture is in conflict with some aspect of the company's direction, performance targets, or strategy, the culture becomes a stumbling block.[24]

How Culture Can Promote Better Strategy Execution   A culture grounded in strategy-supportive values, practices, and behavioral norms adds significantly to the power and effectiveness of a company's strategy execution effort. For example, a culture where frugality and thrift are values widely shared by organization members nurtures employee actions to identify cost-saving opportunities—the very behavior needed for successful execution of a low-cost leadership strategy. A culture built around such business principles as customer satisfaction, fair treatment, operating excellence, and employee empowerment promotes employee behaviors and an esprit de corps that facilitate execution of strategies keyed to high product quality and superior customer service. A culture in which taking initiative, challenging the status quo, exhibiting creativity, embracing change, and teamwork pervade the work climate promotes creative collaboration on the part of employees and organization drive to lead market change—outcomes that are very conducive to successful execution of product innovation and technological leadership strategies.[25]

A tight culture-strategy alignment furthers a company's strategy execution effort in two ways:[26]

1. *A culture that encourages actions supportive of good strategy execution not only provides company personnel with clear guidance regarding what behaviors and results constitute good job performance but also produces significant peer pressure from coworkers to conform to culturally acceptable norms.* The tighter the strategy-culture fit, the more that the culture pushes people to display behaviors and observe operating practices that are conducive to good strategy execution. A strategy-supportive culture thus funnels organizational energy toward getting the right things done and delivering positive organizational results. In a company where strategy and culture are misaligned, some of the very behaviors needed to execute strategy successfully run contrary to the behaviors and values embedded in the prevailing culture. Such a clash nearly always produces resistance from employees who have strong allegiance to the present culture. Culture-bred resistance to the actions and behaviors needed for good execution, if strong and widespread, poses a formidable hurdle that has to be cleared for strategy execution to get very far.

2. *A culture embedded with values and behaviors that facilitate strategy execution promotes strong employee identification with and commitment to the company's vision, performance targets, and strategy.* When a company's culture is grounded in many of the needed strategy-executing behaviors, employees feel genuinely better about their jobs, the company they work for, and the merits of what the company is trying to accomplish. As a consequence, company personnel are more inclined to exhibit some passion and exert their best efforts in making the strategy work, trying to achieve the targeted performance, and moving the company closer to realizing its strategic vision.

This says something important about the task of managing the strategy-executing process: *Closely aligning corporate culture with the requirements for proficient strategy execution merits the full attention of senior executives.* The managerial objective is to create and nurture a work culture that mobilizes organizational energy squarely behind efforts to execute strategy. A good job of culture building on management's part promotes can-do attitudes and acceptance of change, instills strong peer pressures for behaviors conducive to good strategy execution, and enlists more enthusiasm and dedicated effort among company personnel for achieving company objectives.

> **Core Concept**
>
> Because culturally approved behavior thrives and culturally disapproved behavior gets squashed, company managers are well advised to spend time creating a culture that supports and encourages the behaviors conducive to good strategy execution.

The Perils of Strategy-Culture Conflict   Conflicts between behaviors approved by the culture and behaviors needed for good strategy execution send mixed signals to organization members, forcing an undesirable choice. Should organization members be loyal to the culture and company traditions (as well as to their own personal values and beliefs, which are likely to be compatible with the culture) and thus resist or be indifferent to actions and behaviors that will promote better strategy execution? Or should they support the strategy execution effort and engage in actions and behaviors that run counter to the culture?

When a company's culture is out of sync with what is needed for strategic success, the culture has to be changed as rapidly as can be managed—this, of course, presumes that it is one or more aspects of the culture that are out of whack rather than the strategy. While correcting a strategy-culture conflict can occasionally mean revamping strategy to produce cultural fit, more usually it means revamping the mismatched cultural features to produce strategy fit. The more entrenched the mismatched aspects of the culture, the greater the difficulty of implementing new or different strategies until better strategy-culture alignment emerges. A sizable and prolonged strategy-culture conflict weakens and may even defeat managerial efforts to make the strategy work.

Strong versus Weak Cultures

Company cultures vary widely in the degree to which they are embedded in company practices and behavioral norms. Strongly embedded cultures go directly to a company's heart and soul; those with shallow roots provide little in the way of a definable corporate character.

Strong-Culture Companies   A company's culture can be strong and cohesive in the sense that the company conducts its business according to a clear and explicit set of principles and values, that management devotes considerable time to communicating these principles and values to organization members and explaining how they relate to its business environment, and that the values are shared widely across the company—by senior executives and rank-and-file employees alike.[27]

> In a strong-culture company, values and behavioral norms are like crabgrass: deeply rooted and hard to weed out.

Strong-culture companies have a well-defined corporate character, typically underpinned by a creed or values statement. Executives regularly stress the importance of using company values and business principles as the basis for decisions and actions taken throughout the organization. In strong-culture companies, values and behavioral norms are so deeply rooted that they don't change much when a new CEO takes over—although they can erode over time if the CEO ceases to nurture them. And they may not change much as strategy evolves and the organization acts to make strategy adjustments, either because the new strategies are compatible with the present culture or because the dominant traits of the culture are somewhat strategy-neutral and compatible with evolving versions of the company's strategy.

Three factors contribute to the development of strong cultures: (1) a founder or strong leader who establishes values, principles, and practices that are consistent and sensible in light of customer needs, competitive conditions, and strategic requirements; (2) a sincere, long-standing company commitment to operating the business according to these established traditions, thereby creating an internal environment that supports decision making and strategies based on cultural norms; and (3) a genuine concern for the well-being of the organization's three biggest constituencies—customers, employees, and shareholders. Continuity of leadership, small group size, stable group membership, geographic concentration, and considerable organizational success all contribute to the emergence and sustainability of a strong culture.[28]

During the time a strong culture is being implanted, there's nearly always a good strategy-culture fit (which partially accounts for the organization's success). Mismatches between strategy and culture in a strong-culture company tend to occur when a company's business environment undergoes significant change, prompting a drastic strategy revision that clashes with the entrenched culture. A strategy-culture clash can also occur in a strong-culture company whose business has gradually eroded; when a new leader is brought in to revitalize the company's operations, he or she may push the company in a strategic direction that requires substantially different cultural and behavioral norms. In such cases, a major culture-changing effort has to be launched.

One of the best examples of an industry in which strategy changes have clashed with deeply implanted cultures is the electric utility industry. Most electric utility companies, long used to operating as slow-moving regulated monopolies with captive customers, are now confronting the emergence of a vigorously competitive market in wholesale power generation and growing freedom on the part of industrial, commercial, and residential customers to choose their own energy supplier (in much the same way as customers choose their long-distance telephone carriers—an industry that once was a heavily regulated market). These new market circumstances are prompting electric companies to shift away from cultures predicated on risk avoidance, centralized control of decision making, and the politics of regulatory relationships and toward cultures aimed at entrepreneurial risk taking, product innovation, competitive thinking, greater attention to customer service, cost reduction, and competitive pricing.

Weak-Culture Companies   In direct contrast to strong-culture companies, weak-culture companies are fragmented in the sense that no one set of values is consistently preached or widely shared, few behavioral norms are evident in operating practices, and few traditions are widely revered or proudly nurtured by company personnel. Because top executives don't repeatedly espouse any particular business philosophy or exhibit long-standing commitment to particular values or extol particular operating practices and behavioral norms, organization members at weak-culture companies typically lack any deeply felt sense of corporate identity. While employees may have some bonds of identification with and loyalty toward their department, their colleagues, their union, or their boss, a weak company culture breeds no strong employee allegiance to what the company stands for or to operating the business in well-defined ways. Such lack of a definable corporate character results in many employees' viewing their company as just a place to work and their job as just a way to make a living—there's neither passion about the company nor emotional commitment to what it is trying to accomplish. Very often, cultural weakness stems from moderately entrenched subcultures that block the emergence of a well-defined companywide work climate.

As a consequence, *weak cultures provide little or no strategy-implementing assistance* because there are no traditions, beliefs, values, common bonds, or behavioral norms that management can use as levers to mobilize commitment to executing the chosen strategy. While a weak culture does not usually pose a strong barrier to strategy execution, it also provides no support. Absent a work climate that channels organizational energy in the direction of good strategy execution, managers are left with the options of either using compensation incentives and other motivational devices to mobilize employee commitment or trying to establish cultural roots that will in time start to nurture the strategy execution process.

Unhealthy Cultures

The distinctive characteristic of an unhealthy corporate culture is the presence of counterproductive cultural traits that adversely impact the work climate and company performance.[29] The following three traits are particularly unhealthy:

1. A highly politicized internal environment in which many issues get resolved and decisions are made on the basis of which individuals or groups have the most political clout to carry the day.

2. Hostility to change and a general wariness of people who champion new ways of doing things.

3. A "must-be-invented-here" mind-set that makes company personnel averse to looking outside the company for best practices, new managerial approaches, and innovative ideas.

What makes a politicized internal environment so unhealthy is that political infighting consumes a great deal of organizational energy, often with the result that what's best for the company takes a backseat to political maneuvering. In companies where internal politics pervades the work climate, empire-building managers jealously guard their decision-making prerogatives. They have their own agendas and operate the work units under their supervision as autonomous "fiefdoms," and the positions they take on issues are usually aimed at protecting or expanding their turf. Collaboration with other organizational units is viewed with suspicion (What are "they" up to? How can "we" protect "our" flanks?), and cross-unit cooperation occurs grudgingly. When an important proposal moves to the front burner, advocates try to ram it through and opponents try to alter it in significant ways or else kill it altogether. The support or opposition of politically influential executives and/or coalitions among departments with vested interests in a particular outcome typically weigh heavily in deciding what actions the company takes. All this maneuvering takes away from efforts to execute strategy with real proficiency and frustrates company personnel who are less political and more inclined to do what is in the company's best interests.

In less adaptive cultures where skepticism about the importance of new developments and resistance to change are the norm, managers prefer waiting until the fog of uncertainty clears before steering a new course, making fundamental adjustments to their product line, or embracing a major new technology. They believe in moving cautiously and conservatively, preferring to follow others rather than take decisive action to be in the forefront of change. Change-resistant cultures place a premium on not making mistakes, thus prompting managers to lean toward safe, don't-rock-the-boat options that will have only a ripple effect on the status quo, protect or advance their own careers, and guard the interests of their immediate work groups.

Change-resistant cultures encourage a number of undesirable or unhealthy behaviors—avoiding risks, not making bold proposals to pursue emerging opportunities, taking a lax approach to both product innovation and continuous improvement in performing value chain activities, and following rather than leading market change. In change-resistant cultures, word quickly gets around that proposals to do things differently face an uphill battle and that people who champion them may be seen as either something of a nuisance or a troublemaker. Executives who don't value managers or employees with initiative and new ideas put a damper on product innovation, experimentation, and efforts to improve. At the same time, change-resistant companies have little appetite for being first-movers or fast-followers, believing that being in the forefront of change is too risky and that acting too quickly increases vulnerability to costly mistakes. They are more inclined to adopt a wait-and-see posture, carefully analyze several alternative responses, learn from the missteps of early-movers, and then move forward cautiously and conservatively with initiatives that are deemed safe. Hostility to change is most often found in companies with multilayered management bureaucracies that have enjoyed considerable market success in years past and that are wedded to the "we have done it this way for years" syndrome.

When such companies encounter business environments with accelerating change, going slow on altering traditional ways of doing things can be a liability rather than an asset. General Motors, IBM, Sears, and Eastman Kodak are classic examples of companies whose change-resistant bureaucracies were slow to respond to fundamental changes in their markets; clinging to the cultures and traditions that had made them successful, they were reluctant to alter operating practices and modify their business approaches. As strategies of gradual change won out over bold innovation and being an early-mover, all four lost market share to rivals that quickly moved to institute changes more in tune with evolving market conditions and buyer preferences. These companies are now struggling to recoup lost ground with cultures and behaviors more suited to market success—the kinds of fit that caused them to succeed in the first place.

The third unhealthy cultural trait—the must-be-invented-here mind-set—tends to develop when a company reigns as an industry leader or enjoys great market success for so long that its personnel start to believe they have all the answers or can develop them on their own. Such confidence in the correctness of how the company does things and in its skills and capabilities breeds arrogance—there's a strong tendency for company personnel to discount the merits or significance of what outsiders are doing and what can be learned by studying best-in-class performers. Benchmarking and searching for the best practices of outsiders are seen as offering little payoff. Any market share gains on the part of up-and-coming rivals are regarded as temporary setbacks, soon to be reversed by the company's own forthcoming initiatives. Insular thinking, internally driven solutions, and a must-be-invented-here mind-set come to permeate the corporate culture. An inwardly focused corporate culture gives rise to managerial inbreeding and a failure to recruit people who can offer fresh thinking and outside perspectives. The big risk of insular cultural thinking is that the company can underestimate the competencies and accomplishments of rival companies and overestimate its own progress—with a resulting loss of competitive advantage over time.

Unhealthy cultures typically impair company performance. Avon, BankAmerica, Citicorp, Coors, Ford, General Motors, Kmart, Kroger, Sears, and Xerox are examples of companies whose unhealthy cultures during the late 1970s and early 1980s contributed to ho-hum performance on the bottom line and in the marketplace.[30] General Motors, Kmart, and Sears are still struggling to uproot problematic cultural traits and replace them with behaviors having a more suitable strategy-culture fit.

Adaptive Cultures

The hallmark of adaptive corporate cultures is willingness on the part of organization members to accept change and take on the challenge of introducing and executing new strategies.[31] Company personnel share a feeling of confidence that the organization can deal with whatever threats and opportunities come down the pike; they are receptive to risk taking, experimentation, innovation, and changing strategies and practices. In direct contrast to change-resistant cultures, adaptive cultures are very supportive of managers and employees at all ranks who propose or help initiate useful change. Internal entrepreneurship on the part of individuals and groups is encouraged and rewarded.

Core Concept

In adaptive cultures, there's a spirit of doing what's necessary to ensure long-term organizational success provided the new behaviors and operating practices that management is calling for are seen as legitimate and consistent with the core values and business principles underpinning the culture.

Senior executives seek out, support, and promote individuals who exercise initiative, spot opportunities for improvement, and display the skills to implement them. Managers habitually fund product development initiatives, evaluate new ideas openly, and take prudent risks to create new business positions. As a consequence, the company exhibits a proactive approach to identifying issues, evaluating the implications and options, and implementing workable solutions. Strategies and traditional operating practices are modified as needed to adjust to or take advantage of changes in the business environment.

But why is change so willingly embraced in an adaptive culture? Why are organization members not fearful of how change will affect them? Why does an adaptive culture not become unglued with ongoing changes in strategy, operating practices, and behavioral norms? The answers lie in two distinctive and dominant traits of an adaptive culture: (1) Any changes in operating practices and behaviors must *not* compromise core values and long-standing business principles, and (2) the changes that are instituted must satisfy the legitimate interests of stakeholders—customers, employees, shareowners, suppliers, and the communities where the company operates.[32] In other words, what sustains an adaptive culture is that organization members perceive the changes that management is trying to institute as being legitimate and in keeping with the core values and business principles that form the heart and soul of the culture.

Thus, for an adaptive culture to remain intact over time, top management must orchestrate the responses in a manner that demonstrates genuine care for the well-being of all key constituencies and tries to satisfy all their legitimate interests simultaneously. Unless fairness to all constituencies is a decision-making principle and a commitment to doing the right thing is evident to organization members, the changes are not likely to be seen as legitimate and thus be readily accepted and implemented.[33] Making changes that will please customers and/or that protect, if not enhance, the company's long-term well-being is generally seen as legitimate and is often seen as the best way of looking out for the interests of employees, stockholders, suppliers, and communities where the company operates. At companies with adaptive cultures, management concern for the well-being of employees is nearly always a big factor in gaining employee support for change—company personnel are usually receptive to change as long as employees understand that changes in their job assignments are part of the process of adapting to new conditions and that their employment security will not be threatened unless the company's business unexpectedly reverses direction. In cases where workforce downsizing becomes necessary, management concern for employees dictates that separation be handled humanely, making employee departure as painless as possible. Management efforts to make the process of adapting to change fair and equitable for customers, employees, stockholders, suppliers, and communities where the company operates, keeping adverse impacts to a minimum insofar as possible, breeds acceptance of and support for change among all organization stakeholders.

Technology companies, software companies, and today's dot-com companies are good illustrations of organizations with adaptive cultures. Such companies thrive on change—driving it, leading it, and capitalizing on it (but sometimes also succumbing to change when they make the wrong move or are swamped by better technologies or the superior business models of rivals). Companies like Microsoft, Intel, Nokia, Amazon.com, and Dell Computer cultivate the capability to act and react rapidly. They are avid practitioners of entrepreneurship and innovation, with a demonstrated willingness to take bold risks to create altogether new products, new businesses, and new industries. To create and nurture a culture that can adapt rapidly to changing or shifting business conditions, they make a point of staffing their organizations with people who are proactive, who rise to the challenge of change, and who have an aptitude for adapting.

In fast-changing business environments, a corporate culture that is receptive to altering organizational practices and behaviors is a virtual necessity. However, adaptive cultures work to the advantage of all companies, not just those in rapid-change environments. Every company operates in a market and business climate that is changing to one degree or another and that, in turn, requires internal operating responses and new behaviors on the part of organization members. As a company's strategy evolves, an adaptive culture is a definite ally in the strategy-implementing, strategy-executing process as compared to cultures that have to be coaxed and cajoled to change. This constitutes a good argument for why managers should strive to build a strong, adaptive corporate culture.

> A good case can be made that a strongly planted, adaptive culture is the best of all corporate cultures.

Creating a Strong Fit between Strategy and Culture

It is the *strategy maker's* responsibility to select a strategy compatible with the sacred or unchangeable parts of the organization's prevailing corporate culture. It is the *strategy implementer's* task, once strategy is chosen, to change whatever facets of the corporate culture hinder effective execution.

Changing a Problem Culture   Changing a company's culture to align it with strategy is among the toughest management tasks because of the heavy anchor of deeply held values and habits—people cling emotionally to the old and familiar. It takes concerted management action over a period of time to replace an unhealthy culture with a healthy culture or to root out certain unwanted behaviors and instill ones that are more strategy-supportive. *The single most visible factor that distinguishes successful culture-change efforts from failed attempts is competent leadership at the top.* Great power is needed to force major cultural change—to overcome the springback resistance of entrenched cultures—and great power normally resides only at the top.

As shown in Figure 8.4, the first step in fixing a problem culture is to identify those facets of the present culture that are dysfunctional and explain why they pose obstacles to executing new strategic initiatives and achieving company performance targets. Second, managers have to clearly define the desired new behaviors and specify the key features of the culture they want to create. Third, managers have to talk openly and forthrightly to all concerned about problematic aspects of the culture and why and how new behaviors will improve company performance—the case for cultural change has to be persuasive and the benefits of a reformed culture made convincing to all concerned. Finally, and most important, the talk has to be followed swiftly by visible, aggressive actions to promote the desired new behaviors—actions that everyone will understand are intended to produce behaviors and practices conducive to good strategy execution.

> Once a culture is established, it is difficult to change.

The menu of actions management can take to change a problem culture includes the following:[34]

1. Making a compelling case for why the company's new direction and a different cultural atmosphere are in the organization's best interests and why individuals and groups should commit themselves to making it happen despite the obstacles.

Figure 8.4   Changing a Problem Culture

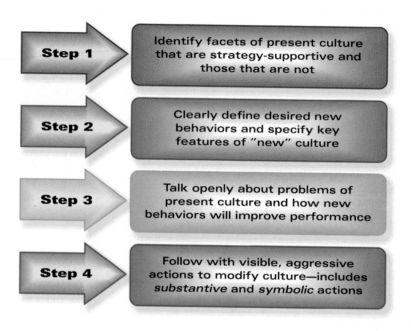

Skeptics have to be convinced that all is not well with the status quo. This can be done by:

- Challenging the status quo with very basic questions: Are we giving customers what they really need and want? Why aren't we taking more business away from rivals? Why do our rivals have lower costs than we do? How can we drive costs out of the business and be more competitive on price? Why can't design-to-market cycle time be halved? Why aren't we moving faster to make better use of the Internet and e-commerce technologies and practices? How can we grow company revenues at 15 percent instead of 10 percent? What can we do to speed up our decision making and shorten response times?

- Creating events where everyone in management is forced to listen to angry customers, dissatisfied strategic allies, alienated employees, or disenchanted stockholders.

2. Repeating at every opportunity the message of why cultural change is good for company stakeholders (particularly customers, employees, and shareholders). Effective culture-change leaders are good at telling stories to convey new values and connect the case for change to organization members.

3. Visibly praising and generously rewarding people who display newly advocated cultural norms and who participate in implementing the desired kinds of operating practices.

4. Altering incentive compensation to reward the desired cultural behavior and deny rewards to those who resist change.

5. Recruiting and hiring new managers and employees who have the desired cultural values and can serve as role models for the desired cultural behavior.

6. Replacing key executives who are strongly associated with the old culture.

7. Revising policies and procedures in ways that will help drive cultural change.

Only with bold leadership and concerted action on many fronts can a company succeed in tackling so large and difficult a task as major cultural change. When only strategic fine-tuning is being implemented, it takes less time and effort to bring values and culture into alignment with strategy, but there is still a lead role for the manager to play in communicating the need for new cultural behaviors and personally launching actions to prod the culture into better alignment with strategy.

Symbolic Culture-Changing Actions   Managerial actions to tighten the strategy-culture fit need to be both symbolic and substantive. Symbolic actions are valuable for the signals they send about the kinds of behavior and performance strategy implementers wish to encourage. The most important symbolic actions are those that top executives take to *lead by example*. For instance, if the organization's strategy involves a drive to become the industry's low-cost producer, senior managers must display frugality in their own actions and decisions: inexpensive decorations in the executive suite, conservative expense accounts and entertainment allowances, a lean staff in the corporate office, scrutiny of budget requests, few executive perks, and so on. If the culture-change imperative is to work harder and smarter to please customers, the CEO can instill greater attention to customer satisfaction by requiring all officers and executives to spend a significant portion of each week talking with customers about their needs.

Another category of symbolic actions includes the ceremonial events organizations hold to designate and honor people whose actions and performance exemplify what is called for in the new culture. Many universities give outstanding-teacher awards each year to symbolize their commitment to good teaching and their esteem for instructors who display exceptional classroom talents. Numerous businesses have employee-of-the-month awards. The military has a long-standing custom of awarding ribbons and medals for exemplary actions. Mary Kay Cosmetics awards an array of prizes—from ribbons to pink automobiles—to its beauty consultants for reaching various sales plateaus.

The best companies and the best executives expertly use symbols, role models, ceremonial occasions, and group gatherings to tighten the strategy-culture fit. Low-cost leaders like Wal-Mart and Nucor are renowned for their spartan facilities, executive frugality, intolerance of waste, and zealous control of costs. Nucor executives make a point of flying coach class and using taxis at airports rather than limousines. Executives sensitive to their role in promoting strategy-culture fits make a habit of appearing at ceremonial functions to praise individuals and groups that get with the program. They honor individuals who exhibit cultural norms and reward those who achieve strategic milestones. They participate in employee training programs to stress strategic priorities, values, ethical principles, and cultural norms. Every group gathering is seen as an opportunity to repeat and ingrain values, praise good deeds, reinforce cultural norms, and promote changes that assist strategy execution. Sensitive executives make sure that current decisions and policy changes will be construed by organization members as consistent with cultural values and supportive of the company's new strategic direction.[35]

Substantive Culture-Changing Actions   While symbolically leading the push for new behaviors and communicating the reasons for new approaches is crucial, strategy implementers have to convince all those concerned that the culture-changing effort is more than cosmetic. Talk and symbolism have to be complemented by substantive actions and real movement. The actions taken have to be credible, highly visible, and unmistakably indicative of the seriousness of management's commitment to new strategic initiatives and the associated cultural changes. There are several ways to accomplish this. One is to engineer some quick successes that highlight the benefits of the proposed changes, thus making enthusiasm for them contagious. However, achieving instant results is usually not as important as having the will and patience to create a solid, competent team psychologically committed to pursuing the strategy in a superior fashion. The strongest signs that management is truly committed to creating a new culture include replacing old-culture traditionalist managers with new-breed managers, changing dysfunctional policies and operating practices, instituting new compensation incentives visibly tied to the achievement of freshly set performance targets, and making major budgetary reallocations that shift substantial resources from old-strategy projects and programs to new-strategy projects and programs.

Implanting the needed culture-building values and behavior depends on a sincere, sustained commitment by the chief executive coupled with extraordinary persistence in reinforcing the culture at every opportunity through both word and deed. Neither charisma nor personal magnetism is essential. However, personally talking to many departmental groups about the reasons for change *is* essential; organizational changes are seldom accomplished successfully from an office. Moreover, creating and sustaining a strategy-supportive culture is a job for the whole management team. Major cultural change requires many initiatives from many people. Senior officers, department heads, and middle managers have to reiterate valued behaviors and translate the organization's core values and business principles into everyday practice. In addition, for the culture-building effort to be successful, strategy implementers must enlist the support of frontline supervisors and employee opinion leaders, convincing them of the merits of practicing and enforcing cultural norms at the lowest levels in the organization. Until a big majority of employees join the new culture and share an emotional commitment to its basic values and behavioral norms, there's considerably more work to be done in both instilling the culture and tightening the strategy-culture fit.

Changing culture to support strategy is not a short-term exercise. It takes time for a new culture to emerge and prevail. Overnight transformations simply don't occur. The bigger the organization and the greater the cultural shift needed to produce a strategy-culture fit, the longer it takes. In large companies, fixing a problem culture and instilling a new set of attitudes and behaviors can take two to five years. In fact, it is usually tougher to reform an entrenched problematic culture than it is to instill a strategy-supportive culture from scratch in a brand-new organization. Sometimes executives succeed in changing the values and behaviors of small groups of managers and even whole departments or divisions, only to find the changes eroded over time by the actions of the rest of the organization—what is communicated, praised, supported, and penalized by an entrenched majority undermines the new emergent culture and halts its progress. Executives, despite a series of well-intended actions to reform a problem culture, are likely to fail at weeding out embedded cultural traits when widespread employee skepticism about the company's new directions and culture-change effort spawns covert resistance to the cultural behaviors and operating practices advocated by top management. This is why management must take every opportunity to convince employees of the need for culture change and communicate to them how new attitudes, behaviors, and operating practices will benefit the interests of organizational stakeholders.

A company that has done a good job of fixing its problem culture is Alberto-Culver—see Company Spotlight 8.2.

COMPANY SPOTLIGHT 8.2

The Culture-Change Effort at Alberto-Culver's North American Division

In 1993, Carol Bernick—vice chairperson of Alberto-Culver, president of its North American division, and daughter of the company's founders—concluded that her division's existing culture had four problems: Employees dutifully waited for marching orders from their bosses, workers put pleasing their bosses ahead of pleasing customers, some company policies were not family-friendly, and there was too much bureaucracy and paperwork. What was needed, in Bernick's opinion, was a culture in which company employees had a sense of ownership and an urgency to get things done, welcomed innovation, and were willing to take risks.

To change the culture, Alberto-Culver's management undertook a series of actions:

- In 1993, a new position, called growth development leader (GDL), was created to help orchestrate the task of fixing the culture deep in the ranks (there were 70 GDLs in Alberto-Culver's North American division). GDLs came from all ranks of the company's managerial ladder and were handpicked for such qualities as empathy, communication skills, positive attitude, and ability to let their hair down and have fun. GDLs performed their regular jobs in addition to taking on the GDL role; it was considered an honor to be chosen. Each GDL mentored about 12 people from both a career and a family standpoint. GDLs met with senior executives weekly, bringing forward people's questions and issues and then, afterward, sharing with their groups the topics and solutions that were discussed. GDLs brought a group member as a guest to each meeting. One meeting each year is devoted to identifying "macros and irritations"—attendees are divided into four subgroups and given 15 minutes to identify the company's four biggest challenges (the macros) and the four most annoying aspects of life at the company (the irritations); the whole group votes on which four deserve the company's attention. Those selected are then addressed, and assignments made for follow-up and results.

- Changing the culture was made an issue across the company, starting in 1995 with a two-hour State of the Company presentation to employees that covered where the company was and where it wanted to be. The State of the Company address was made an annual event.

- Management created ways to measure the gains in changing the culture. One involved an annual all-employee survey to assess progress against cultural goals and to get 360-degree feedback—the 2000 survey had 180 questions, including 33 relating to the performance of each respondent's GDL. A bonfire celebration was held in the company parking lot to announce that paperwork would be cut 30 percent.

- A list of 10 cultural imperatives was formalized in 1998—honesty, ownership, trust, customer orientation, commitment, fun, innovation, risk taking, speed and urgency, and teamwork. These imperatives came to be known internally as HOT CC FIRST.

- Extensive celebrations and awards programs were instituted. Most celebrations are scheduled, but some are spontaneous (an impromptu thank-you party for a good fiscal year). Business Builder awards (initiated in 1997) are given to individuals and teams that make a significant impact on the company's growth and profitability. The best-scoring GDLs on the annual employee surveys are awarded shares of company stock. The company notes all work anniversaries and personal milestones with "Alberto-appropriate" gifts; appreciative company employees sometimes give thank-you gifts to their GDLs. According to Carol Bernick, "If you want something to grow, pour champagne on it. We've made a huge effort—maybe even an over-the-top effort—to celebrate our successes and, indeed, just about everything we'd like to see happen again."

The culture-change effort at Alberto-Culver North America was viewed as a major contributor to improved performance. From 1993, when the effort first began, to 2001, the division's sales increased from just under $350 million to over $600 million and pretax profits rose from $20 million to almost $50 million. Carol Bernick was elevated to chairman of Alberto-Culver's board of directors in 2004.

Source: Reprinted by permission of *Harvard Business Review,* from "When Your Culture Needs a Makeover," by Carol Lavin Bernick, June 2001. Copyright © 2001 by the President and Fellows of Harvard College, all rights reserved.

Table 8.2   THE CONTENT OF COMPANY VALUES STATEMENTS AND CODES OF ETHICS

Topics Commonly Appearing in Values Statements	Topics Commonly Appearing in Codes of Ethics
■ Commitment to such outcomes as customer satisfaction and customer service, quality, product innovation, and/or technological leadership	■ Mandates that company personnel will display honesty and integrity in their actions
■ Commitment to achievement, excellence, and results	■ An expectation that all company personnel will comply fully with all laws and regulations, specifically:
■ Importance of demonstrating such qualities as honesty, integrity, trust, fairness, quality of life, pride of workmanship, and ethics	■ Antitrust laws prohibiting anticompetitive practices, conspiracies to fix prices, or attempts to monopolize
■ Importance of being creative, taking initiative, and accepting responsibility	■ Foreign Corrupt Practices Act
■ Importance of teamwork and a cooperative attitude	■ Securities laws and prohibitions against insider trading
■ Importance of Golden Rule behavior and respect for coworkers	■ Environmental and workplace safety regulations
■ Making the company a great place to work	■ Discrimination and sexual harassment regulations
■ Importance of having fun and creating a fun work environment	■ Prohibitions against giving or accepting bribes, kickbacks, or gifts
■ Duty to stakeholders—customers, employees, suppliers, shareholders, communities where the company operates, and society at large	■ Avoiding conflicts of interest
	■ Fairness in selling and marketing practices
■ Commitment to exercising social responsibility and being a good community citizen	■ Supplier relationships and procurement practices
	■ Acquiring and using competitively sensitive information about rivals and others
■ Commitment to protecting the environment	■ Political contributions, activities, and lobbying
■ Commitment to workforce diversity	■ Avoiding use of company assets, resources, and property for personal or other inappropriate purposes
	■ Responsibility to protect proprietary information and not divulge trade secrets

Grounding the Culture in Core Values and Ethics

A corporate culture grounded in socially approved values and ethical business principles is a vital ingredient in a company's long-term strategic success.[36] Unless a company's executives genuinely care about how the company's business affairs are conducted, the company's reputation and ultimately its performance are put at risk. While there's no doubt that some companies and some company personnel knowingly engage in shady business practices and have little regard for ethical standards, one must be cautious about assuming that a company's core values and ethical standards are meaningless window dressing. Executives at many companies genuinely care about the values and ethical standards that company personnel exhibit in conducting the company's business; they are aware that their own reputations, as well as the company's reputation, hang on whether outsiders see the company's actions as ethical or honest or socially acceptable. At such companies, values statements and codes of ethics matter, and they are ingrained to one degree or another in the company's culture—see Table 8.2 for the kinds of topics that are commonly found in values statements and codes of ethics.

Indeed, at companies where executives are truly committed to practicing the values and ethical standards that have been espoused, *the stated core values and ethical principles are the cornerstones of the corporate culture.* As depicted in Figure 8.5, a company that works hard at putting its stated core values and ethical principles into practice fosters a work climate where company personnel share common convictions

Figure 8.5   The Two Culture-Building Roles of a Company's
Core Values and Ethical Standards

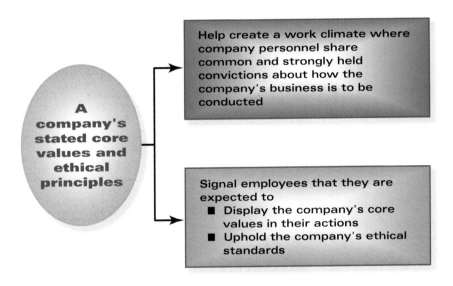

A company's stated core values and ethical principles

Help create a work climate where company personnel share common and strongly held convictions about how the company's business is to be conducted

Signal employees that they are expected to
- Display the company's core values in their actions
- Uphold the company's ethical standards

about how the company's business is to be conducted and where they are expected to act in accord with stated values and ethical standards. By promoting behaviors that mirror the values and ethics standards, a company's stated values and ethical standards nurture the corporate culture in three highly positive ways: (1) They communicate the company's good intentions and validate the integrity and aboveboard character of its business principles and operating methods, (2) they steer company personnel toward both doing the right thing and doing things right, and (3) they establish a "corporate conscience" and provide yardsticks for gauging the appropriateness of particular actions, decisions, and policies (see Figure 8.6).[37]

Companies ingrain their values and ethical standards in a number of different ways.[38] Tradition-steeped companies with a rich folklore rely heavily on word-of-mouth indoctrination and the power of tradition to instill values and enforce ethical conduct. But many companies today convey their values and codes of ethics to stakeholders and interested parties in their annual reports, on their Web sites, and in internal communications to all employees. The standards are hammered in at orientation courses for new employees and in training courses for managers and employees. The trend of making stakeholders aware of a company's commitment to core values and ethical business conduct is attributable to three factors: (1) greater management understanding of the role these statements play in culture building, (2) a renewed focus on ethical standards stemming from the corporate scandals that came to light in 2001–2004, and (3) the growing numbers of consumers who prefer to patronize ethical companies with ethical products.

However, there is a considerable difference between saying the right things (having a well-articulated corporate values statement or code of ethics) and truly managing a company in an ethical and socially responsible way. Companies that are truly

> A company's values statement and code of ethics communicate expectations of how employees should conduct themselves in the workplace.

Figure 8.6   How a Company's Core Values and Ethical Principles Positively Impact the Corporate Culture

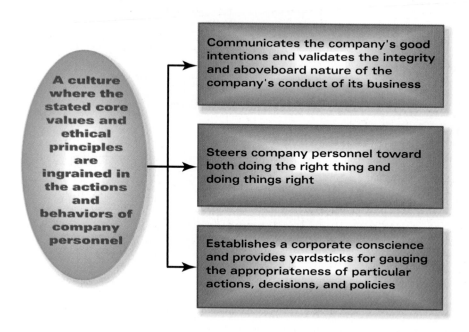

committed to the stated core values and to high ethical standards make ethical behavior *a fundamental component of their corporate culture.* They put a stake in the ground, making it unequivocally clear that company personnel are expected to live up to the company's values and ethical standards—how well individuals display core values and adhere to ethical standards is often part of their job performance evaluations. Peer pressures to conform to cultural norms are quite strong, acting as an important deterrent to outside-the-lines behavior. Moreover, values statements and codes of ethical conduct are used as benchmarks for judging the appropriateness of company policies and operating practices.

At Darden Restaurants—a $5 billion casual-dining company with over 1,300 company-owned Red Lobster, Olive Garden, Bahama Breeze, Seasons 52, and Smokey Bones BBQ Sports Bar restaurants—the core values are operating with integrity and fairness, treating people fairly and with respect, being "of service," engaging in teamwork, promoting innovation and excellence, and welcoming and celebrating workforce diversity. The company's practice of these values has been instrumental in creating a culture characterized by trust, exciting jobs and career opportunities for employees, and a passion to be the best in casual dining.[39]

Once values and ethical standards have been formally adopted, they must be institutionalized in the company's policies and practices and embedded in the conduct of company personnel. Deeply rooting values and ethical standards into how the company conducts its business entails several actions:

■   Incorporating the statement of values and the code of ethics into employee training and educational programs.

- Giving explicit attention to values and ethics in recruiting and hiring to screen out applicants who do not exhibit compatible character traits.

- Having senior executives frequently reiterate the importance and role of company values and ethical principles at company events and in internal communications to employees.

- Making sure that managers, from the CEO down to frontline supervisors, are diligent in stressing the importance of values and ethical conduct and in overseeing the compliance process.

- Periodically having ceremonial occasions to recognize individuals and groups who display the values and ethical principles.

- Instituting ethics enforcement procedures.

In the case of codes of ethics, special attention must be given to sections of the company that are particularly vulnerable—procurement, sales, and political lobbying. Employees who deal with external parties are in ethically sensitive positions and often are drawn into compromising situations. Company personnel assigned to subsidiaries in foreign countries can find themselves trapped in ethical dilemmas if bribery and corruption of public officials are common practices or if suppliers or customers are accustomed to kickbacks of one kind or another. Mandatory ethics training for such personnel is usually desirable.

Structuring the Ethics Compliance and Enforcement Process

If a company's executives truly aspire for company personnel to behave ethically, then procedures for enforcing ethical standards and handling potential violations have to be developed. Even in an ethically strong company, there can be bad apples—and some of the bad apples may even rise to the executive ranks. So it is rarely enough to rely on an ethically strong culture to produce ethics compliance.

The compliance effort must permeate the company, extending to every organizational unit. The attitudes, character, and work history of prospective employees must be scrutinized. Company personnel have to be educated about what is ethical and what is not; this means establishing ethics training programs and discussing what to do in gray areas. Everyone must be encouraged to raise issues with ethical dimensions, and such discussions should be treated as a legitimate topic. Line managers at all levels must give serious and continuous attention to the task of explaining how the values and ethical code apply in their areas. In addition, they must insist that company values and ethical standards become a way of life. In general, instilling values and insisting on ethical conduct must be looked on as a continuous culture-building, culture-nurturing exercise. Whether the effort succeeds or fails depends largely on how well corporate values and ethical standards are visibly integrated into company policies, managerial practices, and actions at all levels.

A company's formal ethics compliance and enforcement mechanisms can entail such actions as forming an ethics committee to give guidance on ethics matters, appointing an ethics officer to head the compliance effort, establishing an ethics hotline or Web site that employees can use to either anonymously report a possible violation or get confidential advice on a troubling ethics-related situation, and having an annual ethics audit to measure the extent of ethical behavior and identify problem areas. Increasing numbers of companies, wary of the damage to their reputations from public exposure of unethical behavior by company personnel, have begun openly encouraging employees to blow the whistle on possible ethical violations via toll-free hotlines, e-mail, and special Web sites. If a company is really serious about enforcing ethical behavior, it probably needs to do four things:[40]

1. Have mandatory ethics training programs for employees.
2. Conduct an annual audit of each manager's efforts to uphold ethical standards and require formal reports on the actions taken by managers to remedy deficient conduct.
3. Require all employees to sign a statement annually certifying that they have complied with the company's code of ethics.
4. Openly encourage company personnel to report possible infractions via anonymous calls to a hotline or posting to a special company Web site.

While these actions may seem extreme or objectionable, they leave little room to doubt the seriousness of a company's commitment to ethics compliance. And most company personnel will think twice about knowingly engaging in unethical conduct when they know their actions will be audited and/or when they have to sign statements certifying compliance with the company's code of ethics. Ideally, the company's commitment to its stated values and ethical principles will instill not only a corporate conscience but also a conscience on the part of company personnel that prompts them to report possible ethical violations. While ethically conscious companies have provisions for disciplining violators, *the main purpose of the various means of enforcement is to encourage compliance rather than administer punishment.* Thus, the reason for openly encouraging people to report possible ethical violations is not so much to get someone in trouble as to *prevent further damage* and heighten awareness of operating within ethical bounds.

As was discussed in Chapter 5, transnational companies face a host of challenges in enforcing a common set of ethical standards because what is considered ethical often varies substantially or subtly from country to country. While there are a number of mostly universal and cross-cultural ethical standards—as concerns honesty, trustworthiness, fairness, avoidance of unnecessary harm to individuals, and respect for the environment—there are shades and variations in what societies generally agree to be "right" and "wrong" based on the prevailing circumstances, local customs, and predominant religious convictions. And certainly there are cross-country variations in the *degree* or *severity* with which certain behaviors are considered unethical.[41] Thus transnational companies have to make a fundamental decision whether to try to enforce common ethical standards and interpretation of what is ethically right and wrong across their operations in all countries or whether to permit selected "rules bending" on a case-by-case basis.

Establishing a Strategy-Culture Fit in Multinational and Global Companies

In multinational and global companies, where some cross-border diversity in the corporate culture is normal, efforts to establish a tight strategy-culture fit are complicated by the diversity of societal customs and lifestyles from country to country. Company personnel in different countries sometimes fervently insist on being treated as distinctive individuals or groups, making a one-size-fits-all culture potentially inappropriate. Leading cross-border culture-change initiatives requires sensitivity to prevailing cultural differences; managers must discern when diversity has to be accommodated and when cross-border differences can be and should be narrowed.[42] Cross-country cultural diversity in a multinational enterprise is more tolerable if the company is pursuing a multicountry strategy and if the company's culture in each country is well aligned with its strategy in that country. But significant cross-country differences in a company's culture are likely to impede execution of a global strategy and have to be addressed.

As discussed earlier in this chapter, the trick to establishing a workable strategy-culture fit in multinational companies is to ground the culture in strategy-supportive values and operating practices that travel well across country borders and strike a chord with managers and workers in many different areas of the world, despite the diversity of local customs and traditions. A multinational enterprise with a misfit between its strategy and culture in certain countries where it operates can attack the problem by reinterpreting or deemphasizing or even abandoning those values and cultural traits that it finds inappropriate for some countries where it operates. Problematic values and operating principles can be replaced with values and operating approaches that travel well across country borders but that are still strategy-supportive. Many times a company's values statement only has to be reworded so as to express existing values in ways that have more universal appeal. Sometimes certain offending operating practices can be modified to good advantage in all locations where the company operates.

Aside from trying to ground the culture in a set of core values and operating principles that have universal appeal, management can seek to minimize the existence of subcultures and cross-country cultural diversity by:

- Instituting training programs to communicate the meaning of core values and explain the case for common operating principles and practices.

- Drawing on the full range of motivational and compensation incentives to induce personnel to adopt and practice the desired behaviors.

- Allowing *some leeway* for certain core values and principles to be interpreted and applied somewhat differently, if necessary, to accommodate local customs and traditions.

Generally, a high degree of cross-country cultural homogeneity is desirable and has to be pursued. Having too much variation in the culture from country to country not only makes it difficult to use the culture in helping drive the strategy execution process but also works against the establishment of a one-company mind-set and a consistent corporate identity.

Key Points

The job of strategy implementation and execution is to convert strategic plans into actions and good results. The test of successful strategy execution is whether actual organization performance matches or exceeds the targets spelled out in the strategic plan. Shortfalls in performance signal weak strategy, weak execution, or both.

In deciding how to implement a new or revised strategy, managers have to determine what internal conditions are needed to execute the strategic plan successfully. Then they must create these conditions as rapidly as practical. The process of implementing and executing strategy involves:

1. Building an organization with the competencies, capabilities, and resource strengths to execute strategy successfully.

2. Allocating ample resources to strategy-critical activities.

3. Ensuring that policies and procedures facilitate rather than impede strategy execution.

4. Instituting best practices and pushing for continuous improvement in how value chain activities are performed.

5. Installing information and operating systems that enable company personnel to carry out their strategic roles proficiently.

6. Tying rewards and incentives directly to the achievement of strategic and financial targets and to good strategy execution.

7. Shaping the work environment and corporate culture to fit the strategy.

8. Exerting the internal leadership needed to drive implementation forward and to keep improving on how the strategy is being executed.

Building a capable organization is always a top priority in strategy execution; three types of organization-building actions are paramount: (1) *staffing the organization*—putting together a strong management team and recruiting and retaining employees with the needed experience, technical skills, and intellectual capital, (2) *building core competencies and competitive capabilities* that will enable good strategy execution and updating them as strategy and external conditions change, and (3) *structuring the organization and work effort*—organizing value chain activities and business processes and deciding how much decision-making authority to push down to lower-level managers and frontline employees.

Building core competencies and competitive capabilities is a time-consuming, managerially challenging exercise that involves three stages: (1) developing the ability to do something, however imperfectly or inefficiently, by selecting people with the requisite skills and experience, upgrading or expanding individual abilities as needed, and then molding the efforts and work products of individuals into a collaborative group effort; (2) coordinating group efforts to learn how to perform the activity *consistently well and at an acceptable cost*, thereby transforming the ability into a tried-and-true *competence* or *capability*; and (3) continuing to polish and refine the organization's know-how and otherwise sharpen performance such that the company becomes *better than rivals* at performing the activity, thus raising the core competence (or capability) to the rank of a *distinctive competence* (or competitively superior capability) and opening an avenue to competitive advantage. Many companies manage to get through stages 1 and 2 in performing a strategy-critical activity but comparatively few achieve sufficient proficiency in performing strategy-critical activities to qualify for the third stage.

Structuring the organization and organizing the work effort in a strategy-supportive fashion has five aspects: (1) deciding which value chain activities to perform internally and which ones to outsource; (2) making internally performed strategy-critical activities the main building blocks in the organization structure; (3) deciding how much authority to centralize at the top and how much to delegate to down-the-line managers and employees; (4) providing for internal cross-unit coordination and collaboration to build and strengthen internal competencies/capabilities; and (5) providing for the necessary collaboration and coordination with suppliers and strategic allies.

A company's culture is manifested in the values and business principles that management preaches and practices, in the tone and philosophy of official policies and procedures, in its revered traditions and oft-repeated stories, in the attitudes and behaviors of employees, in the peer pressures that exist to display core values, in the organization's politics, in its approaches to people management and problem solving, in its relationships with external stakeholders (particularly vendors and the communities in which it operates), and in the atmosphere that permeates its work environment. Culture thus concerns the personality a company has and the style in which it does things.

Changing a company's culture, especially a strong one with traits that don't fit a new strategy's requirements, is one of the toughest management challenges. Changing a culture requires competent leadership at the top. It requires symbolic actions and substantive actions that unmistakably indicate serious commitment on the part of top management. The more that culture-driven actions and behaviors fit what's needed for good strategy execution, the less managers have to depend on policies, rules, procedures, and supervision to enforce what people should and should not do.

To be effective, corporate ethics and values programs have to become a way of life through training, strict compliance and enforcement procedures, and reiterated management endorsements. Moreover, top managers must practice what they preach, serving as role models for ethical behavior, values-driven decision making, and a social conscience.

Exercises

1. Go to www.hermanmiller.com and read what the company has to say about its corporate culture in the careers sections of the Web site. Do you think this statement is just nice window dressing and PR, or—based on what else you can learn about the Herman Miller Company from browsing this Web site—is there reason to believe that management has truly built a culture that makes the stated values and principles come alive?

2. Go to the careers section at www.qualcomm.com and see what Qualcomm, one of the most prominent companies in mobile communications technology, has to say about "life at Qualcomm." Is what's on this Web site just recruiting propaganda, or does it convey the type of work climate that management is actually trying to create? If you were a senior executive at Qualcomm, would you see merit in building and nurturing a culture like that described in the section on life at Qualcomm? Would such a culture represent a tight fit with Qualcomm's high-tech business and strategy (you can get an overview of Qualcomm's strategy by exploring the section for investors and some of the recent press releases)? Is your answer consistent with what is presented in the "Awards and Honors" menu selection in the "About Qualcomm" portion of the Web site?

3. Go to www.jnj.com, the Web site of Johnson & Johnson, and read the "J&J Credo," which sets forth the company's responsibilities to customers, employees, the community, and shareholders. Then read the "Our Company" section. Why do you think the credo has resulted in numerous awards and accolades that recognize the company as a good corporate citizen?

CHAPTER 9

Managing Internal Operations in Ways That Promote Good Strategy Execution

Winning companies know how to do their work better.

—*Michael Hammer and James Champy*

If you talk about change but don't change the reward and recognition system, nothing changes.

—*Paul Allaire, former CEO, Xerox Corporation*

If you want people motivated to do a good job, give them a good job to do.

—*Frederick Herzberg*

You ought to pay big bonuses for premier performance. . . . Be a top payer, not in the middle or low end of the pack.

—*Lawrence Bossidy, CEO, Honeywell International*

Weak leadership can wreck the soundest strategy; forceful execution of even a poor plan can often bring victory.

—*Sun Zi*

Leadership is accomplishing something through other people that wouldn't have happened if you weren't there. . . . Leadership is being able to mobilize ideas and values that energize other people. . . . Leaders develop a story line that engages other people.

—*Noel Tichy*

In Chapter 8 we emphasized why and how the task of executing strategy is facilitated by conscious managerial efforts to strengthen organizational capabilities and instill a strategy-supportive culture. In this chapter we discuss six additional managerial actions that promote the success of a company's strategy execution efforts:

1. Marshaling resources behind the strategy execution effort.

2. Instituting policies and procedures that facilitate strategy execution.

3. Adopting best practices and striving for continuous improvement in how value chain activities are performed.

4. Installing information and operating systems that enable company personnel to better carry out their strategic roles proficiently.

5. Tying rewards and incentives directly to the achievement of strategic and financial targets and to good strategy execution.

6. Exercising strong leadership to drive implementation forward, keep improving on how the strategy is being executed, and attain operating excellence.

Marshaling Resources behind the Drive for Strategy Execution

Early in the process of implementing and executing a new or different strategy, managers need to determine what resources will be needed and then consider whether the current budgets of organizational units are suitable. Plainly, organizational units must have the budgets and resources for executing their parts of the strategic plan effectively and efficiently. Developing a strategy-driven budget requires top management to determine what funding is needed to execute new strategic initiatives and to strengthen or modify the company's competencies and capabilities. This includes careful screening of requests for more people and more or better facilities and equipment, approving those that hold promise for making a cost-justified contribution to strategy execution and turning down those that don't. Should internal cash flows prove insufficient to fund the planned strategic initiatives, then management must raise additional funds through borrowing or selling additional shares of stock to willing investors.

A company's ability to marshal the resources needed to support new strategic initiatives and steer them to the appropriate organizational units has a major impact on the strategy execution process. Too little funding (stemming either from constrained financial resources or from sluggish management action to adequately increase the budgets of strategy-critical organizational units) slows progress and impedes the efforts of organizational units to execute their pieces of the strategic plan proficiently. Too much funding wastes organizational resources and reduces financial performance. Both outcomes argue for managers to be deeply involved in reviewing budget proposals and directing the proper kinds and amounts of resources to strategy-critical organizational units.

A change in strategy nearly always calls for budget reallocations. Units important in the prior strategy but having a lesser role in the new strategy may need downsizing. Units that now have a bigger and more critical strategic role may need more people, new equipment, additional facilities, and above-average increases in their operating

> ### Core Concept
> The funding requirements of a new strategy must drive how capital allocations are made and the size of each unit's operating budgets. Underfunding organizational units and activities pivotal to strategic success impedes execution and the drive for operating excellence.

budgets. Strategy implementers need to be active and forceful in shifting resources, downsizing some areas and upsizing others, not only to amply fund activities with a critical role in the new strategy but also to avoid inefficiency and achieve profit projections. They have to exercise their power to put enough resources behind new strategic initiatives to make things happen, and they have to make the tough decisions to kill projects and activities that are no longer justified.

Visible actions to reallocate operating funds and move people into new organizational units signal a determined commitment to strategic change and frequently are needed to catalyze the implementation process and give it credibility. Microsoft has made a practice of regularly shifting hundreds of programmers to new high-priority programming initiatives within a matter of weeks or even days. At Harris Corporation, where the strategy was to diffuse research ideas into areas that were commercially viable, top management regularly shifted groups of engineers out of government projects and into new commercial venture divisions. Fast-moving developments in many markets are prompting companies to abandon traditional annual or semiannual budgeting and resource allocation cycles in favor of cycles that match the strategy changes a company makes in response to newly developing events.

Just fine-tuning the execution of a company's existing strategy, however, seldom requires big movements of people and money from one area to another. The desired improvements can usually be accomplished through above-average budget increases to organizational units where new initiatives are contemplated and below-average increases (or even small cuts) for the remaining organizational units. The chief exception occurs where all the strategy changes need to be made within the existing budget. Then managers have to squeeze savings out of some areas to fund the new strategic initiatives.

Instituting Policies and Procedures That Facilitate Strategy Execution

Changes in strategy generally call for some changes in work practices and operations. Asking people to alter established procedures always upsets the internal order of things. It is normal for pockets of resistance to develop and for people to exhibit some degree of stress and anxiety about how the changes will affect them, especially when the changes may eliminate jobs. Questions are also likely to arise over what activities need to be rigidly prescribed and where there ought to be leeway for independent action.

As shown in Figure 9.1, prescribing new policies and operating procedures designed to facilitate strategy execution has merit from several angles:

1. *It provides top-down guidance regarding how certain things now need to be done.* New policies and operating practices can help align actions with strategy throughout the organization, placing limits on independent behavior and channeling individual and group efforts along a path in tune with the new strategy. They also help counteract tendencies for some people to resist change—most people refrain from violating company policy or going against recommended practices and procedures without first gaining clearance or having strong justification.

Figure 9.1   How Prescribed Policies and Procedures Facilitate Strategy Execution

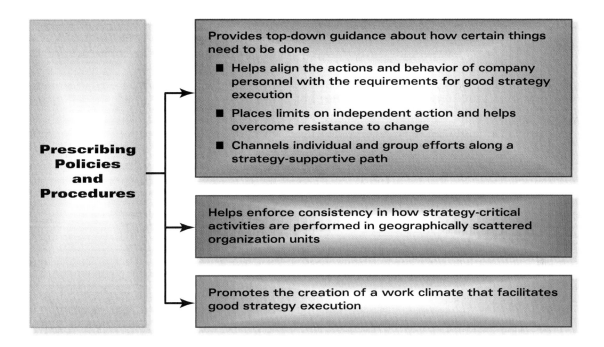

2. *It helps enforce needed consistency in how particular critical activities are performed in geographically scattered operating units.* Eliminating significant differences in the operating practices of different plants, sales regions, customer service centers, or the individual outlets in a chain operation is frequently desirable to avoid sending mixed messages to internal personnel and to customers who do business with the company at multiple locations.

3. *It promotes the creation of a work climate that facilitates strategy execution.* Because dismantling old policies and procedures and instituting new ones invariably alter the internal work climate, strategy implementers can use the policy-changing process as a powerful lever for changing the corporate culture in ways that produce a stronger fit with the new strategy.

Company managers therefore need to be inventive in devising policies and practices that can provide vital support to effective strategy implementation and execution.

In an attempt to steer "crew members" into stronger quality and service behavior patterns, McDonald's policy manual spells out procedures in detail; for example, "Cooks must turn, never flip, hamburgers. If they haven't been purchased, Big Macs must be discarded in 10 minutes after being cooked and French fries in 7 minutes. Cashiers must make eye contact with and smile at every customer." Hewlett-Packard requires R&D people to make regular visits to customers to learn about their problems, talk about new product applications, and in general keep the company's R&D programs customer-oriented.

Core Concept

Well-conceived policies and procedures aid strategy execution; out-of-sync ones are barriers.

Granite Construction, a California company that consistently appears on Fortune's annual list of the "100 Best Companies to Work For," has a strategy aimed at total customer satisfaction and outstanding customer service; to signal both employees and customers that it was deadly serious about these two strategic commitments, it created what it called a "short-pay" policy that appeared on the bottom of every Granite construction invoice: "If you are not satisfied for any reason, don't pay us for it. Simply scratch out the line item, write a brief note about the problem, and return a copy of this invoice along with your check for the balance." Customers do not have to call and complain and are not expected to return the product. They are given complete discretionary power to decide whether and how much to pay based on their satisfaction level. Granite's short-pay policy has worked exceptionally well, providing unmistakable feedback and spurring company managers to correct any problems quickly in order to avoid repeated short payments.[1] Five years after instituting the policy, Granite won the prestigious Malcolm Baldrige National Quality Award. In addition Granite construction has a no-layoff policy (in 82 years, Granite has never had a lay off), provides employees with 12 massages a year, and sends positive customer comments about employees home for families to read.

Thus, wisely constructed policies and procedures help channel actions, behavior, decisions, and practices in directions that promote good strategy execution and push the company to achieve operating excellence. When policies and practices aren't strategy-supportive, they become a barrier to the kinds of attitudinal and behavioral changes strategy implementers are trying to promote. Sometimes people hide behind or vigorously defend long-standing policies and operating procedures in an effort to stall new strategic initiatives or force them to take a different form. Anytime a company alters its strategy, managers should review existing policies and operating procedures, proactively revise or discard those that are out of sync, and formulate new ones to facilitate execution and support the achievement of performance targets.

None of this implies that companies need thick policy manuals to direct the strategy execution process and prescribe exactly how daily operations are to be conducted. Too much policy can erect as many obstacles as wrong policy or be as confusing as no policy. There is wisdom in a middle approach: *Prescribe enough policies to give organization members clear direction in implementing strategy and to place desirable boundaries on their actions; then empower them to act within these boundaries however they think makes sense.* Allowing company personnel to act anywhere between the "white lines" is especially appropriate when individual creativity and initiative are more essential to good strategy execution than standardization and strict conformity. Instituting strategy-facilitating policies can therefore mean more policies, fewer policies, or different policies. It can mean policies that require things to be done a certain way or policies that give employees leeway to do activities the way they think best.

Adopting Best Practices and Striving for Continuous Improvement

Company managers can significantly advance the cause of competent strategy execution by pushing organizational units and company personnel to identify and adopt the best practices for performing value chain activities and, further, insisting on continuous improvement in how internal operations are conducted. One of the most widely used and effective tools for gauging how well a company is executing pieces of its strategy entails benchmarking the company's performance of particular activities and business processes against "best-in-industry" and "best-in-world" performers.[2] It can also be useful to look at "best-in-company" performers of an activity if a company has a number of different organizational units performing much the same function at different locations. Identifying, analyzing, and understanding how top companies or individuals perform particular value chain activities and business processes provides useful yardsticks for judging the effectiveness and efficiency of internal operations and setting performance standards for organizational units to meet or beat.

> **Core Concept**
>
> Managerial efforts to identify and adopt best practices are a powerful tool for promoting operating excellence and better strategy execution.

How the Process of Identifying and Incorporating Best Practices Works

A **best practice** is a technique for performing an activity or business process that at least one company has demonstrated works particularly well. To qualify as a legitimate best practice, the technique must have a proven record in significantly lowering costs, improving quality or performance, shortening time requirements, enhancing safety, or delivering some other highly positive operating outcome. Best practices thus identify a path to operating excellence. For a best practice to be valuable and transferable, it must demonstrate success over time, deliver quantifiable and highly positive results, and be repeatable.

> **Core Concept**
>
> A **best practice** is any practice that at least one company has proved works particularly well.

Benchmarking is the backbone of the process of identifying, studying, and implementing outstanding practices. A company's benchmarking effort looks outward to find best practices and then proceeds to develop the data for measuring how well a company's own performance of an activity stacks up against the best-practice standard. Informally, benchmarking involves being humble enough to admit that others have come up with world-class ways to perform particular activities yet wise enough to try to learn how to match, and even surpass, them. But, as shown in Figure 9.2, the payoff of benchmarking comes from adapting the top-notch approaches pioneered by other companies in the company's own operation and thereby boosting, perhaps dramatically, the proficiency with which value chain tasks are performed.

However, benchmarking is more complicated than simply identifying which companies are the best performers of an activity and then trying to imitate their approaches—

Figure 9.2   From Benchmarking and Best-Practice Implementation to Operating Excellence

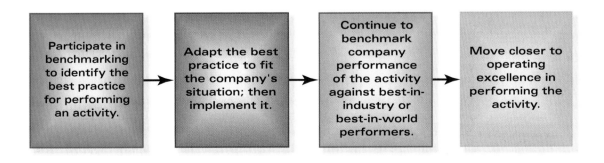

especially if these companies are in other industries. Normally, the outstanding practices of other organizations have to be *adapted* to fit the specific circumstances of a company's own business and operating requirements. Since most companies believe "our work is different" or "we are unique," the telling part of any best-practice initiative is how well the company puts its own version of the best practice into place and makes it work.

Indeed, a best practice remains little more than another company's interesting success story unless company personnel buy into the task of translating what can be learned from other companies into real action and results. The agents of change must be frontline employees who are convinced of the need to abandon the old ways of doing things and switch to a best-practice mind-set. The more that organizational units use best practices in performing their work, the closer a company moves toward performing its value chain activities as effectively and efficiently as possible. This is what operational excellence is all about.

Legions of companies across the world now engage in benchmarking to improve their strategy execution efforts and, ideally, gain a strategic, operational, and financial advantage over rivals. Scores of trade associations and special-interest organizations have undertaken efforts to collect best-practice data relevant to a particular industry or business function and make their databases available online to members—good examples include The Benchmarking Exchange (www.benchnet.com); Best Practices, LLC (www.best-in-class.com); and the American Productivity and Quality Center (www.apqc.org). Benchmarking and best-practice implementation have clearly emerged as legitimate and valuable managerial tools for promoting operational excellence.

Business Process Reengineering, Six Sigma Quality Programs, and TQM: Additional Tools for Promoting Operating Excellence

In striving for operating excellence, many companies have also come to rely on three other potent management tools: business process reengineering, Six Sigma quality control techniques, and total quality management (TQM) programs. Indeed, these three tools have become globally pervasive techniques for implementing strategies keyed to cost reduction, defect-free manufacture, superior product quality, superior customer service, and total customer satisfaction. The following sections describe how business process reengineering, Six Sigma, and TQM can contribute to operating excellence and better strategy execution.

Business Process Reengineering   Companies scouring for ways to improve their operations have sometimes discovered that organizing around traditional functional departments results in higher costs and poses cross-department coordination problems because having pieces of strategically relevant activities and capabilities performed in several different functional departments creates inefficiencies and because no one group or functional manager is thus accountable for optimum performance of the entire activity. Strategy-critical value chain activities where various components are typically scattered across several functional departments include:

- *Filling customer orders accurately and promptly*—a process that cuts across sales (which wins the order), finance (which may have to check credit terms or approve special financing), production (which must produce the goods and replenish warehouse inventories as needed), warehousing (which has to verify whether the items are in stock, pick the order from the warehouse, and package it for shipping), and shipping (which has to choose a carrier to deliver the goods and release the goods to the carrier).[3]

■ *Speeding new products to market*—a cross-functional process involving personnel in R&D, design and engineering, purchasing, manufacturing, and sales and marketing.

■ *Improving product quality*—a process that often involves the collaboration of personnel in R&D, engineering and design, components purchasing from suppliers, in-house components production, manufacturing, and assembly.

■ *Managing the supply chain*—a collaborative process that cuts across such functional areas as purchasing, engineering and design, components purchasing, inventory management, manufacturing and assembly, and warehousing and shipping.

■ *Building the capability to conduct business via the Internet*—a process that involves personnel in information technology, supply chain management, production, sales and marketing, warehousing and shipping, customer service, finance, and accounting.

■ *Obtaining feedback from customers and making product modifications to meet their needs*—a process that involves personnel in customer service and after-sale support, R&D, engineering and design, components purchasing, manufacturing and assembly, and marketing research.

To address the problem of inefficiency and curtail the time and effort that went into coordinating the efforts of different work groups, many companies during the past decade have opted to reengineer the work effort and create *process departments* or *teams*. Pulling the pieces of strategy-critical processes out of the functional silos and creating process departments or cross-functional work groups charged with performing all the steps needed to produce a strategy-critical result is called **business process reengineering.**[4] It involves reorganizing the people who performed the pieces in functional departments into a close-knit group that has charge over the whole process and that can be held accountable for performing the activity in a cheaper, better, and/or more strategy-supportive fashion.

> **Core Concept**
> **Business process reengineering** involves reorganizing the fragmented tasks of a strategy-critical activity into a close-knit group that has charge over the whole process and can be held accountable for performing the activity in a cheaper, better, and/or more strategy-supportive fashion.

When done properly, business process reengineering can produce dramatic operating benefits. In the order-processing section of General Electric's circuit breaker division, elapsed time from order receipt to delivery was cut from three weeks to three days by consolidating six production units into one, reducing a variety of former inventory and handling steps, automating the design system to replace a human custom-design process, and cutting the organizational layers between managers and workers from three to one. Productivity rose 20 percent in one year, and unit manufacturing costs dropped 30 percent. Northwest Water, a British utility, used business process reengineering to eliminate 45 work depots that served as home bases to crews who installed and repaired water and sewage lines and equipment. Now crews work directly from their vehicles, receiving assignments and reporting work completion from computer terminals in their trucks. Crew members are no longer employees but contractors to Northwest Water. These reengineering efforts not only eliminated the need for the work depots but also allowed Northwest Water to eliminate a big percentage of the bureaucratic personnel and supervisory organization that managed the crews.[5]

Since the early 1990s, reengineering of value chain activities has been undertaken at many companies in many industries all over the world, with excellent results being achieved at some companies.[6] While reengineering has produced only modest results in some instances, usually because of ineptness and/or lack of wholehearted commitment, reengineering has nonetheless proven itself as a useful tool for streamlining a company's work effort and moving closer to operational excellence.

Total Quality Management Programs   Total quality management (TQM) *is a philosophy of managing a set of business practices that emphasizes continuous improvement in all phases of operations, 100 percent accuracy in performing tasks, involvement and empowerment of employees at all levels, team-based work design, benchmarking, and total customer satisfaction.*[7] While TQM concentrates on producing quality goods and fully satisfying customer expectations, it achieves its biggest successes when it is extended to employee efforts in *all departments*—human resources, billing, R&D, engineering, accounting and records, and information systems—that may lack pressing, customer-driven incentives to improve. It involves reforming the corporate culture and shifting to a total quality/continuous improvement business philosophy that permeates every facet of the organization.[8] TQM aims at instilling enthusiasm and commitment to doing things right from the top to the bottom of the organization. Management's job is to kindle an organizationwide search for ways to improve, a search that involves all company personnel exercising initiative and using their ingenuity. TQM doctrine preaches that there's no such thing as "good enough" and that everyone has a responsibility to participate in continuous improvement. TQM is thus a race without a finish. Success comes from making little steps forward each day, a process that the Japanese call *kaizen.*

> **Core Concept**
>
> TQM entails creating a total quality culture bent on continuously improving the performance of every task and value chain activity.

TQM takes a fairly long time to show significant results—very little benefit emerges within the first six months. The long-term payoff of TQM, if it comes, depends heavily on management's success in implanting a culture within which TQM philosophies and practices can thrive. TQM is a managerial tool that has attracted numerous users and advocates over several decades, and it can deliver good results when used properly.

Six Sigma Quality Control   *Six Sigma quality control consists of a disciplined, statistics-based procedure aimed at producing not more than 3.4 defects per million iterations for any business process—from manufacturing to customer transactions.*[9] The Six Sigma process of define, measure, analyze, improve, and control (DMAIC) is an improvement system for *existing* processes falling below specification and needing incremental improvement. The Six Sigma process of define, measure, analyze, design, and verify (DMADV) is used to develop *new* processes or products at Six Sigma quality levels. Both Six Sigma processes are executed by personnel who have earned Six Sigma "green belts" and Six Sigma "black belts" and are overseen by personnel who have completed Six Sigma "master black belt" training. According to the Six Sigma Academy, personnel with black belts can save companies approximately $230,000 per project and can complete four to six projects a year.[10]

The statistical thinking underlying Six Sigma is based on the following three principles: All work is a process, all processes have variability, and all processes create data that explain variability.[11] To illustrate how these three principles drive the metrics of DMAIC, consider the case of a janitorial company that wants to improve the caliber of work done by its cleaning crews and thereby boost customer satisfaction. The janitorial company's Six Sigma team can pursue quality enhancement and continuous improvement via the DMAIC process as follows:

- *Define.* Because Six Sigma is aimed at reducing defects, the first step is to define what constitutes a defect. Six Sigma team members might decide that leaving streaks on windows is a defect because it is a source of customer dissatisfaction.

- *Measure.* The next step is to collect data to find out why, how, and how often this defect occurs. This might include a process flow map of the specific ways that cleaning crews go about the task of cleaning a commercial customer's windows. Other metrics may include recording what tools and cleaning products the crews use to clean windows.

- *Analyze.* After the data are gathered and the statistics analyzed, the company's Six Sigma team discovers that the tools and window-cleaning techniques of certain employees are better than those of other employees because their tools and procedures leave no streaked windows—a "best practice" for avoiding window streaking is thus identified and documented.

- *Improve.* The Six Sigma team implements the documented best practice as a standard way of cleaning windows.

- *Control.* The company teaches new and existing employees the best-practice technique for window cleaning. Over time, there's significant improvement in customer satisfaction and increased business.

Six Sigma's DMAIC process is a particularly good vehicle for improving performance when there are *wide variations* in how well an activity is performed.[12] For instance, airlines striving to improve the on-time performance of their flights have more to gain from actions to curtail the number of flights that are late by more than 30 minutes than from actions to reduce the number of flights that are late by less than 5 minutes. Likewise, FedEx might have a 16-hour average delivery time for its overnight package service operation, but if the actual delivery time varies around the 16-hour average from a low of 12 hours to a high of 26 hours such that 10 percent of its packages are delivered over 6 hours late, then it has a huge reliability problem.

A problem tailor-made for Six Sigma occurs in the insurance industry, where it is common for top agents to outsell poor agents by a factor of 10 to 1 or more. If insurance executives offer a trip to Hawaii in a monthly contest to motivate low-performing agents, the typical result is that top agents are motivated to be even more productive, thus making the performance gap even wider. A DMAIC Six Sigma project to reduce the variation in the performance of agents and correct the problem of so many low-performing agents would begin by measuring the performance of all agents, perhaps discovering that the top 20 percent sell seven times more policies than the bottom 40 percent. Six Sigma analysis would then consider such steps as mapping how top agents spend their day, investigating the factors that distinguish top performers from low performers, learning what techniques training specialists have employed in converting low-performing agents into high performers, and examining how the hiring process could be improved to avoid hiring underperformers in the first place.

The next step would be to test proposed solutions—better training methods or psychological profiling to identify and weed out candidates likely to be poor performers—to identify and measure which alternative solutions really work, which don't, and why. Only those actions that prove statistically beneficial are then introduced on a wide scale. The DMAIC method thus entails empirical analysis to diagnose the problem *(design, measure, analyze),* test alternative solutions *(improve),* and then *control* the variability in how well the activity is performed by implementing actions shown to truly fix the problem.

COMPANY SPOTLIGHT 9.1
Whirlpool's Use of Six Sigma to Promote Operating Excellence

Top management at Whirlpool Corporation, the leading global manufacturer and marketer of home appliances in 2003 with production operations in 14 countries and sales in some 170 countries, has a vision of Whirlpool appliances in "Every Home, Everywhere." One of management's chief objectives in pursuing this vision is to build unmatched customer loyalty to the Whirlpool brand. Whirlpool's strategy to win the hearts and minds of appliance buyers the world over has been to produce and market appliances with top-notch quality and innovative features that users will find appealing. In addition, Whirlpool's strategy has been to offer a wide selection of models (recognizing that buyer tastes and needs differ) and to strive for low-cost production efficiency, thereby enabling Whirlpool to price its products very competitively. Executing this strategy at Whirlpool's operations in North America (where it is the market leader), Latin America (where it is also the market leader), Europe (where it ranks third), and Asia (where it is number one in India and has a foothold with huge growth opportunities elsewhere) has involved a strong focus on continuous improvement and a drive for operating excellence. To marshal the efforts of its 68,000 employees in executing the strategy successfully, management developed a comprehensive Operational Excellence program with Six Sigma as one of the centerpieces.

The Operational Excellence initiative, which began in the 1990s, incorporated Six Sigma techniques to improve the quality of Whirlpool products and at the same time lower costs and trim the time it took to get product innovations into the marketplace. The Six Sigma program helped Whirlpool save $175 million in manufacturing costs in its first three years.

To sustain the productivity gains and cost savings, Whirlpool embedded Six Sigma practices within each of its manufacturing facilities worldwide and instilled a culture based on Six Sigma and lean manufacturing skills and capabilities. In 2002, each of Whirlpool's operating units began taking the Six Sigma initiative to a higher level by first placing the needs of the customer at the center of every function—R&D, technology, manufacturing, marketing, and administrative support—and then striving to consistently improve quality levels while eliminating all unnecessary costs. The company has systematically gone through every aspect of its business with the view that company personnel should perform every activity at every level in a manner that focuses on delivering value to the customer and that leads to continuous improvement on how things are done. Whirlpool management believes that the company-wide Six Sigma program and emphasis on continuous improvement has been a major contributor in sustaining the company's global leadership in appliances.

Source: www.whirlpool.com, accessed September 25, 2003.

General Electric, one of the most successful companies implementing Six Sigma training and pursuing Six Sigma perfection, estimated benefits on the order of $10 billion during the first five years of implementation. GE first instituted the use of Six Sigma in 1995 after Motorola and Allied Signal blazed the Six Sigma trail. Since the mid-1990s, thousands of companies and nonprofit organizations around the world have begun utilizing Six Sigma programs to promote operating excellence. Company Spotlight 9.1 describes Whirlpool's use of Six Sigma in its appliance business.

Six Sigma is, however, not just a quality-enhancing tool for manufacturers. At one company, product sales personnel typically wined and dined customers to close their deals.[13] But the costs of such entertaining were viewed as excessively high in many instances. A Six Sigma project that examined sales data found that although face time with customers was important, wining, dining, and other types of entertainment were not. The data showed that regular face time helped close sales but that time could be spent over a cup of coffee instead of golfing at a resort or taking clients to expensive restaurants. In addition, analysis showed that too much face time with customers was counterproductive. A regularly scheduled customer picnic was found to be detrimental to closing sales because it was held at a busy time of year, when customers preferred not to be away from their offices. Changing the manner in which prospective customers were wooed resulted in a 10 percent increase in sales. One of GE's successes was in its Lighting division, where Six Sigma was used to cut invoice defects and disputes by 98 percent, a particular benefit to Wal-Mart, the division's largest customer. GE Capital Mortgage improved the chances of a caller's reaching a "live" GE person from 76 to 99 percent.[14] A Milwaukee hospital used Six Sigma to map the process in which prescriptions originated with a doctor's write-up, were filled by the hospital pharmacy, and then were administered by nurses. DMAIC analysis revealed that most mistakes came from misreading the doctor's handwriting.[15] The hospital implemented a program requiring doctors to type the prescription into a computer, and this slashed the number of errors dramatically.

A company that systematically applies Six Sigma methods to its value chain, activity by activity, can make major strides in improving the proficiency with which its strategy is executed. As is the case with TQM, obtaining managerial commitment, establishing a quality culture, and fully involving employees are the three most intractable challenges encountered in the implementation of Six Sigma quality programs.[16]

The Difference between Business Process Reengineering and Continuous Improvement Programs Like Six Sigma and TQM

Business process reengineering and continuous improvement efforts like TQM and Six Sigma both aim at improved efficiency and reduced costs, better product quality, and greater customer satisfaction. The essential difference between business process reengineering and continuous improvement programs is that reengineering aims at *quantum gains* on the order of 30 to 50 percent or more whereas total quality programs stress *incremental progress*, striving for inch-by-inch gains again and again in a never-ending stream. The two approaches to improved performance of value chain activities and operating excellence are not mutually exclusive; it makes sense to use them in tandem. Reengineering can be used first to produce a good basic design that yields quick, dramatic improvements in performing a business process. Total quality programs like TQM and Six Sigma can then be used as a follow-on to reengineering and/or best-practice implementation, delivering gradual improvements. Such a two-pronged approach to implementing operational excellence is like a marathon race in which you run the first 4 miles as fast as you can and then gradually pick up speed the remainder of the way.

> Business process reengineering aims at one-time quantum improvement; continuous improvement programs like TQM and Six Sigma aim at ongoing incremental improvements.

Capturing the Benefits of Initiatives to Improve Operations

Usually, the biggest beneficiaries of benchmarking and best-practice initiatives, reengineering, TQM, and Six Sigma are companies that view such programs not as ends in themselves but as tools for implementing and executing company strategy more effectively. The skimpiest payoffs occur when company managers seize these programs as something worth trying—novel ideas that could improve things. In most such instances, they result in strategy-blind efforts to simply manage better. There's an important lesson here. Best practices, TQM, Six Sigma quality, and reengineering all need to be seen and used as part of a bigger-picture effort to execute strategy proficiently. Only strategy can point to which value chain activities matter and what performance targets make the most sense. Without a strategic framework, managers lack the context in which to fix things that really matter to business-unit performance and competitive success.

To get the most from initiatives to better execute strategy, managers must have a clear idea of what specific outcomes really matter. Is it a Six Sigma or lower defect rate, high on-time delivery percentages, low overall costs relative to rivals, high percentages of pleased customers and few customer complaints, shorter cycle times, a higher percentage of revenues coming from recently introduced products, or what? Benchmarking best-in-industry and best-in-world performance of most or all value chain activities provides a realistic basis for setting internal performance milestones and longer-range targets.

Then comes the managerial task of building a total quality culture that is genuinely committed to achieving the performance outcomes that strategic success requires.[17] Managers can take the following action steps to realize full value from TQM or Six Sigma initiatives:[18]

1. Visible, unequivocal, and unyielding commitment to total quality and continuous improvement, including a quality vision and specific, measurable objectives for boosting quality and making continuous improvement.

2. Nudging people toward quality-supportive behaviors by:

   a) Screening job applicants rigorously and hiring only those with attitudes and aptitudes right for quality-based performance.

   b) Providing quality training for most employees.

   c) Using teams and team-building exercises to reinforce and nurture individual effort (the creation of a quality culture is facilitated when teams become more cross-functional, multitask-oriented, and increasingly self-managed).

   d) Recognizing and rewarding individual and team efforts regularly and systematically.

   e) Stressing prevention (doing it right the first time), not inspection (instituting ways to correct mistakes).

3. Empowering employees so that authority for delivering great service or improving products is in the hands of the doers rather than the overseers—*improving quality has to be seen as part of everyone's job.*

4. Using online systems to provide all relevant parties with the latest best practices and actual experiences with them, thereby speeding the diffusion and adoption of best practices throughout the organization and also allowing the parties to exchange data and opinions about how to upgrade the prevailing best practices.

5. Preaching that performance can, and must, be improved because competitors are not resting on their laurels and customers are always looking for something better.

Core Concept

The purpose of using benchmarking, best practices, business process reengineering, TQM, Six Sigma, or other operational improvement programs is to improve the performance of critical activities and enhance strategy execution.

If the targeted performance measures are appropriate to the strategy and if all organization members (top executives, middle managers, professional staff, and line employees) buy into a culture of operating excellence, then a company's work climate becomes decidedly more conducive to proficient strategy execution. Benchmarking, best-practices implementation, reengineering, TQM, and Six Sigma initiatives can greatly enhance a company's product design, cycle time, production costs, product quality, service, customer satisfaction, and other operating capabilities—and they can even deliver competitive advantage.[19] Not only do improvements from such initiatives add up over time and strengthen organizational capabilities, but the benefits they produce have hard-to-imitate aspects. While it is relatively easy for rivals to undertake benchmarking, process improvement, and quality training, it is much more difficult and time-consuming for them to instill a deeply ingrained culture of operating excellence (as occurs when such techniques are religiously employed and top management exhibits lasting commitment to operational excellence throughout the organization).

Installing Information and Operating Systems

Company strategies can't be executed well without a number of internal systems for business operations. Southwest, American, Northwest, Delta, and other major airlines cannot hope to provide passenger-pleasing service without a user-friendly online reservation system, an accurate and speedy baggage handling system, and a strict aircraft maintenance program that minimizes equipment failures requiring at-the-gate service and delaying plane departures. FedEx has internal communication systems that allow it to coordinate its over 70,000 vehicles in handling an average of 5.5 million packages a day. Its leading-edge flight operations systems allow a single controller to direct as many as 200 of FedEx's 650 aircraft simultaneously, overriding their flight plans should weather or other special emergencies arise. In addition, FedEx has created a series of e-business tools for customers that allow them to ship and track packages online (either at FedEx's Web site or on their own company intranets or Web sites), create address books, review shipping history, generate custom reports, simplify customer billing, reduce internal warehousing and inventory management costs, purchase goods and services from suppliers, and respond quickly to changing customer demands. All of FedEx's systems support the company's strategy of providing businesses and individuals with a broad array of package delivery services (from premium next-day to economical five-day deliveries) and boosting its competitiveness against United Parcel Service, Airborne Express, and the U.S. Postal Service.

Otis Elevator has a 24-hour centralized communications center called OtisLine to coordinate its maintenance efforts in North America.[20] Trained operators take all trouble calls, input critical information on a computer screen, and dispatch people directly via a beeper system to the local trouble spot. Also, much of the information needed for faulty elevator and escalator repairs is accessed directly from electronic monitors installed on each user's site. The OtisLine system helps keep outage times to less than two and a half hours. All the trouble-call data are automatically relayed to design and manufacturing personnel, allowing them to quickly alter design specifications or manufacturing procedures when needed to correct recurring problems. All customers have online access to performance data on each of their Otis elevators and escalators.

Wal-Mart is generally considered to have the most sophisticated retailing systems of any company in the world. For example, Wal-Mart's computers transmit daily sales data to Wrangler, a supplier of blue jeans; Wrangler then uses a model that interprets the data, and software applications that act on these interpretations, in order to ship specific quantities of specific sizes and colors to specific stores from specific warehouses—the system lowers logistics and inventory costs and leads to fewer stockouts.[21] Domino's Pizza has computerized systems at each outlet to facilitate ordering, inventory, payroll, cash flow, and work control functions, thereby freeing managers to spend more time on supervision, customer service, and business development activities.[22] Most telephone companies, electric utilities, and TV broadcasting systems have online monitoring systems to spot transmission problems within seconds and increase the reliability of their services. At eBay, there are systems for real-time monitoring of new listings, bidding activity, Web site traffic, and page views.

Amazon.com ships customer orders from fully computerized, 1,300- by 600-foot warehouses containing about 3 million books, CDs, toys, and houseware items.[23] The warehouses are so technologically sophisticated that they require about as many lines of code to run as Amazon's Web site does. Using complex picking algorithms, computers initiate the order-picking process by sending signals to workers' wireless receivers, telling them which items to pick off the shelves in which order. Computers also generate data on misboxed items, chute backup times, line speed, worker productivity, and shipping weights on orders. Systems are upgraded regularly, and productivity improvements are aggressively pursued. In 2003 Amazon's six warehouses were able to handle three times the volume handled in 1999 at costs averaging 10 percent of revenues (versus 20 percent in 1999); in addition, they turned their inventory over 20 times annually in an industry whose average was 15 turns. Amazon's warehouse was so efficient and its cost per order filled was so low that one of the fastest-growing and most profitable parts of Amazon's business was using its warehouses to run the e-commerce operations of Toys "R" Us and Target.

In businesses such as public accounting and management consulting, where large numbers of professional staff need cutting-edge technical know-how, companies need well-functioning systems for training and retraining employees regularly and keeping them supplied with up-to-date information. Companies that rely on empowered customer service employees to act promptly and creatively in pleasing customers need state-of-the-art information systems that put essential data in front of employees with a few keystrokes. Many companies have cataloged best-practice information on their intranets to promote faster transfer and implementation organizationwide.[24]

Well-conceived state-of-the-art operating systems not only enable better strategy execution but also strengthen organizational capabilities—perhaps enough to provide a competitive edge over rivals. For example, a company with a differentiation strategy based on superior quality has added capability if it has systems for training personnel in quality techniques, tracking product quality at each production step, and ensuring that all goods shipped meet quality standards. A company striving to be a low-cost provider is competitively stronger if it has a benchmarking system that identifies opportunities to implement best practices and drive costs out of the business. Fast-growing companies get an important assist from having capabilities in place to recruit and train new employees in large numbers and from investing in infrastructure that gives them the capability to handle rapid growth as it occurs. It is nearly always better to put infrastructure and support systems in place before they are actually needed than to have to scramble to catch up to customer demand.

> **Core Concept**
> State-of-the-art support systems can be a basis for competitive advantage if they give a firm capabilities that rivals can't match.

Instituting Adequate Information Systems, Performance Tracking, and Controls

Accurate and timely information about daily operations is essential if managers are to gauge how well the strategy execution process is proceeding. Information systems need to cover five broad areas: (1) customer data, (2) operations data, (3) employee data, (4) supplier/partner/collaborative ally data, and (5) financial performance data.

All key strategic performance indicators have to be tracked and reported as often as practical. Monthly profit-and-loss statements and monthly statistical summaries, long the norm, are fast being replaced by daily statistical updates and even up-to-the-minute performance monitoring that online technology makes possible. Many retail companies have automated online systems that generate daily sales reports for each store and maintain up-to-the-minute inventory and sales records on each item. Manufacturing plants typically generate daily production reports and track labor productivity on every shift. Many retailers and manufacturers have online data systems connecting them with their suppliers that monitor the status of inventories, track shipments and deliveries, and measure defect rates.

Real-time information systems permit company managers to stay on top of implementation initiatives and daily operations and to intervene if things seem to be drifting off course. Tracking key performance indicators, gathering information from operating personnel, quickly identifying and diagnosing problems, and taking corrective actions are all integral pieces of the process of managing strategy implementation and execution and exercising adequate organization control. Telephone companies have elaborate information systems to measure signal quality, connection times, interrupts, wrong connections, billing errors, and other measures of reliability that affect customer service and satisfaction. To track and manage the quality of passenger service, airlines have information systems that monitor gate delays, on-time departures and arrivals, baggage handling times, lost baggage complaints, stockouts on meals and drinks, overbookings, and maintenance delays and failures. Virtually all companies now provide customer-contact personnel with computer access to customer databases so that they can respond effectively to customer inquiries and deliver personalized customer service.

Statistical information gives managers a feel for the numbers, briefings and meetings provide a feel for the latest developments and emerging issues, and personal contacts add a feel for the people dimension. All are good barometers. Managers have to identify problem areas and deviations from plan before they can take actions to get the organization back on course, by either improving the approaches to strategy execution or fine-tuning the strategy. Jeff Bezos, Amazon's CEO, is an ardent proponent of managing by the numbers—as he puts it, "Math-based decisions always trump opinion and judgment. . . . The trouble with most corporations is that they make judgment-based decisions when data-based decisions could be made."[25]

> **Core Concept**
>
> Having good information systems and operating data is integral to the managerial task of executing strategy successfully and achieving greater operating excellence.

Exercising Adequate Controls over Empowered Employees

Another important aspect of effectively managing and controlling the strategy execution process is monitoring the performance of empowered workers to see that they are acting within the specified limits.[26] Leaving empowered employees to their own devices in meeting performance standards without appropriate checks and balances can expose an organization to excessive risk.[27] Instances abound of employees' decisions or behavior having gone awry, sometimes costing a company huge sums or producing lawsuits aside from just generating embarrassing publicity.

Managers can't devote big chunks of their time to making sure that the decisions and behavior of empowered employees stay between the white lines—this would defeat the major purpose of empowerment and, in effect, lead to the reinstatement of a managerial bureaucracy engaged in constant over-the-shoulder supervision. Yet management has a clear responsibility to exercise sufficient control over empowered employees to protect the company against out-of-bounds behavior and unwelcome surprises. Scrutinizing daily and weekly operating statistics is one of the important ways in which managers can monitor the results that flow from the actions of empowered subordinates—if the operating results flowing from the actions of empowered employees look good, then it is reasonable to assume that empowerment is working.

One of the main purposes of tracking daily operating performance is to relieve managers of the burden of constant supervision and give them time for other issues. But managerial control is only part of the answer. Another valuable lever of control in companies that rely on empowered employees, especially in those that use self-managed work groups or other such teams, is peer-based control. Most team members feel responsible for the success of the whole team and tend to be relatively intolerant of any team member's behavior that weakens team performance or puts team accomplishments at risk. Because peer evaluation is such a powerful control device, companies organized into teams can remove some layers of the management hierarchy. This is especially true when a company has the information systems capability to monitor team performance daily or in real time.

Tying Rewards and Incentives to Strategy Execution

> **Core Concept**
>
> A properly designed reward structure is management's most powerful tool for mobilizing organizational commitment to successful strategy execution.

It is important for both organization units and individuals to be enthusiastically committed to executing strategy and achieving performance targets. Company managers typically use an assortment of motivational techniques and rewards to enlist organizationwide commitment to executing the strategic plan. A manager has to do more than just talk to everyone about how important new strategic practices and performance targets are to the organization's well-being. No matter how inspiring, talk seldom commands people's best efforts for long. *To get employees' sustained, energetic commitment, management has to be resourceful in designing and using motivational incentives—both monetary and nonmonetary.* The more a manager understands what motivates subordinates and the more he or she relies on motivational incentives as a tool for achieving the targeted strategic and financial results, the greater will be employees' commitment to good day-in, day-out strategy execution and achievement of performance targets.[28]

Strategy-Facilitating Motivational Practices

Financial incentives generally head the list of motivating tools for trying to gain wholehearted employee commitment to good strategy execution and operating excellence. Monetary rewards generally include some combination of base pay increases, performance bonuses, profit sharing plans, stock awards, company contributions to employee 401(k) or retirement plans, and piecework incentives (in the case of production workers). But successful companies and managers normally make extensive use of such nonmonetary carrot-and-stick incentives as frequent words of praise (or constructive criticism), special recognition at company gatherings or in the company newsletter, more (or less) job security, stimulating assignments, opportunities to transfer to attractive locations, increased (or decreased) autonomy, and rapid promotion (or the risk of being sidelined in a routine or dead-end job). In addition, companies use a host of other motivational approaches to spur stronger employee commitment to the strategy execution process; the following are some of the most important:[29]

■ *Providing attractive perks and fringe benefits*—The various options here include full coverage of health insurance premiums, full tuition reimbursement for work on college degrees, paid vacation time of three or four weeks, on-site child care at major facilities, on-site gym facilities and massage therapists, getaway opportunities at company-owned recreational facilities (beach houses, ranches, resort condos), personal concierge services, subsidized cafeterias and free lunches, casual dress every day, personal travel services, paid sabbaticals, maternity leaves, paid leaves to care for ill family members, telecommuting, compressed workweeks (four 10-hour days instead of five 8-hour days), reduced summer hours, college scholarships for children, on-the-spot bonuses for exceptional performance, and relocation services.

■ *Relying on promotion from within whenever possible*—This practice helps bind workers to their employer and employers to their workers; plus, it is an incentive for good performance. Promotion from within also helps ensure that people in positions of responsibility actually know something about the business, technology, and operations they are managing.

■ *Making sure that the ideas and suggestions of employees are valued and respected*—Research indicates that the moves of many companies to push decision making down the line and empower employees increase employee motivation and satisfaction, as well as boost their productivity. The use of self-managed teams has much the same effect.

■ *Creating a work atmosphere in which there is genuine sincerity, caring, and mutual respect among workers and between management and employees*—A "family" work environment where people are on a first-name basis and there is strong camaraderie promotes teamwork and cross-unit collaboration.

■ *Stating the strategic vision in inspirational terms that make employees feel they are a part of doing something very worthwhile in a larger social sense*—There's strong motivating power associated with giving people a chance to be part of something exciting and personally satisfying. Jobs with noble purpose tend to turn employees on. At Pfizer, Merck, and most other pharmaceutical companies, it is the notion of helping sick people get well and restoring patients to full life. At Whole Foods Market (a natural-foods grocery chain), it is helping customers discover good eating habits and thus improving human health and nutrition.

■ *Sharing information with employees about financial performance, strategy, operational measures, market conditions, and competitors' actions*—Broad disclosure and prompt communication send the message that managers trust their workers. Keeping employees in the dark denies them information useful to performing their job, prevents them from being "students of the business," and usually turns them off.

■ *Having knockout facilities*—An impressive corporate facility for employees to work in usually has decidedly positive effects on morale and productivity.

> **Core Concept**
>
> One of management's biggest strategy-executing challenges is to employ motivational techniques that build wholehearted commitment to operating excellence and winning attitudes among employees.

■ *Being flexible in how the company approaches people management (motivation, compensation, recognition, recruitment) in multinational, multicultural environments*—Managers and employees in countries whose customs, habits, values, and business practices vary from those at the home office often become frustrated with insistence on consistent people-management practices worldwide. But the one area where consistency is essential is conveying the message that the organization values people of all races and cultural backgrounds and that discrimination of any sort will not be tolerated.

For specific examples of the motivational tactics employed by several prominent companies, see Company Spotlight 9.2.

Striking the Right Balance between Rewards and Punishment

While most approaches to motivation, compensation, and people management accentuate the positive, companies also embellish positive rewards with the risk of punishment. At General Electric, McKinsey & Company, several global public accounting firms, and other companies that look for and expect top-notch individual performance, there's an "up-or-out" policy—managers and professionals whose performance is not good enough to warrant promotion are first denied bonuses and stock awards and eventually weeded out. A number of companies deliberately give employees heavy workloads and tight deadlines—personnel are pushed hard to achieve "stretch" objectives and expected to put in long hours (nights and weekends if need be). At most companies, senior executives and key personnel in underperforming units are pressured to boost performance to acceptable levels and keep it there or risk being replaced.

As a general rule, it is unwise to take off the pressure for good individual and group performance or play down the stress, anxiety, and adverse consequences of shortfalls in performance. There is no evidence that a no-pressure/no-adverse-consequences work environment leads to superior strategy execution or operating excellence. As the CEO of a major bank put it, "There's a deliberate policy here to create a level of anxiety. Winners usually play like they're one touchdown behind."[30] *High-performing organizations nearly always have a cadre of ambitious people who relish the opportunity to climb the ladder of success, love a challenge, thrive in a performance-oriented environment, and find some competition and pressure useful to satisfy their own drives for personal recognition, accomplishment, and self-satisfaction.*

However, if an organization's motivational approaches and reward structure induce too much stress, internal competitiveness, and job insecurity and too many unpleasant consequences, the impact on workforce morale and strategy execution can be counterproductive. Evidence shows that managerial initiatives to improve strategy execution should incorporate more positive than negative motivational elements because when cooperation is positively enlisted and rewarded, rather than strong-armed by orders and threats (implicit or explicit), people tend to respond with more enthusiasm, dedication, creativity, and initiative. Something of a middle ground is generally optimal—not only handing out decidedly positive rewards for meeting or beating performance targets but also imposing sufficiently negative consequences (if only withholding rewards) when actual performance falls short of the target. But the negative consequences of underachievement should never be so severe or demoralizing as to impede a renewed and determined effort to overcome existing obstacles and hit the targets in upcoming periods.

COMPANY SPOTLIGHT 9.2

Techniques Companies Use to Motivate and Reward Employees

Companies have come up with an impressive variety of motivational and reward practices to help create a work environment that energizes employees and promotes better strategy execution. Here's a sampling of what companies are doing:

- Google has a sprawling four-building complex known as the Googleplex where the roughly 1,000 employees are provided with free food, unlimited ice cream, pool and Ping-Pong tables, and complimentary massages—management built the Googleplex to be "a dream environment." Moreover, the company allows its employees to spend 20 percent of their work time on any outside activity.

- Lincoln Electric, widely known for its piecework pay scheme and incentive bonus plan, rewards individual productivity by paying workers for each nondefective piece produced. Workers have to correct quality problems on their own time—defects in products used by customers can be traced back to the worker who caused them. Lincoln's piecework plan motivates workers to pay attention to both quality and volume produced. In addition, the company sets aside a substantial portion of its profits above a specified base for worker bonuses. To determine bonus size, Lincoln Electric rates each worker on four equally important performance measures: dependability, quality, output, and ideas and cooperation. The higher a worker's merit rating, the higher the incentive bonus earned; the highest-rated workers in good profit years receive bonuses of as much as 110 percent of their piecework compensation.

- At JM Family Enterprises, a Toyota distributor in Florida, employees get a great lease on new Toyotas and are flown to the Bahamas for cruises on the company yacht, plus the company's office facility has such amenities as a heated lap pool, a fitness center, and a free nail salon.

- Amazon.com hands out Just Do It awards to employees who do something they think will help Amazon *without* getting their boss's permission. The action has to be well thought through but doesn't have to succeed.

- Nordstrom, widely regarded for its superior in-house customer service experience, typically pays its retail salespeople an hourly wage higher than the prevailing rates paid by other department store chains plus a commission on each sale. Spurred by a culture that encourages salespeople to go all-out to satisfy customers and to seek out and promote new fashion ideas, Nordstrom salespeople often earn twice the average incomes of sales employees at competing stores. Nordstrom's rules for employees are simple: "Rule #1: Use your good judgment in all situations. There will be no additional rules."

- At W. L. Gore (the maker of Gore-Tex), employees get to choose what project/team they work on, and each team member's compensation is based on other team members' rankings of his or her contribution to the enterprise.

- At Ukrop's Super Markets, a family-owned chain, stores stay closed on Sunday; the company pays out 20 percent of pretax profits to employees in the form of quarterly bonuses; and the company picks up the membership tab for employees if they visit their health club 30 times a quarter.

- At biotech leader Amgen, employees get 16 paid holidays, generous vacation time, tuition reimbursements up to $10,000, on-site massages, a discounted car wash, and the convenience of shopping at on-site farmers' markets.

- At Synovus, a financial services and credit card company, the company adds 21 percent to employees' salaries with "wealth-building" programs like a 401(k) and profit sharing, plus it holds an annual bass fishing tournament.

- At specialty chip maker Xilinx, new hires receive stock option grants; the CEO responds promptly to employee e-mails, and during hard times management takes a 20 percent pay cut instead of laying off employees.

Source: *Fortune's* lists of the 100 best companies to work for in America, both the February 4, 2002, and January 12, 2004 issues; Jefferson Graham, "The Search Engine That Could," *USA Today*, August 26, 2003, p. B3; and Fred Vogelstein, "Winning the Amazon Way," *Fortune*, May 26, 2003, p.73.

Linking the Reward System to Strategically Relevant Performance Outcomes

The most dependable way to keep people focused on strategy execution and the achievement of performance targets is to generously reward and recognize individuals and groups who meet or beat performance targets and to deny rewards and recognition to those who don't. *The use of incentives and rewards is the single most powerful tool management has to win strong employee commitment to diligent, competent strategy execution and operating excellence.* Decisions on salary increases, incentive compensation, promotions, key assignments, and the ways and means of awarding praise and recognition are potent attention-getting, commitment-generating devices. Such decisions seldom escape the closest employee scrutiny, as they say more about what is expected and who is considered to be doing a good job than about any other factor. Hence, when achievement of the targeted strategic and financial outcomes becomes the dominating basis for designing incentives, evaluating individual and group efforts, and handing out rewards, company personnel quickly grasp that it is in their own self-interest to do their best in executing the strategy competently and achieving key performance targets.[31] Indeed, it is usually through the company's system of incentives and rewards that workforce members emotionally ratify their commitment to the company's strategy execution effort.

> **Core Concept**
>
> A properly designed reward system aligns the well-being of organization members with their contributions to competent strategy execution and the achievement of performance targets.

Strategy-driven performance targets need to be established for every organizational unit, every manager, every team or work group, and perhaps every employee—targets that measure whether strategy execution is progressing satisfactorily. If the company's strategy is to be a low-cost provider, the incentive system must reward actions and achievements that result in lower costs. If the company has a differentiation strategy predicated on superior quality and service, the incentive system must reward such outcomes as Six Sigma defect rates, infrequent need for product repair, low numbers of customer complaints, and speedy order processing and delivery. If a company's growth is predicated on a strategy of new product innovation, incentives should be tied to factors such as the percentages of revenues and profits coming from newly introduced products.

Company Spotlight 9.3 provides two vivid examples of how companies have designed incentives linked directly to outcomes reflecting good strategy execution.

The Importance of Basing Incentives on Achieving Results, Not on Performing Assigned Duties

To create a strategy-supportive system of rewards and incentives, a company must emphasize rewarding people for accomplishing results, not for just dutifully performing assigned tasks. Focusing job-holders' attention and energy on what to *achieve* as opposed to what to *do* makes the work environment results-oriented. It is flawed management to tie incentives and rewards to satisfactory performance of duties and activities in hopes that the by-products will be the desired business outcomes and company achievements.[32] In any job, performing assigned tasks is not equivalent to achieving intended outcomes. Diligently showing up for work and attending to job assignments does not, by itself, guarantee results. As any student knows, the fact that an instructor teaches and students go to class doesn't necessarily mean that the students are learning. The enterprise of education would no doubt take on a different character if teachers were rewarded for the result of student learning rather than for the activity of teaching.

> It is folly to reward one outcome in hopes of getting another outcome.

Nucor and Bank One: Two Companies That Tie Incentives Directly to Strategy Execution

The strategy at Nucor Corporation, now the biggest steel producer in the United States, is to be *the* low-cost producer of steel products. Because labor costs are a significant fraction of total cost in the steel business, successful implementation of Nucor's low-cost leadership strategy entails achieving lower labor costs per ton of steel than competitors' costs. Nucor management uses an incentive system to promote high worker productivity and drive labor costs per ton below rivals'. Each plant's workforce is organized into production teams (each assigned to perform particular functions), and weekly production targets are established for each team. Base pay scales are set at levels comparable to wages for similar manufacturing jobs in the local areas where Nucor has plants, but workers can earn a 1 percent bonus for each 1 percent that their output exceeds target levels. If a production team exceeds its weekly production target by 10 percent, team members receive a 10 percent bonus in their next paycheck; if a team exceeds its quota by 20 percent, team members earn a 20 percent bonus. Bonuses, paid every two weeks, are based on the prior two weeks' actual production levels measured against the targets.

Nucor's piece-rate incentive plan has resulted in labor productivity levels 10 to 20 percent above the average of the unionized workforces of several of its largest rivals, given Nucor a cost advantage over most rivals, and made Nucor workers among the highest-paid in the U.S. steel industry.

At Bank One (recently acquired by JP Morgan Chase), management believed it was strategically important to boost its customer satisfaction ratings in order to enhance its competitiveness vis-à-vis rivals. Targets were set for customer satisfaction, and monitoring systems for measuring customer satisfaction at each branch office were put in place. Then, to motivate branch office personnel to be more attentive in trying to please customers and also to signal that top management was truly committed to achieving higher levels of overall customer satisfaction, top management opted to tie pay scales in each branch office to that branch's customer satisfaction rating—the higher the branch's ratings, the higher that branch's pay scales. Management believed its shift from a theme of equal pay for equal work to one of equal pay for equal performance contributed significantly to its customer satisfaction priority.

Incentive compensation for top executives is typically tied to such financial measures as revenue and earnings growth, stock price performance, return on investment, and creditworthiness and perhaps such strategic measures as market share, product quality, or customer satisfaction. However, incentives for department heads, teams, and individual workers may be tied to performance outcomes more closely related to their strategic area of responsibility. In manufacturing, incentive compensation may be tied to unit manufacturing costs, on-time production and shipping, defect rates, the number and extent of work stoppages due to labor disagreements and equipment breakdowns, and so on. In sales and marketing, there may be incentives for achieving dollar sales or unit volume targets, market share, sales penetration of each target customer group, the fate of newly introduced products, the frequency of customer complaints, the number of new accounts acquired, and customer satisfaction. Which performance measures to base incentive compensation on depends on the situation—the priority placed on various financial and strategic objectives, the requirements for strategic and competitive success, and what specific results are needed in different facets of the business to keep strategy execution on track.

> ### Core Concept
> The role of the reward system is to align the well-being of organization members with realizing the company's vision so that organization members benefit by helping the company execute its strategy competently and fully satisfy customers.

Guidelines for Designing Incentive Compensation Systems

The concepts and company experiences discussed above yield the following prescriptive guidelines for creating an incentive compensation system to help drive successful strategy execution:

1. *Make the performance payoff a major, not minor, piece of the total compensation package.* Payoffs must be at least 10 to 12 percent of base salary to have much impact. Incentives that amount to 20 percent or more of total compensation are big attention getters, likely to really drive individual or team effort; incentives amounting to less than 5 percent of total compensation have comparatively weak motivational impact. Moreover, the payoff for high-performing individuals and teams must be meaningfully greater than the payoff for average performers, and the payoff for average performers meaningfully bigger than that for below-average performers.

2. *Have incentives that extend to all managers and all workers, not just top management.* It is a gross miscalculation to expect that lower-level managers and employees will work their hardest to hit performance targets just so a few senior executives can get lucrative rewards.

3. *Administer the reward system with scrupulous objectivity and fairness.* If performance standards are set unrealistically high or if individual/group performance evaluations are not accurate and well documented, dissatisfaction with the system will overcome any positive benefits.

4. *Tie incentives to performance outcomes directly linked to good strategy execution and financial performance.* Incentives should never be paid just because people are thought to be "doing a good job" or because they "work hard." Performance evaluation based on factors not tightly related to good strategy execution signal that either the strategic plan is incomplete (because important performance targets were left out) or management's real agenda is something other than the stated strategic and financial objectives.

5. *Make sure that the performance targets each individual or team is expected to achieve involve outcomes that the individual or team can personally affect.* The role of incentives is to enhance individual commitment and channel behavior in beneficial directions. This role is not well served when the performance measures by which company personnel are judged are outside their arena of influence.

6. *Keep the time between achieving the target performance outcome and the payment of the reward as short as possible.* Companies like Nucor and Continental Airlines have discovered that weekly or monthly payments for good performance work much better than annual payments. Nucor pays weekly bonuses based on prior-week production levels; Continental awards employees a monthly bonus for each month that on-time flight performance meets or beats a specified percentage companywide. Annual bonus payouts work best for higher-level managers and for situations where target outcome relates to overall company profitability or stock price performance.

7. *Make liberal use of nonmonetary rewards; don't rely solely on monetary rewards.* When used properly, money is a great motivator, but there are also potent advantages to be gained from praise, special recognition, handing out plum assignments, and so on.

8. *Absolutely avoid skirting the system to find ways to reward effort rather than results.* Whenever actual performance falls short of targeted performance, there's merit in determining whether the causes are attributable to subpar individual/group performance or to circumstances beyond the control of those responsible. It can be argued that exceptions should be made in giving rewards to people who've tried hard, gone the extra mile, yet still come up short because of circumstances beyond

their control. The problem with making exceptions for unknowable, uncontrollable, or unforeseeable circumstances is that once good excuses start to creep into justifying rewards for subpar results, the door is open for all kinds of reasons why actual performance failed to match targeted performance. A "no excuses" standard is more evenhanded and certainly easier to administer.

Once the incentives are designed, they have to be communicated and explained. Everybody needs to understand how his or her incentive compensation is calculated and how individual/group performance targets contribute to organizational performance targets. The pressure to achieve the targeted strategic and financial performance and continuously improve on strategy execution should be unrelenting, with few (if any) loopholes for rewarding shortfalls in performance. People at all levels have to be held accountable for carrying out their assigned parts of the strategic plan, and they have to understand that their rewards are based on the caliber of results achieved.

> **Core Concept**
>
> The unwavering standard for judging whether individuals, teams, and organizational units have done a good job must be whether they achieve performance targets consistent with effective strategy execution.

But with the pressure to perform should come meaningful rewards. Without an ample payoff, the system breaks down, and managers are left with the less workable options of barking orders, trying to enforce compliance, and depending on the goodwill of employees.

Performance-Based Incentives and Rewards in Multinational Enterprises   In some foreign countries, incentive pay runs counter to local customs and cultural norms. Professor Steven Kerr cites the time he lectured an executive education class on the need for more performance-based pay and a Japanese manager protested, "You shouldn't bribe your children to do their homework, you shouldn't bribe your wife to prepare dinner, and you shouldn't bribe your employees to work for the company."[33] Singling out individuals and commending them for unusually good effort can also be a problem; Japanese culture considers public praise of an individual an affront to the harmony of the group. In some countries, employees have a preference for nonmonetary rewards—more leisure time, important titles, access to vacation villages, and nontaxable perks. Thus, multinational companies have to build some degree of flexibility into the design of incentives and rewards in order to accommodate cross-cultural traditions and preferences.

Leading the Strategy Execution Process

The litany of managing the strategy process is simple enough: craft a sound strategic plan, implement it, execute it to the fullest, adjust it as needed, and win! But the leadership challenges are significant and diverse. To achieve results, a manager must take on a variety of leadership roles in managing the strategy execution process: resource acquirer and allocator, capabilities builder, motivator, policy maker, policy enforcer, head cheerleader, crisis solver, decision maker, and taskmaster, to mention a few. There are times when leading the strategy execution process entails being authoritarian and hard-nosed, times when it is best to be a perceptive listener and a compromising decision maker, times when matters are best delegated to people closest to the scene of the action, and times when being a coach is the proper role. Many occasions call for the manager in charge to assume a highly visible role and put in long hours guiding the process, while others entail only a brief ceremonial performance with the details delegated to subordinates.

For the most part, leading the strategy execution process has to be top-down and driven by mandates to get things on the right track and show good results. The specifics of leading organization efforts to put a strategy in place and deliver the intended results should start with understanding the requirements for good strategy execution, followed by diagnosing the organization's capabilities and preparedness to execute the necessary strategic initiatives, and then deciding which of several ways to proceed to get things done and achieve the targeted results.[34] In general, leading the drive for good strategy execution and operating excellence calls for several actions on the part of the manager in charge:

1. Staying on top of what is happening, closely monitoring progress, ferreting out issues, and learning what obstacles lie in the path of good execution.

2. Putting constructive pressure on the organization to achieve good results and operating excellence.

3. Leading the development of stronger core competencies and competitive capabilities.

4. Displaying ethical integrity and leading social responsibility initiatives.

5. Pushing corrective actions to improve strategy execution and achieve the targeted results.

Staying on Top of How Well Things Are Going

To stay on top of how well the strategy execution process is going, a manager needs to develop a broad network of contacts and sources of information, both formal and informal. The regular channels include talking with key subordinates, attending presentations and meetings, reading reviews of the latest operating results, talking to customers, watching the competitive reactions of rival firms, exchanging e-mail and holding telephone conversations with people in outlying locations, making on-site visits, and listening to rank-and-file employees. However, some information is more trustworthy than the rest, and the views and perspectives offered by different people can vary widely. Presentations and briefings by subordinates may be colored by wishful thinking or shoddy analysis rather than representing the unvarnished truth. Bad news or problems are sometimes filtered, minimized, or distorted by people pursuing their own agendas; in some cases they are not reported at all, as subordinates delay conveying failures and problems in hopes that they can turn things around in time. Hence, managers have to make sure that they get their information directly from the source and have an accurate feel for the existing situation. They have to confirm whether things are on track, identify problems, learn what obstacles lie in the path of good strategy execution, ruthlessly assess whether the organization has the talent and attitude needed to drive the required changes, and develop a basis for determining what, if anything, they can personally do to move the process along.[35]

Core Concept

Management by walking around (MBWA) is one of the techniques that effective leaders use to stay informed about how well the strategy execution process is progressing.

One of the best ways for executives to stay on top of the strategy execution process is by making regular visits to the field and talking with many different people at many different levels—a technique often labeled **managing by walking around (MBWA).** Wal-Mart executives have had a long-standing practice of spending two to three days every week visiting Wal-Mart's stores and talking with store managers and employees. Sam Walton, Wal-Mart's founder, insisted, "The key is to get out into the store and listen to what the associates have to say." Jack Welch, the highly effective CEO of General Electric from

1980 to 2001, not only spent several days each month personally visiting GE operations and talking with major customers but also arranged his schedule so that he could spend time exchanging information and ideas with GE managers from all over the world who were attending classes at the company's leadership development center near GE's headquarters.

Often, customers and suppliers can provide valuable perspectives on how well a company's strategy execution process is going. Joe Tucci, COO at data-storage leader EMC, when confronted with an unexpected dropoff in EMC's sales in 2001 and not sure whether the downturn represented a temporary slump or a structural market change, went straight to the source for hard information: the CEOs and CFOs to whom CIOs at customer companies reported and to the consultants who advised them. The information he got was eye-opening—fundamental market shifts were occurring and the rules of market engagement now called for major strategy changes at EMC followed by quick implementation.

To keep their fingers on the company's pulse, managers at some companies host weekly get-togethers (often on Friday afternoons) to create a regular opportunity for tidbits of information to flow freely between down-the-line employees and executives. Many manufacturing executives make a point of strolling the factory floor to talk with workers and of meeting regularly with union officials. Some managers operate out of open cubicles in big spaces populated with open cubicles for other personnel so that they can interact easily and frequently with coworkers. Jeff Bezos, Amazon.com's CEO, is noted for his practice of MBWA, firing off a battery of questions when he tours facilities and insisting that Amazon managers spend time in the trenches with their people to avoid abstract thinking and getting disconnected from the reality of what's happening.[36]

Most managers rightly attach great importance to spending time with people at various company facilities and gathering information and opinions firsthand from diverse sources about how well different aspects of the strategy execution process are going. Such contacts give managers a feel for what progress is being made, what problems are being encountered, and whether additional resources or different approaches may be needed. Just as important, MBWA provides opportunities for managers to talk informally to many different people at different organizational levels, give encouragement, lift spirits, shift attention from the old to the new priorities, and create some excitement—all of which generate positive energy and help mobilize organizational efforts behind strategy execution.

Putting Constructive Pressure on the Organization to Achieve Good Results and Operating Excellence

Managers have to be out front in mobilizing organizational energy behind the drive for good strategy execution and operating excellence. Part of the leadership requirement here entails nurturing a results-oriented work climate. A culture where there's constructive pressure to achieve good results is a valuable contributor to good strategy execution and operating excellence. Results-oriented cultures are permeated with a spirit of achievement and have a good track record in meeting or beating performance targets. If management wants to drive the strategy execution effort by instilling a results-oriented work climate, then senior executives have to take the lead in promoting certain enabling cultural drivers: a strong sense of involvement on the part of company personnel, emphasis on individual initiative and creativity, respect for the contribution of individuals and groups, and pride in doing things right.

Organization leaders who succeed in creating a results-oriented work climate typically are intensely people-oriented, and they are skilled users of people-management practices that win the emotional commitment of company personnel and inspire them to do their best.[37] They understand that treating employees well generally leads to increased teamwork, higher morale, greater loyalty, and increased employee commitment to making a contribution. All of these foster an esprit de corps that energizes organization members to contribute to the drive for operating excellence and proficient strategy execution.

Successfully leading the effort to instill a spirit of high achievement into the culture generally entails such leadership actions and managerial practices as:

- Treating employees with dignity and respect. This often includes a strong company commitment to training each employee thoroughly, providing attractive career opportunities, emphasizing promotion from within, and providing a high degree of job security. Some companies symbolize the value of individual employees and the importance of their contributions by referring to them as cast members (Disney), crew members (McDonald's), coworkers (Kinko's and CDW Computer Centers), job owners (Graniterock), partners (Starbucks), or associates (Wal-Mart, Lenscrafters, W. L. Gore, Edward Jones, Publix Supermarkets, and Marriott International). At a number of companies, managers at every level are held responsible for developing the people who report to them.

- Making champions out of the people who turn in winning performances—but doing so in ways that promote teamwork and cross-unit collaboration as opposed to spurring an unhealthy footrace among employees to best one another. Would-be champions who advocate radical or different ideas must not be looked on as disruptive or troublesome. The best champions and change agents are persistent, competitive, tenacious, committed, and fanatical about seeing their idea through to success. It is particularly important that people who champion an unsuccessful idea not be punished or sidelined but, rather, be encouraged to try again—encouraging lots of "tries" is important since many ideas won't pan out.

- Encouraging employees to use initiative and creativity in performing their work. Operating excellence requires that everybody be expected to contribute ideas, exercise initiative, and pursue continuous improvement. The leadership trick is to keep a sense of urgency alive in the business so that people see change and innovation as necessities. Moreover, people with maverick ideas or out-of-the-ordinary proposals have to be tolerated and given room to operate; anything less tends to squelch creativity and initiative.

- Setting stretch objectives and clearly communicating an expectation that company personnel are to give their best in achieving performance targets.

- Using the tools of benchmarking, best practices, business process reengineering, TQM, and Six Sigma quality to focus attention on continuous improvement. These are proven approaches to getting better operating results and facilitating better strategy execution.

- Using the full range of motivational techniques and compensation incentives to inspire company personnel, nurture a results-oriented work climate, and enforce high-performance standards. Managers cannot mandate innovative improvements by simply exhorting people to "be creative," nor can they make continuous progress toward operating excellence with directives to "try harder." Rather, they have to foster a culture where innovative ideas and experimentation with new ways of doing things can blossom and thrive. Individuals and groups need to be strongly encouraged to brainstorm, let their imaginations fly in all directions, and come up with proposals for improving how things are done. This means giving company personnel enough autonomy to stand out, excel, and contribute. And it means that the rewards for successful champions of new ideas and operating improvements should be large and visible.

■ Celebrating individual, group, and company successes. Top management should miss no opportunity to express respect for individual employees and appreciation of extraordinary individual and group effort.[38] Companies like Mary Kay Cosmetics, Tupperware, and McDonald's actively seek out reasons and opportunities to give pins, buttons, badges, and medals for good showings by average performers—the idea being to express appreciation and give a motivational boost to people who stand out in doing ordinary jobs. General Electric and 3M Corporation make a point of ceremoniously honoring individuals who believe so strongly in their ideas that they take it on themselves to hurdle the bureaucracy, maneuver their projects through the system, and turn them into improved services, new products, or even new businesses.

While leadership efforts to instill a results-oriented culture usually accentuate the positive, negative consequences are sometimes needed. Managers whose units consistently perform poorly have to be replaced. Low-performing workers and people who reject the results-oriented cultural emphasis have to be weeded out or at least moved to out-of-the-way positions. Average performers have to be candidly counseled that they have limited career potential unless they show more progress in the form of more effort, better skills, and ability to deliver better results.

Leading the Development of Better Competencies and Capabilities

A third avenue to better strategy execution and operating excellence is proactively strengthening organizational competencies and competitive capabilities. This often requires top management intervention. Senior management usually has to lead the strengthening effort because core competencies and competitive capabilities typically reside in the combined efforts of different work groups, departments, and strategic allies. The tasks of managing human skills, knowledge bases, and intellect and then integrating them to forge competitively advantageous competencies and capabilities is an exercise best orchestrated by senior managers who appreciate their strategy-implementing significance and who have the clout to enforce the necessary networking and cooperation among individuals, groups, departments, and external allies. Stronger competencies and capabilities can not only lead to better performance of value chain activities but also pave the way for better bottom-line results. Also, in today's globalizing economy, strategy leaders are well positioned to spot opportunities to leverage existing competencies and competitive capabilities across geographic borders.

Aside from leading efforts to strengthen existing competencies and capabilities, effective strategy leaders try to anticipate changes in customer-market requirements and proactively build new competencies and capabilities that offer a competitive edge over rivals. Senior managers are in the best position to see the need and potential of new capabilities and then to play a lead role in the capability-building, resource-strengthening process. Proactively building new competencies and capabilities ahead of rivals to gain a competitive edge is strategic leadership of the best kind, but strengthening the company's resource base in reaction to newly developed capabilities of pioneering rivals occurs more frequently.

Displaying Ethical Integrity and Leading Social Responsibility Initiatives

For an organization to avoid the pitfalls of scandal and disgrace and consistently display the intent to conduct its business in a principled manner, the CEO and those around the CEO must be openly and unswervingly committed to ethical conduct and socially redeeming business principles and core values. Leading the effort to operate the company's business in an ethically principled fashion has three pieces. First and foremost, the CEO and other senior executives must set an excellent example in their own ethical behavior, demonstrating character and personal integrity in their actions and decisions. The behavior of senior executives is always watched carefully, sending a clear message to company personnel regarding what the "real" standards of personal conduct are. Moreover, the company's strategy and operating decisions have to be seen as ethical—actions speak louder than words here. Second, top management must declare unequivocal support of the company's ethical code and take an uncompromising stand on expecting all company personnel to conduct themselves in an ethical fashion at all times. This means iterating and reiterating to employees that it is their duty to observe the company's ethical code. Third, top management must be prepared to act as the final arbiter on hard calls; this means removing people from key positions or terminating them when they are guilty of a violation. It also means reprimanding those who have been lax in monitoring and enforcing ethical compliance. Failure to act swiftly and decisively in punishing ethical misconduct is interpreted as a lack of real commitment.

Demonstrating Genuine Commitment to a Strategy of Social Responsibility

As was discussed in Chapter 7, business leaders who want their companies to be regarded as exemplary corporate citizens must not only see that their companies operate ethically but also take a lead role in crafting a social responsibility strategy that positively improves the well-being of employees, the environment, the communities in which they operate, and society at large. The CEO and other senior executives must insist that the company go past the rhetoric and cosmetics of corporate citizenship and employ a genuine strategy of social responsibility. *What separates companies that make a sincere effort to carry their weight in being good corporate citizens from companies that are content to do only what is legally required of them are company leaders who believe strongly that just making a profit is not good enough. Such leaders are committed to a higher standard of performance that includes social and environmental metrics as well as financial and strategic metrics.*

> Companies with socially conscious strategy leaders and a core value of corporate social responsibility move beyond the rhetorical flourishes of corporate citizenship and enlist the full support of company personnel behind social responsibility initiatives.

One of the leadership responsibilities of the CEO and other senior managers, therefore, is to step out front, wave the flag of socially responsible behavior for all to see, marshal the support of company personnel, and transform social responsibility initiatives into an everyday part of how the company conducts its business affairs. Strategy leaders have to insist on the use of social and environmental metrics in evaluating performance, and, ideally, the company's board of directors will elect to tie the company's social and environmental performance to executive compensation—a surefire way to make sure that social responsibility efforts are more than window dressing. To help ensure that it has commitment from senior managers, Verizon Communications ties 10 percent of the annual bonus of the company's top 2,500 managers directly to the achievement of social responsibility targets. One survey found over 60 percent of senior managers believed that a portion of executive compensation should be linked to a company's performance on social and environmental measures. The strength of the commitment from the top—typically a company's CEO and board of directors—ultimately determines whether a company will pursue a genuine, full-fledged strategy of social responsibility that embraces some customized combination of actions to protect the environment (beyond what is required by law), actively participate in community affairs, be a generous supporter of charitable causes and projects that benefit society, and have a positive impact on workforce diversity and the overall well-being of employees.

Leading the Process of Making Corrective Adjustments

The leadership challenge of making corrective adjustments is twofold: deciding when adjustments are needed and deciding what adjustments to make. Both decisions are a normal and necessary part of managing the strategy execution process, since no scheme for implementing and executing strategy can foresee all the events and problems that will arise. There comes a time at every company when managers have to fine-tune or overhaul the approaches to strategy execution and push for better results. Clearly, when a company's strategy execution effort is not delivering desired results and making measurable progress toward operating excellence, it is the leader's responsibility to step forward and push corrective actions.

The *process* of making corrective adjustments varies according to the situation. In a crisis, it is typical for leaders to have key subordinates gather information, identify and evaluate options (crunching whatever numbers may be appropriate), and perhaps prepare a preliminary set of recommended actions for consideration. The organization leader then usually meets with key subordinates and personally presides over extended discussions of the proposed responses, trying to build a quick consensus among members of the executive inner circle. If no consensus emerges and action is required immediately, the burden falls on the manager in charge to choose the response and urge its support.

When the situation allows managers to proceed more deliberately in deciding when to make changes and what changes to make, most managers seem to prefer a process of incrementally solidifying commitment to a particular course of action.[39] The process that managers go through in deciding on corrective adjustments is essentially the same for both proactive and reactive changes: they sense needs, gather information, broaden and deepen their understanding of the situation, develop options and explore their pros and cons, put forth action proposals, generate partial (comfort-level) solutions, strive for a consensus, and finally formally adopt an agreed-on course of action.[40] The time frame for deciding what corrective changes to initiate can take a few hours, a few days, a few weeks, or even a few months if the situation is particularly complicated.

Success in initiating corrective actions usually hinges on thorough analysis of the situation, the exercise of good business judgment in deciding what actions to take, and good implementation of the corrective actions that are initiated. Successful managers are skilled in getting an organization back on track rather quickly; they (and their staffs) are good at discerning what actions to take and in ramroding them through to a successful conclusion. Managers who struggle to show measurable progress in generating good results and improving the performance of strategy-critical value chain activities are candidates for being replaced.

The challenges of leading a successful strategy execution effort are, without question, substantial.[41] But the job is definitely doable. Because each instance of executing strategy occurs under different organizational circumstances, the managerial agenda for executing strategy always needs to be situation-specific—there's no neat generic procedure to follow. And, as we said at the beginning of Chapter 8, executing strategy is an action-oriented, make-the-right-things-happen task that challenges a manager's ability to lead and direct organizational change, create or reinvent business processes, manage and motivate people, and achieve performance targets. If you now better understand what the challenges are, what approaches are available, which issues need to be considered, and why the action agenda for implementing and executing strategy sweeps across so many aspects of administrative and managerial work, then we will look on our discussion in Chapters 8 and 9 as a success.

A Final Word on Managing the Process of Crafting and Executing Strategy   In practice, it is hard to separate the leadership requirements of executing strategy from the other pieces of the strategy process. As we emphasized in Chapter 1, the job of crafting, implementing, and executing strategy is a five-task process with much looping and recycling to fine-tune and adjust strategic visions, objectives, strategies, capabilities, implementation approaches, and cultures to fit one another and to fit changing circumstances. The process is continuous, and the conceptually separate acts of crafting and executing strategy blur together in real-world situations. The best tests of good strategic leadership are whether the company has a good strategy and whether the strategy execution effort is delivering the intended results. If these two conditions exist, the chances are excellent that the company has good strategic leadership.

Key Points

Managers implementing and executing a new or different strategy must identify the resource requirements of each new strategic initiative and then consider whether the current pattern of resource allocation and the budgets of the various subunits are suitable.

Anytime a company alters its strategy, managers should review existing policies and operating procedures, proactively revise or discard those that are out of sync, and formulate new ones to facilitate execution of new strategic initiatives. Prescribing new or freshly revised policies and operating procedures aids the task of strategy execution (1) by providing top-down guidance to operating managers, supervisory personnel, and employees regarding how certain things need to be done and what the boundaries are on independent actions and decisions; (2) by enforcing consistency in how particular strategy-critical activities are performed in geographically scattered operating units; and (3) by promoting the creation of a work climate and corporate culture that fosters good strategy execution.

Competent strategy execution entails visible, unyielding managerial commitment to best practices and continuous improvement. Benchmarking, the discovery and adoption of best practices, reengineering core business processes, and continuous improvement initiatives like total quality management (TQM) or Six Sigma programs all aim at improved efficiency, lower costs, better product quality, and greater customer satisfaction. *These initiatives are important tools for learning how to execute a strategy more proficiently.*

Company strategies can't be implemented or executed well without a number of support systems to carry on business operations. Well-conceived state-of-the-art support systems can not only facilitate better strategy execution but also strengthen organizational capabilities enough to provide a competitive edge over rivals.

Strategy-supportive motivational practices and reward systems are powerful management tools for gaining employee commitment. The key to creating a reward system that promotes good strategy execution is to make strategically relevant measures of performance *the dominating basis* for designing incentives, evaluating individual and group efforts, and handing out rewards. Positive motivational practices generally work better than negative ones, but there is a place for both. There's also a place for both monetary and nonmonetary incentives.

Successful managers do several things in leading the drive for good strategy execution and operating excellence. First, they stay on top of things. They keep a finger on the organization's pulse by spending considerable time outside their offices, listening and talking to organization members, coaching, cheerleading, and picking up important information. Second, they are active and visible in putting constructive pressure on the organization to achieve good results and operating excellence. This entails (1) promoting an esprit de corps that mobilizes and energizes organization members to execute strategy in a competent fashion and deliver the targeted results and (2) championing innovative ideas for improvement and promoting the use of best practices and benchmarking to measure the progress being made in performing value chain activities in first-rate fashion. Third, wise leaders exert their clout in developing competencies and competitive capabilities that enable better execution. Fourth, they serve as a role model in displaying high ethical standards, and they insist that company personnel conduct the company's business ethically and in a socially responsible manner. They demonstrate unequivocal and visible commitment to the ethics enforcement process. Fifth and finally, when a company's strategy execution effort is not delivering good results and the organization is not making measurable progress toward operating excellence, it is the leader's responsibility to step forward and push corrective actions.

Exercises

1. Go to www.google.com and, using the advanced search feature, enter "best practices." Browse through the search results to identify at least five organizations that have gathered a set of best practices and are making the best-practice library they have assembled available to members. Explore at least one of the sites to get an idea of the kind of best-practice information that is available.

2. Using the Internet search engine at www.google.com, do a search on "Six Sigma" quality programs. Browse through the search results and (a) identify several companies that offer Six Sigma training and (b) find lists of companies that have implemented Six Sigma programs in their pursuit of operational excellence. In particular, you should go to www.isixsigma.com and explore the "Six Sigma Q&A" menu option.

3. Using the Internet search engine at www.google.com, do a search on "total quality management." Browse through the search results and (a) identify companies

that offer TQM training, (b) identify some books on TQM programs, and (c) find lists of companies that have implemented TQM programs in their pursuit of operational excellence.

4. Consult the most recent issue of *Fortune* containing the annual "100 Best Companies to Work For" list (usually a late-January or early-February issue). Identify at least 5 (preferably 10) compensation incentives that these companies use to enhance employee motivation and reward employees for good strategic and financial performance.

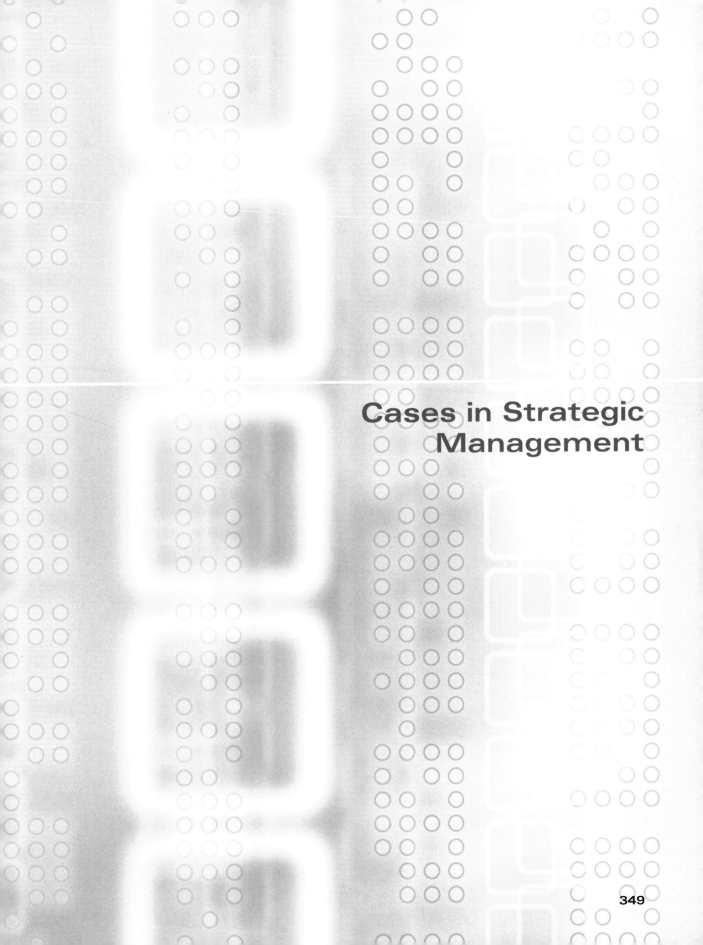

Cases in Strategic
Management

Whole Foods Market in 2005
Mission, Core Values, and Strategy

Arthur A. Thompson
The University of Alabama

Founded in 1980 as a local supermarket for natural and health foods in Austin, Texas, Whole Foods Market had by 2005 evolved into the world's largest retail chain of natural and organic foods supermarkets. The company had 163 stores in the United States, Canada, and Great Britain and 2004 sales of $3.9 billion; revenues had grown at a compound annual rate of 20 percent since 1998. John Mackey, the company's cofounder and CEO, believed that Whole Foods' rapid growth and market success had much to do with its having "remained a uniquely mission-driven company—highly selective about what we sell, dedicated to our core values and stringent quality standards and committed to sustainable agriculture." The company's stated mission was to promote vitality and well-being for all individuals by offering "the highest quality, least processed, most flavorful and naturally preserved foods." But as the company's motto "Whole Foods, Whole People, Whole Planet" implied, its core mission extended well beyond food retailing—see Exhibit 1.

John Mackey's vision was for Whole Foods to become not only a national brand synonymous with natural and organic foods but also the best food retailer in every community it served. In pursuit of this vision, the company's strategic plan aimed at expanding its retail operations to offer the highest-quality and most-nutritious foods to more and more customers and promoting organically grown foods, food safety concern, and sustainability of the entire ecosystem. During its 24-year history, Whole Foods Market had been a leader in the natural and organic foods movement across the United States, helping the industry gain acceptance among growing numbers of consumers. The company's long-term objectives were to have 400 stores and sales of $10 billion by 2010.

The Natural and Organic Foods Industry

The combined sales of natural and organic foods—about $43 billion in 2003—represented 5.5 percent of the roughly $775 billion in total U.S. grocery store sales. *Natural foods* are defined as foods that are minimally processed; largely or completely free of artificial ingredients, preservatives, and other non–naturally occurring chemicals; and as near to their whole, natural state as possible. The U.S. Department of Agriculture's Food and Safety Inspection Service defines *natural food* as "a product containing no artificial ingredient or added color and that is minimally processed." Sales of natural

Exhibit 1   **WHOLE FOODS MARKET'S MOTTO: WHOLE FOODS, WHOLE PEOPLE, WHOLE PLANET**

Whole Foods

We obtain our products locally and from all over the world, often from small, uniquely dedicated food artisans. We strive to offer the highest quality, least processed, most flavorful and naturally preserved foods. Why? Because food in its purest state—unadulterated by artificial additives, sweeteners, colorings and preservatives—is the best tasting and most nutritious food available.

Whole People

We recruit the best people we can to become part of our team. We empower them to make their own decisions, creating a respectful workplace where people are treated fairly and are highly motivated to succeed. We look for people who are passionate about food. Our team members are also well-rounded human beings. They play a critical role in helping build the store into a profitable and beneficial part of its community.

Whole Planet

We believe companies, like individuals, must assume their share of responsibility as tenants of Planet Earth. On a global basis we actively support organic farming—the best method for promoting sustainable agriculture and protecting the environment and the farm workers. On a local basis, we are actively involved in our communities by supporting food banks, sponsoring neighborhood events, compensating our team members for community service work, and contributing at least five percent of total net profits to not-for-profit organizations.

Source: www.wholefoodsmarket.com, November 24, 2004.

foods products had increased at double-digit rates in the 1990s, but growth was running in the single digits in 2001–2004.

Organic foods included fresh fruits and vegetables, meats, and processed foods that had been produced using:

1. Agricultural management practices that promoted a healthy and renewable ecosystem that used no genetically engineered seeds or crops; sewage sludge; or longlasting pesticides, herbicides, or fungicides.

2. Livestock management practices that involved organically grown feed, fresh air, and outdoor access for the animals, and no use of antibiotics or growth hormones.

3. Food processing practices that protected the integrity of the organic product and did not involve the use of radiation, genetically modified organisms, or synthetic preservatives.

In 1990, passage of the Organic Food Production Act started the process of establishing national standards for organically grown products in the United States, a movement that included farmers, food activists, conventional food producers, and consumer groups. In October 2002, the U.S. Department of Agriculture (USDA) officially established labeling standards for organic products, overriding both the patchwork of inconsistent state regulations for what could be labeled as organic and the different rules of some 43 agencies for certifying organic products. The new USDA regulations established four categories of food with organic ingredients, with varying levels of organic purity:

1. *100 percent organic products:* Such products were usually whole foods, such as fresh fruits and vegetables, grown by organic methods—which meant that the

product had been grown without the use of synthetic pesticides or sewage-based fertilizers; had not been subjected to irradiation; and had not been genetically modified or injected with bioengineered organisms, growth hormones, or antibiotics. Products that were 100 percent organic could carry the green USDA organic certification seal, provided the merchant could document that the food product had been organically grown (usually by a certified organic producer).

2. *Organic products:* Such products, often processed, had to have at least 95 percent organically certified ingredients. These could also carry the green USDA organic certification seal.

3. *Made with organic ingredients:* Such products had to have at least 70 percent organic ingredients; they could be labeled "made with organic ingredients" but could not display the USDA seal.

4. *All other products with organic ingredients:* Products with less than 70 percent organic ingredients could not use the word *organic* on the front of a package, but organic ingredients could be listed among other ingredients in a less prominent part of the package.

An official with the National Organic Program, commenting on the appropriateness and need for the new USDA regulations, said, "For the first time, when consumers see the word *organic* on a package, it will have consistent meaning."[1] The new labeling program was not intended as a health or safety program (organic products have not been shown to be more nutritious than conventionally grown products, according to the American Dietetic Association), but rather as a marketing solution. An organic label has long been a selling point for shoppers wanting to avoid pesticides or to support environmentally friendly agricultural practices. However, the new regulations required additional documentation on the part of growers, processors, exporters, importers, shippers, and merchants to verify that they were certified to grow, process, or handle organic products carrying the USDA's organic seal. In 2003, Whole Foods was designated as the first national "Certified Organic" grocer by Quality Assurance International, a federally recognized independent third-party certification organization.

The Organic Trade Association estimated that U.S. sales of organic food products hit $10 billion in 2003, up from $1 billion in 1990, and would reach $30 billion in 2007.[2] In 2004, organic products were sold in about 14,500 natural foods stores in the United States and close to 75 percent of the nation's conventional grocery stores.

According to the USDA, 2000 was the first year in which more organic food was sold in conventional U.S. supermarkets than in the nation's 14,500 natural foods stores. In the past several years, most mainstream supermarkets had been expanding their selections of natural and organic products, which ranged from potato chips to fresh produce to wines, cereals, pastas, cheeses, yogurt, vinegars, beef, chicken, and canned and frozen fruits and vegetables. Fresh produce was the most popular organic product—lettuces, broccoli, cauliflower, celery, carrots, and apples were the biggest sellers. Meat, dairy, and convenience foods were among the fastest-growing organic product categories. Most supermarket chains stocked a selection of natural and organic food items, and both the number and variety of items they carried were growing. Leading supermarket chains like Wal-Mart, Kroger, Publix, Safeway, and Albertson's had created special "health food" sections for nonperishable natural foods and organics in most of their stores as of 2004. Kroger had reopened several of its supermarkets as Fresh Fare stores, offering shoppers items such as sushi, gourmet takeout food, organic produce, and an extensive selection of fine wines and cheeses; there were 20 Fresh Fare stores in California operating under the Ralph's name, and the Fresh Fare concept was being

Exhibit 2   THE 12 LARGEST NORTH AMERICAN SUPERMARKET CHAINS, 2003–2004

Company	Number of Stores	2003 Sales Revenues (in billions)	Share of Total U.S. Grocery Sales ($775 billion)
Wal-Mart Supercenters	1,470	$103.2	13.3%
Kroger	2,519	53.6	6.9
Albertson's	2,541	36.2	4.7
Safeway	1,702	33.6	4.3
Costco Wholesale	420	25.0	3.2
Ahold USA	1,600	23.2	3.0
Sam's Clubs	538	20.4	2.6
Supervalu	1,451	20.3	2.6
Publix Super Markets	806	16.7	2.2
Loblaw	1,031	16.2	n.a.[*]
Delhaize (Food Lion, Kash 'n Karry, Hannaford Bros.)	1,499	15.4	2.0
Winn-Dixie	1,076	11.9	1.5

[*]n.a. = not applicable. Loblaw is a Canadian chain, and market shares are based on U.S. supermarket sales.
Source: www.supermarketnews.com, November 24, 2004.

tested in five Michigan locations. A Kroger official indicated that Fresh Fare was not aimed at the customer who shopped exclusively at upscale natural foods chains like Whole Foods, but rather the customers who already shopped Kroger but might travel to Whole Foods for things like vegetables, meats, and prepared foods. Two chains—upscale Harris Teeter in the southeastern United States and Whole Foods Market—had launched their own private-label brands of organics. Most industry observers expected that, as demand for natural and organic foods expanded, conventional supermarkets would continue to expand their offerings and selection. Exhibit 2 shows 2003–2004 data for the 12 largest supermarket retailers in the United States and Canada.

Leading food processors were showing greater interest in organics as well. Heinz had recently introduced an organic ketchup and owned a 19 percent stake in Hain Celestial Group, one of the largest organic and natural foods producers. Campbell Soup had introduced organic tomato juice. Starbucks, Green Mountain Coffee, and several other premium coffee marketers were marketing organically grown coffees; Odwalla juices were organic; and Tyson Foods and several other chicken producers had introduced organic chicken products. Producers of organically grown beef were selling all they could produce, and sales were expected to grow 30 percent annually through 2008. Safeway, Publix, and Kroger were stocking organic beef and chicken in a number of their stores. Whole Foods was struggling to find organic beef and chicken suppliers big enough to supply all its stores. Lite House organic salad dressings had recently been added to the shelves of several mainstream supermarkets. Major food-processing companies like Kraft, General Mills, Groupe Danone (the parent of Dannon Yogurt), Dean Foods, and Kellogg had all purchased organic food producers in an effort to capitalize on sales-growth opportunities for healthy foods that taste good. Most observers saw the trend toward organics as in its infancy, believing that organic products had staying power in the marketplace and were not a fad marching by in the night.

Organic farmland in the United States was estimated at 2.4 million acres. An estimated 14,000 mostly small-scale farmers were growing organic products in 2004. The amount of certified organic cropland doubled between 1997 and 2001, and livestock pastures increased at an even faster rate. However, less than 1 percent of U.S. farmland was certified organic in 2004. The Rodale Institute, a Pennsylvania-based advocate of organic farming, had set a goal of 100,000 certified organic U.S. farmers by 2013, a number equal to 5 percent of the 2 million U.S. farmers.[3]

Several factors had combined to transform natural foods retailing, once a niche market, into the fastest-growing segment of U.S. food sales:

■ Healthier eating patterns on the part of a populace that was becoming better educated about foods, nutrition, and good eating habits. Among those most interested in organic products were aging affluent people concerned about health and better-for-you foods.

■ Increasing consumer concerns over the purity and safety of food due to the presence of pesticide residues, growth hormones, artificial ingredients and other chemicals, and genetically engineered ingredients.

■ Environmental concerns due to the degradation of water and soil quality.

■ A "wellness," or health-consciousness, trend among people of many ages and ethnic groups.

An August 2004 report by Mintel indicated that 10 percent of consumers purchased organic products frequently enough to be "organically obsessed" and another 34 percent purchased them "at least occasionally." All age groups were at least as likely to buy organics in 2004 as they were in 2002, but the largest increases were among young adults, ages 18 to 24 (49 percent versus 34 percent in 2002), and 55- to 64-year-olds (45 percent, up from 25 percent in 2002).[4] A 2004 survey commissioned by Whole Foods found that 27 percent of Americans were eating more organic products than in 2003, that 54 percent had tried organic foods and beverages, and that nearly 1 in 10 used organic products regularly or several times per week.[5] The higher prices of organic products were the primary barrier for most consumers in trying or using organic products—73 percent of those participating in the Whole Foods survey believed organics were too expensive.

Whole Foods Market

Whole Foods Market was founded in Austin, Texas, when John Mackey, the current CEO, and two other local natural foods grocers in Austin decided the natural foods industry was ready for a supermarket format. The original Whole Foods Market opened in 1980 with a staff of only 19. It was an immediate success. At the time, there were fewer than half a dozen natural foods supermarkets in the United States. By 1991, the company had 10 stores, revenues of $92.5 million, and net income of $1.6 million. Whole Foods became a public company in 1992, with its stock trading on the Nasdaq; Whole Foods stock was added to the S&P Mid-Cap 400 Index in May 2002 and to the Nasdaq-100 Index in December 2002.

Core Values

In 1997, when Whole Foods developed the "Whole Foods, Whole People, Whole Planet" slogan, John Mackey, known as a go-getter with a "cowboy way of doing things," said:

This slogan taps into perhaps the deepest purpose of Whole Foods Market. It's a purpose we seldom talk about because it seems pretentious, but a purpose nevertheless felt by many of our team members and by many of our customers (and hopefully many of our shareholders too). Our deepest purpose as an organization is helping support the health, well-being, and healing of both people (customers and Team Members) and of the planet (sustainable agriculture, organic production and environmental sensitivity). When I peel away the onion of my personal consciousness down to its core in trying to understand what has driven me to create and grow this company, I come to my desire to promote the general well-being of everyone on earth as well as the earth itself. This is my personal greater purpose with the company and the slogan perfectly reflects it.

Complementing the slogan were five core values shared by both top management and company personnel (see Exhibit 3). In the company's 2003 annual report, John Mackey said:

Our core values reflect the sense of collective fate among our stakeholders and are the soul of our company. Our Team Members, shareholders, vendors, community and environment must flourish together through their affiliation with us or we are not succeeding as a business. It is leadership's role to balance the needs and desires of all our stakeholders and increase the productivity of Whole Foods Market. By growing the collective pie, we create larger slices for all of our shareholders.

Growth Strategy

Whole Foods' growth strategy was to expand via a combination of opening its own new store and acquiring existing stores. About 40 percent of the company's store base had come from acquisitions; since 1991, the company had acquired 67 stores through 14 acquisitions (see Exhibit 4). Since the natural foods industry was highly fragmented, consisting of close to 20,000 mostly one-store operations and small and regional chains, Whole Foods' management planned to continue to pursue acquisitions of smaller chains that provided access to desirable locations and markets as well as to experienced team members. However, in the years ahead the company expected to grow more by opening new stores than by acquiring existing stores, chiefly because there were very few natural foods competitors that had stores of the size that Whole Foods was opening.

Store Sizes and Locations

The company's 163 stores had an open format and generated average annual sales of $25 million. Stores opened in fiscal 2004 had average weekly sales of $575,000, close to $30 million annually. Stores more than eight years old averaged about 28,000 square feet, stores less than eight years old averaged about 36,000 square feet, and the company's newest stores ranged between 25,000 and 80,000 square feet (the new stores of supermarket chains like Safeway and Kroger averaged around 55,000 square feet). The three Harry's Farmers Market stores in Atlanta that Whole Foods acquired in 2001 were 75,000–80,000-square-foot stores. Whole Foods' newly opened 58,000-square-foot store on Columbus Circle in New York City was the largest grocery in Manhattan. Whole Foods had a new 62,500-square-foot store in Princeton, New Jersey; a 62,200-square-foot store in Plano, Texas; a 56,000-square-foot store in Bellevue, Washington;

Exhibit 3   WHOLE FOODS MARKET'S CORE VALUES

Our Core Values

The following list of core values reflects what is truly important to us as an organization. These are not values that change from time to time, situation to situation or person to person, but rather they are the underpinning of our company culture. Many people feel Whole Foods is an exciting company of which to be a part and a very special place to work. These core values are the primary reasons for this feeling, and they transcend our size and our growth rate. By maintaining these core values, regardless of how large a company Whole Foods becomes, we can preserve what has always been special about our company. These core values are the soul of our company.

Selling the Highest Quality Natural and Organic Products Available

■ **Passion for Food**
We appreciate and celebrate the difference natural and organic products can make in the quality of one's life.

■ **Quality Standards**
We have high standards and our goal is to sell the highest quality products we possibly can. We define quality by evaluating the ingredients, freshness, safety, taste, nutritive value and appearance of all of the products we carry. We are buying agents for our customers and not the selling agents for the manufacturers.

Satisfying and Delighting Our Customers

■ **Our Customers**
They are our most important stakeholders in our business and the lifeblood of our business. Only by satisfying our customers first do we have the opportunity to satisfy the needs of our other stakeholders.

■ **Extraordinary Customer Service**
We go to extraordinary lengths to satisfy and delight our customers. We want to meet or exceed their expectations on every shopping trip. We know that by doing so we turn customers into advocates for our business. Advocates do more than shop with us, they talk about Whole Foods to their friends and others. We want to serve our customers competently, efficiently, knowledgeably and with flair.

■ **Education**
We can generate greater appreciation and loyalty from all of our stakeholders by educating them about natural and organic foods, health, nutrition and the environment.

■ **Meaningful Value**
We offer value to our customers by providing them with high quality products, extraordinary service and a competitive price. We are constantly challenged to improve the value proposition to our customers.

■ **Retail Innovation**
We value retail experiments. Friendly competition within the company helps us to continually improve our stores. We constantly innovate and raise our retail standards and are not afraid to try new ideas and concepts.

■ **Inviting Store Environments**
We create store environments that are inviting and fun, and reflect the communities they serve. We want our stores to become community meeting places where our customers meet their friends and make new ones.

Team Member Happiness and Excellence

■ **Empowering Work Environments**
Our success is dependent upon the collective energy and intelligence of all of our Team Members. We strive to create a work environment where motivated Team Members can flourish and succeed to their highest potential. We appreciate effort and reward results.

■ **Self-Responsibility**
We take responsibility for our own success and failures. We celebrate success and see failures as opportunities for growth. We recognize that we are responsible for our own happiness and success.

■ **Self-Directed Teams**
The fundamental work unit of the company is the self-directed Team. Teams meet regularly to discuss issues, solve problems and appreciate each others' contributions. Every Team Member belongs to a Team.

■ **Open & Timely Information**
We believe knowledge is power and we support our Team Members' right to access information that impacts their jobs. Our books are open to our Team Members, including our annual individual compensation report. We also recognize everyone's right to be listened to and heard regardless of their point of view.

(continues)

Exhibit 3   (continued)

Team Member Happiness and Excellence   (continued)

- **Incremental Progress**
  Our company continually improves through unleashing the collective creativity and intelligence of all of our Team Members. We recognize that everyone has a contribution to make. We keep getting better at what we do.
- **Shared Fate**
  We recognize there is a community of interest among all of our stakeholders. There are no entitlements; we share together in our collective fate. To that end we have a salary cap that limits the compensation (wages plus profit incentive bonuses) of any Team Member to ten times the average total compensation of all full-time Team Members in the company.

Creating Wealth Through Profits & Growth

- **Stewardship**
  We are stewards of our shareholders' investments and we take that responsibility very seriously. We are committed to increasing long term shareholder value.
- **Profits**
  We earn our profits everyday through voluntary exchange with our customers. We recognize that profits are essential to creating capital for growth, prosperity, opportunity, job satisfaction and job security.

Caring About Our Communities & Our Environment

- **Sustainable Agriculture**
  We support organic farmers, growers and the environment through our commitment to sustainable agriculture and by expanding the market for organic products.
- **Wise Environmental Practices**
  We respect our environment and recycle, reuse, and reduce our waste wherever and whenever we can.
- **Community Citizenship**
  We recognize our responsibility to be active participants in our local communities. We give a minimum of 5% of our profits every year to a wide variety of community and non-profit organizations. In addition, we pay our Team Members to give of their time to community and service organizations.
- **Integrity in All Business Dealings**
  Our trade partners are our allies in serving our stakeholders. We treat them with respect, fairness and integrity at all times and expect the same in return.

Source: www.wholefoodsmarket.com, accessed November 26, 2004.

a 53,000-square-foot store in Torrance, California; and a flagship 80,000-square-foot store in Austin, Texas. In 2004, 92 of the company's 163 stores were 30,000 square feet or larger. It was the company's practice each year to relocate some of its smaller stores to larger sites with improved visibility and parking. Exhibit 5 provides store-related statistics.

Whole Foods sought to locate its new stores in the upscale areas of urban metropolitan centers—88 percent of the U.S. stores were in the top 50 statistical metropolitan areas. In 2004, Whole Foods had stores in 25 states and 33 of the top 50 U.S. metropolitan areas. The company entered Toronto, Canada, in 2002 and expanded into London and Bristol, England, in 2004. In November 2004, the company had 53 stores in varying stages of development, averaging 49,000 square feet. The company expected to open 3 stores before the end of 2004, giving it a total of 166 stores going into 2005.

Most stores were in high-traffic shopping locations, some were freestanding, and some were in strip centers. Whole Foods had its own internally developed model to analyze potential markets according to education levels, population density, and income. After picking a target metropolitan area, the company's site consultant did a comprehensive

Exhibit 4   MAJOR ACQUISITIONS BY WHOLE FOODS MARKET

Year	Company Acquired	Location	Number of Stores	Acquisition Costs
1992	Bread & Circus	Northeast United States	6	$20 million plus $6.2 million in common stock
1993	Mrs. Gooch's	Southern California	7	2,970,596 shares of common stock
1996	Fresh Fields Markets	East Coast and Chicago area	22	4.8 million shares of stock plus options for 549,000 additional shares
1997	Merchant of Vino	Detroit area	6	Approximately 1 million shares of common stock
1997	Bread of Life	South Florida	2	200,000 shares of common stock
1999	Nature's Heartland	Boston area	4	$24.5 million in cash
2000	Food 4 Thought (Natural Abilities, Inc.)	Sonoma County, CA	3	$25.7 million in cash, plus assumption of certain liabilities
2001	Harry's Farmer's Market	Atlanta	3	Approximately $35 million in cash
2004	Fresh & Wild	Great Britain	7	$20 million in cash plus 239,000 shares of common stock

Source: Investor relations section of www.wholefoodsmarket.com, accessed November 18, 2004.

site study and developed sales projections; potential sites had to pass certain financial hurdles. New stores opened 12 to 24 months after a lease was signed.

The cash investment needed to ready a new Whole Foods Market for opening varied with the metropolitan area, site characteristics, store size, and amount of work performed by the landlord; totals ranged from as little as $2 million to as much as $16 million—the average for the past five years was $8.6 million. In addition to the cost of readying a store for operation, it took approximately $750,000 to stock the store with inventory, a portion of which was financed by vendors. Preopening expenses had averaged approximately $600,000 per store over the past five years.

Product Line

Whole Foods' product line included roughly 26,000 food and nonfood items that appealed to both natural foods and gourmet shoppers:

- Fresh produce—fruits; vegetables; displays of fresh-cut fruits; and a selection of seasonal, exotic, and specialty products like cactus pears and cippolini onions.
- Meat and poultry—natural meat, turkey, and chicken products from animals raised on wholesome grains, pastureland, and well water (and not grown with the use of by-products, hormones, or steroids). There were 20 varieties of house-made sausages.
- Fresh seafood—a selection of fresh fish; shrimp; oysters; clams; mussels; homemade marinades; and exotic items like octopus, sushi, and black-tip shark. A portion of the fresh fish selections at the seafood station came from the company's Pigeon Cove and Select Fish seafood processing subsidiaries. Seafood items coming from distant supply sources were flown in to stores to ensure maximum freshness.

Exhibit 5   NUMBER OF STORES IN THE WHOLE FOODS MARKETS CHAIN, 1991–2004, AND SELECTED STORE OPERATING STATISTICS, 2000–2004

Year	Number of Stores at End of Fiscal Year	Year	Number of Stores at End of Fiscal Year
1991	10	1998	87
1992	25	1999	100
1993	42	2000	117
1994	49	2001	126
1995	61	2002	135
1996	68	2003	145
1997	75	2004	163

Store Counts	1997	1998	1999	2000	2001	2002	2003	2004
Beginning of fiscal year	68	75	87	100	117	126	135	145
New stores opened	7	9	9	17	12	11	12	12
Stores acquired	2	6	5	3	0	3	0	7
Relocations and closures	(2)	(3)	(1)	(3)	(3)	(5)	(2)	(1)
End of fiscal year	75	87	100	117	126	135	145	163

	Fiscal Year				
	2000	2001	2002	2003	2004
Store sales (000s)	$1,838,630	$2,272,231	$2,690,475	$3,148,593	$3,864,950
Average weekly sales	$324,710	$353,024	$392,837	$424,095	$482,061
Comparable store sales growth	8.6%	9.2%	10.0%	8.6%	14.9%
Total square footage of all stores, end of year	3,180,207	3,598,469	4,098,492	4,545,433	5,145,261
Average store size, end of year, in square feet	27,181	28,559	30,359	31,348	31,566
Gross margin, all-store average	34.5%	34.8%	34.7%	34.3%	34.8%
Store contribution, all-store average*	9.4%	9.5%	9.6%	9.2%	9.3%

*Defined as gross profit minus direct store expenses, where gross profit equals store revenues less cost of goods sold.
Source: Information posted at www.wholefoodsmarket.com, accessed November 18, 2004.

■ A selection of daily baked goods—breads, cakes, pies, cookies, bagels, muffins, and scones.

■ Prepared foods—soups, canned and packaged goods, oven-ready meals, rotisserie meats, hearth-fired pizza, pastas, pâtés, salad bars, a sandwich station, and a selection of entrées and side foods prepared daily.

■ A worldwide selection of cheeses.

- Frozen foods, juices, yogurt and dairy products, smoothies, and bottled waters.
- A wide selection of bulk items in bins.
- An olive bar (with as many as 24 varieties).
- A selection of chocolates.
- Beer and wine—a wide selection of domestic and imported wines (selections varied from store to store). Organic wines were among those available.
- A coffee and tea bar. The company had its own Allegro brand of specialty and organic coffees and several of the newer stores had in-store coffee-roasting equipment that allowed customers to order any of 20 varieties roasted while they shopped. The tea selections included environmentally correct, premium exotic teas from remote forests.
- A nutrition and body care department containing vitamin supplements, herbs and teas, homeopathic remedies, soaps, natural body care and cosmetics products, yoga supplies, and aromatherapy products. All of these products were proven safe using non–animal testing methods and contained no artificial ingredients.
- Pet products—natural pet foods (including the company's own private-label line), treats, toys, and pest control remedies.
- Grocery and household products—canned and packaged goods, pastas, soaps, cleaning products, and other conventional household items.
- A floral department with sophisticated flower bouquets.
- A 365 Every Day Value line of private-label products that included over 440 items at very competitive price points; a 365 Organic line consisting of 200 items, a 29-item Whole X line of best-of-class premium and superpremium organic products, and a 50-item organic food product line developed for children under the Whole Kids label.
- Educational products (information on alternative health care) and books relating to healing, cookery, diet, and lifestyle. In some stores, there were cooking classes and nutrition sessions.

Perishables accounted for about 65 percent of Whole Foods' sales, considerably higher than the 40–50 percent that perishables represented at conventional supermarkets. Management believed that the company's emphasis on fresh fruits and vegetables, bakery goods, meats, seafood, and other perishables differentiated Whole Foods stores from other supermarkets and attracted a broader customer base. According to John Mackey:

> First-time visitors to Whole Foods Market are often awed by our perishables. We devote more space to fresh fruits and vegetables, including an extensive selection of organics, than most of our competitors. Our meat and poultry products are natural—no artificial ingredients, minimal processing, and raised without the use of artificial growth hormones, antibiotics or animal by-products in their feed. Our seafood is either wild-caught or sourced from aquaculture farms where environmental concerns are a priority. Also, our seafood is never treated with chlorine or other chemicals, as is common practice in the food retailing industry. With each new store or renovation, we challenge ourselves to create more entertaining, theatrical, and scintillatingly appetizing prepared foods areas. We bake daily, using whole grains and unbleached, unbromated flour and feature European-style loaves, pastries, cookies and cakes as well as gluten-free baked goods for those

Exhibit 6   WHOLE FOODS MARKET'S PRODUCT QUALITY STANDARDS AND CUSTOMER COMMITMENTS

Our business is to sell the highest quality foods we can find at the most competitive prices possible. We evaluate quality in terms of nutrition, freshness, appearance, and taste. Our search for quality is a never-ending process involving the careful judgment of buyers throughout the company.

- We carefully evaluate each and every product we sell.
- We feature foods that are free from artificial preservatives, colors, flavors and sweeteners.
- We are passionate about great tasting food and the pleasure of sharing it with each other.
- We are committed to foods that are fresh, wholesome and safe to eat.
- We seek out and promote organically grown foods.
- We provide food and nutritional products that support health and well-being.

Source: 2003 10K Report, p.5 and www.wholefoodsmarket.com, accessed November 27, 2004.

allergic to wheat. We also offer many vegetarian and vegan products for our customers seeking to avoid all animal products. Our cheeses are free of artificial flavors, colors, and synthetic preservatives, and we offer an outstanding variety of both organic cheeses and cheeses made using traditional methods.[6]

One of Whole Foods Market's foremost commitments to its customers was to sell foods that met strict standards and that were of high quality in terms of nutrition, freshness, appearance, and taste. Whole Foods guaranteed 100 percent satisfaction on all items purchased and went to great lengths to live up to its core value of satisfying and delighting customers—see Exhibit 6 for the company's product quality standards. Whole Foods stores had recently broadened its lineup of conventional household products in order to make Whole Foods a one-stop grocery shopping destination where people could get everything on their shopping list. Management was considering whether to include organic clothing in the product offerings at its new flagship store in Austin.

According to one industry analyst, Whole Foods had "put together the ideal model for the foodie who's a premium gourmet and the natural foods buyer. When you walk into a Whole Foods store, you're overwhelmed by a desire to look at everything you see."[7] Because the costs of growing and marketing organic foods ran 25 to 75 percent more than conventionally grown items, prices at Whole Foods were higher than at conventional supermarkets. However, as one analyst noted, "If people believe that the food is healthier and they are doing something good for themselves, they are willing to invest a bit more, particularly as they get older. It's not a fad."[8] Another grocery industry analyst noted that while Whole Foods served a growing niche, it had managed to attract a new kind of customer, one who was willing to pay a premium to dabble in health food without being totally committed to vegetarianism or an organic lifestyle.[9]

Store Description and Merchandising

Whole Foods Market did not have a standard store design. Instead, each store's layout was customized to fit the particular site and building configuration and to best show off the particular product mix for the store's target clientele. Stores had a colorful decor, and products were attractively merchandised (see Exhibit 7). Most stores featured hand-stacked produce, in-store chefs and open kitchens, scratch bakeries, prepared foods stations, European-style charcuterie departments, sampling displays, and ever-changing selections and merchandise displays. Management believed that the extensive and

Exhibit 7   Scenes from Whole Foods Market Stores

attractive displays of fresh produce, seafood, baked goods, and prepared foods in its larger stores appealed to a broader customer base and were responsible for the larger stores showing higher performance than the smaller stores. The acquisition of the three 75,000-plus-square-foot Harry's Market superstores in Atlanta, at which 75 percent of sales were perishables, had provided the company with valuable intellectual capital in creatively merchandising all major perishables categories.

To further a sense of community and interaction with customers, stores typically included sit-down eating areas; customer comment boards; and Take Action centers for customers who wanted information on such topics as sustainable agriculture, organics, the sustainability of seafood supplies and over fishing problems, the environment, and similar issues. A few stores offered valet parking, home delivery, and massages. Management at Whole Foods wanted customers to view company stores as a "third place" (besides home and office) where people could gather, learn, and interact while at the same time enjoying an intriguing food-shopping and eating experience.

The driving concept of Whole Foods' merchandising strategy was to create an inviting and interactive store atmosphere that turned shopping for food into a fun, pleasurable experience. Management was continually experimenting with new merchandising concepts to keep stores fresh and exciting for customers. According to a Whole Foods regional manager, "We take the best ideas from each of our stores and try to incorporate them in all our other stores. We're constantly making our stores better."[10]

Whole Foods got very high marks from merchandising experts and customers for its presentation—from the bright colors of the produce displays, to the quality of the foods and customer service, to the wide aisles and cleanliness. Whole Foods' merchandising skills were said to be a prime factor in its success in luring shoppers back time and again. One retailing consultant said of Whole Foods' new store in Toronto, "The visual and sensory experience is superlative. Today, food is a way of defining who we are and Whole Foods has taken it up a notch."[11] In the Toronto store, biographies of farmers were suspended from the ceiling on placards; a list of Whole Foods' core values and commitments to product quality greeted customers entering the store; a board calling attention to Whole Foods' "Sustainable Seafood Policy" hung above the seafood station; and recipe cards were placed at the end of key aisles. The even newer Columbus Circle store in Manhattan had a 248-seat café where shoppers could enjoy restaurant-quality prepared foods while relaxing in a comfortable community setting; a Jamba Juice smoothie station that served freshly blended-to-order fruit smoothies and juices; a full-service sushi bar by Genji Express where customers sat on bar stools wrapped in Nori seaweed enjoying fresh-cut sushi wrapped in organic seaweed; a walk-in greenhouse showcasing fresh-cut and exotic flowers; a wine shop with more than 700 varieties of wine from both large and small vineyards and family estates; and a chocolate enrobing station in the bakery where customers could request just about anything covered in chocolate.

Marketing and Customer Service

Whole Foods spent less on advertising than did conventional supermarkets, relying primarily on word-of-mouth recommendations from customers. Stores spent most of their marketing budgets on in-store signage and store events such as taste fairs, classes, and product samplings. Store personnel were encouraged to extend company efforts to encourage the adoption of a natural and organic lifestyle by going out into the community and conducting a proactive public relations campaign. Each store also had a separate budget for making contributions to philanthropic activities and community outreach programs. At the corporate level, there was a marketing initiative under way to create greater public awareness of the Whole Foods brand.

Since one of its core values was to satisfy and delight customers (see again Exhibit 3), Whole Foods Market strove to meet or exceed customer expectations on every shopping trip. Competent, knowledgeable, and friendly service was a hallmark of shopping at a Whole Foods Market. The aim was to turn highly satisfied customers into advocates for Whole Foods who talked to close friends and acquaintances about their positive experiences with the company. Store personnel were personable and chatty with shoppers. Customers could get personal attention in every department of the store. When customers asked where an item was located, team members often took them to the spot, making conversation along the way and offering to answer any questions. Team members were quite knowledgeable and enthusiastic about the products in their particular department and tried to take advantage of opportunities to inform and educate customers about natural foods, organics, healthy eating, and food-related environmental issues. They took pride in helping customers navigate the extensive variety to make the best choices. Meat department personnel provided customers with custom cuts, cooking instructions, and personal recommendations.

Store Operations

Depending on store size and traffic volume, Whole Foods stores employed between 70 and 400 team members, who were organized into up to 11 teams, each led by a team leader. Each team within a store was responsible for a different product category or aspect of store operations such as customer service and customer check-out stations. Whole Foods practiced a decentralized team approach to store operations, with many personnel, merchandising, and operating decisions made by teams at the individual store level. Management believed that the decentralized structure made it critical to have an effective store team leader. The store team leader worked with one or more associate store team leaders, as well as with all the department team leaders, to operate the store as efficiently and profitably as possible. Store team leaders were paid a salary plus a bonus based on the store's economic value added (EVA) contribution; they were also eligible to receive stock options.[12] Store team leaders reported directly to one of 10 regional presidents.

Management believed its team members were inspired by the company's mission because it complemented their own views about the benefits of a natural and organic foods diet. In management's view, many Whole Foods team members felt good about their jobs because they saw themselves as contributing to the welfare of society and to the company's customers by selling clean and nutritious foods, by helping advance the cause of long-term sustainable agriculture methods, and by promoting a healthy, pesticide-free environment.

In November 2004, the company had some 27,000 team members, of which approximately 90 percent were full-time. None were represented by unions, although there had been a couple of unionization attempts. John Mackey was viewed as fiercely anti-union and had once said: "The union is like having herpes. It doesn't kill you, but it's unpleasant and inconvenient and it stops a lot of people from becoming your lover."[13] Union leaders were critical of the company's anti-union stance and a Web site, www.wholeworkersunite.org, was devoted to criticizing Mackey, explaining why unionization was good for Whole Foods employees, and compiling instances of the company's anti-union actions. A second Web site, www.michaelbluejay.com, featured postings of "scandals" at Whole Foods.

Whole Foods had been ranked by *Fortune* magazine for seven consecutive years (1998–2004) as one of the top 100 companies to work for in America—Whole Foods was the only national supermarket retailer on the list and one of only 24 companies to make the list every year since its inception. (In scoring companies, *Fortune* places two-thirds weight on responses to a random survey of employees and one-third on its evaluation of a company's benefits and practices.) A team member at Whole Foods' store in Austin, Texas, said, "I really feel like we're a part of making the world a better place. When I joined the company 17 years ago, we only had four stores. I have always loved—as a customer and now as a Team Member—the camaraderie, support for others, and progressive atmosphere at Whole Foods Market."[14] According to the company's vice president of human resources, "Team members who love to take initiative, while enjoying working as part of a team and being rewarded through shared fate, thrive here."

During 2002, team members across the company actively contributed ideas about the benefits they would like the company to offer; the suggestions were compiled and, through three subsequent votes, put into package form. The benefits plan that was adopted for three years was approved by 83 percent of the 79 percent of the team members participating in the benefits vote. Under the adopted plan, each team member could select his or her own benefits package. The resulting health insurance plan that the company put in place in January 2003 involved the company paying 100 percent of the premium for full-time employees and the establishment of company-funded "personal wellness accounts," which team members could use to pay the higher deductibles; any unused balances in a team member's account could roll over and accumulate for future expenses. Whole Foods expected to repeat its benefits vote every three years.

Every year, management gave team members an opportunity to complete a morale survey covering job satisfaction, opportunity and empowerment, pay, training, and benefits. In 2003, the participation rate was 71 percent, higher than any prior year. Of those responding, 86 percent said they almost always or frequently enjoyed their job (up from 82 percent in 2002) and 81 percent said they almost always or frequently felt empowered to do their best work at Whole Foods (up from 80 percent in 2002).

Compensation and Incentives

Whole Foods' management strove to create a "shared-fate consciousness" on the part of team members by uniting the self-interests of team members with those of shareholders. One way management reinforced this concept was through a gain-sharing program that rewarded a store's team members according to their store's contribution to operating profit (store sales less cost of goods sold less store operating expenses)—gain-sharing distributions added 5–7 percent to team member wages. The company also encouraged stock ownership on the part of team members through three other programs:

1. *A team member stock option plan*—Team members were eligible for stock options based on seniority, promotion, or the discretion of regional or national executives. Roughly 85 percent of the company's stock options in 2004 were held by non-executives.

2. *A team member stock purchase plan*—Team members could purchase a restricted number of shares at a discount from the market price through payroll deductions.

3. *A team member 401(k) plan*—Whole Foods Market stock was one of the investment options in the 401(k) plan.

Whole Foods also had a salary cap that limited the compensation (wages plus profit incentive bonuses) of any team member to 10 times the average total compensation of all full-time team members in the company—a policy mandated in the company's core values (see Exhibit 3).

The Use of Economic Value Added

In 1999, Whole Foods adopted an economic value added (EVA) management and incentive system. EVA is defined as net operating profits after taxes minus a charge for the cost of capital necessary to generate that profit; EVA at the store level was based on store contribution (store revenues minus cost of goods sold minus store operating expenses) relative to store investment over and above the cost of capital—average store contribution percentages are shown in Exhibit 5. Senior executives managed the company with the goal of *improving* EVA at the store level and companywide; they believed that an EVA-based bonus system was the best financial framework for team members to use in helping make decisions that created sustainable shareholder value. The teams in all stores were challenged to find ways to boost store contribution and EVA—the team member bonuses paid on EVA improvement averaged 6 percent in 2003.

In 2004, over 500 senior executives, regional managers, and the store leaders were on EVA-based incentive compensation plans. The primary measure for payout was EVA improvement. In fiscal year 2001, the company's overall EVA was a negative $30.4 million, but companywide EVA was $2.6 million in fiscal 2003 and rose to a record $15.6 million in fiscal 2004.

In addition, management used EVA calculations to determine whether the sales and profit projections for new stores would yield a positive and large enough EVA to justify the investment; EVA was also used to guide decisions on store closings and to evaluate new acquisitions.

Purchasing and Distribution

Whole Foods' buyers purchased most of the items retailed in the company's stores from local, regional, and national wholesale suppliers and vendors. In recent years, the company had shifted much of the buying responsibility from the store level to the regional and national levels in order to put the company in a better position to negotiate volume discounts with major vendors and distributors. Whole Foods Market was the largest account for many suppliers of natural and organic foods. United Natural Foods was the company's biggest supplier, accounting for about 18 percent of Whole Foods' purchases in fiscal 2003 and 2004.

Whole Foods owned two produce procurement centers and procured and distributed the majority of its produce itself. However, where feasible, local store personnel sourced produce items from local organic farmers as part of the company's commitment to promote and support organic farming methods. Two subsidiaries, the Pigeon Cove seafood process facility in Massachusetts and Select Fish, a West Coast seafood processing facility, supplied a portion of the company's seafood requirements. A regional seafood distribution facility had recently been established in Atlanta.

The company operated eight regional distribution centers to supply its stores. The largest distribution center in Austin supplied a full range of natural products to the company's stores in Texas, Louisiana, Colorado, Kansas, and New Mexico; the other seven regional centers distributed mainly produce and private-label goods to area stores. Twelve regional bake houses and five regional commissary kitchens supplied area stores with various prepared foods. A central coffee roasting operation supplied stores with the company's Allegro brand of coffees.

Community Citizenship and Social Activism

Whole Foods demonstrated its social conscience and community citizenship in two ways: (1) by donating at least 5 percent of its after-tax profits in cash or products to nonprofit or educational organizations and (2) by giving each team member 20 hours of paid community service hours to use for volunteer work for every 2,000 hours worked. Team members at every store were heavily involved in such community citizenship activities as sponsoring blood donation drives, preparing meals for seniors and the homeless, holding fund-raisers to help the disadvantaged, growing vegetables for a domestic violence shelter, participating in housing renovation projects, and working as delivery people for Meals on Wheels.

Further, John Mackey indicated the company was sincere in living up to its core values as they related to healthy eating habits and protection of ecosystems. In an effort to "walk the talk," Mackey had initiated the gathering of information about key issues that could affect people's health and well-being—the genetic engineering of food supplies, food irradiation practices, and the organic standards process; Whole Foods disseminated this information via in-store brochures, presentations to groups, and postings on its Web site. Mackey had also charged company personnel with developing position statements on sustainable seafood practices (see Exhibit 8), the merits of organic farming, and wise environmental practices. Whole Foods regularly publicized its position statements in its stores and on its Web site, along with the company's commitment to selling only those meats that had been raised without the use of growth hormones, antibiotics, and animal by-products. Company personnel were conscientious in identifying and implementing "green" actions on Whole Foods' part that enhanced the health of the planet's ecosystems. The company's Web site had a "legislative action center" that alerted people to pending legislation on these types of issues and made it easy for them to send their comments and opinions to legislators and government officials.

In 2004, *Business Ethics* named Whole Foods to its "100 Best Corporate Citizens" list.

Whole Foods' Financial Performance

From 1991 to 2004, Whole Foods Market's net income rose at a compound average rate of 40.8 percent. The company had been profitable every year since 1991, when it became a public company, except one. The company's net loss of $4.8 million in 2000 was partly attributable to management's decision to dispose of the company's NatureSmart business, which manufactured and sold (via direct marketing) nutritional supplements; the assets of NatureSmart were written down by $24 million in 2000 to reflect the realizable value of the business, which subsequently was sold for $28 million in May 2001. Also in 2000, Whole Foods incurred a $14 million loss in two affiliated dot-com enterprises (Gaiam.com and WholePeople.com) in which it owned a minority interest. Since 2000, the company had generated sufficient cash flows internally to fund its growth and reduce its long-term debt—long-term debt had dropped from $306 million in 2000 to about $165 million as of October 2004.

The company paid its first quarterly dividend of $0.15 per share in January 2004; the quarterly dividend was increased to $0.19 per share effective in January 2005. Exhibits 9 and 10 present the company's recent statements of operations and consolidated balance sheets.

Exhibit 8   WHOLE FOODS' POSITION ON SEAFOOD SUSTAINABILITY

The simple fact is our oceans are soon to be in trouble. Our world's fish stocks are disappearing from our seas because they have been overfished or harvested using damaging fishing practices. To keep our favorite seafood plentiful for us to enjoy and to keep it around for future generations, we must act now.

As a shopper, you have the power to turn the tide. When you purchase seafood from fisheries using ocean-friendly methods, you reward their actions and encourage other fisheries to operate responsibly.

At Whole Foods Market, we demonstrate our long-term commitment to seafood preservation by:

- Supporting fishing practices that ensure the ecological health of the ocean and the abundance of marine life.
- Partnering with groups who encourage responsible practices and provide the public with accurate information about the issue.
- Operating our own well-managed seafood facility and processing plant, Pigeon Cove Seafood, located in Gloucester, Massachusetts.
- Helping educate our customers on the importance of practices that can make a difference now and well into the future.
- Promoting and selling the products of well-managed fisheries.

Source: www.wholefoodsmarket.com, accessed November 26, 2004.

Exhibit 9   WHOLE FOODS MARKET, STATEMENT OF OPERATIONS, FISCAL YEARS 2002–2004 (in thousands)

	Fiscal Year 2004	Fiscal Year 2003	Fiscal Year 2002
Sales	$3,864,950	$3,148,593	$2,690,475
Cost of goods sold and occupancy costs	2,521,611	2,067,939	1,757,213
Gross profit	1,343,339	1,080,654	933,262
Direct store expenses	983,765	792,536	675,760
Store contribution	359,574	288,118	257,502
General and administrative expenses	119,800	100,693	95,871
Pre-opening and relocation costs	10,459	12,091	12,485
Operating income	229,315	175,334	149,146
Interest expense, net	7,249	8,114	10,384
Investment and other income (loss)	6,456	5,593	2,056
Income before income taxes	228,522	172,813	140,818
Provision for income taxes	91,409	69,126	56,327
Net income	$ 137,113	$ 103,687	$ 84,491
Basic earnings per share	$2.24	$1.76	$1.50
Weighted average shares outstanding	61,324	59,035	56,385
Diluted earnings per share	$2.09	$1.66	$1.40
Weighted average shares outstanding, diluted basis	67,727	65,330	63,340

Source: Company press release, November 10, 2004, and 2004 10K report.

Exhibit 10   WHOLE FOODS MARKET, CONSOLIDATED BALANCE SHEET, FISCAL YEARS 2003–2004 (in thousands)

	September 26, 2004	September 26, 2003
Assets		
Current assets:		
Cash and cash equivalents	$ 198,377	$ 165,779
Restricted cash	23,160	—
Trade accounts receivable	64,972	45,947
Merchandise inventories	152,912	123,904
Prepaid expenses and other current assets	16,702	12,447
Deferred income taxes	28,294	15,607
Total current assets	485,017	363,684
Property and equipment, net of accumulated depreciation and amortization	877,457	718,240
Long-term investments	—	2,206
Goodwill	112,186	80,548
Intangible assets, net of accumulated amortization	24,831	26,569
Other assets	20,302	5,573
Total assets	$1,519,793	$1,196,820
Liabilities and Shareholders' Equity		
Current liabilities:		
Current installments of long-term debt and capital lease obligations	$ 5,719	5,806
Trade accounts payable	90,751	72,715
Accrued payroll, bonus and other employee benefits	100,536	70,875
Dividends payable	9,361	—
Other accrued expenses	124,641	90,188
Total current liabilities	331,008	239,584
Long-term debt and capital lease obligations, less current installments	165,024	162,909
Deferred rent liability	13,566	13,349
Other long-term liabilities	1,581	2,301
Deferred income taxes	20,175	2,501
Total liabilities	531,354	420,644
Shareholders' equity: common stock, no par value, 150,000 and 100,000 shares authorized; 57,988 and 55,114 shares issued; 57,739 and 54,770 shares outstanding	535,107	423,297
Accumulated other comprehensive income	2,053	1,624
Retained earnings	451,279	351,255
Total shareholders' equity	988,439	776,176
Total liabilities and shareholders' equity	$1,519,793	$1,196,820

Source: Company press release, November 10, 2004, and 2004 10K report.

Competitors

The food retailing business was intensely competitive. The degree of competition Whole Foods faced varied from locality to locality, and to some extent from store location to store location within a given locale. Competitors included local, regional, and national supermarkets, along with specialty grocery stores and health and natural foods stores. Most supermarkets had offered at least a limited selection of natural and organic foods, and some had chosen to expand their offerings aggressively. Whole Foods' management believed that it was to the company's benefit for conventional supermarkets to offer natural and organic foods, for two reasons: First, it helped fulfill the company's mission of improving the health and well-being of people and the planet and, second, it helped create new customers for Whole Foods by providing a gateway experience. Management contended that as more people were exposed to natural and organic products, they were more likely to become Whole Foods customers because Whole Foods was the category leader for natural and organic products and because Whole Foods offered the largest selection and most informed customer service at competitive prices.

Whole Foods Market's two biggest competitors in the natural foods and organics segment of the food retailing industry were Wild Oats Markets and Fresh Market. Another competitor with some overlap in products and shopping ambience was Trader Joe's. A small chain, Sunflower Markets, had recently entered the natural and organic foods market with a discount strategy.

Wild Oats Markets, Inc.

Wild Oats Markets, Inc.—a 108-store natural foods chain based in Boulder, Colorado—ranked second behind Whole Foods in the natural foods and organics segment. The company's stores were in 24 states and British Columbia, Canada; stores were operated under four names: Wild Oats Natural Marketplace, Henry's Marketplace, Sun Harvest, and Capers Community Markets. Founded in 1987, Wild Oats had sales of $969 million in 2003, up from $919 million in 2002; it was on track to achieve sales of just over $1 billion in 2004. In 1993 and 1994, Wild Oats was named one of the "500 Fastest-Growing Private Companies in America" by *Inc.* magazine. Interest quickly spread to Wall Street, and in 1996 Wild Oats became a public company traded on the Nasdaq under the symbol OATS. Grocery analysts believed that Wild Oats had close to a 3 percent market share of the natural and organic foods market in 2004, compared to about 12 percent for Whole Foods.

Wild Oats' CEO Perry Odak, formerly the CEO of Ben & Jerry's Homemade until it was acquired by Unilever in 2000, joined the company in 2001 and had launched a turnaround strategy, which was still in progress in 2004. The company's prior CEO and founder, Mike Gilliland, had gone on an aggressive acquisition streak during the late 1990s to expand Wild Oats' geographic coverage; store growth peaked in 1999 with the acquisition of 47 stores. But Gilliland's acquisition binge piled up extensive debt and dropped the company into a money-losing position with too many stores, a dozen different store names, and a dozen different ways of operating. Product selection and customer service were inconsistent from one location to another.

When Odak arrived in March 2001, he streamlined operations; closed 28 unprofitable stores; cut prices; trimmed store staffing by 100 employees; and launched a new, smaller prototype store with a heavier emphasis on fresh food. Merchandising and marketing were revamped. The strategy was to draw in more "crossover" shoppers with lower-priced produce, meat, and seafood, along with a Fresh Look program stressing freshness and affordability to increase store traffic and raise the average purchase above the current $19 level. While the lower prices cut into the company's gross profit margin, management had tried to restore margins by concentrating purchases with fewer vendors and getting better discounts. An agreement was reached in September 2002 for Wild Oats to obtain a substantial part of its store inventories from Tree of Life, one of the leading natural foods distributors. Another of Odak's strategic thrusts was to drive a customer service mind-set throughout the organization via training programs and enhanced employee communication. Odak wanted to position Wild Oats as a resource for value-added services and education about health and well-being. In 2002 Wild Oats sold close to 4.45 million shares at $11.50 to raise capital for opening 58 stores in the next three years (13 in 2003, 20 in 2004, and 25 in 2005) and remodeling a number of existing stores. While both Whole Foods and Wild Oats had stores in some of the same urban areas and were targeting some of the same areas for expansion, Wild Oats was targeting city and metropolitan neighborhoods for its new stores where there were no Whole Foods stores.

Wild Oats' new prototype stores were 22,000 to 24,000 square feet and featured a grocery-store layout in which produce, dairy, meat, seafood, and baked goods were around the perimeters of the store; an expanded produce section at the front of the store; a deli; a sushi bar; a juice-and-java bar; a reduced selection of canned and packaged items; and store-within-a-store sections for supplements and specialty personal care products. So far in 2004, Wild Oats had completed the remodeling of six stores (as part of its overall store remodeling initiative begun in 2003); it opened 12 new stores in 2004 and was planning to open 15 stores in 2005—both new store numbers were below the original target set when new shareholder capital had been raised in 2002.

As was the case at Whole Foods, Perry Odak believed that while conventional supermarkets would continue to expand their offerings of natural and organic products, the competitive threat posed by conventional supermarkets was only moderate because their selection was more limited than what Wild Oats stores offered and because they lacked the knowledge and high level of service provided by a natural foods supermarket. In his view, "they are introducing conventional shoppers to natural brands, which will benefit us in the long run."

Wild Oats' sales in 2004 were adversely affected by conventional grocers' overly aggressive promotional activity in Southern California and by intense competition in Texas. This competition resulted in negative comparable store sales throughout the third quarter in approximately one-third of the company's store base. As a result, comparable store customer traffic in the third quarter of 2004 was a negative 4.1 percent. Wild Oats' management took "aggressive action" in the form of lower prices and additional promotions to rebuild its customer traffic and sales in regions affected by intense competitive activity. But despite all of the moves that had been made under Perry Odak's leadership, the company was still struggling. After reporting losses of $15.0 million in 2000 before Odak became CEO, Wild Oats recorded a loss of $43.9 million in 2001, net income of $6.9 million in 2002, net income of $3.6 million in 2003, and an expected loss of $3.7 to $4.8 million in 2004. Gross margins (sales minus cost of goods sold) at Wild Oats averaged about 28 percent in 2002–2004 versus 35 percent at Whole Foods.

Odak's latest initiatives to improve Wild Oats' performance were to offer Wild Oats–branded products in other retail environments. The company had reached agreement to test two alternative retail concepts. The first—a test in the Chicago market with Peapod, the country's leading Internet grocer—began in October 2004 and involved offering more than 200 private-label products on the Peapod site to consumers in the greater Chicago metropolitan area. The second, to begin by mid-2005, was a three-to-five store test of a Wild Oats–branded store-within-a-store concept with Stop & Shop, the largest food retailer in the northeastern United States. In a June 2004 financial move, Wild Oats sold $100 million in 3.25 percent convertible debentures to private investors; the debentures were convertible into Wild Oats common stock, at the option of the holders, at an initial price of $17.70 per share and could be redeemed starting in May 2011. Management intended to use proceeds of the offering to accelerate its growth plans, fund the repurchase of $25 million in common stock, and finance other "general corporate purposes."

Fresh Market

Fresh Market, headquartered in Greensboro, North Carolina, was a 44-store chain operating in seven southeastern states (Florida, Georgia, North Carolina, South Carolina, Tennessee, Virginia, and Kentucky).[15] The company was founded by Ray Berry, a former vice president with Southland Corporation who had responsibility over some 3,600 7-Eleven stores. The first Fresh Market store opened in 1982 in Greensboro. Berry borrowed ideas from stores he had seen all over the United States and, as the chain expanded, used his convenience-store experience to replicate the store format and shape the product lines. During the 1982–2000 period, Fresh Market's sales revenues grew at a 25.2 percent compound rate, reaching $193 million in 2000; revenues were an estimated $280 million in 2004. Fresh Market's goal was to be the food destination store for people who enjoy cooking and good eating. The company was founded on the premise of getting customers to return again and again by offering quality products at reasonable prices and providing top-notch customer service.

Fresh Market's product line included meats, seafood, fresh produce, fresh baked goods, prepared foods, 40 varieties of coffees, a selection of grocery and dairy items, bulk products, cheeses and deli meats, wine and beer, and floral and gift items. Fresh Market stores averaged 18,000 square feet and were located in neighborhoods near educated, high-income residents. Fresh Market differentiated itself with "upscale grocery boutique" items such as free-range chicken, pick-and-pack spices, gourmet coffees, chocolates, hard-to-get H&H bagels from New York City, Ferrara's New York cheesecake, fresh Orsini parmesan cheese, Acqua della Madonna bottled water, and an extended selection of olive oils, mustards, bulk products (granolas, nuts, beans, dried fruits, spices, and snack mixes), wine, and beer. Stores also stocked a small assortment of floral items and gifts (cookbooks, gift cards, baskets, cutting boards, and gift baskets) and a bare lineup of general grocery products. None of the meats and seafood and few of the deli products were prepackaged, and each department had at least one employee in the area constantly to help shoppers—the idea was to force interaction between store employees and shoppers. Fresh Market's warm lights, classical background music, and terra-cotta-colored tiles made it a cozier place to shop than a typical grocery store. From time to time, stores had cooking classes, wine tastings, and food sampling events. Fresh Market sponsored an annual fund-raiser for the Juvenile Diabetes Research Foundation called the Root Beer Float. The average store had 75 employees, resulting in labor costs about double those of typical supermarkets.

Merchandisers at Fresh Market's headquarters selected the stores' products, but store managers placed orders directly from third-party distributors. According to Berry, Fresh Market didn't have the concentration of stores that would make running its own warehouses profitable; Berry believed some grocers' distribution operations had grown so big that they drove the retail business, rather than the other way around.

Since 2000, the company had opened three to four new stores each year. Expansion was funded by internal cash flows and bank debt. Financial data were not available because the company was privately owned, but Fresh Market's profitability was believed to be above the industry average. Several public companies had shown interest in buying the chain. In 2001 Ray Berry, then age 60, had said, "If I can get what I think the company's worth three years from now, I'll sell it. But I won't sell it for what it's worth today because I'm having too much fun."

Trader Joe's

Based in Pasadena, California, Trader Joe's was a specialty supermarket chain with over 200 stores in Arizona, California, Connecticut, Delaware, Illinois, Indiana, Maryland, Massachusetts, Michigan, Missouri, Nevada, New Jersey, New Mexico, New York, Ohio, Oregon, Pennsylvania, Virginia, and Washington. Management described the company's mission and business as follows:

> At Trader Joe's, our mission is to bring our customers the best food and beverage values and the information to make informed buying decisions. There are more than 2,000 unique grocery items in our label, all at honest everyday low prices. We work hard at buying things right: Our buyers travel the world searching for new items and we work with a variety of suppliers who make interesting products for us, many of them exclusive to Trader Joe's. All our private label products have their own "angle," i.e., vegetarian, Kosher, organic or just plain decadent, and all have minimally processed ingredients.
>
> Customers tell us, "I never knew food shopping could be so much fun!" Some even call us "The home of cheap thrills!" We like to be part of our neighborhoods and get to know our customers. And where else do you shop that even the CEO, Dan Bane, wears a loud Hawaiian shirt.
>
> Our tasting panel tastes every product before we buy it. If we don't like it, we don't buy it. If customers don't like it, they can bring it back for a no-hassle refund.
>
> We stick to the business we know: good food at the best prices! Whenever possible we buy direct from our suppliers, in large volume. We bargain hard and manage our costs carefully. We pay in cash, and on time, so our suppliers like to do business with us.
>
> Trader Joe's Crew Members are friendly, knowledgeable and happy to see their customers. They taste our items too, so they can discuss them with their customers. All our stores regularly cook up new and interesting products for our customers to sample.

Plans called for ongoing development and introduction of new, one-of-a-kind food items at value prices, and continued expansion of store locations across the country.

Prices and product offerings varied somewhat by region and state. Customers could choose from a variety of baked goods, organic foods, fresh fruits and vegetables, imported and domestic cheeses, gourmet chocolates and candies, coffees, fresh salads, meatless entrées and other vegan products, low-fat and low-carbohydrate foods, frozen fish and seafood, heat-and-serve entrées, packaged meats, juices, wine and beer, snack foods, energy bars, vitamins, nuts and trail mixes, and whatever other exotic items the company's buyers had come upon. About 10–15 new, seasonal, or one-time-buy items were introduced each week. Products that weren't selling well were dropped. Trader Joe's had recently worked with its vendors to remove genetically modified ingredients from all of its private-label products. It had also discontinued sale of duck meat because of the cruel conditions under which ducks were grown.

Stores were open, with wide aisles, appealing displays, cedar plank walls, a nautical decor, and crew members wearing colorful Hawaiian shirts. Because of its combination of low prices, emporium-like atmosphere, intriguing selections, and friendly service, customers viewed shopping at Trader Joe's as an enjoyable experience. The company was able to keep the prices of its unique products attractively low (relative to those at Whole Foods, Fresh Market, and Wild Oats) partly because its buyers were always on the lookout for exotic items they could buy at a discount (all products had to pass a taste test and a cost test) and partly because most items were sold under the Trader Joe's label.

Sunflower Markets

Sunflower Markets, out to establish a discount niche in organic and natural foods, entered the market in 2003 with four stores—two in Phoenix, one in Albuquerque, and one in Denver.[16] As of November 2004 the company had opened three additional stores in Arizona and one in Colorado. Based in Longmont, Colorado, Sunflower borrowed parts of its strategy from concepts employed by Trader Joe's and small farmer's-market-type stores. The company's mission statement described its four-pronged strategic approach:

- **We Will Always Offer the Best Quality Food at the Lowest Prices in Town.** "Better-than-supermarket quality at better-than-supermarket prices" is our motto.
- **We Keep Our Overhead Low.** No fancy fixtures or high rent. No corporate headquarters . . . just regular people, like you, looking for the best deals we can find.
- **We Buy Big.** We source directly, we pay our vendors quickly and we buy almost everything by the pallet or truckload. That buying power means big savings for you!
- **We Keep It Simple.** We don't charge our vendors "slotting allowances" or shelf space fees. Just honest-to-goodness negotiating for the lowest possible price and we pass the savings on to you.

The company's tag line was "Serious Food . . . Silly Prices." According to founding partner Mark Gilliland, "The last thing we want to be is another wanna-be Whole Foods." Gilliland was formerly the founder and president of Wild Oats but was forced out when his aggressive expansion strategy put Wild Oats in a financial bind.

Each Sunflower Market had a warehouse-like atmosphere, with no customer service except for check-out personnel. Stores featured many one-of-a-kind items purchased in large lots from brokers. Pallets of goods were placed wherever there was floor space available.

Independent Natural and Health Food Grocers

In 2004 there were approximately 14,000 small, independent retailers of natural and organic foods, vitamins/supplements, and beauty and personal care products in the United States. Most were single-store, owner-managed enterprises. Combined sales of the 14,000 independents were in the $15 billion range in 2004. Two other vitamin/supplement chains, General Nutrition and Vitamin World, dominated the vitamin/supplement segment with about 7,500 store locations. Most of the independent stores had less than 2,500 square feet of retail sales space and generated revenues of less than $1 million annually, but there were roughly 1,000 natural foods and organic retailers with stores in the size range of 4,000 to 12,000 square feet and sales of between $2 million and $5 million annually.

Product lines and range of selection at the stores of independent natural and health foods retailers varied from narrow to moderately broad, depending on a store's market focus and the shopper traffic it was able to generate. Inventories at stores under 1,000 square feet could run as little as $10,000, while those at stores of 10,000 square feet or more might run $400,000. Many of the independents had some sort of deli or beverage bar, and some even had a small dine-in area with a limited health food menu. Revenues and customer traffic at most independent stores were trending upward, reflecting growing buyer interest in natural and organic products.

Endnotes

[1]As quoted in Elizabeth Lee, "National Standards Now Define Organic Food," *Atlanta Journal and Constitution,* October 21, 2002.

[2]Organic Trade Association, "Industry Statistics and Projected Growth," www.ota.com, accessed November 19, 2004.

[3]Press release May 22, 2003, accessed at www.newfarm.org November 24, 2004.

[4]Cited in the Trendspotting section of *Natural Foods Buyer,* Fall 2004, accessed November 26, 2004 at www.newhope.com.

[5]Company press release, October 21, 2004.

[6]Letter to Shareholders, 2003 annual report.

[7]As quoted in Marilyn Much, "Whole Foods Markets: Austin, Texas Green Grocer Relishes Atypical Sales," *Investors Business Daily,* September 10, 2002.

[8]Hollie Shaw, "Retail-Savvy Whole Foods Opens in Canada," *National Post,* May 1, 2002, p. FP9.

[9]See Karin Schill Rives, "Texas-Based Whole Foods Market Makes Changes to Cary, N.C. Grocery Store," *The News and Observer,* March 7, 2002.

[10]As quoted in "Whole Foods Market to Open in Albuquerque, N.M.," *The Santa Fe New Mexican,* September 10, 2002.

[11]As quoted in "Produce That's Picture Perfect," *National Post,* May 9, 2002, p. AL6.

[12]EVA at the store level was based on store contribution (store revenues minus cost of goods sold minus store operating expenses) relative to store investment over and above the cost of capital.

[13]As quoted in John K. Wilson, "Going Whole Hog with Whole Foods," Bankrate.com, posted December 23, 1999. Mackey made the statement in 1991 when efforts were being made to unionize the company's store in Berkeley, California.

[14]Company press release, January 21, 2003.

[15]Much of the information in this section is based on M. E. Lloyd, "Specialty-Grocer Fresh Market Cultivates Upscale Consumers, Reaps Big Returns," *The Wall Street Journal,* February 20, 2001, p. B11b, and information posted at www.freshmarket.com, accessed November 29, 2004.

[16]This section is based on information posted at www.sunflowermarkets.com and in Joe Lewandowski, "Naturals Stores Freshen Their Strategies," *Natural Foods Merchandiser,* January 1, 2004, accessed November 19, 2004, at www.naturalfoodsmerchandiser.com.

Starbucks in 2004
Driving for Global Dominance

Arthur A. Thompson
The University of Alabama

Amit J. Shah
Frostburg State University

Thomas F. Hawk
Frostburg State University

In early 2004 Howard Schultz, Starbucks' founder and chairman of the board, could look with satisfaction on the company's phenomenal growth and market success. Since 1987, Starbucks had transformed itself from a modest nine-store operation in the Pacific Northwest into a powerhouse multinational enterprise with 7,225 store locations, including some 1,600 stores in 30 foreign countries (see Exhibit 1). During Starbucks' early years, when coffee was a 50-cent morning habit at local diners and fast-food establishments, skeptics had ridiculed the notion of $3 coffee as a yuppie fad. But the popularity of Starbucks' Italian-style coffees, espresso beverages, teas, pastries, and confections had made Starbucks one of the great retailing stories of recent history and the world's biggest specialty coffee chain. In 2003, Starbucks made the Fortune 500, prompting Schultz to remark, "It would be arrogant to sit here and say that 10 years ago we thought we would be on the Fortune 500. But we dreamed from day one and we dreamed big."[1]

Having not only positioned Starbucks as the dominant retailer, roaster, and brand of specialty coffees and coffee drinks in North America but also spawned the creation of the specialty coffee industry, top management's strategic intent was now to establish Starbucks as the most recognized and respected brand in the world. Management expected to have 15,000 Starbucks stores by year-end 2005 and 25,000 locations by 2013. In 2003, new stores were being opened at the rate of three a day. Starbucks reported revenues in 2003 of $4.1 billion, up 128 percent from $1.8 billion in fiscal 2000 ending September 30; after-tax profits in 2003 were $268.3 million, an increase of 184 percent from net earnings of $94.6 million in 2000.

Company Background

Starbucks got its start in 1971 when three academics, English teacher Jerry Baldwin, history teacher Zev Siegel, and writer Gordon Bowker—all coffee aficionados—opened Starbucks Coffee, Tea, and Spice in Seattle's touristy Pikes Place Market. The three partners shared a love for fine coffees and exotic teas and believed they could build a clientele in Seattle that would appreciate the best coffees and teas, much like the customer group that had already emerged in the San Francisco Bay area. Baldwin, Siegel, and Bowker each invested $1,350 and borrowed another $5,000 from a bank to open the

Exhibit 1   NUMBER OF STARBUCKS STORE LOCATIONS, 1987–2003

Year	Number of Store Locations	Year	Number of Store Locations
1987	17	1996	1,015
1988	33	1997	1,412
1989	55	1998	1,886
1990	84	1999	2,135
1991	116	2000	3,501
1992	165	2001	4,709
1993	272	2002	5,886
1994	425	2003	7,225
1995	676		

LICENSED LOCATIONS OF STARBUCKS STORES OUTSIDE THE CONTINENTAL UNITED STATES, 2003

Asia-Pacific		Europe–Middle East–Africa		Americas	
Japan	486	Saudi Arabia	29	Canada	53
China	116	United Arab Emirates	27	Hawaii	38
Taiwan	113	Germany	25	Mexico	17
South Korea	75	Kuwait	20	Puerto Rico	3
Philippines	54	Spain	15	Chile	3
Malaysia	37	Switzerland	15	Peru	1
New Zealand	35	Greece	12		
Singapore	35	Lebanon	9		
Indonesia	17	Austria	8		
		Qatar	5		
		Bahrain	4		
		Turkey	4		
		Oman	3		
Total	968		176		113

Source: Company records and reports.

Pikes Place store. The inspiration and mentor for the Starbucks venture in Seattle was a Dutch immigrant named Alfred Peet, who had opened Peet's Coffee and Tea, in Berkeley, California, in 1966. Peet's store specialized in importing fine coffees and teas and dark-roasting its own beans the European way to bring out the full flavors. Customers were encouraged to learn how to grind the beans and make their own freshly brewed coffee at home. Baldwin, Siegel, and Bowker were well acquainted with Peet's expertise, having visited his store on numerous occasions and listened to him expound on quality coffees and the importance of proper bean-roasting techniques.

The Pikes Place store featured modest, hand-built classic nautical fixtures. One wall was devoted to whole-bean coffees, while another had shelves of coffee products. The store did not offer fresh-brewed coffee sold by the cup, but tasting samples were sometimes available. Initially, Siegel was the only paid employee. He wore a grocer's apron, scooped out beans for customers, extolled the virtues of fine, dark-roasted coffees, and functioned as the partnership's retail expert. The other two partners kept their day jobs but came by at lunch or after work to help out. During the start-up period, Baldwin kept the books and developed a growing knowledge of coffee; Bowker served as the "magic, mystery, and romance man."[2] The store was an immediate success, with sales exceeding expectations, partly because of interest stirred by a favorable article in the *Seattle Times*. For most of the first year, Starbucks ordered its coffee beans from Peet's, but then the partners purchased a used roaster from Holland, set up roasting operations in a nearby ramshackle building, and came up with their own blends and flavors.

By the early 1980s, the company had four Starbucks stores in the Seattle area and had been profitable every year since opening its doors. But then Zev Siegel experienced burnout and left the company to pursue other interests. Jerry Baldwin took over day-to-day management of the company and functioned as chief executive officer; Gordon Bowker remained involved as an owner but devoted most of his time to his advertising and design firm, a weekly newspaper he had founded, and a microbrewery that he was launching known as the Redhook Ale Brewery.

Howard Schultz Enters the Picture

In 1981, Howard Schultz, vice president and general manager of U.S. operations for a Swedish maker of stylish kitchen equipment and coffeemakers, decided to pay Starbucks a visit—he was curious about why Starbucks was selling so many of his company's products. The morning after his arrival in Seattle, he was escorted to the Pikes Place store by Linda Grossman, the retail merchandising manager for Starbucks. A solo violinist was playing Mozart at the door, his violin case open for donations. Schultz was immediately taken by the powerful and pleasing aroma of the coffees, the wall displaying coffee beans, and the rows of coffeemakers on the shelves. As he talked with the clerk behind the counter, the clerk scooped out some Sumatran coffee beans, ground them, put the grounds in a cone filter, poured hot water over the cone, and shortly handed Schultz a porcelain mug filled with freshly brewed coffee. After taking only three sips of the brew, Schultz was hooked. He began asking the clerk and Grossman questions about the company, about coffees from different parts of the world, and about the different ways of roasting coffee.

A bit later, he was introduced to Jerry Baldwin and Gordon Bowker, whose offices overlooked the company's coffee-roasting operation. Schultz was struck by their knowledge about coffee, their commitment to providing customers with quality coffees, and their passion for educating customers about the merits of dark-roasted coffees. Baldwin told Schultz, "We don't manage the business to maximize anything other than the quality of the coffee."[3] The company purchased only the finest arabica coffees and put them through a meticulous dark-roasting process to bring out their full flavors. Baldwin explained that the cheap robusta coffees used in supermarket blends burned when subjected to dark roasting. He also noted that the makers of supermarket blends preferred lighter roasts because it allowed higher yields (the longer a coffee was roasted, the more weight it lost).

Schultz was also struck by the business philosophy of the two partners. It was clear that Starbucks stood not just for good coffee but also for the dark-roasted flavor profiles that the founders were passionate about. Top quality, fresh-roasted, whole-bean coffee was the company's differentiating feature and a bedrock value. It was also clear to Schultz that Starbucks was strongly committed to educating its customers to appreciate the qualities of fine coffees. The company depended mainly on word of mouth to get more people into its stores, then built customer loyalty cup by cup as buyers gained a sense of discovery and excitement about the taste of fine coffee.

On his trip back to New York the next day, Howard Schultz could not stop thinking about Starbucks and what it would be like to be a part of the Starbucks enterprise. Schultz recalled, "There was something magic about it, a passion and authenticity I had never experienced in business."[4] The appeal of living in the Seattle area was another strong plus. By the time he landed at Kennedy Airport, he knew in his heart he wanted to go to work for Starbucks. At the first opportunity, Schultz asked Baldwin whether there was any way he could fit into Starbucks. Although the two had established an easy, comfortable personal rapport, it still took a year, numerous meetings at which Schultz presented his ideas, and a lot of convincing to get Baldwin, Bowker, and their silent partner from San Francisco to agree to hire him. Schultz pursued a job at Starbucks far more vigorously than Starbucks pursued hiring Schultz. There was some nervousness about bringing in an outsider, especially a high-powered New Yorker who had not grown up with the values of the company. Nonetheless, Schultz continued to press his ideas about the tremendous potential of expanding the Starbucks enterprise outside Seattle and exposing people all over America to Starbucks coffee. Schultz argued that there had to be more than just the few thousand coffee lovers in Seattle who would enjoy the company's products.

At a meeting with the three owners in San Francisco in the spring of 1982, Schultz once again presented his ideas and vision for opening Starbucks stores across the United States and Canada. He thought the meeting went well and flew back to New York thinking a job offer was in the bag. However, the next day Jerry Baldwin called Schultz and indicated that the owners had decided against hiring him because geographic expansion was too risky and they did not share Schultz's vision for Starbucks. Schultz was despondent, seeing his dreams of being a part of Starbucks' future go up in smoke. Still, he believed so deeply in Starbucks' potential that he decided to make a last ditch appeal; he called Baldwin back the next day and made an impassioned, reasoned case for why the decision was a mistake. Baldwin agreed to reconsider. The next morning Baldwin called Schultz and told him the job of heading marketing and overseeing the retail stores was his. In September 1982, Schultz took over his new responsibilities at Starbucks.

Starbucks and Howard Schultz: The 1982–1985 Period

In his first few months at Starbucks, Howard Schultz spent most of his waking hours in the four Seattle stores—working behind the counters, tasting different kinds of coffee, talking with customers, getting to know store personnel, and learning the retail aspects of the coffee business. By December, Jerry Baldwin concluded that Schultz was ready for the final part of his training, that of actually roasting the coffee. Schultz spent a week getting an education about the colors of different coffee beans, listening for the telltale second pop of the beans during the roasting process, learning to taste the subtle differences among Jerry Baldwin and Gordon Bowker's various roasts, and familiarizing himself with the roasting techniques for different beans.

Schultz made a point of acclimating himself to the informal dress code at Starbucks, gaining credibility and building trust with colleagues, and making the transition from the high-energy, coat-and-tie style of New York to the more casual, low-key ambience of the Pacific Northwest (see Exhibit 2 for a rundown on Howard Schultz's background). Schultz made real headway in gaining the acceptance and respect of company personnel while working at the Pike Place store one day during the busy Christmas season that first year. The store was packed and Schultz was behind the

Exhibit 2   BIOGRAPHICAL SKETCH OF HOWARD SCHULTZ

- Schultz's parents both came from working-class families residing in Brooklyn, New York, for two generations. Neither completed high school.
- Schultz grew up in a government-subsidized housing project in Brooklyn, was the oldest of three children, played sports with the neighborhood kids, developed a passion for baseball, and became a die-hard Yankees fan.
- Schultz's father was a blue-collar factory worker and taxicab driver who held many low-wage, no benefits jobs; his mother remained home to take care of the children during their preschool years, then worked as an office receptionist. The family was hard pressed to make ends meet.
- Schultz had a number of jobs as a teenager—paper route, counter job at luncheonette, an after-school job in the garment district in Manhattan, a summer job steaming yarn at a knit factory. He always gave part of his earnings to his mother to help with family expenses.
- He saw success in sports as his way to escape life in the projects; he played quarterback on the high school football team.
- He was offered a scholarship to play football at Northern Michigan University (the only offer he got) and took it. When his parents drove him to the campus to begin the fall term, it was his first trip outside New York. It turned out that he didn't have enough talent to play football, but he got loans and worked at several jobs to keep himself in school. He majored in communications, took a few business courses on the side, and graduated in 1975 with a B average—the first person in his family to graduate from college.
- He went to work for a ski lodge in Michigan after graduation, then left to go back to New York, landing a sales job at Xerox Corporation. He left Xerox to work for Swedish coffee-equipment maker Hammarplast, U.S.A., becoming vice president and general manager in charge of U.S. operations and managing 20 independent sales representatives.
- He married Sheri Kersch in July 1982; the couple had two children.
- His father contracted lung cancer in 1982 at age 60 and died in 1988, leaving his mother with no pension, no life insurance, and no savings.
- Schultz became a principal owner of Seattle SuperSonics NBA team in 2001; also a principal owner of Seattle Storm of WNBA.
- He owned about 16 million shares of Starbucks in early 2003 and had an estimated net worth of $700 million.

Source: Howard Schultz and Dori Jones Yang, *Pour Your Heart Into It* (New York: Hyperion, 1997).

counter ringing up sales of coffee when someone shouted that a shopper had just headed out the door with some stuff—two expensive coffeemakers it turned out, one in each hand. Without thinking, Schultz leaped over the counter and chased the thief up the cobblestone street outside the store, yelling, "Drop that stuff! Drop it!" The thief was startled enough to drop both pieces he had carried off and ran away. Howard picked up the merchandise and returned to the store, holding the coffeemakers up like trophies. Everyone applauded. When Schultz returned to his office later that afternoon, his staff had strung up a banner that read: "Make my day."[5]

Schultz was overflowing with ideas for the company. Early on, he noticed that first-time customers sometimes felt uneasy in the stores because of their lack of knowledge about fine coffees and because store employees sometimes came across as a little arrogant or superior to coffee novices. Schultz worked with store employees on customer-friendly sales skills and developed brochures that made it easy for customers to learn about fine coffees. However, Schultz's biggest inspiration and vision for Starbucks' future came during the spring of 1983 when the company sent him to Milan, Italy, to attend an international housewares show. While walking from his hotel to the convention center, Schultz spotted an espresso bar and went inside to look around. The cashier beside the door nodded and smiled. The barista behind the counter greeted Howard cheerfully and moved gracefully to pull a shot of espresso for one customer and handcraft a foamy cappuccino for another, all the while conversing merrily with those standing at the counter. Schultz thought the barista's performance was "great theater." Just down the way on a side street, he went in an even more crowded espresso bar where the barista, whom he surmised to be the owner, was greeting customers by name; people were laughing and talking in an atmosphere that plainly was comfortable and familiar. In the next few blocks, he saw two more espresso bars. That afternoon when the trade show concluded for the day, Schultz walked the streets of Milan to explore more espresso bars. Some were stylish and upscale; others attracted a blue-collar clientele. Most had few chairs, and it was common for Italian opera to be playing in the background. What struck Schultz was how popular and vibrant the Italian coffee bars were. Energy levels were typically high, and they seemed to function as an integral community gathering place. Each one had its own unique character, but they all had a barista who performed with flair and maintained a camaraderie with the customers.

Schultz remained in Milan for a week, exploring coffee bars and learning as much as he could about the Italian passion for coffee drinks. Schultz was particularly struck by the fact that there were 1,500 coffee bars in Milan, a city about the size of Philadelphia, and a total of 200,000 in all of Italy. In one bar, he heard a customer order a caffe latte and decided to try one himself—the barista made a shot of espresso, steamed a frothy pitcher of milk, poured the two together in a cup, and put a dollop of foam on the top. Schultz liked it immediately, concluding that lattes should be a feature item on any coffee bar menu even though none of the coffee experts he had talked to had ever mentioned them.

Schultz's 1983 trip to Milan produced a revelation: the Starbucks stores in Seattle completely missed the point. There was much more to the coffee business than just selling beans and getting people to appreciate grinding their own beans and brewing fine coffee in their homes. What Starbucks needed to do was serve fresh brewed coffee, espresso, and cappuccino in its stores (in addition to beans and coffee equipment) and try to create an American version of the Italian coffee bar culture. Going to Starbucks should be an experience, a special treat, a place to meet friends and visit. Re-creating the authentic Italian coffee bar culture in the United States could be Starbucks' differentiating factor.

Schultz Becomes Frustrated

On his return from Italy, Howard Schultz shared his revelation and ideas for modifying the format of Starbucks' stores with Jerry Baldwin and Gordon Bowker. But instead of winning their approval for trying out some of his ideas, Schultz encountered strong resistance. Baldwin and Bowker argued that Starbucks was a retailer, not a restaurant or coffee bar. They feared that serving drinks would put them in the beverage business and diminish the integrity of Starbucks' mission as a purveyor of fine coffees. They pointed out that Starbucks had been profitable every year and there was no reason to rock the boat in a small, private company like Starbucks. But a more pressing reason not to pursue Schultz's coffee bar concept emerged shortly—Baldwin and Bowker were excited by an opportunity to purchase Peet's Coffee and Tea. The acquisition was finalized in early 1984; to fund it, Starbucks had to take on considerable debt, leaving little in the way of financial flexibility to support Schultz's ideas for entering the beverage part of the coffee business or expanding the number of Starbucks stores.

For most of 1984, Starbucks managers were dividing their time between operations in Seattle and the Peet's enterprise in San Francisco. Schultz found himself in San Francisco every other week supervising the marketing and operations of the five Peet's stores. Starbucks employees began to feel neglected and, in one quarter, did not receive their usual bonus due to tight financial conditions. Employee discontent escalated to the point where a union election was called. The union won by three votes. Jerry Baldwin was shocked at the results, concluding that employees no longer trusted him. In the months that followed, he began to spend more of his energy on Peet's operation in San Francisco.

It took Howard Schultz nearly a year to convince Jerry Baldwin to let him test an espresso bar. Baldwin relented when Starbucks opened its sixth store in April 1984. It was the first of the company's stores designed to sell beverages, and it was the first one located in downtown Seattle. Schultz asked for a 1,500-square-foot space to set up a full-scale Italian-style espresso bar, but Baldwin agreed to allocating only 300 square feet in a corner of the new store. The store opened with no fanfare as a deliberate experiment. By closing time on the first day, some 400 customers had been served, well above the 250-customer average of Starbucks' best-performing stores. Within two months the store was serving 800 customers a day. The two baristas could not keep up with orders during the early-morning hours, resulting in lines outside the door onto the sidewalk. Most of the business was at the espresso counter, while sales at the regular retail counter were only adequate.

Schultz was elated at the test results, expecting that Baldwin's doubts about entering the beverage side of the business would be dispelled and that he would gain approval to pursue the opportunity to take Starbucks to a new level. Every day he went into Baldwin's office to show him the sales figures and customer counts at the new downtown store. But Baldwin was not comfortable with the success of the new store, believing that it felt wrong and that espresso drinks were a distraction from the core business of marketing fine arabica coffees at retail. Baldwin rebelled at the thought that people would see Starbucks as a place to get a quick cup of coffee to go. He adamantly told Schultz, "We're coffee roasters. I don't want to be in the restaurant business . . . besides, we're too deeply in debt to consider pursuing this idea."[6] While he didn't deny that the experiment was succeeding, he didn't want to go forward with introducing beverages in other Starbucks stores. Schultz's efforts to persuade Baldwin to change his mind continued to meet strong resistance, although to avoid a total impasse Baldwin finally did agree to let Schultz put espresso machines in the back of possibly one or two other Starbucks stores.

Over the next several months, Schultz made up his mind to leave Starbucks and start his own company. His plan was to open espresso bars in high-traffic downtown locations, serve espresso drinks and coffee by the cup, and try to emulate the friendly, energetic atmosphere he had encountered in Italian espresso bars. Jerry Baldwin and Gordon Bowker, knowing how frustrated Schultz had become, supported his efforts to go out on his own and agreed to let him stay in his current job and office until definitive plans were in place. Schultz left Starbucks in late 1985.

Schultz's Il Giornale Venture

With the aid of a lawyer friend who helped companies raise venture capital and go public, Howard Schultz began seeking out investors for the kind of company he had in mind. Ironically, Jerry Baldwin committed to investing $150,000 of Starbucks' money in Schultz's coffee bar enterprise, thus becoming Schultz's first investor. Baldwin accepted Schultz's invitation to be a director of the new company and Gordon Bowker agreed to be a part-time consultant for six months. Bowker, pumped up about the new venture, urged Howard to take pains to make sure that everything about the new stores—the name, the presentation, the care taken in preparing the coffee—be calculated to lead customers to expect something better than competitors offered. Bowker proposed that the new company be named Il Giornale Coffee Company (pronounced *il jor NAHL ee*), a suggestion that Schultz accepted. In December 1985, Bowker and Schultz made a trip to Italy, where they visited some 500 espresso bars in Milan and Verona, observing local habits, taking notes about decor and menus, snapping photographs, and videotaping baristas in action.

About $400,000 in seed capital was raised by the end of January 1986, enough to rent an office, hire a couple of key employees, develop a store design, and open the first store. But it took until the end of 1986 to raise the remaining $1.25 million needed to launch at least eight espresso bars and prove that Schultz's strategy and business model were viable. Schultz made presentations to 242 potential investors, 217 of whom said no. Many who heard Schultz's hour-long presentation saw coffee as a commodity business and thought that Schultz's espresso bar concept lacked any basis for sustainable competitive advantage (no patent on dark roast, no advantage in purchasing coffee beans, no ways to prevent the entry of imitative competitors). Some noted that coffee couldn't be turned into a growth business—consumption of coffee had been declining since the mid-1960s. Others were skeptical that people would pay $1.50 or more for a cup of coffee, and the company's unpronounceable name turned some off. Being rejected by so many of the potential investors he approached was disheartening for Schultz (some who listened to his presentation didn't even bother to call him back; others refused to take his calls). Nonetheless, Schultz maintained an upbeat attitude and displayed passion and enthusiasm in making his pitch. He ended up raising $1.65 million from about 30 investors, most of which came from nine people, five of whom became directors.

The first Il Giornale store opened in April 1986. It had 700 square feet and was located near the entrance of Seattle's tallest building. The decor was Italian, and the menu had some Italian words. Italian opera music played in the background. The baristas wore white shirts and bow ties. All service was stand-up—there were no chairs. National and international papers were hung on rods on the wall. By closing time on the first day, 300 customers had been served, mostly in the morning hours. But while the core idea worked well, it soon became apparent that several aspects of the format were not appropriate for Seattle. Some customers objected to the incessant opera music, others wanted a place to sit down, and many did not understand the Italian words on the menu. These "mistakes" were quickly fixed, but an effort was made not to compromise the style and elegance of the store. Within six months, the store was serving more than 1,000 customers a day. Regular customers had learned how to pronounce the company's name. Because most customers were in a hurry, it became apparent that speedy service was essential.

Six months after the first Il Giornale opened, a second store was opened in another downtown building. A third store was opened in Vancouver, British Columbia, in April 1987. Vancouver was chosen to test the transferability of the company's business concept outside Seattle. Schultz's goal was to open 50 stores in five years, and he needed to dispel his investors' doubts about geographic expansion early on to achieve his growth objective. By mid-1987 sales at the three stores were running at a rate equal to $1.5 million annually.

Il Giornale Acquires Starbucks

In March 1987 Jerry Baldwin and Gordon Bowker decided to sell the whole Starbucks operation in Seattle—the stores, the roasting plant, and the Starbucks name. Bowker wanted to cash out his coffee business investment to concentrate on his other enterprises;

Baldwin, who was tired of commuting between Seattle and San Francisco and wrestling with the troubles created by the two parts of the company, elected to concentrate on the Peet's operation. As he recalls, "My wife and I had a 30-second conversation and decided to keep Peet's. It was the original and it was better."[7]

Schultz knew immediately that he had to buy Starbucks; his board of directors agreed. Schultz and his newly hired finance and accounting manager drew up a set of financial projections for the combined operations and a financing package that included a stock offering to Il Giornale's original investors and a line of credit with local banks. While a rival plan to acquire Starbucks was put together by another Il Giornale investor, Schultz's proposal prevailed. Within weeks, Schultz had raised the $3.8 million needed to buy Starbucks, and the acquisition was completed in August 1987. The new name of the combined companies was Starbucks Corporation. Howard Schultz, at the age of 34, became Starbucks' president and CEO.

Starbucks as a Private Company: 1987–1992

The Monday morning following the completed acquisition, Howard Schultz returned to the Starbucks offices at the roasting plant, greeted all the familiar faces, and accepted their congratulations. Then he called the staff together for a meeting on the roasting plant floor:

> All my life I have wanted to be part of a company and a group of people who share a common vision . . . I'm here today because I love this company. I love what it represents . . . I know you're concerned . . . I promise you I will not let you down. I promise you I will not leave anyone behind . . . In five years, I want you to look back at this day and say "I was there when it started. I helped build this company into something great."[8]

Schultz told the group that his vision was for Starbucks to become a national company with values and guiding principles that employees could be proud of. He indicated that he wanted to include people in the decision-making process and that he would be open and honest with them.

Schultz believed it was essential, not just an intriguing option, to build a company that valued and respected its people, that inspired them, and that shared the fruits of success with those who contributed to the company's long-term value. His aspiration was for Starbucks to become the most respected brand name in coffee and for the company to be admired for its corporate responsibility. In the next few days and weeks, Schultz came to see that the unity and morale at Starbucks had deteriorated badly in the 20 months he had been at Il Giornale. Some employees were cynical and felt unappreciated. There was a feeling that prior management had abandoned them and a wariness about what the new regime would bring. Schultz decided to make building a new relationship of mutual respect between employees and management a priority.

The new Starbucks had a total of nine stores. The business plan Schultz had presented investors called for the new company to open 125 stores in the next five years— 15 the first year, 20 the second, 25 the third, 30 the fourth, and 35 the fifth. Revenues were projected to reach $60 million in 1992. But the company lacked experienced management. Schultz had never led a growth effort of such magnitude and was just learning what the job of CEO was all about, having been the president of a small company for barely two years. Dave Olsen, a Seattle coffee bar owner whom Schultz had recruited to direct store operations at Il Giornale, was still learning the ropes in managing a multistore operation. Ron Lawrence, the company's controller, had worked as a controller for several organizations. Other Starbucks employees had only the experience of managing or being a part of a six-store organization. When Starbucks' key roaster and coffee buyer resigned, Schultz put Dave Olsen in charge of buying and roasting coffee. Lawrence Maltz, who had 20 years' experience in business, including 8 years as president of a profitable public beverage company, was hired as executive vice president and charged with heading operations, finance, and human resources.

In the next several months, a number of changes were instituted. To symbolize the merging of the two companies and the two cultures, a new logo was created that melded the designs of the Starbucks logo and the Il Giornale logo. The Starbucks stores were equipped with espresso machines and remodeled to look more Italian than Old World nautical. Il Giornale green replaced the traditional Starbucks brown. The result was a new type of store—a cross between a retail coffee bean store and an espresso bar/café—that eventually became Starbucks' signature.

By December 1987, the mood of the employees at Starbucks had turned upbeat. They were buying into the changes that Schultz was making, and trust began to build between management and employees. New stores were on the verge of opening in Vancouver and Chicago. One Starbucks store employee, Daryl Moore, who had started working at Starbucks in 1981 and who had voted against unionization in 1985, began to question the need for a union with his fellow employees. Over the next few weeks, Moore began a move to decertify the union. He carried a decertification letter around to Starbucks stores and secured the signatures of employees who no longer wished to be represented by the union. He got a majority of store employees to sign the letter and presented it to the National Labor Relations Board. The union representing store employees was decertified. Later, in 1992, the union representing Starbucks' roasting plant and warehouse employees was also decertified.

Market Expansion Outside the Pacific Northwest

Starbucks' entry into Chicago proved far more troublesome than management anticipated. The first Chicago store opened in October 1987, and three more stores were opened over the next six months. Customer counts at the stores were substantially below expectations. Chicagoans did not take to dark-roasted coffee as fast as Schultz had hoped. The first downtown store opened onto the street rather than into the lobby of the building where it was located; in the winter months, customers were hesitant to go out in the wind and cold to acquire a cup of coffee. It was expensive to supply fresh coffee to the Chicago stores out of the Seattle warehouse (the company solved the problem of freshness and quality assurance by putting freshly roasted beans in special FlavorLock bags that used vacuum packaging techniques with a one-way valve to allow carbon dioxide to escape without allowing air and moisture in). Rents were higher in Chicago than in Seattle, and so were wage rates. The result was a squeeze on store profit margins. Gradually, customer counts improved, but Starbucks lost money on its Chicago stores until, in 1990, prices were raised to reflect higher rents and labor costs, more experienced store managers were hired, and a critical mass of customers caught on to the taste of Starbucks products.

Portland, Oregon, was the next market the company entered, and Portland coffee drinkers took to Starbucks products quickly. By 1991, the Chicago stores had become profitable and the company was ready for its next big market entry. Management decided on California because of its host of neighborhood centers and the receptiveness of Californians to high-quality, innovative food. Los Angeles was chosen as the first California market to enter. L.A. was selected principally because of its status as a trendsetter and its cultural ties to the rest of the country. L.A. consumers embraced Starbucks quickly, and the *Los Angeles Times* named Starbucks as the best coffee in America even before the first store opened. The entry into San Francisco proved more troublesome because San Francisco had an ordinance against converting stores to restaurant-related uses in certain prime urban neighborhoods; Starbucks could sell beverages and pastries to customers at stand-up counters but could not offer seating in stores that had formerly been used for general retailing. However, the city council was soon convinced by café owners and real estate brokers to change the code. Still, Starbucks faced strong competition from Peet's and local espresso bars in the San Francisco market.

Starbucks' store expansion targets proved easier to meet than Schultz had originally anticipated, and he upped the numbers to keep challenging the organization. Starbucks opened 15 new stores in fiscal 1988, 20 in 1989, 30 in 1990, 32 in 1991, and 53 in 1992—producing a total of 161 stores, significantly above the 1987 objective of 125 stores.

From the outset, the strategy was to open only company-owned stores; franchising was avoided so as to keep the company in full control of the quality of its products and the character and location of its stores. But company-ownership of all stores required Starbucks to raise new venture capital to cover the cost of new store expansion. In 1988 the company raised $3.9 million, in 1990 venture capitalists provided an additional $13.5 million, and in 1991 another round of venture capital financing generated $15 million. Starbucks was able to raise the needed funds despite posting losses of $330,000 in 1987, $764,000 in 1988, and $1.2 million in 1989. While the losses were troubling to Starbucks' board of directors and investors, Schultz's business plan had forecast losses during the early years of expansion. At a particularly tense board meeting where directors sharply questioned Schultz about the lack of profitability, Schultz said:

> Look, we're going to keep losing money until we can do three things. We have to attract a management team well beyond our expansion needs. We have to build a world-class roasting facility. And we need a computer information system sophisticated enough to keep track of sales in hundreds and hundreds of stores.[9]

Schultz argued for patience as the company invested in the infrastructure to support continued growth well into the 1990s. He contended that hiring experienced executives ahead of the growth curve, building facilities far beyond current needs, and installing support systems laid a strong foundation for rapid, profitable growth on down the road. His arguments carried the day with the board and with investors, especially since revenues were growing by approximately 80 percent annually and customer traffic at the stores was meeting or exceeding expectations.

Starbucks became profitable in 1990, and profits increased every year thereafter except for fiscal year 2000. Exhibit 3 provides a financial summary for 1998–2003.

Exhibit 3   FINANCIAL AND OPERATING SUMMARY FOR STARBUCKS CORPORATION, 1998–2003 (dollars in 000s)

	September 30, 2003	September 29, 2002	September 30, 2001	October 1, 2000	October 3, 1999	September 27, 1998
			Fiscal Years Ending[a]			
Results of operations data						
Net revenues						
Retail	$3,449,624	$2,792,904	$2,229,594	$1,823,607	$1,423,389	$1,102,574
Specialty	625,898	496,004	419,386	354,007	263,439	206,128
Total net revenues	$4,075,522	$3,288,908	$2,648,980	$2,177,614	$1,686,828	$1,308,702
Cost of sales and related company costs	1,685,928	1,350,011	1,112,785	961,885	741,010	578,483
Store operating expenses	1,379,574	1,109,782	867,957	704,898	543,572	418,476
Other operating expenses	141,346	106,084	72,406	78,445	51,374	43,479
Depreciation and amortization expenses	237,807	205,557	163,501	130,232	97,797	72,543
General and administrative expenses	244,550	234,581	179,852	110,202	89,681	77,575
Income from equity investors	38,396	33,445	27,740	20,300	—	—
Merger expenses[b]	—	—	—	—	—	8,930
Operating income	$ 424,713	$ 316,338	$ 280,219	$ 212,252	$ 156,711	$ 109,216
Internet-related investment losses			2,940	58,792		
Gain on sale of investment		13,361				
Net earnings	$ 268,346	$ 212,686	$ 180,335	$ 94,564	$ 101,693	$ 68,372
Net earnings per common share—diluted	$ 0.67	$ 0.54	$ 0.46	$ 0.24	$ 0.27	$ 0.19
Cash dividends per share	$ 0	$ 0	$ 0	$ 0	$ 0	$ 0
Balance sheet data						
Current assets	$ 924,029	$ 772,643	$ 593,925	$ 459,819	$ 386,500	$ 337,280
Current liabilities	608,703	462,595	445,264	313,251	251,597	179,475
Working capital	$ 315,326	$ 310,048	$ 148,661	$ 146,568	$ 135,303	$ 157,805
Total assets	$2,729,746	$2,214,392	$1,846,519	$1,491,546	$1,252,514	$ 992,755
Long-term debt (including current portion)	$ 4,354	$ 5,076	$ 6,483	$ 7,168	$ 7,691	$ 1,803
Shareholders' equity	$2,082,427	$1,723,189	$1,375,927	$1,148,399	$ 961,013	$ 794,297

Exhibit 3   (concluded)

	Fiscal Years Ending[a]					
	September 30, 2003	September 29, 2002	September 30, 2001	October 1, 2000	October 3, 1999	September 27, 1998
Store operations data						
Percentage change in comparable store sales[c]						
United States	9%	7%	5%	9%	6%	5%
International	7%	1%	3%	12%	8%	n.a.
Consolidated	8%	6%	5%	9%	6%	5%
Systemwide retail store sales[d]	n.a.	$3,796,000	$2,950,000	$2,250,000	$1,633,000	$1,190,000
Systemwide stores opened during the year						
United States						
Company-operated stores	506	503	498	388	394	352
Licensed stores	315	264	268	342	42	39
International						
Company-operated stores	96	111	149	96	53	35
Licensed stores	284	299	293	177	1,239	48
Total	1,201	1,177	1,208	1,003	612	474
Systemwide stores open at year end[e]						
United States						
Company-operated stores	3,779	3,209	2,706	2,208	1,820	1,622
Licensed stores	1,422	1,033	769	501	159	133
International						
Company-operated stores	767	671	560	411	315	66
Licensed stores	1,257	973	674	381	204	65
Total	7,225	5,886	4,709	3,501	2,498	1,886

[a]The company's fiscal year ends on the Sunday closest to September 30. All fiscal years presented include 52 weeks, except fiscal 1999, which includes 53 weeks.
[b]Merger expenses relate to the business combination with Seattle Coffee Holdings Limited.
[c]Includes only company-operated stores open 13 months or longer.
[d]Systemwide retail sales include sales at company-operated and licensed stores and are believed by management to measure global penetration of Starbucks retail stores.
[e]Systemwide store openings are reported net of closures.
Source: 10-K reports for 2003, 2002, 2000, and 1999 and company press releases (for 2003 data).

Howard Schultz's Strategy to Make Starbucks a Great Place to Work

Howard Schultz deeply believed that Starbucks' success was heavily dependent on customers having a very positive experience in its stores. This meant having store employees who were knowledgeable about the company's products, who paid attention to detail in preparing the company's espresso drinks, who eagerly communicated the company's passion for coffee, and who possessed the skills and personality to deliver consistent, pleasing customer service. Many of the baristas were in their 20s and worked part-time, going to college on the side or pursuing other career activities. The challenge to Starbucks, in Schultz's view, was how to attract, motivate, and reward store employees in a manner that would make Starbucks a company that people would want to work for and that would generate enthusiastic commitment and higher levels of customer service. Moreover, Schultz wanted to send all Starbucks employees a message that would cement the trust that had been building between management and the company's workforce.

One of the requests that employees had made to the prior owners of Starbucks was to extend health care benefits to part-time workers. Their request had been turned down, but Schultz believed that expanding heath care coverage to include part-timers was the right thing to do. His father had recently passed away with cancer and he knew from his own past experience of having grown up in a family that struggled to make ends meet how difficult it was to cope with rising medical costs. In 1988 Schultz went to the board of directors with his plan to expand the company's heath care coverage to include part-timers who worked at least 20 hours a week. He saw the proposal not as a generous gesture but as a core strategy to win employee loyalty and commitment to the company's mission. Board members resisted because the company was unprofitable and the added costs of the extended coverage would only worsen the company's bottom line. But Schultz argued passionately that it was the right thing to do and wouldn't be as expensive as it seemed. He observed that if the new benefit reduced turnover, which he believed was likely, then it would reduce the costs of hiring and training—which equaled about $3,000 per new hire; he further pointed out that it cost $1,500 a year to provide an employee with full benefits. Part-timers, he argued, were vital to Starbucks, constituting two-thirds of the company's workforce. Many were baristas who knew the favorite drinks of regular customers; if the barista left, that connection with the customer was broken. Moreover, many part-time employees were called on to open the stores early, sometimes at 5:30 or 6:00 AM; others had to work until closing, usually 9:00 PM or later. Providing these employees with health care benefits, he argued, would signal that the company honored their value and contribution.

The board approved Schultz's plan, and starting in late 1988 part-timers working 20 or more hours were offered the same health coverage as full-time employees. Starbucks paid 75 percent of an employee's health care premium; the employee paid 25 percent. Over the years, Starbucks extended its health coverage to include preventive care, crisis counseling, dental care, eye care, mental health, and chemical dependency. Coverage was also offered for unmarried partners in a committed relationship. Since most Starbucks' employees were young and comparatively healthy, the company had been able to provide broader coverage while keeping monthly payments relatively low. The value of Starbucks' health care program struck home when one of the company's store managers and a former barista walked into Schultz's office and told him he had AIDS:

I had known he was gay but had no idea he was sick. His disease had entered a new phase, he explained, and he wouldn't be able to work any longer. We sat together and cried, for I could not find meaningful words to console him. I couldn't compose myself. I hugged him.

At that point, Starbucks had no provision for employees with AIDS. We had a policy decision. Because of Jim, we decided to offer health-care coverage to all employees who have terminal illnesses, paying medical costs in full from the time they are not able to work until they are covered by government programs, usually twenty-nine months.

After his visit to me, I spoke with Jim often and visited him at the hospice. Within a year he was gone. I received a letter from his family afterward, telling me how much they appreciated our benefit plan.[10]

In 1994 Howard Schultz was invited to The White House for a one-on-one meeting with President Bill Clinton to brief him on Starbucks' health care program.

The Creation of an Employee Stock Option Plan

By 1991 the company's profitability had improved to the point where Schultz could pursue a stock option plan for all employees, a program he believed would have a positive, long-term effect on the success of Starbucks.[11] Schultz wanted to turn all Starbucks employees into partners, give them a chance to share in the success of the company, and make clear the connection between their contributions and the company's market value. Even though Starbucks was still a private company, the plan that emerged called for granting stock options to all full-time and part-time employees in proportion to their base pay. In May 1991, the plan, dubbed Bean Stock, was presented to the board. Though board members were concerned that increasing the number of shares might unduly dilute the value of the shares of investors who had put up hard cash, the plan received unanimous approval. The first grant was made in October 1991, just after the end of the company's fiscal year in September; each partner was granted stock options worth 12 percent of base pay. Each October since then, Starbucks has granted employees options equal to 14 percent of base pay, awarded at the stock price at the start of the fiscal year (October 1). When the Bean Stock program was presented to employees, Starbucks dropped the term *employee* and began referring to all of its people as *partners* because everyone, including part-timers working at least 20 hours per week, was eligible for stock options after six months. At the end of fiscal year 2003, Starbucks employee stock option plan included 39 million shares in outstanding options; new options for about 10 million shares were being granted annually.[12]

Starbucks became a public company in 1992; its initial public offering (IPO) of common stock in June proved to be one of the most successful IPOs of 1992 and provided the company access to the capital needed to accelerate expansion of its store network. Exhibit 4 shows the performance of the company's stock price since the 1992 IPO.

Starbucks' Stock Purchase Plan for Employees

In 1995, Starbucks implemented an employee stock purchase plan. Eligible employees could contribute up to 10 percent of their base earnings to quarterly purchases of the company's common stock at 85 percent of the going stock price. As of fiscal 2003, about 5.7 million shares had been issued since inception of the plan, and new shares were being purchased at a rate close to 1 million shares annually by some 11,184 active employee participants (out of almost 35,000 employees who were eligible to participate).[13]

Exhibit 4   The Performance of Starbucks' Stock, 1992–2003

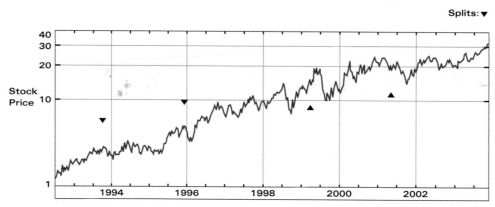

Source: www.finance.yahoo.com.

An employee stock option plan for eligible United Kingdom employees was established in 2002.[14]

The Workplace Environment

Starbucks' management believed that the company's pay scales and fringe benefit package allowed it to attract motivated people with above-average skills and good work habits. Store employees were paid around $9–$12 an hour, several dollars above the hourly minimum wage. Whereas most national retailers and fast-food chains had turnover rates for store employees ranging from 150 to 400 percent a year, the turnover rates for Starbucks' baristas ran about 65 percent. Starbucks' turnover for store managers was about 25 percent, compared to about 50 percent for other chain retailers. Starbucks' executives believed that efforts to make the company an attractive, caring place to work were responsible for its relatively low turnover rates. One Starbucks store manager commented, "Morale is very high in my store among the staff. I've worked for a lot of companies, but I've never seen this level of respect. It's a company that's very true to its workers, and it shows. Our customers always comment that we're happy and having fun. In fact, a lot of people ask if they can work here."[15]

Starbucks' management used annual "Partner View" surveys to solicit feedback from its workforce of over 74,000 people, learn their concerns, and measure job satisfaction. In the latest sample survey of 1,400 employees, 79 percent rated Starbucks' workplace environment favorably relative to other companies they were familiar with, 72 percent reported being satisfied with their present job, 16 percent were neutral, and 12 percent were dissatisfied. But the 2002 survey revealed that many employees viewed the benefits package as only "average," prompting the company to increase its match of 401(k) contributions for those who had been with the company more than three years and to have these contributions vest immediately.

Exhibit 5 contains a summary of Starbucks' fringe benefit program. Starbucks was named by *Fortune* magazine as one of the "100 Best Companies to Work For" in 1998, 1999, 2000, and 2002. Still, in 2003, Starbucks' management was concerned by field reports of stores that were suffering from slumping employee morale and store manager burnout.

Exhibit 5   ELEMENTS OF STARBUCKS' FRINGE BENEFIT PROGRAM

- Medical insurance
- Dental and vision care
- Mental health and chemical dependency coverage
- Short- and long-term disability
- Life insurance
- Benefits extended to committed domestic partners of Starbucks employees
- Sick time
- Paid vacations (first-year workers got one vacation week and two personal days)

- 401(k) retirement savings plan—the company matched from 25% to 150%, based on length of service, of each employee's contributions up to the first 4% of compensation
- Stock purchase plan—eligible employees could buy shares at a discounted price through regular payroll deductions
- Free pound of coffee each week
- 30% product discounts
- Stock option plan (Bean Stock)

Source: Compiled by the case researchers from company documents and other sources.

Starbucks' Corporate Values and Business Principles

During the early building years, Howard Schultz and other Starbucks' senior executives worked to instill some key values and guiding principles into the Starbucks culture. The cornerstone value in the effort "to build a company with soul" was that the company would never stop pursuing the perfect cup of coffee by buying the best beans and roasting them to perfection. Schultz remained steadfastly opposed to franchising, so that the company could control the quality of its products and build a culture common to all stores. He was adamant about not selling artificially flavored coffee beans— "We will not pollute our high-quality beans with chemicals"; if a customer wanted hazelnut-flavored coffee, Starbucks would provide it by adding hazelnut syrup to the drink rather than by adding hazelnut flavoring to the beans during roasting. Running flavored beans through the grinders would leave behind chemical residues that would alter the flavor of beans ground afterward; plus, the chemical smell given off by artificially flavored beans was absorbed by other beans in the store. Furthermore, Schultz didn't want the company to pursue supermarket sales because it would mean pouring Starbucks' beans into clear plastic bins where they could get stale, thus compromising the company's legacy of fresh, dark-roasted, full-flavored coffee.

Starbucks' management was also emphatic about the importance of employees paying attention to what pleased customers. Employees were trained to go out of their way, and to take heroic measures if necessary, to make sure customers were fully satisfied. The theme was "Just say yes" to customer requests. Further, employees were encouraged to speak their minds without fear of retribution from upper management— senior executives wanted employees to be vocal about what Starbucks was doing right, what it was doing wrong, and what changes were needed. Management wanted employees to be involved in and contribute to the process of making Starbucks a better company.

A values and principles "crisis" arose at Starbucks in 1989 when customers started requesting skim (i.e., nonfat) milk in making cappuccinos and lattes. Howard Schultz, who read all customer comments cards, and Dave Olsen, head of coffee quality, conducted taste tests of lattes and cappuccinos made with nonfat milk and concluded they were not as good as those made with whole milk. Howard Behar, recently hired as head of retail store operations, indicated that management's opinions didn't matter;

what mattered was giving customers what they wanted. Schultz took the position that "We will never offer nonfat milk. It's not who we are." Behar, however, stuck to his guns, maintaining that use of nonfat milk should at least be tested—otherwise it appeared as if all the statements management had made about the importance of really and truly pleasing customers were a sham. A fierce internal debate ensued. One dogmatic defender of the quality and taste of Starbucks' coffee products buttonholed Behar outside his office and told him that using nonfat milk amounted to "bastardizing" the company's products. Numerous store managers maintained that offering two kinds of milk was operationally impractical. Schultz found himself in a quandary, torn between the company's commitment to quality and its goal of pleasing customers. One day after visiting one of the stores in a residential neighborhood and watching a customer leave to go to a competitor's store because Starbucks did not make lattes with nonfat milk, Schultz authorized Behar to begin testing.[16] Within six months all 30 stores were offering drinks made with nonfat milk. Currently, about half the lattes and cappuccinos Starbucks sells are made with nonfat milk.

Schultz's approach to offering employees good compensation and a comprehensive benefits package was driven by his belief that sharing the company's success with the people who made it happen helped everyone think and act like an owner, build positive long-term relationships with customers, and do things in an efficient way. He had vivid recollection of his father's employment experience—bouncing from one low-paying job to another, working for employers who offered few or no benefits and who conducted their business with no respect for the contributions of the workforce—and he had no intention of Starbucks being that type of company. He vowed that he would never let Starbucks employees suffer a similar fate, saying:

> My father worked hard all his life and he had little to show for it. He was a beaten man. This is not the American dream. The worker on our plant floor is contributing great value to the company; if he or she has low self-worth, that will have an effect on the company.[17]

The company's employee benefits program was predicated on the belief that better benefits attract good people and keep them longer. Schultz's rationale was that if you treat your employees well, that is how they will treat customers.

Starbucks' Mission Statement

In early 1990, the senior executive team at Starbucks went to an off-site retreat to debate the company's values and beliefs and draft a mission statement. Schultz wanted the mission statement to convey a strong sense of organizational purpose and to articulate the company's fundamental beliefs and guiding principles. The draft was submitted to all employees for review, and several changes were made on the basis of employee comments. The resulting mission statement, which remained unchanged in 2003, is shown in Exhibit 6.

Following adoption of the mission statement, Starbucks' management implemented a "Mission Review" to solicit and gather employee opinions about whether the company was living up to its stated mission. Employees were urged to report their concerns to the company's Mission Review team if they thought particular management decisions were not supportive of the company's mission statement. Comment cards were given to each newly hired employee and were kept available in common areas with other employee forms. Employees had the option of signing the comment cards

Exhibit 6   STARBUCKS' MISSION STATEMENT

Establish Starbucks as the premier purveyor of the finest coffee in the world while maintaining our uncompromising principles while we grow.

The following six guiding principles will help us measure the appropriateness of our decisions:

- Provide a great work environment and treat each other with respect and dignity.
- Embrace diversity as an essential component in the way we do business.
- Apply the highest standards of excellence to the purchasing, roasting, and fresh delivery of our coffee.
- Develop enthusiastically satisfied customers all of the time.
- Contribute positively to our communities and our environment.
- Recognize that profitability is essential to our future success.

Source: www.starbucks.com (accessed November 2003).

or not. Hundreds of cards were submitted to the Mission Review team each year. The company promised that a relevant manager would respond to all signed cards within two weeks. Howard Schultz reviewed all the comments, signed and unsigned.

Starbucks' Store Expansion Strategy

In 1992 and 1993 Starbucks developed a three-year geographic expansion strategy that targeted areas that not only had favorable demographic profiles but also could be serviced and supported by the company's operations infrastructure. For each targeted region, Starbucks selected a large city to serve as a "hub"; teams of professionals were located in hub cities to support the goal of opening 20 or more stores in the hub in the first two years. Once stores blanketed the hub, then additional stores were opened in smaller, surrounding "spoke" areas in the region. To oversee the expansion process, Starbucks created zone vice presidents to direct the development of each region and to implant the Starbucks culture in the newly opened stores. All of the new zone vice presidents Starbucks recruited came with extensive operating and marketing experience in chain store retailing.

Starbucks' strategy in major metropolitan cities was to blanket the area with stores, even if some stores cannibalized another store's business.[18] While a new store might draw 30 percent of the business of an existing store two or so blocks away, management believed that its "Starbucks everywhere" approach cut down on delivery and management costs, shortened customer lines at individual stores, and increased foot traffic for all the stores in an area.

Starbucks' store launches grew steadily more successful. In 2002, new stores generated an average of $1.2 million in first-year revenues, compared to $700,000 in 1995 and only $427,000 in 1990. The steady increases in new-store revenues were due partly to growing popularity of premium coffee drinks and partly to Starbucks' growing reputation. In more and more instances, Starbucks' reputation reached new markets even before stores opened. Moreover, existing stores continued to post sales gains in the range of 2–10 percent annually. In 2003, Starbucks posted same-store sales increases averaging 8 percent (Exhibit 3), the 12th consecutive year the company had achieved sales growth of 5 percent or greater at existing stores. Starbucks' revenues had climbed an average of 20 percent annually since 1992. In a representative week in

2003, about 20 million people bought a cup of coffee at Starbucks; a typical customer stopped at a Starbucks about 18 times a month—no U.S. retailer had a higher frequency of customer visits.[19]

One of Starbucks' core competencies was identifying good retailing sites for its new stores. The company was regarded as having the best real estate team in the coffee bar industry and a sophisticated system for identifying not only the most attractive individual city blocks but also the exact store location that was best; it also worked hard at building good relationships with local real estate representatives in areas where it was opening multiple store locations. The company's site location track record was so good that as of 1997 it had closed only 2 of the 1,500 sites it had opened; its track record in finding successful store locations was still intact as of 2003 (although specific figures were not available).

Exhibit 7 shows a timeline of Starbucks' entry into new market areas, along with other accomplishments, milestones, key events, and awards.

International Expansion

In markets outside the continental United States (including Hawaii), Starbucks had a two-pronged store expansion: either open company-owned and company-operated stores or else license a reputable and capable local company with retailing know-how in the target host country to develop and operate new Starbucks stores. In most countries, Starbucks used a local partner/licensee to help it recruit talented individuals, set up supplier relationships, locate suitable store sites, and cater to local market conditions. Starbucks looked for partners/licensees that had strong retail/restaurant experience, had values and a corporate culture compatible with Starbucks, were committed to good customer service, possessed talented management and strong financial resources, and had demonstrated brand-building skills.

Starbucks had created a new subsidiary, Starbucks Coffee International, to orchestrate overseas expansion and begin to build the Starbucks brand name globally via licensees. (See Exhibit 1 for the number of licensed international stores and Exhibit 7 for the years in which Starbucks entered most of these foreign markets.) Starbucks' management expected to have a total of 10,000 stores in 60 countries by the end of 2005. The company's first store in France opened in early 2004 in Paris. China was expected to be Starbucks' biggest market outside the United States in the years to come. Thus far, Starbucks products were proving to be a much bigger hit with consumers in Asia than in Europe. Even so, Starbucks was said to be losing money in both Japan and Britain; moreover, the Starbucks Coffee International division was only marginally profitable, with 2003 pretax earnings of only $5.5 million on sales of $603 million.

Going into 2004, Schultz believed the company's long-range goal of 25,000 store locations by 2013 was achievable. He noted that Starbucks had only a 7 percent share of the coffee-drinking market in the United States and a 1 percent share internationally. According to Schultz, "That still leaves lots of room for growth. Internationally, we are still in our infancy."[20] Although coffee consumption worldwide was stagnant, coffee was still the second most consumed beverage in the world, trailing only water.[21] Starbucks maintained that it would not franchise, although its foreign stores were frequently opened in partnership with local companies.

Exhibit 7 TIMELINE OF STARBUCKS' ACCOMPLISHMENTS, MILESTONES, KEY EVENTS, AND SELECTED AWARDS, 1987–2003

Year	Accomplishments/Milestones/Key Events/Awards
1987	■ Il Giornale acquires the assets of Starbucks Coffee, Tea, and Spices and changes the company's name to Starbucks Corporation. ■ First stores outside of Seattle are opened in Chicago and Vancouver, British Columbia.
1988	■ Starbucks introduces a mail order catalog, with service to all 50 states.
1990	■ Starbucks expands Seattle headquarters and builds a new coffee bean roasting plant in Seattle.
1990	■ Starbucks' first licensed airport location is opened at Sea-Tac International Airport in partnership with HMS Host. ■ Horizon Air begins serving Starbucks coffee on its flights.
1991	■ Starbucks becomes first privately owned U.S. company to offer a stock option program that includes part-time employees.
1992	■ Starbucks completes an IPO and becomes a public company trading on the Nasdaq National Market under the symbol SBUX.
1993	■ Starbucks enters into an alliance with Barnes & Noble to have Starbucks coffee stores inside B&N's bookstores. ■ Starbucks opens a second roasting plant in Kent, Washington.
1994	■ Starbucks wins contract for its coffees to be served at all Sheraton Hotels. ■ Starbucks expands to Minneapolis, Boston, New York, Atlanta, and Dallas.
1995	■ Starbucks begins selling compact discs of music played in Starbucks stores. ■ United Airlines begins serving Starbucks on its flights. ■ A new $11 million state-of-the-art roasting facility is opened in York, Pennsylvania. ■ A joint venture is formed to open Starbucks stores in Japan. ■ Starbucks expands to Philadelphia, Pittsburgh, Las Vegas, Cincinnati, Baltimore, San Antonio, and Austin.
1996	■ First Starbucks locations are opened in Japan, Hawaii, and Singapore. ■ Starbucks wins an account for Westin Hotels. ■ Starbucks' coffee-flavored ice creams are introduced in partnership with Dreyer's Grand Ice Cream. ■ Starbucks–PepsiCo venture begins selling a bottled version of Starbucks Frappuccino. ■ First Starbucks locations are opened in Rhode Island; Idaho; North Carolina; Arizona; Utah; and Ontario, Canada. ■ Starbucks receives 1996 Corporate Conscience Award for International Human Rights from Council on Economic Priorities.
1997	■ First Starbucks locations are opened in Florida, Michigan, Wisconsin, and the Philippines. ■ Canadian Airlines begins serving Starbucks coffee on its flights. ■ Starbucks Foundation is established to help support local literacy programs in communities where Starbucks has coffeehouses. ■ Starbucks named one of the "Best Companies to Work for in America for People with Disabilities" by *We* magazine.
1998	■ Starbucks enters into an alliance with Kraft Foods to handle the distribution of packaged Starbucks coffee in supermarkets. ■ First Starbucks locations are opened in New Orleans, St. Louis, Kansas City, Portland (Maine), Taiwan, Thailand, New Zealand, and Malaysia. ■ Starbucks enters Great Britain by acquiring 60 Seattle Coffee locations. ■ Starbucks acquires Pasqua, a San Francisco–based coffee retailer. ■ Company Web site, www.starbucks.com, is launched.

(continues)

Exhibit 7   (concluded)

Year	Accomplishments/Milestones/Key Events/Awards
1999	▪ First Starbucks locations are opened in Memphis, Nashville, Saskatchewan, China, Kuwait, South Korea, and Lebanon.
	▪ Tazo, a Portland, Oregon, tea company is acquired, and sales of Tazo teas at Starbucks locations begins.
	▪ Starbucks forms an agreement with Albertson's to open more than 100 Starbucks locations in Albertson's supermarkets beginning in 2000.
2000	▪ Howard Schultz transitions from chairman and CEO to chairman and chief global strategist; Orrin Smith is promoted to president and CEO.
	▪ Starbucks enters into agreement with Host Marriott International to open locations in select properties.
	▪ First Starbucks locations are opened in Dubai, Hong Kong, Shanghai, Qatar, Bahrain, Saudi Arabia, and Australia.
	▪ Starbucks begins marketing Fair Trade Certified coffees.
	▪ Starbucks acquires Hear Music, a San Francisco music company.
	▪ *Interbrand Magazine* names Starbucks as one of the "75 Great Global Brands of the 21st Century."
2001	▪ Starbucks adopts coffee sourcing guidelines developed in partnership with Conservation International and commits to purchase at least 1 million pounds of Fair Trade Certified coffee.
	▪ Starbucks offers $1 million in support to coffee farmers.
	▪ Starbucks begins to offer high-speed wireless Internet access in stores.
	▪ Starbucks begins offering a reloadable Starbucks Card for customers to use in making purchases at Starbucks stores.
	▪ Starbucks opens 300th location in Japan and first stores in Switzerland, Austria, and Israel.
	▪ Howard Schultz is named one of the "Top 25 Best Managers" by *Business Week*.
2002	▪ Starbucks begins selling Fair Trade Certified coffees in select foreign locations.
	▪ Starbucks opens first stores in Oman, Indonesia, Germany, Spain, Puerto Rico, Mexico, Greece, and southern China.
	▪ *Fortune* magazine names Starbucks as one of the "100 Best Companies to Work For" (as it also did in 1998, 1999, and 2000).
	▪ *Business Ethics Magazine* names Starbucks as one of "100 Best Corporate Citizens" (as it also did in 2000 and 2001).
2003	▪ The company introduces the Starbucks Duetto Visa card, which combines Visa card functionality with the reloadable Starbucks Card functionality.
	▪ Starbucks acquires Seattle Coffee Company, consisting of 129 company-operated and franchised Seattle's Best Coffee locations, 21 company-operated Torrefazione Italia locations in the United States and Canada, and distribution of Seattle Coffee in some 12,000 supermarket and retail food locations.
	▪ Starbucks opens its 1,000th store in the Asia Pacific region and its first stores in Turkey, Chile, and Peru; it also announces plans to open stores in France in 2004.
	▪ Starbucks decides to end venture in Israel (a total of six stores) due to challenging operating conditions.
	▪ *Brandweek* ranks Starbucks eighth on its "Super Brand List."
	▪ Starbucks named as one of the "Ten Most Admired Companies in America" in *Fortune* survey.

Source: www.starbucks.com (accessed November 4, 2003).

Employee Training

To accommodate its strategy of rapid store expansion, Starbucks put in systems to recruit, hire, and train baristas and store managers. Starbucks' vice president for human resources used some simple guidelines in screening candidates for new positions: "We want passionate people who love coffee . . . We're looking for a diverse workforce, which reflects our community. We want people who enjoy what they're doing and for whom work is an extension of themselves."[22]

All partners/baristas hired for a retail job in a Starbucks store received at least 24 hours' training in their first two to four weeks. The training topics included coffee history, drink preparation, coffee knowledge (four hours), customer service (four hours), and retail skills; there was also a four-hour workshop titled "Brewing the Perfect Cup." Baristas spent considerable time learning about beverage preparation—grinding the beans, steaming milk, learning to pull perfect (18- to 23-second) shots of espresso, memorizing the recipes of all the different drinks, practicing making the different drinks, and learning how to customize drinks to customer specifications. There were sessions on cash register operations, how to clean the milk wand on the espresso machine, explaining the Italian drink names to customers, selling home espresso machines, making eye contact with customers, and taking personal responsibility for the cleanliness of the store. Everyone was drilled in the Star Skills, three guidelines for on-the-job interpersonal relations: (1) maintain and enhance self-esteem, (2) listen and acknowledge, and (3) ask for help. And there were rules to be memorized: milk must be steamed to at least 150 degrees Fahrenheit but never more than 170 degrees; every espresso shot not pulled within 23 seconds must be tossed; never let coffee sit in the pot more than 20 minutes; always compensate dissatisfied customers with a Starbucks coupon for a free drink.

Management trainees attended classes for 8 to 12 weeks. Their training went much deeper, covering not only coffee knowledge and information imparted to baristas but also the details of store operations, practices and procedures as set forth in the company's operating manual, information systems, and the basics of managing people. Starbucks' trainers were all store managers and district managers with on-site experience. One of their major objectives was to ingrain the company's values, principles, and culture and to pass on their knowledge about coffee and their passion about Starbucks.

When Starbucks opened stores in a new market, it launched a major recruiting effort. Eight to 10 weeks before opening, the company placed ads to hire baristas and begin their training. It sent a Star team of experienced managers and baristas from existing stores to the area to lead the store opening effort and to conduct one-on-one training following the company's formal classes and basic orientation sessions at the Starbucks Coffee School in San Francisco.

Real Estate, Store Design, Store Planning, and Construction

Starting in 1991, Starbucks created its own in-house team of architects and designers to ensure that each store would convey the right image and character. Stores had to be custom-designed because, unlike McDonald's or Wal-Mart, the company bought no real estate and built no freestanding structures; rather, each space was leased in an existing structure, meaning that each store differed in size and shape. Most stores ranged in size from 1,000 to 1,500 square feet and were located in office buildings, downtown and suburban retail centers, airport terminals, university campus areas, and busy neighborhood shopping areas convenient for pedestrian foot traffic and/or drivers. Only a select few were in suburban malls.

Over the years, Starbucks had experimented with a broad range of store formats. Special seating areas were added to help make Starbucks a desirable gathering place where customers could meet and chat or simply enjoy a peaceful interlude in their day. Flagship stores in high-traffic, high-visibility locations had fireplaces, leather chairs, newspapers, couches, and lots of ambience. The company also experimented with drive-through windows in locations where speed and convenience were important to customers and with kiosks in supermarkets, building lobbies, and other public places.

A "stores of the future" project team was formed in 1995 to raise Starbucks' store design to a still higher level and come up with the next generation of Starbucks stores. The vision of what a Starbucks store should be like included such concepts as an authentic coffee experience that conveyed the artistry of espresso making, a place to think and imagine, a spot where people could gather and talk over a great cup of coffee, a comforting refuge that provided a sense of community, a third place for people to congregate beyond work or the home, a place that welcomes people and rewards them for coming, and a layout that could accommodate both fast service and quiet moments. The team researched the art and literature of coffee throughout the ages, studied coffee-growing and coffee-making techniques, and looked at how Starbucks' stores had already evolved in terms of design, logos, colors, and mood. The team came up with four store designs—one for each of the four stages of coffee making: growing, roasting, brewing, and aroma—each with its own color combinations, lighting scheme, and component materials. Within each of the four basic store templates, Starbucks could vary the materials and details to adapt to different store sizes and settings (downtown buildings, college campuses, neighborhood shopping areas). In late 1996, Starbucks began opening new stores based on one of the four formats and color schemes. But as the number of stores increased rapidly between 2000 and 2003, greater store diversity and layout quickly became necessary. Exhibit 8 shows the diverse nature of Starbucks stores in 2003.

To better control average store opening costs, the company centralized buying, developed standard contracts and fixed fees for certain items, and consolidated work under those contractors who displayed good cost-control practices. The retail operations group outlined exactly the minimum amount of equipment each core store needed so that standard items could be ordered in volume from vendors at 20 to 30 percent discounts, then delivered just in time to the store site either from company warehouses or the vendor. Modular designs for display cases were developed. And the whole store layout was developed on a computer, with software that allowed the costs to be estimated as the design evolved. All this cut store opening costs significantly and reduced store development time from 24 to 18 weeks.

In August 2002, Starbucks teamed up with T-Mobile USA, the largest U.S. carrier-owned Wi-Fi service, to experiment with providing Internet access and enhanced digital entertainment to patrons at over 1,200 Starbucks locations. Customers using a Wi-Fi notebook computer while at Starbucks locations equipped with wireless broadband Internet service could surf the Web or take advantage of special Starbucks-sponsored multimedia promotions (e.g., classic blues performances by Howlin' Wolf and Muddy Waters, an array of great blues tunes, and videos of noteworthy musicians sharing how blues music and artists influenced them). The objective was to heighten the "third place" Starbucks experience, entice customers into perhaps buying a second latte or espresso while catching up on e-mail, listening to digital music, putting the finishing touches on a presentation, or accessing their corporate intranet. Since the August 2002 introduction of Wi-Fi at Starbucks, wireless Internet service had been added at 1,200 more stores and the number of accesses was in the millions; internal research showed that the average connection lasted approximately 45 minutes and more than 90 percent of T-Mobile HotSpot accesses were during the off-peak store hours, after 9:00 AM. In October 2003, Starbucks announced that it was expanding Wi-Fi capability to additional locations and would have 2,700 stores equipped with wireless Internet access by year-end.

Exhibit 8   **Scenes from Starbucks Stores**

During the early start-up years, Starbucks avoided debt and financed new stores entirely with equity capital. But as the company's profitability improved and its balance sheet strengthened, Schultz's opposition to debt as a legitimate financing vehicle softened. In 1996 the company completed its second debt offering, netting $161 million from the sale of convertible debentures for use in its capital construction program. This debt was successfully converted into common stock in 1997. Over the next seven years, strong internal cash flows allowed Starbucks to finance virtually all of its store expansion with internal funds; the company had less than $6 million in long-term debt on its balance sheet despite having invested some $1.3 billion in facilities and equipment.

Store Ambience

Starbucks' management viewed each store as a billboard for the company and as a contributor to building the company's brand and image. Each detail was scrutinized to enhance the mood and ambience of the store, to make sure everything signaled "best of class" and reflected the personality of the community and the neighborhood. The thesis was "Everything matters." The company went to great lengths to make sure that the store fixtures, the merchandise displays, the colors, the artwork, the banners, the music, and the aromas all blended to create a consistent, inviting, stimulating environment that evoked the romance of coffee, that signaled the company's passion for coffee, and that rewarded customers with ceremony, stories, and surprise. Starbucks was recognized for its sensitivity to neighborhood conservation with Scenic America's award for excellent design and "sensitive reuse of spaces within cities."

To try to keep the coffee aromas in the stores pure, Starbucks banned smoking and asked employees to refrain from wearing perfumes or colognes. Prepared foods were kept covered so that customers would smell coffee only. Colorful banners and posters kept the look of Starbucks stores fresh and in season. Company designers came up with artwork for commuter mugs and T-shirts in different cities that were in keeping with each city's personality (peach-shaped coffee mugs for Atlanta, pictures of Paul Revere for Boston and the Statue of Liberty for New York). To make sure that Starbucks stores measured up to standards, the company used "mystery shoppers" who posed as customers and rated each location on a number of criteria.

The Product Line at Starbucks

Starbucks stores offered a choice of regular or decaffeinated coffee beverages, a special "coffee of the day," an assortment of made-to-order Italian-style hot and cold espresso drinks, and hot and iced teas. In addition, customers could choose from a wide selection of fresh-roasted whole-bean coffees (which could be ground or not on the premises for take-home in distinctive packages), fresh pastries, juices, coffee-making equipment, coffee mugs and other accessories, and music CDs. From time to time, stores ran special promotions touting Starbucks' special Christmas Blend coffee, shade-grown coffee from Mexico, organically grown coffees, and various rare and exotic coffees from across the world. In 2003, Starbucks began offering customers a choice of using its exclusive Silk soymilk, specifically designed to accentuate its hand-crafted beverages using espresso roast coffee and Tazo Chai teas; the organic, kosher soymilk appealed to some customers as a substitute for milk or skim milk in various coffee and tea beverages.

The company's retail sales mix in 2002 was 77 percent beverages, 13 percent food items, 6 percent whole-bean coffees, and 4 percent coffee-making equipment and accessories.[23] The product mix in each store varied according to the size and location of each outlet. Larger stores carried a greater variety of whole coffee beans, gourmet food items, teas, coffee mugs, coffee grinders, coffee-making equipment, filters, storage containers, and other accessories. Smaller stores and kiosks typically sold a full line of coffee beverages, a limited selection of whole-bean coffees, and a few hardware items.

The idea for selling music CDs (which, in some cases, were special compilations that had been put together for Starbucks to use as store background music) originated with a Starbucks store manager who had worked in the music industry and selected the new "tape of the month" Starbucks played as background in its stores. The manager had gotten compliments from customers wanting to buy the music they heard and suggested to senior executives that there was a market for the company's music tapes. Research through two years of comment cards turned up hundreds asking Starbucks to sell the music it played in its stores. The Starbucks CDs, initially created from the Capitol Records library, proved a significant seller and addition to the product line; some of the CDs were specific collections designed to tie in with new blends of coffee that the company was promoting. In 2000, Starbucks acquired Hear Music, a San Francisco–based company, to give it added capability in enhancing its music CD offerings.

In 2003, in an average week, about 22 million customers patronized Starbucks stores in North America, up from about 5 million in 1998. Stores did about half of their business by 11:00 AM. Loyal customers patronized a Starbucks store 15 to 20 times a month, spending perhaps $50–$75 monthly. Some Starbucks fanatics came in daily. Baristas became familiar with regular customers, learning their names and their favorite drinks. Christine Nagy, a field director for Oracle Corporation in Palo Alto, California, told a *Wall Street Journal* reporter, "For me, it's a daily necessity or I start getting withdrawals."[24] Her standard order was a custom drink: a decaf grande nonfat no-whip no-foam extra-cocoa mocha; when the barista saw her come through the door, Nagy told the reporter, "They just say 'We need a Christine here.'" Since its inception in 2001, 20 million Starbucks customers had purchased the reloadable Starbucks Card that allowed them to pay for their purchases with a quick swipe at the cash register and also to earn and redeem rewards.

In the fall of 2003 Starbucks, in partnership with Bank One, introduced the Duetto Visa card, which added Visa card functionality to the reloadable Starbucks Cards. By charging purchases to the Visa account of their Duetto card anywhere Visa credit cards were accepted, cardholders earned 1 percent back in Duetto Dollars, which were automatically loaded on their Starbucks Card account after each billing cycle. Duetto Dollars could be used to purchase beverages, food, and store merchandise at any Starbucks location. The Duetto card was the latest in an ongoing effort by Starbucks' management to introduce new products and experiences for customers that belonged exclusively to Starbucks; senior executives drummed the importance of always being open to reinventing the Starbucks experience.

So far, Starbucks had spent very little money on advertising, preferring instead to build the brand cup by cup with customers and depend on word of mouth and the appeal of its storefronts.

Joint Ventures

In 1994, after months of meetings and experimentation, PepsiCo and Starbucks entered into a joint venture to create new coffee-related products for mass distribution through

Pepsi channels, including cold coffee drinks in a bottle or can. Howard Schultz saw this as a major paradigm shift with the potential to cause Starbucks' business to evolve in heretofore unimaginable directions; he thought it was time to look for ways to move Starbucks out into more mainstream markets. Cold coffee products had historically met with poor market reception, except in Japan, where there was an $8 billion market for ready-to-drink coffee-based beverages. Nonetheless, Schultz was hoping the partners would hit on a new product to exploit a good-tasting coffee extract that had been developed by Starbucks' recently appointed director of research and development. The joint venture's first new product, Mazagran, a lightly flavored carbonated coffee drink, was a failure; a market test in southern California showed that some people liked it and some hated it. While people were willing to try it the first time, partly because the Starbucks name was on the label, repeat sales proved disappointing.

Despite the clash of cultures and the different motivations of PepsiCo and Starbucks, the partnership held together because of the good working relationship that evolved between Howard Schultz and Pepsi's senior executives. Then Schultz, at a meeting to discuss the future of Mazagran, suggested, "Why not develop a bottled version of Frappuccino?"[25] Starbucks had come up with the new cold coffee drink in the summer of 1995, and it had proved to be a big hot-weather seller; Pepsi executives were enthusiastic. After months of experimentation, the joint venture product research team came up with a shelf-stable version of Frappuccino that tasted quite good. It was tested in West Coast supermarkets in the summer of 1996; sales ran 10 times over projections, with 70 percent being repeat sales. Sales of Frappuccino reached $125 million in 1997 and achieved national supermarket penetration of 80 percent. Starbucks' management believed that the market for Frappuccino would ultimately exceed $1 billion.

In October 1995 Starbucks partnered with Dreyer's Grand Ice Cream to supply coffee extract for a new line of coffee ice cream made and distributed by Dreyer's under the Starbucks brand. The new line, featuring such flavors as Dark Roast Expresso Swirl, JavaChip, Vanilla MochaChip, Biscotti Bliss, and Caffe Almond Fudge, hit supermarket shelves in April 1996, and by July 1996 Starbucks coffee-flavored ice cream was the best-selling superpremium brand in the coffee segment. In 1997, two new low-fat flavors were added to complement the original six flavors, along with two flavors of ice cream bars; all were well received in the marketplace.

In 2003, Starbucks' partnerships with PepsiCo and Dreyer's generated revenues of about $6 million.

Licensed Stores and Specialty Sales

Starbucks had a licensing agreement with Kraft Foods to market and distribute Starbucks' whole-bean and ground coffees in grocery and mass-merchandise channels across the United States. Kraft managed all distribution, marketing, advertising, and promotions and paid a royalty to Starbucks based on a percentage of net sales. Two-thirds of all coffee was sold in supermarkets. Starbucks coffee sold in supermarkets featured distinctive, elegant packaging; prominent positions in grocery aisles; and the same premium quality as that of coffee sold in its stores. Product freshness was guaranteed by Starbucks' FlavorLock packaging, and the price per pound paralleled the prices in Starbucks' retail stores. Flavor selections in supermarkets, however, were more limited than those at Starbucks stores. Starbucks executives recognized that supermarket distribution entailed several risks, especially in exposing Starbucks to first-time customers. Starbucks had built its reputation around the unique retail experience in its stores, where all beverages were properly prepared—it had no control over how customers would perceive Starbucks when they encountered it in grocery aisles. A second risk concerned coffee preparation at home. Rigorous quality control and skilled baristas ensured that store-purchased beverages would measure up, but consumers using poor equipment or inappropriate brewing methods could easily conclude that Starbucks packaged coffees did not live up to their reputation.

Going into 2004, Starbucks coffees were available in some 19,500 supermarkets and warehouse clubs (such as Sam's and Costco) and generated 2003 revenues close to $160 million.

Starbucks had also entered into a limited number of licensing agreements for store locations in areas where it did not have ability to locate its own outlets. The company had an agreement with Marriott Host International that allowed Host to operate Starbucks retail stores in airport locations, and it had an agreement with Aramark Food and Services to put Starbucks stores on university campuses and other locations operated by Aramark. Starbucks received a license fee and a royalty on sales at these locations and supplied the coffee for resale in the licensed locations. All licensed stores had to follow Starbucks' detailed operating procedures and all managers and employees who worked in these stores received the same training given to Starbucks managers and store employees. As of 2003, there were 1,422 licensed or franchised stores in the United States and 1,257 licensed stores internationally. Royalty and license fee revenues from domestic stores generated close to $150 million in revenues in fiscal 2003, with international licensed retail stores accounting for about $250 million in revenues.

Starbucks had a specialty sales group that provided its coffee products to restaurants, airlines, hotels, universities, hospitals, business offices, country clubs, and select retailers. One of the early users of Starbucks coffee was Horizon Airlines, a regional carrier based in Seattle. In 1995, Starbucks entered into negotiations with United Airlines to serve Starbucks coffee on all United flights. There was much internal debate at Starbucks about whether such a move made sense for Starbucks and the possible damage to the integrity of the Starbucks brand if the quality of the coffee served did not measure up. After seven months of negotiation and discussion over coffee-making procedures, United Airlines and Starbucks came up with a mutually agreeable way to handle quality control on 500-plus planes having varying equipment, and Starbucks became the coffee supplier to the 20 million passengers flying United each year. Since then, Starbucks had entered into an agreement to have Starbucks coffee served on Canadian Air flights.

In recent years, the specialty sales group had won the coffee accounts at Sheraton and Westin hotels, resulting in packets of Starbucks coffee being in each room with coffee-making equipment. Starbucks had entered into an agreement with Wells Fargo to provide coffee service at some of the bank's locations in California. A 1997 agreement with U.S. Office Products gave Starbucks an entrée to provide its coffee to workers in 1.5 million business offices. In addition, Starbucks supplied an exclusive coffee blend to Nordstrom's for sale only in Nordstrom stores, operated coffee bars in Barnes & Noble bookstores, and, most recently, had begun coffee bar operations for Chapters, a Toronto book retailer that had sites throughout Canada. In fiscal 2003, Starbucks had approximately 12,800 food-service accounts that generated revenues of about $175 million. Starbucks was in the process of partnering with SYSCO to service the majority of its food-service accounts.

Mail Order Sales

The original Starbucks had begun a small mail order operation in the 1970s to serve travelers who had visited a Seattle store or former store customers who had moved away from Seattle. Sales were solicited by mailing out a simple brochure. In 1988, Starbucks developed its first catalog and began expanding its mail order base to targeted demographic groups. In 1990 a toll-free number was set up. Sales grew steadily as the company's name and reputation began to build. The company's market research indicated that its average mail order customer was a connoisseur, well educated, relatively affluent, well traveled, interested in the arts and cultural events, and usually a loyal buyer of the company's products. As time went on, the cities and neighborhoods where the company's mail order customers were located became beacons the company used to decide where to open new stores.

Starbucks published a mail order catalog that was distributed six times a year and that offered coffee, a selection of candies and pastries, and select coffee-making equipment and accessories. A special gift-giving catalog was mailed to business accounts during the 1997 Christmas holiday season; this practice carried over into 2002. The company also had an electronic store on America Online. In 1997, sales of this division were about $21.2 million, roughly 2 percent of total revenues; almost 50,000 mail order customers were signed up to receive monthly deliveries of Starbucks coffee as of late 1997. The number of mail order consumers steadily increased thereafter, as did sales revenues from online marketing. Starbucks' management believed that its direct response marketing effort helped pave the way for retail expansion into new markets and reinforced brand recognition in existing markets.

However, in 2001–2002 catalog sales fell off as the number of retail stores expanded and as Starbucks coffee began to be sold in supermarkets. The company discontinued its catalog operations in early 2003, along with sales via the company's Web site (online customers could buy selected Starbucks coffees at Amazon.com and several other Web sites).

Coffee Purchasing Strategy

Starbucks personnel traveled regularly to coffee-producing countries—Colombia, Sumatra, Yemen, Antigua, Indonesia, Guatemala, New Guinea, Costa Rica, Sulawesi, Papua, Kenya, Ethiopia, Java, Mexico—building relationships with growers and exporters, checking on agricultural conditions and crop yields, and searching out varieties and sources that would meet Starbucks' exacting standards of quality and flavor. The coffee-purchasing group, working with personnel in roasting operations, tested new varieties and blends of beans from different sources.

Coffee was grown in 70 tropical countries and was the second most traded commodity in the world after petroleum. The global value of the 2000–2001 coffee bean crop was about $5.6 billion. By World Bank estimates, some 25 million small farmers made their living growing coffee. Commodity-grade coffee, which consisted of robusta and commercial-quality arabica beans, was traded in a highly competitive market as an undifferentiated product. Coffee prices were subject to considerable volatility due to weather, economic and political conditions in the growing countries, new agreements establishing export quotas, and periodic efforts to bolster prices by restricting coffee supplies. Starbucks used fixed-price purchase commitments to limit its exposure to fluctuating coffee prices in upcoming periods and, on occasion, purchased coffee futures contracts to provide price protection. In years past, there had been times when unexpected jumps in coffee prices had put a squeeze on Starbucks' margins, forcing an increase in the prices of the beverages and beans sold at retail.

Starbucks sourced approximately 50 percent of its beans from Latin America, 35 percent from the Pacific Rim, and 15 percent from East Africa. Sourcing from multiple geographic areas not only allowed Starbucks to offer a greater range of coffee varieties to customers but also spread the company's risks regarding weather, price volatility, and changing economic and political conditions in coffee-growing countries.

During 2002, a global oversupply of more than 2 billion pounds drove the prices of commodity coffees to historic lows of $0.40–$0.50 per pound. The specialty coffee market, which represented about 10 percent of worldwide production, consisted primarily of high-quality arabica beans. Prices for specialty coffees were determined by the quality and flavor of the beans and were almost always higher than prevailing prices for commodity-grade coffee beans. Starbucks purchased only high-quality arabica coffee beans, paying an average of $1.20 per pound in 2002. Its purchases represented about 1 percent of the world's coffee-bean crop.

Believing that the continued growth and success of its business depended on gaining access to adequate supplies of high-quality coffees on a year-in, year-out basis, Starbucks had been a leader in promoting environmental and social stewardship in coffee-origin countries. Starbucks' coffee-sourcing strategy was to contribute to the sustainability of coffee growers and help conserve the environment. In sourcing green coffee beans, Starbucks was increasingly dealing directly with farmers and cooperatives, and its policy was to pay prices high enough to ensure that small coffee growers, most of whom lived on the edge of poverty, were able to cover their production costs and provide for their families. About 40 percent of Starbucks' purchases were made under three- to five-year contracts, which management believed enabled the company to purchase its future coffee-bean requirements at predictable prices over multiple crop years. Coffee purchases negotiated through long-term contracts increased from 3 percent in 2001 to 36 percent in 2002. Farmers who met important quality, environmental, social, and economic criteria—which Starbucks had developed with the support of Conservation International's Center for Environmental Leadership in Business—were rewarded with financial incentives and preferred supplier status.

Fair Trade Certified Coffee

A growing number of small coffee growers were members of democratically run cooperatives that were registered with Fairtrade Labelling Organizations International; these growers could sell their beans directly to importers, roasters, and retailers at favorable guaranteed "fair-trade" prices. Buyers of Fair Trade Certified coffee beans had to pay a minimum of $1.26 per pound for nonorganic green arabica coffee and $1.41 for organic green arabica coffee. According to TransFair USA, an independent nonprofit organization that licensed Starbucks to sell Fair Trade coffee imported into the United States, the guaranteed prices for Fair Trade coffees boosted earnings for small coffee growers enough to allow them to afford basic health care, education, and home improvements. In 2003, Starbucks marketed Fair Trade Certified coffee at most of its retail stores and through some 350 university and hotel locations that were licensed to sell Starbucks coffees.

Environmental Best Practices

Since 1998, Starbucks had partnered with Conservation International to promote coffee cultivation methods that protected biodiversity and maintained a healthy environment. A growing percentage of the coffees that Starbucks purchased were grown without the use of pesticides, herbicides, or chemical fertilizers; organic cultivation methods resulted in clean ground water and helped protect against degrading of local ecosystems, many of which were fragile or in areas where biodiversity was under severe threat. Another environmental conservation practice involved growing organic coffee under a natural canopy of shade trees interspersed with fruit trees and other crops; this not only allowed farmers to get higher crop yields from small acreages but also helped protect against soil erosion on mountainsides.

Coffee-Roasting Operations

Starbucks considered the roasting of its coffee beans to be something of an art form, entailing trial-and-error testing of different combinations of time and temperature to get the most out of each type of bean and blend. Recipes were put together by the coffee department once all the components had been tested. Computerized roasters guaranteed consistency. Each batch was roasted in a powerful gas oven for 12 to 15 minutes. Highly trained and experienced roasting personnel monitored the process, using both smell and hearing to help check when the beans were perfectly done—coffee beans make a popping sound when ready. Starbucks' standards were so exacting that roasters tested the color of the beans in a blood-cell analyzer and discarded the entire batch if the reading wasn't on target. After roasting and cooling, the coffee was immediately vacuum-sealed in one-way valve bags that let out gases naturally produced by fresh-roasted beans without letting oxygen in—one-way valve technology extended the shelf life of packaged Starbucks coffee to 26 weeks. As a matter of policy, however, Starbucks removed coffees on its shelves after three months and, in the case of coffee used to prepare beverages in stores, the shelf life was limited to seven days after the bag was opened.

In 2003, Starbucks had roasting plants in Seattle and Kent, Washington; York, Pennsylvania; Minden, Nevada; and the Netherlands. In addition to roasting capability, the Kent, Minden, York, and Netherlands plants also had additional space for warehousing and shipping coffees. The roasting plants and distribution facilities in Kent and Seattle supplied stores west of the Mississippi and in the Asia Pacific region. The newly constructed Minden plant/distribution center was used to supply stores in the Mountain West and Midwest. The roasting and distribution facility in York, which could be expanded to 1 million square feet, supplied stores mainly east of the Mississippi. The 70,000-square-foot facility in the Netherlands supplied stores in Europe and the Middle East.

Starbucks' Corporate Social Responsibility Strategy

Howard Schultz's effort to "build a company with soul" included broad-based initiatives to contribute positively to the communities in which Starbucks had stores and to the environment. The guiding theme of Starbucks' social responsibility strategy was "Giving back to our communities is the way we do business." The Starbucks Foundation was set up in 1997 to orchestrate the company's philanthropic activities. Since 1991 Starbucks had been a major contributor to CARE, a worldwide relief and development organization that sponsored health, education, and humanitarian aid programs in almost all of the third world countries where Starbucks purchased its coffee supplies. Stores featured CARE in promotions and had organized concerts to benefit CARE. A second major philanthropic effort involved providing financial support to community literacy organizations. In 1995 Starbucks began a program to improve the conditions of workers in coffee-growing countries, establishing a code of conduct for its growers and providing financial assistance for agricultural improvement projects. In 1997, Starbucks formed an alliance with Appropriate Technology International to help poor, small-scale coffee growers in Guatemala increase their income by improving the quality of their crops and their market access; the company's first-year grant of $75,000 went to fund a new processing facility and set up a loan program for a producer cooperative.

Starbucks had an Environmental Committee that looked for ways not only to reduce, reuse, and recycle waste but also to contribute to local community environmental efforts. A Green Store Task Force looked at how Starbucks stores could conserve on water and energy usage and generate less solid waste. Customers who brought their own mugs to stores were given a 10-cent discount on beverage purchases (in 2002, customers used commuter mugs in making purchases about 12.7 million times). Coffee grounds, which made up a big portion of the waste stream in stores, were packaged and given to customers, parks, schools, and plant nurseries as a soil amendment. Company personnel purchased paper products with high levels of recycled content and unbleached fiber to help Starbucks minimize its environmental footprint. Stores participated in Earth Day activities each year with in-store promotions and volunteer efforts to educate employees and customers about the impacts their actions had on the environment. Suppliers were encouraged to provide the most energy-efficient products within their category and eliminate excessive packaging; Starbucks had recently instituted a Code of Conduct for suppliers of noncoffee products that addressed standards for social responsibility, including labor and human rights. No genetically modified ingredients were used in any food or beverage products that Starbucks served, with the exception of milk (U.S. labeling requirements do not require milk producers to disclose the use of hormones aimed at increasing the milk production of dairy herds).

Starbucks stores participated regularly in local charitable projects of one kind or another, donating drinks, books, and proceeds from store-opening benefits. Employees were encouraged to recommend and apply for grants from the Starbucks Foundation to benefit local community literacy organizations.

On the Fourth of July weekend in 1997, three Starbucks employees were murdered in the company's store in the Georgetown area of Washington, D.C.; Starbucks offered a $100,000 reward for information leading to the arrest of the murderer(s). The company announced that it would reopen the store in early 1998 and donate all future net proceeds of the store to a Starbucks Memorial Fund that would make annual grants to local groups working to reduce violence and aid the victims of violent crimes.

Starbucks felt so deeply about its responsibilities that it even developed an environmental mission statement to expand on its corporate mission statement (see Exhibit 9). In 2002 Starbucks also began issuing an annual "Corporate Social Responsibility Report" (the reports for recent years can be viewed in the Investors section at www.starbucks.com). Going into 2004, Starbucks had received 20 awards from a diverse group of organizations for its philanthropic, community service, and environmental activities.

Exhibit 9   STARBUCKS' ENVIRONMENTAL MISSION STATEMENT

Starbucks is committed to a role of environmental leadership in all facets of our business. We fulfill this mission by a commitment to:

- Understanding of environmental issues and sharing information with our partners.
- Developing innovative and flexible solutions to bring about change.
- Striving to buy, sell, and use environmentally friendly products.
- Recognizing that fiscal responsibility is essential to our environmental future.
- Instilling environmental responsibility as a corporate value.
- Measuring and monitoring our progress for each project.

Starbucks' Excursion into Dot-Com Businesses

In the late 1990s, Howard Schultz became enamored with the potential of the Internet and pushed Starbucks into a series of dot-com investments:

- Cooking.com—a Santa Monica—based e-tailer of kitchenwares, which was still operating in late 2003, although it had not yet earned a profit.

- Living.com, Inc.—an online retailer of furniture and home products in which Starbucks invested $20.3 million. Living.com filed for bankruptcy in mid-2000, even though it had recently been rated as the best online retailer of furniture by e-commerce analyst Gomez.com. Living.com had allied with Amazon.com (which was also an investor) to market its products under the "Home" tab on Amazon's Web site.

- Kozmo.com, Inc.—an Internet start-up that offered fast and free delivery of products such as video games, movies, snacks, and magazines. Starbucks and Kozmo entered into a joint marketing pact in early 2000 that called for Kozmo.com to pay Starbucks $150 million over the next five years for prominent placement in Starbucks shops. Under the terms of the deal, Kozmo would locate "drop boxes" for the return of videos and other items in Starbucks stores throughout the cities where Kozmo operated. Kozmo also agreed to deliver packaged Starbucks coffees, teas, and other products, and look into opportunities to deliver hot beverages. The agreement was a crucial part of Kozmo's planned expansion to 21 U.S. cities by the end of 2000; Kozmo currently offered one-hour delivery of videos, books, magazines, meals, snacks and beverages in the New York, San Francisco, Boston, Seattle, and Washington, D.C., markets. Kozmo, which began operations in March 1998 to deliver videos in the Greenwich Village section of Manhattan, had secured $28 million in venture capital funding in 1999 and reportedly received $60 million from Amazon.com and an additional $30 million from Japanese Internet investor Softbank in January 2000. After burning through some $280 million in capital and getting little interest from consumers, Kozmo closed down operations in April 2001.

- Talk City, Inc.—a 1996 start-up founded by former Apple employees to create chat rooms and online communities on its own Web site as well as for other sites. Starbucks had invested in a $20 million pre-IPO offering of Talk City stock in 1999. Talk City generated most of its revenue from advertising and sponsorships on its sites. Howard Schultz planned to promote Talk City's Web chats at Starbucks stores offering Internet access to patrons. Talk City shut down its Web site and filed for Chapter 7 bankruptcy in August 2002, after changing its name to Live-World in 2001 and then selling its assets to MyESP.com in late 2001. LiveWorld's customers included the Internal Revenue Service, Cisco Systems, Eastman Kodak, Coca-Cola, and Costco; its revenues reached a peak of about $14.8 million, but the company was never profitable, with annual losses running as high as $42 million.

In the fourth quarter of 2000, Starbucks wrote off the full amount of its equity investment in Living.com and the majority of its equity investments in Cooking.com, Kozmo.com, and Talk City—a total of $58.8 million.

The Specialty Coffee Industry

While the market for traditional commercial-grade coffees had stagnated since the 1970s, the specialty coffee segment had expanded as interested, educated, upscale consumers became increasingly inclined to upgrade to premium coffees with more robust flavors. Whereas retail sales of specialty coffees amounted to only $45 million in 1969, by 1994 retail sales of specialty coffees had increased to $2 billion, much of which stemmed from sales in coffee bars or the shops of coffee-bean retailers (like Peet's). The increase was attributed to wider consumer awareness of and appreciation for fine coffee, the emergence of coffee bars featuring a blossoming number of premium coffee beverages, and the adoption of a healthier lifestyle that prompted some consumers to replace alcohol with coffee. Coffee's image changed from one of just a breakfast or after-dinner beverage to a drink that could be enjoyed anytime in the company of others. Many coffee drinkers took to the idea of coffee bars where they could enjoy a high-caliber coffee beverage and sit back and relax with friends or business associates.

Some industry experts expected the gourmet coffee market in the United States to be saturated by 2005. But the international market was much more wide open as of early 2004. The United States, Germany, and Japan were the three biggest coffee-consuming countries.

Competitors

In 2003, there were an estimated 14,000 specialty coffee outlets in the United States, with some observers predicting there would be as many as 18,000 locations selling specialty coffee drinks by 2015. Starbucks' success was prompting a number of ambitious rivals to scale up their expansion plans. No other specialty coffee rival had even as many as 250 stores, but there were at least 20 small local and regional chains that aspired to compete against Starbucks in their local market arenas, most notably Tully's Coffee (98 stores in 4 states), Gloria Jean's (280 mall locations in 35 states and several foreign countries), New World Coffee (30 locations), Brew HaHa (15 locations in Delaware and Pennsylvania), Bad Ass Coffee (about 30 locations in 10 states and Canada), Caribou Coffee (241 locations in 9 states), Second Cup Coffee (the largest chain based in Canada), and Qwiky's (India). While it had been anticipated in the late 1990s that local and regional chains would merge to better position themselves as an alternative to Starbucks, such consolidation had not occurred as of 2003. But numerous retail entrepreneurs had picked up on the growing popularity of specialty coffees and opened coffee bars in high-pedestrian-traffic locations to serve espresso, cappuccino, lattes, and other coffee drinks.

In late 2003, McDonald's announced it would begin opening a new type of store called McCafe featuring premium coffee and made-to-order specialty drinks in a café-style setting, with Internet access also available. Krispy Kreme Doughnuts had recently upgraded the number and quality of the coffee drinks it offered at its locations.

Starbucks also faced competition from nationwide coffee manufacturers such as Kraft General Foods (the parent of Maxwell House), Procter & Gamble (the marketer of Folger's and Millstone brands), and Nestlé, all of which distributed their coffees through supermarkets. There were also dozens of specialty coffee companies that sold whole-bean coffees in supermarkets—brands like Green Mountain, Allegro, Peaberry, Brothers, and Millstone. Because many consumers were accustomed to purchasing their coffee supplies at supermarkets, it was easy for them to substitute whatever specialty coffee brand or brands were featured in their local supermarkets for Starbucks. But despite the upsurge of interest in specialty coffees, the National Coffee Association reported that regular coffee still accounted for 87 percent of all coffee consumed in the United States in 2002; some industry experts believed that this statistic signaled that the gourmet coffee segment was still emerging.

Growing numbers of restaurants were upgrading the quality of the coffee they served. And both General Foods and Procter & Gamble had introduced premium blends of their Maxwell House and Folger's coffees on supermarket shelves, pricing them several dollars below Starbucks' offerings.

Future Challenges

In fiscal 2004, Starbucks planned to open approximately 1,300 new stores worldwide and to have comparable store sales growth of 3 to 7 percent. Top management believed that it could grow revenues by about 20 percent annually and net earnings by 20–25 percent annually for the next three to five years. To sustain the company's growth and make Starbucks one of the world's preeminent global brands, Howard Schultz believed that the company had to challenge the status quo, be innovative, take risks, and adapt its vision of who it was, what it did, and where it was headed. He was pushing Starbucks executives to consider a number of fundamental strategic questions. What could Starbucks do to make its stores an even more elegant "third place" that welcomed, rewarded, and surprised customers? What new products and new experiences could Starbucks provide that would uniquely belong to or be associated with Starbucks? How could Starbucks reach people who were not coffee drinkers? What new or different strategic paths should Starbucks pursue to achieve its objective of becoming the most recognized and respected brand in the world?

Endnotes

[1] As quoted in Cora Daniels, "Mr. Coffee," *Fortune,* April 14, 2003, p. 139.
[2] Howard Schultz and Dori Jones Yang, *Pour Your Heart Into It* (New York: Hyperion, 1997), p. 33.
[3] Ibid., p. 34.
[4] Ibid., p. 36.
[5] As told in ibid., p. 48.
[6] Ibid., pp. 61–62.
[7] As quoted in Jennifer Reese, "Starbucks: Inside the Coffee Cult," *Fortune,* December 9, 1996, p. 193.
[8] Schultz and Yang, *Pour Your Heart Into It,* pp. 101–2.
[9] Ibid., p. 142.
[10] Ibid., p. 129.
[11] As related in ibid., pp. 131–36.
[12] Starbucks annual report, 2002, p. 32.
[13] Ibid.
[14] Ibid.

[15]Ben van Houten, "Employee Perks: Starbucks Coffee's Employee Benefit Plan," *Restaurant Business,* May 15, 1997, p. 85.

[16]As related in Schultz and Yang, *Pour Your Heart Into It,* p. 168.

[17]As quoted in Ingrid Abramovitch, "Miracles of Marketing," *Success* 40, no. 3, p. 26.

[18]Daniels, "Mr. Coffee," p. 140.

[19]Ibid.

[20]Starbucks annual report, 2002, Letter to Shareholders.

[21]Ibid.

[22]Kate Rounds, "Starbucks Coffee," *Incentive* 167, no. 7, p. 22.

[23]Starbucks fiscal 2002 annual report, p. 15.

[24]David Bank, "Starbucks Faces Growing Competition: Its Own Stores," *The Wall Street Journal,* January 21, 1997, p. B1.

[25]As related in Schultz and Yang, *Pour Your Heart Into It,* p. 224.

Netflix in 2004
What Strategic Moves to Make Next?

Braxton Maddox
The University of Alabama

Netflix had a wild ride in 2004. Since its founding in 1997, the pioneering online DVD rental company had reported big increases in the numbers of subscribers and proved to skeptics that its business model for online DVD rentals could be very profitable. But the company's strong performance had a major downside—the online rental market was proving to be so lucrative that Netflix's success and growing reputation had induced both retail giant Wal-Mart and movie rental leader Blockbuster Video to enter the DVD rental market and try to horn in on its bonanza. Amazon.com was expected to enter the DVD rental market in early 2005.

Reed Hastings, founder and CEO of Netflix, stared apprehensively at his company's six-month plummeting stock performance, searching for what to tell waiting analysts about the next strategic moves that Netflix needed to make. For Netflix, the challenges of being a pioneer in a growing industry had just quadrupled. Both Wal-Mart and Blockbuster had entered the competitive arena with the intent of becoming the single dominant player in the business. Hastings speculated about how his company was to survive competitive attack from Wal-Mart and Blockbuster, and be added to the short list of dot-com wonder businesses that made it through the pioneer stages. With large competitors holding enough resources to mount strong, enduring attacks against Netflix, and with the ever-changing aspects of the movie and entertainment industry, Hastings was faced with the challenge of how to sustain Netflix's growth and determine the best ways to protect its industry-leading position against mounting competition from strong rivals.

During the months in which Netflix's online DVD rental service had grown to mainstream use, Netflix had remained a few steps ahead of its closest competitors, but that certainly didn't calm the mind of Reed Hastings. After successfully founding his first company, Pure Software, in 1991, Hastings engineered several acquisitions to make that company one of the 50 largest software companies in the world by 1997. Hastings then founded Netflix in 1997, launched the online subscription service in 1999, and led Netflix to a subscriber base of over 2 million in just four years. (Online service AOL took six years to acquire the same number of subscribers.)

During the third quarter of 2004, despite a rapidly changing industry environment, Netflix reported a stronger-than-expected boost in subscribers of 73 percent (versus 74 percent for the first nine months of 2003). Netflix had become not only one of the very

Prepared under the supervision of Professor A. J. Strickland, The University of Alabama. Copyright © 2004 by Braxton Maddox and A. J. Strickland.

few dot-com success stories but also a highly profitable one, growing substantially in the face of increasingly strong competition.

The strong success of Netflix did not go unnoticed. Since its founding in 1997, Netflix had battled the ever-evolving channels of DVD entertainment and accumulated a steady stream of competitors, the latest and most important of which included retail giant Wal-Mart and movie rental leader Blockbuster Video. So far, Netflix had remained ahead of the game with, among other things, innovative technology and software to help manage its intricate rental system. Netflix had pioneered the online DVD rental industry when DVDs were rare and had developed a strong lead of customers, revenue, and brand recognition. "No one is going to out-hare Netflix," Hastings said. "Our danger is in a tortoise attack. Wal-Mart has the ability to mount such a steady, relentless attack."

In June 2003, Netflix won a patent that covered much of its business model and, management believed, would help it ward off future competitors or at least allow it to demand licensing fees for the service. Mike Schuh of Foundation Capital, one of Netflix's earliest financial backers, noted that the barriers to entry in the online DVD rental market were very low, but the barriers to profitability were extremely high. But, aside from competition from new entrants, Netflix also faced another potent challenge: the likelihood that DVDs would soon no longer be the medium of choice for home entertainment and that customers would instead use high-speed Internet services to begin to download movies directly to their personal computers or television sets.

DVDs

The digital video disc (DVD) player was one of the most successful consumer electronic products of all time (see Exhibit 1). The DVD market was also one of the fastest-growing markets, experiencing unprecedented growth since its debut in 1997 (see Exhibit 2); the growth was largely attributed to dramatically falling component prices. DVD playback had worked its way into a number of electronic devices, and DVD recording was expected to be an essential driver of the DVD market. DVD recorders were forecast to surpass sales of play-only DVD players by 2007, with an expected compound annual growth rate of 126 percent. DVD sales for 2003 were expected to reach $11.4 billion, up 34 percent from 2002 and double those of 2001.

DVD movies were available through a wide variety of channels to the consumer:

- Physical retail store and stand-alone outlet sales such as Wal-Mart and Best Buy.
- Physical retail store rental outlets such as Movie Gallery and Blockbuster Video.
- Web sites of both brick-and-mortar stores and Internet-only retailers such as Amazon.com.
- Online rental services such as Netflix and Wal-Mart's online service.
- PC downloads from Web sites such as Movielink or file-sharing programs such as Kazaa.

Netflix

Netflix was based in Los Gatos, California. As the world's largest online DVD rental service, it had a library of more than 25,000 movies and an inventory of 16 million DVDs. Netflix's business model was simple: Customers signed up for a subscription

Exhibit 1 REVENUES, GROWTH, AND MARKET SHARE FOR DVD AND VHS RENTALS

	1997	1998	1999	2000	2001	2002 E	2003 E	2004 E	2005 E	2006 E
Revenues ($ millions)										
DVD rental	$ 2	$ 22	$ 110	$ 747	$ 2,348	$ 4,218	$ 6,044	$ 7,429	$ 8,548	$ 9,574
VHS rental	8,973	9,634	10,003	9,537	8,471	7,210	5,951	5,043	4,292	3,433
Total rental	$8,975	$9,657	$10,113	$10,284	$10,819	$11,428	$11,995	$12,472	$12,840	$13,007
Growth										
DVD rental	NA	1,259%	396%	577%	214%	80%	43%	23%	15%	12%
VHS rental	NA	7%	4%	–5%	–11%	–15%	–17%	–15%	–15%	–20%
Total rental	NA	8%	5%	2%	5%	6%	5%	4%	3%	1%
% of total rental market										
DVD rental	0%	0%	1%	7%	22%	37%	50%	60%	67%	74%
VHS rental	100%	100%	99%	93%	78%	63%	50%	40%	33%	26%

Exhibit 2 DVD GROWTH AND PENETRATION

	1997	1998	1999	2000	2001	2002 E	2003 E	2004 E	2005 E	2006 E
DVD households (millions)	0.3	1.2	4.6	12.6	24.8	36	45.7	53.6	61.2	69
Growth	—	300%	284%	96%	96%	45%	27%	17%	14%	13%
TV households (millions)	100.2	102.1	103.2	104.8	106	107.2	108.4	109.7	110.9	112.2
Growth	—	2%	1%	2%	1%	1%	1%	1%	1%	1%
DVD penetration	0%	1%	4%	12%	23%	34%	42%	49%	55%	62%

to Netflix and created a "wish list" of all the movies they wanted to see; the list could be changed at any time. Provided the movies were available in Netflix's inventory, the DVDs were shipped to the customer free of charge. The unique aspect about Netflix was that it provided all the benefits of a typical movie rental store but without the hassle of having to return the rentals at a specific time. For a fee of $17.99 each month, customers could rent as many DVDs as they wanted and keep them as long as they wanted—there were no due dates or late fees. The catch was that customers were limited to having only a certain number of DVDs in their possession at a time. The number allowed varied according to the customer's subscription level; Netflix's December 2004 pricing levels were as follows:

$11.99—four DVDs a month, two titles out at a time.

$17.99—unlimited DVDs, three titles out at a time.

$29.99—unlimited DVDs, five titles out at a time.

$47.99—unlimited DVDs, eight titles out at a time.

Netflix prided itself on fast, free service. It could reach 80 percent of its subscribers with overnight delivery and provided prepaid return envelopes for mailing back the DVDs. See Exhibits 3, 4, 5, and 6 for Netflix's financial statements and recent operating statistics.

In a survey by Netflix, customers said they rented twice as many movies per month as they did prior to joining Netflix. New Netflix customers also said they were immediately more satisfied with their home-entertainment experience than they were prior to joining Netflix. And 9 out of 10 customers said they were so satisfied with the service that they recommended it to family and friends.

Netflix's service was full of innovative technology designed to make browsing and selecting movies as easy as possible. One such innovative service was CineMatch, an Oracle database that organized Netflix's library of movies into clusters of similar movies and analyzed how customers rated them after they rented them. Those customers who rated similar movies in similar clusters were then matched as like-minded viewers. When a customer was online, CineMatch looked at the clusters he or she had rented from in the past, determined which movies the customer had yet to rent in that cluster, and recommended only those movies that had been highly rated by matched viewers. "Over 50 percent of our traffic comes via the recommendation system," said Hastings. "It requires a lot of work in real time." CineMatch ran on two Sun 420 systems and could generate thousands of predictions each second. The data set of user ratings was stored on a third system. "The key is the quality of the data we use," said Neil Hunt, Netflix's vice president of e-commerce. "The more data we collect about user preferences, the better the recommendations."

Also to help keep customers happy, Netflix had developed a sophisticated distribution system to speed up mailing times. It already had 29 regional distribution centers across the country and was building more to allow it to achieve overnight delivery of DVDs for 100 percent of its customers. The decentralized distribution system gave Netflix an advantage over both Wal-Mart and Blockbuster. Wal-Mart shipped from seven warehouses, and Blockbuster from a single warehouse, usually getting them to customers within one to three days. But Blockbuster was moving to put systems in place that would allow it to supply customer orders from its local stores to speed delivery—it expected to be able to guarantee 24-hour delivery of DVDs sometime in 2005. Sophistication came with the software Netflix used to keep track of its inventory. Netflix's system allowed the distribution centers to communicate to determine the

Exhibit 3   NETFLIX'S INCOME STATEMENTS, 1999-2003

(in thousands, except per share data)	Year Ended December 31,				
	1999	2000	2001	2002	2003
Statement of operations data					
Revenues:					
Subscription	$ 4,854	$ 35,894	$ 74,255	$150,818	$270,410
Sales	152	—	1,657	1,988	1,833
Total revenues	5,006	35,894	75,912	152,806	272,243
Cost of revenues:					
Subscription	4,217	24,861	49,088	77,044	147,736
Sales	156	—	819	1,092	624
Total cost of revenues	4,373	24,861	49,907	78,136	148,360
Gross profit	633	11,033	26,005	74,670	123,883
Operating expenses:					
Fulfillment	2,446	10,247	13,452	19,366	31,274
Technology and development	7,413	16,823	17,734	14,625	17,884
Marketing	14,070	25,727	21,031	35,783	49,949
General and administrative	1,993	6,990	4,658	6,737	9,585
Restructuring charges	—	—	671	—	—
Stock-based compensation	4,846	9,714	6,250	8,832	10,719
Total operating expenses	30,768	69,501	63,796	85,343	119,411
Operating income (loss)	(30,135)	(58,468)	(37,791)	(10,673)	4,472
Other income (expense):					
Interest and other income	924	1,645	461	1,697	2,457
Interest and other expense	(738)	(1,451)	(1,852)	(11,972)	(417)
Net income (loss)	$(29,949)	$(58,274)	$(39,182)	$ (20,948)	$ 6,512
Net income (loss) per share:					
Basic	$ (10.74)	$ (20.61)	$ (10.73)	$ (0.74)	$ 0.14
Diluted	$ (10.74)	$ (20.61)	$ (10.73)	$ (0.74)	$ 0.10
Weighted-average shares outstanding:					
Basic	2,788	2,828	3,652	28,204	47,786
Diluted	2,788	2,828	3,652	28,204	62,884

fastest way of getting the DVDs to the customers. For example, suppose a customer placed an order for a specific DVD. The system first looked for that DVD at the closest distribution center to the customer. If that distribution center didn't have the DVD in stock, the system then moved to the next closest center and checked there. This continued until the DVD was found and shipped. If the DVD was unavailable anywhere in the system, it was wait-listed. The system then moved to the customer's next choice and the process started all over. And no matter where the DVD was sent from, the system knew to print the return label to the distribution center closest to the customer to reduce return mail times.

Exhibit 4   NETFLIX'S OPERATING PERFORMANCE DURING FIRST NINE MONTHS OF 2004

	Three months Ended			Nine Months Ended	
	September 30, 2003	June 30, 2004	September 30, 2004	September 30, 2003	September 30, 2004
Revenues					
Subscriptions	$71,278	$119,710	$140,414	$189,630	$359,947
Sales	924	611	1,230	1,428	2,388
Total revenues	72,202	120,321	141,644	191,058	362,335
Cost of revenues					
Subscription	38,326	69,604	71,130	103,402	197,178
Sales	322	184	471	494	838
Total cost of revenues	38,648	69,788	71,601	103,896	198,016
Gross profit	33,554	50,533	70,043	87,162	164,319
Operating expenses					
Fulfillment	8,322	14,373	15,013	21,926	40,176
Technology and development	4,738	5,652	6,325	13,044	17,016
Marketing	12,183	20,477	22,525	35,347	69,695
General and administrative	2,678	3,280	4,122	7,019	10,538
Stock-based compensation	2,777	4,134	3,660	6,887	12,229
Total operating expenses	30,698	47,916	51,645	84,223	149,654
Operating income	2,856	2,617	18,398	2,939	14,665
Other income (expense)					
Interest and other income	534	304	579	1,673	1,474
Interest and other expense	(87)	(30)	(52)	(373)	(113)
Net income	$ 3,303	$ 2,891	$ 18,925	$ 4,241	$ 16,026
Net income per share:					
Basic	$0.07	$0.06	$0.36	$0.09	$0.31
Diluted	$0.05	$0.04	$0.29	$0.07	$0.25
Weighted average common shares outstanding:					
Basic	48,172	51,898	52,211	46,990	51,798
Diluted	62,920	64,975	64,449	61,368	64,797

Exhibit 5   SELECTED OPERATING STATISTICS FOR NETFLIX, NINE MONTHS, 2003 VERSUS 2004

	As of Three Months Ended			As of Nine Months Ended	
	Sept. 30, 2003	June 30, 2004	Sept. 30, 2004	Sept. 30, 2003	Sept. 30, 2004
Subscribers					
Subscribers: beginning of period	1,147	1,932	2,093	857	1,487
New trial subscribers: during period	383	583	590	1,127	1,933
New trial subscribers year-to-year change	38.3%	78.3%	54.0%	36.6%	71.5%
New trial subscribers quarter-to-quarter sequential change	17.1%	(23.3%)	1.2%		
Less: Subscriber cancellations: during period	(239)	(422)	(454)	(693)	(1,191)
Subscribers: end of period	1,291	2,093	2,229	1,291	2,229
Subscribers year-to-year change	74.0%	82.5%	72.7%	74.0%	72.7%
Subscribers quarter-to-quarter sequential change	12.6%	8.3%	6.5%		
Free subscribers: end of period	49	69	94	49	94
Free subscribers as percentage of ending subscribers	3.8%	3.3%	4.2%	3.8%	4.2%
Paid subscribers: end of period	1,242	2,024	2,135	1,242	2,135
Paid subscribers year-to-year change	75.4%	83.8%	71.9%	75.4%	71.9%
Paid subscribers quarter-to-quarter sequential change	12.8%	9.9%	5.5%		
Churn	5.2%	5.6%	5.6%	5.5%	5.3%
Subscriber acquisition cost—consolidated	$31.81	$35.12	$38.18	$31.36	$36.06
Subscriber acquisition cost—U.S.	$31.81	$35.12	$36.97	$31.36	$35.69
Margins					
Gross margin	46.5%	42.0%	49.5%	45.6%	45.4%
Operating margin	4.0	2.2	13.0	1.5	4.0
Net margin	4.6	2.4	13.4	2.2	4.4
Expenses as percentage of revenues					
Fulfillment	11.5%	11.9%	10.6%	11.5%	11.1%
Technology and development	6.6	4.7	4.5	6.8	4.7
Marketing	16.9	17.0	15.9	18.5	19.2
General and administrative	3.7	2.7	2.9	3.7	2.9
Operating expenses before stock-based compensation	38.7%	36.4%	33.9%	40.5%	37.9%
Stock-based compensation	3.8	3.4	2.6	3.6	3.4
Total operating expenses	42.5%	39.8%	36.5%	44.1%	41.3%
Year-to-year change					
Total revenues	77.3%	90.4%	96.2%	77.4%	89.6%
Fulfillment	69.6	99.0	80.4	57.5	83.2
Technology and development	19.5	37.1	33.5	22.3	30.5
Marketing	31.0	105.7	84.9	39.8	97.2
General and administrative	43.2	56.7	53.9	45.7	50.1
Operating expenses before stock-based compensation	39.3	87.2	71.9	41.4	77.7
Stock-based compensation	5.9	142.6	31.8	12.6	77.6
Total operating expenses	35.4	90.9	68.2	38.5	77.7

Exhibit 6   NETFLIX'S BALANCE SHEET DATA, 2003–2004

	As of	
	December 31, 2003	September 30, 2004
Assets		
Current assets		
Cash and cash equivalents	$ 89,894	$167,814
Short-term investments	45,297	—
Prepaid expenses	2,231	3,644
Prepaid revenue sharing expenses	905	3,777
Other current assets	619	1,334
Total current assets	138,946	176,569
DVD library, net	22,238	41,503
Intangible assets, net	2,948	1,415
Property and equipment, net	9,772	13,649
Deposits	1,272	1,539
Other assets	836	962
Total assets	$176,012	$235,637
Liabilities and stockholders' equity		
Current liabilities:		
Accounts payable	$ 32,654	$ 47,668
Accrued expenses	11,625	15,840
Deferred revenue	18,324	26,658
Current portion of capital lease obligations	416	164
Total current liabilities	63,019	90,330
Deferred rent	241	487
Capital lease obligations, less current portion	44	—
Total liabilities	63,304	90,817
Commitments and contingencies		
Stockholders' equity:		
Common stock, $0.001 par value; 80,000,000 and 160,000,000 shares authorized at December 31, 2003 and September 30, 2004, respectively; 50,849,370 and 52,303,438 issued and outstanding at December 31, 2003 and September 30, 2004, respectively	51	52
Additional paid-in capital	270,836	285,182
Deferred stock-based compensation	(5,482)	(3,103)
Accumulated other comprehensive income	596	(44)
Accumulated deficit	(153,293)	(137,267)
Total stockholders' equity	112,708	144,820
Total liabilities and stockholders' equity	$176,012	$235,637

Exhibit 7   SELECTED OPERATING STATISTICS FOR BLOCKBUSTER, 1999–2003

	Year Ended December 31				
	1999	2000	2001	2002	2003
Statement of operating data					
Revenues	$4,463.5	$4,960.1	$5,156.7	$ 5,565.9	$5,911.7
Cost of sales	1,762.5	2,036.0	2,420.7	2,358.7	2,389.8
Gross profit	2,701.0	2,924.1	2,736.0	3,207.3	3,521.9
Operating expenses	2,579.3	2,848.4	2,955.6	2,870.1	4,367.1
Operating income (loss)	121.7	75.7	(219.6)	337.1	(845.2)
Interest expense	(119.3)	(16.5)	(78.2)	(49.5)	(33.1)
Interest income	3.2	7.3	6.1	4.1	3.1
Other items, net	(0.2)	1.7	(5.2)	2.9	(0.4)
Income (loss) before income taxes	5.4	(31.8)	(296.9)	294.6	(875.6)
Benefit (provision) for income taxes	(71.8)	(45.4)	56.1	(103.0)	(103.2)
Equity in income (loss) of affiliated companies, net of tax	(2.8)	1.3	0.5	(2.2)	(0.7)
Income (loss) before cumulative effect of change in accounting principle	(69.2)	(75.9)	(240.3)	189.4	(979.5)
Cumulative effect of change in accounting principle, net of tax	—	—	—	(1,817.0)	(4.4)
Net loss	$ (69.2)	$ (75.9)	$ (240.3)	$(1,677.6)	$ (983.9)
Cash flow data					
Cash flows provided by operating activities	$1,142.8	$1,320.8	$1,395.1	$ 1,451.2	$1,416.1
Cash flows used for investing activities	(1,258.1)	(1,056.8)	(945.2)	(1,303.5)	(1010.4)
Cash flows provided by/(used for) financing activities	137.2	(187.2)	(441.2)	(199.2)	(335.5)
Other data					
Depreciation	$ 220.5	$ 279.0	$ 246.6	$ 232.1	$ 255.5
Amortization of intangibles	171.8	180.1	177.1	1.7	2.4
Impairment of goodwill and other long-lived assets	—	—	—	—	1,304.9
Margins					
Rental margin[a]	66.0%	64.4%	57.7%	66.1%	70.0%
Merchandise margin[b]	21.0%	21.4%	18.9%	17.1%	19.8%
Gross margin[c]	60.5%	59.0%	53.1%	57.6%	59.6%
Worldwide store data					
Same-store revenues increase (decrease)	8.3%	5.6%	2.5%	3.1%	(2.2)%
Company-operated stores at end of year	5,879	6,254	6,412	6,907	7,105
Franchised and joint venture stores at end of year	1,274	1,423	1,569	1,638	1,762
Total stores at end of year	7,153	7,677	7,981	8,545	8,867

[a]Rental gross profit (rental revenues less cost of rental revenues) as a percentage of rental revenues.
[b]Merchandise gross profit (merchandise sales less cost of merchandise sold) as a percentage of merchandise sales.
[c]Gross profit as a percentage of total revenues.

Blockbuster Video

Blockbuster Video was the world leader in the videocassette, DVD, and video game rental industry, holding a 65 percent market share of the $8.5 billion market. (See Exhibit 7 for the company's income statements, 1999–2003.) It had revenues of more than $5.9 billion in 2003—80 percent of which came from the United States. Founded in Dallas, Texas, in 1985, Blockbuster had grown to almost 8,900 company-operated and franchised stores worldwide—with more than 2,600 stores outside the United States. Analysts predicted the movie/video game rental market would grow to more than $30 billion by 2006, and Blockbuster planned to be "the complete source" for movies and games, both rental and retail.

In an increasing focus on retail, Blockbuster had developed innovative programs and expanded its in-store movie, DVD, and video game selection, including everything from the newest releases to a wide collection of older titles in a number of genres. One such innovative program was developed in September of 2000, when Blockbuster began to market the pay-per-view service DIRECTV in 3,800 of its stores. After the initial success of the alliance, Blockbuster co-branded with DIRECTV in July 2001 and thus established its presence in the pay-per-view movie industry. The Blockbuster pay-per-view service offered 44 movie selections a day to subscribers.

Blockbuster also began investigating the online DVD rental market. In 2002 it acquired Film Caddy, one of Netflix's smaller competitors. Blockbuster felt that online rental was a niche market but was nonetheless focused on a program it planned to roll out the following year that would integrate online and in-store rentals. In late 2004, in a move to better compete with Netflix, Blockbuster discontinued its practice of charging late fees on DVD rental returns. Blockbuster ran extensive ads for several weeks touting its new no-late-fee policy. To help compensate for the estimated $250 to $300 million that late fees were expected to contribute to Blockbuster's revenues in 2005, management planned to lower its ongoing marketing, operating, and promotional costs.

Wal-Mart

Wal-Mart Stores, Inc., was the world's largest retailer, with $256.3 billion in sales in fiscal 2004. The company employed more than 1.4 million associates at over 4,700 stores worldwide, and about 140 million people in 11 countries shopped Wal-Mart's stores each day. Wal-Mart had developed a rental DVD offer nearly identical to that of Netflix—DVDs, priced at $15.54 for unlimited service—in October 2002 and implemented it in June 2003 through Walmart.com. Wal-Mart was still offering unlimited DVD rentals at $15.54 monthly in December 2004, but had a two-DVD limit at any one time. Its envelopes and movie selections were also nearly identical to Netflix's. Wal-Mart's policy was not to reveal the number of DVD subscribers it had, but one market researcher expected that at the end of 2003 Walmart.com would have, at most, about a fifth of the number of Netflix subscribers.

Wal-Mart was planning to open more distribution centers for DVD rentals at other Wal-Mart facilities to cut its delivery times to subscribers. Wal-Mart was also still working out the remaining bugs with its online software, whereas Netflix had already spent several years debugging its software.

Movie Gallery

Movie Gallery was formed in 1985 by Joe Malugen and Harrison Parrish in Dothan, Alabama. It began operating in southern Alabama and the Florida panhandle through its wholly owned subsidiary M.G.A., Inc. By 1992 the company had annual revenues of $6 million and a total of 37 stores. Movie Gallery grew through the acquisition of various mom-and-pop video stores and in 1994 had reached a total of 73 stores and annual revenues of $12 million.

In August of 1994, to further its growth, Movie Gallery completed an initial public offering (IPO) of its stock. The revenue received from this IPO was used to purchase video chains, mainly in the Southeast. The company then raised more public funds to continue the acquisition of stores to add to the Movie Gallery name. As a result of this intense expansion, Movie Gallery had grown to over 850 stores by way of more than 100 separate acquisitions and employed more than 6,000 associates in more than 24 states. This aggressive approach took off with no looking back.

From 1996 through 1998 Movie Gallery focused its attention away from expansion and toward fine-tuning internal aspects of the company. Because Movie Gallery was essentially a conglomerate of different mom-and-pop and chain stores, the company focused on implementing the Movie Gallery culture and philosophy. The goals were to assimilate all the different movie stores and to differentiate Movie Gallery from the rest of the major movie rental stores. In 1999 the company once again undertook intense expansion, announcing the plans to construct 100 new stores and acquiring Blowout Entertainment, which added 88 more stores to the chain. By the end of the year, Movie Gallery had revenues of $276 million and some 950 stores in 31 states, plus it created a Web site for customers to review its movie lineups and newly available releases. In 2000, Movie Gallery opened 100 new stores and relocated 25 stores.

Movie Gallery kicked off 2001 by winning the honor of Retailer of the Year (Large Chain) from the Video Software Dealers Association. It followed by completing its largest single-chain acquisition to date, buying Video Update, an international video rental company. The acquisition of 100 retail stores in five Canadian provinces expanded Movie Gallery's store base by 30 percent and gave the company an international presence.

Heading into 2005, Movie Gallery was the third largest video specialty retailer in the United States, with over 2,000 stores in all 50 states and seven Canadian provinces and 2003 revenues of nearly $700 million. Exhibit 8 shows Movie Gallery's income statements for 2000–2003. Movie Gallery had not launched an online DVD rental service, but its large and diverse geographic spread and its ambitions to be "the dominant entertainment source for video and video game rental and sale in rural and secondary markets in the United States" made it a likely entry candidate.

Walt Disney's Movies on Demand

A popular criticism of the Netflix business model was that, even though they could have a number of movies always at their disposal, customers had to wait at least a day to receive newly ordered DVDs. A strong upcoming threat against Netflix was the new technology of movies on demand. There were a number of ways companies could market this new idea, and one of these was being pioneered by entertainment titan Walt Disney. The service, called MovieBeam, could transmit a digital-quality movie to a receiver manufactured by Samsung. The movie was then stored on the receiver's hard drive, a process that allowed the customer the opportunity to watch the movie on his or

Exhibit 8   MOVIE GALLERY'S PERFORMANCE, FISCAL YEARS 2002–2004 (in thousands, except per share data)

	Fiscal Year Ended		
	January 6, 2002	January 5, 2003	January 4, 2004
Operating results			
Revenues	$369,131	$528,988	$692,395
Adjusted EBITDA	61,581	82,260	109,416
Net income	14,356	20,934	49,436
Plus (minus) reconciling items (after tax)			
Amortization policy change	—	16,741	3,634
Stock option compensation	4,919	1,367	903
Legal settlement	—	2,400	—
Supply contract amendment	954	—	—
Early debt extinguishment	177	—	—
Adjusted net income	$ 20,406	$ 41,442	$ 53,973
Net income per diluted share (GAAP basis)	$0.53	$0.67	$1.48
Plus (minus) reconciling items (after tax)			
Amortization policy change	—	0.53	0.11
Stock option compensation	0.18	0.04	0.03
Legal settlement	—	0.08	—
Supply contract amendment	0.04	—	—
Early debt extinguishment	0.01	—	—
Adjusted net income per diluted share	$0.75	$1.32	$1.62
Weighted average diluted shares outstanding	27,220	31,436	33,370
Financial position			
Cash and cash equivalents	$ 16,349	$ 39,526	$ 53,720
Rental inventory, net	88,424	82,880	102,479
Total assets	270,132	363,574	464,289
Long term debt, less current maturities	26,000	—	—
Stockholders' equity	162,182	259,051	320,116

her own schedule. MovieBeam's prices included a $6.99 monthly equipment service fee and a viewing fee of $3.99 each for new releases and $2.49 each for older titles. The viewing fee entitled the customer unlimited viewing of the title for 24 hours. MovieBeam had access to films released by DreamWorks, MGM, Miramax, New Line Cinema, Sony Pictures, Universal Studios, Warner Bros. Entertainment, Twentieth Century Fox, and Walt Disney Pictures.

Movielink's Downloadable Movies

Another way consumers could watch movies on demand was by downloading the movies directly to their personal computers (PCs). One company that provided this service was MovieLink, formed in August 2001 as a joint venture between Metro-Goldwyn-Mayer Studios, Paramount Pictures, Sony Pictures, Warner Bros., and Universal Studios. Headquartered in Santa Monica, California, MovieLink had become the leading online movie download delivery service.

The download service offered customers with broadband Internet connections a wide selection of movies. After browsing the selection of movies, customers registered and rented movies using a valid credit card. There were no late fees or return times, and MovieLink did not require a subscription or membership. Instead, each movie was independently priced by the content provider and charged per rental. MovieLink also offered a downloadable program, MovieLink Manager, to help customers manage downloads, which could then be viewed with Windows Media Player or the RealOne Player. Customers could also easily connect their PCs to their TVs with an S-Cable, RCA composite connection, wireless connection, or cable connection to view the movies on a bigger screen, thus eliminating the problem of having to sit in front of a computer to watch a movie at home.

DVD Recorders

In addition to having the ability to copy and burn CDs and DVDs on a personal computer, consumers also now had the option to copy DVDs with new home theater DVD recorders. About the size of a VHS or DVD player, these drives allowed the user to quickly burn a digital copy of the DVD on a blank disc. Users could record live TV programs as well. Information from the original DVD or other audiovisual input was stored on an internal hard drive, ranging anywhere from 80 to 120 gigabytes, and could then be burned to the blank DVD.

Piracy in the Movie Industry

In the late 1990s music sales were booming. This was of course before the advent of the infamous Napster and numerous other file-sharing Web sites that together cost the worldwide music industry an estimated $2.6 billion in sales in 2002. The technology used to pirate music files over the Internet was also allowing people to easily pirate movies. Web sites such as Kazaa, Morpheus, and iMesh were being used more and more to download movies that sometimes weren't even released in theaters yet. With the pirates just scratching the surface of the $65-billion-a-year film and TV business, entertainment companies were striving for ways to protect themselves from becoming the victims of the next wave of piracy attacks. Some 600,000 films were being downloaded illegally every day, costing film companies hundreds of millions in lost video sales. Fortunately, movie and TV companies still had a little time to work. Downloading movies was still quite a large endeavor, requiring a couple of hours per movie. And only about 27 percent of the country's 66 million Internet users had the necessary broadband connections to accomplish downloading a movie in that amount of time. But the growing trend of ripping and burning movies to DVDs was quickly becoming an underground industry that by late 2003 cost the film studios an estimated $3 billion in lost DVDs sales.

It wasn't that film and entertainment companies wanted to keep movie downloads from happening—as Brian Roberts of Comcast noted, "We would certainly like to be able to make our content available in a digital world . . . but we need to feel secure that we're going to get paid for it." This was vitally important to film companies, for which DVD and home video sales were the major sources of revenues, even over theater revenues. The early success of online music stores such as Apple Computer Inc.'s iTunes provided much optimism among entertainment companies. These stores offered a large library of music files that customers could download at 99 cents per song. More than 5 million songs were sold by iTunes in the first two months of its operation—evidence that consumers were willing to accept limits on copyrights of music, and possibly movies, if the price was right.

Online Rental Market Trends

Despite mounting competitive threats, Netflix's managers had remained optimistic about the future, believing that key market trends were working in favor of a strong, sustained demand for Netflix's DVD rental service:

- Consumers were becoming more comfortable with the Internet.

- With growing adoption of broadband technology and high-speed Internet access, consumers were able to do more on the Internet than ever before.

- As the Internet continued to evolve, reaching consumers online in new innovative ways provided strong advantages.

- As hardware improved and the costs came down, the growth of DVD use as the preferred medium choice for at-home entertainment was accelerating quickly (see again Exhibit 2).

- As ownership of DVDs had become more mainstream, so had Netflix's subscriber base. Women made up over half of Netflix's subscribers, and the average household income of new subscribers had fallen by approximately half over two years—indicating that online DVD rental was reaching a wider socioeconomic range.

Netflix and Reed Hastings had their goals set: "Our vision is to change the way people access and view the movies they love. To accomplish that, on a large scale, we have to set a long-term goal to acquire 5 million subscribers in the U.S., or 5 percent of the U.S. TV households over the next four to seven years." According to one securities analyst, "Blockbuster's the real challenge for Netflix and the challenge for the market because Blockbuster sees its core business starting to deteriorate on a year over year basis . . . Blockbuster's clearly on the defensive here, and they will try to have impact on this market."

Netflix's Strategic Responses during 2004

The entry of Blockbuster, along with Netflix and Wal-Mart, had produced a three-way race for online rental market supremacy. John Antioco, CEO of Blockbuster, said, "Our mission right now is to transform Blockbuster from a place you go to rent movies to a place you go to rent or buy movies or games new or used, pay by the day, pay by the month, online or in-store." While Blockbuster didn't reveal how many customers it currently had signed up for its online service, John Antioco noted that "after six weeks, we had more subscribers than Netflix had in a year and a half of existence." Furthermore, there were continuing strong rumors that Amazon would likely enter the online rental business in a few months.

In response to all the recent events, Netflix halted expansion into Britain and Canada and dropped its monthly subscription price from $21.99 to $17.99 starting November 1, 2004—a move that precipitated a price war with Blockbuster. At this price,

Netflix believed it could continue to grow its subscriber base but it would only be breaking even. After Netflix's price drop, Blockbuster responded with a price drop from $19 to $17.50 per month. Since Netflix's price reduction announcement, investors had become nervous not only about Netflix's profitability but also about whether it had the market staying power against such formidable competitors. CEO Reed Hastings commented, "They're certainly gunning for us and us for them." Harry Katica, with Aperion Group LLC, said "Any type of aggressive pricing is temporary. I don't think any of these businesses can survive at $17 a month."

Netflix's business future was thus questionable—at least investors thought so, as evidenced by the drop in the company's stock price from around $35 as late as July 2004 to just $12 in mid-December 2004. Several questions Hastings needed to answer kept looming overhead. How could Netflix sustain itself and grow given the sudden rise of such strong competition? What financial resources would the company have when it was just breaking even after the price cut? If Netflix managed to remain the market leader, how could it gain a sustainable competitive advantage to enable it to ward off a significant competitive attack in the future? And, more immediately, what was Hastings going to say to the analysts about the details of just how Netflix was going to adjust its strategy to try to protect its market-leading position against such formidable competition?

From KaZaA to Skype

N. Rajshekar
ICFAI Business School

Kalyani Vemuri
ICFAI Business School

I knew it was over when I downloaded Skype. When the inventors of KaZaA are distributing for free a little program that you can use to talk to anybody else, and the quality is fantastic, and it's free—it's over. The world will change now inevitably.[1]
—Michael Powell, Chairman, The U.S. Federal Communications Commission

Skype has gone from 5,000 users to 120,000 users in two months. Is it going to replace the PSTN overnight? No, but it's certainly a very interesting thing to watch.[2]
—Joe Glynn, Vice President of product strategy at Qwest

Niklas Zennström and Janus Friis, who invented Kazaa the on-line file-sharing program in 2000, entered the Internet telephony–Voice over Internet Protocol (VoIP) market with their new service, Skype. After analyzing the existing VoIP services, Zennström and Friis found that one of the reasons why VoIP technology hadn't made a big impact on the mainstream market was a technical snag that they felt Skype could avoid. Skype launched in August 2003, used the same peer-to-peer (P2P) infrastructure (Exhibit 1) that was the basis of Kazaa. Since there was no need for an expensive central infrastructure to maintain the service, the creators could offer Skype for free. Users could simply download Skype and make PC-to-PC calls, without requiring any telephone and paying just for the Internet service.

From August 2003 to January 2004, Skype (still in its beta/test version) had been downloaded close to 6 million times. Registered users totaled 2.4 million. On an average, 11 new users signed up every minute. According to the company, apart from an initial glitch when Skype went from 0 to 60,000 downloads in one week (Kazaa took three months to achieve that figure), it hadn't experienced any serious technical problems. It also claimed that its network had handled nearly 170,000 concurrent users from 170 countries.[3] Venture capitalists put in $25 million in the venture.[4] All eyes were on Skype, especially in the wake of the big telecom companies (AT&T, Qwest) and cable companies like Time Warner announcing heavy investments in VoIP (Exhibit 2).[5]

Exhibit 1   How Does P2P Work?

How does P2P work?

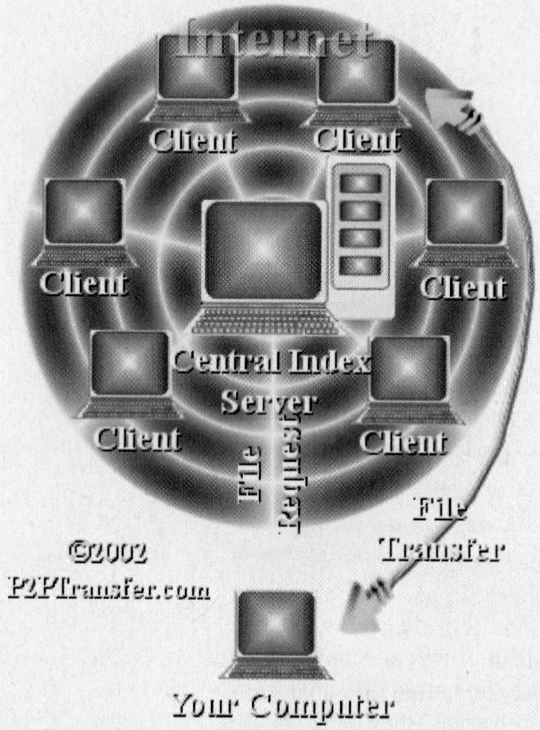

This is what happens when you search for a file:

1. You open the utility. Either the program checks for an Internet connection, or you must connect before opening.

2. If it finds a connection, you are logged onto the central server. The main purpose of this central server is to keep an index of all the users currently online and connect them to each other. It does not contain any of the files itself.

3. You type in the name of the file you are looking for.

4. The utility on your computer queries the index server for other computers online that have the file you have requested. Whenever a match is found, the central server informs your computer where to find the requested file.

5. When the server replies, the server builds a list of these systems in the results window.

6. You click on the file(s) that interest you and then choose Download.

7. Your copy of the program attempts to establish a connection with the system hosting the file you have selected.

8. If a connection is successfully made, the file begins downloading.

9. Once the file is downloaded, the host computer breaks the connection with your system.

Source: www.p2ptransfers.com.

Founding Kazaa

Zennström was working for Tele2, a Swedish telecom company when he met Friis. Zennström had graduated in engineering and business from Sweden's Uppsala University. When Tele2 sent him to Denmark to build its ISP business there, he advertised in a few newspapers for people to join his team. Friis, who was working for a rival company, responded and was hired. Their collaboration continued till late 1992, when both quit Tele2 and started brainstorming for new ideas.

During his days at Tele2, Zennström noticed that watching movies or listening to music online needed large bandwidths.[6] Both wanted to see if P2P technologies could help avoid that by making files stored locally on subscribers' computers accessible to other subscribers who needed them. Napster had already made P2P and music file swapping a very popular phenomenon that raised the ire of music companies. In late 2002, a U.S. judge ruled that Napster had to stop illegal music sharing, a ruling that contributed to the eventual shutdown of that service.[7] Zennström and Friis clearly

Exhibit 2   MAJOR PLAYERS IN THE VOIP MARKET IN 2004

Cable Companies		
Company	**Location**	
Time Warner Cable	Stamford, Conn.	This subsidiary of Time Warner (parent of *Fortune*'s publisher) launched VoIP service in Maine in 2003 and is planning a nationwide rollout this year. It's rumored to be an IPO candidate as a way for parent Time Warner to buy out 18% investor Comcast.
Cox Communications	Atlanta	Cox offers VoIP in one cable market, Roanoke, Va. The company also provides digital phone service—including traditional circuit-switching technology—in other markets, where it pays phone companies to carry some calls. Cox customers pay between $9.99 and $15.89 a month for their first line.
Cablevision Systems	Bethpage, N.Y.	Cablevision offers "Optimum Voice" VoIP service to high-speed Internet customers for unlimited calling in the United States and Canada at $34.95 a month. Its target market will initially include its 1 million–plus cable-modem customers; the product launched in September 2003.

Telcos		
Company	**Location**	
AT&T	Bedminster, N.J.	Ma Bell is starting small. It announced plans late last year for business and residential VoIP services in major cities in 2004, with rollout in "selected metropolitan markets" during the first quarter. VoIP is seen as a defensive move. No specifics have been released, VoIP is unlikely to have a big near-term impact on the stock.
Verizon	New York City	The country's largest telco says it plans to build the nation's biggest "converged network," which includes VoIP. It made a splash with a five-year deal to buy equipment from Nortel. It intends to begin offering DSL customers VoIP equipment and service during the second quarter. No prices have been announced.

Pure Plays		
Company	**Location**	
Net2Phone	Newark	A VoIP pioneer, it's currently focused on selling wholesale VoIP service to cable companies (although it generates its revenues by selling mundane phone cards at convenience stores and such). At one point during the bubble it traded at over $90. It now trades at $8, up from $3 in April 2003.
Vonage	Edison, N.J.	The biggest independent, Vonage offers national VoIP service. Monthly rates range from $15 to $35, and the company has signed up 97,000 customers. The service works with any cable modem or DSL connection. Founded by entrepreneur Jeffrey Citron, Vonage is a probable IPO by 2005.
8×8	Santa Clara, Calif.	A former chip company, 8×8 began offering its "Packet8" VoIP service nationwide in 2002. For $19.95, plus a $29.95 activation fee, customers get unlimited local and long-distance calling in the United States and Canada. Though the company had fewer than 10,000 customers by December, the stock has shot from 17 cents to $5 in a year.

Source: Adam Lashinsky, "Leaping Into the VoIP," *Fortune*, January 26, 2004.

opined that a true P2P system is one in which all nodes in a network join together dynamically to participate in traffic routing, processing and executing bandwidth intensive tasks that would otherwise require central servers.[8] Both knew that there was great potential in P2P, but lacked a clear business plan and the necessary programming skills.

Zennström then turned to a team of four Estonian programmers he had once hired for Tele2. These programmers understood what the entrepreneurs wanted and created Kazaa. Kazaa's software enabled file sharing just like Napster, but that was where the similarity ended. Napster functioned in a way that its servers maintained a catalog of what files were present on which users' computers. As the number of users increased, Napster had to add more servers to update the catalog. These servers later established in court that Napster was directly involved in sharing of copyrighted material.[9]

The Estonian programmers avoided this issue by creating the FastTrack software. FastTrack enabled computers that were logged on to Kazaa to interact with each other and find the ones that had the best processing speeds and Net connections, called supernodes.[10] There is about one supernode per a few hundred clients. These supernodes then started hosting the catalog. As the number of users increased, so did the supernodes. Simply put, the whole system ensured that Kazaa had no information of what exactly was being swapped and therefore no evidence that Kazaa was directly involved in any kind of illegal trading.

Kazaa had become the most downloaded program in the world in 2000, with more than 315 million copies downloaded by users from around the world.[11] They licensed FastTrack to services like Morpheus and Grokster, other P2P programs to bring in revenues and planned to cut licensing deals with entertainment companies. However, on October 2, 2002, the Motion Picture Association and the Recording Industry of America (RIAA) member companies—including Bertelsmann, Disney, MGM, and Time Warner—filed a lawsuit against Kazaa, Grokster, and Streamcast (maker of Morpheus). In order to avoid the complex legal tangles, Zennström and Friis started a company called Joltid, transferred the source code of Kazaa there, and sold the worldwide licensing rights of Kazaa to Sharman Networks, an Australian company.[12] The RIAA later slapped lawsuits against Sharman, which were unresolved by February 2004.

Skype

In June 2002, Zennström and Friis were contemplating their next venture and, according to Friis, were specifically considering those industries that were ready for a disruptive technology. "We wondered what we could do now, what would be big. We wanted to do something that could reach millions of people. During our discussions, we determined that telephony was extremely well suited for a peer-to-peer disruption. The key metrics? It was centralized and expensive," said Friis.[13] "The telephony market is characterized both by what we think is rip-off pricing and reliance on heavily centralized infrastructure. We just couldn't resist the opportunity to help shake this up a bit," he added.[14]

Internet-based telephony, a low-cost alternative to traditional telecom services, hadn't taken off yet in a big way by 2003, Zennström and Friis thought, because of lower sound quality, firewalls, and the use of Network Address Translation (which renders over 50% of residential computers unable to communicate using VoIP software)[15] and the unfriendly user interface (see Exhibit 3).

Exhibit 3   WHAT IS NETWORK ADDRESS TRANSLATION?

For a computer to communicate with other computers and Web servers on the Internet, it must have an IP address. An IP address (IP stands for Internet Protocol) is a unique 32-bit number that identifies the location of your computer on a network. Basically, it works like your street address—as a way to find out exactly where you are and deliver information to you.

Network Address Translation allows a single device, such as a router, to act as an agent between the Internet (or "public network") and a local (or "private") network. This means that only a single, unique IP address is required to represent an entire group of computers.

Developed by Cisco, Network Address Translation is used by a device (firewall, router, or computer) that sits between an internal network and the rest of the world. NAT has many forms and can work in several ways: Static NAT, Dynamic NAT, etc.

Implementing dynamic NAT automatically creates a firewall between your internal network and outside networks, or between your internal network and the Internet. NAT only allows connections that originate inside the stub domain. Essentially, this means that a computer on an external network cannot connect to your computer unless your computer has initiated the contact. You can browse the Internet and connect to a site, and even download a file; but somebody else cannot latch onto your IP address and use it to connect to a port on your computer.

Source: http://computer.howstuffworks.com

VoIP service providers like Vonage, Net2Phone, and 8*8 had to centralize and route calls through firewalls. This ran up the costs of maintaining the network proportionally to the number of users. For example, it cost Vonage nearly $400 to add a new customer. For Skype, it was one-tenth of a cent.[16]

Skype initially offered only PC-to-PC calling, combining the features of both Instant Messaging (IM) and VoIP (Exhibits 4 and 5). For example, a user can both speak and text-chat with different users simultaneously. Skype, claimed the creators, was as simple to use as an IM tool and didn't require special technical knowledge. The hardware requirements to use Skype were 400-MHz CPU, 128MB of RAM, 10MB of hard drive space, microphone, sound card, and speakers/headphones. A broadband Internet connection ensured superior quality, but Skype worked even on dial-up lines of 33.6 Kbps. It worked on Windows 2000 or XP, but Zennström and Friis were working on making it compatible with other operating systems. They were also working on providing other features like conferencing and voice mail.[17] One upside of Skype was the security it provided to its users. Calls made over Skype were encrypted end-to-end using 256 bit AES,[18] the level of encryption usually used by several government agencies. It was difficult to intercept and decrypt such calls.[19] Hence, some observers opined that Skype provided better security than ordinary telephones and other VoIP services.

Business Model

Skype did not announce any plans for charging its services yet. But Zennström was confident that "there was multibillion dollars in potential for Skype." "We're not here to try to make some small business," he said.[20] The creators insisted that since Skype did not have to invest in expensive infrastructure, its basic services would be kept free. "We have zero costs of getting new users and zero costs of running traffic. Our costs are only business development and software development."[21] But it would charge for "added features like voicemail, connections to regular phones, or placing targeted ads on the main window."[22] The creators believed that a large base of users would provide Skype with customers who would opt for premium features and pay for them. They were banking on the use of premium features by a number of customers to bring in a greater part of the revenues.

Exhibit 4   Pop-up of Skype

Source: Dave Salvator, "Review Skype Voice Chat," www.extremetech.com, October 17, 2003.

Zennström's initial focus was on growth. Bessemer Venture Partners and Silicon Valley venture capitalist Bill Draper, two of the early investors in Skype, supported his vision and were confident that it was going to be the "next great company." The founders hadn't spent a single cent on marketing. Kazaa's immense popularity and the fact that both users needed to install Skype contributed to the initial quick adoption of the service. Friis did not believe in putting up features like "Invite a friend to use this service." He firmly believed that such artificial methods do not work. "The product has to be fundamentally viral in itself," he said.[23] The only apparent marketing was in the form of deals with broadband providers to offer Skype's services to customers.

Two other factors seemed to be strongly in favor of Skype's success:

■ ***Growing broadband and Wi-Fi penetration:*** By February 2004, nearly 50 million U.S. homes, or 38 percent of all home Internet users, used broadband. Reports said that the global number of broadband subscribers grew 72 percent in 2002 to about 62 million. Even in a smaller country like Korea, 21 percent of the population had access to broadband. Broadband services were commercially avail-

Exhibit 5 **Skype versus All the Rest**

	Skype	Net2Phone	MSN Messenger, ICQ, AIM, Yahoo Messenger	Other Standard VoIP Clients
Works with ANY firewall/NAT setup —nothing to configure	✓	⊘	⊘	⊘
Unlimited FREE calls to users of same application	✓	⊘	✓	Sometimes
Sound quality	★★★ Better than phones	★ Worse than phones	★ Worse than phones	★ Worse than phones
Secure and encrypted communications	✓	⊘	⊘	⊘
100% ad-free	✓	⊘	⊘	Sometimes

Source: www.skype.com.

able in about 82 out of 200 economies worldwide—almost all of them in the developed world, they said.[24] Analysts expected that broadband would become one of the fastest growing communications services. Also, the expected spurt in high-speed wireless Internet, called Wi-Fi, and Wi-Fi chips would make the Net access wider to laptops, PDAs, and cellphones. Zennström predicted there would be "a migration from circuit-switched telephony services to Internet telephony."[25]

■ **Regulation:** The Federal Communications Commission (FCC),[26] a United States government agency, regulates interstate and international communications by radio, television, wire, satellite, and cable. All circuit-switched telephony players like AT&T contribute to a universal service fund, which helps subsidize phone service for rural and low-income U.S. consumers and Net access for schools and libraries.[27] There had been a lot of debating on whether VoIP service providers should be made to contribute to the fund, and hence, subject to FCC's regulation.

In a statement in January 2004, Kevin Martin, the FCC commissioner, agreed that "Voice over IP raised a lot of regulatory issues that couldn't be simplified into one set of problems, because VoIP services vary quite dramatically."[28] However, Martin added that one effective way to determine whether a user should contribute to the universal fund was to see if he used a telephone number. He explained further, "A telephone number, after all, is a key to the public system telephone network. So if you were using voice over IP that works from PC-to-PC, you would not contribute to the universal service fund. But if you use one of the services that do give you a telephone number, like Vonage, you would pay."[29] Skype, being a PC-to-PC telephony service, would then be exempt from such a regulatory commitment.

Competition

Zennström was candid when it came to defining his competition. Rather than instant messaging clients, he claimed his real competitors were telecom companies. "We see our competitors as being Deutsche Telecom, British Telecom, AT&T, and Verizon." The telecom companies expressed mixed reactions to VoIP and Skype. Tadanobu Okada, director of R&D for NTT Communications Corp., for example, said that VoIP will cost his company "one trillion yen" in 2004 and that NTT was not happy about the current IP phone business at all. A spokesperson for MCI, however, dismissed Skype as a serious competitor. "Skype is for the younger generation, kids on campus—it's not for the mainstream."[30] "Providing voice services of high quality and reliability isn't an easy thing to do," said David Young, director of technology policies at the nation's biggest telecom company, Verizon.[31]

Independent analysts like Dave Burstein, publisher of *DSL Prime,* a telecom-industry newsletter, relegated Skype to a probable profitable player in what for big phone companies would be a marginal niche. "It'll be a cottage industry," echoed Jeff Kagan, an independent telecommunications industry analyst. "Skype will never threaten the traditional phone companies that have billions of revenue, but it is going to be a grass roots success story."[32]

Skype's Challenges

One of the biggest challenges facing Skype was the rapid entry of telecom majors like AT&T and cable companies like Time Warner into the VoIP market. Unlike Skype, they worked with regular phones and did not need a PC. Experts thought that the necessity of both Skype users to have PCs with broadband was an impediment to Skype's becoming a primary communication tool. Also, with telecom companies slashing their calling rates, the no-cost factor would not be very appealing to users, they added.[33]

AT&T was confident that it would garner the Benjamin's portion of the VoIP market. "What Skype is doing is like a toy," said Hussein Eslambolchi, AT&T's chief technology officer and president of AT&T Labs. "They will realize they can't scale it, they don't have a brand like the AT&T brand, and they don't have the local footprint, which we have. It's going to be very hard to compete with someone like AT&T."[34]

Apart from the stiff competition, Skype also faced a potential tussle with the FBI because "traffic over Skype is strongly encrypted and distributed over wide-ranging sources, it could hamper authorities' ability to wiretap."[35] Zennström said that Skype would work with the authorities in whatever jurisdiction it was subject to, but insisted that Skype was just a software that wasn't different from e-mail or chat.[36]

While pioneers like Vinton Cerf had predicted the inevitable rise in the popularity of VoIP,[37] the future of Skype depended heavily on factors like superior quality, number of users switching to VoIP, adaptability to corporate needs, and interoperability between different kinds of services.

Endnotes

[1]Daniel Roth, "Catch Us If You Can," www.fortune.com, January 26, 2004.
[2]"Skype Spooks Operators," www.boardwatch.com
[3]"Skype Rings Jingle Bells," www.lightreading.com, December 24, 2003.
[4]Op. cit., "Catch Us If You Can".

[5]"For Whom the VoIP Bell Tolls," www.businessweek.com, January 6, 2004.
[6]"Bandwidth is defined as the amount of data that can be transmitted in a fixed amount of time. For digital devices, the bandwidth is usually expressed in bits per second (bps) or bytes per second," www.pcwebopedia.com.
[7]Kevin J. Delaney, "Kazaa's Founder Peddles Software to Speed File Sharing," www.wsjclassroom.com, September 8, 2003.
[8]www.skype.com
[9]Op. cit., "Catch Us If You Can."
[10]Declan McCullagh, "Skype's VoIP Ambitions," http://news.com.com, December 2, 2003.
[11]Ibid.
[12]Ibid.
[13]Eric Hellweg, "The Skype Is Calling," www.technologyreview.com, November 19, 2003.
[14]Op. cit., "Why VoIP Is Music to Kazaa's Ear?"
[15]www.webopedia.com
[16]Op. cit., "Catch Us If You Can."
[17]www.skype.com
[18]Ibid.
[19]"Skype Security," www.filesharingwatch.com.
[20]Op. cit., "Catch Us If You Can."
[21]Amey Stone, "Phone Service the Zero-Cost Way," www.businessweek.com, January 6, 2004.
[22]Op. cit., "Catch Us If You Can."
[23]Op. cit., "Skype's VoIP Ambitions."
[24]"High-Speed Web Access Growing," www.news24.com, September 18, 2003.
[25]Op. cit., "Skype's VoIP Ambitions."
[26]www.fcc.gov
[27]"Skype-ing Work," http://education.guardian.co.uk.
[28]"New Rules for the New Telecom," www.businessweek.com, January 6, 2004.
[29]Ibid.
[30]Op. cit., "Skype Spooks Operators."
[31]Op. cit., "For Whom the VoIP Bell Tolls."
[32]"Skype: Net Telephony as File-Trading," www.businessweek.com, January 6, 2004.
[33]Op. cit., "The Skype Is Calling."
[34]Op. cit., "Catch Us If You Can."
[35]www.dailywireless.org
[36]Op. cit., "Skype's VoIP Ambitions."
[37]Op. cit., "For Whom the VoIP Bell Tolls."

Competition in the Digital Music Industry in 2005

Louis Marino
The University of Alabama

Katy Beth Jackson
The University of Alabama

When Shawn Fanning dropped out of Northeastern University in January 1999 to work full-time on his idea of developing a software program that allowed Internet users to search for digital music and then share that music with other users, his parents and many of his friends were skeptical of his career choice. However, when 3,000 copies of the program had been downloaded within a few days of its June 1 release, Fanning, nicknamed "Napster" for his curly, or nappy, hair,[1] knew he was onto something. However, even in his most optimistic scenarios Fanning did not foresee that his creation would revolutionize the digital music industry, resulting in sales of $270 million in 2004, including both online subscription services and downloads, and spawning worldwide sales of 24 million MP3 players (for a total of $3 billion) in 2003.[2] While the growth from 1999 to 2004 was impressive, experts predicted that both the online digital music and the MP3 player industry would continue to grow as more households signed up for high-speed Internet services, more music titles became available for legitimate online purchase, and the price of memory used in MP3 players continued to fall. The fundamental challenge facing industry participants was how best to position themselves in the face of rapid technological change and the continued evolution of consumer preferences.

The Roots of Digital Music: File Sharing

Music file-sharing programs first gained real popularity and widespread attention in the late 1990s when music fans found that they could download a free copy of file-sharing software online and begin downloading music singles within minutes. At first music file sharing was limited to technologically sophisticated music lovers. However, this all changed when Napster surfaced and became a huge success. Internet users visiting the Napster Web site could download the actual file-sharing program and then launch it on their desktop, which automatically connected them to a central support system that coordinated all the users of Napster into a network, and then searched for and downloaded song titles. Just being signed into the central hub made each user capable of sending out music files as well as receiving them (i.e., uploading the files to others users' computers). These users could download as many songs as they liked, burn them onto as many CDs as they wished, and even transfer them to their portable digital music players (commonly called MP3 players regardless of their format)—all without paying a cent.

This activity quickly drew the attention of the music industry and its trade group representative, the Recording Industry Association of America (RIAA), which strongly protested against what it considered to be blatant music stealing, in essence, piracy. What followed was a fairly long legal battle in a case called *A&M Records et al.* v. *Napster,* filed in December 1999 by several prominent record companies. Ultimately, Napster was found guilty of copyright infringement—even though the software did not itself directly distribute copyrighted music files, it did facilitate distribution to the general public. The court ordered Napster to remove all copyrighted material from its central database, in effect ordering the company to cease operations. Unfortunately for the music industry and the RIAA, the shuttering of Napster was largely a hollow victory since by the time the legal battle with Napster had ended, dozens more software programs like its own had sprung up to replace it, but a few had made a couple of important changes. A new era of file-sharing programs, called peer-to-peer (P2P) networks, had emerged. Some of the more popular P2P companies were Kazaa, Morpheus, Grokster, and Lime Wire.

The essential difference between P2P networks and their Napster predecessor was that they were true peer-to-peer networks—there was no central database keeping track of all the users and facilitating the music file searches for those users. When computer users signed on to a P2P program, they were automatically recognized by all the other users on an individual basis. In that way music files were truly downloaded and uploaded from one computer to another; there was no routing the transaction through a central receiving database. That feature made the newer P2P programs much harder to shut down; even if a court had ordered them to do so, compliance was not guaranteed.

Once again, the RIAA and the music industry took action, but they had a much tougher fight on their hands and did not win as many resounding victories as they had won with Napster. Some courts had not ordered P2P networks to shut down because the networks could actually have legitimate uses: Besides sharing illegally obtained music tracks, users could also share personal documents, photos, and other such files. And because of the decentralization of the post-Napster programs, it was much more difficult for a court to determine that Kazaa, for instance, was guilty of copyright infringement. Some of the P2P networks employed the legal defense that they designed their programs to ensure users privacy by preventing the distributors of the software from knowing exactly what types of files their users were sharing on the network. Therefore, according to the defense, it followed that they could not be held legally responsible if the users happened to be exchanging pirated music. This defense proved successful in some instances and led the RIAA to employ a different judicial tactic.

In 2003 the RIAA began targeting individuals who had downloaded or uploaded more than 1,000 songs from a file-sharing program. It filed lawsuits against 216 people, ranging in age from 12 to 60, and it continued its legal assault on music pirates, seeking as many as 75 to 100 subpoenas a day against individuals who broke copyright laws. The RIAA sued pirates for between $750 and $150,000 per song and sought sentences of up to five years in jail. However, the RIAA settled for much more lenient dollar amounts and no jail time in most cases. In its efforts to prevent the most active file sharers from accessing the services, the music industry targeted universities, for two reasons: First, students were prime candidates for downloading free music because of tight budget constraints. Second, universities provided students with access to a broadband network, which made downloading large music and video files much faster and easier. The RIAA began imploring schools to stress to their students the significance and illegality of their actions with respect to P2P networks.

Exhibit 1   WHO DOWNLOADED MUSIC?*

- Pirates tended to be students and young adults.
- 50% of all Web users ages 18 to 29 had downloaded music.
- 27% of all Web users ages 30 to 49 regularly downloaded music.
- 12% of all Web users ages 50 and older downloaded music.
- 32% of male Web users downloaded music; 26% of females did so.
- 37% of African American Web users regularly downloaded music.
- 35% of Hispanics downloaded music.
- 28% of online whites downloaded music.

*The study only reflects information provided by people 18 and older; none of the nearly 30 million Americans ages 12 to 17 were surveyed.

Source: Chris Cobbs, "Majority of Online Music Pirates Don't Care About Possible Charges, Study Says," *Knight Ridder Tribune Business News,* August 1, 2003, p. 1.

While the RIAA's actions could be seen as extreme, the association felt they were justified because of the impact file sharing had had on legitimate music sales. According to RIAA data, since 2000 unit shipments of recorded music had fallen 31 percent and revenues dropped by 22 percent in 2003 alone—declines attributed almost exclusively to file sharing.[3] The RIAA estimated that in 2004 about 60 million Americans were still downloading music for free on the Internet and about 40 million of those were concerned about the copyright laws that protected the music they were downloading.[4] The RIAA estimated that these individuals downloaded about 2.6 billion copyrighted files (mostly music) each month, and that the music industry would lose $4.7 billion in worldwide revenues by 2008 if this activity was not stopped. The profile of a typical music downloader is shown in Exhibit 1.

Shortly after the RIAA began its legal battles, it became apparent that legal action would not be enough to allow the recording industry to completely recover, even if the association could somehow win all of its cases. Observers noted that there was definitely a lesson to be learned from file sharing and declining music sales: the traditional business model used by the music industry was going to have to be revised or changed completely. One writer asked, "Does the RIAA really grasp the significance of 20 million consumers choosing to download music with Napster?"[5] In other words, consumers obviously liked the idea of being able to get music on a per-song basis. As this realization became increasingly clear, in 2000 and 2001 the digital music industry reluctantly began an evolutionary shift in which the major recording studios launched efforts to make legitimate music available online.

The Evolution of Digital Music: Legal Online Sources

Even before Napster began its meteoric rise, major recording studios recognized the need to develop online music offerings. However, concerned about protecting artists' intellectual property, the labels were hesitant to make recordings available online unless they could ensure strong digital rights management (DRM). The industry recognized that any legal music files would need to be encoded in such a way that the consumer had to pay for the file in order to be allowed to play the file on a computer, burn the file to a CD readable in a traditional CD player, or copy the file to an MP3 player. In 2000, Sony

Corporation's Sony Music Entertainment group began selling music singles for $2.49 each through Internet downloading methods. Other companies first considered subscription music services that might entail, for example, having users pay a set fee each month for the ability to download and listen to music files from their computers. Early subscription services would generally not allow files to be burned to a CD or transferred to a digital player. Other early contenders, such as MP3.com, Inc., offered subscriptions that enabled users to upload their own music files to the MP3.com Web site, which would then act as a sort of storage facility that would allow the user to access his or her music files from any PC that had an Internet connection.

By 2001 most of the major record labels were either offering subscription-based services with limited downloading and sharing capabilities, or they were in the process of developing such a service. RealNetworks, a pioneer in offering on-demand, real-time audio over the Internet (a process known as streaming), partnered with three of the owners of major music studios and record labels—Bertelsmann AG, AOL Time Warner, and the EMI Group—to form MusicNet, a platform that allowed distribution affiliates such as AOL and RealOne Music to offer the record labels' content for streaming and for limited download. Similarly, in 2001 Sony and Vivendi collaborated to offer a service similar to MusicNet, but without an intermediary, through a service known as Pressplay. Pressplay was offered through distribution affiliates such as MP3.com, Roxio, Yahoo, and MSN. However, both MusicNet and Pressplay were limited in that they offered songs only from their labels. In 2001 the selection of songs available for streaming improved when Rhapsody, a streaming-only service launched by Listen.Com, signed agreements with all five major labels. The five labels readily agreed to work with Rhapsody since the service did not offer file downloading. However, in October 2002, Rhapsody began offering CD burning for 75,000 titles from its 250,000-song library.

While Rhapsody, MusicNet, and Pressplay were hailed as steps in the right direction, critics argued that the major labels were too focused on DRM and had not gone far enough. For example, MusicNet allowed subscribers to download or stream 100 songs a month, but not to burn the songs to CDs or download them to portable MP3 players. Additionally, users who canceled their MusicNet subscriptions could no longer access the downloaded music. Pressplay was somewhat better in that it allowed users to get 300 streams (similar to listening to a radio for a period of time) and to burn music to CDs, but only 30 songs a month—to be chosen from a very narrow selection of the label's records. Also, users could burn only two songs from a given artist in a month. Rhapsody users could choose from a broader selection but were also limited to burning CDs only; they could not copy songs to portable MP3 players. Not surprisingly, these limitations sparked many complaints early on, with users claiming that there were more restrictions than actual service. At this point in the evolution of legal digital music, many critics doubted that fans would be drawn away from free (but illegal) download services.[6]

The slow adoption of the early legitimate online digital music services forced industry members to realize that any successful fee-based service would have to contain features similar to those of the enormously popular file-sharing software; a wide selection of music, a relatively easy-to-use interface, the ability to burn CDs, and the ability to transfer music to portable MP3 players. Apple was one of the first companies to grasp the necessary mix of consumer preferences; its 2003 launch of iTunes dramatically changed the scope of legitimate music download services.

When iTunes was launched, Apple's CEO, Steve Jobs, said, "This will go down in history as a turning point for the music industry. This is landmark stuff. I can't overestimate it!"[7] Consistent with Jobs's observation, Apple was one of the first companies to

Exhibit 2   DIGITAL AUDIO FILE FORMATS

Format	Comments
AA	Audible, the format used by Audible.com, was designed for spoken audio content such as audiobooks and talk radio programs, including National Public Radio. Many portable music players support AA.
AAC	Advanced Audio Coding, developed by Dolby Laboratories, was best known as the format used in iPods. Apple and Real used their own digital rights management (DRM) technology to secure AAC downloads for iTunes and Real Rhapsody. The iPod was the only player that accepted copy-protected AAC files, and those files were accepted only from the iTunes Music Store.
FLAC	Free Lossless Audio Codec, an open-source format that used a clever algorithm to preserve every 1 and 0 found in the uncompressed file. Though not widely implemented, lossless formats such as FLAC were popular with music lovers who prized sound quality.
MP3	Motion Pictures Experts Group Layer 3 (soon abbreviated to MP3) was the Kleenex of digital music—MP3 became shorthand for all portable players whether or not they used this format. The eMusic online music store and most file-sharing networks used MP3.
MP3Pro	From Thomson/RCA (the company that licensed MP3 to manufacturers and developers), MP3Pro sounded better than MP3 at the same bit rate. However, it hadn't been widely adopted by manufacturers other than RCA.
OGG	Ogg Vorbis was the underdog of file formats. It sounded great, and because it was open source there were no licensing fees when it was used to encode or play music. Although it was not as widespread as AAC, MP3, or WMA in players or online music services, OGG had the potential to gain traction as consumers grew more sophisticated in their digital audio usage and developers looked for ways to cut down on licensing costs.
WAV/AIFF	Uncompressed audio was similar to a standard audio CD. For the most part, WAVs were found on Windows machines, while AIFFs were used on Macs.
WMA	Windows Media Audio, Microsoft's format, sounded better than MP3 at the same bit rate. Some WMA files included copy protection, but others did not. Most players supported WMA, and online music stores such as Napster and Wal-Mart used secure WMA.

Source: "MP3 Player Buying Guide: How Does an MP3 Player Work?" www.reviews.cnet.com/4520-7964_7-5134106-1.html?tag=tnav, accessed December 16, 2004.

convince all five major record labels to give it the right to sell song titles individually and allow buyers to do almost anything they wanted with the purchased files, and probably the first such service that gained widespread popularity (as well as market share).

The record labels were willing to work with Apple due to the company's marketing abilities; its assurance that it was trying to offer music pirates a legitimate alternative; and, perhaps most important, its development of the Advanced Audio Coding (AAC) technology, also known as Fairplay, which made the songs compatible only with the Apple iPod device and provided strong DRM capabilities. For example, the AAC technology prevented individual songs from being burned to a CD more than 10 times. Other music encoding standards such as MP3 existed, as shown in Exhibit 2, but Apple's AAC was considered to be one of the most sophisticated DRM tools so far devised. Apple's iTunes was hungrily accepted by online music fans and quickly became the clear market leader.

In response to iTunes' success, many other major players found themselves scrambling to join the new frenzy of the digital music market. However, some of the previously existing subscription-based services still held out in 2003 against allowing their users to transfer files to a CD or portable digital music device. For example, the CEO of MusicNet claimed that portable devices "haven't caught on yet."[8] However, Apple's growing success encouraged the subscription services to begin offering customers

Exhibit 3   SUMMARY OF LEADING ONLINE MUSIC SERVICES AS OF JANUARY 1, 2005

Music Store	Number of Songs	Format*	Bit Rate	Download	On-Demand Streaming	Free Radio	Premium Radio
iTunes	1,000,000	ACC	128	✓		✓	
MSN Music	1,000,000	WMA	160	✓		✓	✓
MusicMatch	800,000	WMA	160	✓	✓	✓	✓
Napster	700,000	WMA	128	✓	✓		✓
RealPlayer	800,000	RAX	192	✓		✓	✓
Sony Connect	500,000	ATRAC3	128, 256	✓		✓	
Virgin	1,000,000	WMA	128	✓	✓	✓	✓
Wal-Mart	400,000	WMA	128	✓			

Source: Digital Music Services Review, www.mp3.com/tech/services_comparison_delivery.php, accessed December 17, 2004.

more flexible alternatives. Users of these services still had to pay the monthly fee to hear as many songs as they liked, but if they wanted to burn a particular music file or place it on their digital player, they could pay an extra fee (such as $1) and buy the right to do so. In 2003 AOL offered another option: users paid $8.95 a month for the right to listen to songs online and an additional $9 per month for the ability to burn a maximum of 10 songs onto a CD (no transfers to portable players allowed). Rhapsody offered a music listening service for $10 per month, plus $1 to burn a song; again, no portable players were allowed. PressPlay was the only subscription service that allowed users to transfer any songs (up to 10) to either a CD or an MP3 player. The first direct competition for Apple came in 2003 with BuyMusic.com, a service that offered music downloads to users of Windows-based PCs ranging anywhere from $0.79 to $1.14 per song, with the buyer owning the file for good. That was especially significant at the time because iTunes was not available to PC users at first, although a later edition was.

At the start of 2005, the online music market was dominated by a few major players, Apple chief among them, but a number of potent competitors—such as Microsoft, MusicMatch, Napster, RealNetworks, Sony, Virgin, and Wal-Mart—were using diverse strategies to sell music in their online music stores. See Exhibit 3 for a summary of the leading online music services.

iTunes

Apple's commitment to avoiding piracy issues was one of the reasons the major record labels agreed to allow the company to launch iTunes. Begun in April 2003, iTunes allowed customers to buy songs for $0.99 or albums for $9.99 and offered a free, limited Internet radio service. While the store was originally only available to Mac users, it had become available to PC users by October 2003. However, songs downloaded from the site could only be uploaded to an iPod, Apple's portable MP3 player. Likewise, iPod owners who wanted to purchase music online could do so only at the iTunes site because of the proprietary file format used in the iPod and by the iTunes store. In 2004, RealNetworks introduced a new technology known as Harmony that allows iPod users to also purchase music from the Real Player Music Store.

Like the iPod itself, iTunes featured a clean, uncluttered appearance and was lauded by critics for its simplicity of design and ease of use. The store offered over 1 million titles from over 600 labels. As of January 1, 2005, it had claimed 200 million downloads since its April 2003 launch date,[9] with about 2.5 million downloads being added to that number each week. Those amounts placed Apple far above even the closest competition, with some researchers estimating the company's share of the market at 70 percent of all legitimate single-song downloads. However, Apple did not offer music streaming over the Internet, and some industry experts believed that the fact that songs could be played only on iPods would hinder iTunes' long-term growth potential.

MSN Music

In October 2004, Microsoft launched MSN Music, its entry into the online music market. MSN Music users could purchase songs that, with Windows Media Player 10, could be played on up to five Windows PCs, burned to CD up to seven times, and transferred to an unlimited number of Windows Media Audio compatible portable audio devices. Like the other legitimate online music stores, MSN Music did not offer tracks in open formats such as MP3 due to concerns about DRM. It did, however, offer a library of over 1 million songs (although only 620,000 were available at the launch) from all of the major labels, and over 3,000 independent labels (through a partnership with Garageband.com), and had exclusively signed a number of artists, such as the rock group AC/DC. Individual tracks cost $0.99, and entire albums could be purchased for between $7.92 and $9.90, with most albums selling for $8.91. MSN downloads were available in a higher quality (160 kilobits per second [Kbps], with some as high as 256 Kbps) than those from most other music stores (128 Kbps), and the site offered a relatively unique search function that was intuitive and easy to use. MSN Music also offered a free, limited Internet radio service as well as premium radio service, but it did not offer on-demand streaming. While analysts acknowledged that Microsoft's entry into the digital music scene was late, many believed that the move was intended to help extend the Microsoft franchise and to help transform the MSN portal into a multimedia hub. Observers agreed that Microsoft was likely to continue the music store even if it did not prove profitable.[10]

MusicMatch

MusicMatch was launched in 1997 and acquired in 2004 by leading global Internet company Yahoo. MusicMatch offered an easy-to-use, award-winning software known as the MusicMatch Jukebox, which had over 60 million registered users who could listen to live radio available on the Internet, stream MusicMatch channels, create individual playlists that could be streamed on demand, or purchase songs through the MusicMatch music store. As of January 1, 2005, MusicMatch offered about 800,000 songs. Buyers could listen to a 30-second segment of any song prior to purchasing it and then buy an individual song download for $0.99 or an entire album for $9.99. Once consumers purchased a song or an album and downloaded the tracks—encoded in Windows Media Audio (WMA)—they could burn the music onto as many CDs as they liked (it was assumed that they would not distribute those CDs to friends or family but would instead keep them only for personal use), load the music onto any PC-compatible MP3 player (excluding the iPod), and place those songs on a maximum of three personal computers at one time. The three-computer limit was an antipiracy measure—if a user tried to load the same song onto a fourth computer, the software would recognize the action and disallow it until one of the first three computers was inactivated and the fourth activated for the first time. Antipiracy measures such as these were one of the main reasons the major record companies agreed to sell music in the MusicMatch store. Customers who did not want to purchase individual songs could stream music online from radio stations or from proprietary MusicMatch channels, or create play lists of individual songs that they could store and stream on demand.

To increase its customer base, MusicMatch formed a number of partnerships with computer makers such as Dell, Gateway, and Hewlett-Packard to make MusicMatch the default media player on specific computer lines such as Dell Dimension PCs and Dell Inspiron notebooks. MusicMatch would co-brand the MusicMatch jukebox with its partners, thus allowing the partners to enter the online market and giving MusicMatch, a relatively small company, the benefit of being linked to very large, successful companies such as Dell. Although the financial details of the deals were not disclosed, it was likely that the partners received a percentage of the profit from each MusicMatch purchase, thus providing them with a steady stream of income. MusicMatch also partnered with a number of MP3 player manufacturers such as RCA, Samsung, Creative, and Diamond Multimedia to make MusicMatch the default music management software for MP3 players such as Creative's Nomad, RCA's Lyra, and Samsung's Yepp.

Napster

Though Napster was closed down by a U.S. federal court order in 2001, few industry experts believed that this valuable Internet brand would remain dormant for long. In 2002, Roxio, a leader in CD and DVD authoring, compiling, and burning bought the Napster brand name. To support online music distribution, Roxio then purchased Pressplay from Universal for $12.5 million, along with 3.9 million shares of Roxio common stock, for a total price of approximately $39.5 million in 2003 and relaunched Napster as a paid music service later that year. In its legitimate incarnation, Napster offered 700,000 full-length songs that customers could access through either a subscription service or Napster Light. The subscription service charged $9.95 per month for the ability to download and listen to songs and radio stations online, both Internet radio stations and 50 of Napster's own stations. There was no contract; customers simply paid for each month as long as they wanted to continue to be able to listen to any music they had downloaded using Napster. If customers wanted to be able to burn the music to a CD or transfer it to a device, they had to purchase the song for an additional fee of $0.99 for single songs (which could go as low as $0.80 per song when multiple tracks were purchased at the same time) and $9.99 for albums. Napster's songs were compatible with over 60 Windows Media Audio–compatible MP3 players including those from Rio, Samsung, Creative, iRiver, and Dell.

In an effort to retain its original peer-to-peer feeling, Napster allowed subscribers to join its online community. Members could view other subscribers' music collections, playlists, and music tracks and copy playlists they liked to their own library. If they found one user in particular with whom they shared a similar taste in music, Napster's service allowed them to save that member's name and information so they could continue to examine his or her playlist for interesting songs. Napster's other option, Napster Light, was purely a music purchase venue with no subscription fees. Users of this service paid only $0.99 per song or $9.95 and up for albums; they then owned the music and could use it in any legal manner they chose. When it began its offerings, Napster was relatively unique in that no other major online music store offered both subscription and nonsubscription sales.

Napster also actively sought to differentiate its business model by partnering with the Campus Action Network (CAN) to actively pursue relationships with universities that were facing increasing scrutiny from the RIAA for music sharing among college students. By January 1, 2005, Napster offered legitimate online music downloading services in partnership with universities such as Cornell, Eastern Michigan University, George Washington University, Middlebury College, North Carolina State University, University of Miami, University of North Carolina, University of Rochester, University of Southern California, the University of Tennessee at Knoxville, Vanderbilt University, and Wright State University. Students at these universities had access to Napster's unlimited subscription features for a significantly reduced price.

Real Player Music Store

Founded in 1995, RealNetworks, the parent of the Real Player Music Store, was a pioneer in Internet media. It was the first company to allow users to stream real audio on demand and one of the earliest to allow users of its software to easily copy music from and to CDs. By 1998, 42 million copies of RealNetworks' software application RealPlayer had been downloaded and more than 400,000 Web sites used the company's services. In 1999 RealNetworks released its RealJukebox, which allowed users to copy, manage, and play digital music on their PCs from all of the major formats including MP3, Windows Media, and Sony's ATRAC3. A premium version of the software allowed users to copy, or "burn," music from their computers to a CD that could be played in a portable music player or on another PC.

In August 2000, RealNetworks introduced one of the first online music subscription services, providing subscribers with a diverse offering of radio stations, news, music video, and third-party games. Notably, users could not stream or download songs with this service in 2000. In 2001, RealNetwork unveiled the RealOne Player, which was compatible with most major audio and video encoding standards, including Windows Media, Apple's QuickTime, and MP3. In April 2003, RealNetworks acquired Listen.com, the company that had launched the Rhapsody subscription service in 2001 and began offering downloads in 2002.

In January 2004, RealNetworks upgraded its software to RealPlayer 10 and later that year introduced a new technology named Harmony, which allowed users to play music downloaded from the Real Music Store on more than 100 portable music devices, including the Apple iPod and devices from Sony, Creative, iRiver, Rio, and Samsung. Harmony was especially noteworthy since no other music store had succeeded in making its music compatible with the iPod; the software that made this possible won an award as the Digital Music Innovation of the Year in 2004. To highlight Harmony's launch, RealNetworks had a three-week sale during which customers could download songs for only $0.49. RealNetworks reportedly sold 3 million songs during this sale and noted a 50 percent increase in sales following the promotion.

Apple threatened to sue RealNetworks and later made statements to the effect that Harmony's introduction was a form of piracy. Apple even accused Real of using the "ethics of a hacker to break into the iPod."[11] By 2005 Apple had taken action against Harmony by making specific changes to the iPod's software to prevent Harmony from operating. Apple was expected to make similar changes to other models, but it was unlikely that Apple would be able to "Harmony-proof" previously released versions of the iPod. In fact, in response to Apple's move to block Harmony's compatibility with future iPods, a Real spokesperson commented that the company was working to make Harmony once again compatible with Apple's iPods.

By January 1, 2005, RealNetworks' Rhapsody and premium radio services had over 625,000 paying subscribers, and over 1.55 million subscribers for its full range of services, including games, movies, and music. Rhapsody subscribers had access to over 800,000 songs, and the Real Player Music Store allowed users to download over 700,000 songs; customers could purchase individual songs for $0.99 or an entire album for $9.99. One notable exception to the pricing was that, through a partnership with *Rolling Stone,* songs that appeared on *Rolling Stone*'s top 10 list could be downloaded from the Real Music Store for only $0.49. In the music store customers purchased only what they wanted, with no subscription fees, and they could transfer purchased songs to a portable device, burn them to a CD, or simply listen to the music on their computer. Like Napster, RealNetworks was partnering with CAN and universities to make legitimate online music available to students at a steeply discounted price. RealNetworks first introduced its university program in the fall of 2004 with pilot programs at the University of California Berkeley and the University of Minnesota. The initial program was successful and was expanded to include other universities, though not as many as Napster.

Sony Connect

Sony, a relatively late entrant in the online digital music market, launched its online music store, Sony Connect, in April 2004. Sony Connect offered 500,000 songs at a price of $0.99 per song or $9.99 for most albums. In a move questioned by many analysts, music offered by Sony Connect was formatted in Sony's proprietary ATRAC3 format and could only be played in Sony's Network Walkman and other Sony MP3 players. Downloads from Sony Connect could not be played on any non-Sony portable MP3 players, but industry experts believe that Sony planned eventually to make Connect compatible with other players and products. Through the use of Sony's SonicStage music player, users could listen to a free radio service and to tracks downloaded from Sony Connect on up to three computers, copy music purchased from Sony Connect to an unlimited number of Sony MP3 players, or burned up to 10 times on CDs that could be played in ATRAC3 compatible CD players. Some analysts such as Rob Enderle from The Enderle Group in San Jose, California, were not optimistic about Sony's long-term success in the digital music business. When asked his opinion Enderle stated, "I give this store very little chance of being successful, given Sony's poor history in this space, the proprietary nature of the store's technology, and the entrenched competition it will face."[12]

Virgin Digital Music

Virgin, begun in October 2004, became the first major record store retailer to develop an online music presence. Virgin's offerings included a music store, a streaming service, and an Internet radio service, all of which were powered by music wholesaler MusicNet. Virgin Digital Music was Virgin's online store that offered access to over 1 million songs and allowed customers to purchase individual tracks for $0.99 or entire albums for prices ranging from around $7.00 to over $20.00 depending on the number of songs and on artists' requirements. The songs purchased from this service were encoded in Windows Media format and were compatible with over 60 MP3 players, similar to Napster. Virgin's subscription service, the Virgin Digital Music Club, offered subscribers access to over 1 million songs for $7.95 a month and included access to Virgin's Internet radio service, Radio Free Virgin. Subscribers could download their favorite tracks from the Digital Music Club and could play them later, offline on their PCs. However, when subscribers canceled their subscriptions to the Digital Music Club, they could no longer access the music they had downloaded from the club. Finally, customers could access either a free version of Radio Free Virgin, which offered a number of online radio stations, or a premium version, which offered over 60 radio stations. Analysts believed that Virgin's online offerings would be a test to see whether there was any benefit in pairing a traditional music store and an online music store. They also believed that Virgin's powerful brand name coupled with the company's substantial financial position would offer the partnership the best possible chance for success.

Wal-Mart

Consistent with this giant retailer's strategy of selling consumer products at low prices, Wal-Mart offered online music at a discounted rate of $0.88 per song and most albums for $9.44. For consumers who purchased a significant amount of music online, that price discount could make quite a difference. Wal-Mart did not offer a separate music player, as did Real and Napster, but would use any media player the user had chosen as the default. Nor did Wal-Mart offer online radio services or on-demand streaming. The company's 400,000-song library was offered in Windows Media Audio format. Downloaded songs could be transferred to any portable MP3 player, transferred to up to three computers, and burned to CD up to 10 times. Wal-Mart also offered an upgraded music service that required an Internet Explorer plug-in (a software application) that allowed users to more easily buy, download, organize, and burn purchased music using a single interface. This plug-in made Wal-Mart's technology easier to use, as consumers no longer had to buy the music from Wal-Mart, manually add it to their computer's music library, and then manually burn a CD using yet another software program. Wal-Mart's discounted price and ease of use were seen as its two key advantages in this highly competitive market.

MP3 Players

The growth in the availability of digital music was facilitated by and, in turn, facilitated the sale of portable digital audio players. As of January 1, 2005, there were over 100 manufacturers of MP3 players, ranging from market leaders such as Apple, Sony, Creative, and iRiver to small manufacturing firms in China. According to CNET.COM, a leading computer and electronics Web site, there were four basic types of MP3 players, including hard-drive-based players, micro-hard-drive-based players, flash-based players, and MP3 CD players.[13] The hard-drive-based players were high-capacity players ranging from 10 gigabytes (GB) to 60 GB and could hold as many as 17,000 songs. The downside to these players was that they tended to be larger and heavier than others, had rechargeable batteries that users could not easily replace themselves, and had moving parts that made them less suited for use during physical activity (e.g., jogging or working out). Micro-hard-drive-based players were more compact than hard-drive players but offered a larger capacity than flash-based players. These players were more costly in a dollar-per-megabyte comparison than hard-drive players but suffered from many of the same disadvantages of the larger players, such as the moving parts and rechargeable battery. The flash-based players ranged in size from 32 megabytes (MB) to 1 GB. This was the original MP3 player design, and the players' lack of moving parts and small size made them the most suitable for physical activity. However, these

Exhibit 4   TOP MP3 PLAYERS BY TYPE

Hard-Drive-Based Players	Micro-Hard-Drive-Based Players	Flash-Based MP3 Players	CD Players
■ Apple iPod (20 GB)	■ Apple iPod Mini (4 GB)	■ iRiver 795 (512 MB)	■ iRiver SlimX iMP-550
■ Dell Digital Jukebox DJ (20 GB)	■ Rio Carbon (5 GB)	■ Creative MuVo TX FM (512 MB)	■ Panasonic SL-CT800
■ Creative Zen Touch (20 GB) ■ JetAudio iAudio M3 (20 GB) ■ iRiver iHP-120 (20 GB) ■ Rio Nitrus (1.5 GB)	■ Apple iPod Mini (4 GB) ■ Rio Nitrus (1.5 GB) ■ Creative Nomad MuVo2 (4 GB)	■ iRiver iFP-390T ■ Creative Muvo Slim (256 MB) ■ iRiver iFP-790 ■ Creative Muvo TX FM ■ Jens of Sweden MP 300 ■ JetAudio iAudio 4 (512 MB) ■ Rio Cali (256 MB)	■ iRiver SlimX iMP-400 ■ iRiver SlimX iMP-350 ■ Rio Volt SP250

Source: "MP3 Player Buying Guide: What Are My Choices?" www.reviews.cnet.com/4520-7964_7-5134106-1.html?tag=tnav, accessed December 16, 2004.

players were limited to 1 GB and had the highest per-megabyte cost. The final type was MP3 CD players, which looked like traditional portable CD players but could read MP3s from CDs. These players were the least expensive and used inexpensive write/rewrite (R/RW) CDs. However, these players were the largest of the MP3 players and were not suitable for physical activity. A list of the top MP3 players by type is shown in Exhibit 4.

Along with the physical characteristics, the MP3 player market could also be segmented by the type of end user. CNET.COM identified six MP3 user profiles on the basis of user needs and preferences: the commuter, the fitness freak, the traveler, the audiophile, the file hoarder, and the audio recorder. A list of the profiles and the top players by user profile is presented in Exhibit 5.

Exhibit 5   MP3 USER PROFILES AND TOP BRANDS

Profile	Top Players
Commuters Commuters require a portable player. Commuters who commute by car need a hard-drive-based model. Those who commute via subway or bus should shop for a compact flash-based player.	■ Apple iPod (20 GB) ■ River SlimX iMP-550 ■ Cowon iAudio CW300 (256 MB) ■ Rio Carbon (5 GB) ■ Audible Otis ■ Dell Digital Jukebox DJ (15 GB)
Fitness Freaks Fitness Freaks who spend a lot of time in the gym need an MP3 player that can keep pace. It should be compact and easy to operate with one hand. The best player for Fitness Freaks is a flash-based model (with up to 1 GB of storage) that can also withstand tough workouts better than hard-drive-based players.	■ iRiver iFP-390T (256 MB) ■ Cowon iAudio CW300 (256 MB) ■ Rio S35S ■ Creative Nomad MuVo NX (128 MB) ■ Rio Cali (256 MB)
Travelers Travelers need an MP3 player that will enhance their trips with music yet doesn't add undue weight to their carry-on. For those who travel with the same laptop that stores their music, a compact flash-based player is the way to go, otherwise they need a high-capacity player that will hold all or most of their music.	■ Apple iPod (40 GB) ■ Apple iPod Mini (4 GB) ■ Etymotic ER-6 Isolator ■ Sony MDR-NC11 ■ Creative Nomad MuVo2 (4 GB) ■ Creative Zen Touch (20 GB)
Audiophiles Audiophiles prize sound quality above all other factors. Audiophiles should choose high-enough bit rates and look for lossless codecs in their MP3 players.	■ Apple iPod (15 GB) ■ Apple iPod Mini (4 GB) ■ Creative Labs Nomad Jukebox 3 (20 GB) ■ iRiver iFP-390T (256 MB) ■ Rio Karma (20 GB) ■ Cowon iAudio CW300 (256 MB)
File Hoarders File hoarders need enormous capacity: at least 40 GB but maybe even more.	■ Apple iPod (40 GB) ■ Creative Labs Nomad Jukebox 3 (40 GB) ■ Rio Karma (20 GB) ■ iRiver iFP-599T (1 GB) ■ Creative Nomad Zen (60 GB)
Audio Recorders Audio recorders need to capture audio, from either live music sessions or interviews, and to convert music from CDs, tapes, and vinyl records to digital formats such as MP3, WAV, or WMA.	■ Creative Labs Nomad Jukebox 3 (40 GB) ■ iRiver iFP-390T (256 MB) ■ iRiver iHP-120 (20 GB) ■ Archos AV320 Video Recorder ■ Philips HDD100

Source: "What Kind of MP3 User Am I?" www.reviews.cnet.com/4520-7964_7-5134106-1.html?tag=tnav, accessed December 16, 2004.

Exhibit 6 MARKET SHARES AND MP3 PLAYER SALES IN 2004

Company	Market Share (%)	Revenue (% of total in market)
Apple (iPod)	17.7	35.9
iRiver	14.1	11.9
RCA (Lyra)	13.6	8.7
Rio	13.5	11.7
Creative	7.9	8.6

Source: Steve Traiman, "Goin' Digital," *Billboard*, May 1, 2004, pp. 45, 47, 73.

Apple: The iPod and the iPod Mini

In fiscal year 2003, Apple Computer reported net revenues of $6.2 billion (up 8.1 percent from 2002) and net income of $69 million. For much of the company's history, Apple had been very good at being the first company to introduce a concept or a new product but then struggled to maintain control of its market share in that product line. Although Apple didn't introduce the first portable MP3 player (Rio did in 1999), it did introduce the first to gain widespread attention and popularity—the iPod in October 2001. The iPod supports the MP3 digital music standard as well as Apple's proprietary Advanced Audio Coding (AAC) format sold in the iTunes Music Store.

When Apple launched the iPod, many critics did not give the product much of a chance for success as its launch came about one month after the September 11 terrorist attacks and it carried a fairly hefty price tag of $399. However, the success of the iPod had reached phenomenal proportions. According to one article, "It is now a fashion statement, and any other MP3 player is considered 'Brand X' for many consumers."[14] Industry experts agreed that the iPod's success has revolutionized the portable music industry in a manner similar to the Sony Walkman in 1980.

Although iPods accounted for approximately 17.7 percent of the overall MP3 player market in 2004, as shown in Exhibit 6, they accounted for around 71 percent of hard-drive-based players, the fastest-growing segment of MP3 players.[15] In 2004 the iPod was available in three base models: the iPod Mini, a 4-GB hard drive model that held 1,000 songs and cost about $249; a 20-GB iPod that could hold 5,000 songs and retailed for about $299; and the 40-GB iPod, which held 10,000 songs and sold for $399. Apple also offered an iPod photo in 40-GB ($499) and 60-GB ($599) sizes that allowed users to store and view pictures as well as music and a limited edition 20-GB iPod ($349) that was co-branded with the band U2.

All of Apple's iPods featured a thumb wheel, a concept that Apple first introduced in MP3 players, which served as the tool for scrolling through play lists and other menus on the iPod interfaces. When comparing the iPod with other competing products, most critics agreed that Apple's simple and elegant interface was superior to most competitors' and made the product especially attractive to consumers new to the MP3 player industry and willing to pay a premium for the simplicity. Another fairly unique feature was that the iPod included a calendar, a contact list, and a to-do list. These features allowed the iPods to meet their owners' music and personal digital assistant (PDA) needs, so they did not have to carry two separate units to accomplish both tasks. The iPod also featured some unique antipiracy software: if the iPod was connected to a foreign computer (one that it didn't recognize) and the user tried to transfer music files either to or from the computer, the software would give the user a choice—either stop the transfer or proceed with it knowing that the newly transferred music would delete every file already on the iPod, essentially overwriting it and replacing it. While users were not favorably inclined toward this feature, it drew praise from the music industry and allowed iTunes (Apple's music store) to offer music from all of the major labels. The only significant complaints users had regarding the iPod were the relatively short battery life of only about 10 hours and the frequency with which the rechargeable batteries had to be replaced.

As of December 2004, Apple had stated its intention to maintain its investments in innovation and to defend its leadership position in the MP3 player industry. However, the company had no intentions to develop a multimedia player that played and recorded video as well as MP3s.

Dell: The Digital Jukebox

Headquartered in Round Rock, Texas, Dell was known for its build-to-order, sell-direct business model in personal computers and servers. In fiscal year 2004, Dell reported net revenues of $41.4 billion (a 17 percent increase from 2003) and net income of $2.6 billion. A longtime supplier of customized PCs, Dell was a relatively new entrant in the personal electronics market. In October 2003, Dell introduced its Dell Digital Jukebox (Dell DJ), a personal, portable MP3 player, to compete head-to-head against the Apple iPod and other MP3 players.

Dell DJ users could either download music from the Internet to the device, or they could "rip" tracks from the CD collection they already owned and load them onto the Dell DJ. The DJ was both physically and technically similar to the iPod and was available in two hard-drive models. The 15-GB Dell DJ held over 3,700 songs (128 bit rate) and sold for $199, while the 20-GB model held about 5,000 songs compressed at the same bit rate and sold regularly for $279 (but was occasionally sold by Dell for as low as $229). The DJ also claimed 20 hours of battery life with continuous play, although some consumers found that the DJ could last up to 23 hours of play.[16] The DJ also allowed the user to record sound, like any other voice recorder, while the iPod users had to purchase a kit that allowed external sound recording.

Although a relatively late entrant to the MP3 player market, Dell had long recognized consumers' interest in, and demand for, electronics that catered to digital music fans. As early as 1999, Dell began offering PC customization features such as a CD-recordable disk drive, specialized software for managing a digital music library, and of course the jukebox software necessary to play all the digital music on the PC. Dell saw its recent forays into computer peripherals and other electronics such as the Dell DJ as a natural extension of their product line. Dell was committed to building a relatively diversified product line to afford the company a more constant and steady stream of income than the company realized on personal computers alone. Overall, Dell's product rated well against Apple and other competitors, especially given the size and strength of the company and its success in other electronics areas. Although some critics argued that the Dell DJ was not as aesthetically pleasing or quite as easy to use as the iPod, the device was considered a very solid contender in the MP3 player market. With Dell's almost $100 price advantage, huge battery-power advantage, and greater flexibility concerning where users could shop for their digital music, many consumers were expected to decide the iPod was not worth the extra cash and lack of options.

The Sony Network Walkman

In fiscal year 2004, Sony Corporation had $72.1 billion in revenue (up 0.3 percent from 2003) and $851 million in net income, but the company's net revenues specifically derived from the audio electronics segment had fallen every year since fiscal year 2002. In the 1980s, Sony revolutionized mobile music technology when it introduced the Walkman, a portable cassette tape player that spawned dozens of imitations and look-alikes. Prior to 2004, Sony had been active in the digital music industry but had resisted selling portable players that were MP3 compatible. Sony argued that its proprietary compression technology Acoustic Transform Adaptive Coding (ATRAC3) was superior to MP3. In August 2004, Sony relented and released its first hard-drive-based MP3-compatible player. The company also planned to release an MP3-compatible flash player by year's end and to allow users of some earlier hard-drive-based players to upgrade to MP3 compatibility for a fee of $20. However, by this time roles were reversed and Sony was viewed as one of the imitators in the digital music industry.

The 20-GB Network Walkman sold for $399 and held 13,000 songs (compressed at a bit rate of 48 Kbps). The Network Walkman came in a few other flash-based models, which were less expensive and stored significantly fewer songs on between 128 and 512 MB of embedded memory. In late 2004, Sony launched the 40-GB VAIO Pocket Digital Music Player ($499), which allowed users to download photos as well as music. In comparison to the iPod, the 20-GB Walkman was about 10 percent smaller, was one-third lighter, and had a much better battery life (up to 30 hours).[17] However, critics generally viewed the Network Walkman as somewhat inferior to other MP3 players. Some consumers found the user interface to be confusing and difficult to use, and the accompanying computer software for unloading and managing the music was thought to be weaker than the competition's. Critics believed that these perceived weaknesses, coupled with the company's price premium and late entry to the digital music market, indicated that the company would encounter significant trouble in overcoming the competition.

RCA's Lyra

RCA-branded products were owned and manufactured by Thomson Worldwide, which had $10.2 billion in revenue in fiscal year 2003 (about a 17 percent decrease from 2002) and net income of $31 million. The RCA division of Thomson released a portable MP3 player called the Lyra in 1999. By 2004 the company was offering a relatively broad family of players, including flash players (ranging from 64 MB to 256 MB with secure digital expansion slots); hard-drive players (both 20-GB and 40-GB capacity); the Lyra Audio/Video Jukebox, a portable multimedia player that allowed audio and video recording and playback; and a CD player with MP3 playback. RCA's players supported either MP3 or WMA music files, which allowed users to shop for music from any online music store that supported those formats and made the Lyra models more versatile and flexible than the iPod or the Network Walkman.

Like all the other MP3 players with internal hard drives, the RCA players could store any type of information (not just music files), similar to a computer hard drive. The product shipped with MusicMatch Jukebox software, which users could install on their computer to allow music to be loaded and unloaded from their MP3 player. MusicMatch software also played the music on the PC itself and allowed users to convert and transfer music from their own CDs to their MP3 players. Another differentiating feature of the Lyra products was that they acted as radio tuners as well as MP3 players. This feature allowed the user to listen to radio stations and to record directly from the radio to the Lyra's hard drive. The recording could be saved as an MP3 file and later transferred to the user's computer. Finally, like the other MP3 players in the market, the Lyra models included equipment that allowed the unit to be used in a vehicle. A notable difference between RCA and its competitors was that, so far, the company had not launched an online music store and had not disclosed plans to do so.

Rio: Carbon, Nitrus, and Karma

Rio, owned by Digital Networks North America, introduced the very first portable MP3 player, the Rio 300, in 1998. In 2004 Rio produced three different hard-drive MP3 players, all of which were WMA and MP3 compatible. The Rio Carbon sold for around $249 and was a 5-GB player (competitive with the iPod Mini) that held about 2,500 songs compressed at 128 Kbps. The unit could be charged through an electrical outlet or through a computer's USB port, and the rechargeable battery's life was claimed to be 20 hours. The Carbon also allowed voice recordings, like the Dell Digital Jukebox, and was supported on either PC or Mac operating systems.

Rio's Karma was a 20-GB player similar to the Dell DJ and sold for $299. Rio claimed that this unit could hold up to 5,000 MP3 song files compressed at 128 Kbps and that the rechargeable lithium ion battery would last up to 15 hours. The Karma was designed to be attached to a home stereo system or to a computer's speaker system for easy listening ability.

Finally, Rio's Nitrus was a 1.5-GB model that sold for $169, held about 375 MP3 music files, and had a rechargeable battery with a 16-hour battery life. Even smaller than the iPod Mini, the Rio Nitrus was yet another alternative for users who needed to take only a limited amount of music with them but still wanted quality and reliability from a hard-drive MP3 player. Based on battery life and price, critics believed that Rio's units were equal or superior to the other players available. Like RCA, Rio did not operate an online music store.

Creative: Nomad Zen Xtra

Creative reported 2003 revenues of $701 million (down 12.9 percent from 2002) and net income of $23.4 million. Creative offered the broadest and most diverse array of MP3 players, including hard disk/micro drive players such as the Zen Micro, the Zen Touch, and the Nomad Jukebox Zen, flash drive players such as the MuVo, and digital MP3 players such as the Rhomba. Creative also offered the Zen multimedia center which leveraged the Windows Media Center Edition software and allowed users to listen to, record, and play back WMAs and MP3s, movies, and television shows, as well as to view photos.

Creative's hard disk players differentiate themselves slightly from the competition by offering the Nomad Zen Xtra, a 60-GB hard-drive player that held up to 16,000 songs (128 Kbps) and sold for $369. Creative also offered a 30-GB model for $239 and a 40-GB model for $269. The two smaller models competed directly with the iPod based on price, and the largest model on its hard-drive size. Like the other hard-drive models, the Nomad Zen Xtra players doubled as external hard drives and could carry any type of files, not just music or MP3 files. The rechargeable battery claimed a life of up to 14 hours, and the player could serve as an alarm clock that would wake the user to the sound of music. Creative's players allowed users to slow down a song while it is playing without ruining the pitch or to speed up an audio file (such as a book) without making it sound nonsensical.[18] Downsides to the Creative products were that the car adapter kit had to be purchased separately and the user had to purchase online music from other sources.

Creative offered a wide variety of flash drives under the MuVo brand, ranging from the Creative MuVo Micro N200, which claimed a 15-hour battery life and included an FM tuner and the ability to record from the tuner, ranged in size from 128 MB to 1 GB, and came in "8 fun and vibrant colors" (according to the company's marketing literature), to the Nomad MuVo, which could be used as a USB drive and had a 12-hour battery life on one AAA battery.

Creative's digital MP3 players were compatible with both WMA and MP3, as were the company's other players. The Rhomba Nx featured an FM tuner and MP3 encoding and ranged in size from 128 MB to 512 MB. The 20-GB Nomad Jukebox 3, which was targeted to audiophiles, included a second battery bay boosting the player's life to 22 hours with both batteries installed.

iRiver: H140 and H120

iRiver Inc. was owned by Reigncom Ltd., which reported in 2003 sales growth of over 182 percent from 2002. In 2004 iRiver produced hard-drive-based players, flash-based players, portable multimedia players, and CD players. The two hard-drive MP3 players were the H320 ($329, 20 GB, enhanced 3-D audio, and a 16-hour rechargeable battery) and the H340 (40 GB, $429). The H300 series was an improvement over the company's H100 series and included a full-color screen, MP3, WMA, ASF, and OCG compatibility; the ability to record from the player's FM radio; the ability to view photos; and the ability to store and transfer data files. The screens of the units included a significant amount of information about the song currently playing, as well as the status of the machine, such as volume and battery levels. Furthermore, the user interface of the iRiver models was very versatile, allowing users to customize the buttons and the method of scrolling through the music. Music, sound, and recording quality were great enough that one article found the H140 to be "the best player in the 20GB-plus class" of MP3 players.[19] Like RCA, Rio, and Creative, iRiver users could shop for music at almost any online store other than Sony's or Apple's.

Like creative, iRiver offered a broad array of flash-based players. These players ranged from the iFP-880 with 128 MB; to the iFP-999 ($299.99), with 1 GB; to the iFP-1095, with 512 MB and a built-in 0.3 megapixel digital camera. These payers featured an integrated digital FM tuner; the ability to record from the tuner; a built-in voice recorder; MPS, WMA, OCG, and ASF compatibility; and up to 40 hours of battery life. Some of the players, such as the iFP-999, included a rechargeable battery, while the iFP-880 used one AA battery.

iRiver's portable multimedia players included the PMC-120 (20 GB), based on the Windows Media Center interface, and the PMP-120 (20 GB) and 140 (40 GB), which used a proprietary technology. Each of these players allowed users to connect to their home entertainment system and to play music and video files. The PMC-120 also allowed users to connect seamlessly to the Windows Media Player. These players had an average battery life of 5 hours when showing video and 14 hours with audio.

A summary of the product specifications of the top brands of MP3 players is shown in Exhibit 7.

Market Trends

Heading into 2005, several key trends were emerging in the digital music and MP3 player industries. One significant trend was that the influx of competition experienced by both markets was expected to continue for the foreseeable future. Competition was expected to come from music industry sources that were currently not actively involved in online sales as well as companies that had not traditionally been involved in music or personal electronics, similar to the entry of MSN and Wal-Mart over the past two years

Exhibit 7   PRODUCT SPECIFICATIONS FOR THE TOP BRANDS

Company/ Model Name	Size of Hard Drive (GB)	Size of Unit (h, w, d in inches)	Weight of Unit (ounces)	Battery Life (hours)	Songs Held (128 Kbps)	Retail Price
Apple iPod	20	4.1 × 2.4 × 0.57	5.6	12	5,000	$299
Apple iPod	40	4.1 × 2.4 × 0.69	6.2	12	10,000	$399
Apple iPod Mini	4	3.6 × 2.0 × 0.5	3.6	8	1,000	$249
Dell Digital Jukebox	15	4.1 × 2.7 × 0.86	7.61	20	3,700	$199
Dell Digital Jukebox	20	4.1 × 2.7 × 0.86	7.61	20	5,000	$229
Sony Network Walkman	20	3.625 × 2.5 × 0.5625	3.8	25	Under 5,000	$399
RCA Lyra RD 2850	20	3.4 × 2.9 × 0.97	5.3	10	5,000	$349
RCA Lyra RD 2840	40	4.5 × 3.2 × 0.9	9.6	10	10,000	$299
Rio Nitrus	1.5	2.4 × 3 × 0.6	2.0	16	375	$169
Rio Carbon	5	3.3 × 2.5 × 0.6	3.2	20	2,500	$249
Rio Karma	20	3.0 × 2.7 × 1.1	5.5	15	5,000	$299
Creative Nomad Zen Xtra	30	3.0 × 4.4 × 0.86	7.0	14	7,500	$239
Creative Nomad Zen	40	3.0 × 4.4 × 0.86	7.0	14	10,000	$269
Creative Nomad Zen	60	3.0 × 4.4 × 0.86	7.0	14	16,000	$369
iRiver H120	20	4.1 × 2.4 × 0.75	5.6	16	5,000	$329
iRiver H140	40	4.1 × 2.4 × 0.04	6.5	16	10,000	$429

Source: Compiled from product data available from manufacturer's Web sites and from www.amazon.com, accessed December 17, 2004.

into online music sales. Additionally, firms such as RealNetworks were using their platforms to develop new distribution channels with partners such as Comcast Cable and Charter Cable, which provided broadband Internet access. One segment of the market that was not expected to directly enter the online music market was the major record labels, other than Virgin music. Industry experts agreed that the investments necessary for the labels to enter the industry on the scale necessary to provide a sufficient payback would be difficult for the labels to make given their declining financial position. Further, experts doubted that other labels would be willing to share their catalogs with a direct competitor. Additionally, firms in the online music market were increasingly trying to differentiate their products through the use of exclusive distribution agreements; the addition of unique independent labels to a service; and in some cases, such as RealNetworks' Rhapsody, offering a full-service music player that allowed customers to find, download, burn, and stream songs and manage digital music collections. These full-service music players were seen as a significant opportunity to increase consumer switching costs since users would lose access to music downloaded, but not purchased, in these services and to any subscription specific playlists they had developed.

Streaming was expected to become increasingly important to the industry as the number of homes in the United States and worldwide gained access to broadband Internet connections and wireless connectivity increased. Some industry experts predicted that, as wireless connectivity increased, giving users access to their music almost anywhere, subscription services that offered on-demand streaming would overtake individual song sales. This trend would be especially welcomed by companies offering on-demand streaming since the subscription services had a significantly higher profit margin than did single-song sales. However, one of the most significant challenges

Exhibit 8   DEMAND FOR MUSIC SUBSCRIPTIONS AND DOWNLOADS IN 2003

Type of Consumer (number sampled)	Subscriptions	Downloads	Will Not Pay For Music
Music aficionados (357)	21%	25%	46%
Free-music fans (514)	13	19	60
CD purists (280)	10	16	71
Passive populace (746)	7	10	79

Source: Robyn Greenspan, "Paid Music Downloading, MP3 Player Sales Double," www.internetnews.com, posted December 9, 2003, accessed December 16, 2004.

faced by the music industry was convincing users to pay for music. A 2003 survey conducted by Jupiter Research revealed that most consumers were not interested in paying for either subscription-based services or downloads—see Exhibit 8.

One segment of the population that continued to have a voracious appetite for online music was college students. Unfortunately, college students were widely believed to be the main users of illegal file-sharing software. In fact, several of the lawsuits filed by the RIAA against pirates involved college students and named the students' universities in the suits. One reason colleges were such a common place to find music pirates was that, especially before cable and DSL connections became common, many students for the first time had access to a large bandwidth and could download songs in less than two minutes. In response to all of the illegal action, the music industry formed the Joint Committee of the Higher Education and Entertainment Companies, a partnership whereby the music industry provides colleges with information about educational and technological solutions to their file-sharing problems.

In response to these efforts, many universities began partnering with online music services to make legitimate online music available to students for free, or for a significantly reduced cost. Pennsylvania State University was one of the first to offer online music to all enrolled students through the legal form of Napster in January of 2004. The project was financed by the university's technology budget and allowed students to download and listen to an unlimited number of songs on up to three computers. In order to burn a song to a CD or transfer the song to a portable player, the student had to pay $0.99 or buy the whole album for $9.99.[20] It was estimated that in August 2004 approximately 25 of the nation's 3,300 colleges offered music to their students on campus networks.[21] Companies actively partnering with universities in developing legitimate online music services for their students included Cdigiz (a Denver-based company that ran digital music, video, and educational services for colleges), Napster, Rhapsody, and Ruckus Network. While colleges were actively working to facilitate legitimate music services, music piracy still occurred due to the lower cost of sharing music on P2P networks and the broader selection available on illicit services.

One final trend that had become evident by January 1, 2005, was that digital music was beginning to appear in some unusual places, such as restaurants or as an option in new cars. For example, in 2002 the Ford Ranger had an option of a Pioneer sound package with a radio, CD player, and an MP3 player. Additionally, Alpine, the stereo company, introduced a new product in January 2004 that was an interface adapter that would convert some of its compatible stereo units into a controller for Apple's iPod. That means that the owner could simply plug his or her iPod into the Alpine stereo face and would be able to control the iPod from the buttons on the stereo. Kenwood was also considering options similar to this and had planned to expand its ideas beyond just the iPod. Digital music was also appearing in restaurants. Starbucks and Hewlett-Packard joined to offer not only Wi-Fi Internet access but also a CD-burning service. Customers could burn full albums or personalized compilations of five songs for $6.95 and $1 for every additional song. Starbucks initially offered the service in 2004 to 10 of its Seattle-area locations but was expected to expand that to 2,500 locations over the next two years. Another partnership was developing between McDonald's and Sony's Connect. Under this deal, McDonald's customers would be able to receive free downloads from Connect when they purchased certain menu items, which would give them access to a redemption code they could use online at Sony's store to obtain a free song. Digital music was beginning to crop up in somewhat unlikely places and was expected to continue to do so as the industry grew and matured.

Growth and increasing competition in the MP3 player market was being driven by the increasing availability of online music; fallen memory prices, especially in flash memory and micro hard drives; and technological innovations that allowed manufacturers to produce smaller players that held more music. In the MP3 player segment, hard-drive players were becoming increasingly common and many companies were beginning to offer products very similar to Apple's at a much lower cost. Although Apple had three different versions of the iPod, each one had at least one direct competitor. Among the major strengths Apple retained were its early entry to the market and many loyal fans; in fact, for many people, the word *iPod* was synonymous with *MP3 player*. However, analysts predicted that micro-hard-drive players, such as the iPod Mini and the Rio Carbon, would outsell hard-drive players (e.g., iPod and Creative Zen) in the near future but that the fastest growth would come in the flash-based player segment, an area in which Apple did not have a presence.

As MP3 players increasingly became a part of everyday life, they were also changing from being mere music players to becoming status symbols. MP3 players were being seen as the new toy for the young and old alike to sport in their daily lives, and generally, the smaller, lighter, and "prettier" models were the most popular. Apple's product design and color schemes were nearly famous for their elegance and simplicity; the original iPod (about the size of a box of cigarettes) had distinctive white headphones that were easily distinguished and the Mini's colorful pastel models (about the size of a credit card) were equally unique and popular. Said one article, "iPod has become so popular it is now a fashion statement."[22] The popularity of those players was partly the fault of Apple's excellent marketing scheme and partly because many very famous celebrities were photographed or seen with an Apple player, or happened to mention their iPod during an interview.[23] Other players were literally being incorporated as fashion. For example, Oakley, a sunglasses maker, was about to introduce a line of sunglasses called Oakley Thump, which had tiny MP3 players built in and were to be priced between $395 and $495.[24] As another example of these tiny wearable players, Virgin had one so small that it could be worn as a necklace. MP3 players were becoming more fashion-oriented for several reasons, including the fact that they were actually worn on the body, which made their appearance important, and that MP3 players are extremely popular with younger consumers, a group that often demanded that products looked just as good as they functioned.

A final trend driving change in the MP3 player industry was that increasing technological convergence was encouraging MP3 player manufacturers to increase their players' multifunctional usage capabilities. Many of the competing models available in 2004 could be used not only for managing and listening to music but also as PDAs with, for example, calendar/appointment books, data storage devices, and alarm clocks. Almost any MP3 player that used hard-drive technology could be used to actually store any type of data files, not just music. The iPods could even be used as an external hard drive when attached to a computer and also had photo storage capabilities. Other features of the iPod included an alarm clock, to-do lists, a calendar, an appointment book, games, and voice recording (with the purchase of an accessory). Dell's Digital Jukebox, while it offered built-in sound recording ability, notably lacked any other type of special features such as a calendar or an appointment book. Creative's Nomad line of players all had the ability to function as alarm clocks that could wake their owner to the sound of music. Many of the competing players also offered sound recording abilities and some had other unique features, such as a built-in radio tuner and sound manipulating hardware.

Heading into 2005, it was evident that the fates of the digital music and MP3 player industries were inextricably linked. However, what was not as certain was who the major players would be in the next five years and how the companies in each segment should position themselves to anticipate and meet rapidly evolving technologies and consumer preferences.

In February 2005, in a move to stem market share erosion and combat mounting competition from rivals, Apple announced $50 price cuts on two iPod mini models. The suggested retail price of Apple's 4GB iPod mini was cut to $199 (from $249), and the suggested retail price of the 6GB mini was reduced from $299 to $249. In addition, Apple introduced two new iPod photo models with 2-inch color LDC screens, a 30GB model retailing for about $349 and a 60GB model retailing for about $449. The 60GB iPod photo model had sufficient capacity for a whole music library—about 15,000 songs and full album cover art—or it could hold roughly 25,000 photos.

Endnotes

[1]"Special to the Globe and Mail," *Globe and Mail,* December 23, 1999.
[2]"Usage Models Drive Adoption For The Next Wave of MP3 Players & Digital Audio Services," www.instat.com, December 18, 2004.
[3]Jared Wade, "The Music Industry's War on Piracy," *Risk Management* 51, no. 2 (February 2004), p. 10.
[4]"By the Numbers," *Network Magazine* 18, no. 10 (October 2003), p. 16.
[5]Clinton Wilder, "Music Industry's Long, Strange Trip." *Information Week,* August 21, 2000, p. RB16.
[6]Lim Chong, "Still Far from Music to the Ears," *Computimes Malaysia,* December 10, 2001, p. 1.
[7]Devin Leonard, "Songs in the Key of Steve," *Fortune,* May 12, 2003, p. 54.
[8]Ibid.
[9]Steve Traiman, "Goin' Digital," *Billboard,* May 1, 2004, pp. 45, 47, 73.
[10]J. Borland and J. Hu, "MSN Music: It's Really About Windows," *CNET News.com,* www.cnet.com, August 30, 2004.
[11]Keith O'Brien, "Apple Blasts RealNetworks' New Digital-Music Software," *PRweek,* August 9, 2004, p. 2.
[12]J. C. Perez, "Sony Spins New Online Music Store," *PC World.com,* May 5, 2004.
[13]"MP3 Player Buying Guide: What Are My Choices?" www.reviews.cnet.com/4520-7964_7-5134106-1.html?tag=tnav, accessed December 16, 2004.
[14]Steve Smith, "iPod's Lessons," *Twice,* July 26, 2004, p. 12.
[15]"The Meaning of iPod," *The Economist,* June 12, 2004, p. TQ14.
[16]Peter Rojas, "Feeding Power-Hungry Gadgets," *Money* 33, no. 5 (May 2004), pp. 131–32.
[17]Walter S. Mossberg, "The Mossberg Solution: Sony's iPod Killer," *The Wall Street Journal,* July 28, 2004, p. D1.
[18]Bill Machrone, "New Music Players Gun for the iPod," *PC Magazine,* August 17, 2004, pp. 34–35.
[19]Ibid.
[20]Wade, "The Music Industry's War on Piracy."
[21]Jefferson Graham, "Students Score Music Perks as Colleges Fight Piracy," *USA Today,* August 24, 2004.
[22]Smith, "iPod's Lessons."
[23]Steven Levy, "iPod Nation," *Newsweek,* July 26, 2004, pp. 42–50.
[24]Paul Hansell, "Battle of Form (and Function) in MP3 Players," *New York Times,* October 4, 2004.

Competition in the Bottled Water Industry in 2004

John E. Gamble
University of South Alabama

Bottled water was among the world's most attractive beverage categories in 2003, with global sales exceeding 38 billion gallons that year and annual growth averaging more than 10 percent between 1998 and 2003. Bottled water had long been a widely consumed product in Western Europe and Mexico, where annual per capita consumption approached or exceeded 40 gallons in 2003, but until the mid-1990s bottled water had been somewhat of a novelty or prestige product in the United States. In 1990 approximately 2.2 billion gallons of bottled water were consumed in the United States and per capita consumption approximated 9 gallons. U.S. per capita consumption had grown to more than 22 gallons by 2003 and was expected to grow to 26 gallons by 2005. The rising popularity of bottled water in the United States during the late 1990s and early 2000s had allowed the United States to become the world's largest market for bottled water, with annual volume sales of nearly 6.4 billion gallons in 2003. In 2004, emerging markets in Asia and South America seemed to be replicating the impressive growth of bottled water in the United States, with annual growth rates exceeding 20 percent. Exhibit 1 presents bottled water statistics for the 10 largest country markets for bottled water in 2003.

The growing popularity of bottled water in the United States was attributable to concerns over the safety of municipal drinking water, an increased focus on fitness and health, and the hectic on-the-go lifestyles of American consumers. The convenience, purity, and portability of bottled water made it the natural solution to consumers' dissatisfaction with tap water and carbonated beverages. The U.S. bottled water market, like most markets outside the United States, was characterized by fierce competitive rivalry as the world's bottled water sellers jockeyed for market share and volume gains. Both the global and U.S. bottled water markets had become dominated by a few international food and beverage producers like Coca-Cola, PepsiCo, and Nestlé, but included many small regional sellers that were required to either develop low-cost production and distribution capabilities or use differentiation strategies keyed to some unique product attributes. In 2004, competitive rivalry continued to ratchet upward as sellers developed innovative product variations, entered into strategic agreements to strengthen positions in established markets, and acquired smaller sellers to gain footholds in rapidly growing emerging markets. Industry analysts and observers believed the recent moves undertaken by the world's largest sellers of bottled water would alter the competitive dynamics of the bottled water industry and would mandate that certain players modify their current strategic approaches to competition in the industry.

Exhibit 1   **LEADING COUNTRY MARKETS FOR BOTTLED WATER, 1998 AND 2003 (in millions of gallons)**

2003 Rank	Country	1998	2003	CAGR* (1998–2003)
1	United States	4,130.7	6,395.0	9.1%
2	Mexico	2,873.0	4,354.7	8.7
3	Brazil	1,521.8	2,840.1	17.8
4	China	934.6	2,805.8	24.6
5	Italy	2,038.7	2,791.0	6.5
6	Germany	2,169.1	2,727.2	4.7
7	France	1,733.2	2,351.4	6.3
8	Indonesia	722.2	1,963.3	22.1
9	Thailand	1,014.4	1,302.5	5.1
10	Spain	981.1	1,213.9	4.4
All others		5,340.7	9,278.4	11.7
Worldwide total		23,189.5	38,023.3	10.4

*Compound average growth rate
Source: Beverage Marketing Corporation, as reported by the International Bottled Water Association, 2004.

Industry Conditions in 2004

Even though it was already the world's largest market for bottled water, the United States remained among the faster-growing markets for bottled water since per capita consumption of bottled water fell substantially below consumption rates in Western Europe, the Middle East, and Mexico. Bottled water consumption in the United States also lagged per capita consumption of soft drinks by a wide margin, but in 2003 bottled water surpassed coffee, tea, milk, and beer to become the second largest beverage category in the United States. In 2003, the carbonated-soft-drink industry accounted for sales of more than $19 billion, but concerns about sugar consumption and other nutrition and fitness issues had encouraged many U.S. consumers to transition from consuming soft drinks to consuming bottled water. Whereas the soft drink market had grown by less than 1 percent annually between 1998 and 2003, the market for bottled water had continued to grow at annual rates near 10 percent during the same time period. In 2004, 70 percent of U.S. households purchased bottled water at least once a year, whereas 90 percent of U.S. households purchased carbonated soft drinks at least once a year. Exhibits 2, 3, and 4 illustrate the growing popularity of bottled water among U.S. consumers during the 1990s and through 2003.

Almost one-half of bottled water consumed in the United States in 1990 was delivered to homes and offices in returnable five-gallon containers and dispensed through coolers. At that time, only 186 million gallons of water was sold in one-liter or smaller single-serving polyethylene terephthalate (PET) bottles. In 2002, bottled water sold in one-liter or smaller PET containers accounted for 36.2 percent of industry volume and 50.8 percent of dollar sales, and had grown by 29.1 percent annually between 1995 and 2001. The unit sales of bottled water packaged in PET containers grew by an additional 33 percent between 2002 and 2003. In 2002, the sales of water sold in five-gallon containers or one- or two-and-a-half-gallon high-density polyethylene (HDPE) containers accounted for 60.9 percent of gallonage, but only 43.3 percent of dollar sales.

**Exhibit 2   PER CAPITA CONSUMPTION OF BOTTLED WATER
BY COUNTRY MARKET, 1998, 2003**

2003 Rank	Country	Per Capita Consumption (in gallons)		CAGR*
		1998	2003	
1	Italy	35.9	48.1	7.6%
2	Mexico	29.2	41.5	9.2
3	France	29.5	39.1	7.3
4	United Arab Emirates	28.1	38.1	7.9
5	Belgium-Luxembourg	30.7	35.1	3.4
6	Germany	26.4	33.1	5.8
7	Spain	25.1	30.2	4.7
8	Switzerland	23.8	25.4	1.6
9	Lebanon	16.2	25.3	11.8
10	Saudi Arabia	18.9	23.3	5.4
11	Cyprus	17.2	22.8	7.3
12	Austria	19.8	22.7	3.5
13	United States	15.3	22.6	10.2
14	Czech Republic	15.4	22.2	9.6
15	Portugal	17.2	20.6	4.6
	Global average	3.9	6.0	11.4

*Compound average growth rate
Source: Beverage Marketing Corporation, as reported by the International Bottled Water Association, 2004.

**Exhibit 3   VOLUME SALES AND DOLLAR VALUE OF THE U.S. BOTTLED
WATER MARKET, 1991–2003**

Year	Volume Sales (in millions of gallons)	Annual Change	Industry Revenues (in millions of dollars)	Annual Change
1991	2,355.9	2.1%	$2,512.9	−0.6%
1992	2,486.6	5.5	2,658.7	5.8
1993	2,689.4	8.2	2,876.7	8.2
1994	2,966.4	10.3	3,164.3	10.0
1995	3,226.9	8.8	3,521.9	11.3
1996	3,495.1	8.3	3,835.4	8.9
1997	3,794.3	8.6	4,222.7	10.1
1998	4,130.7	8.9	4,666.1	10.5
1999	4,583.4	11.0	5,314.7	13.9
2000	4,904.4	7.0	5,809.0	9.3
2001	5,372.1	9.5	6,880.0	18.4
2002	5,950.7	10.8	7,794.0	13.3
2003	6,395.9	7.5	8,319.0	6.7

Source: Beverage Marketing Corporation, as reported by *Bottled Water Reporter,* April/May 2002, and *Business Wire,* April 8, 2004.

Exhibit 4   U.S. PER CAPITA CONSUMPTION OF BOTTLED WATER, 1991–2003

Year	Per Capita Consumption (in gallons)	Annual Change
1991	9.3	—
1992	9.8	5.4%
1993	10.5	7.1
1994	11.5	9.5
1995	12.2	6.1
1996	13.1	7.4
1997	14.1	7.6
1998	15.3	8.5
1999	16.8	9.8
2000	17.8	6.0
2001	19.3	8.5
2002	21.2	9.8
2003	22.6	6.6

Source: Beverage Marketing Corporation, as reported by *Bottled Water Reporter,* April/May 2002, and *Business Wire,* April 8, 2004.

Convenience and portability were appealing features of smaller, single-serving PET containers since consumers could purchase chilled water from a convenience store that could be drunk immediately. Beginning in 2001, consumers also began to prefer PET containers for home use as the take-home PET market for the first time exceeded the volume sales of chilled PET water sold for immediate consumption. Water packaged in PET containers sold through take-home channels accounted for 28 percent of industry sales volume in 2001, but was expected to account for more than one-half of industry growth between 2002 and 2007.

The convenience and portability of bottled water were two of a variety of reasons U.S. consumers were increasingly attracted to bottled water. An increased emphasis on healthy lifestyles and improved consumer awareness of the need for proper hydration led many consumers to shift traditional beverage preferences toward bottled water. Bottled water consumers frequently claimed drinking more water improved the appearance of their skin and gave them more energy. Bottled water analysts also believed many health-conscious consumers drank bottled water because it was a symbol to others that they were interested in health.

A certain amount of industry growth was attributable to increased concerns over the quality of tap water provided by municipal water sources. Consumers in parts of the world with inadequate water treatment facilities relied on bottled water to provide daily hydration needs, but tap water in the United States was very pure by global standards—municipal water systems were regulated by the U.S. Environmental Protection Agency (EPA) and were required to comply with the provisions of the Safe Drinking Water Act Amendments of 2001. Consumer concerns over the quality of drinking water in the United States emerged in 1993 when 400,000 residents of Milwaukee, Wisconsin, became ill with flu-like symptoms and almost 100 immune-impaired residents died from waterborne bacterial infections. Throughout the 1990s and into the early 2000s, the media sporadically reported cases of municipal water contamination, such as in 2000 when residents of Washington, D.C., became ill after the city's water filtration process caused elevated levels of suspended materials in the water. Consumer attention to the purity of municipal water was also heightened in 2000 when the EPA proposed revising the standard for arsenic content in tap water as specified by the Safe Drinking Water Act Amendments of 1996 from 50 to 10 parts per billion (ppb). Prior to the congressional discussion of acceptable arsenic levels in drinking water, most Americans were unaware that any arsenic was present in tap water.

Even though some consumers were concerned about the purity of municipal water, most consumers' complaints with tap water centered on the chemical taste of tap water, which resulted from treatment processes that included the use of chlorine and other chemicals such as fluoride. In a tap-water tasting in Atlanta hosted by *Southpoint* magazine, judges rated municipal water on taste and found some cities' waters very palatable. Water obtained from the municipal source in Memphis was said to have "a refreshing texture" and tap water from New Orleans was commended for its "neutrality." However, other municipal systems did not fare as well with the judges—some of whom suggested that Houston's water tasted "like a chemistry lab," while others said Atlanta's municipal water was akin to "a gulp of swimming pool water."[1] However, there were positive attributes to the chemicals added to tap water, as chlorine was necessary to kill any bacteria in the water and fluoride had contributed greatly to improved dental health in the United States. In addition, tap water had been shown to be no less healthy than bottled water in a number of independent studies, including a study publicized in Europe that was commissioned by the World Wide Fund for Nature and conducted by researchers at the University of Geneva.

Bottled water producers in the United States were required to meet the standards of both the EPA and the U.S. Food and Drug Administration (FDA). Like all food and beverage products sold in the United States, bottled water was subject to such food safety and labeling requirements as nutritional labeling provisions and General Good Manufacturing Practices (GMPs). Bottled water GMPs were mandated under the 1962 Kefauver-Harris Drug Amendments to the Federal Food, Drug and Cosmetic Act of 1938 and established specifications for plant construction and design, sanitation, equipment design and construction, production and process controls, and record keeping. The FDA required bottled water producers to test for the presence of bacteria at least weekly and on an annual basis test for inorganic contaminants, trace metals, minerals, pesticides, herbicides, and organic compounds. Bottled water was also regulated by state agencies that conducted inspections of bottling facilities and certification of testing facilities to ensure bottled water was bottled under federal GMPs and was safe to drink.

Bottled water producers were also required to comply with the FDA's Standard of Identity, which required bottlers to include source water information on their products' labels. Water labeled as "spring water" must have been captured from a borehole or natural orifice of a spring that naturally flows to the surface. "Artesian water" could be extracted from a confined aquifer (a water-bearing underground layer of rock or sand) where the water level stood above the top of the aquifer. "Sparkling water" was required to have natural carbonation as it emerged from the source, although carbonation could be added to return the carbon dioxide level to what was evident as the water emerged from the source. Even though sparkling water was very popular throughout most of Europe and the Middle East, it was purchased on at least one occasion per year by less than 20 percent of U.S. households. Typical households purchasing sparkling water were made up of middle-aged childless couples earning $70,000 or more.

The FDA's definition of "mineral water" stated that such water must have at least 250 parts per million (ppm) of total dissolved solids, and its standards required water labeled as "purified" to have undergone distillation, deionization, or reverse osmosis to remove chemicals such as chlorine and fluoride. "Drinking water" required no additional processing beyond what was required for tap water, but could not include flavoring or other additives that accounted for more than 1 percent of the product's total weight. Both "drinking water" and "purified water" had to clearly state that the water originated "from a community water system" or "from a municipal source."

Bottled water producers could also voluntarily become members of the International Bottled Water Association (IBWA) and agree to comply with its Model Code, which went beyond the standards of the EPA, FDA, or state agencies. The Model Code allowed fewer ppm of certain organic and inorganic chemicals and microbiological contaminants than FDA, EPA, or state regulations and imposed a chlorine limitation on bottled water. Neither the FDA nor the EPA limited chlorine content. IBWA members were monitored for compliance through annual, unannounced inspections administered by an independent third-party organization.

Distribution and Sale of Bottled Water

Consumers could purchase bottled water in nearly any location in the United States where food was also sold. Supermarkets, supercenters, natural foods stores, and wholesale clubs all stocked large inventories of bottled water, and most convenience stores dedicated at least one stand-up cooler to bottled water. Bottled water could also be purchased in most delis and many restaurants, from vending machines, and at sporting events and other special events like concerts, outdoor festivals, and carnivals. Bottled water could also be delivered directly to consumers' homes or offices. In 2003, home and office delivery (HOD) accounted for 17 percent of bottled water sales, while take-home channels accounted for 54 percent of sales and immediate consumption channels accounted for 29 percent of industry sales.

The distribution of bottled water varied according to the producer and the distribution channel. Typically, bottled water was distributed to large grocers and wholesale clubs directly by the bottled water producer, while most producers used third parties like beer and wine distributors or food distributors to make sales and deliveries to convenience-store buyers. Similarly, food-service distributors usually handled landing accounts with restaurants and delis and making necessary deliveries to keep the account properly stocked. Most distributors made deliveries of bottled water to convenience stores and restaurants along with their regular scheduled deliveries of other foods and beverages.

Because of the difficulty for food-service distributors to restock vending machines and provide bottled water to special events, Coca-Cola and PepsiCo were able to dominate such channels since they could make deliveries of bottled water along with their deliveries of other beverages. Coca-Cola and PepsiCo's vast beverage distribution systems made it easy for the two companies to make Dasani and Aquafina available anywhere Coke or Pepsi could be purchased. In addition, the two cola giants almost always negotiated contracts with sports stadiums, universities, and school systems that made one of them the exclusive supplier of all types of non-alcoholic beverages sold in the venue for some specified period. Under such circumstances, it was nearly impossible for other brands of bottled water to gain access to the account.

PepsiCo's and Coca-Cola's soft drink businesses also aided the two companies in making Aquafina and Dasani available in supermarkets, supercenters, wholesale clubs, and convenience stores. Soft-drink sales were important to all types of food stores since soft drinks made up a sizable percentage of the store's sales and since food retailers frequently relied on soft-drink promotions to generate store traffic. Coca-Cola and PepsiCo were able to encourage their customers to purchase items across their product lines to ensure prompt and complete shipment of key soft-drink products. As a diversified food products company, PepsiCo had exploited the popularity of its soft drinks, Gatorade sports drinks, Frito-Lay snack foods, and Tropicana orange juice in persuading grocery accounts to purchase not only Aquafina but also other new brands such as FruitWorks, SoBe, Lipton's Iced Tea, and Starbucks Frappuccino.

Since most supermarkets, supercenters, and food stores usually carried only three to five branded bottled waters plus a private-label brand, bottled water producers other than Coke and Pepsi were required to compete aggressively on price to gain access to shelf space. Market surveys indicated that wholesale prices for branded bottled water ranged from $3.50 to $7.00 per case—depending on the appeal of the product and the competitive strength of the seller. Some supermarkets and other grocery chains required bottled water suppliers to pay slotting fees in addition to offering low prices to gain shelf space. Grocers expected to pay less for private-label products and typically required private-label suppliers to prepare bids offering both purified and spring water in various sized packages. Contracts were awarded to the low bidder and typically rebid annually or biannually. Natural foods stores might also require annual contracts and slotting fees but were much more willing than traditional supermarkets to pay higher wholesale prices for products that could contribute to the store's overall level of differentiation. In fact, most natural foods stores would not carry brands found in traditional supermarkets.

Convenience stores were also aggressive in pressing bottled water producers and food distributors for low prices and slotting fees. Most convenience stores carried only two to four brands of bottled water beyond what was distributed by Coca-Cola and Pepsi, and required bottlers to pay annual slotting fees of $300 to $400 per store in return for providing 5 to 10 bottle facings on a cooler shelf. Food and beverage distributors usually paid the bottlers of lesser-known brands $3.75 to $4.25 per case, while popular national brands commanded wholesale prices in the range of $5.00 to $6.00. Some bottlers offered to provide retailers with rebates of approximately 25 cents per case to help secure distributors for their brand of bottled water. Food distributors also asked their bottled water suppliers to sponsor annual trade shows, hosted by the food distributor, at which participating vendors (including bottled water producers) would offer discounts of approximately 25 cents per case to convenience-store customers willing to commit to large quarterly purchases. Food and beverage distributors usually allowed bottled water producers to negotiate slotting fees and rebates directly with convenience store buyers.

There was not as much competition among bottled water producers to gain shelf space in delis and restaurants since volume was relatively low—making per unit distribution costs exceedingly high unless other beverages were delivered along with bottled water. PepsiCo and Coca-Cola were among the better-suited bottled water producers to economically distribute water to restaurants since they likely provided fountain drinks to such establishments.

Water sold in returnable five-gallon containers by such companies as Culligan, Danone Waters, and Vermont Pure Holdings was delivered to home and office users directly by bottled water producers. These producers usually specialized in the home and office delivery (HOD) segment but might also sell a PET product through convenience and supermarket channels. Retail pricing to bulk water purchasers ranged from $5 to $7 per five-gallon container. Consumers of bulk water were also required to rent a cooler at $10 to $15 per month. Most bulk water sellers used a delivery route system with scheduled visits for deliveries of water and empty container pickup.

Suppliers to the Industry

The suppliers to the bottled water industry included municipal water systems, spring operators, bottling equipment manufacturers, deionization, reverse osmosis, and filtration equipment manufacturers, cooler manufacturers, sellers of racking systems, manufacturers of PET and HDPE bottles and plastic caps, label printers, and secondary packaging suppliers. Most packaging supplies needed for the production of bottled water were readily available for a large number of suppliers. Large bottlers able to commit to annual purchases of more than 5 million PET bottles could purchase bottles for as little as 5 cents per bottle, while regional bottlers purchasing smaller quantities of bottles or only making one-time purchases of bottles could expect to pay a much as 15 cents per bottle. Suppliers of secondary packaging—like cardboard boxes, shrink-wrap, and six-pack rings—and suppliers of printed film or paper labels were numerous and aggressively competed for the business of large bottled water producers.

Bottling equipment used for water purification and filling bottles was manufactured and marketed by about 50 different companies in the United States. About 10 manufacturers offered a complete line of filling equipment, filtration equipment, distillation equipment, deionization equipment, bottle washers, labeling equipment, packaging equipment, and reverse osmosis equipment, with others specializing in a few equipment categories. A basic bottle-filling line could be purchased for about $125,000, while a large state-of-the-art bottling facility could require a capital investment of more than $100 million. Bottlers choosing to sell spring water could expect to invest about $300,000 for source certification, road grading, and installation of pumping equipment, fencing, holding tanks, and disinfecting equipment. Bottlers that did not own springs were also required to enter into lease agreements with spring owners that typically ranged from $20,000 to $30,000 per year. Companies selling purified water merely purchased tap water from municipal water systems at industrial rates prior to purifying and bottling the water for sale to consumers. Sellers of purified water were able not only to pay less for water they bottled but also to avoid spring water's inbound shipping costs of 5 to 15 cents per gallon since water arrived at the bottling facility by pipe rather than by truck.

Key Competitive Capabilities in the Bottled Water Industry

Bottled water did not enjoy the brand loyalty of soft drinks, beer, or many other food and beverage products but was experiencing some increased brand loyalty with 10 to 25 percent of consumers looking for a specific brand and an additional two-thirds considering only a few brands acceptable. Because of the growing importance of brand recognition, successful sellers of bottled water were required to possess well-developed brand-building skills. Most of the industry's major sellers were global food companies—having built respected brands in soft drinks, dairy products, chocolates, and breakfast cereals prior to entering the bottled water industry. PepsiCo, Coca-Cola, and Nestlé were the most successful sellers at building consumer loyalty in the United States, according to a 2002 brand loyalty study conducted by NFO WorldGroup. The survey found that consumers of Aquafina (PepsiCo's brand) were rather loyal, as the brand accounted for 77 percent of regular Aquafina consumers' total bottled water purchases. Nestlé Waters' brands also commanded a 77 percent brand loyalty rating, while Dasani (Coca-Cola's brand) accounted for 62 percent of bottled water consumed by frequent Dasani purchasers. Brands offered by other bottled water sellers achieved far lower levels of brand loyalty.

Bottled water sellers also needed to have efficient distribution systems to supermarket, wholesale club, and convenience store channels to be successful in the industry. It was imperative for bottled water distributors (whether direct store delivery by bottlers or delivery by third parties) to maximize the number of deliveries per driver since distribution included high fixed costs for warehouses, trucks, handheld inventory tracking devices, and labor. It was also critical for distributors and bottlers to provide on-time deliveries and offer responsive customer service to large customers in the highly price-competitive market. Price competition also mandated high use of large-scale plants to achieve low production costs. Volume and market share were also key factors in keeping marketing expenses at an acceptable per-unit level.

Recent Trends in the Bottled Water Industry

As the U.S. per capita consumption of bottled water grew to more than 22 gallons in 2003 and the annual growth rate of bottled water sales in the United States slowed, industry analysts became concerned that price competition in the bottled water industry might mirror that of the carbonated-soft-drink industry. Fierce price competition could be expected to bring volume gains but result in flat or declining revenues for the bottled water industry. Coca-Cola, Nestlé, and PepsiCo's use of discounted 12–24-bottle multipacks helped boost unit volume in the United States during 2003, but as of mid-2004, none of the industry's chief participants had relied primarily on price to increase volume.

The world's largest sellers of bottled water appeared to be positioning for industry maturity by purchasing smaller regional brands. Nestlé had acquired bottle water producers in Poland, Hungary, Russia, Greece, France, and Saudi Arabia between 2000 and 2002. Danone Waters had made a number of acquisitions in attractive global markets and had also entered into strategic alliances and joint ventures to increase penetration of selected emerging and developed markets. By 2003, the four largest sellers of bottled water (Nestlé Waters, Danone Waters, PepsiCo, and Coca-Cola) accounted for 34 percent of worldwide bottle sales by volume and 41 percent of worldwide bottled water sales in value.

Industry consolidation created a more globally competitive environment, in which the top sellers met each other in almost all of the world's markets. Danone and Nestlé had long competed against each other in most country markets, but PepsiCo and Coca-Cola were also becoming global sellers as they moved into new international markets. Exhibits 5 and 6 indicate the degree of industry consolidation in the U.S. bottled water market in 2003.

The introduction of enhanced waters or functional waters was the most important product innovation since bottled water gained widespread acceptance in the United States, with most sellers in 2004 having introduced variations of their products that included vitamins, carbohydrates, electrolytes, and other supplements. The innovation seemed to be a hit with some consumers, as the market for enhanced bottled waters expanded from $20 million in 2000 to $230 million in 2002. One of the earliest enhanced waters was Energy Brands' Glaceau Vitamin Water, which was launched in 2000. In 2004, Glaceau Vitamin Water came in 20 flavor and supplement varieties that promised mental stimulation, physical rejuvenation, and overall improved health. Glaceau retailed for about $1.49 per bottle. Glaceau was the best-selling brand of enhanced water in 2000 and 2001, but fell to the number two position in the segment, with 27.3 percent market share, in 2002. Sales of PepsiCo's Propel Fitness Water grew by 440 percent during 2002 to make it the leading brand of enhanced water, with

Exhibit 5 TOP 10 U.S. BOTTLED WATER MARKETERS, 2003

Rank	Company	Leading Brands	Wholesale Sales (in millions)	Market Share	2003 Growth
1	Nestlé Waters	Poland Spring, Deer Park, Arrowhead, Zephyrhills, Ozarka, Ice Mountain	$2,695.0	32.4%	10.0%
2	Coca-Cola	Dasani, (Evian and Dannon from Danone JV)	1,254.0	15.1	63.9
3	PepsiCo	Aquafina	936.0	11.3	11.7
4	Suntory Water Group (DS Waters PET)	Crystal Springs, Sierra Springs, Hinckley Springs, Kentwood Springs, Sparkletts	487.3	5.9	−2.8
5	Crystal Geyser	Alpine Spring, private label	375.0	4.5	38.9
6	Danone Waters (DS Waters HOD)	Home and office delivery	294.8	3.5	−61.7
7	Dr Pepper/7UP Bottling	Deja Blue	172.5	2.1	16.3
8	Culligan International	Culligan	116.0	1.4	−3.4
9	Micropack Bottled Water	Vermont Pure	74.6	0.9	4.0
10	Glacier Water	Glacier	70.0	0.8	−1.4

Source: Beverage Marketing Corporation, as reported by *Beverage World,* April 15, 2004.

Exhibit 6 TOP 10 U.S. BOTTLED WATER BRANDS, 2003

Rank	Brand	Parent Company	Wholesale Sales (in millions)	Market Share	2003 Growth
1	Aquafina	PepsiCo	$936.0	11.3%	11.7%
2	Dasani	Coca-Cola	834.0	10.0	9.0
3	Poland Springs	Nestlé Waters	649.4	7.8	4.5
4	Arrowhead	Nestlé Waters	546.1	6.6	19.6
5	Deer Park	Nestlé Waters	356.5	4.3	14.6
6	Crystal Geyser	Crystal Geyser	335.0	4.0	24.1
7	Ozarka	Nestlé Waters	236.1	2.8	12.6
8	Zephyrhills	Nestlé Waters	215.2	2.6	6.5
9	Ice Mountain	Nestlé Waters	206.7	2.5	24.3
10	Evian	Danone Waters	145.0	1.7	−24.1

Source: Beverage Marketing Corporation, as reported by *Beverage World,* April 15, 2004.

annual sales of approximately $100 million. Coca-Cola, Nestlé, and Danone Waters waited until late 2003 to develop and launch their brands of enhanced waters. Coke's Dasani NutriWater, which was still confined to test markets in 2004, was said to improve metabolism and fight free radicals, while Nestlé Waters' Vittel + Energy and Danone Waters' Volvic Revive were mineral-water-based sports drinks.

Bottled water producers were optimistic about the prospects of selling vitamin-enhanced waters since marketing research had shown that consumers (especially female baby boomers) were interested in increasing their intakes of vitamins, since enhanced waters were more easily differentiated than purified or spring water, and since enhanced waters carried retail prices as much as 40 percent higher than those of purified water. Enhanced waters also offered higher margins than those of typical bottled waters. Even though enhanced waters offered potential benefits, there were some features of enhanced waters that might cause consumers to limit their consumption of such products, including the need for sweeteners to disguise the taste of added vitamins and supplements. Calorie contents for enhanced waters ranged from 20 calories per 16-ounce serving for Propel to 100 calories per 16-ounce serving for Glaceau. In addition, some medical researchers had suggested that consumers would need to drink approximately 10 bottles of enhanced water each day to meet minimum dietary requirements for the vitamins promoted on the waters' labels.

Profiles of the Leading Bottled Water Producers

Nestlé Waters

Nestlé was Switzerland's largest industrial company and the world's largest food company, with 2003 sales of 88 billion Swiss francs (approximately $70 billion). The company was broadly diversified into 10 food and beverage categories that were sold in almost every country in the world under such recognizable brand names as Nescafé, Taster's Choice, Perrier, Vittel, Carnation, PowerBar, Friskies, Alpo, Nestea, Libby's, Stouffer's, and of course Nestlé. The company produced bottled water in as early as 1843, but its 1992 acquisition of Perrier created the foundation of what has made Nestlé Waters the world's largest seller of bottled water, with 77 brands in 130 countries. In 2003, Nestlé recorded bottled water sales of 8.1 billion Swiss francs (approximately $6.4 billion) and was the global leader in the bottled water industry, with 17 percent worldwide market share in 2002. Nestlé Waters was the number one seller of bottled water in the United States and Canada, with a 31.6 percent market share in 2002, and the number-one seller in Europe, with a 16.5 percent market share. Nestlé was also aggressive in its attempts to build market-leading positions in emerging markets in the Middle East, Asia, and Africa through the introduction of global Nestlé products and acquisitions of established local brands in most geographic regions of the world. Nestlé Waters achieved organic sales growth of 21.5 percent in Africa and the Middle East during 2002 and 21.7 percent in Asia and the Pacific during the year. The company acquired nearly 19 bottled water producers between 2001 and 2003. Including the sales of acquisitions, Nestlé Waters held market shares of 7.1 percent in Africa and the Middle East and 3.7 percent in Asia/Pacific region at year-end 2002.

The company's bottled water portfolio in 2004 included 2 global brands (Nestlé Pure Life and Nestlé Aquarel), 5 international premium brands (Perrier, Vittel, Contrex, Acqua Panna, and S. Pellegrino), and 70 local brands. Nestlé Pure Life was a purified water product developed in 1998 for emerging markets and other markets in which spring water was not an important differentiating feature of bottled water. Nestlé Aquarel was developed in 2000 for the European market and markets that preferred still spring water over purified water or sparkling spring water. Nestlé's other waters marketed in Europe were either spring water with a higher mineral content or sparkling waters such as Perrier and S. Pellegrino. Almost all brands marketed outside of Europe were either spring water or mineral water with no carbonation. Its brands in the United States included Pure Life, Aberfoyle, Arrowhead, Ice Mountain, Calistoga, Deer Park, Great Bear, Zephyrhills, Ozarka, and Poland Springs.

Nestlé Waters management believed its broad brand portfolio was among its key resource strengths since its 70 local brands accounted for 75.7 percent of sales in 2002. In addition the sales of Nestlé Waters' local brands achieved organic growth of 8.6 percent in 2002. The company's five premium international brands accounted for 21.8 percent of 2002 sales and grew by 8 percent during 2002. Pure Life and Aquarel, Nestlé's two global brands, accounted for only 2.5 percent of the water division's 2002 sales, but grew by 68.3 percent during the year. Nestlé Waters' management expected Pure Life and Aquarel to account for a greater percentage of the company's bottled water sales as it launched Pure Life in new international markets such as the United States, Canada, Turkey, Egypt, and Uzbekistan and Aquarel in Hungary, Finland, Switzerland, and Denmark. The company was also expanding Aquarel in HOD-sized containers throughout western Europe.

Nestlé also expected to increase its sales and market share through innovations in packaging and water enhancements. Nestlé Waters developed Vittel + Energy to enter the rapidly growing enhanced water segment of the industry. The company also created fruit-flavored varieties of Vittel and Contrex that might appeal to children. Other enhanced waters developed by Nestlé included Nestlé Wellness, which was based on Aquarel and included plant extracts, ginseng, and 5 percent fruit extracts, and Nestlé Harmony, which was based on Pure Life and included natural fiber to stimulate natural protections during digestion. Nestlé Wellness was initially launched in Germany, and Nestlé Harmony made its debut in China.

Packaging innovations included a new packaging design for Acqua Panna's international launch that would make the traditional European brand better accepted in North America, Asia, and other international markets. Also, Nestlé Waters redesigned the packages of many of its local brands and international brands such as Contrex, Vittel, and Perrier. Perrier's new PET container was the most-talked-about packaging innovation in the bottled water industry in 2004, since Perrier had been packaged in its distinctive green glass bottles for 141 years. The new PET bottle retained the curved shape and green color of Perrier's tradition bottles and included two layers of plastic separated by a nylon barrier to prevent Perrier's natural carbonation from permeating the surface of the container. The change in packaging was part of a strategy to revitalize the prestigious brand, which had experienced annual sales declines since the mid-1990s. Perrier's sales declined by 7 percent in 2003 alone, and industry participants believed Nestlé might sell the brand because of its poor performance in the marketplace and its high production costs associated with restrictive labor contracts in France. The new plastic bottle was intended to better match the on-the-go lifestyles of young consumers than heavy one-liter glass containers. Nestlé would still package Perrier in glass bottles for consumers who preferred the brand's traditional packaging for dinner parties and other formal settings.

Home and office delivery (HOD) was becoming a more important component of Nestlé's strategy—especially in Europe. The company's acquisitions in the United States had provided it with experience in HOD, which, although it provided lower margins, did provide additional volume and scale. Since 2000, Nestlé had made eight acquisitions in the HOD segment to grow from no presence to the leading position in Europe, with a 32 percent market share in 2003. Nestlé's market-leading positions in Europe and the United States in HOD and PET channels allowed it to earn the status

Exhibit 7   VALUE CHAIN COMPARISON FOR THE BOTTLED WATER OPERATIONS OF NESTLÉ, PEPSICO, AND COCA-COLA

	Nestlé Waters	PepsiCo	Coca-Cola
Retailer price per case	$8.44	$8.52	$8.65
Retailer margin	35.0%	17.5%	17.6%
Wholesale price per case	$5.49	$7.03	$7.13
Wholesale sales	$5.49	$7.03	$7.13
Support revenue	0.00	0.41	0.52
Total bottler revenue	$5.49	$7.44	$7.65
Expenses			
Water	$0.01	$1.67	$1.70
PET bottles	1.03	1.16	1.16
Secondary packaging	0.61	0.68	0.68
Closures	0.21	0.23	0.23
Labor/manufacturing	0.70	0.70	0.77
Depreciation	0.07	0.08	0.08
Total cost of goods sold	2.63	4.52	4.62
Gross profit	$2.86	$2.92	$3.03
S,G,&A	2.29	2.25	2.53
EBITA	$0.57	$0.67	$0.50
EBITA margin	10.4%	9.0%	6.5%

Source: Goldman Sachs Global Equity Research, as reported by *Beverage World,* April 2002.

of low-cost leader in the United States. Exhibit 7 illustrates Nestlé Waters' cost and wholesale pricing advantages relative to Coca-Cola and PepsiCo in U.S. markets. Nestlé Waters' management stated in mid-2002 that it expected to double the division's revenues by 2010.

Danone Waters

Groupe Danone was established in 1966 through the merger of two of France's leading glass makers, who foresaw the oncoming acceptability of plastic as a substitute to glass containers. The management of the newly merged company believed that, rather than shift its focus to the manufacture of plastic containers, the company should enter markets for products typically sold in glass containers. Groupe Danone's diversification outside of glass containers began in 1969 when the company acquired Evian—France's leading brand of bottled water. Throughout the 1970s and 1980s, Groupe Danone acquired additional food and beverage companies that produced beer, pasta, baby food, cereals, sauces, confectionery, dairy products, and baked goods. In 1997, the company slimmed its portfolio of businesses to dairy products, bottled water, and a baked goods division producing cereal, cookies, and snacks. In 2004, Groupe Danone was a leading global food company, with annual sales of €13.1 billion. It was the world's largest producer of dairy products, the number two producer of cereal, cookies, and baked snacks, and the largest seller of bottled water by volume (Nestlé was the world's largest bottled water producer based on dollar sales).

The Group's Danone Waters unit included three of the world's best-selling brands of water—Aqua, Evian, and Volvic. Danone Waters also marketed country-specific brands such as Villa del Sur in Argentina, Wahaha in China, and Dannon in the United States. Danone Waters also had recently developed enhanced or functional waters for markets in Western Europe and North America. The company's Volvic Touch of Fruit and Volvic Revive were targeted primarily toward 18- to 35-year-old women.

Danone recorded worldwide bottled water sales of €3.5 billion in 2003. The company's bottled water sales had declined by approximately 25 percent between 2000 and 2002 before growing by nearly 10 percent during 2003. Like Nestlé, Danone had made a number of acquisitions of regional bottled water producers during the late 1990s and early 2000s. During 2002, Danone acquired a controlling interest in Poland's leading brand of bottled water for an undisclosed amount and purchased Canada's Sparkling Spring brand of waters for an estimated $300–$400 million. The company also entered into a joint venture with Kirin Beverage Company to strengthen its distribution network in Japan and embarked on a partnership with the Rachid Group, an Egyptian firm, to accelerate its development of market opportunities in North Africa and the Near and Middle East. During 2003 and 2004, Groupe Danone acquired three HOD bottled water sellers in Mexico. Danone had also made offers to acquire the leading seller of bottled water in Serbia and an HOD seller in Spain in late 2004.

Danone Waters' sales and market share began to decline in the United States beginning in 2000, when Coca-Cola bottlers began distributing Dasani rather than distributing only Evian and other non-Coke brands. Prior to the introduction of Dasani, about 60 percent of Evian's U.S. distribution was handled by Coca-Cola bottlers. Danone relied on Pepsi bottlers and independent bottlers for distribution to markets not handled by Coca-Cola. With Coca-Cola bottlers' attention directed toward the sale of Dasani, Evian lost shelf space in many convenience stores, supermarkets, delis, restaurants, and wholesale clubs.

Danone Waters and Coca-Cola entered into two new strategic partnerships in mid-2002 that made Coca-Cola the exclusive distributor of Evian and Dannon in the United States and Canada. The two companies entered into a distribution agreement in April 2002 whereby Coca-Cola agreed to distribute Evian along with Dasani to convenience stores, supermarkets, and other retail locations serviced by Coca-Cola's bottling operations. The two companies also began a joint venture in June 2002 that made Coke responsible for the production, marketing, and distribution of Dannon in the United States. Coca-Cola provided Danone an up-front cash payment in return for 51 percent ownership of the joint venture. Danone contributed its five plants and other bottled water assets located in the United States to the joint venture. Coca-Cola also held the license for the use of the Dannon brand in the United States.

Danone's HOD businesses were not included in the agreement with Coca-Cola and were combined with Suntory Water Group's assets to form DS Waters in 2003. The combination of Danone Waters' and Suntory Waters assets made the joint venture the largest HOD distributor in the United States and North America. The joint venture agreement made Suntory and Danone equal partners in the company and provided Suntory with an option to sell 50 percent of its interest in the venture to Groupe Danone after three years and the remaining 50 percent interest to Danone after five years.

Danone's 50 percent interest in DS Waters made it the leader in the United States and broader North American HOD market, while a similar agreement with Swiss-based Eden Springs made it the second largest HOD water seller in Europe. The Danone–Eden Springs joint venture gave Danone Waters geographic coverage in 18

European countries, with number one positions in France, Spain, Switzerland, Finland, Norway, and Sweden and a 20 percent share of the entire European HOD market. Groupe Danone held a 53.2 percent interest in the joint venture.

The Coca-Cola Company

The Coca-Cola Company was the world's leading manufacturer, marketer, and distributor of non-alcoholic beverage concentrates, with 300 brands worldwide. The company produced soft drinks, juice and juice drinks, sports drinks, water, and coffee and was best known for Coca-Cola, which had been called the world's most valuable brand. In 2003, the company sold more than 19.4 billion cases of beverages worldwide to record revenues of approximately $21 billion. Coca-Cola's net income for 2003 was more than $4.3 billion. Seventy percent of Coke's revenues were generated outside of North America, with five international markets (Germany, Brazil, United Kingdom, Japan, and Mexico) each contributing more than $1 billion per year to Coca-Cola's consolidated revenues. The company also sold more than $1 billion worth of beverages in the United States each year.

Along with the universal appeal of the Coca-Cola brand, Coca-Cola's vast global distribution system—which included independent bottlers, bottlers partially owned by Coca-Cola, and company-owned bottlers—made Coke an almost unstoppable international powerhouse. Coca-Cola held market-leading positions in most countries in the cola segment of the soft-drink industry, and the strength of the Coca-Cola brand aided the company in gaining market share in most other soft-drink segments such as the lemon-lime and diet segments. The company had also been able to leverage Coke's appeal with consumers to gain access to retail distribution channels for new beverages included in its portfolio such as Minute Maid orange juice products, Powerade isotonic beverages, and Dasani purified water.

The Coca-Cola Company did not market and distribute its own brand of bottled water until mid-1999, when it introduced Dasani. The company created a purified water that included a combination of magnesium sulfate, potassium chloride, and salt to re-create what Coke researchers believed were the best attributes of leading spring waters from around the world. The Dasani formula was a closely guarded secret and was sold to bottlers, just as the company sold its Coke concentrate to bottlers. The Dasani name was developed by linguists who suggested the dual a's gave a soothing sound to the name, the s conveyed crispness and freshness, and the i ending gave a foreign ring to the name. Dasani was supported with an estimated $15 million advertising budget during its first year on the market and was distributed through all retail channels where Coke was available. Coca-Cola's U.S. advertising budget for Dasani was $18.8 million in 2003. Coca-Cola's marketing expertise and vast U.S. distribution system allowed Dasani to become the second largest brand of water sold in the United States by 2001—a position it continued to hold in 2004.

In late 2002, Coca-Cola was testing four varieties of enhanced bottled waters in New York; Cincinnati, Ohio; and Charleston, South Carolina. The Dasani NutriWater line included a lemon tangerine flavor that promoted "bone strength" with added calcium, magnesium, and B vitamins; pear cucumber for "balancing" that included B and C vitamins; mandarin orange for "immunity" with vitamin C and zinc; and a multivitamin wild berry variety that included B, C, and E vitamins. Each of the varieties of NutriWater had about 20 calories per 16-ounce serving. Coke's new product retailed for $1.19 to $1.39 per 16-ounce container in test markets. Dasani NutriWater's national rollout was expected for early 2003 but had been delayed because of production problems.

Coca-Cola's 2002 joint venture with Danone Waters allowed Coca-Cola to jump to the rank of second largest bottled water producer in the United States. The joint venture and Evian distribution agreement provided Coke with bottled water products at all price points, with Dasani positioned as an upper-mid-priced product, Evian as a premium-priced bottled water, and Dannon as a discount-priced water. Coke management believed the addition of Dannon would allow the company to protect Dasani's near-premium pricing while gaining spring water brands that could be marketed nationally to challenge Nestlé's regional brands in the spring water segment. The editor of *Beverage Digest* noted that the Coca-Cola–Danone Waters joint venture would take Coke into several new bottled water markets, including private-label and spring water markets, and said the deal "has the potential of significantly altering the landscape of the bottled water business in the U.S."[2]

Even though the joint venture allowed Coca-Cola's sales of bottled water to increase from $765 million in 2002 to $1.3 billion in 2003, the three-tier strategy seemed to be failing in some regards since Coke's three water brands had collectively lost 2.6 market share points during the first six months of 2004. Coca-Cola's loss of market share seemed to be attributable, to some degree, to Nestlé's 25-plus percent growth during 2004 and to the growing popularity of private-label brands, whose sales had increased by more than 60 percent during 2004. However, some lost market share for the three brands combined might have been a result of weak support for Evian and Dannon brands. Beverage industry analysts believed it was unlikely that Coke's 2003 advertising budget of $800,000 for Evian would return the brand to its previous top-five ranking in the United States.

Coca-Cola produced and market bottled water in foreign countries under local brand names, such as Bon Aqua in the German market and NaturAqua in Hungary, but began efforts to make Dasani an international brand early 2004 with expansion into Africa, Brazil, and the United Kingdom. Coca-Cola's management chose the United Kingdom as the company's entry point to western Europe, with launches planned for 20 additional European countries by mid-2004. Dasani bottled and marketed in England would be purified water, similar to what was sold in the United States, but the company chose to use spring water in country markets with strong preferences for spring water such as in Germany and France. Consumers in the United Kingdom also tended to prefer spring water over purified water—so much so that the UK press pummeled Coke for planning to sell filtered tap water at premium prices—but Coca-Cola's management believed that purified water, or polished water as it would be called in UK markets, would be found palatable by consumers.[3]

Coca-Cola supported the March 2004 launch of Dasani in the United Kingdom with a $3.2 million advertising budget and a 4-million-bottle sampling campaign, but voluntarily recalled all Dasani bottles from retailers' shelves just two weeks after the launch. The recall was predicated on test results performed by the company that indicated the bottles were tainted with bromate—a cancer-causing agent. Bromate became introduced to the product when calcium, a mandatory ingredient of bottled waters sold in the United Kingdom, was added to Coca-Cola's proprietary formula of minerals used to distinguish Dasani from other bottled waters. The bromate levels present in Dasani exceeded regulatory limits in the United Kingdom but met standards for purity on the European continent. Nevertheless, Coke management believed it best to recall the product and discontinue immediate plans to distribute Dasani not only in the United Kingdom but also in all other European markets. Even though some in the business press viewed the situation as one of the great "marketing disasters" of all time and suggested that Coke should abandon the Dasani brand in Britain, others believed that

Dasani could be reintroduced after some modest respite.[4] Coca-Cola's acquisition of a spring in Derbyshire, England, in June 2004 seemed to support the notion that Dasani might be reintroduced to European consumers.

PepsiCo, Inc.

In 2004, PepsiCo was the world's fourth largest food and beverage company, with sales of about $27 billion. The company's brands were sold in more than 200 countries and included such well-known names as Lay's, Tostitos, Mountain Dew, Pepsi, Doritos, Lipton Iced Tea, Gatorade, Quaker, and Cracker Jack. Six of PepsiCo's products were among the top 15 products sold in U.S. supermarkets. PepsiCo also produced and marketed Aquafina—the best-selling brand of bottled water in the United States between 2002 and 2004.

PepsiCo had made attempts to enter the bottled water market in as early as 1987, when it purchased a spring water company, but its attempts were unsuccessful until its 1997 introduction of Aquafina. After experimenting with spring water and sparkling water for several years, Pepsi management believed it would be easier to produce a national brand of bottled water that could use its water purification facilities used in its soft-drink bottling plants. Pepsi management also believed the company could distinguish its brand of purified bottled water from competing brands by stripping all chlorine and other particles out of tap water that might impart an unpleasant taste or smell. PepsiCo began testing a filtration process for Aquafina in 1994 when it installed $3 million worth of reverse osmosis filtration equipment in its Wichita, Kansas, bottling plant to further purify municipal water used to make soft drinks. The system pushed water through a fiberglass membrane at very high pressure to remove chemicals and minerals before further purifying the water using carbon filters. The water produced by Pepsi's process was so free of chemicals that the company was required to add ozone gas to the water to prevent bacteria growth.

Pepsi sold the purification process to its bottlers, who were responsible for the production and distribution of Aquafina. PepsiCo marketed the product nationally and supported the brand with advertising expenditures of $15 million in 2000, $20 million in 2001, $40 million in 2002, and $25 million in 2003. PepsiCo also developed innovative supermarket displays for Aquafina, employed celebrities to endorse the product, and negotiated contracts to make Aquafina the official beverage of sports organizations such as the Professional Golfers' Association of America and Major League Soccer.

PepsiCo was slowly moving into international bottled water markets, with its most notable effort occurring in Mexico. In late 2002, PepsiCo's bottling operations acquired Mexico's largest Pepsi bottler, Pepsi-Gemex SA de CV, for $1.26 billion. Gemex not only bottled and distributed Pepsi soft drinks in Mexico but also was Mexico's number one producer of purified water. The company's Electropura was sold only in one-gallon and larger HDPE containers, but it was expected that Pepsi management would eventually introduce bottled water in small PET containers in the Mexican bottled water market.

PepsiCo launched its Aquafina Essentials enhanced water line in the United States during the summer of 2002. The line retailed for a suggested price of $1.49 per 20-ounce bottle and included four varieties. Multi-V was a watermelon-flavored beverage containing 25 percent of the daily requirement for Vitamins B6, B12, C, E, Pantothenic Acid, and Niacin. Daily-C was a citrus blend fortified with 100 percent of the daily requirement for Vitamin C. B-Power had a wild berry flavoring and provided 25 percent of the daily requirement of Vitamins B6, B12, Pantothenic Acid, and Niacin. The line filled out by Aquafina Essentials Calcium+, with a tangy tangerine-pineapple flavoring and 25 percent of the daily requirement for calcium and folic acid. The Essentials line was PepsiCo's second attempt at functional waters. It had attempted to add calcium to Aquafina without any flavoring in 2000, but the company's director of beverage research and development said the beverage's taste was like "chewing on chalk."[5]

PepsiCo's Propel fitness water was another enhanced water the company introduced in 2002 that had grown rapidly to become the number one brand of enhanced water in the United States, with a 44 percent market share in 2003. Propel was a lightly flavored Gatorade product that included B vitamins and antioxidants (vitamins C and E) and had only 20 calories per 16-ounce serving. The combined sales of Aquafina, Aquafina Essentials, and Propel made up 5 percent of PepsiCo's total 2003 beverage sales of $7.8 billion.

DS Waters

DS Waters was a 50-50 joint venture owned by Groupe Danone and Suntory Limited. Suntory was a diversified Japanese consumer products company with 2002 sales of 816 billion yen (approximately $7.3 billion). The company was Japan's largest producer and distributor of alcoholic and non-alcoholic beverages and was among Japan's largest food distributors. The company also competed in the pharmaceutical and publishing industries and operated restaurants, bars, and sports clubs in Japan. The company's businesses in the United States included independent Pepsi-Cola bottling operations, a resort management group, Suntory Pharmaceuticals, and Suntory Water Group. In 2002, Suntory Water Group was the fourth largest producer and distributor of bottled water in the United States, with annual sales of approximately $500 million. Suntory Water Group's bottled spring water was available nationwide under such regional brands as Alhambra, Crystal Springs, Sierra Springs, Hinckley Springs, Kentwood Springs, Belmont Springs, and Sparkletts. Suntory's brands were distributed to supermarkets and convenience stores but were only modestly differentiated and therefore forced to compete primarily on price to gain shelf space.

The company's HOD business maintained delivery fleets in 20 of the top 25 U.S. HOD regions and was supported by the company's Water.com Web site, which allowed consumers to purchase bulk water and water bottled in PET containers for direct delivery. The 2003 joint venture with Groupe Danone that created DS Waters resulted in a stronger leader in the North American HOD segment, with annual sales of $810 million (HOD and PET distribution channels combined); earnings before interest, taxes, depreciation, and amortization (EBITDA) of $146 million; and 1.7 million home and office customers. The joint venture was also expected to provide cost savings of $40 million between 2004 and 2006 from synergies in administration, distribution, production, and purchasing activities.

Other Sellers

In addition to the industry's leading sellers of bottled water, there were hundreds of regional and specialty brands of bottled water in the United States. Most of these companies were privately held bottlers with distribution limited to small geographic regions that competed aggressively on price to make it onto convenience-store and supermarket shelves as third-tier brands. Many of these bottlers also sought out private-label contracts with discounters and large supermarket chains to better ensure full capacity utilization and to achieve sufficient volume to purchase bottles and other packaging at lower prices.

Another group of small bottlers such as Fiji, Aspen Pure, Voss, Penta, and Trinity Springs used differentiating features to avoid the fierce price competition at the low end of the market and sold in the superpremium segment, where bottled water retailed from $1.50 to $2.25 per 16-ounce PET container. Superpremium brands were most often sold in natural foods stores, with Trinity Springs leading in the channel in 2003. Trinity's differentiation was based on its water source, which was a 2.2-mile-deep artesian well located in the Trinity Mountains of Idaho. Trinity claimed its water was incomparable in natural purity since it entered the aquifer 16,000 years ago as rain and snow and was heated at temperatures of 300 degrees Fahrenheit by the earth's core before emerging back to the surface through crystal-lined granite faults in the mountain. Trinity Springs' Natural Mineral Supplement bottled water had a high mineral content to provide needed minerals to consumers' diets and was naturally alkaline, which could help offset the effects of acidic foods and wine. Trinity Natural Mineral Supplement was not marketed as a bottled water because bottled water was required to undergo some type of disinfection or purification in five states where Trinity was sold. The company's Trinity Geothermal Bottled Water was partially distilled to lower the natural mineral levels of water flowing from its springs and, according to the company, was best suited for those who made Trinity their primary source of water consumed throughout the day.

Penta was the number two bottled water brand sold in natural foods stores in 2003. Its differentiation was based on a proprietary purification system that the company claimed removed 100 percent of impurities from tap water. The company had also built brand recognition through product placements in motion pictures, music videos, and more than 25 television series. Penta also sponsored a large number of triathlons across the United States and was endorsed by a wide variety of entertainers and professional athletes. In 2004, Penta was distributed in more than 3,000 health food stores in 49 U.S. states. Penta was also available in England and Canada. Fiji was the third best-selling brand of superpremium water sold in natural foods stores in 2003, but was also sold in many supermarkets and drugstores across the United States. Fiji was sourced from a Pacific island aquifer and was also very popular in Hollywood. Like Penta, Fiji received considerable exposure from its placement in network television series and motion pictures.

The superpremium bottled water segment had attracted new entrants every year during the early 2000s. Voss, a new brand to the market, was sourced from a deep aquifer in Norway and was sold only in upscale spas and resorts. Another new entrant was PowerWater, which was distilled and superoxygenated with medical-grade oxygen. PowerWater was targeted toward active, health-conscious consumers. Another superpremium brand, Eon, claimed to "accelerate cellular absorption while enhancing the body's oxygenation" through its proprietary reverse osmosis technology.[6] Eon was sold only in Texas and California in 2004. Aspen Pure, another new entrant to the bottled water industry that had achieved notable successes in gaining access to retail distribution, was founded in 2002 but began to grow rapidly in 2003 when a cofounder of Pizza Hut became a substantial investor in the company. The company's identification with Aspen, Colorado, and the product's attractive packaging were the primary sources of the brand's differentiation. Aspen Pure was bottled at the source of a Rocky Mountain spring near Aspen, Colorado, and was packaged in a distinctively shaped bottle that pictured Aspen's twin Maroon Bells mountains. Relative to other premium waters, Aspen Pure was priced moderately at 79 to 89 cents for a 24-ounce bottle and 69 to 79 cents for a half-liter bottle. In 2004 Aspen Pure was sold in more than 600 locations in

Colorado, including restaurants, natural foods stores, and supermarkets. Aspen Pure was also sold in nine additional states. Many other superpremium brands of bottled water were sold in the United States during 2004, with each attempting to support its premium pricing with some unique characteristic.

Endnotes

[1]As quoted in "The Taste of Water," Bottled Water Web, www.bottledwaterweb.com/watertaste.htm.

[2]"Coca-Cola Water Deal Creates a Stir," *Atlanta Journal-Constitution,* June 18, 2002, p. 1D.

[3]"Reaching for the Water Margin," *Marketing Week,* March 4, 2004, p. 22.

[4]"Dasani Debacle Spills Over, Stunts Coke's European Plans," *Atlanta Journal-Constitution,* March 25, 2004.

[5]"Pepsi, Coke Take Opposite Tacks in Bottled Water Marketing Battle," *The Wall Street Journal,* April 18, 2002, p. A1.

[6]As quoted in *Beverage Aisle,* May 15, 2004.

Dell, Inc., in 2005
A Winning Strategy?

Arthur A. Thompson
The University of Alabama

John E. Gamble
University of South Alabama

In 1984, at the age of 19, Michael Dell invested $1,000 of his own money and founded Dell Computer with a simple vision and business concept—that personal computers (PCs) could be built to order and sold directly to customers. Michael Dell believed his approach to the PC business had two advantages: (1) bypassing distributors and retail dealers eliminated the markups of resellers, and (2) building to order greatly reduced the costs and risks associated with carrying large stocks of parts, components, and finished goods. Between 1986 and 1993 the company worked to refine its strategy, build an adequate infrastructure, and establish market credibility against better-known rivals. In the mid and late 1990s, Dell's strategy started to click into full gear. By 2003, Dell's sell-direct and build-to-order business model and strategy had provided the company with the most efficient procurement, manufacturing, and distribution capabilities in the global PC industry and had given Dell a substantial cost and profit margin advantage over rival PC vendors. And by late 2004 Dell seemed well on its way to solidifying its market standing as the global leader in PCs.

Dell had a market-leading 33 percent share of PC sales in the United States in the first nine months of 2004, comfortably ahead of Hewlett-Packard (19.5 percent), IBM (5.1 percent), and Gateway (4.7 percent). Dell had moved ahead of IBM into second place during 1998 and then overtaken Compaq Computer as the U.S. sales leader in the third quarter of 1999. Its market share leadership in the United States had widened every year since 2000. Dell had overtaken Compaq as the global market leader in 2001. But when HP, the third-ranking PC seller in the world, acquired Compaq, the second-ranking PC vendor in 2002, Dell found itself in a tight battle with HP for the top spot globally. Dell was the world leader in unit sales in the first and third quarters of 2002, and HP was the sales leader in the second and fourth quarters. However, Dell opened a clear market share gap over HP in 2003–2004. In the United States, Dell had the number one PC market share in every customer segment in the three months ending October 2004. However, Dell trailed HP in PC sales outside the United States; HP's non-U.S. share had been in the 12.5 to 13.8 percent range since late 2001, with Dell's share climbing from about 7.5 percent in late 2001 to 11 percent in 2004. Exhibit 1 shows the shifting domestic and global sales and market share rankings in PCs during 1998–2004.

Since the late 1990s, Dell had also been driving for industry leadership in servers. In 2004 Dell was the number one domestic seller of servers, with close to a 33 percent market share (up from about 3–4 percent in the mid-1990s). It was number two in the world in server shipments, with a 24.5 percent share in the third quarter of 2004, within striking distance of global market leadership. Dell was the leader in servers in the three largest server markets—the United States, Japan, and China. In the mid-to-late 1990s, a big fraction of the servers sold were proprietary machines running on customized Unix operating systems and carrying price tags ranging from $30,000 to $1 million or more. But a seismic shift in server technology, coupled with growing cost-consciousness on the part of server users, produced a radical shift away from more costly, proprietary, Unix-based servers during 1999–2004. In 2003–2004, about 8 out of 10 servers sold carried price tags below $10,000, were based on standardized components and technology, and ran on either Windows or Linux operating systems. The overall share of Unix-based servers shipped in 2003–2004 was under 10 percent, down from about 18 percent in 1997. Dell's rise to prominence in servers came from its focus on low- and mid-range servers that used standard technology.

In addition, Dell was making market inroads in other product categories. Its sales of data storage devices had grown to over $2 billion annually, aided by a strategic alliance with EMC, a leader in the data storage. In 2001–2002, Dell began selling low-cost data-routing switches—a product category in which Cisco Systems was the dominant global leader. In late 2002 Dell introduced a new line of handheld PCs—the Axim X5—to compete against the higher-priced products of Palm, HP, and others; the Axim offered a solid but not trendsetting design, was packed with features, and was priced roughly 50 percent below the best-selling models of rivals. Starting in 2003, Dell began marketing Dell-branded printers and printer cartridges, product categories that provided global leader HP with the lion's share of its profits—Dell was on track to sell over 5 million printers and generate more than $1 billion in imaging and printing revenues in 2004. Also in 2003, Dell began selling flat-screen LCD TVs and retail-store systems, including electronic cash registers, specialized software, services, and peripherals required to link retail-store checkout lanes to corporate information systems. Dell's recently introduced MP3 player, the Dell DJ, was number two behind the Apple iPod. Dell added plasma screen TVs to its TV product line in 2004. Since the late 1990s, Dell had been marketing CD and DVD drives, printers, scanners, modems, monitors, digital cameras, memory cards, data storage devices, and speakers made by a variety of manufacturers.

So far, Dell's foray into new products and businesses had proved to be profitable. According to Michael Dell, "We believe that all our businesses should make money. If a business doesn't make money, if you can't figure out how to make money in that business, you shouldn't be in that business."[1] In 2003 and 2004, Dell earned a profit in each of its product categories, customer segments, and geographic markets. Dell products were sold in more than 170 countries, but sales in 60 countries accounted for about 95 percent of total revenues.

Company Background

At age 12, Michael Dell was running a mail-order stamp-trading business, complete with a national catalog, and grossing $2,000 a month. At 16 he was selling subscriptions to the *Houston Post,* and at 17 he bought his first BMW with money he had earned. He enrolled at the University of Texas in 1983 as a premed student (his parents wanted him to become a doctor), but he soon became immersed in computers and started selling PC components out of his college dormitory room. He bought random-access memory

Exhibit 1   U.S. AND GLOBAL MARKET SHARES OF LEADING PC VENDORS, 1998–2004

A. U.S. Market Shares of the Leading PC Vendors, 1998–2003

2003 Rank	Vendor	First Nine Months of 2004 Shipments (in 000s)	First Nine Months of 2004 Market Share	2003 Shipments (in 000s)	2003 Market Share	2002 Shipments (in 000s)	2002 Market Share
1	Dell	14,011	33.1%	16,319	30.9%	13,324	27.90%
	Compaq*	—	—	—	—	—	—
2	Hewlett-Packard*	8,256	19.5	10,851	20.6	8,052	16.8
3	IBM	2,170	5.1	2,748	5.2	2,531	5.3
4	Gateway	1,991	4.7	1,987	3.8	2,725	5.7
5	Apple	n.a.	n.a.	1,675	3.2	1,693	3.5
	Others	15,954	37.6	19,158	36.3	19,514	40.8
	All vendors	42,382	100.0%	52,739	100.0%	47,839	100.0%

B. Worldwide Market Shares of the Leading PC Vendors, 1996–2003†

2003 Rank	Vendor	First Nine Months of 2004 Shipments (in 000s)	First Nine Months of 2004 Market Share	2003 Shipments (in 000s)	2003 Market Share	2002 Shipments (in 000s)	2002 Market Share
1	Dell	22,999	18.4%	25,833	16.9	20,672	15.2%
	Compaq*	—	—	—	—	—	—
2	Hewlett-Packard*	19,796	15.8	25,009	16.4	18,432	13.6
3	IBM	7,478	6.0	9,000	5.9	7,996	5.9
4	Fujitsu Siemens	5,142	4.1	6,375	4.2	5,822	4.3
5	Toshiba	n.a.	n.a.	5,080	3.3	n.a	n.a
	Others	69,753	55.7	81,271	53.3	78,567	57.8
	All vendors	125,168	100.0%	152,568	100.0%	136,022	100.0%

n.a. = Not available.

*Compaq was acquired by Hewlett-Packard in May 2002. The 2002 data for Hewlett-Packard include both Compaq-branded and Hewlett-Packard-branded PCs for the last three quarters of 2002 plus only Hewlett-Packard-branded PCs for Q1 2002. Compaq's worldwide PC shipments during Q1 2002 totaled 3,367,000 units; its U.S. PC shipments during Q1 2002 totaled 1,280,000 units.

†Includes branded shipments only and excludes original equipment manufacturer (OEM) sales for all manufacturers; shipments of Compaq PCs for last three quarters of 2002 included in 2002 figures for Hewlett-Packard.

Source: International Data Corp.

(RAM) chips and disk drives for IBM PCs at cost from IBM dealers, who at the time often had excess supplies on hand because they were required to order large monthly quotas from IBM. Dell resold the components through newspaper ads (and later through ads in national computer magazines) at 10–15 percent below the regular retail price.

By April 1984 sales were running about $80,000 per month. Michael decided to drop out of college and form a company, PCs Ltd., to sell both PC components and PCs under the brand name PCs Limited. He obtained his PCs by buying retailers' surplus stocks at cost, then powering them up with graphics cards, hard disks, and memory before reselling them. His strategy was to sell directly to end users; by eliminating the retail markup, Dell's new company was able to sell IBM clones (machines that copied the functioning of IBM PCs using the same or similar components) about 40

A. U. S. Market Shares of the Leading PC Vendors, 1998–2003

| 2001 | | 2000 | | 1999 | | 1998 | |
Shipments (in 000s)	Market Share	Shipments (in 000s)	Market Share	Shipments (in 000s)	Market Share	Shipments (in 000s)	Market Share
10,817	23.5%	9,645	19.7%	7,492	16.6%	4,799	13.2%
5,341	11.6	7,761	15.9	7,222	16	6,052	16.7
4,374	9.5	5,630	11.5	3,955	8.8	2,832	7.8
2,461	5.3	2,668	5.5	3,274	7.2	2,983	8.2
3,219	7.0	4,237	8.7	4,001	8.9	3,039	8.4
1,665	3.6	n.a	n.a.	n.a	n.a.	n.a.	n.a.
23,509	51.0	18,959	38.8	19,248	42.6	16,549	45.6
46,051	100.0%	48,900	100.0%	45,192	100.0%	36,254	100.0%

B. Worldwide Market Shares of the Leading PC Vendors, 1996–2003[†]

| 2001 | | 2000 | | 1999 | | 1998 | |
Shipments (in 000s)	Market Share	Shipments (in 000s)	Market Share	Shipments (in 000s)	Market Share	Shipments (in 000s)	Market Share
17,231	12.9%	14,801	10.6%	11,883	10.5%	7,770	8.5%
14,673	11	17,399	12.5	15,732	14	13,266	14.5
9,309	7	10,327	7.4	7,577	6.7	5,743	6.3
8,292	6.2	9,308	6.7	9,287	8.2	7,946	8.7
6,022	4.5	6,582	4.7	n.a	n.a.	n.a.	n.a.
n.a	n.a	n.a.	n.a	n.a	n.a	n.a	n.a
73,237	54.9	80,640	58	62,258	55.2	50,741	55.5
133,466	100.0%	139,057	100.0%	112,726	100.0%	91,442	100.0%

percent below the price of IBM's best-selling PCs. The discounting strategy was successful, attracting price-conscious buyers and generating rapid revenue growth. By 1985, the company was assembling its own PC designs with a few people working on six-foot tables. The company had 40 employees, and Michael Dell worked 18-hour days, often sleeping on a cot in his office. By the end of fiscal 1986, sales had reached $33 million.

During the next several years, however, PCs Ltd. was hampered by growing pains—specifically, a lack of money, people, and resources. Michael Dell sought to refine the company's business model; add needed production capacity; and build a bigger, deeper management staff and corporate infrastructure while at the same time keeping costs low. The company was renamed Dell Computer in 1987, and the first international offices were opened that same year. In 1988 Dell added a sales force to serve large customers, began selling to government agencies, and became a public company—raising $34.2 million in its first offering of common stock. Sales to large customers quickly became the dominant part of Dell's business. By 1990 Dell Computer had sales of $388 million, a market share of 2–3 percent, and a research and development (R&D) staff of over 150 people. Michael Dell's vision was for Dell Computer to become one of the world's top three PC companies.

Thinking its direct sales business would not grow fast enough, in 1990–93, the company began distributing its computer products through Soft Warehouse Superstores (now CompUSA), Staples (a leading office products chain), Wal-Mart, Sam's Club, and Price Club (now Price/Costco). Dell also sold PCs through Best Buy stores in 16 states and through Xerox in 19 Latin American countries. But when the company learned how thin its margins were in selling through such distribution channels, it realized it had made a mistake and withdrew from selling to retailers and other intermediaries in 1994 to refocus on direct sales. At the time, sales through retailers accounted for only about 2 percent of Dell's revenues.

In 1993, further problems emerged: Dell reportedly lost $38 million in a risky foreign-currency hedging, quality difficulties arose with certain PC lines made by the company's contract manufacturers, profit margins declined, and buyers were turned off by the company's laptop PC models. To get laptop sales back on track, the company took a charge of $40 million to write off its laptop line and suspended sales of laptops until it could get redesigned models into the marketplace.

Because of higher costs and unacceptably low profit margins in selling to individuals and households, Dell did not pursue the consumer market aggressively until sales to individuals at the company's Internet site took off in 1996 and 1997. It became clear that PC-savvy individuals, who were buying their second and third computers, wanted powerful computers with multiple features; did not need much technical support; and liked the convenience of buying direct from Dell, ordering exactly what they wanted, and having it delivered to their door within a matter of days. In early 1997, Dell created an internal sales and marketing group dedicated to serving the individual consumer segment and introduced a product line designed especially for individual users.

By late 1997, Dell had become a low-cost leader among PC vendors by wringing greater and greater efficiency out of its direct sales and build-to-order business model. Since then, the company had continued driving hard to reduce its costs and, by late 2004, was considered the lowest-cost producer among all the leading vendors of PCs and servers. The company was a pioneer and an acknowledged world leader in incorporating e-commerce technology and use of the Internet into its everyday business practices. Michael Dell's goal was to stitch Dell's business together with its supply partners and customers in real time such that all three appeared to be part of the same organizational team.[2]

In its fiscal year ending January 30, 2004, Dell Computer posted revenues of $41.4 billion, up from $3.4 billion in the year ending January 29, 1995—a nine-year compound average growth rate of 32 percent. Over the same period, profits were up from $140 million to $2.62 billion—a 38.5 percent compound average growth rate. Dell expected to achieve close to $50 billion in sales in its fiscal year ending January 2005. A $100 investment in Dell's stock at its initial public offering in June 1988 would have been worth about $52,000 in December 2004. Based on 2003 data, Dell ranked number 31 on the Fortune 500, number 93 on the Fortune Global 500, and number 6 on the Fortune Global "most admired" list. In late 2004, Dell Computer had over 53,000 employees worldwide, up from 16,000 at year-end 1997; over 50 percent of Dell's employees were located in countries outside the United States, and this percentage was growing. The company's headquarters and main office complex was in Round Rock, Texas (an Austin suburb). The company changed its name from Dell Computer to Dell, Inc., in 2003 to reflect the company's growing business base outside of PCs. Exhibits 2 and 3 provide information about Dell's financial performance and geographic operations.

Michael Dell

In the company's early days Michael Dell hung around mostly with the company's engineers. He was so shy that some employees thought he was stuck up because he never talked to them. But people who worked with him closely described him as a likable young man who was slow to warm up to strangers.[3] He was a terrible public speaker and wasn't good at running meetings. But Lee Walker, a 51-year-old venture capitalist brought in by Michael Dell to provide much-needed managerial and financial experience during the company's organization-building years, became Michael Dell's mentor, built up his confidence, and was instrumental in turning him into a polished executive.[4] Walker served as the company's president and chief operating officer during the 1986–1990 period; he had a fatherly image, knew everyone by name, and played a key role in implementing Michael Dell's marketing ideas. Under Walker's tutelage, Michael Dell became intimately familiar with all parts of the business, overcame his shyness, learned to control his ego, and turned into a charismatic leader with an instinct for motivating people and winning their loyalty and respect.

When Walker had to leave the company in 1990 because of health reasons, Dell turned to Morton Meyerson, former CEO and president of Electronic Data Systems, for advice and guidance on how to transform Dell Computer from a fast-growing medium-sized company into a billion-dollar enterprise. Though sometimes given to displays of impatience, Michael Dell usually spoke in a quiet, reflective manner and came across as a person with maturity and seasoned judgment far beyond his age. His prowess was based more on an astute combination of technical knowledge and marketing know-how than on being a technological wizard. In 1992, at the age of 27, Michael Dell became the youngest CEO ever to head a Fortune 500 company; he was a billionaire at the age of 31.

By the late 1990s, Michael Dell had become one of the most respected executives in the PC industry. Media journalists had described him as "the quintessential American entrepreneur" and "the most innovative guy for marketing computers." He was a much-sought-after speaker at industry and company conferences. His views and opinions about the future of PCs, the Internet, and e-commerce practices carried considerable weight both in the PC industry and among executives worldwide. Once pudgy and bespectacled, in early 2005, 40-year-old Michael Dell was physically fit, considered good-looking, wore contact lenses, ate only health foods, and lived in a three-story 33,000-square-foot home on a 60-acre estate in Austin, Texas, with his wife and four children. He owned about 9 percent of Dell's common stock, worth over $9 billion.

Michael Dell was considered a very accessible CEO and a role model for young executives because he had done what many of them were trying to do. He delegated authority to subordinates, believing that the best results came from turning "loose talented people who can be relied upon to do what they're supposed to do." Business associates viewed Michael Dell as an aggressive personality, an extremely competitive risk taker who had always played close to the edge. He spent about 30 percent of his time traveling to company operations and meeting with customers. In a typical year, he would make two or three trips to Europe and two trips to Asia.

Exhibit 2 SELECTED FINANCIAL STATEMENT DATA FOR DELL INC., FISCAL YEARS
1998–2004 (in millions, except per share data)

	Fiscal Year Ended	
	January 30, 2004	January 31, 2003
Results of operations		
Net revenue	$41,444	$35,404
Cost of revenue	33,892	29,055
Gross margin	7,552	6,349
Operating expenses:		
Selling, general and administrative	3,544	3,050
Research, development and engineering	464	455
Special charges	—	—
Total operating expenses	4,008	3,505
Operating income	3,544	2,844
Investment and other income (loss), net	180	183
Income before income taxes, extraordinary loss, and cumulative effect of change in accounting principle	3,724	3,027
Provision for income taxes	1,079	905
Net income	$ 2,645	$ 2,122
Earnings per common share:		
Basic	$1.03	$0.82
Diluted	$1.01	$0.80
Weighted average shares outstanding:		
Basic	2,565	2,584
Diluted	2,619	2,644
Cash flow and balance sheet data		
Net cash provided by operating activities	$ 3,670	$ 3,538
Cash, cash equivalents, and investments	11,922	9,905
Total assets	19,311	15,470
Long-term debt	505	506
Total stockholders' equity	$ 6,280	$ 4,873

*Includes effect of $59 million adjustment due to the cumulative effect of a change in accounting principle.
Source: Dell, Inc., 2004 10-K and 1999 annual report.

In mid-2004, Michael Dell, the company's first and only CEO, transferred his title of CEO to Kevin Rollins, the company's president and chief operating officer. Dell remained as chairman of the board. Dell and Rollins had run the company for the past seven years under a shared leadership structure. The changes were primarily ones of title, not of roles or responsibilities.

Dell Computer's Strategy

The core of Dell Computer's strategy during 2002–2004 was to use its strong capabilities in supply chain management, low-cost manufacturing, and direct sales capabilities to expand into product categories where it could provide added value to its

	Fiscal Year Ended				
	February 1, 2002	February 2, 2001	January 28, 2000	January 29, 1999	February 1, 1998
	$31,168	$31,888	$25,265	$18,243	$12,327
	25,661	25,455	20,047	14,137	9,605
	5,507	6,443	5,218	4,106	2,722
	2,784	3,193	2,387	1,788	1,202
	452	482	374	272	204
	482	105	194	—	—
	3,718	3,780	2,955	2,060	1,406
	1,789	2,663	2,263	2,046	1,316
	(58)	531	188	38	52
	1,731	3,194	2,451	2,084	1,368
	485	958	785	624	424
	$ 1,246	$ 2,177*	$ 1,666	$ 1,460	$ 944
	$0.48	$0.84	$0.66	$0.58	$0.36
	$0.46	$0.79	$0.61	$0.53	$0.32
	2,602	2,582	2,536	2,531	2,631
	2,726	2,746	2,728	2,772	2,952
	$ 3,797	$ 4,195	$ 3,926	$ 2,436	$ 1,592
	8,287	7,853	6,853	3,181	1,844
	13,535	13,670	11,560	6,877	4,268
	520	509	508	512	17
	$ 4,694	$ 5,622	$ 5,308	$ 2,321	$ 1,293

customers in the form of lower prices. Its standard pattern of attack was to identify an IT product with good margins; figure out how to build it (or else have it built by others) cheaply enough to be able to significantly underprice competitive products; and then market the new product to Dell's steadily growing customer base and watch the market share points, incremental revenues, and incremental profits pile up.

Dell management believed it had the industry's most efficient business model. The company's strategy was built around a number of core elements: a cost-efficient approach to build-to-order manufacturing, partnerships with suppliers aimed at squeezing cost savings out of the supply chain, direct sales to customers, award-winning customer service and technical support, pioneering use of the Internet and e-commerce technology, and product-line expansion aimed at capturing a bigger share of the dollars its customers spent for IT products and services.

Exhibit 3   DELL'S GEOGRAPHIC AREA PERFORMANCE, FISCAL YEARS 2000–2004
(in millions of dollars)

	Fiscal Year Ended				
	January 30, 2004	January 31, 2003	February 1, 2002	February 2, 2001	January 28, 2000
Net revenues					
Americas					
Business	$21,888	$19,394	$17,275	$18,969	$15,160
U.S. consumer	6,715	5,653	4,485	3,902	2,719
Total Americas	28,603	25,047	21,760	22,871	17,879
Europe	8,495	6,912	6,429	6,399	5,590
Asia-Pacific-Japan	4,436	3,445	2,979	2,618	1,796
Total net revenues	$41,444	$35,404	$31,168	$31,888	$25,265
Operating income					
Americas					
Business	$ 2,124	$ 1,945	$ 1,482	$ 1,999	$ 1,800
U.S. consumer	400	308	260	253	204
Total Americas	2,594	2,253	1,742	2,252	2,004
Europe	637	388	377	347	359
Asia-Pacific-Japan	313	203	152	169	94
Special charges	—	—	(482)	(105)	(194)
Total operating income	$ 3,544	$ 2,844	$ 1,789	$ 2,663	$ 2,263

Source: Dell, Inc., 10-K reports, 2004 and 2001.

Cost-Efficient Build-to-Order Manufacturing

Dell built its computers, workstations, and servers to order; none were produced for inventory. Dell customers could order custom-equipped servers and workstations based on the needs of their applications. Desktop and laptop customers ordered whatever configuration of microprocessor speed, random-access memory, hard disk capacity, CD or DVD drives, fax/modem/wireless capabilities, graphics cards, monitor size, speakers, and other accessories they preferred. The orders were directed to the nearest factory. In 2004 Dell had assembly plants in Austin, Texas; Nashville, Tennessee; Limerick, Ireland; Xiamen, China; Penang, Malaysia; and El Dorado do Sul, Brazil; a seventh manufacturing plant was being constructed in North Carolina. At all locations, the company had the capability to assemble PCs, workstations, and servers; Dell assembled its data storage products at its Austin, Limerick, and Penang plants. In 2002–2004, typical orders were built and delivered in three to five days.

Until 1997, Dell operated its assembly lines in traditional fashion with workers performing a single operation. An order form accompanied each metal chassis across the production floor; drives, chips, and ancillary items were installed to match customer specifications. As a partly assembled PC arrived at a new workstation, the operator, standing beside a tall steel rack with drawers full of components, was instructed what to do by little red and green lights flashing beside the drawers. When the operator was finished, the drawers containing the used components were automatically replenished from the other side, and the PC chassis glided down the line to the next workstation. However, Dell had reorganized its plants in 1997, shifting to "cell manufacturing" techniques whereby a team of workers operating at a group workstation (or cell) assembled an entire PC according to customer specifications. The shift to cell manufacturing reduced Dell's assembly times by 75 percent and doubled productivity per square foot of assembly space. Assembled computers were first tested and then loaded with the desired software, shipped, and typically delivered five to six business days after the order was placed.

At Dell's newest plant on its Austin manufacturing campus, the cell manufacturing approach had been abandoned in favor of an even more efficient assembly-line approach. Workers at the new plant in 2004 could turn out close to 800 desktop PCs per hour on three assembly lines that took half the floor space of the older cell manufacturing process, where production had run about 120 units per hour. Although the new Austin plant was originally designed for production of 400 units per hour, management believed that it would be able to boost hourly production to 1,000 units per hour. The gains in productivity were being achieved partly by redesigning the PCs to permit easier and faster assembly, partly by innovations in the assembly process, and partly by reducing the number of times a computer was touched by workers during assembly and shipping by 50 percent. At both Dell's Austin plant and its plant in Ireland, workers could assemble a PC in two to three minutes. Moreover, just-in-time inventory practices that left pallets of parts sitting around everywhere had been tweaked to just-in-the-nick-of-time delivery by suppliers of the exact parts needed every couple of hours; double-decker conveyor belts moved parts and components to designated assembly points. Newly assembled PCs were routed on conveyors to shipping, where they were boxed and shipped to customers the same day.

Dell was regarded as a world-class manufacturing innovator and a pioneer in how to mass-produce a customized product—its methods were routinely studied in business schools worldwide. Most of Dell's PC rivals—notably IBM and HP/Compaq—had given up on trying to produce their own PCs as cheaply as Dell and shifted to outsourcing their PCs from contract manufacturers. Dell management believed that its in-house manufacturing delivered about a 6 percent cost advantage versus outsourcing. Dell's build-to-order strategy meant that the company had no in-house stock of finished goods inventories and that, unlike competitors using the traditional value chain model, it did not have to wait for resellers to clear out their own inventories before it could push new models into the marketplace—resellers typically operated with 30 to 60 days inventory of prebuilt models (see Exhibit 4). Equally important was the fact that customers who bought from Dell got the satisfaction of having their computers customized to their particular liking and pocketbook.

Quality Control

All assembly plants had the capability to run testing and quality control processes on components, parts, and subassemblies obtained from suppliers, as well as on the finished products Dell assembled. Suppliers were urged to participate in a quality certification program that committed them to achieving defined quality specifications. Quality control activities were undertaken at various stages in the assembly process. In addition, Dell's quality control program included testing of completed units after assembly, ongoing production reliability audits, failure tracking for early identification of problems associated with new models shipped to customers, and information obtained from customers through its service and technical support programs. All of the company's plants had been certified as meeting ISO 9002 quality standards.

Exhibit 4   Comparative Value Chain Models of PC Vendors

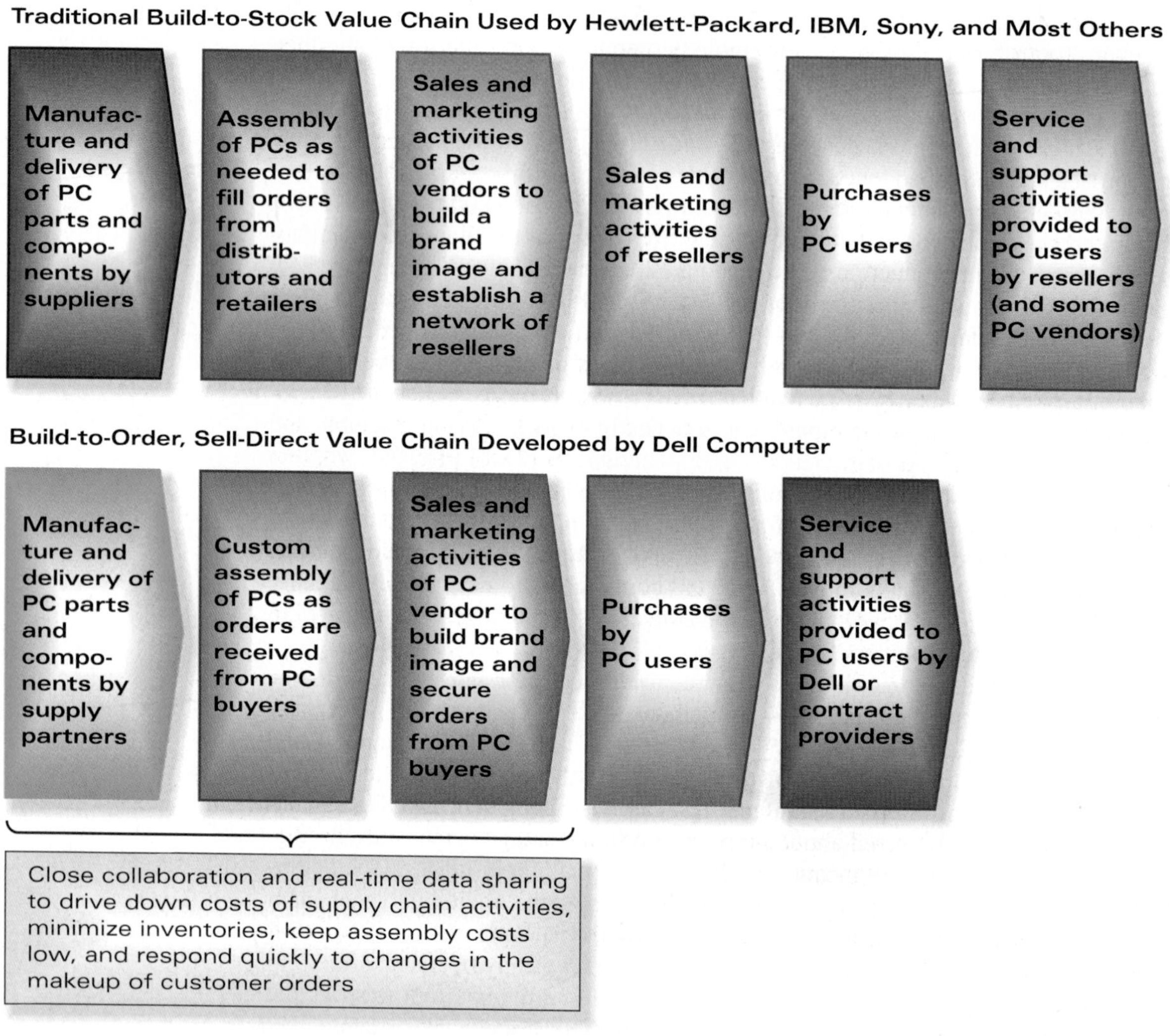

Traditional Build-to-Stock Value Chain Used by Hewlett-Packard, IBM, Sony, and Most Others

Manufacture and delivery of PC parts and components by suppliers	Assembly of PCs as needed to fill orders from distributors and retailers	Sales and marketing activities of PC vendors to build a brand image and establish a network of resellers	Sales and marketing activities of resellers	Purchases by PC users	Service and support activities provided to PC users by resellers (and some PC vendors)

Build-to-Order, Sell-Direct Value Chain Developed by Dell Computer

Manufacture and delivery of PC parts and components by supply partners	Custom assembly of PCs as orders are received from PC buyers	Sales and marketing activities of PC vendor to build brand image and secure orders from PC buyers	Purchases by PC users	Service and support activities provided to PC users by Dell or contract providers

Close collaboration and real-time data sharing to drive down costs of supply chain activities, minimize inventories, keep assembly costs low, and respond quickly to changes in the makeup of customer orders

Partnerships with Suppliers

Michael Dell believed that it made much better sense for the company to partner with reputable suppliers of PC parts and components than to integrate backward and get into parts and components manufacturing on its own. He explained why:

> If you've got a race with 20 players all vying to make the fastest graphics chip in the world, do you want to be the twenty-first horse, or do you want to evaluate the field of 20 and pick the best one?[5]

Dell management evaluated the various makers of each component; picked the best one or two as suppliers; and then stuck with those suppliers as long as they maintained their leadership in technology, performance, quality, and cost. Management believed that long-term partnerships with reputable suppliers had at least five advantages. First, using name-brand processors, disk drives, modems, speakers, and multimedia components enhanced the quality and performance of Dell's PCs. Because of varying performance among different brands of components, the brand of the components was quite important to customers concerned about performance and reliability. Second, because Dell partnered with suppliers for the long term and because it committed to purchase a specified percentage of its requirements from each supplier, Dell was assured of getting the volume of components it needed on a timely basis even when overall market demand for a particular component temporarily exceeded the overall market supply. Third, Dell's long-run commitment to its suppliers made it feasible for suppliers to locate their plants or distribution centers within a few miles of Dell assembly plants, putting them in position to make deliveries daily or every few hours, as needed. Dell supplied data on inventories and replenishment needs to its suppliers at least once a day—hourly in the case of components being delivered several times daily from nearby sources.

Fourth, long-term supply partnerships facilitated having some of the supplier's engineers assigned to Dell's product design teams and being treated as part of Dell. When new products were launched, suppliers' engineers were stationed in Dell's plants; if early buyers called with a problem related to design, further assembly and shipments were halted while the supplier's engineers and Dell personnel corrected the flaw on the spot.[6] Fifth, long-term partnerships enlisted greater cooperation on the part of suppliers to seek new ways to drive costs out of the supply chain. Dell openly shared its daily production schedules, sales forecasts, and new model introduction plans with vendors. Dell also did a three-year plan with each of its key suppliers and worked with suppliers to minimize the number of different stock-keeping units of parts and components in its products and to identify ways to drive costs down.

Commitment to Just-in-Time Inventory Practices

Dell's just-in-time inventory emphasis yielded major cost advantages and shortened the time it took for Dell to get new generations of its computer models into the marketplace. New advances were coming so fast in certain computer parts and components (particularly microprocessors, disk drives, and wireless devices) that any given item in inventory was obsolete in a matter of months, sometimes quicker. Moreover, rapid-fire reductions in the prices of components were not unusual—for example, Intel regularly cut the prices on its older chips when it introduced newer chips, and it introduced new chip generations about every three months. In 2003–2004, component costs declined an average of 0.5 percent weekly.[7] Michael Dell explained the competitive and economic advantages of minimal component inventories:

> If I've got 11 days of inventory and my competitor has 80 and Intel comes out with a new chip, that means I'm going to get to market 69 days sooner. In the computer industry, inventory can be a pretty massive risk because if the cost of materials is going down 50 percent a year and you have two or three months of inventory versus eleven days, you've got a big cost disadvantage. And you're vulnerable to product transitions, when you can get stuck with obsolete inventory.[8]

For a growing number of parts and components, Dell's close partnership with suppliers was allowing it to operate with no more than two hours of inventory.

Dell's supplier of CRT monitors was Sony. Because the monitors Sony supplied with the Dell name already imprinted were of dependably high quality (a defect rate of fewer than 1,000 per million), Dell didn't even open up the monitor boxes to test them at its Reno, Nevada, monitor distribution center.[9] Utilizing sophisticated data exchange systems, Dell arranged for its shippers (Airborne Express and United Parcel Service) to pick up computers at U.S. assembly plants, then pick up the accompanying monitors at its Reno distribution center and deliver both to the customer simultaneously. The savings in time and cost were significant. Dell had been working hard for the past several years to refine and improve its relationships with suppliers and its procedures for operating with smaller inventories.

In fiscal year 1995, Dell averaged an inventory turn cycle of 32 days. By the end of fiscal 1997 (January 1997), the average was down to 13 days. In fiscal 1998 Dell's inventory averaged 7 days, which compared very favorably with Gateway's 14-day average, Compaq's 23-day average, and the estimated industrywide average of over 50 days. In fiscal years 1999 and 2000, Dell operated with an average of six days' supply in inventory; the average dropped to five days' supply in fiscal year 2001, four days' supply in 2002, and three days' supply in 2003 and 2004.

Dell's Direct Sales Strategy and Marketing Efforts

With thousands of phone, fax, and Internet orders daily and ongoing field sales force contact with customers, the company kept its finger on the market pulse, quickly detecting shifts in sales trends, design problems, and quality glitches. If the company got more than a few of the same complaints, the information was relayed immediately to design engineers who checked out the problem. When design flaws or components defects were found, the factory was notified and the problem corrected within a few days. Management believed Dell's ability to respond quickly gave it a significant advantage over PC makers that operated on the basis of large production runs of variously configured and equipped PCs and sold them through retail channels. Dell saw its direct sales approach as a totally customer-driven system, with the flexibility to transition quickly to new generations of components and PC models.

Dell's Customer-Based Sales and Marketing Focus
Whereas many technology companies organized their sales and marketing efforts around product lines, Dell was organized around customer groups. Dell had placed managers in charge of developing sales and service programs appropriate to the needs and expectations of each customer group. Up until the early 1990s, Dell operated with sales and service programs aimed at just two market segments—high-volume corporate and governmental buyers, and low-volume business and individual buyers. But as sales took off in 1995–97, these segments were subdivided into finer, more homogeneous categories that by 2000 included global enterprise accounts, large and midsize companies (over 400 employees), small companies (under 400 employees), health care businesses (over 400 employees), federal government agencies, state and local government agencies, educational institutions, and individual consumers. Many of these customer segments were further subdivided—for instance, in education, there were separate sales and marketing programs for K–12 schools; higher education institutions; and personal-use purchases by faculty, staff, and students.

Dell's largest global enterprise accounts were assigned their own dedicated sales force—for example, Dell had a sales force of 150 people dedicated to meeting the needs of General Electric's facilities and personnel scattered across the world. Dell's sales to individuals and small businesses were made by telephone, fax, and the Internet. It had call centers in the United States, Canada, Europe, and Asia with toll-free lines; customers could talk with a sales representative about specific models, get information faxed or mailed to them, place an order, and pay by credit card. The Asian and European call centers were equipped with technology that routed calls from a particular country to a particular call center. Thus, for example, a customer calling from Lisbon, Portugal, was automatically directed to a Portuguese-speaking sales rep at the call center in Montpelier, France.

Dell in Japan   With a market share of about 10 percent, Dell was the number three provider of computer systems in Japan (behind NEC and Toshiba); in 2002 Dell had the fifth highest dollar market share, at 7.7 percent. Other competitors in Japan included Sony, Fujitsu, Hitachi, IBM, Sharp, and Matshusita. Counting units sold, however, Dell was number one in business desktop computers and was number two in entry-level and midrange servers. Dell's 2004 sales in Japan were up about 30 percent, in a market where overall sales were flat. Dell's technical and customer support for PCs, servers, and network storage devices was ranked the best in Japan in 2002 and 2003. Dell had 1,100 personnel in Japan and was tracking Japanese buying habits and preferences with its proprietary software. The head of Dell's consumer PC sales group in Japan had installed 34 kiosks in leading electronics stores around Japan, allowing shoppers to test Dell computers, ask questions of staff, and place orders—close to half the sales were to people who did not know about Dell prior to visiting the kiosk. Dell believed that it was more profitable than any other PC-server vendor selling in the Japanese market. Dell's profit margins in Japan were higher than those in the U.S. market, and sales were rising briskly.

Dell in China   Dell Computer entered China in 1998 and achieved faster growth there than in any other foreign market it had entered. The market for PCs in China was the third largest in the world, behind the United States and Japan, and was on the verge of being the second largest. PC sales in China were growing 20–30 percent annually and, with a population of 1.4 billion people (of which some 400 million lived in metropolitan areas where computer use was growing rapidly), the Chinese market for PCs was expected to become the largest in the world by 2010.

The market leader in China was Lenovo, a local company formerly called Legend, which had a 26.4 percent share in 2004. Other major local PC producers were Founder (10.3 percent share) and Great Wall (8.7 percent share). Dell had an 8.1 percent share and expected to overtake Great Wall and move into third place in 2004. Dell's shipments in China rose 60 percent in fiscal 2004 (four times the rest of the industry) and its revenues were up 40 percent, making China Dell's fourth largest market. Other competitors in China included IBM, Hewlett-Packard, Toshiba, Acer, and NEC Japan. All of the major contenders except Dell relied on resellers to handle sales and service; Dell sold directly to customers in China just as it did elsewhere.

Dell's primary target market in China consisted of large corporate accounts. Management believed that many Chinese companies would find the savings from direct sales appealing, that they would like the idea of having Dell build PCs and servers to their requirements and specifications, and that—once they became a Dell customer—they would like the convenience of Internet purchases and the company's growing array of products and services. Dell recognized that its direct sales approach put it at a short-term disadvantage in appealing to small business customers and individual consumers. According to an executive from rival Lenovo, "It takes two years of a person's savings to buy a PC in China. And when two years of savings is at stake, the whole family wants to come out to a store to touch and try the machine."[10] But Dell believed that over time, as Chinese consumers became more familiar with PCs and more comfortable with making online purchases, growing numbers of small business customers and consumers would become comfortable with placing Internet and telephone orders. In 2002, about 40 percent of Dell's sales in China were over the Internet.

Dell in Latin America In 2002 PC sales in Latin America exceeded 5 million units. Latin America had a population of 450 million people. Dell management believed that in the next few years PC use in Latin America would reach 1 for every 30 people (one-tenth the penetration in the United States), pushing annual sales up to 15 million units. The company's plant in Brazil, the largest market in Latin America, was opened to produce, sell, and provide service and technical support for customers in Brazil, Argentina, Chile, Uruguay, and Paraguay.

Using Dell Direct Store Kiosks to Access Individual Consumers In 2002 Dell began installing Dell Direct Store kiosks in a variety of retail settings. The kiosks did not carry inventory, but customers could talk face-to-face with a knowledgeable Dell sales representative, inspect Dell's products, and order them on the Internet while at the kiosk. The idea for using kiosks had begun in Japan, where Dell sales reps were encountering resistance to Dell's direct sales approach from individual buyers—Japanese consumers were noted for wanting to carefully inspect different PC brands in stores before making a purchase. When kiosks were installed in Japanese retail settings, they proved quite popular and helped generate a big boost in Dell's share of PC sales to consumers in Japan. The success of kiosks in Japan had inspired Dell to try them in the United States. About 60 kiosks were in place at U.S. locations during the 2002 holiday sales season. Dell began placing Dell Direct Store kiosks in selected Wal-Mart and Sears stores in 2003 and had a total of 80 kiosks at various locations in December 2004.

Customer Service and Technical Support

Service became a feature of Dell's strategy in 1986 when the company began providing a year's free onsite service with most of its PCs after users complained about having to ship their PCs back to Austin for repairs. Dell contracted with local service providers to handle customer requests for repairs; on-site service was provided on a next-day basis. Dell also provided its customers with technical support via a toll-free phone number and e-mail. Dell received 500,000 to 600,000 e-mail messages and 6 to 8 million phone calls annually requesting service and support. Dell was aggressively pursuing initiatives to enhance its online technical support tools and reduce the number and cost of telephone support calls. The company was adding Web-based customer service and support tools to make a customer's online experience pleasant and satisfying. In 2003–2004, over 50 percent of Dell's technical support activities were conducted via the Internet.

Bundled service policies were a major selling point for winning corporate accounts. If customers preferred to work with their own service provider, Dell supplied the provider of choice with training and spare parts needed to service customers' equipment. Recently, Dell had instituted a First Call Resolution initiative to strengthen its capabilities to resolve customer inquiries or difficulties on the first call; First Call Resolution percentages were made an important measure in evaluating the company's technical support performance.

Value-Added Services Dell kept close track of the purchases of its large global customers, country by country and department by department—and customers themselves found this purchase information valuable. Dell's sales and support person-nel used their knowledge about a particular customer's needs to help that customer plan PC purchases, to configure the customer's PC networks, and to provide value-added services. For example, for its large customers Dell loaded software and placed ID tags on newly ordered PCs at the factory, thereby eliminating the need for the cus-tomer's IT personnel to unpack the PC, deliver it to an employee's desk, hook it up, place asset tags on the PC, and load the needed software from an assortment of CD-ROMs and diskettes—a process that could take several hours and cost $200–$300.[11] While Dell charged an extra $15 or $20 for the software-loading and asset-tagging ser-vices, the savings to customers were still considerable—one large customer reported savings of $500,000 annually from this service.[12]

Premier Pages   Dell had developed customized, password-protected Web sites called Premier Pages for close to 50,000 corporate, governmental, and institutional customers worldwide. These Premier Pages gave customers' personnel online access to information about all Dell products and configurations the company had purchased or that were currently authorized for purchase. Employees could use Premier Pages to (1) obtain customer-specific pricing for whatever machines and options the employee wanted to consider, (2) place an order online that would be electronically routed to higher-level managers for approval and then on to Dell for assembly and delivery, and (3) seek advanced help desk support. Customers could also search and sort all invoices and obtain purchase histories. These features eliminated paper invoices, cut ordering time, and reduced the internal labor customers needed to staff corporate purchasing and accounting functions. Customer use of Premier Pages had boosted the productiv-ity of Dell salespeople assigned to these accounts by 50 percent. Dell was providing Premier Page service to thousands of additional customers annually and adding more features to further improve functionality.

www.dell.com   Dell operated one of the world's highest-volume Internet com-merce sites, with nearly 8 billion page requests annually at 81 country sites in 28 lan-guages/dialects and 26 currencies. Dell began Internet sales at its Web site (www.dell.com) in 1995, almost overnight achieving sales of $1 million a day. By early 2003, over 50 percent of Dell's sales were Web-enabled—and the percentage was increasing, especially for sales to small businesses and consumers. Dell's Web site sales exceeded $60 million a day in 2004, up from $35 million daily in early 2000 and $5 million daily in early 1998. Its Web site averaged over 6 million visits weekly in the third quarter of 2004.

At the company's Web site, prospective buyers could review Dell's entire product line in detail, configure and price customized PCs, place orders, and track orders from manufacturing through shipping. The closing rate on sales at Dell's Web site was 20 percent higher than that on sales inquiries received via telephone. Management be-lieved that enhancing www.dell.com to shrink transaction and order fulfillment times, increase accuracy, and provide more personalized content resulted in a higher degree of "e-loyalty" than traditional attributes like price and product selection.

On-Site Services   Corporate customers paid Dell fees to provide technical sup-port, on-site service, and help with migrating to new IT technologies. Services were one of the fastest-growing part of Dell, accounting for almost $4 billion in sales in 2002 and close to $6 billion in fiscal 2003. Dell's service business was split about 50–50 between what Michael Dell called close-to-the-box services and management and professional services—but the latter were growing faster, at close to 25 percent annually. Dell estimated that close-to-the-box support services for Dell products represented about a $50 billion market, whereas the market for management and professional services (IT life-cycle services, deployment of new technology, and solutions for greater IT productivity) was about $90 billion. IT consulting services were becoming more standardized, driven primarily by growing hardware and software standardization, reduction in on-site service requirements (partly because of online diagnostic and support tools, growing ease of repair and maintenance, increased customer knowledge, and increased remote management capabilities), and declines in the skills and know-how that were required to perform service tasks on standardized equipment and install new, more standardized systems.

Dell's strategy in services, like its strategy in hardware products, was to bring down the cost of IT consulting services for its large enterprise customers. The providers of on-site service, technical support, and other types of IT consulting typically charged premium prices and realized hefty profits for their efforts. According to Michael Dell, customers who bought the services being provided by Dell saved 40 to 50 percent over what they would have paid other providers of IT services.

Top management expected services to play an expanding role in the company's growth. Kevin Rollins, Dell's president and CEO in 2004, indicated the company's business model "isn't just about making cheap boxes, it's also about freeing customers from overpriced relationships" with such vendors as IBM, Sun Microsystems, and Hewlett-Packard.[13] While a number of Dell's corporate accounts were large enough to justify dedicated on-site teams of Dell support personnel, Dell generally contracted with third-party providers to make the necessary onsite service calls. Customers notified Dell when they had problems; such notices triggered two electronic dispatches—one to ship replacement parts from Dell's factory to the customer sites, and one to notify the contract service provider to prepare to make the needed repairs as soon as the parts arrived.[14] Bad parts were returned so that Dell could determine what went wrong and how to prevent such problems from happening again. Problems relating to faulty components or flawed components design were promptly passed along to the relevant supplier for correction.

Customer Forums   In addition to using its sales and support mechanisms to stay close to customers, Dell periodically held regional forums for its best customers. The company formed Platinum and Gold Councils composed of its largest customers in the United States, Europe, Japan, and the Asia-Pacific region; regional meetings were held every six to nine months.[15] Some regions had two meetings—one for chief information officers and one for technical personnel. At the meetings, which frequently included a presentation by Michael Dell, Dell's senior technologists shared their views on the direction of the latest technological developments, what the flow of technology really meant for customers, and Dell's plans for introducing new and upgraded products over the next two years. There were also breakout sessions on topics of current interest. Dell found that the information gleaned from customers at these meetings assisted the company in forecasting demand for its products.

Pioneering Leadership in Use of the Internet and E-Commerce Technology

Dell was a leader in using the Internet and e-commerce technologies to squeeze greater efficiency out of its supply chain activities, to streamline the order-to-delivery process, to encourage greater customer use of its Web site, and to gather and use all types of information. In a 1999 speech to 1,200 customers, Michael Dell said:

The world will be changed forever by the Internet . . . The Internet will be your business. If your business isn't enabled by providing customers and suppliers with more information, you're probably already in trouble. The Internet provides a dramatic reduction in the cost of transactions and the cost of interaction among people and businesses, and it creates dramatic new opportunities and destroys old competitive advantages. The Internet is like a weapon sitting on a table ready to be picked up by either you or your competitors.[16]

Dell's use of its Web site and various Internet technology applications had proved instrumental in helping the company become the industry's low-cost provider and drive costs out of its business. Internet technology applications were a cornerstone of Dell's collaborative efforts with suppliers. The company provided order-status information quickly and conveniently over the Internet, thereby eliminating tens of thousands of order-status inquiries coming in by phone. It used its Web site as a powerful sales and technical support tool. Few companies could match Dell's competencies and capabilities in the use of Internet technology to improve operating efficiency and gain new sales in a cost-efficient manner.

Expansion into New Products

Dell's recent expansion into data storage hardware, switches, handheld PCs, printers, and printer cartridges represented an effort to diversify the company's product base and to use its competitive capabilities in PCs and servers to pursue revenue growth opportunities. Michael Dell explained why Dell had decided to expand into products and services that complemented its sales of PCs and servers:

We tend to look at what is the next big opportunity all the time. We can't take on too many of these at once, because it kind of overloads the system. But we believe fundamentally that if you think about the whole market, it's about an $800 billion market, all areas of technology over time go through a process of standardization or commoditization. And we try to look at those, anticipate what's happening, and develop strategies that will allow us to get into those markets. In the server market in 1995 we had a 2 percent market share, today we have over a 30 percent share, we're number 1 in the U.S. How did that happen? Well, first of all it happened because we started to have a high market share for desktops and notebooks. Then customers said, oh yes, we know Dell, those are the guys who have really good desktops and notebooks. So they have servers, yes, we'll test those, we'll test them around the periphery, maybe not in the most critical applications at first, but we'll test them here. [Then they discover] these are really good and Dell provides great support . . . and I think to some extent we've benefited from the fact that our competitors have underestimated the importance of value, and the power of the relationship and the service that we can create with the customer.

And, also, as a product tends to standardize there's not an elimination of the requirement for custom services, there's a reduction of it. So by offering some services, but not the services of the traditional proprietary computer company, we've been able to increase our share. And, in fact, what tends to happen is customers embrace the standards, because they know that's going to save them costs. Let me give you an example . . . about a year ago we entered into the data networking market. So we have Ethernet switches, layer 2 switches. So if you have PCs and servers, you need switches; every PC attaches to a switch, every server attaches to a switch. It's a pretty easy sale, switches go along with computer systems. We looked at this market and were able to come up with products that are priced about $2\frac{1}{2}$ times less than the market leader today, Cisco, and as a result the business has grown very, very quickly. We shipped 1.8 million switch ports in a period of about a year, when most people would have said that's not going to work and come up with all kinds of reasons why we can't succeed.[17]

As Dell's sales of data-routing switches accelerated in 2001–2002 and Dell management mulled whether to expand into other networking products and Internet gear, Cisco elected to discontinue supplying its switches to Dell for resale as of October 2002. Dell's family of PowerConnect switches—simple commodity-like products generally referred to as layer 2 switches in the industry—carried a price of $20 per port, versus $70–$100 for comparable Cisco switches and $38 for comparable 3Com switches.

Michael Dell and Kevin Rollins saw external storage devices as a growth opportunity because the company's corporate and institutional customers were making increasing use of high-speed data storage and retrieval devices. Dell's PowerVault line of storage products had data protection and recovery features that made it easy for customers to add and manage storage and simplify consolidation. The PowerVault products utilized standardized technology and components (which were considerably cheaper than customized ones), allowing Dell to underprice rivals and drive down storage costs for its customers by about 50 percent. Dell's competitors in storage devices included Hewlett-Packard (HP) and IBM.

Some observers saw Dell's 2003 entry into the printer market as a calculated effort to go after HP's biggest and most profitable business segment and believed the Dell offensive was deliberately timed to throw a wrench into HP's efforts to resolve the many challenges of successfully merging its operations with those of Compaq. One of the reasons that Dell had entered the market for servers back in 1995 was that Compaq Computer, then its biggest rival in PCs, had been using its lucrative profits on server sales to subsidize charging lower prices on Compaq computers and thus be more price-competitive against Dell's PCs—at the time Compaq was losing money on its desktop and notebook PC business. According to Michael Dell:

Compaq had this enormous profit pool that they were using to fight against us in the desktop and notebook business. That was not an acceptable situation. Our product teams knew that the servers weren't that complicated or expensive to produce, and customers were being charged unfair prices.[18]

Dell management believed that HP was doing much the same thing in printers and printer products, where it had a dominant market share worldwide and generated about 75 percent of its operating profits. Dell believed HP was using its big margins on printer products to subsidize selling its PCs at prices comparable to Dell's, even though Dell had costs that were about 8 percent lower than HP's. HP's PC operations were either in the red or barely in the black during most of 2003–2004, while Dell consistently had profit margins of 8 percent or more on PCs. Dell's entry and market success in printer products had put pricing pressure on HP in the printer market and had helped erode HP's share of the printer market worldwide from just under 50 percent to around 46 percent. Kevin Rollins believed that Dell's decision to enter the printer market as a head-to-head rival of HP served two purposes:

Any strategist is going to try to develop a strategy that is going to help them and hurt competitors. Our whole vision here was to do both: improve the revenues and profits of our own business, and at the same time put our competitors at a disadvantage.[19]

To further keep the pricing pressure on HP in 2003, Dell had priced its new Axim line of handheld PCs at about 50 percent less than HP's popular iPaq line of handhelds, and Dell's storage and networking products also carried lower prices than comparable HP products. Dell management believed the company's entry into the printer market would add value for its customers. Michael Dell explained:

> We think we can drive down the entire cost of owning and using printing products. If you look at any other market Dell has gone into, we have been able to significantly save money for customers. We know we can do that in printers; we have looked at the supply chain all the way through its various cycles and we know there are inefficiencies there. I think the price of the total offering when we include the printer and the supplies . . . can come down quite considerably.[20]

When Dell announced it had contracted with Lexmark to make printers and printer and toner cartridges for sale under the Dell label beginning in 2003, HP immediately discontinued supplying HP printers to Dell for resale at Dell's Web site. Dell had been selling Lexmark printers for two years and since 2000 had resold about 4 million printers made by HP, Lexmark, and other vendors to its customers. Lexmark designed and made critical parts for its printers but used offshore contract manufacturers for assembly. Gross profit margins on printers (sales minus cost of goods sold) were said to be in single digits in 2002–2004, but the gross margins on printer supplies were in the 50–60 percent range—brand-name ink cartridges for printers typically ran $25 to $35.

Dell's Entry into the White-Box PC Segment

In 2002 Dell announced it would begin making so-called white-box (i.e., unbranded) PCs for resale under the private labels of retailers. PC dealers that supplied white-box PCs to small businesses and price-conscious individuals under the dealer's own brand name accounted for about one-third of total PC sales and about 50 percent of sales to small businesses. According to one industry analyst, "Increasingly, Dell's biggest competitor these days isn't big brand-name companies like IBM or HP, it's white-box vendors." Dell's thinking in entering the white-box PC segment was that it was cheaper to reach many small businesses through the white-box dealers that already served them than by using its own sales force and support groups to sell and service businesses with fewer than 100 employees. Dell believed its low-cost supply chain and assembly capabilities would allow it to build generic machines cheaper than white-box resellers could buy components and assemble a customized machine. Management forecast that Dell would achieve $380 million in sales of white-box PCs in 2003 and would generate profit margins equal to those on Dell-branded PCs. Some industry analysts were skeptical of Dell's move into white-box PCs because they expected white-box dealers to be reluctant to buy their PCs from a company that had a history of taking their clients. Others believed this was a test effort by Dell to develop the capabilities to take on white-box dealers in Asia and especially in China, where the sellers of generic PCs were particularly strong.

Other Elements of Dell's Business Strategy

Dell's strategy had two other elements that assisted the company's drive for industry leadership: R&D and advertising.

Research and Development   Dell's R&D focus was to track and test new developments in components and software, ascertain which ones would prove most useful and cost-effective for customers, and then design them into Dell products. Management believed that it was Dell's job on behalf of its customers to sort out all the new technology coming into the marketplace and help steer customers to options and solutions most relevant to their needs. The company talked to its customers frequently about "relevant technology," listening carefully to customers' needs and problems, and endeavoring to identify the most cost-effective solutions.

Dell was a strong advocate of incorporating standardized components in its products so as not to tie either it or its customers to one company's proprietary technology and components, which almost always carried a price premium and increased costs for its customers. Dell actively promoted the use of industrywide standards and regularly pressed its suppliers of a particular part or component to agree on common standards. Dell executives saw standardized technology as beginning to take over the largest part of the $800 billion spent annually on IT—standardization was particularly evident in servers, storage, networking, and high-performance computing. One example of the impact of standardized technology was at the University of Buffalo, where Dell had installed a 5.6 teraflop cluster of about 2,000 Dell servers containing 4,000 microprocessors that was being used to decode the human genome. The cluster of servers, which were the same as those Dell sold to its business customers, had been installed in about 60 days at a cost of a few million dollars and represented the third most powerful supercomputer in the world. High-performance clusters of PCs and servers were replacing mainframe computers and custom-designed supercomputers because of their much lower cost. Amerada Hess, attracted by Dell's use of standardized and upgradable parts and components, installed a cluster of several hundred Dell workstations and allocated about $300,000 a year to upgrade and maintain it; the cluster had replaced an IBM supercomputer that cost $1.5 million a year to lease and operate. Studies conducted by Dell indicated that, over time, products incorporating standardized technology delivered about twice the performance per dollar of cost as products based on proprietary technology.

Dell's R&D group included over 3,000 engineers, and its annual R&D budget was $450 to $470 million. The company's R&D unit also studied and implemented ways to control quality and to streamline the assembly process. About 15 percent of Dell's 800 U.S. patents were ranked "elite."

Advertising   Michael Dell was a strong believer in the power of advertising and frequently espoused its importance in the company's strategy. His competitive zeal resulted in the company's being the first to use comparative ads, throwing barbs at Compaq's higher prices. Although Compaq won a lawsuit against Dell for making false comparisons, Michael Dell was unapologetic, arguing that the ads were very effective: "We were able to increase customer awareness about value."[21] He insisted that the company's ads be communicative and forceful, not soft and fuzzy. The company regularly had prominent ads describing its products and prices in such leading computer publications as *PC Magazine* and *PC World*, as well as in *USA Today, The Wall Street Journal,* and other business publications.

Dell's Performance in 2004

During the first nine months of 2004, Dell's revenues and unit shipments grew 2–3 times faster than the industry average. Despite steadily eroding average selling prices—

$1,540 in fiscal 2004, down from $1,640 in 2003; $1,700 in 2002; $2,050 in 2001; $2,250 in 2000; and $2,600 in 1998—Dell's revenues were climbing as the company gained volume and market share in virtually all product categories and geographic areas where it competed. Worldwide revenues, which reached $35.7 billion in the first nine months of fiscal 2005, were expected to run about 20 percent higher than fiscal 2004 levels and total about $48–$50 billion for the full year. Dell's sales increases were strongest in Europe and in notebook PCs.

During the November 2002–January 2003 period (the fourth quarter of Dell's 2003 fiscal year), the company posted its best-ever quarterly product shipments, revenues, and operating profits. Management indicated that Dell's global market share in PCs in the last quarter of fiscal 2003 was almost 3 points higher than in its fiscal 2002 fourth quarter, and its U.S. share was 5 points higher—in servers, Dell's market share was over 3 points higher. Unit shipments were up by 25 percent, and shipments in China, France, Germany, and Japan increased a combined 39 percent, with server sales in those countries up by 47 percent.

Market Conditions in the Information Technology Industry in Late 2004

Analysts expected the $800 billion worldwide IT industry to grow roughly 10 percent in 2004, following a single-digit increase in 2003, a 2.3 percent decline in 2002, and close to a 1 percent decline in 2001—corporate spending for IT products accounted for about 45 percent of all capital expenditures of U.S. businesses. From 1980 to 2000, IT spending had grown at an average annual rate of 12 percent and then flattened. The slowdown in IT spending reflected a combination of factors: sluggish economic growth worldwide that was prompting businesses to delay IT upgrades and hold on to aging equipment longer, overinvestment in IT in the 1995–99 period, declining unit prices for many IT products (especially PCs and servers), and a growing preference for lower-priced, standard-component hardware that was good enough to perform a variety of functions using off-the-shelf Windows or Linux operating systems (as opposed to relying on proprietary hardware and customized Unix software). The selling points that appealed most to IT customers were standardization, flexibility, modularity, simplicity, economy of use, and value.

Exhibit 5 shows actual and projected PC sales for 1980–2005 as compiled by industry researcher International Data Corporation (IDC). According to Gartner Research, the billionth PC was shipped sometime in July 2002; of the billion, an estimated 550 million were still in use. Nearly 82 percent of the 1 billion PCs that had been shipped were desktops, and 75 percent were sold to businesses. With a world population of 6 billion, most industry participants believed there was ample opportunity for further growth in the PC market. Computer usage in Europe was half of that in the United States, even though the combined economies of the European countries were a bit larger than the U.S. economy. Growth potential for PCs was particularly strong in China, India, several other Asian countries, and portions of Latin America. Forrester Research estimated that the numbers of PCs in use worldwide would approach 1.3 billion by 2010, up from 575 million in 2004, with the growth being driven by the emerging markets in China, India, and Russia. IDC had predicted that notebook PC sales would grow from 26.9 percent of PC shipments in 2003 to 37.3 percent in 2007.

Currently, there was growing interest in notebook computers equipped with wireless capability; many businesses were turning to notebooks equipped with wireless

Exhibit 5   WORLDWIDE SHIPMENTS OF PCS, 1980–2005

Year	PCs Shipped (in millions)	Year	PCs Shipped (in millions)
1980	1	1999	113
1985	11	2000	139
1990	24	2001	133
1995	58	2002	136
1996	69	2003	153
1997	80	2004*	177
1998	91	2005*	195

*Forecast data.

Source: International Data Corp.

data communications devices to improve worker productivity and keep workers connected to important information. The emergence of Wireless Fidelity (Wi-Fi) networking technology, along with the installation of wireless home and office networks, was fueling the trend. Wi-Fi systems were being used in businesses, on college campuses, in airports, and other locations to link users to the Internet and to private networks. Three other devices—flat-panel LCD monitors, DVD recorder drives, and portable music players like Apple's iPod—were also stimulating sales of new PCs.

The Server Market

At the same time, forecasters expected full global build-out of the Internet to continue, which would require the installation of millions of servers. But since 2000 IT customers had been switching from the use of expensive high-end servers running customized Unix operating systems to the use of low-cost servers running on standardized Intel/Windows/Linux technologies; the switch to stands-based servers had caused a slowdown in dollar revenues from server sales despite rapidly increasing unit volume. A number of industry observers believed that the days of using expensive, proprietary Unix-based servers were numbered. The Unix share of the server operating system market (based on unit shipments) was said to have decreased by nearly 50 percent over the past five years, whereas Windows and Linux servers had tripled in use. As of the third quarter of 2004:

- IBM held the number one spot in the worldwide server systems market based on dollar revenues, with a 31.7 percent market share. HP had the number two spot, with a 26.8 percent share.

- Sun and Dell tied for third place in server revenues, with 10.2 percent and 10.1 percent shares, respectively. Dell had experienced strong 14.1 percent year-over-year revenue growth while Sun's revenues were flat.

- In terms of unit shipments, HP was the number one vendor worldwide and Dell was number two, with a 24.5 percent share. HP had been the unit volume leader in server shipments for 10 consecutive quarters, but Dell had narrowed the gap considerably.

- HP had the number one spot in Linux servers, with a 26.9 percent market share based on revenue, while IBM was second, with 20.5 percent, and Dell was third, with 17.4 percent. Overall, 31.7 percent of the servers shipped in the third quarter of 2004 were Linux-based.

Competing Value Chain Models in the Global PC Industry

When the personal computer industry first began to take shape in the early 1980s, the founding companies manufactured many of the components themselves—disk drives, memory chips, graphics chips, microprocessors, motherboards, and software. Subscribing to a philosophy that mandated in-house development of key components, they built expertise in a variety of PC-related technologies and created organizational units to produce components as well as handle final assembly. While certain noncritical items were typically outsourced, if a computer maker was not at least partially vertically integrated and produced some components for its PCs, then it was not taken seriously as a manufacturer. But as the industry grew, technology advanced quickly in so many directions on so many parts and components that the early personal computer manufacturers could not keep pace as experts on all fronts. There were too many technologies and manufacturing intricacies to master for a vertically integrated manufacturer to keep its products on the cutting edge.

As a consequence, companies emerged that specialized in making particular components. Specialists could marshal enough R&D capability and resources to either lead the technological developments in their area of specialization or else quickly match the advances made by their competitors. Moreover, specialist firms could mass-produce the component and supply it to several computer manufacturers far cheaper than any one manufacturer could fund the needed component R&D and then make only whatever smaller volume of components it needed for assembling its own brand of PCs. Thus, in the early 1990s, such computer makers as Compaq Computer, IBM, Hewlett-Packard, Sony, Toshiba, and Fujitsu-Siemens began to abandon vertical integration in favor of a strategy of outsourcing most components from specialists and concentrating on efficient assembly and marketing their brand of computers. They adopted the build-to-stock value chain model shown in the top section of Exhibit 4. It featured arm's-length transactions between specialist suppliers, manufacturer/assemblers, distributors and retailers, and end users. However, a few others, most notably Dell and Gateway, employed a shorter value chain model, selling directly to customers and eliminating the time and costs associated with distributing through independent resellers. Building to order avoided (1) having to keep many differently equipped models on retailers' shelves to fill buyer requests for one or another configuration of options and components, and (2) having to clear out slow-selling models at a discount before introducing new generations of PCs (for instance, HP's retail dealers had an average of 43 days of HP products in stock as of October 2004). Direct sales eliminated retailer costs and markups (retail dealer margins were typically in the range of 4 to 10 percent).

Because of Dell's success in using its business model and strategy to become the low-cost leader, most other PC makers in 2002–2004 were endeavoring to emulate various aspects of Dell's strategy, but with only limited success. Nearly all vendors were trying to cut days of inventory out of their supply chains and reduce their costs of goods sold and operating expenses to levels that would make them more cost-competitive with Dell. In an effort to cut their assembly costs, IBM, HP, and several others had begun outsourcing assembly to contract manufacturers and refocused their internal efforts on product design and marketing. Virtually all vendors were trying to minimize the amount of finished goods in dealer/distributor inventories and shorten the time it took to replenish dealer stocks. Collaboration with contract manufacturers was increasing to develop the capabilities to build and deliver PCs equipped to customer specifications within 7 to 14 days, but these efforts were hampered by the use of Asia-based contract manufacturers—delivering built-to-order PCs to North American and European customers within a two-week time frame required the use of costly air freight from Asia-based assembly plants.

While most PC vendors would have liked to adopt Dell's sell-direct strategy for at least some of their sales, they confronted big channel conflict problems: if they started to push direct sales hard, they would almost certainly alienate the independent dealers on whom they depended for the bulk of their sales and service to customers. Dealers saw sell-direct efforts on the part of a manufacturer whose brand they represented as a move to cannibalize their business and to compete against them. However, Dell's success in gaining large enterprise customers with its direct sales force had forced growing numbers of PC vendors to supplement the efforts of their independent dealers with direct sales and service efforts of their own. During 2003–2004, several of Dell's rivals were selling 15 to 25 percent of their products direct.

Profiles of Selected Competitors in the PC Industry

This section presents brief profiles of three of Dell's principal competitors. Exhibit 6 summarizes Dell's principal competitors in the various product categories where it competed and the sizes of these product markets.

Exhibit 6   DELL'S PRINCIPAL COMPETITORS AND DELL'S ESTIMATED MARKET SHARES BY PRODUCT CATEGORY, 2004

Product Category	Dell's Principal Competitors	Estimated Size of Worldwide Market, 2003–2004 (in billions)	Dell's Worldwide Share, 2004
PCs	Hewlett-Packard (maker of both Compaq and HP brands); IBM, Gateway, Apple, Acer, Sony, Fujitsu-Siemens (in Europe and Japan), Legend (in China)	$175	18.5%
Servers	Hewlett-Packard, IBM, Sun Microsystems, Fujitsu	$50	~10%
Data storage devices	Hewlett-Packard, IBM, EMC, Hitachi	$40	~10%
Networking switches and related equipment	Cisco Systems, Enterasys, Nortel, 3Com	$58	2–3%
Handheld PCs	Palm, Sony, Hewlett-Packard, Toshiba, Casio	$4	~2–3%
Printers and printer cartridges	Hewlett-Packard, Lexmark, Canon, Epson	~$50	~7%
Cash register systems	IBM, NCR, Wincor Nixdorf, Hewlett-Packard, Sun Microsystems	$4 (in North America)	~1–2%
Services	Accenture, IBM, Hewlett-Packard, many others	$350	~2–3%

Source: Compiled by the case authors from a variety of sources, including International Data Corp. and www.dell.com.

Hewlett-Packard

In one of the most contentious and controversial acquisitions in U.S. history, Hewlett-Packard shareholders voted by a narrow margin in early 2002 to approve the company's acquisition of Compaq Computer, the world's second largest full-service global computing company (behind IBM) and a company with 2001 revenues of $33.6 billion and a net loss of $785 million. Compaq had passed IBM to become the world leader in PCs in 1995 and remained in first place until it was overtaken by Dell in late 1999. Compaq had acquired Tandem Computer in 1997 and Digital Equipment Corporation in 1998 to give it capabilities, products, and service offerings that allowed it to compete in every sector of the computer industry.[22] When Compaq purchased it, Digital was a troubled company with high operating costs, an inability to maintain technological leadership in high-end computing, and a nine-year string of having either lost money or barely broken even.[23]

The acquisitions gave Compaq a product line that included PCs, servers, workstations, mainframes, peripherals, and such services as business and e-commerce solutions, hardware and software support, systems integration, and technology consulting. In 2000, Compaq spent $370 million to acquire certain assets of Inacom Corporation that management believed would help Compaq reduce inventories, speed cycle time, and enhance its capabilities to do business with customers via the Internet. Carly Fiorina, who became HP's CEO in 1999, explained why the acquisition of Compaq was strategically sound:

> With Compaq, we become No. 1 in Windows, No. 1 in Linux and No. 1 in Unix . . . With Compaq, we become the No. 1 player in storage, and the leader in the fastest growing segment of the storage market—storage area networks. With Compaq, we double our service and support capacity in the area of mission-critical infrastructure design, outsourcing and support . . . Let's talk about PCs . . . Compaq has been able to improve their turns in that business from 23 turns of inventory per year to 62—100 percent improvement year over year— and they are coming close to doing as well as Dell does. They've reduced operating expenses by $130 million, improved gross margins by three points, reduced channel inventory by more than $800 million. They ship about 70 percent of their commercial volume through their direct channel, comparable to Dell. We will combine our successful retail PC business model with their commercial business model and achieve much more together than we could alone. With Compaq, we will double the size of our sales force to 15,000 strong. We will build our R&D budget to more than $4 billion a year, and add important capabilities to HP Labs. We will become the No. 1 player in a whole host of countries around the world—HP operates in more than 160 countries, with well over 60 percent of our revenues coming from outside the U.S. The new HP will be the No. 1 player in the consumer and small- and medium-business segments . . . We have estimated cost synergies of $2.5 billion by 2004 . . . It is a rare opportunity when a technology company can advance its market position substantially and reduce its cost structure substantially at the same time. And this is possible because Compaq and HP are in the same businesses, pursuing the same strategies, in the same markets, with complementary capabilities.

However, going into 2005 the jury was still out on whether HP's acquisition of Compaq was the success that Carly Fiorina had claimed it would be. The company's only real bright spot was its $24 billion crown jewel printer business, which still reigned as the unchallenged world leader (largely because of a highly productive $1 billion investment in printer R&D). But the rest of HP's businesses were underachievers. Its PC and server businesses were struggling, losing money in most quarters and barely breaking even in others—and HP was definitely losing ground to Dell in PCs and low-priced servers. In servers, HP was being squeezed on the low-end by Dell's low prices and on the high-end by strong competition from IBM. Most observers saw IBM as overshadowing HP in corporate computing—high-end servers and IT services. In data storage and technical support services, HP had been able to grow revenues but profit margins and total operating profits were declining. While HP had successfully cut annual operating costs by $3.5 billion—beating the $2.5 billion target set at the time of the Compaq acquisition, the company's operating margins in the first nine months of 2004 were a skimpy 5.3 percent, well below the 8–10 percent targets expected when the Compaq deal was finalized.[24] And the company had missed its earnings forecasts in 7 of the past 20 quarters.

With the company's stock price stuck in the $18–$23 price range, impatient investors had recently begun clamoring for the company to break itself up and create two separate companies, one for its printer business and one for all the rest of the businesses (PCs, servers, storage devices, digital cameras, calculators, and IT services). A Merrill Lynch analyst had estimated that the total value of HP's business would be 25–45 percent greater if split into printing and nonprinting operations.[25] In fact, HP's board of directors was actively considering breaking up the company into smaller pieces, but so far had taken no action. Carly Fiorina had expressed opposition to a breakup, arguing that HP's broad product/business lineup paid off in the form of added sales and lower costs. In an August 2004 speech, she said, "We think we have a unique opportunity, because we have leadership positions and intellectual property at every stage of the value chain."[26]

HP reported total revenues of $79.9 billion and net profits of $3.5 billion for fiscal 2004, versus total revenues of $73.1 billion and earnings of $2.5 billion in 2003. However, a substantial portion of the increase in net earnings in 2004 was due to cutbacks in R&D spending and a lower effective tax rate. Moreover, the company's EPS of $1.16 in 2004 was substantially below the EPS of $1.80 reported in 2000. Exhibit 7 shows the performance of HP's four major business groups. In February 2005, with HP's financial performance continuing to lag and mounting differences with the company's board of directors, Carly Fiorina resigned her post as HP's CEO.

IBM

IBM was seen as a "computer solutions" company and had the broadest and deepest capabilities in customer service, technical support, and systems integration of any company in the world. IBM's Global Services business group was the world's largest information technology services provider, with sales of $42.6 billion in 2003. In addition to its IT services business, IBM had 2003 hardware sales of $28.2 billion and software sales of $12.2 billion. IBM conducted business in 170 countries and had total sales of $89 billion and earnings of $7.6 billion in 2003. Once the world's undisputed king of computing and information processing, IBM was struggling to remain a potent contender in PCs, servers, storage products, and other hardware-related products. Since the early 1990s, IBM had been steadily losing ground to competitors in product categories it had formerly dominated. Its recognized strengths—a potent brand name, global distribution capabilities, a position as the longtime global leader in mainframe computers, and strong capabilities in IT consulting services and systems integration—had proved insufficient in overcoming buyer resistance to IBM's premium prices.

Exhibit 7   PERFORMANCE OF HEWLETT-PACKARD'S FOUR MAJOR BUSINESS GROUPS,
FISCAL YEARS 2001–2004 (in billions of dollars)

	Printing and Imaging	Personal Computing Systems*	Enterprise Systems*	HP Services
2004 (fiscal year ending October 31)				
Net revenue	$24,199	$24,622	$16,074	$13,778
Operating income (loss)	3,847	(210)	28	1,263
2003 (fiscal year ending October 31)				
Net revenue	$22,623	$21,228	$15,379	$12,305
Operating income (loss)	3,570	19	(54)	1,372
2002 (fiscal year ending October 31)*				
Net revenue	$20,447	$21,895	$16,194	$12,326
Operating income (loss)	3,345	(372)	(664)	1,369
2001 (fiscal year ending October 31)*				
Net revenue	$19,602	$26,710	$20,205	$12,802
Operating income (loss)	2,103	(728)	(579)	1,617

*Results for 2001 and 2002 represent the combined results of both HP and Compaq Computer.

Source: 2003 10-K report and company press release, November 16, 2004.

Many of its former customers had turned to lower-priced vendors—the old adage "No one ever got fired for selecting IBM products" no longer applied. IBM's revenues had hovered in the $81 to $89 billion range for the past five years. The company's only remaining strength in IT hardware was in high-end servers.

IBM's Troubles in PCs   IBM's market share in PCs was in a death spiral—it had lost more market share in the 1990s than any other PC maker. Once the dominant global and U.S. market leader, with a market share exceeding 50 percent in the late 1980s and early 1990s, IBM was fast becoming an also-ran in PCs, with a global market share of only 6 percent in 2004 (see Exhibit 1). Its last stronghold in PCs was in laptop computers, where its ThinkPad line was a consistent award winner on performance, features, and reliability. The vast majority of IBM's laptop and desktop sales were to large enterprises that had IBM mainframe computers and had been long-standing IBM customers. IBM's PC group had higher costs than rivals, making it virtually impossible to match rivals on price and make a profit. IBM distributed its PCs, workstations, and servers through reseller partners, but used its own sales force to market to large enterprises. IBM competed against rival hardware vendors by emphasizing confidence in the IBM brand and the company's longstanding strengths in software applications, IT services and support, and systems integration capabilities. IBM had responded to the direct sales inroads Dell had made in the corporate market by allowing some of its resellers to economize on costs by custom-assembling IBM PCs to buyer specifications.

The Sale of IBM's PC Business to Lenovo in Late 2004   In December 2004, IBM agreed to sell its PC business to Lenovo Group Ltd., the number one computer maker in China, in a $1.75 billion business deal that made Lenovo the world's third biggest PC maker, with a global market share of about 8.7 percent, and that also gave IBM an 18.9 percent ownership interest in Lenovo. The head of IBM's PC operations was slated to become CEO of Lenovo, with Lenovo's current CEO (who did not speak English) assuming the role of chairman. Lenovo announced it would move its corporate headquarters from Beijing to New York City.

The new company was expected to have about $12 billion in annual sales and about 20,000 employees, including about 10,000 IBM employees who would be a part of the new company—about 2,500 of the IBM employees scheduled to become part of Lenovo were in North Carolina, about half were in China, and the rest were scattered around the world. Prior to the deal, Lenovo had annual sales of about $3 billion and IBM's PC business had annual sales close to $9 billion; IBM's PC business lost $258 million in 2003. IBM had about a 6 percent share of the PC market in China. The new company had the rights to use the IBM name on its PCs for a maximum of five years, but Lenovo indicated it would consider co-branding after 18 months. The new company planned to continue to sell its PCs through the efforts of an internal sales force for large accounts and its network of distributors and retail outlets.

Lenovo had little reputation for innovation, and it usually followed the technology lead of Intel and Microsoft, the PC industry's standard setters. It was regarded as a made-in-China-for-China producer of PCs. It had previously tried to enter the PC market outside China without success and was under competitive pressure in its home market, particularly from Dell (which was said to have lower costs). However, the company's original parent, the government's Chinese Academy of Sciences, was still a major shareholder, which gave Lenovo access to loans from state banks.

Some observers believed that one of management's major challenges would be integrating the cultures of the operations. Twice daily at Lenovo's headquarters, the sound system broadcast "Number Six Broadcast Exercises," a set of stretches and knee bends—participation was voluntary but highly encouraged.[27] The company song was played every morning at eight o'clock and sung by workers at the start of widely attended meetings. Lenovo employees who were late to meetings had to stand behind their chairs for one minute (as an attempt to humiliate them into being punctual). Employees' activities were strictly monitored; time spent outside the work area during work hours had to be accounted for, and deductions were made from employees' paychecks if the explanations were unsatisfactory. Most employees were young and had worked at Lenovo since graduating from college; few spoke English and most had never met a foreigner.

Gateway

Gateway, a San Diego–based company (recently relocated from South Dakota), had 2003 revenues of $3.4 billion (down from $4.2 billion in 2002) and a net loss of $515 million (bigger than the loss of $298 million in 2002). It was the fourth largest seller of PCs in the U.S. market and one of the top 10 sellers worldwide. However, as shown in Exhibit 1, its unit sales and market share had been sliding since 2000. Gateway's all-time peak revenues were $9.6 billion in 2000 and its peak-year profits were $428 million.

In 2001–2002, Gateway's top management tried to reverse the company's deteriorating market position; the turnaround initiatives included:

- Closing its retail stores in Canada, Europe, the Middle East, Africa, and the Asia-Pacific region, along with 70 underperforming U.S. retail locations.

- Combining its consumer and business sales organization into a single unit.

- Focusing its sales and marketing efforts on consumers, small and medium-sized businesses, educational institutions, and government.

- Consolidating its manufacturing operations and call center operations to pave the way for a 50 percent cutback in its workforce in 2001. Manufacturing operations in Ireland and Malaysia were closed, and all production was moved to the company's two existing plants in South Dakota and Virginia. Further cutbacks to reduce the workforce from 14,000 to 11,500 employees were announced in early 2002.

■ Supplementing its sell-direct distribution strategy by stocking a limited inventory of prebuilt Gateway PCs in its retail stores that customers could take home immediately.

■ Improving its offering of digital cameras, music, and videos and actively marketing broadband Internet services to its customers via alliances with a number of cable broadband Internet access providers.

■ Introducing a sleek new line of desktop and notebook PCs with industry-leading features.

■ Refreshing its spotted-cow box logo, used since 1998.

■ Selling consumer electronics products made by other manufacturers in its retail stores, including digital cameras, MP3 players, and high-end plasma-screen TVs.

The 2001–2002 initiatives failed to reverse the decline. In 2003, further efforts were made to stem Gateway's slide in the marketplace (which was mainly due to stiff competition from Dell):

■ The entire product line was refreshed and expanded, with 118 Gateway-branded products in 22 categories being introduced.

■ The company concentrated its sales efforts in PCs on the government and education segments.

■ Back-office operations were streamlined to reduce costs.

Then in January 2004, Gateway acquired eMachines, Inc., for 50 million shares of Gateway common stock and $30 million in cash. A $1.1 billion producer of low-end computers, eMachines had distribution capabilities in Japan, Great Britain, and parts of western Europe. The two companies had combined sales of $4.5 billion in 2003. Gateway management believed the eMachines acquisition would allow Gateway to better compete in the low end of the PC market and also give it the resources and competitive strength to reenter markets outside the United States. As part of the deal, the founder and CEO of eMachines, Wayne Inouye, became the CEO of Gateway, with Ted Waitt, Gateway's founder and former CEO, functioning as chairman.

Gateway's revenue decline continued in the first half of 2004. The company had a net loss of $561 million on sales of $2.6 billion during the first nine months of 2004, but management expected that the company to become profitable in the fourth quarter on sales of about $1 billion. Gateway sold 931,000 units in the third quarter of 2004, its highest volume in 14 quarters. Management had forecast sales of $4 billion in 2005 and earnings of $50–$60 million.

Dell's Future Prospects

In a February 2003 article in *Business 2.0,* Michael Dell said, "The best way to describe us now is as a broad computer systems and services company. We have a pretty simple system. The most important thing is to satisfy our customers. The second most important thing is to be profitable. If we don't do the first one well, the second one won't happen."[28] For the most part, Michael Dell was not particularly concerned about the efforts of competitors to copy many aspects of Dell's build-to-order, sell-direct strategy. He explained why on at least two separate occasions:

The competition started copying us seven years ago. That's when we were a $1 billion business . . . And they haven't made much progress to be honest with you. The learning curve for them is difficult. It's like going from baseball to soccer.[29]

I think a lot of people have analyzed our business model, a lot of people have written about it and tried to understand it. This is an 18½-year process . . . It comes from many, many cycles of learning . . . It's very, very different than designing products to be built to stock . . . Our whole company is oriented around a very different way of operating . . . I don't, for any second, believe that they are not trying to catch up. But it is also safe to assume that Dell is not staying in the same place. You know, this past year we've driven a billion dollars of cost out of our supply chain, and certainly next year we plan to drive quite a bit of cost out as well.[30]

On two other occasions, Michael Dell spoke about the size of the company's future opportunities:

When technologies begin to standardize or commoditize, the game starts to change. Markets open up to be volume markets and this is very much where Dell has made its mark—first in the PC market in desktops and notebooks and then in the server market and the storage market and services and data networking. We continue to expand the array of products that we sell, the array of services and, of course, expand on a geographic basis. The way we think about it is that there are all of these various technologies out there . . . What we have been able to do is build a business system that takes those technological ingredients, translates them into products and services and gets them to the customer more efficiently than any company around.[31]

This year [2004], we're roughly a $50 billion business. We have only six percent market share in an $800 billion market. There are enormous opportunities for us to grow across multiple dimensions in terms of products, with servers, storage, printing, and services representing a huge realm of expansion for us. There's geographic expansion and market share expansion back in the core business. The primary focus for us is picking those opportunities, seizing on them, and making sure we have the talent and the leadership growing inside the company to support all that growth. We have the goal of reaching $60 billion and we're tracking about a year ahead of plan. And there's also a network effect here. As we grow our product lines and enter new markets, we see a faster ability to gain share in new markets versus ones we've previously entered. Printing is a great example; it's also a great example of a market where people are either underestimating us or wondering if we'll succeed. In the U.S. market where all-in-one inkjets are the fastest growing part of the market, we already have 20 percent of the market. We just introduced color laser printers. You can pay only $449 for a color networked laser printer that offers industry-leading price performance for both the hardware and printing supplies. That's a huge new opportunity for us that's highly-related to computing. Our first full year in [the printer] business, we hit a billion dollars of revenue—that's pretty good for a startup.[32]

Going into 2005, Dell Computer had a war chest of over $12 billion in cash and liquid investments that it could deploy in its pursuit of attractive revenue growth opportunities.

Endnotes

[1]As quoted in "Dell Puts Happy Customers First," *Nikkei Weekly,* December 16, 2002.

[2]Joan Magretta, "The Power of Virtual Integration: An Interview with Dell Computer's Michael Dell," *Harvard Business Review,* March–April 1998, p. 75.

[3]"Michael Dell: On Managing Growth," *MIS Week,* September 5, 1988, p. 1.

[4]"The Education of Michael Dell," *Business Week,* March 22, 1993, p. 86.

[5]As quoted in Magretta, "The Power of Virtual Integration," p. 74.

[6]Ibid., p. 75.

[7]Speech by Michael Dell at University of Toronto, September 21, 2004; posted at www.dell.com and accessed December 15, 2004.

[8]Ibid., p. 76.

[9]Ibid.

[10]Quoted in Neel Chowdhury, "Dell Cracks China," *Fortune,* June 21, 1999, p. 121.

[11]Magretta, "The Power of Virtual Integration," p. 79.

[12]"Michael Dell Rocks," *Fortune,* May 11, 1998, p. 61.

[13]Quoted in Kathryn Jones, "The Dell Way," *Business 2.0,* February 2003.

[14]Kevin Rollins, "Using Information to Speed Execution," *Harvard Business Review,* March–April 1998, p. 81.

[15]Magretta, "The Power of Virtual Integration," p. 80.

[16]Keynote speech given on August 25, 1999, in Austin, Texas, at Dell's DirectConnect Conference and posted at www.dell.com.

[17]Remarks by Michael Dell, Gartner Fall Symposium, Orlando, Florida, October 9, 2002; posted at www.dell.com.

[18]Remarks by Michael Dell at the University of Toronto, September 21, 2004; posted at www.dell.com.

[19]Quoted in Adam Lashinsky, "Where Dell Is Going Next," *Fortune,* October 18, 2004, p. 116.

[20]Quoted in the *Financial Times* Global News Wire, October 10, 2002.

[21]"The Education of Michael Dell," p. 85.

[22]"Can Compaq Catch Up?" *Business Week,* May 3, 1999, p. 163.

[23]More information on Digital's competitive position can be found in "Compaq-Digital: Let the Slimming Begin," *Business Week,* June 22, 1998.

[24]Ben Elgin, "Carly's Challenge," *Business Week,* December 13, 2004, p. 101.

[25]Ibid.

[26]Ibid., p. 102.

[27]Julie Chao, "Chinese Computer Maker Lenovo Shoots for Leadership in the World," *Atlanta Journal-Constitution,* December 14, 2004, pp. F1, F8.

[28]*Business 2.0,* February 2003; posted at www.business2.com.

[29]Comments made to students at the University of North Carolina and reported in the *Raleigh News & Observer,* November 16, 1999.

[30]Remarks by Michael Dell, Gartner Fall Symposium, Orlando, Florida, October 9, 2002; posted at www.dell.com.

[31]Remarks by Michael Dell, MIT Sloan School of Management, September 26, 2002, and posted at www.dell.com.

[32]Remarks by Michael Dell, University of Toronto, September 21, 2004, and posted at www.dell.com.

easyCar.com

John J. Lawrence
University of Idaho

Luis Solis
Instituto de Empresa

In 2003 easyCar.com had become the fastest-growing rental car company in Europe by offering a minimal selection of cars that could be booked at low daily rates via the company's Web site. Its mission was "to offer you outstanding value for money. To us value for money means a reliable service at a low price. We achieve this by simplifying the product we offer, and passing on the benefits to you in the form of lower prices."[1]

EasyCar was a member of the easyGroup family of companies, founded by the flamboyant Greek entrepreneur Stelios Haji-Ioannou, who was known simply as Stelios to most. Stelios founded low-cost air carrier easyJet.com in 1995 after convincing his father, a Greek shipping billionaire, to loan him the £5 million to start the business.[2] (Note: In January 2003, £1 = €1.52 = U.S.$1.61.) EasyJet was one of the early low-cost, no-frills air carriers in the European market and was built on a foundation of simple point-to-point flights, Internet-only flight reservations, and the aggressive use of yield management policies. The company proved highly successful, and as a result Stelios expanded the easyJet business model to industries with characteristics similar to the airline industry. One such business was easyCar, which was founded in 2000 with a £10 million initial investment.

EasyCar's business model was quite different than that of traditional rental car companies. EasyCar rented only a single vehicle type at each location it operated, while most of its competitors rented a wide variety of vehicle types. EasyCar did not work with agents—over 95 percent of its bookings were made through the company's Web site, with the remainder of bookings being made directly through the company's phone reservation system (at a cost to the customer of €0.95/minute for the call). Most rental car companies worked with a variety of intermediaries, with their own Web sites accounting for less than 10 percent of their total booking.[3] And like easyJet, easyCar managed rental rates in an attempt to have its fleet rented out 100 percent of the time and to generate the maximum revenue from its rentals. EasyCar's information system constantly evaluated projected demand and expected utilization at each site, and adjusted price accordingly. Because of its aggressive pricing, easyCar was able to achieve a fleet utilization rate in excess of 90 percent[4]—much higher than other major rental car companies. Industry leader Avis Europe, for example, had a fleet utilization rate of 68 percent.[5]

EasyCar's business model was showing signs of success by fiscal year-end 2002, when it broke even on revenues of £27 million[6] after losing £7.5 million on revenues of £18.5 million in 2001.[7] Pleased with the company's early performance, Stelios announced the company would open an average of two new sites a week through 2003 and 2004 to reach a total of 180 sites by the end of 2004.[8] Stelios expected new locations would allow easyCar to quadruple revenues to £100 million in revenue and earn profits of £10 million by year-end 2004 in preparation for a planned initial public offering (IPO) that same year. The company's management and financial advisers projected the IPO might yield as much as £250 million to fund future growth in the European rental car market.[9]

The Rental Car Industry in Western Europe

The western European rental car industry consisted of many different national markets that were only semi-integrated. While there were many companies that competed within this industry, a handful of companies held dominant positions, either across a number of national markets or within one or a few national markets. Industry experts saw the sector as ripe for consolidation.[10] Several international companies—notably Avis, Europcar, and Hertz—had strong positions across most major European markets. Within most countries, there was also a primarily national or regional company that had a strong position in its home market and perhaps moderate market share in neighboring markets. Sixt was the market leader in Germany, for example, while Atesa (in partnership with National) was the market leader in Spain. Generally these major players accounted for more than half of the market. In Germany, for example, Sixt, Europcar, Avis, and Hertz had a combined 60 percent of the €2.5 billion German rental car market.[11] In Spain, the top five firms accounted for 60 percent of the €920 million Spanish rental car market. Generally, these top firms targeted both business and vacation travelers and offered a wide range of vehicles for rent. Exhibit 1 provides basic information on these market-leading companies.

Exhibit 1   INFORMATION ON EASYCAR'S MAJOR EUROPEAN COMPETITORS, 2002

	easyCar	Avis Europe	Europcar	Hertz	Sixt
Number of rental outlets	46	3,100	2,650	7,000	1,250
2002 fleet size	7,000	120,000	220,000	700,000	46,700
Number of countries	5	107	118	150	50
Largest market	United Kingdom	France	France	United States	Germany
Who owns company	EasyGroup/ Stelios Haji-loannou	D'Ieteren (Belgium) is majority shareholder	Volkswagen AG	Ford Motor Company	Publicly traded
European revenues	€41 million	€1.25 billion	€1.12 billion	€910 million	€600 million
Company Web site	www.easycar .com	www.avis-europe.com	www.europcar .com	www.hertz.com	ag.sixt.com

Source: Information in this table came from each company's Web site and online annual reports. European revenues are for vehicle rental in Europe and are estimated on the basis of market share estimates for 2001 from Avis Europe's Web site.

In addition to these major companies in each market, there were many smaller rental companies operating in each market. In Germany, for example, there were over 700 smaller companies,[12] while in Spain there were more than 1,600 smaller companies. Many of these smaller companies operated at only one or a few locations and were particularly prevalent in tourist locations. Also operating in the sector were a number of brokers, like Holiday Autos. Brokerage companies did not own their own fleet of cars but instead managed the excess inventory of other companies and matched customers with rental companies with excess fleet capacity.

Overall, the rental car market could be thought of as composed of two broad segments, a business segment and a tourist/leisure segment. Depending on the market, the leisure segment represented somewhere between 45 and 65 percent of the overall market, and a large part of this segment was very price-conscious. The business segment made up the remaining 35 to 55 percent of the market. It was less price-sensitive than the tourist segment and more concerned about service quality, convenience, and flexibility.

The Growth of easyCar

EasyCar opened its first location in London, in April 2000, under the name easyRentacar. In the same week, easyCar opened locations in Glasgow and Barcelona. All three locations were popular easyJet destinations. Vehicles initially could be rented for as low as €15 a day plus a one-time car preparation fee of €8. Each of these locations had a fleet consisting entirely of Mercedes A-class vehicles, which was the smallest car manufactured by the German automaker. It was the only vehicle that easyCar rented at the time. Exhibit 2 presents images of easyCar's Spanish home page, an A-class model, and its Mercedes MPV rental fleet.

EasyCar had signed a deal with Mercedes, amid much fanfare, at the Geneva Motor Show earlier in the year to purchase a total of 5,000 A-class vehicles. The vehicles, which came with guaranteed buy-back terms, cost easyCar's parent company a little over £6 million.[13] Many in the car rental industry were surprised by the choice, expecting easyCar to rely on less expensive compact models.[14] In describing the acquisition of the 5,000 Mercedes vehicles, Stelios had said:

> The choice of Mercedes reflects the easyGroup brand. EasyRentacar will use brand new Mercedes cars in the same way that easyJet uses brand new Boeing aircraft. We do not compromise on the hardware, we just use innovation to substantially reduce costs. The car hire industry is where the airline industry was five years ago, a cartel feeding off the corporate client. EasyRentacar will provide a choice for consumers who pay out of their own pockets and who will not be ripped off for traveling mid-week.[15]

EasyCar quickly expanded to other locations, focusing first on those locations popular with easyJet customers, including Amsterdam, Geneva, Nice, and Malagra. By July 2001, a little over a year after its initial launch, easyCar had fleets of Mercedes A-class vehicles in 14 locations in the United Kingdom, Spain, France, and the Netherlands. At this point, EasyCar secured £27 million from a consortium of Bank of Scotland Corporate Banking and NBGI Private Equity to further expand its operations. The package consisted of a combination of equity and loan stock.

While easyCar added a few sites in the second half of 2001 and early 2002, volatile demand in the wake of the September 11, 2001, terrorist attacks forced easyCar to roll out new rental locations somewhat slower than originally expected.[16] Growth acceler-

Exhibit 2   Images of easyCar's Spanish Home Page, A-Class Mercedes Rental Car, and Its Mercedes MPV Rental Fleet

Source: easyCar.com's Web site, accessed October and November 2004.

ated, however, in the spring of 2002. Between May 2002 and January 2003, EasyCar opened 30 new locations, going from 18 to 48 sites. This acceleration in growth also coincided with a change in easyCar's policy regarding the makeup of its fleet. By May 2002, easyCar's fleet consisted of 6,000 Mercedes A-class vehicles across 18 sites. Beginning in May, however, easyCar began to stock its fleet with other types of vehicles. It still maintained its policy of offering only a single type of vehicle at each location, but now the vehicle the customer received depended on the location. The first new vehicle easyCar introduced was the Vauxhall Corsa. According to Stelios,

Vauxhall Corsas cost easyCar £2 a day less than Mercedes A-Class so we can pass this saving on to customers. Customers themselves will decide if they want to pay a premium for a Mercedes. EasyGroup companies benefit from economies of scale where relevant but we also want to create contestable markets among our suppliers so that we can keep the cost to our customers as low as possible.[17]

By January 2003, EasyCar was also using Ford Focuses (4 locations), Renault Clios (3 locations), Toyota Yarises (3 locations), and Smart cars (2 locations) in addition to the Vauxhall Corsas (7 locations) and the Mercedes A-Class vehicles (28 locations). Plans called for a further expansion of the fleet, from the 7,000 vehicles that easyCar had in January to 24,000 vehicles across 180 rental sites by the end of 2004.[18]

In addition to making vehicles available at more locations, easyCar had also changed its policies for 2003 to allow rentals for as little as one hour, and with as little as one hour's notice of rental. By making this change, Stelios felt that easyCar could be a serious competitor to local taxis, buses, trains, and even car ownership. EasyCar expected that if it made car rental simple enough and cheap enough, that some people living in traffic-congested European cities who only used their car occasionally would give up the costs and hassles of car ownership and simply hire an easyCar when they needed a vehicle. Tapping into this broader transportation market would help the company reach its ambitious future sales goals.

Facilities

In January 2003 easyCar had facilities in a total of 17 cities in five European countries, as shown in Exhibit 3. It primarily located its facilities near bus and train stations in the major European cities, seeking out sites that offered lower lease costs. It generally avoided prime airport locations, as the cost for space at, and in some cases near, airports was significantly higher than most other locations. When easyCar did locate near an airport, it generally chose sites off the airport, in order to reduce the cost of the lease. Airport locations also tended to require longer hours to satisfy customers arriving on late flights or departing on very early flights. EasyCar kept its airport locations open 24 hours a day, whereas its other locations were generally only open from 7:00 AM to 11:00 PM.

The physical facilities at all locations were kept to a minimum. In many locations, easyCar leased space in an existing parking garage. Employees worked out of a small, self-contained cubicle within the garage. The cubicle, depending on the location, might be no more than 15 square meters and included little more than a small counter and a couple of computers at which staff processed customers as they came to pick up or return their vehicles. EasyCar also leased a number of spaces within the garage for its fleet of cars. However, because easyCar's vehicles were rented 90 percent of the time, only 15 to 20 spaces were required at an average site, which had a fleet of about 150 cars.[19] To speed up the opening of new sites, easyCar had equipped a number of vans with all the needed computer and telephone equipment to run a site.[20] From an operational perspective, it could open a new location by simply leasing 20 or so spaces in a parking garage, hiring a small staff, driving a van to the location, and adding the location to the company's Web site. Depending on the fleet size at a location, easyCar typically had only one or two people working at a site at a time.

Exhibit 3   EASYCAR LOCATIONS IN JANUARY 2003

Country	City	Number	Number Near an Airport
France	Nice	1	1
France	Paris	8	0
Netherlands	Amsterdam	3	1
Spain	Barcelona	2	0
Spain	Madrid	2	0
Spain	Majorca	1	1
Spain	Malagra	1	1
Switzerland	Geneva	1	1
United Kingdom	Birmingham	2	0
United Kingdom	Bromley	1	0
United Kingdom	Croydon	1	1
United Kingdom	Glasgow	2	1
United Kingdom	Kingston-upon-Thames	1	0
United Kingdom	Liverpool	2	1
United Kingdom	London	15	0
United Kingdom	Manchester	2	1
United Kingdom	Waterford	1	0
Total	5 Countries, 17 Cities	46	9

Source: www.easyCar.com, January 2003.

Vehicle Pickup and Return Processes

Customers arrived to a site to pick up a vehicle within a prearranged one-hour period. They selected this time slot when they booked the vehicles. EasyCar adjusted the first day's rental price according to the pickup time. Customers who picked their cars up earlier in the day or at popular times were charged more than were customers picking up their cars later in the day or at less busy times. Customers were required to bring a printed copy of their contract, along with the credit card they used to make the booking and identification. Given the low staffing levels, customers occasionally had to wait 30 minutes or more to be processed and receive their vehicles, particularly at peak times of the day. Processing a customer began with the employee accessing the customer's contract online. If the customer was new to the site, the basic policies and possible additional charges were briefly explained. The employee then made copies of the customer's identification and credit card and took a digital photo of the customer. The customer put down an €80 refundable deposit, signed the contract, and drove the car away.

All vehicles were rented with more or less empty fuel tanks, with the exact level dependent on how much gasoline was left in the vehicle when the previous renter returned it. Customers were provided with a small map of the immediate area around the rental site, showing the locations and hours of nearby gas stations. Customers could return vehicles with any amount of gas in them as long as the low-fuel indicator light in the vehicle was not on. Customers who returned vehicles with the low-fuel indicator light on were charged a fueling fee of €16.

Customers were also expected to return the vehicle within a prearranged one-hour period, which they also selected at the time of booking. While customers did not have to worry about refueling the car before returning it, they were expected to thoroughly clean the car. This clean car policy was implemented in May 2002 as a way to further reduce the price customers could pay for their vehicle. Prior to this change, all customers paid a fixed preparation fee of €11 each time they rented a vehicle (up from the €8 preparation fee when the company started operations in 2000). The new policy reduced this up-front preparation fee to €4 but required customers to either return the vehicle clean or pay an additional cleaning fee of €16. In order to avoid any misunderstanding, easyCar provided customers with an explicit description of what constituted a clean car, both for the interior and the exterior. It had to be apparent, for example, that the exterior of the car had been washed. The maps showing nearby gas stations also showed nearby car washes. While easyCar had received some bad press in relation to the policy,[21] 85 percent of customers returned their vehicles clean as a result of it.

When a customer returned the vehicle, an easyCar employee would check to make sure that the vehicle was clean and undamaged and that the low-fuel indicator light was not on. The employee would also check the kilometers driven. The customer would then be notified of any additional charges. These charges would be subtracted from the €80 deposit and the difference refunded to the customer's credit card (or, if additional charges exceeded the €80 deposit, the customer's credit card would be charged the difference).

Pricing

EasyCar's low pricing was a major point of distinction from rival car rental companies. EasyCar advertised prices as low as €5 a day plus a per rental preparation fee of €4. Prices, however, varied by the location and dates of the rental, by when the booking was made, and by what time the car was to be picked up and returned. EasyCar's systems constantly evaluated projected demand and expected use at each site, and adjusted price accordingly. Achieving the €5 a day rate usually required customers to book well in advance, and these rates were typically available only on weekdays. Weekend rates, when booked well in advance, typically started a few euros higher than the weekday rates. As a given rental date approached, however, the price typically went up significantly as easyCar approached 100 percent fleet use for that day. Rates could triple overnight if there was sufficient booking activity. Generally, however, easyCar's price was less than half that of its major competitors. EasyCar, unlike most other rental car companies, required customers to pay in full at the time of booking, and once a booking was made, it was nonrefundable.

EasyCar's base price covered only the core rental of the vehicle—the total price customers paid was in many cases much higher and depended on how the customer reserved, paid for, used, and returned the vehicle. EasyCar's price was based on customers booking through the company's Web site and paying for their rental with their easyMoney credit card. EasyMoney was the easyGroup's credit and financial services company. Customers who chose to book through the company's phone reservation system were charged an additional €0.95 a minute for the call, and those who used other credit cards were charged €5 extra. All vehicles had to be paid for by a credit or debit card—cash was not accepted. The base rental price allowed customers to drive vehicles 100 kilometers per day—additional kilometers were charged at a rate of €0.12 per kilometer. In addition, customers were expected to return their cars clean and on time.

Customers who returned cars that did not meet easyCar's standards for clean were charged a €16 cleaning fee. Those who returned their cars late were immediately charged €120 and subsequently charged an additional €120 for each subsequent 24-hour period in which the car was not returned. EasyCar explained the high late fee as representing the cost that the company would likely incur in providing another vehicle to the next customer. Customers wishing to make any changes to their bookings were also charged a change fee of €16. Changes could be made either before the rental started or during the rental period, but were limited to changing the dates, times, and location of the rental, and were subject to the prices and vehicle availability at the time the change was made. If the change resulted in an overall lower price for the rental, however, no refund was provided for the difference.

Beginning in 2003, for an additional charge of €4 a day, all customers were also required to purchase loss/damage insurance that eliminated the customer's liability for loss or damage to the vehicle (excluding damage to the tires or windshield of the vehicle). Through 2002, customers were able to choose whether or not to purchase additional insurance from easyCar to eliminate any financial liability in the event that the rental vehicle was damaged. The cost of this optional insurance had been €6 a day, and approximately 60 percent of easyCar's customers had purchased it. Those not purchasing this insurance either had assumed the liability for the first €800 in damages personally or had had their own insurance through some other means (e.g., some credit card companies provide this insurance to their cardholders at no additional charge for short-term rentals paid for with the credit card).

EasyCar's Web site attempted to make all of these additional charges clear to customers at the time of the booking. EasyCar had received a fair amount of bad press when it first opened for business after many renters complained about having to pay undisclosed charges when they returned their cars.[22] In response, easyCar had revamped its Web site in an effort to make these charges more transparent to customers and to explain the logic behind many of them.

Promotion

EasyCar's promotional efforts through 2002 had focused primarily on posters and press advertising. Posters were particularly prevalent in metro systems and bus and train stations in cities where easyCar had operations. All of this advertising focused on easyCar's low price. According to founder Stelios:

> You will never see an advert for an easy company offering an experience—it's about price. If you create expectations you can't live up to, then you will ultimately suffer as a result.[23]

The company allocated £1.43 million to advertising in 2002.[24]

EasyCar also promoted itself by displaying its name, phone number, and Web address prominently on the doors and rear window of its entire fleet of vehicles, and took advantage of free publicity when the opportunity presented itself. An example of seeking out such publicity occurred when Hertz complained that easyCar's comparative advertising campaign in the Netherlands that featured the line "The best reason to use easyCar.com can be found at hertz.nl" violated Dutch law that required comparative advertising to be exact, not general. In response, Stelios and a group of easyCar employees, dressed in orange boiler suits and with a fleet of easyCar vehicles, protested outside the Hertz Amsterdam office with signs asking "What is Hertz frightened of?"[25]

In an effort to help reach its goal of quadrupling sales in the next two years, easy-Car had recently hired Jennifer Mowat into the new position of commercial director to take over responsibility for easyCar's European marketing. Mowat had previously been eBay's UK country manager and had recently completed an MBA in Switzerland. Previously, Stelios and easyCar's managing director, Andrew Fitzmaurice, had handled the marketing function themselves.[26] As part of this stepped-up marketing effort, easy-Car also planned to double its advertising budget for 2003, to £3 million, and to begin to advertise on television. The television advertising campaign was to feature easy-Car's founder, Stelios.[27]

Legal Challenges

EasyCar faced several challenges to its approaches. The most significant dealt with a November 2002 ruling made by the Office of Fair Trading (OFT) that easyCar had to grant customers seven days from the time they made a booking to cancel their booking and receive a full refund. The OFT was a UK governmental agency responsible for protecting UK consumers from unfair and/or anticompetitive business practices. The ruling against easyCar was based on the 2000 Consumer Protection Distance Selling Regulations. These regulations stipulated that companies that sell at a distance (e.g., by Internet or phone) must provide customers with a seven-day cooling-off period, during which time customers can cancel their contracts with the company and receive a full refund. The law exempted accommodation, transportation, catering, and leisure service companies from this requirement. The OFT's ruling concluded that easyCar did not qualify as a transportation service company because the consumer had to drive them-selves, and therefore they were not receiving a transport service, just a car.[28]

EasyCar had appealed the OFT's decision to the UK High Court on the grounds that it was indeed a transportation service company and was entitled to an exemption from this requirement. EasyCar was hopeful that it would eventually win this legal challenge. EasyCar had argued that this ruling would destroy the company's book-early-pay-less philosophy and could lead to a tripling of prices.[29] Chairman Stelios was quoted as saying:

> It is very serious. My fear is that as soon as we put in the seven-day cooling off periods our utilization rate will fall from 90% to 65%. That's the difference be-tween a profitable company and an unprofitable one.[30]

EasyCar was also concerned that prolonged legal action on this point could interfere with its plans for a 2004 IPO.

The OFT, for its part, had also applied to the UK High Court for an injunction to make the company comply with the ruling. Other rental car companies were generally unconcerned about the ruling, because few offered big discounts for early bookings or nonrefundable bookings.[31]

EasyCar's new policy of posting the pictures of customers whose cars were 15 days or more overdue was also drawing legal criticism. EasyCar had recently received public warnings from lawyers that this new policy might violate data protection, libel, privacy, confidentiality, and human rights laws.[32] Of particular concern to some lawyers was the possibility that easyCar might post the wrong person's picture, given the large number of customers the company dealt with.[33] Such a mistake could open the company to costly libel suits. The policy of posting the pictures of overdue cus-tomers on the easyCar Web site, initiated in November 2002, was designed to reduce the losses associated with customers renting a vehicle and never returning it. The costs were significant, according to Stelios:

> These cars are expensive, £15,000 each, and we have 6,000 of them. At any given time we are looking for as many as several tens which are overdue. If we don't get one back, it's a write-off. We are writing off an entire car, and it's uninsurable.[34]

Stelios was also convinced of the legality of the new policy. In a letter to the editor responding to the legal concerns raised in the press, Stelios said:

> From a legal perspective, we have been entirely factual and objective and are merely reporting the details of the overdue car and the person who collected it. In addition, our policy is made very clear in our terms and conditions and the photo is taken both overtly and with the consent of the customer . . . I estimate the total cost of overdue cars to be 5 percent of total easyCar costs, or 50p on every car rental day for all customers. In 2004, when I intend to float easyCar, this cost will amount to £5 million unless we can reduce our quantity of overdue cars.[35]

In the past, easyCar had simply provided pictures to police when a rental was 15 or more days overdue. It was hoped that posting the picture would both discourage drivers from not returning vehicles and shame those drivers who currently had overdue cars into returning them. In fact, the first person whose photo was posted on the easyCar Web site did indeed return his car two days later. The vehicle was 29 days late.[36]

The Future

At the end of 2002, Stelios had stepped down as the CEO of easyJet so that he could devote more of his time to the other easyGroup companies, including easyCar. He had three priorities for the new year. One was to turn around the money-losing easyInternetCafe business, which Stelios had described as "the worst mistake of my career."[37] The 22-store chain had lost £80 million in the last two years. Stelios's second priority was to oversee the planned launch of another new easyGroup business, easyCinema, in the spring of 2003. And the third was to oversee the rapid expansion of the easyCar chain so that it would be ready for an initial public offering by year-end 2004.

Endnotes

[1]www.easyCar.com

[2]"The Big Picture—an Interview with Stelios," *Sunday Herald* (UK), March 16, 2003.

[3]"Click to Fly," *The Economist*, May 13, 2004.

[4]E. Simpkins, "Stelios Isn't Taking It Easy," *Sunday Telegraph* (UK), December 15, 2002.

[5]Avis Europe plc 2002 annual report, p. 10, http://ir.avis-europe.com/avis/reports, accessed August 16, 2004.

[6]"Marketing: Former eBay UK Chief Lands Top easyCar Position," *Financial Times* Information Limited, January 9, 2003.

[7]T. Burt, "EasyCar Agrees Deal with Vauxhall," *Financial Times*, April 30, 2002, p. 24.

[8]Simpkins, "Stelios Isn't Taking It Easy."

[9]N. Hodgson, "Stelios Plans easyCar Float," *Liverpool Echo*, September 24, 2002.

[10]"Marketing Week: Don't Write Off the Car Rental Industry," *Financial Times* Information Limited, September 26, 2002.

[11]"EasyCar Set to Shake Up German Car Rental Market," European Intelligence Wire, February 22, 2002.

[12]Ibid.

[13]Hodgson, "Stelios Plans easyCar Float."

[14]A. Felsted, "EasyCar Courts Clio for Rental Fleet," *Financial Times*, February 11, 2002, p. 26.

[15]EasyCar.com news release, March 1, 2000, www.easyCar.com.

[16]T. Burt, "EasyCar Agrees Deal with Vauxhall."

[17]EasyCar.com news release, May 2, 2002, www.easyCar.com.

[18]"Marketing Week: EasyCar Appoints Head of European Marketing," *Financial Times* Information Limited, January 9, 2003.

[19]Simpkins, "Stelios Isn't Taking It Easy."

[20]Ibid.

[21]J. Hyde, "Travel View: Clearing Up on the Extras," *The Observer* (UK), July 7, 2002.

[22]J. Stanton, "The Empire That's Easy Money," *Edinburgh Evening News*, November 26, 2002.

[23]"The Big Picture."

[24]"EasyCar Appoints Head of European Marketing."

[25]EasyCar.com news release, April 22, 2002, www.easyCar.com.

[26]"EasyCar Appoints Head of European Marketing."

[27]"Campaigning: EasyGroup Appoints Publicist for easyCar TV Advertising Brief," *Financial Times* Information Limited, January 31, 2003.

[28]J. Macintosh, "EasyCar Sues OFT amid Threat to Planned Flotation," *Financial Times,* November 22, 2002, p. 4.

[29]"EasyCar Appoints Head of European Marketing."

[30]Mackintosh, "EasyCar Sues OFT amid Threat.

[31]Ibid.

[32]B. Sherwood & A. Wendlandt, "EasyCar May Be in Difficulty over Naming Ploy," *Financial Times*, November 14, 2002, p. 2.

[33]Ibid.

[34]"E-Business: Internet Fraudsters Fail to Steal Potter Movie's Magic & Other News," *Financial Times* Information Limited, November 19, 2002.

[35]S. Haji-Ioannou, "Letters to the Editor: Costly Effect of Late Car Return," *Financial Times,* November 16, 2002, p. 10.

[36]M. Hookham, "How Stelios Nets Return of His Cars," *Daily Post* (Liverpool, UK), November 14, 2002.

[37]S. Bentley, "The Worst Mistake of My Career, by Stelios" *Financial Times*, December 24, 2002.

KFC and the Global Fast-Food Industry in 2003–2004

Jeffrey A. Krug
Appalachian State University

KFC Corporation was the world's largest chicken restaurant chain and third largest fast-food chain in 2004. It held more than 51 percent of the U.S. market in terms of sales and operated more than 12,200 restaurants in 99 countries. KFC was one of the first fast-food chains to go international in the late 1950s and is one of the world's most recognizable brands. KFC's early international strategy was to grow its company and franchise restaurant base throughout the world. By early 2004, however, KFC had refocused its international strategy on several high growth markets that included China, Canada, the United Kingdom, Australia, South Africa, Malaysia, Thailand, Mexico, Korea, and Indonesia. KFC planned to base much of its growth in these markets on company-owned restaurants, which gave KFC greater control over product quality, service, and restaurant cleanliness. In other international markets, KFC planned to grow primarily through franchises, which were operated by local business-people who understood the local market better than KFC. Franchises enabled KFC to more rapidly expand into smaller countries that could support only a small number of restaurants. KFC planned to more aggressively expand its company-owned restaurants into other major international markets in Europe and Latin America in the future. Latin America was an appealing area for investment because of the size of its markets and geographical proximity to the United States. Mexico was of particular interest because of the North American Free Trade Agreement (NAFTA), a free-trade zone between Canada, the United States, and Mexico that went into effect in 1994. McDonald's, Burger King, and Wendy's, however, were rapidly expanding into other countries in Latin America, most notably Argentina, Chile, Brazil, and Venezuela. KFC's task in Latin America was to develop an effective strategy for further penetrating the Latin American market.

Company History

Fast-food franchising was still in its infancy in 1952 when Harland Sanders began his travels across the United States to speak with prospective franchisees about his "Colonel Sanders Recipe Kentucky Fried Chicken." By 1960, "Colonel" Sanders had granted KFC franchises to more than 200 take-home retail outlets and restaurants across the United States. He had also established a number of franchises in Canada. By 1963, the number of KFC franchises had risen to more than 300 and revenues topped $500 million. The Colonel celebrated his 74th birthday the following year and was eager to lessen the load of running the day-to-day operations of his business. He sold his business to two Louisville businessmen—Jack Massey and John Young Brown Jr.—for $2 million. The Colonel stayed on as a public relations man and goodwill ambassador for the company. During the next five years, Massey and Brown concentrated on growing KFC's franchise system across the United States. In 1966, they took KFC public and the company was listed on the New York Stock Exchange. By the late 1960s, a strong foothold had been established in the United States. Massey and Brown then turned their attention to international markets. In 1969, a joint venture was signed with Mitsuoishi Shoji Kaisha, Ltd., in Japan and the rights to operate franchises in England were acquired. Subsidiaries were later established in Hong Kong, South Africa, Australia, New Zealand, and Mexico. By 1971, KFC had established 2,450 franchises and 600 company-owned restaurants in 48 countries.

Heublein, Inc.

In 1971, KFC entered into negotiations with Heublein, Inc., to discuss a possible merger. The decision to pursue a merger was partially driven by Brown's desire to pursue other interests, which included a political career (Brown was elected governor of Kentucky in 1977). Several months later, Heublein acquired KFC. Heublein was in the business of producing vodka, mixed cocktails, dry gin, cordials, beer, and other alcoholic beverages. It had little experience, however, in the restaurant business. Conflicts quickly erupted between Colonel Sanders and Heublein management. In particular, Colonel Sanders was distraught over poor quality control and restaurant cleanliness. By 1977, new restaurant openings had slowed to only 20 a year. Few restaurants were being remodeled and service quality had declined. To combat these problems, Heublein sent in a new management team to redirect KFC's strategy. A "back-to-the-basics" strategy was implemented and new restaurant construction was halted until existing restaurants could be upgraded and operating problems eliminated. A program for remodeling existing restaurants was implemented, an emphasis was placed on cleanliness and service, marginal products were eliminated, and product consistency was reestablished. This strategy enabled KFC to gain better control of its operations, and it was soon again aggressively building new restaurants.

R. J. Reynolds Industries, Inc.

In 1982, R. J. Reynolds Industries, Inc. (RJR), acquired Heublein and merged it into a wholly owned subsidiary. The acquisition of Heublein was part of RJR's corporate strategy of diversifying into unrelated businesses such as energy, transportation, food, and restaurants to reduce its dependence on the tobacco industry. Tobacco had driven RJR's sales since its founding in North Carolina in 1875. Sales of cigarettes and tobacco products, however, while profitable, were declining as consumption continued to fall in the United States. Reduced consumption was largely the result of increased awareness among Americans of the negative health consequences of smoking.

RJR, however, had little more experience in the restaurant business than did Heublein when it acquired KFC 11 years earlier. In contrast to Heublein, which tried to actively manage KFC using its own managers, RJR allowed KFC to operate autonomously. RJR believed that KFC's executives were better qualified to operate the business than its own managers; therefore, KFC's top management team was left largely intact. In doing so, RJR avoided many of the operating problems that plagued Heublein during its ownership of KFC. In 1985, RJR acquired Nabisco Corporation for $4.9 billion. The acquisition of Nabisco was an attempt to redefine RJR as a world leader in the consumer foods industry. Nabisco sold a variety of well-known food products such as Oreo cookies, Ritz crackers, Planters peanuts, Life Savers candies, and Milk-Bone dog biscuits. RJR subsequently divested many of its nonconsumer food businesses. It sold KFC to PepsiCo, Inc., one year later.

PepsiCo, Inc.

PepsiCo, Inc., was formed in 1965 with the merger of the Pepsi-Cola Co. and Frito-Lay Inc. The merger created one of the largest consumer products companies in the United States. Pepsi-Cola's traditional business was the sale of soft-drink concentrates to licensed independent and company-owned bottlers that manufactured, sold, and distributed Pepsi-Cola soft drinks. Pepsi-Cola's best known trademarks were Pepsi-Cola, Diet Pepsi, and Mountain Dew. Frito-Lay manufactured and sold a variety of leading snack foods such as Lay's potato chips, Doritos tortilla chips, Tostitos tortilla chips, and Ruffles potato chips.

PepsiCo believed the quick-service restaurant business complemented its consumer product orientation. The marketing of fast food relied on many of the same competencies, capabilities, and marketing approaches as soft drinks and snack foods. Pepsi-Cola and Lay's potato chips, for example, could be marketed in the same television and radio segments, which provided higher returns for each advertising dollar. Restaurant chains also provided an additional outlet for the sale of Pepsi soft drinks. PepsiCo believed it could take advantage of numerous synergies by operating the three businesses under the same corporate umbrella. PepsiCo also believed that its management skills could be transferred among the three businesses. This practice was compatible with PepsiCo's policy of frequently moving managers among its business units as a means of developing future executives. PepsiCo's acquisition of KFC in 1986 followed earlier acquisitions of Pizza Hut and Taco Bell. The three restaurant chains were the market leaders in the chicken, pizza, and Mexican categories.

Following the acquisition of KFC, PepsiCo initiated sweeping changes. It announced that the franchise contract would be changed to give PepsiCo greater control over KFC franchisees and to make it easier to close poorly performing restaurants. Staff at KFC was reduced to cut costs and many KFC managers were replaced with PepsiCo managers. Soon after the acquisition, KFC's new personnel manager, who had just relocated from PepsiCo's New York headquarters, was overheard in the KFC cafeteria saying, "There will be no more home grown tomatoes in this organization." Rumors spread quickly among KFC employees about their opportunities for advancement within KFC and PepsiCo. Harsh comments by PepsiCo managers about KFC, its people, and its traditions, several restructurings that led to layoffs throughout KFC, the replacement of KFC managers with PepsiCo managers, and conflicts between KFC and PepsiCo's corporate cultures created a morale problem within KFC. KFC's culture was built largely on Colonel Sanders's laid-back approach to management. Employees enjoyed good job security and stability. A strong loyalty had been created over the years as a result of the Colonel's efforts to provide for his employees' benefits, pension, and other non-income needs. In addition, the southern environment in Louisville resulted in a friendly, relaxed atmosphere at KFC's corporate offices.

PepsiCo's culture, in contrast, was characterized by a strong emphasis on performance. Top performers expected to move up through the ranks quickly. PepsiCo used its KFC, Pizza Hut, Taco Bell, Frito Lay, and Pepsi-Cola divisions as training grounds for its executives, rotating its best managers through the five divisions on average every two years. This practice created pressure on managers to demonstrate their management skills within short periods to maximize their potential for promotion. This practice reinforced feelings among KFC managers that they had few opportunities for advancement within the new company. One PepsiCo manager commented, "You may have performed well last year, but if you don't perform well this year, you're gone, and there are 100 ambitious guys with Ivy League MBAs at PepsiCo's headquarters in New York who would love to have your job." An unwanted effect of this performance-driven culture was that employee loyalty was lost and turnover was higher than in other companies.

Kyle Craig, president of KFC's U.S. operations, commented on PepsiCo's relationship with KFC:

> The KFC culture is an interesting one because it was dominated by a lot of KFC folks, many who have been around since the days of the Colonel. Many of those people were very intimidated by the PepsiCo culture, which is a very high performance, high accountability, highly driven culture. People were concerned about whether they would succeed in the new culture. Like many companies, we have had a couple of downsizings which further made people nervous. Today, there are fewer old KFC people around and I think to some degree people have seen that the PepsiCo culture can drive some pretty positive results. I also think the PepsiCo people who have worked with KFC have modified their cultural values somewhat and they can see that there were a lot of benefits in the old KFC culture.
>
> PepsiCo pushes their companies to perform strongly, but whenever there is a slip in performance, it increases the culture gap between PepsiCo and KFC. I have been involved in two downsizings over which I have been the chief architect. They have been probably the two most gut-wrenching experiences of my career. Because you know you're dealing with peoples' lives and their families, these changes can be emotional if you care about the people in your organization. However, I do fundamentally believe that your first obligation is to the entire organization.

A second problem for PepsiCo was its poor relationship with KFC franchisees. A month after becoming president and chief executive officer in 1989, John Cranor addressed KFC's franchisees in Louisville to explain the details of the new franchise contract. This was the first contract change in 13 years. It gave PepsiCo greater power to take over weak franchises, relocate restaurants, and make changes in existing restaurants. In addition, restaurants would no longer be protected from competition from new KFC units and PepsiCo would have the right to raise royalty fees on existing restaurants as contracts came up for renewal. After Cranor finished his address, there was an uproar among the attending franchisees, who jumped to their feet to protest the changes. KFC's franchise association later sued PepsiCo over the new contract. The contract remained unresolved until 1996, when the most objectionable parts of the contract were removed by KFC's new president and CEO, David Novak. A new contract was ratified by KFC's franchisees in 1997.

PepsiCo's Divestiture of KFC, Pizza Hut, and Taco Bell

PepsiCo's strategy of diversifying into three distinct but related markets—soft drinks, snack foods, and fast-food restaurants—created one of the world's largest food companies and a portfolio of some of the world's most recognizable brands. Between 1990 and 1996, PepsiCo's sales grew at an annual rate of more than 10 percent, surpassing $31 billion in 1996. PepsiCo's growth, however, masked troubles in its fast-food businesses. Operating margins (profit after tax as a percent of sales) at Pepsi-Cola and Frito Lay averaged 12 and 17 percent, respectively. During the same period, margins at KFC, Pizza Hut, and Taco Bell fell from an average of more than 8 percent in 1990 to a little more than 4 percent in 1996. Declining margins in the fast-food chains reflected increasing maturity in the U.S. fast-food industry, intense competition, and the aging of KFC and Pizza Hut's restaurant bases. As a result, PepsiCo's restaurant chains absorbed nearly one-half of PepsiCo's annual capital spending during the 1990s but generated less than one-third of PepsiCo's cash flows. This meant that cash had to be diverted from PepsiCo's soft drink and snack food businesses to its restaurant businesses. This reduced PepsiCo's corporate return on assets, made it more difficult to compete effectively with Coca-Cola, and hurt its stock price. In 1997, PepsiCo decided to spin off its restaurant businesses into a new company called Tricon Global Restaurants, Inc. The new company was based in KFC's headquarters in Louisville, Kentucky.

PepsiCo's objective was to reposition itself as a beverage and snack food company, strengthen its balance sheet, and create more consistent earning growth. PepsiCo received a one-time distribution from Tricon of $4.7 billion, $3.7 billion of which was used to pay off short-term debt. The balance was earmarked for stock repurchases. In 1998, PepsiCo acquired Tropicana Products, which controlled more than 40 percent of the U.S. chilled orange juice market. Because of the divestiture of KFC, Pizza Hut, and Taco Bell, PepsiCo sales fell by $11.3 billion and assets fell by $7.0 billion. Profitability, however, soared. Operating margins rose from 11 percent in 1997 to 14 percent in 1999, and return on assets rose from 11 percent in 1997 to 16 percent in 1999. By focusing on high-cash-flow market leaders, PepsiCo raised profitability while decreasing its asset base. In 2001, PepsiCo acquired the Quaker Oats Company, which included Gatorade. Gatorade and Tropicana were moved into a separate division to increase efficiencies. By 2003, PepsiCo sales exceeded $25 billion annually.

Yum! Brands, Inc.

The spin-off created a new, independent, publicly held company called Tricon Global Restaurants, Inc. The new company managed the KFC, Pizza Hut, and Taco Bell franchise systems. David Novak became Tricon's new CEO and moved quickly to create a new culture within the company. One of his primary objectives was to reverse the long-standing friction between management and franchisees that was created under PepsiCo ownership. Novak announced that PepsiCo's top-down management system would be replaced by a new management emphasis on providing support to the firm's franchise base. Franchises would have greater independence, resources, and technical support. Novak symbolically changed the name on the corporate headquarters' building in Louisville to "KFC Support Center" to drive home his new philosophy.

Exhibit 1   Yum! Brands, Inc., Organizational Chart, 2004

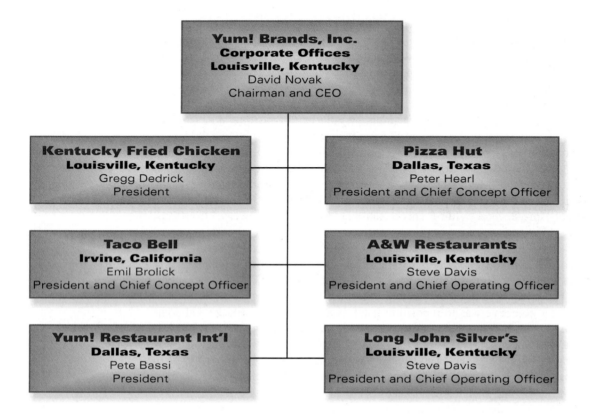

In 2002, Tricon announced the acquisition of Long John Silver's and A&W All-American Food Restaurants. The acquisition, which increased Tricon's worldwide system to 32,500 restaurants, signaled Tricon's decision to aggressively promote a multibranding strategy that combined two brands in one restaurant and attracted a larger consumer base by offering them a broader menu selection in one location. One week after it announced the acquisition, shareholders approved a corporate name change to Yum! Brands, Inc. The new name reflected the company's expanding portfolio of fast-food brands (see Exhibit 1). In 2003, Novak announced the acquisition of Pasta Bravo, a made-to-order pasta and salad concept based in California. The acquisition followed several months of test marketing of the multibranding of Pasta Bravo and Pizza Hut.

Novak also initiated a plan to reduce the company-owned restaurant base by either closing poorly performing restaurants or selling company restaurants to individual franchisees. In 1997, 38 percent of the restaurant base (KFC, Pizza Hut, and Taco Bell) was company-owned. By early 2004, company-owned restaurants had declined to 23 percent of the total. The long-term goal was to reduce the company base to 20 percent. The firm's new emphasis on supporting individual franchisees had an immediate effect on morale. In 1997, the year of the divestiture, the company recorded a loss of $111 million in net income. In 2003, net income was estimated at $585 million on estimated sales of $8.3 billion, a return on sales of about 7 percent.

Fast-Food Industry

The National Restaurant Association (NRA) estimated that U.S. food-service sales increased by 4.3 percent, to $408 billion, in 2002. More than 858,000 restaurants made up the U.S. restaurant industry and employed almost 12 million people. Sales were highest in the full-service, sit-down sector, which grew 4.5 percent, to $147 billion. Fast-food sales grew at a slower rate, rising about 3.7 percent, to $115 billion. The fast-food sector was increasingly viewed as a mature market. As U.S. incomes rose during the late 1990s and early 2000s, more consumers frequented sit-down restaurants that offered better service and a more comfortable dining experience. Together, the full-service and fast-food segments made up about 64 percent of all U.S. food-service sales.

Major Fast-Food Segments

Eight major segments made up the fast-food segment of the restaurant industry: sandwich chains, pizza chains, family restaurants, grill buffet chains, dinner houses, chicken chains, nondinner concepts, and other chains. Sales data for the leading restaurant chains in each segment are shown in Exhibit 2. Most striking is the dominance of McDonald's, which had sales of more than $20 billion in 2002. McDonald's accounted for 13 percent of the sales of the top 100 chains. To put McDonald's dominance in perspective, the second largest chain—Burger King—held less than 6 percent of the market.

Sandwich chains made up the largest segment of the fast-food market. McDonald's controlled 33 percent of the sandwich segment, while Burger King ran a distant second, with a 14 percent market share. Sandwich chains, however, were struggling because of continued price discounting that lowered profits. The threat of obesity lawsuits and increased customer demand for more healthy food items and better service lowered demand for the traditional hamburger, fries, and soft-drink combinations. Per store sales declined most at Hardee's, Carl's Jr., McDonald's, and Jack in the Box, the segment's best-known hamburger chains. In contrast, per store sales increased sharply at Quiznos, Taco Bell, Schlotsky's, Subway, and Wendy's. These chains made in-roads by offering more healthy food items. Wendy's promoted its leadership in gourmet salads, while Subway heavily advertised its low-fat sandwiches. Taco Bell rolled out a new "fresco" menu that replaced cheese and sour cream on most menu items with fat-free salsa. To meet health trends, McDonald's introduced premium salads and Burger King introduced a new line of low-fat, grilled chicken sandwiches. In contrast, Hardee's introduced a new "Thickburger" menu that included Angus burgers weighing one-third, one-half, and two-thirds of a pound in an attempt to distinguish itself from other hamburger chains.

Dinner houses made up the second largest and fastest-growing fast-food segment. Sales in the dinner house segment increased by more than 9 percent in 2002, surpassing the average increase of 4 percent among other segments. Much of the growth in dinner houses came from new unit construction, a marked contrast with the other fast-food segments, which have slowed U.S. construction because of market saturation. Much of the new unit construction took place in new suburban markets and small towns. Applebee's, Red Lobster, Outback Steakhouse, and Chili's Grill & Bar dominated the dinner house segment. Each chain generated sales of more than $2 billion in 2002. The fastest-growing dinner houses, however, were chains generating less than $600 million in sales, such as Texas Road House, P. F. Chang's China Bistro, and The Cheesecake Factory. Each of these chains increased sales by more than 20 percent.

Exhibit 2   TOP U.S. FAST-FOOD RESTAURANT CHAINS BASED ON 2002 REVENUES
($ in millions)

Rank	Sandwich Chains	Sales	Share
1	McDonald's	$20,306	33.3%
2	Burger King	8,350	13.7
3	Wendy's	6,953	11.4
5	Subway	5,230	8.6
6	Taco Bell	5,200	8.5
12	Arby's	2,695	4.4
17	Jack in the Box	2,240	3.7
18	Sonic Drive-In	2,205	3.6
19	Dairy Queen	2,190	3.6
24	Hardee's	1,700	2.8
	Other chains	3,980	6.5
	Total segment	$61,049	100.0%

Rank	Dinner Houses	Sales	Share
9	Applebee's	$ 3,183	15.2%
14	Red Lobster	2,360	11.3
15	Outback Steakhouse	2,271	10.9
16	Chili's Grill & Bar	2,240	10.7
21	Olive Garden	1,940	9.3
23	T.G.I. Friday's	1,746	8.3
33	Ruby Tuesday	1,255	6.0
55	Bennigan's	681	3.3
62	Romano's Mac. Grill	639	3.1
63	Hooters	629	3.0
	Other chains	3,985	19.0
	Total segment	$20,928	100.0%

Rank	Pizza Chains	Sales	Share
7	Pizza Hut	$ 5,100	43.4%
10	Domino's	2,927	24.9
22	Papa John's	1,749	14.9
37	Little Caesars	1,150	9.8
80	Chuck E. Cheese's	460	3.9
95	Round Table Pizza	374	3.2
	Total segment	$11,761	100.0%

Rank	Chicken Chains	Sales	Share
8	KFC	$4,800	50.7%
31	Chick-fil-A	1,373	14.5
34	Popeyes	1,215	12.8
51	Church's	720	7.6
61	Boston Market	641	6.8
97	El Pollo Loco	364	3.8
99	Bojangles'	347	3.7
	Total segment	$9,460	100.0%

Rank	Family Restaurants	Sales	Share
20	Denny's	$2,120	22.2%
27	IHOP	1,461	15.3
29	Cracker Barrel	1,406	14.7
43	Bob Evans	876	9.2
46	Perkins	798	8.3
48	Waffle House	768	8.0
	Other chains	2,133	22.3
	Total segment	$9,561	100.0%

Rank	Other Dinner Chains	Sales	Share
49	Long John Silver's	$ 756	23.5%
52	Disney Theme Parks	705	21.9
54	Panera Bread Co.	688	21.4
67	Old Country Buffet	574	17.8
74	Captain D's Seafood	497	15.4
	Total segment	$3,219	100.0%

Rank	NonDinner Chains	Sales	Share
11	Dunkin' Donuts	$2,700	34.6%
13	Starbucks	2,478	31.7
32	7-Eleven	1,335	17.1
47	Krispy Kreme	772	9.9
72	Baskin-Robbins	523	6.7
	Total segment	$7,808	100.0%

Rank	Grill Buffet Chains	Sales	Share
36	Golden Corral	$1,157	46.3%
44	Ryan's	812	32.5
71	Ponderosa	532	21.3
	Total segment	$2,501	100.0%

Source: *Nation's Restaurant News.* Sales rankings for contract and hotel chains not included.

Increased growth among dinner houses came at the expense of sandwich chains, pizza and chicken chains, grilled buffet chains, and family restaurants. "Too many restaurants chasing the same customers" was responsible for much of the slower growth in these other fast-food categories. Sales growth within each segment, however, differed from one chain to another. In the family segment, for example, Denny's (the segment leader) and Shoney's continued to shut down poorly performing restaurants while IHOP, Bob Evans, and Cracker Barrel expanded their bases. In the pizza segment, Pizza Hut, Little Caesars, and Papa John's closed underperforming restaurants while Chuck E. Cheese's added more restaurants. The hardest hit segment was grilled buffet chains. Declining sales caused both Sizzlin' and Western Sizzlin' to drop out of the list of top 100 chains, leaving only three chains in the top 100 (Golden Grill, Ryan's, and Ponderosa). Dinner houses, because of their more upscale atmosphere and higher-ticket items, were better positioned to take advantage of the aging and wealthier U.S. population. Even dinner houses, however, faced the prospect of market saturation and increased competition in the near future.

Chicken Segment

KFC continued to dominate the chicken segment with sales of $4.8 billion in 2002 and estimated sales of $5.0 billion in 2003 (see Exhibit 3). Its nearest competitor, Chick-fil-A, ran a distant second with sales of $1.4 billion. KFC's leadership in the U.S. market was so extensive that it had fewer opportunities to expand its U.S. restaurant base, which was only growing at about 1 percent per year. Despite its dominance, KFC was slowly losing market share as other chicken chains increased sales at a faster rate. KFC's share of chicken segment sales fell from 64 percent in 1993 to less than 51 percent in 2003, a 10-year drop of 14 percent (see Exhibit 4). During the same period, Chick-fil-A and Boston Market increased their combined market share by 11 percent. In the 1990s, many industry analysts predicted that Boston Market would challenge KFC for market leadership. Boston Market was a new chain that emphasized roasted rather than fried chicken. It successfully created the image of an upscale deli offering healthy, "home-style" alternatives to fried chicken. To distinguish itself from more traditional fast food, it refused to construct drive-throughs and established most of its units outside of shopping malls rather than at major city intersections.

On the surface, it appeared that Boston Market and Chick-fil-A's market share gains were achieved by taking customers away from KFC. Another look at the data, however, reveals that KFC's sales have grown at a stable rate during the last 10 years. Boston Market, rather than drawing customers away from KFC, appealed to new consumers who did not regularly frequent KFC and wanted nonfried chicken alternatives. Boston Market was able to expand the chicken segment beyond its traditional emphasis on fried chicken by offering nonfried chicken products that appealed to this new consumer group. After aggressively growing its restaurant base through 1997, however, Boston Market fell on hard times as it was unable to handle mounting debt problems. It soon entered bankruptcy proceedings. McDonald's acquired Boston Market in 2000. The acquisition followed earlier acquisitions of Donatos Pizza in 1999 and Chipotle Mexican Grill in 1998. McDonald's hoped the acquisitions would help it expand its U.S. restaurant base, as there were few opportunities to expand the McDonald's concept. Chick-fil-A's early strategy was to establish sit-down restaurants in shopping malls. As more malls added food courts, however, malls became less enthusiastic about allocating separate store space to restaurants. As a result, Chick-fil-A began to open smaller units in shopping mall food courts and to build freestanding

Exhibit 3   TOP CHICKEN CHAINS, 1997–2002

	1997	1998	1999	2000	2001	2002	Growth Rate
Sales ($ millions)							
KFC	$4,000	$4,200	$4,300	$4,400	$ 4,700	$ 4,800	4%
Chick-fil-A	643	764	943	1,082	1,242	1,373	16%
Popeyes	720	843	986	1,077	1,179	1,215	11%
Church's	574	620	705	699	721	720	5%
Boston Market	1,197	929	855	685	640	641	−12%
El Pollo Loco	235	245	275	305	339	364	9%
Bojangles'	229	250	270	298	333	347	9%
Total	$7,598	$7,851	$8,334	$ 8,546	$ 9,154	$ 9,460	5%
U.S. restaurants							
KFC	$5,092	$5,105	$5,231	$ 5,364	$ 5,399	$ 5,472	1%
Chick-fil-A	749	812	897	958	1,014	1,074	8%
Popeyes	945	1,066	1,165	1,248	1,327	1,380	8%
Church's	1,070	1,105	1,178	1,217	1,242	1,232	3%
Boston Market	1,166	889	858	712	657	653	−11%
El Pollo Loco	243	261	270	279	293	306	5%
Bojangles'	258	255	265	278	280	292	3%
Total	$9,551	$9,493	$9,864	$10,056	$10,212	$10,409	2%
Sales per unit ($ 000s)							
KFC	$ 781	$ 823	$ 822	$ 820	$ 871	$ 877	2%
Chick-fil-A	859	941	1,051	1,130	1,225	1,278	8%
Popeyes	762	790	847	863	889	880	3%
Church's	536	561	598	574	581	584	2%
Boston Market	1,027	1,045	997	962	974	982	−1%
El Pollo Loco	967	939	1,019	1,094	1,157	1,190	4%
Bojangles'	888	980	1,020	1,072	1,189	1,188	6%
Total	$ 796	$ 827	$ 845	$ 850	$ 896	$ 909	3%

Source: *Nation's Restaurant News.*

restaurants that competed head-to-head with existing chicken chains. Despite market share gains by Boston Market and Chick-fil-A, however, KFC's customer base has remained loyal to the KFC brand because of its unique taste.

The maturation of the U.S. fast-food industry increased the intensity of competition within the chicken segment. While Chick-fil-A and Popeye's continued to grow new restaurants at a fast pace, other chains focused their strategies on new product introductions, product launches beyond fried chicken, and intensive marketing campaigns. All chains attempted to differentiate themselves based on unique product and customer characteristics. KFC used animated images of the Colonel to drive home its home-style image. Recent product introductions included Popcorn Chicken, Honey BBQ Chicken, and Spicy BBQ Wings. Popeyes continued to re-image its restaurants with its "Heritage" design, which included a balcony over the drive-through, Cajun-style murals, and new signage. It recently introduced a Chicken Strip Po' Boy sandwich to expand its New Orleans–style menu of spicy chicken, jambalaya, etouffée, and gumbo. Bojangles' also promoted a Cajun decor but focused more heavily on core chicken products such as its Cajun Fried Chicken, Cajun Filet Sandwich, and Buffalo Bites. El Pollo Loco

Exhibit 4   COMPARATIVE MARKET SHARES OF TOP CHICKEN CHAINS, 1993–2002

	KFC	Chick-fil-A	Popeyes	Church's	Boston Market	Pollo Loco	Bojangles'	Total
1993	64.2%	7.5%	10.7%	8.3%	2.9%	3.2%	3.2%	100.0%
1994	60.7	7.8	10.6	8.0	6.6	3.1	3.2	100.0
1995	56.6	7.7	10.1	7.7	11.6	3.0	3.3	100.0
1996	54.2	7.9	9.3	7.3	15.3	3.0	3.0	100.0
1997	52.5	8.5	9.5	7.6	15.8	3.1	3.0	100.0
1998	53.4	9.7	10.7	7.9	11.8	3.1	3.2	100.0
1999	51.6	11.3	11.8	8.5	10.3	3.3	3.2	100.0
2000	51.4	12.7	12.6	8.2	8.0	3.6	3.5	100.0
2001	51.3	13.6	12.9	7.9	7.0	3.7	3.6	100.0
2002	50.8	14.5	12.8	7.6	6.8	3.8	3.7	100.0
10-year change	−13.4%	7.0%	2.1%	−0.7%	3.9%	0.6%	0.5%	0.0%
5-year compound annual growth rate (CAGR)	−2.6%	7.6%	2.1%	−1.0%	10.0%	2.1%	1.5%	0.0%

served marinated, flame-broiled chicken and other Mexican food entrées such as chicken burritos, tostada salads, and chicken nachos. Church's emphasized its "made-from-scratch," southern-style fried chicken and side dishes such as corn on the cob, fried okra, and macaroni and cheese. It was testing new products—such as batter-fried fish, fried thigh filets, and fried fruit pies—that would be introduced later in 2004. Chick-fil-A continued to focus on its pressure-cooked and char-grilled skinless chicken breast sandwiches. It focused on introducing salads and more portable menu items such as the recently introduced Cool Wrap Chicken Sandwich.

Trends in the Restaurant Industry

A number of demographic and societal trends influenced the demand for food eaten outside of the home. During the last two decades, rising incomes, greater affluence among a greater percentage of American households, higher divorce rates, and the fact that people married later in life contributed to the rising number of single households and the demand for fast food. More than 50 percent of women worked outside of the home, a dramatic increase since 1970. This number was expected to rise to 65 percent by 2010. Double-income households contributed to rising household incomes and increased the number of times families ate out. Less time to prepare meals inside the home added to this trend. Countering these trends, however, was a slower growth rate of the U.S. population and an overpopulation of fast-food chains that increased consumer alternatives and intensified competition.

Baby boomers 35 to 50 years of age constituted the largest consumer group for fast-food restaurants. Generation X'ers (ages 25 to 34) and the "mature" category (ages 51 to 64) made up the second and third largest groups. As consumers aged, they became less enamored with fast food and were more likely to trade up to more expensive restaurants such as dinner houses and full-service restaurants. Sales of many Mexican restaurants, which were extremely popular during the 1980s, began to slow as Japanese, Indian, and Vietnamese restaurants became more fashionable. Ethnic foods were rising in popularity as U.S. immigrants, who constituted 13 percent of the U.S. population in early 2004, looked for establishments that sold their native foods.

Labor was the top operational challenge of U.S. restaurant chains. Restaurants relied heavily on teenagers and college-age workers. Twenty percent of all employed teenagers worked in food service, compared to only 4 percent of all employed men over the age of 18 and 6 percent of all employed women. As the U.S. population aged, fewer young workers were available to fill food-service jobs. The short supply of high school and college students also meant those students had greater opportunities outside of food service. Turnover rates were notoriously high. The National Restaurant Association estimated that about 96 percent of all fast-food workers quit within a year, compared to about 84 percent of employees in full-service restaurants.

Labor costs made up about 30 percent of the fast-food chain's total costs, second only to food and beverage costs. To deal with the decreased supply of employees in the 16-to-24 age category, many restaurants were forced to hire lower-quality workers, which affected service and restaurant cleanliness. To improve quality and service, restaurants increasingly hired elderly employees who were interested in returning to the workforce. To attract more workers, especially the elderly, restaurants offered health insurance, noncontributory pension plans, and profit-sharing benefits that were generally not given only 10 years before. To combat high turnover rates, restaurants also turned to better training programs and mentoring systems, which paired new employees with more experienced ones. Mentoring systems were particularly helpful in increasing the learning curve of new workers and providing better camaraderie among employees.

Intense competition in the mature restaurant industry made it difficult for restaurants to increase prices sufficiently to cover the increased cost of labor. Consumers made decisions about where to eat partially based on price. As a result, profit margins were squeezed. To reduce costs, restaurants eliminated low-margin food items, increased portion sizes, and improved product value to offset price increases. Restaurants also attempted to increase consumer traffic through discounting, by accepting coupons from competitors, by offering two-for-one specials, and by making limited-time offerings.

Technology was increasingly used to lower costs and improve efficiencies. According to the National Restaurant Association, restaurant operators viewed computers as their number one tool for improving efficiency. Computers were used to improve labor scheduling, accounting, payroll, sales analysis, and inventory control. Most restaurant chains also used point-of-sale systems that recorded the selected menu items and gave the cashier a breakdown of food items and the ticket price. These systems reduced serving times and cashier accuracy. Other chains like McDonald's and Carl's Jr. converted to new food preparation systems that allowed them to prepare food more accurately and a variety of sandwiches using the same process.

Higher costs and poor availability of prime real estate was another trend that negatively affected profitability. A plot of land suitable for a freestanding restaurant cost between $1.5 and $2.5 million. Leasing was a less costly alternative to buying. Nevertheless, market saturation decreased per store sales as newer units cannibalized sales from existing units. As a result, most food chains began to expand their U.S. restaurant bases into alternative distribution channels in hospitals, airports, colleges, highway rest areas, gas stations, shopping mall food courts, and large retail stores or by dual branding with other fast-food concepts.

The Global Fast-Food Industry

As the U.S. market matured, more restaurants turned to international markets to expand sales. Foreign markets were attractive because of their large customer bases and comparatively little competition. McDonald's, for example, operated 46 restaurants for every 1 million U.S. residents. Outside of the United States, it operated only one restaurant for every 3 million residents. McDonald's, KFC, Burger King, and Pizza Hut were the earliest and most aggressive chains to expand abroad, beginning in the 1960s. By early 2004, at least 35 chains had expanded into at least one foreign country. McDonald's operated more than 13,000 U.S. units and 17,000 foreign units in the 119 countries. With the acquisition of A&W and Long John Silver's, however, Yum! Brands became the world's largest restaurant chain in 2003. It operated more than 21,000 U.S. and close to 33,000 non-U.S. KFC, Pizza Hut, Taco Bell, A&W, and Long John Silver's restaurants in 88 countries. Because of their early expansion abroad, McDonald's, KFC, Burger King, and Pizza Hut had all developed strong brand names and managerial expertise operating in international markets. This made them formidable competitors for fast-food chains investing abroad for the first time. Subway, TCBY, and Domino's were more recent global competitors but were expanding more aggressively than McDonald's or KFC. By 2003, each was operating in more than 65 countries.

Exhibit 5 lists the world's 35 largest restaurant chains. The global fast-food industry had a distinctly American flavor. Twenty-eight chains (80 percent of the total) were headquartered in the United States. U.S. chains had the advantage of a large domestic market and ready acceptance by the American consumer. European firms had less

Exhibit 5　THE WORLD'S 35 LARGEST FAST-FOOD CHAINS IN 2004

	Franchise	Corporate Headquarters	Home Country	Countries
1.	McDonald's	Oakbrook, Illinois	United States	121
2.	KFC	Louisville, Kentucky	United States	99
3.	Pizza Hut	Dallas, Texas	United States	92
4.	Subway Sandwiches	Milford, Connecticut	United States	74
5.	TCBY	Little Rock, Arkansas	United States	67
6.	Domino's Pizza	Ann Arbor, Michigan	United States	65
7.	Burger King	Miami, Florida	United States	58
8.	T.G.I. Friday's	Dallas, Texas	United States	53
9.	Baskin Robbins	Glendale, California	United States	52
10.	Dunkin' Donuts	Randolph, Massachusetts	United States	40
11.	Wendy's	Dublin, Ohio	United States	34
12.	Chili's Grill & Bar	Dallas, Texas	United States	22
13.	Dairy Queen	Edina, Michigan	United States	22
14.	Little Caesars Pizza	Detroit, Michigan	United States	22
15.	Popeyes	Atlanta, Georgia	United States	22
16.	Outback Steakhouse	Tampa, Florida	United States	20
17.	A&W Restaurants	Lexington, Kentucky	United States	17
18.	PizzaExpress	London, England	United Kingdom	16
19.	Carl's Jr.	Anaheim, California	United States	14
20.	Church's Chicken	Atlanta, Georgia	United States	12
21.	Taco Bell	Irvine, California	United States	12
22.	Hardee's	Rocky Mt., North Carolina	United States	11
23.	Applebee's	Overland Park, Kansas	United States	9
24.	Sizzler	Los Angeles, California	United States	9
25.	Arby's	Ft. Lauderdale, Florida	United States	7
26.	Denny's	Spartanburg, South Carolina	United States	7
27.	Skylark	Tokyo	Japan	7
28.	Lotteria	Seoul	Korea	5
29.	Taco Time	Eugene, Oregon	United States	5
30.	Mos Burger	Tokyo	Japan	4
31.	Orange Julius	Edina, Minnesota	United States	4
32.	Yoshinoya	Tokyo	Japan	4
33.	IHOP	Glendale, California	United States	3
34.	Quick Restaurants	Brussels	Belgium	3
35.	Red Lobster	Orlando, Florida	United States	3

Source: Case writer research.

success developing the fast-food concept because Europeans were more inclined to frequent midscale restaurants, where they spent several hours enjoying multicourse meals in a formal setting. KFC had trouble breaking into the German market during the 1970s and 1980s because Germans were not accustomed to buying take-out or ordering food over the counter. McDonald's had greater success penetrating the German market because it made a number of changes to its menu and operating procedures to appeal to German tastes. German beer, for example, was served in all of McDonald's restaurants in Germany. In France, McDonald's used a different sauce on its Big Mac sandwich that appealed to the French palate. KFC had more success in Asia and Latin America, where chicken was a traditional dish.

Aside from cultural factors, international business carried risks not present in the domestic market. Long distances between headquarters and foreign franchises made it more difficult to control the quality of individual restaurants. Large distances also caused servicing and support problems. Transportation and other resource costs were higher than in the domestic market. In addition, time, cultural, and language differences increased communication and operational problems. As a result, most restaurant chains limited expansion to their domestic market as long as they were able to meet profit and growth objectives. As companies gained greater expertise abroad, they turned to profitable international markets as a means of expanding restaurant bases and increasing sales, profits, and market share. Worldwide demand for fast food was expected to grow rapidly during the next two decades as rising per capita incomes worldwide made eating out more affordable for greater numbers of consumers. In addition, the development of the Internet was quickly breaking down communication and language barriers. Greater numbers of children were growing up with computers in their homes and schools. As a result, teenagers in Germany, Brazil, Japan, and the United States were equally likely to be able to converse about the Internet. The Internet also exposed more teenagers to the same companies and products, which enabled firms to quickly develop global brands and a worldwide consumer base.

Kentucky Fried Chicken Corporation

Marketing Strategy

Many of KFC's problems during the 1980s and 1990s surrounded its limited menu and inability to quickly bring new products to market. The popularity of its Original Recipe Chicken allowed KFC to expand through the 1980s without significant competition from other chicken chains. As a result, new product introductions were not a critical part of KFC's business strategy. KFC suffered one of its most serious setbacks in 1989 as it prepared to introduce a chicken sandwich to its menu. KFC was still experimenting with the chicken sandwich concept when McDonald's rolled out its McChicken sandwich. By beating KFC to the market, McDonald's developed strong consumer awareness for its sandwich. This significantly increased KFC's cost of developing awareness for its own sandwich, which KFC introduced several months later. KFC eventually withdrew the sandwich because of low sales. Today, about 95 percent of chicken sandwiches are sold through traditional hamburger chains.

KFC's focus on fried chicken ("chicken-on-the-bone") had become a serious problem by the 1990s as the U.S. fast-food industry matured. In order to expand sales, restaurant chains began to diversify their menus to include noncore products, thereby cutting into the business of other fast-food segments. For example, hamburger and pizza chains, family restaurants, and dinner houses all introduced a variety of chicken items such as chicken sandwiches and chicken wings to expand their consumer base. This made it difficult for KFC to increase per-unit sales. By 2003, McDonald's boasted a menu that included hamburgers, chicken sandwiches, fish sandwiches, burritos, a full line of breakfast items, ice cream, and milkshakes. By diversifying its menu, McDonald's was able to raise annual sales to $1.5 million per restaurant. This compared with KFC's average restaurant sales of $883,000. In 2003, Yum! Brands conducted market research showing that customers preferred multiple menu offerings over single-concept menus like chicken or pizza by a six-to-one margin.

KFC's short-term strategy was to diversify its menu. It rolled out a buffet that included over 30 dinner, salad, and dessert items. The buffet was most successful in rural locations and suburbs but less successful in urban areas, where restaurant space was limited. It then introduced Colonel's Crispy Strips and a line of chicken sandwiches that complemented its core fried chicken products. More recent product innovations include Popcorn Chicken, Chunky Chicken Pot Pie, and Twisters (a flour tortilla filled with chunks of chicken). To increase brand awareness for these new products, KFC introduced a new television campaign featuring a cartoon caricature of Colonel Sanders stating "I'm a Chicken Genius!" It also featured Jason Alexander from the television sitcom *Seinfeld* promoting Popcorn Chicken using the slogan "There's fast food, then there's KFC." Sandwiches and other noncore items, however, cannibalized sales of KFC's core chicken products. Most important, the new products did little to address the consumer's desire for greater menu variety beyond chicken.

Multibrand Strategy

By 2000, the company began to open "two-in-one" units that sold both KFC and Taco Bell or KFC and Pizza Hut in the same location. Most of KFC's sales (64 percent) and Pizza Hut's sales (61 percent) were driven by dinner, while most of Taco Bell's sales (50 percent) were driven by lunch. The combination of KFC and Taco Bell was a natural success because it increased per-unit sales simply by filling up counter space left empty by KFC at lunch or Taco Bell at dinner. It became increasingly apparent, however, that the real value of combining restaurant concepts was in attracting greater numbers of consumers who wanted more menu variety. The acquisition of A&W and Long John Silver's in 2002 provided additional opportunities to create a variety of combinations of five highly differentiated fast-food category leaders. By 2003, Yum! Brands had opened 1,975 multibrand restaurants worldwide that included KFC/Taco Bell, KFC/A&W, Taco Bell/Pizza Hut, and A&W/Long John Silver's. The company believed there was potential for opening 13,000 multibrand restaurants in the United States alone. The increase in per-unit sales that resulted from multibranding meant that new restaurants could be opened in more expensive locations and lower population areas than were profitable with stand-alone restaurants.

International Operations

KFC's early experience operating abroad put it in a strong position to take advantage of the growing trend toward global expansion. By early 2004, 56 percent of KFC's restaurants were located outside of the United States. KFC was the most global of the five brands managed by Yum! Brands, Inc. The other brands had a significantly smaller percentage of their restaurant base outside of the United States—Pizza Hut (37 percent), Taco Bell (4 percent), Long John Silver's (2 percent), and A&W (22 percent). Historically, franchises made up a large portion of KFC's international restaurant base because franchises were owned and operated by local entrepreneurs who had a deeper understanding of local language, culture, customs, law, financial markets, and marketing characteristics. Franchising was also a good strategy for establishing a presence in smaller countries like Grenada, Bermuda, and Suriname, whose small populations could only support a single restaurant. The costs of operating company-owned restaurants were prohibitively high in these smaller markets. Of the 7,000 KFC restaurants located outside of the United States, 77 percent were franchisees, licensed restaurants, or joint ventures. In larger markets such as Mexico, China, Canada, Australia, Puerto Rico, Korea, Thailand, and the United Kingdom, there was a stronger emphasis on building company-owned restaurants. By coordinating purchasing, recruiting, training, financing, and advertising in these larger markets, fixed costs could be spread over a larger restaurant base. KFC could also maintain tighter control over product quality and customer service.

Latin American Strategy

KFC operated 650 restaurants in Latin America in 2003 (Exhibit 6). Its primary presence was in Mexico, Puerto Rico, and the Caribbean. KFC established subsidiaries in Mexico and Puerto Rico in the late 1960s and expanded through company-owned restaurants. Franchises were used to penetrate countries in the Caribbean whose market size prevented KFC from profitably operating company-owned restaurants. Subsidiaries were later established in the Virgin Islands, Venezuela, and Brazil. KFC had planned to expand into these regions using company-owned restaurants. The Venezuelan subsidiary, however, was later closed because of the high costs of operating the small subsidiary. KFC had opened eight restaurants in Brazil but closed them by 2000 because it lacked the cash flow needed to support an expansion program in that market.

Exhibit 6   **LATIN AMERICA RESTAURANT COUNT IN 2003: MCDONALD'S, BURGER KING, WENDY'S, AND KFC**

	McDonald's	Burger King	Wendy's	KFC
Mexico	261	154	16	274
Puerto Rico	112	163	46	97
Caribbean Islands	29	55	20	134
Central America	99	104	38	32
Subtotal	501	476	120	537
% total	31%	82%	68%	83%
Colombia	25	0	3	9
Ecuador	10	13	0	39
Peru	10	12	0	25
Venezuela	129	20	33	5
Other Andean	45	6	0	5
Andean region	219	51	36	83
% total	14%	9%	25%	13%
Argentina	203	25	21	0
Brazil	584	0	0	0
Chile	70	23	0	30
Paraguay + Uruguay	28	6	0	0
Southern cone	885	54	21	30
% total	55%	9%	15%	5%
Latin America	1,605	581	143	650
% total	100%	100%	100%	100%

Franchises were opened in other markets that had good growth potential such as Chile, Ecuador, and Peru. In 2003, KFC signed a joint venture agreement with a Brazilian partner that had a deeper understanding of the Brazilian market. KFC hoped the joint venture would help it reestablish a presence in Brazil.

KFC's early entry into Latin America gave it a leadership position over McDonald's in Mexico and the Caribbean. It also had an edge in Ecuador and Peru. KFC's Latin America strategy represented a classic internationalization strategy. It first expanded into Mexico and Puerto Rico because of their geographical proximity as well as political and economic ties to the United States. KFC then expanded its franchise system throughout the Caribbean, gradually moving away from its U.S. base as its experience in Latin America grew. Only after it had established a leadership position in Mexico and the Caribbean did it venture into South America. McDonald's pursued a different strategy. It was late to expand into the region. Despite a rapid restaurant construction program in Mexico during the 1990s, McDonald's still lagged behind KFC. Therefore, McDonald's initiated a first-mover strategy in Brazil and Argentina, large markets where KFC had no presence. By 2003, 55 percent of McDonald's restaurants in Latin America were located in the two countries. Wendy's pursued a different strategy. It first expanded into Puerto Rico, the Caribbean, and Central America because of their geographical proximity to the United States. Wendy's late entry into Latin America, however, made it difficult to penetrate Mexico, where KFC, McDonald's, and Burger King had already established strong positions. Wendy's announced plans to build 100 Wendy's restaurants in Mexico by 2010; however, its primary objective was to establish strong positions in Venezuela and Argentina, where most U.S. fast-food chains had not yet been established.

Country Risk Assessment in Latin America

Latin America comprised some 50 countries, island nations, and principalities that were settled primarily by the Spanish, Portuguese, French, Dutch, and British during the 1500s and 1600s. Spanish was spoken in most countries, the most notable exception being Brazil, where the official language was Portuguese. Catholicism was the major religion, though Methodist missionaries successfully exported Protestantism into many regions of Latin America in the 1800s, most notably on the coast of Brazil. Despite commonalities in language, religion, and history, however, political and economic policies differed significantly from one country to another. Frequent changes in governments and economic instability increased the uncertainty of doing business in the region.

Most U.S. and Canadian companies realized that they could not overlook the region. Geographical proximity made communications and travel easier, and the North American Trade Agreement (NAFTA) eliminated tariffs on goods shipped between Canada, Mexico, and the United States. A customs union agreement signed in 1991 (Mercosur) between Argentina, Paraguay, Uruguay, and Brazil eliminated tariffs on trade among those four countries. Other countries such as Chile had also established free-trade policies that were stimulating strong growth. The primary task for companies investing in the region was to accurately assess the different risks of doing business in Latin America and to select the proper countries for investment. Miller (1992) developed a framework for analyzing country risk that was a useful tool for evaluating different countries for future investment. He argued that firms must examine country, industry, and company factors to fully assess country risk. *Country factors* addressed the risks associated with changes in the country's political and economic environment that potentially affected the firm's ability to conduct business. They included:

1. *Political risk* (e.g., war, revolution, changes in government, price controls, tariffs and other trade restrictions, appropriation of assets, government regulations, and restrictions on the repatriation of profits).

2. *Economic risk* (e.g., inflation, high interest rates, foreign exchange rate volatility, balance of trade movements, social unrest, riots, and terrorism).

3. *Natural risk* (e.g., rainfall, hurricanes, earthquakes, and volcanic activity).

Industry factors addressed changes in industry structure that inhibited the firm's ability to successfully compete in its industry. They included:

1. *Supplier risk* (e.g., changes in quality, shifts in supply, and changes in supplier power).

2. *Product market risk* (e.g., consumer tastes and availability of substitute products).

3. *Competitive risk* (e.g., rivalry among competitors, new market entrants, and new product innovations).

Company factors examined a company's ability to control its internal operations. They included:

1. *Labor risk* (e.g., labor unrest, absenteeism, employee turnover, and labor strikes).

2. *Supplier risk* (e.g., raw material shortages and unpredictable price changes).

3. *Trade secret risk* (e.g., protection of trade secrets and intangible assets).

4. *Credit risk* (e.g., problems collecting receivables).

5. *Behavioral risk* (e.g., control over franchise operations, product quality and consistency, service quality, and restaurant cleanliness).

Mexico

Many U.S. companies considered Mexico to be one of the most attractive investment locations in Latin America. Mexico's population of 105 million exceeded one-third of that of the United States. It was three times larger than Canada's 32 million. Prior to 1994, Mexico levied high tariffs on many goods imported from the United States. Other goods were regulated by quotas and licensing requirements that made Mexican goods more expensive. As a result, many U.S. consumers purchased less-expensive products from Asia or Europe. In 1994, the long-awaited North American Free Trade Agreement (NAFTA) between Canada, the United States, and Mexico went into effect. NAFTA eliminated tariffs on goods traded among the three countries and created a trading bloc with a larger population and gross domestic product than the European Union. The elimination of tariffs led to an immediate increase in trade between Mexico and the United States. In 1995, only one year after NAFTA was signed, Mexico posted its first balance of trade surplus in six years. A large part of that surplus was attributed to greater exports to the United States. By 2003, almost 85 percent of Mexico's exports were purchased by U.S. consumers. In turn, about 68 percent of Mexico's total imports came from the United States.

U.S. investment in Mexico also increased significantly after NAFTA was signed, largely in the Maquiladoras located along the U.S.–Mexican border. With the elimination of import tariffs, U.S. firms could produce or assemble goods and transport them back into the United States more quickly and at significantly less cost than they could transport goods from Asia or Europe. Mexico's largest exports to the United States were automobiles, automobile parts, crude oil, petroleum products, and natural gas. A large portion of Mexico's automobile and auto part production was produced in U.S.-owned plants. The cost of transporting automobiles back into the United States was more than offset by the lower cost of labor in Mexico. In 2003, about 2,600 U.S. firms operated in Mexico and accounted for 60 percent of all foreign direct investment in that country.

Despite the benefits, many Mexican farmers and unskilled workers strongly opposed NAFTA and U.S. investment. The day after NAFTA went into effect, rebels rioted in the southern Mexican province of Chiapas on the Guatemalan border. After four days of fighting, Mexican troops drove the rebels out of several towns the rebels had earlier seized. Around 150 people were killed. The Mexican government negotiated a cease-fire with the rebels; however, armed clashes between rebel groups protesting poverty and lack of land rights continued to be a problem. Another protest followed the signing of NAFTA when 30 to 40 masked men attacked a McDonald's restaurant in the tourist section of Mexico City. The men threw cash registers to the floor, smashed windows, overturned tables, and spray-painted "No to Fascism" and "Yankee Go Home" on the walls.

Most Mexicans (70 percent) lived in urban areas such as Mexico City, Guadalajara, and Monterrey. Mexico City's population of 18 million made it one of the most populated areas in Latin America. Many U.S. firms had operations in or around Mexico City. The fast-food industry was well developed in Mexico's cities. The leading U.S. fast-food chains already had significant restaurant bases in Mexico, most importantly KFC (274 restaurants), McDonald's (261), Pizza Hut (174), Burger King (154), and Subway (71). Mexican consumers readily accepted the fast-food concept. Chicken was also a staple product in Mexico and helped explain KFC's wide popularity. Mexico's large population and ready acceptance of fast-food represented a significant opportunity for fast-food chains. Competition, however, was intense.

Despite Mexico's relative economic stability during the late 1990s and early 2000s, Mexico had a history of high inflation, foreign exchange controls, and government regulations. These often affected foreign firms' ability to make a profit. In 1989, President Salinas attempted to reduce high inflation by controlling the peso–dollar exchange rate, allowing the peso to depreciate by only one peso per day against the dollar. He also instituted price and wage controls. Firms like KFC were unable to raise prices and were closely monitored by Mexican authorities. However, smaller firms that supplied KFC and other U.S. firms with raw materials continued to charge higher prices to compensate for inflation. KFC was soon operating at a loss, setting off heated debate in PepsiCo's headquarters. PepsiCo's finance group wanted to halt further restaurant construction in Mexico until economic stability improved. PepsiCo's marketing group wanted to continue expansion despite losses to protect its leading market share in Mexico. PepsiCo's marketing group eventually won the debate, and KFC continued to build new restaurants in Mexico during the period.

When Ernesto Zedillo became Mexico's president in December 1994, one of his objectives was to continue the stability of prices, wages, and exchange rates achieved by ex-president Carlos Salinas. This stability, however, was achieved primarily on the basis of price, wage, and foreign exchange controls. While giving the appearance of stability, an overvalued peso continued to encourage imports that exacerbated Mexico's balance of trade deficit. At the same time, Mexican exports became less competitive on world markets. Anticipating a devaluation of the peso, investors began to move capital into U.S. dollar investments. On December 19, 1994, Zedillo announced that the peso would be allowed to depreciate by an additional 15 percent per year against the dollar. Within two days, continued pressure on the peso forced Zedillo to allow the peso to float freely against the dollar.

By mid-January 1995, the peso had lost 35 percent of its value against the dollar and the Mexican stock market had plunged 20 percent. By the end of the year, the peso had depreciated from 3.1 pesos per dollar to 7.6 pesos per dollar. In order to thwart a possible default by Mexico, the U.S. government, International Monetary Fund, and World Bank pledged $25 billion in emergency loans. Shortly thereafter, Zedillo announced an emergency economic package called the *pacto* that included lower government spending, the sale of government-run businesses, and a wage freeze. By 2000, there were signs that Mexico's economy had stabilized. Interest rates and inflation, however, remained higher than in the United States, putting continuous pressure on the peso. This led to higher import prices and exacerbated inflation. In sum, optimism about future prospects for trade and investment in Mexico was tempered by concern about continued economic stability.

Brazil

Mexico's geographical proximity and membership in NAFTA partially explained why many U.S. firms with little experience in Latin America expanded to Mexico first. Mexico's close proximity to the United States minimized travel and communication problems and NAFTA reduced the complexity of establishing production in Mexico and importing goods back into the United States. Many firms overlooked the potential of Brazil. Brazil, with a population of 182 million, was the largest country in Latin America and fifth largest country in the world. Its land base was as large as the United States and bordered 10 countries. It was the world's largest coffee producer and largest exporter of sugar and tobacco. In addition to its abundant natural resources and strong export position in agriculture, Brazil was a strong industrial power. Its major exports were airplanes, automobiles, and chemicals. Its gross domestic product of $1.3 trillion was larger than Mexico's and the largest in Latin America (see Exhibit 7). Some firms did view Brazil as one of the most important emerging markets, along with China and India.

In 1990, U.S. president George Bush initiated negotiations on a Free Trade Area of the Americas (FTAA) that would eliminate tariffs on trade within North, Central, and South America. The FTAA would create the world's largest free-trade area with a combined gross domestic product of $13 trillion and 800 million consumers. In 1994, the presidents of 33 countries met with President Bush to negotiate details of the free-trade agreement to go into effect by 2005. Many Brazilians opposed the FTAA because they feared Brazilian companies could not compete with more efficient U.S. firms. Brazil imposed high tariffs of between 10 and 35 percent on a variety of goods imported from the United States such as automobiles, automobile parts, computers, computer parts, engines, and soybeans. Other Brazilian firms, however, stood to gain substantially. To protect U.S. producers from lower-cost Brazilian goods, the United States imposed tariffs of between 10 and 350 percent on imported Brazilian sugar cane, tobacco, orange juice concentrate, soybean oil, and women's leather footwear. The FTAA would eliminate these tariffs. This would give U.S. consumers the opportunity to buy Brazilian products at significantly lower prices.

Brazil played a leading role in negotiating trade and investment arrangements with other countries in Latin America. In 1991, Brazil, Argentina, Uruguay, and Paraguay signed an agreement to form a common market (Mercosur) that eliminated internal

Exhibit 7   LATIN AMERICA—SELECTED ECONOMIC AND DEMOGRAPHIC DATA, 2002-2003

	United States	Canada	Mexico	Colombia	Venezuela	Peru	Brazil	Argentina	Chile
2003 population (millions)	290.3	32.2	104.9	41.7	24.7	28.4	182.0	38.7	15.7
Growth rate	0.9%	0.9%	1.4%	1.6%	1.5%	1.6%	1.5%	1.1%	1.1%
Population data: origin									
European (non-French origin)	65.1%	43.0%	9.0%	20.0%	21.0%	15.0%	55.0%	97.0%	95.0%
European (French origin)		23.0							
African	12.9			4.0	10.0		6.0		
Mixed African and European				14.0		37.0	38.0		
Latin American (Hispanic)	12.0								
Asian	4.2	6.0							
Amerindian or Alaskan native	1.5	2.0	30.0	1.0	2.0	45.0			3.0
Mixed Amerindian and Spanish			60.0	58.0	67.0				
Mixed African and Amerindian				3.0					
Other	4.3	26.0	1.0			3.0	1.0	3.0	2.0
Total	100.0%	100.0%	100.0%	100.0%	100.0%	100.0%	100.0%	100.0%	100.0%
Economic data (2002)									
Gross domestic product ($ billion)	$10,400	$923	$900	$268	$133	$132	$1,340	$391	$151
Per capital income ($U.S.)	$37,600	$29,400	$9,000	$6,500	$5,500	$4,800	$7,600	$10,200	$10,000
Real GDP growth rate	2.5%	3.4%	1.0%	2.0%	−8.9%	4.8%	1.0%	−14.7%	1.8%
Inflation rate	1.6	2.2	6.4	6.2	31.2	0.2	8.3	41.0	2.5
Unemployment rate	5.8	7.6	3.0	17.4	17.0	9.4	6.4	21.5	9.2
Literacy rate	97.0	97.0	92.2	92.5	93.4	90.9	86.4	97.0	96.2

Source: U.S. Central Intelligence Agency, *The World Factbook.* Demographic data is 2003 estimate; economic data as of year-end 2002.

tariffs on goods traded among member countries and established a common external tariff. By 1995, 90 percent of trade among member countries was free from trade restrictions. Member countries were allowed to impose tariffs on a limited number of products considered to be a threat to sensitive domestic industries. The hope was to expand Mercosur to include other countries in the region. Chile and Bolivia, for example, were offered associate memberships. Chile, however, later withdrew because it wanted to negotiate future membership in NAFTA. Like NAFTA, the signing of Mercosur had a dramatic effect on trade among its members. Argentina quickly became Brazil's second-largest trading partner after the United States, while Brazil became Argentina's largest trading partner. Brazilian officials made it clear that making Mercosur successful was their highest priority and that the Free Trade Area of the Americas might have to wait. Many believed Brazil was the major stumbling block to establishing the FTAA by 2005.

Historically, the Brazilian government used a variety of tariffs and other restrictions on imports to encourage foreign investment in Brazil. The most highly visible example was automobiles that were taxed at rates up to 100 percent during the 1980s and 1990s. By 2003, almost all global automobile companies, including General Motors, Mercedes-Benz, Toyota, Volkswagen, Honda, Fiat, and Peugeot were producing cars in Brazil for the Brazilian market. During the 1980s, the Brazilian government attempted to stimulate domestic production in a number of technology industries like computers through an outright prohibition on imports. An example was Texas Instruments (TI), a major computer manufacturer with semiconductor operations in São Paulo. TI was prohibited from using its own computers in its Brazilian production facilities. Instead, it was forced to use slower, less efficient Brazilian computers. The Brazilian government later eliminated such restrictions after it became clear that Brazilian computer firms were unable to compete head-to-head with global computer firms. Strong government regulations and the tendency of the Brazilian government to change regulations from year to year eventually caused TI to withdraw from Brazil, even though its plant was profitable.

During the 1980s and early 1990s, Brazil battled sustained cycles of high inflation and currency instability. Between 1980 and 1993, inflation averaged more than 400 percent per year. Brazil's government attempted to reduce inflation through a variety of new currency programs, price and wage controls, and the policy of indexation, which adjusted wages and contracts based on the inflation rate. In 1994, President Cardoso introduced the Real Plan, which restructured Brazil's currency system. The cruzeiro was eliminated and replaced with a new currency called the real. The real was pegged to the U.S. dollar in an attempt to break the practice of indexation. By 1997, inflation had dropped to under 7 percent. Brazil's ability to successfully peg the real against the dollar was made possible in large part by the large foreign investment flows into Brazil during this period. The inflow of dollars boosted Brazil's dollar reserves, which could be used to buy the real on currency markets, thereby stabilizing the value of the real against the dollar.

By 1998, however, investors began to pull investments out of Brazil. Many investors were increasingly concerned about Brazil's growing budget deficit and pension system crisis. Pension benefits represented almost ten percent of Brazil's gross domestic product. Almost half of Brazil's retirement payments went to retired civil servants who made up only 5 percent of all retired Brazilians. The heavy demand on public funds for pension benefits diminished Brazil's ability to use fiscal and monetary policy to support economic development and promote stability. The Brazilian Central Bank attempted to reduce the outflow of investment capital by raising interest rates;

however, dwindling dollar reserves finally reached a crisis in 1999, when Brazil abandoned its policy of pegging the real. The real was subsequently allowed to float against the dollar. The real depreciated by almost 50 percent against the dollar in 1999.

The fast-food industry in Brazil was less developed than in Mexico or the Caribbean. This was partly the result of the structure of the fast-food industry that was dominated by U.S. restaurant chains. U.S. chains expanded farther away from their home base as they gained experience operating in Latin America. As firms gained a foothold in Mexico and Central America, it was a natural progression to move into South America. McDonald's understood the importance of the Brazilian market and was early to expand there. By 2003, it was operating 584 restaurants. Many restaurant chains such as Burger King, Pizza Hut, and KFC built restaurants in Brazil in the early to mid-1990s but eventually closed them because of poor sales. In one example, Pizza Hut opened a restaurant in a popular restaurant section of Goiânia, a city of more than 1 million people about a two-hour drive from Brasília, Brazil's capital. When the restaurant opened, long lines of Brazilian customers wrapped around the block waiting to try Pizza Hut for the first time. Within a few weeks, the lines were gone. Pizza Hut had opened a freestanding restaurant identical to those it operated in the United States. U.S. consumers were accustomed to waiting until a table was opened, sitting down and eating their meal, and leaving. Brazilian consumers did not mind waiting. However, they were accustomed to sitting outside with friends, socializing with a drink and hors d'oeuvres until a table was ready. Pizza Hut restaurants didn't accommodate this facet of Brazilian culture. Rather than change the structure of its operations, Pizza Hut sold the restaurant to Habib's, a popular Brazilian restaurant chain that sold Arab food.

Another problem was eating customs. Brazilians normally ate their big meal in the early afternoon. This could last two hours. It normally included salad, meat, rice and beans, dessert, fruit, and coffee. In the evening, it was customary to have a light meal such as a soup or small plate of pasta. Brazilians rarely ate food with their hands, preferring to eat with a knife and fork. This included food like pizza, which Americans typically ate with their hands. They also were not accustomed to eating sandwiches. If they did eat sandwiches, they wrapped the sandwich in a napkin. U.S. fast-food chains catered to a different kind of customer, one who wanted more than soup but less than a full sit-down meal. U.S. fast-food chains such as McDonald's were more popular in larger cities such as São Paulo and Rio de Janeiro, where business people were in a hurry. In smaller cities, however, traditional customs of eating were still popular. Food courts were well developed in Brazil's shopping malls. They included a variety of sit-down restaurants, fast-food restaurants, and kiosks. In the United States, in contrast, food courts consisted primarily of fast-food restaurants. U.S. restaurant chains were, therefore, faced with a daunting task of changing Brazilians' eating habits—or convincing Brazilians of the attractiveness of fast food, American style. The risk of not penetrating the Brazilian market, however, was significant given the size of Brazil's economy and McDonald's already significant presence.

Risks and Opportunities

KFC faced difficult decisions surrounding the design and implementation of an effective Latin American strategy over the next 20 years. It wanted to sustain its leadership position in Mexico and the Caribbean but also looked to strengthen its position in other regions in South America, particularly in Brazil. Limited resources and cash flow limited KFC's ability to aggressively expand in all countries simultaneously. KFC also faced the task of adapting its entry strategy to overcome barriers to entry in countries where it had little presence such as Argentina, Paraguay, Uruguay, and Venezuela. In Brazil, KFC hoped a joint venture partner would help overcome cultural barriers that forced it to withdraw in 2000. How should KFC expand its restaurant base in Latin America given differences in consumer acceptance of the fast-food concept, intensity of competition, and culture? Should KFC open company-owned restaurants or rely on franchises to grow its restaurant base? In which markets should KFC approach joint venture partners as a means of more effectively developing the KFC concept? Could KFC approach markets like Brazil and Argentina cautiously in light of McDonald's and Wendy's aggressive first-mover advantages in those countries, or should KFC proceed more aggressively? Last, in which countries should KFC establish subsidiaries that actively managed multiple restaurants in order to exploit synergies in purchasing, operations, and advertising? A country subsidiary that was supported by resources from KFC headquarters in Louisville could only be justified if KFC had a large restaurant base in the targeted country. KFC's Latin American strategy required considerable analysis and thought about how to most efficiently use its resources. It also required an in-depth analysis of country risk and selection of the right country portfolio.

References

General References

Direction of Trade Statistics. Washington, DC: International Monetary Fund.
International Financial Statistics. Washington, DC: International Monetary Fund.
Miller, Kent D. "A Framework for Integrated Risk Management in International Business." *Journal of International Business Studies* 23, no. 2 (1992), pp. 311–31.
Quickservice Restaurant Trends. Washington, DC: National Restaurant Association.
Standard & Poor's Industry Surveys. New York: Standard & Poor's.
The World Factbook. Washington, DC: U.S. Central Intelligence Agency.

Periodicals

FIU Hospitality Review. Miami, FL: FIU Hospitality Review.
IFMA Word. Chicago: International Foodservice Manufacturers Association.
Independent Restaurant. Madison, WI: EIP.
Journal of Nutrition in Recipe & Menu Development. Binghamton, NY: Food Product Press.
Nation's Restaurant News. New York: Lebhar-Friedman, www.nrn.com.
Restaurant Business. New York: Bill Communications, www.restaurant.biz.com.
Restaurants & Institutions. New York: Cahners, www.restaurantsandinstitutions.com.
Restaurants USA. Washington, DC: National Restaurant Association, www.restaurant.org.

Associations

National Restaurant Association, 1200 17th St. NW, Washington, DC 20036-3097, (202) 331-5900, www.restaurant.org.
International Franchise Association, 1350 New York Ave. NW, Suite 900, Washington, DC 20005-4709, (202) 628-8000, www.franchise.org.

Books

Alfino, Mark, John S. Caputo, and Robin Wynyard (eds.), *McDonaldization Revisited*. Greenwood Publishing Group, 1998.
Baldwin, Debra Lee. *Taco Titan: The Glen Bell Story*. Summit, 1999.
Cathy, S. Truett. *It's Easier to Succeed than to Fail*. Nashville, TN: Oliver-Nelson Books, 1989.
Greising, David. *I'd Like the World to Buy a Coke: The Life and Leadership of Roberto Goizueta*. New York: John Wiley & Sons, 1999.
Hogan, David Gerard. *Selling 'Em by the Sack: White Castle and the Creation of American Food*. New York: New York University Press, 1999.
Kentucky Fried Chicken Japan Ltd.: International Competitive Benchmarks and Financial Gap Analysis. Icon Group Ltd., 2000.

Kentucky Fried Chicken Japan Ltd.: Labor Productivity Benchmarks and International Gap Analysis. Icon Group Ltd., 2000.

Kroc, Ray, and Robert Anderson. *Grinding It Out: The Making of McDonald's.* New York: St. Martins, 1990.

Lechner, Frank, and John Boli (eds.), *The Globalization Reader.* Blackwell, 2000.

Love, John F. *McDonald's Behind the Arches.* New York: Bantam Books, 1986, 1995, 1999.

Ritzer, George. T*he McDonaldization of Society: An Investigation into the Changing Character of Contemporary Social Life.* Pine Forge Press, 1995.

————. *The McDonald's Thesis: Explorations and Extensions.* Sage, 1998.

Thomas, R. David. *Dave's Way: A New Approach to Old-Fashioned Success.* Berkley Publishing Group, 1992.

Watson, James L., ed. *Golden Arches East: McDonald's in East Asia.* Palo Alto, CA: Stanford University Press, 1998.

Web Pages

Boston Market Corporation, www.bostonmarket.com.
Burger King Corporation, www.burgerking.com.
Bojangles', www.bojangles.com.
Chick-fil-A, www.chickfila.com.
Churchs Chicken, www.churchs.com.
McDonald's Corporation, www.mcdonalds.com.
Popeyes Chicken & Biscuits, www.popeyes.com.
Yum! Brands, Inc., www.yum.com.
Wendy's International Incorporated, www.wendys.com.

CASE 10

Krispy Kreme Doughnuts in 2005
Are the Glory Days Over?

Arthur A. Thompson
The University of Alabama

Amit J. Shah
Frostburg State University

We think we're the Stradivarius of doughnuts.
— Scott Livengood, president, chairman, and CEO of Krispy Kreme

In early 2004, Krispy Kreme's prospects appeared bright. With 357 Krispy Kreme stores in 45 states, Canada, Great Britain, Australia, and Mexico, the company was riding the crest of customer enthusiasm for its light, warm, melt-in-your-mouth doughnuts. During the past 4 years, consumer purchases of Krispy Kreme's doughnut products had taken off, with sales reaching 7.5 million doughnuts a day. Considerable customer excitement—approaching frenzy and cult status—often surrounded the opening of the first store in an area. When a new Krispy Kreme opened in Rochester, New York, in 2000, more than 100 people lined up in a snowstorm before 5:00 AM to get some of the first hot doughnuts coming off the conveyor line; within an hour there were 75 cars in the drive-through lane. Three TV stations and a radio station broadcast live from the store site. The first Krispy Kreme store in Denver, which opened in 2001, grossed $1 million in revenues in its first 22 days of operation; commonly had lines running out the door with a one-hour wait for doughnuts; and, according to local newspaper reports, one night had 150 cars in line for the drive-through window at 1:30 AM. Opening day was covered by local TV and radio stations, and off-duty sheriff's deputies were brought in to help with traffic jams for a week following the store's grand opening.

The first Minnesota store, just outside of Minneapolis, had opening-week sales of $480,693—the company record for fiscal 2002. In July 2003, the first store to open in the Massachusetts market—in Medford, outside Boston—had a record opening-day revenue of $73,813 and a record opening-week sales volume of $506,917. Sales exceeded $2 million in the first seven weeks. At the June 2003 opening of the company's first store in Australia, in the outskirts of Sydney, some customers camped overnight in anticipation of the opening and others waited in line for hours to experience their first Krispy Kreme hot doughnut. The store, about an hour from downtown Sydney, attracted more than 500,000 customers from Sydney in its first six months of operations. In South Bend, Indiana, one exuberant customer camped out in the parking lot for 17 days to be the first in line for the grand opening of that city's first Krispy Kreme store.

To capitalize on all the buzz and customer excitement, Krispy Kreme had been adding new stores at a record pace throughout 2002–2003. The company's strategy and business model were aimed at adding a sufficient number of new stores and boosting sales at existing stores to achieve 20 percent annual revenue growth and 25 percent annual growth in earnings per share. In the just-completed 2004 fiscal year, total company revenues rose by 35.4 percent, to $665.6 million, compared with the $491.5 million in fiscal 2003. Net income in fiscal 2004 increased by 70.4 percent, from $33.5 million to $57.1 million. Krispy Kreme's stock price had increased eightfold since the company went public in April 2000, giving the company a high profile with investors and Wall Street analysts. In February 2004, Krispy Kreme stock was trading at 30 times the consensus earnings estimates for fiscal 2005, a price/earnings ratio that was justified only if the company continued to grow 20 to 25 percent annually.

A number of securities analysts doubted whether Krispy Kreme's strategy and growth potential would continue to push the company's stock price upward. According to one analyst, "The odds are against this stock for long-term success." Another commented, "I think the market is overly optimistic about the long-term opportunities of the growth of the doughnut business." A third said, "Single-product concepts only have so many years to run." Indeed, restaurants with quick-service products presently had the slowest revenue growth of any restaurant type. The Krispy Kreme bears were particularly concerned about reports from franchisees that, as the number of Krispy Kreme stores expanded in choice markets, average-store sales were slowing and newly opened stores were not performing as well as the first one or two stores. After the initial buying frenzy at high-profile store openings in a major market, the buzz tended to fade as the fourth, fifth, and sixth outlets opened; moreover, new stores started to cannibalize sales from existing stores, thus moderating the potential for new stores to boost overall sales. Several franchisees in California, Michigan, New York, Canada, and a few other places were said to be in financial difficulty because of overexpansion and disappointing sales at newly opened stores.

Company Background

In 1933, Vernon Rudolph bought a doughnut shop in Paducah, Kentucky, from Joe LeBeau. His purchase included the company's assets and goodwill, the Krispy Kreme name, and rights to a secret yeast-raised doughnut recipe that LeBeau had created in New Orleans years earlier. Several years thereafter, Rudolph and his partner, looking for a larger market, moved their operations to Nashville, Tennessee; other members of the Rudolph family joined the enterprise, opening doughnut shops in Charleston, West Virginia, and Atlanta, Georgia. The business consisted of producing, marketing, and delivering fresh-made doughnuts to local grocery stores. Then, during the summer of 1937, Rudolph decided to quit the family business and left Nashville, taking with him a 1936 Pontiac, $200 in cash, doughnut-making equipment, and the secret recipe; after some disappointing efforts to find another location, he settled on opening the first Krispy Kreme Doughnuts shop in Winston-Salem, North Carolina. Rudolph was drawn to Winston-Salem because the city was developing into a tobacco and textiles hub in the Southeast, and he thought a doughnut shop would make a good addition to the thriving local economy. Rudolph and his two partners, who accompanied him from Nashville, used their last $25 to rent a building across from Salem College and Academy. With no money left to buy ingredients, Rudolph convinced a local grocer to lend them what they needed, promising payment once the first doughnuts were sold. To deliver the doughnuts, he took the backseat out of the 1936 Pontiac and installed a delivery rack. On July 13, 1937, the first Krispy Kreme doughnuts were made at Rudolph's new Winston-Salem shop and delivered to grocery retailers.

Soon afterward, people began stopping by the shop to ask if they could buy hot doughnuts. There were so many requests that Rudolph decided to cut a hole in the shop's wall so that he could sell doughnuts at retail to passersby. Krispy Kreme doughnuts proved highly popular in Winston-Salem, and Rudolph's shop prospered. By the late 1950s, Krispy Kreme had 29 shops in 12 states, with each shop having the capacity to produce 500 dozen doughnuts per hour.

In the early 1950s, Vernon Rudolph met Mike Harding, who was then selling powdered milk to bakeries. Rudolph was looking for someone to help grow the business, and Harding joined the company as a partner in 1954. Starting with six employees, the two began building an equipment department and a plant for blending doughnut mixes. They believed the key to Krispy Kreme's expansion was to have control over each step of the doughnut-making process and to be able to deliver hot doughnuts to customers as soon as they emerged from the frying and sugar-glazing process. In 1960, they decided to standardize all Krispy Kreme shops with a green roof, a red-glazed brick exterior, a viewing window inside, an overhead conveyor for doughnut production, and bar stools—creating a look that became Krispy Kreme's trademark during that era.

Harding focused on operations, while Rudolph concentrated on finding promising locations for new stores and getting bank financing to support expansion into other southeastern cities and towns. Harding became Krispy Kreme's president in 1958, and he became chief executive officer when Rudolph died in 1973. Under Rudolph and then Harding, Krispy Kreme's revenues grew from less than $1 million in 1954 to $58 million by the time Harding retired in 1974. Corporate headquarters remained in Winston-Salem.

In 1976, Beatrice Foods bought Krispy Kreme and proceeded to make a series of changes. The recipe was changed, and the company's script-lettered signs were altered to produce a more modern look. As customers reacted negatively to Beatrice's changes, business declined. A group of franchisees, led by Joseph McAleer, bought the company from Beatrice in 1982 in a $22 million leveraged buyout. The new owners quickly reinstated the original recipe and the original script-lettered signs. Sales rebounded, but with double-digit interest rates in the early 1980s, it took years to pay off the buyout debt, leaving little for expansion.

To grow revenues, the company relied mainly on franchising "associate" stores, opening a few new company-owned stores—all in the southeastern United States—and boosting store volume through off-premise sales. Associate stores operated under a 15-year licensing agreement that permitted them to use the Krispy Kreme system within a specific geographic territory. They paid royalties of 3 percent of on-premise sales and 1 percent of all other branded sales (to supermarkets, convenience stores, charitable organizations selling doughnuts for fund-raising projects, and other wholesale buyers); no royalties were paid on sales of unbranded or private-label doughnuts. The primary emphasis of the associate stores and many of the company stores was on wholesaling both Krispy Kreme doughnuts and private-label doughnuts to local groceries and supermarkets. Corporate revenues rose gradually to $117 million in 1989 and then flattened for the next six years.

New Leadership and a New Strategy

In the early 1990s, with interest rates falling and much of the buyout debt paid down, the company began experimenting cautiously with expanding under Scott Livengood, the company's newly appointed president and chief operating officer. Livengood, 48, joined Krispy Kreme's human relations department in 1978 three years after graduating from the University of North Carolina at Chapel Hill with a degree in industrial relations and a minor in psychology. Believing strongly in the company's product and long-term growth potential, he rose through the management ranks, becoming president and chief operating officer in 1992, a member of the board of directors in 1994; president and CEO in 1998; and president, CEO, and chairman of the board in 1999.

Shortly after becoming president in 1992, Livengood became increasingly concerned about stagnant sales and shortcomings in the company's strategy: "The model wasn't working for us. It was more about selling in wholesale channels and less about the brand." He and other Krispy Kreme executives, mindful of the thousands of "Krispy Kreme stories" told by passionate customers over the years, concluded that the emphasis on off-premise sales did not adequately capitalize on the enthusiasm and loyalty of customers for Krispy Kreme's doughnuts. A second shortcoming was that the company's exclusive focus on southeastern U.S. markets unnecessarily handcuffed efforts to leverage the company's brand equity and product quality in the rest of the U.S. doughnut market. The available data also indicated that the standard 7,000-plus-square-foot stores were uneconomic to operate in all but very high-volume locations.

By the mid-1990s, with fewer than 100 franchised and company-owned stores and corporate sales stuck in the $110–$120 million range for six years, company executives determined that it was time for a new strategy and aggressive expansion outside the Southeast. Beginning in 1996, Krispy Kreme began implementing a new strategy to reposition the company, shifting the focus from a wholesale bakery strategy to a specialty retail strategy that promoted sales at the company's own retail outlets and emphasized the "hot doughnut experience" so often stressed in customers' Krispy Kreme stories. Doughnut sizes were also increased. The second major part of the new strategy was to expand the number of stores nationally using both area franchisees and company-owned stores. In preparing to launch the strategy, the company tested several different store sizes, eventually concluding that stores in the 2,400- to 4,200-square-foot range were better suited for the company's market repositioning and expansion plans.

The franchising part of the strategy called for the company to license territories, usually defined by metropolitan statistical areas, to select franchisees with proven experience in multi-unit food operations. Franchisees were expected to be thoroughly familiar with the local area market they were to develop and also to have the capital and organizational capability to open a prescribed number of stores in their territory within a specified period. The minimum net worth requirement for franchise area developers was $750,000 per store or $5 million, whichever was greater. Area developers paid Krispy Kreme a franchise fee of $20,000 to $40,000 for each store they opened. They also were required to pay a 4.5 percent royalty fee on all sales and to contribute 1.0 percent of revenues to a company-administered advertising and public relations fund. Franchisees were expected to strictly adhere to high standards of quality and service.

By early 2000, the company had signed on 13 area developers operating 33 Krispy Kreme stores and committed to open another 130 stores in their territories within five years. In addition, the company was operating 61 stores under its own management. Sales had zoomed to $220 million, and profits were a record $6 million.

After a decision was made to take the company public in April 2000, Krispy Kreme spent much of late 1999 and early 2000 preparing for an initial public offering (IPO) of the company's stock. The old corporate structure, Krispy Kreme Doughnut Corporation, was merged into a new company, Krispy Kreme Doughnuts, Inc. The new company planned to use the proceeds from its IPO to remodel or relocate older company-owned stores, to repay debt, to make joint venture investments in franchised stores, and to expand its capacity to make doughnut mix.

The IPO of 3.45 million shares was oversubscribed at $21 per share, and when the stock began trading in April under the ticker symbol KREM, the price quickly rose. Krispy Kreme was the second-best-performing stock among all IPO offerings in the United States in 2000. The company's stock began trading on the New York Stock Exchange in May 2001 under the symbol KKD.

Between early 2000 and early 2004, the company increased the number of Krispy Kreme stores from 144 to 357, boosted doughnut sales from an average of 3 million a day to an average of 7.5 million a day, and began the process of expanding internationally—opening its first factory store in Europe, located in the world-renowned department store Harrods of Knightsbridge, London (with plans for another 25 stores in Britain and Ireland by 2008), and continuing expansion in Australia, Canada, and Mexico. In fiscal 2004, Krispy Kreme captured an estimated 30.6 percent of the market for packaged doughnut sales, compared with 23.9 percent in fiscal 2003 and 6.4 percent in fiscal 2002.

Exhibit 1 presents a summary of Krispy Kreme's financial performance and operations for fiscal years 2000–2004.

Krispy Kreme's Business Model and Strategy

Krispy Kreme's business model involved generating revenues and profits from three sources:

- Sales at company-owned stores.
- Royalties from franchised stores and franchise fees from new store openings.
- Sales of doughnut mixes, customized doughnut-making equipment, and coffees to franchised stores.

Exhibit 2 shows revenues, operating expenses, and operating income by business segment.

The company was drawn to franchising because it minimized capital requirements, provided an attractive royalty stream, and put responsibility for local store operations in the hands of successful franchisees who knew the ins and outs of operating multi-unit chains efficiently. Krispy Kreme had little trouble attracting top-quality franchisees because of the attractive economics of its new stores (see Exhibit 3).

Krispy Kreme had developed a vertically integrated supply chain whereby it manufactured the mixes for its doughnuts at company plants in North Carolina and Illinois and also manufactured proprietary doughnut-making equipment for use in both company-owned and franchised stores. The sale of mixes and equipment, referred to as "KK manufacturing and distribution" by the company, generated a substantial fraction of both revenues and earnings (Exhibit 2).

Many of the stores built prior to 1997 were designed primarily as wholesale bakeries, and their formats and site locations differed considerably from the newer stores being located in high-density areas where there were lots of people and high traffic counts. In order to improve on-premise sales at these older stores, the company was implementing a program to either remodel them or close and relocate them to sites that could better attract on-premise sales. In new markets, the company's strategy was to focus initial efforts on on-premise sales at its stores and then leverage the interest

Exhibit 1   FINANCIAL STATEMENT DATA FOR KRISPY KREME DOUGHNUTS, FISCAL YEARS 2000–2004 (dollar amounts in thousands, except per share data)

	Fiscal Years Ending				
	Jan. 30, 2000	Jan. 28, 2001	Feb. 3, 2002	Feb. 2, 2003	Feb. 1, 2004
Statement of operations data					
Total revenues	$220,243	$300,715	$394,354	$491,549	$665,592
Operating expenses	190,003	250,690	316,946	381,489	507,396
General and administrative expenses	14,856	20,061	27,562	28,897	36,912
Depreciation and amortization expenses	4,546	6,457	7,959	12,271	19,723
Arbitration award	—	—	—	9,075	(575)
Income from operations	10,838	23,507	41,887	59,817	102,086
Interest expense, (income), net, and other adjustments	1,232	(276)	(659)	5,044	7,409
Income (loss) before income taxes	9,606	23,783	42,546	54,773	94,677
Provision for income taxes	3,650	9,058	16,168	21,295	37,590
Net income	$ 5,956	$ 14,725	$ 26,378	$ 33,478	$ 57,087
Net income per share:					
Basic	$0.16	$0.30	$0.49	$0.61	$0.96
Diluted	$0.15	0.27	0.45	0.56	0.92
Shares used in calculation of net income per share:					
Basic	37,360	49,184	53,703	55,093	59,188
Diluted	39,280	53,656	58,443	59,492	62,388
Balance sheet data					
Current assets	$ 41,038	$ 67,611	$101,769	$141,128	$138,644
Current liabilities	29,586	38,168	52,533	59,687	53,493
Working capital	11,452	29,443	49,236	81,441	85,151
Total assets	104,958	171,493	255,376	410,487	660,664
Long-term debt, including current maturities	22,902	—	4,643	60,489	137,917
Total shareholders' equity	$ 47,755	$125,679	$187,667	$273,352	$452,207
Cash flow data					
Net cash provided by operating activities	$ 8,498	$ 32,112	$ 36,210	$ 51,036	$ 95,553
Net cash used for investing activities	(11,826)	(67,288)	(52,263)	(94,574)	(186,241)
Net cash provided by (used for) financing activities	(398)	39,019	30,931	53,837	79,514
Cash and cash equivalents at end of year	3,183	7,026	21,904	32,203	21,029

Source: Company SEC filings and annual reports.

generated in Krispy Kreme products to secure supermarket and convenience store accounts and grow packaged sales.

So far, the company had spent very little on advertising to introduce its product to new markets, relying instead on local media publicity, product giveaways, and word of mouth. In almost every instance, local newspapers had run big features headlining the opening of the first Krispy Kreme stores in their area; in some cases, local radio and TV stations had sent news crews to cover the opening and conduct on-the-scene interviews. The grand opening in Austin, Texas, was covered live by five TV crews and

Exhibit 2   KRISPY KREME'S PERFORMANCE BY BUSINESS SEGMENT, FISCAL YEARS 2000–2004 (in thousands)

	Fiscal Years Ending				
	Jan. 30, 2000	Jan. 20, 2001	Feb. 3, 2002	Feb. 2, 2003	Feb. 1, 2004
Revenues by business segment					
Company store operations	$164,230	$213,677	$266,209	$319,592	$441,868
Franchise operations	5,529	9,445	14,008	19,304	23,848
KK Manufacturing and Distribution	50,484	77,593	114,137	152,653	193,129
Total	$220,243	$300,715	$394,354	$491,549	$665,592*
Operating income by business segment (before depreciation and amortization)					
Company store operations	$ 18,246	$ 27,370	$ 42,932	$ 58,214	$ 83,724
Franchise operations	1,445	5,730	9,040	14,319	19,043
KK Manufacturing and Distribution	7,182	11,712	18,999	26,843	39,345
Total	$ 10,838	$ 23,507	$ 41,887	$ 59,817	$102,086*
Unallocated general and administrative expenses	$ (16,035)	$ (21,305)	$ (29,084)	$ (30,484)	$ (38,564)
Depreciation and amortization expenses					
Company store operations	$ 3,059	$ 4,838	$ 5,859	$ 8,854	$ 14,392
Franchise operations	72	72	72	108	173
KK Manufacturing and Distribution	236	303	507	1,723	3,006
Corporate administration	1,179	1,244	1,521	1,586	1,653
Total	$ 4,546	$ 6,457	$ 7,959	$ 12,271	$ 19,723*

*Totals include operations of Montana Mills, a business that was acquired in April 2004 and divested during fiscal 2005.

Source: Company SEC filings and annual reports.

Exhibit 3   ESTIMATED KRISPY KREME STORE ECONOMICS AS OF 2001

Store revenues	$3,600,000
Cash flow (after operating expenses)	960,000
Cash flow margin	27%
Owner's equity investment to construct store	$1,050,000
Cash flow return on equity investment	91%

Source: As estimated by Deutsche Bank Alex. Brown.

four radio station crews (there were 50 people in line at 11:30 PM the night before the 5:30 AM store opening). At the first San Diego store opening, there were five remote TV trucks on the scene; radio reporters were out interviewing customers camped out in their pickup trucks in the parking lot; and a nationally syndicated radio show broadcast "live" at the site. It was common for customers to form lines at the door and at the drive-through window well before the initial day's 5:30 AM grand opening, when the HOT DOUGHNUTS NOW sign was first turned on. In a number of instances, there were traffic jams at the turn in to the store—a Buffalo, New York, traffic cop said, "I've never seen anything like this . . . and I mean it." As part of the grassroots marketing effort surrounding new-store openings, Krispy Kremes were typically given away at public events as a treat for participants—then, as one franchisee said, "the Krispy Kremes seem to work their own magic and people start to talk about them."

Krispy Kreme had originally financed its expansion strategy with the aid of long-term debt. However, the April 2000 IPO raised enough equity capital to completely pay off the long-term debt outstanding as of fiscal 2001. Since then the company had borrowed about $50 million on a long-term basis to help fund its rapid growth during 2002–2004. When the company went public, it ceased paying dividends to shareholders; currently all earnings were being retained and reinvested in growing the business.

Company Operations

Products and Product Quality

Doughnuts   Krispy Kreme produced nearly 50 varieties of doughnuts, including specialty doughnuts offered at limited times and locations. By far the biggest seller was the company's signature "hot original glazed" doughnut made from Joe LeBeau's original yeast-based recipe. Exhibit 4 shows the company's doughnut varieties as of September 2003. Exhibit 5 indicates the nutritional content for a representative selection of Krispy Kreme doughnuts.

Company research indicated that Krispy Kreme's appeal extended across all major demographic groups, including age and income. Many customers purchased doughnuts by the dozen for their office, clubs, and family. According to one enthusiastic franchisee:

> We happen to think this is a very, very unique product which has what I can only describe as a one-of-a-kind taste. They are extremely light in weight and texture. They have this incredible glaze. When you have one of the hot original doughnuts as they come off the line, there's just nothing like it.

In 2003, Krispy Kreme ranked number one in Restaurants and Institutions' Choice in Chains category, beating number-two-ranked Starbucks.

Exhibit 4   VARIETIES OF KRISPY KREME DOUGHNUTS

■ Original Glazed	■ Powdered Blueberry Filled
■ Chocolate Iced	■ Chocolate Iced Cake
■ Chocolate Iced with Sprinkles	■ Dulce de Leche
■ Maple Iced	■ Sugar Coated
■ Chocolate Iced Creme Filled	■ Glazed Cruller
■ Glazed Creme Filled	■ Powdered Cake
■ Traditional Cake	■ Glazed Devil's Food
■ Apple Fritter	■ Chocolate Iced Cruller
■ Powdered Strawberry Filled	■ Cinnamon Bun
■ Chocolate Iced Custard Filled	■ Glazed Blueberry
■ Raspberry Filled	■ Glazed Sour Cream
■ Lemon Filled	■ Caramel Kreme Crunch
■ Cinnamon Apple Filled	

Source: www.krispykreme.com, September 22, 2003.

The company received several thousand e-mails and letters monthly from customers. By all accounts, most were from customers who were passionate about Krispy Kreme products, and there were always some from people pleading for stores to be opened in their area. Exhibit 6 presents sample comments from customers and franchisees. According to Scott Livengood:

> You have to possess nothing less than a passion for your product and your business because that's where you draw your energy. We have a great product . . . We have loyal customers, and we have great brand equity. When we meet people with a Krispy Kreme story, they always do it with a smile on their faces.

Coffee   Krispy Kreme had recently launched strategic initiatives to improve the caliber and appeal of its on-premise coffee and beverage offerings, aligning them more closely with the hot doughnut experience in its stores. The first move came in early 2001 when Krispy Kreme acquired Digital Java, Inc., a small Chicago-based coffee company that sourced and roasted premium quality coffees and that marketed a broad line of coffee-based and noncoffee beverages. Scott Livengood explained the reasons for the acquisition:

> We believe the Krispy Kreme brand naturally extends to a coffee and beverage offering that is more closely aligned with the hot doughnut experience in our stores. Vertical integration of our coffee business provides the capability to control the sourcing and roasting of our coffee. Increasing control of our supply chain will help ensure quality standards, recipe formulation, and roast consistency. With this capability, one of our first priorities will be the research and benchmarking necessary to develop premier blends and roasts of coffee which will help make Krispy Kreme a coffee destination for a broader audience.

Exhibit 5   NUTRITIONAL CONTENT OF SELECTED VARIETIES OF KRISPY KREME DOUGHNUTS

Product	Calories	Calories from Fat	Total Fat		Saturated Fat		Carbohydrates		Sugars (grams)
			Grams	% Daily Value*	Grams	% Daily Value*	Grams	% Daily Value*	
Original Glazed	200	110	12	18	3	15	22	7	10
Chocolate Iced Glazed	250	110	12	19	3	15	33	11	21
Maple Iced Glazed	240	110	12	18	3	15	32	11	20
Powdered Blueberry Filled	290	150	16	25	4	21	32	11	14
Chocolate Iced Creme Filled	350	190	21	32	5	25	39	13	23
Glazed Creme Filled	340	180	20	31	5	24	39	13	23
Traditional cake	230	120	13	20	3	15	25	8	9
Glazed Cruller	240	130	14	22	3.5	17	26	9	14
Cinnamon Bun	260	140	16	24	4	20	28	9	13
Glazed Devil's Food	340	160	18	28	4.5	21	42	14	27

*Based on a 2,000-calorie diet.
Source: www.krispykreme.com, September 22, 2003.

Exhibit 6   SAMPLE COMMENTS FROM KRISPY KREME CUSTOMERS AND FRANCHISEES

Customer comments:

- "I ate one and literally it brought a tear to my eye. I kid you not."
- "Oh my gosh, this is awesome. I wasn't even hungry, but now I'm going to get two dozen."
- "We got up at 3 o'clock this morning. I told them I would be late for work. I was going to the grand opening."
- "They melt in your mouth. They really do."
- "Krispy Kreme rocks."
- "It's hot, good and hot. The way a doughnut should be."
- "The doughnut's magnificent. A touch of genius."
- "I love doughnuts, but these are different. It's terrible for your weight because when you eat just one, you feel like you've barely tasted it. You want more. It's like popcorn."*
- "When you bite into one it's like biting into a sugary cloud. It's really fun to give one to someone who hasn't had one before. They bite into one and just exclaim."†

Franchisee comments:

- "Krispy Kreme is a 'feel good' business as much as it is a doughnut business. Customers come in for an experience which makes them feel good—they enjoy our doughnuts and they enjoy the time they spend in our stores watching the doughnuts being made."
- "We're not selling doughnuts as much as we are creating an experience. The viewing window into the production room is a theater our customers can never get enough of. It's fun to watch doughnuts being made and even more fun to eat them when they're hot off the line."
- "Southern California customers have responded enthusiastically to Krispy Kreme. Many of our fans first came to Krispy Kreme not because of a previous taste experience but rather because of the 'buzz' around the brand. It was more word of mouth and publicity that brought them in to sample our doughnuts. Once they tried them, they became loyal fans who spread the word that Krispy Kreme is something special. . . We witness the excitement everyday, especially when we're away from the store and wearing a hat or shirt with the Krispy Kreme logo. When people see the logo, we get the big smile and are always asked. 'When will we get one in our neighborhood?'. . . The tremendous local publicity coupled with the amazing brand awareness nationwide has helped us make the community aware of our commitment to support local charities. Our fund-raising program, along with product donations to schools, churches, and other charitable organizations have demonstrated our real desire to give back. This commitment also impacts our employees who understand firsthand the value of supporting the needy as well as the worthy causes in our neighborhoods."
- "In all my many years of owning and operating multiple food franchise businesses, we have never been able to please—until Krispy Kreme—such a wide range of customers in the community. Its like an old friend has come to town when we open our doors: we're welcomed with open arms . . . Quite frankly, in my experience, publicity for Krispy Kreme is like nothing I have ever seen. It is truly unprecedented."

*As quoted in "Winchell's Scrambles to Meet Krispy Kreme Challenge," *Los Angeles Times,* September 30, 1999, p. C1.

†As quoted in Greg Sukiennik, "Will Dunkin' Donuts Territory Take to Krispy Kreme?" The Associated Press State & Local Wire, April 8, 2001.

Source: Krispy Kreme's 2000 and 2001 annual reports, except for two quotes noted above.

Beyond coffee, we intend to offer a full line of beverages including espresso-based drinks and frozen beverages. We believe we can substantially increase the proportion of our business devoted to coffee specifically and beverages generally by upgrading and broadening our beverage offering.

Since the acquisition of Digital Java, coffee sales at Krispy Kreme stores had increased nearly 40 percent due to expanded product offerings and upgraded quality. In 2003, Krispy Kreme was marketing four types of coffee: Smooth, Rich, Bold, and Robust

Decaf—all using coffee beans from the top 5 percent of the world's growing regions. Beverage sales accounted for about 10 percent of store sales, with coffee accounting for about half of the beverage total and the other half divided among milk, juices, soft drinks, and bottled water. In the years ahead, Krispy Kreme hoped to increase beverage sales to about 20 percent of store sales.

Store Operations

Each store was designed as a "doughnut theater" where customers could watch the doughnuts being made through a 40-foot glass window (see Exhibit 7). New stores ranged in size between 2,400 and 4,200 square feet. Stores had a drive-through window and a dining area that would seat 50 or more people—a few of the newer and larger stores had special rooms for hosting Krispy Kreme parties. Store decor was a vintage 1950s look with mint green walls and smooth metal chairs; some of the newest stores had booths (see Exhibit 8). A typical store employed about 125 people, including about 65 full-time positions. Approximately half of on-premise sales occurred in the morning hours and half in the afternoon and evening. Many stores were open 24 hours a day, with much of the doughnut making for off-premise sales being done between 6:00 PM and 6:00 AM. Production was nearly always under way during peak instore traffic times. In several large metropolitan areas, however, the doughnut making for off-premise sales was done in a central commissary specially equipped for large-volume production, packaging, and local-area distribution.

Each doughnut took about one hour to make. After the ingredients were mixed into dough, the dough was rolled and cut. The pieces went into a 12-foot-tall machine where each piece rotated on a wire rack for 33 minutes under high humidity and a low heat of 126 degrees to allow the dough to rise. When the rising process was complete, the doughnuts moved along a conveyor to be fried on one side, flipped, fried on the other side, and drained. Following all this came inspection. Doughnuts destined to be glazed were directed through a waterfall of warm, sugary topping; the others were directed to another part of the baking section to be filled and/or frosted. Exhibit 8 depicts the mixing, rising, frying, draining, and glazing parts of the process. Depending on store size and location, a typical day's production ranged between 4,000 and 10,000 dozen doughnuts.

Each producing store featured a prominent HOT DOUGHNUTS NOW neon sign (Exhibit 8) signaling customers that freshly made original glazed doughnuts were coming off the bakery conveyor belt and were available for immediate purchase. Generally, the signs glowed from 6:00 to 11:00 AM and then came on again during the late afternoon into the late-night hours.

Depending on the store location, Krispy Kreme's original glazed doughnuts sold for 60 to 75 cents each, or $4.50 to $7.50 per dozen; a mixed dozen usually sold for about 50 cents extra. Some stores charged a small premium for hot doughnuts coming right off the production line. Customers typically got a $1.00-per-dozen discount on purchases of two or more dozen.

Stores generated revenues in three ways:

- On-premise sales of doughnuts.
- Sales of coffee and other beverages.
- Off-premise sales of branded and private-label doughnuts to local supermarkets, convenience stores, and fund-raising groups. Krispy Kreme stores actively promoted sales to schools, churches, and civic groups for fund-raising drives.

Exhibit 7   Making the Doughnuts

Mixing Ingredients   Rising   Frying and Flipping

Inspection and Draining   Drying and Entering Glazing

Inspection and Draining   Packaging

Exhibit 8   Representative Krispy Kreme Stores and Store Scenes

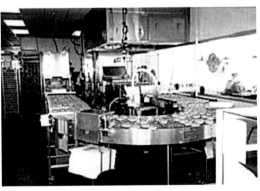

The company had developed a highly effective system for delivering fresh doughnuts, both packaged and unpackaged, to area supermarket chains and convenience stores. Route drivers had the capability to take customer orders and deliver products directly to retail accounts where they were typically merchandised either from Krispy Kreme–branded displays or from bakery cases (as unbranded doughnuts). The popularity of Krispy Kreme's stores had prompted many area supermarkets to begin stocking a selection of Krispy Kreme products in either branded display cases or in dozen and half-dozen packages.

The franchisee for Krispy Kreme stores in San Francisco had arranged to sell a four-pack of Krispy Kremes for $5 at San Francisco Giant baseball games at Pacific Bell Park—Krispy Kreme sold out of 2,100 packs by the third inning of the first game and, despite increasing supplies, sold out again after the fourth and sixth innings of the next two games; stadium vendors were supplied with 3,450 four-packs for the fourth game. The franchisee of the Las Vegas stores had a Web site that allowed customers to place orders online before 2:00 PM and have them delivered to their place of work by a courier service.

A Texas franchisee built a new 18,000-square-foot production and distribution center to supply Metroplex supermarkets, convenience stores, and other area retailers with Krispy Kreme 12-packs because newly opened Krispy Kreme stores did not have the baking capacity to keep up with both on-premise and off-premise demand; there were similar franchiser-operated wholesale baking and distribution centers in Nashville, Cincinnati, Atlanta, Chicago, and Philadelphia. Several of these centers had established delivery capability to supply Krispy Kremes to retailers in outlying areas deemed too small to justify a stand-alone Krispy Kreme store.

In 2004, about 20,000 supermarkets, convenience stores, truck stops, and other outside locations sold Krispy Kreme doughnuts. A growing number of these locations had special Krispy Kreme display cases, stocked daily with trays of different varieties for shoppers to choose from; these stand-alone cases could be placed in high-traffic locations at the end of an aisle or close to the check-out register.

The cost of opening a new store was around $2 million (including the standard package of equipment purchased from Krispy Kreme), but new store construction could range as high as $2.5 million in locations with high land and/or building costs. The initial franchise fee per unit was $40,000. Site selection was based on household density, proximity to both daytime employment and residential centers, and proximity to other retail traffic generators. A record number of new stores were opened in fiscal 2004—42 company-owned stores and 39 franchised stores. Plans were in place to open 75 new stores in the upcoming fiscal 2005 year.

Weekly sales at newly opened stores could run anywhere from $100,000 to $500,000 the first couple of weeks a new store was open. Weekly sales tended to moderate to around $40,000 to $50,000 after several months of operation, but Krispy Kreme management expected new stores to have annual sales averaging more than $3 million in their first year of operation. In fiscal 2003, sales at all of the company's 276 stores (which included those open less than a year) averaged $2.82 million. In fiscal 2004, sales at all 357 stores averaged $2.76 million—slightly lower than in 2003, chiefly because of the larger number of new store openings (roughly half of the 86 new stores were open less than six months). Exhibit 9 provides data on store operations.

Exhibit 9   STORE OPERATIONS DATA, KRISPY KREME DOUGHNUTS, FISCAL YEARS 1998–2004

	1998	2000	2001	2002	2003	2004
Systemwide sales (000s)	$203,439	$318,854	$448,129	$621,665	$778,573	$984,895
Number of stores at end of period:						
Company-owned	58	58	63	75	99	141
Franchised	62	86	111	143	177	216
Systemwide total	120	144	174	218	276	357
Increase in comparable store sales:						
Company-owned	11.5%	12.0%	22.9%	11.7%	12.8%	13.6%
Franchised	12.7%	14.1%	17.1%	12.8%	11.8%	10.2%
Average weekly sales per store:						
Company-owned (000s)	$42	$54	$69	$72	$76	$73
Franchised (000s)	$23	$38	$43	$53	$58	$56

Source: Company annual reports and 10K reports.

Krispy Kreme Manufacturing and Distribution

All the doughnut mix and equipment used in Krispy Kreme stores was manufactured and supplied by the company, partly as a means of ensuring consistent recipe quality and doughnut making throughout the chain and partly as a means of generating sales and profits from franchise operations. Revenues of the Krispy Kreme Manufacturing and Distribution (KKM&D) unit had averaged about 30 percent of total Krispy Kreme revenues for the past three years and contributed 38 to 45 percent of annual operating income (Exhibit 2). The company's line of custom stainless-steel doughnut-making machines ranged in capacity from 230 to 600 dozen doughnuts per hour. Franchisees paid Krispy Kreme about $770,000 for the standard doughnut-making equipment package in 2003–2004 (up from about $500,000 in the late 1990s); the price increase was due partly to increased equipment capacity and partly to longer equipment durability. Increased doughnut sales at franchised stores also translated into increased revenues for KKM&D from sales of mixes, sugar, and other supplies to franchisees.

Krispy Kreme had recently opened a state-of-the-art 187,000-square-foot manufacturing and distribution facility in Effingham, Illinois, dedicated to the blending and packaging of prepared doughnut mixes and to distributing mixes, equipment, and other supplies to stores in the Midwest and the western half of North America. This facility had significantly lowered Krispy Kreme's unit costs and provided triple the production capacity of the older plant in Winston-Salem.

Training

Since mid-1999, Krispy Kreme had invested in the creation of a multimedia management training curriculum. The program included classroom instruction, computer-based and video training modules, and in-store training experiences. The online part of the training program made full use of graphics, video, and animation, as well as seven different types of test questions. Every Krispy Kreme store had access to the training over the company's intranet and the Internet; employees who registered for the course could access the modules from home using their Internet connection. Learners' test results were transferred directly to a Krispy Kreme human resources database; learners were automatically redirected to lessons where their test scores indicated that they had not absorbed the material well on the first attempt. The online course was designed to achieve 90 percent mastery from 90 percent of the participants and could be updated as needed.

The course for managers had been recast into a program suitable for hourly employees. The course could also be divided into small pieces and customized to fit individual needs. In 2003, Krispy Kreme intensified its focus on leadership development by establishing the Learning Initiative Program as well as the Performance Management System. In 2003, 18 employees attended the Krispy Kreme Leadership Institute to increase their capacities in senior management areas.

Growth Potential

In 2003 and continuing into early 2004, Krispy Kreme management expressed confidence that the company was still in its infancy. The company's highest priority was on expanding into markets with over 100,000 households; management believed these markets were attractive because the dense population characteristics offered opportunities for multiple store locations, gave greater exposure to brand-building efforts, and afforded multi-unit operating economies. However, the company believed that secondary markets with fewer than 100,000 households held significant sales and profit potential—it was exploring smaller-sized store designs suitable for secondary markets. In 2002, Krispy Kreme CEO Scott Livengood stated, "We are totally committed to putting full factory stores in every town in the U.S." Krispy Kreme's management further believed the food-service and institutional channel of sales offered significant opportunity to extend the brand into colleges and universities, business and industry facilities, and sports and entertainment complexes. Management had stated that the company's strong brand name, highly differentiated product, high-volume production capability, and multichannel market penetration strategy put the company in a position to become the recognized leader in every market it entered.

Expansion into Foreign Markets   In December 2000, the company hired Donald Henshall, 38, to fill the newly created position of president of international development; Henshall was formerly managing director of new business development with the London-based Overland Group, a maker and marketer of branded footwear and apparel. Henshall's job was to refine the company's global strategy, develop the capabilities and infrastructure to support expansion outside the United States, and consider inquiries from qualified parties wanting to open Krispy Kreme stores in foreign markets. Outside of the United States, Krispy Kreme stores had opened in Canada, Australia, Mexico, and Great Britain. Krispy Kreme and its franchisees planned to open 39 new stores in Canada, 30 in Australia and New Zealand, 20 in Mexico, and 25 in Great Britain and Ireland in the coming years. So far, sales had been very promising at the foreign locations that had been opened, and franchise agreements were in the works for further global expansion.

As of May 2001, the company had stopped accepting franchise applications for U.S. locations, indicating that there were no open territories. By 2003, it had stopped accepting franchise applications in Canada, Mexico, Western Europe, and Australia, indicating that franchise contracts were already under way and that Krispy Kreme would be opening in these areas soon. According to Scott Livengood, "Krispy Kreme is a natural to become a global brand. Looking at our demographics, we appeal to a very broad customer base. We receive lots of interest on a weekly basis to expand into international locations and we are confident our brand will be received extremely well outside the U.S."

The Montana Mills Acquisition

Krispy Kreme's chief strategic move in 2003 was to acquire Montana Mills Bread Company, a Rochester, New York–based bakery operation with 11 retail locations. The acquisition price was 1.2 million shares of Krispy Kreme stock (worth roughly $50 million). The Montana Mills chain of neighborhood bakeries featured fresh stone-ground flour, a highly visual presentation of the baking process in full view of the customer, and customer sampling with large slices of a variety of fresh-baked breads. In explaining why the acquisition was made, Scott Livengood, Krispy Kreme's Chairman and CEO, said:

> This acquisition is a natural outgrowth of the development of Krispy Kreme over the past five years. As I have indicated previously, we view Krispy Kreme Doughnuts, Inc., first and foremost as a set of unique capabilities which include the abilities to explore and nurture our customers' passion for and connection to a brand, create an effective franchise network, vertically integrate to provide a complete range of products and services to a system-wide store network serving flour-based, short shelf life products, and deliver these products daily across multiple channels. Applying these core organizational competencies to the development of a second concept has the potential to create significant leverage.
>
> The opportunity to create a wholesome, fresh-baked bakery and café concept the "Krispy Kreme way" is obviously unique to Krispy Kreme. I have long considered how to capitalize on this opportunity. In Montana Mills, we found the perfect foundation for this new concept—passionate bread bakers who have created a fiercely loyal customer following around a wide variety of fresh-baked goods, bread-baking theater, and sampling of large slices of bread. I have personally observed this passion that each Montana Mills employee carries for their customers and their breads. This is a great platform on which to build. We will work closely with the Montana Mills team as we try to add value to an already outstanding concept.
>
> I expect we will spend in the range of two years fully developing the concept I described. As we have indicated regarding our international expansion, we will always try to prepare for any type of expansion well before we need the growth. We want the time to do it right. For this concept, I think that time is now.

In fiscal 2004, Montana Mills generated revenues of $6.7 million and had operating expenses of $8.7 million, thus generating an operating loss of $2.0 million.

Industry Environment

By some estimates, the U.S. doughnut industry was a $5 to $6 billion market in 2003–2004. Americans consumed an estimated 10 to 12 billion doughnuts annually—over three dozen per capita. In 2002, doughnut industry sales rose by about 13 percent. According to a study done by Technomic, a marketing research specialist in foods, doughnut shops were the fastest-growing dining category in the country in 2002–2003.

In 2002, estimated sales at outlets specializing in doughnuts rose by about 9 percent, to about $3.6 billion. Growth in packaged doughnut sales at supermarkets, convenience stores, and other retail outlets had been quite small in the past five years. The proliferation of bakery departments in supermarkets had squeezed out many locally owned doughnut shops and, to some extent, had constrained the growth of doughnut chains. Doughnuts were a popular item in supermarket bakeries, with many customers finding it more convenient to buy them when doing their regular supermarket shopping as opposed to making a special trip to local bakeries. Doughnut aficionados, however, tended to pass up doughnuts in the grocery store, preferring the freshness, quality, and variety offered by doughnut specialty shops. Most patrons of doughnut shops frequented those in their neighborhoods or normal shopping area; it was unusual for them to make a special trip of more than a mile or two for doughnuts.

Small independent doughnut shops usually had a devoted clientele, drawn from neighborhood residents and regular commuters passing by on their way to and from work. A longtime employee at a family-owned shop in Denver said, "Our customers are very loyal to us. Probably 80 percent are regulars."[1] Owners of independent shops seemed to believe that new entry by popular chains like Krispy Kreme posed little competitive threat, arguing that the market was big enough to support both independents and franchisers, that the Krispy Kreme novelty was likely to wear off, and that unless a doughnut franchiser located a store close to their present location the impact would be minimal at worst. A store owner in Omaha said, "Our doughnut sales increased when Krispy Kreme came to town. We benefit every time they advertise because doughnuts are as popular as ever."[2]

As of early 2004, there was little indication the low-carbohydrate, weight-watching craze that had swept the United States and other countries in recent years had cut much into sales. Industry observers and company officials attributed this in part to doughnuts being an affordable indulgence, easy to eat on the run, and in part to the tendency of many people to treat themselves occasionally. Doughnuts were readily available almost anywhere.

The three leading doughnut chains were Krispy Kreme; Dunkin' Donuts, with worldwide 2002 sales of $2.7 billion, 5,200 outlets worldwide (3,600 in the United States), and close to a 45 percent U.S. market share based on dollar sales volume; and Tim Hortons (160 outlets and 2002 U.S. sales of $115 million, plus 2,300 Canadian outlets with 2002 sales of $536 million).

Krispy Kreme's Chief Competitors

Dunkin' Donuts

Dunkin' Donuts was the largest coffee and baked-goods chain in the world, selling 4.4 million donuts and 1.8 million cups of coffee daily. The quick-service restaurant chain was owned by British-based Allied Domecq PLC, a diversified enterprise whose other businesses included the Baskin-Robbins ice cream chain, ToGo's Eateries (sandwiches), and an assortment of alcoholic beverage brands (Kahla, Beefeater's, Maker's Mark, Courvoisier, Tia Maria, and a host of wines). In 2004, Allied Domecq's Dunkin' Donuts chain had total sales approaching $4 billion, almost 6,200 franchised outlets in 40 countries (including 4,418 in the United States), and comparable store sales growth of 4.4 percent in the United States. About 83 percent of the chain's total sales were in the United States. In New England alone, Dunkin' Donuts operated 1,200 stores, including 600 in the Greater Boston area, where the chain was founded in 1950. Starting in 2000, Dunkin' Donuts franchisees could open co-branded stores that included Baskin Robbins and ToGo. Dunkin' Donuts ranked 9th in *Entrepreneur* magazine's annual Franchise Top 500 for 2005.

The key thrust of Dunkin' Donuts' strategy was to expand into those geographic areas in the United States where it was underrepresented. In areas where there were clusters of Dunkin' Donuts outlets, most baked items were supplied from centrally located kitchens rather than being made on-site. Despite its name, Dunkin' Donuts put more emphasis on coffee and convenience than on doughnuts. According to one company executive, "People talk about our coffee first. We're food you eat on the go. We're part of your day. We're not necessarily a destination store." Roughly half of all purchases at Dunkin' Donuts included coffee without a doughnut.[3] Dunkin' Donuts menu included doughnuts (50 varieties), muffins, bagels, cinnamon buns, cookies, brownies, Munchkins doughnut holes, cream cheese sandwiches, nine flavors of fresh coffee, iced coffees, and a lemonade Coolatta.

In 2004, Coolatta was being promoted in collaboration with MTV in a campaign called "Route to Cool." Dunkin' Donuts also had a new "express donuts" campaign to promote the sale of boxed donuts—12-packs containing the top six flavors. This campaign was being supported by advertising based on the theme "Who brought the donuts?" In addition, the chain was emphasizing coffee sales by the pound and had recently broadened its coffee offerings to include cappuccino, latte, espresso, and iced coffees.

The nutritional content of Dunkin' Donuts' 50 doughnut varieties ranged between 200 and 340 calories, between 8 and 19 grams of fat, between 1.5 and 6 grams of saturated fat, and between 9 and 31 grams of sugars; its cinnamon buns had 540 calories, 15 grams of fat, 4 grams of saturated fat, and 42 grams of sugars. Whereas Krispy Kreme's best-selling original glazed doughnuts had 200 calories, 12 grams of fat, 3 grams of saturated fat and 10 grams of sugar, the comparable item at Dunkin' Donuts had 180 calories, 8 grams of fat, 1.5 grams of saturated fat, and 6 grams of sugar. Several Dunkin' Donuts customers in the Boston area who had recently tried Krispy Kreme doughnuts reported that Krispy Kremes had more flavor and were lighter.[4]

Dunkin' Donuts had successfully fended off competition from national bagel chains and Starbucks. When national bagel chains, promoting bagels as a healthful alternative to doughnuts, opened new stores in areas where Dunkin' Donuts had stores, the company responded by adding bagels and cream cheese sandwiches to its menu offerings. Dunkin' Donuts had countered threats from Starbucks by adding a wider variety of hot and cold coffee beverages—and whereas coffee drinkers had to wait for a Starbucks barista to properly craft a $3 latte, they could get coffee and a doughnut on the fly at Dunkin' Donuts for less money. Quick and consistent service was a Dunkin' Donuts forte. Management further believed that the broader awareness of coffee created by the market presence of Starbucks stores had actually helped boost coffee sales at Dunkin' Donuts. In markets such as New York City and Chicago where there were both Dunkin' Donuts and Krispy Kreme stores, sales at Dunkin' Donuts had continued to rise. In commenting on the competitive threat from Krispy Kreme, a Dunkin' Donuts vice president said:

> We have a tremendous number of varieties, a tremendous level of convenience, tremendous coffee and other baked goods. I think the differentiation that Dunkin' enjoys is clear. We're not pretentious and don't take ourselves too seriously, but we know how important a cup of coffee and a donut or bagel in the morning is. Being able to deliver a great cup of coffee when someone is on their way to something else is a great advantage.[5]

In 2003, Couche-Tard, Canada's largest convenience store operator, bought control of the Dunkin' Donuts name in Quebec as well as the 104 Dunkin' Donuts outlets located there. Couche-Tard planned to double the number of outlets within five years to better compete with Tim Hortons and Krispy Kreme.

Tim Hortons

Tim Hortons, a subsidiary of Wendy's International, was one of North America's largest coffee and fresh-baked-goods chains, with almost 2,400 restaurants across Canada and a steadily growing base of 200 locations in key markets within the United States. In April 2004, Tim Hortons acquired 42 Bess Eaton coffee and doughnut restaurants throughout Rhode Island, Connecticut, and Massachusetts, which it planned to convert to the Tim Hortons brand and format. Tim Hortons had systemwide sales of around $3.0 billion in 2003, equal to annual sales of about $1.3 million per store. Same-store sales were up about 4.7 percent in 2003 and, during the first nine months of 2004, were up 10.1 percent in the United States and 7.7 percent in Canada. In Canada, the Tim Hortons chain was regarded as something of an icon—it was named for a popular Canadian-born professional hockey player who played for the Toronto Maple Leafs, Pittsburgh Penguins, and Buffalo Sabers; Horton was born in 1930, started playing hockey when he was five years old, and died in an auto accident while on the Buffalo Sabers. A recent survey of Canadian consumers rated Tim Hortons as the best managed brand in Canada.

The Tim Hortons division of Wendy's relied heavily on franchising—only 57 of the 2,527 Tim Hortons outlets at year-end 2003 were company-owned. Franchisees paid a royalty of 3 to 6 percent of weekly sales to the parent company, depending on whether they leased the land and/or buildings from Tim Hortons and on certain other conditions; in addition, franchisees paid fees equal to 4 percent of monthly gross sales to fund advertising and promotional activities undertaken at the corporate level. Franchisees were also required to purchase such products as coffee, sugar, flour and shortening from a Tim Hortons subsidiary; these products were distributed from five warehouses located across Canada and were delivered to the company's Canadian restaurants primarily by its fleet of trucks and trailers. In the United States, both company and franchised stores purchased ingredients from a supplier approved by the parent company.

Tim Hortons used outside contractors to construct its restaurants. The restaurants were built to company specifications as to exterior style and interior decor. The standard Hortons restaurant being built in 2003–2004 consisted of a freestanding production unit ranging from 1,150 to 3,030 square feet. Each included a bakery capable of supplying fresh baked goods throughout the day to several satellite Tim Hortons within a defined area. Tim Hortons locations ranged from full standard stores with in-store baking facilities, to combo units with Wendy's and Tim Hortons under one roof, to carts and kiosks in shopping malls, highway outlets, universities, airports, and hospitals. Most full-standard Tim Hortons locations offered 24-hour drive-through service. Tim Hortons promoted its full-standard stores as neighborhood meeting places and was active in promoting its products for group fund-raisers and community events.

The menu at each Tim Hortons unit consisted of coffee, cappuccino, teas, hot chocolate, soft drinks, soups, sandwiches, and fresh baked goods such as doughnuts, muffins, pies, croissants, tarts, cookies, cakes, and bagels. In recent years, the chain had expanded its lunch menu to include a bigger variety of offerings. One of the chain's biggest drawing cards was its special blend of fresh-brewed coffee, which was also sold in cans for customers' use at home. About half of the purchases at Tim Hortons included coffee without a doughnut. Tim Hortons had the number one in market share in Canada during breakfast, was number one in the afternoon/early evening snack category, and had a strong number two position at lunch with a menu featuring six sandwiches.

Executives at Tim Hortons did not feel threatened by Krispy Kreme's expansion into Canada and those parts of the United States where it had stores (Michigan, New York, Ohio, Kentucky, Maine, and West Virginia). According to David House, Tim Hortons president, "We really welcome them. Anyone who draws attention to doughnuts can only help us. It is a big market and a big marketplace. I would put our doughnut up against theirs any day."[6] A Canadian retailing consultant familiar with Tim Hortons and Krispy Kreme said, "This is the Canadian elephant and the U.S. mouse. Listen, if there's anything where Canadians can kick American butt, it is in doughnuts."[7] Another Canadian retailing consultant said, "It [Krispy Kreme] is an American phenomenon. These things are sickeningly sweet."[8]

Canada was reputed to have more doughnut shops per capita than any other country in the world. Aside from Tim Hortons, other chains in Canada featuring doughnuts included Dunkin' Donuts, Robin's Donuts, Country Style, and Coffee Time. Tim Hortons management had a goal of opening 500 Tim Hortons stores in the United States over the next three years, mostly in the Northeast and Great Lakes regions, and a longer-term goal of growing to about 3,500 outlets in Canada.

Winchell's Donut House

Winchell's, founded by Verne Winchell in 1948, was owned by Shato Holdings, Ltd., of Vancouver, Canada. In 2000, there were approximately 600 Winchell's units located in 10 states west of the Mississippi River, along with international franchises in Guam, Saipan, Korea, Egypt, Saudi Arabia, and New Zealand. Since then, Winchell's Doughnut House had lost steam and closed two-thirds of its locations. In 2003, there were 200 units in 12 states, plus locations in Guam, Saipan, New Zealand, and Saudi Arabia. Winchell's was the largest doughnut chain on the West Coast. To combat Krispy Kreme's entry into Southern California, where Winchell's had a brand awareness of 97 percent, Winchell's had launched a Warm 'n Fresh program for all outlets in 2000. The program entailed having fresh glazed doughnuts in display cases that were replaced every 15 to 20 minutes between 6:00 and 9:00 AM daily. A flashing red light on display cases signaled that a fresh batch of glazed doughnuts was available. Winchell's was offering customers a Warm 'n Fresh doughnut between 6:00 and 11:00 AM daily.

As of September 2003, a "Winchell's dozen" of 14 doughnuts sold for $5.99 and a double dozen (28) sold for $9.99. A single donut sold for about 60 cents, and many stores regularly ran a special of two donuts and a cup of coffee for $1.99. Winchell's bakery offerings included 20 varieties of doughnuts and 14 flavors of muffins, as well as croissants, bagels (breakfast bagel sandwiches were available at select locations), éclairs, tarts, apple fritters, and bear claws. It served three varieties of its "legendary" coffees—Dark Roast Supreme, Legendary Blend, and Legendary Decaf—all using only 100 percent arabica beans (considered by many to be the finest coffee beans in the world). Other beverages included regular and frozen cappuccino, soft drinks, milk, and juices.

Winchell's corporate goal for the next five years was to triple its sales. In 2003–2004 it was actively seeking franchisees in 14 western and midwestern states. Winchell's charged a franchise fee of $7,500 and required franchisee to be able to invest

$75,000 of unborrowed funds; the cost of new stores depended on such factors as store size, location, style of decor, and landscaping. A 5 percent royalty and a 3 percent advertising fee were charged on net sales.

LaMar's Donuts

Headquartered in Englewood, Colorado, LaMar's was a small, privately held chain that had 32 corporate-owned and franchised doughnut shops open or under development in 10 states; 8 stores were in the Denver area. Ray LaMar opened the original LaMar's Donuts in 1960 on Linwood Avenue in Kansas City and quickly turned the shop into a local institution. On a typical day, lines started forming before 6:00 AM and, by closing time about 11,000 donuts would be sold. Based on the doughnut shop's success and reputation, Ray and his wife, Shannon, decided in the early 1990s to franchise LaMar's. Hundreds of LaMar's devotees applied for the limited number of franchises made available in the Kansas City area; 15 were granted over a few months. But little became of the initial franchising effort and, in 1997, Franchise Consortium International, headed by Joseph J. Field, purchased a majority interest in LaMar's Franchising, renamed the company LaMar's Donuts International, moved the company's headquarters to a Denver suburb, and began laying the groundwork for a national expansion program.

LaMar's stores were typically located along neighborhood traffic routes. Average unit sales were $500,000 in 2003, and management expected that the average would increase to $750,000 in a few years. At one point, Fields expressed an objective of having 1,200 stores in operation by 2013, but so far LaMar's expansion was far slower than had been anticipated.

LaMar's utilized a secret recipe to produce "artisan quality" doughnuts that were handmade daily with all-natural ingredients and no preservatives. Day-old doughnuts were never sold at the shops but were donated at day's end to the needy. In addition to 75 varieties of doughnuts, LaMar's menu included gourmet coffee and cappuccino. LaMar's had recently partnered with Dazbog Coffee Company in Denver, Colorado, and created over a dozen customized specialty coffee blends under the LaMar's Old World Roast label. Beans were hand-picked from Costa Rica and then slow-roasted in an authentic Italian brick fire oven. Coffee products at LaMar's shops included cappuccinos, espressos, lattes, iced coffee drinks, and chai teas.

The company used the tag line "Simply a better doughnut." Joe Fields said, "People come in and try the product and they are surprised. They are wowed, in a very different way than Krispy Kreme. They say, 'Oh my God, this is the best doughnut I've had in my life.'" The Zagat Survey, a well-known rater of premier dining spots nationwide, described LaMar's doughnuts as "extraordinary; fit for kings." *Gourmet* magazine, in search of the country's favorite doughnut, conducted a nationwide poll; the winner was a LaMar's doughnut. LaMar's Donuts has been named Best in the Country by the John Walsh Show, a one-hour daily nationally syndicated television program. Several newspapers had named LaMar's doughnuts as tops in their market area.

Unexpected Developments at Krispy Kreme in 2004

In March 2004, Krispy Kreme's management announced that it expected the company to have diluted earnings per share of $1.16 to $1.18 for fiscal 2005 (up from $0.92 in fiscal 2004) and systemwide comparable store sales growth in the mid-to-high single digits. Executives estimated that systemwide sales would increase approximately 25 percent in fiscal 2005 (ending January 29, 2005) and that approximately 120 new stores would be opened systemwide, including 20 to 25 smaller doughnut-and-coffee-shop stores, during the next 12 months. But as 2004 progressed, Krispy Kreme's business prospects went from rosy to stark within a matter of months.

Developments at Krispy Kreme in May 2004

In a May 7, 2004, press release that caught investors by surprise, CEO Scott Livengood said:

> For several months, there has been increasing consumer interest in low-carbohydrate diets, which has adversely impacted several flour-based food categories, including bread, cereal and pasta. This trend had little discernable effect on our business last year. However, recent market data suggests consumer interest in reduced carbohydrate consumption has heightened significantly following the beginning of the year and has accelerated in the last two to three months. This phenomenon has affected us most heavily in our off-premises sales channels, in particular sales of packaged doughnuts to grocery store customers.

Sales at Krispy Kreme's franchised stores were approximately evenly split between on-premises and off-premises sales, while approximately 60 percent of company-owned store sales were off-premises. As a consequence of the falloff in sales at external outlets, sales at Krispy Kreme stores open at least 18 months grew only 4 percent, well below the 9 percent realized in preceding quarter. Due to the lower-than-expected off-premise sales at company stores, Livengood said the company was lowering its earnings guidance for the first quarter of fiscal 2005 to about $0.23 per share, down from about $0.26 per share. The company went on to announce in the same press release that it was

- Divesting its recently acquired Montana Mills operation. The plan was to close the majority of the Montana Mills store locations, which were underperforming, and pursue a sale of the remaining Montana Mills stores. Management indicated the Montana Mills divesture would entail write-offs of approximately $35 to $40 million in the first quarter on its Montana Mills investment and would likely involve further write-offs of $2 to $4 million in subsequent quarters.

- Closing six underperforming factory stores—four in older retail locations in below-average retail trade areas and two commissaries.

- Lowering its guidance for fiscal 2005 diluted earnings per share from continuing operations, excluding asset impairment and other charges described below, to between $1.04 and $1.06, approximately 10 percent lower than prior forecasts. Including the Montana Mills charges, diluted earnings per share from continuing operations were estimated to be between $0.93 and $0.95 for fiscal 2005.

In the hours following the announcement, the company's stock price was hammered in trading—dropping about 20 percent.

On May 25, 2004, Krispy Kreme reported a $24.4 million loss for the first quarter of fiscal 2005, blaming (1) trendy low-carb diets such as Atkins and South Beach for a decline in its sales in grocery stores and (2) a $34 million write-off of its investment in Montana Mills. The stock price was down 37 percent since the May 7 lower earnings announcement and was trading at about $20.

At the company's annual stockholders' meeting on May 26, 2004, executives said the company was slowing down expansion plans and had plans to counter consumer interest in low-carbohydrate foods by adding a sugar-free doughnut to its product lineup. Management also announced that the company would soon (1) introduce a chocolate-flavored glazed doughnut; mini rings that were 40 percent smaller than regular doughnuts; and crushed-ice drinks in raspberry, latte, and double chocolate flavors and (2) begin selling bags of the company's own brand of coffee in whole-bean and ground form in grocery stores alongside Krispy Kreme doughnut displays. The company said it planned to go forward with overseas expansion. The overseas expansion was concentrated in Asia; 25 new stores were being planned for South Korea, and on the horizon were stores in Japan, China, Indonesia, the Philippines, and the Persian Gulf.

Developments at Krispy Kreme in July–August 2004

In late July 2004, the company announced that the U.S. Securities and Exchange Commission was launching an inquiry into the company's accounting practices regarding certain franchise buybacks. A *Wall Street Journal* article in May had detailed questionable accounting in the $32.1 million repurchase of a struggling seven-unit franchise in Michigan that was behind on its payments for equipment, ingredients, and franchise fees, along with questionable accounting for another reacquired franchise in southern California.

In late August 2004, Krispy Kreme reported its second-quarter fiscal 2005 results:

- Systemwide sales increases of 14.8 percent as compared with the prior year's second quarter.

- An 11.5 percent increase in company revenue to $177.4 million (versus $159.2 million in the second quarter of the prior year)—company store sales increased 18.7 percent to $123.8 million, revenues from franchise operations grew 13.7 percent to $6.8 million, and KKM&D revenues decreased 4.1 percent to $46.9 million (principally because of lower equipment sales to franchisees opening new stores).

- Very small comparable store sales increases—sales at company-owned increased 0.6 percent, and systemwide sales (at both company-owned and franchised stores) increased only 0.1 percent.

- A decline in operating income from continuing operations for the second quarter of fiscal 2005 to $6.2 million, or $0.10 per diluted share, versus $13.4 million, or $0.22 per diluted share, in the second quarter of fiscal 2004.

- Twenty-two new Krispy Kreme factory/retail stores in 12 new markets, and 10 new doughnut-and-coffee-shop stores. Six company-owned factory/retail stores and three doughnut-and-coffee shops were closed during the quarter.

Commenting on the Krispy Kreme's second quarter performance, Scott Livengood, said:

> Although we are disappointed with the second-quarter financial results, we are optimistic about the long-term growth potential of the business. We are focusing our efforts and resources on initiatives that improve long-term business prospects. We have core strategies with supporting initiatives, a leading consumer brand and great people to address the current challenges. Krispy Kreme has proven over its 67-year history an ability to overcome challenges, and I am confident in our ability to restore our business momentum.[9]

Top management indicated that systemwide sales should grow approximately 15 percent for fiscal 2005 and approximately 10 percent in the last two quarters of the year but declined to provide updated earnings estimates. The company said it had scaled back expansion plans and would only open approximately 75 new stores systemwide (60 factory/retail stores and 15 doughnut-and-coffee shops) during fiscal 2005.

Developments at Krispy Kreme in November–December 2004

In November 2004, Krispy Kreme reported that the company lost $3.0 million in the third quarter of fiscal 2005. Total revenues for the quarter, which included sales from company stores, franchise operations and KKM&D, were up only 1.4 percent to $170.1 million (versus $167.8 million in the third quarter of fiscal 2004). Third-quarter systemwide sales at both company-owned and franchised stores were up 4.7 percent over the third quarter of fiscal 2004. The sales increases were well below the 10 percent gains that management had forecast in August.

During the quarter, 13 company-owned factory/retail stores and two doughnut-and-coffee shop stores were opened, and seven company owned factory/retail stores and two doughnut-and-coffee shop stores were closed. There were total 429 Krispy Kreme stores systemwide at the end of October 2004, consisting of 393 factory/retail stores and 36 doughnut-and-coffee shops. There were plans to open approximately 10 new stores systemwide in the fourth quarter of fiscal 2005.

Exhibit 10 shows the declining performance of Krispy Kreme's stores during the first three quarters of fiscal 2005. Exhibits 11 and 12 shows selected financial statistics for Krispy Kreme Doughnuts during the first nine months of fiscal 2005 compared to the first nine months of fiscal 2004.

Management declined to provide systemwide sales and earnings guidance for the fourth quarter of fiscal 2005 and withdrew its previous estimates of 10 percent systemwide sales growth made in August. Commenting on the company's performance,

Exhibit 10   QUARTERLY OPERATING PERFORMANCE OF KRISPY KREME STORES, FISCAL YEARS 2004–2005

	Fiscal Year 2004				Fiscal Year 2005		
	Q1	Q2	Q3	Q4	Q1	Q2	Q3
Average sales per week							
Company stores	$77.4	$74.4	$73.0	$69.1	$67.9	$63.1	$58.4
Area developer stores	58.0	61.2	60.3	58.7	59.2	54.3	49.9
Associate stores	52.4	48.7	45.9	42.6	46.7	43.9	41.7
Franchised store average	56.2	57.3	56.3	54.3	56.0	51.6	47.9
Systemwide average	64.1	63.7	62.7	60.1	60.7	56.3	52.2
Change in comparable store sales							
Company stores	15.4%	15.6%	13.3%	10.7%	5.2%	0.6%	−6.2%
Systemwide	11.2%	11.3%	9.5%	9.1%	4.0%	0.1%	−6.4%
Increase in systemwide sales	24.4%	27.6%	28.6%	25.5%	24.2%	14.8%	4.7%

Source: Company press releases of quarterly earnings results.

Exhibit 11 **FINANCIAL STATEMENT DATA FOR KRISPY KREME DOUGHNUTS, FIRST NINE MONTHS OF FISCAL 2004 VERSUS FIRST NINE MONTHS OF FISCAL 2005**
(dollar amounts in thousands, except per share)

	Nine Months ending November 2, 2003	Nine Months ending October 31, 2004
Statement of operations data		
Total revenues	$475,598	$531,941
Operating expenses	359,820	430,613
General and administrative expenses	27,362	34,928
Depreciation and amortization expenses	13,473	19,496
Arbitration award	(525)	—
Impairment charge and store closing costs	—	14,865
Income from operations	$ 75,468	$ 32,039
Interest expense, (income), net, and other expenses and adjustments	6,410	5,424
Income (loss) from continuing operations before income taxes	69,058	26,615
Provision for income taxes	27,488	11,543
Income from continuing operations	41,570	15,072
Discontinued operations	(907)	(36,741)
Net income (loss)	$ 40,663	$ (21,669)
Diluted earnings (loss) per share		
Income (loss) from continuing operations	$0.67	$0.24
Discontinued operations	(0.01)	(0.58)
Net income (loss) per share	$0.66	$(0.34)
Diluted shares outstanding	61,975	63,441
Balance sheet data		
Cash and cash equivalents	$ 39,287	$ 17,213
Receivables	62,454	73,416
Inventories	29,717	32,287
Payables and accrued expenses	52,101	67,820
Long-term debt and other long-term obligations, including current maturities	149,142	170,509
Total assets	$629,431	$675,897
Total shareholders' equity	$428,188	$437,568

Source: Company press releases, November 21, 2003, and November 22, 2004.

Scott Livengood said, "Clearly we are disappointed with our third-quarter results. We are focused on addressing the challenges facing the Company and regaining our business momentum." Early in the fourth fiscal quarter, Krispy Kreme sold its remaining Montana Mills assets for what management described as "a modest amount."

In December 2004, Krispy Kreme announced that it had identified accounting errors related to its acquisition of two franchises that could reduce net income for fiscal 2004 by 2.7 percent to 8.6 percent. It was as yet unclear whether the company would have to restate its fiscal year 2004 results. A special committee of the company's board of directors was investigating the accounting problems. The company's outside auditor, PricewaterhouseCoopers LLP, said it refused to complete reviews of Krispy

Exhibit 12 KRISPY KREME'S PERFORMANCE BY BUSINESS SEGMENT, FIRST NINE MONTHS OF FISCAL 2004 VERSUS FIRST NINE MONTHS OF FISCAL 2005 (in thousands)

	Nine Months ending November 2, 2003	Nine Months ending October 31, 2004
Revenues by business segment		
Company store operations	$317,158	$369,593
Franchise operations	17,555	20,060
KK Manufacturing and Distribution	140,885	142,288
Total	$475,598*	$531,941
Operating income by business segment (before depreciation and amortization)		
Company store operations	$ 61,969	$ 41,797
Franchise operations	13,721	14,694
KK Manufacturing and Distribution	27,824	26,706
Total	103,514*	83,197
Unallocated general and administrative expenses	$ (28,571)	$ (36,293)

*Totals do not include operations of Montana Mills, a business which was acquired in April 2004 and divested during fiscal 2005; nine-month revenues for Montana Mills were $4,481,000, and the operating loss at Montana Mills was $1,408,000.

Source: Company press releases, November 21, 2003, and November 22, 2004.

Kreme's financial performance for the first six months of 2005 until the special committee completed its probe of the bookkeeping problems.

In late December 2004, Krispy Kreme's stock was trading in the $10–$13 range, well below the $40 high attained in March 2004. Then in January 2005 developments at Krispy Kreme implied the company's situation was getting even worse. The board of directors forced Scott Livengood to retire and hired two outsiders with expertise in turning around troubled companies to run Krispy Kreme; Stephen Cooper was named CEO and Steven Panagos was appointed president and COO. Both executives were "on loan" from Kroll Zolfo Cooper, a company best known for presiding over the remains of Enron and rejuvenating Sunbeam and Polaroid—Cooper was chairman of KZC and Panagos was a managing director. The two new executives were assisted by a team of professionals from KZC, with KZC being paid $440,000 per month for its services. Along with the management changes, Krispy Kreme also announced that average weekly sales at factory stores were down 18 percent systemwide and down 25 percent at company-owned stores for the eight weeks ending December 26, 2004 (as compared to the same weeks in 2003). By mid-February 2005, Krispy Kreme's stock price was trading at around $6.00 per share.

Endnotes

[1]As quoted in "Dough-Down at the Mile High Corral," *Rocky Mountain News,* March 25, 2001, p. 1G.

[2]As quoted in "Hole-ly War: Omaha to Be Battleground for Duel of Titans," *Omaha World Herald,* September 7, 1999, p. 14.

[3]According to information in Hermione Malone, "Krispy Kreme to Offer Better Coffee as It Tackles New England," *Charlotte Observer,* March 16, 2001.

[4]"Time to Rate the Doughnuts: Krispy Kreme Readies to Roll into N.E. to Challenge Dunkin' Donuts," *Boston Globe,* February 21, 2001, p. D1.

[5]As quoted in Malone, "Krispy Kreme to Offer Better Coffee."

[6]As quoted in "Can Krispy Kreme Cut It in Canada?" *Ottawa Citizen,* December 30, 2000, p. H1.

[7]As quoted in ibid.

[8]As quoted in ibid.

[9]Company press release, August 26, 2004.

Atkins Nutritionals
Market-Driven Business Model

Hansa Iyengar
ICFAI Business School

N. Rajshekar
ICFAI Business School

In the 20th century, changing lifestyles and food habits had led to an enormous increase in the number of people suffering from obesity worldwide, with the number of obese adults increasing from 200 million in 1995 to 300 million in 2000.[1] As a result, obesity-related health problems increased at unprecedented rates, which led to more research that were focused on the causes and cures of obesity. Public awareness about the health benefits of having an optimal body weight to stay fit also increased from the mid-1950s onward (see Exhibit 1).

To cater to an ever-increasing demand for techniques of losing weight, Dr. Robert Atkins, who was a private medical practitioner in New York, promulgated a diet plan theory in his book *Dr. Atkins' Diet Revolution* in the early 1970s, and named it the Atkins diet.[2] The increasing popularity of the Atkins diet led to a subsequent increase in the demand for low-carbohydrate (low-carb) diet foods. This prompted Dr. Atkins to start his own company, Atkins Nutritionals, which produced a wide array of food products and nutritional supplements that were based on the low-carb theory and triggered off what was popularly known as the Atkins revolution (see Exhibit 2).

Prompted by the runaway success of Atkins, many other companies started jumping on to the low-carb bandwagon toward the end of the 1990s and introduced product ranges of their own. Many diet plans and "lose-weight-quick" diet or food fads also began flooding the market.[3] Despite tough competition and rising concerns about the health risks associated with prolonged usage of the Atkins diet, the company remained optimistic about its future since global obesity levels were predicted to reach record highs in the 21st century.

Increasing Global Obesity and Diet-Foods Market

Popular interest in nutrition was fostered by the increasing awareness of the health properties of foods in the early 20th century. During the First World War, this interest, coupled with a concern about food shortages, led to the growth of many of the dietary or food fads. One of the first food fads was the "back-to-nature" diet advocated by Sylvester Graham during the early part of the 20th century, which held that all

Exhibit 1 BODY MASS INDICATOR TABLE

BMI	19	20	21	22	23	24	25	26	27	28	29	30	31	32	33	34	35
Height (inches)							Body Weight (pounds)										
58	91	96	100	105	110	115	119	124	129	134	138	143	148	153	158	162	167
59	94	99	104	109	114	119	124	128	133	138	143	148	153	158	163	168	173
60	97	102	107	112	118	123	128	133	138	143	148	153	158	163	168	174	179
61	100	106	111	116	122	127	132	137	143	148	153	158	164	169	174	180	185
62	104	109	115	120	126	131	136	142	147	153	158	164	169	175	180	186	191
63	107	113	118	124	130	135	141	146	152	158	163	169	175	180	186	191	197
64	110	116	122	128	134	140	145	151	157	163	169	174	180	186	192	197	204
65	114	120	126	132	138	144	150	156	162	168	174	180	186	192	198	204	210
66	118	124	130	136	142	148	155	161	167	173	179	186	192	198	204	210	216
67	121	127	134	140	146	153	159	166	172	178	185	191	198	204	211	217	223
68	125	131	138	144	151	158	164	171	177	184	190	197	203	210	216	223	230
69	128	135	142	149	155	162	169	176	182	189	196	203	209	216	223	230	236
70	132	139	146	153	160	167	174	181	188	195	202	209	216	222	229	236	243
71	136	143	150	157	165	172	179	186	193	200	208	215	222	229	236	243	250
72	140	147	154	162	169	177	184	191	199	206	213	221	228	235	242	250	258
73	144	151	159	166	174	182	189	197	204	212	219	227	235	242	250	257	265
74	148	155	163	171	179	186	194	202	210	218	225	233	241	249	256	264	272
75	152	160	168	176	184	192	200	208	216	224	232	240	248	256	264	272	279
76	156	164	172	180	189	197	205	213	221	230	238	246	254	263	271	279	287

(A BMI below 18.5 is considered underweight, 18.5–24.9 is normal, 25.0–29.9 overweight, and 30 and above obese.)

Source: International Obesity Task Force, www.iotf.org.

Exhibit 2 TIMELINE OF THE ATKINS REVOLUTION

1972	Dr. Robert Atkins publishes the first edition of Dr. Atkins' Diet Revolution.
1977	Dr. Atkins publishes Dr. Atkins' Super Energy Diet about the effects of unstable blood sugar.
1978	Dr. Atkins begins to develop a line of nutritional formulations for patients.
1984	He expands and renames private practice to the Atkins Center for Complementary Medicine.
1989	Complementary Formulations, Inc., a mail-order distributor of food and vitamin products, is established by Dr. Atkins.
1996	Complementary Formulations mails its first catalog of vitamins and supplements.
1996	Atkins Online is launched at www.atkins.com.
1997	Dr. Atkins's *New Diet Revolution* begins its five-year run on the *New York Times* best-seller list.
1997	Complementary Formulations introduces its first controlled-carbohydrate food product, the Atkins Advantage Bar in Chocolate Macadamia Nut flavor.
1998	Complementary Formulations is renamed to Atkins Nutritionals, Inc.
1999	The Dr. Robert C. Atkins Foundation is established.
2002	Dr. Atkins's *New Diet Revolution* remains on the best-seller list for 285 weeks, becoming the number one best-selling Avon paperback of all time.
2002	Dr. Atkins's books reach the milestone of 15 million copies sold.
2003	*Atkins for Life,* published by St. Martin's Press, is released.
2003	Dr. Atkins dies as a result of complications from severe head trauma suffered in an accident.

Source: Compiled by IBS-CDC from www.atkins.com.

Exhibit 3   OVERWEIGHT AND OBESITY—HEALTH CONSEQUENCES

Overweight and obese individuals (BMI of 25 and above) are at increased risk for physical ailments such as

- High blood pressure, hypertension
- High blood cholesterol, dyslipidemia
- Type 2 (non-insulin-dependent) diabetes
- Insulin resistance, glucose intolerance
- Hyperinsulinemia[a]
- Coronary heart disease
- Angina pectoris[b]
- Congestive heart failure
- Stroke
- Gallstones
- Cholescystitis[c] and cholelithiasis[d]
- Gout
- Osteoarthritis
- Obstructive sleep apnea[e] and respiratory problems
- Some types of cancer (such as endometrial, breast, prostate, and colon)
- Complications of pregnancy
- Poor female reproductive health (such as menstrual irregularities, infertility, irregular ovulation)
- Bladder control problems (such as stress incontinence)
- Uric acid nephrolithiasis[f]
- Psychological disorders (such as depression, eating disorders, distorted body image, and low self-esteem)

[a]A condition in which the level of insulin in the blood is higher than normal.

[b]A recurring pain or discomfort in the chest that happens when some part of the heart does not receive enough blood. It is a common symptom of coronary heart disease (CHD), which occurs when vessels that carry blood to the heart become narrowed and blocked due to atherosclerosis.

[c]Inflammation of the gallbladder.

[d]A condition characterized by gallstones present in the gallbladder itself.

[e]Cessation of breathing for ten or more seconds during sleep.

[f]The presence of kidney stones (calculi) in the kidney.

Source: "Overweight and Obesity—Health Consequences," Centers for Disease Control, www.cdc.gov, 1998.

processed foods were devoid of nutritional value. This fad prevailed in the 21st century in the form of "fruitarianism," whose followers shunned all processed and cooked food. Food fads were based on certain beliefs that attributed good or harmful qualities to food. One of the major beliefs was that particular foods contained properties that could cure diseases; for example, it was widely held that garlic had the potential to prevent and cure certain types of cancer. Other beliefs involved opinions that certain foods were harmful and that certain foods passed on special health benefits. Most of these fads claimed substantially more benefits than proven scientifically, and each of them had a devoted set of followers.

Increasingly luxurious lifestyles led to a sharp rise in the number of people living sedentary lives toward the end of the 20th century. Absence of strenuous physical activity coupled with increasing consumption of food rich in calories, led to a large chunk of the population becoming overweight and obese. The rising obesity problem caused serious concern over the potential health risks associated with it (Exhibit 3).

Exhibit 4 **GLOBAL OBESITY STATISTICS (2003)**

Country	% Men	% Women
Finland	19.0%	19.0%
Russia	10.8	27.9
England	17.0	20.0
Germany	17.2	19.3
Czech Republic	16.3	20.2
Scotland	15.9	17.3
Belgium	12.1	18.4
Spain	11.5	15.2
Sweden	10.0	11.9
France	9.6	10.5
Denmark	10.0	9.0
Netherlands	8.4	8.3
Italy	6.5	6.3
United States	19.5	25.0
Australia	18.0	18.0

Source: International Obesity Task Force, www.iotf.org, 2003.

This led to the introduction of a flurry of exercise schedules and dietary fads that promised to make the follower lean and healthy.

The 1950s and 1960s saw *fitness* becoming a household word. In 1996, body mass index (BMI) became the global standard for the calculation of obesity levels.[4] Surveys held by the World Health Organization (WHO) based on BMI in 2000 showed that 1 billion people worldwide were overweight, and of these, 300 million were obese.[5] Global levels of obesity (Exhibit 4) and related diseases had increased at alarming rates. A survey by the International Obesity Task Force (IOTF)[6] forecast that by 2010 at least one in four adults in the United Kingdom would be obese.[7] Another survey predicted that by 2010, 40 percent of all Americans would be obese and that by 2040, this would increase to encompass more than 80 percent of the U.S. populace.[8]

Concerns about obesity taking on epic proportions led to intensive research focused on determining the causes and the related health hazards of obesity. Public awareness regarding the benefits of weight control also increased.

Dieting and diet foods became exceedingly popular as an alternative technique to lose weight without strenuous physical activity. As a result, many companies like Kellogg, Heinz, and Nestlé started manufacturing low-calorie diet foods and beverages like food bars, shakes and diet candy. One of the most popular diet fads of the late 20th century was the Atkins diet, and diet foods made by Atkins Nutritionals based on Dr. Atkins's diet plan were one of the best-selling weight-loss products. The market for weight-loss products in the United States was estimated to be around $4.5 billion in 2003, with 26 percent of women and 11 percent of men controlling their diet.[9] The global market for weight-loss supplements, foods, and beverages was predicted to grow from $19.2 billion in 1999 to $23.9 billion by 2004.[10]

The Atkins Nutritional Approach and Atkins Nutritionals, Inc.

In 1972, Dr. Robert Atkins published his best-selling book *Dr. Atkins' Diet Revolution*, which advocated a diet low in carbohydrates and high in protein and fat content as being ideal for weight loss. Atkins's approach was based on a "lifetime nutritional philosophy," focusing on the consumption of nutrient-dense unprocessed foods and vital nutrient supplementation. The Atkins diet restricted processed or refined carbohydrates such as high-sugar foods, breads, pasta, cereal, and starchy vegetables. The diet was supplemented with multivitamins and an oil or fatty acid formula to make up for the missing nutrients. The approach was based on four main principles that helped the follower of the diet in reducing weight to healthy levels and maintaining it (Exhibit 5).

Dr. Atkins founded Atkins Complimentary Formulations Inc. in 1989 (name changed to Atkins Nutritionals in 1998) to provide controlled-carbohydrate foods, natural supplements, herbs, and minerals to a growing population of people who followed the Atkins diet. Initially, Atkins produced only nutritional supplements, but in 1997 the company started manufacturing low-carbohydrate food products along with the supplements (Exhibit 6).

In 2002, sales of Atkins products were worth $100 million.[11] With midyear sales reaching $75 million in June 2003, it was estimated that the figures would double by the year end.[12] Industry experts estimated that 30 million Americans were on a low-carb diet in 2003.[13] To cater to the increasing demand, Atkins launched 70 new products in 2003, bringing the total number of its products to 115 (Exhibit 7). The president and COO of Atkins, Scott Kabak, said, "We're being very aggressive in launching

Exhibit 5   THE FOUR PRINCIPLES OF THE ATKINS NUTRITIONAL APPROACH

■ **The Atkins Primary Principle for Weight Loss**

Both carbohydrate and fat provide fuel for the body's energy needs. Carbohydrate is the first fuel to be metabolized. However, when the intake of digestible carbohydrates is sufficiently restricted (without caloric restriction), the body converts from the primary metabolic pathway of burning carbohydrate to burning fat as its main energy source. This results in weight loss.

■ **The Atkins Primary Principle for Weight Maintenance**

For each individual there is a tightly regulated carbohydrate threshold below which fat burning and weight loss occurs. However, if the individual's carbohydrate intake exceeds this threshold, carbohydrate burning predominates, allowing fat to be accumulated, resulting in weight gain. Therefore, each individual has a level of carbohydrate intake at which weight is maintained.

■ **The Atkins Primary Principle for Disease Prevention**

By following an individualized controlled carbohydrate nutritional approach that lowers carbohydrate intake resulting in lower insulin production, people at high risk for or diagnosed with certain chronic illnesses like cardiovascular diseases, diabetes, and hypertension can see improvement in clinical parameters.

■ **The Atkins Primary Principle for Good Health**

By adhering to a controlled carbohydrate nutritional approach, an individual who chooses to eat nutrient-dense foods (including adequate fiber, healthy fats, and supplementation as needed) is more likely to meet his nutritional needs and promote good health than he would by following a calorie-restricted, fat-deficient diet.

Source: Atkins Nutritionals, Inc., www.atkins.com.

products and expect to continue to be for the foreseeable future."[14] By the end of 2003, the Atkins diet had become extremely popular, with 3 million people in the United Kingdom and 30 percent of the population of the United States following it.[15] Catering to popular demand, many restaurants, such as TGI Friday (owned by the Carlson Restaurants Worldwide), also began to offer low-carb menus to their customers, and many Web sites providing low-carb recipes emerged.

The Road Ahead for Atkins

Despite the immense popularity of the Atkins diet, the scientific community raised a lot of arguments regarding the potential long-term health risks of following a low-carb diet. Doctors from the American Heart Association warned that following the Atkins diet was harmful in the long run since diets rich in fats and proteins led to high levels of cholesterol and increase in the risks of kidney diseases, osteoporosis, and colon and breast cancer.

Exhibit 6   THE ATKINS RANGE OF FOOD PRODUCTS

Atkins Advantage range

The Advantage range includes the Atkins Advantage Bars. The most popular Atkins food by far, these satisfying and nutritious bars were available in 11 great flavors, and were formulated with a focus on protein, including soy, and healthy natural fats. Advantage bars were a delicious quick snack or, in a pinch, an on-the-go meal.

The Atkins Breakfast Bars provided a delicious, nutritious breakfast and were available in several breakfast-favorite flavors such as Cherry Almond Danish and Creamy Cinnamon Bun, these bars were a great alternative to muffins and other sugary treats.

Atkins Ready-to-Drink Shakes and Shake Mixes were ready-to-drink shakes with no sugar added. Alternatively, a person could whip up his or her own shake with Atkins Shake Mix.

Atkins Endulge range

The Atkins Endulge Bar was a chocolate candy filled with the decadent taste of chocolate but none of the added sugar and hydrogenated oil found in other chocolate bars.

Atkins Kitchen range

The Atkins Quick & Easy mixes helped controlled-carb followers stock their kitchen with useful items. Atkins Bake Mix could be used as a controlled-carb, all-purpose substitute for flour. Atkins Pancake & Waffle Mix and Atkins Sugar Free Pancake Syrup together offered a tasty controlled-carb breakfast alternative. The Atkins Quick & Easy Muffin/Bread Mixes made other delicious alternatives.

The Kitchen brand also included Atkins Sugar Free Syrups. These flavored syrups could be added to coffee, tea, or soda water, or used in controlled-carb recipes for baked goods, marinades, and desserts.

Atkins Bakery range

Atkins' Bread used selective ingredients and advanced food technology to create a product that tastes as good or better than traditional bread did. The cornstarch used was a special low-glycemic version, and inulin (a natural extract of chicory root) was used to add fiber and body. Both this cornstarch and inulin had a minimal impact on blood sugar.

Nutritional supplements

Atkins also manufactured a range of nutritional supplements to supplement the diet with nutrients that were missing. The nutritional products range included basic enzymes, essential oils, and antioxidants.

Source: Compiled by IBS-CDC from www.atkins.com.

Exhibit 7 NEW PRODUCTS FROM ATKINS NUTRITIONALS

Atkins Endulge ice cream bars, ice cream pints, and premium ice cream cups
Super Premium Ice Cream Bars, pints and cups in four flavors: Chocolate Fudge, Vanilla Fudge Swirl, Chocolate Fudge Swirl on Peanut Butter Swirl.

Atkins entrées
Delicious frozen entrées give you great taste and real convenience.

Caramels—milk and dark chocolate coated

Carb Counters cookie mixes
To make scrumptious, all-natural cookies and control your carbs.

Celebration Cake—chocolate and butter-cream
Layer cake in chocolate and almond flavors, topped with authentic French butter-cream icing and surrounded by chopped almonds!

Celebration Cake—icing kit
Add your own individual touch to any cake with this ready-to-use butter-cream icing kit in blue, pink or green. Top your Celebration cake (sold separately) with this spectacular icing.

Chocolate truffle torte
Flavored with rich natural chocolate and cocoa butter, and there's no flour or added sugar.

Chocolate-covered cookie dough bites
Sweet and delicious, bite-size morsels to satisfy the sweet tooth.

Donut mixes

Flatbread crackers
Wheat-free flatbread crackers are made with protein-rich soy, almond, and hazelnut flours. Available in eight versatile and delicious flavors.

Soft peanut and almond brittle
Soft Peanut Brittle or our Soft Almond Brittle, made with premium dry-roasted nuts coated in a unique soft-textured brittle that's easy on your teeth.

Soup mixes
New Dine 'n Dash soup mixes in four flavors are delicious and easy to prepare.

Soy nuts
This is the perfect healthy snack with an appealing crunch.

Sunny Butter
This creamy, delicious sunflower seed butter spread gives the taste of peanut butter without the carbs or potential allergies. Sunny Butter is made from the finest natural sunflower seeds.

Teriyaki beef strips
Teriyaki Beef Strips are gourmet beef snacks with no added sugar. The marinade is teriyaki sauce sweetened with sucralose.

Source: Compiled by IBS-CDC from www.atkins.com.

Apart from the health risks involved in adhering to the Atkins diet, Atkins Nutritionals also faced tough challenges from competitors like Kraft Foods, which planned to cut the carbohydrate content in its range of cookies, hot dogs, and cheese products. Other companies, like Low Carb Solutions, Carbolite Foods Inc., Heinz, and Kellogg planned to launch their own brands of low-carb products. Competition was also expected from major players like Nestlé's line of Stouffers' Lean Cuisine, and Unilever's Slim-Fast Foods that promoted a range of weight-loss products of their own. Chocolate maker Hershey's launched its line of One Gram Sugar Carb bars. Food make Sara Lee launched a version of low-carb bread, while CarbSense Foods Inc. introduced a low-carb tortilla chip, and beer maker Anheuser-Busch launched its low-carb beer (Exhibit 8).

Exhibit 8 LOW-CARB PRODUCTS OF ATKINS'S COMPETITORS

Products from Low Carb Solutions

- Line of 100% whole wheat bread; multigrain bread; raisin bread; and hamburger, hot dog, and cheese buns
- Baja Bob's piña colada, margarita, and sweet & sour mixes
- Ross chocolate bars, Asher's chocolate bars and truffles
- LeBon sugar-free gummie bears, toffees, hard candies, and wine gums
- No-sugar, low-carb pudding mixes, frozen dessert mixes, mousse mixes, cheesecake mixes, and the popular Thick 'n' Thin Pizza Crusts and mixes
- Carbosave crackers
- La Tortilla Factory 6-inch tortilla shells
- Hot and cold cereals
- Sugar-free hot chocolate
- Steel's sauces, ketchups, jams, syrups
- DaVinci syrups
- Jok'n' Al jams, jellies, sauces and pie fillings
- Walden Farms calorie-free, no-carb veggie dips, marinara, scampi sauces, and salad dressings
- Botanical ICE diet juices and carbonated water
- Protein powders and bars

Products from Carbolite Foods

Carbolite foods offer a range of low-carb products that are sold under the Carbolite and Carborite brands. These products include low-carb sugar-free soft-serve ice cream; soy shakes, a zero-carb bake mix and low-carb bread mix; low-carb zero-sugar snack bars; a line of candies that includes jelly beans, citrus slices, chocolate-covered almonds, chewy fruits, and chewy mints; high-protein shakes, bars, candy, snacks, chips, crackers, desserts, breads, and shake mixes.

Nestlé's Stouffer's Lean Cuisine Products

Category	Product
Beef/veal	Meat lasagna
	Oriental beef stirfry
Chicken/turkey	Chicken & vegetables
	Chicken à l'orange
	Chicken cacciatore
	Chicken carbonara
	Chicken chow mein
	Chicken fettuccine
	Chicken in wine sauce
	Chicken Parmigiana
	Chicken with peanut sauce
	Glazed chicken
	Honey mustard chicken
	Sweet & sour chicken
Pasta	Cheese cannelloni
	Italian cheese ravioli

Source: Compiled by IBS-CDC from www.carbolitedirect.com, www.lowcarbsolutions.ca, and www.nestle.ca.

Exhibit 9 POPULAR DIET PLANS AND FADS

Diet Plans

South Beach

Miami cardiologist Arthur Agatston crafted the diet a few years ago to help heart patients.

How it works: Some carbohydrates are good, as in cereals and wheat breads. Bad carbs—biscuits, pasta, and such—should be avoided. The diet also cites good fats and bad fats. Users cut out bad carbs first and reintroduce banned foods later.

Claim to fame: Users lose 8 to 10 pounds in the first two weeks.

Alcohol: Beer is a bad carb. Wine and some whiskeys are acceptable. Red wine is a recommended option.

Dr. Phil's Ultimate Weight Solution

Created by Texan Phil McGraw, TV talk-show host and friend of Oprah Winfrey.

How it works: Users focus on eating habits, feelings about food and their environment. They find the reasons for failed weight loss attempts of the past and change them while eating better and exercising.

Claim to fame: Weight loss is a lifestyle change, not a temporary fix, Dr. Phil preaches.

Alcohol: Alcohol consumption is not directly addressed in the book.

Zone

Created by Barry Sears, a former researcher and biochemist.

How it works: Users arrange their eating to include a specific balance of 40 percent low-fat proteins, 30 percent carbohydrates in the form of fiber-rich fruits and vegetables and 30 percent fat. Proteins are eaten at each meal, and carbs are allowed in portions twice the size of protein portions. "Unfavorable carbohydrates," the book says, are foods like pasta, bananas and bagels that should be eaten in small portions.

Claim to fame: The diet is billed as the "revolutionary life plan to put your body in total balance for permanent weight loss."

Alcohol: Allowed as long as it's consumed with the appropriately portioned protein chaser.

Diet Fads

Hollywood 48-hour miracle diet programs

The Hollywood 48-hour miracle diet programs have been advertised heavily on television, on radio, and in print. These fad diets are some of the latest fads among diet product manufacturers. They promise you'll lose up to 10 pounds in 48 hours by drinking a liquid derived from plant juices. These fad diets consist of mostly liquids and have very few calories.

Grapefruit diet programs

There are several versions of grapefruit fad diets. All of them require that you eat half a grapefruit before every meal. The idea behind these types of fad diets is to induce natural fat-burning enzymes that are supposedly found in grapefruits. However, there is no scientific proof that grapefruit contains fat-burning enzymes.

Scarsdale diet programs

The Scarsdale diet program is similar to the popular low-carbohydrate fad diets only they incorporate lots of grapefruit and sugar-free products. These particular fad diets recommend that you take appetite suppressant pills. The idea is to lose up to one pound per day by following a low-carbohydrate plan based on chemical reactions rather than portion control. Snacking is not allowed, and meals consist of limited amounts of fresh fruits and vegetables with unlimited amounts of protein.

Cabbage soup diet programs

Cabbage soup fad diets are based on fat-burning soup that contains reduced calories. According to the plan, the more soup you eat, the more weight you will lose. This allows unlimited amounts of cabbage soup, and promises you will lose 10 to 15 pounds in one week.

Pritikin diet program

The Pritikin plan, developed by Nathan Pritikin, is more of a lifestyle modification program rather than a diet. It focuses on eating habits instead of the amount of food you actually consume. The idea behind these fad diets is to curb appetite cravings by eating foods that are high in fiber. There is no calorie counting, food weighing, or measuring with this plan. Overall this is one of the least destructive fad diets to hit the scene.

Source: Compiled by IBS-CDC from www.hoovers.com, "From Bread to Beer, High-Carb Foods Get a Low-Carb Makeover," January 11, 2004, and www.weight-loss-diet-center.com.

New diet plans and weight-loss therapies that promised "instant results" also began to flood the market (Exhibit 9). Tough competition existed in the form of weight-loss drugs like Pondimin, Redux (manufactured by Wyeth-Ayerst Laboratories), and Xenical (made by Hoffman La Roche), along with weight-loss clinics like Weight Watchers International, and natural remedies from companies like Herbalife.

Despite rising concerns about health risks involved in following Atkins over a prolonged duration and increasing competition, the management of Atkins Nutritionals remained confident about the future prospects of the company. As Scott Kabak remarked, "This is not a diet but a lifestyle. There's no ceiling to this business."[16]

Endnotes

[1]International Obesity Task Force, www.iotf.org.

[2]Dr. Atkins advocated a diet that was low in carbohydrate content and high on protein and fats. The idea was to derive the required calories from fats rather than carbohydrates, since the body converted unused carbohydrates into fat reserves, which led to weight-related problems and obesity.

[3]Food faddism was defined as a dietary practice based on an exaggerated belief in the effects of food or nutrition on health and disease.

[4]BMI = Weight in pounds/(Height in inches) ^{2} * 703. A person with BMI of 25 or more is termed overweight or obese.

[5]World Health Organization, www.who.int.

[6]IOTF is a part of the International Association for the Study of Obesity (IASO) and collaborates with the WHO in surveys related to obesity worldwide.

[7]Lyndel Costain, "Your Weight—Obesity Statistics," www.bbc.co.uk.

[8]Nancy Hellmich, "Obesity Predicted for 40% of America," www.usatoday.com, October 13, 2003.

[9]"The US Market for Weight Loss Eating and Product Trends," www.marketresearch.com, January 1, 2004.

[10]"Market for Weight Loss Products to Total Nearly $24 Billion by 2004," www.bccresearch.com, April 24, 2000.

[11]Michelle Leder, "Is the Atkins Brand Toast?" www.inc.com, December 2003.

[12]Daisy Whitney, "Atkins Nutritionals Opens Aurora Facility," www.denverpost.com, October 19, 2003.

[13]Leder, "Is the Atkins Brand Toast?"

[14]Ibid.

[15]"Weight Watchers Bursts at Seams—Thanks to Atkins," www.atkins-diet.cc, September 30, 2003.

[16]Leder, "Is the Atkins Brand Toast?"

Kodak at a Crossroads
The Transition from Film-Based to Digital Photography

Boris Morozov
University of Nebraska at Omaha

Rebecca J. Morris
University of Nebraska at Omaha

It's not clear with Kodak if they can successfully compete in the digital world. Are they a buggy whip manufacturer?[1]
David Winters, chief investment officer, Franklin Mutual Advisers, Inc.

It's a challenging strategy, there's no question about it. This is about our belief in where the company can go, and in our ability to bring growth back to the company in the next three or four years.[2]
Daniel Carp, CEO, Eastman Kodak Company

On September 25, 2003, Eastman Kodak Company's CEO, Daniel Carp, announced to investors that, after a three-year decline in sales, the company would stop making major investments in its consumer film business and devote its resources to becoming a "digital-oriented growth company." By the end of trading on the day of the announcement, Kodak's stock fell to an 18-year low. Institutional investors criticized Kodak's announced strategy, expressing annoyance at the company's intention to invest in ink-jet printing, a business dominated by Hewlett-Packard.[3] People at the company's meeting said that Carp did not provide enough detail on how the strategy would affect earnings before 2006.[4] Investment analyst Shannon Cross expressed the concerns of many investors, saying, "There are so many questions with regard to Kodak's future strategy . . . The track record we've seen out of management in terms of being able to hit targets and implement a strategy has been pretty spotty."[5]

Since January 1, 2000, when Carp took over as chief executive of Kodak, the company's revenues and net income had declined, its shares had dropped by 66 percent, and Standard & Poor's (S&P) had cut Kodak's credit rating by five grades.[6] Kodak had reduced its workforce by 49 percent since 1989, cutting 7,300 employees in 2002.[7] Plans were announced to eliminate up to 6,000 jobs in 2003 to stem future losses, cutting Kodak's traditional photography divisions in Rochester, New York, to fewer workers than the firm had employed during the Great Depression.[8] Kodak's income statements for 1993 through 2003 are presented in Exhibit 1. The company's balance sheets for the 11-year period ending 2003 are presented in Exhibit 2.

Despite investing over $4 billion in digital research and related technologies since the early 1990s, Kodak was characterized as a firm struggling to find its footing in the world of digital photography. Analysts gave Kodak only two to three years to find its

An earlier version of this case was anonymously peer reviewed and accepted by the North American Case Research Association (NACRA) for presentation at its annual meeting, October 7–9, 2004, Sedona, Arizona. Copyright ©2004 by Boris Morozov and Rebecca J. Morris. All rights reserved.

Exhibit 1 EASTMAN KODAK'S INCOME STATEMENT, 1993–2003 ($ in millions except per share)

	2003	2002	2001	2000	1999	1998	1997	1996	1995	1994	1993
Sales	$13,317	$12,835	$13,234	$13,994	$14,089	$13,406	$14,538	$15,968	$14,980	$13,557	$16,364
Cost of goods sold	8,130	7,391	7,749	7,105	6,731	6,372	6,986	7,423	7,046	6,442	6,952
Gross profit	5,187	5,444	5,485	6,889	7,358	7,034	7,552	8,545	7,934	7,115	9,412
SG&A expense	3,339	3,260	3,333	3,747	3,986	4,119	4,956	5,438	5,039	4,570	6,290
Operating income before depreciation	1,848	2,184	2,152	3,142	3,372	2,915	2,596	3,107	2,895	2,545	3,122
Depreciation and amortization	830	818	919	889	918	853	828	903	916	883	1,111
Operating profit	1,018	1,366	1,233	2,253	2,454	2,062	1,768	2,204	1,979	1,662	2,011
Interest expense	148	173	219	178	142	110	131	112	108	177	635
Nonoperating income (expense)	(23)	(66)	(29)	96	141	210	57	209	109	(143)	18
Special Items	(651)	(164)	(888)	(39)	(344)	(56)	(1,641)	(745)	(54)	(340)	(538)
Pretax income	196	963	97	2,132	2,109	2,106	53	1,556	1,926	1,002	856
Total income taxes	(66)	153	32	725	717	716	48	545	674	448	381
Minority interest	24	17	(11)	—	—	—	5	—	—	—	—
Income before extraordinary items	238	793	76	1,407	1,392	1,390	5	1,011	1,252	554	475
Extraordinary items	0	0	0	0	0	0	0	0	0	(266)	(2,182)
Discontinued operations	27	(23)	0	0	0	0	0	277	0	269	192
Adjusted net income	$265	$770	$76	$1,407	$1,392	$1,390	$5	$1,288	$1,252	$557	($1,515)
EPS excluding extraordinary items and discontinued operations	$0.83	$2.72	$0.26	$4.62	$4.38	$4.30	$0.01	$3.00	$3.67	$1.65	$1.44
EPS including extraordinary items and discontinued operations	$0.92	$2.64	$0.26	$4.62	$4.38	$4.30	$0.01	$3.82	$3.67	$1.66	($4.62)
EPS diluted; excluding extraordinary items and discontinued operations	$0.83	$2.72	$0.26	$4.59	$4.33	$4.24	$0.01	$3.00	$3.58	$1.63	$1.44
EPS diluted; including extraordinary items and discontinued operations	$0.92	$2.64	$0.26	$4.59	$4.33	$4.24	$0.01	$3.82	$3.58	$1.63	($4.62)
EPS basic from operations	$2.37	$2.77	$2.37	$4.73	$5.09	$4.42	$3.52	$4.50	$3.77	$2.40	$2.60
EPS diluted from operations	$2.37	$2.77	$2.37	$4.70	$5.03	$4.37	$3.46	n.a.	n.a.	n.a.	n.a.
Dividends per share	$1.15	$1.80	$1.77	$1.76	$1.76	$1.76	$1.76	$1.60	$1.60	$1.60	$2.00
Common shares for basic EPS (in millions)	286.5	291.5	290.6	304.9	318.0	323.3	327.4	337.4	341.5	335.7	328.3
Common shares for diluted EPS (in millions)	286.6	291.7	291.0	306.6	321.5	327.8	331.9	n.a.	n.a.	n.a.	n.a.

Source: Eastman Kodak 2003 annual report.

Exhibit 2   EASTMAN KODAK'S BALANCE SHEET, 1993–2003 ($ in millions)

	2003	2002	2001	2000	1999	1998	1997	1996	1995	1994	1993
Assets											
Cash and equivalents	$ 1,261	$ 578	$ 451	$ 251	$ 393	$ 500	$ 752	$ 1,796	$ 1,811	$ 2,068	$ 1,966
Net receivables	2,389	2,234	2,337	2,653	2,537	2,527	2,271	2,738	3,145	3,064	3,463
Inventories	1,075	1,062	1,137	1,718	1,519	1,424	1,252	1,575	1,660	1,480	1,913
Other current assets	730	660	758	869	995	1,148	1,200	856	693	1,071	679
Total current assets	5,455	4,534	4,683	5,491	5,444	5,599	5,475	6,965	7,309	7,683	8,021
Gross property and equipment	13,277	13,288	12,982	12,963	13,289	13,482	12,824	12,585	12,652	12,299	13,311
Accumulated depreciation	8,183	7,868	7,323	7,044	7,342	7,568	7,315	7,163	7,275	7,007	6,945
Net property and equipment	5,094	5,420	5,659	5,919	5,947	5,914	5,509	5,422	5,377	5,292	6,366
Investments at equity	426	382	360	0	2	3	25	31	74	@CF	@CF
Other investments	310	53	85	—	—	—	—	—	—	338	187
Intangibles	1,678	981	948	947	982	1,232	548	581	536	616	4,312
Deferred charges	1,147	972	482	0	0	0	0	0	0	0	0
Other assets	708	1,027	1,145	1,855	1,995	1,985	1,588	1,439	1,181	1,039	1,439
Total assets	$14,818	$13,369	$13,362	$14,212	$14,370	$14,733	$13,145	$14,438	$14,477	$14,968	$20,325
Liabilities and shareholder equity											
Long-term debt due in one year	$ 457	$ 387	$ 156	$ 150	$ 2	$ 78	$ 3	$ 245	$ 0	$ 0	$ 350
Notes payable	489	1,055	1,378	2,056	1,161	1,440	608	296	586	371	305
Accounts payable	834	720	674	817	940	947	943	966	799	703	737
Taxes payable	654	584	544	572	612	593	567	603	567	1,701	420
Accrued expenses	1,696	1,739	1,635	1,358	1,460	1,289	1,080	1,160	731	616	609
Other current liabilities	1,177	892	967	1,262	1,594	1,831	1,976	2,147	1,960	2,344	2,489
Total current liabilities	5,307	5,377	5,354	6,215	5,769	6,178	5,177	5,417	4,643	5,735	4,910
Long-term debt	2,302	1,164	1,666	1,166	936	504	585	559	665	660	6,853
Deferred taxes	81	52	81	61	59	69	64	102	97	95	79
Minority interest	45	70	84	93	98	128	24				
Other liabilities	3,819	3,929	3,283	3,249	3,596	3,866	4,134	3,626	3,951	4,461	5,127
Total liabilities	$11,554	$10,592	$10,468	$10,784	$10,458	$10,745	$9,984	$9,704	$9,356	$10,951	$16,969

Exhibit 2   (concluded)

	2003	2002	2001	2000	1999	1998	1997	1996	1995	1994	1993
Eastman Kodak equity	$38,324	$38,323	$38,322	$36,861	$36,495	$36,130	$35,765	$35,400	$35,034	$34,669	$34,304
Total preferred stock	0	0	0	0	0	0	0	0	0	0	0
Common stock	978	978	978	978	978	978	978	978	974	966	948
Capital surplus	842	849	849	871	889	902	914	910	803	515	213
Retained earnings	7,296	6,840	6,834	7,387	6,850	6,052	5,141	6,006	5,277	4,493	4,234
Less: treasury stock	5,852	5,890	5,767	5,808	4,805	3,944	3,872	3,160	1,933	1,957	2,039
Common equity	3,264	2,777	2,894	3,428	3,912	3,988	3,161	4,734	5,121	4,017	3,356
Total equity	3,264	2,777	2,894	3,428	3,912	3,988	3,161	4,734	5,121	4,017	3,356
Total liabilities and equity	$14,818	$13,369	$13,362	$14,212	$14,370	$14,733	$13,145	$14,438	$14,477	$14,968	$20,325

Source: Eastman Kodak 2003 annual report.

way or find itself fading into history. "The question is, can Kodak come up with the new products, the new insights that make sense out of digital?" asked a marketing professor from the Rochester Institute of Technology. "They have to be able to execute fast. They've got to differentiate themselves because they're going very heavily into a commodity market."[9]

The switch by consumers to digital photography was coming much faster than expected, and Kodak's traditional film, papers, and photofinishing businesses were declining. By the end of 2003, analysts expected that digital cameras would begin to outsell film cameras for the first time in the United States. The digital photography industry was fast-paced and crowded, offering razor-thin profit margins. Kodak was clearly at a crossroads. Would the strategy announced on September 25, 2003, position the company for growth, or would the company continue to decline?

Kodak's Challenges in 2003

With the slogan "You press the button, we do the rest," George Eastman put the first simple camera into the hands of consumers in 1888. In so doing, he changed an awkward and intricate process into something easy to use and accessible to nearly everyone. Since that time, the Eastman Kodak Company had led the way with an abundance of new products and processes to make photography simpler, more useful, and more enjoyable. However, in 2003, Kodak's CEO, Daniel Carp, faced challenges similar to those George Eastman faced over a century before: How to make the process of printing the picture even easier in an era of digital technologies.

The economy was in a recession in 2003, major market indexes were still at a low level, and investors were cautious. As a result of an unfavorable economic situation, shareholder wealth had been cut to a portion of what it was during the phenomenal technology-based run-up of the market in the late 1990s. The bursting of the technology bubble proved that the absence of a strong profit-generating business model could not be replaced with information technology solutions.

Kodak's moves paralleled those at many companies whose comfortable business models were threatened by rapid changes in information technology. When asked whether Kodak had moved into digital photography soon enough, Carp replied, "I saw my first digital camera inside Kodak in 1982. Today, we're arguably one of the top three providers of digital cameras in the U.S. So we did the right thing. At the same time, we shouldn't have walked away from the historical film businesses before they turned down, because it would have destroyed value."[10]

Under slumping economic and competitive market conditions, Kodak faced tough pressure from its existing competitors as well as from new rivals in the area of digital photography. Kodak coined the term *infoimaging* to describe the use of technology to combine images and information—a development that held the potential to profoundly change how people and businesses communicated.[11] Infoimaging was a $385 billion industry composed of devices (digital cameras and personal data assistants); infrastructure (online networks and delivery systems for images); services; and media (software, film, and paper) that enabled people to access, analyze, and print images.

Although the company had invested $4 billion in digital research and related technologies and spent many years perfecting its digital cameras,[12] Kodak's status as an iconic brand was threatened by the technological shift away from its cash-cow business of traditional film and film processing. In July 2003, Kodak reported flat sales and a 60 percent drop in second-quarter profits.

When announcing the latest rounds of workforce reductions in July 2003, Carp expressed his perspective on Kodak's challenges: "I think we're at the point where we have to get on with reality. The consumer traditional business is going to begin a slow decline, though it's not going to fall off a cliff." Was Kodak closer to the edge of the cliff than Carp thought? Could Kodak survive and thrive in the digital shift? Or would Kodak fade from history like a piece of film exposed to the light?

Growth in Digital Photography

Three years into the 21st century, the digital camera market was expanding at a fast pace. This was a major transfer from the previous decade of consumer photography as a largely mature market. Color film photography (also known as traditional photography) was a technology rich in history and closely tied to the art world. Eastman Kodak popularized color photography after the introduction of Kodachrome slide film in 1935.[13] Color print photography using 35-millimeter film grew rapidly in 1961 after the introduction of Kodacolor II print film.[14]

Demand for Digital Cameras

Digital photography was catching on fast in mainstream America as digital camera prices fell and image quality increased. The number of U.S. households owning a digital camera passed 1 million in 1997. By 2002, more than 23 million households owned digital cameras—this represented a 57 percent increase over 2001. Demand for digital cameras was expected to continue to increase, with more than 33 million households expected to own a digital camera in 2003. Exhibit 3 shows the growth in digital cameras and the decline in the number of households owning traditional film cameras. The 2.6 percent decline in traditional film cameras in 2002 was attributed in part to the growing demand for digital cameras and the rising popularity of one-time-use cameras. Market research projected continued further declines in traditional camera ownership.[15] Declines were also projected for sales of traditional film (down by 4 percent) and film processing (down by 3 percent) in 2003.

Although digital photography was making significant inroads with the mass market, technically sophisticated users were adopting digital technology at a higher rate. Among Internet-connected U.S. households, the estimate was that 60 percent had converted to digital cameras by the end of 2002.

Digital cameras generated a significant portion of industry revenues, accounting for $2.96 billion in revenues for 2002. This figure represented an increase of 22 percent over 2001 revenues. Revenues for traditional film, film processing, and traditional cameras had declined during this same period, as shown in Exhibit 4.

Industry experts predicted that the consumer shift to digital photography would be nearly complete by 2008, with sales of digital cameras nearly replacing sales of traditional film cameras such as 35-millimeter film cameras.[16] One-time-use cameras would continue to be popular, thus providing continued, although reduced, demand for film processing services.

What made digital cameras so attractive for consumers? Digital cameras gave users capabilities that were not possible with traditional cameras. Experts attributed the growth in digital photography to four factors—instant preview, sleek design, features, and price.[17] The technology of digital cameras allowed users to instantly view the shots they had taken and reshoot until they were satisfied with the results. The sleek design of many

Exhibit 3   **Number of Households Owning Cameras, 1996–2003 (in millions)**

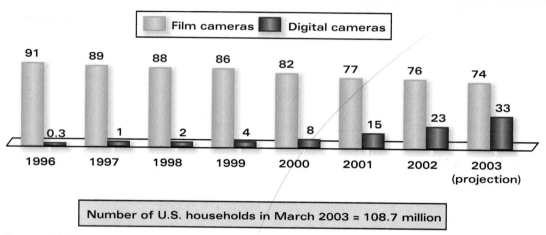

Number of U.S. households in March 2003 = 108.7 million

Source: PMA Marketing Research.

Exhibit 4   **Consumer Photographic Market Revenue, 2000–2002 (in billions of $)**

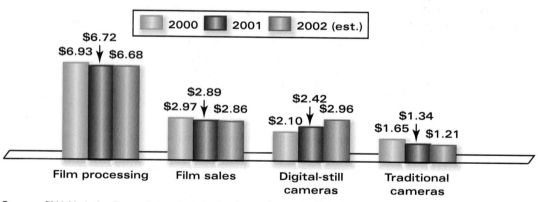

Source: PMA Marketing Research; www.pmai.org/pdf/0403_pixels_to_prints.pdf.

digital cameras made carrying one a fashion statement or a must-have item for teenagers and young professionals. Camera features also allowed digital users to capture short movies and to manipulate the images using photo-editing software that often came bundled with the camera. Price declines had made digital cameras much more affordable.

Michelle Slaughter, director of digital photography trends at InfoTrends Research Group, described digital cameras as an "essential communications device" for consumers.[18] "Consumers are becoming accustomed to the immediacy of digital photography and are integrating digital photos into their daily communications with friends and family and for work. As a result, digital cameras have a higher intrinsic value to consumers than film cameras. This, in turn, paves the way for digital camera sales to exceed film camera sales," predicted Slaughter.

Exhibit 5   PERCENTAGE OF CONSUMERS WHO BOUGHT DIGITAL CAMERAS IN 2002

By Age	
Age Group	**Percent**
18–24	9%
25–34	25
35–54	50
55 or older	17

By Income	
Household Income	**Percent**
Less than $25,000	6%
$25,000–$49,999	19
$50,000–$74,999	23
$75,000 or more	52

Source: *American Demographics*, July 1, 2003, p. 6.

Although the price of digital cameras had declined sharply, the average price of a digital camera was still significantly more expensive than for 35-millimeter cameras. In 2002, the average price for a digital camera was $328.[19] When compared with an average price of $137 for a 35-millimeter camera, it was no surprise that more than half of digital camera buyers were in households where the annual income was $75,000 or more. Half of the digital camera buyers in 2002 were between the ages of 35 and 54. Buyers in this age group and income bracket were in the prime segment for capturing family photos and often traveled more frequently than those in other age groups and income brackets. Age and income statistics for digital camera buyers in 2002 are shown in Exhibit 5.

Although market research showed that men tended to purchase digital cameras more frequently than women (58 percent versus 42 percent), women tended to be the primary users of the equipment.[20] Women were described as the preservers of family memories and were increasingly using digital cameras to capture birthday parties, holiday celebrations, or family vacations. Women were becoming more likely to spur the decision to buy a digital camera for the household.[21] Women with children were described as the "most photo active consumers"[22] and were expected to lead the demand for services such as digital printing.

Digital Printing Trends

Early adopters of digital photography consistently cited sending photos by e-mail as the number one reason for taking pictures with digital cameras.[23] Although mothers might e-mail friends and family the latest batch of baby photos, showing them off to a crowd gathered around a computer screen did not provide the same gratification and ease of use as looking at photos in an album. Consumers saw the ability to preview digital photos and to print only those they wanted as one of the strengths of the medium.

Exhibit 6   DESTINATION OF DIGITAL PICTURES AFTER CAPTURE

Picture Destination	Year		
	2000	2001	2002
Save, store, or keep	63%	68%	71%
E-mail	16	13	13
Print	12	14	20

Source: Photomarketing Association International, April 2003.

Few digital images were ever actually printed on paper. In 2000, only 12 percent of all digital images taken were printed. By 2002, this had increased to 20 percent of images taken.[24] Trends in the destination for digital images are shown in Exhibit 6.

The low ratio of printed photos to digital images was a big problem for companies wanting to profit from the printing process. According to analysts' estimations, companies such as Hewlett-Packard (HP), Lexmark, Canon, Seiko Epson, Olympus, and Eastman Kodak made almost nothing on the printers they sold. The money and profits were in the materials used to make prints. For instance, in summer 2003, HP saw profit margins of about 65 percent on ink-jet paper and ink, and roughly 30 percent margins on laser printing supplies.[25]

Consumers had a wide variety of options to choose from in obtaining prints from digital images. Digital photographers printed 2.1 billion images from digital cameras in 2003. Of these, 77 percent were printed with home printers, 6.4 percent were ordered from online photo services, 8.7 percent were made at a local retailer, and 3.6 percent were made using digital self-service kiosks. Consumers reported using "some other means" to produce 4.2 percent of all digital prints in 2003.[26]

Most consumers used their personal computers and home printers for printing their digital pictures; however, these were often perceived as lower-quality, more time-consuming, and more expensive than traditional film prints. More than half of digital camera users indicated they would print more digital images if they could make high-quality prints on their home printers.[27] Almost as many also indicated the printing of digital images at home would need to be easier and less time-consuming. Consumers often got confused while transferring pictures from their digital cameras to their computers. "There are so many ways for people to get into trouble when they try to print photos at home," said Kristy Holch, a principal at InfoTrends Research Group.

Online photo services provided another option. Services such as Snapfish, Shutterfly, and Ofoto allowed consumers to upload their photos; preview, crop, and manipulate them; and obtain high-quality snapshots by mail. Pictures could further be shared online with friends and relatives via online albums. Custom calendars, cards, books, and mouse pads could be ordered with the customer's photos. Prints were priced significantly less than those printed at home at 19–29 cents per print versus the 62-cent cost of a print made on a Kodak Easyshare printer.[28] Disadvantages to online photo services included slow photo uploads (especially for consumers with dial-up Internet connections) and the four to six days it took to receive the prints by mail.

In September 2003, 18.4 million people visited online photography sites that could be used for sharing and printing, according to Nielsen//Net Ratings. Yahoo! Photos had 4.7 million unique visitors, followed by the Time Warner AOL unit, You've Got Pictures, with 2.7 million. Ofoto and Snapfish each had 1.67 million users, and Kodak's online site drew 1.5 million.

Exhibit 7   Annual Change in Unit Sales of Film Rolls, One-Time-Use Cameras, and Film Processing, 1999–2003

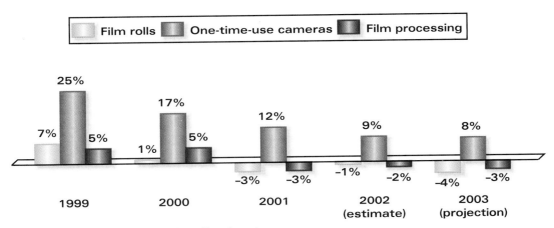

Note: Film processing includes both film rolls and one-time-use cameras.
Source: PMA Monthly Processing Surveys.

Local retailers such as Costco, Wal-Mart, and Walgreens provided another option for obtaining prints of digital images; however, these services failed to catch on with consumers. Many consumers did not realize that they could drop off their digital camera's memory card at the photo counter for printing. Others were reluctant to entrust the expensive memory cards to film processors. Retailers attempted to resolve these problems by adding self-service photo printing kiosks in their stores. Consumers could use the kiosks to edit photos and make their own prints from digital memory cards. Retailers launched advertising emphasizing ease of use and the immediacy of prints from the kiosks to overcome consumer's lack of awareness of this option. Expectations for growth in print volume at self-service kiosks were strong. "As digital camera users begin to use photo kiosks, print volumes on photo kiosks will increase dramatically," reported Kerry Flatley, a research analyst.[29] "Digital camera customers . . . will use photo kiosks as a high-volume source for their original photo prints," Flatley stated.

Impact on Demand for Traditional Film

The widespread adoption of digital photography had taken a toll on demand for traditional film and film processing. The volume of prints made from traditional films in 2002 declined by 700,000 over 2001 volumes. During the same time, digital prints grew by 1.3 million units. Digital images accounted for 6.1 percent of the total volume of prints made in 2002, up from only 2.4 percent in 2001.[30] Film sales were expected to decline by 4 percent in 2003, as shown in Exhibit 7.

One-time-use cameras were popular with consumers due to their convenience and low price, although the growth had slowed from 25 percent in 1999 to 8 percent in 2003. Film processing, which included both film rolls and one-time-use cameras, had declined significantly over the period from 1999 to 2003 due to the decrease in the use of traditional film among digital camera owners and the economic slowdown.

Other Digital Imaging Options

Another interesting market situation was developing—photo-capable cell phones. According to a survey done by experts in September 2003, more cell phones with integrated digital cameras than other types of digital cameras were sold in the first half of the year.[31] The research group Strategy Analytics stated that 25 million camera phones were purchased by consumers worldwide in the first half of 2003, compared with only 20 million digital still cameras.

"This is a milestone event, but it is just the first step towards the industry goal of getting a camera phone in every pocket," said Neil Mawston, senior analyst at Strategy Analytics' Global Wireless Practice. Mobile operators wanted to get customers to send picture messages regularly over their recently enhanced networks, in hopes of replicating the surprise success of text messaging. As the market for voice calls was becoming more competitive, nonvoice data revenues could prove vital for operators' profitability.

However, security and privacy concerns among companies represented one potential problem for the camera phone market. Besides, Strategy Analytics said, camera phones represented no major threat to the digital still camera market because the difference in picture quality between the two technologies was too great. A Canon marketing director expressed the view of most camera manufacturers when it called even the two-megapixel camera phone just a "distraction." "It's good to have mobile phone cameras," the marketing director said, "but their functionalities are limited in terms of storage, picture quality, zooming functionality, and power supply. Consumers will still go for the 'real camera' even though they have camera phones. Cameras on phones are just add-ons to give phones more functionalities."[32]

The Economist reported that camera phones might create a "nightmare scenario" for the traditional photography industry by hastening the decline of printed photos.[33] As camera phones improved, consumers might view on-screen images on phones, PCs, televisions, or even by beaming photos to a wireless-enabled picture frame. If this came to pass, "printing could become a niche, like film is expected to," said Chris Chute of the telecommunications consulting firm IDC.[34] Increased popularity of on-screen photo viewing would prove damaging for the photography industry, which depended on revenues from film processing and printing. Digital photography was threatening the first source of revenue. If camera phones caught on, cell phone operators could capture the second source, earning revenues by charging users for transmitting images.

Global Trends in Photography

Income distribution among countries influenced the sales of the cameras around the world. While sales of digital cameras were booming in developed countries like the United States and Japan, consumers from emerging economies such as China bought more traditional cameras.

China was developing into a center of photography—and was doing so more rapidly than anyone would have expected only a few years ago. More than 5 million cameras were sold in China in 2002, and 400,000 of those were digital models (see Exhibit 8). This figure was set to increase, and Chinese consumers were expected to buy more than 3 million digital cameras by 2005. However, there were also other reasons why China was so important for the photographic and imaging sector, since every market segment was still growing in this country, not just the one for digital devices.

Exhibit 8   Camera Sales in China, 2000–2002, with Projections for 2003–2005

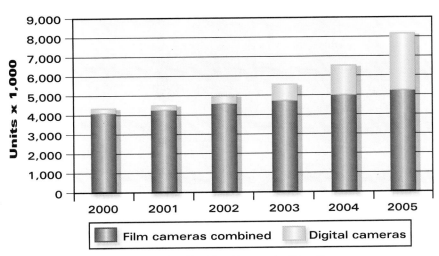

Source: www.prophoto-online.de/photokina/photokinanewsEnglish.pdf.

A large amount of additional sales potential remained unexploited in China. China's per capita consumption of film in 2003 was a mere 0.1 a year, compared to an average of 3.1 in Europe and 3.6 in the United States. China was still a long way from reaching market saturation even though film sales were rapidly increasing. Revenues from digital camcorders, photographic paper, data projectors, scanners, and printers were growing rapidly as well.

Competitive Standings and Digital Strategies

In the segment of traditional photography, Kodak's main brand competitors were Canon, Sony, and Fuji, with Fuji being the biggest competitor. According to analysts' estimations, Kodak's competitors in the digital photography industry were Sony, HP, and Fuji.

Eastman Kodak captured 18.3 percent of the digital market, compared with the 15.3 percent share it had captured in the first six months of 2003. Sony led the market with a 21.5 percent share, with Canon, Fuji, HP, and Nikon following, with 14.7 percent, 8.7 percent, 7 percent, and 5.7 percent, respectively.[35] The market shares are shown in Exhibit 9.

Although Kodak was a major player in the photography market (both digital and traditional), it was far from being the biggest (see Exhibit 10). Eastman Kodak's earnings before interest, taxes, depreciation, and amortization (EBITDA) of $1.2 billion were just a fraction of its closest competitor Fuji's of $3.11 billion. Competitors Sony and Canon had EBITDA figures of $7.06 and $6.05 billion, respectively.

Sony

Sony had been on the digital wave since the mid-1990s, when it introduced its first PlayStation.[36] Nobuyuki Idei, chairman and CEO, played a key role in moving Sony

Exhibit 9   Market Shares in Digital Imaging

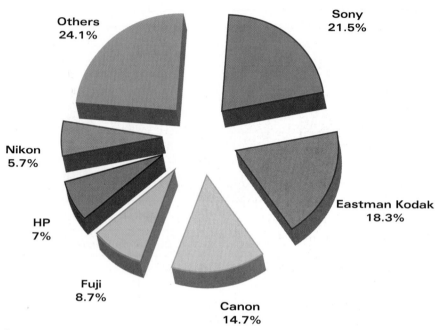

Source: "Digital Imaging's Winners and Losers," *Forbes,* August 9, 2004.

Exhibit 10   COMPETITOR COMPARISON FOR 2003

	Kodak	Canon	Fuji	Sony
Market capitalization	$8.32 billion	$43.19 billion	$15.80 billion	$36.56 billion
Employees	70,000	98,873	72,569	161,100
Revenue growth	−3.00%	11.80%	0.4%	9.10%
Gross margin	32.17%	50.31%	41.64%	25.28%
EBITDA	$1.20 billion	$6.05 billion	$3.11 billion	$7.06 billion
Operating margins	2.79%	14.21%	6.20%	1.25%
Net income	$238 million	$2.62 billion	$532 million	$170 million
Earnings per share	$0.83	$2.948	$1.036	$0.09
Price/earnings ratio	35x	17x	30x	440x

Source: Company annual reports and Web sites.

into the digital network era by emphasizing the integration of audiovisual and information technology products. He was responsible for Sony's image campaign "Do you dream in Sony?" and helped coin the term "digital dream kids."[37]

Sony was a Japanese consumer electronics and multimedia giant. The firm produced music, movies, and television shows as well as the devices to bring them to the consumer. The electronics division produced videogame consoles, personal digital assistants, DVD and MP3 players, digital camcorders, digital cameras, computers, and car audio products.

A team of developers gathered at a Sony laboratory in 1995 to "develop a digital still camera filled with enjoyment."[38] Sony's Cyber-Shot cameras were developed as the first "self-shooting" digital still cameras. Unburdened by a legacy in traditional film, developers relied on Sony's experience as a leading consumer technology company to develop a full line of digital cameras targeted to men and women between the ages of 25 and 55. Sony positioned its cameras at a premium or fair price based on cutting-edge technology and design. "You'll never see Sony offer a $99 camera," predicted one senior digital imaging analyst.[39] Sony's digital cameras ranged from about $180 for a point-and-shoot model to just under $1,000 for an advanced-featured Pro model.

Canon

Japan's Canon Inc. had come a long way since its days as a producer of cheap cameras. Much of Canon's success against its archrival had come on the watch of the company's president, Fujio Mitarai. A nephew of a Canon founder, Mitarai spent 23 years working in New York before returning to Japan in 1995 to head the company. Canon operated in the document reproduction markets producing copiers, fax machines, and scanners. Canon's optical segment produced diverse products such as television broadcast lenses and semiconductor manufacturing equipment. The camera division produced camcorders, binoculars, lenses, and digital cameras. Canon was relatively late to the market with its digital products, but the products it had introduced were hits.[40]

On November 21, 2001, Canon U.S.A. Inc., a subsidiary of Canon Inc., launched a marketing campaign featuring its PowerShot digital cameras and Bubble Jet printers working in concert to showcase Canon's leadership in digital photo solutions for the 2001 holiday season.[41] "The camera and printer are the stars of this 'production' number from beginning to end. Canon has a 60-year history in optics/lens technology for cameras, as well as creating its own printing technology—a combination our competitors cannot claim. By showcasing the 'digital duet' of our digital cameras and printers, we show the viewer that Canon products create picture perfect results that are unmatched by our competition," said Rick Booth, assistant director of advertising for the Canon Photographic Products Group.

Canon offered digital cameras for a wide variety of users at different price points. A simple point-and-shoot model was priced at slightly less than $200, while a professional-level digital single-lens reflex (SLR) camera sold for almost $8,000.

Fuji

Fuji, a longtime rival of Kodak, offered a complete portfolio of imaging, information, and document products, services, and e-solutions to retailers, consumers, professionals, and business customers. Fuji had been digital since 1998, when it introduced the first digital camera. "Fuji's solution was to start a suite of online options to share, order, pay for and collect digital photos," Dane Anderson of IDC, pointed out. By the summer of 2003, Fuji had developed a program for digital photography called Image Intelligence. This integrated system of digital image-processing software technologies came from the culmination of nearly 70 years of imaging expertise.

Fuji's traditional film, photo paper, developing chemicals, and nondigital printers accounted for 42 percent of the firm's 2003 sales. Experts expected the percentage of sales due to traditional photography to shrink to 31 percent by 2006.[42]

Fuji had introduced digital minilabs in the market. A minilab offered a service similar to that of traditional picture printing—consumers could print their digital photos by dropping off their digital memory cards and returning later to pick up finished prints. With more than 5,000 labs in the marketplace, Fuji had about 60 percent of the U.S. digital minilab market, including deals to put machines in 2,500 Wal-Mart and about 800 Walgreens outlets. Those two chains handled about 40 percent of the U.S. photo-processing market.

Hewlett-Packard (HP)

HP provided consumer and business customers with a full range of technology-based products, including personal computers, servers, storage devices, networking equipment, and software. The company also included an information technology service organization that was among the world's largest. Known primarily by consumers for its dominance in computer printers, HP expanded into the digital imaging segment as a way to continue to fuel demand for HP printers and ink cartridges.

HP's breadth also provided an important advantage to consumers, according to HP vice president Chris Morgan. "We think consumers are going to want their products to be interoperable. Digital photography is a natural extension given our strength in computing and image processing," said Morgan. Consumers will "want to move content from camera to computer to email or DVD, from camcorder to computer to TV, or just skip the computer and go directly from device to playback system. That plays to our advantage. Not only are we the No. 1 consumer computer company in the world, we think that our understanding of big-business ecosystems will be a powerful advantage in helping us develop these solutions," he continued.[43]

Prices for HP's digital cameras ranged from about $100 to $400. As part of the firm's strategy to provide interoperable solutions that allowed consumers to connect various devices, HP offered several different camera and photo printer bundles and camera and docking station bundles.[44]

HP had a personal computer dubbed PhotoSmart, which had a built-in docking slot for uploading photos only from HP's latest digital cameras and unified photo software that handled downloading, storing, exchanging, and printing photos.

HP was also trying to get more people to share digital pictures electronically because that got more people making prints. HP's Instant Share software allowed consumers to preprogram e-mail addresses and photo-sharing Web sites into their cameras. After making pictures, users specified where they wanted the images sent, and the pictures were mailed the next time the camera was connected to the PC.

Nikon

Nikon was well known for its traditional photography products—35-millimeter cameras, lenses, and other consumer optical products. Nikon also produced equipment used in the manufacturing of semiconductors and a broad range of other optical products such as binoculars, microscopes, eyewear, and surveying equipment. Imaging products such as camera equipment comprised 57.6 percent of Nikon's net sales in 2003.[45]

Nikon targeted amateur photographers with its line of Coolpix cameras. These cameras ranged in price from about $140 to $850. The Coolpix line offered a full range of stylish and simple-to-use cameras designed to appeal to the first-time user and the more advanced photography hobbyist. Nikon also offered a line of digital single lens reflex (SLR) cameras that targeted advanced and professional photographers who wanted multifeatured, easy-to-use digital cameras. Digital SLR cameras permitted the use of interchangeable lenses and were designed to provide sharper, clearer images at faster shutter speeds than other digital cameras. Nikon digital SLR cameras ranged in price from $900 (camera body only) to well over $1,200. Nikon used the trademarked phrase "Nikon . . . If the picture matters, the camera matters" in the marketing of its cameras.[46]

Kodak's Photography Unit

Eastman Kodak was primarily engaged in developing, manufacturing and marketing traditional and digital imaging products, services, and solutions for consumers, professionals, health care providers, and other commercial customers. The company operated in four segments: components, health imaging (18 percent of company's total revenue), commercial imaging (11 percent of total sales), and photography (70 percent of revenue).

The photography segment included traditional and digital product offerings for consumers, professional photographers, and the entertainment industry. This segment combined traditional and digital photography and photographic services in all its forms—consumer, advanced amateur, and professional. Kodak manufactured and marketed various components of these systems, including films (consumer, professional, and motion picture); photographic papers; processing services; photofinishing equipment; photographic chemicals; and cameras (including one-time-use and digital).

Product and service offerings included kiosks and scanning systems to digitize and enhance images, digital media for storing images, and a network for transmitting images. In addition, other digitization options were available to stimulate more pictures in use, adding to the consumption of film and paper. These products served different groups of customers, including amateur photographers as well as professional, motion picture, and television customers. Technically, Eastman Kodak provided the services of picture creation to everyone who requested it, adjusting these services for specific groups of consumers.

Since Kodak's bread-and-butter unit was its photography unit, the company's stock price heavily depended on this unit's performance. The firm's stock price declined from more than $80 to $20 per share (see Exhibit 11) as revenues from traditional photography declined. In June 2003, Standard & Poor's (S&P) Rating Service placed Kodak on a CreditWatch, with negative implications, expressing concerns that economic, competitive, and leisure travel pressures would continue to impair Kodak's sales and earnings.[47] S&P analysts expressed concern that Kodak's transition to digital imaging would hurt future profitability for the firm by reducing high-margin film sales. Kodak's migration to digital technologies might also require additional restructuring as the firm adapted to evolving market conditions.

Kodak's restructuring actions prior to 2003 were primarily of a tactical nature. Three modifications between 1999 and 2003 indicated that the company's traditional film and photography businesses, while still hugely important as a source of cash, were becoming less of a central focus in a world where images were increasingly captured as bytes and bits. These modifications signaled management's attempt to keep up with the market, meaning that Eastman Kodak was losing the role of market maker.

Exhibit 11   Eastman Kodak's Stock Price, January 1999–September 2003

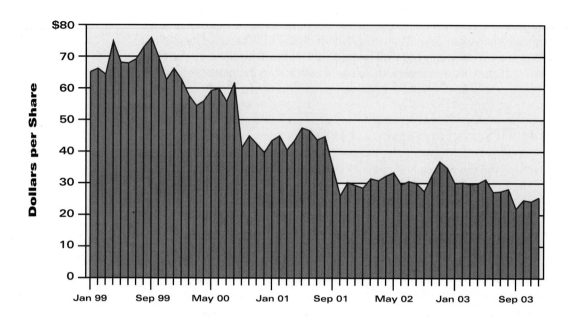

Tough Choices for a Traditional Photography Company

Although it did not announce a change to a digital strategy until 2003, Eastman Kodak was moving toward this objective through acquisitions of smaller companies successful in the digital area. "Digital imaging is going to be like the cellular telephone business," George Fisher, Kodak's then CEO, predicted in 1997. "Highly competitive, very high growth, good profits for the leader, but not for the followers."[48]

In general, Kodak's performance in the new market conditions was varied. In some areas it was successful; in others it was not. Kodak's president and chief operating officer, Antonio Perez, had conceded that the company was behind the curve in printers, an area it regarded as key to its future digital profits. This was not for lack of effort. A joint attempt in 2000 to introduce a desktop photo ink-jet printer with Lexmark flopped, partly because the product's direct-to-camera interface never caught on. Most consumers made their digital prints via PC-to-printer links. Kodak said its newly introduced system for docking a thermal printer with a PC, designed for greater ease of use, was faring much better, and would generate a respectable $100 million in sales in 2003, its first year.

Kodak entered the market segment of digital minilabs. However, due to technical problems, it suffered some losses. Kodak purchased machines made by a manufacturing partner that broke down frequently, printed pictures of poor quality, and frustrated customers. Fuji's rival Frontier machines, meanwhile, were gaining market share. Kodak changed its minilab partner to Noritsu Koki Company of Japan. As result of this change, Kodak mentioned that the machines had been well received.

Phogenix, a joint venture between HP and Kodak to develop smaller digital photo printers for retail outlets, crumbled in May 2003 because the technology had already become obsolete by the time the machines were brought to market. In a joint statement, Matthias Freund, chairman of the Phogenix board of directors and chief operating officer of Kodak's Consumer Imaging Products and Services business, and Mary Peery, member of the Phogenix board of directors and senior vice president of HP's Digital Imaging & Publishing business, said, "Both HP and Kodak believe the technology being developed by Phogenix continues to offer a viable solution for on-site digital photo processing. However, based on the anticipated return on invested capital for the parent companies, each company has separately decided to focus its own investments on other opportunities."[49]

The Phogenix labs, small enough to fit in stores typically unequipped to house typical automated film-developing machines, would have cost retailers about $40,000 but could produce only about 250 prints an hour, compared with more than 1,000 for Fuji's Noritsu minilab. Fuji's system cost $139,000 to $245,000, analysts estimated.

Kodak had had some notable digital successes. Kodak's popular EasyShare cameras were the second best-selling digital cameras in the United States in the first half of 2003, behind only those of Sony. After successfully focusing on the lower end of the camera market, Kodak was planning to begin selling more-expensive digital cameras aimed at tech-savvy shutterbugs. The company was diversifying its product line's depth and width, aiming at new segments of the market.

Finally, Kodak believed it had a strong management team. CEO Daniel Carp was considered to have good leadership skills. He was helped by other specialists, known for their extensive experience in the digital photography industry. Executive by executive, he replaced a top management cadre steeped in the ways of traditional photography with a team that had almost a pure digital pedigree. Except for Carp, almost every senior executive was from outside the company. Carp's management team was composed from new hires from Lexmark, HP, General Electric, and Olympus Optical.

Shift from Traditional Photography to Digital Photography

On September 25, 2003, Kodak unveiled its digitally oriented strategy. "We are acting with the knowledge that demand for traditional products is declining, especially in developed markets," Carp said. "Given this reality, we are moving fast—as digital markets demand—to transform our business portfolio, with an emphasis on digital commercial markets. The digital world is full of opportunity for Kodak, and we intend to lead it, as we have led innovation in the imaging industry for more than a century."[50]

Kodak was among the last photographic giants to announce its digital plans. The truly global scale of Kodak's operations represented an additional complexity for Kodak. While some parts of the world were outgrowing the shoes of traditional photography (e.g., developed countries like the United States, western European countries, and Japan), other parts of the world still exhibited growth opportunities for old film production.

Kodak recognized that, on the one hand, there were growth opportunities in areas that provided 30 percent profit margins (traditional film). These opportunities were in unstable emerging economies of countries like China, India, and the Russian Federation. On the other hand, opportunities in new digital photography looked better than those in traditional photography. The expected growth rate of the digital photography industry was about 26 percent until 2012. However, pursuing these opportunities would require substantial capital investment of up to $3 billion (according to stock analysts).

Daniel Carp's PowerPoint presentation for the September announcement showed that Kodak's new strategy would be based on three pillars—commercial imaging, health imaging, and consumer imaging.[51] Additional pillars under construction were ink-jet printers, commercial workflow management, and flat-panel displays.

The digital and film imaging strategy focused on four components:[52]

1. Manage the traditional film business for cash and manufacturing share leadership
2. Lead in distributed output
3. Grow the digital capture business
4. Expand digital imaging services.

Under the first of these components, Kodak planned to reduce costs in its traditional film businesses and cut back on marketing expenditures for film (shifting instead to processing). The firm would continue to offer premium, high-margin products such as Perfect Touch processing and High Definition film in developing markets, while establishing leadership in emerging markets such as China and Russia.

Leading in distributed output referred to Kodak's plan to capture more of the demand for digital prints, whether produced in retail locations or at home. Kodak's plan called for the development of improved minilabs and kiosks that could print images faster, and for an increase of 50,000 kiosks by 2004. Kodak's home output strategy centered on the printer dock that allowed Kodak EasyShare users to transfer images directly from their cameras to a printer through a docking station. Users could then select and print images without a PC. Increasing use of Kodak's online photo service, Ofoto, was also a part of this strategy.

The digital capture business component referred to the further development of Kodak's digital cameras. Kodak intended to obtain a top-three worldwide market position for digital cameras by 2006. This goal would be reached by becoming the industry standard for ease of use and by moving to more sophisticated cameras.

Kodak planned to expand its digital imaging services by expanding the products and services offered through Ofoto to include items such as picture frames, calendars, and photo albums. Kodak also planned to develop kiosks that could print images from mobile phones. Rollout of this product had already begun in Asia and Europe and was expected to be ready for the U.S. market by the end of the fourth quarter of 2003.

On October 22, 2003, about 60 institutional shareholders met in New York City to examine other strategy alternatives, objecting to Carp's "risky" strategy of investing $3 billion into emerging digital markets.[53] Investors attending the meeting controlled about 25 percent of Kodak's stock. They felt that Kodak had been struggling with the transition to digital photography for almost 10 years and that, while it had enjoyed some success, the progress had not been enough, especially given the billions of dollars that had already been spent. Investors pushed for radical cost cuts to quickly boost earnings but had not yet come to an agreement about any long-term strategies for Kodak.

Carp argued that the cost-cutting plans touted by the investors "really aren't viable, practical options" and that Kodak had few alternatives other than slashing its dividends and pouring its resources into digital technologies.[54] Herbert A. Denton, president of Providence Capital, the host for the meeting, said, "We want them

[Kodak] to let us under the tent and really show us why this strategy is best."[55] Was Carp's strategy best? Would Kodak's transition to a digital strategy be enough to help it reach its goal of becoming a $20 billion company by 2010?[56]

Endnotes

[1]C. Wolf, "Kodak Stock Plummets as Dividend Cut: Slashed by 72%," *Bloomberg News,* September 26, 2003, p. FP03.

[2]Ibid.

[3]C. H. Deutsch, "Some Positive News Aside, Kodak's Quarterly Profit Falls 63%," *New York Times,* October 23, 2003, p. C9.

[4]Wolf, "Kodak Stock Plummets."

[5]B. Dobbin, "Kodak Works Through Profit Drop," *Times Union,* October 23, 2003, p. E4.

[6]Wolf, "Kodak Stock Plummets."

[7]Ibid.

[8]Ibid.

[9]Dobbin, "Kodak Works Through Profit Drop."

[10]"What It 'Boils Down To' for Kodak," *Business Week,* November 23, 2003.

[11]www.kodak.com.

[12]"Kodak Struggles to Find Its Focus," *Leader-Post,* July 28, 2003, p. B5.

[13]"Milestones—The Chronology," http://kodak.com/US/en/corp/kodakHistory/1930_1959.shtml, accessed December 6, 2004.

[14]A. Mutz, "Digital Photography Fundamentals and Trends," www.codesta.com/knowledge/technical/digital_photography/printable_version.aspx, March 26, 1993 (accessed December 6, 2004).

[15]Photo Marketing Association International, "The Path From Pixels to Print: The Challenge of Bringing Digital Imaging to the Mass Market," from www.pmai.org/pdf/0403_pixels_to_prints.pdf, April 2003 (accessed November 22, 2004).

[16]InfoTrends Research Group, "Digital Cameras Will Nearly Replace Film Cameras by 2008," press release, www.infotrends-rgi.com/home/Press/itPress/2003/6.25.03.html, June 25, 2003 (accessed November 29, 2004).

[17]I. Ismail, "Digital Photography Is Hot," *New Straits Times Press* (Malaysia), June 7, 2004, p. 9.

[18]InfoTrends Research Group, "Worldwide Consumer Digital Camera Sales to Reach Nearly 53 Million in 2004," press release, www.infotrends-rgi.com/home/press/itPress/2003/11.19.03.html, November 19, 2003 (accessed November 29, 2004).

[19]S. Yin, "Picture This," *American Demographics,* July 1, 2003, p. 6.

[20]Photo Marketing Association International, "The Path From Pixels to Print."

[21]"Digital Camera Ownership Moving Deeper into Mainstream Market, According to New InfoTrends/CAP Ventures Study," *Business Wire,* October 12, 2004.

[22]Photo Marketing Association International, "The Path From Pixels to Print."

[23]Ibid.

[24]Ibid.

[25]A. Ferrari, "The Push for More Digital Photo Prints," www.forbes.com/2003/10/30/cx_af_1030printing.html, October 30, 2003 (accessed December 6, 2004).

[26]R. A. Dalton Jr., "In a Tech World, It's a Snap," *Newsday,* September 26, 2004, p. E6.

[27]Photo Marketing Association International, "The Path From Pixels to Print."

[28]Dalton, "In a Tech World, It's a Snap."

[29]InfoTrends Research Group, "New Wave of Photo Kiosk and Digital Print Solutions Driven by Digital Photography," press release, www.infotrends-rgi.com/home/Press/itPress/2002/5.20.02.html, May 20, 2002 (accessed November 30, 2004).

[30]Photo Marketing Association International, "The Path From Pixels to Print."

[31]"Camera Phones Outselling Digital Cameras—Report," www.forbes.com/newswire/2003/09/26/rtr1092489.html, September 26, 2003 (accessed December 6, 2004).

[32]Ismail, "Digital Photography Is Hot."

[33]"Mobile Snaps," *The Economist,* July 3, 2003.

[34]Ibid.

[35]A. Ferrari, "Digital Imaging's Winners and Losers," www.forbes.com/infoimaging/2004/08/09/cx_af_0809imagingupdate_ii.html, August 9, 2004 (accessed December 3, 2004).

[36]"Sony History," www.sony.ca/sonyca/view/english/corporate/corporate_sonyhistory1.shtml (accessed December 6, 2004).

[37]"Executive Biographies," www.sony.com/SCA/bios/idei.shtml (accessed December 6, 2004).

[38]"Cybershot: The Roots," www.sony.net/Products/cybershot/the_roots_01.html (accessed December 6, 2004).

[39]B. S. Bulik, "Sony, Kodak Lead U.S. Battle for Share in Digital Cameras," *Advertising Age* 75, no. 22 (May 31, 2004).

[40]P. Klebinkov and B. Fulford, "Canon on the Loose," www.forbes.com/global/2001/0723/036_3.html, July 23, 2001 (accessed December 6, 2004).

[41]"New Canon Marketing Campaign Highlights 'Digital Duet' of Digital Cameras and Printers," *Business Wire,* November 21, 2001 (accessed via Lexis/Nexis November 30, 2004).

[42] "Fuji's Digital Picture Is Developing Fast," www.businessweek.com/print/magazine/content/04_08/b3871064. htm, February 23, 2004 (accessed November 29, 2004).

[43] "HP's Strategy: Connect 'Device Islands,'" www.businessweek.com/technology/content/dec2003/tc2003129_2679_tc137.htm, December 9, 2003 (accessed November 29, 2004).

[44] "Digital Cameras," www.shopping.hp.com (accessed November 29, 2004).

[45] "Nikon Portfolio," www.nikon.co.jp/main/eng/portfolio/index.htm (accessed November 29, 2004).

[46] Nikon Web site, www.nikonusa.com/home.php (accessed November 29, 2004).

[47] "Kodak Debt Placed on CreditWatch Negative," www.businessweek.com/print/investor/content/jun2003/pi20030619_9134_pi036.htm?chan=pi&, June 19, 2003 (accessed November 29, 2004).

[48] S. N. Chakravarty, "How an Outsider's Vision Saved Kodak," www.forbes.com/forbes/1997/0113/ 5901045a_3.html, January 13, 1997 (accessed December 6, 2004).

[49] "HP, Kodak to Dissolve Phogenix Venture," www.printondemand.com/MT/archives/000142.html, May 23, 2003 (accessed December 6, 2004).

[50] Kodak press release, www.kodak.com/eknec/PageQuerier.jhtml?pq-path=2709&pq-locale=en_US&gpcid=0900688a8022df48, September 25, 2003 (accessed November 29, 2004).

[51] "Kodak Strategy Review," http://media.corporate-ir.net/media_files/IROL/11/115911/Reports/Carp_Sept25.pdf, September 25, 2003 (accessed December 6, 2004).

[52] "Kodak Strategy Review: Digital and Film Imaging," http://media.corporate-ir.net/media_files/IROL/11/115911/Reports/Masson_sept25.pdf, September 25, 2003 (accessed December 6, 2004).

[53] W. Symonds, "Not Exactly a Kodak Moment," *Business Week,* November 24, 2003, p. 44.

[54] Ibid.

[55] C. H. Deutsch, "Some Positive News Aside, Kodak's Quarterly Profit Falls 63%," *The New York Times,* October 23, 2003, p. C9.

[56] Kodak press release, www.kodak.com/eknec/PageQuerier.jhtml?pq-path=2709&pq-locale=en_US&gpcid=0900688a8022df48, September 25, 2003 (accessed November 29, 2004).

Adam Aircraft

Carl Hedberg
Babson College

John Hamilton
Babson College

William Bygrave
Babson College

As the sleek, six-seat Adam A500 performed a graceful arc overhead, Babson College MBA John Hamilton, vice president of marketing for Adam Aircraft Industries (AAI), had to smile. Earlier that morning, he had read an article describing the difficulties and pitfalls associated with designing, building, and certifying new aircraft. In the last 30 years, there were countless examples of start-up aircraft manufacturers that had tried and failed to deliver new products to the small and midsized aircraft markets. In fact, the only two start-up companies that had recently succeeded had been builders of very basic, single-engine aircraft.

Like most MBAs, John had been taught to analyze companies based on all the standard metrics: the management team, product viability and appeal, market demand, capitalization, and financing potential. While Adam Aircraft appeared to be a winner on all counts—including the progress it was making in the lengthy and complex certification process—the company did not have the many millions of dollars it would need to bring its products to market and reach positive cash flow.

Talking with some of his peers in venture capital, John had come to understand that private equity investors were a fickle bunch. The vast majority preferred to invest in biotechnology, telecommunications, and other industries with historically well-defined harvest potential. Following the market correction in 2000, the flow of venture capital had significantly diminished, and investments outside of these core industries had all but ceased.

John had grown up in a family of aviators. He had been a licensed pilot for over 18 years. Since flying machines were not only his vocation but also his passion, he had to wonder whether this love was clouding his analysis. The market was clearly desperate for products like the plane performing flawlessly overhead, but did Adam Aircraft have

Carl Hedberg and John Hamilton prepared this case under the supervision of Professor William Bygrave, Babson College, as a basis for class discussion rather than to illustrate either effective or ineffective handling of an administrative situation. Funding provided by the F. W. Olin Graduate School and the gift of the class of 2003, and the Frederic C. Hamilton Chair for Free Enterprise.

what it took to succeed where so many had failed? Could it continue to advance toward certification and full-production capability, or would the challenges that lay ahead slow it down enough to increase its burn rate to a level that would discourage even the most ardent investor?

John did know that in less than five years company founder Rick Adam had orchestrated the fabrication of two flying prototypes—the A500 twin piston and the A700 jet—at a speed of design and production that had turned heads in all sectors of the aviation industry. Certification on both models was expected in the coming year—two years ahead of a number of well-funded competitors. With their third product—the A600 twin turboprop—nearly ready to fly, Adam Aircraft had become the one to watch in 2004.

John zipped up against the cold December wind and tracked the A500 as it snapped a sharp wing-turn on its approach to their home field at Centennial Airport in Englewood, Colorado. Another successful flight test. He smiled; definitely the one to watch . . .

The Entrepreneur

George Adam Sr. had been a career Air Force officer who had flown B-17 and B-29 bombers during World War II. His son Rick, born in 1946, grew up on Air Force bases and had always expected to follow his father into the military cockpit. When a color-vision deficiency kept him out of the Air Force Academy flight program, he joined the Army, attended West Point Academy, and then switched his commission to the Air Force.

Rick specialized in computer science, and as an Air Force captain he ran the Real Time Computer Centers at the Kennedy Space Center and at Vandenberg Air Force Base. During that time he earned his MBA at Golden Gate University, and later, as a civilian, he found his way to Wall Street. At Goldman Sachs he ran the IT department as a general partner. In 1993, Rick left Goldman to start his own business: New Era of Networks, an enterprise application integration software developer. The wildly successful company went public and grew to a market capitalization of over $1 billion. It was later acquired by the Sybase Corporation.

All the while, Rick had never lost sight of his first love, and in the early 1990s he learned to fly. Since his business required lots of travel, he was able to log over a thousand pilot-hours in just a few years by flying himself to meetings. He started in an old Skymaster, moved into a 1978 Mitsubishi MU2, and ultimately got type-rated in a 1993 Citation jet. While Rick had had the opportunity and the personal wealth to progress quickly as a pilot, he recognized that the majority of owner-operators weren't as fortunate:

> As a pilot you have to go in steps; you can't get ahead of yourself. So, as you log more and more hours in the air, you can begin to fly increasingly more complex airplanes. The problem is that when you are ready to make the move from a single to a twin-engine aircraft, there are very few products to choose from. Most of the aircraft are based on old designs, which makes them tough to fly and expensive to own and operate.
>
> One of the most popular production twin-engine planes on the market is the Beechcraft Baron—introduced in 1961! Because they quit building their more capable pressurized twins in the mid-80s, and stopped innovating at the same time, the old Baron is still their frontline light twin—and a new one costs over a million dollars. See, as the volume of orders has gone down, the prices have continued to climb (see Exhibit 1).

Exhibit 1   **Annual New U.S. Manufactured General Aviation Unit Shipments/Billings, 1974–2002**

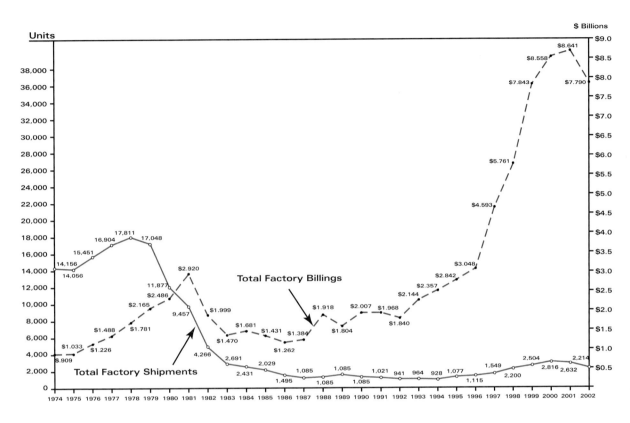

Source: *General Aviation Manufacturers Association (GAMA) Statistical Databook 2002.*

Rick added that the alternative to buying a new version of an old design was far worse:

> Demand for used planes is huge, because they are cheaper than new ones, and, since nothing has changed in the industry, pilots can buy something that may have been manufactured in the 70s or 80s, but it looks like a new plane. Right now the average age of a general aviation[1] aircraft is over 30 years (see Exhibit 2), and it's getting one year older every year.
>
> And frankly, these airplanes become unsafe. If you look at the accident rate in aircraft, it climbs dramatically with age. So even though there are strict regulations on maintaining these aircraft, it's hard to keep an old plane in good shape. Systems like the wiring just get to a point where they are too old to be reliable.

The more Rick thought about this aging factor, the more certain he became that the only solution would be an entirely new generation of general aviation products. It wasn't long before he had begun to evaluate the commercial viability of such a venture.

Exhibit 2   AVERAGE AGE OF U.S. GENERAL AVIATION FLEET IN 2002

Aircraft Type	Engine Type	Seats	Average Age in Years
Single-engine	Piston	1–3	36
		4	33
		5–7	28
		8+	43
	Turboprop	All	12
	Jet	All	31
Multi-engine	Piston	1–3	36
		4	33
		5–7	33
		8+	37
	Turboprop	All	26
	Jet	All	28
All aircraft			31

Source: *General Aviation Manufacturers Association (GAMA) Statistical Databook 2002.*

Spotting the Opportunity

Almost immediately upon joining the ranks of experienced aviators, Rick began to contemplate the type of effort that would be required to deliver a new plane to the marketplace:

> Every time I went to a cocktail party or barbeque, all the pilots would go off into a corner and start talking pilot stuff. And since everybody was moaning about the lack of new products, I became convinced that there was a huge demand. So in the early 90s I started developing strategies for launching a new aircraft company.
>
> Now, I have launched a few entrepreneurial ventures, and when you think there is a big opportunity, you make sure to stop and evaluate why it hasn't been done before. Why isn't anyone pursuing this opportunity? What do I know, or what do I see that nobody else is seeing? Very often, entrepreneurial opportunities occur when a series of prior developments makes it possible to accomplish the once unachievable. You reach a point where you finally have all the ingredients to make it happen.

To illustrate, Rick referred to the electronic organizer on the table:

> There were at least a dozen attempts to bring out handheld devices ahead of the PalmPilot. The most notable was Jerry Kaplan's GO Corporation. Kaplan saw the opportunity, had the right idea, and raised $50 million in funding back in the early 90s. But since the chips weren't small enough, the displays weren't big enough, and the batteries weren't powerful enough, his product looked like a brick. He spent 50 million bucks and failed, simply because his great idea was ahead of the prevailing technology.

In a similar way, the Beechcraft Corporation was ahead of its time when, in the late 1970s, it set out to develop a new class of business aircraft. The five-and-a-half-year,

Exhibit 3   The Beechcraft Starship

The Beechcraft Starship, a twin-turboprop pusher design, was the first all-composite pressurized airframe ever certified by the FAA. The task was larger than simply developing an all-new aircraft. Beech had to master an innovative technology, work hand-in-hand with FAA regulators, build a new manufacturing facility, and train a specialized workforce. Much of this effort was concentrated on areas the industry had not addressed before. The company built 53 Starships in all before ceasing production in the early 1990s.

$300-million development program resulted in the federally certified Starship (see Exhibit 3). The futuristic craft was the world's first pressurized, all-composite business turboprop.[2] Many in the industry had high hopes that the Starship would usher in a new age of modern propeller-driven aircraft, but that was not to be.

Developed by Scaled Composites, a cutting-edge aircraft design enterprise founded by visionary Burt Rutan,[3] the Starship project brought about the development of Federal Aviation Authority (FAA) standards for the construction of composite aircraft. Unfortunately for Beechcraft, this was a very long and difficult process resulting in an aircraft that was heavier and more expensive than predicted. As a result, the Starship's performance was only marginally better than the existing fleet—and yet its price was far higher. Despite its commercial failure, this project was the first in a series of events that would begin to spark new life into the long-ailing general aviation aircraft industry in America.

A Convergence of Factors

Between 1978 and 1992, the general aviation industry had suffered a 95 percent unit sales decline and the loss of over 100,000 jobs. Over that same period, general aviation (GA) manufacturers had spent as much to defend product liability suits as they had spent to develop new aircraft in the 30 years following the Second World War.

When Congress enacted the General Aviation Revitalization Act (GARA) in 1994 to protect aircraft builders from lawsuits on planes that were older than 18 years, it revitalized an industry nearly wiped out by two decades of what lawmakers were calling lawsuit abuse and trial lawyer profiteering.

The 1990s also brought about enormous advances in computing power and computer-aided design and modeling (CAD/CAM) software. Airframe geometry could now reside in the computer, with all of its internal structures defined electronically as three-dimensional models. By the end of that decade, expensive wind tunnels and physical scale models were being replaced by computational fluid dynamics software. Manufacturing and tooling capabilities had made great strides as well.

Rick said that after a couple of kit manufacturers[4] managed to achieve commercial certification for their composite designs, he figured that the time was right:

> In the early 90s, all the innovation was being done in composites and kits. Then Lancair and Cirrus announced that they were going to take what they had learned and build production airplanes. Everybody who loves flying was rooting for them, hoping they would make it, and sure enough, they both got certified.
>
> I'm watching this process and realizing that while there were quite a few single-engine, nonpressurized, fixed-gear start-ups out there, nobody had yet brought an innovative product into the middle market. It was real clear to me that pilots wanted a new twin, and once I had seen the success that the composite guys had down in single engines, I came to the conclusion it could be done in the twin-engine area.

By the latter half of the 1990s, a number of well-financed firms were competing to introduce a personal jet into this middle-market space by 2006. Rick looked at these projects and wondered: Would it be possible to design a single airframe that could accommodate jet engines as well as twin pistons? He didn't have the answer, but he knew who would.

The Project Begins

Although he was still running his software venture, in 1998 Rick decided to put up a million dollars to get into the aviation business. At the same time, he brought in a talented partner: former FAA trial attorney John Knudsen, an experienced aviator with a career in the U.S. Navy as a carrier-based attack pilot. Understanding that a commercially viable new design—whether it was a jet or a twin piston—would have to blend superior performance capabilities with curb appeal, Rick said that they contacted the best in the business:

> We met with Burt Rutan and showed him some requirements, definitions, and preliminary designs for a twin piston. Since carbon fiber lends itself to much more aerodynamic shapes than you can get with aluminum construction—I told him to make it look as much like a jet as possible.
>
> As always, he had some wild stuff and he had some stuff that was more middle of the road. We narrowed four or five design concepts down to an in-line, front and back engine configuration, with twin booms to get to the tail.

If this plane was going to be the step up for single-engine pilots that Rick was envisioning, they understood that ease of operation would be critical. With this in mind, they chose a centerline thrust arrangement, since, compared to twins with the power plants mounted on the wings, the push-pull design significantly reduced the difficulty of flying with one engine not functioning. Having settled on what he felt was an exciting airframe, Rick noted that they had no desire to conquer more than one frontier at a time:

Exhibit 4   The M-309

Named for Burt Rutan's 309th completed design, the Model 309 was built with the aim of delivering a very safe twin-engine aircraft that would give good performance and benign single engine handling qualities. The pressurized cabin was designed to carry a pilot and five passengers.

The central goal of this program was to develop an aerodynamically refined aircraft. However, there were several features that were more representative of a full-production airplane. For example, there were several major structural components that had been produced as single-cure parts. The outboard wings, horizontal tail, elevator, rudders, and flaperons had no secondary bonds in their primary structure. This allowed for a lighter, stronger, and safer structure due to the significant elimination of fasteners and secondary bonds.

Source: www.scaled.com.

The Eclipse 500 project has raised $400 million so far in its effort to build a light business jet. They tried to develop a new airframe and a new engine at the same time. The engine didn't work, and now they are two years off schedule.

I'm a raging incrementalist; the way to innovate is to take one step at a time. We chose power plants, avionics, and construction methods that had previously been certified by the FAA for other planes; our only major innovation initially will be with the shape of the airframe. I figured that once we had that done, we could innovate on something else later on. It's just so tough to bring a certified new airplane to market; we had to be very careful to avoid adding layers of complexity—and lots of time and money.

The team at Scaled Composites began work on the conceptual designs for Adam Aircraft in May of 1999, and cut the first tool in late August.[5] When the M-309 (see Exhibit 4) lifted off on its maiden flight in March 2000, it marked the most rapid manned-aircraft development program in the company's history.

Despite the price tag, Rick understood that this "experimental" was a one-of-a-kind, hand-built model that would serve only as a research vehicle. Conventional evidence suggested that the development of an FAA-certified version of the M-309 would take a few years, at least a couple more flying test planes, millions of engineering man-hours, and hundreds of millions of dollars. Rick was determined, however, to make sure that his aircraft company was anything but conventional.

Research and Innovation

With the M-309 outfitted with an array of data collection equipment, the AAI team proceeded to log over 300 flight hours in 2000 as they scrutinized the full range of the craft's aerodynamic characteristics and performance capabilities. Rick explained that with regard to understanding the commercial viability of the plane, their destinations were often just as important as their in-flight calculations:

> We collected aerodynamic data as we flew the M-309 to air shows around the country, and that gave us the opportunity to survey the market and listen to what potential customers had to say. We completely reengineered the original design. For example, we increased the size of the empennage,[6] and also moved the door for easier access to the cabin. By the fall of 2000, I had come to the conclusion that there was a significant market for this kind of aircraft.

Rick, who was self-funding most of the start-up costs, had been busy recruiting a top-tier management group. Nearly everyone on his 10-member executive staff was an accomplished pilot, and collectively they had many years of experience from all corners of the aviation industry, including Boeing, Beechcraft, Martin Marietta, Cirrus, Lancair, Scaled Composites, Eclipse, the U.S. military, and the FAA.

In December, Adam Aircraft established its home base at Centennial Field, just south of Denver. As they got down to the business of fitting the factory in advance of tooling design for the first production model, now called the Adam A500, Rick said that because of the direct relationship between time to market and project cost, they had no choice but to innovate:

> I had recently heard from an industry expert that the standard budget for a new airplane project is about $250 million. Since there has been so little success in this industry to date, it would be nearly impossible to raise that kind of money for a start-up airplane company like ours. That's a long way from $250 million, but still, we knew that the only way we could make financing achievable was by cutting development costs by at least 75 percent.

He added that to accomplish such a feat would require not only brilliant engineering but also the development of a culture unheard of in aviation manufacturing:

> Being a lifetime computer guy, speed and innovation seem very natural to me. We knew right off that time was not our friend; either we get this plane up and certified quickly, or we'd attract competitors and run out of money. One of the first things we did was to institute the kind of 24-hour scheduling that we had used to run our data centers and networks.
>
> Our people now work 12-hour, overlapping shifts; three-day weeks, with voluntary overtime on Sundays. So while our competitors are putting in five shifts in a calendar week, we are getting up to 21—in addition to high morale and very low attrition.

Over the past few decades, powerful aircraft builders like McDonnell Douglas, Lockheed, and Boeing had developed highly sophisticated modeling design tools that

Exhibit 5   **Five Axis Tooling Mill**

Fabricating the Air-Stair door tool out of dense foam material

were powered by multimillion-dollar mainframe computers. The PC age had put those capabilities into the hands of small shops like Adam Aircraft. For an off-the-shelf cost of about $3,000 per system, the company was able to set up a 40-station CAD/CAM engineering center with all the capabilities of the big guys. Rick said that by tying this powerful design architecture into the tooling mill downstairs (see Exhibit 5), the company was able to add efficiencies by keeping the entire design process in-house:

> With aluminum technology, you design the part, and then you bid it out for tooling. You award the tooling—which typically costs over a million dollars— and six to nine months later, the tool comes back. If it's wrong or you want to make a design change, you have to start all over. Because we have our own tooling mill, we can do it fast the first time, and more importantly, continue to modify the tool quickly until we get it right.

The management team understood that merely coupling rapid application development with a 24/7 working environment would not provide enough of an edge to develop the full line of airplanes they were envisioning. Rick explained that for that to happen, they would need to adopt a computer industry concept that, if successful, would change the face of general aviation manufacturing forever:

> PCs are developed around a common set of rules as to how the parts interact with each other. That way, you can change the keyboard, the disc drive, the

screen, whatever you want, and it won't tear up your memory or your software; that's called modular architecture.

There has been little progress in modular architecture in airplanes—until now. We are building enormous modularity into our design so we can do things like move the wing location, modify the cabin size, change the power plants; all kinds of things. What that means is that we will bring this first plane to certification status for about $50 million bucks. For another 10 million, we'll adjust the modules slightly and get a jet. For another 5 million, we'll get a turbo prop.[7]

Detractors felt that this was wishful thinking, and pointed out that the modular architecture approach could potentially compromise performance. Some noted that since each power plant system would have different weight and structural characteristics, installing all three on essentially the same airframe could cause center-of-gravity problems. In addition, critics felt that using a single-wing and empennage design would mean that two of the planes, or maybe even the whole line of products, would fly at less than optimum performance.

The AAI team felt that they were on top of those challenges with innovations like their "smart tunnel," a device that enabled engineers to shift the wing location on the fuselage in order to control the range of the aircraft's center of gravity. The team felt that this technology and other specialized systems they were devising would give AAI engineers the means to modify the underlying airframe to accommodate a wide range of engine choices and configurations. In addition, they felt that this engineering strategy would enable them to leverage their research and development spending over at least three commercially viable aircraft designs. Time would tell.

Working with the FAA

Throughout 2001, all manner of government and industry groups had visited the plant to witness the A500 project as it came together very nearly on schedule, and on budget. Predictably, the one group that would not be offering praise or extra points for speed of design and assembly was the Federal Aviation Authority.

The task of the FAA was to see to it that the Type Certification (TC) approval process (see Exhibit 6) proceeded in a careful and thorough manner. The complex system of inspections and testing was similar to what health care companies faced with the Federal Drug Administration (FDA). Like the FDA, the FAA required exhaustive proof that products were safe before they could be marketed to consumers. In the aviation industry, that regulatory oversight translated into lots of time and money. While it was true that successful new entrants like Lancair and Cirrus had helped pave the way for subsequent efforts, Rick said that getting through the regulatory process would still be one of AAI's greatest challenges:

Although the FAA is constantly working to improve the aircraft certification process, for good reason it is designed to be extremely arduous. Nevertheless, we do have a number of advantages over our predecessors. For example, as opposed to submitting aircraft designs on paper, we can now send designs to the FAA electronically. By doing this, we save a ton of time and, most importantly, are assured of the highest degree of accuracy in our documentation process.

By the time the A500 had been cleared for its inaugural flight in July of 2002, a second test aircraft was already under construction (see Exhibit 7), and fabrication of

Exhibit 6   FAA TYPE CERTIFICATION PROCESS

Familiarization Meeting

Meeting to establish a partnership with the applicant. It is an opportunity to develop mutual understanding of the type certification process as it applies to the applicant's design. It's highly recommended as a beginning point in the process.

Formal Application

Applicant's formal application for a Type Certification (TC) includes a cover letter, Form 8110-2, and a three-view drawing.

Preliminary Type Certification Board

At this initial formal meeting, the project team collects data about the technical aspects of the project and the applicant's proposed certification basis and identifies other information needed to start developing the Certification Program Plan. Special-attention items are also identified at this time.

Certification Program Plan (CPP)

A key document, the Certification Plan addresses:

- The proposed FAA certification basis.
- Noise and emission requirements.
- Issue papers.
- Special conditions, exemptions, and equivalent level of safety findings.
- Means of compliance.
- Compliance checklists and schedules.
- Use of delegations/designees.

Technical Meetings

Held throughout the project, technical meetings (e.g., specialist and interim TC meetings) cover a variety of subjects. Team members may:

- Approve test plans and reports.
- Review engineering compliance findings.
- Close out issue papers.
- Review conformity inspections.
- Review minutes of board meetings.
- Revise the Certification Program Plan.
- Issue new FAA policy guidance.
- Review airworthiness limitations.
- Review instructions for continued airworthiness.

Preflight Type Certification Board

Discussions at the preflight TC board center on the applicant's flight test program, including conformity inspections and engineering compliance determinations.

Type Inspection Authorization (TIA)

Prepared on FAA Form 8110-1, the TIA authorizes conformity and airworthiness inspections and flight tests to meet certification requirements. The TIA is issued when examination of technical data required to TC is completed or has reached a point where it appears that the product will meet pertinent regulations.

Conformity Inspections and Certification Flight Tests

Conformity inspections ensure that the product conforms with the design proposed for type certification. Flight tests are conducted in accordance with the requirements of the TIA.

Aircraft Evaluation Group (AEG) Determinations

The AEG works with certification engineers and FAA flight test pilots to evaluate the operational and maintenance aspects of certificated products through such activities as:

Flight Standardization Board (FSB)

- Pilot type rating.
- Pilot training checking, currency requirements.
- Operational acceptability.

(continued)

Exhibit 6 (continued)

> Flight Operations Evaluation Board (FOEB)
> ■ Master minimum equipment list (MMEL).
> Maintenance Review Board (MRB)
> ■ Maintenance instructions for continued airworthiness.
>
> **Final Type Certification Board**
>
> When the applicant has met all certification requirements, the ACO schedules the final formal TC board. The board wraps up any outstanding items and decides on the issuance of the TC.
>
> **Type Certificate**
>
> The certifying ACO issues the TC when the applicant completes demonstration of compliance with the certification basis. The TC data sheet is part of the TC and documents conditions and limitations to meet FAR requirements.
>
> **Postcertification Activities**
>
> This includes the Type Inspection Report (TIR)—to be completed within 90 days of issuance of the unique technical requirements and lessons learned—the Certification Summary Report (CSR), and the Postcertification Evaluation, which closes out the TC project and provides the foundation for continued FAA airworthiness monitoring activities such as service bulletins, revisions to type design, malfunction/defect reports, and Certificate Management for the remainder of the aircraft's life cycle.

parts for a third had begun as well. Comprising the entire testing fleet, these three aircraft would each undergo a series of exhaustive flight and static tests—many requiring the construction of customized systems and fixtures (see Exhibit 8). If all proceeded as planned, AAI expected to achieve certification for the A500 by the first half of 2004.

The Customers

When AAI flew its A500 to the Experimental Aircraft Association's (EAA) AirVenture Convention in Oshkosh, Wisconsin, that summer, the company brought along a full-size mockup of the plane's cockpit and fully appointed interior. Vice President of Marketing John Hamilton noted that Oshkosh was an excellent show since it attracted buyers from all the major markets for its $895,000 twin piston:

> There are two basic markets for aircraft like the A500; owner-flown, and professionally flown. The owner-flown market is just that. The owner of the aircraft is also the pilot in command. In the professionally flown market, non-owners fly the aircraft. It sounds like a silly distinction but it makes a difference in how you market the aircraft.
>
> I would say between 70 and 80 percent of our A500 customers will be owner-operators. These folks are evaluating our aircraft from the pilot's seat. They will be very tuned in to things like the performance of the aircraft, its handling characteristics, and the electronic systems in the instrument panel. In addition, because they also manage the scheduled maintenance requirements, they will be very sensitive to serviceability.
>
> Marketing to the professionally flown segment is a bit different since they are more focused on the needs of their client-passengers. They'll be interested in things like how comfortable the seating is, how much baggage area is available, whether the plane has a toilet or an entertainment system. They'll also want a pressurized cabin so they can fly over weather, a plane that looks and feels safe and substantial—and a plane that is appealing to the eye.

Exhibit 7   Fuselage Construction of the A-500 SN002

Vacuum bag on fuselage tool

Laying up the carbon material into the tail boom tool

Exhibit 8   **Custom-Built Static Test Rig**

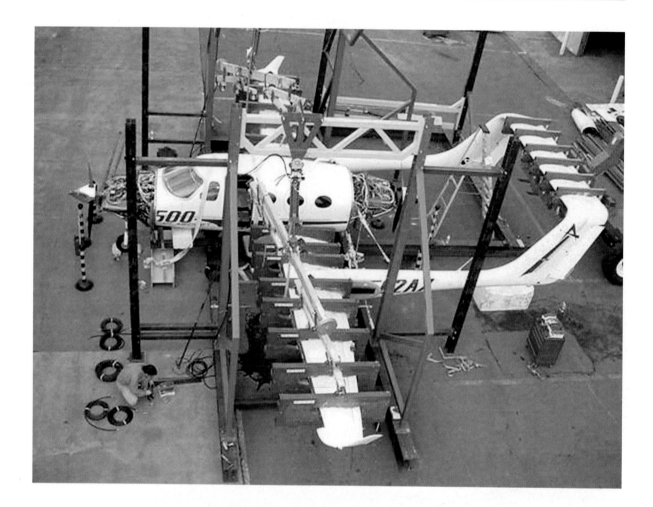

In addition, John emphasized that aviation consumers of all types demanded top service and easily maintainable aircraft:

> You've got to have absolute first-rate service. Customers can't have difficulty getting parts or finding somebody to work on their airplane.
>
> Pilots are also hesitant to adopt something that is new. We're not Cessna, we're not Beechcraft, and we're not Piper. Those guys have been around forever, and they've built a ton of airplanes.
>
> That's why with everything we do—from delivery, to flight training, to service and parts—we have to prove to our customers that there is a very compelling reason why they should adopt this new aircraft.

John added that the company's unique design modularity would play an important role in serviceability:

> One feature of the A500 that customers will love is how easy it is to access the systems on the aircraft that need to be inspected and or replaced. A great deal of engineering work has been performed to dramatically reduce the amount of

time it takes maintenance personnel to complete the necessary service tasks. This will result in reduced downtime and lower costs of operation. Going the extra mile for owners in this area will pay substantial dividends in customer satisfaction.

Eyeing the Future

In October 2002, the company announced its plan to introduce the next aircraft. The company also indicated that due to the modular systems, the A700, a six- to eight-seat stretched-fuselage twin-jet, would share 80 percent part commonality with the A500. Some critics doubted Rick's assertion that since the A700 would present only an incremental development challenge for his talented engineers, AAI would be able to build a flying model within a year.

Ten months after completing preliminary design work, the A700 jet shocked and amazed the general aviation world by making a surprise appearance at the 2003 EAA AirVenture event. Industry dignitaries such as Secretary of Transportation Norman Minetta and FAA administrator Marion Blakey welcomed the aircraft with words of support and congratulations. The aviation press was buzzing; if the company was able to hold to its schedule and achieve FAA certification for the A700 in the fourth quarter of 2004, the $1.995 million craft would be the first to market in this emerging, closely watched segment (see Exhibit 9).

John explained that this keen interest in light jets was directly related to the need for more efficient transportation solutions:

> The average mission is less than a two-hour flight, with three and a half people on board—meaning nearly every business jet in America is oversized for what it does.
>
> This emerging personal jet segment is based on the same concept that Japanese automakers used to take on Detroit 30 years ago. With gas prices going up, why not build a car which was more suitably sized to the average driver's need? Reducing the size and weight of the machine dramatically improved its operating efficiency. We're building a smaller and lighter aircraft designed for the most common trip length and passenger load to deliver optimal efficiency in the twin-jet category.

In addition to the benefits of an incremental improvement in the efficiency of twin-engine jets, personal jet aircraft were being viewed by some as the solution to the gridlock in the hub-and-spoke airline system. Rick Adam described one official's views on the subject:

> Dr. Bruce Holmes at NASA[8] has performed extensive studies of the transportation system and has concluded that the best way to increase capacity in the air is by directing more traffic to the 5,000 underutilized regional airports in this country. Regional travelers would fly point-to-point out of small airports and never enter the hub and spoke system unless they plan to fly across the country or abroad.
>
> Because this air taxi system would require a massive fleet of aircraft to achieve network coverage, the price of the aircraft and its operating cost are critical components to the success of the system. Aircraft like the A700 could get the cost per seat mile down to a level where the average business traveler could afford the service.

Exhibit 9   VERY LIGHT JET SEGMENT: COMPETITOR PROFILES

Manufacturer	Product	List ($000)	Seats	Cruise Speed	First Delivery	Orders to Date (11/03)	Home Base
Avocet	Pro-Jet	2,000	6–8	420	Late 2006	200	Westport, Connecticut
Cessna	Citation Mustang	2.295	6	391	Late 2006	300+	Wichita, Kansas
Safire	Safire Jet	1,395	6	437	2006	300+	Miami, Florida
Eclipse	Eclipse 500	950	3–6	432	2006	2,060	Albuquerque, New Mexico

We don't need the air taxi model to take off for the A700 to be a successful project, but it would certainly provide a fantastic upside to our company.

With two distinct models flying, Rick and his company now had a real story to tell. CFO Mike Smith observed that for outside investors and municipal development groups, one of the most attractive aspects of the AAI plan was that the economics seemed entirely within the range of possibility:

We could break even right out of this facility [at Centennial Field] by adding roughly 100 production people to our current staff of 150. With the A500, the current overhead breaks even at somewhere between 35 and 40 planes a year, and the jet would be roughly a third of that. We have a component capacity for about 100 planes a year, and an assembly capacity for about 40 or 50. The great thing about this company is at just 50 airplanes a year, we're making money. So far we have taken deposits for over 50 twin pistons.[9] Once we are certified, we anticipate a surge in orders.

By late 2003 the planes had appeared on a host of aviation magazine covers (see Exhibit 10) and in a wide range of business publications including the *New York Times, The Wall Street Journal,* and *Forbes* magazine. Nearly all seemed to be anticipating a significant American success story.

The Critical Juncture

Heading out for a meeting over in Boulder, John fired up his twin-engine Beechcraft as the A500 crossed his path on its way back to the hanger for further testing. As he taxied out in preparation for take-off, John recalled an earlier meeting with a reporter from an aviation magazine. When she had asked him whether he thought much about the possibility of failure, he prefaced his response with a story:

You know, we were speaking with some guys in the airborne fire-fighting business. They currently use airplanes that are roughly in the A500 class to fly lead-in for fire-fighting tankers. These spotter planes fly low and left of the tankers, and tell those pilots where to make the drop.

They asked if we could put a window overhead on the A500 so their lead pilots could have good visibility of the tanker high and right. They told us that none of the established competitors they had spoken with would even consider that kind of modification. Our engineers told him that it would take us about a week to figure that out.

The point is, that's why I don't spend much time thinking about the business risk of this venture. Adam Aircraft has been surprising the experts and our potential customers from the very beginning; there is no reason to assume we won't continue to do so.

As John lifted off and banked north toward Boulder, he realized that his thrill of flying had never waned since he was a kid. Although he loved his 30-year-old Beech, he knew it wouldn't last forever—and there were a bunch of pilots just like him out there waiting for something new. He felt certain that Adam Aircraft would be the one to answer that call.

Exhibit 10   Magazine cover: AAI's A700 and A500

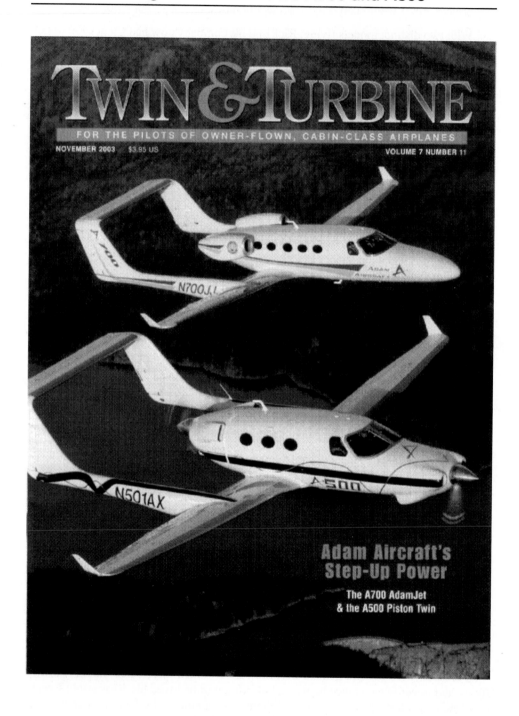

Endnotes

[1]General aviation (GA) is a term comprising all of aviation other than government and scheduled air transport (commercial airlines), and includes privately owned aircraft, charter services, business-owned aircraft, and many more types of working aircraft that are not, strictly speaking, for transportation. Although a large part of GA consists of recreational flying, an equally large part involves important commercial activities such as flight training, shipping, surveying, agricultural application, air taxi, charter passenger service, corporate flying, emergency transport, and firefighting.

[2]An easy-to-understand composite material would be an adobe brick; wet mud and straw—mixed together and dried. The result is a material stronger than either mud or straw. Composite airframes typically consisted of a carbon, graphite, or glass fiber reinforcing material, and an epoxy resin binder. Alone, these substances had very little strength, but when combined and properly cured, they became a composite structure that was very strong. Since this construction process lent itself to fluid design, composite airframes were often sleeker and more pleasing to the eye than their aluminum counterparts.

[3]As a schoolboy, Burt Rutan had designed award-winning model aircraft, and by age 16 had learned to fly. After receiving a bachelor's degree in aeronautical engineering from Cal Poly, he worked for the U.S. Air Force as a Flight Test Project Engineer at Edwards Air Force Base in California. In 1972, at age 29, he founded Rutan Aircraft Factory, which sold plans and kits for Rutan-designed aircraft. His science-fiction-like aircraft designs were considered risky by established aircraft manufacturers, who made sure that the regulators of the Federal Aviation Administration were aware of their concerns. While he successfully sold a number of different unique designs, he became frustrated by the litigious regulatory environment and substantial liability claims that had put many private aircraft manufacturers out of business. In 1982, Rutan chose to leave the homebuilt industry in favor of larger-scale designs for companies. His new firm was Scaled Composites.

[4]Kit planes were considered experimental by the Federal Aviation Administration. This designation was originally intended for aircraft designers who wanted to do research, or for amateur pilots who wanted to learn about aerodynamics as they built their own planes. Because these aircraft were barred from commercial use, the FAA felt that there was no need to impose its exhaustive and very expensive certification process on this class of aircraft.

[5]In composite engineering, a tool was the master mold that the composite material was layered into before being vacuum-compressed, and then oven-cured—a process known as thermosetting—at 240 degrees.

[6]The empennage, commonly called the tail assembly, was the rear section of the body of the airplane. Its main purpose was to provide stability to the aircraft.

[7]Turboprops were designed to carry high passenger (or cargo) loads over relatively short distances (under 300 miles or so). Short-field take-off and landing capabilities, and the ability to use kerosene instead of aviation fuel, had contributed to the popularity of turboprops, particularly in developing countries.

[8]Dr. Bruce Holmes led the Small Aircraft Transportation System Program (SATS) unit at NASA. SATS was a driving force in the incubation of innovative technologies necessary to bring affordable, on-demand flight service by small aircraft in near-all-weather conditions to small community airports.

[9]Initial deposits to secure a delivery position for an A-500 were between $50,000 (non-escrowed) and $100,000 (escrowed). An additional $50,000 progress payment would be due at aircraft type certification, with an additional $100,000 progress due six months prior to the scheduled delivery date of the aircraft. The balance would be due upon delivery.

Creating Customer Value at Rocky Mountain Fiberboard

John J. Lawrence
University of Idaho

Doug Haines
University of Idaho

Michelle O'Neill
University of Idaho

In early 2002, Luke Waterman stared at the year-end 2001 financials for Rocky Mountain Fiberboard (RMF). The company, which produced strawboard—an environmentally friendly substitute for wood-based particleboard—had lost $1.9 million on sales of $1.7 million in its third year of operations. RMF had over $4.5 million in debt and payables of over $800,000; internal cash flows were negative, requiring the owners to come up with cash infusions of approximately $42,000 per month just to keep operations going. Clearly, the small northern Idaho company needed to make substantial changes to survive.

The financials might hold the key to understanding what to do next, Luke thought, but he was distracted today. From the window of his office, Luke could see 20 wall panels that had just been unloaded into the plant. The wall panels came from Quickstart Building System's southern Idaho plant, which Luke Waterman and Frank Lewis, the president of RMF's board of directors, had just visited. They were considering partnering with Quickstart and had visited to learn more about the firm's product: prefabricated wall panels made primarily from oriented strand board (OSB), a variety of particleboard that oriented wood fibers in lengthwise and crosswise layers rather than in a random pattern.

Quickstart's wall panels could speed up on-site construction of homes with similar floor plans, and the company had a market among developers of such housing developments. Quickstart's owner was looking for a business interested in either producing wall panels under some type of license agreement or buying the production line and becoming a partner of the wall panel business. While there were a few challenges to overcome, Luke believed RMF's strawboard could replace OSB in the interior of the wall panels, thereby creating demand for strawboard.

Sitting in his rural Idaho office, Luke wondered whether the wall panels represented the opportunity that could save RMF or were just another distraction for the company that already had too many things that needed to be done. Looking into the plant, Luke could see beyond the wall panels that had just been unloaded to where the production equipment sat idle for lack of orders. Production, when running, was plagued with a number of quality problems that resulted in as much as 20 percent of production on some days having to be downgraded. RMF had a large inventory of second-quality, or shop-grade, boards. The company had a hard enough time finding customers for its first-quality boards, let alone for these shop-grade boards.

Luke was frustrated and more than a little nervous. He had been associated with RMF for just a year, and he had come into the organization as simply a marketing intern and part-time undergraduate business student at a nearby university. Recently he had been asked to take over the general manager position at RMF, and he wanted to find a way to turn the company around and save the jobs that the plant created—jobs that were needed in the local community. Luke was a member of the American Indian tribe that co-owned RMF, and it was his position as a trusted member of the tribal community, combined with his business education and experience with the organization, that had led to his being asked to assume the general manager position. While Luke was a little older than the typical undergraduate student and had some previous work experience, he was still in the process of finishing up his senior year of university coursework and felt somewhat overwhelmed by the task he now faced. "What have I gotten myself into?" Luke thought to himself. "Last year I was a full-time student with a marketing internship at RMF, and this year I am the general manager of a business that's in crisis."

Company Background

Rocky Mountain Fiberboard was established in March 1999 as a joint venture between Bluegrass Growers, Inc. (BGI), and a Northwest American Indian tribe. BGI processed and marketed bluegrass seed for inland producers in the Northwest and was owned and managed by a group of bluegrass farming families in eastern Washington. The American Indian tribe was a sovereign Indian nation located on its own reservation in northern Idaho.

RMF was established in an effort to find at least a partial solution to the dilemma of coping with the waste straw from the harvest of bluegrass seed in eastern Washington and northern Idaho. Until recently, the bluegrass straw left over after the seed harvest was burned in the field. Burning not only was an efficient way to deal with the straw residue but also promoted high bluegrass yields in subsequent years and helped prevent disease and pest problems. However, burning also created significant air-quality problems during late summer and early fall. Citizen groups protested the burning on the basis of health and quality-of-life arguments. People with respiratory problems and elderly people were affected the most, and during heavy burning public health officials recommended that such people remain indoors. Meanwhile, bluegrass farmers argued that field burning was critical to their being able to grow bluegrass seed profitably. Not surprisingly, this became a very emotional issue for many people in the region and polarized some communities.

In the face of pressure from various citizen groups, the state of Washington banned field burning in 1996. Bluegrass farmers then resorted to cutting and baling the bluegrass straw to remove it. Thus, along with reduced yields and higher incidences of pest infestation and disease, bluegrass seed farmers began incurring baling costs of approximately $25 per ton. Further, farmers were faced with figuring out how to use or dispose of the residual straw.

BGI hired an agronomist, Adam Davis, to help devise a plan to use the growing piles of baled straw and recover the cost of baling the straw each year. It was Adam's idea to create a strawboard production business and market the strawboard as an environmentally friendly, or green, alternative to traditional wood-based particleboard. An informal business plan was quickly developed. Preliminary research reported that strawboard plants in North Dakota and Kansas regularly sold out of their production runs and that there were no strawboard plants in the Pacific Northwest. These facts led Adam to believe that a strawboard plant in the Pacific Northwest would have to compete primarily against wood-based particleboard. He felt that a small strawboard plant could compete successfully against particleboard producers, despite their larger size, because of strawboard's superior product characteristics (see the next section for a discussion of these characteristics) and because a small plant would be more flexible and could produce smaller runs of specialty items, which could be sold at higher prices. Adam also felt that, if run efficiently, a small strawboard plant could have lower production costs than the much larger particleboard competitors, particularly if good used equipment could be located.

After some searching Adam eventually found a Canadian broker who knew of two used strawboard production lines available from a company in Australia that was getting out of the strawboard business, in part because the Asian currency crisis of 1997 had caused a partial collapse of the market. Having found the equipment and without conducting further market research, Adam then approached a neighboring American Indian tribe to see if it would be interested in becoming a partner in the venture. The tribe operated a very successful casino operation on its reservation but was also known to be interested in further economic development that would lead to greater diversification of the reservation's economy. The tribe had decided to put 25 percent of its casino profits into such economic development efforts.

After listening to Adam's presentation on strawboard production, the tribe agreed to partner with BGI to create Rocky Mountain Fiber. The initial agreement gave 50 percent of the ownership to the tribe and 50 percent to BGI. Another agreement allowed the percentage ownership, which was based on the notion of "sharing units," to vary according to the level of resources each organization put into the venture over time. A five-member board of directors was established to oversee the operation of RMF. Three of the directors were from BGI, and two were from the tribe. Frank Lewis, of BGI, was named the president of the board. Adam Davis was appointed to be general manager of RMF. The new entity's mission statement read as follows:

> Rocky Mountain Fiberboard is a joint venture created for the purpose of fabricating particleboard from bluegrass, wheat and other grain straw residue from Eastern Washington and Northern Idaho. Rocky Mountain Fiberboard was established in March of 1999 in an effort to find a solution to the unused straw residue.

RMF signed a 20-year lease agreement with the tribe to use a tribe-owned warehouse in Idaho as RMF's manufacturing facility. To acquire the necessary equipment, primarily the two used production lines from Australia, RMF borrowed $4.5 million from Northwest Farm Credit Service in the form of a 10-year note payable. The loan was collateralized by a first lien position on the leasehold interest in real property and a first security interest in all equipment and machinery. In addition, the U.S. Department of Agriculture (USDA) guaranteed $3.5 million of the loan, while BGI and the tribe guaranteed the remaining $1 million at $500,000 each.

The production equipment was dismantled in Australia, containerized, and shipped to Idaho for reassembly. Rich Stanley, a former production supervisor with the Australian company from which the equipment was purchased, went to Idaho to help set up the equipment and train RMF employees on its use and maintenance. Adam Davis soon recognized that Rich's knowledge and experience with the equipment would be extremely valuable to RMF. To entice Rich to stay on with RMF, Adam offered him the position of production manager despite Rich's limited managerial experience and training. Rich accepted, the equipment was set up with his help, and in July of 1999 RMF produced its first unit of strawboard.

RMF Strawboard

Strawboard was produced from two ingredients: straw (composing approximately 96 percent of RMF's panels by weight) and methylene diphenyl diisocyanate (MDI) resin (the remaining 4 percent of the panels). It had functional characteristics similar to traditional wood particleboard and thus competed with particleboard in the market. Compared to particleboard, strawboard had several favorable characteristics. Bluegrass straw produced fibers that were longer than the wood fibers in traditional particleboard. With the straw fibers chemically bonded by the MDI resin, bluegrass strawboard was stronger and more stable than wood particleboard, which used a urea-formaldehyde resin that simply provided the wood fibers a place to sit, as opposed to chemically bonding them. In addition, the bluegrass fibers possessed a natural resin, which when combined with the MDI resin provided superior moisture resistance. As a result, bluegrass strawboard absorbed less moisture and expanded much less than particleboard.

Another positive characteristic of strawboard was that it could be considered green, and that appealed to certain consumer segments. An important selling point for strawboard, then, was that it was "tree-free." Also, using bluegrass straw to produce the board eliminated the need to burn leftover straw, reducing air pollution. Finally, the resin used specifically in strawboard, MDI, did not release fumes once it was formed into the board, whereas the urea-formaldehyde resin used in particleboard did release fumes.

Strawboard was also literally green. The product itself had a slight green tinge and an odor similar to that of a freshly mowed lawn, only not as strong. Both the color and the odor became insignificant, however, several weeks after the board was produced. Luke recalled that, early on, some freshly produced strawboard panels had been provided to prospective RMF customers who, unfortunately, reacted negatively to the smell.

Strawboard could be used in almost any application that used particleboard, including underlayment, shelving, home and office furniture, countertops, and cabinets. Indeed, in many such applications (e.g., countertops) a laminate was placed on the strawboard or particleboard so that the final customer did not even see the actual board. Retail customers could use strawboard for any home improvement project or other home use that might otherwise require particleboard. Strawboard could even be used in some home construction applications.

RMF's Competitive Strategy and Market Opportunities

RMF's original strategy had been to exploit strawboard's green attributes and the lack of strawboard competitors in the Pacific Northwest. Luke Waterman felt that markets for green products should still be the most receptive to strawboard and would offer the greatest opportunity for obtaining price premiums over traditional particleboard. He therefore decided to focus his research on such green markets. RMF could pursue these markets through either manufacturers interested in using green materials in their products or through building material distributors or retailers who featured such products. Before going further into either of these areas, Luke first decided he needed an understanding of the green markets' end users.

Luke found that the "Green Gauge Report," published annually by Roper-Starch, provided a reasonable overview of the U.S. public's interests and intentions with respect to buying green products.[1] This report classified people into five broad categories, from "true-blue greens" to "basic browns." True-blue greens, who represented about 11 percent of the population, were the most proactively green group in the United States. They recycled, composted, wrote letters to their congressional representatives, and volunteered to help with environmental causes. These people tended to be the ones most likely to go out of their way to buy green products. The research indicated, however, that true-blue greens were willing to pay only about 7 percent more, on average, for green products compared to a competing nongreen product. One other group also tended to buy green products: the "greenback greens." These people, while less likely to make lifestyle changes in support of a better environment, were more willing to contribute financially. They did this both by donating money to environmental organizations as well as by paying more for environmentally friendly products—up to 20 percent more, on average. This group, however, represented only about 5 percent of the U.S. population. Luke did note that both greenback greens and true-blue greens were somewhat more likely to live in the West than in other regions of the country.

With this basic understanding of U.S. consumers' disposition toward green products, Luke began to study the retail market for green products, in particular green building materials. He found an interesting article in *Environmental Building News* that provided a useful profile of green building material retailers.[2] It turned out that there were only a small number of general building material retailers nationwide that specialized in green products but that they tended to be concentrated in Colorado, the Pacific Northwest, and California—which meant that RMF was the closest strawboard manufacturer to the majority of these outlets. The article indicated that most of these retailers regularly invested significant time in educating their clients about green building materials and that many had branched into green building design and consulting. Luke found this very promising, as he knew that educating consumers about the desirable properties of strawboard was a significant challenge for both RMF and the strawboard industry generally.[3] Many of these retailers were also making use of the Internet to extend their customer base beyond their local business. The article also indicated that there were about 60 specialized green building material retailers that focused on only a very narrow range of products (e.g., energy conservation products or certified lumber). A complete directory of green building material retailers—the GreenSpec directory—was published by the Environmental Building News organization.

Both the general and specialized green building material retailers tended to receive a premium price for their products relative to comparable nongreen building materials, although Luke had been unable to ascertain an average price premium. Luke did know that the one green building material retailer that was carrying RMF's strawboard—the Environmental Home Center in Seattle—was selling it at about a 20 percent price premium over comparable retail particleboard. Luke also knew that a few larger building-product chains were beginning to carry a few products that could be considered green, but these chains were generally not making the stocking of such items a priority and were not doing much to educate their customers about the items' benefits. While these chains also charged a small premium for green products, Luke knew they were reluctant to stock green products that were significantly more expensive than nongreen alternatives.

On the manufacturing side, Luke felt that furniture manufacturers represented the most promising target group of RMF customers. Furniture makers used a lot of particleboard to make less-expensive home furniture and office furniture, particularly tables, bookshelves, cabinets, and dressers. The particleboard was either painted or, more commonly, laminated or veneered. Since laminates adhered to strawboard extremely well, strawboard was ideally suited for these applications. Luke felt there were opportunities to sell strawboard either to true green furniture manufacturers or to more mainstream furniture manufacturers that might be leaning toward using green materials in some of their products.

Having found several lists of green furniture manufactures, Luke estimated that there were well over 100 such organizations spread around the United States. As was the case with building supply retailers, these companies tended to be small, and many specialized in either one type of furniture (e.g., garden furniture, office furniture) or one type of material (e.g., reclaimed lumber, recycled plastics). Without too much searching, Luke was able to find a handful that were already using a competitor's strawboard in their furniture. Baltix, in Long Lake, Minnesota, for example, was using strawboard in a variety of desks, bookshelves, filing cabinets, and office dividers. Luke found similar companies using strawboard to produce office furniture in Illinois and in Ontario, Canada. The most interesting and perhaps most promising green furniture company was Brandrud Furniture, in Seattle, Washington. Brandrud had been in business since 1955 but had been using green materials only in the last five or six years. Brandrud had, however, found that such materials worked well, and it currently used some green materials in almost all of its products. It was making extensive use of strawboard to build the interior frames of many of its furniture pieces. Brandrud's current source of strawboard was Isobord, in Alberta, Canada.

As one of the projects he had done during his marketing internship at RMF, Luke had looked at the more mainstream furniture manufacturers. At that time, he had developed a model to help identify those furniture companies that would have the greatest potential interest in RMF's strawboard. The model was based primarily on four screening factors: (1) how the company positioned itself in terms of quality (a company that positioned itself as high quality was more attractive to RMF); (2) to what extent the company positioned itself as green; (3) to what extent the company appeared to use particleboard in its products; and (4) how close the company was geographically to RMF. Luke had obtained data on over 80 U.S. furniture manufacturers and ranked each according to his model to separate good prospects from those that seemed unlikely candidates to use RMF's strawboard.

One of the top-scoring companies was Herman Miller, Inc., the Zealand, Michigan, office furniture manufacturer that frequently showed up on *Fortune* magazine's list of most-admired companies. Luke had contacted Herman Miller partly to assess the validity of his model. Herman Miller had expressed some interest in the strawboard because of its green qualities but had also voiced concerns about the environmental safety of MDI resin. It had asked for certain testing to be done before it would seriously consider using the strawboard in its products.

While the MDI resin had been certified in general as a result of tests completed by its manufacturer, separate Environmental Protection Agency (EPA) certification was recommended for each unique application involving MDI and formaldehyde resins. Resins could give off toxic fumes and were regarded as hazardous materials unless the particular combination of fibers and bonding processes rendered them environmentally benign. Luke knew that the cost of testing had prevented RMF from certifying its use of MDI resin. However, in his research, Luke discovered that lack of funding for certification was a common problem for the strawboard industry generally.[4] Even so, all strawboard was currently being made with MDI or an equivalent resin, and many customers accepted the safety of MDI in strawboard without special EPA certification.

The Production Process

In general, strawboard production required straw to be cut, combined with resin, deposited on a metal plate, and then cured using a combination of heat and pressure.

Production started with the straw. The BGI/RMF joint venture agreement required BGI to provide straw to RMF in exchange for sharing units. The sharing units represented an equity investment in the joint venture by BGI. Expecting to at least cover the cost of baling the straw, BGI valued the straw at $25 a ton when RMF opened in 1999. However, because RMF was unable to produce earnings distributions for the partners and since no long-term pricing contracts were in place, BGI had begun valuing the straw at $40–$42 a ton by 2001. BGI had recognized that charging a higher selling price to a company that could not pay cash and instead "paid" by allocating sharing units only resulted in BGI's gaining additional ownership in a money-losing operation. As a result, BGI stopped providing straw in spring of 2002. RMF then began purchasing straw for a comparable price from Oregon Hay Products, Inc., located in northeastern Oregon. RMF had never attempted to acquire straw from other sources or through a competitive bidding process.

To be used in the production process, the straw needed to be dry and free from deterioration, such as mildew. Because bluegrass seed was harvested and the leftover straw baled only once a year in the late summer, the storage conditions largely determined how much deterioration occurred. Most farmers stored straw bales in large piles under tarps. RMF acquired straw throughout the year in bales measuring four by four by eight feet, which it stored outside its facility under tarps. RMF's inspection assured the quality of incoming bales, but outside storage at its facility led to significant straw deterioration, causing RMF to dispose of approximately 15 percent of the straw it purchased. Furthermore, outdoor storage contributed to greater variability in moisture content of the straw, which made it more difficult to achieve consistently high-quality boards in production. RMF had plans for a straw storage facility that would help overcome these problems but did not currently have the capital to build such a facility.

The actual processing of the straw began by loading a bale onto a machine that broke up the bale. The straw then traveled along a conveyor specially built to remove contaminants. Next, it was gravity-fed into a hammer mill and cut to the required length. From the hammer mill, the straw was blown through a ductwork system to a cut-straw storage bin. This first part of the production process was performed outside RMF's building. A diagram of the production process is shown in Exhibit 1.

Augers brought the cut straw inside, where RMF had two separate, identical production lines. The production lines were among the first built by the equipment manufacturer that made them and were smaller, less flexible, and less automated than current models. The two lines combined had the capacity to produce approximately 12 million square feet of ¾-inch strawboard annually when operating 24 hours a day, 7 days a week. The capacity increased with decreasing board thickness such that the combined capacity for ¼-inch strawboard was approximately 38 million square feet.

Exhibit 1   Schematic of RMF's Production Process

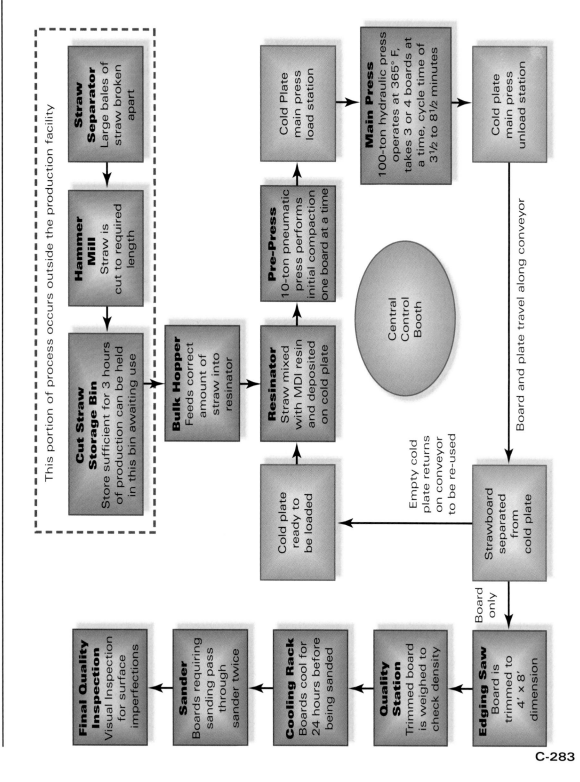

C-283

The incoming cut straw went first into a bulk hopper. From this hopper a 200-pound batch of straw was fed into a chamber, called a resinator, where it was mixed with resin. From the resinator the mixture traveled up an inclined belt that dropped it onto a "cold plate." A cold plate was simply a polished piece of metal on which the straw/resin mixture would be pressed into a board. Increasing or decreasing the speed of the track on which the cold plates traveled controlled the amount of straw/resin mixture deposited. An operator checked the weight of each board to ensure that the correct amount of straw/resin mixture had been deposited and adjusted the track speed if there was either too much or too little.

The filled cold plate went into a 10-ton pneumatic prepress, where initial compaction of the material occurred. From the prepress the boards were moved to the main press, a 100-ton hydraulic device. The time in the main press was a function of the board thickness and ranged from 3.5 minutes for ¼-inch boards to 8.5 minutes for the ¾-inch boards. From the main press the boards traveled along a track to a station where an operator removed each board from its cold plate and pushed it into an edging saw that trimmed the board to its required four-by-eight-foot size. After edging, the completed board was again weighed and, if acceptable, went to cooling racks. However, if a board was too light or too heavy, the inspector marked it as such and signaled to the operator in the central control booth. In response, the operator might adjust the speed of the track on which the cold plates were loaded.

Once the boards had cooled, they were inspected again for quality. Two problems were typically uncovered at this point. One, the surfaces of some of the boards had imperfections. Typically these were attributed to imperfections in either the main platens of the 100-ton main press (top-side imperfections) or the cold plates (bottom-side imperfections). Both the press platens and the cold plates needed replacing. Ideally, press platens needed to be replaced once every five to seven years, while the cold plates needed replacing about once every two years. RMF had put off replacing this equipment in order to conserve capital. New press platens would cost about $50,000 per line, and a new set of cold plates would cost $30,000. The other typical problem was that the edges of some of the boards had imperfections. This occurred because the boards were trimmed to size before they had cooled completely, which resulted in a rough cut. While ideally the boards would be allowed to cool before they were trimmed, the cooling racks were sized for trimmed rather than untrimmed boards. The boards with significant surface irregularities or edge damage were either downgraded to be sold at a discount or designated as salvage boards and set aside to be reground into new boards.

The final step in the process was sanding. Unsanded boards were extremely smooth—too smooth to create a good bond with the various glues that furniture manufacturers used to attach laminate—so sanding was performed to create a rougher surface. The sanding process took off about a millimeter of material from both the top and bottom of the board, so boards that were to be sanded were made slightly thicker to meet width specifications once sanded. Although not all customers required their boards to be sanded, currently a few customers did. After the boards were sanded there was a final, visual quality inspection. While the sander could eliminate some minor imperfections caused by the aging press platens and cold plates, the sander, because of its age and limited capability, was equally likely to create surface imperfections in the boards. Boards that came out of the sander with surface irregularities had to be downgraded. The firm also had the capability to cut the four-by-eight-foot sheets into smaller sizes as desired by customers, although this was rarely requested.

Approximately 10 percent of all boards produced had to be downgraded or designated as salvage at some point in the process. Downgraded boards were structurally sound but had soft spots, surface irregularities, or nicks on the edges, whereas salvage boards contained defects that affected the board's structural integrity. Total downgrade and salvage rates varied greatly from day to day. Only 2 percent of the boards were downgraded on good days, but on bad days, 20 percent or more of the production was downgraded. Generally the quality problems were greatest with the ¾-inch boards. From a quality standpoint, RMF had been fortunate in 2001—about 80 percent of its sales were ¼-inch boards and only about 15 percent of its sales were of the more problematic ¾-inch boards.

Compounding the quality problems in production was the disposition of the downgraded and salvage boards. Finding customers for downgraded boards had proved challenging because most customers willing to purchase downgraded boards were extremely price-sensitive and, as such, were more likely to purchase downgraded particleboard, which was cheaper than downgraded strawboard. Because of this, almost 55 percent of the inventory RMF held was in downgraded boards. Salvage boards, in contrast, were set aside to be reground to make new boards. RMF, however, did not own the necessary grinding equipment to do this. As a result, one end of RMF's facility was full of salvage boards that had been accumulating since the business opened in 1999, awaiting possible regrinding at some future time.

The Situation in February 2002

Circumstances by February 2002 had reached a state of crisis. Pricing issues had continually frustrated RMF during its three years in business. The original informal business plan that Adam Davis assembled had a sales strategy that called for initially pricing at a discount relative to wood-based products to attract customers and then increasing the price over time. However, market prices for particleboard peaked in January 2000 at $275 and then dropped steadily to $235 in January 2002.[5] RMF attributed the decline in prices generally to the slowing economy during these three years and an apparent oversupply of particleboard. Falling prices for particleboard and other wood-based alternatives to strawboard made it very difficult for RMF to increase its price much over time.

Also, sales had also declined steadily over the last year, from 1.5 million square feet per month in the first quarter of 2001 to less than 200,000 square feet per month in January 2002. Only a single customer remained who could be considered a steady customer—a distributor in the Seattle area who regularly bought ¾-inch boards. RMF absorbed the shipping costs for this customer to better encourage the customer to remain with the company. Previously, prices for all customers were quoted free on board (FOB)–factory.

As a result of the steep decline in sales, RMF had laid off the majority of its employees. Out of 30 employees in the summer of 2001, only 6 remained on payroll and had fixed annual salaries. In addition to Luke, the company currently employed an office manager, a production manager, two production team leaders, and a quality control inspector. An organizational chart is shown in Exhibit 2. These few employees performed all work necessary to supply the remaining customer in Seattle and handle what few orders came through from elsewhere. Susie Nelson, the office manager, handled a variety of tasks, including accounting and human resource management functions and secretarial support. Rich Stanley, the former production supervisor from Australia, was the production manager. Working with the two remaining team leaders and quality control inspector, Rich operated the production equipment when there were orders and worked to refurbish the production equipment (to the extent possible without investing

Exhibit 2   Rocky Mountain Fiberboard Organizational Chart, February 2002

significant capital) when there were not. The marketing manager's position was currently open. The most recent marketing manager had been fired several months ago because he had taken little action to pursue and follow up with potential customers. RMF had had several people in this position since the business opened, but none seemed effective. RMF had primarily recruited people from the particleboard industry, and Luke had found these individuals to have difficulty shifting away from the "price is everything" marketing approach used in the commodity-based particleboard industry. Luke and Susie were picking up the marketing responsibilities where they could.

Compounding RMF's marketing and operations problems was the financial situation, which had become extremely tenuous. The company's 2001 balance sheet, income statement, and cost of goods manufactured statements are shown in Exhibits 3, 4, and 5, respectively. By this time, the company reported an annual net loss of almost $2 million and the owners had incurred equity losses of just over $600,000. In addition, RMF had long-term debt of $4.6 million, of which $950,000 was due in 2002. In an attempt to head off possible bankruptcy, RMF had approached its principal lender, Farm Credit Services, at the end of 2001 to work out a debt-relief schedule. As part of that plan, RMF had applied through Farm Credit Services to the USDA to have the $3.5 million portion of the loan that the USDA backed converted into a grant. The grant conversion program was designed to help troubled businesses that had obtained USDA-backed loans reduce their debt and increase their chance of survival. The grant conversion process came with some expectation that the business would continue to operate as a going concern. The USDA, working with Farm Credit Services, was expected to make a decision on RMF's grant application by late March or early April. On the basis of conversations with Farm Credit Services employees, Luke expected

Exhibit 3   ROCKY MOUNTAIN FIBERBOARD'S BALANCE SHEET,
YEAR ENDED DECEMBER 31, 2001

Assets	
Current assets	
Cash	$ 41,941
Accounts receivable	30,663
Finished goods inventory	96,265
Raw materials inventory	7,109
Total current assets	$ 175,978
Long-term assets	
Property, plant, and equipment	$5,415,252
Less: accumulated depreciation	799,269
Total property, plant, and equipment	4,615,983
Total net intangible assets	69,011
Total long-term assets	$4,684,994
Total assets	$4,860,972
Liabilities and Owners' Equity	
Current liabilities	
Accounts payable	$ 851,845
Current portion of long-term debt	953,005
Total current liabilities	$1,804,850
Long-term debt	3,658,380
Total liabilities	$5,463,230
Owners' equity	
Sharing units—the tribe	$1,285,334
Sharing units—BGI	1,014,000
Retained earnings	(972,423)
Year-to-date earnings (losses)	(1,929,169)
Total owners' equity	$ (602,258)
Total liabilities and owners' equity	$4,860,972

that at least $3 million of the loan would be converted into a grant, significantly improving RMF's debt situation.

From Luke's perspective, RMF appeared to have three options. Option 1 was to try to turn around the business while remaining focused purely on strawboard. To do this, Luke knew the company would need to find new customers. Option 2 was to team up with the firm Luke and Frank had just visited, Quickstart Building Systems, to produce wall panels comprised of OSB and strawboard. This would allow RMF to further differentiate its product from traditional particleboard. Option 3 was to simply shut the business down and perhaps declare bankruptcy.

To better analyze each of these options and understand the competitive potential for RMF's product, Luke knew he needed to learn more about the strawboard industry in general, and RMF's competitors in particular. Similarly, Luke thought it would be helpful to know more about the particleboard industry since RMF was trying to sell a

Exhibit 4   ROCKY MOUNTAIN FIBERBOARD'S 2001 INCOME STATEMENT

Sales	$ 1,767,435
Sales returns and allowances	(51,262)
Freight charges	(354,601)
Net sales	$ 1,361,572
Cost of goods sold	
Finished goods inventory, December 31, 2000	$ 113,200
Cost of goods manufactured	2,623,831
Total cost of finished goods available for sale	$ 2,737,031
Less: finished goods inventory, December 31, 2001	96,265
Cost of goods sold	$ 2,640,766
Gross margin	$(1,279,194)
Operating expenses	
Selling expenses	$ 6,742
Marketing expenses	2,301
Product research expenses	25,210
Administrative expenses	255,856
Total operating expenses	$ 290,109
Operating profit (loss)	$(1,569,303)
Net interest expense	(359,866)
Profit (loss) before taxes	$(1,929,169)
Net income (loss)	$(1,929,169)

substitute for traditional particleboard. Luke also felt that he needed to have more information about the marketplace opportunities for strawboard. After doing this research, Luke hoped that he would understand why RMF's original business strategy was not working and why the firm was in such trouble now.

Industry Situation and Evaluation of Competitors

Luke identified three other companies in North America that produced strawboard: PrimeBoard, Inc., in Wahpeton, North Dakota; Prairie Forest Products, in Hutchinson, Kansas; and Isobord Enterprises in Elie, Manitoba, Canada. All three of these competitors were significantly larger than RMF and produced particleboard primarily out of wheat straw, which had properties similar to bluegrass straw. All three also promoted strawboard's green characteristics in addition to its superior qualities relative to particleboard.

PrimeBoard, Inc.

PrimeBoard was the oldest manufacturer of strawboard in North America. The privately held company had begun operations in 1995. PrimeBoard's plant employed 70 people and produced approximately 30 million square feet of strawboard in 2001. The

Exhibit 5   ROCKY MOUNTAIN FIBERBOARD, STATEMENT OF COST OF GOODS MANUFACTURED, 2001

Direct materials used		
Materials inventory, December 31, 2000		
Straw	$ 0	
Resin	37,440	
Release agent	1,005	
Propane and nitrogen	2,413	
	$ 40,858	
Direct materials purchased		
Straw	$ 425,346	
Resin	560,928	
Release agent	42,864	
Propane and nitrogen	94,178	
	$1,123,316	
Less: purchase discounts	2,317	
	$1,120,999	
Cost of direct materials available for use	$1,161,857	
Less: materials inventory, December 31, 2001		
Straw	$ 0	
Resin	0	
Release agent	2,400	
Propane and nitrogen	4,709	
	$ 7,109	
Cost of direct materials	$1,154,748	
Direct labor used		
Production labor	$ 611,519	
Quality control/inspection labor	19,620	
Packaging materials	37,023	
Straw storage and supplies	7,550	
Cost of direct labor	$ 675,712	
Manufacturing overhead		
Equipment repair and maintenance	$ 131,701	
Plant electricity	69,912	
Production employee taxes, benefits, and insurance	120,560	
Contract management	41,600	
Depreciation, building, and plant equipment	320,615	
Building and equipment lease payments	43,706	
Miscellaneous factory consumables	36,196	
Miscellaneous factory supplies and services	15,372	
Off-cut and waste straw disposal	9,568	
Training	4,141	
Cost of manufacturing overhead	$ 793,371	
Cost of goods manufactured	$2,623,831	

plant could produce boards in thicknesses from ⅜ inch to 1¼ inches and had sufficient capacity to produce as much as 60 million square feet of strawboard per year. That was five times RMF's capacity of approximately 12 million square feet of strawboard per year.

Prairie Forest Products

Prairie Forest, another privately held company, had opened its strawboard plant in 1997. It operated 24 hours a day, 7 days a week, and produced approximately 20 million square feet of strawboard in 2001. The company focused mainly on producing ⁷⁄₁₆-inch and ⅝-inch boards. Prairie was in the process of installing a second production line that would effectively double its capacity.

Isobord Enterprises

Isobord was perhaps the most significant threat to RMF among the strawboard producers because of its recent acquisition by Dow Chemical. Isobord began production in 1998 with a $100 million plant that had the capacity to produce 144 million square feet of ¾-inch strawboard per year. The plant produced boards that ranged in thickness from ½ inch to ¾ inch. Isobord products were sold through conventional wood particleboard distribution channels, as well as directly to some large manufacturers. Still, the company had run into financial trouble and declared bankruptcy in February of 2001. Dow acquired the company out of bankruptcy in May of 2001. At the time of the acquisition, Brad Money, the Dow executive charged with running the business, was quoted as saying, "We have always believed in the product, and we continue to believe that it has the potential for strong commercial appeal with consumers and contractors."[6] At the same time, a Home Depot spokesperson predicted that the acquisition would be "a strong factor in bringing environmentally conserving wood replacement panels more into the mainstream with consumers."[7]

Other Producers and Competitors

Even though Luke found only three other strawboard producers, RMF's competition consisted of traditional wood particleboard producers, too, since RMF was trying to replace their product. Indeed, Luke was more hopeful about prospects when he found that particleboard accounted for as much as 18 percent of the total wood- and agrifiber-based products produced in the United States.[8] Luke identified the leaders of the wood industry that produced particleboard among other wood products. Two of the top U.S. producers of particleboard were Georgia-Pacific and Louisiana-Pacific. Boise Cascade and Potlatch were other important competitors that had plants nearby RMF in the Northwest (see Exhibit 6).

Georgia-Pacific was a diversified wood and paper company headquartered in Atlanta, Georgia, that offered consumer goods, building materials, chemicals, and other industrial products. In fact, wood products represented less than 8 percent of the company's $25 billion annual revenue. However, Georgia-Pacific was the top producer of industrial panels, which included particleboard. It had no particleboard plants in the northwest. In contrast, Louisiana-Pacific was headquartered in Portland, Oregon, and was a more focused wood products company, with $2.4 billion in sales. Relative to RMF, Louisiana-Pacific's closest particleboard plant was in Missoula, Montana, and it accounted for 43 percent of the company's particleboard capacity.

Exhibit 6   WOOD PRODUCTS COMPETITORS

Company	Sales (millions of $)		Particleboard (¾-inch basis)	
	Total	Wood Products	Production (millions of sq. ft.)	Capacity (millions of sq. ft.)
Georgia-Pacific	$25,016	$1,998	967	1,362
Louisiana-Pacific	2,360	2,312	488	1,000
Boise Cascade	7,420	2,400	198	200
Potlatch	1,752	518	67	70

Source: http://ccbn.tenkwizard.com.

A company closer regionally was Boise Cascade, based in Boise, Idaho. Even though Boise Cascade was one of the nation's largest wood products companies, with sales of $2.4 billion, it was not a leader in particleboard, and its only particleboard plant was in LaGrande, Oregon. The plant ran at 99 percent of its 200-million-square-foot capacity for a ¾-inch basis.

Potlatch Corporation, another nearby competitor, had $1.8 billion in annual sales, of which $500 million was in wood products. Potlatch's particleboard plant had a capacity of 70 million square feet of ¾-inch board and ran at 96 percent of capacity. Though almost seven times larger than RMF's plant, the Potlatch plant was about one-third the size of Boise Cascade's. This niche size reflected Potlatch's belief that "competitiveness in this industry is largely based on individual mill efficiency, rather than the number of mills operated, and on the availability of resources on a facility-by-facility basis."[9]

In conducting this study of the industry and RMF's competitors, Luke had uncovered a number of challenges facing RMF, and to some extent, the strawboard industry in general. One challenge was that even though strawboard was theoretically stronger and offered better moisture resistance than wood particleboard, these advantages were not widely understood by the general public and had been difficult to communicate to RMF's early prospective customers. Luke had realized in the course of his research that educating customers about the various properties of strawboard was a challenge mainly because the market in general remained undeveloped due to the small size of the strawboard industry. It constituted less than 0.5 percent of the total wood- and agrifiber-based products produced in the United States.[10]

The industry's small size and undeveloped market also meant that prices were generally negotiated for individual sales or contracts, leaving Luke unable to find industrywide strawboard prices to use as benchmarks. Instead, to get an idea of the appropriateness of RMF's pricing for its most popular size, $300 per thousand square feet for ¾-inch boards, he compared it to the January price of ¾-inch particleboard, the substitute product against which RMF was competing. Luke determined that RMF's price was more than 25 percent greater. Even though strawboard was stronger, more moisture resistant, and environmentally friendlier than particleboard, Luke wondered whether it could justify such a premium given the challenges RMF faced educating its customers.

Luke also came to realize that leading companies in the wood industry had "deep financial pockets." Moreover, they typically owned vast forest resources, ones that could withstand seasonal weather and be harvested nearly year-round. In contrast, residual straw was harvested annually and its quality was highly susceptible to the timing of rain and temperature fluctuations, which could result in highly variable raw material input quality and cost.[11] Luke had also found that one of RMF's strawboard competitors, Isobord Enterprises, took a somewhat novel approach to dealing with straw acquisition. It didn't actually purchase straw, but instead purchased the right to go on to farmers' fields to remove the straw itself after harvest. Isobord then used a fleet of 38 tractors to bale and remove the straw from farmers' fields, giving it greater control of straw quality and cost.[12]

While straw represented the primary ingredient in strawboard by weight, the resin used in the production of strawboard actually presented a greater competitive challenge to the industry because of its cost. MDI, the resin used for strawboard, was three to five times more expensive than the urea-formaldehyde resins used in particleboard.[13] Luke knew of three separate development projects focused on finding alternate resins for use in strawboard. One involved a consortium of European companies that had developed a patented means to process the straw such that the same urea-formaldehyde resins used in particleboard could be used in strawboard. The last that Luke had heard, the consortium planned to license the use of this technology beginning in the first half of 2002. A second alternative on the horizon was the use of soy-based resins. A small start-up company in Iowa had developed and tested soy-based resins in both particleboard and strawboard, and the evidence was that the resins would work with either. The company was in the process of building a production facility, which it expected to complete later in the spring. The resins were to be priced comparable to urea-formaldehyde resins. Finally, a Canadian research laboratory had reportedly developed a substitute urea-formaldehyde type of resin that would work with straw. It was unclear if or when this resin would be available, or how it would be priced.

Evaluation of Alternatives

With the information he had gathered on RMF's strawboard competitors, the characteristics of the particleboard industry, and the market opportunities for strawboard, Luke Waterman believed he was ready to consider RMF's alternatives. He saw three strategic options.

Option 1: Focus on Strawboard

Turning around the business while remaining focused on strawboard production would at a minimum require finding new customers and solving some of the quality problems RMF had been experiencing in production. The lack of customers seemed the more pressing need. Luke was unsure whether RMF should continue to pursue a variety of customers in the long term, but felt in the short term that the company should focus on either building-supply retailers or furniture manufacturers. Luke felt that furniture manufacturers might represent the most promising target group of customers.

Luke had been encouraged by Herman Miller's interest, but he knew that he lacked the marketing resources to follow up on the furniture manufacturer's requests for certification testing or even continue contacting other companies that scored high on his model. Luke also wanted to approach potential green-leaning furniture customers with care because he felt that there was a lot of education that needed to occur for them to accept strawboard. In particular, Luke felt that RMF needed to approach these companies' marketing managers rather than their purchasing managers. He believed that if the marketing managers were convinced of the quality and environmental benefits of strawboard, they would make this an element of the marketing and design programs at their own company and essentially force designers to specify strawboard in their products. Alternatively, if RMF went directly to purchasing managers, Luke was afraid he would have to compete head-to-head with wood particleboard solely on the basis of price, and he knew this was a competition he could not win.

To pursue this marketing strategy, Luke needed to obtain some additional financial resources not only to hire and support a marketing person but also to conduct any tests that potential customers might need. Some money would also be needed to address the quality problems on the operations side, as these problems not only were costing RMF money but had also cost it several customers over the last year. The company needed an infusion of cash to make these strategic investments. Luke knew that BGI didn't have additional resources to put into the company and that his tribe's leaders were concerned about putting significant additional resources into it without a more concrete plan to achieve profitability.

Option 2: Partner with Quickstart Building Systems

At the end of 2001, RMF had retained the services of Stanford Financial, a financial consulting company, to find additional equity investors that might help RMF with its present situation. Stanford Financial had initially approached the tribe on behalf of another client, Quickstart Building Systems. Quickstart, which manufactured wall panels, was looking for a company interested in acquiring its current production line or entering into some type of partnership. The tribe referred Stanford Financial to RMF, both because RMF might make a logical partner for the wall panel business (at least as a possible supplier of strawboard for the wall panels) and because RMF might benefit from the services that Stanford Financial could provide. After initial discussions, RMF retained Stanford Financial to help it find a way out of its financial dilemma and agreed to pay the company a fee for its services. Stanford Financial had since recommended to RMF that it effectively merge with Quickstart.

Quickstart was building its wall panels on a semi-automated production line in Burley, Idaho, and was in the process of acquiring new, more fully automated equipment. Quickstart's owner was looking for either (1) a business interested in acquiring or leasing the Burley facility's existing semi-automated equipment, moving it to its own facility, and using it to produce wall panels under some type of license agreement, or (2) a partner to merge operations with and share the ownership and management of an expanded wall panel business.

The wall panels themselves consisted of a core of rigid spars and ribs sandwiched between two large sheets of oriented strand board (OSB). The wall panels included insulation and electrical conduits and could be used for both internal and external walls, including bearing walls. Quickstart produced both standard-size and custom panels. They could be used in single-family homes, apartment complexes, duplexes, and commercial buildings. Quickstart's owner felt that the primary customer group for wall panels would be contractors who built housing developments comprising many identical or nearly identical homes. The panels reduced the cost of construction relative to traditionally framed homes because they allowed significant labor savings. Indeed, Quickstart estimated that the use of the wall panels produced a 56 percent savings in home construction costs compared to a traditionally framed home. Further, according to Quickstart's promotional material, almost anyone, regardless of construction skills, could build with them. To date, Quickstart wall panels had been used in the construction of about 25 homes in a Seattle-area housing development and in several Habitat for Humanity homes in the Boise area.

Quickstart had indicated that the production of such panels was highly profitable. The attraction for RMF was that wall panels represented both a way to add greater value to its strawboard product and the potential for a better price. While the cost for RMF to produce these panels out of strawboard might be higher than Quickstart's costs, since strawboard cost more than OSB, RMF could probably price the boards comparably to Quickstart's and simply operate with a reduced profit margin. However, this partly depended on how much of a royalty Quickstart would expect on each panel sold.

Luke knew there were clearly some challenges to overcome if RMF was to pursue the wall panel opportunity. Some of these challenges were technical. RMF's strawboard was not approved for exterior surfaces. Therefore, while interior panels could be built entirely from strawboard, exterior panels would have to be built from either OSB or a combination of OSB and strawboard—that is, the strawboard could be used for the ribs and spars and/or for the interior side of the wall panel. In addition to the issue of the exterior rating, many of Quickstart's current panels used boards larger than the four-by-eight-foot size that RMF could produce. Another potential technical problem was the fact that strawboard did not hold screws quite as well as OSB, although it was unclear whether or not this represented a significant problem.

There were also potential economic and business challenges with the wall panel option. The wall panels were very bulky, and freight costs were a large unknown. Luke wondered if RMF could get the panels to customers for a reasonable cost. Luke also wondered about the acceptance of wall panels made out of strawboard. OSB was the established material, and it was stronger than strawboard, so Luke was concerned that customers might choose OSB panels over strawboard panels despite the latter's environmental benefits. The strawboard panels would have the advantage that a laminate could be applied to them, but Luke wasn't sure this would be a valuable attribute.

There were also significant production challenges associated with the wall panels. Wall panels were produced by an assembly process, which was fairly different from RMF's current process used to produce strawboard. Luke knew there was still work to be done to improve the production of strawboard and wondered about the complexity that would come from adding a second manufacturing process. The wall panel equipment, if operating at full capacity, also would require more strawboard than RMF's current processes could produce.

Option 3: Close the Business and Declare Bankruptcy

If the loan-to-grant conversion for which RMF had applied through Farm Credit Services was not approved by the USDA, RMF faced the possibility of filing for Chapter 11 bankruptcy. Luke knew very little about such a process. He did know, however, that even if RMF didn't make a lot of money, both the tribe and BGI wanted the firm to be an ongoing business because of their unique motivations for starting the venture. Namely, the tribe had struggled to diversify the reservation economy to make it less reliant on the casino and accompanying hotel/resort the tribe ran, and BGI wanted to find an economical solution to the bluegrass straw disposal problem resulting from the burning bans imposed in Washington in 1996.

Luke was somewhat unclear on the implications to both BGI and the tribe of a bankruptcy declaration. For example, RMF had entered into a 20-year lease on the Idaho warehouse with the tribe. Luke was unsure what would happen to the remaining 17 years of this lease in bankruptcy court. Likewise, Luke was unsure how bankruptcy would affect either BGI's or the tribe's ability to raise capital for future ventures. In total, he knew he did not understand the issues well enough to fully evaluate bankruptcy as an alternative. But he knew it might need to be considered—the tribe didn't want to keep putting $42,000 each month into a business that didn't have the potential to turn around.

The Decision

Luke turned away from the window and back toward the financials. He needed to put together a sound recommendation that he could present to both RMF's board of directors and the tribal council regarding what should be done about RMF. Could RMF survive as a business producing strawboard? he wondered. He believed in the product, but he knew that wasn't enough. Somehow RMF would have to make money with the product or at least break even. Could RMF achieve that? Even if it could, what about servicing the current debt load? He felt that maybe some further review of the financials would help him sort out the questions. Luke wanted to avoid dragging things out and sinking more money into the business if things ultimately couldn't be turned around. If the business was shut down, Luke wanted that decision to be based on a sound analysis of the business's long-term potential, not just on the current crisis that was requiring additional input of resources by the owners. Luke knew that whatever decision was made, he would need to develop a plan to implement it. Luke also knew a lot of people were depending on him to make the right decision.

Endnotes

[1] "Green Gauge Report—2000," Roper Starch Worldwide, New York.
[2] "Getting the Right Stuff: A Guide to Building Material Retailers," *Environmental Building News* 10, no. 4 (April 2001).
[3] Keith E. Gorzell, "Finding an Economic and Environmental Balance to the Technology of Producing Building Materials from Agricultural Crop Residue," 2001.
[4] Ibid.
[5] www.randomlengths.com.
[6] M. McCoy, "Dow Picks Up Plywood Stand-In," *Chemical & Engineering News,* May 28, 2001, p. 11.
[7] Ibid.
[8] Terry Sellers, "Wood Adhesive Innovations and Applications in North America," *Forest Products Journal* 51, no. 6 (2001), pp. 12–22.
[9] Potlatch 10-K405 report, year ended December 31, 2001 (filed March 27, 2002).
[10] Sellers, "Wood Adhesive Innovations."
[11] Gorzell, "Finding an Economic and Environmental Balance."
[12] R. Christianson, "Wheat Field of Dreams," *Wood & Wood Products,* November 1999.
[13] Sellers, "Wood Adhesive Innovations."

Electronic Arts and the Global Video Game Industry

Arthur A. Thompson
The University of Alabama

Going into 2004, Electronic Arts (EA) was the world's leading independent developer, publisher, and marketer of video games. EA developed games for play on all the leading home video game consoles (Sony's PlayStation and PlayStation 2, Microsoft's Xbox, and Nintendo's GameCube); on handheld devices such as Nintendo's Game Boy Advance; on personal computers; and online. In 2002, more than 22 EA games sold over 1 million units each, including Madden NFL Football 2003, NBA Live 2003, FIFA Soccer 2003, Harry Potter and the Chamber of Secrets, The Sims, Medal of Honor Frontline, and James Bond 007 Nightfire. EA released sequels of its popular sports titles annually. When Madden NFL Football 2004 was introduced in August 2003, it sold 2 million copies in three weeks at retail prices of $50 a copy; in the same three-week period, the new release of NCAA Football 2004 sold over 1 million copies. Players were expected to spend, conservatively, an average of 100 hours testing their skills over the course of the season and often beyond.

EA's chairman and CEO, Lawrence Probst, believed EA was on course to become the "biggest and best entertainment company in the world," eventually surpassing Disney (2002 revenues of $25.3 billion), Viacom (2002 revenues of $24.6 billion), and Time Warner (2002 revenues of $42 billion). Founded in 1982, EA earned $2.5 billion in revenues at the end of fiscal 2003 (March 31), and the company expected to post revenues of $2.9 billion in its fiscal year ending March 31, 2004. Probst saw two factors at work that gave EA tremendous growth potential in the years just ahead. One growth driver was the rapidly mushrooming number of households across the world that had high-speed Internet access, which allowed gamers to play video games over the Internet. The second growth driver was expected to come in 2005–2006 when Sony, Microsoft, and Nintendo were to launch the supercharged, next-generation versions of their game-playing platforms—the new consoles were expected to be as much as 1,000 times more powerful than the versions presently on the market. Probst and other EA executives believed that broadband connections and powerful game-playing consoles gave EA the opening it needed to take video games to heights far beyond what consumers could experience with movies and TV entertainment. Probst said, "There are a lot of potential growth drivers over the next five-, six-, seven-year period. And we think we're going to keep this business growing faster than the movie business, faster than the music business or any other form of entertainment business. So yeah, we're very bullish."[1]

Exhibit 1   ACTUAL AND PROJECTED SIZE OF THE GLOBAL MARKET FOR VIDEO GAMES, 2002–2010 (in millions)

	2002	2003	2007	2010
Console hardware	$ 7,187	$ 6,047	$ 6,445	$ 5,358
Console software (both sales and rentals)	14,922	16,449	13,969	13,077
Handheld hardware	1,307	1,501	1,925	1,206
Handheld software (both sales and rentals)	2,326	2,238	2,693	1,602
PC software (both sales and rentals)	3,707	3,806	3,135	2,617
Broadband	290	497	2,137	4,106
Interactive TV	133	249	1,955	4,130
Mobile phones	243	587	3,783	6,928
Total	$30,115	$31,374	$36,042	$39,024

Source: Informa Media Group, "Game Industry Dynamics, Data, Figures, and Forecasts," news release, www.gii.co.jp/press/fi14850_en.shtml, accessed November 14, 2003.

In October 2003, EA formally launched EA Sports Nation, an online service that would allow tens of thousands of broadband-enabled gamers to compete against one another individually or in teams across the Internet. Sports enthusiasts could choose among such EA games as Madden NFL Football 2004, NCAA Football 2004, NASCAR Thunder, Tiger Woods PGA Tour, NBA Live 2004, NHL Hockey 2004, FIFA Soccer 2004, and MVP Baseball 2004. EA Sports Nation had tournaments, leagues, rankings, laddering systems, and stats to entice network-enabled PlayStation 2 gamers to buy a sports game, log on to Sports Nation, pick an opponent, and test their skills. The pricing structure for EA Sports Nation was still being evaluated, but EA executives saw huge global revenue potential in attracting subscribers with not only the competitive challenge of online play and tournaments but also the prospect of winning cash or other attractive prizes. Probst said, "Our goal is to generate hundreds of thousands, and hopefully millions, of registered users playing EA Sports products online. We think that's pretty compelling and a pretty powerful vision."[2]

The Video Game Industry

In 2003, the video game industry represented a $31 billion global market (see Exhibit 1), up sharply from about $10 billion in 1995. The industry consisted of makers of video game consoles, handheld players, and arcade machines; game developers who developed games for play on both personal computers (PCs) and various kinds of video game machines; retailers of video game players and video games; and companies that had Web sites for online game play. Video and computer games were an unforeseen by-product of advancing chip technology. Faster chip processing speeds and growing graphics capabilities opened the way for game developers to put players in the midst of all kinds of action-filled situations. During the 1990s, video game developers created increasingly sophisticated, multifeatured games that allowed players to compete in a host of sports and racing events, pilot supersonic fighter jets and spacecraft to defend against all manner of enemies, and enter mystical worlds to untangle ancient webs of treachery and deceit.

Retail video game sales soared to record levels in the 1990s, with annual sales in the billions. From 1985 to 1994, Nintendo and Sega dominated the market for video game consoles, with combined market shares of around 90 percent. The two rivals sparred back and forth in an escalating battle for market leadership. Then in 1995, competitive rivalry in video games took on a new dimension when Sony entered the market with its new PlayStation. Nintendo and Sega, the longtime industry leaders, found themselves in a fierce battle with Sony, and other small-share console makers scrambled to generate enough sales to survive. There was a huge industry shakeout. By 1998, Sony emerged as the undisputed leader worldwide. In the United States, Sony's PlayStation captured a 70 percent market share, with Nintendo at 26 percent and Sega at only 4 percent. All other video console makers faded into oblivion and Sega, unable to make any headway in regaining lost market share, exited the market for video consoles in 2001 and turned its full attention to developing video games. The entry of Microsoft's Xbox in 2002 made the video console business a fierce three-way contest.

Total sales of PlayStation 2 were expected to reach 100 million units by 2005, making the PlayStation 3 the odds-on favorite to keep Sony as the market leader in video game hardware. But despite PlayStation 2's market dominance, Microsoft's Xbox and Nintendo were expected to gain market share and become significantly more competitive as concerned both their hardware and the number of attractive games that could be played on their equipment. Microsoft was projected to be particularly strong in Europe, a region that was less emphasized by Sony and Nintendo.

In 2003 game developers were riding the crest of a software sales wave for current-generation consoles (PlayStation 2, Xbox, and GameCube). The wave of video game sales was expected to peak in 2004 before slackening off in the run-up to the expected launch of next-generation consoles in 2005–2006. Video game industry sales were projected to reach nearly $39 billion worldwide by 2010 (Exhibit 1). Some observers were predicting that the global video game market was on track to rival the movie, music, and television industries; according to a writer for *Fortune*, "Music sales have been falling in recent years, the moviegoing experience hasn't changed that much since *Gone with the Wind*, and network TV is on the skids."[3]

The Players of Video Games

About 250 to 300 million people worldwide were very active or frequent players of video games; game enthusiasts usually owned consoles, handheld players, or PCs and spent five or more hours weekly playing video games. Perhaps another 100 million people were infrequent players, playing them occasionally on arcade machines in malls and other retail locations, on their own PCs during idle moments or as a diversion, on the consoles and handheld players of friends and acquaintances, or on personal digital assistants (PDAs) and cell phones. The majority of video game players were preteens, teenagers, and young adults (between the ages of 20 and 40). The average age of game players was rising, as people who became game players as a preteen or teenager continued to play in their adult years. And, to broaden the appeal of video games for adults, game developers were creating a growing number of games with mature content. The average American was expected to spend 75 hours annually playing video games, more than double the amount spent gaming in 1997 and more than was spent watching rented movies on DVDs or videocassettes.[4]

Hard-core gamers purchased 10–15 new games annually and were also among those most attracted to playing games online. IDC, a Massachusetts-based research firm, estimated that North American households owned 75 million game consoles such as the PlayStation, Xbox, and GameCube. A study by the Pew Internet and American Life Project found that 70 percent of college students played video games at least

Exhibit 2   REASONS PEOPLE PLAY VIDEO GAMES, 2002

It's fun	87.3%
They're challenging	71.4
Like to play with friends/family	42.4
Lots of entertainment for the price	35.6
Like to keep up with the latest technology	18.9
Interested in the stories	17.9
Like the music and/or the celebrities involved	15.5
I do the same thing in real life	13.1

Source: 2002 survey of 1,500 households, conducted by Interactive Digital Software Association, www.idsa.com, accessed November 13, 2003.

occasionally in 2002 and that 100 percent of college students responded affirmatively when asked if they had *ever* played video games. The study said, "Computer, video, and online games are woven into the fabric of life for college students. Gaming is a part of growing up in the U.S."[5]

Still, there were drawbacks to playing video games. Not everyone had the patience to learn complex controls or wanted to spend the 20 to 30 hours it took to navigate a game successfully. Exhibit 2 presents the primary reasons people played video games, and Exhibit 3 provides game player demographics and other video game–related statistics.

Industry Growth

A number of factors had contributed to growth of the video game industry during the 1990–2003 period:[6]

■ *Broader game content*—In 2003, video gaming offered entertainment for the masses, with games involving sports, racing, action, adventure, edutainment, shooting, fighting, and a host of children's games and family entertainment games.

■ *The evolution of video game consoles into multifaceted entertainment devices*— People could play DVD movies and music on game machines, expanding the entertainment value for families.

■ *People who started out playing games in the 1980s were staying in the market and playing in their 30s and 40s*—Demographic research indicated that growing numbers of young adults were continuing to play video games past their teenage and college years. Sports games involving professional and college sports and NASCAR racing were appealing to adults, as were games with mature content.

■ *There had been quantum leaps in the quality of both graphics and play*—Moreover, another huge leap was coming in next-generation consoles scheduled for introduction in 2005–2006. The chip designs in next-generation video game consoles featured a revolutionary new architecture that packed the processing power of a hundred 2003-style PCs onto a single chip and, further, tapped the resources of additional computers using high-speed Internet connections. The next-generation consoles, expected to retail for about $300, would have the ability to render real-life images, record TV shows, surf the Internet in 3-D, play music, and run movielike video games.

Exhibit 3   VIDEO GAME–PLAYING STATISTICS, U.S HOUSEHOLDS, 2002–2003

- An estimated 50 percent of the U.S. population, about 145 million people, played computer and video games in 2003, with the average player spending about 6.5 hours a week playing games.
- 17% of all game players in the United States in 2003 were over age 50, up from 13% in 2000. The average game player in the United States in 2003 was 29 years old.
- Boys ages 6 to 17 represented 21% of gamers in the United States and spent an average of 7.3 hours a week playing games; girls between the ages of 6 and 17 represented 12% of gamers.
- Men ages 18 and over represented 38% of all gamers.
- 40% of game players in the United States were female; women ages 18 and older made up 26% of the game-playing population in the United States.
- The average number of U.S. family members who play PC games regularly (5 or more hours per week) is 1.6, while for console games about 2 people per household play regularly.
- 31% of the most frequent game players in the United States reported playing games online in 2002, up from 24% in 2001.
- Age and gender of U.S. most frequent game players—PCs versus consoles in 2002:

	PC Players	Console Players
Age		
36 + years	40%	19%
18–35 years	26	36
Under 18 years	34	45
Gender		
Male	62%	72%
Female	38	28

- About 37% of American households either with game consoles or with PCs that are used to play games reported in 2002 they also played games on mobile devices like handheld game players, personal digital assistants (PDAs), and cell phones.
- Age and gender of U.S. buyers of consoles versus PC games in 2002:

	PC Game Buyers	Console Game Buyers
Age		
18 + years	96%	86%
Gender		
Male	45%	46%
Female	55	54

(continued)

- *Growing ability on the part of video game developers to capitalize on expanding action movies into popular video games*–Game developers and Hollywood movie studios were becoming increasingly aware of the merits of working hand-in-hand on projects like a Harry Potter, Spider-Man, Lord of the Rings, or James Bond movie that had both the action component and widespread interest (especially among teenagers) to make a good game. Releasing a game in conjunction with a hit movie could increase sales by three or four times. Sometimes, film stars recorded dialogue for video games and special scenes were filmed specifically for

Exhibit 3 (concluded)

■ Best-selling video games by type of genre, 2001–2002:

Game Categories	2001 PC and Console Games	2002 PC Games	2002 Console Games
Sports	22.2%	6.3%	19.5%
Action	19.8	—	25.1
Strategy/role-playing	17.6	35.4	7.4
Racing	16.7	4.4	16.6
Fighting	5.7	0.1	6.4
Shooting	9.1	11.5	5.5
Family	3.6	9.6	—
Child	3.4	15.9	—
Adventure	—	—	5.1
Edutainment	—	—	7.6

Note: The categories were redefined between 2001 and 2002.

■ Computer and video game sales by rating, 2001–2002:

	2001	2002
Everyone	62.3%	55.7%
Teen	24.6	27.6
Mature	9.9	13.2
Early Childhood	2.1	3.5

■ In 2002, 16 of the top 20 best-selling console games and 18 of the top 20 best-selling PC games were rated Everyone or Teen.

■ In 2001, U.S. sales equaled 141.5 million video games, 58.8 million computer games, and 25.1 million "edutainment" games, equal to an average of almost 2 games per U.S. household.

Sources: "Essential Facts about the Computer and Video Game Industry," Interactive Digital Software Association, 2002, www.idsa.com, accessed November 12, 2003; and 2003 ESA poll of 806 adults reported in August 26, 2003, press release at www.theesa.com.

use in a game. Game designers would take a movie script and add to the storyline, making it more mission-rich and multifaceted than what appeared on-screen.

■ *The growing capability to play games online, often in head-to-head competition with other online players*—Online gaming had allowed game designers to extend their storylines by providing new chapters, adding new missions, and introducing new characters, thus hooking enthusiasts into playing through a never-ending story. Sequels of sports games with the latest player rosters and team schedules spurred continuing interest on the part of online players. Most observers contended that online gaming gave game developers a wider vista of game-designing options than any other prior technology.

The growth in interactive entertainment was expected to continue as game-playing hardware and software continued to improve, hardware and broadband penetrated more homes, and technology continued to evolve in ways that brought more game-

Exhibit 4   WORLDWIDE SALES OF PC AND VIDEO GAMES, 1996–2002

Year	Unit Volume (in millions)	Dollar Sales (in billions)
1996	105	$3.7
1997	133	4.4
1998	181	5.5
1999	215	6.1
2000	219	6.0
2001	225	6.3
2002	255	6.9

Sources: "Essential Facts about the Computer and Video Game Industry," Interactive Digital Software Association, 2002, www.idsa.com, accessed November 12, 2003; and press release at www.theesa.com, accessed November 13, 2003.

playing experiences into the reach of more consumers. By 2007 players were expected to be playing a yet-to-be released breed of games on a new breed of powerful game-playing consoles. Forecasters at DFC Intelligence expected the successors to PlayStation 2, Xbox, and GameCube to be the fastest-selling video game systems ever and to offer quantum leaps in graphics quality and game-playing interest. Exhibit 4 shows worldwide sales of PC and video game software for the 1996–2002 period.

Video Game Prices

The most popular video games retailed for about $50 in 2003. However, prices varied according to the games' popularity, length of time of the market, and the age and popularity of the console for which they were developed. It had been the experience of the industry for game prices to decline once a generation of consoles had been in the market for a significant period of time; this was mainly due to the increasing number of game titles competing for acceptance by game players. The prices of games for older 16-bit and 32-bit consoles in 2003 were considerably lower than the prices of games for the newer 64-bit and 128-bit consoles (see Exhibit 5).

Some industry observers were predicting that rising costs would soon drive the prices of games with a triple-A rating to $59.99. According to an analyst at NPD Group, "There just doesn't seem to be negative reaction to game prices. Even if one publisher took the chance to lower the price of a triple-A game, it could bias the consumer that it's a lesser game." About 750 new games were expected to hit the market between mid-2003 and mid-2004. If past sales statistics held true, the top 50 to 60 games would account for 50 percent of total sales, and half of those might be able to command a $60 price if publishers took a chance on raising prices. Industry observers were predicting that overall prices for games would fall in 2004 and 2005 as more new titles were introduced and the total number of titles competing for buyer attention grew; however, hit titles were expected to continue to command premium prices.

The Costs of Developing a New Video Game

In the early 1980s, a game for an 8-bit Nintendo game player could be developed for less than $100,000. In the early 1990s, game publishers customarily spent around $300,000 to develop a game for Nintendo's Super NES, Sega's Genesis, or PCs. In 1996, a typical PlayStation game cost just under $1 million to develop and retailed for $49. In 2003, development costs for a PlayStation 2 or Xbox game usually ran from

Exhibit 5   AVERAGE RETAIL PRICES OF VIDEO GAMES, 1995–2002

Type of Console	1995	1996	1997	1998	1999	2000	2001	2002
16-bit (1989 debut)								
Sega Genesis	$41	$29	$21	$14	$13	$10	$10	$ 7
Super Nintendo	43	41	29	22	17	11	10	9
32-bit (1995 debut)								
PlayStation	53	49	39	35	31	28	23	18
Sega Saturn	55	47	35	20	11	5	14	6
64-bit (1996 debut)								
Nintendo 64	—	65	61	51	46	42	38	28
128-bit (2000 debut)								
GameCube	—	—	—	—	—	—	50	46
Xbox	—	—	—	—	—	—	50	45
PlayStation 2	—	—	—	—	—	49	48	41

Sources: The NPD Group/NPD FunWorld, and www.msnbc.com/news.

$2 million to $7 million per title, and the game retailed for $49.99. However, some game titles could entail development costs upward of $30 million. Development costs were rising for several reasons:

■ Games for the current 128-bit consoles required at least 40 times as many lines of code to fully exploit their capabilities as did the prior-generation 64-bit consoles.

■ Costs went up when a game had to be reworked or when developers decided to push the technology envelope a bit further and add new or more elaborate features. Game developers often did not know how long it would take or what it would cost to program some games because aspects of many new games had never been done before and it took several rounds of programming to create the desired effects.

■ It was taking ever bigger and more talented development teams to push the limits of each new generation of consoles. As a consequence, talented game developers were becoming a more and more valuable resource, commanding ever higher salaries and bonuses. As the industry moved to PlayStation 3 and Xbox 2, most industry observers believed that a large and capable staff of game developers would become an even more important key success factor.

■ Payments for licensed content or the use of intellectual property owned by others (for rights to use certain characters or celebrities in games or to tie in with hit movies), coupled with the need for special film crews and backdrops to stage certain scenes (the Matrix game had an hour of exclusive video footage), could cost game publishers an additional $1 to $10 per game unit.

Some observers were predicting that costs to develop hit games for next-generation game consoles could *average* as high as $20 million.

Royalties Paid to Console Manufacturers   Sony, Nintendo, and Microsoft, aside from creating their own games with in-house staff, licensed independent game developers to create software for use with their respective game-playing systems. The license agreements gave the platform manufacturer the right to set the fee structure that developers had to pay in order to publish games for their platforms. The customary royalty was about $8 per unit on newly released games, but the royalty payment typically decreased as game prices fell. The license agreement also gave manufacturers an assortment of controls in other areas. Typically, the game developer was required to submit a prototype for evaluation and approval that included all artwork to be used in connection with packaging and marketing of the product. The console manufacturer had final approval over all games for its consoles (sometimes limiting the number of games approved in a given time frame) and could specify the dates on which new games could be released. In many cases, console manufacturers also controlled the manufacture of the game cartridges or CDs, in which case the developer had to provide the platform manufacturer with a purchase order for the number of units to be manufactured and an irrevocable letter of credit for 100 percent of the purchase price.

All these requirements tended to increase developer lead times and costs for getting a new game to market. This was especially true when platform manufacturers opted to bring out next-generation platforms with capabilities that entailed more demanding specifications. Moreover, when next-generation platforms were introduced, platform manufacturers required a new license of developers, giving them an opportunity to alter the fee structure and impose new terms and conditions on licensees. Next-generation platforms posed two other risks to game developers. If manufacturers were delayed in introducing next-generation platforms, then the introduction of their new games was delayed as well. And if a manufacturer's new platform met with poor reception in the marketplace, then the accompanying games of developers had shorter-than-expected life cycles.

In addition, as online capabilities emerged for video game platforms, platform manufacturers had control over the financial terms on which online game play would be offered to players. In 2003, both Microsoft and Sony provided online capabilities for Xbox and PlayStation 2, respectively. In each case, compatibility code and the consent of the platform manufacturer were required before a game developer could include online capabilities in their games for Xbox and PlayStation consoles. This tended to put the strategies and business models of Microsoft and Sony in direct competition with the strategies and business models of independent game developers, like Electronic Arts, that had their own online game-playing businesses and were promoting their PC-based video games to game enthusiasts for play online.

Marketing and Distribution Costs

Competition for shelf space and efforts to make games top sellers had prompted game publishers to boost their advertising. In 2002 industry advertising was about 65 percent higher than in 2002. In 2003 advertising budgets for video games were at record levels. EA had even scheduled ads for its Madden NFL Football game for *Monday Night Football*. With more than 500 titles for PlayStation, 200 titles for Xbox, and 150 titles for GameCube, retailers struggled to find shelf space for even the most popular titles. Wal-Mart, for example, generally stocked only about 80–90 games, and it was the leading retailer of video game consoles, with about an 18 percent market share of the combined sales of GameCube, Xbox, and PlayStation consoles. Other key retailers in North America were Best Buy, Circuit City, Toys "R" Us, and Target. In many instances, retailers demanded hefty slotting fees to stock lesser-known or slower-selling games. The shelf life of the average video game was about five weeks, even with expensive in-store merchandising campaigns; the most popular video games had a shelf life of about 120 days.

Exhibit 6   REPRESENTATIVE VALUE CHAIN FOR VIDEO GAMES, 2002

	PC CD-ROM	Console DVD
Retail price	$39.99	$49.99
Retailer margin	8.00	10.00
Wholesale received by publisher	$31.99	$39.99
Publisher costs		
Manufacturing/packaging	$3.00	$3.00
Hardware royalty fee (paid to console maker)	$0.00	$8.00
Licensed content royalties	$0–$6.00	$0–$10.00
Margin for game development and programming, marketing, other costs, and profit	$22.99–$28.99	$18.99–$28.99

Sources: Wedbush Morgan Securities, and www.msnbc.com/news/924871.asp.

Game publishers promoted their games in several ways:

- Television, print, radio, outdoor, and Internet ads.
- Company Web sites.
- In-store promotions, displays, and retailer-assisted cooperative advertising.
- Trade shows.
- Product sampling through demonstration soft-ware.
- Consumer contests and promotions.

Television advertising was often required to create mass-market demand for an altogether new game; a minimal TV advertising campaign for a game cost about $2 million.

In 2002, the top 20 best-selling video games accounted for about 22 percent of the sales of video games in North America. About 50 percent of annual video game sales occurred in the fourth quarter of the calendar year; many holiday shoppers considered video game hardware and software to be ideal gifts. Exhibit 6 shows a representative value chain for video games.

Mobile Gaming

Nintendo was the dominant market leader in handheld game devices, having sold more than 150 million Game Boys in various forms since 1989. Mobile gaming was highly popular in Japan and South Korea; the two countries represented an estimated 64 percent of the global market for mobile games. However, mobile gaming was growing rapidly in China, the United States, Britain, Germany, France, and Italy. The Game Boy business in the United States in 2003 was expected to be a $1 billon market (including sales of both hardware and software). The telecom segment of the mobile gaming market in Japan and South Korea in 2003 was estimated at $400 million. Forecasts of the size of the mobile gaming market in 2006 (including games played on cell phones as well as portable devices) varied widely, ranging from as little as $1.65 billion to as much as $38 billion. While mobile gaming had historically been a favorite pastime of preteens and teenagers, the advent of game-capable cell phones and more sophisticated handheld devices like Nintendo's Game Boy SP were expected to spur increases in mobile gaming among the young-adult population in the years ahead.

Online Gaming

The worldwide online game segment was expected to grow from $875 million in 2002 to over $5 billion in 2008.[7] Online game playing was projected to reach 35 billion hours in 2008 and include about 200 million people, distributed about equally across North America, Europe, and Asia. Forecasters expected the growth to be driven not only by PC-based subscriptions but also by the rapidly growing number of video game console systems with online capability. By 2008, the installed base of online-capable video game systems was projected to exceed 100 million worldwide. The other major factor driving online game playing was increased broadband penetration. Broadband capability in households began to rise sharply in 2002, especially in South Korea and Japan, where the growing base of broadband users was producing big gains in online game playing. Some forecasters believed online games would be the "killer application" that spurred households to upgrade their connections from modems to broadband. However, in 2003 it was still uncertain just how much online game playing would translate into revenues and profits for game developers like EA. Revenues came from annual or monthly subscription fees, "pay-to-play" fees, and onsite advertising.

While it had been demonstrated that a highly popular online video game could generate $100 million in annual revenues with a 50 percent operating profit margin, such success was the exception rather than the rule. Many online game services had failed and others had built a large user base that produced little or no revenue. Moreover, there was a serious glut of online games presently on the market. In late 2003, there were close to 1.2 million PlayStation and Xbox game players using high-speed Internet connections to play online. In August and September 2003, close to 300,000 people registered to compete online with Madden NFL 2004 and NCAA Football 2004; on Sunday, September 14, the number of simultaneous online players of Madden NFL 2004 hit 7,000 and then hit progressively higher peaks as the season unfolded. Some 250,000 people were paying $10 a month to enjoy a virtual world called EverQuest (www.everquest.com); EverQuest enthusiasts were spending an average of 20 hours a week at the site in mid-2003. For its part, EA had invested close to $300 million to build its online division (called EA.com); when it launched The Sims Online site in anticipation of attracting perhaps a million people to sign up, only 10,000 of the several million buyers of the popular game were motivated to register and form Sims communities; EA had also failed with its Earth and Beyond online game site. Of EA's five "persistent state world products," which allowed players across the world to gather to play online, only the Ultima Online site was considered to be a financial success.

One of the keys to success in online gaming was easy interaction among the players—making it simple to chat with other players, heckle opponents, talk trash, or cooperate with other players to complete certain tasks and missions. Sony Online strived to evoke four core human emotions in its online games: exploration, fantasy fulfillment, social interaction, and acquisition. Gamers enjoyed being part of an online gaming community that allowed them to hang out, chat, engage in head-to-head duels, and check statistics showing their skills versus those of other players.

Microsoft's Xbox Live   Microsoft introduced a subscription-based online game-playing service dubbed Xbox Live in November 2002. About 350,000 starter kits were sold in the first 120 days, double original sales expectations. The $50 starter kits, which included a one-year subscription to Xbox Live, enabled gamers with a high-speed Internet connection to play multiplayer Xbox Live games with other gamers logged on to the Xbox Live site. The Xbox, with a built-in hard drive and

Ethernet connection, was the only video game system built from the ground up for on-line gaming—PlayStation 2 users had to buy network adapters for their consoles (Sony had sold about 1 million adapters for its PlayStation consoles). Xbox Live enabled gamers to find their gaming acquaintances online, talk to other players during game play through the Xbox Communicator headset, check out the latest game-paying statistics and achievement levels, download new difficulty levels and characters to their hard drives, and play online. Xbox Live offered gamers a unique ID, called a Gamertag, for use across its service; a Friends list that let gamers find their friends on-line and invite them to a game; and Matchmaking, which let players find opponents of similar skill levels. In a recent survey, Microsoft discovered that downloadable content was considered the most desired feature of Xbox Live by 82 percent of its users.

In late 2003 the subscription fee for Xbox Live was $49.99 for 12 months, and the price of the Xbox Starter Kit had increased to $69.99 (which included a 12-month subscription, an Xbox Communicator voice headset, and a full version of the game MechAssault). Gamers could also get a free two-month trial for Xbox Live by purchasing a specially marked Xbox Live–enabled game in retail stores (the free trial could be extended on a monthly basis for $5.99). All Xbox Live users had to enter credit card and billing information in signing up for the service.

Microsoft's strategy called for no royalties or share of subscription fees to be paid to game developers for any game played on Xbox Live. It wanted to fully control the gaming experience at Xbox Live and retain all monies collected—a policy that had prompted EA to refuse to program online play capability into any of its Xbox games, thereby preventing Xbox owners from using their consoles to play EA games on Xbox Live. EA, however, had inked a deal with Sony to make nine of its sports games compatible for online play using the PlayStation 2; Sony's online strategy was to give game makers the autonomy to establish the online environment in which the action took place for their games (even though the player was using a PlayStation 2), control the play using their own servers, and dictate subscription fees at their sites. This contrasted sharply with Microsoft's practice of keeping all revenues from online play of games via an Xbox console. Nintendo had an online policy similar to Sony's, allowing game developers to promote and manage their own online services and not to take a percentage of revenues or charge a royalty for the use of their consoles in online play.

Sales of Current-Generation Video Game Consoles

As of September 2003, Sony had sold 60 million PlayStation 2 consoles since October 2000; of these, 14.2 million were in Japan, 26.4 million were in North America, and 19.4 million were in Europe, the Middle East, Africa, and Australia. The original PlayStation had sold about 37.5 million units in its first three years on the market, and forecasters expected that PlayStation 2 sales would reach 100 million in 2005. As of July 2003, Microsoft had sold 9.4 million Xbox consoles since its November 2001 launch and expected to have an installed base of 14.5 to 16 million worldwide by June 2004. Xbox sales in North America equaled 6.2 million units (about 66 percent of the total), followed by Europe with 2.2 million units (23 percent), and the Asia-Pacific region with nearly 1 million units (11 percent). Worldwide sales of Nintendo's Game-Cube were approaching 20 million in the fall of 2003, but were running behind projections; to spur console sales, Nintendo cut its console price from $149 to $99 in September 2003, tripling its volume and prompting Microsoft and Sony to cut the prices of their consoles from $199 to $179.99 in November 2003. Console makers expected to sell a combined 15 million units in the U.S. market in 2003.

Since 1989, Nintendo had sold over 150 million handheld Game Boys in various versions—over 35 million of its Game Boy Advance players had been sold in 2002–2003 alone. Nearly 40 percent of those who played Game Boy Advance and the flip-top SP version were older than 18, and 20 percent were over 30.

Designs and Capability of the Next-Generation Consoles

The design for Sony's PlayStation 3 called for putting 72 microprocessors on a single chip—8 IBM PowerPC processors, each of which controlled 8 additional auxiliary processors. This would allow the PlayStation 3 to process a trillion math operations a second, the equivalent of 100 Intel Pentium 4 chips and a speed 1,000 times faster than the processing power of the PlayStation 2. Sony envisioned that its PlayStation 3 would have the capability to simultaneously handle a wide range of electronic tasks in the home—recording a TV program, playing music, and managing home appliances, thus functioning as an in-the-home server and turning video game consoles into "a new class of beast." Microsoft envisioned much the same capability for its next-generation Xbox, and Nintendo had indicated that its new console would not lag behind Sony's on technology. There was reason to expect the capabilities of the next-generation PlayStation, Xbox, and GameCube consoles to be relatively similar because Sony, Microsoft, and Nintendo had all selected IBM to supply IBM PowerPC microprocessors for their next-generation consoles. Furthermore, programming games for these next-generation consoles was expected to be far more complicated and lengthy than for the current generation of consoles because programmers would have to keep track of all the tasks being performed by 72 processors.

Competition

The software segment of the video game industry was highly competitive, characterized by the continuous introduction of new games and updated game titles and the development of new technologies for creating and playing games. The developers of software games ranged from small companies with limited resources to large corporations with significantly greater resources for developing, publishing, and marketing video game software. Independent game developers like Electronic Arts, Activision, Take-Two Interactive, Capcom, Eidos, Acclaim Entertainment, Sega, Lucas Arts, Infogrames, THQ, Konami, Namco, Vivendi Universal, Midway Games, and 3DO competed not only with each other but also with Sony, Microsoft, and Nintendo, each of which published games for their respective consoles. Sony, Nintendo, and Microsoft licensed a number of companies to develop and publish games that operated on their consoles. Competition among game developers was based on game features and product quality, timing of game releases, access to distribution channels and retailer shelf space, brand-name recognition, marketing effectiveness, and price. Software developers also competed with other forms of entertainment (movies, television, music, and sports) for the leisure time and discretionary spending of consumers.

Small game developers were struggling. They were more capital constrained, had less predictable revenues and cash flows, lacked product diversity, and were forced to spread fixed costs over a smaller revenue base—factors that were prompting the industry to consolidate to a smaller number of larger developers. Such companies as Acclaim Entertainment, 3DO, Midway Games, and Vivendi Universal's game division had been up for sale at various times but had been unable to convince potential buyers that the value of their development teams and aging brands outweighed the risks of taking on their entire enterprise, given that they were either losing money or barely breaking even. As a result, many of the troubled game developers were either cutting operations to the bone or trying to turn their operations around with new infusions of cash from investors and renewed efforts to come up with a best-selling game. Square and Enix, two Japanese game developers, had merged in early 2003 to form what was one of the biggest game developing companies in Japan.

Sega In 2003, Sega, which had withdrawn from competing in the segment for video game consoles in 2001 to focus exclusively on developing video games, had failed to attract a buyer for its video game business; acquisition discussions had been broken off with several companies and Sega was making a major push to establish itself in sports games. Sega had teamed with ESPN to introduce a series of sports games with the ESPN label—ESPN NFL Football, ESPN NHL Hockey, and ESPN NBA Basketball. Prior to its ESPN branding approach, Sega had promoted its sports games under the 2K brand, using such titles as NFL 2K3, NBA 2K3, NCAA College Football 2K3, and so on. To differentiate its sports games from those of Electronic Arts, Sega was creating a situation in which the player would see the game through the eyes of a participant as opposed to watching the game with a bird's-eye view of the playing field. Many analysts expected that Sega's ESPN series would prove to be the primary competition for EA Sports in the sports genre. Other games in Sega's lineup included Shinobi, Super Monkey Ball, Fantasy Star Online, The House of the Dead, Bass Fishing Duel, and Panzer Dragoon.

Activision Founded in 1979 and headquartered in Santa Monica, California, Activision's mission was to be one of the largest, most profitable, most well-respected interactive entertainment companies in the world. Activision posted net revenues of $864 million for the fiscal year ended March 31, 2003, almost double the $434 million reported for fiscal 1999; Activision had a net income of $66.2 million in 2003, versus a net of $14.9 million in 1999. The company was expecting revenues close to $1 billion in the year ending March 31, 2004. Activision had operations in the United States, Canada, the United Kingdom, France, Germany, Italy, Japan, Australia, Scandinavia, and the Netherlands. Activision's strategy was grounded in three elements:

- The company developed and published games for (1) a wide range of product categories, including action, adventure, action sports, racing, role-playing, simulation, and strategy, and (2) target audiences ranging from game enthusiasts and children to mass-market consumers and "value-priced" buyers. It was concentrating on games for PlayStation 2, Xbox, GameCube, Game Boy handheld devices, and PCs. The company typically released its console products for use on multiple platforms in order to reduce the risks associated with any single platform, leverage its costs over a larger installed base, and increase unit sales.

- Activision focused its development and publishing activities principally on products that were, or had the potential to become, "franchise properties" with sustainable consumer appeal and brand recognition. It had acquired the rights to publish products based on Star Trek, various Disney films such as Toy Story 2 and Marvel Comics' properties such as Spider-Man, X-Men, Blade, Iron Man, and Fantastic Four. The company had signed long-term agreements with a number of action sports athletes in skateboarding, biking, surfing, snowboarding, and wakeboarding, and established the Activision O2 brand as the dominant brand in the action sports category.

- To try to ensure a high success rate of new product releases, Activision's management relied on a formal control process for the selection, development, production, and quality assurance of its products called the Greenlight Process. This process included in-depth reviews of each project at five intervals during their development by a team that included several of the company's highest-ranking operating managers and sales and marketing personnel. Projects that were deemed less promising were either discontinued early in the development phase or revamped before additional development costs were incurred. New games were often developed using a combination of internal and external development resources; when an external developer was used, that developer usually produced the same game for multiple platforms and also produced sequels to the original game.

Activision was modifying its acquisition strategy to focus on (1) increasing its development capacity through the acquisition of or investment in select experienced development firms and (2) expanding its intellectual property library through licenses and strategic relationships with intellectual property owners. Having completed 13 acquisitions since 1997, Activision believed that it had successfully diversified its operations, channels of distribution, development talent pool, and library of titles. But management believed that success down the road would be driven in part by the company's ability to capture greater economies of scale.

Activision's biggest competitive strength was in games based on superheroes such as Spider-Man, animated characters such as Shrek, and skateboard legend Tony Hawk. It was the market leader in action sports games; during the 1995–April 2002 period, it had number 3 and number 7 of the top 15 best-selling action sports titles. The company's franchise title was its Tony Hawk skating series, the latest version of which was Tony Hawk's Pro Skater 4. Other action sports titles included Mat Hoffman's Pro BMX 2, Kelly Slater's Pro Surfer, Shaun Murray's Pro Wakeboarder, Wreckless, True Crime: Streets of LA, Street Hoops, X-Men: Next Dimension, Tenchu 3: Wrath of Heaven, and X-Men: Wolverine's Revenge.

Activision was the third-ranked publisher of games for Nintendo's Game Boy software. For the week ending November 9, 2003, Activision's critically acclaimed first-person action game Call of Duty was the best-selling PC-based video game in North America, the United Kingdom, Scandinavia, Germany, and Australia.

Activision was scaling back its releases of new games to devote more attention to its better-selling high profile titles. Management had decided that the glut of over 500 recently released titles made it advantageous for Activision to focus its development and marketing resources on high-quality titles that stood a much better chance of winning space on retailers' shelves. However, many software publishers were also putting more emphasis on sequels to previous hits. Senior management was monitoring developments in online game play and was developing plans to enter the online segment in the near future. Robert Kotick, Activision's CEO said, "The thing I'm most excited about is prize play and cash play. When you reward people, that's going to open up a whole new universe of revenue. It's the gaming component of gaming."[8]

Acclaim Entertainment   Founded in 1987, Acclaim developed, published, marketed, and distributed games for PlayStation 2, Xbox, GameCube, Game Boy and, to a lesser extent, PC systems. It had six software development studios in the United States and the United Kingdom that developed its games, and it also contracted with independent software developers to create software products. Through its subsidiaries in North America, the United Kingdom, Germany, France, Spain, and Australia, Acclaim distributed its games directly to retailers and other outlets in North America, Europe, Australia, and New Zealand; but in Japan and other parts of the Pacific Rim, Acclaim relied on regional distributors. Acclaim had contracted to distribute a limited number of games developed by third parties, and it had a small operation that developed and published strategy guides relating to its software products and, from time to time, issued certain "special edition" comic magazines to support some of its games.

Acclaim's development time for a new game ranged from 12 to 36 months, and the average development cost for new titles ranged from $2 million to $8 million. Acclaim had spent $8 million and three years developing its Turok: Evolution (shooting) game for the PlayStation, Xbox, and GameCube platforms and spent another $8 million to market and promote the title in the marketplace. Other Acclaim "franchise" titles included All-Star Baseball, NBA Jam, Alias, and Gladiator: Sword of Vengance; among its lesser titles were three wrestling games (WWF Warzone, Legends of Wrestling, and WWF Attitude), Jeremy McGrath Supercross (motocross), Aggressive Inline (skating), Dave Mirra BMX XXX, and NFL QB Club. Close to 50 new titles had been released in the September 2002–November 2003 period. Most were targeted at males in the 15 to 35 age range.

Acclaim had lost money for the past two years. It reported a loss of $4.5 million on revenues of $269 million in the fiscal year ending August 31, 2002; for the seven-month period September 1, 2002, through March 31, 2003 (during which the company converted to a fiscal year ending March 31), Acclaim posted a $68 million loss on sales of almost $102 million. For the first six months of fiscal 2004 (April 2003 through September 2003), Acclaim had revenues of $74 million and a loss of $22 million. As of late fall 2003, the company was working with creditors to improve its financial condition and reduce a working capital deficit of $67 million; if sales did not improve in the 2003 holiday season, management expected to have to curtail some aspects of the company's operations starting in early 2004.

THQ THQ was one of the world's fastest-growing video game publishers, with a diverse portfolio of game titles and a number two ranking among the independent game publishers, behind Electronic Arts. In 2003, it had more than 70 products in development across the action, racing, puzzle, wrestling, kids, action-adventure, and platform game genres. THQ's England, Germany, France, Korea, and Australia offices distributed games to retailers in more than 77 countries. The company had nearly 400 programmers, artists, and designers spread across six studios and a minority interest in wrestling game developer Yuke's Company, Ltd., of Japan. THQ's strategic priorities were to build a well-diversified product portfolio across brand, genre, and platform; establish strong technology and internal development capabilities; expand its global product development capabilities; grow its international sales; and pursue opportunities in wireless gaming. THQ's revenues and profits for the 2000–2002 period were as follows:

	2002	2001	2000
Net sales	$480,529,000	$378,992,000	$347,003,000
Net income	$ 12,994,000	$ 36,013,000	$ 18,189,000

The decline in profitability in 2002 was due to sharply higher costs for software development and for sales and marketing. For 2003, management was forecasting revenues of about $570 million and earnings of close to $28 million.

THQ had the strongest lineup of wrestling games of any game developer. It introduced over 40 new games for various platforms in 2002, including Britney's Dance Beat, 2 Rugrats titles, Jimmy Neutron vs. Jimmy Negatron, Scooby Doo! Night of 100 Frights, MX Superfly, 6 wrestling titles, 4 racing titles, and 23 Game Boy Advance titles. THQ was the leading independent publisher of games for Game Boy Advance, with roughly a 20 percent market share of all GBA games sold. GBA games accounted for about one-fourth of THQ's revenues.

Sony   Sony had revenues of $62.3 billion in 2002 ($20 billion in North America) and had 161,000 employees worldwide. The profits of Sony's video game division accounted for over 50 percent of Sony's total profits in 2001–2002, much of which came from the Sony Computer Entertainment America (SCEA) division. The head of SCEA was considered one of the most powerful executives in Hollywood. About one of three U.S. households owned a PlayStation. Sony had introduced its PlayStation 2 in Japan in March 2000, in North America in October 2000, and in Europe in November 2000. The PlayStation 2 was a 128-bit DVD-based system that was Internet and cable ready, as well as backward compatible for games published for the PlayStation.

Sony developed about 10–15 percent of the games developed for PlayStation 2. Sony game developers had created several best-selling titles-Gran Turismo (action racing), Rise to Honor (martial arts adventure), Twisted Metal (combat racing), Cool Boarders, Jet Ski X$_2$O, NFL Gameday, NBA Shootout, NCAA Gamebreaker (basketball), NHL Faceoff, World Tour Soccer, and SOCOM II: U.S. Navy SEALs (a Mature-labeled game that was the sequel to the number one–rated online game in 2002).

Sony had attracted about 25,000 European online gamers three months after launching its service in June 2003. The company's Sony Online Entertainment (SOE) division created, developed, and provided online games for the personal computer, on-line, and console markets. SOE's games ranged from simple card and trivia games to more strategic, tactical, and role-playing "persistent interactive worlds." More than 13 million people had registered at SOE's award-winning Web site, The Station (www.station.com), and the division was striving to become the premier Internet gaming destination. Sony launched a multimillion-dollar marketing blitz in North America during the 2003 holiday season to expand the PlayStation 2 gaming experience among mass-market consumers, specifically targeting new users, gift-givers, and children.

Nintendo   Nintendo launched its GameCube console in Japan in September 2001, in North America in November 2001, and in Europe in May 2002. The GameCube employed 128-bit technology and played games that were manufactured on a proprietary optical disk. During the six-month period from April through September 2003, Nintendo sold 890,000 GameCube consoles worldwide, well below expectations. Strong sales of Game Boy hardware and software, however, pushed Nintendo's revenues for the period up 1.6 percent, from 208 billion yen to 211 billion yen. Despite posting a loss of 2.9 billion yen for the six-month period, Nintendo said it was on track to achieve revenues of 550 billion yen and profits of 60 billion yen for its fiscal year ending March 31, 2004. Company officials hoped that the worldwide price cuts for the GameCube in September–October 2003 would enable it to meet its objective of selling 6 million GameCubes by the end of the fiscal year. About 74 percent of Nintendo's sales were outside Japan.

In 2003 Nintendo had introduced the Game Boy Advance SP, a new, foldable version of its popular Game Boy Advance with features that were appealing to adults. The makeover was intended to make the Game Boy more competitive with a raft of new handheld models coming on the market—the PlayStation Portable; Nokia's N-Gage (a cell phone that played video games); and the Zodiac, a Palm-compatible game system developed by Tapwave, a company founded by former Palm executives. Nintendo had recently reduced its royalty on Game Boy Advance games by about $3, to a range of $7 to $11, to help lower the price of Game Boy software and to give independent game developers a bigger financial incentive to create and publish new games for Game Boy Advance.

Nintendo released new versions of three of its biggest franchise games for Game-Cube in 2002 and 2003—Mario Sunshine, Metroid Prime, and The Legend of Zelda. Other important Nintendo games for GameCube and Game Boy were Pokémon; Super Mario Brothers; Donkey Kong; Super Smash Brothers (head-to-head fighting); Disney's Magical Quest; and the Starfox, Mario Kart, and Final Fantasy series. The most popular title played on GameCube was Resident Evil, developed by Capcom.

Industry observers believed that Nintendo's aggressive pricing of its consoles, coupled with its efforts to bundle games with its hardware and its strong relationships with game developers, would prove beneficial in boosting Nintendo's market share over the long term.

Microsoft   Microsoft launched the Xbox in North America in November 2001, in Japan in February 2002, and in Europe in March 2002. While Microsoft was far from thrilled with unit sales of its Xbox consoles going into the 2003 holiday season, executives saw the industry as a marathon rather than a sprint when it came to global market leadership. The Xbox was firmly entrenched as the number two-selling console in North America and Europe in 2003, but it trailed both Sony and Nintendo in Japan, South Korea, and the rest of the Asia-Pacific region. Management expected the Xbox to narrow the gap on Sony's PlayStation and become a stronger number two when the next-generation consoles were introduced. Microsoft was using Xbox Live and the online capabilities of its Xbox console to differentiate itself from rivals and build market share. Microsoft executives saw Xbox Live as the key to its future in Japan, where sales of Xbox had not met expectations.

Microsoft had announced plans to spend $2 billion during the 2003–2007 period to build and promote Xbox Live. Xbox Live had been introduced in 14 European markets and had attracted around 100,000 European subscribers as of late 2003. Worldwide, Microsoft had an estimated 500,000 Xbox Live subscribers in late 2003 and 50 Xbox titles available for online play at Xbox Live. In early 2003 Xbox Live was hosting about 3 million game sessions weekly; more than 15.7 million hours of play had been logged in the first three months of operation.

The most popular game on Xbox was Halo: Combat Evolved, developed by Bungie, which debuted with the Xbox in November 2001 and had sold over 3 million copies. A sequel, Halo 2, originally scheduled for release in time for the 2003 holiday season, was scheduled to ship in 2004. Games that had Xbox Live capability included Microsoft's NFL Fever 2003, Counterstrike, Midtown Madness 3, MechAssault, and Whacked; Infogrames' Unreal Championship; and LucasArts' Star Wars Galaxies. So far, Microsoft's lineup of internally developed games (which also included Kung Fu Chaos, NBA Inside Drive, Brute Force, and Crimson Skies) had not proved as popular as those of Sony, Nintendo, or Electronic Arts.

In the year ending June 30, 2003, Microsoft reported consolidated revenues of $32.2 billion and net income of $10 billion, and it had cash and short-term investments of $49 billion.

Electronic Arts

Electronic Arts began operations in 1982 in California and over the years grew from being a niche technology venture into a full-fledged entertainment company. EA maintained its headquarters in Redwood City. In 2003, it had about 4,000 employees, of whom 1,700 were outside the United States, and management had plans to add 1,200 new staff, mostly game developers. EA's revenues had more than doubled since 1999

Exhibit 7   SUMMARY OF ELECTRONIC ARTS' FINANCIAL PERFORMANCE, FISCAL YEARS 1999–2003 (in thousands of dollars, except for per share data)

	Fiscal Year Ending March 31				
	2003	2002	2001	2000	1999
Statement of operations data					
Net revenues	$2,482,244	$1,724,675	$1,322,273	$1,420,011	$1,221,863
Cost of goods sold	1,072,802	814,783	664,991	710,974	630,827
Gross profit	$1,409,442	$ 909,892	$ 657,282	$ 709,037	$ 591,036
Operating expenses:					
Marketing and sales	$ 332,453	$ 241,109	$ 185,336	$ 188,611	$ 163,407
General and administrative	130,859	107,059	104,041	92,418	76,219
Research and development	400,990	380,564	376,179	255,694	196,137
Amortization of intangibles	7,482	25,418	19,323	11,989	5,880
Charge for acquired in-process technology	–	–	2,719	6,539	44,115
Restructuring charges	15,102	7,485	–	–	–
Asset impairment charges	66,329	12,818	—	—	–
Total operating expenses	$ 953,215	$ 774,453	$ 687,598	$ 555,251	$ 485,758
Operating income (loss)	$ 456,227	$ 135,439	$ (30,316)	$ 153,786	$ 105,278
Interest and other income, net	5,222	12,848	16,886	16,028	13,180
Income (loss) before provision for income taxes and minority interest	$ 461,449	$ 148,287	$ (13,430)	$ 169,814	$ 118,458
Provision for income taxes	143,049	45,969	(4,163)	52,642	45,414
Income (loss) before minority interest	$ 318,400	$ 102,318	$ (9,267)	$ 117,172	$ 73,044
Minority interest in consolidated joint ventures	(1,303)	(809)	(1,815)	(421)	(172)
Net income (loss)	$ 317,097	$ 101,509	$ (11,082)	$ 116,751	$ 72,872
Net income per share-diluted	$2.17	$0.71	$ (0.08)	$0.88	$0.58
Balance sheet data at fiscal year end					
Cash and cash equivalents	$ 949,995	$ 552,826	$ 419,812	$ 246,265	$ 242,208
Short-term investments	637,623	244,110	46,680	93,539	70,614
Marketable securities	1,111	6,869	10,022	236	4,884
Working capital	1,340,261	699,561	478,701	440,021	333,256
Long-term investments	–	–	8,400	8,400	18,400
Total assets	2,359,533	1,699,374	1,378,918	1,192,312	901,873
Total liabilities	570,876	452,982	340,026	265,302	236,209
Minority interest	3,918	3,098	4,545	3,617	2,733
Total stockholders' equity	1,784,739	1,243,294	1,034,347	923,393	662,931

Source: 2003 10K report.

(see Exhibit 7). The slight dip in fiscal 2001 revenues was due to the transition to the new-generation consoles in 2000–2001—many gamers postponed the purchase of new games in the months leading up to the introduction of new consoles, preferring to wait until more sophisticated games for the new consoles were released. EA reported a loss in fiscal 2001 because of heavy start-up expenditures for the EA.com segment of the company's business and low initial revenues from online operations (see Exhibit 8).

Exhibit 8   EA'S FINANCIAL PERFORMANCE BY BUSINESS SEGMENT, FISCAL YEARS 2001–2003 (in thousands)

	2003	2002	2001
Operations of "EA Core" (or non-online) business segment			
Net revenues	$2,400,669	$1,647,502	$1,280,172
Cost of goods sold	1,056,385	797,894	650,330
Gross profit	$1,344,284	$ 849,608	$ 629,842
Total operating expenses	730,747	563,146	506,427
Operating income (loss)	$ 613,537	$ 286,462	$ 123,415
Identifiable assets	$2,287,743	$1,529,422	$1,167,846
Capital expenditures	58,328	38,406	51,460
Operations of EA.com business segment			
Net revenues	$ 81,575	$ 77,173	$ 42,101
Cost of goods sold	16,417	16,889	14,661
Gross profit	$ 65,158	$ 60,284	$ 27,440
Total operating expenses	222,468	211,307	181,171
Operating income (loss)	$ (157,310)	$ (151,023)	$ (153,731)
Identifiable assets	$ 71,790	$ 169,952	$ 211,072
Capital expenditures	780	13,112	68,887

Note: EA defined its two business segments as EA Core (which included all non-online operations worldwide) and EA.com (which consisted of all online activities worldwide). Beginning in March 2003, EA consolidated the operations of EA.com into its core business operations and eliminated the distinction between the two segments.

Source: 2003 10K report, pp. 110–12.

EA's near-term goal was to be the market leader of games played on the current generation of 128-bit consoles. Toward this end, EA was investing heavily in the development of tools and technologies that would facilitate the creation of new games for the existing (and future) game-playing platforms, spending $401 million for research and development (R&D) in fiscal 2003, $380.6 million in fiscal 2002, and $376.2 million in fiscal 2001. In fiscal 2004, EA planned to introduce games for six platforms: PlayStation 2, GameCube, Xbox, Game Boy Advance, PlayStation, and PCs. In the prior fiscal year, EA had introduced games for seven platforms: PlayStation 2, GameCube, Xbox, Game Boy Advance, Game Boy Color, PlayStation, PCs, and online play. Over the past 20 years, EA had published games for 42 different platforms.

Foreign sales were expected to account for a significant and growing portion of EA's revenues. Exhibit 9 shows the geographic distribution of EA's sales in 2001, 2002, and 2003.

EA's Creative Process

EA's game design staff consisted of digital animators, programmers, and creative individuals who in many instances had backgrounds in television, the music industry, and the movie industry and were attracted by the creative opportunities in video games and EA's attractive compensation packages of high pay and stock options. Developing a game from scratch was about an 18-month process. To create a new game, small teams of EA game developers put together quick prototypes to demonstrate one small scene

Exhibit 9   EA'S FINANCIAL PERFORMANCE BY GEOGRAPHIC AREA, FISCAL YEARS
2001–2003 (in thousands)

	Fiscal Years Ending March 31		
	2003	**2002**	**2001**
North America			
Revenues from unaffiliated customers	$1,435,718	$1,093,244	$ 831,924
Operating income (loss)	216,491	8,328	(31,996)
Capital expenditures	47,955	39,259	103,048
Identifiable assets	1,764,103	1,325,939	1,034,625
Europe			
Revenues from unaffiliated customers	$ 878,904	$ 519,458	$ 386,728
Operating income (loss)	230,101	121,058	(8,914)
Capital expenditures	9,894	10,350	15,535
Identifiable assets	544,782	333,825	300,196
Japan			
Revenues from unaffiliated customers	$ 80,053	$ 58,597	$ 52,582
Operating income (loss)	4,601	3,401	7,437
Capital expenditures	384	871	660
Identifiable assets	22,800	18,175	23,733
Asia-Pacific (excluding Japan)			
Revenues from unaffiliated customers	$ 87,569	$ 53,376	$ 51,039
Operating income (loss)	4,927	2,277	2,962
Capital expenditures	875	1,038	1,104
Identifiable assets	27,848	21,435	20,364

Source: 2003 10K report, p. 113.

that represented the "creative center" of a potential game, usually focusing on the activity that would make the game fun to play.[9] If greenlighted, the team fleshed out the idea and created comiclike storyboards of every scene, much like moviemakers would illustrate a script. State-of-the-art tools were used to allow for more cost-effective product development and to efficiently convert games designed on one game platform to other platforms.

EA had two major design studios—one in Vancouver, British Columbia, and one in Los Angeles—and smaller design studios in San Francisco, Orlando, London, and Tokyo. The dispersion of design studios helped EA to design games that were specific to different cultures—for example, the London studio took the lead in designing the popular FIFA Soccer game to suit European tastes and to replicate the stadiums, signage, and team rosters. No other game software company had EA's ability to localize games or to launch games on multiple platforms in multiple countries in multiple languages. EA's Harry Potter and the Chamber of Secrets was released simultaneously in 75 countries, in 31 languages, and on seven platforms.[10]

Every 90 days, a large group of managers and executives would gather in EA's Milestones theater to listen to game developers update their works in progress. If a game did not come across as promising, EA pulled the plug on further work. According to John Riccello, the company's chief operating officer, "We double down on things that work. We tend to stop things that don't work." Only a few new original games made it through to production and distribution each year. In fiscal 2003, a team of employees that had developed one of EA's hit Medal of Honor products was hired away by a competitor.

In the course of creating a number of its games, EA acquired intellectual property and other licensed content from sports leagues, player associations, performing artists, movie studios, music studios, and book authors. Many of its games included the likenesses or voices of various artists, sports personalities, and cartoon characters, along with the musical compositions and performances of film stars and musicians. J. K. Rowling, the author of the Harry Potter books, had written portions of the script for EA's three Harry Potter games.

EA's policy was to make games that it could be proud of, which meant that it stayed away from games with profanity, sex, crime, and violence. While some of EA's rivals—like Take-Two Interactive, whose best-selling Grand Theft Auto: Vice City game involved doing drug deals, blowing up cars, consorting with a prostitute, and then hacking her to death—were willing to create violent or sexually suggestive games, EA had a firm policy of not creating games for mature audiences. The chief guardians of this policy were Lawrence Probst and Ruth Kennedy, EA's general counsel. When EA's developers were creating the DefJam Vendetta wrestling title, Probst, at the urging of Kennedy, vetoed several scenes that he and Kennedy felt were objectionable. In 1998, EA acquired Westwood Studios, which had developed a best-selling game called Thrill Kill for Sony's PlayStation; Thrill Kill was a four-player fighting game that featured beheadings, dismemberment, and lots of blood-spilling action. Several members of EA senior management, including Kennedy, did not believe that Thrill Kill belonged in the EA lineup; Probst agreed and axed the game. Web sites sprang up protesting the move, the game industry press screamed censorship, and there were even grumblings within the company. Even though the decision cost EA millions in lost revenues, Probst declared, "I don't regret it for a minute. EA will not publish games with gratuitous sex and violence."[11] But while gore and raunchy graphics were forbidden, EA did include trash talk in its sport games. During the past 20 years, EA had won over 700 awards for outstanding software in the United States and Europe.

EA's Relationships with the Three Major Console Manufacturers

Approximately 37 percent of EA's revenues in fiscal 2003 were derived from software sales for Sony's PlayStation 2, and it derived about 4 percent of its revenues from sales of games for the original PlayStation (see Exhibit 10). EA released 19 new titles worldwide for PlayStation 2 in fiscal 2003, compared to 18 titles in fiscal 2002; 6 titles were released for PlayStation in fiscal 2003 versus 5 in fiscal 2002. Management expected that sales of EA games for PlayStation 2 would continue to grow in fiscal 2004 but at a slower rate; sales of PlayStation games were expected to continue to decline. Under terms of an agreement in 2000, EA was authorized to develop and distribute DVD-based software for the PlayStation 2; however, the agreement called for Sony to supply PlayStation 2 DVDs for its products. Likewise, under terms of an amended 1994 agreement, EA was authorized to develop and distribute CD-based software for the PlayStation, with all PlayStation CDs being sourced from Sony. In May 2003, EA and Sony announced that EA would make many of its sports games available for Sony's PlayStation 2 online service. EA considered that its relationship with Sony was good.

EA derived about 7 percent of its 2003 revenues from GameCube software. It released 17 titles worldwide for GameCube play in 2003, versus 5 titles in 2002.

Exhibit 10   EA'S REVENUES BY PRODUCT LINE, FISCAL YEARS 2001–2003 (in thousands)

Revenue Source	2003	2002	2001	Percent Change 2002–2003	Percent Change 2001–2002
Games for Sony PlayStation 2	$ 910,693	$ 482,882	$ 258,988	89%	86%
Games for PCs	499,634	456,292	405,256	9	13
Games for Microsoft Xbox	219,378	78,363	–	180	n.a.
Games for Nintendo GameCube	176,656	51,740	–	241	n.a.
Games for Sony PlayStation	99,951	189,535	309,988	(47)	(39)
Games for Nintendo Game Boy Advance	79,093	43,653	–	81	n.a.
Online subscriptions	37,851	30,940	28,878	22	7
Advertising	31,988	38,024	6,175	(16)	516
Games for Nintendo Game Boy Color	26,293	38,026	–	(31)	n.a.
License, original equipment manufacture, and other	24,948	46,210	90,710	(46)	(49)
Co-publishing and distribution	375,759	269,010	222,278	40	21
Total	$2,482,244	$1,724,675	$1,322,273	44%	30%

Source: 2003 10K report.

Revenues from games for GameCube were expected to increase in fiscal 2004 as the installed base of GameCube consoles grew. As per a 2001 licensing agreement, EA was authorized to distribute Nintendo's proprietary optical disks containing EA game software for GameCube consoles, but Nintendo supplied EA with all the optical disks. EA management believed that it had a strong working relationship with Nintendo.

About 9 percent of EA's fiscal 2003 revenues came from sales of games for Microsoft's Xbox, up from 5 percent in fiscal 2002. The revenue gains were due to a growing installed base of Xbox consoles, plus the Xbox's being available for a full 12 months compared to only 5 months in fiscal 2002. EA introduced 16 new titles for play on the Xbox in fiscal 2003 versus 10 new games in fiscal 2002. Under terms of a licensing agreement entered into with Microsoft in late 2000, EA was authorized to develop and distribute DVD-based video games to play on the Xbox; unlike its agreements with Sony and Nintendo, it was not compelled to source its DVDs from Microsoft. However, EA's relationship with Microsoft was strained in 2003; Microsoft's policy of not allowing EA (or any other game developer) to earn any revenues from online play of Xbox games had prompted EA management, after months of back-and-forth negotiations, to refuse to program online functionality into its Xbox games. It was unclear to what extent the absence of online capability in EA's games for the Xbox would impact the sales of EA's Xbox games.

EA's Suppliers

Electronic Arts used four types of suppliers:

- The console makers (Sony and Nintendo) that supplied the CDs, DVDs, or optical disks on which EA then installed its video games designed for PlayStation, GameCube, and Game Boy consoles.
- Companies that pressed the CDs, DVDs, and optical disks containing its games.

- Companies that printed its game instruction booklets.

- Companies that packaged the disks and printed game instructions on the jewel cases and boxes for shipping to customers.

In many cases, EA was able to negotiate volume discounts and it was the company's practice to have multiple sources of supply for all the functions that were outsourced to suppliers. The costs to press a disk and print game instruction booklets were typically less than $1 per unit.

EA kept only a small inventory of its games on hand because (1) it could obtain additional supplies and fill retailer orders from replenished inventories within two to three weeks and (2) historically, most sales of a particular game occurred 60–90 days after initial release.

EA's Marketing and Distribution

Electronic Arts marketed its products worldwide under four brand logos: EA Sports, EA Sports Big, EA Games, and Pogo (see Exhibit 11). In fiscal 2003, EA introduced 70 new game titles under its four brands in North America, plus localized versions of its products in the rest of the world; it also distributed about 34 titles that it co-published with or distributed for other parties. In addition to releasing new versions of its popular sports titles annually, EA also released "expansion packs" for previously published games that provided additional characters, storylines, settings, and missions—for example, six expansion packs had been issued for The Sims, the best-selling PC game of 2000, 2001, and 2002. Games that were popular enough to justify sequels or expansion packs were viewed by EA as "franchise titles." The Sims, which was essentially a digital dollhouse, was EA's all-time best-selling game, achieving sales of 27 million copies in three years and luring addicted players, who included housewives and investment

Exhibit 11   EXAMPLES OF INTERACTIVE SOFTWARE GAMES MARKETED UNDER ELECTRONIC ART'S FOUR MAJOR BRANDS

- **EA Sports**—Madden NFL 2004, NCAA Football 2004, FIFA Soccer 2004, NBA Live 2004, NHL 2004 (hockey), MVP Baseball 2004, Rugby 2004, NCAA March Madness 2004 (basketball), Tiger Woods PGA Tour 2004, and NASCAR Thunder.

- **EA Sports Big**—Def Jam Vendetta (wrestling), SSX 3 (snowboarding), NFL Street, and NBA Street Volume 2 (basketball).

- **EA Games**—Harry Potter and the Chamber of Secrets, The Lord of the Rings: The Two Towers, James Bond 007 in Nightfire, The Sims, Superstar, Sim City 4, Need for Speed: Underground, Hot Pursuit 2, Harry Potter: Quidditch World Cup, Medal of Honor Rising Sun, Freedom Fighters, Command & Conquer Generals, Battlefield 1942: Secret Weapons of World War II.

- **Pogo**—Games marketed under this brand were electronic card games, puzzle games, and word games such as First Class Solitaire, Tumble Bees, Poppit!, Turbo 21, Word Whomp, Jungle Gin, and Sci-Fi Slots. These games, as well as many others, were available for play online at www.pogo.com, www.ea.com, and certain online services provided by America Online. At www.pogo.com, players won cash prizes and could also pay fees to enter tournaments or subscribe to Club Pogo ($4.99 per month or $29.99 per year) to become eligible for even larger prizes and awards. Club Pogo offered subscribers exclusive games with enhanced graphics, sound, and player features and a variety of ways to win big prizes and drawings.

Source: Company reports and press releases.

bankers. EA's first two Harry Potter games—both of which involved months of collaboration between EA and the producers, artists, and engineers of the movie and were released worldwide on the same day as the movie was released—had generated $500 million in revenues for EA. Sales of Harry Potter and the Chamber of Secrets, published on seven platforms, accounted for approximately 10 percent of EA's fiscal 2003 revenues, and sales of Harry Potter and the Sorcerer's Stone, published on four platforms, accounted for 12 percent of EA's fiscal 2002 revenues. Some 33 EA games had sold over 1 million copies worldwide.

The retail selling prices in North America of EA's games, excluding older titles marketed as Classics, typically ranged from $30 to $50. Classics titles had retail prices from $10 to $30. Outside North America, prices varied widely based on local market conditions. EA expected that in fiscal 2004 the premium prices of its hit titles would remain firm but that prices for its other games would be lower than in fiscal 2003, in line with the tendency for overall game prices to decline once current-generation consoles had been on the market for several years (see again Exhibit 5).

A big part of EA's marketing effort was devoted to promoting the EA Sports brand. EA saw the sports segment of the video game market as particularly attractive. Sports games were appealing to males between the ages of 16 and 40 because they had nearly photo-realistic graphics and gave game-playing sports fans the chance to carry on rivalries that were the trademark of professional and collegiate teams. Sports games were regularly endorsed by the biggest stars in professional sports, which helped spur sales (as well as providing big name sports stars with lucrative endorsement contracts). According to EA's vice president of marketing, from a marketing positioning standpoint, EA preferred to think of itself "as a sports company that makes games as opposed to a game company that makes sports games. EA Sports is as much a culture as it is a product."[12]

In the past few years, EA had begun trimming its lineup of video games, eliminating many of the slow sellers and concentrating its efforts on creating "franchise" games that could achieve sales of millions of copies. In 2000 EA released 68 new titles, and in 2002 only 58 titles were released. Lawrence Probst indicated that EA's strategy was to "focus on doing fewer things and doing them better and getting more leverage out of the titles we ship." Roughly 70 percent of EA's revenues came from new releases of existing games.

Electronic Arts used a field sales organization and a group of telephone sales representatives to market its games directly to retailers; these two channels accounted for 95 percent of sales in North America. In markets where direct sales were uneconomical, EA utilized specialized and regional distributors and rack jobbers to gain retail access. Games were made available on a disk (usually a CD or DVD) or a cartridge that was packaged and sold in retail stores or through EA's online store.

In fiscal 2003, EA's games were available in approximately 80,000 retail locations worldwide, including mass-market retailers like Wal-Mart, electronics specialty stores like Best Buy, and game software specialty stores like Electronics Boutique. Over 66 percent of EA's sales in the United States were made to six retailers (Wal-Mart, Toys "R" Us, Target, Best Buy, Circuit City, and Kmart), and in Europe over 40 percent of sales were made to 10 retailers. Worldwide, Wal-Mart was EA's biggest customer, accounting for 12 percent of EA's total sales. EA's largest distribution relationship was with Sony in Japan; 60 percent of the sales of EA's PlayStation and PlayStation 2 games in Japan were made through Sony.

Because the video game business was becoming increasingly "hits driven," EA had found it necessary to boost its budgets for marketing and advertising, particularly

TV advertising. Sales and marketing expenditures had increased from $163.4 million in fiscal 1999 to $332.4 million in fiscal 2003 and had averaged 13–14 percent of sales each year since 1999.

EA's business was highly seasonal. Sales were highest in the calendar year-end holiday season (about 40–50 percent of the annual total) and lowest in the April–May–June period. Orders were typically shipped upon receipt, resulting in little or no order backlog.

EA's Co-Publishing and Distribution Activities with Other Game Developers

In 2003, EA was distributing 34 co-publishing and distribution titles. Co-published titles were games conceived and developed by other game developers for which EA provided production assistance and marketing and distribution services. Some of the games were published and marketed under one of EA's three primary brands (EA Games, EA Sports, and EA Sports Big). The distribution titles were games published by another game developer and delivered to EA as ready-to-market products; EA provided only distribution services for these games.

Electronic Arts and America Online

In 1999, EA and America Online entered into a five-year agreement for EA to be AOL's exclusive provider of a broad aggregation of online games and interactive entertainment for AOL's Game Channel. EA managed all of the content of the Game Channel and had the latitude to sell its games to AOL subscribers and users. The terms of the five-year agreement resulted in AOL paying EA $21.3 million and ultimately receiving 477,350 shares of EA's common stock in return.

Endnotes

[1] As quoted in Peter Lewis, "The Biggest Game in Town," *Fortune*, September 15, 2003, p. 140.

[2] As quoted in ibid., p. 138.

[3] Ibid., p.135.

[4] Ibid.

[5] Ibid.

[6] Paul A. Paterson, "Synergy and Expanding Technology Drive Booming Video Industry," *TD Monthly* 2, no. 8 (August 2003), accessed at www.toydirectory.com/monthly/Aug2003 on November 15, 2003.

[7] Based on research conducted by DFC Intelligence and reported in a press release, June 25, 2003, at www.dfcint.com.

[8] As quoted in Lewis, "The Biggest Game in Town," p. 138.

[9] Dean Takahashi, "Electronic Arts Grows to $2.5 Billion in Annual Sales," *San Jose Mercury News*, May 5, 2003.

[10] Associated Press, "Electronic Arts, A Powerhouse Well-Attuned to Public Tastes," news release, August 18, 2003.

[11] As quoted in Ashby Jones, "The Rules of the Game," *Corporate Counsel* 3, no. 7 (July 1, 2003), pp. 72 ff. (accessed December 4, 2003 at www.law.com/jsp/cc/pubarticleCC.jsp?id= 1055463668855).

[12] As quoted in "Sports, Racing Games Are Powerhouse of Video Games World," www.Kiplinger.com, July 17, 2003.

CASE 16

eBay

In a League by Itself

Louis Marino
The University of Alabama

Patrick Kreiser
The University of Alabama

 On September 20, 2000, eBay's top management surprised the financial community by announcing ambitious objectives of $3 billion in annual revenues by year-end 2005, a gross margin target above 80 percent, and target operating margins of 30–35 percent. Given that eBay's 2000 annual revenues were only $400 million, the $3 billion annual revenue target implied a compound annual growth rate of 50 percent from the end of 2000 through 2005—an objective some analysts criticized as too aggressive. Other analysts, however, wondered if the revenue target was ambitious enough, since online auction sales were forecast to reach $54.3 billion by 2007 and since eBay was far and away the dominant player in the online auction market.

But in early 2004 eBay was well on its way to meeting the 2005 goals it set for itself in 2000. In January 2004, eBay reported 2003 revenues of $2.17 billion and a gross margin of 81 percent. If the company could grow its revenues by 40 percent in 2004, it could reach its $3 billion annual revenue goal a year ahead of the 2005 target date. However, analysts were becoming increasingly concerned about whether eBay could sustain its phenomenal growth (see Exhibit 1), given that almost one-third of all U.S. Internet users were already registered on eBay and that eBay could expect stiffening competition from other ambitious online auction sites and e-tailers as it pursued its growth initiatives.

Building on the vision of its founder, Pierre Omidyar (pronounced oh-*mid*-ee-ar), eBay was initially conceived as an online marketplace that would facilitate a person-to-person trading community based on a democratized, efficient market in which

Exhibit 1   SELECTED INDICATORS OF eBAY'S GROWTH, 1996–2003

	1996	1997	1998	1999	2000	2001	2002	2003
Number of registered users (in millions)	0.041	0.341	2.2	10.0	22.0	42.4	61.7	94.9
Active users (in millions)	NA	NA	NA	NA	NA	18.0	27.7	41.2
Gross merchandise sales (in millions)	$7	$95	$745	$2,800	$5,400	$9,300	$14,900	$24,000
Number of auctions listed (in millions)	0.29	4.4	33.7	129	264	423	638	971

everyone could have equal access through the same medium, the Internet. Leveraging a unique business model and the growing popularity of the Internet, eBay had dominated the online auction market since its beginning in the mid-1990s and had grown its business to include over 94.9 million registered users from more than 150 countries heading into 2004. The auction site's diverse base of registered users in early 2004—which ranged from high school and college students looking to make a few extra dollars, to Fortune 500 companies such as IBM selling excess inventory, to large government agencies like the U.S. Postal Service selling undeliverable parcels—differed greatly from its original user base of individuals and small companies.

The Growth of E-Commerce and Online Auctions

The concepts underlying the Internet were first conceived in the 1960s, but it wasn't until the 1990s that the Internet garnered widespread use and became a part of everyday life. The *Computer Industry Almanac* estimated that by the end of 2002 there were approximately 665 million Internet users worldwide in over 150 countries and that number would grow to over 1 billion users worldwide by 2005.[1] While the top 15 countries accounted for more than 70 percent of the computers in use, slightly less than one-fourth of these Internet users (160.7 million) resided in the United States, and the United States' share as a percentage of total Internet users worldwide was falling. The highest areas of Internet usage growth were expected to be in developing countries in Asia, Latin America, and Eastern Europe with increasing access through new technologies such as Web-enabled cell phones. However, it was expected that total growth rates would not exceed 20 percent annually in the future.

Forrester Research forecast that worldwide e-commerce revenues would be $6.79 trillion in 2004 and that online retail would grow at a 19 percent annual rate between 2003 and 2008 to reach $229.9 billion, of which 25 percent, or $57.5 billion, was expected to come from online auction sales. It was also predicted that North America would account for 51.5 percent of total e-commerce sales in 2004, with the Asia-Pacific region accounting for 24.3 percent, Western Europe accounting for 22.5 percent, and Latin America accounting for 12.1 percent of total sales. Within the business-to-consumer segment, eBay's primary area of operation, U.S. e-commerce accounted for over 65 percent of all Internet transactions in 1999 but was expected to account for only about 38 percent in 2003 and potentially less in the future, due to rapid expansion in other parts of the world. Asia was expected to grow especially rapidly following the 2001 decision to include China in the World Trade Organization. In 2002, Germany, the United Kingdom, France, and Italy accounted for 70 percent of the e-commerce revenues in Western Europe, but this share was expected to decline as business-to-business e-commerce in Europe was expected to triple from 2003 to 2006. Exhibit 2 displays the expected total growth in worldwide e-commerce between 1999 and 2004.

Key Success Factors in Online Retailing

It was relatively easy to create a Web site that functioned like a retail store; the more significant challenge was for an online retailer to generate traffic to the site in the form of both new and returning customers. To reach new customers, some online retailers part-

Exhibit 2   ESTIMATED GROWTH IN GLOBAL E-COMMERCE 1999–2004

	1999	2000	2001	2002	2003	2004
Estimated value of e-commerce transactions	$170 billion	$657 billion	$1.23 billion	$2.23 trillion	$3.98 trillion	$6.79 trillion

Source: Forrester Research.

nered with search engines—such as Google, MySimon, or StreetPrices—that allowed customers to compare prices for a given product from many retailers. Other tactics employed to build traffic included direct e-mail, online advertising at portals and content-related sites, and some traditional advertising such as print and television advertising. For customers who found their way to a site, most online retailers endeavored to provide extensive product information, include pictures of the merchandise, make the site easily navigable, and have enough new things happening at the site to keep customers coming back. (A site's ability to generate repeat visitors was known as *stickiness.*) For new Internet users, retailers had to help them overcome their nervousness about using the Internet itself to shop for items customers generally bought in stores. Web sites had to appease concerns about the possible theft of credit card numbers and the possible sale of personal information to marketing firms. Online retailing also had severe limitations in the case of those goods and services people wanted to see in person to verify their quality. From the retailer's perspective, there was the issue of collecting payment from buyers who wanted to use checks or money orders instead of credit cards.

Online Auctions

The first known auctions were held in Babylon around 500 BC. In AD 193, the entire Roman Empire was put up for auction after the emperor Pertinax was executed. Didius Julianus bid 6,250 drachmas per royal guard and was immediately named emperor of Rome. However, Julianus was executed only two months later, suggesting that he may have been the first-ever victim of the winner's curse (bidding more than the good would cost in a nonauction setting).

Auctions have endured throughout history for several reasons. First, they give sellers a convenient way to find a buyer for something they would like to dispose of. Second, auctions are an excellent way for people to collect difficult-to-find items, such as certain Beanie Babies or historical memorabilia, that have a high value to them personally. Finally, auctions are one of the "purest" markets that exist for goods, in that they bring buyers and sellers into contact to arrive at a mutually agreeable price. As technological advances led to the advent and widespread adoption of the Internet, this ancient form of trade found a new medium.

Online auctions worked in essentially the same way as traditional auctions, the only difference being that the auction process occurred over the Internet rather than at a specific geographic location with buyers and sellers physically present. There are three basic categories of online auctions:

1. Business-to-business auctions, typically involving equipment and surplus merchandise.

2. Business-to-consumer auctions, in which businesses sold goods and services to consumers via the Internet. Many such auctions involved companies interested in selling used or discontinued goods, or liquidating unwanted inventory.

3. Person-to-person auctions, which gave interested sellers and buyers the opportunity to engage in competitive bidding.

Since eBay's pioneering of the person-to-person online auction process in 1995, the number of online auction sites on the Internet had grown to well over 2,750 by the end of 2001. Forrester Research predicted that 6.5 million customers would use online auctions in 2002.

Online auction operators could generate revenue in four principal ways:

1. Charging sellers for listing their good or service.

2. Charging a commission on all sales.

3. Selling advertising on their Web sites.

4. Selling their own new or used merchandise via the online auction format.

More recently, however, online auction sites had also added a fifth revenue-generation option that allowed buyers to purchase the desired good without waiting for an auction to close:

5. Selling their own goods or allowing other sellers to offer their goods in a fixed-price format.

Most sites charged sellers either a fee or a commission and sold advertising to companies interested in promoting their goods or services to users of the auction site.

Online Auction Users

Participants in online auctions could be grouped into six categories: (1) bargain hunters, (2) hobbyist/collector buyers, (3) professional buyers, (4) casual sellers, (5) hobbyist/collector sellers and (6) corporate and power sellers.

Bargain Hunters   Bargain hunters viewed online auctions primarily as a form of entertainment; their objective usually was to find a great deal. Bargain hunters were thought to make up only 8 percent of active online users but 52 percent of eBay visitors. To attract repeat visits from bargain hunters, industry observers said, sites must appeal to them on both rational and emotional levels, satisfying their need for competitive pricing, the excitement of the search, and the desire for community.

Hobbyist and Collector Buyers   Hobbyists and collectors used auctions to search for specific goods that had a high value to them personally. They were very concerned with both price and quality. Collectors prized eBay for its wide variety of product offerings.

Professional Buyers   As the legitimacy of online auctions grew, a new type of buyer began to emerge: the professional buyer. Professional buyers covered a broad range of purchasers, from purchasing managers acquiring office supplies to antiques and gun dealers purchasing inventory. Like bargain hunters, professional buyers were looking for a way to help contain costs; and like hobbyists and collectors, some professional buyers were seeking unique items to supplement their inventory. The primary difference between professional buyers and other types, however, was their affiliation with commercial enterprises. With the growth of online auction sites dedicated to business-to-business auctions, professional buyers were becoming an increasingly important element of the online auction landscape.

Casual Sellers　Casual sellers included individuals who used eBay as a substitute for a classified ad listing or a garage sale to dispose of items they no longer wanted. While many casual sellers listed only a few items, some used eBay to raise money for some new project.

Hobbyist and Collector Sellers　Sellers who were hobbyists or collectors typically dealt in a limited category of goods and looked to eBay as a way to sell selected items in their collections to others who might want them. Items ranged from classic television collectibles, to hand-sewn dolls, to coins and stamps. The hobbyists and collectors used a range of traditional and online outlets to reach their target markets. A number of the sellers used auctions to supplement their retail operations, while others sold exclusively through online auctions and in fixed-price formats such as Half.com.

Power and Corporate Sellers　Power sellers were typically small to medium-sized businesses that favored eBay as a primary distribution channel for their goods and often sold tens of thousands of dollars' worth of goods every month on the site. One estimate suggested that while these power sellers accounted for only 4 percent of eBay's population, they were responsible for 80 percent of eBay's total business.[2] Individuals who were power sellers could often make a full-time job of the endeavor.

As with the evolution of buyers, commercial enterprises were becoming an increasingly important part of the online auction industry. These commercial enterprises generally achieved power-seller status relatively rapidly. On eBay, for example, some of the new power sellers were familiar names such as IBM, Compaq, and the U.S. Postal Service (which sells undeliverable items on eBay under the user name usps-mrc).

Pierre Omidyar and the Founding of eBay

Pierre Omidyar was born in Paris, France, to parents who had left Iran decades earlier. The family emigrated to the United States when Omidyar's father began a residency at Johns Hopkins University Medical Center. Omidyar attended Tufts University, where he met his future wife, Pamela Wesley, who came to Tufts from Hawaii to get a degree in biology. Upon graduating in 1988, the couple moved to California, where Omidyar, who had earned a bachelor of science degree in computer science, joined Claris, an Apple Computer subsidiary in Silicon Valley, and wrote a widely used graphics application, MacDraw. In 1991, Omidyar left Claris and cofounded Ink Development (later renamed eShop), which became a pioneer in online shopping and was eventually sold to Microsoft in 1996. In 1994 Omidyar joined General Magic as a developer services engineer and remained there until mid-1996, when he left to pursue full-time development of eBay.

Internet folklore has it that eBay was founded solely to allow Pamela to trade Pez dispensers with other collectors. While Pamela was certainly a driving force in launching the initial Web site, Pierre had long been interested in how one could establish a marketplace to bring together a fragmented market. Pierre saw eBay as a way to create a person-to-person trading community based on a democratized, efficient market where everyone could have equal access through the same medium, the Internet. Pierre set out to develop his marketplace and to meet both his and Pamela's goals. In 1995 he launched the first online auction under the name of Auctionwatch at the domain name of www.eBay.com. The name *eBay* stood for "electronic Bay area," coined because Pierre's initial concept was to attract neighbors and other interested San Francisco Bay area residents to the site to buy and sell items of mutual interest. The first auctions charged no fees to either buyers or sellers and contained mostly computer equipment (and no Pez dispensers). Pierre's fledgling venture generated $1,000 in revenue the first month and an additional $2,000 the second. Traffic grew rapidly, however, as word about the site spread in the Bay area and a community of collectors emerged, using the site to trade and chat—even some marriages resulted from exchanges in eBay chat rooms.[3]

By February 1996 the traffic at Pierre Omidyar's site had grown so much that his Internet service provider informed him that he would have to upgrade his service. When Omidyar compensated for this by charging a listing fee for the auction, and saw no decrease in the number of items listed, he knew he was on to something. Although he was still working out of his home, Omidyar began looking for a partner and in May asked his friend Jeffrey Skoll to join him in the venture. While Skoll had never cared much about money, his Stanford master of business administration degree provided the firm with the business background that Omidyar lacked. With Omidyar as the visionary and Skoll as the strategist, the company embarked on a mission to "help people trade practically anything on earth."

Their concept for eBay was to "create a place where people could do business just like in the old days—when everyone got to know each other personally, and we all felt we were dealing on a one-to-one basis with individuals we could trust."

In eBay's early days, Omidyar and Skoll ran the operation alone, using a single computer to serve all of the pages. Omidyar served as CEO, chief financial officer, and president, while Skoll functioned as copresident and director. It was not long until Omidyar and Skoll grew the company to a size that forced them to move out of Pierre Omidyar's living room, due to the objections of Pamela, and into Skoll's living room. Shortly thereafter, the operations moved into the facilities of a Silicon Valley business incubator for a time until the company settled in its current facilities in San Jose, California. Exhibits 3 and 4 present eBay's recent financial statements.

eBay's Transition to Professional Management

From the beginning Pierre Omidyar intended to hire a professional manager to serve as the president of eBay: "[I would] let him or her run the company so . . . [I could] go play."[4] In 1997 both Omidyar and Skoll agreed that it was time to locate an experienced professional to function as CEO and president. In late 1997 eBay's headhunters came up with a candidate for the job: Margaret (Meg) Whitman, then general manager for Hasbro, Inc.'s preschool division. Whitman had received her bachelor of arts degree in economics from Princeton and her master of business administration from the Harvard Business School; her first job was in brand management at Procter & Gamble. Her experience also included serving as the president and CEO of FTD, the president of Stride Rite Corporation's Stride Rite Division, and as the senior vice president of marketing for the Walt Disney Company's consumer products division.

Exhibit 3 eBAY'S INCOME STATEMENTS, 1996–2002 (in thousands, except per share figures)

	1996	1997	1998	1999	2000	2001	2002	2003
Net revenues	$32,051	$41,370	$ 86,129	$224,724	$431,424	$748,821	$1,214,100	$2,165,096
Cost of net revenues	6,803	8,404	16,094	57,588	95,453	134,816	213,876	416,058
Gross profit	$25,248	$32,966	$ 70,035	$167,136	$335,971	$614,005	$1,000,224	$1,749,038
Operating expenses:								
Sales and marketing	$13,139	$15,618	$ 35,976	$ 96,239	$166,767	$253,474	$ 349,650	$ 567,565
Product development	28	831	4,640	24,847	55,863	75,288	104,636	159,315
General and administrative	5,661	6,534	15,849	43,919	73,027	105,784	171,785	304,703
Patent litigation expense	—	—	0	0	2,337	—	—	29,965
Payroll taxes on stock options	—	—	0	0	2,337	2,442	4,015	9,590
Amortization of acquired intangibles	—	—	805	1,145	1,443	36,591	15,941	50,659
Merger-related costs	—	—	0	4,359	1,550	0	0	0
Total operating expenses	$18,828	$22,983	$ 57,270	$170,509	$300,977	$473,579	$ 646,027	$1,119,797
Income (loss) from operations	$ 6,420	$ 9,983	$ 12,765	$ (3,373)	$ 34,994	$140,426	$ 354,197	$ 629,241
Interest and other income (expense), net	(2,607)	(1,951)	1,799	23,833	46,337	41,613	49,209	37,803
Interest expense	—	—	(2,191)	(2,319)	(3,374)	(2,851)	(1,492)	(4,314)
Impairment of certain equity investments	—	—	0	0	0	(16,245)	(3,781)	(1,230)
Income before income taxes and minority interest	$ 3,813	$ 8,032	$ 12,373	$ 18,141	$ 77,957	$162,943	$ 398,133	$ 661,500
Provision for income taxes	(475)	(971)	(4,789)	(8,472)	(32,725)	(80,009)	(145,946)	(206,738)
Minority interests in consolidated companies	—	—	(311)	(102)	3,062	7,514	(2,296)	(7,578)
Net income	$ 3,338	$ 7,061	$ 7,273	$ 9,567	$ 48,294	$ 90,448	$ 249,891	$ 447,184
Net income per share:								
Basic	$ 0.39	$ 0.29	$ 0.07	$ 0.04	$ 0.19	$ 0.34	$ 0.43	$ 0.69
Diluted	0.07	0.08	0.03	0.04	0.17	0.32	0.43	0.67
Weighted-average shares:								
Basic	8,490	24,428	104,128	217,674	251,776	268,971	574,992	638,288
Diluted	45,060	84,775	233,519	273,033	280,346	280,595	585,640	656,657

Source: Company financial documents.

Exhibit 4   eBAY'S CONSOLIDATED BALANCE SHEETS, 1997–2003 (in thousands)

					Year Ended December 31		
	1997	1998	1999	2000	2001	2002	2003
Assets							
Current assets:							
Cash and cash equivalents	$3,723	$ 37,285	$219,679	$ 201,873	$ 523,969	$1,109,313	$1,381,513
Short-term investments	—	40,401	181,086	354,166	199,450	89,690	340,576
Accounts receivable, net	1,024	12,425	36,538	67,163	101,703	131,453	225,871
Funds receivable	—	—	—	—	—	41,014	79,893
Other current assets	220	7,479	22,531	52,262	58,683	96,988	118,029
Total current assets	$4,967	$ 97,590	$459,834	$ 675,464	$ 883,805	$1,468,458	$2,145,882
Long-term investments	—	—	—	—	286,998	470,227	934,171
Restricted cash and investments	—	—	—	—	129,614	134,644	127,432
Property and equipment, net	652	44,062	111,806	125,161	142,349	218,028	601,785
Goodwill	—	—	—	—	187,829	1,456,024	1,719,311
Investments	—	—	373,988	—	—	—	—
Deferred tax assets	—	—	5,639	—	21,540	84,218	—
Intangible and other assets, net	—	7,884	12,675	23,299	26,394	292,845	291,553
Total assets	$5,619	$149,536	$963,942	$1,182,403	$1,678,529	$4,040,226	$5,820,134
Liabilities and stockholders' equity							
Current liabilities:							
Accounts payable	$252	$ 9,997	$ 31,538	$ 31,725	$ 33,235	$ 47,424	$ 64,633
Funds payable and amounts due to customers	—	—	—	—	—	50,396	106,568
Accrued expenses and other current liabilities	—	6,577	32,550	60,882	94,593	199,323	356,491
Deferred revenue and customer advances	128	973	5,997	12,656	15,583	18,846	28,874
Debt and leases, current portion	258	4,047	12,285	15,272	16,111	2,970	2,840
Income taxes payable	169	1,380	6,455	11,092	20,617	67,265	87,870

(continued)

C-329

Exhibit 4   (concluded)

	Year Ended December 31						
	1997	1998	1999	2000	2001	2002	2003
Deferred tax liabilities, current	—	1,682	—	—	—	—	—
Other current liabilities	128	5,981	7,632	5,815	—	—	—
Total current liabilities	$1,124	$ 24,656	$ 88,825	$ 137,442	$ 180,139	$ 386,224	$ 647,276
Debt and leases, long-term portion	305	18,361	15,018	11,404	12,008	13,798	124,476
Deferred tax liabilities, long-term	—	—	—	—	3,629	27,625	79,238
Other liabilities	157	—	—	6,549	15,864	22,874	33,494
Minority interests	—	—	—	—	37,751	33,232	39,408
Total liabilities	$1,586	$ 48,998	$111,475	$ 168,643	$ 249,391	$ 483,753	$ 923,892
Series B redeemable convertible preferred stock and Series B warrants	3,018	—	—	—	—	—	—
Total stockholders' equity	1,015	100,538	852,467	1,013,760	1,429,138	3,556,473	4,896,242
	$5,619	$149,536	$963,942	$1,182,403	$1,678,529	$4,124,444	$5,820,134

Source: Company financial documents.

When first approached by eBay, Whitman was not especially interested in joining a company that had fewer than 40 employees and less than $6 million in revenues the previous year. It was only after repeated pleas that Whitman agreed to meet with Omidyar in Silicon Valley. After a second meeting, Whitman realized the company's enormous growth potential and agreed to give eBay a try. According to Omidyar, Meg Whitman's experience in global marketing with Hasbro's Teletubbies, Playskool, and Mr. Potato Head brands made her "the ideal choice to build upon eBay's leadership position in the one-to-one online trading market without sacrificing the quality and personal touch our users have grown to expect."[5] In addition to convincing Whitman to head eBay's operations, Omidyar had been instrumental in helping bring in other talented senior executives and in assembling a capable board of directors. Notable members of eBay's board of directors included Scott Cook, the founder of Intuit, a highly successful financial software company, and Fred D. Anderson, executive vice president and chief financial officer of Apple.

How an eBay Auction Worked

eBay endeavored to make it very simple to buy and sell goods. In order to sell or bid on goods, users first had to register at the site. Once they registered, users selected both a user name and a password. Unregistered users were able to browse the Web site but were not permitted to bid on any goods or list any items for auction.

On the Web site, search engines helped customers determine what goods were currently available. When registered users found an item they desired, they could choose to enter a single bid or to use automatic bidding (called proxy bidding). In automatic bidding the customer entered an initial bid sufficient to make him or her the high bidder, and then the bid would be automatically increased as others bid for the same object until the auction ended and either the bidder won or another bidder surpassed the original customer's maximum specified bid. Regardless of which bidding method they chose, users could check bids at any time and either bid again, if they had been outbid, or increase their maximum amount in the automatic bid. Users could choose to receive e-mail notification if they were outbid.

Once the auction had ended, the buyer and seller were each notified of the winning bid and were given each other's e-mail address. The parties to the auction would then privately arrange for payment and delivery of the good.

Fees and Procedures for Sellers

Buyers on eBay were not charged a fee for bidding on items, but sellers were charged an insertion fee and a "final value" fee; they could also elect to pay additional fees to promote their listing. Listing, or insertion, fees ranged from 30 cents for auctions with opening bids, minimum values, or reserve prices of between $0.01 and $0.99, to $4.80 for auctions with opening bids, minimum values, or reserve prices of $500 and up. Final value fees ranged from 1.25 to 5 percent of the final sale price and were computed according to a graduated fee schedule in which the percentage fell as the final sales price rose. As an example, in a basic auction with no promotion, if the item had brought an opening bid of $200 and eventually sold for $1,500, the total fee paid by the seller would be $35.48—the $3.60 insertion fee plus $31.88. The $31.88 was based on a fee structure of 5 percent of the first $25 (or $1.25), 2.5 percent of the additional amount between $25.01 and $1,000 (or $24.38), and 1.25 percent of the additional amount between $1,000.01 and $1,500 (or $6.25). Auction fees varied for special categories of goods such as passenger vehicles in eBay Motors that were charged a $40 transaction fee when the first successful bid was placed and a $100 insertion fee for residential, commercial, and other real estate.

Sellers could also customize items by adding photographs and featuring their item in a gallery. Sellers could indicate a photograph in the item's description if they posted the photograph on a Web site and provided eBay with the appropriate Web address. Items could be showcased in the Gallery section with a catalog of pictures rather than text. A seller who used a photograph in his or her listing could have this photograph included in the Gallery section for 25 cents or featured there for $19.95. A Gallery option was available in all categories of eBay, but fees varied between categories and the prominence of the gallery. For example, a simple gallery listing cost 25 cents, whereas a featured gallery listing, which included a periodic listing in the featured section above the general gallery, cost $19.95. In the eBay Motors gallery, options could cost as much as $99.95.

To make doing business on eBay more attractive to potential sellers, the company introduced several features. To receive a minimum price for an auction, the seller could specify an opening bid or set a reserve price on the auction. If the bidding did not top the reserve price, the seller was under no obligation to sell the item to the highest bidder and could relist the item at no additional cost. For items with a reserve price between $0.01 and $49.99, the fee was $1.00; between $50.00 and $199.99, the fee was $2.00; and for over $200, the fee was 1 percent of the reserve price. If the seller wished, he or she could also set a Buy It Now price that allowed bidders to pay a set amount for a listed item. The fee for this service was $1.00. If the Buy It Now price was met, the auction would end immediately.

As of June 11, 2001, new sellers at eBay were required to provide both a credit card number and bank account information to register. While eBay admitted that these requirements are extreme, it argued that they helped protect everyone in the community against fraudulent sellers and ensured that sellers were of legal age and were serious about listing the item on eBay.

How Transactions Were Completed

Under the terms of eBay's user agreement, if a seller received one or more bids above the stated minimum, or reserve, price, the seller was obligated to complete the transaction, although eBay had no enforcement power beyond suspending a noncompliant buyer or seller from using the company's service. In the event the buyer and seller were unable to complete the transaction, the seller notified eBay, which then credited the seller the amount of the final value fee.

When an auction ended, the eBay system validated that the bid fell within the acceptable price range. If the sale was successful, eBay automatically notified the buyer and seller via e-mail; the buyer and seller could then either work out the transaction details independent of eBay or use eBay's checkout and payment services to complete the transaction. In its original business model, at no point during the process did eBay take possession of either the item being sold or the buyer's payment. In an effort to increase revenues, eBay expanded its offerings to facilitate buyers' payments by first offering services that accepted credit card payments and electronic funds transfers on behalf of the seller and then purchasing PayPal, the leading third-party online payment facilitator in 2003. To make selling easier, eBay also had alliances with two leading shippers, the U.S. Postal Service and United Parcel Service (UPS). Both of these shippers had centers on eBay that would allow sellers to calculate postage and to print postage-paid labels. However, the buyer and seller still had to independently arrange shipping terms, with buyers typically paying for shipping. Items were sent directly from the buyer to the seller unless an independent escrow service was arranged to help ensure security.

To encourage sellers to use eBay's ancillary services the company offered an automated checkout service to help expedite communication, payment, and delivery between buyers and sellers.

Feedback Forum

In early 1996 eBay pioneered a feature called Feedback Forum to build trust among buyers and sellers and to facilitate the establishment of reputations within its community. Feedback Forum encouraged individuals to record comments about their trading partners. At the completion of each auction, both the buyer and seller were allowed to leave positive, negative, or neutral comments about each other. Individuals could dispute feedback left about them by annotating comments in question.

By assigning values of $+1$ for a positive comment, 0 for a neutral comment, and -1 for a negative comment, each trader earned a ranking that was attached to his or her user name. A user who had developed a positive reputation over time had a color-coded star symbol displayed next to his or her user name to indicate the amount of positive feedback. The highest ranking a trader could receive was "over 100,000," indicated by a red shooting star. Well-respected high-volume traders could have rankings well into the thousands.

Users who received a sufficiently negative net feedback rating (typically a -4) had their registrations suspended and were thus unable to bid on or list items for sale. Buyers could review a person's feedback profile before deciding to bid on an item listed by that person or before choosing payment and delivery methods. A sample user profile is shown in Exhibit 5.

The terms of eBay's user agreement prohibited actions that would undermine the integrity of the Feedback Forum, such as leaving positive feedback about oneself through other accounts or leaving multiple negative comments about someone else through other accounts. The Feedback Forum had several automated features designed to detect and prevent some forms of abuse. For example, feedback posted from the same account, positive or negative, could not affect a user's net feedback rating by more than one point, no matter how many comments an individual made. Furthermore, a user could make comments only about his or her trading partners in completed transactions. Prior to 2004, once a feedback comment was made, it could not be altered. However, as of February 9, 2004, the system was changed in response to suggestions by community members to all users to mutually withdraw feedback about each other. Withdrawn feedback would no longer impact a user's feedback rating.

The company believed its Feedback Forum was extremely useful in overcoming users' initial hesitancy about trading over the Internet, since it reduced the uncertainty of dealing with an unknown trading partner. However, there was growing concern among sellers and bidders that feedback might be positively skewed, as many eBayers chose not to leave negative feedback for fear of unfounded retribution that could damage their carefully built reputations.

Exhibit 5   A Sample Feedback Forum Profile

home | pay | sign out | services | site map | help ⑦

| Browse | Search | Sell | My eBay | Community | Powered By IBM |

← Back to My eBay   Home > Services > Feedback Forum > **Member Profile**   Why does this page look different?

Member Profile: nuggett12 (50 ★)

Feedback Score:	**50**	Recent Ratings:				Member since: May-17-99
Positive Feedback:	**100%**		Past Month	Past 6 Months	Past 12 Months	Location: United States
Members who left a positive:	50	⊕ positive	0	16	21	▪ ID History
Members who left a negative:	0	◎ neutral	0	0	0	▪ Items for Sale
All positive feedback received:	56	⊖ negative	0	0	0	Contact Member

Learn about what these numbers mean.   Bid Retractions (Past 6 months): 0

| **All Feedback Received** | From Buyers | From Sellers | Left for Others |

56 feedback received by nuggett12   page 1 of 3

Comment	From	Date / Time	Item #
⊕ Super transaction! Lightning FAST payment! Thanks! Come back again soon :)	Seller fussypants (fpdotcomm@aol.com) (1382 ★)	Jan-06-04 18:25	2976322019
⊕ FAST PAYMENT!! GREAT EBAY'R!! THANKS!!	Seller cheribook (cheriberri5@aol.com) (645 ★)	Dec-11-03 10:35	2207627646
⊕ Very prompt and courteous buyer, great to deal with, Thanks!	Seller network482 (sales@shopoem.com) (11742 ☆)	Nov-28-03 01:04	3057703028
⊕ Very prompt and courteous buyer, great to deal with, Thanks!	Seller network482 (sales@shopoem.com) (11742 ☆)	Nov-28-03 01:04	3058162337
⊕ very good transaction	Seller hoefker@earthlink.net (hoefker@earthlink.net) (35 ☆) no longer a registered user	Nov-27-03 11:48	3061637655
⊕ FAST PAY!!! EXCELLENT!!! PLEASURE TO DO BUSINESS WITH! AAAAA+++++	Seller rafaelos (lancergroup@yahoo.com) (3907 ★)	Nov-25-03 08:22	2968729737
⊕ Very prompt and courteous buyer, great to deal with, Thanks!	Seller network482 (sales@shopoem.com) (11742 ☆)	Nov-14-03 08:38	3058162328
⊕ Very prompt and courteous buyer, great to deal with, Thanks!	Seller network482 (sales@shopoem.com) (11742 ☆)	Nov-14-03 08:38	3057561133
⊕ a+	Seller mountainairvideo (firebaseutah@aol.com) (1817 ★) 🎖	Nov-10-03 11:12	243650630174
⊕ Quick payment, and easy to deal with. Fine buyer!	Seller dumbells101 (91 ★)	Oct-27-03 06:29	2863059214
⊕ A very easy and fast transaction. Couldn't ask for a better buyer.	Seller cornshedprofits (1459 ★)	Oct-06-03 03:05	243633243688
⊕ Fast payment enjoed working with you.....	Seller mmddaa@msn.com (82 ★)	Sep-21-03 20:35	3627701979
⊕ Smooth transaction!	Seller phoenix_trading_co (23518 ☆)	Sep-02-03 13:47	3044067884
⊕ Smooth transaction!	Seller phoenix_trading_co (23518 ☆)	Sep-02-03 13:42	3044088621
⊕ Great seller! Delivered promptly! Smooth transaction.	Buyer bama-tarheels (3)	Aug-25-03 11:44	2186695578
⊕ Prompt payment and good communication	Seller rjpedigo (35 ☆)	Aug-17-03 14:53	3040479706
⊕ I highly recommend this seller.	Buyer jessievanderhoff (6)	Jul-21-03 11:48	3033456370
⊕ Customer is A+! We appreciate your business and fast payment!	Seller restaurant.com (100851 ★)	Apr-14-03 13:14	2922961668
⊕ Customer is A+! We appreciate your business and fast payment!	Seller restaurant.com (100851 ★)	Apr-14-03 13:14	2922958665
⊕ Worthwhile in every way. A+	Seller genuine_oem (29204 ☆)	Feb-10-03 21:41	1949802659
⊕ EXCELLENT eBayer, GREAT customer service, DEFFINATELY do bus. with again! AAAA++	Buyer brendon800 (81 ★)	Feb-09-03 18:01	2156921953
⊕ Very understanding. I Would have great confidence buying from this seller.	Buyer longinternational (142 ☆)	Feb-01-03 18:44	2156940759
⊕ Item as described & functioning. Shipping excellent. Will do business again!	Buyer brkidsman (11 ☆)	Dec-10-02 07:25	1789511721
⊕ AN EXAMPLE OF A GOOD EBAYER _ HIGHLY RECOMMENDED _ AAAAAAA++++++	Seller shilito34 (1338 ★)	Oct-03-02 15:12	1772433194
⊕ Super quick payment and very patient. My apologies for being late...	Seller dane_mel (107 ☆)	Sep-13-02 09:00	243618255866

Source: www.ebay.com, February 4, 2004.

eBay's Strategy to Sustain Its Market Dominance

Meg Whitman assumed the helm of eBay in February 1998 and began acting as the public face of the company. In an effort to stay in touch with her customers, Whitman hosted an auction on eBay herself. She found the experience so enlightening that she required all of eBay's managers to sell on eBay. Pierre Omidyar stepped back to become chairman of eBay's board of directors and focused his time and energy on overseeing eBay's strategic direction and growth, business model and site development, and community advocacy. Jeff Skoll, who became the vice president of strategic planning and analysis, concentrated on competitive analysis, new business planning and incubation, the development of the organization's overall strategic direction, and supervision of customer support operations.

The Move to Go Public

eBay's initial public offering (IPO) took place on September 24, 1998, with a starting price of $18 per share. The IPO exceeded that price and closed the day up 160 percent at $47. The IPO generated $66 million in new capital for the company and was recognized by several investing publications. The success of the September 1998 offering led eBay to issue a follow-up offering in April 1999 that raised an additional $600 million. As a qualification to the IPOs, eBay's board of directors retained the right to issue as many as 5 million additional shares of preferred stock with no further input from the current shareholders in case of a hostile takeover attempt.

eBay's Business Model

According to eBay's Meg Whitman, the company could best be described as a dynamic, self-regulating economy. Its business model was based on creating and maintaining a person-to-person trading community in which buyers and sellers could readily and conveniently exchange information and goods. The company's role was to function as a value-added facilitator of online buyer–seller transactions by providing a supportive infrastructure that enabled buyers and sellers to come together in an efficient and effective manner. Success depended not only on the quality of eBay's infrastructure but also on the quality and quantity of buyers and sellers attracted to the site; in management's view, this entailed maintaining a compelling trading environment, a number of trust and safety programs, a cost-effective and convenient trading experience, and strong community affinity. By developing the eBay brand name and increasing the customer base, eBay endeavored to attract a sufficient number of high-quality buyers and sellers necessary to meet the organization's goals. The online auction format meant that eBay carried zero inventory and could operate a marketplace without the need for a traditional sales force.

eBay's business model was built around three profit centers: the domestic business (auction operations within the United States), international business (auction operations outside of the United States), and payments (e.g., PayPal). It was estimated that, in 2003, U.S. operations accounted for 31.7 percent of revenue growth, international's share was 34.6 percent, and the remaining 33.8 percent was from payments (see Exhibit 6).

Specific elements of eBay's business model that the company particularly recognized as key to its success included:[6]

Exhibit 6   SHARE OF eBAY TRANSACTION REVENUE GROWTH, 2001–2008

	2001(a)	2002(a)	2003(e)	2004(e)	2005(e)	2006(e)	2007(e)	2008(e)
U.S.	62.8%	48.0%	31.7%	39.1%	31.7%	32.5%	32.5%	32.7%
International	32.6	36.9	34.6	35.9	41.6	42.0	38.7	38.7
Payments	4.7	15.1	33.8	25.0	26.7	25.5	28.8	28.6
	100.0%	100.0%	100.0%	100.0%	100.0%	100.0%	100.0%	100.0%

1. The fact that it was the largest online trading forum, with a critical mass of buyers, sellers, and items listed for sale.

2. Its compelling and entertaining trading environment, which had strong values, established rules, and procedures that facilitated communication and trade between buyers and sellers.

3. Established trust and safety programs such as SafeHarbor. This program provided guidelines for trading, aided in resolving disputes, and warned and suspended (both temporarily and permanently) users who violated eBay's rules.

4. Cost-effective, convenient trading.

5. Strong community affinity.

6. An intuitive user interface that was easy to understand, arranged by topics, and fully automated.

In implementing its business model, eBay employed three main competitive tactics. First, it sought to build strategic partnerships in all stages of its value chain, creating an impressive portfolio of over 250 strategic alliances with companies such as America Online (AOL), Yahoo, IBM, Compaq, and Walt Disney. Second, it actively sought customer feedback and made improvements on the basis of this information. Third, it actively monitored both its external and internal environments for developing opportunities. One way eBay executives kept in touch with internal trends was by hosting online town hall meetings and by visiting cities with large local markets. The feedback gained from these meetings was used to adopt and adjust practices to keep customers satisfied.

eBay's Strategy

eBay's strategy to sustain growth rested on five key elements:[7]

1. *Broaden the existing trading platform* within existing product categories, across new product categories, through geographic expansion, both domestic and international, and through introduction of additional pricing formats such as fixed price sales.

2. *Foster eBay community affinity* by instilling a vibrant, loyal eBay community experience, seeking to maintain a critical mass of frequent buyers and sellers with a vested interest in the eBay community.

3. *Enhance features and functionality* by continually updating and enhancing the features and functionality of the eBay and Half.com Web sites to ensure continuous improvement in the trading experience.

4. *Expand value-added services* to include end-to-end personal trading service by offering a variety of pre- and post-trade services to enhance the user experience and make trading easier.

5. *Continue to develop U.S. and international markets* that employ the Internet to create an efficient trading platform in local, national, and international markets that can be transformed into a seamless, truly global trading platform.

Broadening the Existing Trading Platform   Efforts intended to broaden the eBay trading platform concentrated on growing the content within current categories, broadening the range of products offered according to user preferences, and developing regionally targeted offerings. Growth in existing product categories was facilitated by deepening the content within the categories through the use of content-specific chat rooms and bulletin boards as well as targeted advertising at trade shows and in industry-specific publications.

To broaden the range of products offered, eBay developed new product categories, introduced specialty sites, and developed eBay stores. Over 2,000 new categories were added between 1998 and 2000, and by 2003 eBay offered over 27,000 categories of items (greatly expanded from the original 10 categories in 1995). Ten of these categories had gross merchandise sales of over $1 billion, including eBay Motors ($7.5 billion), Consumer Electronics ($2.6 billion), Computers ($2.4 billion), Books/Movies/Music ($2.0 billion), Clothing and Accessories ($1.8 billion), Sports ($1.8 billion), Collectibles ($1.5 billion), Toys ($1.5 billion), Home and Garden ($1.3 billion), and Jewelry and Gemstones ($1.3 billion).

Significant new product categories and specialty sites developed since eBay's early days included:

- eBay Motors, which began as a category and was developed when eBay noticed that an increasing number of automobile transactions were taking place on its site. In 2002, eBay Motors sold more than $3 billion worth of vehicles and parts and was the largest online marketplace for buying and selling autos as of mid-2003. According to Meg Whitman, "One month, we saw the miscellaneous category had a very rapid growth rate, and someone said we have to find out what's going on. It was the buying and selling of used cars. So we said, maybe what we should do is give these guys a separate category and see what happens. It worked so well that we created eBay Motors."[8] In partnership with AutoTrader.com this category was later expanded to a specialty site.

- The LiveAuctions specialty site, which allowed live bidding via the Internet for auctions occurring in brick-and-mortar auction houses around the world. Through an alliance with Icollector.com, eBay users had access to more than 300 auction houses worldwide. Auction houses that participated in this agreement were well rewarded, as more than 20 percent of their sales went to online bidders. One auction broadcast on the LiveAuctions site, held in February 2001, featured items from a rare Marilyn Monroe collection including a handwritten note from Monroe that listed her reasons for divorcing her first husband.

- The eBay Business marketplace, launched in 2002, which allowed business-related items to be sold in one location. Items such as office technology, wholesale lots, and marketplace services were offered at this destination. By the end of 2002, over 500,000 items were listed in eBay Business each week and more than $1 billion in annualized gross merchandise sales occurred across these categories.

- eBay's Real Estate category, launched to foster eBay's emerging real estate marketplace. The offerings within this category were significantly enhanced by eBay's August 2001 acquisition of Homesdirect, which specialized in the sale of foreclosed properties owned by government agencies such as Housing and Urban

Development and the Department of Veterans Affairs (formerly known as the Veterans Administration). The company estimated that a parcel of land was sold through the Real Estate category every 45 minutes during 2002.

Other notable moves to broaden the platform included the following:

- The Application Program Interface (API) and Developers Program was launched to allow other companies to use eBay's commerce engine and technology to build new sites.

- Starting in 1999, eBay launched over 60 regional sites to offer a more local flavor to eBay's offerings. These regional sites focused on the 50 largest metropolitan areas in the United States. Regional auction sites were intended to encourage the sale of items that were prohibitively expensive to ship, items that tended to have only a local appeal, and items that people preferred to view before purchasing. To supplement the regional sites, in mid-2001 eBay began offering sellers the option of having their items listed in a special seller's area in the classified sections of local newspapers. Sellers could highlight specific items, their eBay store, or their user ID in these classifieds.

- In June 2001 eBay introduced eBay stores to complement new offerings, to make it easier for sellers to build loyalty and for buyers to locate goods from specific sellers and to prevent sellers from driving bidders to the seller's own Web site. In an eBay store the entirety of a seller's auctions would be listed in one convenient location. These stores could also offer a fixed-price option from a seller and the integration of a seller's Half.com listings with their auction listings. While numerous sellers of all sizes moved to take advantage of eBay stores, the concept was especially appealing to large retailers such as IBM, Hard Rock Café, Sears, and Handspring that were moving to take advantage of eBay's reach and distribution power.

- In May 2002 eBay reached an agreement with Accenture to develop a service intended to allow large sellers to more efficiently sell their products. These sellers were able to use a wide range of tools, such as high-volume listing capabilities, expanded customer service and support, and payment and fulfillment processes.

- A fixed-price format was established through the acquisition of Half.com and allowed eBay to compete more directly with online sellers such as Amazon.com. Half.com was a fixed-price, person-to-person format that enabled buyers and sellers to trade books, CDs, movies and video games at prices starting at generally half of the retail price. Like eBay, Half.com offered a feedback system that helped buyers and sellers to build a solid reputation. eBay intended to eventually fully integrate both Half.com's listings and the feedback system into eBay's current site.

Fostering eBay Community Affinity   From its founding, eBay considered developing a loyal, vivacious trading community to be a cornerstone of its business model. This community was nurtured through open and honest communication and was built on five basic values that eBay expected its members to honor:

- We believe people are basically good.
- We believe everyone has something to contribute.
- We believe that an honest, open environment can bring out the best in people.
- We recognize and respect everyone as a unique individual.
- We encourage you to treat others the way that you want to be treated.[9]

The company recognized that these values could not be imposed by fiat. According to Omidyar,

> As much as we at eBay talk about the values and encourage people to live by those values, that's not going to work unless people actually adopt those values. The values are communicated not because somebody reads the Web site and says, "Hey, this is how we want to treat each other, so I'll just start treating people that way." The values are communicated because that's how they're treated when they first arrive. Each member is passing those values on to the next member. It's little things, like you receive a note that says, "Thanks for your business."[10]

Consistent with eBay's desire to stay in touch with its customers and be responsive to their needs, the company flew in 10 new sellers every few months to hold group meetings known as Voice of the Customer. The company noted that 75–80 percent of new features were originally suggested by community members.

An example of eBay values in action took place when eBay introduced a feature that referred losing bidders to similar auctions from other eBay sellers, eliciting a strong outcry from the community. Sellers demanded to know why eBay was stealing their sales, and one longtime seller went so far as to auction a rare eBay jacket so that he could use the auction as a forum to complain about "eBay's new policy of screwing the folks who built them."[11] This caught the attention of Omidyar and Whitman, who met with the seller in his home for 45 minutes. After the meeting eBay changed its policy.

Recognizing that many new users might not get the most out of their eBay experience, and hoping to introduce new entrepreneurs to the community, the company created eBay University in August 2000. The university traveled across the country to hold two-day seminars in various cities. These seminars attracted between 400 and 500 people, who each paid $25 for the experience. Courses offered ranged from freshmen-level classes that introduced buying and selling on eBay to graduate-level classes that taught the intricacies of bulk listing and competitive tactics. eBay University was so successful that the company partnered with Evoke Communications to offer an online version of the classes. While community members gained knowledge from these classes, so did eBay. The company kept careful track of questions and concerns and used them to uncover areas that needed improvement.

A second important initiative to make the eBay community more inclusive was aimed at the fastest-growing segment of the U.S. population, adults 50 and older. In an effort to bridge the digital divide for seniors, eBay launched the Digital Opportunity Program for Seniors and set a goal of training and bringing online 1 million seniors by 2005. Specific elements of this plan included partnering with SeniorNet, the leading nonprofit computer technology trainer of seniors, and donating $1 million to this organization for training and establishing 10 new training facilities by 2005, developing a volunteer program for training seniors, and creating a specific area on eBay for Senior Citizens (www.ebay.com/seniors).

To foster a sense of community among eBay users, the company employed tools and tactics designed to promote both business and personal interactions between consumers, to foster trust between bidders and sellers, and to instill a sense of security among traders. Interactions between community members were facilitated through the creation of chat rooms based on personal interests. These chat rooms allowed individuals to learn about their chosen collectibles and to exchange information about items they collected.

To manage the flow of information in the chat rooms, eBay employees went to trade shows and conventions to seek out individuals who had knowledge about and a passion for either a specific collectible or a category of goods. These enthusiasts would act as community leaders or ambassadors; they were never referred to as employees but were compensated $1,000 a month to host online discussions with experts.

Although personal communication between members fostered a sense of community, as eBay's community grew from "the size of a small village to a large city" additional measures were necessary to ensure a continued sense of trust and honesty among users.[12] One of eBay's earliest trust-building efforts was the 1996 creation of the Feedback Forum, described earlier.

Unfortunately, the Feedback Forum was not always sufficient to ensure honesty and integrity among traders. eBay estimated that far less than 1 percent of the millions of auctions completed on the site involved some sort of fraud or illegal activity, but some users, like Clay Monroe, disagreed. Monroe, a Seattle-area trader of computer equipment, estimated that "ninety percent of the time everybody is on the up and up . . . [but] . . . ten percent of the time you get some jerk who wants to cheat you." Fraudulent or illegal acts perpetrated by sellers included misrepresentation of goods; trading in counterfeit goods or pirated goods that infringed on others' intellectual property rights; failure to deliver goods paid for by buyers; and shill bidding, whereby sellers would use a false bidder to artificially drive up the price of a good. Buyers could manipulate bids by placing an unrealistically high bid on a good to discourage other bidders and then withdraw their bid at the last moment to allow an ally to win the auction at a bargain price. Buyers could also fail to deliver payment on a completed auction.

Recognizing that fraudulent activities represented a significant danger to eBay's future, management took the Feedback Forum a step further in 1998 by launching the SafeHarbor program to provide guidelines for trade, provide information to help resolve user disputes, and respond to reports of misuse of the eBay service. The SafeHarbor initiative was expanded in 1999 to provide additional safeguards and to actively work with law enforcement agencies and members of the trading community to make eBay more secure. New elements of SafeHarbor included:

- Free insurance, with a $25 deductible for transactions under $200 and further protection for buyers and sellers who used PayPal.
- Cooperation with local law enforcement agencies to identify and prosecute fraudulent buyers and sellers.
- Enhancements to the Feedback Forum such as listing whether the user was a buyer or a seller in a transaction.
- A partnership with SquareTrade, an online dispute resolution service.
- A partnership with Escrow.com to promote the use of escrow services on purchases over $500.
- A new class of verified eBay users with an accompanying icon.
- Easy access to escrow services.
- Tougher policies relating to nonpaying bidders and shill bidders.
- Clarification of which items were not permissible to list for sale (such as items associated with Nazi Germany, the Ku Klux Klan, or other groups that glorified hate, racial intolerance, or racial violence).
- A strengthened antipiracy and anti-infringement program known as the Verified Rights Owner program (VeRO), and the introduction of dispute resolution services.

The use of verified buyer and seller accounts was viewed as especially significant because it allowed eBay to ensure that suspended users did not open new eBay accounts under different names. User information was verified through Atlanta-based Equifax, Inc. To further ensure that suspended users didn't register new accounts with different identities, eBay partnered with Infoglide to use a similarity search technology to examine new registrant information.

To implement these new initiatives, eBay increased the number of positions in its SafeHarbor department from 24 to 182, including full-time employees and independent contractors. It also organized the department around the functions of investigations, community watch, and fraud prevention. The investigations group was responsible for examining reported trading violations and possible misuses of eBay. The fraud prevention group mediated customer disputes over such things as the quality of the goods sold. If a written complaint of fraud was filed against a user, eBay generally suspended the alleged offender's account, pending an investigation. Despite all of these initiatives, innovative thieves were developing new ways to cheat honest bidders and sellers as quickly as eBay could identify and ban them from the system, and many eBayers still viewed this as one of the most significant threats to the eBay community.

The community watch group worked with over 100 industry-leading companies, ranging from software publishers to toy manufactures to apparel makers, to protect intellectual property rights. To ensure that illegal items were not being sold and sale items listed did not violate intellectual property rights, this SafeHarbor group automated daily keyword searches on auction content. Offending auctions were closed and the seller was notified of the violation. Repeated violations resulted in suspension of the seller's account.

As eBay expanded its categories to include Great Collections and the new automobile categories, new safeguards were introduced to meet the unique needs of these areas. In the eBay Great Collections category, the company partnered with Collector's Universe to offer authentication and grading services for specific products such as trading cards, coins, and autographs. In the automobile area, one of eBay's fastest-growing segments, eBay partnered with Saturn to provide users with access to a nationwide automobile brand and offered a free limited one-month or 1,000-mile warranty, free purchase insurance up to $20,000 with a $500 deductible, and a special escrow service (Secure Pay) designed for the needs of automotive buyers and sellers.

Expanding Value-Added Services   Since its earliest days, eBay had realized that to be successful, its service had to be both easy to use and convenient to access. Recognizing this, the company continuously sought to add services to fill these needs by offering a variety of pre- and post-trade services to enhance the user experience and provide an end-to-end trading experience. Early efforts in this direction included alliances with:

- Leading shipping services (USPS and UPS).
- Two companies that helped guarantee that buyers would get what they paid for (Tradesafe and I-Escrow).
- The world's largest franchiser of retail business, communications, and postal service centers (Mailboxes, Etc.).
- The leader in multicarrier Web-based shipping services for e-commerce (iShip.com).

To facilitate person-to-person credit card payments, eBay acquired PayPal, a company that specialized in transferring money from one cardholder to another, in October

2002. Using the newly acquired capabilities of PayPal, eBay was able to offer sellers the option of accepting credit card payments from other eBay users. At the end of 2002, PayPal was available to users in 38 countries, including the United States. eBay's objective was to make credit card payment a "seamless and integrated part of the trading experience."[13] The company expected that net revenues from the payments segment of PayPal would be approximately $300 to $310 million in 2003.

Developing U.S. and International Markets

As competition increased in the online auction industry, eBay began to seek growth opportunities in international markets in an effort to create a global trading community. While international buyers and sellers had been trading on eBay for some time, there were no facilities designed especially for the needs of these community members. In entering international markets, eBay considered three options: it could build a new user community from the ground up, acquire a local organization, or form a partnership with a strong local company. In realizing its goals of international growth, eBay employed all three strategies.

In late 1998, eBay's initial efforts at international expansion into Canada and the United Kingdom relied on building new user communities. The first step in establishing these communities was creating customized home pages for users in those countries. These home pages were designed to provide content and categories locally customized to the needs of users in specific countries, while providing them with access to a global trading community. Local customization in the United Kingdom was facilitated through the use of local management, grassroots and online marketing, and participation in local events.[14] In February 1999 eBay partnered with PBL Online, a leading Internet company in Australia, to offer a customized Australian and New Zealand eBay home page. When the site went live in October, 1999 transactions were denominated in Australian dollars and, while buyers could bid on auctions anywhere in the world, they could also search for items located exclusively in Australia. Further, local chat boards were designed to facilitate interaction between Australian users, and country-specific categories, such as Australian coins and stamps as well as cricket and rugby memorabilia, were offered.

To further expand its global reach, eBay acquired Germany's largest online person-to-person trading site, Alando.de AG, in June 1999. eBay's management handled the transition of service in a manner calculated to be smooth and painless for Alando.de AG's users. While users would have to comply with eBay rules and regulations, the only significant change for Alando.de AG's 50,000 registered users was that they would have to go to a new URL to transact their business.

To establish an Asian presence, in February 2000 eBay formed a joint venture with NEC to launch eBay Japan. According to the new CEO of eBay Japan, Merle Okawara, an internationally renowned executive, NEC was pleased to help eBay in leveraging the tried-and-trusted eBay business model to provide Japanese consumers with access to a global community of active online buyers and sellers. In customizing the site to the needs of Japanese users, eBay wrote the content exclusively in Japanese and allowed users to bid in yen. The site had over 800 categories ranging from internationally popular categories (such as computers, electronics, and Asian antiques) to categories with a local flavor (such as Hello Kitty, Pokémon, and pottery). The eBay Japan site also debuted a new merchant-to-person concept known as Supershops, which allowed consumers to bid on items listed by companies.

In 2001, eBay expanded into South Korea through an acquisition of a majority ownership position in the country's largest online trading service, Internet Auction Co.

Ltd., and into Belgium, Brazil, Italy, France, the Netherlands, Portugal, Spain, and Sweden through the acquisition of Europe's largest online trading platform, iBazar. Further expansion in 2001 included the development of a local site in Singapore, and an equity-based alliance with the leading online auction site for the Spanish and Portuguese-speaking communities in Latin America, MercadoLibre.com, that would give eBay access to Argentina, Chile, Colombia, Ecuador, Mexico, Uruguay, and Venezuela.

At the end of 2003 eBay had a presence in 28 countries, including Australia, Austria, Belgium, Canada, China (through an investment in the Chinese company Eachnet), France, Germany, Ireland, Italy, the Netherlands, New Zealand, Singapore, South Korea, Spain, Sweden, Switzerland, Taiwan, Great Britain, and Latin America (through an investment in MercadoLibre.com) and held the top online auction position in every country except Taiwan, where it was a close number two to Yahoo. eBay perceived this rapid international expansion as one of the keys to attaining its goal of having $3 billion in annual revenues by 2005. Growth opportunities were especially appealing in Asia (due to rapid increases in Internet access) and Europe. The company's international business grew by 165 percent in 2002, and its largest international markets were Germany (where 75 percent of eBay users were classified as active users), the United Kingdom, and South Korea. At the end of 2002, the company said:

> [We are] going to invest heavily in international expansion, to tap the huge potential that appears to be the hallmark of Germany, the UK, and Korea and so many of the other markets that we've entered. And we're going to do all of this with the same financial discipline we have always shown by staying true to our strategy of balancing returns with appropriate investment to capitalize on the company's long-term opportunities.[15]

How eBay's Auction Site Compared with Those of Rivals

Auction sites varied in a number of respects: their inventory, the bidding process, extra services and fees, technical support, functionality, and sense of community. Since its inception eBay had gone to great lengths to make its Web site intuitive, easy to use by both buyers and sellers, and reliable. Efforts to ensure ease of use ranged from narrowly defining categories (to allow users to quickly locate desired products) to introducing services designed to personalize a user's eBay experience. Two specific services developed by eBay and launched in 1998 to increase personalization were My eBay and About Me. My eBay gave users centralized access to confidential, current information regarding their trading activities. From his or her My eBay page a user could view information pertaining to his or her current account balances with eBay; feedback rating; the status of any auctions in which he or she was participating, as either a buyer or a seller; and auctions in favorite categories. In October, eBay introduced the About Me service, which allowed users to create customized home pages that could be viewed by all other eBay members and could include elements from the My eBay page such as user ratings or items the user had listed for auction, as well as personal information and pictures. This service not only increased customer ease of use but also contributed to the sense of community among the traders; one seller stated that the About Me service "made it easier and more rewarding for me to do business with others."[16] New features and services added in 2000 included new listing functions that could make an auction

Exhibit 7   PERFORMANCE METRICS FOR ONLINE AUCTION FIRMS

	Customer Experience Metrics				
	Reliability	Efficiency			Consistency
	Percent Error Rate	Average Transaction Length (seconds)	Minimum Transaction Length (seconds)	Maximum Transaction Length (seconds)	Variability of Transaction Length (seconds)
Amazon Auctions	0.52%	5.68	3.39	47.1	3.60
BidVille	0.62	3.90	0.05	71.1	3.77
eBay	3.97	13.20	7.34	97.5	6.01
ePier	1.02	7.29	4.70	83.0	5.99
uBid	11.76	5.95	3.05	185.0	8.39
Yahoo Auctions	2.38	10.94	2.97	112.0	4.37

Source: Benchmark Study of Online Auction Performance August–September 2003, www.empirix.com.

stand out, including Highlight and Feature Plus, as well as a feature that allowed sellers to cross-list their products in two categories, a tool to set prequalification guidelines for bidders, a new imaging and photo hosting service that made it easier for sellers to include pictures of their goods, and the introduction of the Buy It Now tool.

Throughout its history eBay had struggled to balance its explosive growth with its technological infrastructure. To counter several significant service outages the company had faced in its early days, eBay hired Maynard Webb, a premier software engineer and troubleshooter who was working at Gateway Computer. Webb took swift action, forming alliances with key vendors such as Sun, IBM, and Microsoft, and outsourcing its technology and Web site operations to Exodus Communications and Abovenet. These outsourcing agreements were intended to allow Exodus and Abovenet to "manage network capacity and provide a more robust backbone" while eBay focused on its core business.[17] While eBay still experienced minor outages when it changed or expanded services (for example, a system crash coincided with the introduction of the original 22 regional Web sites), system downtime decreased. However, the stability of the system under eBay's explosive growth and continuous introduction of new features was a continuing management concern.

In 2003 Empirix conducted a benchmark study of online auction site performance that measured key performance metrics for six leading auction sites. This study included three customer experience metrics: efficiency (how long transactions were in seconds), consistency (how much the transaction lengths varied), and reliability (how often transactions were completed successfully). Results indicated that Amazon.com had the best performance, BidVille had the shortest transaction length, and eBay's Web applications were slower and more error prone than rivals' (see Exhibit 7).

eBay's Main Competitors

eBay considered the ability to attract buyers, the volume of transactions and selection of goods, customer service, and brand recognition to be the most important competitive factors in the online auction industry. In addition to these principal factors, eBay was also attempting to compete along several other dimensions: sense of community, system reliability, reliability of delivery and payment, Web site convenience and accessibility, level of service fees, and quality of search tools.[18]

Exhibit 8   CUSTOMER SERVICE RANKINGS (scores out of 100)

Sector/Company	1999	2000	2001	2002
E-commerce				
E-commerce retail	n.a.	78	77	83
Yahoo, Inc.	74	73	76	78
Amazon.com, Inc.	n.a.	84	84	88
Online Auctions Overall	n.a.	72	74	77
eBay	n.a.	80	82	82
uBid, Inc.	n.a.	67	69	70
Portals/search engines				
Yahoo, Inc.	74	73	76	78
Google, Inc.	n.a.	n.a.	80	82
Retail				
Overall retail	73.3	72.9	74.8	74.6
Target	74	73	77	78
Sears	71	73	76	75
Wal-Mart	72	73	75	74

Source: American Customer Satisfaction Index, www.theacsi.org.

Early in eBay's history the company's main rivals could be considered classified advertisements in newspapers, garage sales, flea markets, collectibles shows, and other venues such as local auction houses and liquidators. As eBay's product mix and selling techniques evolved, the company's range of competitors did as well. The broadening of eBay's product mix beyond collectibles to include practical household items, office equipment, toys, and so on brought the company into more direct competition with brick-and-mortar retailers, import/export companies, and catalog and mail order companies. Further, with the acquisition of Half.com, the introduction of eBay stores, and the growing percentage of fixed-price and Buy It Now sales as a percentage of eBay's revenue, eBay considered itself to be competing in a broad sense with a number of other online retailers, such as Wal-Mart, Kmart, Target, Sears, JCPenney, and Office Depot. In competing with these larger sellers, eBay began to adopt some of their tools, such as the use of gift certificates. The company also felt that it was competing with a number of specialty retailers, such as Christie's (antiques), KB Toys (toys), Blockbuster (movies), Dell (computers), Foot Locker (sporting goods), Ticketmaster (tickets), and Home Depot (tools).[19] In 2003 eBay begin experiencing competition from new sources, including portals (such as Yahoo) and search providers (such as Google and Overture) that sought to become primary launch pads for online shopping. Exhibit 8 displays eBay's customer service rankings as compared to a variety of rivals' customer service rankings.

eBay management saw traditional competitors as inefficient because their fragmented local and regional nature made it expensive and time-consuming for buyers and sellers to meet, exchange information, and complete transactions. Moreover, the competitors suffered from three other deficiencies: (1) They tended to offer limited variety and breadth of selection as compared to the millions of items available on eBay, (2) they often had high transaction costs, and (3) they were information inefficient in the sense that buyers and sellers lacked a reliable and convenient means of setting prices for sales or purchases. By the same token, eBay's management saw its online auction format as competitively superior to these rivals because (1) it facilitated buyers and sellers meeting, exchanging information, and conducting transactions; (2) it allowed buyers and sellers to bypass traditional intermediaries and trade directly, thus lowering costs; (3) it provided global reach to greater selection and a broader base of participants; (4) it permitted trading at all hours and provided continuously updated information; and (5) it fostered a sense of community among individuals with mutual interests.

Even with the strengthening competition, analysts estimated that eBay controlled approximately 85 percent of the consumer-to-consumer online auction market and 64 percent of total online auction revenue share. The most significant competitors to eBay's auction business included Amazon Auctions, Yahoo Auctions, and uBid. Two of the smaller competitors in the online auction industry included BidVille (an auction site with no listing fees and no final value fees) and ePier (60,000 members as of January, 2004). Both of these had closely copied eBay's look and fee structure and touted themselves as "alternatives to eBay."

Amazon.com Auctions   Amazon.com's business strategy was to "be the world's most customer-centric company where customers can find and discover anything they may want to buy online."[20] With its customer base of 35 million users in over 150 countries and a very well-known brand name, Amazon.com was considered the closest overall competitive threat to eBay, especially as eBay expanded its business model beyond its traditional auction services. Analysts estimated that Amazon.com had a 5–7 percent share of all online retail sales, but Hitwise, an Internet competitive intelligence service, found that for the week ending September 20, 2003, eBay had a 93.6 percent share of all Web traffic to auction sites while Amazon.com had only a 1.1 percent share.

Amazon was created in July 1995 as an online bookseller and had rapidly transitioned into a full-line, one-stop-shopping retailer with a product offering that included books, music, toys, electronics, tools and hardware, lawn and patio products, video games, software, and a mall of boutiques (called z-shops). Amazon.com was the Internet's number one music, video, and book retailer. One of the distinctive features customers appreciated about Amazon.com was the extensive reviews available for each item. These product reviews were written both by professionals and by regular users who had purchased a specific product. The company's 2003 net sales were estimated between $6.2 and $6.7 billion, up almost 58.9 percent from 2002. In 2002 Amazon.com generated its first profit from operations—$64.1 million—and in 2003 operating profits increased substantially from 2002 (as seen in Exhibit 9). One significant weakness analysts noted in Amazon's financials was that the company's free shipping policies, put in place to draw more customers, had cut deeply into profitability.

By 2003 Amazon's management felt that it was time to strike a better balance between cost control and growth in executing a strategy intended to enhance Amazon's position as leader in retail e-commerce. An indication of the company's success was the rise in Amazon's customer base from 14 million to 20 million during 2000 and to 35 million by 2003. The company invested more than $300 million in infrastructure in 1999 and opened two international sites, www.amazon.co.uk (the United Kingdom) and www.amazon.de (Germany), and later added www.amazon.ca (Canada), www.amazon.co.jp (Japan) and www.amazon.fr (France). These sites, along with Amazon.com, were among the most popular online retail domains in Europe. By 2004 international sales had grown to over $2 billion from just $168 million in 1999 and accounted for 38 percent of all Internet sales.

Some analysts felt that in expanding its position both internationally and abroad Amazon had conceded the top spot in online auction to eBay and was looking to explore other avenues. Amazon often used strategic alliances to support its innovative expansion

Exhibit 9   AMAZON.COM'S OPERATING RESULTS, 1996–2003

Year	Income or (Loss) from Operations (in millions)
1996	$ (6.2)
1997	(31.0)
1998	(124.5)
1999	(720.0)
2000	(863.9)
2001	(412.3)
2002	64.1
2003	400.0 (est)

initiatives. For example, the company had agreements with Borders Books to allow customers to pick up Amazon.com book orders in-store, as well as e-commerce partnerships with Ashford.com, Drugstore.com, CarsDirect.com, and Sotheby's (a leading auction house for art, antiques, and collectibles), and opened a co-branded toy and video game store online with Toysrus.com. During 2003, the company announced an agreement with the band Pearl Jam to sell the group's music directly to fans through Amazon's Advantage program. By 2003 Amazon.com had over 550,000 active third-party sellers on its site and 350 branded sellers, most of them selling through shops rather than auctions. These third-party sellers accounted for over 22 percent of U.S. sales. To further expand the company's reach, in September 2003 Amazon established an independent unit called A9 that was charged with creating the best shopping search tool for Amazon's use and for use by other companies and third-party Web sites. To compete with eBay's fixed-price formats, Amazon began including links on product pages that allowed customers to view identical new and used items from third-party sellers.

uBid.com   uBid's mission statement was to "be the most recognized and trusted business-to-consumer marketplace, consistently delivering exceptional value and service to its customers and supplier partners."[21] According to the company, "uBid delivers to the customer both the cost savings of an auction and the customer care of popular brand name retail e-commerce sites, making uBid a destination point for consumer share of wallet as they capitalize on the benefits of this high performance hybrid business model."[22] As such, uBid considered itself to be in direct competition with eBay, although a distant second, especially to that portion of eBay's business that was derived from large corporations and smaller companies wanting to sell their products through an auction format. The company's business model centered on offering brand-name merchandise, often refurbished and closeout, at a deep discount in a relatively broad range of categories from leading brand-name manufacturers such as Sony, Hewlett-Packard, IBM, Compaq, AMD, Minolta, and over 1,000 other suppliers. Categories included Computer and Office; Consumer Electronics; Music, Movies & Games; Jewelry & Gifts; Travel & Events; Home & Garden; Sports; Toys & Hobbies; Apparel; Collectibles; and Everything Else. The merchandise was offered in both an online auction format in which prices started at $1.00 and through uBid's fixed-price superstore. The merchandise was sourced from corporate partners and from uBid's own operations, which included a 400,000-square-foot warehouse and refurbishment center, and their current parent company Petters Group Worldwide, and from small and medium-sized companies who were members of uBid's Certified Merchant Program.

Although uBid had offered consumer-to-consumer auctions at one time, the company had discontinued this option as of 2002 due to the costs associated with policing fraud and concerns over product quality.

Founded in April 1997, uBid offered an initial public offering on the Nasdaq in December 1998. The company had experienced significantly increased revenues every year since its inception through 2000, but it had never captured the share of the auction market that its founders hoped was possible, although it at one time had a 14.7 percent share of revenues in the online auction market. In mid-2000 uBid was sold to CGMI Networks, and then it was sold again to Petters Group Worldwide in 2003. With each sale the number of workers employed by uBid fell and the product mix was changed in an attempt to find a niche market that would insulate the company from the competitive power of eBay.

Yahoo Auctions   Yahoo.com, the first online navigational guide to the Web, launched Yahoo Auctions in 1998. Yahoo.com offered services to nearly 200 million users every month in North America, Europe, Asia, and Latin America. The Web site was available in 24 countries and 12 languages. Yahoo reported net revenues of $1.11 billion in 2000 (up 88 percent from 1999) and net income of $290 million. Yahoo's user base grew from 120 million to over 180 million during 2000. In December 2000 Yahoo's traffic increased to an average of 900 million page views per day (up 94 percent from 1999). Yahoo had entered into numerous alliances and marketing agreements to generate additional traffic at its site and was investing in new technology to improve the site's performance and attractiveness.

Its auction services were provided to users free of charge in the early days, and the number of auctions listed on Yahoo increased from 670,000 to 1.3 million during the second half of 1999. However, when Yahoo decided to start charging users a listing fee in January 2001, listings fell from over 2 million to about 200,000.[23] Yahoo Auctions also offered many extra services to its users. For example, the Premium Sellers Program was designed to reward the sellers that were consistently at the top of their category. These Premium Sellers were allowed enhanced promotions, premium placement, and direct access to customer support. In recognition of the fall in listings due to the listing fee instituted in January, Yahoo Auctions announced a revamped performance-based pricing model for its U.S. auctions in November 2001. In this system, which was relatively similar to eBay's, listing fees were reduced and sellers were charged according to the value of an item sold. In response to this change the number of listings rose to more than 500,000 by December 7, 2001.

While Yahoo had significant reach throughout the world, including over 25 local auction sites internationally, by 2004 Yahoo Auctions had reduced its international operations from 16 countries to 7 (Brazil, Canada, Hong Kong, Japan, Mexico, Singapore, and Taiwan). In 2002 alone Yahoo conceded its auction sites in France, Germany, Italy, Spain, and the United Kingdom and Ireland and promoted eBay's sites in each of those countries via banner ads and text links. In 2003 Yahoo sold its Australian site as well. However, in 2004 Yahoo began offering auctions in China through a joint venture with a dominant Chinese Web portal, Sina, indicating that it had not completely abandoned the international auction market. Further reinforcing Yahoo's commitment to online retail, in July 2003 Yahoo acquired Overture, which was the leading provider of commercial search as of the end of the first quarter of 2003 with more than 88,000 advertisers globally as well as an extensive affiliate distribution network. Many of the sellers who advertised on Overture also advertised on eBay, and some analysts estimated that the amount of sales by merchants through the combination of Yahoo's and Overture's offerings would total between one-half to two-thirds of that available on eBay.

eBay's New Challenges

Heading into 2004, eBay faced two fundamental challenges:

1. How could eBay continue to grow at its current pace given the maturing of its domestic market?

2. As eBay's business model evolved to include more fixed-price sales, could it transfer its competitive advantage in the online auction industry into the more general area of online retail?

Throughout its climb to become the undisputed leader of the online auction industry, eBay had faced each new challenge with an eye on its founding values and an ear for community members. Omidyar said, "What we do have to be cautious of, as we grow, is that our core is the personal trade, because the values are communicated person-to-person. It can be easy for a big company to start to believe that it's responsible for its success. Our success is really based on our members' success. They're the ones who have created this, and they're the ones who will create it in the future. If we lose sight of that, then we're in big trouble."[24] The company applied this perspective in response to significant customer concerns regarding the growing presence of corporate sellers on eBay.

Omidyar and Whitman recognized the importance of eBay's culture and were aware of the potential impact rapid growth and the evolution of the product line could have on this valued asset. When asked about the importance of the culture Omidyar said, "If we lose that, we've pretty much lost everything."[25] Whitman agreed with the importance of eBay's culture, but she did not see the influx of larger retailers and liquidators as a significant problem. Even as these sellers grew to account for 5 percent of eBay's total business in 2004 (from 1 percent in 2001), these large sellers received no favorable treatment. Whitman stated, "There are no special deals. I am passionate about creating this level playing field."[26] While this view was applauded by the smaller sellers, some larger sellers viewed these policies as overly restrictive.

Continued Growth

By virtually any measure, eBay's growth had been outstanding. However, this impressive track record, coupled with the progress they had made in reaching their stated goals had created high expectations among investors. These lofty expectations began to cause some concern among analysts as eBay's domestic core market of online auction sales began to show some warning signals. For example, in 2003 the average conversion rate (the number of auctions that were completed successfully) was approximately 51 percent, a rate that had held steady over the last two years. However, supply imbalances threatened this key metric. In many categories, as the number of sellers grew, supply was beginning to outstrip demand. One of the few categories in which demand outstripped supply was eBay Motors, which had an average of 11 bids from seven unique users for each sale. Further, almost half of eBay's registered users were from the United States and represented almost one-third of all U.S. Internet users. With the U.S. online auction market maturing and eBay maintaining the dominant market share, analysts were concerned with how much more penetration eBay could achieve.

In response to these concerns, eBay cited new trends indicating that even in the United States the company was reaching new customers and had room to grow. One of the trends eBay saw as particularly promising was the increasing use of eBay's 28,000 registered Trading Assistants and the emergence of drop-off eBay consignment services.

Exhibit 10   eBAY'S LARGEST AUCTION CATEGORIES, BY ANNUALIZED GROSS MERCHANDISE SALES, FOURTH QUARTER 2003 (in millions)

	Fourth-Quarter 2003	Market Penetration
Motors	$7,500	< 1%
Consumer electronics	2,600	1–4%
Computers	2,400	1–3%
Books, movies, music	2,000	~ 3%
Clothing and accessories	1,800	< 1%
Sports	1,800	2–5%
Collectibles	1,500	2–3%
Toys	1,500	~ 5%
Home and garden	1,100	< 1%

Source: Corporate reports, Lehman Brothers estimates, www.lehman.com.

Trading Assistants were experienced eBay sellers who, for a fee, would help users sell their items on eBay. Extending this service, drop-off consignment services began to spring up as early as 2000. These consignment services, such as AuctionDrop, Quick-Drop, and Picture-It-Sold, would take physical possession of a customer's items, typically those with an eBay value of over $50, and sell them on eBay for a fee equal to between 30 and 40 percent of the item's final sale price. The company was encouraged by these activities because they reached sellers who would not normally use the Internet.

eBay also challenged the theory that the maturity of its markets was based on the company's total market penetration in key categories. For example, eBay argued that it had significant market opportunity in areas such as eBay Motors, where its $6.7 billion in gross merchandise sales accounted for less than 1 percent of the value of all vehicles sold in the United States. Based on this model, none of eBay's largest categories had a market penetration of 5 percent (see Exhibit 10).

Evolution of the Business Model

There was little concern that any company could seriously threaten eBay in its core auction business in the near future, but with the increasing use of tools such as gift certificates, the growing importance of fixed-price sales, the purchase of Half.com, and the growing popularity of Buy It Now, eBay came into more direct competition with retailers such as Amazon.com, with e-commerce solutions, and with the likes of Microsoft. Some analysts also thought that search engines such as Google that were directing customers to clients who paid to have their sites prominently featured in the search engine's results would also become a competitor in the near future, but Meg Whitman dismissed this possibility, saying, "We see Google and Yahoo search and MSN search . . . as actually enablers of our business," she said. "We think both natural search and paid search are allies of ours."[27] When asked about how the evolution of eBay's business model influenced the company's sphere of competition, Whitman said,

> If we were a retailer, we'd be the 27th-largest in the world. So our sellers are competing [with retailers] for consumer dollars. If you're thinking about buying a set of golf clubs or a tennis racket or a jacket or a pair of skis, you decide

whether you're going to do that at eBay, at Wal-Mart, a sporting-goods store, or Macy's. I would define our competition more broadly than ever before.[28]

The threat of these competitors increased as fixed-price sales comprised an ever-increasing percentage of eBay's total sales and growth. By the end of 2003, fixed-price trading accounted for 28 percent of eBay's gross merchandise sales (the dollar value of merchandise sold) and was expected to experience continued growth throughout the foreseeable future.

The Future

Heading into 2004, eBay was almost certain to reach the aggressive growth targets it had set for itself in 2000—and its stock price reflected this belief (see Exhibit 11). In fact, most analysts forecast that eBay would meet these goals a year early. The main question that plagued investors was, How would the company continue its phenomenal growth rate? In considering future moves eBay had a few issues to address. First, how should it prioritize its efforts? Was additional expansion in the international markets the highest priority? If so, where? Alternatively, should eBay focus on further broadening its offerings to include more categories, more specialty sites, and more sellers? How much emphasis should be put on fixed-price options? If the company chose to continue expanding its fixed-price offerings, how could it position itself vis-à-vis established online retailers, and how could it defend itself against new, more diverse competitors such as paid search engines?

Finally, eBay was facing increasing dissatisfaction by some of its largest corporate sellers. Some corporate sellers were experiencing significant difficulty with selling a large volume of goods on the site while maintaining a sufficient profit margin.

Exhibit 11   eBay's Stock Price Performance, March 2003–February 2004

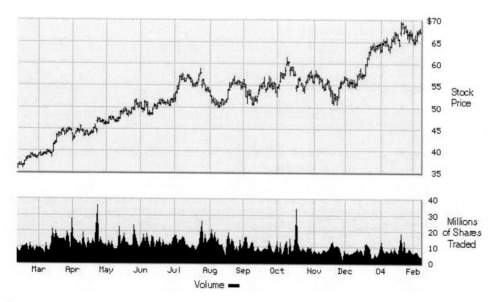

Source: www.bigcharts.com, February 9, 2004.

According to Walt Shill, the former chief of Return-Buy, a company that liquidated unsold merchandise for electronics retailers and manufacturers, eBay didn't have enough buyer demand to absorb significant quantities of a single good, such as a specific brand and model of a digital camera, in a short period of time, as eBay was "two inches deep and miles wide."[29] Whitman acknowledged this problem and stated that, for sellers wishing to "move a thousand of the same computer in a day, eBay may not be one of the most effective channels."[30] This problem, coupled with eBay's fairness policy, was causing many large sellers such as Motorola and Circuit City to abandon selling on eBay and to search for additional sales outlets. According to Scott Wingo, CEO of ChannelAdvisor, a leading provider of auction and marketplace management software that was partially owned by eBay, eBay would need to reconsider its level-playing-field policy, which prohibited giving special perks or fee discounts to big sellers if it wanted to attract large businesses and keep growing at its current rate.[31]

When eBay posted its 2003 results in early 2004, it was apparent to most industry observers that it would easily reach its stated goals a year early. Perhaps the only significant concern among analysts and investors was whether eBay could continue its growth without stretching itself too thin, especially given Meg Whitman's philosophy:

> You really need to do things 100 percent. Better to do 5 things at 100 percent than 10 things at 80 percent. Because the devil in so much of this is in the detail and while we have to move very, very fast, I think you are not well served by moving incredibly rapidly and not doing things that well.[32]

Endnotes

[1] www.c-i-a.com, press releases, April 2001 and July 2001.
[2] Claire Tristram, "'Amazoning' Amazon," www.contextmag.com, November 1999.
[3] Quentin Hardy, "The Radical Philanthropist," *Forbes*, May 1, 2000, p. 118.
[4] "Billionaires of the Web," *Business 2.0*, June 1999.
[5] eBay press release, May 7, 1998.
[6] Company 10K filing with the Securities and Exchange Commission, March 3, 2001, pp. 4–6.
[7] eBay company 10K, filed March 28, 2001.
[8] "Q&A with eBay's Meg Whitman," *BusinessWeek E.Biz*, December 3, 2001.
[9] http://pages.ebay.com/help/community/values.html, January 1, 2002.
[10] "Q&A with eBay's Meg Whitman."
[11] Ibid.
[12] Tristram, "'Amazoning' Amazon."
[13] eBay press release, May 18, 1999.
[14] eBay 10K, filed March 30, 2000.
[15] 2002 eBay annual report.
[16] Ann Pearson, in an eBay press release dated October 15, 1998.
[17] eBay press release, October 8, 1999.
[18] Ibid.
[19] eBay 10Q annual report, November 14, 2001.
[20] 2000 Amazon annual report.
[21] www.ubid.com/about/companyinfo.asp.
[22] Ibid.
[23] Troy Wolverton , "eBay Seeks to Sail into New Territory," CNET News.com, July 19, 2001.
[24] "Q&A with eBay's Pierre Omidyar," *BusinessWeek E.Biz*, December 3, 2001.
[25] "The People's Company," *BusinessWeek E.Biz*, December 3, 2001.
[26] "Queen of the Online Flea Market," Economist.com, December 30, 2003.
[27] Ben Berkowitz, "eBay to Experiment Again with Local Auction Sites," www.usatoday.com, February 24, 2004.
[28] "Meg Whitman on eBay's Self-Regulation," *Business Week Online*, August 18, 2003.
[29] Nick Wingfield, "As eBay Grows, Site Disappoints Some Big Vendors," *The Wall Street Journal*, February 26, 2004.
[30] Ibid.
[31] Ibid.
[32] "What's Behind the Boom at eBay?" *Business Week Online*, May 21, 1999.

Google's Strategy—The Quest for a Technology-Based Competitive Advantage

John E. Gamble
University of South Alabama

In 2004, Internet searches were the second most common online activity after e-mail. Advertisers spent an estimated $3.2 billion on paid search Internet ads in 2004—168 percent more than spending for such ads in 2003. Expenditures on paid search advertising were expected to grow to $4.3 billion in 2005 and to $5.2 billion in 2006. Advertisers believed that search-based ads were particularly effective because they were highly targeted to what Internet users were immediately searching for. In 2004, Google was the leading search engine on the Web and provider of search-based ads because of Internet users' faith in the search engine. The company did not collect information on search users, placed ads discreetly on its page listing search results, and did not intersperse paid search results with nonpaid search results. Perhaps Google's most important feature was its capability to retrieve highly relevant results to search queries, made possible by its innovative PageRank technology.

When an Internet user entered a search query at Google.com, from a Google toolbar or deskbar, or requested a search at a Web site that licensed Google's search appliance, the search engine performed a computation of an equation involving 500 million variables and 2 billion terms to generate a list of best-matching search results. The results were generated in a fraction of a second and pulled from billions of Web sites that were constantly downloaded onto Google's farm of more than 10,000 personal computers. Many Internet users found Google's search results more relevant than results generated by competing search engines because of this equation, which assessed how well the search terms matched and, most important, how many other Web sites pointed to a site. Google cofounder Larry Page suggested that Google's technology was superior to other search technologies: "You're asking the whole Web who's the greatest site to ask about this subject."[1]

Internet users' preference for Google's search results allowed the company to establish accounts with more than 100,000 advertisers, which had produced 2003 net revenues of nearly $1.5 billion and profits of more than $105 million. The company executed a successful initial public offering (IPO) in August 2004 that brought in an investment of $1.7 billion. In its first reporting period as a public company, Google recorded revenues of more than $2.1 billion for the nine-month period ending September 30, 2004. Analysts expected Google to earn more than $300 million in profits by year-end 2004.

Google's stock price nearly doubled between its IPO and the release of its first financial statements. However, Google's stock price began to drop markedly in early November 2004 when Microsoft unveiled the preview-version of its MSN Search product. Microsoft had spent more than $100 million and taken 20 months to try to build a search engine that matched Google's most important features and surpassed its capabilities with direct links to MSN Encarta and other sites for searches written in plain language. In addition, Microsoft intended to incorporate MSN Search capabilities into Outlook and Internet Explorer upon the official launch of the search engine in early 2005. In addition, many technology sector analysts believed that MSN Search would ultimately be integrated into Microsoft Office and other Microsoft applications.

Google also faced growing competition from Yahoo, which had developed its own search capabilities in 2003 and severed its three-year agreement with Google in July 2004. Some technology sector analysts were also worried that Google's business model, which relied primarily on revenues from search-based ads, would limit its growth potential. Some suggested the company should consider adopting strategies used by Yahoo, AOL, MSN, and others that would allow it to evolve into a Web portal or at least to collect user information to better target ads to Internet users.

Company History

The development of Google's search technology began in January 1996 when Stanford University computer science graduate students Larry Page and Sergey Brin collaborated to develop a new search engine. They named the new search engine BackRub because of its ability to rate Web sites for relevancy by examining the number of back links pointing to them. The approach for assessing the relevancy of Web sites to a particular search query used by other Web sites at the time was based on examining and counting metatags and keywords. By 1997, the search accuracy of BackRub had allowed it to gain a loyal following among Silicon Valley Internet users. Yahoo cofounder David Filo was among the converted, and in 1998 he convinced Sergey Brin and Larry Page to leave Stanford to focus on making their search technology the backbone of a new Internet company.

BackRub would be renamed Google, which was a play on the word *googol*—a mathematical term for a number represented by the numeral 1 followed by 100 zeros (or 10^{100}). Brin and Page's adoption of the new name reflected their mission to organize the seemingly infinite amount of information on the Internet. In August 1998, a Stanford professor arranged for Brin and Page to meet at his home with a potential angel investor to demonstrate the Google search engine. The investor, who had been a founder of Sun Microsystems, was immediately impressed with Google's search capabilities but was too pressed for time to hear much of its inventors' informal presentation. The investor stopped the two during the presentation and suggested, "Instead of us discussing all the details, why don't I just write you a check?"[2] The two partners held the investor's $100,000 check made payable to Google Inc. for two weeks while they scrambled to set up a corporation with that name and open a corporate bank account. The two officers of the freshly incorporated company went on to raise a total of $1 million in venture capital from family, friends, and other angel investors by the end of September 1998.

Even with a cash reserve of $1 million, Brin and Page ran Google on a shoestring budget. The two partners built the main servers from discounted computer components, and its four employees operated out of a garage owned by a friend of the founders. By year-end 1998 Google's beta version was handling 10,000 search queries per day and *PC* magazine had named the company to its list of top 100 Web sites and search engines for 1998.

The new company recorded successes at a lightning-fast pace, with the search kernel answering more than 500,000 queries per day and Red Hat agreeing to become the company's first search customer in early 1999. Google attracted an additional $25 million in funding from two leading Silicon Valley venture capital firms by midyear 1999 to support further growth and enhancements to Google's search technology. Google began to add employees, bringing the number up to 39 by the end of 1999, and to accrue key customers for its search functionality. Customers like AOL/Netscape and Virgilio, the leading online portal in Italy, helped push search requests to more than 3 million per day.

In 2000, Google Inc. grew to 60 employees; introduced wireless search technology; provided search services for new Web portal customers in the United States, Europe, and Asia; launched search capabilities in 10 non-English languages; expanded its index of ranked Web sites to 1.3 billion URLs; was called the "Best Bet Search Engine" by *PC World;* and was named by *Yahoo! Internet Life* magazine as the "Best Search Engine on the Internet." Yahoo signed an agreement to make Google its default search provider, which helped make Google the largest search engine on the Web, with more than 100 million daily searches. Also that year, the company introduced the Google Toolbar browser plug-in, which allowed computer users to search the Internet without first visiting a Google-affiliated Web portal or Google's home page. Among its most important innovations in 2000 was the development of keyword-targeted advertising that provided the company with an additional revenue source beyond fees for licensing its search appliance to other Web sites.

In 2001, Google signed agreements with such wireless providers as Sprint PCS, Cingular, and AT&T that gave mobile phone users access to Google's index of Web pages. It then acquired Deja.com, which provided Google with the Internet's largest archive of searchable messages posted on Usenet discussion boards. Google also expanded search capabilities to 28 languages—allowing it to establish licensing agreements with 130 Web portals and destination sites in Latin American, Asian, Middle Eastern, and European countries. New capabilities enabled Google users to search an index of 250 million images, review and search daily news, search more than 1,100 mail-order catalogs, and search for any published phone number in the United States. The company's search-based advertising program expanded to include small businesses and individuals with a self-service advertising system that gave small advertisers the capability to set up ads online and pay Google by credit card on a per-click basis. The expansion of advertising-based revenue allowed Google to increase annual revenues from $220,000 in 1999 to more than $86 million in 2001 and end the year with a profit of nearly $7 million.

Google's rapid growth in services and revenues made it obvious to Sergey Brin and Larry Page that the company needed executive-level management with experience in managing a large, rapidly growing company. In March 2001, the two asked Novell's CEO and chairman, Eric Schmidt, to chair Google's board of directors. Four months later, Google's founders and board asked Schmidt to become CEO of the company, which moved Page to president of products and Brin to president of technology. Schmidt was brought in to introduce formal processes, procedures, and financial systems to the almost anarchic business environment that resulted from Google's unorthodox corporate culture. Employees at the company's Googleplex headquarters in Mountain View, California, had been encouraged to work on pet projects that might be unrelated to work assignments, bring dogs to work, and engage in biweekly hockey games where checking higher-ups was fair game. Also, prior to Schmidt's arrival, important strategy and operating issues were settled by upper-level management during weekly two-hour meetings that rarely had an agenda and wandered from topic to topic. Google's board wanted Schmidt to bring a sufficient level of structure to the company to prepare it for an IPO, while avoiding a cumbersome bureaucracy that would limit Google's ability to sustain its technological advantage. Schmidt commented just prior to Google's registration for a public offering that his instruction from the board was "Don't screw this up now, Eric. This is a really, really good starting point . . . So it doesn't require some gross change."[3]

In a March 2004 interview with *The Wall Street Journal* Eric Schmidt stated, "You do not want to take big-company structures and apply them to small companies. You want to evolve small-company structures on a need-appropriate basis."[4] Even though Schmidt was made Google's CEO, both Page and Brin were acutely involved in strategy making, forming what was described by the three as a "triumvirate."[5] When asked about the roles of the two founders in decision making, Schmidt, who many business journalists suggested should have been given the title of chief operating officer instead of CEO, commented, "Whenever we have something important, two people have to agree . . . Now, often the two are the founders. When it's managerial things, things Larry and Sergey aren't as focused on, we try to get two of the vice presidents to agree."[6]

Under Eric Schmidt's leadership as CEO, Google continued to add new features, such as Google Compute, parcel tracking, flight information, vehicle identification number searches, Google News, Froogle, Google Deskbar, Local Search, and Gmail. In 2002 Google launched Google Labs, which allowed users to examine Google's latest technology while it was still under development. Google was recognized in 2001 by Searchenginewatch.com with numerous technical awards like Outstanding Search Service, Best Image Search Engine, Best Design, Most Webmaster-Friendly Search Engine, and Best Search Feature. Google was also named the 2002 Brand of the Year by Interbrand and the number one business-to-business Web site by *BtoB Magazine* in 2003. Also in 2003, the company acquired Pyra Labs, the developer of Blogger—a self-publishing tool for users of online journals called weblogs (blogs). By mid-2004, Google's index included 4.28 billion Web pages, was available to 63 domains and in 88 languages, and boasted more than 100,000 active advertisers.

The Initial Public Offering

Two and a half years after Eric Schmidt arrived at Google to institute formal policies, procedures, and controls to ensure that Google did not collapse under the pressures of its accelerated growth rate, the company filed its Form S-1 Registration Statement for an initial public offering (IPO) of common stock. Google's April 29, 2004, IPO registration became the most talked-about planned offering involving an Internet company since the dot-com bust of 2000. Analysts estimated Google's potential market value to be as high as $36 billion on the basis of the company's revenue growth; projected 2004 gross margin and earnings before interest, taxes, depreciation, and amortization (EBITDA) margin of 85 percent and 61 percent, respectively; and revenue, gross profit, and EBITDA multiples of competing firms such as Yahoo. The registration announced Google's intention to raise as much as $3.6 billion from the issue of 25.7 million shares through an unusual Dutch auction.

Among Google's key tenets was "You can make money without doing evil."[7] The choice of a Dutch auction stemmed from this philosophy since Dutch auctions allowed potential investors, regardless of size, to place bids for shares. Small investors were typically locked out of participating in IPOs since brokers handling such trades favored institutional investors or individual investors with large portfolio balances or frequent trades. After a period when investors could bid for Google shares over the Internet, the Dutch auction set the clearing price for Google shares at the lowest bid that allowed all shares to be sold. On the day the IPO was finalized, any potential investor bidding the clearing price or higher was granted shares at the clearing price. A Dutch auction would also be favorable to Google since it involved considerably lower investment banking and underwriting fees and little or no commissions for brokers.

Google's financial advisers initially believed the company's shares would fetch between $108 and $135 per share, but the clearing price was ultimately set at $85 after it became apparent that the Dutch auction process would not generate sufficient demand for the company's shares. The poor demand was caused by a number of factors, which included institutional investors' uneasiness with placing a bid absent satisfactory pricing guidance; individual investors' unfamiliarity with the auction process; and, even though 28 brokerage firms were involved in the underwriting syndicate, brokers' unwillingness to help clients purchase shares when few or no commissions were involved. Google had planned to close the auction on August 17, 2004, but instead asked the Securities and Exchange Commission for a one-day extension to evaluate how many shares should be offered when it became clear demand for its shares was much lower than anticipated. The company and its financial advisers decreased the number of shares offered from 25.7 million to 19.6 million to establish an $85 clearing price—making shares available to bidders on August 18 and making August 19 the first day of trading for Google shares.

The lower clearing price caused Sergey Brin and Larry Page to reduce the number of shares they personally planned to sell on August 19 by one-half and caused Google's two major venture capital investors to abandon plans to sell 4.5 million shares when trading began. Still, Google's $1.7 billion IPO easily surpassed Barnesandnoble.com's 1999 IPO of $431 million to become the largest Internet IPO ever. In addition, Google's initial offering was the 25th largest U.S. IPO of all time and made the company's $23 billion market capitalization roughly equivalent to that of General Motors Corporation.

Google's shares appreciated by 18 percent during the first day of trading, making both Brin and Page about $600 million richer by the end of the day and each worth approximately $3.8 billion. Also, an estimated 900 to 1,000 Google employees were worth at least $1 million, with 600 to 700 holding at least $2 million in Google stock. On average, each of Google's 2,292 staff members held approximately $1.7 million in company stock, excluding the holdings of the top five executives. Stanford University also enjoyed a $179.5 million windfall from its stock holdings granted for its early investment in Brin and Page's search engine. Some of Google's early contractors and consultants also profited handsomely from forgoing fees in return for stock options in the company. One such contractor was Abbe Patterson, who took options for 4,000 shares rather than a $5,000 fee for preparing a PowerPoint presentation and speaking notes for one of Brin and Page's first presentations to venture capitalists. After two splits and four days of trading, her 16,000 shares were worth $1.7 million.[8] Exhibit 1 tracks the performance of Google's common shares between August 19, 2004, and November 8, 2004.

Exhibit 1   Performance of Google Inc.'s Stock Price, August 19, 2004, to November 8, 2004

(a) Trend in Google Inc.'s Common Stock Price

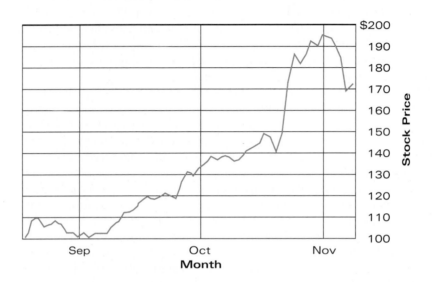

(b) Performance of Google Inc.'s Stock Price versus the S&P 500 Index

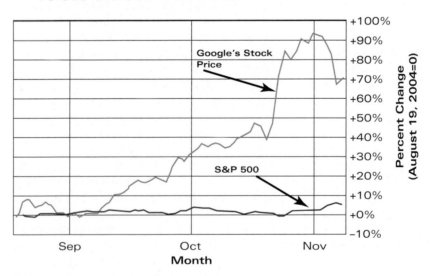

Google's Business Model

When Google secured its $25 million round of venture capital funding, the business press became very interested in the company and its approach to generating revenues and providing a return to investors. Page and Brin left the press bewildered when their explanation of Google's business plan didn't fit the general model for Internet companies. Page and Brin explained that Google would generate revenues by licensing its search engine to other Web publishers and would not strive become a Web portal or e-commerce site. Also, Google would not advertise and was not interested in selling its technology to a large Internet portal such as AOL. Business journalists discounted Google's ability to ever generate adequate revenues from licensing fees to cover expenses and also expected Google to quickly burn through its investment capital as other Internet companies had done. Little did the press understand that the capital needed for computer equipment necessary to perform Google's complex calculations was far less than that of other search engines because of Brin and Page's ability to weave together a network of low-cost personal computers that performed as well as a supercomputer. Also, Google's operating expenses were held down by its frugal culture that, for example, called for three to four employees, or Googlers, to share a work space. In addition, Google would soon add a second revenue source from keyword-targeted search advertising.

As Google's revenues grew dramatically during 2001, outsiders began to understand Google's business model but were still perplexed by Brin and Page's insistence that Google forgo revenue opportunities that other Internet companies had pursued. Google's business model generated revenue from only two sources: (1) the licensing fees it charged to supply search capabilities to other Internet sites and wireless telephone companies, and (2) the advertising fees it charged for providing highly targeted text-only sponsor links adjacent to its search results. Page and Brin insisted that the company would only sell discreet text ads placed near search results and never mix paid keyword-based ads with legitimate search results even though the practice was standard among search engine companies. Also, Google would not place banner ads on its Web site, nor would it sell pop-up ads.

In 2004, Google's advertising programs included AdWords, which charged customers on a cost-per-click (CPC) basis, so that the customer paid for the ad only when an Internet user clicked on it. Google maintained a direct sales force that marketed AdWords to large advertisers such as General Motors, Sony, and L. L. Bean. Full-service account teams helped large advertisers set up accounts, design campaigns, and monitor click-through rates. Small advertisers could also participate in the program by setting up an account at Google.com for a $5 fee and entering a credit card for CPC charges. There were no minimum advertising expenditures required, and agreements could be terminated at any time by the advertiser. CPC pricing was determined by an auction-based pricing model that allowed advertisers to assign dollar values to keywords. The minimum cost per click was 5 cents. The ad's placement on the Web page was determined by the value the advertiser assigned to a keyword and the click-through rate of the ad. Therefore, advertisers who bid higher prices for particular keywords, and whose ads were clicked on more frequently, were displayed more prominently.

Google's AdSense program allowed Web publishers to share in the advertising revenues generated by Google's CPC text ads. The AdSense program served content-relevant Google text ads to pages of Google Network Web sites. For example, an Internet user reading an article about the shortage of Splenda, an artificial sweetener popularized by the Atkins Diet, at Foxnews.com would see two Google text ads by mail-order sellers of Splenda embedded in the article. Google Network members did not pay a fee to participate in the program and received the majority of advertising dollars generated from the ads. Owners of dormant domain names could also participate in the AdSense program.

Advertising was the far more important component of Google's business model, generating 77 percent of Google's revenues in 2001, 92 percent of revenues in 2002, 95 percent of revenues in 2003, and 99 percent of revenues in the first nine months of fiscal 2004. No single advertiser had ever accounted for more than 3 percent of Google's net revenues, and no Google Network member had accounted for more than 5 percent of net AdSense revenues.

The following table presents a breakdown of Google's revenues by source:

	2003	2002	2001
Advertising revenues			
Google Web sites	$772,192	$306,977	$66,932
Google Network Web sites	144,411	12,278	—
Total advertising revenues	916,603	319,255	66,932
Licensing and other revenues	45,271	28,593	19,494
Net revenues	$961,874	$347,848	$86,426

Source: Google Inc., Form S1, filed April 29, 2004.

Exhibit 2 provides Google's consolidated income statements for 1999 through the first nine months of fiscal 2004. Google's balance sheets for 2002 through the nine months ending September 30, 2004, are presented in Exhibit 3. The company's consolidated statements of cash flows for 2001 through the first nine months of fiscal 2004 are presented in Exhibit 4.

Google's Products and Services

Google believed that the purpose of its business was to organize the world's information and make it easily accessible to Internet users. The company made three key commitments to its users: (1) to provide the most relevant search results possible, (2) to provide the most relevant and useful advertising, and (3) never to stop working to improve the user experience. Approximately 600 of Google's 2,000 employees in 2004 were involved in research and development and were encouraged to devote 20 percent of their time to individual projects. In fact, many of Google's most important features, such as AdSense and Google News, had begun as independent research projects.

WebSearch

Google's PageRank search technology was a protected trade secret that evaluated the relevancy of a Web site to a search on the basis of the link structure of the site. PageRank counted the number of Web sites pointing to a specified site that might be a possible match to a search request and also evaluated the importance of sites pointing to a possible site match. Each site pointing to a site that might be a match to a search query counted as a vote for that site, but the votes of Web pages deemed to be important were given greater weight and were more influential in choosing a search match.

Exhibit 2 GOOGLE INC. CONSOLIDATED INCOME STATEMENTS, 1999–2003, WITH COMPARISON OF FIRST NINE MONTHS OF 2004 TO FIRST NINE MONTHS OF 2003 (in thousands, except per share amounts)

	Fiscal Year Ending December 31					First Nine Months	
	2003	2002	2001	2000	1999	2004	2003
Consolidated statements of operations data							
Revenues	$1,465,934	$439,508	$ 86,426	$19,108	$ 220	$2,157,722	$953,759
Costs and expenses:							
Cost of revenues	625,854	131,510	14,228	6,081	908	1,003,874	374,986
Research and development	91,228	31,748	16,500	10,516	2,930	138,190	62,771
Sales and marketing	120,328	43,849	20,076	10,385	1,677	170,193	79,164
General and administrative	56,699	24,300	12,275	4,357	1,221	87,857	36,415
Stock-based compensation*	229,361	21,635	12,383	2,506	—	219,215	144,377
Non-recurring portion of settlement of disputes with Yahoo	—	—	—	—	—	201,000	—
Total costs and expenses	1,123,470	253,042	75,462	33,845	6,736	1,820,329	697,713
Income (loss) from operations	342,464	186,466	10,964	(14,737)	(6,516)	337,393	256,046
Interest income (expense) and other, net	4,190	(1,551)	(896)	47	440	2,668	1,183
Income (loss) before income taxes	346,654	184,915	10,068	(14,690)	(6,076)	340,061	257,229
Provision for income taxes	241,006	85,259	3,083	—	—	145,042	178,835
Net income (loss)	$ 105,648	$ 99,656	$ 6,985	($14,690)	($6,076)	$ 195,019	$ 78,394
Net income (loss) per share:							
Basic	$0.77	$0.86	$0.07	($0.22)	($0.14)	$1.14	$0.58
Diluted	$0.41	$0.45	$0.04	($0.22)	($0.14)	$0.73	$0.31
Number of shares used in per share calculations:							
Basic	137,697	115,242	94,523	67,032	42,445	170,511	134,820
Diluted	256,638	220,633	186,776	67,032	42,445	268,394	254,664

*Stock-based compensation, consisting of amortization of deferred stock-based compensation and the fair value of options issued to non-employees for services rendered, is allocated as follows:

Cost of revenues	$ 8,557	$ 1,065	$ 876	$ 167	—	$ 9,618	$ 5,821
Research and development	138,377	8,746	4,440	1,573	—	134,222	82,115
Sales and marketing	44,607	4,934	1,667	514	—	39,156	30,530
General and administrative	37,820	6,890	5,400	252	—	36,219	25,911
	$229,361	$21,635	$12,383	$2,506	—	$219,215	$144,377

Sources: Google Inc. Form S-1 filed April 29, 2004; Google Financial Release, October 21, 2004.

Exhibit 3   GOOGLE INC. CONSOLIDATED BALANCE SHEETS, 2003 AND FIRST NINE MONTHS OF 2004
(in thousands, except par value)

	December 31 2003	September 30 2004
Assets		
Current assets:		
Cash and cash equivalents	$148,995	$ 344,469
Short-term investments	185,723	1,513,887
Accounts receivable, net of allowance of $2,297, $4,670 and $5,611	154,690	233,057
Income taxes receivable	—	115,070
Deferred income taxes	22,105	48,455
Prepaid revenue share, expenses, and other assets	48,721	105,273
Total current assets	560,234	2,360,211
Property and equipment, net	188,255	362,609
Goodwill	87,442	101,815
Intangible assets, net	18,114	43,660
Prepaid revenue share, expenses and other assets, non-current	17,413	20,223
Total assets	$871,458	$2,888,518
Liabilities, redeemable convertible preferred stock warrant, and stockholders' equity		
Current liabilities:		
Accounts payable	$ 46,175	$ 49,557
Accrued compensation and benefits	33,522	53,841
Accrued expenses and other current liabilities	26,411	44,185
Accrued revenue share	88,672	101,973
Deferred revenue	15,346	21,888
Income taxes payable	20,705	—
Current portion of equipment leases	4,621	3,026
Total current liabilities	235,452	274,470
Long-term portion of equipment leases	1,988	63
Deferred revenue, long-term	5,014	6,344
Liability for stock options exercised early, long-term	6,341	7,206
Deferred income taxes	18,510	—
Other long-term liabilities	1,512	11,412
Commitments and contingencies		
Redeemable convertible preferred stock warrant	13,871	—

(continues)

Exhibit 3 (continued)

	December 31 2003	September 30 2004
Stockholders' equity:		
Convertible preferred stock, $0.001 par value, issuable in series: 166,896, 164,782, and 164,782 shares authorized at December 31, 2002 and 2003, and June 30, 2004; 70,432, 71,662, and 79,099 shares issued and outstanding at December 31, 2002 and 2003, and June 30, 2004; no shares issued and outstanding pro forma; aggregate liquidation preference of $40,815 and $62,458 at December 31, 2003, and June 30, 2004	44,346	—
Class A and Class B common stock, $0.001 par value: 700,000 shares authorized, 145,346, 160,866, and 165,012 shares issued and outstanding, excluding 3,281, 11,987, and 10,203 shares subject to repurchase at December 31, 2002 and 2003, and June 30, 2004, and 244,111 shares outstanding pro forma	161	273
Additional paid-in capital	725,219	2,497,299
Note receivable from officer/stockholder	(4,300)	—
Deferred stock-based compensation	(369,668)	(292,690)
Accumulated other comprehensive income	1,660	(2,230)
Retained earnings	191,352	386,371
Total stockholders' equity	$588,770	$2,589,023
Total liabilities, redeemable convertible preferred stock warrant, and stockholders' equity	$871,458	$2,888,518

Sources: Google Inc. Form S-1 filed April 29, 2004; Google Financial Release, October 21, 2004.

Exhibit 4   GOOGLE INC. CONSOLIDATED STATEMENTS OF CASH FLOWS, 2001–2003, WITH COMPARISON OF FIRST NINE MONTHS OF 2004 TO FIRST NINE MONTHS OF 2003 (in thousands)

	Fiscal Year Ending December 31			Nine Months Ending September 30	
	2003	2002	2001	2004	2003
Operating activities					
Net income	$105,648	$99,656	$ 6,985	$ 195,019	$ 78,394
Adjustments to reconcile net income to net cash provided by operating activities:					
Depreciation and amortization of property and equipment	43,851	17,815	9,831	85,620	28,203
Amortization of warrants and warrants	11,198	11,168	4,351	10,393	8,975
In-process research and development	11,618	—	—	950	11,618
Stock-based compensation	229,361	21,635	12,383	219,215	144,377
Tax benefits from exercise of warrants	—	—	—	144,971	—
Nonrecurring portion of settlement of disputes with Yahoo	—	—	—	201,000	—
Changes in assets and liabilities, net of effects of acquisitions:					
Accounts receivable	(90,385)	(43,877)	(11,736)	(78,361)	(54,574)
Income taxes, net	(6,319)	11,517	2,398	(182,415)	8,120
Prepaid revenue share, expenses and other assets	(58,913)	(5,875)	(22)	(54,134)	(29,156)
Accounts payable	36,699	5,645	1,643	3,369	35,175
Accrued expenses and other liabilities	31,104	15,393	4,207	42,148	15,545
Accrued revenue share	74,603	13,100	—	13,301	57,991
Deferred revenue	6,980	9,088	1,049	7,871	4,234
Net cash provided by operating activities	395,445	155,265	31,089	608,947	308,902
Investing activities					
Purchases of property and equipment	(176,801)	(37,198)	(13,060)	(259,915)	(120,310)
Purchase of short-term investments	(316,599)	(93,061)	(26,389)	(2,877,309)	(105,229)
Maturities and sales of short-term investments	219,404	20,443	11,460	1,548,334	130,149
Purchases of other investments	—	—	—	(4,999)	—
Acquisitions, net of cash acquired	(39,958)	—	—	10,833	(39,958)
Change in other assets	—	99	(1,102)	—	—
Net cash used in investing activities	(313,954)	(109,717)	(29,091)	(1,604,722)	(135,348)

(continues)

Exhibit 4 (continued)

| | Fiscal Year Ending December 31 | | | Nine Months Ending September 30 | |
	2003	2002	2001	2004	2003
Financing activities					
Proceeds from issuance of convertible preferred stock, net	—	—	1,042	—	—
Proceeds from exercise of stock options, net	15,476	2,262	988	10,159	10,649
Proceeds from exercise of warrants	—	—	—	21,944	—
Net proceeds from initial public offering				$1,161,466	
Payments of notes receivable from stockholders			34	4,300	
Payments of principal on capital leases and equipment loans	(7,386)	(7,735)	(4,503)	(3,521)	(3,435)
Net cash provided by (used in) financing activities	8,090	(5,473)	(2,439)	$ 1,194,328	4,214
Effect of exchange rate changes on cash and cash equivalents	1,662	—	—	(3,079)	(104)
Net increase (decrease) in cash and cash equivalents	91,243	40,075	(441)	195,474	177,664
Cash and cash equivalents at beginning of year	57,752	17,677	18,118	148,995	57,752
Cash and cash equivalents at end of period	$ 148,995	$ 57,752	$17,677	$ 344,469	$235,416

Sources: Google Inc. Form S-1 filed April 29, 2004; Google Financial Release, October 21, 2004.

Google's WebSearch technology also used text matching, as did many other search engines, but Google's search engine not only counted the number of times keywords appeared on a page but also examined the proximity of multiple search terms on a page. The combination of Google's text-matching capabilities and PageRank technology gave users the most relevant search results possible in 2004.

Key features of Google's WebSearch, available at Google.com or affiliated sites, included advanced search functionality that allowed users to restrict results to languages, countries, or Web sites; spell checking; and Web page translation from French, German, Italian, Portuguese, and Spanish into English and vice versa. In addition, WebSearch users could obtain stock quotes, street maps, telephone numbers, and flight information, and could track parcels shipped by FedEx, UPS, and the U.S. Postal Service by entering requested information in the Google search box. Users could also use the search box to solve math problems or convert units of measurement and could look up vehicle identification numbers, patent numbers, Federal Aviation Administration airplane registration numbers, and product codes. The Google WebSearch function included a dictionary that enabled users to obtain definitions of words entered in the search box.

In late 2004, Google users could search the company's ever-growing index of images found across the Web (880 million at one count) and review the latest news from nearly 10,000 sources. Google's Toolbar allowed users to add a search bar to their browsers that made it easy to search from any site on the Web. The Toolbar also helped block pop-up ads, highlighted search terms, and had a secure auto-fill feature for completing Web forms. Froogle, Google's price-comparison feature, allowed users in search of specific products to locate e-commerce sites or local stores. Gmail was an e-mail service offered by Google that gave account holders 1 megabyte of storage space. Google Groups enabled participation in Internet discussion groups, while Blogger made it easy for users to instantly publish personal weblogs. Google provided access to the full content of 6,600 mail-order catalogs, many of which did not have e-commerce Web sites. Google also provided local results to search queries and contracted with more than 500 freelance researchers who could respond to requests for information submitted to Google Answers. Archived answers to various questions were available to Google users for free, while unique requests involved a fee payable to the researcher.

Google Search Appliance

Google's search technology could be integrated into a third party's Web site or intranet if search functionality was important to the customer. The Google Search Appliance could be installed within one day and could search both public Web pages and local intranets to return relevant results for search users. The search appliance was available in three models tailored to the size of the organization and its search requirements. The model GB-1001 was designed for departments or midsized companies and could be licensed at prices beginning at $32,000. The GB-5005 was developed for companies needing searches for companywide intranets or customer-facing Web sites, with prices beginning at $230,000. The GB-8008 was best suited for global business units and could be implemented at prices beginning at $600,000.

AdWords

Google AdWords allowed advertisers to create text-based ads that would appear alongside Google search results either independently through Google's automated tools or with the assistance of Google's marketing teams. AdWords users could evaluate the effectiveness of their advertising expenditures with Google through the use of performance reports that tracked the effectiveness of each ad. Google also offered a keyword targeting program that suggested synonyms for keywords entered by advertisers; a traffic estimator that helped potential advertisers anticipate CPC charges; and multiple payment options that included charges to credit cards, debit cards, and monthly invoicing. Google accepted payment for ads in 48 currencies.

Larger advertisers were offered additional services to help run large, dynamic advertising campaigns. Such assistance included the availability of specialists with expertise in various industries to offer suggestions for targeting potential customers, offer suggestions in identifying relevant keywords, and help develop ads that would increase click-through rates and purchase rates. Google also offered its large advertising customers bulk posting services that helped launch and manage campaigns including ads using hundreds or thousands of keywords.

Even though all advertisers were allowed to bid on keywords to achieve a more prominent placement, ads that were infrequently selected by Internet users moved to a less visible placement—regardless of the amount of the advertiser's bid for a keyword. Ads that were frequently clicked on by Internet users moved up the list, ensuring that the most relevant ads always had a good placement on Google's site.

Google also allowed users to pay a CPC rate lower than their bid price if their bid was considerably more than the next highest bid. For example, an advertiser who bid 75 cents per click for a particular keyword would only be charged 51 cents per click if the next highest bid was only 50 cents. The AdWords discounter ensured that advertisers paid only one cent more than the next highest bid, regardless of the actual amount of their bid.

AdSense

Google's AdSense program enabled Google Network partners to serve targeted ads from AdWords advertisers on their Web pages by matching keyword-based ads to the context of the Web publisher's pages. During the first nine months of fiscal 2004, 82 percent of advertising revenue generated from such ads was paid to Google Network Web publishers. The program was also available to almost any Web site and used an automated system similar to what small AdWords advertisers used to allow small Web sites to participate in the AdSense program. Google offered customized personal services for Web sites with more than 20 million page views per month.

In 2004 Google had 23 sales and development offices in 11 countries to better serve the needs of Internet users and advertisers outside of the United States. The company's focus on service to international customers had allowed it to increase international net revenues from 14 percent of total revenues in 2001 to 30 percent of revenues during the first quarter of 2004.

Google's Internet Rivals

Google's ability to sustain its competitive advantage among search companies was a function of its ability to maintain strong relationships with Internet users, advertisers, and Web sites. In 2004, Internet users went to Google to search for information more often than to any other site with search capabilities. The following table shows the breakdown of U.S. Internet searches among Web sites offering search capabilities in June 2004:

Search Company	% of Searches
Google	34.5%
Yahoo	28.2
MSN	14.1
AOL/Netscape	12.9
Ask Jeeves	5.8
Others	4.5
Total	100.0%

Source: ComScore, as reported by *The Wall Street Journal Online,* August 11, 2004.

There was nothing that would prevent Internet users from abandoning Google to use a better search technology. Google's status in 2004 as the search engine of choice for most Internet users allowed its AdWords program to attract advertisers and its AdSense program attract Google Network members that would display Google ads. The development of a better search engine could lead to rapid erosion of advertising revenues for Google. Google management believed its primary competitors to be Microsoft and Yahoo, but it also competed with a host of Internet portals and Web publishers for a share of Internet advertising dollars. AOL used Google's search appliance to perform Web searches, while rival search company Ask Jeeves developed its search capabilities internally. Exhibit 5 presents a listing of the 10 most visited Web sites in June 2004. A brief profile of the leading Internet companies is provided in Exhibit 6.

Yahoo

Yahoo was founded in 1994 and was the leading Internet destination worldwide in 2004. Almost any information available on the Internet could be accessed through Yahoo's Web portal. Visitors could anonymously access content categorized by Yahoo or set up an account with Yahoo to maintain a personal calendar and e-mail account, check the latest news, check local weather, obtain maps, check TV listings, track a

Exhibit 5   TOP 10 INTERNET SITES OVERALL, JUNE 2004*

Rank	Site
1	Yahoo sites
2	MSN/Microsoft sites
3	Time Warner Network (AOL, Netscape, ICQ, Moviefone, MapQuest, CompuServe)
4	Google sites
5	eBay
6	Ask Jeeves
7	Terra Lycos
8	About/Primedia
9	Amazon sites
10	Monster Worldwide

*U.S. only, measured by unique visitors.
Source: ComScore Media Metrix.

Exhibit 6   PROFILES OF LEADING INTERNET COMPANIES

	2003 Revenues	2003 Net Earnings	Primary Business	Other Businesses
InterActiveCorp	$6.33 billion	$154.3 million	26 e-commerce sites including Expedia.com, Hotels.com, Hotwire.com, Ticketmaster.com, Match.com, LendingTree.com, and Home Shopping Network (HSN.com)	—
Amazon.Com Inc.	$5.26 billion	$35.3 million	Internet retailer	—
EBay Inc.	$2.17 billion	$441.8 million	Online auctions	Half.com fixed-price Internet retailer, Pay Pal payment processing service
Yahoo Inc.	$1.625 billion	$237.9 million	Search-based and Web-page-based advertising	High-speed Internet access partnership with SBC, shopping sites, e-mail service, webcasts
Ask Jeeves Inc.	$107.3 million	$26 million	Search-based advertising	—

Source: *The Wall Street Journal Online*, April 29, 2004.

stock portfolio, maintain a golf handicap, keep an online photo album, or search personal ads or job listings. Yahoo also hosted Web sites for small businesses and Internet retailers. Yahoo had established an alliance with SBC Communications to offer dial-up and broadband access to Internet users. The company's broad range of services made it a key rival to just about any company with an Internet presence. Internet service providers (ISPs), business-to-consumer e-commerce sites, business-to-business e-commerce companies, content providers, Web portals, and those who provided paid search advertising were all directly affected by the competitive moves of Yahoo.

Yahoo was among Google's earliest customers for its search appliance, but the company initiated moves to distance itself from Google when it acquired Inktomi for $235 million in December 2002 and Overture Services for $1.6 billion in July 2003. Both Inktomi and Overture were developers of search technologies that would allow Yahoo to internally control its search capabilities. Yahoo began to replace Google with its own search capabilities in February 2004, and the two partners officially became rivals in July 2004 when they formally ended their relationship.

Yahoo recorded revenues and earnings of $1.625 billion and $237.9 million, respectively, during 2003. The company's third-quarter 2004 revenues of $907 million represented a 154 percent increase over the same period in 2003 and marked its sixth consecutive quarter of record revenues.

MSN Search

After 20 months in development, Microsoft launched a preview version of its search engine in November 2004. Microsoft had spent more than $100 million developing Microsoft's MSN Search (www.search.msn.com) to enter the market for search-based advertising. MSN Search was closely modeled after Google with its home page very similar in appearance to the clean, uncluttered look of Google. Also, Microsoft's search engine returned results and text-only ads in 11 languages that looked like those offered by Google. When MSN Search was previewed, its index included 5 billion Web sites. MSN Search could perform some tasks Google was unable to carry out, such as answering plain-language questions like "When did Virginia become a state?," linking to Microsoft's online Encarta encyclopedia to answer questions, and linking to MSN Music for those wishing to purchase MP3s of specific songs. MSN Search matched Google features such as local searching, had a calculator built into its search box, and performed measurement conversions. However, the initial reviews of MSN Search found that its search results were not as relevant as those retrieved by Google and that MSN Search included more paid ads than Google. The final version of MSN Search would launch in early 2005, and most believed that MSN Search would be integrated into Outlook, Internet Explorer, and other Microsoft applications soon afterward. Microsoft expected MSN Search to allow the company to double its 2004 advertising revenue of $360 million within five years.

AOL/Netscape

AOL/Netscape, owned by Time Warner Inc., generated 2003 revenues of $8.6 billion from its ISP business, advertising sales, and sales of services to its ISP customers. More than 30 million households in the United States and Europe subscribed to AOL, Netscape, or CompuServe in 2004 to gain dial-up access to the Internet. AOL also offered a service for broadband users with third-party broadband access. The company owned destination sites such as Moviefone.com, ICQ.com, Mapquest.com, AOL Instant Messenger, and Love.com—which together attracted over 100 million unique visitors each month. AOL's exposure to vast numbers of Internet users allowed it to market banner ads and other forms of advertising to large companies that might also advertise on Time Warner cable channels or magazines. Time Warner generated advertising revenues of $787 million in 2003 from its Internet properties, which was a substantial decline from its Internet advertising revenues of $1.3 billion in 2002. Some of AOL/Netscape's loss of advertising revenues was attributable to Time Warner's decreased Internet advertising for its cable operations, television programming, and publishing, but to some extent the decline was a result of consumers switching from AOL's premium dial-up services to broadband or low-priced dial-up ISPs. AOL/Netscape was a Google search partner and had not attempted to develop its own search capabilities.

Ask Jeeves

Ask Jeeves was founded in 1996 and retrieved search results using its Teoma plain-language search technology. Initially, the company provided plain-language search results only, but as Google became more dominant in the industry it attempted to clone the look and functionality of Google. In late 2004, Ask Jeeves offered features almost identical to those of Google and, like MSN Search, had attempted to make its home page look as much like Google.com as possible. Internet users could access Ask Jeeves's search engine through Askjeeves.com, Ask.com, Ask.co.uk, Iwon.com, Excite.com, Myway.com, Mysearch.com, and Ajkids.com. A major point of distinction between Ask Jeeves and Google was Ask Jeeves's paid inclusion program, which allowed advertisers to include their uniform resource locators (URLs) among search results. However, Ask Jeeves discontinued paid inclusion advertising in late 2004. The company anticipated 2004 revenues to approximate $260 million, which would amount to a 143 percent increase over 2003 revenues. The company projected that 2005 revenues would approach $500 million. Ask Jeeves was given an honorable mention for Outstanding Search and Best Search Feature in the 2004 Search Engine Watch Awards.

Google's Performance as a Public Company

Google's influx of cash generated from the proceeds of its IPO and its subsequent growth worried Internet companies beyond its key search rivals. It was believed that Google's Froogle feature would decrease traffic to Internet retailers like Amazon.com and eBay since users could perform price comparisons from Google. Amazon.com replaced Google with a search engine called A9 for searches on its site just prior to Google's IPO. In addition, Internet companies were not quite sure how Google would use its additional $1.7 billion capitalization from the IPO since it held a cash balance of $550 million prior to the IPO. Google's only response to such concerns was "We currently have no specific plans."[9]

In late 2004, Google released the beta version of Google Desktop Search, which allowed users to search their computers for e-mails, files, Web histories, music, photos, and chat logs. Google Desktop Search was far superior to Microsoft Windows' search option since it could search an entire hard drive in a fraction of a second. Searching for a file through the standard Windows feature could take several minutes and might not return any results if the file name was not spelled correctly. There was also speculation that Google would make acquisitions to expand free services to users such as tools for photo organization and sharing.

Google continued to expand its index of Web sites and announced it had increased its index to 8.1 billion sites upon Microsoft's November 11, 2004, launch of the preview version of MSN Search. Google had expanded to 95 international domains and was available in 97 languages by late 2004. All strategies seemed to be working flawlessly, and the company's third-quarter revenues increased by 105 percent over the same period in 2003. The Google Network was continuing to grow, with AdSense revenues increasing 120 percent between the third quarter of 2003 and the third quarter of 2004. Google's net income increased from $20.4 million in the third quarter of 2003 to $52.0 million in the third quarter of 2004. The net income included the after-tax effects of a noncash and nonrecurring settlement charge of $119 million and a tax benefit of $46 million related to stock-based compensation charges. The settlement charge resulted from a two-year-old lawsuit brought against Google by Yahoo for a patent infringement. Google settled the suit by granting Yahoo 2.7 million shares of stock in return for dropping the suit.

Endnotes

[1] As quoted in "High-Tech Search Engine Google Won't Talk about Business Plan," *The Wall Street Journal Online,* June 14, 1999.

[2] As quoted in Google's Corporate Information, www.google.com/corporate/history.html.

[3] As quoted in "The Grownup at Google," *The Wall Street Journal Online,* March 29, 2004, p. B1.

[4] Ibid.

[5] Google Inc. Form S-1, p. 2.

[6] Ibid.

[7] As listed under "Our Philosophy," Google Corporate Information, www.google.com/corporate/tenthings.html.

[8] As reported in "For Some Who Passed on Google Long Ago, Wistful Thinking," *The Wall Street Journal Online,* August 23, 2004.

[9] As quoted in "Nice Problem: How Will Google Use $2 Billion?" *The Wall Street Journal Online,* August 17, 2004.

Vincor and the New World of Wine

Paul W. Beamish
The University of Western Ontario

On September 16, 2002, Donald Triggs, chief executive officer (CEO) of Vincor International Inc. (Vincor) was preparing for the board meeting to discuss the possible acquisition of Goundrey Wines, Australia. Vincor had embarked upon a strategic internationalization plan in 2000, acquiring R. H. Phillips and Hogue in the United States. Although Vincor was the largest wine company in Canada and the fourth largest in North America, Triggs felt that to be a major player, Vincor had to look beyond the region. The acquisition of Goundrey Wines in Australia would be the first step. Convincing the board would be difficult, as the United States was a close and attractive market where Vincor had already spent more than US$100 million on acquisitions. In contrast, Australia was very far away.

The Global Wine Industry

Wine-producing countries were classified as either New World producers or Old World producers. Some of the largest New World producers were the United States, Australia, Chile, and Argentina. The largest of the Old World producers were France, Italy, and Spain (see Exhibit 1). The world's top 10 wine exporters accounted for more than 90 percent of the value of international wine trade. Of those top 10, half were in western Europe, and the other half were New World suppliers, led by Australia (see Exhibit 2).

France

France had been a longtime world leader in the production of wine, due to historical and cultural factors. France was the top producer of wine in the world (see Exhibit 1). The French had developed the vins d'appellation d'origine contrôlée (AOC) system

Exhibit 1   TOP 10 PRODUCERS OF WINE IN THE WORLD, 2001

Country	Wine Production* (million liters)	Share of World Production (%)
France	5,330	19.9%
Italy	5,090	19.0
Spain	3,050	11.4
United States	1,980	7.4
Argentina	1,580	5.9
Australia	1,020	3.8
Germany	900	3.4
Portugal	770	2.9
South Africa	650	2.4
Chile	570	2.1
World	27,491	

*Does not include juice and musts (the expressed juice of fruit and especially grapes before and during fermentation: also the pulp and skins of the crushed grapes).

Note: 1 liter = 0.26 gallon; each case contains 12,750 mil bottles = 9 liters.

Source: G. Dutruc-Rosset, *Extract of the Report on World Vitiviniculture*, June 24, 2002.

Exhibit 2   TOP 10 EXPORTERS OF WINE IN THE WORLD, 2001

Country	Wine Production* (million liters)	Share of World Exports (%)
Italy	1,830	26.5%
France	1,580	22.9
Spain	990	14.4
Australia	380	5.5
Chile	310	4.5
United States	300	4.3
Germany	240	3.5
Portugal	200	2.9
South Africa	180	2.6
Moldavia	160	2.3
World	6,897	

Source: G. Dutruc-Rosset, *Extract of the Report on World Vitiviniculture*, June 24, 2002.

centuries ago to ensure that the quality of wine stayed high. There were many regions in which quality grapes could be grown in France. Some of their better known appellations were Bordeaux, Burgundy, and Champagne. France was the second largest exporter of wine (see Exhibit 2).

Italy

Italy, like France, also had a very old and established wine industry that relied on the appellation method to control the quality. Italy was the second largest producer of wine in the world (see Exhibit 1) and the largest exporter (see Exhibit 2).

Australia

Grape vines were first introduced to Australia in 1788. The wine "industry" was born in the 1860s when European immigrants added the skilled workforce necessary to develop the commercial infrastructure. The Australian wine industry grew after 1960 with the development of innovative techniques to make higher quality wine while keeping costs down. Australia was the sixth largest producer of wine in the world (see Exhibit 1). Australia had 5.5 percent of the total export market and was ranked fourth in the world for its export volume (see Exhibit 2).

Chile

The first vines were introduced to Chile in the 16th century. Due to political and economic instability, the wine industry was not able to develop and take on a global perspective until 1979 when Chile began to focus on the exporting of natural resources to strengthen its economy. Despite being only the 10th largest producer, Chile had 4.5 percent of the total export market and was ranked fifth in the world (see Exhibit 2).

Argentina

Argentina had a long history of making wine. However, the quality of the wine from Argentina was never as high, due to the small area of land that was capable of producing high-quality grapes. Argentina was the fifth largest producer of wine in the world (see Exhibit 1), but did not feature in the top 10 exporters of wine.

All of the countries, with the exception of Argentina, were capable of shipping brands that could compete at a wide range of price points. The French wines typically were capable of competing in the higher price classes, and could retail for more than US$100 per bottle.

Major World Markets

After a 2.2 percent gain in 2001, the global wine market was estimated to have increased another 1.2 percent in 2002 to 2.55 billion cases, according to *The Global Drinks Market: Impact Databank Review and Forecast 2001 Report*. Wine consumption was projected to expand by 120 million cases by 2010. Most of the growth was expected to come from major wine-consuming nations, such as the United States, United Kingdom, Australia, and South Africa, as well from less developed wine markets, such as China and Russia.

Wine imports were highly concentrated. The 10 top importing countries accounted for all but 14 percent of the value of global imports in the late 1980s. In 2001, half the value of all imports were purchased by the three biggest importers: the United Kingdom (19 percent), the United States (16 percent), and Germany (14 percent).

France and Italy were the number one and two countries in the world for per capita consumption (see Exhibit 3). However, the consumption rate in France was relatively stagnant, while Italy was showing a decrease. Italy, unlike France, had a very small market for imported wines. The import market sizes for France and Italy were, respectively, 13.4 percent and 2.8 percent in 2001, based on volume.

The United Kingdom's wine market was considered to be the "crucible" for the global wine market (*Wine Market Report*, May 2000). The United Kingdom had very small domestic wine production and good relationships with many of the wine-producing countries in the world. This coupled with the long history of wine consumption, resulted

Exhibit 3   TOP 10 WINE-CONSUMING NATIONS, 2001

Country	Wine Consumption (millions liters)	Share of World Consumption (%)
France	3,370	15.4%
Italy	3,050	13.9
United States	2,133	9.7
Germany	1,966	9.0
Spain	1,400	6.4
Argentina	1,204	5.5
United Kingdom	1,010	4.6
China	580	2.6
Russia	550	2.5
Romania	470	2.1
World	21,892	

Source: G. Dutruc-Rosset, *Extract of the Report on World Vitiviniculture,* June 24, 2002.

in an open and competitive market. The United Kingdom was ranked number seven for consumption in 2001, with a trend of increasing consumption. The United Kingdom wine market was dominated by Old World country imports; however, New World imports had grown as Australian wines replaced French wines as the number one import (see Figure 1).

Other Countries

In 2001, Canada was ranked number 30 in the world for per capita consumption with an increasing trend. Japan had seen a steady increase in the size of its imported wine market. Asia presented a great opportunity for wine producers around the world because it had populous markets that had yet to be tapped.

Figure 1   Share of United Kingdom Wine Market, by Country

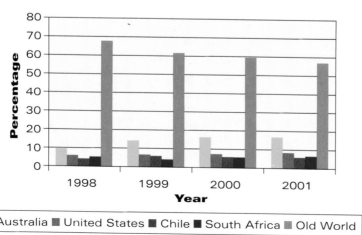

Source: Vincor International files.

The U.S. Wine Industry

The international image of the U.S. wine industry until the mid-1970s was that of a low-quality jug wine producer. This changed in 1976 during a blind wine-tasting contest in France where California wines from Napa Valley beat out several well-established European wines for the top honors. From that time forward, there has been a focus on developing high-quality wines that could compete in the international market from the northern California appellations, such as Napa Valley and Sonoma County. The United States was the fourth largest producer of wine (1.98 billion liters) in 2001 (see Exhibit 1), with California wines accounting for 90 percent of production volume. There were more than 3,000 wineries in all 50 states. The nation's top wine-producing states were California, New York, Washington, and Oregon.

The United States saw huge gains in the total volume and value of its wine exports, increasing from US$85 million in 1988 to US$548 million in 2002. The major markets for U.S. wines included the United Kingdom, Canada, and Japan. Together they represented 66 percent of the total export market value for the United States (see Exhibit 4).

The United States was the third largest wine market in the world, consuming 2.13 billion liters a year in 2001. It was also one of the biggest untapped wine markets in the world; 7 percent of the U.S. population accounted for 86 percent of the country's wine consumption. The total wine market in the United States in 2001 was $21.1 billion with an average growth rate of 6 percent since 1994. Of this, approximately $10 billion were sales of New World wines.

Exhibit 4   U.S. WINE EXPORTS, TOP COUNTRIES (by dollar value in 2002)

Country Ranking by 2002 Dollar Value	Value ($000)	Volume (liters 000)
United Kingdom	$188,895	95,446
Canada	92,571	50,348
Japan	81,199	32,342
Netherlands	53,201	26,388
Belgium	18,791	10,884
France	13,326	5,943
Germany	11,818	8,634
Ireland	10,153	5,380
Switzerland	7,199	3,914
Denmark	5,710	3,933
Mexico	5,001	3,705
Taiwan	4,868	2,736
South Korea	3,865	2,439
China	3,370	2,537
Singapore	3,002	1,822
Sweden	2,782	1,145
Hong Kong	2,393	1,140

Source: Wine Institute and Ivey International using data from U.S. Dept. of Commerce, USA Trade Online. History revised. Numbers may not total exactly due to rounding.

While California wines dominated the domestic market (67 percent market share) due to the ideal growing conditions and favorable marketing and branding actions taken by some of California's larger wineries, imports were on the rise. The United States had one of the most open markets in the world for wine, with low barriers to entry for imports. Imports represented 530 million liters for a 25 percent share of the market. By 2002, wine imports grew by 18 percent (see Figures 2 and 3).

Wine was the most popular alcoholic beverage in the United States after beer, which accounted for 67 percent of all alcohol consumed. The table wine category represented 90 percent of all wine by volume, dessert wine was 6 percent, and sparkling wine accounted for 4 percent. U.S.-produced table wine held an 83 percent share of the volume and 78 percent of the value. Premium wine ($7 and more per 750 ml bottle)

Figure 2   United States Wine Markets 1998 to 2001

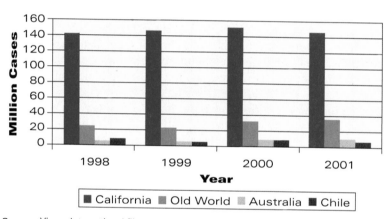

Source: Vincor International files.

Figure 3   United States Wine Market Growth Rates

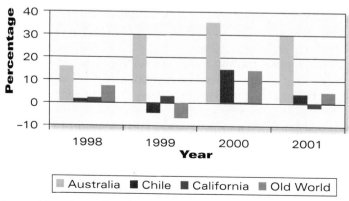

Source: Vincor International files.

sales increased 8 percent over 2001, accounting for 30 percent of the volume but a sizeable 62 percent of winery revenues. Everyday value-priced wines selling for less than $7 per bottle grew about 1.5 percent by volume. This segment represented 70 percent of all California table wine shipments and 38 percent of the value.

The United States wine industry was fragmented with the largest producer, E. & J. Gallo, supplying 30 percent and no other producer supplying more than 15 percent by volume in 2002.

In the United States, a law mandated the implementation of a three-tier distribution system. The wine producers were required to sell to a wholesaler, who then sold to an established customer base of grocery stores, liquor stores, hotels, and restaurants. Wineries were capable of using a two-tier distribution system, which allowed wineries to sell directly to the customers through gift shops located at the winery. The role of the distribution channel was growing and taking on greater strategic importance as the trend toward international and domestic consolidation grew.

The Canadian Wine Industry

Canadians had been making wine for more than two centuries, but Canada's modern-day success in the production of high-quality vinifera-based wines went back only a quarter century. The signing of the North American Free Trade Agreement in 1988, together with a ruling under the General Agreement on Tariffs and Trade (GATT) required Canada to abandon the protection it offered its wine industry. While many producers felt threatened, many more responded by reaffirming their belief in their capacity to produce premium wines, and redoubled their efforts to prove it. New vineyards were planted with only the finest varieties of grapes: Chardonnay, Riesling, Sauvignon Blanc, Pinot Gris, Gewürztraminer, Pinot Noir, Cabernet Sauvignon, Merlot, and others.

During 1988, the Vintners Quality Alliance (VQA) was launched in Ontario, culminating six years of voluntary initiatives by the leaders of Ontario's wine industry. This group set the standards, to which they agreed to comply, to elevate the quality of Canadian wines and provide quality assurances to the consumer. British Columbia adopted similar high standards in 1990, under the VQA mark.

The 1990s was a decade of rapid growth. The number of commercial wineries grew from about 30 in 1990 to more than 100 by the end of the decade, and consumers began to recognize the value represented by wines bearing the VQA medallion. Canadian vintners continued to demonstrate that fine grape varieties in cooler growing conditions could possess complex flavors, delicate yet persistent aromas, tightly focused structure, and longer aging potential than their counterparts in warmer growing regions of the world.

In Canada, despite increasing import competition, sales of Canadian quality wines were increasing as consumers moved up the quality and price scale (see Figure 4).

Canadian quality wines began to capture both domestic and international recognition not only in sales but also by garnering an impressive list of significant wine awards, beginning in 1991 when Inniskillin won the Grand Prix d'Honneur for its 1989 icewine at the prestigious VinExpo, in Bordeaux, France. New access for Canadian wines, especially icewine, in the European market, and expanding market opportunities in the United States and Asia were giving Canadian wines greater market exposure.

Figure 4   **Sales of Canadian Wines (in millions of Canadian $)**

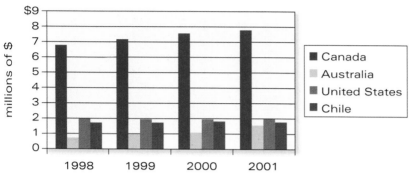

Source: Vincor International files.

The Australian Wine Industry

The Australian wine industry was structured to be able to deliver large quantities of high quality branded wine to the world's major markets, at costs less than many of their Old World and New World competitors. Since Australia had a very limited domestic market (population of only 17 million), the wineries realized that if the industry was to continue to grow it would have to do so internationally.

As a result, Australian wineries had gained, and were expected to continue to gain, market share. Growth had been in exports as well as domestic sales (see Exhibits 5 and 6). Australia had recently overtaken France as the largest exporter to the United Kingdom, where 7 of the top 10 wine brands were Australian. Exports to North America had grown at 27 percent by volume in 2001. Consumption of Australian wine in Canada was up 24 percent and in the United States consumption was up 35 percent. The growth trends were expected to continue. Export growth had been driven by sales of premium red wine, which accounted for 53 percent of Australia's wine exports.

Domestic wine consumption had grown from 296 million liters in 1991 to 398 million liters in 2001, an annual growth rate of 4 percent. The Australian domestic market was relatively unregulated compared to North America, although alcohol taxes were high (42 percent). Wineries were allowed to have their own retail outlets and sell directly to retailers or on-premise customers. The 7,500 licensed liquor retail outlets, accounted for 56 percent of wine sales while the 28,000 licensed on-premise outlets accounted for 44 percent of wine sales.

Although there were 1,300 wineries in Australia, the industry was the most concentrated of any major wine region, with 80 percent of production being accounted for by four players: Southcorp Wine, Beringer Blass, BRL Hardy, and Orlando Wyndham. The large wineries had their own sales forces, as well as warehouses in the major markets.

Southcorp Wines was Australia's largest winery and vineyard owner, with sales of AUD$1.5 billion. Beringer Blass was owned by the Fosters Group and had wine revenues of approximately AUD$800 million (7 million cases). The purchase of Beringer (for AUD$2.6 billion) provided the company with significant growth and U.S. market access.

Exhibit 5   AUSTRALIA WINERIES

	1998 to 1999	2000 to 2001
Wineries (number)	1,150	1,318
Hectares under vine	122,915	148,275
Wine grape production	793	1,035
Wine consumption	373	398
Wine exports		
Million liters	216	339
AUD$ million	$991	$1,614
Wine imports		
Million liters	24	13
AUD$ million	$114	$92

Source: Vincor International files.

Exhibit 6   TOP EXPORT MARKETS FOR AUSTRALIAN WINES, 2001

	Million Liters	AUD$ Million
United Kingdom	183	$ 762
United States	78	457
Canada	17	106
New Zealand	23	83
Germany	13	55
Other	61	301
All markets	375	$1,764

Source: Vincor International files.

BRL Hardy had revenues of more than AUD$700 million. The company had several top brands and a very strong U.K. market position. A recent joint venture in the United States with Constellation brands had improved their United States market access. Orlando Wyndham was owned by Pernod Ricard, a French publicly traded spirits company.

Trends in the Global Wine Industry

Wine was unique among alcoholic beverages in that its top 25 brands represented only 7 percent of the global market. In 2002, Martini vermouth was the world's most widely distributed wine, while Gallo's E. & J. Wine Cellars was the largest-selling brand, at 25 million cases annually, with most of those sales in the United States.

Globally, vermouth and other fortified wines were projected to continue their long-term decline, but this would be more than offset by expected growth in table wines, which accounted for more than 90 percent of total wine consumption. The hottest sales category was Australian wines, with brands such as Rosemount Estate, Jacob's Creek, and Lindemans showing double-digit growth rates.

The North American market was expected to exhibit annual growth rates of 3 percent. There were positive demographics with the 20-to-39 age group having a per

Exhibit 7   THE WINE MARKET—CANADA, FISCAL 2002

	Retail Price	% by Volume	Change from Prior Year	% by Sales
Popular	< $7	33%	−5%	20%
Premium	$ 7–$10	35	5	30
Superpremium	$10–$15	24	19	33
Ultrapremium	$15–$20	6	31	15
Specialty	> $20	2	45	6

Source: Vincor International files.

Exhibit 8   THE U.S. MARKET FOR CALIFORNIA WINE, FISCAL 2002

	Retail Price	% by Volume	Change from Prior Year	% by Sales
Jug	< $3	36%	−4%	12%
Premium	$3–$ 7	36	−2	27
Superpremium	$7–$15	18	8	28
Ultrapremium	> $15	10	3	33

*Total U.S. table wine market +1%; imports +9%; states other than California +4%.
Source: Vincor International files.

capita consumption at 7.9 liters and the 40+ age group having a per capita of 14.0 liters. The ongoing trends were a shift in consumer preference to red wines and premium wines (see Exhibits 7 and 8).

The global wine market was consolidating in terms of its retail, wholesale, and production operations. One key to success seemed to be distribution and marketing. Globalization was also altering the structure of firms both within the wine industry and among those distributing and retailing wine. Rapid growth in supermarkets and in concentration among distributors was driving wine companies into mergers and acquisitions to better meet the needs of those buyers and their customers. Since information about the various niches and the distribution networks in foreign markets was expensive to acquire, new alliances between wine companies were being explored with a view to capitalizing on their complementarities in such knowledge.

Recent examples of such alliances included the purchase by the owner of Mildara Blass (Fosters Brewing Group) of Napa Valley–based Beringer, the alliance between Southcorp/Rosemount and California's Mondavi, BRL Hardy's joint venture with the second largest U.S. wine company, Constellation Brands (to operate as Pacific West Partners) and the purchase by New Zealand's biggest wine firm (Montana) of the country's second largest winery (Corbans). See Exhibit 9 for the 10 largest wine companies worldwide.

Vincor International Inc.

Vincor International Inc. (Vincor) was formed as a combination of a number of Canadian wineries: Barnes Wines, Brights Wines, Cartier Wines, Inniskillin Wines, and Dumont over the period from 1989 to 1996. Vincor began operations in 1989 with a

Exhibit 9   TOP 10 WINE COMPANIES AND SALES IN 2002 (US$)

Company	Country	Wine Sales ($ million)
E. & J. Gallo Winery	United States	$1,500
Foster's Group	Australia	818
Seagram	Canada	800
Constellation Brands	United States	712
Southcorp	Australia	662
Castel Freres	France	625
Diageo	Britain	590
Henkell & Sonlein	Germany	528
Robert Mondavi	United States	506

Note: Excludes France's LVMH, which earned more than 75 percent of its $1.6 billion in wine sales from champagne.
Source: Direction des Etudes/Centre Français du Commerce Exterieur.

**Exhibit 10   VINCOR'S SIGNIFICANT LEGAL SUBSIDIARIES, 2001
(all wholly owned)**

Subsidiary	Jurisdiction of Incorporation
Hawthorne Mountain Vineyards (2000) Ltd	Canada
The Hogue Cellars, Ltd	Washington
Inniskillin Wines Inc.	Ontario
Inniskillin Okanagan Vineyards Inc.	British Columbia
R. H. Phillips, Inc.	California
Spagnol's Wine & Beer Making Supplies Ltd	Canada
Sumac Ridge Estate Winery (2000) Ltd.	Canada
Vincor (Quebec) Inc.	Quebec

Source: Company files.

management buyout of Ridout Wines (Ridout) from John Labatt Ltd. The Ridout management team, led by Allan Jackson, Peter Graigner, and John Hall, sought out Donald Triggs to lead the purchase and become CEO. They raised more than Cdn$2 million in equity, largely from personal finances, and borrowed $25 million to buy out Ridout. The new company was renamed Cartier Wines and Beverages.

Vincor had grown in three stages to become Canada's largest wine company in 2002. The first stage of growth had been a leveraged buyout (LBO) in turbulent times 1989 to 1995, followed by a period of consolidation and rationalization—Building Canada's Wine Company (1990 to 2000). The third stage of growth was Building an International Wine Company (2000 onward).

The first stage had seen the formation of Vincor and wine company acquisitions. From 1995 to 2000, Vincor acquired eight wineries; integrated its sales, marketing, production and accounting; and merged two wine kit companies. This led to economies of scale and a 21 percent market share in 2000.

During this period, Vincor developed Canada's first premium wine brands: Jackson-Triggs, Inniskillin, and Sawmill Creek. The Canadian wine market had seen a shift from popular (less than $7 retail price) to premium ($7 to $10 retail price), leading Vincor to start focusing on the premium and superpremium ($10 to $15 retail price) segments. They developed vineyards and recapitalized wineries to support premium growth. Product coverage was also achieved in the growing ultrapremium ($15 to $20 retail price) and specialty (more than $20 retail price) segments. The year 2000 saw Vincor at a strategic crossroad. Triggs recalled:

> We were faced with three options. We could choose to be a cash cow by further developing our dominant Canadian position. A second option was to develop a diversified Canadian beverage conglomerate. A third option was to expand to the United States and perhaps beyond.
>
> We went for option 3. The move was driven by opportunities as well as threats. In terms of opportunities, the global trend was one of strong growth and premiumisation. There was an industry consolidation favoring global brands. The market was fragmented with the largest player only having one percent market share. The markets for New World wine were growing. The dynamics in the U.S. market were highly profitable with very high profit margins. We were already number 5 in North America and number 22 globally.
>
> On the risk side, wine was an agricultural industry and as such susceptible to changing weather conditions. A diversified portfolio in terms of production and markets would only be an asset.

Triggs and Vincor decided to go international. The company's mission statement was drafted to reflect the new strategic plan:

> To become one of the world's top-10 wine companies, producing Vincor-owned New World, premium branded wines, which are marketed and sold through Vincor-controlled sales and distribution systems in all major premium wine consuming regions.

Where Were the Big Markets?

According to Triggs:

> The United States was the largest market with New World wine sales of $10 billion followed by the United Kingdom and Australia at $3.7 billion each. Canada and the rest of Europe were next at $700 million. Japan was the sixth largest with sales of about $500 million. To be a New World market player, Vincor needed to be in five to six markets.

In 2002, the company's strategy was formulated for each region. In Canada, the aim was to build share in premium segments, to develop export capability and to generate cash and improve return on capital employed. In the United States, Vincor decided to focus on portfolio migration to high-end superpremium, enhancement of sales capability, product innovation and a shift to consumer marketing. Vincor's international strategy was to develop new geographic markets for core brands, specifically for icewine, a signature product for Canada that had attained world recognition. It was a luxury product in terms of pricing and margins and one of the top five wine brands in select Asian duty-free stores. The U.S. launch was in F'01 in 1,850 high-end restaurants. By 2002, Inniskillin was being sold in 3,300 premium restaurants across the United States. The European launch of Inniskillin was slated for F'02.

U.S. Acquisitions

R. H. Phillips

On October 5, 2000, Vincor acquired R. H. Phillips, a leading California estate winery, which produced a range of superpremium wines. The aggregate purchase price, including acquisition costs, was US$56.7 million. In addition, R. H. Phillips' debt of US$33.8 million was assumed and refinanced by the company. The Phillips acquisition and the refinancing of the assumed debt were funded entirely through borrowing from the company's senior lender.

R. H. Phillips was established in 1981 by John and Karl Giguiere. It was located in the Dunnigan Hills Viticultural Region near the wine regions of Napa and Sonoma. R. H. Phillips specialized in the production of superpremium wines, marketing its products under the brands R. H. Phillips, Toasted Head, EXP, and Kempton Clark. Its wines were sold throughout the United States and in several other countries, including Canada. In 2001, its brands generated sales revenues of approximately US$25 million for Vincor. Its wines were distributed across the United States by a network of 13 sales executives, distributors, and brokers.

The Phillips acquisition established a presence for Vincor in the U.S. wine market, in addition to adding strong brands, which were well positioned in the superpremium category, one of the fastest-growing segments of the wine market. With its national network of distributors and sales professionals, R. H. Phillips provided a platform for future acquisitions in the United States (such as the Hogue acquisition), while also facilitating the marketing of Vincor's products in the United States.

The Hogue Cellars

On September 1, 2001, Vincor acquired Hogue Cellars for US$36.3 million. Hogue was the second largest wine producer in Washington state, well known for its superpremium wine. Hogue was a family controlled and family operated winery founded in 1982 by Mike and Gary Hogue.

The Washington state wine industry had emerged as the second largest producer of premium wines in the United States, after California. Hogue produced red varietals, including Cabernet Sauvignon, Merlot, and Syrah, as well as white varietals, including Chardonnay, Sauvignon Blanc, Riesling, and Pinot Gris. In 2001, sales of Hogue-produced premium wine were 415,400 cases. In addition to its owned brands, Hogue was the U.S. agent for Kim Crawford wines of New Zealand and Heritage Road wines from Brian McGuigan wines of Australia.

The Hogue acquisition added 11 salespeople nationally and immediately increased Vincor's annual U.S. sales volume to more than 1 million cases and its annual U.S. revenues to more than US$60 million.

Integration with R. H. Phillips

Vincor's management believed that Hogue was an excellent complement to the R. H. Phillips portfolio, as Hogue was primarily a superpremium brand, with approximately 88 percent of its volume in the superpremium category. The strength of the Hogue product range lay in different varietals from the R. H. Phillips range. Different appellations greatly reduced portfolio overlap, as the character and taste of the wines were clearly

Exhibit 11   VINCOR CONSOLIDATED FINANCIALS, 1998 TO 2002 (CDN$ millions)

	Fiscal Years					Average Annual Growth	
	1998	1999	2000	2001	2002	2001–2002	1998–2002
Revenue	$206.4	$253.2	$268.2	$294.9	$376.6	27.7%	17.7%
EBITDA	28.1	35.0	37.9	49.5	70.5	42.4%	26.1%
% revenue	13.60%	13.80%	14.10%	16.80%	18.70%		
Net income	10.8	11.7	13.3	14.3	26.9	40.1%	25.6%
Average capital employed	$145.5	$191.6	$222.1	$310.4	$468.2		
ROCE (EBIT)	14.50%	13.80%	12.70%	13.10%	12.50%		
Funds employed							
Receivables	$ 30.4	$ 33.3	$ 35.7	$ 37.4	$ 55.1		
Inventory	65.1	83.1	70.7	125.9	175.6		
Working capital	57.8	73.3	67.9	111.9	184.9		
Net fixed assets	45.2	60.0	73.3	165.9	178.8		
Other assets	59.8	87.1	82.7	133.4	161.5		
Funds employed	162.8	220.4	223.9	411.2	525.2		
Turnover	1.2x	1.1x	1.2x	.7x	.7x		
Financing							
Debt (net)	$ 50.9	$ 92.5	$ 80.5	$254.5	$110.1		
Deferred tax	9.6	12.1	14.1	11.4	18.3		
Equity	102.3	115.8	129.3	145.3	396.8		
Financing	162.8	220.4	223.9	411.2	525.2		

Note: EBITDA—Earnings Before Interest, Taxes, Depreciation and Amortization
Source: Company files.

distinct. Given the price and quality positioning of both businesses, customers were similar and opportunity existed to improve the efficiency and effectiveness of the sales force, while simultaneously developing incremental sales for all brands in the combined portfolio. Vincor incurred expenses of US$4 million from the integration of Hogue and R. H. Phillips and from transaction costs related to the Hogue acquisition. It was management's objective that the integration of Hogue and R. H. Phillips would result in the realization of annual synergies of US$2.8 million.

Vincor in 2002

In 2002, Vincor was Canada's largest producer and marketer of wines, with leading brands in all segments of the market in Canada. Vincor had a 22 percent market share and sales of Cdn$376.6 million (see Exhibit 11 for Financials). Andrés Wines Ltd., the second largest winery in Canada, had approximately an 11 percent market share. Vincor was North America's fourth largest wine producer in terms of volume and the world's 22nd largest wine producer in terms of revenue.

The company had wineries in British Columbia, Ontario, Quebec, New Brunswick, California, and Washington state, marketing wines produced from grapes grown in the

Niagara Peninsula of Ontario, the Okanagan Valley of British Columbia, the Dunnigan Hills of California, the Columbia Valley of Washington state, and other countries. The company's California and Washington wines were available throughout the United States and in parts of Canada. (See Exhibit 10 for Corporate Structure.)

Canada's government liquor distribution systems and the company's 165-store Wine Rack chain of retail stores sold Vincor's well-known and industry-leading brands: Inniskillin, Jackson-Triggs, Sumac Ridge, Hawthorne Mountain, R. H. Phillips, Toasted Head, Hogue, Sawmill Creek, Notre Vin Maison, Entre-Lacs, L'Ambiance, Caballero de Chile, Bellini, Spumante Bambino, President Canadian Champagne, Okanagan Vineyards, Salmon Harbor, and other table, sparkling, and fortified wines, Vex and the Canada Cooler brands of coolers, and the Growers and Vibe brands of cider.

In the United States, R. H. Phillips, Toasted Head, EXP, Kempton Clark and Hogue wine brands were distributed through a national network of more than 127 distributors, supported by eight brokers and 40 sales managers. The company's icewines were sold in the United States through a dedicated team of sales managers and internationally, primarily through the duty-free distribution channel. The company had seven employees outside of Canada engaged full-time in the sale of icewine.

Vincor's portfolio had evolved as per Table 1.

Table 1   EVOLUTION OF VINCOR'S PORTFOLIO—TABLE WINE

	Fiscal 1995 % by Volume	% by $	Fiscal 2002 % by Volume	% by $
Popular	83%	80%	47%	28%
Premium	17	20	53	72

Source: Company files.

The company's objectives in 2002 were to obtain a top quartile return on capital employed (ROCE) of 16 percent to 20 percent and to achieve sales of Cdn$1 billion and an earnings per share (EPS) of more than 15 percent. At the time these objectives were to be met as per Table 2.

Table 2   COMPANY SALES OBJECTIVES (CDN$ millions)

	Current	5 Years
Canada	$300	$ 400
United States	100	200
Icewine	15	50
Acquisitions	0	350
Total	$415	$1,000

Source: Company files.

Goundrey Wines Pty. Ltd.

Goundrey Wines was one of the pioneer winery operations in Western Australia. The Goundrey family had established the vineyard in 1972, and the first vintage was produced in 1976. By 1995, the business had grown to approximately 17,000 cases in

Exhibit 12   GOUNDREY FINANCIALS, FOR YEARS ENDING
                JUNE 30 (in 000s of AUD$)

	1999	2000	2001
Sales (000)	$16,280	$21,509	$20,942
EBITDA	3,102	6,014	3,548
EBITDA % sales	19.1%	28.0%	16.9%

Source: Company files.

annual sales and was sold to Perth businessman Jack Bendat. Bendat expanded both the vineyards and the winery to reach 2002 sales levels of 250,000 cases annually and revenues of AUD$25 million. Goundrey was one of the largest wineries in Western Australia selling under two labels, Goundrey and Fox River (see Exhibit 12 for financials).

Bendat was 77 years old, and health and family concerns had resulted in his recent decision to sell the business. Vincor believed it would be able to purchase the assets of Goundrey for AUD$46 million plus working capital at close (estimated at AUD$16.5 million) plus transaction costs of AUD$2 million for an enterprise value of AUD$64.5 million.

The majority of the Goundrey brand volume (85 percent) was sold in the $15 to $30 superpremium segment of the Australian market. The ultrapremium segment ($30 to $50) accounted for 7 percent of sales and the premium ($10 to $15) for the remaining 8 percent. The company's sales were almost entirely in the domestic market with 3 percent export sales. When asked what was Goundrey's export strategy, Bendat said, "I answer the phone."

Goundrey employed its own sales force in Queensland and New South Wales, with a total of 13 sales reps and four sales managers in two states. In other states, Goundrey had appointed distributors. In all regions, Goundrey was the most important winery for the distributor. Goundrey had tighter control of its distribution capability in Australia than most of its competitors. Goundrey consumption was running at more than 26 percent year over year growth.

Located 350 km south of Perth, the winery could process 3,500 tons of grapes. The winery also had its own bottling capability, enabling it to support an export business where each export market has different labeling requirements.

Triggs felt the Goundrey acquisition would be an important strategic move for Vincor. He saw several major advantages. First, the acquisition would be a significant step in achieving Vincor's strategy of converting from a North American to a global player. The Australian wine industry had captured market share in the world's new wine markets and was poised to continue to do so. Second, the Western Australia region had an established reputation for super- and ultrapremium wines. Although the grape harvest was a mere 4 percent of the Australian total, more than 25 percent of Australia's superpremium wines were sourced from that state. Third, the company had developed its own sales force in Queensland and New South Wales. Triggs wanted the proposal to go through.

CASE 19

Coca-Cola's Marketing Challenges in Brazil
The *Tubaínas* War

David Gertner
Pace University

Rosane Gertner
Pace University

Dennis Guthery
Thunderbird—The Garvin School of International
Management

Introduction

For about a decade, the Coca-Cola Company's Brazilian subsidiary tried to stop the growth of *tubaínas* (too-bah-ee'-nas). The word *tubaínas* designates numerous brands of fairly inexpensive, carbonated, and rather sweet beverages sold throughout Brazil. For more than half a century, hundreds of micro, and a few medium-size, manufacturers produced and distributed the so-called *tubaínas* on a local or regional basis.

Brazil was Coca-Cola's third largest operation and, after Mexico, the company's second largest international market. Until the mid-1990s, *tubaínas'* combined market share did not pose a threat to Coca-Cola. However, in the next decade, due to important environmental changes, *tubaínas'* sales steadily grew in Brazil, making inroads into Coca-Cola's business and jeopardizing the company's profitability.

Rather than the cola war (the name given to Coke versus Pepsi competition in many countries), the real issue for the Brazilian subsidiary of the Coca-Cola Company has been the *tubaínas* war. Over the years, Coca-Cola attempted different strategies to undercut *tubaínas'* growth. Pepsi-Cola, Coca-Cola's notorious contender, ranked fourth among the best-selling soda brands in Brazil. However, Pepsi also gained market share, thanks to its partnership with Brazilian beverage manufacturer AmBev and the successful launch of Pepsi Twist in 2003.

Background

Mr. Brian Smith, a University of Chicago graduate and a close colleague of Coca-Cola's world vice-president Brian Dyson, arrived in Brazil in August 2002 to assume

Exhibit 1   MEXICO AND BRAZIL INDICATORS

Indicator	Mexico	Brazil
Area (sq km)	1,972,550	8,511,965
Population*	104,907,991	182,032,604
GDP** (Purchasing power parity)	US$900 billion	US$1.34 trillion
GDP real growth rate**	1%	1%
GDP per capita (Purchasing power parity)	US$9,000	US$7600
Median age***	23.8 years	27 years
Life expectancy at birth***	72.3 years	71.13 years

*July 2003 est.

**2002 est.

***2003 est.

Sources: *2003 CIA World Fact Book,* http://www.cia.gov/cia/publications/factbook/geos/mx.html and http://www.cia.gov/cia/publications/factbook/geos/br.html, viewed on October 17, 2003.

the presidency of the Brazilian subsidiary of the Coca-Cola Company. Mr. Smith was the third president of Coca-Cola in Brazil since 1997 (that is, in just a six-year period).[1]

Coca-Cola expected Mr. Smith to lead the Brazilian subsidiary to the position of largest overseas operation, surpassing Mexico.[2] To fulfill this goal, Mr. Smith's assignment was to improve the subsidiary's profitability and regain Coca-Cola's market share. Although challenging, Coke's performance could be improved, as Brazil's socioeconomic conditions were similar to Mexico's and the country's population was nearly 80 percent larger than that of Mexico (see Exhibit 1).

In spite of Brazil being a large market and Coca-Cola's third largest operation, average consumption of Coke in the country was relatively low. Brazilians consumed only 144 bottles, each 237 ml (8 ounces), per person annually. In the USA, the largest of Coca-Cola's markets, per capita soda consumption was 462 bottles annually. In Mexico, the company's number two market, per capita consumption was 402 bottles annually. In terms of profitability, the Brazilian market position was even more critical. Mexico was Coca-Cola's second market, both in sales and profitability. Brazil was Coca-Cola's third market in sales and ranked a worrisome 20th position in profitability.[3,4] This disappointing rank might have been due to the local subsidiary's decision to keep lowering Coca-Cola's prices in Brazil to prevent *tubaínas'* growth. Since the 1950s, Coca-Cola's price in Brazil had dropped nearly 30 percent.[5]

For many years, competition from *tubaínas* frustrated Coca-Cola Company's growth plans in the Brazilian market. According to beverage sector experts, Coca-Cola's strategies to stop *tubaínas'* market growth in Brazil either failed to revert market share lost or, when they did succeed, eroded the company's profitability.

Economic Stabilization and Consumer Behavior in Brazil

In the mid-1990s, after a long period of high inflation and economic stagnation, the successful Brazilian economic stabilization plan, known as *Plano Real,* restored the purchasing power of the low-income segment of the population. This upturn allowed many Brazilians to purchase consumer goods formerly inaccessible to them, such as cookies, yogurt, snacks, cereals, and personal care products. As a result, during the second half of the 1990s, numerous segments of the economy underwent tremendous prosperity. Several product categories experienced fantastic sales growth. For example, per capita consumption of soda shot up 60 percent between 1994 and 1999.[6]

Brazilians categorized in the Social Class C group were the most benefited by the economic stabilization that occurred in the 1990s. The Brazilian Market Research Association, ABIPEME, developed a social class classification that was widely adopted by local researchers, marketers, and advertising agencies. The scheme combines income, education, and material possessions to define five social classes—A, B, C, D, and E. Classes A and B members possess the highest levels of income, education, and purchasing power, and tend to be more sophisticated consumers. Classes D and E lack purchasing power and struggle to afford even the very basic goods and services. Class C consumers have been described as typical workers in the lower middle class, and comprise 12.6 million Brazilian households. Their monthly family income ranges between four and ten times the minimum wage (*salário mínimo*). Class C accounts for 28 percent of total national consumption.[7]

According to a market study conducted by the local branch of the Boston Consulting Group (BCG), in spite of the fact that price affects 38 percent of the food-related purchase decisions and 31 percent of other products, quality seems to be the main factor that guides Class C Brazilians' buying decisions.[8] The study pointed out that brand was the least important factor in the food purchase decisions of Class C. The BCG report concluded that brand influence was restricted to 13 percent of the occurrences examined. The highest level of influence was observed in the personal care category, where brands impact 22 percent of the decisions.[9] The BCG report also noted that very few Class C consumers could be considered brand loyalists. They often switch among a few brands. When no evident difference in the perceived quality exists. Class C consumers tend to favor lower-priced products. The lack of importance of branding among Class C Brazilian consumers was supported by market data showing that, between 1998 and 2000, 63 percent of the market leaders in 157 product categories lost market share in Brazil.[10]

In Brazil, for nearly a decade, consumer habits observed among the massive segment of Class C consumers resulted in significant market share losses for brand leaders in several categories. The phenomenon of cheap local products stealing market share of leading global consumer goods was a trend not restricted to Brazil and to the soda market. It has been similarly detected in numerous markets, mostly in developing economies across different product categories. These products have been widely referred to as B brands.

The Soda Market

According to drink consultancy Zenith International, soft-drink sales have grown globally an average of 5 percent a year. The company's "Global Soft Drink Report 2002" states that, in 2001, consumers around the world drank 412,000 million liters of soft drinks, which represents 67.5 liters per capita.[11] Carbonated drinks accounted for 45 percent of the total soft drink sales. Zenith has projected soft drink sales growth to remain around 5 percent through 2006, compared to 3 percent for alcohol, 2 percent for milk, and 1 percent for hot beverages.

For more than a century, the Coca-Cola Company has reigned as the supreme soft drink market leader. The company sells its products in more than 200 countries. In the U.S., Coca-Cola and Pepsi hold, respectively, 44 percent and 31 percent market shares.[12] Overseas, Coca-Cola sells about three times Pepsi's volume. The distance between the two cola war contenders increased up to 2003: Coke Classic grew 30 percent worldwide during the 1990s, while Pepsi's volume went up only 2 percent.[13]

Americans, Mexicans, and Germans were the world's heaviest soda consumers. The U.S. alone, with less than 5 percent of the world's population, consumed 27 percent of the world's soft drink volume total.[14] However, soft drink growth opportunities were mainly found in large developing economies, such as China, India, and Brazil.[15] While Coca-Cola expanded its sales 3 percent a year in the U.S., overseas the annual growth was around 7 percent.[16] The highest market growth rates were observed in Latin America and in Asian countries, such as China (29%), India (17%), and the Philippines (16%).

The Coca-Cola Company— Brazilian Division

The Coca-Cola Company, which operates in more than two hundred countries as of 2001, initiated business in Brazil in 1942. Coca-Cola's Brazilian division comprises Coca-Cola Indústrias Ltda., Recofarma Indústrias do Amazonas Ltda., and 39 bottling plants operated by 16 independently managed companies. Coca-Cola's Brazilian division employed 25,000 people and generated another 250,000 indirect jobs. The company's products were available at nearly one million points of sale. The largest commercial fleet in the country, comprised of 9,000 vehicles, supplied these outlets.[17]

The Brazilian subsidiary of the Coca-Cola Company owned and distributed a broad product mix in Brazil. Coca-Cola's combined sales accounted for approximately 50 percent of the soft drink market (2003). This figure roughly translated into a per capita annual consumption of 34.2 liters of Coca-Cola products.[18] Product lines included bottled water, iced tea, juices, and energy drinks (see Exhibit 2). The company's closest competitor in the Brazilian soft-drink market was AmBev, which held nearly 17 percent of the Brazilian soft-drink market share (see AmBev section ahead). All other manufacturers' sales totaled 33 percent of the Brazilian soft-drink market[19] (see Exhibit 3).

As of 2003, the Coca-Coca brand (regular and diet) was the leader in the Brazilian soft drink market with 35.6 percent of market share. The cola flavor accounted for 45 percent of the Brazilian soft-drink market.[20] Coca-Cola's closest competitor was Guaraná Antarctica, with 7.9 percent of market share. *Guaraná* was the generic name of a very popular flavor of soft drink in Brazil that competed with cola drinks. The flavor was named after a small red fruit native to the Amazon region, *guaraná*, known for its energy-enhancing qualities. Antarctica was a leading beer and soft drink brand owned by AmBev, Coca-Cola's major competitor in Brazil. Another Coca-Cola company brand, Fanta, available in Brazil in several flavors, was ranked third in the Brazilian soft drink market, with 7.1 percent market share.[21]

Although Coca-Cola's sales steadily grew in Brazil, the brand's market share decreased after 1996 due to the competition from AmBev products and from the hundreds of low-priced *tubaínas*.

The Brazilian Soft Drink Market

Brazil was among the top ten largest economies in the world in 2004. The country had approximately 180 million inhabitants, living on a territory larger than the continental USA. Brazil was sometimes referred to as the "Latin American Titan" and was a major

Exhibit 2   COCA-COLA COMPANY—PRODUCT MIX IN BRAZIL

Product	Brands
Soft drinks	Coca-Cola, Kuat, Fanta, Sprite
Bottled waters	Schweppes, Bonaqua
Fruit-based drinks	Kapo
Energy drinks	Burn
Teas	Nestea

Source: Coca-Cola Company, http://www.cocacolabrasil.com.br/nossasmarcas/nossasmarcas.asp, viewed on May 10, 2004.

Exhibit 3   MARKET SHARE OF SOFT DRINKS* IN BRAZIL—YEAR 2003

Month	Coca-Cola	AMBEV	Others
January	50.6%	16.5%	32.9%
February	50.5	16.1	33.4
March	50.2	15.8	34.0
April	48.9	16.7	34.4
May	48.8	17.2	34.0
June	49.0	17.4	33.6
July	50.4	16.7	32.9
August	50.7	16.5	32.8
September	50.1	16.4	33.5
October	50.6	16.4	33.0
November	50.4	16.7	32.9
December	50.1	17.2	32.7

*Bottled water, juices, juice-flavored drinks, sports drinks, teas, and soft drinks.

Source: ABIR—Associação Brasileira das Indústrias de Refrigerantes e de Bebidas Não Alcoólicas (Brazilian Association of Soft Drink and Non-Alcoholic Beverages Manufacturers), http://www.abir.org.br/article.php3?id_article=117, viewed on April 11, 2004.

investment destination of global companies, particularly manufacturers of mass consumer goods.

In Brazil, soft drinks were sold in a variety of containers—containers made of glass, PET, and aluminum, with capacities that varied from 200 ml to 2.5 liters (see Exhibit 4). There were more than 3,500 brands of soft drinks in Brazil, manufactured in more than 700 plants, according to ABIR, The Brazilian Association of Soft Drink and Non-Alcoholic Beverages Manufacturers, an entity that represented producers of soft drinks, bottled water, juices, teas, and sport drinks.[22] Nonalcoholic drink sales in Brazil underwent intensive growth for over two decades. In 1986, the size of the Brazilian market was slightly below 4.9 billion liters. In 1994, Brazilians consumed an estimated 6.44 billion liters of nonalcoholic drinks. Ten years later, in 2003, nonalcoholic drink consumption leaped up to 11.6 billion liters.[23] In 2004, ABIR forecast sales to go back to 2002 levels, that is, close to 12 billion liters[24] (see Exhibit 5). Data summarizing the soft drink market specifically revealed continued growth into the future. Brazilian per capita soft drink consumption was 82.8 liters in 1998 and grew to 95.3 liters in 2003. Per capita consumption was forecasted to grow to 104.9 liters by 2008[25] (see Exhibit 6).

Exhibit 4   PERCENTAGE OF SOFT DRINK SALES IN BRAZIL BY TYPE OF CONTAINER,
JULY–DECEMBER, 2003

Container	Jul	Aug	Sep	Oct	Nov	Dec
Returnable bottle—Up to 300 ml	5.5%	5.6%	5.7%	5.5%	5.4%	5.4%
Disposable bottle—Up to 300 ml	1.0	1.0	1.0	1.0	1.0	1.0
Disposable bottle—500 ml	0.1	0.1	0.1	0.1	0.1	0.1
Returnable bottle—600 ml	3.2	3.2	3.3	3.3	3.2	3.0
Disposable bottle—Up to 600 ml	3.5	3.4	3.4	3.4	3.5	3.4
Disposable bottle—1 liter	1.8	1.8	1.8	1.8	1.7	1.7
Returnable bottle—1 to 1.25 liters	1.5	1.5	1.6	1.7	1.7	17
Disposable bottle—1.5 liters	1.3	1.3	1.2	1.1	1.3	1.3
Disposable bottle—2 to 2.5 liters	73.0	73.2	72.9	73.0	72.5	72.7
Can—350 ml	8.8	8.6	8.7	8.9	9.3	9.5
Other containers	0.3	0.3	0.3	0.2	0.3	0.2
Total (%)	100.0%	100.0%	100.0%	100.0%	100.0%	100.0%

Source: ABIR, http://www.abir.org.br/article.php3?id_article=125, viewed on April 11, 2004.

Exhibit 5   SALES OF NON-ALCOHOLIC BEVERAGES* IN BRAZIL,
1986–2003

Year	Volume (1,000 liters)	Change from Prior Year
1986	4,895,835	
1987	5,305,593	8.37%
1988	5,095,788	−3.95
1989	5,800,108	13.82
1990	5,769,264	−0.53
1991	5,978,175	3.62
1992	5,147,758	−13.89
1993	5,615,803	9.09
1994	6,440,397	14.68
1995	9,146,041	42.01
1996	9,861,493	7.82
1997	10,574,528	7.23
1998	11,029,351	4.30
1999	11,052,303	0.21
2000	11,516,598	4.20
2001	11,585,868	0.60
2002	11,968,630	3.30
2003	11,571,945	−3.31

*Bottled water, juices, juice-flavored drinks, sports drinks, teas, and soft drinks.
Source: ABIR-Associação Brasileira das Indústrias de Refrigerantes e de Bebidas Náo Alcoólicas (Brazilian Association of Soft Drink and Non-Alcoholic Beverages Manufacturers), http://www.abir.org.br/article.php3?id_article=118, viewed on April 11, 2004.

Exhibit 6   PER CAPITA CONSUMPTION OF ALL SOFT DRINKS (as sold), 1998–2003 WITH PROJECTIONS FOR 2004–2008

Year	Per Capita Consumption in Liters
1998	82.8
1999	84.3
2000	89.6
2001	92.3
2002	93.9
2003	95.3
2004	97.6
2005	99.4
2006	101.2
2007	103.1
2008	104.9

Source: Euromonitor Market Study, "Soft Drinks in Brazil," April 2004, Table 5 and Table 16.

Exhibit 7   BRAZILIAN SOFT DRINK MARKET PERCENTAGES BY FLAVOR, 1999–2003

Flavor	1999	2000	2001	2002	2003
Cola	39.1%	39.3%	39.6%	40.5%	41.8%
Guaraná	25.2	25.8	25.2	24.2	23.9
Orange	13.6	13.3	13.2	12.2	11.4
Lemon	6.8	6.5	6.2	5.9	5.6
Grape	2.7	2.4	2.9	3.1	2.9
Tutti-Frutti	1.2	1.0	1.0	1.1	1.2
Apple	0.0	0.0	0.1	1.0	0.9
Tonic	0.7	0.8	0.8	0.7	0.7
Citric	0.0	0.0	0.1	0.6	0.4
Others	3.5	3.1	2.2	2.4	2.7
Diet/Light	7.3	7.9	8.4	8.3	8.4
TOTAL	100.0%	100.0%	100.0%	100.0%	100.0%

Source: ABIR in, http://www.abir.org.br/article.php3?id_article=126, viewed on April 11, 2004.

Cola was the Brazilians' favorite flavor (41.8% in 2003), followed directly by *guaraná* (23.9%) and orange (11.4%)[26] (see Exhibit 7).

In spite of the 1990s impressive growth rates, nonalcoholic beverage market analysts argued that the volume of nonalcoholic drinks sales in Brazil, 11,571,945 liters in 2003,[27] was still rather small compared to the market potential. Observers believed the Brazilian soft drink market could be easily expanded by simply improving and expanding distribution.

Although the majority of the Brazilian population resided in urban areas located on the country's Atlantic coastline, several million Brazilians still lived in thousands of small communities spread throughout the country. Due to the small size of these markets, and to cost and accessibility-related issues, few consumer products reached some of these faraway communities.

Supermarkets, which were the primary distribution channel for sodas in most countries, accounted for only a quarter of the category sales in Brazil. Additionally, nearly half of the soft drink volume was sold refrigerated and was consumed at or near the point of sale. Soft drink vending machines were not widely available in Brazil up to 2004.[28]

The Competition—AmBev

Coca-Cola's main Brazilian competitor was AmBev, Companhia de Bebidas das Americas (American Beverage Company—NYSE: ABV and Aback). The company was formed from a merger in July 1999 of Brahma and Antarctica, two leading Brazilian beer and soft drink manufacturers. By then, both companies had realized the threats and opportunities posed by globalization and decided to join forces. With the merger, AmBev became the fifth largest beer manufacturer,[29] the seventh largest world beverage manufacturer, and Latin America's largest beverage company. AmBev held nearly 70 percent of the Brazilian beer market and 17 percent of the Brazilian soft drink market.[30] AmBev aggressively expanded into several Latin American and Caribbean markets, where the company developed impressive market shares, such as in Argentina (77%), Bolivia (99%), Paraguay (94%), and Uruguay (99%).[31]

AmBev's assets included 49 facilities, located both in Brazil and overseas. AmBev had 18,000 employees. The company owned numerous bottling facilities, malt production factories, concentrate plants, and a *guaraná* farm. The company's product mix comprised various brands of beers, soft drinks, bottled water, iced tea, and isotonic beverages. Some of AmBev's most popular brands were Brahma, Antarctica, Skol, and Bohemia (see Exhibit 8). One of AmBev's major competitive advantages was its superior distribution structure. AmBev's products reached more than one million points of sales, located in over six thousand Brazilian municipalities, covering most of the extremely large Brazilian territory.

In March 2004, Interbrew, the world's third largest brewer, manufacturer of Beck's, Stella Artois, Labatt, and other brands sold in 140 countries, and AmBev, the world's fifth largest brewer, announced a global alliance that resulted in the creation of a new beverage corporation by the name of InterbrewAmBev. The new company's 2003 sales totaled US$11.9 billion, which made it the largest brewery company in the world by sales revenue. InterbrewAmBev controlled 14 percent of the world's beer consumption. In 2003, the company sold 195 million hectoliters of beer and 25 million hectoliters of soda.[32]

AmBev was the second largest company in the Brazilian soft drink market. The company bottled and distributed numerous brands of bottled water, isotonic drinks, and sodas. The company's Guaraná Antarctica brand was second to Coca-Cola in the Brazilian soft drink market. Guaraná Antarctica was exported to several countries, and in 2002, it began production and distribution in Europe.

Ambev's and Pepsi's Partnership

Pepsi Cola had been available in Brazil for over 50 years. However, the cooperation between AmBev and Pepsi began in 1997, when Brahma signed a 20-year franchise contract to produce and distribute Pepsi products in Brazil.[33] By 2004, AmBev was the largest Pepsi-Cola bottler outside the U.S. Besides AmBev's handling of Pepsi's

Exhibit 8   AMBEV'S PRODUCT LINE IN BRAZIL, 2004

Product	Brands
Soft drinks	Guaraná Antarctica
	Pepsi
	Sukita
	Club Soda
	Tônica Antarctica
	Guaraná Brahma
	7-Up
	Limão Brahma
	Soda Limonada Antarctica
	Teen
	Mountain Dew
Beers	Skol
	Brahma
	Antarctica
	Bohemia
	Kroneabier
	Caracu
	Miller
	Polar
	SerraMalte
	Carlsberg
Bottled water	Agua Fratelli Vita
Isotonic drinks	Gatorade
	Marathon
Teas	Lipton Ice Tea

Source: AMBEV, http://www.ambev.com.br/produtos, viewed May 10, 2004.

bottling and distribution in Brazil, the two companies cooperated in several other Latin American countries, including Peru and Guatemala, in addition to the Caribbean.[34]

Before AmBev, a company called Baesa handled as much as 80 percent of Pepsi's volume in Brazil.[35] In the mid-1990s, when Brahma bought Baesa, the company was facing a difficult financial situation. In spite of Pepsi's significant marketing investments, the brand failed to appeal to younger upper-middle class consumers as planned.[36]

By then, Pepsi distribution in Brazil was also rather limited and concentrated, mainly in the southern states of the country. Additionally, Baesa failed to compete with cheaper brands of soft drinks widely available in the Brazilian market, despite its efforts to increase productivity and lower costs. When AmBev took over Baesa, Pepsi finally gained access to new points of sales, especially restaurants, where AmBev had a strong position.[37] Reciprocally, Pepsi helped AmBev to distribute its Guaraná Antarctica in overseas markets. Pepsi's plan even included testing the product in the huge U.S. market.[38]

Pepsi's product mix in Brazil included Pepsi-Cola, Pepsi Light, Teem, Diet Teem, Seven-Up, and Diet Seven-Up. Some of these brands were available exclusively in southern Brazilian states. In 2002, Pepsi-Cola introduced Mountain Dew, targeting young Brazilians.[39] After the partnership with AmBev started, Pepsi grew steadily in the Brazilian market. Between 2001 and 2002, 60,000 points of sales began to sell Pepsi products. Pepsi's products were then found in nearly 600,000 Brazilian outlets.

As of 2003, the Pepsi-Cola brand held approximately 6 percent of the Brazilian soft drink market. Pepsi-Cola became the fourth best-selling brand, after Coca-Cola, Guaraná Antarctica, and Fanta. In the cola segment, Pepsi was ranked number two. The brand's cola market share grew from 9.7 percent in December 2002 to 12.2 percent in October 2003.

While soft drink sales shrank 2 percent in Brazil in 2003, Pepsi sales grew by 28 percent. Most of the growth was attributed to the launch of the new Pepsi Twist (lemon-flavored Pepsi). The product was well received by Brazilian consumers, already used to ordering iced cola drinks with a slice of lime. Pepsi Twist was launched in a differentiated bottle, taller and easier to handle. The success encouraged Pepsi to bring other products into the Brazilian market to capture future sales.[40]

The *Tubaínas'* Competitive Pressure

Tubaínas[41] was an old trademark registered by the Ferráspari Company, located in Jundiaí, São Paulo.[42] The name Tubaína initially branded a candy. Later, the company introduced a soft drink under the same brand name. Ferráspari's Tubaína was still a popular brand in the interior of São Paulo state, especially in Campinas and its vicinities. The distribution of the product had recently been expanded to neighboring areas in Minas Gerais state.[43]

In the 1940s and 1950s, the Ferráspari Company granted other soda manufacturers permission to use the term *tubaína* as a suffix preceding the brand name, believing that such a decision would help to promote its own brand. Therefore, *tubaínas* became a common designation for a number of small brands of carbonated soft drinks, mainly sold in the interior of São Paulo state.

Later on, *tubaínas* became a general term for low-profile soft drinks. These local or regional products were sold everywhere in Brazil, from the north to the south of the country (see Exhibits 9 and 10). *Tubaínas* sold at prices significantly lower than nationally marketed soft drink brands, such as Coca-Cola's and AmBev's products. Some beverage industry experts referred to them as "liquid candy." *Tubaínas* tended to be quite sweet, were offered in different flavors, such as *guaraná*, tutti-frutti, orange, tangerine, grape, and gooseberry, and came in different colors, such as pink or yellow.[44]

About twenty independent manufacturers of *tubaínas* were members of ABIR, the Brazilian Association of Soft Drink Manufacturers. However, it was believed that there were more than seven hundred manufacturers of *tubaínas* in Brazil.[45] This universe spanned from very small manufacturers, who did not have a legal business nor paid taxes, to quite structured companies with regional coverage, considerable revenues, and sizable market shares.

Despite the fact that some *tubaínas* manufacturers had been in business for nearly seventy years, market reports ignored their existence until the early 1990s. This situation radically changed in the following years. Still, no individual *tubaína* had more than 1.5 percent of the total Brazilian soft drink market.[46] ABIR director Carlos Cabral Menezes estimated that *tubaínas'* combined market share was 32 percent. His educated guess was that *tubaínas* generated sales of nearly US$1.5 billion in 2001.[47]

By 2004, some *tubaínas* manufacturers owned modern plants and had adopted the latest bottling technologies. While, in the past, most *tubaínas* were primarily distributed through small points of sales in poor neighborhoods, several brands were now

Exhibit 9   SAMPLE OF *TUBAÍNAS* BRANDS

Manufacturer/Brand	Location	Market Introduction
Celina	Rio Grande do Sul	1894
Agua da Serra/Fanni/Gasosão	Santa Catarina	1976
Cirylla (originally Distilléria Urso)	Rio Grande do Sul	1910
Ciryllinha	Rio Grande do Sul	1960
Frutty	Minas Gerais	1950
Conquista	Paraná	1960s
Papuan	Santa Catarina	1979
Itamarati	São Paulo	1950
Poty	São Paulo	1951
Mineirinho	Rio de Janeiro	1946
Flexa	Rio de Janeiro	N.A.
Cini	Paraná	1904
Fruki	Rio Grande do Sul	1998
Xereta	São Paulo	N.A.
Baré	Pernambuco	N.A.
Frevo	Pernambuco	1997
Maracaná/Marasuco	N.A.	N.A.
Kiko-Cola	São Paulo	N.A.
Convenção	São Paulo	1951
Fricote	Bahia	N.A.
Garoto	Pará	N.A.

Source: *2K Para Viagem,* http://www.revista2k.com.br/vida/tubaina/imprima.htm, viewed on October 15, 2003.

available in the leading supermarket chains, located in the largest Brazilian metropolitan areas. *Tubaínas* manufacturers, who had historically relied on cheap prices to attract consumers, were increasingly investing in quality control, product development, packaging, branding, advertising, and marketing. Some brands had gained consumers' trust and loyalty.

In spite of some brands' success, most had limited distribution. For example, the brand Convenção only focused on the markets of São Paulo and Rio de Janeiro. Hugo Cini, another successful *tubaínas,* was based in Paraná state, in southern Brazil. In 1999, it was the number two brand in the capital city of Curitiba.[48] In the Brazilian Northeast, the region with the country's lowest income, *tubaínas'* market share was the highest, over 40 percent.[49]

Some *tubaínas* manufacturers became quite successful business cases. For example, Refrigerantes Xereta, a company located in Tietê, São Paulo, in southeastern Brazil, was in the market for more than thirty years. To avoid the price war in the two-liter PET segment, the company introduced its soft drink, Xereta, in aluminum cans, and launched Xeretinha (Little Xereta), in 250 ml PET containers. Xereta was then the third best-selling brand in its region, one of the wealthiest in the country, competing with market leaders Coca-Cola and Guaraná Antarctica. TV host and singer Xuxa, one

Exhibit 10   BRAZILIAN POPULATION BY REGION

Region	Population, Census 2000	% Region/Country Population, Census 2000
Southeast	72,297,351	42.6%
South	25,089,783	14.8%
North	12,893,561	7.6%
Northeast	47,975,416	28.2%
Central West	11,616,745	6.8%
TOTAL	169,872,856	100.0%

Source: http://www.terravista.pt/Enseada/1347/mapado.htm, viewed on June 1, 2004.

of the most popular Brazilian showbiz celebrities, endorsed the Xereta brand. The Xereta Company also manufactured Wal-Mart's and Carrefour's private brands of soft drinks.[50] Nearly 30 percent of canned Xereta was exported to Mercosur countries. The product was even sold in improbable markets such as the U.S., Lebanon, and China.[51]

In 1996, DGB (Distribuidora Guararapes de Bebidas), a leading distributor of beer and sodas in the northeast of Brazil, lost the rights to distribute Brahma's products (AmBev's brand). Thus, the company decided to develop its own line of soft drinks, Frevo, named after a traditional pop rhythm mainly played and danced during Carnaval. Frevo sodas were lower priced than traditional competitors. This rather sweet beverage was available in four flavors: *guaraná*, orange, lemon, and cola. The advertising promoted the slogan, "Taste ours, it is better." After only two years in the market, Frevo gained 25 percent of market share in Recife, Pernambuco state, one of Brazil's largest metropolitan areas. Production increased from 1.1 million liters to 21.4

million. Frevo distributed in seven of the nine states of the northeast region. DGB's revenue quadrupled compared to its distribution days for Brahma.[52]

Xereta and Frevo were only two amongst numerous *tubaínas* success stories. Bebidas Dom, a nearly forty-year-old operation in São Paulo's interior, achieved impressive market growth, mostly through word of mouth. Since 1993, Cotuba, another *tubaína,* produced by Refrigerantes Arco Iris, a company founded in 1958 in São José do Rio Preto, São Paulo, was the second-best-selling brand in the northwestern region of the state. The U.S. and Japan were among Cotuba's export markets.[53] The Timbalada brand was promoted in association with soccer, the most popular sport in Brazil. Numerous other brands of *tubaínas,* such as Frutty, Bacana, and 15, have winning stories as well.[54]

Leading national and global soft drink manufacturers were challenged by small, no-frills, no-advertising brands in markets other than Brazil. In Chile, soft drink bottlers experienced analogous problems—low-priced soft drink companies increased their market share.[55] In Peru, Indústrias Amano's performance surprised much larger competitors, such as Coca-Cola and Pepsi. This was accomplished with virtually no investments in marketing communications. Its extremely low-priced Kola Real captured 20 percent of Peru's soda market. The product was the number one soda brand among the lower-income segment in Peru, the brand's home country.[56] Indústrias Amano rolled out Kola Real to neighboring countries, such as Ecuador and Venezuela. In Mexico, Kola Real was introduced as Big Cola, gaining 4 percent of the market.[57] The brand was well accepted even by consumers in wealthy neighborhoods, such as Polanco, in Mexico's capital. Competing with Coca-Cola, Kola Real became one of the leading brands in the local Sam's Club store.

While equivalent stories can be found in several markets, they more often took place in developing economies, where informal businesses were easier to start and grow. Moreover, global brands losing market share to the so-called B brands were observed across many product categories. Their impact in the Brazilian market is briefly discussed ahead.

B Brands in Brazil

B brands attacked established brands in territory they had ruled for ages. Like guerrillas, these brands were fast, flexible, and fought the enemy in diverse and inhospitable battlefields. They had very lean operations, allowing them to offer products for about half the price of their traditional competitors.

Between 1998 and 2000, Brazilian brand leaders in 157 product categories lost 63 percent of market share, according to an A. C. Nielsen/CBPA study.[58] The study indicated that the most affected categories were beverages, candies and sweet confections, and house-care products. An additional threat faced by leading brands in Brazil was the rapid proliferation of private brands. By 2003, product introductions by leading Brazilian supermarket chains, such as Pão de Açucar, Carrefour, Sonae, Bompreço, and Sendas, increased the number of private brands to nearly 13,000—twice as many as in 1999. The dispute for shelf space with established brands increased significantly and continually. A. C. Nielsen estimated that by 2003, private brand sales would reach US$2.8 billion, approximately 17 percent of supermarket sales in Brazil.[59]

A major problem for established brands in Brazil was the unfair competition from companies that had no legal existence and from those who were legally registered but did not pay taxes. Marco Aurélio Eboli, a vice president of the Brazilian Coca-Cola bottler Spal, estimated that in Brazil, 90 percent of the 750 regional brands of soft drinks did not pay the taxes they ought.[60] Emerson Kapaz, a Brazilian businessman who investigated the nonpayment of taxes by firms in several sectors, affirmed that taxes amounted to 40 percent of the final soft drink sales price.[61] This was a major reason why *tubaínas* could compete on the basis of price. In fact, the so-called unofficial side of the Brazilian economy was quite large. Sebrae, the Brazilian Micro- and Small-Business Support Service, estimated it comprised approximately 12 million micro-companies in 2003, up from 9 million in 1997.[62]

Another important issue in the competitive Brazilian market that seemed to impact the share of traditional brands regarded the relative use of promotional tools. To fight price competition, several leading brands increased their trade promotional activities. According to the top Brazilian advertising agency, Talent, investments in media were reduced in roughly two-thirds of the product categories during the 1990s. Some argued that during that time, traditional brands should have invested to stay at the forefront of consumers' tastes.[63]

Coca-Cola Fights Back against *Tubaínas*

When Coca-Cola's market share started to decline in Brazil by 1996, the company took several actions to fight back. In 1999, when Coca-Cola's share in Brazil dropped to 48 percent, the local subsidiary froze its products' prices. In the northeast region, Coca-Cola cut its prices from 1.80 to 1.25 Brazilian reals (R$), attempting to stop *tubaínas'* growth. The company promoted changes in its distribution channels, such as buying back franchisee operations. Although these types of actions brought the share back to the 50 percent historic level, the Company's headquarters disliked the negative effect on profitability.[64]

Another way the Brazilian subsidiary of the Coca-Cola Company attempted to rectify dwindling sales was by the expansion of the number of brands offered in the market. For example, the *guaraná* market became a huge segment to take over. It increased from 3.6 percent to 28.1 percent in the years 1995–2000.[65] In 2001, Coca-Cola expanded the output of its soft drink Guaraná Kuat. They also renovated production facilities and planted 200 hectares of *guaraná,* the Amazonian fruit used to flavor Kuat. Further expansions and plantings were to follow. All of this was done to confront the hard-hitting competition from other *guaraná* brands, such as AmBev's Antarctica.[66] Kuat secured 11 percent of the *guaraná* market in Brazil, compared to Antarctica's 28 percent share.[67] Coca-Cola also expanded Fanta's mix by incorporating new flavors, such as citrus and strawberry.[68] Such efforts helped combined sales of Fanta to approach Guaraná Antarctica's market share.

Coca-Cola somehow also ventured into the *tubaínas'* territory. It has been said that Coca-Cola's Brazilian subsidiary took over a few competitors in order to stop *tubaínas'* growth. Buying competitive brands, though, could not prevent former owners from reentering the market or new competitors from emerging. In Maranhão, a state located in northeastern Brazil, Coca-Cola's own bottler distributed a *tubaína* called Jesus. The brand claims to hold 20 percent of that regional market. The product was named after its creator, Jesus Norberto Gomes. Like Coca-Cola, the drink originated as a medicine.[69] The sweet, shocking-pink beverage, with a cherry taste and touch of cinnamon, sold in a retro-styled bottle, was one of the most popular beverages in the local market.[70]

Lastly, Coca-Cola attempted to build closer ties with Brazilian consumers to improve its image and garner good will. The local subsidiary increasingly sponsored and participated in local, regional, and national events and celebrations, such as São João, Festival Parintins, Revolução Farroupilhas, and Brazil's most popular festivity, Carnaval.[71]

Coca-Cola vs. *Tubaínas*—The Unfair Competition Controversy

The Coca-Cola Company's Brazilian subsidiary claimed to be deeply harmed by *tubaínas'* unfair competition. It advocated that the price advantage held by *tubaínas* was only possible through tax evasion practices, overlooked by the Brazilian authorities. In 1998, a two-liter bottle of *tubaínas* could be bought for as low as fifty cents, compared to as much as one dollar and fifty cents for the same volume of Coca-Cola. As other multinational companies that operated in the Brazilian market did, Coca-Cola lobbied to persuade state and federal lawmakers and tax agencies to exert a more rigid control over its competitors' operations and market practices.[72]

In August 2003, Coca-Cola's role in the *tubaínas* war switched from victim to villain. Mr. Laerte Codonho, owner of Dolly, a *tubaína* brand that had experienced substantial growth, filed a formal complaint against the Coca-Cola Company before the Brazilian Council of Economic Rights, CADE (*Conselho Administrativo de Direito Econômico*). Coca-Cola was accused of economic abuse and unfair business practices, the same criticism the company had always held against emergent soft drink brands. Mr. Codonho claimed that the giant soft-drink manufacturer threatened smaller competitors, bribed public authorities to indict the *tubaínas* for tax evasion, and coerced retailers to restrain them from selling *tubaínas*. Coca-Cola was also accused of sabotage and espionage. Dolly's owner charged the company with the public distribution of copies of an e-mail stating that Dolly soft drinks caused cancer. The Coca-Cola Company promptly distributed a press release refuting all the allegations, affirming that all were entirely false, and totally inconsistent with Coca-Cola's ethical behavior.[73] Accusations continued, and the matter came under investigation by both Brazilian and American authorities.[74] Dolly paid for outdoor advertising that insinuated that Coca-Cola used coca leaves as an ingredient. Coke pursued the matter in court and won a judgment which called for Dolly to cease and desist the insinuation, and imposed a R$100,000 fine for each billboard should Dolly resume the false allegation.[75]

The Return of Returnable Bottles

For nearly a decade, competition from inexpensive brands of sodas, *tubaínas,* deeply affected not only Coca-Cola's sales in Brazil, but also its profitability. Coca-Cola tried a number of strategies to stop *tubaínas'* market growth in Brazil. Although some of the attempted strategies in the past produced good results, none really curtailed market share loss and profitability erosion. To carry out a new strategy to recoup the company's market share and profitability, Coca-Cola Company headquarters appointed Brian Smith as president of the Brazilian subsidiary in 2002.

The new Coca-Cola weapon to confront *tubaínas* consisted of reintroducing Coca-Cola in returnable glass bottles, which had been discontinued about a decade earlier in favor of the more convenient disposable plastic bottles and aluminum cans. However, compared to the same period in 2002, while sales of the Coca-Cola Company's Brazilian subsidiary fell 6 percent in the first half of 2003, sales of soft drinks in returnable bottles went up 10 percent. Coca-Cola returnable bottles were priced closer to *tubaínas,* and, therefore, appealed and became accessible to Class C and D consumers. "If consumers could buy Coca-Cola for almost the same price of *tubaínas,* they would certainly favor Coca-Cola," believed Adalberto Viviani, from Concept, a food and beverage consultancy in São Paulo.

By September 2003, Coca-Cola in glass returnable bottles (1.25 liters and 200 ml) was already available in 4,000 sales outlets on the outskirts of Rio de Janeiro, and in popular vicinities in the state of Minas Gerais. Coca-Cola planned to expand distribution to nearly 7,000 points of sale by the end of 2003. Coca-Cola also reintroduced the product in small 200 ml bottles to be consumed at the points of sale.[76]

The reintroduction of Coca-Cola in returnable bottles elicited mixed reactions in the Brazilian market. The strategy was welcomed by glass manufacturer Cisper, a company that expected to increase sales by 20 percent simply by supplying bottles to Coca-Cola. On the other hand, some large retailers were not so sure about Coca-Cola's move. Nelson Sendas, of Grupo Sendas, a leading Brazilian supermarket chain, stated that returnable bottles posed a major operational problem for both retailers and consumers. In his opinion, the company was moving backward.[77]

Giovanni Fiorentino, a strategy consultant, also shared his concerns that costs associated with transporting, cleaning, and storing bottles could null any apparent savings. Other experts also doubted that the use of returnable bottles could reduce Coca-Cola's prices by 25 percent as the company desired. Coca-Cola's president refuted allegations that the price reductions were actually subsidized by the Company, and that the real objective was to obtain consumers' loyalty once they bought the bottles. Mr. Smith declared that the real objective was to increase Coca-Cola's profitability in Brazil.[78]

At the end of 2003, returnable bottles accounted for less than 10 percent of soft drink sales in Brazil, and there were no signs of significant growth in market share (see Exhibit 4).

The Future

Going into 2004, Coca-Cola showed encouraging signs. In a partnership with Norsa, a company owned by Tasso Jereissati, a nationally known businessman and state governor, Coca-Cola regained control of distribution in several northeastern states, such as Ceará, Bahia, Piauí, and Rio Grande do Norte.[79] As a result, Coca Cola's market share reached 44.5 percent in November 2003, up from 42 percent in November 2002, which led the operational profit to grow by 40 percent.[80] At the same time, the *tubaínas'* share dropped from 42.8 to 38.8 percent. Norsa's president, Augusto Parada, stated that Coca-Cola should offer northeastern consumers products at all possible tastes and price levels ("*Coca-cola para todos os gostos e todos os bolsos*"). As a result, Coca-Cola was found in supermarkets in 237 ml disposable glass bottles at R$0.82, and 2.5 liter PET bottles for R$2.59. Additionally, at snack bars and grocery stores, consumers could buy a 200 ml returnable bottle of Coca-Cola and pay only R$0.50 (less than US$.20).[81]

Brazilian consumers were the ones who benefited the most from the *tubaínas* war. In the Brazilian market, sodas were offered in a much broader range of flavors, packaging, and price than prior to 2003.

The market became even more competitive in 2003 with the entry of RC Cola into Brazil. Real Bebidas, based in the state of Minas Gerais, signed a master franchise agreement to produce and distribute RC for twenty years, extendable for another ten years. The group responsible for launching RC Cola in Brazil hired Renato Barcellos, a Brazilian engineer who served the Coca-Cola Company's business in the northeast region. In blind tests conducted in the U.S. with RC Cola, Coca-Cola, and Pepsi-Cola, a larger number of consumers preferred the taste of RC Cola. Based on that, one of the strategies to be adopted to promote RC Cola in Brazil was to offer sampling of the product in supermarkets. Counting on RC taste qualities and Mr. Barcellos' market expertise and experience, RC Cola's franchisee expected to gain 5 percent of the Brazilian soft drink market within the first three years of operation.[82]

RC soon appeared in the leading supermarkets of Belo Horizonte, one of Brazil's largest cities. In addition, RC was being produced and distributed in five northeastern states. Real Bebidas had partners and plans to launch RC in São Paulo and Rio de Janeiro. RC was sold in two liter, one liter, and 600 ml PET bottles, as well as 350 ml cans. The products were launched with initial prices 10–15 percent lower than Coke. Concurrent with the launch of RC, Bebidas Real launched PIT, a fruit-flavored soft drink line with guarana, grape, orange, and lemon flavors.[83]

Endnotes

[1]"Rumo ao Passado: Coca-Cola Apela Para Garrafas de Vidro," *Revista Exame,* Setembro 04, 2003, http://oeconomista.com/wm/wmview.php?ArtID=544, viewed on October 15, 2003.

[2]Ibid.

[3]Ibid.

[4]Rutkowski, Lauro, "Coca aposta no Brasil," *Correiro Braziliense,* Brasília, quinta-feria, 09 de maio de 2002, http://www2.correioweb.com.br/cw/EDICAO_20020509/pri_eco_090502_165.htm, viewed on October 7, 2003.

[5]Morais, Jomar, "Frevo Arretado," *Revista Exame,* June 2, 1999, www.planetajota.jor.br/tubaina.htm, viewed on February 3, 2004.

[6]"At Twice the Volume of Water, Soda Still Saturates," *The World Paper,* http://www.worldpaper.com/2002/oct02/water4.html, viewed on October 17, 2003.

[7]Blecher, Nelson, "A Invasão das Marcas Talibás: Por que as marcas líderes estão perdendo participação de mercado para produtos populares e baratos," *Revista Exame,* 757, http://www.gb.com.br/materia_gb29.html, in September 15, 2003.

[8]Ibid.

[9]Ibid.

[10]Ibid.

[11]"Global Soft Drinks 2002," *Zenith International,* http://www.the-infoshop.com/study/roc14659_softdrinks.html, viewed on October 20, 2003.

[12]Going Global: Coca-Cola Dominates, http://weblog.wtob.ws/archives/002120.html.

[13]Ibid.

[14]Global Soft Drinks 2002.

[15]Going Global: Coca-Cola Dominates.

[16]Ibid.

[17]http://www.cocacolabrasil.com.br/quemsomos/negocio/negocio.pdf, viewed on June 1, 2004.

[18]http://www.cocacolabrasil.com.br/quemsomos/negocio/negocio.asp, viewed on October 20, 2003.

[19]ABIR—Associação Brasileira das Indústrias de Refrigerantes e de Bebidas Não Alcoólicas (Brazilian Association of Soft Drink and Non-Alcoholic Beverages Manufacturers), http://www.abir.org.br/article.php3?id_article=117, viewed on April 11, 2004.

[20]Morais, "Frevo Arretado."

[21]Simão, Juliana, "A Terra da Fanta, "Assorev—Associaçáo das revendas AMBEV do Estado do Rio de Janeiro, http://www.adiscrj.com.br, viewed on October 15, 2003.

[22]ABIR Statistics, http://www.abir.org.br/rubrique.php3?id_rubrique=4, viewed on April 11, 2004.

[23]ABIR Statistics, http://www.abir.org.br/article.php3?id_article=118, viewed on April 11, 2004.

[24]Ibid.

[25]Euromonitor Market Study, "Soft Drinks in Brazil (April 2004)," Table 5 and Table 16.

[26]ABIR Statistics, http://www.abir.org.br/article.php3?id_article=126, viewed on April 11, 2004.

[27]ABIR Statistics, http://www.abir.org.br/article.php3?id_article=118, viewed on April 11, 2004.

[28]"Coming of Age: Latin American Soft Drinks," *Beverage Industry,* 89 (7): 13+, July 1998. ISSN: 0148-6187 Stagnito Publishing Company.

[29]http://www.corporate-ir.net/ireye/ir_site.zhtml?ticker=25240&script=2100, viewed on May 02, 2004.

[30]http://www.AMBEV.com.br/empresa, viewed on February 01, 2004.

[31]Press Release—AmBev and Interbrew Establish InterbrewAmBev—The World's Premier Brewer, http://www.mz-ir.com/ambev/popup/popup_eng.htm, in http://www.ambev.com.br/english/investidores, viewed on May 10, 2004.

[32]http://www.ambev.com.br/english/investidores.

[33]Ibid.

[34]Ibid.

[35]"Coming of Age: Latin American Soft Drinks."

[36]Business Latin America, "Baesa, New Pepsi?" March 29, 1999.

[37]Fritsch, Peter, "Brazilian Brewery Merger Gets the Go-Ahead—Blend of Brahma Paulista Will Rank No. 3 in the World," *Wall Street Journal;* New York; March 31, 2000.

[38]Penteado, Claudia, "Brazil Drink Marketers Aim for a Guaraná World," *Advertising Age International,* Dec 1999.

[39]*Pepsi Traz Mountain Dew Para Jovens Brasileiros,* http://ambev.com.br/imprensa/press_release/ano2002/0023/imprimir, viewed on April 12, 2004.

[40]Teixeira, Alexandre, "A Gota que faltava," *Isto É,* December 03, 2003, in http://www.terra.com.br/istoedinheiro/327/negocios/327_gota_faltava.htm, viewed on May 02, 2004.

[41]Also known and registered as *tubaírna,* with an "r."

[42]"Tubaínas Mudam de Cara e Já Controlam 32% do Mercado," *Revista Recall,* Edição 49, in http://fonte.jor.br?pagina_indice.asp?iditem=149, viewed on September 15, 2003.

[43]Ibid.

[44]*2K Para Viagem.* http://www.revista2k.com.br/vida/tubaina/imprima.htm, viewed on October 15, 2003.

[45]Tubaínas mudam de cara e já controlam 32% do mercado.

[46]Penteado, Claudia, "The Little Drinks That Took on Coca-Cola." *Advertising Age International,* October 5, 1998, p10, 3/5p, 2c.

[47]Tubaínas mudam de cara e j controlam 32% do mercado.

[48]Dyer, Geoff, "The Americas: Brazil's Regional Drink Makers Slake Thirst for Value: The Tax Regime and Growing Demand Have Penalized Leading Brands," ISSN: 0307-1766, *The Financial Times London Edition,* June 16, 1999.

[49]Teixeira, Alexandre, "A Virada Arretada Da Coca-Cola Quarta-Feira," *Isto ...,* January 14, 2004, http://www.terra.com.br/istoedinheiro/332/negocios/332_virada_coca.htm, viewed on May 02, 2004.

[50]Tubaínas mudam de cara e já controlam 32% do mercado.

[51]Ibid.

[52]Torreão, Luciana. Lucros borbulhantes e refrescantes. Prevista Pronews, June 2003, nº. 45, http://www.revistapronews.com.br/.

[53]Tubaínas mudam de cara e já controlam 32% do mercado.

[54]Ibid.

[55]"Generic and B Brands conquer 7% of soda market," *Santiago Times,* January 8, 2002.

[56]Luhnow, David, "A Low-Budget Cola Shakes Up Markets South of the Border," *The Wall Street Journal Eastern Edition,* October 27, 2003, Vol. 242, Issue 83, pA1, 2p.

[57]Luhnow, David.

[58]Blecher, Nelson.

[59]Blecher, Nelson.

[60]Vasconcellos, Carlos, *"Pirataria, A Ponta Do Iceberg,"* Revista Update, http://www.amcham.com.br/revista/revista2003-01-16a/materia2003-01-17a, viewed on October 15, 2003.

[61]http://www.unafisco-sp.org.br/Secao.asp?IdNot=2506&IdSec=50.

[62]Vasconcellos, Carlos.

[63]Tubaínas mudam de cara e já controlam 32% do mercado.

[64]Rumo ao Passado: Coca-Cola Apela Para Garrafas De Vidro.

[65]"Taste Trends: Mexico and Brazil: Changing Competitive Landscapes," Latin American Equity Research, July 3, 2002, New York.

[66]AFX Asia, "Coca-Cola Brazil Targets Bigger Share of Guaraná-Based Soft Drinks Market," November 7, 2001.

[67]"There's a Liter of Subtility in Soft Drink Wars," Gazeta Mercantil Online (Brazil), June 14, 2002.

[68]Terra da Fanta.

[69]Penteado, Claudia.

[70]"Coca-Cola Investe Para Comercializar Guaraná Jesus Preferência," Mala Direta E Banco De Dados Evangélicos, in http://www.preferencia.com.br/porque_anunciar.htm, viewed on October 15, 2003.

[71]Rutkowski, Lauro.

[72]Barcellos, Marta, "Multinacionais baixam preço para competir," *Sala de Imprensa,* http://www.procter.com.br/materia_multinacionais.htm, viewed on October 15, 2003.

[73]Rumo ao Passado: Coca-Cola Apela Para Garrafas De Vidro.

[74]Gonçales, Marli, *"Dolly x Coca-Cola—Novas Denúncias,"* CMI Brasil, Centro De Mídia Independente, http://www.midiaindependente.org/pt/blue//2003/09/262669.shtml, May 9, 2003, viewed on October 15, 2003.

[75]http://oglobo.globo.com/jornal/colunas/ancelmo.asp, viewed on July 9, 2004.

[76]Rumo ao Passado: Coca-Cola Apela Para Garrafas de Vidro.

[77]Ibid.

[78]Ibid.

[79]Teixeira, Alexandre, "A Virada Arretada Da Coca-Cola Quarta-Feira."

[80]Ibid.

[81]Ibid.

[82]*Patrícia Cançado,* "A Sede Da RC Cola," *Isto É,* Jan 21, 2004, http://www.terra.com.br/istoedinheiro/333/-negocios/333_sede_rc_cola.htm, viewed on May 05, 2004.

[83]RC Cola Chega ao Brasil com Boa Aceitacao, http://www.odebate.com.br/noticias.asp?ID=20284, viewed on May 24, 2004.

Harley-Davidson in 2004

John E. Gamble
University of South Alabama

Roger Schäfer
University of South Alabama

Harley-Davidson's management had much to be proud of as the company wrapped up its Open Road Tour centennial celebration, which began in July 2002 in Atlanta, Georgia, and ended on the 2003 Memorial Day Weekend in Harley's hometown of Milwaukee, Wisconsin. The 14-month Open Road Tour was a tremendous success, drawing large crowds of Harley owners in each of its five stops in North America and additional stops in Australia, Japan, Spain, and Germany. Each stop along the tour included exhibits of historic motorcycles, performances by dozens of bands as diverse as Lynyrd Skynyrd, Earl Scruggs, and Nickelback, and brought hundreds of thousands of Harley enthusiasts together to celebrate the company's products. The Ride Home finale brought 700,000 biker-guests from four points in the United States to Milwaukee for a four-day party that included concerts, factory tours, and a parade of 10,000 motorcycles through downtown Milwaukee. The company also used the Open Road Tour as a platform for its support of the Muscular Dystrophy Association (MDA), raising $7 million for the MDA during the 14-month tour. Photos from the Open Road Tour and Harley's new V-Rod model are presented in Exhibit 1.

Harley-Davidson's centennial year was also a year to remember for the company's being named to *Fortune*'s annual list "The 100 Best Companies to Work For" and judged third in automotive quality behind Rolls-Royce and Mercedes-Benz by Harris Interactive, a worldwide market research and consulting firm best known for the Harris Poll. Consumer loyalty to Harley-Davidson motorcycles was unmatched by almost any other company. As a Canadian Harley dealer explained, "You know you've got strong brand loyalty when your customers tattoo your logo on their arm."[1] The company's revenues had grown at a compound annual rate of 16.6 percent since 1994 to reach $4.6 billion in 2003—marking its 18th consecutive year of record revenues and earnings. In 2003, the company sold more than 290,000 motorcycles, giving it a commanding share of the market for motorcycles in the 651+ cubic centimeters (cc) category in the United States and the leading share of the market in the Asia/Pacific region. The consistent growth had allowed Harley-Davidson's share price to appreciate by more than 15,000 percent since the company's initial public offering in 1986. In January 2004, the company's CEO, Jeffrey Bleustein, commented on the centennial year and the company's prospects for growth as it entered its second century:

> We had a phenomenal year full of memorable once-in-a-lifetime experiences surrounding our 100th Anniversary. As we begin our 101st year, we expect to grow the business further with our proven ability to deliver a continuous stream of exciting new motorcycles, related products, and services. We have set a new goal for the company to be able to satisfy a yearly demand of 400,000 Harley-Davidson motorcycles in 2007. By offering innovative products and services, and

Exhibit 1   **Photos from Harley-Davidson's Open Road Tour and Its VRSC V-Rod**

Source: Harley-Davidson Web site.

by driving productivity gains in all facets of our business, we are confident that we can deliver an earnings growth rate in the mid-teens for the foreseeable future.[2]

However, not everyone was as bullish on Harley-Davidson's future, with analysts pointing out that the company's plans for growth were too dependent on aging baby boomers. The company had achieved its record growth during the 1990s and early 2000s primarily through the appeal its image held for baby boomers in the United

Exhibit 2   SUMMARY OF HARLEY-DAVIDSON'S FINANCIAL PERFORMANCE, 1994–2003
(in thousands, except per share amounts)

	2003	2002	2001
Income statement data			
Net sales	$4,624,274	$4,090,970	$3,406,786
Cost of goods sold	2,958,708	2,673,129	2,253,815
Gross profit	1,665,566	1,417,841	1,152,971
Operating income from financial services	167,873	104,227	61,273
Selling, administrative and engineering	(684,175)	(639,366)	(551,743)
Income from operations	1,149,264	882,702	662,501
Gain on sale of credit card business	—	—	—
Interest income, net	23,088	16,541	17,478
Other income (expense), net	(6,317)	(13,416)	(6,524)
Income from continuing operations before provision for income taxes and accounting changes	1,166,035	885,827	673,445
Provision for income taxes	405,107	305,610	235,709
Income from continuing operations before accounting changes	760,928	580,217	437,746
Income (loss) from discontinued operations, net of tax	—	—	—
Income before accounting changes	760,928	580,217	437,746
Cumulative effect of accounting changes, net of tax	—	—	—
Net income (loss)	$ 760,928	$ 580,217	$ 437,746
Weighted average common shares:			
Basic	302,271	302,297	302,506
Diluted	304,470	305,158	306,248
Earnings per common share from continuing operations:			
Basic	$2.52	$1.92	$1.45
Diluted	$2.50	$1.90	$1.43
Dividends paid	$0.195	$0.135	$0.115
Balance sheet data			
Working capital	$1,773,354	$1,076,534	$ 949,154
Current finance receivables, net	1,001,990	855,771	656,421
Long-term finance receivables, net	735,859	589,809	379,335
Total assets	4,923,088	3,861,217	3,118,495
Short-term finance debt	324,305	382,579	217,051
Long-term finance debt	670,000	380,000	380,000
Total debt	994,305	762,579	597,051
Shareholders' equity	2,957,692	2,232,915	1,756,283

Source: Harley-Davidson, Inc., 2003, 2002, and 1998 10Ks.

States. Some observers wondered how much longer boomers would choose to spend recreational time touring the country by motorcycle and attending motorcycle rallies. The company had yet to develop a motorcycle that appealed in large numbers to motorcycle riders in their 20s or cyclists in Europe, both of whom preferred performance-oriented bikes over cruisers or touring motorcycles. Another concern of analysts watching the company was Harley-Davidson's short-term oversupply of certain models brought about by the 14-month production run for its 100th anniversary models. The

2000	1999	1998	1997	1996	1995	1994
$2,943,346	$2,482,738	$2,087,670	$1,762,569	$1,531,227	$1,350,466	$1,158,887
1,979,572	1,666,863	1,414,034	1,176,352	1,041,133	939,067	800,548
963,774	815,875	673,636	586,217	490,094	411,399	358,339
37,178	27,685	20,211	12,355	7,801	3,620	—
(485,980)	(427,701)	(360,231)	(328,569)	(269,449)	(234,223)	(204,777)
514,972	415,859	333,616	270,003	228,446	180,796	153,562
18,915	—	—	—	—	—	—
17,583	8,014	3,828	7,871	3,309	96	1,682
(2,914)	(3,080)	(1,215)	(1,572)	(4,133)	(4,903)	1,196
548,556	420,793	336,229	276,302	227,622	175,989	156,440
200,843	153,592	122,729	102,232	84,213	64,939	60,219
347,713	267,201	213,500	174,070	143,409	111,050	96,221
—	—	—	—	22,619	1,430	8,051
347,713	267,201	213,500	174,070	166,028	112,480	104,272
$ 347,713	$ 267,201	$ 213,500	$ 174,070	$ 166,028	$ 112,480	$ 104,272
302,691	304,748	304,454	151,650	150,683	149,972	150,440
307,470	309,714	309,406	153,948	152,925	151,900	153,365
$1.15	$0.88	$0.70	$1.15	$0.95	$0.74	$0.64
$1.13	$0.86	$0.69	$1.13	$0.94	$0.73	$0.63
$0.098	$0.088	$0.078	$0.135	$0.110	$0.090	$0.070
$ 799,521	$ 430,840	$ 376,448	$ 342,333	$ 362,031	$ 288,783	$ 189,358
530,859	440,951	360,341	293,329	183,808	169,615	—
234,091	354,888	319,427	249,346	154,264	43,829	—
2,436,404	2,112,077	1,920,209	1,598,901	1,299,985	980,670	676,663
89,509	181,163	146,742	90,638	8,065	—	—
355,000	280,000	280,000	280,000	250,000	164,330	—
444,509	461,163	426,742	391,572	285,767	185,228	10,452
1,405,655	1,161,080	1,029,911	826,668	662,720	494,569	433,232

effect of the extended production period shortened the waiting list for most models from over a year to a few months and left some models on showroom floors for immediate purchase. The combined effects of a market focus on a narrow demographic group, the difficulty experienced in gaining market share in Europe, and short-term forecasting problems led to a sell-off of Harley-Davidson shares going into 2004. Exhibit 2 presents a summary of Harley-Davidson's financial and operating performance for 1994–2003. Its market performance for 1994 through January 2004 is presented in Exhibit 3.

Exhibit 3   Monthly Performance of Harley-Davidson, Inc.'s Stock Price, 1994 to January 2004

(a) Trend in Harley-Davidson, Inc.'s Common Stock Price

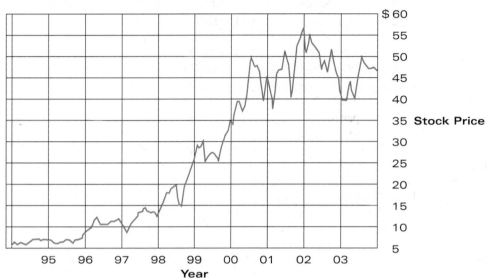

(b) Performance of Harley-Davidson, Inc.'s Stock Price Versus the S&P 500 Index

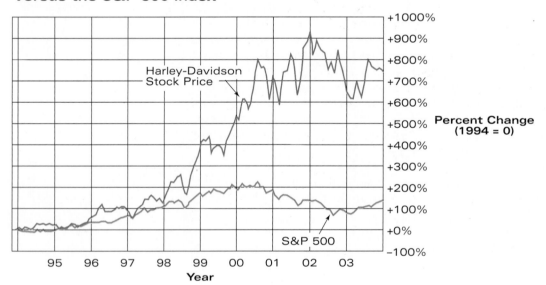

Company History

Harley-Davidson's history began in Milwaukee, Wisconsin, in 1903 when 20-year-old Arthur Davidson convinced his father to build a small shed in their backyard where Arthur and 21-year-old William Harley could try their hand at building a motorcycle. Various types of motorized bicycles had been built since 1885, but the 1901 development of a motorcycle with an integrated engine by a French company inspired Davidson and Harley to develop their own motorcycle. The two next-door neighbors built a two-horsepower engine that they fit onto a modified bicycle frame. At first the motorcycle could not pull itself and a rider up a steep hill, but after some additional tinkering, the first Harley-Davidson motorcycle could run as fast as 25 miles per hour. Milwaukee residents were amazed as Harley and Davidson rode the motorcycle down local streets, and by the end of the year the partners were able to produce and sell three of their motorcycles. Walter Davidson joined his brother and William Harley during the year to help assemble and race the company's motorcycles. In 1905, a Harley-Davidson motorcycle won a 15-mile race in Chicago with a time of 19:02, and by 1907 the company had developed quite a reputation in motorcycle racing with numerous wins in Milwaukee-area races. In 1907, another Davidson brother, William, joined the company and the company began adding dealers. Harley-Davidson's dealers helped the company sell 150 motorcycles in 1907.

In 1909, Harley-Davidson developed a more powerful seven-horsepower motorcycle engine to keep its edge in racing, an innovation that turned out to define the look of the company's motorcycles for the next century. Twin cylinders joined at a 45-degree angle became a trademark Harley-Davidson engine design characteristic and created a distinctive "potato-potato-potato" sound. Harley designed his V-twin engine with two pistons connected to a single crankpin, whereas later designs used crankpins for each piston. The single-crankpin design had been called an inferior design because it caused the pistons to come into firing positions at uneven intervals, which produced an uneven cadence in sound and excessive vibrations. Nevertheless, the vibrations and distinctive rumble of a Harley engine were accepted by the market in the early 1900s and continued to appeal to motorcyclists in the early 2000s.

The stronger engine allowed the company to produce 17,000 motorcycles for the U.S. military during World War I and become the largest motorcycle producer in the world in 1920, with 2,000 dealers in 67 countries. A number of features that make up Harley-Davidson's image originated during the 1920s, including the teardrop gas tank, the "Hog" nickname, and the "Flathead" engine design. Harley-Davidson was one of two U.S. motorcycle companies to survive the Great Depression—the other being Indian—by relying on exports and sales to police departments and the U.S. military. The 1930s saw Harley-Davidson win more races and develop additional elements of its differentiated image, including the art deco eagle design painted on its gas tanks, three-tone paint, and the "Knucklehead" engine rocker boxes. Harley-Davidson's 1936 EL model, or "Knucklehead," became its first highly styled motorcycle and formed the foundation of style elements that remained present in the highly demanded 2004 Softail Fat Boy. The company suspended production of civilian motorcycles in 1941 to produce almost 90,000 motorcycles for the U.S. military during World War II.

The recreational motorcycle market grew dramatically after World War II, as ex-GIs purchased motorcycles and led enthusiasm for riding. Harley-Davidson introduced new models for enthusiasts, including the Hydra-Glide in 1949, the K-model in 1952, the Sportster in 1957, and the Duo-Glide in 1958. The combination of racing success

(Harley-Davidson riders won 18 of 24 races and set six new racing records in 1950 alone) and innovative new Harley-Davidson models led to rival company Indian's demise in 1953. Harley-Davidson would remain the sole U.S. manufacturer of motorcycles until 1998, when the Indian brand was revived.

Harley-Davidson continued to win races throughout the 1960s, but its reputation began to erode soon after its acquisition by American Machine and Foundry Company (AMF) in 1969. Harley-Davidson under AMF was known for its leaking engines, unreliable performance, and poor customer service. At one point during AMF's ownership of the company, more than one-half of its bikes had to be repaired before leaving the factory. The company attempted to offset its declining sales of road bikes with the introduction of dirt bikes and snowmobiles in the early 1970s, but by the late 1970s AMF lost faith in the acquisition and slated it for divestiture. When no buyers for the company emerged, 13 executives engineered a leveraged buyout of Harley-Davidson in 1981. Harley-Davidson struggled under the heavy debt load and came within four hours of bankruptcy in 1985, before then-CEO Richard Teerlink was able to convince new creditors to step in and restructure Harley with less costly financing terms. Teerlink also launched a restructuring program that updated manufacturing methods, improved quality, and expanded the model line.

U.S. tariffs imposed on 651+ cc Japanese motorcycles also aided Harley-Davidson in gaining financial strength and competitiveness in the heavyweight segment of the U.S. motorcycle industry. Harley-Davidson completed an initial public offering in 1985 and petitioned the International Trade Commission to terminate tariffs on Japanese heavyweight motorcycles in 1987 when its market share in the U.S. heavyweight category had improved to 25 percent from 16 percent in 1985. In 1998, the company purchased Wisconsin-based Buell Motorcycle, a performance brand using Harley-Davidson engines that began as a venture between Erik Buell and Harley-Davidson in 1992. Harley-Davidson opened its 358,000-square-foot Kansas City, Missouri, plant in 1998 to produce Sportster, Dyna Glide, and V-Rod models and built an assembly plant in Brazil in 1999 to aid in its Latin American expansion. The new capacity allowed Harley-Davidson to set production records each year during the early 2000s to reach 290,000 units by year-end 2003.

Overview of the Motorcycle Industry

Demand for motorcycles in developed countries such as the United States, Germany, France, Spain, and Great Britain, grew dramatically at the end of World War II as veterans who enjoyed riding motorcycles during the war purchased their own bikes upon return to civilian life. Groups of enthusiasts began to form motorcycle clubs that allowed them to socialize and participate in rallies and races. Two of the earliest motorcycle rallies in the United States were the Daytona Bike Week and the Sturgis Rally. The first Daytona 200, which occurs during Bike Week, was run in 1937 on a 3.2-mile beach and road course. The first Sturgis, South Dakota, race took place in 1938 when nine participants raced a half-mile track and performed such stunts as jumping ramps and crashing through plywood walls. These and other such events grew dramatically in popularity beginning in the 1970s, with both Daytona Bike Week and the Sturgis Rally each drawing over 200,000 bikers in 2003. The Sturgis Rally was said to be among the most raucous motorcycle rallies in the United States, with plenty of public drunkenness and lewd behavior accompanying the seven days of races. Such behavior was common enough that the Rally Web site (www.sturgis.com) provided the fines and bonds associated with such offenses as indecent exposure, disorderly conduct, open container in public, and possession of controlled substances.

The rowdy and rebellious image of bikers is traced to some of the motorcycle clubs that began after World War II. The outlaw image of cyclists first developed in 1947 when *Life* magazine photographers captured images of an impromptu rally at Hollister, California, by a motorcycle group calling themselves the Boozefighters. The group became quite rowdy during their motorcycling exhibition, but *Life* reporters embellished the story significantly, claiming the Boozefighters descended on the town and proceeded to terrorize its residents by drag-racing down the main street, tossing beer bottles, and riding motorcycles through the front doors of the town's saloon. The imagery of the drunken Fourth of July attack on the town became etched deeper into the minds of the world when the story became the subject of *The Wild One,* a 1954 movie starring Marlon Brando. When asked by a local resident what he was rebelling against, Brando's character, Johnny, replied, "Whaddya got?"[3] The general public came to dislike bikers because of incidents like the one in Hollister and because of the Hollywood treatment of the event, but the Hells Angels made many people fearful of bikers and put motorcycle gangs under the close scrutiny of law enforcement at local, state, and federal levels.

The Hells Angels were established in 1948 in Fontana, California, by a group of young cyclists who had read of the Hollister rampage and wished to start their own outlaw biker group. The Hells Angels, who took their name and symbols from various World War II flying units, became notorious during the 1960s when they became linked to drug trafficking and other organized crime activities. Sonny Barger, a founder of the Oakland, California, chapter in the late 1950s, became the United States' most infamous biker after organizing a disastrous security effort for the 1969 Rolling Stones concert in Altamont at which one concertgoer was stabbed and killed by Hells Angels members. Barger, who had been convicted of attempted murder, possession of narcotics with intent to sell, and assault with a deadly weapon, commented in an interview with the British Broadcasting Corporation (BBC) that he pressed a pistol into Keith Richards' ribs and ordered him to continue to play after the Rolling Stones' guitarist threatened to end the show because of Hells Angels' rough tactics with fans.[4]

The Hells Angels and rival motorcycle clubs like the Pagans, the Banditos, and the Outlaws, rode only Harleys, which hurt Harley-Davidson's image with the public in the 1960s. Honda successfully exploited Harley's outlaw image with the slogan "You meet the nicest people on a Honda" to become the largest seller of motorcycles in the United States during the late 1960s and early 1970s.[5] The image of the Hells Angels had spilled over to the entire industry and contributed to declines in motorcycle demand in the United States and Europe during the 1960s before a new Hollywood film resurrected interest in motorcycles. *Easy Rider* (1969) portrayed bikers as less villainous rebels and appealed greatly to young people in the United States and Europe. The movie eventually gained cult status and helped charge a demand for motorcycles that began in the 1970s and continued through 2003. The red-white-and-blue 1951 Harley "Captain America" chopper ridden by Peter Fonda's Wyatt character helped Harley-Davidson break the outlaw image and come to represent less malevolent rebellion.

Industry Conditions in 2003

In 2003, more than 950,000 motorcycles were sold in the United States and 28 million motorcycles were in operation worldwide. The industry was expected to grow by approximately 5 percent annually through 2007 with light motorcycles, mopeds, and scooters accounting for most of the expected growth. A general increase in incomes in such emerging markets as China, India, and Southeast Asia was the primary force expected to drive industry growth. Demand growth for the heavyweight motorcycle category had outpaced smaller motorcycles in the United States during the 1990s and into 2003, but analysts projected that demand for larger motorcycles would decline as the population aged and became less able to travel on two-wheelers. In 2002, demand for heavyweight motorcycles in the United States grew by 17 percent compared to an industrywide growth rate of 10 percent.

The industry was segmented into various groups on the basis of engine size and vehicle style. Mopeds, scooters, and some small motorcycles were equipped with engines having displacements of 50 cubic centimeters (cc) or less. These motorbikes were best suited for urban areas where streets were narrow and parking was limited or for developing countries where personal incomes were limited and consumers could make only small investments in transportation. Motorcycles used for basic transportation or for motocross events were typically equipped with engines ranging from 125 cc to 650 cc. Larger street bikes required more power and usually had engines over 650 cc. Large motorcycles with engine displacements greater than 651 cc accounted for the largest portion of demand in North America and Europe as riders increasingly chose motorcycles with more horsepower and better performance. Exhibit 4 presents registrations of 651+ cc motorcycles in the United States, Europe, and Asia/Pacific for 1998–2003. Even though Europe had fewer registrations of 651+ cc motorcycles than the United States, it was the world's largest market for motorcycles, with 1.1 million registrations of 125+ cc motorcycles in 2002. Registrations of motorcycles with engine displacements greater than 125 cc in the largest European markets are presented in Exhibit 5.

Segmentation within the 651+ cc Category

Motorcycles in the 651+ cc segment were referred to as heavyweights and were grouped into four categories. Standard heavyweight motorcycles were designed for low-cost transportation and lacked many of the features and accessories of more expensive classes of heavyweights. Performance bikes had streamlined styling, low-profile fairings, and seat and handlebar configurations that required the rider to lean forward; they were characterized by responsive handling, rapid acceleration, and high top-end speeds. Custom motorcycles ranged from motorcycles with a custom paint scheme to highly personalized bikes painted with murals or other designs, chromed frames and other components, and accessories not found on stock motorcycles. The chopper, among the more unusual custom styles, was limited only by designers' imaginations but typically had extended forks, high handlebars, a narrow front tire, and a rigid "hardtail" frame design that lacked rear shocks and was stretched longer than normal motorcycles. Another notable feature of custom choppers was that they were almost always built from stock Harley-Davidson motorcycles, sometimes retaining only the engine.

Custom bikes were the largest segment of the U.S. heavyweight market for motorcycles and had become a curiosity for noncyclists. The Discovery Channel regularly aired two programs dedicated to the topic of choppers and other custom vehicles. The names of two custom motorcycle shops, West Coast Choppers (WCC) and Orange County Choppers, frequently made the Internet search engine Lycos's list of 50 most-searched terms. Jesse James, a descendent of the famous American Old West outlaw and owner of West Coast Choppers, also made Lycos's list of most searched terms. WCC charged between $60,000 and $150,000 for its custom motorcycles, which were usually sold to celebrities such as movie stars, professional athletes, and rock musicians.

Exhibit 4   MARKET SHARES OF THE LEADING PRODUCERS OF MOTORCYCLES BY
GEOGRAPHIC REGION FOR THE HEAVYWEIGHT SEGMENT, 1998–2003
(engine displacement of 651+ cc)

	2003	2002	2001	2000	1999	1998
New U.S. registrations (thousands of units)						
Total market new registrations	461.2	442.3	394.3	340	275.6	227.1
Harley-Davidson new registrations	228.4	209.3	177.4	155.1	134.5	109.1
Buell new registrations	3.5	2.9	2.6	4.2	3.9	3.2
Total company new registrations	231.9	212.2	180.0	159.3	138.4	112.3
Percentage market share						
Harley-Davidson motorcycles	49.5%	47.5%	45.0%	45.6%	48.8%	48.1%
Buell motorcycles	0.8	0.7	0.7	1.2	1.4	1.4
Total Harley-Davidson	50.3%	48.2%	45.7%	46.8%	50.2%	49.5%
Honda	18.4%	19.8%	20.5%	18.5%	16.4%	20.3%
Suzuki	9.8	9.6	10.8	9.3	9.4	10.0
Kawasaki	6.7	6.9	8.0	9.0	10.3	10.1
Yamaha	8.5	8.9	7.9	8.4	7.0	4.2
Other	6.3	6.6	7.1	8.0	6.7	5.9
Total	100.0%	100.0%	100.0%	100.0%	100.0%	100.0%
New European registrations (thousands of units)						
Total market new registrations	323.1	303.5	292.1	293.4	306.7	270.2
Total Harley-Davidson new registrations	26.3	20.1	19.6	19.9	17.8	15.7
Percentage market share						
Total Harley-Davidson	8.1%	6.6%	6.7%	6.8%	5.8%	5.8%
Honda	16.7	21.0	17.4	21.8	22.2	24.1
Yamaha	16.0	17.7	16.4	17.3	18.0	16.3
BMW	15.3	15.1	15.1	13.0	13.0	13.4
Suzuki	15.5	14.8	16.5	14.3	15.4	17.2
Other	28.4	24.8	27.9	26.8	25.6	23.2
Total	100.0%	100.0%	100.0%	100.0%	100.0%	100.0%
New Asia/Pacific registrations (thousands of units)						
Total market new registrations	58.9	63.9	62.1	62.7	63.1	69.2
Total Harley-Davidson new registrations	15.2	13.0	12.7	12.2	11.6	10.3
Percentage market share						
Total Harley-Davidson	25.8%	21.3%	20.4%	19.5%	18.5%	14.8%
Honda	17.8	19.1	17.3	20.4	22.4	28.0
Kawasaki	13.8	15.8	15.6	18.9	19.0	22.1
Yamaha	11.4	13.6	15.8	17.0	19.0	16.0
Suzuki	10.7	10.1	12.8	10.4	9.3	7.9
Other	20.5	20.1	18.1	13.8	11.8	11.2
Total	100.0%	100.0%	100.0%	100.0%	100.0%	100.0%

Source: Harley-Davidson, Inc., 10Ks and annual reports.

Exhibit 5   REGISTRATIONS OF NEW MOTORCYCLES IN MAJOR EUROPEAN MARKETS, 1998–2003 (engine displacement of 125+ cc)

Country	1998	1999	2000	2001	2002	2003
Germany	175,937	187,192	170,636	158,270	145,369	138,712
Italy	79,400	103,800	122,085	126,400	129,261	130,224
France	88,500	109,105	103,900	106,802	113,852	N/A
Great Britain	84,500	98,186	93,634	91,543	93,557	N/A
Spain	35,600	39,200	38,052	31,829	35,252	N/A

N/A = Not available.
Sources: Association des Constructeurs Européens de Motocycles, Brussels; Industrieverband Motorrad Deutschland e.V.

Touring bikes were set apart from other categories by creature comforts and accessories that included large fairings, storage compartments, CD players, cruise control, and other features typically found on cars rather than on motorcycles. Touring bikes were popular in the United States since many baby boomers wished to enjoy biking, but with some comfort. Comfortable saddles, upright riding positions, and other features found on touring bikes were especially welcomed by those who took cross-country or other long-distance journeys on their motorcycles. Custom and touring motorcycles were less popular outside of the United States since cyclists in other countries were more likely to travel only short distances and did not necessarily identify with the individualist or outlaw image associated with heavyweights in the United States. The largest segment of the heavyweight motorcycle category outside the United States was the performance bike category since most riders in other countries preferred sleek styling and were more interested in speed and handling rather than in comfort and tradition. In addition, motorcyclists in Europe and Asia tended to choose performance bikes over motorcycles in the custom and touring categories because of the high relative prices of such motorcycles. Exhibit 6 presents a regional comparison of motorcycle registrations by heavyweight category for 1998 through 2002.

Competition in the Global Motorcycle Industry

Rivalry in the motorcycle industry centered on performance, styling, breadth of product line, image and reputation, quality of after-the-sale service, and price. Most motorcycle manufacturers had good reputations for performance and styling with the greatest variance between brands occurring in pricing, variety of models, and quality of dealer service. Most cyclists preferred not to purchase specific brands, even if they were attracted to specific models, if the company's dealers did not have trained mechanics or had a reputation for shoddy workmanship or poor parts availability. There was also a great degree of price variability in the industry with comparable models of Japanese motorcycles typically carrying retail prices far below that of U.S.- or European-made motorcycles.

Exhibits 7 and 8 illustrate the difficulty U.S. and European manufacturers had experienced in attracting price-sensitive buyers in Europe. The Japanese producers were able to offer high-performance motorcycles at prices below those of Harley-Davidson, Ducati, Triumph, or Moto Guzzi. BMW had achieved considerable success in Europe, especially in Germany, because of exceptional performance and reputation, a strong dealer network, and regional loyalty to the brand.

Exhibit 6 **REGIONAL COMPARISON OF THE 651+ CC MOTORCYCLE MARKET BY SEGMENT,* 1998–2002 (percent of units registered)**

	1998	1999	2000	2001	2002
United States					
Custom	58.4%	57.7%	56.6%	58.9%	60.3%
Touring	20.4	21.7	21.1	20.3	20.2
Performance	19.4	18.9	20.4	19.1	17.3
Standard	1.8	1.8	2.0	1.7	2.2
	100.0%	100.0%	100.0%	100.0%	100.0%
Europe					
Custom	22.8%	20.2%	17.6%	17.8%	13.8%
Touring	5.3	5.5	5.2	5.2	4.8
Performance	59.8	58	61.7	59.8	61.2
Standard	12.1	16.3	15.5	17.2	20.2
	100.0%	100.0%	100.0%	100.0%	100%
Asia/Pacific					
Custom	18.3%	28.6%	26.7%	23.9%	n/a
Touring	3.9	4.7	3.7	7.2	n/a
Performance	76.1	64.5	66.2	65.5	n/a
Standard	1.7	2.2	3.5	3.4	n/a
	100.0%	100.0%	100.0%	100.0%	n/a

*Category definitions:

Custom: Characterized by "American styling." Often personalized by accessorizing.

Touring: Designed primarily for long trips, with an emphasis on comfort, cargo capacity, and reliability. Often have features such as two-way radios (for communication with passenger), stereo, and cruise control.

Performance: Characterized by quick acceleration, top speed, and handling. Commonly referred to as "sport bikes."

Standard: A basic, no-frills motorcycle with an emphasis on low price.

Source: Harley-Davidson, Inc., 2003 and 2002 10K reports.

Motorcycle manufacturers, like automobile manufacturers, maintained relationships with suppliers to produce or assemble components such as upholstery, tires, engine parts, brake parts, wiring harnesses, shocks, and rims. Almost without exception, the manufacturer designed and manufactured its engines and frames. Design and assembly of motorcycles took place in the manufacturers' home country, and completed motorcycles were exported to country markets where dealer networks had been established.

Consumers typically evaluated brands by talking to other cyclists, reading product reviews, perusing company Web sites, noting ads in print and other media, and noting a manufacturer's performance in competitive events. Typically, consumers had some ability to negotiate prices with dealers, but most preferred to buy from dealers with good service departments, large parts inventories, and attractive financing programs. Similarly, strong motorcycle dealers preferred to represent manufacturers with good reputations and strong consumer demand, responsive customer service and parts delivery, formal training programs for service technicians, and financing divisions that offered competitive rates and programs.

Consumers purchased motorcycles for various reasons. Some individuals, especially in developing countries, were looking for low-cost transportation. Lightweight motorcycles, mopeds, and scooters were priced inexpensively compared to cars and

Exhibit 7   MARKET SHARES OF THE LEADING SELLERS OF MOTORCYCLES IN GERMANY, 2001–2003 (engine displacement of 125+ cc)

Brand	2001 Market Share	2002 Market Share	2003 Market Share
BMW	16.0%	18.1%	19.5%
Suzuki	21.7	20.3	19.2
Yamaha	16.3	16.0	15.9
Honda	16.8	17.3	15.5
Kawasaki	11.1	10.7	10.6
KTM	3.1	3.8	4.4
Harley-Davidson	3.6	3.7	4.2
Ducati	2.8	2.8	2.9
Triumph	2.5	1.8	2.0
Aprilia	1.7	1.5	1.4
Moto Guzzi	0.6	0.7	0.9
Buell	0.4	0.3	0.6
MV/Cagiva	1.2	0.8	0.6
MZ	0.5	0.4	0.3
Sachs	0.3	0.2	0.2
Other	1.4	1.6	1.9
Total	100.0%	100.0%	100.0%

Sources: Kraftfahrtbundesamt; Industrieverband Motorrad Deutschland e.V.

Exhibit 8   BEST-SELLING MOTORCYCLE MODELS IN GERMANY, NOVEMBER 2003

Rank	Brand	Model	Manufacturers' Recommended Price (USD)	Year-to-Date 2003 Registrations	Heavyweight Classification
1	BMW	R 1150 GS	$14,500	6.242	Enduro/Touring
2	Suzuki	GSF 1200 (KL)	7,399	4.023	Performance
3	BMW	F 650 GS	8,190	3.524	Enduro/Touring
4	Suzuki	SV 650	6,299	3.444	Standard
5	Yamaha	FZS 600	6,499	3.294	Standard
6	Suzuki	GSF 600	6,299	3.182	Standard
7	Suzuki	GSX-R 1000	10,599	2.836	Performance
8	Kawasaki	Z1000	8,499	2.825	Performance
9	BMW	R 1150 RT	16,290	2.607	Touring
10	BMW	R 1150 R	9,990	2.539	Performance

Sources: Kraftfahrtbundesamt; Industrieverband Motorrad Deutschland e.V.

used far less gasoline. However, motorcycles provided no protection from the elements and were used only for fair-weather transportation by most riders who also owned a car. In the United States and Europe, most consumers who purchased a motorcycle also owned a car and preferred to travel by motorcycle on weekends or other times they were not working. Some in Europe did choose to commute to and from work on motorcycles when weather permitted because of limited parking available in large European cities and the high cost of fuel. Many motorcycle owners, particularly so in the United States, looked at riding as a form of recreation and had given up other sports or hobbies to spend time touring on motorcycles. Many middle-aged bikers in the United States had purchased motorcycles after giving up sports and activities requiring more athleticism or endurance.

Regulation and Legal Challenges

The motorcycle industry was subject to laws and regulations in all countries where motorcycles were operated. The European Parliament and the European Council included motorcycles in their agreement to reduce exhaust gas values during their March 2002 meeting. The agreement required producers of motorcycles and scooters to reduce pollutants by 60 percent for all new cycles produced after April 2003. A further 60 percent reduction would be required for motorcycles produced after January 2006. Demand for motorcycles in Europe was impacted to a great degree by the implementation of the euro in 2002; prices of motorcycles increased substantially in some countries when the currency exchange took effect. For instance, because Germany's currency was much stronger than that of many other European Union countries, prices of most products and services increased in Germany after the change to the euro since the euro attempted to equalize the differences between currencies. The difficulty in obtaining a driver's license for motorcycles in some European countries also affected demand for motorcycles. German laws required separate automobile and motorcycle licenses for riders of motorcycles larger than 125 cc, and France required those applying motorcycle licenses to have first held an automobile license for two years. Austria's licensing laws were the most restrictive, requiring applicants to first hold an automobile license for five years and to complete six training sessions prior to obtaining a motorcycle license. Motorcycles that produced excessive noise were also under attack in most European countries.

In the United States, motorcycle producers were subject to certification by the Environmental Protection Agency (EPA) for compliance with emission and noise standards, as well as agencies in some states imposing more stringent noise and emission standards. The California Air Resources Board (CARB) had outlined new tailpipe emission standards that would go into effect in 2004 and 2008. The EPA developed new emission standards that would go into effect in 2006 and 2010 to match national standards with those in California. Motorcycle producers in the United States were also required to meet the product safety standards imposed by the National Highway Traffic Safety Administration (NHTSA).

Also in the United States, many motorcyclists found that their health insurance providers excluded coverage for any injuries sustained while on a motorcycle. The American Motorcyclists Association (AMA) had successfully petitioned the U.S. Senate to pass a bill in October 2003 that would prohibit insurance companies from denying coverage to someone hurt while riding a motorcycle, a snowmobile, or an all-terrain vehicle. Insurance companies had based their policies on NHTSA statistics that found motorcycling to be much more dangerous than traveling by car. While traffic fatalities per 100 million vehicle miles traveled hit a historic low in 2002, motorcycle fatalities had increased for a fifth consecutive year, to reach 3,244 deaths. There were 42,815 traffic fatalities in 2002 involving occupants of automobiles. Fatalities involving motorcyclists ages 50 and older increased by 26 percent during 2002—a higher rate of increase than any other age demographic. State legislatures in some states where helmets were optional had attempted to force motorcyclists who chose not to wear helmets to become mandatory organ donors. However, the AMA and its membership had successfully stopped all such attempts to pass mandatory organ donor laws.

Harley-Davidson's Strategy for Competing in the Motorcycle Industry

Harley-Davidson was reincorporated in 1981 after it was purchased from AMF by 13 of its managers through a leveraged buyout (LBO). The management team's main focus at the time was to preserve jobs, but its members soon realized the company would need to be rebuilt from the ground up to survive. The company's market share in the United States had fallen to 3 percent, primarily because its products were unreliable and had poorer performance relative to less-expensive Japanese motorcycles. In addition, its network of dealers ran greasy, run-down shops that many people didn't feel comfortable visiting. Upon assessing the company's situation, the management team concluded that a strong allegiance to the Harley brand by many bikers was the company's only resource strength. However, when managers began to meet with customers, they found that longtime Harley riders felt cheated by the company and were angry about the lack of attention to product quality and customer service under AMF ownership. Some of the most loyal Harley riders refused to call models produced in the 1970s Harleys, preferring to label them as AMFs. After the LBO, Harley management tried to win over previous customers by attending any function at which motorcyclists congregated. The company's director of communications at the time commented in a 2003 interview with a trade publication, "At first we found that our customers didn't like us, and they didn't trust us."[6] However, the distrust subsided when Harley owners saw their suggestions being implemented by the company.

Harley-Davidson's turnaround strategy including improving product quality by adopting Japanese management practices, abandoning a reliance on advertising in favor of promotions at motorcycle rallies, and improving its dealer network to broaden its appeal to new customers. After hearing complaints about dealers from Harley riders at rallies and other bike events, Harley-Davidson conducted a pilot program with two dealers in Milwaukee that called for the dealers to build clean, attractive stores to showcase the company's improved motorcycles and display apparel and other merchandise that cyclists might wish to purchase. The two dealerships recaptured their investments within 18 months, while other dealers struggled. The pilot program led to new or remodeled dealerships across the Harley-Davidson network and helped the company enter into a new product category. Harley showrooms offered a large assortment of clothing items and accessories—for example, leather jackets, T-shirts, helmets, and boots—in addition to new motorcycles. In 2003 Harley-Davidson introduced 1,200 new clothing items and licensed its name to more than 100 manufacturers making everything from Harley-Davidson Edition Ford F-150 pickups to Harley Barbie dolls. Apparel and accessories were so important to the company and its dealers that in 2003 every dealer had a fitting room.

Cultivating Loyalty through HOG Membership

After Harley-Davidson's product quality issues had been resolved, the company focused on cultivating the mystique of Harley ownership. The company formed Harley

Owners Groups (HOGs) in 1983 to provide Harley owners with local chapters through which they could socialize and ride with other owners. Harley-Davidson established HOGs in cities where dealers were located, but did not interfere with HOG operations or try to use the organization in a self-serving way. The company's primary interest in setting up the chapters was to give motorcycle buyers a sense of community. Management understood that once new owners came to feel they belonged to the Harley community, they would bring new buyers to the company without any encouragement from Harley-Davidson.

The company provided each new Harley buyer with a free membership to a HOG where they could not only meet other area bikers but also learn the ins and outs of the biker world. HOGs also organized rides, raised money for charities, and participated in nationwide HOG events. Owners were required to renew their free memberships each year to ensure that only active participants would be on chapter roles. The HOG organization started with 33,000 members in 1983 and had grown to 793,000 members in 1,200 chapters in 2003. The company sponsored about 100 HOG rallies in 2003, with thousands of additional events organized by local chapters.

Harley's Image and Appeal with Baby Boomers

Even though Harley sold many motorcycles to construction workers, mechanics, and other blue-collar workers, Harley riders included a great many accountants, lawyers, bankers, and corporate executives. In 2003, Harley-Davidson's typical customer was a 46-year-old male earning $78,000 per year. The company had successfully added upscale consumers to its list of customers without alienating traditional bikers. Some of the more traditional bikers did complain about the new breed of "bean counter Harley owners," sometimes calling them "rubbers"—rich urban bikers. Such concern had been calmed to some degree by William G. Davidson's continuing involvement with the company. "Willie G." was the grandson of the company's cofounder and, as chief designer, had designed every motorcycle for the company since the 1960s. Willie G. was an "old-school" biker himself and rationalized the company's alliance with upscale baby boomers with comments such as "There's a lot of beaners, but they're out on the motorcycles, which is a beautiful thing."[7]

Part of the appeal of HOG membership was that new motorcyclists could experience freedom of the open road, much like a Hells Angel might, if only during occasional weekends when the weather was nice. Some middle-aged professionals purchased Harleys because riding was an opportunity to recreate and relax without being reminded of their daily responsibilities. Belonging to an HOG or other riding group was different from joining a country club or other club dominated by upper-income families; as the CEO of a Fortune 500 company explained, "Nobody cares what anybody else does. We share a common bond of freedom on a bike." This same Harley owner claimed that after a few hours of riding, he forgets he's a CEO.[8] Another affluent Harley owner suggested that Harley owners from all walks of life shared the brotherhood of the open road: "It doesn't matter if you make $10,000 a year or $300,000."[9] Others suggested that Harley ownership gave you an identity and provided you with a close group of friends in an increasingly anonymous culture.

However, other Harley owners were lured by the appeal of Harley-Davidson's outlaw image. The editor of *AARP Magazine* believed that baby boomers purchased Harleys because of a desire to feel "forever young."[10] The *AARP Magazine* editor said that riding a Harley helped take boomers back to a time when they had less responsibility. "You saw 'Easy Rider.' As a kid, you had a bit of a wild period in the '70s and you associate the motorcycle with that. But you got married. You had kids and a career. Now you can afford this. It's a safe way to live out a midlife crisis. It's a lot safer than running off with a stewardess."[11] In fact, many of Harley-Davidson's competitors have claimed that Harley sells lifestyles, not motorcycles. Harley-Davidson CEO Jeffrey Bleustein commented on the appeal of the company's motorcycles by stating, "Harley-Davidson stands for freedom, adventure, individual expression and being a little on the edge, a little bit naughty. People are drawn to the brand for those reasons."[12]

The desire to pose as a Hells Angel, Peter Fonda's Wyatt character, or Brando's Johnny helped Harley-Davidson sell more than 290,000 motorcycles and over $200 million in general merchandise in 2003. Many of Harley-Davidson's 1,400 dealers dedicated as much as 75 percent of their floor space to apparel and accessories, with most suggesting that between 25 and 40 percent of their annual earnings came from the sale of leather jackets, chaps, boots, caps, helmets, and other accessories. One dealer offered her opinion of what drove merchandise sales by commenting, "Today's consumer tends to be a little more affluent, and they want the total look."[13] The dealer also said that approximately 5 percent of the dealership's apparel sales were to non–bike owners who wanted the biker image. Even though some high-income baby boomers wanted to be mistaken from a distance for Hells Angels' "1 percenters"—the most rebellious 1 percent of the population—for most it was all show. When looking out at the thousands of leather-clad bikers attending Harley-Davidson's 2003 Memorial Day centennial celebration in Milwaukee, a Harley owner said, "The truth is, this is mostly professional people . . . People want to create an image. Everybody has an alter side, an alter ego. And this is a chance to have that."[14]

Another Harley owner who had ridden his Heritage Softail from his home in Sioux Falls, South Dakota, to attend the centennial event commented on his expectations for revelry during the four-day celebration by pointing out, "Bikers like to party pretty big. It's still a long way to go before you forget the image of the Hells Angels."[15] However, weekend bikers were quite different from the image they emulated. The Hells Angels continued to be linked to organized crime into 2003, with nine Hells Angels members being convicted in September 2003 of drug trafficking and murdering at least 160 people, most of whom were from rival gangs.[16] Similarly, Hells Angels organizations in Europe had been linked to drug trafficking and dozens of murders.[17] Fifty-seven Angels in the United States were arrested in December 2003 for crimes such as theft of motorcycles, narcotics trafficking, and firearms and explosives trafficking following a two-year investigation of the motorcycle club by the Bureau of Alcohol, Tobacco, Firearms and Explosives.[18]

Harley-Davidson balanced its need to promote freedom and rebellion against its need to distance the company from criminal behavior. Its Web site pointed out that "the vast majority of riders throughout the history of Harley-Davidson were law-abiding citizens," and the company archivist proposed, "Even those who felt a certain alienation from society were not lawless anarchists, but people who saw the motorcycle as a way to express both their freedom and their identity."[19] When looking at the rows of Harleys glistening in the sun in front of his Southern California roadside café, the long-time proprietor of one of the biggest biker shrines in the United States commented, "There used to be some mean bastards on those bikes. I guess the world has changed."[20] A Harley-Davidson dealer commented that dealers considered hardcore bikers "1 percenters" because they made up less than 1 percent of a dealer's annual sales. The dealer found that very affluent buyers made up about 10 percent of sales, with the remainder of customers making between $40,000 and $100,000 per year.[21]

Harley-Davidson's Product Line

Unlike Honda and Yamaha, Harley-Davidson did not produce scooters and mopeds, nor did it manufacture motorcycles with engine displacements less than 651 cc. In addition, Harley-Davidson did not produce dirt bikes or performance bikes like those offered by Kawasaki and Suzuki. Of the world's major motorcycle producers, BMW produced bikes that most closely resembled Harley-Davidson's traditional line, although BMW also offered a large number of performance bikes. In 2004, Harley-Davidson's touring and custom motorcycles were grouped into five families: Sportster, Dyna Glide, Softail, Touring, and the VRSC V-Rod. The Sportster, Dyna Glide, and VRSC models were manufactured in the company's Kansas City, Missouri, plant, while Softail and Touring models were manufactured in York, Pennsylvania. Harley-Davidson considered the Sportster, Dyna Glide, and VRSC models custom bikes, while Softails and Touring models fell into the Touring industry classification. Sportsters and Dyna Glides each came in four model variations, while Softails came in six variations and Touring bikes came in seven basic configurations. The VRSC V-Rod came in two basic styles. Harley-Davidson produced three models of its Buell performance bikes in its East Troy, Wisconsin, plant. In 2004, Harley Sportsters carried retail prices ranging from $6,495 to $8,675; Dyna Glide models sold at price points between $11,995 and $16,580; VRSC V-Rods sold between $16,895 and $17,995; Softails were offered between $13,675 and $17,580; and the Road King and Electra Glide touring models sold at prices between $16,995 and $20,405. Consumers could also order custom Harleys through the company's Custom Vehicle Operations (CVO) unit, started in 1999. Customization and accessories on CVO models could add as much as $10,000 to the retail price of Harley-Davidson motorcycles. Images of Harley-Davidson's five product families and CVO models can be viewed at www.harley-davidson.com.

Honda, Kawasaki, Suzuki, and Yamaha had all introduced touring models that were very close replicas of Harley Sportsters, DynaGlides, Road Kings, and Electra Glides. The Japanese producers had even copied Harley's signature V-twin engine and had tuned their dual-crankpin designs in an attempt to copy the distinctive sound of a Harley-Davidson engine. However, even with prices up to 50 percent less on comparable models, none of the Japanese producers had been able to capture substantial market share from Harley-Davidson in the United States or in their home markets. (Refer back to Exhibit 4 for a breakdown of market shares in the heavyweight segment in the U.S., Europe, and Asia/Pacific regions.) Indian Motorcycle Corporation had experienced similar difficulties gaining adequate market share in the U.S. heavyweight segment and ceased its operations for a second time in September 2003.

Harley-Davidson's difficulties in luring buyers in the performance segment of the industry were similar to challenges that Japanese motorcycle producers had encountered in their attempts to gain market share in the custom and touring categories of the U.S. heavyweight motorcycle segment. Harley-Davidson had co-developed and later purchased Buell to have a product that might appeal to motorcyclists in the United States who were in their 20s and did not identify with the *Easy Rider* or Hells Angels images or who did not find Harley-Davidson's traditional styling appealing. Harley management also believed that Buell's performance street-racer-style bikes could help it gain market share in Europe, where performance bikes were highly popular. The Buell brand competed exclusively in the performance category against models offered by Honda, Yamaha, Kawasaki, Suzuki, and lesser-known European brands such as Moto Guzzi, Ducati, and Triumph. Buell prices began at $4,595 for its Blast model to better compete with Japanese motorcycles on price as well as on performance and styling. Buell's Lighting and Firebolt models were larger, faster motorcycles and retailed for between $9,000 and $11,000. The VSRC V-Rod, with its liquid-cooled, Porsche-designed engine, was also designed to appeal to buyers in the performance segment of the industry, both in the United States and Europe.

As of 2004, Harley-Davidson had not gained a significant share of the performance motorcycle segment in the United States or Europe. Some industry analysts criticized Harley-Davidson's dealers for the lackluster sales of V-Rod and Buell models since most dealers did little to develop employees' sales techniques. Demand for Harleys had exceeded supply since the early 1990s, and most dealers' sales activities were limited to taking orders and maintaining a waiting list. In addition, most Harley-Davidson dealers had been able to charge $2,000 to $4,000 over the suggested retail price for new Harley-Davidson motorcycles, although most dealers had begun to sell Harleys at sticker price in 2003. Harley-Davidson's revenues by product group are shown below:

HARLEY-DAVIDSON REVENUES BY PRODUCT GROUP (in millions)

	2003	2002	2001
Harley-Davidson motorcycles	$3,621.5	$3,161.0	$2,671.3
Buell motorcycles	76.1	66.9	61.7
Total motorcycles	3,697.6	3,227.9	2,733.0
Motorcycle Parts and Accessories	712.8	629.2	509.6
General Merchandise	211.4	231.5	163.9
Other	2.5	2.4	0.3
Net revenue	$4,624.3	$4,091.0	$3,406.8

Source: Harley-Davidson, Inc., 2002 and 2003 annual reports.

The number of Harley-Davidson and Buell motorcycles shipped annually between 1998 and 2003 is presented in Exhibit 9.

Distribution and Sales in North America, Europe, and Asia/Pacific

Harley-Davidson's dealers were responsible for operating showrooms where motorcycles could be examined and test-ridden, stocking parts and accessories that existing owners might need, operating service departments, and selling biking merchandise such as apparel, boots, helmets, and various Harley-Davidson-branded gift items. Some Harley owners felt such strong connections to the brand that they either gave or asked for Harley gifts for birthdays, weddings, and anniversaries. Some Harley owners had even been married at Harley-Davidson dealerships or at HOG rallies. Harley-Davidson dealers were also responsible for distributing newsletters and promoting rallies for local HOG chapters. The 10,000-member Buell Riders Adventure Group (BRAG) was also supported by Harley-Davidson dealers.

Harley mechanics and other dealership personnel were trained at the Harley-Davidson University (HDU) in Milwaukee, where they took courses in such subjects as retail management, inventory control, merchandising, customer service, diagnostics, maintenance, and engine service techniques. More than 17,000 dealership employees took courses at the company's university in 2002. Harley-Davidson also provided in-dealership courses through its Web-based distance learning program. In 2002, HDU

Exhibit 9 ANNUAL SHIPMENTS OF HARLEY-DAVIDSON AND BUELL MOTORCYCLES, 1998–2003

	2003	2002	2001	2000	1999	1998
Harley-Davidson						
Sportster	57,165	51,171	50,814	46,213	41,870	33,892
Custom*	151,405	141,769	118,303	100,875	87,806	77,434
Touring	82,577	70,713	65,344	57,504	47,511	39,492
	291,147	263,653	234,461	204,592	177,187	150,818
Domestic	237,656	212,833	186,915	158,817	135,614	110,902
International	53,491	50,820	47,546	45,775	41,573	39,916
	291,147	263,653	234,461	204,592	177,187	150,818
Buell						
Buell (exc. Blast)	8,784	6,887	6,436	5,043	7,767	6,334
Buell Blast	1,190	4,056	3,489	5,416	—	—
	9,974	10,943	9,925	10,189	7,767	6,334

*Custom includes Softail, Dyna Glide, and VRSC.
Source: Harley-Davidson, Inc., 2002 and 2003 annual reports.

held 665 instructor-led classes, 115 online classes, and had participation in their courses by 96 percent of the company's dealers.

The company also held demo rides in various locations throughout the United States, and many Harley dealers offered daily rentals designed to help novices decide whether they really wanted a motorcycle. Some dealers also rented motorcycles for longer periods to individuals who wished to take long-distance trips. Harley-Davidson motorcycles could also be rented from third parties like EagleRider—the world's largest renter of Harleys, with 29 locations in the United States and Europe. Harley-Davidson's Riders Edge motorcycle training courses were also offered by quite a few dealers in North America, Europe, and Asia/Pacific. The company had found that inexperienced riders and women were much more likely to purchase motorcycles after taking a training course. Harley-Davidson management believed the 25-hour Riders Edge program had contributed to the company's increased sales to women, which had increased from 2 percent of total sales prior to the adoption of the program to 9 percent in 2003.

In 2003, Harley-Davidson motorcycles were sold by 644 independently owned and operated dealerships across the United States. Buell motorcycles were also sold by 436 of these dealers. There were no Buell-only dealerships, and 81 percent of Harley dealers in the United States sold Harley-Davidson motorcycles exclusively. The company also sold apparel and merchandise in about 50 nontraditional retail locations such as malls, airports, and tourist locations. The company's apparel was also available seasonally in about 20 temporary locations in the United States where there was significant tourist traffic. The company also had three nontraditional merchandise outlets in Canada, where it had 76 independent dealers and one Buell dealership. Thirty-two of its Canadian Harley dealers also sold Buell motorcycles.

Harley-Davidson had 161 independent dealers in Japan, 50 dealers and three distributors in the Australian/New Zealand market and seven other dealers scattered in smaller East and Southeast Asian markets. Only 73 of Harley-Davidson's Asia/Pacific

Exhibit 10   HARLEY-DAVIDSON'S NET REVENUES AND LONG-LIVED ASSETS BY BUSINESS GROUP AND GEOGRAPHIC REGION, 2000–2003

	2003	2002	2001	2000
Motorcycles net revenue				
United States	$3,807,707	$3,416,432	$2,809,763	$2,357,972
Europe	419,052	337,463	301,729	285,372
Japan	173,547	143,298	141,181	148,684
Canada	134,319	121,257	96,928	93,352
Other foreign countries	89,649	72,520	57,185	57,966
	$4,624,274	$4,090,970	$3,406,786	$2,943,346
Financial services income				
United States	$260,551	$199,380	$172,593	$132,684
Europe	8,834	4,524	1,214	655
Canada	10,074	7,596	7,738	6,796
	$279,459	$211,500	$181,545	$140,135
Long-lived assets				
United States	$1,400,772	$1,151,702	$1,021,946	$856,746
Other foreign countries	41,804	36,138	33,234	27,844
	$1,442,576	$1,187,840	$1,055,180	$884,590

Source: Harley-Davidson, Inc., 2002 and 2003 10Ks.

also sold Buell motorcycles. The company also had two dealers that sold Buell but not Harley-Davidson motorcycles. Harley-Davidson motorcycles were sold in 17 Latin American countries by 32 dealerships. The company did not have a dealer for its Buell motorcycles in Latin America, but had 13 retail stores carrying only apparel and merchandise in the region.

The company's European distribution division based in the United Kingdom served 32 countries in Europe, the Middle East, and Africa. The European region had 436 independent dealers, with 313 choosing to also carry Buell motorcycles. Buell motorcycles were also sold in Europe by 10 dealers that were not Harley dealers. Harley-Davidson also had 26 nontraditional merchandise retail locations in Europe.

Exhibit 10 presents the company's revenues by geographic region, along with the division of assets in the United States and abroad and a breakdown of financial services revenues by region. The company's financial services unit provided retail financing to consumers and wholesale financial services to dealers, including inventory floor plans, real estate loans, computer loans, and showroom remodeling loans.

Challenges Confronting Harley-Davidson as It Entered Its Second Century

As Harley-Davidson entered its second century in 2004, the company not only celebrated a successful centennial celebration that brought more than 700,000 of Harley's most loyal customers to Milwaukee but also a successful year with record shipments, revenues, and earnings. New capacity had allowed the company's shipments to increase to more than 290,000 units, which drove annual revenues to $4.6 billion and net earnings to nearly $761 million. The company's planned 350,000-square-foot expansion of its York, Pennsylvania, plant would allow the company to increase production to 400,000 units by 2007. However, there was some concern that the company might not need the additional capacity.

Some market analysts had begun to believe Harley-Davidson's stock was approaching its apex because of the aging of its primary baby boomer customer group. Between 1993 and 2003, the average age of the company's customers had increased from 38 to 46. The average age of purchasers of other brands of motorcycles in 2003 was 38. Some analysts suspected, that within the next 5 to 10 years, fewer baby boomers would be interested in riding motorcycles and Harley's sales might begin to decline. Generation X buyers were not a large enough group to keep Harley's sales at the 2003 level, which would cause the company to rely on Generation Y (or echo boomer) consumers. However, most Generation Y motorcyclists had little interest in the company's motorcycles and did not identify with the *Easy Rider* or outlaw biker images that were said to appeal to baby boomers. The company's V-Rod motorcycle had won numerous awards for its styling and performance, but its $17,000-plus price tag kept most 20-year-olds away from Harley showrooms. Similarly, Buell motorcycles were critically acclaimed in terms of performance and styling but had been unable to draw performance-minded consumers in the United States or Europe away from Japanese street-racing-style bikes to any significant degree.

Europe was the largest market for motorcycles overall, and the second largest market for heavyweight motorcycles, but Harley-Davidson had struggled in building share in the region. In some ways the company's 6+ percent market share in Europe was impressive since only 4.8 percent of motorcycles purchased in 2002 were touring cycles and custom cycles accounted for only 13.8 percent of motorcycles sold in Europe during 2002. The V-Rod's greatest success was in Europe, but neither the V-Rod nor any other HD model had become one of the top-10 best-selling models in any major European market.

There was also some concern that Harley-Davidson's 14-month production run had caused an unfavorable short-term production problem since the company's waiting list, which required a two-year wait in the late 1990s, had fallen to about 90 days beginning in mid-2003. The overavailability of 2003 models had caused Harley-Davidson's management to adopt a 0 percent down payment financing program that began at midyear 2003 and would run through February 2004. When asked about the program during a television interview, Harley-Davidson CEO Jeffery Bleustein justified it by noting, "It's not zero percent financing, as many people understood it to be, its zero dollars down, and normal financing. The idea there was to get the attention of some of the people who aren't riding Harleys and are used to a world of other motorcycles where there's always a financing program of some sort going on. We just wanted to get their attention."[22] By year-end 2003, dealer inventories had declined to about 2,000 units and many dealers again began charging premiums over list price, but not the $2,000–$4,000 premiums charged in prior years.

Endnotes

[1] As quoted in "Analyst Says Harley's Success Had Been to Drive into Buyers' Hearts," *Canadian Press Newswire*, July 14, 2003.
[2] As quoted in January 21, 2004, press release.
[3] As quoted in "Wings of Desire," *The Independent*, August 27, 2003.
[4] As quoted in "Born to Raise Hell," *BBC News Online*, August 14, 2000.

[5]"Wheel Life Experiences," *Whole Pop Magazine Online.*

[6]As quoted in "Will Your Customers Tattoo Your Logo?" *Trailer/Body Builders,* March 1, 2003, p. 5.

[7]As quoted in "Will Harley-Davidson Hit the Wall?" *Fortune,* July 22, 2002.

[8]As quoted in "Even Corporate CEOs Buy Into the Harley-Davidson Mystique, *Milwaukee Journal-Sentinel,* August 24, 2003.

[9]As quoted in "Harley-Davidson Goes Highbrow at Annual Columbia, S.C., H.O.G. Rally," *The State,* September 26, 2003.

[10]As quoted in "Even Corporate CEOs."

[11]Ibid.

[12]As quoted in "Milwaukee-Based Harley-Davidson Rides into Future with Baby Boomers Aboard," *The News-Sentinel,* August 5, 2003.

[13]As quoted in "Harley-Davidson Fans Sport Motorcycle Style," *Detroit Free Press,* August 28, 2003.

[14]As quoted in "Bikers Go Mainstream 100 Years On," *Global News Wire,* September 11, 2003.

[15]Ibid.

[16]"Nine Montreal Hells Angels Sentenced to 10 to 15 Years in Prison," *CNEWS,* September 23, 2003.

[17]"Hells Angels: Easy Riders or Criminal Gang?," *BBC News,* January 2, 2004.

[18]"Feds Raid Hells Angels' Clubhouses," *CBSNews.com,* December 4, 2003.

[19]As quoted in "Wings of Desire," *Global News Wire,* August 27, 2003.

[20]Ibid.

[21]Interview with Mobile, Alabama, Harley-Davidson dealership personnel.

[22]As quoted in a CNNfn interview conducted on *The Money Gang,* June 11, 2003..

Globalizing Volkswagen
Creating Excellence on All Fronts

Z. Jan Kubes
International Institute for Management Development

George Rädler
International Institute for Management Development

Is there room for Volkswagen? As its market shrinks, Europe seems to have one car-maker too many. Could it be troubled Volkswagen? (. . .) The biggest danger is that with its problems at home and abroad, VW will have to abandon any notion of becoming a global car maker.

—*The Economist*, August 28, 1993: 59

No doubt about it: Volkswagen CEO Ferdinand Piëch engineered one of Europe's greatest turnarounds ever. The grandson of auto pioneer Ferdinand Porsche inherited a loss of more than $1 billion and declining market share in 1993. With a battery of new models, Piëch seized European market share from Ford Motor Company and General Motors Corp. Including its Audi, Skoda and Seat brands, VW now has almost 19 percent of Western European car sales, up from a low of 15 percent in 1994. Profits last year topped $1.2 billion on sales of $71.4 billion.

—*Business Week*, November 22, 1999: 20

When Dr. Ferdinand Piëch took over as CEO of the Volkswagen Group (VW) in early 1993, things did not look good: Customers complained about high prices, the main factory in Wolfsburg, Germany was only breaking even at utilization rates above 100 percent, and Japanese competitors enjoyed a cost advantage of up to €2,500 per car in their newly built plants in the UK. 1992 ended with profits down 85 percent.

By 2001 the situation looked totally different. VW was the market leader in Europe, China, and South America (refer to Exhibit 1 for market data); sales of the VW brand in the United States had increased sevenfold between 1993 and 2001. Overall, VW was the world's fourth-largest car company offering 65 models (up from 30), reported record profits, and newly acquired luxury brands created growth potential. At home, VW engaged in unusual ventures: "Autostadt," a €420 million auto theme park, followed by a revolutionary €180 million car plant and event center in the heart of Dresden.

With Piëch stepping down in April 2002, how could VW maintain spectacular results, clearly outperforming the competition?

Exhibit 1   KEY MARKETS OF THE VOLKSWAGEN GROUP (all brands)

	Deliveries 2001 (units)	Change over 2000 (%)	Share of Passenger Car Market 2001 (%)	Share of Passenger Car Market 2000 (%)
Worldwide	5,083,547	+0.4	12.4	12.2
Western Europe	2,980,144	−0.6	18.9	18.7
Germany	988,762	−3.6	30.2	29.8
Spain	348,744	+3.1	23.4	23.2
Italy	312,036	+1.7	12.3	11.8
Great Britain	307,944	+16.4	11.8	11.2
France	280,434	+3.4	11.4	11.2
Central/Eastern Europe	329,790	+10.0	15.4	14.0
Czech Republic	98,471	+3.1	61.6	60.9
Poland	71,775	−3.7	20.8	14.8
North America	669,495	+1.8	6.6	6.3
United States (import market)	439,784	+0.7	10.1	10.4
Canada	49,463	+0.7	5.7	5.8
Mexico	180,248	+5.1	25.8	27.8
South America/Africa	555,106	+3.8	22.7	23.1
Brazil	436,824	+7.1	28.6	29.9
Argentina	28,165	−41.9	18.5	17.9
South Africa	57,888	+13.2	22.9	21.4
Asia-Pacific	461,054	+7.2	5.4	5.3
China	358,879	+6.9	51.3	53.2
Japan (import market)	68,514	+6.3	27.3	26.5

Source: Volkswagen annual report 2001, p. 24.

Background: The 1990s and Beyond in the Car Industry[1]

In 1990 the Massachusetts Institute of Technology (MIT) published a report on car manufacturing. The report ("The Machine that Changed the World") presented the findings of a five-year study on efficient car manufacturing around the globe. The findings were revolutionary. Due to lean production, just in time (JIT), and kanban, Japanese factories were on average 35 percent more efficient than their European counterparts. This was a considerable figure, as purchasing and manufacturing accounted for 63 percent of the value chain (refer to Exhibit 2 for the value chain). This report indeed changed the world of automotive manufacturing as non-Japanese manufacturers tried to catch up with these skills. They were soon transferred to many other industries.

During the 1990s the car industry had been characterized by a high rate of innovation in products and processes. Customers were increasingly looking for lifestyle/niche models. Until 1987 the car market had been grouped into 9 segments, but by 1997 it consisted of 26 segments. Some market researchers could already foresee 50 or more segments by the year 2005. In fact, light commercial vehicles (minivans, jeeps, and pick-up trucks) accounted for half of all vehicles sold in the United

Exhibit 2   **Value Chain**

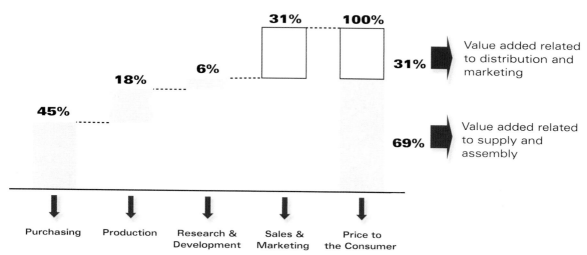

Source: McKinsey, ATKearney, IMD Research.

States. Customers also demanded more efficient engines; e.g., diesel engines grew from 14 percent of the European market in 1990 to 30 percent within 10 years (even reaching above 60 percent in France). The increasing variety of models had put pressure on dealers, since they had to carry higher inventory levels.

In order to offer more body styles, car companies had to reduce development times for models. At the same time, car companies increasingly relied on outsourcing. This strengthened the position of suppliers in relation to car companies, and in the case of high pressure diesel injections, the leading supplier controlled 85 percent of the world market. McKinsey had already asked in 1996: "Are automobiles the next commodity?" The consulting firm noticed a strong convergence in performance and quality among vehicles; e.g., defects per car in the United States decreased from eight in 1981 to one or two in 1995.[2] Competing consultants recommended that car companies look beyond the traditional business of making cars. Services around the car such as financing and insurance provided much higher profits (refer to Exhibit 3 for profit pools in the auto industry). The potential for car-related services was considerable. By 2001, almost 50 percent of new cars sold in Germany were registered in the name of a legal entity—either a corporation or a leasing/financing company. McKinsey estimated all revenues from a car over a 10-year period: In addition to the purchase price of $30,000, it had another $40,000 in revenues over the same period (refer to Exhibit 4 for revenue streams over 10 years). Some car manufacturers even went beyond car-related services. DaimlerChrysler, among others, offered retail banking, too.

For car manufacturers, this environment was difficult. The low profitability, overcapacity, and huge R&D expenditures forced many companies to exit the industry by merging or selling. By 1998, only 17 independent manufacturers remained in the world (down from 42 in 1960) and the industry had become truly global with maturing markets in Europe, North America, Japan. In response, car companies tried to move into higher margin premium markets (refer to Exhibit 5 for average margins and average prices), but even they became crowded (refer to Exhibit 6 for production rates for premium brands). Only emerging markets in South America, Eastern Europe, and Asia

Exhibit 3   Profit Pools in the Auto Industry

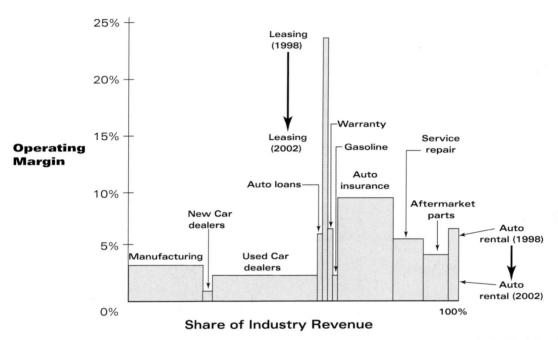

Note: The original numbers were published in 1998. A weak market for used cars considerably lowered the profitability of leasing and rental income.

Source: Adapted from: Gadiesh, Orit and James L. Gilbert. "Profit Pools: A Fresh Look at Strategy." *Harvard Business Review,* May–June 1998: 142.

were expected to produce considerable growth up to the year 2010, but the overall market estimates varied between 58.6 million units and 77.3 million units (refer to Exhibit 7 for estimated market sizes by 2010). In addition, the development of new technologies (e.g., fuel cells, telematics) was very costly and could only be financed by several players. As a result, it was not unusual for the survivors to cooperate with their competitors; e.g., Peugeot was building a joint factory with Toyota while developing a new engine with BMW. Such combinations were not uncommon in the car industry. Many observers saw the car industry as a model of the modern, networked company: "Car makers look at each other as competitors, partners, friends and role models."

Volkswagen AG (VW)

Early Beginnings

VW traced its beginnings back to Austrian-born Ferdinand Porsche. He started his career as an engineer designing cars for Mercedes-Benz in Stuttgart, Germany. In 1930 he set up his own vehicle development center and this was the foundation of the Porsche AG, a leading sports car maker.

In 1934 Porsche started to develop a small car with an air-cooled rear-mounted engine. This project was financed by the National Socialist government, since it saw the unique mandate to build a "people's car"—Volkswagen (VW). In 1938 the government

Exhibit 4   Revenue Streams over 10 Years

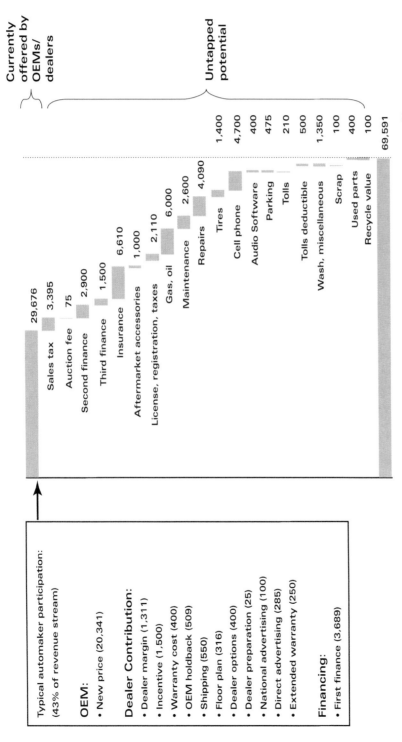

Source: Ealey, Lance and Luis Troyano-Bermudez. "The Automotive Industry: A 30,000-mile Checkup." *McKinsey Quarterly* 2000, Issue 1: 74.

Exhibit 5   **Average Margins and Average Price, 1994–1999**

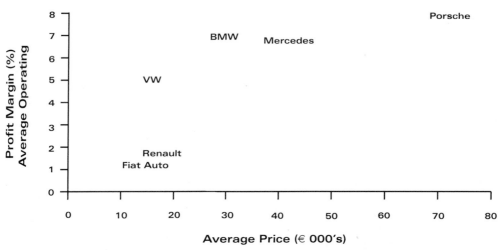

Source: Blair-Smith, Andrew, Graham Philips, Clive Wiggins, and Robert Ashton. "Global Auto Consolidation." *Commerzbank Securities,* September 14, 2000: 13.

Exhibit 6   **Production Rates for Premium Brands in 2000 (in 000s units)**

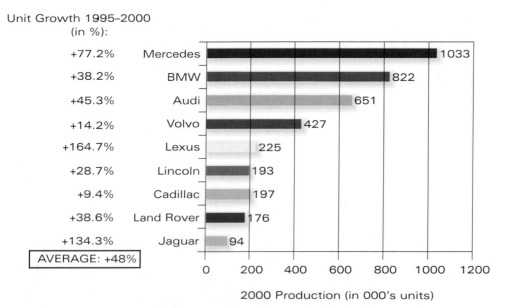

Note: 2000 numbers for Mercedes, BMW and the 1995 numbers (unit growth) of Volvo are sales figures.

Source: Company records; Automotive News Market; Automotive News Europe; IMD Research; Muller, Joann and David Welch. "Ford's Gamble on Luxury." *Business Week,* March 15, 2001: 65.

Exhibit 7   **Growth Estimates (1999 actual vs. 2010 low/high estimate in million units) Passenger Cars (PC) and Light Commercial Vehicles (LCV)**

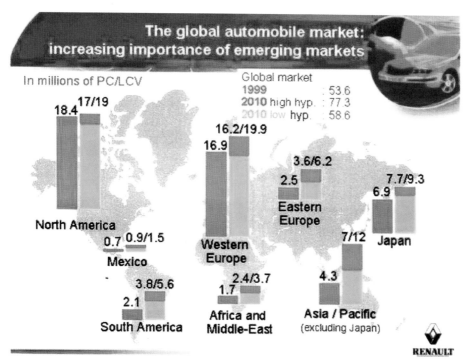

Source: Renault.

laid the foundations of the factory in Wolfsburg, around 90 km outside Hanover. But before the plant started producing cars, it was turned over to war-time production of military vehicles and airplane maintenance.

In 1945 the British military government assumed control as a temporary trustee for the next four years. It ordered the production of the "Beetle" passenger cars as planned before the war. However, the quality of the cars was below standard and, in 1948, Heinrich Nordhoff, an engineer, took over. Nordhoff improved quality and focused on exporting cars; by 1951 the company was exporting to 29 countries.

During the 1950s sales continued to increase and completely-knocked-down (CKD*) production sites were set up in Brazil and Ireland. Driven by strong export sales to over 100 countries, the millionth Beetle rolled off the assembly line in 1955. Further CKD production sites in Australia and South Africa as well as a domestic plant in Brazil were opened. Volkswagen do Mexico was founded in 1964.

Acquiring Production Capacity

Sales of Beetles continued to rise, necessitating the establishment of new plants in Germany. The increasing buying power of customers led Nordhoff to add to the range a station wagon and sedan based on the Beetle. In 1964 Nordhoff purchased the unprofitable

---

*CKD involved packaging the parts for each car together before sending them to a factory for final assembly.

Auto Union (Audi) from Daimler-Benz. The acquisition of Audi was seen as a fast way to increase VW's production capacity. By the time Nordhoff died in 1968, VW was the world's fourth-largest car company, but over 75 percent of the production was limited to the Beetle. The name VW was synonymous with the global success of one model, the Beetle.[3] However, after 30 years even this model had become outdated.

Kurt Lotz, Nordhoff's successor, had no automotive background:

> His objective was to expand VW's product line by acquiring NSU Motoren-werke, which held patent rights to a rotary Wankel engine. He also formed a joint venture with Porsche for the VW Porsche. Within three years, Lotz had stretched VW from a single-model company to a company with a wide range. VW was selling cars with air-cooled, water-cooled and Wankel engines. They were located in the front, middle or rear, some tied to front-wheel drives and others to rear-wheel drives.[4]

Overall, the complexity of the manufacturing process made it virtually impossible to reap economies of scale. Following poor financial results, Lotz was ousted in 1971 and replaced by Rudolf Leiding, the former head of Audi and VW Brazil. Leiding fully integrated the acquired companies into VW and concentrated on water-cooled engines. Moreover, he prepared for the time after the Beetle with the introduction of the Golf, Passat, Polo, and Scirocco. However, the oil crisis and an increasingly strong Deutschmark led to the biggest loss of any German company in 1974 and Leiding resigned.

During the 1970s VW had a hard time because of the global recession. In response to the oil crisis, it offered its first diesel engine in 1978. The company also opened its first factory in the United States. Toni Schmücker ran the company between 1975 and 1982, when he had a heart attack.

Further International Expansion

Under the stewardship of Dr. Carl Hahn, VW set the stage for further international expansion. Hahn steered the company into the Chinese market in 1983, and entered into a 75 percent capital purchase in Seat and subsequently acquired the company and 30 percent of Skoda in the Czech Republic in 1991 (eventually raised to 100 percent). Hahn remembered:

> Next to making profits, our mandate was to motorize our country and large parts of Europe, to provide employment to tens of thousands of people. Even today [1991] we provide 20 percent of the employment in [our home state of] Lower Saxony and 50 percent of its exports.[5]

Between 1982 and 1992, the number of cars produced by the Volkswagen Group increased from 2 million units to 3.4 million units. However, by the early 1990s it became clear that VW was once again having serious financial problems. The loss could only be covered with financial reserves from previous years.

Ownership Structure

VW had been partly privatized in the 1960s, with 60 percent of the company being sold to the public. The federal government and the state of Lower Saxony held equal parts of the remaining 40 percent. The state had two members—one of whom was usually the premier—on the supervisory board of VW. Due to this tight connection with politics, VW has often been accused of a conflict of interest.

Table 1   PIËCH'S CAREER PATH

1937	Born in Vienna, Austria, to Anton and Louise Piëch. His mother was the daughter of Ferdinand Porsche, and his father later became plant manager of VW's first plant in Wolfsburg.
1963	Graduates from Zurich's Technical Institute (ETH) and joins Porsche as an engine tester.
1968	Promoted to head of development at Porsche. Porsche wins the Manufacturer's Championships in 1969, 1970, 1971.
1972	Blocked from becoming Porsche's CEO and joins Audi as director of special projects in R&D.
1975	Promoted to head of R&D at Audi. Established Audi as a technology leader with innovations such as the quattro all-wheel drive and world-beating aerodynamics.
1988	Promoted to CEO of Audi.
1993	Promoted to CEO of VW.

Source: "Hard Driving Boss." *Business Week,* October 5, 1998, p. 53.

Always Full Speed Ahead:
Ferdinand Piëch

With Hahn's retirement, and the continuing deterioration of VW's financial performance, Piëch was a natural choice for the position of CEO. In his previous job at Audi, Piëch had been head of R&D since 1975, before becoming CEO 13 years later.

Piëch was widely recognized in the industry as the mastermind who had successfully repositioned Audi as an acclaimed technology leader. Audi's worldwide slogan "Vorsprung durch Technik" (Advance through Technology) was a credible promise of the brand. Under Piëch's leadership, Audi offered technological innovations at breakneck speed: all-wheel drive, 10-year corrosion warranties, record drag coefficients, turbo-charged diesel engines and all-aluminum bodies originated from Audi and made it the envy of the industry.

Despite its heavy investment in technology, Audi became a highly profitable business. Although Audi recorded only €8.5 billion in sales in 1992 (compared with VW's €25.5 billion), both companies contributed similar profits to the VW Group.

Piëch was also well known for his "closeness" to products and customers. He did not have a chauffeur, drove to work himself, and often got first-hand information from the dealers personally. Although Piëch was described as intense, unpredictable and quirky, he still got the job (refer to Table 1 for Piëch's major career steps).

Piëch Arrives in Wolfsburg

The difficult situation at VW became apparent, and as early as 1992 a German business magazine reported:

> VW is in crisis. Return on sales is negative, the accounting system is chaotic and fixed costs are rising a lot faster than sales.[6]

When Piëch arrived in Wolfsburg in early 1993 he knew he faced a challenging set of issues:

- Customers were increasingly complaining about the high prices of VW and Audi.

- VW produced 30 models on 16 platforms. The main plant in Wolfsburg—similar in size to the city-state of Monaco—only made money when it worked overtime. Japanese competitors and their newly built factories in the United Kingdom posed a serious threat to established players like VW. In fact, benchmarking studies revealed that the most efficient Japanese plants in Europe could produce the VW Golf model €2,500 more cheaply than VW itself.

- At any one time 8 percent of the employees were sick. About 30,000 workers were estimated to be surplus to requirements. As most factories were in poorly developed areas, it seemed impossible to lay the workers off. VW had never had layoffs before and the retirement age was already down to 55.

- There was little integration among the brands; e.g., both Audi and VW independently developed a similar six-cylinder engine at the same time.

- In the United States, unit sales of VW had fallen from 600,000 in 1970 to fewer than 50,000 units in 1993.

- In Asia, except for China, VW commanded less than 2 percent market share.

Piëch recalled the situation in 1993: "We did not do our homework and had to catch up in record time."[7] As a first step he hired Jose Ignazio Lopez (Super Lopez), the former purchasing boss of General Motors (GM). Lopez had started his career at Opel before transferring to GM in Detroit, where he was referred to as the "Hangman of Detroit" because he squeezed suppliers too hard. His sudden departure to VW started a legal battle, as Lopez was accused of leaking confidential material. VW later settled with GM by agreeing to purchase parts valued at $1 billion.

Although Piëch faced many challenges, he could also see some light at the end of the tunnel. After all, VW had the image of producing high quality cars and innovative turbocharged diesel engines (TDI) and it was supported by an excellent sales network. Nevertheless, the year 1993 would be remembered for a long time: It was the worst recession in 30 years for the European car industry. Automobile production in Europe fell from 12.9 million units to 11.2 million units and VW posted a financial loss of €992 million.

Volkswagen in 2001

The company in 2001 was barely recognizable from the company Piëch had taken over eight years earlier (refer to Exhibits 8 to 11 for detailed financial data). He transformed the once almost bankrupt manufacturer into a powerful global player. Under Piëch's stewardship, the VW Group added prestigious brands such as Bentley, Bugatti, Lamborghini and a minority stake in Scania trucks, while turning former "loser" brands such as Skoda and Seat into respected players.

For the second time—2000 was the first—the company sold over 5 million cars worldwide and its world market share increased to 12.4 percent (up from 9 percent in 1994). At the same time, VW recorded its highest profits in history: After-tax profits for 2001 reached €2.9 billion. Even after VW introduced a share buyback program in 2000, market capitalization did not reflect these previously unimaginable profits (refer to Table 2 for the after-tax profits and market capitalization).

VW's success was based on several factors. *Euromoney* wrote:

> Overall the product and the product know-how that VW has is definitely the strength of the company. The firm has been particularly strong in providing

Exhibit 8   VOLKSWAGEN GROUP FINANCIAL AND OPERATING STATISTICS, 1992–2001

	1992	1993	1994	1995	1996	1997	1998	1999	2000	2001
Sales (€ billion)	€43.666	€39.158	€40.924	€45.055	€51.192	€57.901	€68.637	€75.167	€83.127	€88.540
Change over previous year	12%	−10%	5%	10%	14%	13%	19%	10%	14%	7%
Domestic sales	46%	45%	41%	39%	36%	35%	35%	32%	29%	28%
Foreign sales	54%	55%	59%	61%	64%	65%	65%	68%	71%	72%
Sales (million units)	€ 3.433	€ 2.962	€ 3.108	€ 3.607	€ 3.994	€ 4.250	€ 4.748	€ 4.923	€ 5.161	€ 5.083
Change over previous year	6%	−14%	5%	16%	11%	6%	12%	4%	5%	−1.5%
Domestic sales	€ 1.211	€ 0.914	€ 0.901	€ 0.937	€ 0.958	€ 0.993	€ 1.153	€ 1.104	€ 1.019	€ 0.988
Foreign sales	€ 2.222	€ 2.048	€ 2.207	€ 2.670	€ 3.036	€ 3.257	€ 3.595	€ 3.819	€ 4.142	€ 4.095
Cost of materials (as a % of sales)	64%	62%	60%	59%	61%	60%	63%	62%	62%	N/A
Labor cost (as a % of sales)	24%	25%	23%	22%	21%	18%	17%	16%	16%	N/A
Workforce (000s)	€ 273	€ 253	€ 238	€ 257	€ 261	€ 275	€ 294	€ 306	€ 324	€ 322
Net Earnings (€ million)	75	(990)	77	172	347	696	1,147	844	2,614	2,926
Dividend (€ million)	34	34	55	106	161	246	316	327	506	550

Note: Starting in 2000, VW decided to use the International Accounting Standard (IAS).
Source: VW annual report 2000: 108/109; VW annual report 2001: 142/143.

Exhibit 9   VOLKSWAGEN AG: OVERVIEW OF THE DIFFERENT BRANDS, 2000–2001

Volkswagen Passenger Cars

	2000	2001	Change
Production (000s units)	1,999	1,923	−3.8%
Workforce (000s)	126.7	126.2	−0.4
Revenue (€ bn)	45.230	47.888	+5.9
Operating result (€ bn)	1.993	2.238	+12.3
Return on sales	4.4%	4.7%	—

Volkswagen Commercial Vehicles Brand

	2000	2001	Change
Production (000s units)	247	215	−12.8%
Workforce (000s)	18.0	18.3	+1.4
Revenue (€ bn)	4.562	4.280	−6.2
Operating result (€ mn)	433	296	−31.7
Return on sales	9.5%	6.9%	—

Audi Brand

	2000	2001	Change
Production (000s units)	651	727	+11.7%
Workforce (000s)	50.2	50.6	+0.8
Revenue (€ bn)	19.952	22.032	+10.4
Operating result (€ bn)	1.138	1.421	+24.9
Return on sales	5.7%	6.4%	—

Seat Brand

	2000	2001	Change
Production (000s units)	516	480	−7.0%
Workforce (000s)	17.2	16.5	−4.4
Revenue (€ bn)	6.711	6.339	−5.5
Operating result (€ mn)	−47	63	—
Return on sales	−0.7%	1.0%	—

Skoda Brand

	2000	2001	Change
Production (000s units)	451	461	+2.2%
Workforce (000s)	23.9	22.8	−4.9
Revenue (€ bn)	4.090	4.754	+16.2
Operating result (€ mn)	185	230	+24.3
Return on sales	4.5%	4.8%	—

Rolls-Royce/Bentley Brand

	2000	2001	Change
Production (in units)	1,938	1,781	−8.1%
Workforce (000s)	2.5	2.6	+3.6
Revenue (€ mn)	418	422	+1.0
Operating result (€ mn)	−68	−48	—
Return on sales	−16.3%	−11.1%	—

Note: Revenue of VW Passenger Cars includes revenues from Volkswagen's European distribution companies. Revenue of Audi includes revenue of AUTOGERMA S.p.A., the Italian distributor.

Source: Volkswagen AG, annual report 2001.

Exhibit 10 **Volkswagen AG's Operating Profit by Division in 2001**

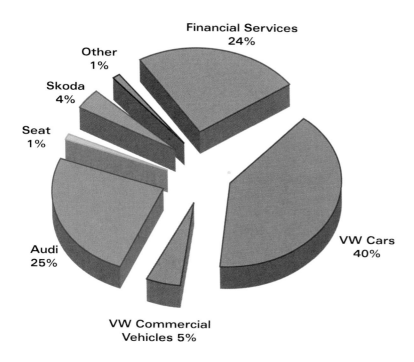

VW Group Operating Profit: €5.4 B

Source: Morgan Stanley.

excellent car interiors that attract European consumers. Further, Volkswagen's reputation and brand are impressive. On average the company's selling prices are several percent better compared to other volume car competitors.

One of the company's best traits is its geographical reach. VW may be a dominant European player, but it has also infiltrated many other regions. It maintains a leading position in China. It has also succeeded in North America. VW is enjoying an incredible degree of success there.

In fact, 2001 was another record year. Deliveries to customers were up in many areas. Some of the increases were quite dramatic: In the United States, sales almost tripled between 1997 and 2001. Some of the acquired brands turned out to be star performers:

■ Skoda increased its sales from 172,000 units in 1991 to 465,000 units in 2001 with an export rate reaching 81 percent in the same year.

■ Seat, after a massive loss in 1994, was finally on the road to profitability with a positive contribution to the Group.

■ Bentley was enjoying strong sales growth. The production of Bentley grew from 414 units in 1998 to 1,550 units in 2000. In 2002 Bentley proudly announced the British Queen as a new customer. The "royal" Bentley used liquid natural gas and could travel at 200 km/h plus.

But how had VW achieved such a great turnaround?

Exhibit 11   VOLKSWAGEN AG: BALANCE SHEET, 2000–2001
(in millions of €)

	2000	2001
Assets		
Intangible assets	€ 5,355	€ 6,596
Tangible assets	19,726	21,735
Investments in group companies accounted for using the equity method	3,088	3,398
Other financial assets	1,128	601
Total noncurrent assets	29,297	32,330
Leasing and rental assets	4,783	7,284
Inventories	9,335	9,945
Financial services receivables	32,553	36,087
Trade receivables	5,058	5,141
Other receivables and assets	3,821	3,938
Securities	3,886	3,610
Cash and cash equivalents	2,156	4,285
Total current assets	56,809	63,006
Deferred tax assets	1,377	1,426
Prepayment and deferred charges	299	378
Total assets	**€92,565**	**€104,424**
Equity and liabilities		
Subscribed capital	€ 1,071	€ 1,087
Capital reserve	4,296	4,415
Revenue reserve	13,690	14,546
Accumulated profits	2,314	3,947
Total equity and reserves	21,371	23,995
Minority interests	49	53
Provisions	21,128	21,782
Deferred tax liabilities	2,095	2,299
Non-current borrowings	8,383	12,750
Current borrowings	26,201	30,044
Trade payables	7,435	7,055
Other payables	5,699	6,161
Total other liabilities	47,718	56,010
Deferred income	204	285
Total equity and liabilities	**€92,565**	**€104,424**

Source: VW annual report 2001, p. 77.

Table 2   VOLKSWAGEN GROUP'S AFTER-TAX PROFITS AND MARKET CAPITALIZATION, 1993–2001 (in millions)

	1993	1994	1995	1996	1997	1998	1999	2000	2001
After-tax profits	€ (992)	€ 77	€ 172	€ 347	€ 696	€ 1,147	€ 844	€ 2,614	€ 2,926
Market capitalization	7,100	7,000	8,000	11,200	19,700	26,000	20,800	18,800	16,000

VW's Transformation

The Plan

Piëch's recovery plan for VW involved avoiding costly duplication of investment, cutting down parts proliferation within the Group, and rationalizing the production of different models of vehicles. It was clear that any strategy he proposed had to be in line with future developments in the car industry. The increased variety of models would further increase costs of development, procurement, and production due to increased complexity.

Selecting an Appropriate Strategy

Car makers had only three options: to use similar parts, badge engineering, or platforms. With similar parts, it was questionable whether the required savings could be achieved. Badge engineering—selling a similar car under different brands (e.g., Chrysler Voyager minivan and Dodge Caravan minivan)—was seen as not acceptable, as VW still had a price premium in the market, so necessary distinctions had to be made between the different brands. VW settled on the use of platforms, since they led to shorter development times, lower development costs, and economies of scale in procurement (refer to Exhibit 12 for an overview of the A-platform). The platforms accounted for around 60 percent of the total cost of a car. By 1998 as much as 47 percent of the product range was built on platforms and this gradually increased to 80 percent by 2000 (refer to Table 3 for production volumes per platform).

Although the platform strategy sounded great in theory, other car companies had experienced difficulty with it. GM had been putting many cars on a few platforms, with the result that a lot of them looked and drove alike. VW claimed that it would apply greater attention to detail than any other manufacturer had done before.

Because each car was designed by a different brand group, the body shapes, the position of the steering wheel, the seats, the engine and gearbox software, the suspension systems and anything felt by the driver were different. A market research study in 2000 revealed that 75 percent of German customers were unaware of the platform concept. Respondents who knew of the concept tended to think of it positively, since it made high quality vehicles more affordable.[9]

Breaking with Old Traditions

The platform approach was not enough for VW. When Piëch started in 1993, the Polo replacement was being finalized. The Polo was traditionally seen as the little brother of the Golf. The Golf was a highly profitable product line but the Polo was not. So everything was done not to harm the Golf while maintaining the Polo as an entry model. Piëch's approach was that both cars were built in the same factory and thus had to provide a similar profit contribution.

World-Class Manufacturing

With the platform strategy, VW had implemented a global manufacturing system, and foreign employment levels had increased from 41 percent of the total in 1993 to 51 percent in 2001 (refer to Exhibit 13 for an overview of plants). The similarity of the platforms allowed for short set-up times in factories and thereby greatly improved flexibility.

Exhibit 12   VW's A-Platform

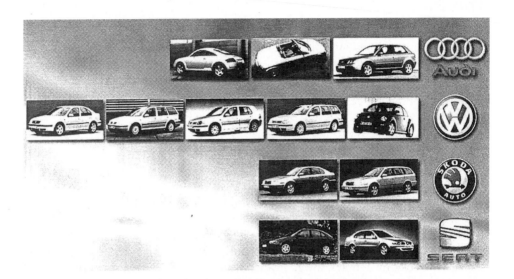

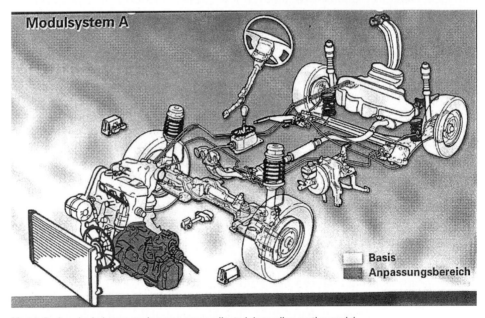

Note: Darker shaded parts are in some cases adjusted depending on the model.

Source: Volkswagen.

Underutilized plants could pick up production from other plants. In order to increase profit contributions from factories, Piëch was willing to finance innovative approaches:

- *Audi Engine Plant in Hungary:* What initially started as an engine plant for Audi soon became a component supplier for the VW Group. In 2000 the company produced over 1 million engines, over 50,000 Audi TT, and became Hungary's

Table 3   PLATFORM OVERVIEW (production in 000s units in 2000)[8]

Platform	Volkswagen	Audi	Seat	Skoda	Total
A00	Lupo (97)		Arosa (28)		125
A0	Polo (433)	A2 (32)	Cordoba (95)		
			Ibiza (199)	Fabia (176)	935
A	Golf (819)				
	Bora/Jetta (370)				
	New Beetle (149)	A3 (136)			
		TT (57)	Leon (92)		
			Toledo (59)	Octavia (154)	1,836
B/C	Passat (384)				
	Sharan (52)				
	Ford Galaxy* (50)	A4 (230)			
		A6 (181)	Alhambra (24)	Superb	921
D	Phaeton	A8 (13)			

Note: This statistic does not include production in South America and Asia.

*VW also produces the Ford Galaxy. Initially, Ford and VW had a joint venture in Portugal, before VW acquired Ford's stake.

Exhibit 13   Global Production Overview

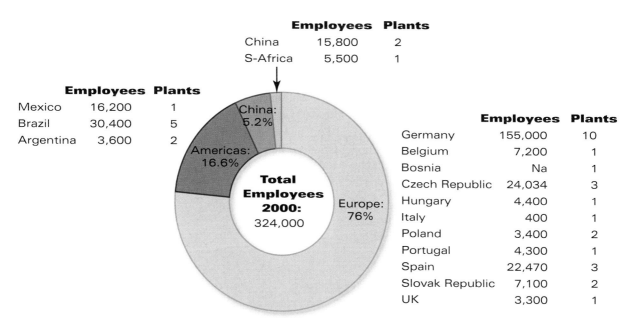

Note: Independent, locally owned assembly plants existed in Indonesia, Malaysia, Philippines, and Thailand.

Source: Volkswagen, "Ideas on the Move 2001": 24/25.

biggest exporter. The mix of highly skilled labor at competitive rates, proximity to German plants, and the high quality levels made it possible to manage the growth.

■ *Skoda Plant in Mlada Boleslav, Czech Republic:* This Skoda plant was at the forefront of supplier integration in Europe. Skoda had six integrated suppliers on-site (makers of carpets, seats, exhaust systems, rear axles, bumpers, dashboards and instrument panels) and this plant was considered to be one of the most cost-effective plants in Europe. According to the Economist Intelligence Unit (EIU),[10] VW was able to increase the output from 10.1 cars per employee in 1994 to around 30 in 1998, a fairly high figure for a European company.

■ *VW Plant in Resende, Brazil:* This plant was the most innovative factory in the world. Inaugurated in 1996, the factory pioneered the use of pure modular consortia to produce 30,000 truck and bus chassis per year. The plant was set up with seven leading suppliers and they were responsible for managing sub-suppliers and the final assembly process on the line. At Resende, VW managed only the final quality control and had a total of 40 employees on the shop floor, another 160 engineers in product development and a few in sales and marketing. In all, there were 1,350 workers at the plant.[11]

■ *Modular manufacturing system:* VW announced this new system in 2000. The company identified 11 modules, e.g., braking and steering systems, which could be shared among different platforms. The electric motors to adjust both outside mirrors were the first modules to be identical in all cars of the VW Group, reaching a total capacity of about 10 million units.

■ *Flexible production schedule in Germany:* VW was working together with the unions to introduce a more flexible production schedule. The plan called for aligning production and sales. In the past, cars were often stocked for months before they could be sold during the peak season in the spring and summer. The first half of the year accounted for two-thirds of annual sales. This tied up working capital and made the company vulnerable to changing market trends and tastes. The proposed system required employees to work up to 48 hours per week in the peak season, and significantly less during other periods, thus keeping average work time over a year. This would greatly improve the flexibility and efficiency of production (refer to Exhibit 14 for examples of the flexibility cascade).

■ *5000 × 5000 program:* VW started this program to fulfill its promise to reduce the unemployment rate in Wolfsburg by 50 percent. VW offered to hire 5,000 unemployed workers and guaranteed them a fixed salary of DM 5,000 (€2,550). However, the workers had to agree to meet certain quality levels. This implied that they would work until the required quality level was met.

Top managers at Volkswagen realized that manufacturing excellence was not enough; the company also needed global sales.

Worldwide Sales

In 2001 VW's biggest markets were in Europe excluding Germany (40.5 percent of sales), followed by Germany (27.7%) and North America (20.1%). Asia/Oceania and South America each accounted for 5 percent of sales, and Africa for 1.2 percent.

Exhibit 14   Flexibility Cascade

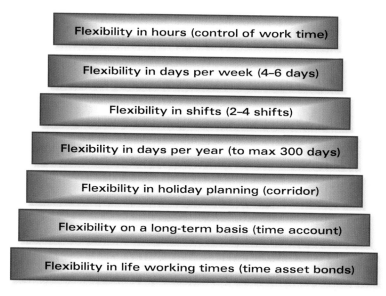

Flexibility in hours (control of work time)

Flexibility in days per week (4–6 days)

Flexibility in shifts (2–4 shifts)

Flexibility in days per year (to max 300 days)

Flexibility in holiday planning (corridor)

Flexibility on a long-term basis (time account)

Flexibility in life working times (time asset bonds)

Source: Volkswagen.

North America

The region included the NAFTA countries—the United States, Canada, and Mexico. Since 1993, VW had experienced a great turnaround in North America, with massive growth. In 1993 VW sold only 49,000 units in the United States and commanded less than 1 percent of the American import market (rising to 2 percent by 1997). The highly successful launch of the New Beetle boosted other VW models, too. By 2000 VW commanded over 5 percent of the American import market, putting it in the lead among European brands. Dr. Jens Neumann, board member for legal affairs and the North America region, explained the success in NAFTA:

> Since 1993 we have been able to record double digit increases in almost every year, on account of improved positioning and strong new models, such as the New Beetle, which inspired an entirely new generation of American customers. In the US market, [2000] was our best year since 1973 with 355,000 units sold; Jetta grew strongly to 144,000 units. We sold 84,000 Passats and the New Beetle remained strong with more than 81,000 units.[12]

VW operated a large plant in Mexico with an annual capacity of 425,000 units. Vehicles were also imported from Brazil and Europe.

Asia

VW's Asian activities were heavily concentrated in China, where the company greatly benefited from first-mover advantages, having assembled the first model there back in 1983. VW commanded over 51 percent of the Chinese market and had successfully set up local production sites. Moreover, it was able to convince many suppliers to relocate to China in order to comply with local-content rules.

Exhibit 15   AUTO MANUFACTURER MARKET SHARES IN WESTERN EUROPE, 1994–2000

	1994	1995	1996	1997	1998	1999	2000
Total market size (million units)	11.9	12.0	12.8	13.4	14.4	15.1	14.7
Market shares (%)							
VW Group	15.8%	16.7%	17.2%	17.1%	18.0%	18.8%	18.7%
GM Group	12.9	13.0	12.5	12.1	11.5	11.5	10.8
PSA Group	12.8	12.0	11.9	11.3	11.4	12.1	12.8
Ford Group	13.5	13.8	13.2	13.1	11.8	11.7	10.8
Fiat Group	10.7	10.9	11.2	11.7	10.9	9.5	10.0
Japanese	11.0	10.7	10.8	11.7	11.9	11.5	11.4
Renault	11.0	10.3	10.1	9.9	10.7	11.0	10.6
BMW	3.3	3.3	3.4	3.2	3.1	3.2	3.4
Rover	3.3	3.1	2.9	2.9	2.6	1.5	1.3
DaimlerChrysler	3.5	3.4	3.6	3.7	5.1	5.6	6.2
Korean	—	—	1.9	2.1	2.7	3.2	3.4
Other	2.2	2.9	1.3	1.0	0.4	0.3	0.6

Source: Melich, Gregory. "Global Automotive September 2001." Morgan Stanley 2001: 9.

Europe

The European market was highly competitive and the American car companies, in particular, were facing considerable difficulties there. Ford Europe was struggling with high-cost production bases in Britain and Germany. Moreover, the company was slow to add new products. Its popular Fiesta was sold for 10 years, exceeding the industry average by 3 years. The higher margin Scorpio misjudged the taste of consumers and was stopped only a few years after its introduction. Ford saw its market share fall from 13.5 percent in 1994 to 10.8 percent in 2000 (refer to Exhibit 15 for historic market share development in Western Europe). During the 1990s, Ford lost around $2.7 billion in Europe. As a result, the company reduced its European production capacity from 2.3 million units to 1.6 million units by early 2001. The situation was improving with the arrival of popular models such as the Focus and Mondeo, and Ford Europe had a net profit of $28 million in 2000.

In the early 1990s Opel, the European division of GM, was one of the most profitable car manufacturers in the world. GM decided to use Opel globally as an entry brand in developing countries in Asia, Latin America, and Eastern Europe. So Opel was trimmed to achieve cost efficiency, and quality in the European market suffered. Market share fell from 12.9 percent in 1994 to 10.8 percent in 2000. In order to move cars, the company had to discount heavily, leading to a loss of €680 million in 2001.

VW's Success Formula: Keeping the Brands Distinct

The challenge was to benefit from economies of scale while keeping the brands separate. Dr. Robert Büchelhofer, board member for sales and marketing, explained:

Table 4   BRAND IMAGES

Audi	Challenging the conventional
Bentley	Gentleman's sporty touring car
Bugatti	Masterpiece of automotive engineering
Lamborghini	Uncompromising sports car
Seat	Auto Emocion (automotive emotion)
Skoda	Creative solutions for smart customers
VW	The benchmark for automotive values

We can serve all important car markets with credible brands. Skoda with its value-for-money approach is as plausible as Bentley in the top segment of the automotive hierarchy. We are likely to have the most experience with multi-branding. We have learned a lot from our mistakes. Every brand has a high degree of independence. The independence is reduced when the results are not OK.

In the future, Piëch wanted to offer a full product range, from a tiny 3-liter (fuel-consumption) Lupo to a 16-cylinder Bugatti with 1,001 horsepower. The iron-willed Piëch wanted to distance VW from its mass-market heritage and mold a brand with Mercedes-like reputation and margins. Moving upmarket was key and within the space of just three months in 1998, VW bought Rolls-Royce Motor Cars for $640 million—only to lose the rights to the coveted Rolls brand to BMW; put down some $110 million for Italian sports car maker Lamborghini; bought Cosworth, the British engine manufacturer, for $178 million; and snapped up Bugatti. For each brand, VW developed a distinct image (refer to Table 4 for examples).

In order to deliver these different brand images, the company invested heavily in downstream activities.

New Ways of Distribution

As early as the mid-1990s, VW and Audi had decided on the physical differentiation of VW and Audi dealerships—long before their competitors. In the past both dealerships had generally been under one roof, but it was increasingly difficult to sell and keep VWs and Audis in the same location. The price range of the products had just become too large. A marketing executive explained:

> The increasing fragmentation of the markets is the biggest challenge for the automotive industry. The challenge to manufacturers is to meet this demand and still have sufficient margins. The differentiation and redesign has cost dealers €3.5 billion. Worldwide over 11,000 Audi and VW dealers have been targeted, of which almost 90 percent have now been completed. And with an average retail mark-up of some 12–17 percent, motor vehicle distribution is low-cost in comparison with many other industries. The figures show how much confidence our dealers have in the brands.

As brand loyalty and purchasing decisions were driven by sympathy and emotions, VW explored opportunities to build its own delivery center and theme park in Wolfsburg. It soon decided to create a facility that would go far beyond anything a conventional delivery center could offer to the visitor. The "Autostadt" team took its

Exhibit 16 Autostadt in Wolfsburg

Source: Volkswagen AG.

inspiration from the great museums of the world and examined what companies in quite different business areas had created. The result was a €420 million facility that opened its doors in summer 2000.

The two 48-meter-high glass "Auto Towers," resembling engine cylinders, were the focal point of Autostadt, where cars ready for delivery were stored (refer to Exhibit 16 for a picture of Autostadt). The towers could handle 1,000 cars daily. A multimedia museum featured displays on the history of cars and the future of mobility; simulators and models demonstrated modern production processes. Each brand of the VW Group had its own pavilion. A manager explained:

> VW has gone to immense trouble to create a fascinating "world of encounter" located somewhere between emotive vision and reality. Passing on to the brand pavilions, [visitors] can then investigate "the souls" of the individual Group brands, their mystique and heritage. It is this unusual alternation between emotive and rational styles of communication that accounts for Autostadt's specific attraction. Entertainment to a very high standard, the thrill of discovery, an opportunity to see familiar things in an entirely new and possibly unexpected light are among the things that make a visit not only memorable but also of lasting personal value.

After strolling through the different pavilions, visitors could stop at the numerous Mövenpick restaurants or stay at the Ritz-Carlton hotel.

Initially many financial analysts thought Autostadt was excessive—they did not see the value and thought that the project cost of €420 million was astronomical. In comparison, Opel spent about €60 million on its theme park. Journalists shared the concern. *Fortune* wrote in 1998:

> Autostadt is VW's effort to turn Wolfsburg, the company's sleepy hometown, into a throbbing tourist mecca. It'll take some doing; Wolfsburg (pop. 120,000) is hardly known for its charm.[13]

In its first year of operation, Autostadt attracted more than 2 million visitors, twice the number initially expected. By its second year, Autostadt recorded on average 6,000 visitors per day and had become Germany's second most popular theme park, with each customer paying €14.

Moving Upmarket

From VW's point of view, the company needed something in its range above the highly successful redesigned Passat. The new Passat sold 400,000 units annually, about twice the volume of its initial model. Given VW's loyalty rate of 74 percent, the company needed something to extend the range. As customers were continually trying to upgrade, the Phaeton was supposed to fill that need. The car was expected to cost around €55,000 and VW hoped that a success in its luxury-car strategy would add some glitter to its mass-market products.

The Phaeton aimed to boost the company's share in the premium-car market, in direct competition with Mercedes, BMW and, to a certain extent, Audi. The company planned to launch its VW Phaeton brand in late 2001. However, being a latecomer to the market caused some headaches. A brand manager for the Phaeton explained:

> Nobody is waiting for a luxury car from Volkswagen. We have to be better than our competitors if we want to be successful—and we have to be different.[14]

In fact, VW decided that such an important and prestigious vehicle could be built only somewhere with special flair. The *Financial Times* reported:

> As Dresden, according to the Austrian Mr Piëch, is Germany's most beautiful city, it could only be built there. The project—especially the extraordinary all-glass assembly plant—has attracted widespread attention. The "factory of glass" (it even has a glass ceiling) breaks conventions by being in the city centre at a time when most carmakers are moving to greenfield sites.[15]

The plant aimed to set new records. Each vehicle would be built to its future owner's individual specification. For the first time, customers would be able to monitor the car's progress on the Internet, from placing the order until production was scheduled. On request, they could watch the decisive stages in the car's manufacture on the spot (refer to Exhibit 17 for a picture of the Transparent Factory). At the plant, fitted with hardwood floors, they would be greeted by workers wearing white suits to emphasize their precision jobs. The plant would have a capacity of about 30,000 to 40,000 units.

Many competitors in the top league did not think VW would make it in the premium sector. They questioned VW's ability to create the image by acquiring brands and multiplying the number of cylinders. As early as 1999 Piëch explained:

> A few years ago many people did not think we could sell the Audi A8 [Audi's top model]. However, we became established players in the premium segment. Measured by market share, Audi beats BMW in Germany and Europe. A few years ago BMW surpassed Daimler [Mercedes-Benz]. Times change. Whoever is the fastest will win. We always drive at full speed.[16]

VW tried to counter these concerns by stressing product features of the car (strongest diesel engine ever built and air conditioning with no drafts) and a prominent first customer: German chancellor Gerhard Schröder.

Exhibit 17   Transparent Factory in Dresden

Source: Volkswagen AG.

However, VW's move into the highly profitable luxury market was not limited to the Phaeton. It had joined forces with Porsche to develop an SUV, which Porsche branded as a Porsche Cayenne and which VW branded as a Touareg.

Financial Services

Financial services proved to be a highly profitable business for car companies, and VW was no exception. In 2001 this division produced profits of €552 million, making a considerable contribution to overall profits. VW realized the potential of financial services beyond car financing and soon expanded its offerings:

- *Retail customers:* Classic car credits, leasing and insurance services.

- *Fleet customers:* Fleet leasing and management for all cars. This included fleet analysis and consulting, accident management, direct communication with the drivers. Some of these services were also offered through the Europcar rental agency, a fully owned subsidiary of VW.

- *Dealer services:* Financing of inventory, working capital loans, investment loans and insurance services.

- *Volkswagen Bank:* Products included credit cards, bank accounts, mortgages, online and telephone banking. In Germany, VW Bank had over 500,000 customers and this made it the third biggest direct bank. International expansion began.

Overall, the company saw a big potential for financial services. Norbert Massfeller, the managing director of Volkswagen Bank, explained: "We have a database with four million customers. We can target them individually and hence our acquisition cost for new customers is much lower than for the competition."[17]

"Piëch Seems to Make Up His Own Rules in Life"[18]

Piëch's success was fueled by engineering know-how, a passionate love of cars and enormous wealth. His family owned one of the biggest businesses in Austria and a 34 percent stake in Porsche. That background, some argue, gave him a psychological advantage in confrontations with ordinary mortals for whom job loss was a financial threat.

When Piëch arrived in Wolfsburg, he soon realized that he had 30,000 employees too many. Rather than laying them off and sending whole regions into an economic freefall, he decided to introduce a four-day workweek. Workers had their annual worktime reduced by 20 percent and received 16 percent less salary. This way he could keep the employees until the recession lifted. Piëch frequently visited the plants and talked to employees. At the plant level his was known "to be tough, but extremely reliable." He even supported the formation of a global union council within VW. It seemed that Piëch had more difficulties with his top managers.

Management Style

After arriving in Wolfsburg, Piëch cut the salary of board members by 20 percent and shrank VW's management board to just five members, from nine before he took the job. Except for the CFO, Bruno Adelt, all board members were new, a couple having followed him from Audi. At Audi Piëch had strongly encouraged open communication among board members. He introduced glass walls in board members' offices and every board member had to name a top executive who could replace him in case of absence. Proposals for board meetings were limited to two pages. When he moved to VW he did the same.

Journalists often described Piëch's management style as one of fear and brutality. Piëch answered: "Do you really think we could be successful if this was my management style?" He definitely did not back down from a fight. In 1993 many managers saw the prototype of the New Beetle as an unaffordable plaything when it arrived from VW's California design studio. But Piëch, whose grandfather had conceived the Beetle, bowled over the critics and drove it to popular acclaim. He consolidated power and swept out top managers who did not follow his lead.

Piëch explained his management tools:

> I believe that my grandfather was a genius. He was not so much a great inventor, I'm also not a big inventor, but he was good at finding the right people.

Finding the right people was also key for Piëch. He commented:

> When I took over in 1993, we had a real problem in Mexico with the launch of the Golf. Although the cars were built according to the same specifications as in Europe, the pre-production cars did not pass our internal quality requirements. This was not the fault of the workers, but of the managers. In the old system, incapable executives were disposed of by sending them on foreign assignments. I recognized this and changed it accordingly. The old guard was asked to leave for early retirement while new managers were sent abroad with the guarantee of returning to HQ within three to five years—in a higher position.[19]

In his role as the CEO of VW, he believed in open competition between the brands. The different brands were free to make their decisions, as long as they were

Exhibit 18   Volkswagen's Product Portfolio

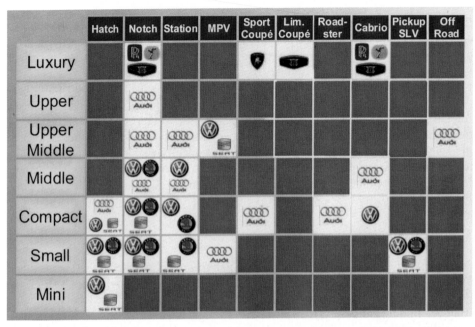

Source: Volkswagen AG.

	VW	Audi	Seat	Skoda	Bentley	Lamborghini	Bugatti
Mini-car	Lupo		Arosa				
Small car	Polo	A2	Ibiza/Cordoba	Fabia			
Compact	Golf/Beetle	A3	Leon/Toledo	Octavia			
Middle class	Passat	A4		Superb			
Upper middle class		A6					
Upper class	Phaeton	A8					
Luxury					Arnage		
Sports cars		RS 4				Murcielago	Veyron
Coupes	Bora	TT			Continental		
Convertibles	Golf	TT C			Azare		
Vans	Sharan		Alhambra				
SUVs	Touareg	A6 Allroad					

Source: Volkswagen.

producing good results (refer to Exhibit 18 for the different market and model segments). Piëch explained:

> I have learned to lead federally like the Swiss do with their cantons. This is a big difference between how VW and other competitors are led. Others lead out of their headquarters and it is holy what comes out of there. We lead in a more

Exhibit 19   VW Group's Purchasing Organization

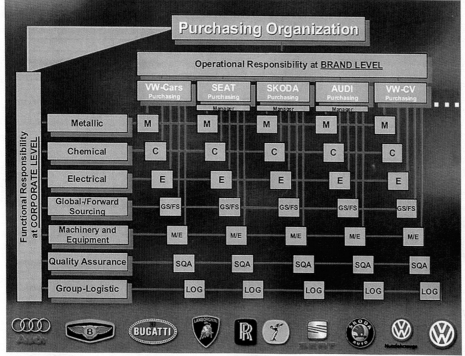

Source: Volkswagen.

decentralized way, and we let our brands do whatever they like as long as they bring in 6.5 percent [return on sales]. But in the principle of finance, we are like other companies. Only a direct line works.

To focus everyone on profitability, VW required new projects to be self-financing. Changes to the platform could only be made with approval of the board. And Piëch monitored VW's purchasing list for pricing that seemed too high. The purchasing volume stood at €57.98 billion in 2000, with the biggest volume at VW (66%), followed by Audi (20%). The department was structured as a matrix in order to reap maximum synergies (refer to Exhibit 19 for the purchasing organization).

By 1998 Piëch held personal responsibility for R&D, production, purchasing, quality and the VW brand. Piëch explained how he got everything done:

I only spend a few hours per week in my office. The life of a company does not happen here. It happens out there, in the development department, on the race track, in the design studio—there you get an impression of what is going on. It is management by asking questions, probing, clarifying, connecting, always putting time pressure on people and never remaining non-committal.[20]

Within the daughter companies, Piëch installed his colleagues from the corporate executive board as chairmen. CFO Adelt controlled Seat, Neumann (legal) controlled Skoda and Büchelhofer (sales and marketing) was chairman at Audi. The board met every Monday at HQ. This system worked well, but Piëch hinted at the difficulty of running seven brands (plus Rolls-Royce and a minority stake in Scania trucks). As Piëch was expected to retire in 2002, he increased the board by four members, who took over responsibilities previously held by Piëch. VW also decided on a new organizational structure as of 2002. The newly appointed CEO, Dr. Bernd Pischetsrieder, would run four brands (VW, Skoda, Bentley, Bugatti) while Dr. Martin Winterkorn would run the remaining three brands—Audi, Seat, and Lamborghini (refer to Exhibit 20 for the evolution of the executive board). Piëch would stay on as chairman of the Group.

Culture

When Piëch arrived in Wolfsburg, he complained bitterly that nobody had suffered when the company was losing money. He rapidly overhauled the culture by making the brands much more responsible for their actions. All top managers had to meet once or twice a month in secret locations around the world. Said Hartz, board member for HR: "The most important thing for board members is to test products. If you have a company just looking at finances, you should lead a bank." CFO Adelt added: "We don't play golf. We build Golf."

When managers gathered to test cars, they also swapped ideas about what worked best in which cars, and they competed to sell each other technologies they were developing. Piëch commented:

> The way we handle our culture is unique. In other car companies, a leading brand or a group streamlines the others. Here, it is an open market, you put your ideas out, and the other brands can accept it or not.

Piëch had to overcome many critics, who wanted only Audi and Volkswagen to have access to the newest technology. But Piëch was adamant on this point:

> Every new model needs the latest technology available. This was also true for the VW Group. Seat and Skoda could only succeed by getting the best from the Group. VW had 11,000 employees in R&D and Audi another 8,000—Seat and Skoda had only a small portion of that. But this is also about strategic issues. You can only run this place when you offer the advantages also to the smaller companies in the Group. Then they will accept HQ and the Group.[21]

The companies in the Group benefited a lot from this component availability; e.g., customers of the Skoda Octavia could choose from nine different engines, with the top engine reaching 275 horsepower (up from 75 horsepower a few years earlier).

Future Challenges

On April 15, 2002, Piëch was sitting in his office preparing for the shareholder meeting the next day in Hamburg. This was his last meeting and he decided to drive the 200 kilometers to Hamburg in the newest prototype, the so-called Batmobile. This little black car was the first car with a fuel consumption of less than 1 liter per 100 kilometers and capable of traveling at 120 kilometers per hour. A few years back Piëch had publicly announced that this was feasible. Once again he delivered.

**Exhibit 20   VW Group's Executive Board Structure 1993–2001
(arrows indicate additions in 2000)**

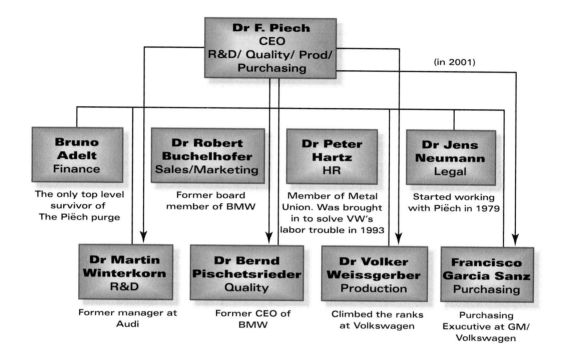

New Structure Starting 2002

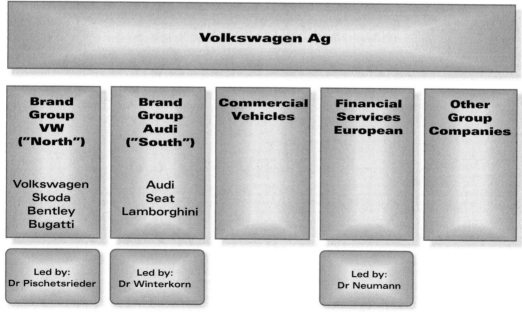

Source: Volkswagen.

As he stared at the towers of Autostadt, he reflected on his nine years and three months in office. He was wondering how history would evaluate his team's performance in terms of:

- Finances.
- Product/segment strategy.
- Globalization.
- Business systems.

He was also wondering how the VW approach to structure, people, systems and stakeholder management would be assessed. The main competitors were gearing up and VW could not afford to become complacent. Already in early 2002, Peugeot was producing the best-selling car in Europe, as the VW Golf was reaching maturity.

Endnotes

[1] For a more detailed background, see Rädler, George, Z. Jan Kubes, and Ulrich Steger, *The Global Automotive Industry*. IMD Case No. IMD-3-0911, 2001.

[2] Ealey, Lance and Luis Troyano-Bermudez. "Are Automobiles the Next Commodity?" *McKinsey Quarterly*, 4/1996: 66.

[3] See Edisis, Wayne and Malcolm Salter, *The Volkswagen Group*. Harvard Business School Case No. 9-385-333, 1985, for a detailed overview of the historic development of Volkswagen. Parts of this historic overview originate from this source.

[4] Ibid.

[5] Avishai, Bernard. "A European Platform for Global Competition: An Interview with VW's Carl Hahn." *Harvard Business Review*, July–August 1991: 4.

[6] Hillebrand, Walter. "Die Erben sehen rot." *Manager Magazin*, 4/1992: 35 ff.

[7] Hillebrand, Walter and Frank A. Linden. "Die Jagd ist auf." *Manager Magazin*, 12/1993: 129.

[8] Borland, Tom, Georges Dieng, and Louis Bailoni. "Volkswagen." *ABN AMRO*, August 8, 2001: 15.

[9] "Plattformstrategie wenig bekannt." *Handelsblatt*, September 12, 2000.

[10] Economist Intelligence Unit (EIU), "Inside Skoda's Mlada Boleslav Plant: A Thriving Operation." *Motor Business Europe*, 1st Quarter 2000: 86.

[11] For further information on the Skoda plant and Resende, please refer to "Outsourcing in the Automotive Industry: From JIT to Modular Consortia" by Robert S. Collins, Kimberly A. Bechler & Silvio R.I. Pires, *M2000 Executive Report*, No. 21, May 1997.

[12] Neumann, Jens. "Dresdner Kleinwort Wasserstein: New York German Investment Seminar." Speakers' Notes, January 22, 2001: 6.

[13] Guyon, Janet. "Those Irrepressible Germans: VW's Theme Park." *Fortune*, September 28, 1998.

[14] *Automotive News International*, May 8, 2000.

[15] Simonian, Haig. "Critics Deride Dresden's Heart of Glass." *Financial Times*, July 27, 1999.

[16] Hawranek, Dietmar and Richard Rickelmann. "Immer auf Vollgas." *Der Spiegel*, 6/1999: 94.

[17] "Banken, Brillen, Briefbeschwerer." *Focus*, April 15, 2002: 234–238.

[18] "Hard Driving Boss." *Business Week*, October 5, 1998.

[19] Piëch, Ferdinand. *Auto. Biographie*. Hoffmann und Campe Verlag, Hamburg, 2002: 181.

[20] Piëch, Ferdinand. *Auto. Biographie*. Hoffmann und Campe Verlag, Hamburg, 2002: 235/236.

[21] Piëch, Ferdinand. *Auto. Biographie*. Hoffmann und Campe Verlag, Hamburg, 2002: 211.

adidas-Salomon

John E. Gamble
University of South Alabama

Adidas-Salomon was the world's second largest sporting goods company, with 2003 revenues of €6.3 billion. Nearly 80 percent of its revenues came from the sale of adidas branded athletic footwear and apparel, but the company competed in a variety of sporting goods equipment segments. Adidas had broadened its diversification base in sporting goods via a 1998 acquisition of diversified sporting goods producer Salomon SA. Salomon had several businesses that adidas management viewed as attractive—its Salomon ski division was the leading producer of ski equipment; TaylorMade Golf was the second largest seller of golf equipment; and Mavic was the leading producer of high-performance bicycle wheels and rims. Other Salomon businesses included Bonfire snowboard apparel and Cliché skateboard equipment. Adidas management believed the Salomon acquisition would give it the products and brands it needed to better compete with industry leader Nike, which had grown from $4.8 billion in revenues in 1995 to $9.2 billion in 1997.

But the Salomon acquisition had so far failed to do much in the way of boosting adidas-Salomon's performance, chiefly because of declining industry attractiveness in winter sports and golf equipment and because of integration problems with the Salomon and TaylorMade business units. Not until 2003, five years after the acquisition, had adidas-Salomon's earnings per share returned to the level that shareholders had enjoyed in 1997. And the company's stock price in 2004 was still trading below levels that had prevailed in 1998, just months after the Salomon acquisition (see Exhibit 1). The Salomon ski equipment division recorded a €7 million operating loss for the first nine months of 2004, and operating profits were down 29.9 percent in the Taylor-Made–adidas Golf division—since their acquisition in 1998, both divisions had struggled at various times to deliver good earnings. And these two divisions were the crown jewels that had made acquiring Salomon so attractive back in 1998.

Adidas-Salomon made a $126 million offer for Top-Flite Golf in August 2003 to strengthen its golf equipment business, but it lost out to rival Callaway Golf Company, which topped adidas-Salomon's offer. Callaway's acquisition of Top-Flite mirrored a general consolidation trend in the sporting goods industry—industry leader Nike had acquired three sporting goods businesses in 2003 and 2004. Industry analysts believed that rapidly growing private sporting goods companies—like technical ski wear

Exhibit 1   Performance of adidas-Salomon's Stock Price, 1997–2004

(a) Trend in adidas-Salomon's Common Stock Price

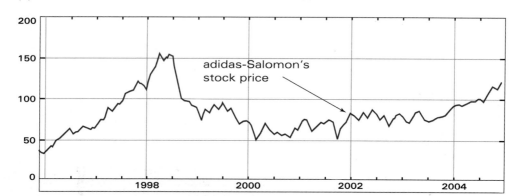

(b) Performance of adidas-Salomon's Stock Price Versus the DAX 30 Index

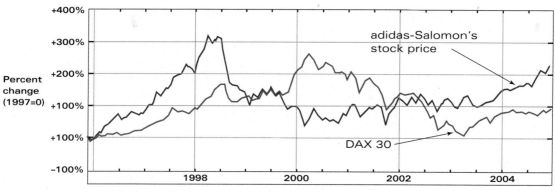

Source: www.finance.yahoo.com, accessed December 21, 2004.

producer Spyder, athletic undergarment maker Under Armour, and basketball shoe maker And 1—were likely targets for takeover by diversified sporting goods sellers like Nike or adidas-Salomon.

Adidas-Salomon discounted rumors that it was pursuing And 1 to boost its position in the U.S. basketball shoe category. When asked about the company's plans for further diversification, adidas-Salomon CEO Herbert Hainer responded:

> If your question is referring to whether we have an acquisition in mind or not, I can definitely say: No. Because I still believe and have said this several times before: Our portfolio of brands still has a lot of organic growth potential. We can grow the top-line for the next few years at the rate of 3–5 percent. Therefore we are definitely not looking at major acquisitions at the moment.[1]

Exhibit 2 shows some of adidas-Salomon's golf, winter sports, and cycling products in 2004. A summary of adidas-Salomon financial performance during 1995–2003 is presented in Exhibit 3.

Exhibit 2   A Sampling of Salomon, Mavic, and TaylorMade Golf Products

Source: adidas-Salomon AG Investor Day 2004 presentation, October 5, 2004.

Exhibit 3 FINANCIAL SUMMARY FOR ADIDAS-SALOMON, 1995–2003 (in millions, except per share amounts and financial ratios)

	2003	2002	2001	2000	1999	1998	1997	1996	1995
Net sales	€ 6,267	€ 6,523	€ 6,112	€ 5,835	€ 5,354	€ 5,065	€ 3,425	€ 2,408	€ 1,790
Gross profit	2,814	2,819	2,601	2,528	2,352	2,124	1,437	960	710
Operating profit	490	477	475	437	482	416	316	192	129
Income before taxes	438	390	376	347	398	319	346	227	151
Net income	€260	€229	€208	€182	€228	€205	€237	€161	€125
Basic earnings per share	€5.72	€5.04	€4.60	€4.01	€5.02	€4.52	€5.22	€3.54	€2.76
Total assets	€ 4,183	€ 4,261	€ 4,183	€ 4,018	€ 3,587	€ 3,206	€ 2,224	€ 1,288	€909
Inventories	1,164	1,190	1,273	1,294	1,045	975	821	556	431
Working capital	1,433	1,455	1,485	1,417	1,096	(327)	11	284	175
Net total borrowings	946	1,498	1,679	1,791	1,591	1,655	738	174	208
Shareholders' equity	1,356	1,081	1,015	815	680	463	717	489	295
Dividend payout	45.5%	45.4%	41.7%	41.7%	41.7%	38.1%	38.1%	25.4%	5.8%
Return on capital employed	18.3%	16.8%	16.7%	17.0%	20.7%	20.5%	35.8%	35.2%	35.0%
SG&A expenses as a percent of sales	35.6%	34.4%	33.3%	34.5%	33.8%	32.7%	31.8%	30.9%	31.3%
Interest coverage	8.4	6.4	4.9	4.6	6.1	4.8	21.2	14.1	8.8

Source: adidas-Salomon 2003 annual report.

Company History

In 1920, 20-year-old German baker-by-trade Adolph Dassler began making simple canvas shoes in the rear of his family's small bakery located in the North Bavarian town of Herzogenaurach. Dassler, a sports enthusiast, had little interest in working as a baker and wanted to make shoes for athletes competing in soccer, tennis, and track and field events. Adolph (nicknamed Adi) Dassler thought that proper footwear might improve an athlete's performance and began to study ways to improve athletic shoe design to give athletes wearing his shoes an edge in competitive events.

In 1924, Adi Dassler's brother, Rudolph, joined him in shoemaking to establish Gebrüder Dassler Schuhfabrik (Dassler Brothers Shoe Factory), a new company specializing in innovative sports shoes. The two brothers realized that athletes should have shoes designed specifically for their respective sport and developed a variety of styles. In 1925, the Dasslers made their first major innovation in athletic shoe design when they integrated studs and spikes into the soles of track and field shoes. The Dassler brothers also developed other key innovations in footwear such as the arch support. Many of the standard features of today's athletic footwear were developed by the Dassler brothers, with Adi Dassler alone accumulating 700 patents and property rights worldwide by the time of his death in 1978.

The Dasslers were also innovators in the field of marketing—giving away their shoes to German athletes competing in the 1928 Olympic Games in Amsterdam. By the 1936 Olympic Games in Berlin, most athletes—including Jesse Owens, who won four gold medals in the Berlin games—would compete only in Gebrüder Dassler shoes. By 1937, Dassler was making 30 different styles of shoes for athletes in 11 sports. All of the company's styles were distinguished from other brands by two stripes applied to each side of the shoe.

The Dasslers' sports shoe production ceased during World War II when Gebrüder Dassler Schuhfabrik was directed to produce boots for the armed forces of Nazi Germany. Adi Dassler was allowed to remain in Herzogenaurach to run the factory, but Rudolph (or Rudi) Dassler was drafted into the army and spent a year in an Allied prisoner-of-war camp after being captured. Upon the conclusion of the war, Rudi Dassler was released by the Allies and returned to Herzogenaurach to rejoin his family. The Dasslers returned to production of athletic shoes in 1947, but the company was dissolved in 1948 after the two brothers entered into a bitter feud. Rudi Dassler moved to the other side of the small village to establish his own shoe company, Puma Schuhfabrik Rudolph Dassler. With the departure of Rudi Dassler, Adi renamed the company adidas—a combination of the first three letters of his nickname and the first three letters of his last name. Adi Dassler also applied an additional stripe to the sides of adidas shoes and registered the three-stripe trademark in 1949.

The nature of the disagreement between the brothers was never known for certain, but the two never spoke again after their split and the feud became the foundation of both organizations' cultures while the two brothers were alive. The two rival companies were highly competitive, and both discouraged employees from fraternizing with cross-town rivals. An adidas spokesperson described the seriousness of the feud by stating, "Puma employees wouldn't be caught dead with adidas employees," and continuing, "It wouldn't be allowed that an adidas employee would fall in love with a Puma employee."[2]

Adi Dassler kept up his string of innovations with molded rubber cleats in 1949 and track shoes with screw-in spikes in 1952. He expanded the concept to soccer shoes in

1954 with screw-in studs, an innovation partially credited for Germany's World Cup Championship that year. By 1960, adidas was the clear favorite among athletic footwear brands, with 75 percent of all track and field athletes competing in the Olympic Games in Rome wearing adidas shoes. The company began producing soccer balls in 1963 and athletic apparel in 1967. The company's dominance in the athletic footwear industry continued through the early 1970s with 1,164 of the 1,490 athletes competing in the 1972 Olympic Games in Munich wearing adidas shoes. In addition, when jogging became popular in the United States in the early 1970s, adidas was the leading brand of consumer jogging shoe. Also, T-shirts and other apparel bearing adidas's trefoil logo were popular wardrobe items for U.S. teenagers during the 1970s.

At the time of Adi Dassler's death in 1978, adidas remained the worldwide leader in athletic footwear, but the company was rapidly losing market share in the United States to industry newcomer Nike. The first Nike shoes appeared in the 1972 U.S. Olympic Trials in Eugene, Oregon, and had become the best-selling training shoe in the United States by 1974. Both Adi Dassler and his son, Horst, who took over as adidas's chief manager after Adi's death, severely underestimated the threat of Nike. With adidas perhaps more concerned with cross-town adversary Puma, Nike pulled ahead of its European rivals in the U.S. athletic footwear market by launching new styles in a variety of colors and by signing recognizable sports figures to endorsement contracts. Even though Nike was becoming the market leader in U.S. athletic footwear market, adidas was able to retain its number one ranking among competitive athletes, with 259 gold medal winners in the 1984 Olympic Summer Games in Los Angeles wearing adidas products (compared to only 65 Olympic athletes wearing Nike shoes). However, at the time of Horst Dassler's unexpected death in 1987, Nike was the undisputed leader in the U.S. athletic footwear market, with more than $1 billion in annual sales.

Adidas's performance spiraled downward after the death of Horst Dassler, with no clear direction from the top and quality and innovation rapidly deteriorating. By 1990, adidas had fallen to number eight in the U.S. athletic footwear market and held only a 2 percent share of the market. A number of management and ownership changes occurred between 1987 and 1993, when a controlling interest in the company was acquired by a group of investors led by French advertising executive Robert Louis-Dreyfus. Louis-Dreyfus launched a dramatic turnaround of the company—cutting costs, improving styling, launching new models such as the Predator soccer shoe, and creating new promotional events like the adidas Predator Cup tournament for young soccer players in Germany. The turnaround was also aided by a trend among teenagers that re-popularized 1970s styles and teens' preference for niche brands that weren't likely to be purchased by adults. At year-end 1994, adidas had increased its annual sales in the United States by 75 percent from the prior year and improved its market share enough to become the third largest seller of athletic footwear in the United States—trailing only Nike and Reebok.

The company's turnaround continued in 1995 as adidas went public and recorded annual sales of nearly €1.8 billion. In 1996, adidas outfitted more than 6,000 athletes in the Olympic Games held in Atlanta and supplied the official matchball for the European Soccer Championship. Louis-Dreyfus's turnaround strategy also included a push in 1997 to sign athletes such as Kobe Bryant, Anna Kournikova, and David Beckham to offset the appeal of Nike's Michael Jordan with athletic footwear and apparel consumers in the United States. The company's mid-1990s image revival was also aided when celebrities such as Madonna and Elle MacPherson appeared in magazines or on television wearing adidas shoes without any prompting from the company.

Even though the company's turnaround had produced outstanding results, with sales and earnings growing at annual rates of 38.3 percent and 37.5 percent, respectively, between 1995 and 1997, the company was a distant number three in the worldwide athletic footwear and apparel industry. Nike's 1997 revenues of $9.2 billion were nearly three times greater than that of adidas, and Nike continued to grow at a fast pace as it expanded into more international markets. In addition, Nike had begun to diversify outside of athletic footwear and apparel with the 1988 acquisition of Cole-Haan and the 1995 acquisition of Bauer hockey equipment; it was even rumored in 1997 that Nike was eyeing French ski maker Skis Rossignol SA. In late 1997, Louis-Dreyfus and the family owners of Salomon SA, a French sports equipment manufacturer, agreed to a $1.5 billion buyout that would diversify adidas beyond footwear and apparel and into ski equipment, golf clubs, bicycle components, and winter sports apparel. The acquisition would also give adidas a stronger sales platform in North America and Asia—two markets where adidas was still struggling.

The Salomon SA Acquisition

Adidas's $1.5 billion acquisition of Salomon SA allowed it to surpass Reebok to become the world's second largest sporting goods company, with projected 1998 sales of nearly €5.1 billion. Nike remained the leader of the $90 billion global sporting goods industry, but the acquisition added the number one winter sports equipment producer, the second largest golf equipment company, and the leading producer of performance bicycle wheels and rims to adidas's lineup of businesses. The acquisition was a move toward achieving Robert Louis-Dreyfus's vision of building "the best portfolio of sports brands in the world."[3]

The price of adidas's shares fell upon the announcement of the acquisition over concerns about the price adidas had agreed to pay for Salomon and how the company might finance the acquisition. There was also some concern among investors that adidas did not have expertise in manufacturing sports equipment since its apparel and footwear were produced by contract manufacturers. A Merrill Lynch analyst suggested the Salomon acquisition might prove troublesome for adidas since other athletic shoe companies had "dabbled in the hard goods segment, but they have been unsuccessful to date in making inroads."[4] Other analysts were quite bullish on adidas's acquisition of Salomon, with a Frankfurt fund manager commenting, "This is a positive link because Salomon is strong where adidas is weak. The business mix fits well together."[5] Some were even as bold to suggest, as did a fund manager controlling 500,000 shares of adidas stock in 1997, that "Adidas' goal is to be the number-one sports equipment company in the world and I think they're going to get there. They will overtake Nike in the early 21st century."[6]

Adidas shareholders approved the merger in December 1997. The new company would be named adidas-Salomon AG upon approval of the acquisition by the German federal cartel office. Louis-Dreyfus elected to finance 100 percent of the purchase with debt but was not concerned with adidas's ability to service the debt since the company's annual free cash flow in 1997 was projected to be more than €200 million. Upon approval of the acquisition during the shareholders meeting, adidas's supervisory board extended Robert Louis-Dreyfus's management contract through 2003. Adidas's 1997 results (prior to the integration of Salomon) reached record levels, with the company's annual revenues increasing 42 percent from the prior year as a result of footwear sales growing by 32 percent and apparel sales increasing by 55 percent.

Gains were recorded for all geographic regions, with North American sales increasing by 66 percent during 1997, sales in Europe increasing by 31 percent, and Asia/Pacific revenues growing by 38 percent between 1996 and 1997.

Coming off its banner 1997 year, adidas-Salomon owned a collection of businesses in 1998 that included adidas-branded athletic footwear and apparel, Salomon skis and bindings, Mavic bicycle rims and wheels, Bonfire snowboard apparel, Cliché skateboard equipment, and TaylorMade golf clubs. Louis-Dreyfus expected the new business units to boost adidas's pretax profits by 20 to 25 percent in 1998 and by an additional 20 percent in 1999. He believed 2000 would be the first year shareholders would see the full potential of the acquisition. However, with adidas taking control of Salomon just as the winter sports equipment and golf equipment industries were becoming less attractive, Louis-Dreyfus's projections never materialized. Intensifying competitive conditions in the United States, along with the Asian financial crisis, led to losses at TaylorMade and Salomon at midyear 1998. The signs of a slowdown in the ski equipment industry actually appeared in early 1997, and the poor performance of Salomon and TaylorMade in 1998 led to a net loss of $164 million for adidas-Salomon during the first nine months of its fiscal year. To make matters worse, the integration of Mavic, Salomon, Bonfire, Cliché, and TaylorMade was not going as smoothly as Louis-Dreyfus and adidas's shareholders had expected. The poor performance of the Salomon and TaylorMade business units led to the resignation of the president of Salomon in August 1998, with Louis-Dreyfus announcing he would "devote the majority of his time" to turning around the Salomon businesses.[7]

Adidas's core footwear and apparel business performed commendably during 1998 to contribute to a net profit of €205 million for the fiscal year. In early 1999, adidas-Salomon management announced that synergies from the merger would amount to less than one-half of what was initially projected. By the summer of 1999, adidas-Salomon's share price had declined by more than a third from its early-1998 high and most large investors believed that adidas had bitten off more than it could chew with the acquisition.[8] Robert Louis-Dreyfus attempted to deflect criticism by commenting that "the sporting goods markets do not seem to be in good shape."[9] Louis-Dreyfus also suggested that the steep falloff in adidas-Salomon's shares was attributable to an investment preference for growth-oriented technology companies by institutional investors in the United States.[10] In November 1999, Herbert Hainer, the head of adidas-Salomon's marketing efforts in Europe and Asia, was appointed vice chairman and chief operating officer of the company. In January 2000, the company's chief financial offer was dismissed. Robert Louis-Dreyfus announced in early 2000 that he too would step down from adidas-Salomon and rejoin his family's business France in early 2001. Herbert Hainer was tapped as his replacement to run the diversified sporting goods company.

Under Hainer's leadership, adidas-Salomon implemented a program called Growth and Efficiency to cut costs; introduced new apparel and footwear products; increased the company's advertising; signed additional athletes to endorsement contracts; and supplied apparel, equipment, and footwear to more than 3,000 athletes competing in 26 sports during the 2000 Olympic Games in Sydney, Australia. Hainer also reorganized the company's apparel and footwear around three broad categories: adidas Sport Performance, which met the demands of competitive athletes; adidas Sport Heritage, a casual line that drew on the company's classic models for inspiration; and adidas Sport Style, which was developed for casual wear and light training. The company also expanded into company-owned retail stores in 2001 with its first adidas Originals store opening in Berlin in September, followed by stores in Tokyo, Amsterdam, and Paris by year-end. In December 2001, Hainer added to the company's lineup of sports businesses with the acquisition of Arc'Teryx, the producer of technical winter sports apparel. Adidas-Salomon recorded sales of €6.1 billion in 2001 and ended the year as the top performer in the DAX 30.

The company was the best-performing stock in the DAX 30 again in 2002. Its sales and earnings increases were aided by the introduction of new products like its ClimaCool footwear, which featured 360-degree ventilation; its a³ footwear line, which featured a mechanical cushioning system; and new Sport Style apparel items, developed by Japanese clothing designer Yohji Yamamoto. Also, adidas- and Salomon-branded products were used by more than 50 percent of athletes competing in the 2002 Winter Olympics in Salt Lake City and athletes using adidas-Salomon equipment won 191 medals during the company's first appearance in the Winter Games.

In 2003, adidas opened additional company-owned stores, including a factory store in Herzogenerauch, and restructured its debt with a €400 million convertible bond that offered a 15-year term and a more favorable rate than the original debt financing that accompanied the Salomon acquisition. Fiscal 2003 revenues and earnings per share had increased to €6.3 billion and €5.72, respectively.

adidas-Salomon's Corporate Strategy in 2004

Adidas-Salomon's corporate strategy had diversified the company beyond general athletic footwear and apparel to winter sports products, skateboard equipment, golf equipment, and bicycle components. The company's chief managers believed that adidas-Salomon's portfolio represented the world's leading collection of sports brands. Adidas-Salomon's businesses were organized under three units based around the company's core brands—adidas, Salomon, and TaylorMade–adidas Golf. Innovation and excellence in strategy execution were common themes in all of adidas-Salomon's three business segments. The company expected its product design teams to develop at least one major product innovation per year in each product category. In 2004, TaylorMade Golf introduced its r7 Quad driver, a first-of-its-kind product that incorporated four movable weights. The movable weights allowed golfers to make adjustments to the club that could produce six different ball flight trajectories. The adidas Sport Performance group introduced its Roteiro soccer ball, which was the industry's first thermal-bonded soccer ball. Also, the adidas Sport Performance group and the Salomon group collaborated to develop footwear featuring the Ground Control System, which adjusted for uneven ground. Adidas T-Mac 4 laceless basketball shoes were another innovation developed by the Sport Performance group in 2004.

Adidas-Salomon also relied heavily on ongoing brand-building activities to further differentiate adidas, TaylorMade, and Salomon from competing brands of sporting goods. Partnerships with major sporting events around the world and with notable athletes competing in winter sports, track and field, soccer, basketball, tennis, and golf were critical to creating a distinctive image with consumers. Exhibit 4 shows some of the company's print ads for its products used in 2004. The company also attempted to provide its retailers with superior customer service, including on-time deliveries, since the retailer was a crucial element of the sporting goods industry value chain. Efficient supply chain management and manufacturing efficiencies were also vital to the success of the company since poor product quality might discourage repeat sales to consumers.

Exhibit 4   Print Advertisements for adidas Sport Performance and TaylorMade Golf

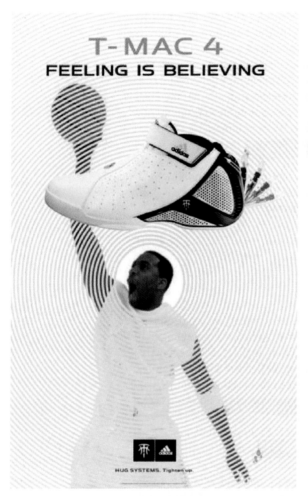

Source: adidas-Salomon AG Investor Day 2004 presentation, October 5, 2004.

Even though the majority of adidas-Salomon products were produced by contract manufacturers, the company employed more than 100 quality control officers to monitor supplier standards.

Adidas-Salomon management expected visible improvements in operating margins each year and anticipated that the company would achieve an overall 10 percent operating profit margin in 2006. Increased profitability in Europe, strong top-line and bottom-line growth in Asia, and steady growth in North America were expected to deliver sought-after gains in operating profit margins. The company's chief managers believed that operational efficiency coupled with product innovation would allow it to attain number one or number two positions in each sporting goods segment where it competed.

adidas Footwear and Apparel

Adidas footwear and apparel was organized under three categories according to the clothing needs of the consumer. The adidas Sport Performance group developed sports shoes and attire suitable for use by athletes in running, football and soccer, basketball, tennis, and general training. Adidas held number one or number two positions globally in these athletic categories and maintained its advantage primarily through innovations like its ClimaCool 360-degree footwear ventilation system, its a^3 energy management system, and endorsements by individual athletes or league sponsorships. Tim Duncan, Kevin Garnett, and Tracy McGrady were among the latest NBA athletes to endorse adidas footwear and apparel. In soccer, not only players such as David Beckham and Zinedine Zidane but also entire clubs endorsed adidas soccer shoes and clothing. In 2004, adidas was the official sponsor for the German national women's team and UEFA soccer league teams in Munich, Amsterdam, Milan, and Madrid. Also, the adidas Roteiro was the official match ball for all UEFA games. Adidas was also the official supplier to 18 National Olympic Committees competing in the 2004 Olympic Games in Athens and fully equipped athletes from 45 nations competing in 26 of the 28 disciplines included in the Olympics.

The company's Sport Heritage group, established in 2000, designed new styles of shoes and apparel that were very similar to performance-oriented styles of the 1970s. Although athletes in the early 2000s would not compete in products based on 1970s technology, many teenagers and urban trend-followers liked the look of adidas's older products. Adidas limited distribution of its Sport Heritage products to avoid dilution of the brand.

Like those who purchased Sport Heritage products, few purchasers of adidas Sport Style products were likely to wear such products while engaged in athletic endeavors. The Y-3 collection of sportswear, which was designed by Yohji Yamamoto, was based on athletic styles but would be only marginally suitable for sports. Most of the Y-3 line was best suited for consumers looking for trendy and comfortable casual wear with a mild sports influence. The line was launched in 2003 and adidas-Salomon management believed the division could eventually account for €100 million in sales.

North America   The North American market for sporting goods showed virtually no growth between 2000 and 2004 and was characterized by fierce competition among manufacturers and deep promotional discounting by retailers. All of adidas's brand-building efforts and product innovations were directed toward building on its number four ranking in North America. In 2003, adidas held an 8.8 percent market share, behind Nike, with a 37.6 percent market share; Reebok, with a 13 percent market share; and New Balance, with an 11.4 percent market share. Adidas management's emphasis was on slower, profitable growth rates, but the company did expect revenue growth rates to approach 10 percent in 2005 and exceed 10 percent in 2006. Revenue growth in North America was the key to achieving adidas's goal of becoming the leading sports brand in the world since the United States was the world's largest market for all types of sports gear, including soccer, which had 18 million participants in 2004.

To achieve its revenue growth objectives, adidas developed new styles and models in all three of its segments; placed a strong emphasis on basketball; established marketing partnerships with college sports teams, major league soccer, and major league baseball teams; and improved retailer relations. Further, it expanded distribution to additional sporting goods stores, mall-based stores, department stores, urban distribution locations, and company-owned stores. Adidas also hoped to encourage retailers to create shop-within-a-shop merchandising sections and provide permanent wall space for adidas shoes. In 2004, Foot Locker agreed to give adidas's Kevin Garnett shoes permanent wall space in its best locations and feature the sub-brand in its television and print ads. Adidas also planned to expand distribution into additional urban retail stores that might not be a part of a large chain but that were close to urban consumers. The company estimated the U.S. urban retail market for athletic footwear and apparel to be over $6 billion. Finally, adidas planned to open company-owned retail stores in Las Vegas, New York, Chicago, and San Francisco in 2005 and in Portland, Boston, Washington, Philadelphia, Los Angeles, and Atlanta in 2006.

Europe   Growth plans in Europe were focused on building on adidas's number one ranking in the region through its sponsorship of youth and professional soccer and continued support for running. The European athletic footwear and apparel market was growing at a modest rate, but retailers in Europe had relied even more on promotional pricing than retailers in North America. Prices for children's apparel had declined by 10 percent during 2004 and prices of adult apparel had decreased by 8.5 percent between 2003 and 2004. Adidas believed that its emphasis on product innovation and its strong brand loyalty would help protect the company from margin erosion due to price competition. It also planned to increase its number of retailers in Europe by 25 percent between 2004 and 2006, with most new locations coming in emerging-country markets. Additional company-owned stores were planned for Europe during 2005 and 2006.

Asia   In 1999, adidas held a 6 percent market share in Japan, but its market share had grown to 18 percent in 2004 and its management expected a 20–24 percent market share in Japan by 2006. Adidas's increase in market share had come mainly at the expense of local brands such as Asics and Mizuno. In 2004, Japan accounted for 50 percent of athletic apparel sales in Asia, but adidas and other consumer goods companies were directing considerable efforts to building brand awareness in China and other emerging Asian markets. The region's growth in gross domestic product was projected to be the highest in the world between 2005 and 2010, with much of the growth resulting from domestic-driven demand rather than exports. The size of the middle class in the region was also expected to grow dramatically in the region by 2010, with China's middle class growing from 60 million in 2002 to 160 million by 2010. Adidas management estimated that every 1 percent increase in consumption by China's population translated into a $70 billion increase in sales of consumer goods. Adidas expected the 2008 Olympic Games in Beijing to generate interest in athletic footwear and apparel in China.

The company was rapidly adding retail stores to ensure that its products were available for purchase by China's growing consumer base. The company was adding more than 40 stores per month in urban locations in China since 55 percent of the country's population was expected to migrate from the countryside to cities by 2012. In 2004, adidas had more than 150 retail locations in only 1 province of China but expected to have more than 150 retail locations in 10 provinces by the 2008 Olympics. In 2004, adidas's revenues of more than €100 million made it the number two brand of athletic footwear and apparel in China. Nike was the leading seller of athletic goods in China. Adidas management expected to double its sales in China by 2008.

Salomon

Like athletic footwear and apparel, the winter sports industry was mature, with the market declining by 3.1 percent during the 2003–2004 ski season. The 2003–2004 decline followed a 3.6 percent decline during the 2002–2003 season and a 1.8 percent decline in the 2001–2002 season. Some categories within the winter sports industry were declining at a more rapid pace, with the snowboard industry falling from €428.9 million in 2000–2001 to €344.5 million in 2003–2004. Nordic (cross-country) skiing was the only bright spot in the industry, with a 3.1 percent growth rate during the 2003–2004 ski season. The total value of worldwide winter sports equipment market in 2004 was €1.5 billion.

Revenue increases for most winter sporting goods producers had come from adding summer outdoor-inspired apparel and footwear to their product lines. Salomon was the number one producer of winter sports equipment with a number one position in alpine (downhill) ski boots and high-end skis, a number two position in alpine skis overall and snowboard boots, and a number three position in snowboards. The company held an 80 percent market share in Nordic (cross-country) ski systems. The Salomon business group also included Mavic, which was the number one brand of performance bicycle wheels and rims. The performance bicycle category was also mature, but it was growing a modest rate because of the popularity of road racing in the United States and Europe. Other businesses in the portfolio included Bonfire, the producer of snowboard apparel, Arc'Teryx, which produced technical winter sports apparel, and Cliché, the maker of skateboard equipment and apparel.

The businesses included in the Salomon division used competitive approaches similar to those of adidas-branded products. The division was committed to innovation in products in its snow, outdoor, and asphalt categories and attempted to benefit from synergies with the core adidas business when feasible. An example of such cross-division strategic fit was Salomon and adidas's collaboration on the development of the Ground Control System running shoe. Shoes using the design were marketed under both the adidas and the Salomon brand names and were sold in different retail channels. The division also exploited adidas's apparel design expertise in its development of winter sports, cycling, and skateboard apparel. The collaboration between adidas and Salomon brands in apparel design had contributed to a 400 percent increase in soft goods sales for the division since 1995.

In 2004, sales for the Salomon group were nearly evenly split between winter sports hard goods and other products. The Salomon group was undertaking efforts to increase soft goods sales to 50 percent of the group's sales by expanding apparel lines, developing dedicated soft goods sales forces for each brand, and developing advertising targeting women since studies had shown a large percentage of winter sports apparel purchases were made by women.

Christain Finell, Salomon's chief manager, suggested Salomon's revenue growth in 2005 would be limited to single digits. He noted, "50% of our sales are still linked to winter sports hardware. And there is of course always big fluctuation potential when it comes to snow conditions."[11] The division head believed increasing revenue contribution of soft goods would help Salomon's sales growth potential since apparel lines could be developed for all four seasons and winter apparel was purchased by nonskiers as well as skiers.

Improvement in operating margins was also a strategic priority at Salomon since top-line growth was limited. Since 2001, the division had shifted hardware production from France to Eastern Europe and Asia, developed a new production process in skis that lowered materials costs, reduced production time, and lowered labor costs per unit. In addition, Salomon had reduced total employment between 2002 and 2004 through early retirements and an increased reliance on temporary employees. The effect of Salomon's cost-cutting efforts had reduced operating expenses for the division from €234 million in 2001 to €201 million in 2003.

Even with Salomon management's efforts to improve operating margins for the division, there were some characteristics of the winter sports industry that precluded options that might be pursued in other industries. When asked by an investment banker why Salomon didn't shift all production to Asia, Finell responded, "The reason for this is that the main part of our business in winter sports is done in Europe. We believe it makes much more sense to have our production close to our customers. Also most of the relevant raw materials are found in Europe and not in Asia. And lead times are relatively long in this business. So by adding both the lead time and additional transportation costs it doesn't make sense to shift the production to Asia."[12]

TaylorMade Golf

TaylorMade Golf was the second largest producer in the $5.5 billion golf equipment industry. The industry had experienced little growth since 1999, when golf's chief governing body in the United States began to ban from play any golf clubs that it deemed performed too well. Golf equipment sales had grown dramatically during the mid to late 1990s as golf equipment manufacturers like Callaway Golf Company, Titleist, Ping, and TaylorMade Golf introduced better-performing clubs that were more forgiving of recreational golfers' poor swing characteristics. Professional golfers using the technologically advanced equipment saw improvements in their games as well—particularly in driving distance. The United States Golf Association (USGA) began to believe that these new high-tech clubs provided a springlike or trampoline effect and developed a coefficient of restitution (COR) limitation that would prevent any such effect for golf equipment sold in the United States. Golf equipment manufacturers scoffed at the idea that clubs could produce a timed springlike effect that could help propel the ball forward but nevertheless were obliged to discontinue research and development projects that would produce clubs exceeding a COR of 0.83.

By 2000, most golf club manufacturers had reached the 0.83 COR limitation and were compelled to find new approaches to innovation. In 2002, golf club manufacturers began to produce larger clubheads that provided a larger hitting area and produced a higher launch angle that allowed a golf ball to carry more distance. As clubhead size began to increase, the USGA also limited the size of clubs that could be sold in the United States. In 2004, there was only modest differentiation among golf clubs until TaylorMade introduced its r7 Quad Driver. The driver was unique in that it allowed golfers to reposition movable weights screwed into the clubhead. The golfer could move the weights to provide a higher or lower launch angle and cause the flight path to pull to the left or fade to the right. The new innovation spurred 8 percent growth in driver sales for the year, making TaylorMade the number one producer of drivers and metalwoods. Prior to TaylorMade's introduction of the r7 Quad driver, Callaway Golf had held the number one position in the industry sine 1991.

Annual growth rates between 1999 and 2003 for irons and golf balls had ranged between −6 percent and 4 percent. Prior to the launch of the r7, growth in driver sales had ranged between −3 percent and 4 percent during the 1999 and 2003 period. The number of rounds played in the United States reached a peak at 518.4 million in 2000 and had declined by approximately 2.0 percent annually because of a lack of interesting new products to draw consumers to golf and because of the growing expense of golf. During golf's period of dramatic growth in the mid to late 1990s, many resort-quality golf courses were added across the United States. However, most of these courses charged between $75 and $150 per round because of the considerable initial investments made in the courses and high operating expenses.

Having concluded that it would be unwise to count on growth of the game, TaylorMade management expected to increase sales primarily through market share gains. TaylorMade believed it could increase market share through endorsement contracts with touring professionals on the PGA Tour and other professional tours and through new product innovations like the movable weight system used in its r7 driver. TaylorMade management also wished to achieve revenue growth by increasing sales in Asia. The company had successfully increased its sales in Asia from 13 percent of sales in 1999 to 31 percent of sales in 2004 and the United States accounted for only 52 percent of sales in 2004 versus 69 percent of sales in 1999. TaylorMade CEO Mark King designated Asia as a high-priority market: "Asia is very, very profitable as a region. The main reason is because the selling prices in Asia for golf equipment are higher than in any other place in the world. So the margins there are very, very strong. Profitability in North America is also very strong. The only area that we are struggling in right now a little bit is in Europe."[13] In addition, USGA rules did not apply to play in Asia and most golf club manufacturers produced models with high COR ratings for sale in Asia.

Even though TaylorMade had become the number one brand of metalwoods worldwide, its market share in irons was about one-half that of industry leader, Callaway Golf Company, and its market share in putters was negligible. The division's sales of Maxfli golf balls, which was acquired by adidas-Salomon in 2002, accounted for less than 5 percent of industry sales. Segment leader Titleist had held a 70 percent or greater market share in golf balls for decades. King commented on Maxfli's lackluster performance by saying, "The golf ball category itself is difficult. Prior to buying the Maxfli brand we really had no ability to compete in golf balls. We do today. And we have a wonderful sub-brand under Maxfli, called The Noodle, of which we sell about 2 million dozen balls globally. For us to be successful we need to be a little bit more competitive at the premium end which is something we have been working on in terms of new technologies for golf balls, which should be launched in [2005]."[14] In addition, King stated, "We are working on all phases of our golf ball situation, our technology, and our supply chain," to make the newly acquired business profitable by 2005.[15]

Like Salomon, TaylorMade attempted to benefit from adidas's core competencies in footwear and apparel design. The company offered a full line of adidas-branded golf apparel and footwear that was sold in golf shops in North America, Europe, and Asia. The division expected double-digit annual growth rates in apparel and footwear revenues. Exhibit 5 presents TaylorMade Golf's market share in metalwoods, irons, and footwear. Exhibit 6 presents key financial data for each of adidas-Salomon's operating divisions between 1998 and 2003. The company's financial data by geographic region for 1998–2003 are presented in Exhibit 7. Income statements for and balance sheets for 2002–2003 are provided in Exhibits 8 and 9, respectively.

adidas-Salomon's Performance and Opportunities in Late 2004

At the end of the first nine months of 2004, adidas-Salomon's revenues and net income had increased by 6 percent and 26.1 percent, respectively. The adidas unit led the growth, with a 7 percent increase in revenues and a 34.1 percent increase in operating profit compared to the same period in 2003. Sales of the Salomon group grew by 5 percent, but the unit had recorded a €7 million operating loss for the first nine months of

Exhibit 5   Market Shares of Leading Sellers of Metalwoods, Irons, and Golf Footwear, January 2002–July 2004

Metalwoods

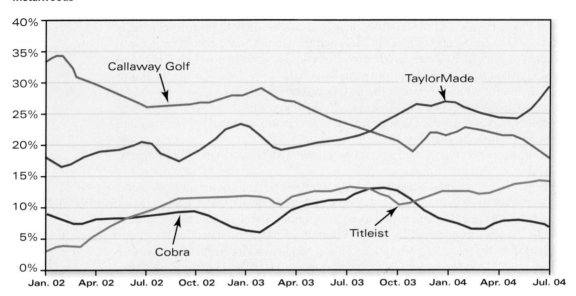

Irons

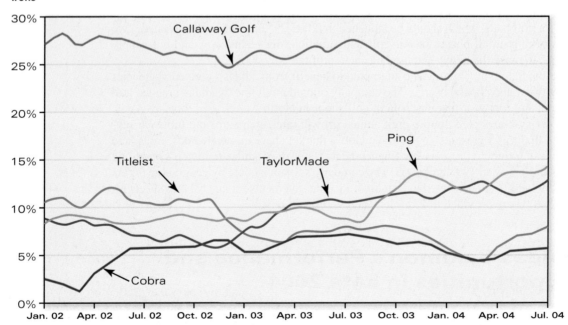

Source: adidas-Salomon AG Investor Day 2004 Presentation, October 5, 2004.

Exhibit 5   (concluded)

Footwear

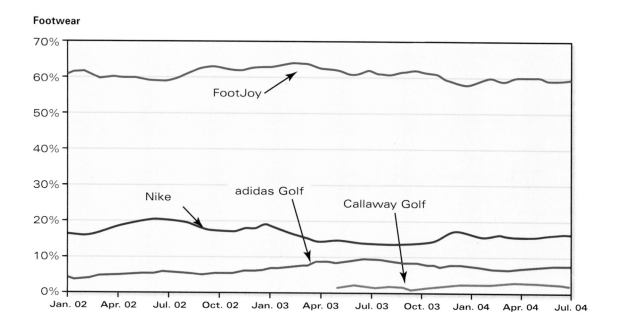

2004. TaylorMade–adidas Golf sales for the first nine months of fiscal 2004 grew by 4 percent, while operating profits declined by 29.9 percent from the first nine months in 2003.

As the 2004 holiday season approached, adidas held a 55 percent market share in soccer shoes in the United States compared to Nike's 33 percent market share. However, in the overall U.S. cleated-shoe segment, Nike led adidas by a 48 percent to 23 percent margin. Adidas was not a contender in the basketball category, in which Nike held a 70 percent market share. Adidas, Nike, and New Balance were all tied, with about 20 percent market share each, in the tennis category. Nike, Asics, New Balance, and Reebok all recorded gains in the running category during the first nine months of 2004, but analysts suggested that adidas missed out on growth in the category because its new technologies had not been a hit with consumers. Sales of casual sports shoes similar to those included in the adidas Heritage and adidas Sport Style lines were up 30 percent during the first nine months of 2004 although adidas did not make the list of top four brands in the category. The category was expected to grow by 40 percent in 2005 to displace running as the second largest category of athletic shoes in the United States.

The company was hopeful that its new T-MAC HUG basketball shoe and adidas 1 running shoe would lead to market share gains in the United States. The T-MAC HUG was a laceless design, while the adidas 1 was the first running shoe with an embedded microprocessor. The microprocessor evaluated the runner's weight, the terrain, and

Exhibit 6   ADIDAS-SALOMON FINANCIAL DATA BY OPERATING SEGMENT, 1998–2003

Brands	2003	2002	2001	2000	1999	1998
adidas						
Net sales	€ 4,950	€ 5,105	€ 4,825	€ 4,672	€ 4,427	€ 4,316
Gross profit	2,008	2,004	1,845	1,907	1,827	1,818
Operating profit	365	343	352	391	431	412
Operating assets	2,172	2,294	1,954	2,286	1,987	1,730
Capital expenditures	63	84	113	93	105	102
Amortization and depreciation, excluding goodwill amortization	63	57	52	45	48	38
Salomon						
Net sales	€ 658	€ 684	€ 714	€ 703	€ 587	€ 487
Gross profit	264	279	313	296	233	188
Operating profit	35	39	63	61	32	6
Operating assets	521	581	679	566	533	598
Capital expenditures	18	18	38	24	17	20
Amortization and depreciation, excluding goodwill amortization	7	7	7	7	5	7
TaylorMade Golf						
Net sales	€ 637	€ 707	€ 545	€ 441	€ 327	€ 263
Gross profit	290	345	281	221	160	118
Operating profit	67	74	63	44	30	20
Operating assets	391	433	316	219	156	99
Capital expenditures	12	49	16	12	10	16
Amortization and depreciation, excluding goodwill amortization	9	7	6	4	4	2
Headquarters/consolidation						
Net sales	€ 22	€ 27	€ 28	€ 19	€ 10	€ —
Gross profit	252	191	162	104	—	—
Operating profit	23	21	(3)	(59)	(14)	(22)
Operating assets	1,104	953	1,234	947	903	782
Capital expenditures	29	22	20	16	—	—
Amortization and depreciation, excluding goodwill amortization	17	26	25	23	6	6

Source: adidas-Salomon annual reports.

speed to vary the compression in the heel of the shoe with the use of mechanical shock-absorbing components. Adidas 1 running shoes were scheduled for a December 2004 launch and would retail for $250. The company also had high expectations for its new Equipment line of footwear and apparel that would be targeted to men ages 25 and up and its Stella McCartney designer line for women, which would both make their debuts in the spring of 2005.

Adidas-Salomon's CEO, Herbert Hainer, had told participants invited to the company's 2004 Investor Day series of strategy presentations that the company had no immediate interest in pursuing further diversification, but consolidation in the industry

Exhibit 7   ADIDAS-SALOMON FINANCIAL DATA BY GEOGRAPHIC REGION, 1998–2003

Regions	2003	2002	2001	2000	1999	1998
Europe						
Net sales	€ 3,365	€ 3,200	€ 3,066	€ 2,860	€ 2,723	€ 2,774
Gross profit	1,383	1,268	1,153	1,171	1,133	1,127
Operating profit	534	471	444	454	382	357
Operating assets	1,428	1,396	1,419	1,107	1,167	1,114
Capital expenditures	44	56	74	55	40	35
Amortization and depreciation, excluding goodwill amortization	30	27	24	22	20	19
North America						
Net sales	€ 1,562	€ 1,960	€ 1,818	€ 1,907	€ 1,826	€ 1,784
Gross profit	552	742	697	729	731	713
Operating profit	92	162	161	177	234	276
Operating assets	778	969	945	862	848	666
Capital expenditures	22	82	68	54	26	29
Amortization and depreciation, excluding goodwill amortization	21	20	17	16	12	11
Asia						
Net sales	€ 1,116	€ 1,166	€ 1,010	€ 875	€ 663	€ 383
Gross profit	525	562	481	416	301	156
Operating profit	191	189	170	129	96	26
Operating assets	447	505	743	455	390	201
Capital expenditures	12	16	15	17	18	9
Amortization and depreciation, excluding goodwill amortization	14	15	12	10	5	3
Latin America						
Net sales	€ 179	€ 163	€ 178	€ 171	€ 126	€ 112
Gross profit	70	65	73	72	50	43
Operating profit	25	24	16	23	15	11
Operating assets	93	79	98	109	75	66
Capital expenditures	1	1	2	3	3	2
Amortization and depreciation, excluding goodwill amortization	1	1	2	2	1	1
Headquarters/consolidation						
Net sales	€ 45	€ 34	€ 40	€ 23	€ 34	€ 12
Gross profit	284	182	197	140	—	—
Operating profit	(352)	(369)	(316)	(346)	(239)	(254)
Operating assets	1,442	1,312	978	1,485	1,108	1,162
Capital expenditures	43	15	28	16	45	63
Amortization and depreciation, excluding goodwill amortization	30	34	35	29	25	19

Source: adidas-Salomon annual reports.

Exhibit 8   ADIDAS-SALOMON INCOME STATEMENTS, 2002–2003
(in thousands, except per share data)

	2003	2002
Net sales	€ 6,266,800	€ 6,523,419
Cost of sales	3,453,132	3,704,269
Gross profit	2,813,668	2,819,150
Selling, general and administrative expenses	2,228,135	2,245,383
Depreciation and amortization (excluding goodwill)	95,519	97,147
Operating profit	490,014	476,620
Goodwill amortization	44,809	45,396
Royalty and commission income	42,153	46,006
Financial expenses, net	49,170	87,116
Income before taxes	438,188	390,114
Income taxes	166,712	147,862
Net income before minority interests	271,476	242,252
Minority interests	(11,391)	(13,681)
Net income	€ 260,085	€ 228,571
Basic earnings per share (in euros)	€ 5.72	€ 5.04
Diluted earnings per share (in euros)	€ 5.72	€ 5.04

Source: adidas-Salomon annual reports.

was continuing at a rapid pace at year-end 2004. K2—which was well known for its line of ski and snowboard equipment but also owned Shakespeare fishing gear, Stearns life vests, and Rawlings baseball equipment—had recently expanded its lineup of winter sports companies with the acquisitions of Volkl Sports, Marker, and Marmut. Also, after acquiring Converse basketball shoes and Hurley skateboard equipment in 2003, Nike acquired Starter athletic apparel in August 2004. Some industry analysts believed that adidas-Salomon was considering the purchase of privately owned And 1 to strengthen its position in the U.S. basketball market. And 1, a highly differentiated brand of basketball shoes popular with serious athletes, had grown from $1 million in sales in 1993 to $160 million in 2003. The company also held a 4.2 percent share of the U.S. men's basketball footwear category in 2003.

Endnotes

[1] As quoted in a Q&A session during the adidas-Salomon 2004 Investor Day, October 5, 2004.
[2] As quoted in "The Brothers Dassler Fight On," *Deutsche Welle,* dw-world.de.
[3] As quoted in "Adidas Foots $1.5B to Buy Sporting Firm, *USA Today,* September 17, 1997.
[4] As quoted in "Sporting Goods Consolidation Off to the Races," *Mergers & Acquisitions Report,* November 10, 1997.
[5] As quoted in "Adidas to Buy Salomon, a French Sports Company," *New York Times,* September 17, 1997.
[6] As quoted in "Dreyfus Launches adidas into Foot Race with Nike," *Financial Post,* September 17, 1997.
[7] As quoted in "Adidas-Salomon Unveils Top-Tier Reshuffle," *Financial Times,* August 5, 1998.
[8] As quoted in "Sports Goods/Shareholders Criticize Salomon Takeover," *Handesblatt,* May 21, 1999.
[9] As quoted in "Salomon Purchase Was a Mistake," *Frankfurter Allgenmeine Zeitung,* May 21, 1999.
[10] "Sports Goods/Shareholders."
[11] As quoted in a Q&A session during the adidas-Salomon 2004 Investor Day, October 5, 2004.
[12] Ibid.
[13] Ibid.
[14] Ibid.
[15] Ibid.

Exhibit 9   ADIDAS-SALOMON BALANCE SHEETS, 2002–2003
             (in thousands)

	December 31,	
	2003	2002
Assets		
Cash and cash equivalents	€ 189,503	€ 67,455
Short-term financial assets	89,411	8,501
Accounts receivable	1,075,092	1,292,667
Inventories	1,163,518	1,189,933
Other current assets	259,427	267,435
Total current assets	2,776,951	2,825,991
Property, plant and equipment, net	344,554	365,756
Goodwill, net	591,045	638,742
Other intangible assets, net	103,797	115,495
Long-term financial assets	88,408	87,474
Deferred tax assets	178,484	169,692
Other noncurrent assets	104,569	57,661
Total noncurrent assets	1,410,857	1,434,820
Total assets	€ 4,187,808	€ 4,260,811
Liabilities, minority interests, and shareholders' equity		
Accounts payable	€ 592,273	€ 668,461
Income taxes	157,764	112,461
Accrued liabilities and provisions	454,573	450,748
Other current liabilities	139,095	148,959
Total current liabilities	1,343,705	1,380,629
Long-term borrowings	1,225,385	1,574,046
Pensions and similar obligations	105,264	98,959
Deferred tax liabilities	65,807	51,398
Other noncurrent liabilities	35,278	18,907
Total noncurrent liabilities	1,431,734	1,743,310
Minority interests	56,579	55,513
Shareholders' equity	1,355,790	1,081,359
Total liabilities, minority interests, and shareholders' equity	€ 4,187,808	€ 4,260,811

Source: 2003 adidas-Salomon annual report.

News Corp in 2004
The DirecTV Acquisition and Beyond

Ravi S. Madapati
ICFAI Knowledge Center

> *For News Corporation, completing this transaction would mark the culmination of our longtime pursuit of satellite TV distribution in the U.S. and provide the missing link in an unprecedented global satellite television platform.*
>
> —Rupert Murdoch[1]

Rupert Murdoch, 71, News Corp's chairman, seemed to be on top of the world in early 2004. The U.S. Federal Communications Commission (FCC) had approved News Corp's bid to purchase a controlling interest in the General Motors (GM) subsidiary Hughes Electronics Corporation (Hughes) on December 19, 2003.[2] Under the terms of the $6.6 billion deal, Hughes would become an independent company. News Corp, with a 34 percent stake in the company, would become the largest single shareholder in Hughes, giving it a controlling interest in the company. The deal would give News Corp control of Hughes's DirecTV satellite television service (DirecTV), which serviced 11 million homes in the United States. The U.S. Department of Justice announced it would not be challenging the acquisition.

The DirecTV deal was closed at a time when News Corp was performing well in what seemed to be a beleaguered media industry. Most media companies were still recovering from the expensive mistakes they had committed during the halcyon days of the Internet. Top-management squabbles were also common in other leading media companies. News Corp, on the other hand, had made its Internet forays carefully. News Corp's top management also seemed to be working in unison.

Background Note

News Corp was one of the largest media companies in the world, with total assets (as of June 30, 2003) of $67 billion and total annual revenues of about $30 billion (see Exhibit 1). News Corp had diversified global operations in the United States, Canada, the United Kingdom, Australia, Latin America, and the Pacific Basin. These included the production and distribution of motion pictures and television programming; television, satellite, and cable broadcasting; the publication of newspapers, magazines, and books; the production and distribution of promotional and advertising products and services; the development of digital broadcasting; the development of conditional access and subscriber management systems; and the creation and distribution of popular online programming.

Exhibit 1   **NEWS CORP FINANCIALS, 2001–2003 (in billions of $)**

	Year Ended June 30		
	2003	**2002**	**2001**
Revenues	$29,913	$29,014	$25,578
Operating income	4,352	3,542	3,093
Associated entities, before other items	(159)	(314)	(162)
Income before other items	1,898	1,217	1,282
Other items, net	(90)	(13,179)	(2,028)
Net profit	1,808	(11,962)	(746)
Earnings per share			
Income before other items	$0.36	$0.23	$0.30
Net profit	$0.34	$(2.43)	$(0.19)
Financial position			
Assets	$67,747	$71,441	$84,961
Debt	$12,429	$15,441	$18,805

Source: News Corp annual report, 2003.

Exhibit 2   **NEWS CORP'S GLOBAL REACH**

Region	TV Households (millions)	Percent Covered by News Corp
Africa	31	0%
United States and Canada	116	0
Europe	213	20
Latin America	92	80
Asia and Australia	407	100

Source: *Fortune*, February 3, 2003.

News Corp dominated the newspaper industry in Australia and owned approximately one-third of newspapers and BSkyB (satellite television) in Britain. News Corp owned 80.6 percent of the Fox Entertainment Group, which made movies under the name Twentieth Century Fox and television programs under the Fox Network. News Corp also owned HarperCollins publishing and the *New York Post.* Its television reach extended to millions of homes worldwide (see Exhibit 2). In addition to these holdings, News Corp owned the LA Dodgers (a popular baseball team), the National Rugby League, Broadsystem, and Fox Interactive. News Corp had successfully ventured into the Internet market as well, with its LineOne Service (see Exhibit 3).

News Corp's global presence had been built over a period of five decades starting from a single newspaper business in a small Australian town in 1952. After studying at Oxford and working at the Daily Express in London, Murdoch returned to Australia in 1952, when he inherited the *Adelaide News* from his father, Sir Keith Murdoch. Murdoch first focused on revamping the *News,* then the *Mirror* in Sydney and later on the *Sun* in London. In the 1970s, he turned the *New York Post* from a serious, stagnant paper into a provocative, popular paper. Murdoch acquired the *Times* and the *Sunday Times* in London in the 1980s. He took on Hollywood by purchasing Twentieth

Exhibit 3   THE NEWS CORP EMPIRE

Filmed Entertainment	Television	Cable	Magazines
Twentieth Century Fox	BSkyB	Fox Movie Channel	*Inside Out*
Twentieth Century Fox Español	Fox Broadcasting Company	Fox News Channel	*Donna Hay*
Twentieth Century Fox International	Fox Sports Australia	Fox Sports Digital	*News America*
Twentieth Century Fox Television	Fox Television Stations	Fox Sports Enterprises	*Marketing*
Fox Searchlight Pictures	FOXTEL	Fox Sports En Español	*SmartSource*
Fox Studios Australia	SkyPerfecTV!	Fox Sports Net	*The Weekly Standard*
Fox Studios Baja	Star	Fox Sports World	*Gemstar: The TV Guide*
Fox Studios LA	Stream	FX	
Fox Television Studios		Los Angeles Dodgers	
		National Geographic Channel	
		Speed Channel	

Newspapers	Books	Other Assets
Australasia (a few)	HarperCollins	Broadsystem
Daily Telegraph	Regan Books	Festival Records
Herald Sun	Zondervan	Fox Interactive
Sunday Mail		Mushroom Records
Sunday Tasmanian		National Rugby League
Sunday Times		NDS
Advertiser		News Interactive
Australian		News Outdoor
United Kingdom (a few)		Nursery World
News International		
News of the World		
Sun		
Sunday Times		
United States		
New York Post		

Source: News Corp, corporate Web site.

Century Fox and Fox TV that same year. In Asia, Murdoch purchased Star TV in the early 1990s. In 1990, News Corp merged the ailing Sky with BSB to form British Sky Broadcasting (BSkyB), which became one of the largest media businesses in the United Kingdom by the end of the century.

News Corp went public in Australia in 1973 and in the United States in 1985. Between 1985 and 1991, News Corp grew sevenfold, from an asset base of A$3.5 billion to A$24 billion. By this time, News Corp had borrowed from 146 different financial institutions in 10 different currencies. In 1991, the short-term debt was A$2.3 billion and News Corp found itself unable to meet its interest payments on occasions. As a result, it could not refinance its loans.

The turn of events forced News Corp into a restructuring mode. A consortium of 146 banks, led by Citibank, agreed to sign new agreements to cover the outstanding debt of News Corp by the end of 1991. News Corp managed to escape from potential bankruptcy. Notwithstanding the crisis, Murdoch boldly continued to expand his global empire. After emerging from the financial crises in the early 1990s, Murdoch maintained the group's momentum, acquiring more companies and entering new markets.

In 2002, News Corp provided for its investors the third highest returns among major blue-chip companies in the United States, trailing only Wal-Mart and Berkshire Hathaway and ahead of General Electric, Coca-Cola, Disney, Intel, and 3M.

Publishing

He regarded journalism really as a branch of the entertainment business.
—Alan Watkins, British Columnist on Murdoch[3]

Murdoch had inherited his passion for newspapers from his father, Sir Keith Murdoch. Just before his death, Sir Keith used all his savings to increase his stake in the *Adelaide News,* which he bequeathed to his only son.

The young Murdoch was aggressive almost from the beginning. As soon as he took control of the *Adelaide News,* which was then outsold 2 to 1 by its bigger rival *Adelaide Advertiser,* he wrote to the *Advertiser* and made clear his intentions about taking it head-on. Following a two-year circulation battle and significant expenses for both papers, the *Advertiser* agreed to merge with the *Adelaide News* under Murdoch's leadership.

Murdoch then targeted the United Kingdom's newspaper market. In 1968, he acquired a controlling interest in *News of the World,* Britain's most sensational Sunday paper. Murdoch overhauled the company's laid-back management style, forced out the editor and other senior managers, and installed his chosen people. Murdoch cut costs, made the operations leaner, and encouraged more politically outspoken editorials. Subsequently, Murdoch purchased the *Daily Herald* and relaunched the *Sun,* in order to target upwardly mobile young people.

Murdoch had always believed that he could not build a media empire without a strong presence in the United States. Backed by the cash flows of his British papers, he purchased two financially weak newspapers, the *Express* and the *News of Texas,* along with the Sunday special editions of these papers in 1973. Just as in England, the *Express* and the *News of Texas* were relaunched with more sensational content and strong promotions. In 1976, Murdoch bought the ailing tabloid the *New York Post.*

In 1981, Murdoch bought the *Times* and the *Sunday Times* of London, two of the most respected newspapers in the United Kingdom. By 1985, the *Times* had a 30 percent market share and approached the circulation of the leader, the *Guardian.* The *Sunday*

Times, with a circulation in excess of 4 million copies at that time, was the world's largest Sunday newspaper.

By 1988, News Corp had become the world's largest English-language newspaper publisher. During the year, Murdoch purchased the Triangle Group for $3 billion in a cash deal. The Triangle Group had various publications, including *TV Guide, Seventeen, Good Food,* and the *Racing Form.* The largest media acquisition in corporate history at that time made News Corp the largest publisher of consumer magazines in the United States.

In 1990, News Corp acquired the publishing company HarperCollins and later added other publishing companies, including William Morrow, Avon Books, Amistad Press, and Fourth Estate, making it one of the leading publishers in the world.

Entertainment

By the 1980s, Murdoch was looking seriously at entertainment. He eyed the United States, long considered to be the entertainment capital of the world. Murdoch believed that a serious integrated media company had to be involved in entertainment, of which movies were a vital part.

Fox Television

After a few futile attempts to purchase Time Warner, News Corp acquired a 50 percent stake in Twentieth Century Fox for $250 million in 1985. Fox had a formidable library, which included hits like *The Sound of Music* and *Star Wars.* Eight months later, News Corp purchased the remaining 50 percent of Fox for $325 million. Fox targeted the international market, which by 1997 generated 60 percent of the studio's revenues.

After purchasing Fox, Murdoch turned to television. He thought that Metromedia, an independent television station with a presence in seven major metropolitan markets in the United States, would be a good fit. He believed that he could launch a fourth broadcast television network competing with American Broadcasting Company (ABC), Central Broadcasting Corporation (CBS), and National Broadcasting Corporation (NBC). News Corp's purchase of Metromedia for $2 billion not only was the second largest media acquisition in corporate history but also made News Corp the first company to integrate its newspaper interest with television programs.

In 1986, News Corp launched the Fox Television Network, an audacious move, considering that the big three networks of ABC, CBS, and NBC together controlled 93 percent of viewership. After its launch, Fox Television targeted a younger audience with racy, provocative shows. Some of its early shows were *Married with Children,* a show full of lewd dialogue and sexual references; *A Current Affair,* which featured tabloid news stories; and *America's Most Wanted,* which featured violent crimes. By 1990, almost 50 percent of the Fox Television audience was between the ages of 12 and 34, compared to 37 percent for ABC, 31 percent for NBC, and 25 percent for CBS.

In the early 1990s, Fox struggled with many show cancellations due to falling viewership. Paramount (owned by Viacom) and Warner Bros. announced they would launch their broadcast networks. Murdoch fought back by outbidding his rivals for the exclusive rights of National Football Conference (NFC). His offer of $395 million was $100 million more than that of the nearest competitor, CBS. Murdoch thought that this price was worth paying to get Fox entrenched in people's minds. It forced cable operators to air Fox. Eventually Fox established itself in the market.

Encouraged by the turnaround of Fox, Murdoch started acquiring local television stations. In 1996, News Corp acquired New World Communication, which owned several television stations, for $3.4 billion. With this, the television stations of News Corp combined together reached 40 percent of the U.S. viewership.

In 1993, Fox launched FX, an entertainment channel aimed at the youth. FX used the production facilities of Twentieth Century Fox studios. From 1996, Murdoch started leveraging the Fox brand into new cable channels such as sports, entertainment, news, family shows, and movies. By this time, Viacom had acquired the CBS network, Nickelodeon, and Movie Channel/Showtime cable channels; Time Warner acquired Home Box Office (HBO), a very popular movie channel, Cinemax, and CNN; Disney acquired the ABC network and the popular sports channel ESPN.

News Corp launched Fox Sports cable channel in 1997, after acquiring 21 local and regional sports channels. Unlike ESPN, Fox Sports programming was offered at both local and national levels. In 1999, Fox Sports acquired the exclusive rights to air NASCAR (one of the most popular racing sports in the United States). By the beginning of the new millennium, Fox Sports was among the top sports channels in the United States. By 2001, FX was the fastest-growing cable network in the United States.

Against a backdrop of declining television news channels, Fox News was launched in 1996. Fox News aired round-the-clock fresh news and innovative content. It created a tremendous stir when it was launched. But the major obstacle Fox News faced was in convincing cable operators to air another news channel. Murdoch launched an aggressive campaign to target cable operators. He offered huge cash incentives to all those operators who aired Fox News. This move was unprecedented in television history and effectively preempted Disney from launching its own news channel. And in a year, with the exception of Time Warner's cable operators, most operators agreed to air Fox News.

Since Time Warner owned CNN and MSNBC, it made sure Fox News was not aired, leading to a highly publicized feud between Time Warner and News Corp. Murdoch's *New York Post* carried articles in favor of Fox News and launched an aggressive campaign to turn public opinion against Time Warner and its CNN. By 1998, Warner had to relinquish its stand amidst growing public disenchantment and Fox News was aired to 9 million households. By the end of 2001, Fox News was ahead of CNN in weekly ratings. Murdoch ensured that it got additional resources for gaining a complete domination of the market.

Star

In the early 1990s, having conquered most of the developed markets, Murdoch set his sights on Asia. As Asian markets opened to Western companies, many Asian countries were launching private television channels. The most famous of these was Star. Viewed by approximately 3 billion people in Asia and the Middle East, Star was owned by the Li family of China. In 1993, Murdoch paid $525 million to acquire a 64 percent stake in Star. News Corp faced many challenges and upheavals over the next few years in the form of increasing competition and regulatory restrictions. By 1996, Star had lost $100 million. But by the end of the decade, Star had become highly popular in India and China. This turnaround was achieved with the help of innovative programs and aggressive marketing. In India, Star made the hugely popular *Kaun Banega Crorepati* (*Who Wants to Become a Millionaire?*) featuring superstar Amitabh Bachchan, which became an instant hit. By 2000, Star had 42 of the top 50 shows in India. Similarly, Star's joint venture channel in China, Phoenix, became profitable by 2000.

Sky Television

Murdoch realized that unlike cable, satellite could reach more homes. In the mid-1980s, Murdoch paid $10 million for a controlling interest in Sky Television (Sky), a pan-European channel that aired common programs to several European countries. By 1987, Murdoch had spent £40 million on Sky, which reached nearly 12 million homes in 20 European countries. But Sky was a company in trouble and was losing about £4 million per week in 1989.

In 1990, after prolonged negotiations, BSB, a television channel, merged into a single company, British Sky Broadcasting (BSkyB). This merger was designed to stem losses and maximize profits. Between 1989 and 1992, the combined entity incurred losses of about $1.2 billion. As BSkyB introduced better programs and aired soccer matches exclusively, it achieved a turnaround by the end of 1992 and revenues rose to £385 million. By 1993, BSkyB reached financial stability. Over the next four years, the company developed new content and innovative programs. By 1997, 25 percent of British homes were subscribers to the channel. Sky became the first digital television channel in the world. By June 2002, BSkyB had 6.1 million subscribers and recorded a 20 percent increase in revenues over 2001.

The DirecTV Acquisition

Don't worry. We don't want to take over the world. We just want a piece of it.

—Rupert Murdoch[4]

Television programs were delivered by cable or through satellite (see Exhibit 4). Cable television beamed programming content through cables to the subscribers' homes. Satellite television beamed programming content by satellites orbiting in the sky and did not require any cable connection.

DirecTV, a leading provider of direct broadcast satellite services, had been promoted by Hughes, a subsidiary of General Motors (GM), in 1995. Attractive sports content, together with aggressive marketing that included free installation resulted in rapid penetration of DirecTV. By 2000, DirecTV had acquired more than 9.5 million subscribers to become the largest satellite-based provider of television content in the United States. DirecTV offered more than 225 programming channels to 60 million homes in about 40 cities in the United States. All this caught the attention of Murdoch, who had been looking for a satellite platform in the United States since the early 1980s, when his plans for a venture called Skyband did not take off.

Murdoch realized DirecTV would add the strategic U.S. market to his worldwide network of satellite distribution that included BSkyB in Britain, Star TV in Asia, Foxtel in Australia, SkyTel in Latin America, and Stream in Italy. DirecTV would eliminate dependence on cable distribution in the U.S. market. With a satellite platform, Murdoch would have a strategy weapon to protect his fast-growing cable networks, which included Fox News, Fox Sports, National Geographic, and Speed Channel, which carried motor sports. DirecTV gave Murdoch the missing link in News Corp's worldwide satellite-distribution system, creating the global media empire he had always dreamed of. As press reports put it, the DirecTV acquisition made Murdoch "a general in both the content and distribution camps."[5]

Murdoch first attempted to acquire DirecTV in September 2000 when he made an offer of $22 billion for a 35 percent stake in the company. GM was eager to sell its noncore subsidiary, so that it could focus on automobiles. But negotiations between

Exhibit 4   CABLE TELEVISION VERSUS SATELLITE TELEVISION

	Cable TV	Satellite TV
Popularity	Very popular, and although satellite was rapidly growing, cable remained popular.	Very popular, had impacted cable's growth significantly
Equipment	Required a set-top box for digital services.	Satellite dish and receivers.
Transmission and reception quality	Cable's basic and expanded basic services were all analog but could be upgraded to digital cable. However, when upgraded, the analog channels remained analog even though one had digital equipment.	100% digital, which in general meant better quality reception. However, TV reception could be subjected to interference from heavy rain, snow, or nearby trees.
Programming	Digital cable could support up to 260 channels, option packages along with pay per view services. Cable TV had more local and community channel options. Cable players were a bit behind in HDTV services.	Satellite TV had more channels than cable providers. It offered more international and sports programming. HDTV channels were available, like HBO and ShowTime.
Pricing	Cable TV had several additional costs such as franchise fees, taxes, plus costs for any pay per view services, and equipment costs. Local channels were included.	Usually if all of the costs of cable were added, satellite TV saved money. In general, one got more channels per dollar spent. However, local channel packages were not included. Normally it required higher initial costs, but if one committed to 12 months of services one could get free equipment and installation.
Interactive services support	Digital cable provided an electronic program guide. In general, had fewer interactive features.	Had some great features that were not available on cable. For example, personal video recording (PVR), which allowed one to pause and even rewind live, broadcasts. Also had features like the electronic program guide, instant weather and video on demand.
Online customer services	Both cable and satellite offered online services such as viewing current and prior statements, adding packages, and making payments to one's account. They also provided online user manuals and installation guides.	

Source: www.dish-network-vs-direct-tv.com.

News Corp and DirecTV proceeded slowly and were further hampered by a 25 percent decline in the stock of Hughes Electronics in February 2001. In April 2001, Murdoch reduced his bid for a 30 percent stake and got Microsoft to commit $3 billion in cash for the deal. In August 2001, EchoStar surprised everyone by announcing an unsolicited $32.3 billion bid for an outright acquisition of DirecTV. EchoStar and DirecTV together commanded about 92 percent of the U.S. satellite pay-TV market. Murdoch lobbied intensely and succeeded in getting the merger blocked on antitrust grounds.

Finally in April 2003, News Corp acquired GM's 19.9 percent stake in Hughes and a further 14.1 percent from public shareholders and GM's pension and other benefit plans. Following the completion of the acquisition, Murdoch became chairman of Hughes, while News Corp's former co–chief operating officer, Chase Carey, became the president and chief executive officer. The public shareholders as well as GM's pension and other benefit plans owned all of GM's common stock, which represented 80.1 percent of the economic interest in Hughes Electronics. GM retained a 19.9 percent stake in Hughes. Murdoch had plans to add 1 million subscribers a year, using DirecTV. Fox TV Stations were expected to let DirecTV viewers choose their angle on their television sets at sports events or create their own video newsmagazines.[6]

Acquisition of DirecTV gave News Corp considerable bargaining power. At any given time, as many as one in five U.S. households would be tuned in to a show of News Corp. DirecTV was also expected to fortify Murdoch's own channels against competition from Comcast and Time Warner. Industry analysts predicted that News Corp would be able to drive down the prices of entertainment and sports programming. With so many viewers hooked up to DirecTV, no programming producer would risk not being in News Corp's system. Hence, producers would accept the prices News Corp fixed. At the same time, Murdoch would have the leverage to force his cable and satellite rivals to carry his programs at premium prices. Murdoch's aggressive marketing tactics would facilitate this process. There were strong rumors that Murdoch might even distribute set-top boxes at a very low price to attract subscribers to DirecTV.

In response, cable and media rivals such as Comcast and Time Warner were moving to increase their own distribution networks. Comcast acquired AT&T Broadband in 2003 for $54 billion. AT&T Broadband owned regional sports rights, telephony and two-way Internet interactivity over cable lines. Comcast was also seeking to enhance its partnership with News Corps rival programmers such as Viacom.

But News Corp's position had been weakened by some compromises made while closing the DirecTV deal. The FCC had already banned large cable operators from discriminating against rival programmers, and Murdoch had volunteered to follow those rules. So News Corp could not use the muscle power of DirecTV to benefit News Corp. News Corp also had to submit to arbitration, if cable operators accused it of using its most popular channels as bargaining tools. But these restrictions were temporary as they expired in six years. By then News Corp would have about 6 million more subscribers according to company projections.

Cable had an important advantage over satellite. Cable offered high-speed, two-way Net access, including phone capability. Satellite was still mostly a one-way service. By the end of 2003, both systems (satellite and cable) were engaged in intense competition to be big players in new consumer technologies such as the digital video recorder (DVR), high-definition TV, and a host of other products that were reshaping home entertainment. In many ways, Comcast, the number one cable system in the United States, was the only rival that came close to matching the power of News Corp. Comcast had even made a hostile bid to take over Walt Disney in February 2004 for $56 billion.

After closing the AT&T Broadband deal, Comcast had pursued various deals to strengthen its distribution network. Comcast had held firm on fees for pricey cable channels, won favorable deals for equipment, and put pressure on Hollywood to change its long-standing movie-release tradition so that it could get movies ahead of video stores and sell them over cable. News Corp clearly had more programming. But Comcast had launched various initiatives to strengthen its content. It had partnered with Radio One to launch a new channel targeting African Americans and acquired TechTV to cater to video gamers. In December 2003, Comcast struck a deal with Chicago's major sports teams—Chicago Bulls, Cubs, White Sox, and Blackhawks—to create a new sports channel, leaving Murdoch's Fox Sports Chicago with no big draws. Comcast had also struck a deal with Viacom channels, such as MTV and Nickelodeon to supply content to Comcast's 21 million subscribers for as long as five years.

Comcast realized that News Corp was a formidable rival. Comcast CEO Brian Roberts admitted, "[Rupert] has broadcast, news, sports, movies, cable channels, and now distribution. You'd have to be crazy to not take that seriously. That's going to cause a lot of people to reassess their businesses."[7]

As rivalry increased, consumers seemed to be the big winners. Cable companies in the past had rolled out new offerings such as video on demand, telephony, and

Exhibit 5   News Corp's Global Distribution Empire

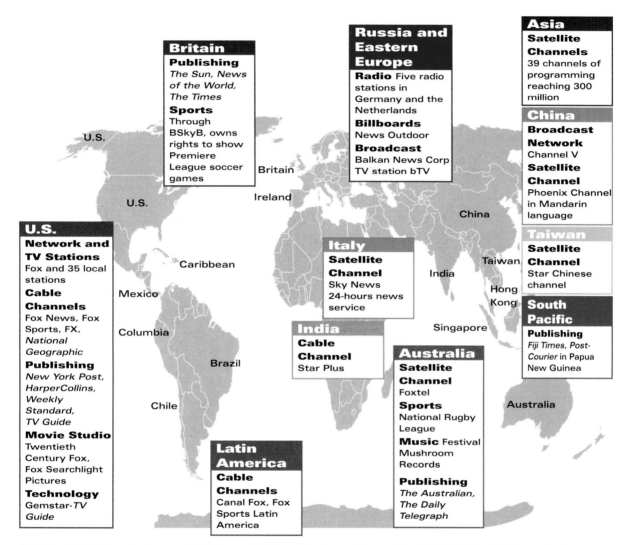

Britain
Publishing
The Sun, News of the World, The Times
Sports
Through BSkyB, owns rights to show Premiere League soccer games

Russia and Eastern Europe
Radio Five radio stations in Germany and the Netherlands
Billboards News Outdoor
Broadcast Balkan News Corp TV station bTV

Asia
Satellite Channels
39 channels of programming reaching 300 million

China
Broadcast Network Channel V
Satellite Channel Phoenix Channel in Mandarin language

Taiwan
Satellite Channel Star Chinese channel

U.S.
Network and TV Stations
Fox and 35 local stations
Cable Channels
Fox News, Fox Sports, FX, *National Geographic*
Publishing
New York Post, HarperCollins, Weekly Standard, TV Guide
Movie Studio
Twentieth Century Fox, Fox Searchlight Pictures
Technology
Gemstar-*TV Guide*

Italy
Satellite Channel Sky News 24-hours news service

India
Cable Channel Star Plus

Australia
Satellite Channel Foxtel
Sports National Rugby League
Music Festival Mushroom Records
Publishing *The Australian, The Daily Telegraph*

South Pacific
Publishing *Fiji Times, Post-Courier* in Papua New Guinea

Latin America
Cable Channels Canal Fox, Fox Sports Latin America

U.S. Britain Ireland China Caribbean Taiwan India Hong Kong Mexico Columbia Singapore Brazil Chile Australia

Source: Reprinted from the January 26, 2004 issue of *Business Week* by special permission. © 2004 McGraw-Hill Companies, Inc.

high-definition channels by spending more than $75 billion to upgrade their systems for the two-way technology that still eluded satellite. With News Corp breathing down their necks, many were scrambling to launch their services quickly so that customers did not defect. Meanwhile, Murdoch's old nemesis EchoStar, which had 9 million subscribers on its network, was gearing up to block News Corp's advances.

Future Outlook

With DirecTV, Murdoch had captured access to 12 million subscribers in the United States, marking a pivotal turn in his 50-year rise from a newspaperman from Australia

Exhibit 6   News Corp. Financials, By Segment, 2002–2003 (in millions of $)

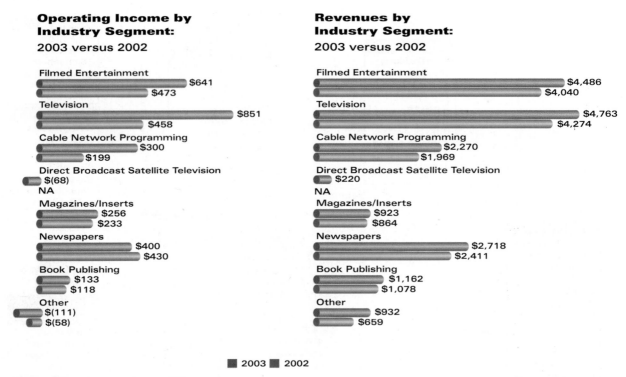

Operating Income by Industry Segment:
2003 versus 2002

Filmed Entertainment — $641 / $473
Television — $851 / $458
Cable Network Programming — $300 / $199
Direct Broadcast Satellite Television — $(68) / NA
Magazines/Inserts — $256 / $233
Newspapers — $400 / $430
Book Publishing — $133 / $118
Other — $(111) / $(58)

Revenues by Industry Segment:
2003 versus 2002

Filmed Entertainment — $4,486 / $4,040
Television — $4,763 / $4,274
Cable Network Programming — $2,270 / $1,969
Direct Broadcast Satellite Television — $220 / NA
Magazines/Inserts — $923 / $864
Newspapers — $2,718 / $2,411
Book Publishing — $1,162 / $1,078
Other — $932 / $659

■ 2003   ■ 2002

Source: News Corp annual report, 2003.

to one of the world's most powerful businessmen. By early 2004, Murdoch oversaw a media empire with businesses that generated $30 billion a year and reached out to just about every corner of the world (see Exhibit 5). No other media company controlled such a mix of programming and the means to deliver it to households as News Corp did.

Financially and operationally, 2003 had been the single most successful year in the history of News Corp (see Exhibit 6). The company's operating income rose 36 percent, to $2.5 billion. Backed by huge financial resources, News Corp had plans to add more channels and programs in its television business. This included a history channel, a business channel to compete with CNBC and programs similar to the sensational *Temptation Island.* News Corp believed speed was its weapon in new product development. TV shows like *That 70s Show, The Simpsons,* and *King of the Hill* continued to generate revenues. In Asia, News Corp's Star TV celebrated its first full year of operating profitability while the company's National Geographic Channel had expanded to 43 million homes in the United States alone. Meanwhile, News Corp's movie studio, Twentieth Century Fox, had recorded revenues of $641 million, up 36 percent from 2002, with big hits such as *X2: X-Men United, Daredevil,* and *Ice Age.*

While there was some criticism of Murdoch's aggressive, interventionalist management style and his attempts to perpetuate dynastic rule, few doubted his ability to build on News Corp's awesome competitive position (see Exhibit 7). At 72, Murdoch showed no signs of fatigue. As he remarked, "I intend to be around as long as my brain holds out, and my mother is doing very well at 95."[8]

Exhibit 7   NEWS CORP'S BOARD OF DIRECTORS AND MANAGEMENT COMMITTEE

Directors	Executive Management Committee	
K. Rupert Murdoch AC Chairman and Chief Executive	Rupert Murdoch Chairman and Chief Executive News Corporation	John Hartigan Chief Executive News Limited
Geoffrey C. Bible Chase Carey Peter Chernin Kenneth E. Cowley AO David F. DeVoe Roderick I. Eddington Dr. Aatos J. Erkko KBE Andrew S. B. Knight Graham Kraehe AO James R. Murdoch Lachlan K. Murdoch Thomas J. Perkins Stanley S. Shuman Arthur M. Siskind	Tony Ball Chief Executive British Sky Broadcasting	David Hill Chairman and Chief Executive Officer Fox Sports Television Group
	Paul Carlucci Chairman and Chief Executive Officer News America Marketing	Les Hinton Executive Chairman News International plc
	Peter Chernin President and Chief Operating Officer News Corporation	James Murdoch Chairman and Chief Executive Officer STAR Group
	David DeVoe Senior Executive Vice President and Chief Financial Officer News Corporation	Lachlan Murdoch Deputy Chief Operating Officer News Corporation
	Anthea Disney Executive Vice President, Content News Corporation	Abe Peled Chief Executive Officer NDS
	Jane Friedman President and Chief Executive Officer HarperCollins	Martin Pompadur Executive Vice President News Corporation
	James Gianopulos Chairman Fox Filmed Entertainment	Thomas Rothman Chairman Fox Filmed Entertainment
	Gary Ginsberg Executive Vice President, Investor Relations and Corporate Communications News Corporation	Jeff Shell Chief Executive Officer Gemstar-TV Guide International
		Arthur Siskind Senior Executive Vice President and Group General Counsel News Corporation
	Sandy Grushow Chairman Fox Television Entertainment Group	Mitchell Stern Chairman and Chief Executive Officer Fox Television Stations

Source: News Corp annual report, 2003.

Endnotes

[1] News Corp., annual report 2003, "Chief Executive's Review."
[2] "FCC Approves DirecTV Acquisition," IDG News Service, www.itworld.com, December 22, 2003.
[3] Stuart Crainer, *Business the Rupert Murdoch Way* (Capstone Publishing, 1999), p. 10.
[4] "Rupert's World," *BusinessWeek,* January 26, 2004.
[5] Ibid.
[6] Ibid.
[7] Ibid.
[8] Ibid.

Bibliography

Anand, Bharat, and Kate Attea. "News Corporation." Harvard Business School Case, June 19, 2002.

Baker, Russ. "Murdoch's Mean Machine." *Columbia Business Review,* June 1999.

Cassy, John. "Untouchable BBC Angers Murdoch." *The Guardian,* November 2002.

Chenoweth, Neil. *Rupert Murdoch: The Untold Story of the World's Greatest Media Wizard.* Crown Publications, 2002.

"Comrade Murdoch." *The Economist,* June 17, 1995.

Crainer, Stuart. *Business the Rupert Murdoch Way* (Capstone Publishing, 1999).

"Crossed Wires." *The Economist,* December 12, 1996.

Doward, Jamie. "Sun King Rising in the East." *The Observer,* January 2003.

Gajilan, Arlyn Tobias. "They Coulda Been Contenders." *Fortune Small Business,* September 9, 2002.

"The Gambler's Last Throw." *The Economist,* September 9, 1996.

Greenslade, Roy. "Their Masters Voice." *The Guardian,* February 2003.

Grover, Ronald, and Tom Lowry. "Rupert's World." *BusinessWeek,* January 26, 2004.

Günter, Mark. "Murdoch's Prime Time." *Fortune,* February 17, 2003.

Günter, Mark. "A Rival for Rupert." *Fortune (Asia),* March 3, 2003.

Günter, Marc. "The Rules According to Rupert." *Fortune,* October 26, 1998.

Hagerty, Bill. "Interview with Rupert Murdoch." *British Journalism Review* 10, no. 4 (1999).

Helyar, John. "Media Strike Out." *Fortune,* March 17, 2003.

News Corp annual reports, 2002 and 2003.

News Corp Web site, www.newscorp.com.

Randall, Jeff. "The Fallout from ITV Digital Collapse." BBC, May 2002.

Rapoport, Carla. "Linking the World with TV." *Fortune,* Autumn/Winter 1993.

"Rupert Laid Bare." *The Economist,* March 20, 1999.

"Rupert's Misses." *The Economist,* March 7, 1999.

"Rupert the Invincible." *The Economist,* August 17, 2002.

Shawcross, William. *Murdoch: The Making of a Media Empire.* Simon & Schuster, 1992.

Snoddy, Raymond. "News Corp Bid for Direct TV Expected Today. *Time Online,* April 2003.

"Star Woes." *The Economist,* November 4, 1998.

"Still Rocking." *The Economist,* November 23, 2002.

Robin Hood

Joseph Lampel
New York University

It was in the spring of the second year of his insurrection against the High Sheriff of Nottingham that Robin Hood took a walk in Sherwood Forest. As he walked he pondered the progress of the campaign, the disposition of his forces, the Sheriff's recent moves, and the options that confronted him.

The revolt against the Sheriff had begun as a personal crusade. It erupted out of Robin's conflict with the Sheriff and his administration. However, alone Robin Hood could do little. He therefore sought allies, men with grievances and a deep sense of justice. Later he welcomed all who came, asking few questions and demanding only a willingness to serve. Strength, he believed, lay in numbers.

He spent the first year forging the group into a disciplined band, united in enmity against the Sheriff and willing to live outside the law. The band's organization was simple. Robin ruled supreme, making all important decisions. He delegated specific tasks to his lieutenants. Will Scarlett was in charge of intelligence and scouting. His main job was to shadow the Sheriff and his men, always alert to their next move. He also collected information on the travel plans of rich merchants and tax collectors. Little John kept discipline among the men and saw to it that their archery was at the high peak that their profession demanded. Scarlock took care of the finances, converting loot to cash, paying shares of the take, and finding suitable hiding places for the surplus. Finally, Much the Miller's son had the difficult task of provisioning the ever-increasing band of Merrymen.

The increasing size of the band was a source of satisfaction for Robin, but also a source of concern. The fame of his Merrymen was spreading, and new recruits were pouring in from every corner of England. As the band grew larger, their small bivouac became a major encampment. Between raids the men milled about, talking and playing games. Vigilance was in decline, and discipline was becoming harder to enforce. "Why," Robin reflected, "I don't know half the men I run into these days."

The growing band was also beginning to exceed the food capacity of the forest. Game was becoming scarce, and supplies had to be obtained from outlying villages. The cost of buying food was beginning to drain the band's financial reserves at the very moment when revenues were in decline. Travelers, especially those with the most to lose, were now giving the forest a wide berth. This was costly and inconvenient to them, but it was preferable to having all their goods confiscated.

Robin believed that the time had come for the Merrymen to change their policy of outright confiscation of goods to one of a fixed transit tax. His lieutenants strongly resisted this idea. They were proud of the Merrymen's famous motto: "Rob the rich and give to the poor." "The farmers and the townspeople," they argued, "are our most important allies. How can we tax them, and still hope for their help in our fight against the Sheriff?"

Robin wondered how long the Merrymen could keep to the ways and methods of their early days. The Sheriff was growing stronger and becoming better organized. He now had the money and the men and was beginning to harass the band, probing for its weaknesses. The tide of events was beginning to turn against the Merrymen. Robin felt that the campaign must be decisively concluded before the Sheriff had a chance to deliver a mortal blow. "But how," he wondered, "could this be done?"

Robin had often entertained the possibility of killing the Sheriff, but the chances for this seemed increasingly remote. Besides, killing the Sheriff might satisfy his personal thirst for revenge, but it would not improve the situation. Robin had hoped that the perpetual state of unrest, and the Sheriff's failure to collect taxes, would lead to his removal from office. Instead, the Sheriff used his political connections to obtain reinforcement. He had powerful friends at court and was well regarded by the regent, Prince John.

Prince John was vicious and volatile. He was consumed by his unpopularity among the people, who wanted the imprisoned King Richard back. He also lived in constant fear of the barons, who had first given him the regency but were now beginning to dispute his claim to the throne. Several of these barons had set out to collect the ransom that would release King Richard the Lionheart from his jail in Austria. Robin was invited to join the conspiracy in return for future amnesty. It was a dangerous proposition. Provincial banditry was one thing, court intrigue another. Prince John had spies everywhere, and he was known for his vindictiveness. If the conspirators' plan failed, the pursuit would be relentless, and retributions swift.

The sound of the supper horn startled Robin from his thoughts. There was the smell of roasting venison in the air. Nothing was resolved or settled. Robin headed for camp promising himself that he would give these problems his utmost attention after tomorrow's raid.

Dilemma at Devil's Den

Allen Cohen
Babson College

Kim Johnson
Babson College

My name is Susan, and I'm a business student at Mt. Eagle College. Let me tell you about one of my worst experiences. I had a part-time job in the campus snack bar, The Devil's Den. At the time, I was 21 years old and a junior with a concentration in finance. I originally started working at the Den in order to earn some extra spending money. I had been working there for one semester and became upset with some of the happenings. The Den was managed by contract with an external company, College Food Services (CFS). What bothered me was that many employees were allowing their friends to take free food, and the employees themselves were also taking food in large quantities when leaving their shifts. The policy was that employees could eat whatever they liked free of charge while they were working, but it had become common for employees to leave with food and not to be charged for their snacks while off duty as well.

I felt these problems were occurring for several reasons. For example, employee wages were low, there was easy access to the unlocked storage room door, and inventory was poorly controlled. Also, there was weak supervision by the student managers and no written rules or strict guidelines. It seemed that most of the employees were enjoying freebies, and it had been going on for so long that it was taken for granted. The problem got so far out of hand that customers who had seen others do it felt free to do it whether they knew the workers or not. The employees who witnessed this never challenged anyone because, in my opinion, they did not care and they feared the loss of friendship or being frowned upon by others. Apparently, speaking up was more costly to the employees than the loss of money to CFS for the unpaid food items. It seemed obvious to me that the employees felt too secure in their jobs and did not feel that their jobs were in jeopardy.

The employees involved were those who worked the night shifts and on the weekends. They were students at the college and were under the supervision of another student, who held the position of manager. There were approximately 30 student employees and 6 student managers on the staff. During the day there were no student managers; instead, a full-time manager was employed by CFS to supervise the Den. The employees and student managers were mostly freshmen and sophomores, probably because of the low wages, inconvenient hours (late weeknights and weekends), and the duties of the job itself. Employees were hard to come by; the high rate of employee turnover indicated that the job qualifications and the selection process were minimal.

The student managers were previous employees chosen by other student managers and the full-time CFS day manager on the basis of their ability to work and on their length of employment. They received no further formal training or written rules beyond what they had already learned by working there. The student managers were briefed on how to close the snack bar at night but still did not get the job done properly. They received authority and responsibility over events occurring during their shifts as manager, although they were never actually taught how and when to enforce it! Their increase in pay was small, from a starting pay of just over minimum wage to an additional 15 percent for student managers. Regular employees received an additional nickel for each semester of employment.

Although I only worked seven hours per week, I was in the Den often as a customer and saw the problem frequently. I felt the problem was on a large enough scale that action should have been taken, not only to correct any financial loss that the Den might have experienced but also to help give the student employees a true sense of their responsibilities, the limits of their freedom, respect for rules, and pride in their jobs. The issues at hand bothered my conscience, although I was not directly involved. I felt that the employees and customers were taking advantage of the situation whereby they could "steal" food almost whenever they wanted. I believed that I had been brought up correctly and knew right from wrong, and I felt that the happenings in the Den were wrong. It wasn't fair that CFS paid for others' greediness or urges to show what they could get away with in front of their friends.

I was also bothered by the lack of responsibility of the managers to get the employees to do their work. I had seen the morning employees work very hard trying to do their jobs, in addition to the jobs the closing shift should have done. I assumed the night managers did not care or think about who worked the next day. It bothered me to think that the morning employees were suffering because of careless employees and student managers from the night before.

I had never heard of CFS mentioning any problems or taking any corrective action; therefore, I wasn't sure whether they knew what was going on, or if they were ignoring it. I was speaking to a close friend, Mack, a student manager at the Den, and I mentioned the fact that the frequently unlocked door to the storage room was an easy exit through which I had seen different quantities of unpaid goods taken out. I told him about some specific instances and said that I believed that it happened rather frequently. Nothing was ever said to other employees about this, and the only corrective action was that the door was locked more often, yet the key to the lock was still available upon request to all employees during their shifts.

Another lack of strong corrective action I remembered was when an employee was caught pocketing cash from the register. The student was neither suspended nor threatened with losing his job (nor was the event even mentioned). Instead, he was just told to stay away from the register. I felt that this weak punishment happened not because he was a good worker but because he worked so many hours and it would be difficult to find someone who would work all those hours and remain working for more than a few months. Although a customer reported the incident, I still felt that management should have taken more corrective action.

The attitudes of the student managers seemed to vary. I had noticed that one in particular, Bill, always got the job done. He made a list of each small duty that needed to be done, such as restocking, and he made sure the jobs were divided among the employees and finished before his shift was over. Bill also stared down employees who allowed thefts by their friends or who took freebies themselves; yet I had never heard of an employee being challenged verbally, nor had anyone ever been fired for these actions. My friend Mack was concerned about theft, or so I assumed, because he had taken some action about locking the doors, but he didn't really get after employees to work if they were slacking off.

I didn't think the rest of the student managers were good motivators. I noticed that they did little work themselves and did not show much control over the employees. The student managers allowed their friends to take food for free, thereby setting bad examples for the other workers, and allowed the employees to take what they wanted even when they were not working. I thought their attitudes were shared by most of the other employees: not caring about their jobs or working hard, as long as they got paid and their jobs were not threatened.

I had let the "thefts" continue without mention because I felt that no one else really cared and may even have frowned upon me for trying to take action. Management thus far had not reported significant losses to the employees so as to encourage them to watch for theft and prevent it. Management did not threaten employees with job loss, nor did they provide employees with supervision. I felt it was not my place to report the theft to management, because I was just an employee and I would be overstepping the student managers. Also, I was unsure whether management would do anything about it anyway—maybe they did not care. I felt that talking to the student managers or other employees would be useless, because they were either abusing the rules themselves or were clearly aware of what was going on and just ignored it. I felt that others may have frowned upon me and made it uncomfortable for me to continue working there. This would be very difficult for me, because I wanted to become a student manager the next semester and did not want to create any waves that might have prevented me from doing so. I recognized the student manager position as a chance to gain some managerial and leadership skills, while at the same time adding a great plus to my resume when I graduated. Besides, as a student manager, I would be in a better position to do something about all the problems at the Den that bothered me so much.

What could I do in the meantime to clear my conscience of the freebies, favors to friends, and employee snacks? What could I do without ruining my chances of becoming a student manager myself someday? I hated just keeping quiet, but I didn't want to make a fool of myself. I was really stuck.

Wal-Mart Stores, Inc.
A New Set of Challenges

Arthur A. Thompson
The University of Alabama

 In early 2004, Wal-Mart's president and CEO, H. Lee Scott, was bullish not only about Wal-Mart's growth prospects but also about its ability to deal with critics who were challenging the company's seemingly virtuous business model of relentlessly wringing cost efficiencies out of its supply chain and providing customers with everyday low prices. Scott and other members of Wal-Mart's highly regarded management team, as well as members of founder Sam Walton's family, could look with justifiable pride on the company's remarkable journey from humble beginnings in the 1960s as a folksy discount retailer in the boondocks of Arkansas to what in 2004 was a $260 billion retailing juggernaut in the early stages of globalizing its operations from its headquarters in Bentonville, Arkansas (which was now served by two daily nonstop flights to New York's LaGuardia Airport). Wal-Mart's growth over the past four decades was unprecedented:

	1962	1970	1980	1990	2000	2004
Sales	$1.4 million	$31 million	$1.2 billion	$26 billion	$191 billion	$256 billion
Profits	$112,000	$1.2 million	$41 million	$1 billion	$6.3 billion	$9.0 billion
Stores	9	32	276	1,528	4,188	4,906

Just as unprecedented was Wal-Mart's impact on general merchandise retailing and the attraction its stores had to shoppers. During 2003, about 140 million people in 11 countries shopped Wal-Mart's almost 4,700 stores every week. More than half of American shoppers visited a Wal-Mart at least once a month, and one-third went once a week—in 2002 an estimated 82 percent of American households made at least one purchase at Wal-Mart.[1] Since the early 1990s, the company had gone from dabbling in supermarket sales to taking the number one spot in grocery retailing worldwide. In the United States, Wal-Mart was the biggest employer in 21 states, and it employed 1.4 million people worldwide, far more than any other company.[2] It was the largest retailer in Canada and Mexico, as well as in the United States and the world as a whole. On November 28, 2003, Wal-Mart set a one-day sales record of $1.52 billion in the United States and over $1.6 billion worldwide—figures bigger than the gross domestic products of 36 countries.

Wal-Mart's performance and prominence in the retailing industry had resulted in numerous awards. By the turn of the century, it had been named "Retailer of the Century" by *Discount Store News,* made the *Fortune* magazine lists of "Most Admired Companies in America" and "100 Best Companies to Work for in America," and been included on the *Financial Times'* "Most Respected in the World" list. In 2000, Wal-Mart was ranked fifth on *Fortune*'s list of the "Global Most Admired Companies." In 2002, Wal-Mart became number one on the Fortune 500 list of the largest companies in America and also on *Fortune*'s Global 500 list. Wal-Mart topped Fortune's 2003 list of "Most Admired Companies in America" and was recognized as the "Largest Corporate Cash Giver" by *Forbes* magazine based on the *Chronicle of Philanthropy*'s survey of sales and cash donations for 2002—Wal-Mart's cash contributions to some 80,000 organizations increased in 2002 to $136 million, up 17 percent from 2001; in addition, customers and associates raised another $70 million at Wal-Mart's stores and clubs. Wal-Mart received the 2002 Ron Brown Award, the highest presidential award recognizing outstanding achievement in employee relations and community initiatives. In 2003, American Veterans Awards gave Wal-Mart its "Corporate Patriotism Award."

Wal-Mart's success had made the Walton family (Sam Walton's heirs and living relatives) the wealthiest in the world—in 2003, five Walton family members controlled about 1.75 billion shares of Wal-Mart stock worth about $93 billion. Increases in the value of Wal-Mart's stock over the years had made hundreds of Wal-Mart employees, retirees, and shareholders millionaires or multimillionaires. Since 1970, when Wal-Mart shares were first issued to the public, the company's stock had split 11 times. A $1,650 investment in Wal-Mart stock in 1970 (100 shares purchased at the initial offer price of $16.50) equated to 204,800 shares worth $10.8 million as of December 2003.

Company Background

Sam Walton graduated from the University of Missouri in 1940 with a degree in economics and took a job as a management trainee at J. C. Penney Company. His career with Penney's ended with a call to military duty in World War II. When the war was over, Walton decided to purchase a franchise and open a Ben Franklin retail variety store in Newport, Arkansas, rather than return to Penney's. Five years later, when the lease on the Newport building was lost, Walton decided to relocate his business in Bentonville, Arkansas, where he bought a building and opened Walton's 5 & 10 as a Ben Franklin–affiliated store. By 1960 Walton was the largest Ben Franklin franchisee, with nine stores.

In 1961 Walton started to become concerned about the long-term competitive threat to variety stores posed by the emerging popularity of giant supermarkets and discounters. An avid pilot, he took off in his plane on a cross-country tour to study the changes in stores and retailing trends, then put together a plan for a discount store of his own. Walton went to Chicago to try to interest Ben Franklin executives in expanding into discount retailing; when they turned him down, he decided to go forward on his own because he believed deeply in the retailing concept of offering significant price discounts to expand sales volumes and increase overall profits. The first Wal-Mart Discount City opened July 2, 1962, in Rogers, Arkansas. The store was successful, and Walton quickly began to look for opportunities to open stores in other small towns and to attract talented people with retailing experience to help him grow the business. Although he started out as a seat-of-the-pants merchant, he had great instincts, was quick to learn from other retailers' successes and failures, and was adept at garnering ideas for improvements from employees and promptly trying them out. Sam Walton incorporated his business as Wal-Mart Stores in 1969. When the company went public in 1970 and sold 300,000 shares at $16.50 each to help finance its rapid growth, it had 38 stores and sales of $44.2 million. In 1979, with 276 stores, 21,000 employees, and operations in 11 states, Wal-Mart became the first company to reach $1 billion in sales in such a short time.

As the company grew, Sam Walton proved to be an effective and visionary leader. His folksy demeanor and his talent for motivating people, combined with a very hands-on management style and an obvious talent for discount retailing, produced a culture and a set of values and beliefs that kept Wal-Mart on a path of continuous innovation and rapid expansion. Moreover, Wal-Mart's success and Walton's personable style of leadership generated numerous stories in the media that cast the company and its founder in a positive light. As Wal-Mart emerged as the premier discount retailer in the United States in the 1980s, an uncommonly large cross-section of the American public came to know who Sam Walton was and to associate his name with Wal-Mart. Sam Walton's folksy personality, unpretentious manner, and interest in people and their feelings caused people inside and outside the company to hold him in high esteem. Regarded by many as "the entrepreneur of the century" and "a genuine American folk hero," he enjoyed a reputation of being not only a community-spirited man who was concerned for his employees but also a devoted family man who epitomized the American dream and demonstrated the virtues of hard work.

Just before Sam Walton's death in 1992, his vision was for Wal-Mart to become a $125 billion company by 2000. But his handpicked successor, David D. Glass, beat that target by almost two years. Under Glass's leadership (1988–2000), Wal-Mart's sales grew at an average annual compound rate of 19 percent, pushing revenues up from $20.6 billion to $165 billion. When David Glass retired in January 2000, H. Lee Scott was chosen as Wal-Mart's third president and CEO. In the four years that Scott had been CEO, Wal-Mart's sales had grown over $100 billion, matching the company's growth in its first 35 years. Even though there were Wal-Mart stores in all 50 states and 10 foreign countries in 2004, Scott and other senior executives believed there were sufficient domestic and foreign growth opportunities to permit the company to grow at double-digit rates for the foreseeable future and propel Wal-Mart's revenues past $500 billion by 2010.

Exhibit 1 provides a summary of Wal-Mart's financial and operating performance for the 1993–2004 fiscal years.

Yet, while a report by the prominent Boston Consulting Group said, "The world has never known a company with such ambition, capability, and momentum," in 2003 there were growing signs that the continued growth and influence of the "Beast of Bentonville" was breeding a backlash among competing retailers, organized labor, community activists, and so-called cultural progressives. Wal-Mart was drawing increasing flak from organized labor about the company's low wages and anti-union posture. It was confronting some 6,000 lawsuits on a variety of issues, including one claiming that it discriminated against female employees.

Wal-Mart's Strategy

The hallmarks of Wal-Mart's strategy were multiple store formats, low everyday prices, wide selection, a big percentage of name-brand merchandise, a customer-friendly store environment, low operating costs, innovative merchandising, a strong emphasis on customer satisfaction, disciplined expansion into new geographic

Exhibit 1   FINANCIAL AND OPERATING SUMMARY, WAL-MART STORES, FISCAL YEARS
1993–2004 (in billions, except earnings per share data)

	Fiscal Year Ending January 31					
	2004	2003	2002	2001	2000	1993
Financial and operating data						
Net sales	$256.3	$244.5	$217.8	$191.3	$165.0	$55.5
Net sales increase	12%	12%	14%	16%	20%	26%
Domestic comparable store sales increase*	5%	5%	6%	5%	8%	11%
Cost of sales	198.7	191.8	171.6	150.3	129.7	44.2
Operating, selling, general and administrative expenses	44.9	41.0	36.2	31.6	27.0	8.3
Interest costs, net	0.8	0.9	1.2	1.2	0.8	0.3
Net income	$ 9.0	$ 8.0	$ 6.7	$ 6.3	$ 5.4	$ 2.0
Earnings per share of common stock (diluted)	$2.07	$1.81	$1.49	$1.40	$1.20	$0.44
Balance sheet data						
Current assets	$ 34.2	$30.5	$27.9	$26.6	$24.4	$10.2
Net property, plant, equipment, and capital leases	55.2	51.9	45.8	40.9	36.0	9.8
Total assets	104.9	94.7	83.5	78.1	70.3	20.6
Current liabilities	37.4	32.6	27.3	28.9	25.8	6.8
Long-term debt	17.5	16.6	15.7	12.5	13.7	3.1
Long-term obligations under capital leases	3.0	3.0	3.0	3.2	3.0	1.8
Shareholders' equity	43.6	39.3	35.1	31.3	25.8	8.6
Financial ratios						
Current ratio	0.9	0.9	1.0	0.9	0.9	1.5
Return on assets	8.6%	9.2%	8.5%	8.7%	9.5%	11.1%
Return on shareholders' equity	20.6%	21.6%	20.1%	22.0%	22.9%	25.3%
Other year-end data						
Number of domestic Wal-Mart Discount stores	1,478	1,568	1,647	1,736	1,801	1,848
Number of domestic Wal-Mart Supercenters	1,471	1,258	1,066	888	721	34
Number of domestic Sam's Clubs	538	525	500	475	463	256
Number of domestic Neighborhood Markets	64	49	31	19	7	—
Number of international stores	1,355	1,288	1,170	1,070	1,004	10

*Defined as sales at stores open a full year that have not been expanded or relocated in the past 12 months.
Source: Wal-Mart annual reports for 2003 and 2004.

markets, and in many cases using acquisitions to enter foreign markets. On the outside
of every Wal-Mart store in big letters was the message "We Sell for Less." The company's advertising tag line reinforced the low-price theme: "Always low prices. Always." Major merchandise lines included housewares, consumer electronics, sporting
goods, lawn and garden items, health and beauty aids, apparel, home fashions, paint,
bed and bath goods, hardware, jewelry, automotive repair and maintenance, toys and
games, and groceries.

Multiple Store Formats

In 2004, Wal-Mart was seeking to meet customers' needs with four different retail concepts: Wal-Mart discount stores, Supercenters, neighborhood markets, and Sam's Clubs:

- *Discount stores*—These stores ranged from 40,000 to 125,000 square feet, employed an average of 150 people, and offered as many as 80,000 different items, including family apparel, automotive products, health and beauty aids, home furnishings, electronics, hardware, toys, sporting goods, lawn and garden items, pet supplies, jewelry, housewares, prescription drugs, and packaged grocery items. Discount stores had sales in the $30 to $50 million range, depending on store size and location.

- *Supercenters*—Supercenters, which Wal-Mart started opening in 1988 to meet a demand for one-stop family shopping, joined the concept of a general merchandise discount store with that of a full-line supermarket. They ranged from 109,000 to 220,000 square feet, employed between 200 and 550 associates, had about 36 general merchandise departments, and offered up to 150,000 different items, at least 30,000 of which were grocery products. In addition to the value-priced merchandise offered at discount stores and a large supermarket section with 30,000+ items, Supercenters contained such specialty shops as vision centers, tire and lube expresses, a fast-food restaurant, portrait studios, one-hour photo centers, hair salons, banking, and employment agencies. Typical Supercenters had annual sales in the $80–$100 million range.

- *Sam's Clubs*—A store format that Wal-Mart launched in 1983, Sam's was a cash-and-carry, members-only warehouse that carried about 4,000 frequently used, mostly brand-name items in bulk quantities along with some big-ticket merchandise. The product lineup included fresh, frozen, and canned food products, candy and snack items, office supplies, janitorial and household cleaning supplies and paper products, apparel, CDs and DVDs, and an assortment of big-ticket items (TVs, tires, large and small appliances, watches, jewelry, computers, camcorders, and other electronic equipment). Stores were approximately 110,000 to 130,000 square feet in size, with most goods displayed in the original cartons stacked in wooden racks or on wooden pallets. Many items stocked were sold in bulk quantity (five-gallon containers, bundles of a dozen or more, and economy-sized boxes). Prices tended to be 10–15 percent below the prices of the company's discount stores and Supercenters since merchandising costs and store operation costs were lower. Sam's was intended to serve small businesses, churches and other religious organizations, beauty salons and barber shops, motels, restaurants, offices, local schools, families, and individuals looking for great prices on large-volume quantities or big-ticket items. Annual member fees were $30 for businesses and $35 for individuals—there were 46 million members in 2003. Sam's stores employed about 125 people each and had annual sales averaging $63 million. A number of Sam's stores were located adjacent to a Supercenter or discount store.

- *Neighborhood markets*—Neighborhood markets—the company newest store format, launched in 1998—were designed to appeal to customers who just needed groceries, pharmaceuticals and general merchandise. They were always located in markets with Wal-Mart Supercenters so as to be readily accessible to Wal-Mart's food distribution network. Neighborhood Markets ranged from 42,000 to 55,000 square feet, employed 80–100 people each, and featured fresh produce, deli foods, fresh meat and dairy items, health and beauty aids, one-hour photo and traditional photo developing services, drive-through pharmacies, stationery and paper goods, pet supplies, and household supplies—about 28,000 items in total.

Domestically, during 2004 Wal-Mart planned to open approximately 50 to 55 new discount stores, 220 to 230 new Supercenters, 25 to 30 new neighborhood markets, and 35 to 40 new Sam's Clubs. Relocations or expansions of existing discount stores accounted for approximately 140 of the new Supercenters, and approximately 20 of the Sam's Clubs were relocations or expansions.

Internationally, Wal-Mart planned to open 130 to 140 units in the 10 countries where it already had stores; of these, 30 were expected to be relocations or expansions. In 2004 Wal-Mart expected to spend $18 million to open three new stores in eastern China, an area where French retailer Carrefour (the world's second largest retailer behind Wal-Mart) and Germany's Metro AG had stores; Wal-Mart had opened 31 stores in 15 cities across the country since 1996.

Exhibit 2 shows the number of Wal-Mart stores in each state and country. There were still many locations in the United States that were underserved by Wal-Mart stores. Inner-city sections of New York City had no Wal-Mart stores of any kind because ample space with plenty of parking was unavailable at a reasonable price. Wal-Mart's first Supercenter in all of California opened in 2003 at a three-story location in downtown Los Angeles that had escalators sized for shopping carts. There were no Supercenters in New Jersey, Rhode Island, Vermont, or Hawaii, and only 1 in Massachusetts and 2 in Connecticut (versus 155 in Texas, 87 in Florida, 58 in Missouri, 52 in North Carolina, 49 in Alabama, and 47 in Louisiana).

Wal-Mart's various domestic and international stores were served by 108 regional general merchandise and food distribution centers. Five additional distribution centers averaging over 1 million square feet of space were planned for 2004.

Wal-Mart's Geographic Expansion Strategy

One of the most distinctive features of Wal-Mart's domestic strategy was the manner in which it expanded outward into new geographic areas. Whereas many chain retailers achieved regional and national coverage quickly by entering the largest metropolitan centers before trying to penetrate less-populated markets, Wal-Mart always expanded into adjoining geographic areas, saturating each area with stores before moving into new territory. New stores were usually clustered within 200 miles of an existing distribution center so that daily deliveries could be made cost-effectively; new distribution centers were added as needed to support store expansion into additional areas. In the United States, the really unique feature of Wal-Mart's geographic strategy had involved opening stores in small towns surrounding a targeted metropolitan area before moving into the metropolitan area itself—an approach Sam Walton had termed "backward expansion." Wal-Mart management believed that any town with a shopping-area population of 15,000 or more was big enough to support a Wal-Mart Discount Store and that towns of 25,000 could support a Supercenter. Once stores were opened in towns around the most populous city, Wal-Mart would locate one or more stores in the metropolitan area and begin major market advertising.

By clustering new stores in a relatively small geographic area, Wal-Mart could spread advertising expenses for breaking into a new market across all the area stores, a tactic the company used to keep its advertising costs under 1 percent of sales (compared to 2 or 3 percent for other discount chains). Don Soderquist, Wal-Mart's retired

Exhibit 2   WAL-MART'S STORE COUNT, JANUARY 2003

State	Discount Stores	Super-centers	Sam's Clubs	Neighborhood Markets
Alabama	34	49	9	2
Alaska	6	0	3	0
Arizona	24	17	10	0
Arkansas	35	43	4	6
California	133	0	30	0
Colorado	17	29	14	0
Connecticut	27	2	3	0
Delaware	3	3	1	0
Florida	66	87	37	1
Georgia	42	61	20	0
Hawaii	6	0	1	0
Idaho	5	11	1	0
Illinois	81	33	27	0
Indiana	42	42	14	0
Iowa	27	24	7	0
Kansas	29	23	6	0
Kentucky	34	41	5	0
Louisiana	35	47	12	0
Maine	12	9	3	0
Maryland	32	5	13	0
Massachusetts	41	1	3	0
Michigan	48	14	22	0
Minnesota	34	9	12	0
Mississippi	21	41	5	1
Missouri	56	58	14	0
Montana	5	6	1	0
Nebraska	10	11	3	0
Nevada	11	7	5	0
New Hampshire	19	6	4	0
New Jersey	30	0	8	0
New Mexico	6	18	5	0
New York	52	22	18	0
North Carolina	47	52	17	0
North Dakota	8	0	2	0
Ohio	70	28	26	0
Oklahoma	41	40	7	12
Oregon	24	3	0	0
Pennsylvania	50	43	20	0
Rhode Island	8	0	1	0
South Carolina	22	37	9	0
South Dakota	6	4	2	0
Tennessee	33	57	15	2
Texas	117	155	68	24

(continues)

Exhibit 2   (concluded)

State	Discount Stores	Super-centers	Sam's Clubs	Neighborhood Markets
Utah	6	15	7	1
Vermont	4	0	0	0
Virginia	21	52	13	0
Washington	29	6	2	0
West Virginia	8	20	3	0
Wisconsin	49	20	11	0
Wyoming	2	7	2	0
U.S. totals	1,568	1,258	525	49
International/Worldwide				
Argentina	0	11	0	0
Brazil	0	12	8	2[a]
Canada	213	0	0	0
China	0	20	4	2
Germany	0	94	0	0
S. Korea	0	15	0	0
Mexico	472[b]	75	50	0
Puerto Rico	9	1	9	33[c]
United Kingdom	248[d]	10	0	0
International totals	942	238	71	37
Grand totals	2,510	1,496	596	86

[a] Brazil includes Todo Dias.
[b] Mexico includes 118 Bodegas, 50 Suburbias, 44 Superamas, 260 Vips.
[c] Puerto Rico includes 33 Amigos.
[d] United Kingdom includes 248 ASDA Stores.

senior vice chairman, explained why the company preferred its backward expansion strategy:

> Our strategy is to go into smaller markets first before we hit major metro areas because you've got a smaller population base to convince over. So you begin to get the acceptance in smaller markets and the word begins to travel around and people begin to travel further and further to get to your stores.[3]

In the small towns Wal-Mart entered, it was not unusual for a number of local businesses that carried merchandise similar to Wal-Mart's lines to fail within a year or two of Wal-Mart's arrival. Wal-Mart's low prices tended to attract customers away from apparel shops, general stores, pharmacies, sporting goods stores, shoe stores, hardware stores, supermarkets, and convenience stores operated by local merchants. The "Wal-Mart effect" in small communities was so potent that it had spawned sometimes fierce local resistance to the entry of a new Wal-Mart among both local merchants and area residents wanting to preserve the economic vitality of their downtown areas and protect against the invasion of what they considered to be an unsightly Wal-Mart store and parking lot. Consulting firms formed that specialized in advising local retailers on how to survive the opening of a Wal-Mart.

For the past several years, Wal-Mart had been driving hard to expand its geographic base of stores outside the United States through a combination of new store construction and acquisition. Acquisition of general merchandise or supermarket chains had been a part of Wal-Mart's entry and/or store expansion strategy in Canada, Mexico, Brazil, Japan, Puerto Rico, China, and Great Britain. International sales accounted for 16.7 percent of total sales in fiscal 2003, and the percentage was expected to rise in the coming years. Wal-Mart stores in China had some of the highest traffic counts of any stores in the world. Wal-Mart's entry into Japan via minority ownership of Japan's fifth largest supermarket chain, Seiyu, had stirred a retailing revolution among Japanese retailers to improve their merchandising, cut their costs, lower their prices, and streamline their supply chains. Prior to buying a minority stake in Seiyu in 2002 (with an option to increase its ownership to 67 percent by 2007), Wal-Mart had studied the Japanese market for four years. It planned to spend most of 2003–2004 getting Seiyu stores and its Japanese supply chain ready for a full-scale assault on penetrating the Japanese market with a lineup of both supermarket and general merchandise products. Sales at Wal-Mart's nearly 1,300 international stores averaged about $31 million per store in fiscal 2003; the company's international division had 2003 total sales of $40.7 billion (up 15 percent) and operating profits of $2.0 billion (up almost 56 percent).

But as Wal-Mart grew more global, management intended to "remain local" in terms of the goods it carried and in some of the ways it operated. Most store managers and senior managers in its foreign operations were natives of the countries where Wal-Mart operated; many had begun their careers as hourly employees. Wal-Mart did, however, have a program that allowed stores in different areas to exchange best practices.

Everyday Low Prices

While Wal-Mart did not invent the concept of everyday low pricing, it had done a better job than any other discount retailer in executing the strategy. The company was widely seen by consumers as being the lowest-priced general merchandise retailer in its market. Recent studies showed that prices of its grocery items were 8 to 27 percent below those of such leading supermarket chain competitors as Kroger (which used the City Market brand in the states west of the Mississippi), Safeway, and Albertson's, after making allowances for specials and loyalty cards. In-store services were also bargain-priced—customers could wire money for a flat $12.95 (versus a fee of $50 to wire $1,000 at Western Union) and could purchase money orders for 46 cents (versus 90 cents charged by the U.S. Postal Service). Wal-Mart touted its low prices on its storefronts ("We Sell for Less"), in advertising, on signs inside its stores, and on the logos of its shopping bags. Some economists believed that Wal-Mart's everyday low prices had reduced inflationary pressures economywide, allowing all U.S. consumers to benefit from the Wal-Mart effect. The well-known financier Warren Buffet said, "You add it all up and they have contributed to the financial well-being of the American public more than any other institution I can think of."[4]

Merchandising Innovations

Wal-Mart was unusually active in testing and experimenting with new merchandising techniques. From the beginning, Sam Walton had been quick to imitate good ideas and merchandising practices employed by other retailers. According to the founder of Kmart, Sam Walton "not only copied our concepts; he strengthened them. Sam just took the ball and ran with it."[5] Wal-Mart prided itself on its "low threshold for change," and much of management's time was spent talking to vendors, employees, and customers to get ideas for how Wal-Mart could improve.

Suggestions were actively solicited from employees. Most any reasonable idea was tried; if it worked well in stores where it was first tested, then it was quickly implemented in other stores. Experiments in store layout, merchandise displays, store color schemes, merchandise selection (whether to add more upscale lines or shift to a different mix of items), and sales promotion techniques were always under way. Wal-Mart was regarded as an industry leader in testing, adapting, and applying a wide range of cutting-edge merchandising approaches. In 2003 Wal-Mart was testing the merits of an in-store candy department featuring an assortment mainly targeted to children, with bulk candy from Brach's, Jelly Belly, and M&M, plus a wide range of novelty and licensed items and coin-operated kiddie rides.

Advertising

Wal-Mart relied less on advertising than most other discount chains did. The company distributed only one or two circulars per month and ran occasional TV ads, relying primarily on word of mouth to communicate its marketing message. Wal-Mart's advertising expenditures ran about 0.3 percent of sales revenues, versus 1.5 percent for Kmart and 2.3 percent for Target. Wal-Mart spent $676 million on advertising in fiscal 2003, $618 million in fiscal 2002, and $574 million in fiscal 2001. Wal-Mart's spending for radio and TV advertising was said to be so low that it didn't register on national ratings scales. Most Wal-Mart broadcast ads appeared on local TV and local cable channels. Wal-Mart did no advertising for its Sam's Club stores. The company often allowed charities to use its parking lots for their fund-raising activities.

Distribution

Over the years, Wal-Mart's management had turned the company's centralized distribution systems into a competitive edge—the company's low distribution costs and cost-effective supply chain management practices were a big reason why its prices were low. Wal-Mart got an early jump on competitors in distribution efficiency because of its rural store locations. Whereas other discount retailers relied on manufacturers and distributors to ship directly to their mostly metropolitan-area stores, Wal-Mart found that its rapid growth during the 1970s was straining suppliers' ability to use independent trucking firms to make frequent and timely deliveries to its growing number of rural store locations. To improve the delivery of merchandise to its stores, the company in 1980 began to build its own centralized distribution centers and to supply stores from these centers with daily deliveries by its own truck fleet. Wal-Mart added new distribution centers when new outlying stores could no longer be reliably and economically supported from an existing center.

The Competitive Environment

Discount retailing was an intensely competitive business. Competition among discount retailers centered on pricing, store location, variations in store format and merchandise mix, store size, shopping atmosphere, and image with shoppers. Wal-Mart's primary competitors were Kmart and Target in general merchandise retailing, and in superstores that also included a full-line supermarket, Super Target stores and Super Kmart stores. Wal-Mart also competed against category retailers like Best Buy and Circuit City in electronics; Toys "R" Us in toys; Goody's in apparel; Bed, Bath, and Beyond in household goods; and Kroger, Albertson's, and Safeway in groceries.

Surveys of households comparing Wal-Mart with Kmart and Target indicated that Wal-Mart had a strong competitive advantage. According to *Discount Store News:*

> When asked to compare Wal-Mart with Kmart and Target, the consensus of households is that Wal-Mart is as good or better. For example, of the households with a Wal-Mart in the area, 59 percent said that Wal-Mart is better than Kmart and Target; 33 percent said it was the same. Only 4 percent rated Wal-Mart worse than Kmart and Target . . . When asked why Wal-Mart is better, 55 percent of the respondents with a Wal-Mart in their area said lower/better prices . . . Variety/selection and good quality were the other top reasons cited by consumers when asked why Wal-Mart is better. Thirty percent said variety; 18 percent said good quality.[6]

The two largest competitors in the warehouse club segment were Costco and Sam's Clubs; BJ's Wholesale Club, a smaller East Coast chain, was the only other major U.S. player in this segment.[7] For the year ended August 31, 2003, Costco had U.S. sales of $34.4 billion at 312 stores versus $32.9 billion at 532 stores for Sam's. The average Costco store generated annual revenues of $112 million, almost double the $63 million average at Sam's. Costco catered to affluent households with upscale tastes and located its stores in mostly urban areas. Costco's 42 million members averaged 11.4 store visits annually and spent an average of $94 per visit, which compared favorably with averages of 8.5 visits and expenditures of $78 at Sam's. Costco was the nation's biggest retailer of fine wines ($600 million annually) and roasted chickens (55,000 rotisserie chickens a day). While its product line included food and household items, sporting goods, vitamins, and various other merchandise, its big attraction was big-ticket luxury items (diamonds and plasma TVs) and the latest gadgets at bargain prices (Costco capped its markups at 14 percent). Costco had beaten Sam's in being the first to sell fresh meat and produce (1986 versus 1989), to introduce private-label items (1995 versus 1998), and to sell gasoline (1995 versus 1997). Costco offered its workers good wages and fringe benefits (full-time hourly workers made about $40,000 after four years).

Wal-Mart's rapid climb to become the largest supermarket retailer had triggered heated price competition in the aisles of most supermarkets. Wal-Mart's three major rivals—Kroger, Albertson's, and Safeway—along with a host of smaller regional supermarket chains, were scrambling to cut costs, narrow the price gap with Wal-Mart, and otherwise differentiate themselves so as to retain their customer base and grow revenues. Continuing increases in the number of Wal-Mart Supercenters meant that the majority of rival supermarkets would be within 10 miles of a Supercenter by 2010. Wal-Mart had recently concluded that it took fewer area residents to support a Supercenter than the company had thought; management believed that Supercenters in urban areas could be as little as four miles apart and still attract sufficient store traffic. Kroger had announced plans to cut its costs by $500 million by January 31, 2004, to put it in better position to match Wal-Mart's lower prices on grocery items. Supermarket industry observers were speculating that either Albertson's (which was already closing underperforming stores and struggling to maintain current revenues) or Safeway (which had its hands full trying to digest a series of acquisitions of regional supermarket chains) would not survive a coming shakeout among the weaker supermarket competitors.

Wal-Mart's Approaches to Strategy Execution

To implement and execute its strategy, Wal-Mart put heavy emphasis on getting the lowest possible prices from its suppliers, forging close working relationships with key suppliers in order to capture win–win cost savings throughout its supply chain, keeping its internal operations lean and efficient, paying attention to even the tiniest details in store layouts and merchandising, making efficient use of state-of-the-art technology, and nurturing a culture that thrived on hard work, constant improvement, and pleasing customers, especially passing cost savings on to customers in the form of low prices.

Wal-Mart's Use of Cutting-Edge Technology

Wal-Mart began using computers to maintain inventory control on an item basis in its distribution centers and stores in 1974. Wal-Mart began testing point-of-sale scanners in 1981 and then committed to systemwide use of scanning bar codes in 1983—a move that improved checkout times by 25–30 percent. In 1984, Wal-Mart developed a computer-assisted merchandising system that allowed each store to tailor the product mix to its own market circumstances and sales patterns. Between 1985 and 1987 Wal-Mart installed the nation's largest private satellite communication network, which allowed two-way voice and data transmission between headquarters, the distribution centers, and the stores and one-way video transmission from Bentonville's corporate offices to distribution centers and to the stores; the system was less expensive than the previously used telephone network. The video system was used regularly by company officials to speak directly to all employees at once.

In 1989 Wal-Mart established direct satellite links with about 1,700 vendors supplying close to 80 percent of the goods sold by Wal-Mart; these links allowed the use of electronic purchase orders and instant data exchanges. Wal-Mart also used the satellite system's capabilities to develop a credit card authorization procedure that took five seconds, on average, to authorize a purchase, speeding up credit check-out by 25 percent compared to the prior manual system. In the early 1990s, through pioneering collaboration with Procter & Gamble, Wal-Mart instituted an automated reordering system that notified suppliers as their items moved through store checkout lanes; this allowed suppliers to track sales and inventories of their products (so they could plan production and schedule shipments accordingly).

Throughout the 1990s Wal-Mart continued to invest in information technology and online systems, usually being a first-mover among retailers in upgrading and improving its capabilities as new technology was introduced. By 2003 the company had developed and deployed sophisticated information technology systems and online capability that not only gave it real-time access to detailed figures on most any aspect of its operations but also made it a leader in cost-effective supply chain management. It could track the movement of goods through its entire value chain—from the sale of items at the cash register backward to stock on store shelves, in-store backup inventory, distribution center inventory, and shipments en route. Moreover, Wal-Mart collaborated with its suppliers to develop data-sharing capabilities aimed at streamlining the supply of its stores, avoiding both stockouts and excess inventories, identifying slow-selling items that might warrant replacement, and spotting ways to squeeze costs out of the supply chain. The company's Retail Link system allowed suppliers to track their wares through Wal-Mart's value chain, get hourly sales figures for each item, and monitor gross margins on each of their products (Wal-Mart's actual selling price less what it paid the supplier).

In mid-2003 Wal-Mart informed its suppliers that they would have to convert to electronic product code (EPC) technology based on radio frequency identification (RFID) systems by 2005. EPCs involved a new product numbering standard that went beyond identifying products. Every single item that rolled off a manufacturing line was embedded with an electronic tag containing a unique number. EPCs offered users significant time savings and enhanced their ability to update online databases—identifying where and when a case or pallet of goods arrived, for example—in supply chain logistics applications. EPC tags could be read by RFID scanners when brought into range of a tag reader—unlike bar codes, they did not have to be directly in the line of sight of the scanner. Wal-Mart's management expected EPC scanning would eventually be built into warehouse bin locations and store shelves, allowing the company to locate and track items throughout the supply chain in real time. With EPC and RFID capability, every single can of soup or DVD or screwdriver in Wal-Mart's supply chain network or on its store shelves could then be traced back to where and when it was made, where and when it arrived at the store, and where and when it was sold (or turned up missing). Further, EPCs linked to an online database provided a secure way of sharing product-specific information with supply chain partners. Wal-Mart management believed that EPC technology, in conjunction with the expanding production of RFID-capable printers/encoders, had the potential to revolutionize the supply chain by providing more accurate information about product movement, stock rotation, and inventory levels; it was also seen as a significant tool for preventing theft and dealing with product recalls. An IBM study indicated that EPC tagging would reduce stockouts by 33 percent, while an Accenture study showed that EPC/RFID technology could boost worker productivity by 5 percent and shrink working capital and fixed capital requirements by 5 to 30 percent.

The attention Wal-Mart management placed on using cutting-edge technology and the astuteness with which it deployed this technology along its value chain to enhance store operations and continuously drive down costs had, over the years, resulted in Wal-Mart's being widely regarded as having the most cost-effective, data-rich information technology systems of any major retailer in the world. So powerful had Wal-Mart's influence been on retail supply chain efficiency that its competitors (and many other retailers as well) had found it essential to follow Wal-Mart's lead and pursue "Wal-Martification" of their retail supply chains.[8]

Relationships with Suppliers

Wal-Mart was far and away the biggest customer of virtually all of its suppliers (see Exhibit 3). Wal-Mart's scale of operation allowed it to bargain hard with suppliers and get their bottom prices. It looked for suppliers who were dominant in their category (thus providing strong brand-name recognition), who could grow with the company, who had full product lines (so that Wal-Mart buyers could both cherry-pick and get some sort of limited exclusivity on the products the company chose to carry), who had the long-term commitment to R&D to bring new and better products to retail shelves, and who had the ability to become more efficient in producing and delivering what it supplied.

Procurement personnel spent a lot of time meeting with vendors and understanding their cost structure. By making the negotiation process transparent, Wal-Mart buyers soon learned whether a vendor was doing all it could to cut down its costs and quote Wal-Mart an attractively low price. Wal-Mart's purchasing agents were dedicated to getting the lowest prices they could, and they did not accept invitations to

Exhibit 3   THE SCALE OF WAL-MART'S PURCHASES FROM SELECTED SUPPLIERS AND ITS MARKET SHARES IN SELECTED PRODUCT CATEGORIES

Supplier	Percent of Total Sales to Wal-Mart	Product Category	Wal-Mart's U.S. Market Share*
Tandy Brands Accessories	39%	Dog food	36%
Dial	28	Disposable diapers	32
Del Monte Foods	24	Photographic film	30
Clorox	23	Shampoo	30
Revlon	20–23	Paper towels	30
RJR Tobacco	20	Toothpaste	26
Procter & Gamble	17	Pain remedies	21
		CDs, DVDs, and videos	15–20
		Single-copy sales of magazines	15
Although sales percentages were not available, Wal-Mart was also the biggest customer of Disney, Campbell Soup, Kraft, and Gillette.		Although market shares were not available, Wal-Mart was also the biggest seller of toys, guns, diamonds, detergent, video games, socks, and bedding.	

*Based on sales through food, drug, and mass merchandisers.

Sources: Jerry Useem, "One Nation Under Wal-Mart," *Fortune,* March 3, 2003, p. 66; and Anthony Bianco and Wendy Zellner, "Is Wal-Mart Too Powerful?" *Business Week,* October 6, 2003, p. 102.

be wined or dined by suppliers. The marketing vice president of a major vendor told *Fortune* magazine:

> They are very, very focused people, and they use their buying power more forcefully than anybody else in America. All the normal mating rituals are verboten. Their highest priority is making sure everybody at all times in all cases knows who's in charge, and it's Wal-Mart. They talk softly, but they have piranha hearts, and if you aren't totally prepared when you go in there, you'll have your ass handed to you.[9]

All vendors were expected to offer their best price without exception; one consultant that helped manufacturers sell to retailers observed, "No one would dare come in with a half-ass price."[10]

Even though Wal-Mart was tough in negotiating for absolute rock-bottom prices, the price quotes it got were still typically high enough to allow suppliers to earn a profit. Being a Wal-Mart supplier generally meant having a stable and dependable enough sales base to operate production facilities in a cost-effective manner. Moreover, once Wal-Mart decided to source from a vendor, then it worked closely with the vendor to find *mutually beneficial* ways to squeeze costs out of the supply chain. Every aspect of a supplier's operation got scrutinized—how products got developed, what they were made of, how costs might be reduced, what data Wal-Mart could supply that would be useful, how sharing of data online could prove beneficial, and so on. Nearly always, as they went through the process with Wal-Mart personnel, suppliers saw ways to prune costs or otherwise streamline operations in ways that enhanced their profit margins. In 1989 Wal-Mart became the first major retailer to embark on a program urging vendors to develop products and packaging that would not harm the environment. In addition, Wal-Mart expected its vendors to contribute ideas about how to make its stores more fun insofar as their products were concerned. The maker of Power Rangers products, for example, had created the world's largest inflatable structure—a 5,000-cubic-foot moon—which toured Wal-Mart parking lots.[11] Coca-Cola had routed its

Los-Angeles-to-Atlanta Olympic Torch Run past as many Wal-Mart stores as possible. Those suppliers that were selected as "category managers" for such product groupings as lingerie or pet food or school supplies were expected to educate Wal-Mart on everything that was happening in their respective product category.

Some 200 vendors had established offices in Bentonville to work closely with Wal-Mart on a continuing basis—most were in an area referred to locally as "Vendorville." Vendors were encouraged to voice any problems in their relationship with Wal-Mart and to become involved in Wal-Mart's future plans. Top-priority projects ranged from using more recyclable packaging to working with Wal-Mart on merchandise displays and product mix to tweaking the just-in-time ordering and delivery system to instituting automatic reordering arrangements to coming up with new products with high customer appeal. Most recently, one of Wal-Mart's priorities was working with vendors to figure out how to localize the items carried in particular stores and thereby accommodate varying tastes and preferences of shoppers in different areas where Wal-Mart had stores. Most vendor personnel based in Bentonville spent considerable time focusing on which items in their product line were best for Wal-Mart, where they ought to be placed in the stores, how they could be better displayed, what new products ought to be introduced, and which ones ought to be rotated out.

A 2003 survey conducted by Cannondale Associates found that manufacturers believed Wal-Mart was the overall best retailer with which to do business—the fifth straight year in which Wal-Mart was ranked number one.[12] Target was ranked second, and Costco was ranked seventh. The criteria for the ranking included such factors as clearest company strategy, best store branding, best buying teams, most innovative consumer marketing/merchandising, best supply chain management practices, best overall business fundamentals, and best practice management of individual product categories. One retailing consultant said, "I think most [suppliers] would say Wal-Mart is their most profitable account."[13] While this might seem surprising because of Wal-Mart's enormous bargaining clout, the potentially greater profitability of selling to Wal-Mart stemmed from the practices of most other retailers to demand that suppliers pay sometimes steep slotting fees to win shelf space and their frequent insistence on supplier payment of such extras as in-store displays, damage allowances, handling charges, penalties for late deliveries, rebates of one kind or another, allowances for advertising, and special allowances on slow-moving merchandise that had to be cleared out with deep price discounts; further, most major retailers expected to be courted with Super Bowl tickets, trips to the Masters golf tournament, fancy dinners at conventions and trade shows, or other perks in return for their business. All of these extras represented costs that suppliers had to build into their prices. At Wal-Mart everything was boiled down to one price number, and no "funny-money" extras ever entered into the deal.[14]

Most suppliers viewed Wal-Mart's single bottom-line price and its expectation of close coordination as a win–win proposition, not only because of the benefits of cutting out all the funny-money costs and solidifying their relationship with a major customer but also because what they learned from the collaborative efforts and mutual data-sharing often had considerable benefit in the rest of their operations. Many suppliers, including Procter & Gamble, liked Wal-Mart's supply chain business model so well that they had pushed their other customers to adopt similar practices.[15]

Wal-Mart's Standards for Suppliers   In the 1990s Wal-Mart began establishing standards for its suppliers, with particular emphasis on foreign suppliers that had a history of problematic wages and working conditions. Management believed that suppliers' practices regarding workers' hours; child labor; discrimination based on race, religion, or other factors; workplace safety, and compliance with local laws and regulations could be attributed to Wal-Mart and could affect its reputation with customers and shareholders. To mitigate the potential for being adversely affected by the manner in which its suppliers conducted their business, Wal-Mart had established a set of supplier standards and set up an internal group to see that suppliers were conforming to the published ethical standards and business practices of Wal-Mart itself.

The company's supplier standards had been through a number of changes as the concerns of Wal-Mart management evolved over time. Suppliers' factories were monitored regularly, and in February 2003 Wal-Mart took direct control of foreign factory audits. Wal-Mart had factory certification teams based in offices in Dubai, Singapore, India, and China; the offices were staffed with more than 100 Wal-Mart employees dedicated to monitoring foreign factory compliance with the company's supplier standards. All suppliers were asked to sign a document certifying their compliance with the standards and were required to post a version of the supplier standards in both English and the local language in each production facility servicing Wal-Mart.

Distribution Center Operations

Throughout the 1980s and 1990s, Wal-Mart had pursued a host of efficiency-increasing actions at its distribution centers. The company had been a global leader in automating its distribution centers and expediting the transfer of incoming shipments from manufacturers to its fleet of delivery trucks, which made daily deliveries to surrounding stores. Prior to automation, bulk cases received from manufacturers had to be opened by distribution center employees and perhaps stored in bins, then picked and repacked in quantities needed for specific stores, and finally loaded onto trucks for delivery to Wal-Mart stores—a manual process that was error-prone and sometimes slow. Using state-of-the-art technology, Wal-Mart had automated many of the labor-intensive tasks, gradually creating an ever-more-sophisticated and cost-efficient system of conveyors, bar-coding, and handheld computers, along with other devices with the capability to quickly sort incoming shipments from manufacturers into smaller, store-specific quantities and route them to waiting trucks to be sent to stores to replenish sold merchandise. Often, incoming goods from manufacturers being unloaded at one section of the warehouse were immediately sorted into store-specific amounts and conveyed directly onto waiting Wal-Mart trucks headed for those particular stores—a large portion of the incoming inventory was in a Wal-Mart distribution center an average of only 12 hours. Distribution center employees had access to real-time information regarding the inventory levels of all items in the center and used the different bar codes for pallets, bins, and shelves to pick up items for store orders. Handheld computers also enabled the packaging department to get accurate information about which items to pack for which store and what loading dock to convey them to.

Truck Fleet Operations

Wal-Mart operated a fleet of 3,500+ company-owned trucks to get goods from its 100+ distribution centers to its almost 5,000 stores. Wal-Mart hired only experienced drivers who had driven more than 300,000 accident-free miles with no major traffic violations. Distribution centers had facilities where drivers could shower, sleep, eat, or attend to personal business while waiting for their truck to be loaded. A truck dispatch coordinator scheduled the dispatch of all trucks according to the available time of drivers and estimated driving time between the distribution center and the designated store. Drivers were expected to pull their trucks up to the store dock at the scheduled time (usually late afternoon or early evening) even if they arrived early; trucks were unloaded by store personnel during nighttime hours, with a two-hour gap between each new truck delivery (if more than one was scheduled for the same night).

In instances where it was economical, Wal-Mart trucks were dispatched directly to a manufacturer's facilities, picked up goods for one or more stores, and delivered them directly, bypassing the distribution center entirely. Manufacturers that supplied certain high-volume items or even a number of different items sometimes delivered their products in truckload lots directly to some or many of Wal-Mart's stores.

Store Construction and Maintenance

Wal-Mart management worked at getting more mileage out of its capital expenditures for new stores, store renovations, and store fixtures. Ideas and suggestions were solicited from vendors regarding store layout, the design of fixtures, and space needed for effective displays. Managers had open-air offices that could be furnished economically, and store designs featured a maximum of display space that could be rearranged and refurbished easily. Wal-Mart claimed that the design and aisle width at its new Supercenters would accommodate 100 million shoppers a week. Because Wal-Mart insisted on a high degree of uniformity in the new stores it built, the architectural firm Wal-Mart employed was able to use computer modeling techniques to turn out complete specifications for 12 or more new stores a week. Moreover, the stores were designed to permit quick, inexpensive construction as well as to allow for low-cost maintenance and renovation. All stores were renovated and redecorated at least once every seven years. If a given store location was rendered obsolete by the construction of new roads or the opening of new shopping locations, then the old store was abandoned in favor of a new store at a more desirable site. In 2003, Wal-Mart stores were being expanded or relocated at the rate of 100–200 annually.

In keeping with the low-cost theme for facilities, Wal-Mart's distribution centers and corporate offices were also built economically and furnished simply. The offices of top executives were modest and unpretentious. The lighting, heating, and air-conditioning controls at all Wal-Mart stores were connected via computer to Bentonville headquarters, allowing cost-saving energy management practices to be implemented centrally and freeing store managers from the time and worry of trying to hold down utility costs. Wal-Mart mass-produced a lot of its displays in-house, not only saving money but also cutting the time needed to roll out a new display concept to as little as 30 days. The company also had a group that disposed of used fixtures and equipment via auctions at the store sites where the surplus existed—a calendar of upcoming auctions was posted on the company's Web site.

Wal-Mart's Approach to Providing Superior Customer Service

Wal-Mart tried to put some organization muscle behind its pledge of "Satisfaction Guaranteed" and do things that would make customers' shopping experience at Wal-Mart pleasant. Store managers challenged store associates to practice what Sam Walton called "aggressive hospitality." A "greeter" was stationed at store entrances to welcome customers with a smile, thank them for shopping at Wal-Mart, assist them in getting a shopping cart, and answer questions about where items were located. Clerks and checkout workers were trained to be courteous and helpful and to exhibit a "friendly, folksy attitude." All store associates were called on to display the "10-foot attitude" and commit to a pledge of friendliness: "I solemnly promise and declare that every customer that comes within ten feet of me, I will smile, look them in the eye, and greet them." Wal-Mart's management stressed five themes in training and supervising store personnel:

1. Think like a customer.
2. Sell what customers want to buy.
3. Provide a genuine value to the customer.
4. Make sure the customer has a good time.
5. Exceed the customer's expectations.

In all stores, efforts were made to present merchandise in easy-to-shop shelving and displays. Floors in the apparel section were carpeted to make the department feel homier and to make shopping seem easier on customers' feet. Store layouts were constantly scrutinized to improve shopping convenience and make it easier for customers to find items. Store employees wore blue vests to make it easier for customers to pick them out from a distance. Fluorescent lighting was recessed into the ceiling to create a softer impression than exposed fluorescent lighting strips. Yet nothing about the decor conflicted with Wal-Mart's low-price image; retailing consultants considered Wal-Mart to be very adept at sending out an effective mix of signals concerning customer service, low prices, quality merchandise, and friendliness. Wal-Mart's management believed that the effort the company put into making its stores more user-friendly and inviting caused shoppers to view Wal-Mart in a more positive light. A reporter for *Discount Store News* observed:

> The fact is that everything Wal-Mart does from store design to bar coding to lighting to greeters—regardless of how simple or complex—is implemented only after carefully considering the impact on the customer. Virtually nothing is done without the guarantee that it benefits the customer in some way . . . As a result Wal-Mart has been able to build loyalty and trust among its customers that is unparalleled among other retail giants.[16]

The Culture at Wal-Mart in 2003

Wal-Mart's culture in 2003 continued to be deeply rooted in Sam Walton's business philosophy and leadership style. Mr. Sam, as he had been fondly called, had been not only Wal-Mart's founder and patriarch but also its spiritual leader—and still was in many respects. Four key core values and business principles underpinned Sam Walton's approach to managing:[17]

■ Treat employees as partners, sharing both the good and bad about the company so that they will strive to excel and participate in the rewards. (Wal-Mart fostered the concept of partnership by referring to all employees as "associates," a term Sam Walton had insisted on from the company's beginnings because it denoted a partnerlike relationship.)

■ Build for the future, rather than just immediate gains, by continuing to study the changing concepts that are a mark of the retailing industry and be ready to test and experiment with new ideas.

■ Recognize that the road to success includes failing, which is part of the learning process rather than a personal or corporate defect or failing. Always challenge the obvious.

■ Involve associates at all levels in the total decision-making process.

Sam Walton practiced these principles diligently in his own actions and insisted that other Wal-Mart managers do the same. Up until his health failed badly in 1991, he spent several days a week visiting the stores, gauging the moods of shoppers, listening to employees discuss what was on their minds, learning what was or was not selling, gathering ideas about how things could be done better, complimenting workers on their efforts, and challenging them to come up with good ideas.

The values, beliefs, and practices that Sam Walton instilled in Wal-Mart's culture and that still carried over in 2003 were reflected in statements made in his autobiography:

> Everytime Wal-Mart spends one dollar foolishly, it comes right out of our customer's pockets. Everytime we save a dollar, that puts us one more step ahead of the competition—which is where we always plan to be.

> One person seeking glory doesn't accomplish much; at Wal-Mart, everything we've done has been the result of people pulling together to meet one common goal.

> I have always been driven to buck the system, to innovate, to take things beyond where they've been.

> We paid absolutely no attention whatsoever to the way things were supposed to be done, you know, the way the rules of retail said it had to be done.

> My role has been to pick good people and give them the maximum authority and responsibility.

> I'm more of a manager by walking and flying around, and in the process I stick my fingers into everything I can to see how it's coming along . . . My appreciation for numbers has kept me close to our operational statements, and to all the other information we have pouring in from so many different places.

> The more you share profit with your associates—whether it's in salaries or incentives or bonuses or stock discounts—the more profit will accrue to your company. Why? Because the way management treats the associates is exactly how the associates will then treat the customers. And if the associates treat the customers well, the customers will return again and again.

> The real challenge in a business like ours is to become what we call servant leaders. And when they do, the team—the manager and the associates—can accomplish anything.

> There's no better way to keep someone doing things the right way than by letting him or her know how much you appreciate their performance.

> I like my numbers as quickly as I can get them. The quicker we get that information, the quicker we can act on it.

> The bigger we get as a company, the more important it becomes for us to shift responsibility and authority toward the front lines, toward that department manager who's stocking the shelves and talking to the customer.

> We give our department heads the opportunity to become real merchants at a very early stage of the game . . . we make our department heads the managers of their own businesses . . . We share everything with them: the costs of their goods, the freight costs, the profit margins. We let them see how their store ranks with every other store in the company on a constant, running basis, and we give them incentives to want to win.

We're always looking for new ways to encourage our associates out in the stores to push their ideas up through the system . . . Great ideas come from everywhere if you just listen and look for them. You never know who's going to have a great idea.

A lot of bureaucracy is really the product of some empire builder's ego . . . We don't need any of that at Wal-Mart. If you're not serving the customers, or supporting the folks who do, we don't need you.

I believe in always having goals, and always setting them high . . . The folks at Wal-Mart have always had goals in front of them. In fact, we have sometimes built real scoreboards on the stage at Saturday morning meetings.

You can't just keep doing what works one time, because everything around you is always changing. To succeed, you have to stay out in front of that change.[18]

Walton's success flowed from his cheerleading management style, his ability to instill the principles and management philosophies he preached into Wal-Mart's culture, the close watch he kept on costs, his relentless insistence on continuous improvement, and his habit of staying in close touch with both consumer and associates. It was common practice for Walton to lead cheers at annual shareholder meetings, store visits, managers' meetings, and company events. His favorite was the Wal-Mart cheer:

Give me a W!
Give me an A!
Give me an L!
Give me a Squiggly!
   (Here, everybody sort of does the twist.)
Give me an M!
Give me an A!
Give me an R!
Give me a T!
What's that spell?
Wal-Mart!
Whose Wal-Mart is it?
My Wal-Mart!
Who's number one?
The Customer! Always!

In 2003, the Wal-Mart cheer was still a core part of the Wal-Mart culture and was used throughout the company at meetings of store employees, managers, and corporate gatherings in Bentonville to create a "whistle while you work" atmosphere, loosen everyone up, inject fun and enthusiasm, and get sessions started on a stimulating note. While the cheer seemed corny to outsiders, once they saw the cheer in action at Wal-Mart they came to realize its cultural power and significance. And much of Sam Walton's cultural legacy remained intact in 2003, most especially among the company's top decision makers and longtime managers. As a *Fortune* writer put it:

Spend enough time inside the company—where nothing backs up a point better than a quotation from Walton scripture—and it's easy to get the impression that the founder is orchestrating his creation from the beyond.[19]

The Three Basic Beliefs Underlying the Wal-Mart Culture in 2003

Wal-Mart top management stressed three basic beliefs that Sam Walton had preached since 1962:

1. *Treat individuals with respect and dignity*—Management consistently drummed the theme that dedicated, hardworking, ordinary people who teamed together and who treated each other with respect and dignity could accomplish extraordinary things. Throughout company literature, comments could be found referring to Wal-Mart's "concern for the individual." Such expressions as "Our people make the difference," "We care about people," and "People helping People" were used repeatedly by Wal-Mart executives and store managers to create and nurture a family-oriented atmosphere among store associates.

2. *Service to customers*—Management stressed that the company was nothing without its customers. Management emphasized that, to satisfy customers and keep them coming back again and again, the company had to build their trust in its pricing philosophy—Wal-Mart customers had to always find the lowest prices with the best possible service. One of the standard Wal-Mart mantras preached to all associates was that the customer was boss. Associates in stores were urged to observe the rule regarding the "10-foot attitude."

3. *Strive for excellence*—The concept of striving for excellence stemmed from Sam Walton's conviction that prices were seldom as low as they needed to be and that product quality was seldom as high as customers deserved. The thesis at Wal-Mart was that new ideas and ambitious goals made the company reach further and try harder—the process of finding new and innovative ways to push boundaries and constantly improve made the company better at what it did and contributed to higher levels of customer satisfaction. Wal-Mart managers at all levels spent much time and effort motivating associates to offer ideas for improvement and to function as partners. It was reiterated again and again that every cost counted and that every worker had a responsibility to be involved.

These three beliefs were supplemented by several supporting cultural themes and practices:

- Go all-out to exceed customers' expectations and make sure that customers have a good time shopping at Wal-Mart. Every associate repeatedly heard "The customer is boss and the future depends on you."

- Practice Sam Walton's 10 rules for building a business. Management had distilled much of Sam Walton's business philosophy into 10 rules (see Exhibit 4); these were reiterated to associates and used at meetings to guide decision making and the crafting and executing of Wal-Mart's strategy.

- Observe the Sundown Rule: Answer requests by sundown on the day they are received. Management believed this working principle had to be taken seriously in a busy world in which people's job performance depended on cooperation from others.

Wal-Mart's culture had unusually deep roots at the headquarters complex in Bentonville. The numerous journalists and business executives who had been to Bentonville and spent much time at Wal-Mart's corporate offices uniformly reported being impressed with the breadth, depth, and pervasive power of the company's culture. Jack Welch, former CEO of General Electric and a potent culture builder in his own right, noted that "the place vibrated" with cultural energy. There was little evidence that the

Exhibit 4   Sam Walton's 10 Rules for Building a Business

Rule 1: Commit to your business. Believe in it more than anybody else. I think I overcame every single one of my personal shortcomings by the sheer passion I brought to my work. I don't know if you're born with this kind of passion, or if you can learn it. But I do know you need it. If you love your work, you'll be out there every day trying to do it the best you possibly can, and pretty soon everybody around will catch the passion from you—like a fever.

Rule 2: Share your profits with all your Associates, and treat them as partners. In turn, they will treat you as a partner, and together you will all perform beyond your wildest expectations. Remain a corporation and retain control if you like, but behave as a servant leader in a partnership. Encourage your Associates to hold a stake in the company. Offer discounted stock, and grant them stock for their retirement. It's the single best thing we ever did.

Rule 3: Motivate your partners. Money and ownership alone aren't enough. Constantly, day-by-day, think of new and more interesting ways to motivate and challenge your partners. Set high goals, encourage competition, and then keep score. Make bets with outrageous payoffs. If things get stale, cross-pollinate; have managers switch jobs with one another to stay challenged. Keep everybody guessing as to what your next trick is going to be. Don't become too predictable.

Rule 4: Communicate everything you possibly can to your partners. The more they know, the more they'll understand. The more they understand, the more they'll care. Once they care, there's no stopping them. If you don't trust your Associates to know what's going on, they'll know you don't really consider them partners. Information is power, and the gain you get from empowering your Associates more than offsets the risk of informing your competitors.

Rule 5: Appreciate everything your Associates do for the business. A paycheck and a stock option will buy one kind of loyalty. But all of us like to be told how much somebody appreciates what we do for them. We like to hear it often, and especially when we have done something we're really proud of. Nothing else can quite substitute for a few well-chosen, well-timed, sincere words of praise. They're absolutely free—and worth a fortune.

Rule 6: Celebrate your successes. Find some humor in your failures. Don't take yourself so seriously. Loosen up, and everybody around you will loosen up. Have fun. Show enthusiasm—always. When all else fails, put on a costume and sing a silly song. Then make everybody else sing with you. Don't do a hula on Wall Street. It's been done. Think up your own stunt. All of this is more important, and more fun, than you think, and it really fools the competition. "Why should we take those cornballs at Wal-Mart seriously?"

Rule 7: Listen to everyone in your company. And figure out ways to get them talking. The folks on the front lines—the ones who actually talk to the customer—are the only ones who really know what's going on out there. You'd better find out what they know. This really is what total quality is all about. To push responsibility down in your organization, and to force good ideas to bubble up within it, you must listen to what your Associates are trying to tell you.

Rule 8: Exceed your customers' expectations. If you do, they'll come back over and over. Give them what they want—and a little more. Let them know you appreciate them. Make good on all your mistakes, and don't make excuses—apologize. Stand behind everything you do. The two most important words I ever wrote were on that first Wal-Mart sign, "Satisfaction Guaranteed." They're still up there, and they have made all the difference.

Rule 9: Control your expenses better than your competition. This is where you can always find the competitive advantage. For 25 years running—long before Wal-Mart was known as the nation's largest retailer—we ranked No. 1 in our industry for the lowest ratio of expenses to sales. You can make a lot of different mistakes and still recover if you run an efficient operation. Or you can be brilliant and still go out of business if you're too inefficient.

Rule 10: Swim upstream. Go the other way. Ignore the conventional wisdom. If everybody else is doing it one way, there's a good chance you can find your niche by going in exactly the opposite direction. But be prepared for a lot of folks to wave you down and tell you you're headed the wrong way. I guess in all my years, what I heard more often than anything was: a town of less than 50,000 population cannot support a discount store for very long.

Source: www.walmartstores.com, accessed December 18, 2003.

culture in Bentonville was any weaker in 2003 than it had been 12 years earlier when Sam Walton personally led the culture-building, culture-nurturing effort.

But Wal-Mart executives nonetheless were currently facing a formidable challenge in sustaining the culture in the company's distribution centers and especially in its stores. Annual turnover rates in Wal-Mart's stores were running about 45 percent in 2002–2003 and had run as high as 70 percent in 1999 when the economy was booming and the labor market was tight. Such high rates of turnover among the company's worldwide workforce of 1.4 million, coupled with the fact that Wal-Mart would need to add another 800,000 new employees from 2004 to 2008 (including 47,000 management positions) to staff its new stores and distribution centers, made keeping the culture intact outside Bentonville a Herculean task. No other company in all of business history had been confronted with cultural indoctrination of so many new employees in so many locations in such a relatively short time.

Soliciting Ideas from Associates

Associates at all levels were expected to be an integral part of the process of making the company better. Wal-Mart store managers usually spent a portion of each day walking around the store checking on how well things were going in each department, listening to associates' comments, soliciting suggestions, discussing how improvements could be made, and praising associates who were doing a good job. Store managers frequently asked associates what needed to be done better in their department and what could be changed to improve store operations. Associates who believed that a policy or procedure detracted from operations were encouraged to challenge and change it. Task forces to evaluate ideas and plan out future actions to implement them were common, and it was not unusual for the person who developed the idea to be appointed the leader of the group. An assistant store manager explained the importance of getting employees to suggest ways to boost sales:

> We are encouraged to be merchants. If a sales clerk, a checker or a stockman believes he can sell an item and wants to promote it, he is encouraged to go for it. That associate can buy the merchandise, feature it, and maintain it as long as he can sell it.[20]

That same assistant store manager, when he accidentally ordered four times as many Moon Pies for an in-store promotion as intended, was challenged by the store manager to be creative and figure out a way to sell the extra inventory. The assistant manager's solution was to create the first World Championship Moon Pie Eating Contest, held in the store's parking lot in the small town of Oneonta, Alabama. The promotion and contest drew thousands of spectators and was so successful that it became an annual store event.

Listening to employees was a very important part of each manager's job. All of Wal-Mart's top executives relied on a concept known as management by walking around; they visited stores, distribution centers, and support facilities regularly, staying on top of what was happening and listening to what employees had to say about how things were going. Senior managers at Wal-Mart's Bentonville headquarters believed that visiting stores and listening to associates was time well spent because a number of the company's best ideas had come from Wal-Mart associates—Wal-Mart's use of people greeters at store entrances was one of those ideas.

Compensation and Incentives

New hourly associates at U.S. Wal-Mart stores were paid anywhere from $1 to $6 above the minimum wage, depending on the type of job, and could expect to receive a raise within the first year at one or both of the semiannual job evaluations. Typically, at least one raise was guaranteed in the first year if Wal-Mart planned to keep the individual on the staff. The other raise depended on how well the associate worked and improved during the year. At the store level, only the store manager was salaried; all other associates, including the department managers, were considered hourly employees. A 2003 study by *Forbes* found that Wal-Mart employees earned an average hourly wage of $7.50, which translated to an annual income of $18,000. Store clerks generally earned the least—one study showed that sales clerks earned an average of $8.23 an hour and $13,861 annually in 2001.[21] Workers that unloaded trucks and stocked store shelves could earn anywhere from $25,000 to $50,000.

Part-time jobs were most common among sales clerks and checkout personnel in the stores where customer traffic varied appreciably during days of the week and months of the year. New full-time and part-time associates became eligible for health care benefits after a six-month wait and a one-year exclusion for preexisting conditions. As of 2003, about 60 percent of the roughly 800,000 U.S. Wal-Mart associates signed up for coverage (compared with an average of 72 percent for the whole retailing industry); many Wal-Mart associates did not sign up for health care coverage because another household member already had family coverage at his or her place of employment. Worker premiums for coverage were as little as $13 every two weeks with an annual deductible of $1,000, but associates could opt for plans with a higher premium and a lower deductible.[22] The health care benefit package covered 100 percent of most major medical expenses above $1,750 in employee out-of-pocket expenses and entailed no lifetime cap on medical cost coverage (a feature offered by fewer than 50 percent of U.S. employers). The company's health benefits also included dental coverage, short- and long-term disability, an illness protection plan, and business travel accident insurance. But to help control its health care costs for associates, Wal-Mart's plan did not pay for flu shots, eye exams, child vaccinations, chiropractic services, and certain other treatments allowed in the plans of many companies; further, Wal-Mart did not pay any health care costs for retirees. Due to Wal-Mart management's recent efforts to control costs for health care benefits, the company's health care costs compared very favorably with those of other organizations:[23]

	Average Cost per Eligible Employee	
	2001	**2002**
U.S. employees of a cross-section of large, medium, and small companies	$4,924	$5,646
Employees of wholesale/ retail stores	4,300	4,834
Wal-Mart employees (estimated)	3,000	3,500

Wal-Mart's package of fringe benefits for full-time employees (and some part-time employees) also included:

■ Vacation and personal time.

■ Holiday pay.

■ Jury duty pay.

■ Medical and bereavement leave.

■ Military leave.

■ Maternity/paternity leave.

■ Confidential counseling services for associates and their families.

■ Child care discounts for associates with children (through four national providers).

■ GED reimbursement/scholarships for associates and their spouses.

Wal-Mart associates received 10 percent off selected merchandise and Sam's Club associates received a Sam's Club membership card at no cost.

According to management, some 60 percent of associates indicated that a major reason they joined Wal-Mart was the benefits. In addition to compensation and fringe benefits, Wal-Mart had installed an extensive system of incentives that allowed associates to share monetarily in the company's success.

The Profit-Sharing Plan   Wal-Mart maintained a profit-sharing plan for full- and part-time associates; individuals were eligible after one year and 1,000 hours of service. Annual contributions to the plan were tied to the company's profitability and were made at the sole discretion of management and the board of directors. Employees could contribute up to 15 percent of their earnings to their 401(k) accounts. Wal-Mart's contribution to each associate's profit-sharing account became vested at the rate of 20 percent per year beginning the third year of participation in the plan. After seven years of continuous employment the company's contribution became fully vested; however, if the associate left the company prior to that time, the unvested portions were redistributed to all remaining employees. The plan was funded entirely by Wal-Mart, and most of the profit-sharing contributions were invested in Wal-Mart's common stock. The company had contributed more than $2.7 billion toward associates' profit-sharing and 401(k) accounts since 1972. Company contributions to the plan totaled $98.3 million in 1991, $129.6 million in 1992, and $166 million in 1993 but had risen significantly over the last decade—annual contributions to 401(k) and profit-sharing worldwide amounted to $663 million in fiscal 2003, $555 million in fiscal 2002, and $486 million in fiscal 2001. Associates could begin withdrawals from their account upon retirement or disability, with the balance paid to family members upon death.

Stock Purchase and Stock Option Plans   A stock purchase plan was adopted in 1972 to allow eligible employees a means of purchasing shares of common stock through regular payroll deduction or annual lump-sum contribution. Prior to 1990, the yearly maximum under this program was $1,500 per eligible employee; starting in 1990 the maximum was increased to $1,800 annually. The company contributed an amount equal to 15 percent of each participating associate's contribution. Longtime employees who had started participating in the early years of the program had accumulated stock worth over $100,000. About one-fourth of Wal-Mart's employees participated in the stock purchase plan in 1993, but this percentage had since declined because many new employees opted not to participate.

In addition to regular stock purchases, certain employees qualified to participate in stock option plans; options expired 10 years from the date of the grant and could be exercised in nine annual installments. In 2003 there were over 59 million shares reserved for issuance under stock option plans. The value of options granted in recent years was substantial: $96 million (1990), $128 million (1991), $143 million (1992), and $235 million (1993).

Sales Contests and Other Incentive Programs   Associate incentive plans were in place in every store, club, distribution center, and support facility. Associates received bonuses for "good ideas," such as how to reduce shoplifting or how to improve merchandising. Wal-Mart instituted a shrinkage bonus in 1980. If a store held losses from theft and damage below the corporate goal, every associate in that store was eligible to receive up to $200. As a result, Wal-Mart's shrinkage ran about 1 percent, compared to an industry average of 2 percent. One of Wal-Mart's most successful incentive programs involved in-store sales contests that allowed departments within the store to do a special promotion and pricing on items they themselves wanted to feature. Management believed these contests boosted sales, breathed new life into an otherwise slow-selling item, and helped keep associates thinking about how to help bolster sales. In 1999 (the most recent year for which data were available), Wal-Mart paid $500 million in incentive bonuses based on store and individual performance to 525,000 full- and part-time employees.

On the basis of data provided by Wal-Mart associates, *Fortune* had included Wal-Mart on its list of the "100 Best Companies to Work For" for four of the six years from 1998 to 2003. Wal-Mart was the largest U.S. employer of African Americans and Hispanics.

However, in 2003, Wal-Mart was faced with a federal lawsuit filed by six female employees claiming that the company discriminated against women in pay, promotions, training, and job assignments—plaintiffs' attorneys were seeking class-action status for the lawsuit on behalf of all past and present female workers at Wal-Mart's U.S. stores and wholesale clubs. According to data from various sources, while two-thirds of Wal-Mart's hourly employees were women, less than 15 percent held store manager positions. There were also indications of pay gaps between male and female employees. The differences increased up the corporate ladder for the same positions, beginning with full-time hourly women employees making 6.2 percent less than their male counterparts, and female senior vice presidents making 50 percent less than men in the same position. According to a study conducted by the plaintiffs as part of their discrimination lawsuit and based on an analysis of Wal-Mart's payroll data, female workers at Wal-Mart between 1996 and 2001 earned 4.5 to 5.6 percent less than men doing similar jobs and with similar experience levels. The pay gap allegedly widened higher up the management ladder. The study found that male management trainees made an average of $23,175 a year, compared with $22,371 for women trainees. At the senior vice president level, the average male made $419,435 a year, whereas the four female senior vice presidents earned an average of $279,772.

Training

Top management was committed to providing all associates state-of-the-art training resources and development time to help achieve career objectives. The company had a number of training tools in place, including classroom courses, computer-based learning, distance learning, corporate intranet sites, mentor programs, satellite broadcasts, and skills assessments. In November 1985 the Walton Institute of Retailing was opened in affiliation with the University of Arkansas. Within a year of its inception every Wal-Mart manager from the stores, the distribution facilities, and the general office were expected to take part in special programs at the Walton Institute to strengthen and develop the company's managerial capabilities.

Management Training   Wal-Mart store managers were hired in one of three ways. Hourly associates could move up through the ranks from sales to department manager to manager of the check lanes into store management training—more than 65 percent of Wal-Mart's managers had started out as hourly associates. Second, people with outstanding merchandising skills at other retail companies were recruited to join the ranks of Wal-Mart managers. And third, Wal-Mart recruited college graduates to enter the company's training program. Store management trainees went through an intensive on-the-job training program of almost 20 weeks and then were given responsibility for an area of the store. Trainees who progressed satisfactorily and showed leadership and job knowledge were promoted to an assistant manager, which included further training in various aspects of retailing and store operations. Given Wal-Mart's contin-ued store growth, above-average trainees could progress to store manager within five years. Through bonuses for sales increases above projected amounts and company stock options, the highest-performing store managers earned well into six figures annually.

Associate Training   Wal-Mart did not provide a specialized training course for its hourly associates. Upon hiring, an associate was immediately placed in a position for on-the-job-training. From time to time, training films were shown in associates' meet-ings. Store managers and department managers were expected to train and supervise the associates under them in whatever ways were needed. As one associate put it, "Mostly you learn by doing. They tell you a lot; but you learn your job every day."

Respect for the individual, one of the company's three core values, was reinforced throughout the training process for both managers and associates. Wal-Mart had been ranked among *Training* magazine's "Top Training 100" companies in 2001 and 2002.

Meetings and Rapid Response

The company used meetings both as a communication device and as a culture-building exercise. In Bentonville, there were Friday merchandising meetings and Saturday-morning meetings at 7:30 AM to review the week. The weekly merchandising meeting included buyers and merchandising staff headquartered in Bentonville and various re-gional managers who directed store operations.

David Glass, Wal-Mart's former CEO, explained the purpose of the Friday mer-chandise meetings:

> In retailing, there has always been a traditional, head-to-head confrontation be-tween operations and merchandising. You know, the operations guys say, "Why in the world would anybody buy this? It's a dog, and we'll never sell it." Then the merchandising folks say, "There's nothing wrong with that item. If you guys were smart enough to display it well and promote it properly, it would blow out the doors." So we sit all these folks down together every Friday at the same table and just have at it.
>
> We get into some of the doggonedest, knock-down drag-outs you have ever seen. But we have a rule. We never leave an item hanging. We will make a de-cision in that meeting even if it's wrong, and sometimes it is. But when the peo-ple come out of that room, you would be hard-pressed to tell which ones oppose it and which ones are for it. And once we've made that decision on Friday, we expect it to be acted on in all the stores on Saturday. What we guard against around here is people saying, "Let's think about it." We make a decision. Then we act on it.[24]

At the Saturday-morning meetings—a Wal-Mart tradition since 1961—top offi-cers, merchandising and regional managers, and other Bentonville headquarters' staff (about 100 people in all) gathered to exchange ideas on how well things were going and talk about any problems relating to the week's sales, store performance, special promotion items, store construction, distribution centers, transportation, supply chain activities, and so on. As with the Friday merchandise meetings, decisions were made about what actions needed to be taken.

The store meetings and the Friday/Saturday meetings in Bentonville, along with the in-the-field visits by Wal-Mart management, created a strong bias for action. A *Fortune* reporter observed, "Managers suck in information from Monday to Thursday, exchange ideas on Friday and Saturday, and implement decisions in the stores on Monday."[25]

Wal-Mart's Future: Mounting Flak from Several Directions

Sam Walton had engineered the development and rapid ascendancy of Wal-Mart to the forefront of the retailing industry—the discount stores and Sam's Clubs were strategic moves that he directed. His handpicked successor, David Glass, had directed the hugely successful move into Supercenters and grocery retailing, as well as presiding over the company's growth into the world's largest retailing enterprise; the neighborhood market store format also came into being during his tenure as CEO. H. Lee Scott, Wal-Mart's third CEO, had the challenge of globalizing Wal-Mart operations and continuing the long-term process of saturating the U.S. market with Supercenters and adding other types of stores in those areas that were underserved.

But as 2003 unfolded, it was apparent that Scott had to deal with a growing number of issues and obstacles that were being thrown in Wal-Mart's path, some of which were embarrassing or threatening. Not only was the company faced with over 6,000 active lawsuits, ranging from antitrust and consumer issues to torts claims (like a customer suffering injury from falling in a store or being in a collision with a Wal-Mart truck). A couple of the lawsuits had potentially serious consequences—like the one alleging the company discriminated against women, which had potential to turn into the largest sex-bias class action ever, and a second alleging that associates were forced to work unpaid overtime. But Wal-Mart was also getting flak from other quarters, forcing management to devote more time and attention to putting out brushfires than to growing and operating the business (as had been the case during the David Glass era):

- Wal-Mart had to temporarily stop selling guns at its 118 stores across California following what California's attorney general said were hundreds of violations of state laws. Investigations by California authorities revealed that six Wal-Mart stores had released guns before the required 10-day waiting period, failed to verify the identity of buyers properly, sold illegally to felons, and committed other violations. Wal-Mart cooperated with governmental officials and agreed to immediately suspend firearms sales until corrective action could be taken and store associates properly trained on state firearms laws.

- In New York, Wal-Mart had run afoul of the state's 1988 toy weapons law. The toy guns Wal-Mart sold had an orange cap at the end of the barrel but otherwise looked real, thus violating New York laws banning toy guns with realistic colors such as black or aluminum and not complying with New York's requirement that toy guns have unremovable orange stripes along the barrel. Investigators from the state attorney general's office shopped 10 Wal-Marts in New York state from Buffalo to Long Island and purchased toy guns that violated the law at each of them. The president of New York's State Police Investigators Union said, "Without clear markings, it is extremely difficult to tell the difference between a toy gun and a real weapon." Wal-Mart acknowledged that its toy guns did not have all of the state-required markings, but the company maintained that it need only comply with federal law, which requires an orange cap on the end of the barrel. Wal-Mart had sold more than 42,000 toy guns in the state during the past two and a half years. If the state of New York prevailed in its halt of toy gun sales at Wal-Mart, it could seek damages equal to $1,000 for each illegal toy gun sold since April 1, 1997.

- Immigration authorities were investigating certain Wal-Mart managers for knowingly hiring janitorial contractors who were using illegal immigrants to clean stores. In a series of predawn raids on October 23, 2003, federal agents had arrested nearly 250 illegal immigrants after cleaning shifts at 61 Wal-Mart stores in 21 states; agents also searched a manager's office at Wal-Mart's Bentonville headquarters and took 18 boxes of documents relating to cleaning contractors dating back to March 2000.[26] Federal officials reportedly had wiretaps showing that Wal-Mart officials knew its contractors were furnishing illegal cleaning crews. Several weeks later, Wal-Mart was notified that it had been included in a federal grand jury probe of the contractors. Wal-Mart, however, was indignant about the charges, saying that Wal-Mart managers at many levels knew about the problem of illegal workers in its stores and had been cooperating with federal authorities in the investigations for almost three years. Wal-Mart indicated that it had helped federal investigators tape conversations between some of its store managers and employees of the cleaning contractors suspected of using illegal immigrants; that it revised its written contracts with cleaning contractors in 2002 to include language that janitorial contractors were complying with all federal, state, and local employment laws (because of the information developed in 2001); and that it had begun bringing all janitorial work in-house rather than outsourcing such services in 2003 because outsourcing was more expensive—in October 2003 fewer than 700 Wal-Mart stores used outside cleaning contractors, down from almost half in 2000.

■ United Food and Commercial Workers (UFCW) was exerting all the pressure it could to force Wal-Mart to raise its wages and benefits for associates to levels that would be comparable to union wages and benefits at unionized supermarket chains. A UFCW spokeswoman in Southern California, where union members were striking supermarket chains to protest efforts to trim health care costs, said:

> Their productivity is becoming a model for taking advantage of workers, and our society is doomed if we think the answer is to lower our standards to Wal-Mart's level. What we need to do is to raise Wal-Mart to the standard we have set using the supermarket industry as an example so that Wal-Mart does not destroy our society community by community.[27]

Wal-Mart's labor costs were said to be 20 percent less than those at unionized supermarkets.[28] In Dallas, 20 supermarkets had closed once Wal-Mart had saturated the area with its Supercenters. According to one source, for every Wal-Mart Supercenter opened in the next five years, two other supermarkets would be forced to close, thus casting some doubt on whether Wal-Mart's entry into a community resulted in a net increase in jobs and tax revenues.[29] One trade publication estimated that Wal-Mart's plans to open more than 1,000 Supercenters in the United States in the 2004–2008 period would boost Wal-Mart's grocery and related revenues from $82 billion to $162 billion, thus increasing its market share in groceries from 19 percent to 35 percent and its share of pharmacy and drugstore-related sales from 15 percent to 25 percent.[30]

■ Opponents of "big-box" retailers had battled against Wal-Mart's efforts to locate new stores in such states as Vermont and California. Oakland officials had recently voted to limit stores with full-service supermarkets to 100,000 square feet or 2.5 acres—a move deliberately aimed at blocking Wal-Mart's plan to open 187,000-square-foot Supercenters in the Oakland area. In Contra Costa County, near San Francisco, county supervisors enacted an ordinance prohibiting any retail outlet larger than 90,000 square feet from devoting more than 5 percent of its floor space to food or other nontaxable goods—Wal-Mart gathered enough signatures to force a referendum in March 2004, but the referendum lost due mainly to certain tactics Wal-Mart employed as opposed to citizens' rejection of Wal-Mart Supercenters.[31] Restrictive zoning codes, vocal opponents of big-box retailers (most of whom were desirous of protecting local businesses from the competition of Wal-Mart's every-day low prices), high land costs in urbanized areas, and combative labor unions were major reasons why in 2003 Wal-Mart had more stores in rural and less urban-ized areas compared to major metropolitan areas. Saturating major metropolitan ar-eas with Supercenters, Sam's Clubs, and neighborhood markets was crucial to Wal-Mart's strategy of sustaining its double-digit growth rate in the United States.

■ An article by newspaper reporter Jon Talton in the August 17, 2003 issue of Phoenix's *Arizona Republic* slammed Wal-Mart on several fronts:

> Fair play is a heartland value. But Wal-Mart is known for clear-cutting the retail landscape. Competing national stores won't even consider locating within three miles of a Wal-Mart Supercenter, and local retailers go out of business. Suppliers are bullied for "everyday low prices," with the result being that many have been forced from business.
>
> Speaking of fair, you're the nation's largest employer, with a million "associates." But relatively few work 40-hour weeks, and a union cashier at Safeway or Albertson's can make twice as much as one of your check-ers. Nor is it easy for someone making seven bucks an hour to afford your "pay-for-it-yourself" benefits.

■ Wal-Mart had been criticized for refusing to stock CDs or DVDs with parental warning stickers (mostly profanity-laced hip-hop music) and for either pulling cer-tain racy magazines (*Maxim, Stuff,* and *FHM*) from its shelves or obscuring their covers. Critics contended that Wal-Mart made no effort to survey shoppers about how they felt about such products but rather that it responded in ad hoc fashion to complaints lodged by a relative handful of customers and by conservative outside groups.[32] Wal-Mart had also been the only one of the top 10 drugstore chains to refuse to stock Preven, a morning-after contraceptive introduced in 1999, because company executives did not want its pharmacists to have to grapple with the moral dilemma of abortion.

■ In Colorado, the UFCW accused Wal-Mart of harassing workers to keep them from joining its local in Denver and elsewhere. According to the complaint filed with the National Labor Relations Board, Wal-Mart managers at a Denver store threatened, intimidated, and illegally monitored employees who were organizing. Similar complaints had previously been filed in Florida and Texas. A Wal-Mart spokesman denied the charge concerning the Denver store and noted that similar complaints at other locations had been dismissed without a hearing. Even so, Wal-Mart, which had an official policy of being strongly opposed to unionization, had seen the number of complaints about its efforts to prevent unionization grow in re-cent years—so far, 17 complaints had been filed in 12 states.

A Web site called Walmartwatch.com had sprung up to collect and publicize re-ports of misbehavior and wrongful conduct on the part of Wal-Mart management and the company's growing economic power and influence. A union-affiliated Web site (www.nlcnet.org), run by the National Labor Committee, was also disseminating anti–Wal-Mart information.

H. Lee Scott was understandably concerned about the raft of issues that threatened to mar Wal-Mart's reputation and raise questions about the company's efforts to secure the lowest prices for its customers. He recognized that the company's size and market standing made it an attractive target for critics; as he put it, "In the past we were judged by our aspirations. Now, we're going to be judged by our exceptions."[33] Scott had launched his own investigations into the sex-bias claims and the use of illegal workers and vowed that there would be zero tolerance on Wal-Mart's part for misbehavior:

> Wal-Mart does not and will not tolerate illegal workers in any capacity. Whatever we find, we would be shocked if a Wal-Mart executive were ever involved in the hiring of illegal workers.
>
> What we can't do is give people the fuel to attack us. I have a responsibility that is twofold: to make sure we're not doing the wrong thing, and to make sure that we are trying to communicate that this is a quality company.[34]

However, despite concerns in some quarters over Wal-Mart's growing size and economic influence, Scott believed the company could grow to be two or three times its present size.

Endnotes

[1]Anthony Bianco and Wendy Zellner, "Is Wal-Mart Too Powerful?" *Business Week,* October 6, 2003, p. 102.

[2]Jerry Useem, "One Nation Under Wal-Mart," *Fortune,* March 3, 2003, p. 66. © 2004 Time Inc. Reprinted with permission.

[3]*Discount Store News,* December 18, 1989, p. 162.

[4]As quoted in Useem, "One Nation Under Wal-Mart," p. 68.

[5]As quoted in Bill Saporito, "What Sam Walton Taught America," *Fortune,* May 4, 1992, p. 105.

[6]*Discount Store News,* December 18, 1989, p. 168.

[7]The information in this paragraph is drawn from John Helyar, "The Only Company Wal-Mart Fears," *Fortune,* November 24, 2003, pp. 158-66.

[8]Paul Lightfoot, "Wal-Martification," *Operations and Fulfillment,* June 1, 2003, posted at www.opsandfulfillment.com.

[9]As quoted in *Fortune,* January 30, 1989, p. 53.

[10]As quoted in Useem, "One Nation Under Wal-Mart," p. 68.

[11]Ibid., p. 74.

[12]Reported in a *DSN Retailing Today Online* editorial by Tony Lisanti, November 10, 2003.

[13]As quoted in Useem, "One Nation Under Wal-Mart," p. 74.

[14]Ibid.

[15]Ibid.

[16]*Discount Store News,* December 18, 1989, p. 161.

[17]Sam Walton with John Huey, *Sam Walton: Made in America* (New York: Doubleday, 1992), p. 12.

[18]Ibid., pp. 10, 12, 47, 63, 115, 128, 135, 140, 213, 226-229, 233, 246, 249-254, and 256.

[19]Useem, "One Nation Under Wal-Mart," p. 72.

[20]*Discount Store News,* December 18, 1989, p. 83.

[21]According to documents filed in a lawsuit against the company and cited in Bianco and Zellner, "Is Wal-Mart Too Powerful?" p. 102.

[22]Bernard Wysocki Jr. and Ann Zimmerman, "Wal-Mart Cost-Cutting Finds a Big Target in Health Benefits," *The Wall Street Journal,* September 30, 2003, p. A16.

[23]Ibid., p. A1.

[24]Walton with Huey, *Sam Walton,* pp. 225-26.

[25]Saporito, "What Sam Walton Taught America," p. 105.

[26]Ann Zimmerman, "After Huge Raid on Illegals, Wal-Mart Fires Back at U.S.," *The Wall Street Journal,* December 19, 2003, pp. A1, A10.

[27]As quoted in Lorrie Grant, "Retail Giant Wal-Mart Faces Challenges on Many Fronts," *USA Today,* November 11, 2003, p. B2. Copyright 2003, *USA Today.* Reprinted with permission.

[28]Bianco and Zellner, "Is Wal-Mart Too Powerful?" p. 103.

[29]Ibid.

[30]Ibid., p. 108.

[31]Ibid.

[32]Ibid., pp. 104, 106.

[33]Useem, "One Nation Under Wal-Mart," p. 78.

[34]Grant, "Retail Giant Wal-Mart Faces Challenges on Many Fronts," p. B1.

Michelin China

Katherine Xin
China Europe International Business School

Vladimir Pucik
International Institute for Management Development

Liu Shengjun
China Europe International Business School

Inna Francis
International Institute for Management Development

Michelin— the world-leading French-based tire maker—like many multinationals in the 1980s and 1990s, was attracted to China by the size and diversity of its marketplace. Michelin started selling tires to China in 1988. Eager to establish an infrastructure that would help to capture business opportunities, Michelin set up its first joint venture (JV) in Shenyang in 1996. When a bigger opportunity emerged in Shanghai in 2001, to create the one of the largest tire production sites in China, Michelin was ready to exploit it. Analysts were predicting that China's tire sector would grow by 30 percent annually between 2000 and 2005 and demand would reach 108 million tires by 2010. Demand for radial tires[1] was expected to grow even faster—more than tripling between 2000 and 2005 and reaching 100 percent market penetration for the passenger car market and 40 percent for the truck market.

> *Michelin is here to stay and grow with the market. Our strategy from the start has been to manufacture the same quality tires in China as we did around the world.*
> —Eric Jugier, CEO and Chairman, Michelin China

It was clear that there were major gains to be made in China, but there were also risks and challenges. The main challenge was managing cultural differences and instilling Michelin's culture in China. According to Jugier:

> Revamping the facilities to turn out Michelin-quality tires was not just a matter of money. It was also a matter of nerves. We had to address the question whether we should adapt Michelin's management practices to Chinese culture or whether we should instead implement Michelin's global management policies in China.

Michelin in China

A leader in world tire technology, Michelin operated nearly 80 manufacturing facilities worldwide and controlled around 20 percent of the global tire market.

In March 2001, after 18 months of negotiations, Michelin signed a $200 million deal with the Shanghai Tire & Rubber Co. Ltd (STRC) to form a foreign invested Joint Stock Company (JSC)—Shanghai Michelin Warrior Tire Co. Ltd (SMW)—in which Michelin had a 70 percent stake.

STRC was China's largest tire manufacturer, with 5 percent market share in that country and annual capacity of 5 million passenger and light truck tires, besides its radial truck tire factory and bias truck tire facilities. In its passenger and light truck factory, it employed about 2,700 people and had sales of around $80 million in 2000. It also had land-use rights, and the right to use the Warrior brand, known in the Chinese market since 1947.

Although STRC was publicly listed on the Shanghai stock exchange in 1992, the company's culture was dominated by the state-owned enterprise (SOE) mentality (refer to Exhibit 1). The US$28 million raised from the listing were put into building apartment blocks and an office tower, which failed to make a profit after the Shanghai real estate market crashed in 1994. After a series of unsuccessful acquisitions, STRC was showing a loss of $56.7 million in 2000.

To save the company, the Shanghai government appointed a new president. Fan Xian, who had breathed new life into Shanghai Soap—the state-owned cosmetics company. Fan Xian became the driving force behind the JSC with Michelin:

> Many people disagreed on merging with Michelin. They thought it was a pity to marry their daughter to a stranger.[3] But the alliance offered us an opportunity to learn from Michelin's world-class technology, craftsmanship, management, and marketing skills and sharpen the competitive edge of Chinese tire producers.

In April 2001 Jugier, formerly vice president of passenger car and light truck tires at Michelin Asia-Pacific, became chairman and general manager of SMW. Fan Xian was appointed as a vice chairman.

While the legal teams worked to set up control mechanisms, three other teams supported SMW in operations, communications, and business development. Michelin was able to leverage its JV experience in Shenyang to continue uninterrupted production of Warrior brand tires immediately after the JSC negotiations. Just 12 months later, SMW began shipping Michelin-branded tires as well.

Exhibit 1   STATE-OWNED ENTERPRISES (SOEs)

SOEs were typically large firms in strategic industries, such as energy, automobile and steel, that were owned directly by the central government. Although some were profitable, many lost money and relied on government subsidies. The government required SOEs to provide an expensive array of benefits for workers and their families, including housing, health care, pensions, vacations, and education. An SOE could be losing money because of this "welfare burden," because the government was forcing it to charge artificially low prices for its products, or often because its management was incompetent or even corrupt. Many SOEs have in effect been privatized by issuing shares of stock and by having some or all of their welfare obligations moved to other entities. If the government remained the dominant shareholder, however, there was rarely any improvement in performance. The outcome could be very different when the new owners were private investors or foreign firms that negotiated for the right to radically restructure the SOEs.

When Jugier, a candid and sanguine chairman, recalled his early days in Shanghai, his restraint was evident when he described it as a "difficult year." The market challenges and risks called for a strong national executive team. Since the majority of managers in China had limited exposure to modern management concepts, Michelin sent a dozen expatriates at the beginning. A technical team led the refurbishing and replacement of equipment, the institution of new processes and the deployment of new technologies. Other overseas staff worked to restructure distribution, train retailers on merchandising and product knowledge, install a market tracking system, further strengthen the Warrior brand support, and wrestle with customers unaccustomed to paying on time. The expertise of these expatriates was required to lay the foundation for future operations.

The Michelin expatriates realized that the management of human resources was one of the biggest challenges facing the group. The fact that Chinese values and beliefs were different from their own could result in costly misunderstandings. If successfully managed, however, the differences in culture could complement each other and lead to better and faster knowledge transfer within the company.

In order to facilitate the integration process, Michelin kept the original management team. To minimize cultural conflict, Michelin emphasized the importance of nourishing local management talent. Jugier commented:

> From the very beginning, we were clear-headed about both the shortcomings and advantages of joint venture. That's why expatriates that joined in were mostly experts rather than managers.

Compared with the integration of marketing, sales, and production, the integration of people was Michelin's biggest challenge. Eric's vision was to integrate all Chinese employees into "one big Michelin family."

Michelin's Culture

The culture at Michelin was based on five fundamental values: (1) respect for customers; (2) respect for people; (3) respect for shareholders; (4) respect for facts;[4] and (5) respect for the environment (refer to Exhibit 2). All group decisions were taken in light of these values.

Respect for people was considered the key factor in Michelin's powerful innovation ability (see Exhibit 3). The company encouraged managers to delegate in a spirit of trust, providing employees with freedom of initiative and action. There was no established and predetermined job path, no road straight to the top, and no lists of jobs to fill in. Michelin people always had the opportunity to let their talents and interests guide their careers. All Michelin employees could pursue opportunities outside their formal education:

> From your first day you will be given responsibility. An induction scheme and a personalized training and development program will be designed so as to develop and enhance personal and professional effectiveness and to foster individual growth and career progression. Career structures are not set in stone. At Michelin, anything is possible.[5]

Michelin aimed to achieve balanced development for both the company and employees through its distinctive career management system (see Exhibit 4). It was not uncommon to find a Michelin manufacturing engineer exploring a new career in product

Exhibit 2   THE FIVE VALUES OF THE MICHELIN GROUP

The very core of the company's mission is to serve its customers; our long-term existence and growth depend on the long-term satisfaction of our customers. Our primary responsibility is to provide our customers with safe products, suitable for their intended use, of high manufacturing quality. Likewise, the services we provide aim for the highest levels of quality in terms of reliability, customer expectations, and compliance with deadlines and costs.

We intend to continue the Michelin Group's global expansion through the development of good relations which are mutually beneficial for all our stakeholders be they our employees, our industrial and commercial partners, public authorities, nongovernmental organizations, the media or local communities where we are implanted.

Respecting shareholders therefore means fully recognizing their role and the risks they take, involving them in the life of the Company and striving to meet their long-term expectations.

It is our responsibility to provide our customers with ever more environmentally friendly products and services. Accordingly, our permanent innovation policy focuses on enhancing the environmental performance of mobility.

Respecting facts demands objectivity and intellectual honesty, above and beyond opinions and preconceived ideas.

Source: Michelin Performance and Responsibility Charter.

Exhibit 3   Michelin's Innovation History

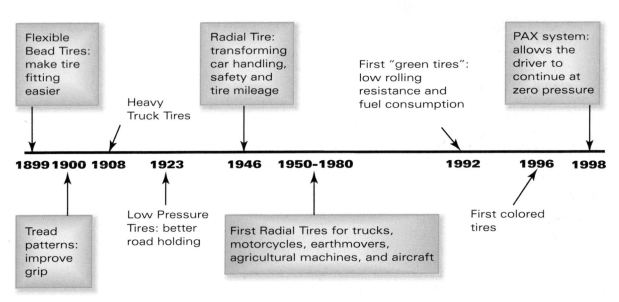

Source: www.michelin.com.

development, or a production supervisor moving into sales, or an information systems professional seeking a new direction in marketing.

As a worldwide organization, Michelin offered a wide range of career opportunities at an international level, encouraging transfers between activities, sites, services, and entities domestically and internationally. The mobility was perceived as an opportunity to transmit and reinforce Michelin values and culture throughout the group.

Exhibit 4   Career Management Model

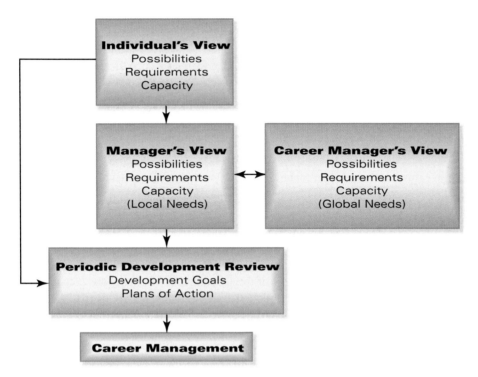

Source: Company information.

International mobility was encouraged—12 percent of the company's 4,500 managers were involved in expatriate assignments and usually spent three to five years abroad.

Based on the group's five values, Michelin created a Performance and Responsibility Charter. Its purpose was to measure and reduce the gap between the group's values and their implementation. To a large extent, the charter took existing practices from the Michelin culture and translated them into management principles. Edouard Michelin, managing partner and CEO of the Michelin Group, noted:

> A company's performance is not assessed only in terms of its economic results. It is also measured by its ability to develop its employees and to take its place harmoniously in the communities and society around it.

To emphasize the equality between managers and workers, Michelin carved the following slogan into a stone: Nobody owns the talents! Christian Tschann, former president of Michelin Asia-Pacific and now president of Michelin Europe, commented:

> François Michelin—the company patriarch who was at the helm of the business for 45 years—believed in avoiding too much control over people and allowing for a culture where it is possible to admit mistakes, where individuality, tenacity and strength of character can grow and where intellectual conformity is avoided. Michelin prides itself in being a company that is "willing to dare." We encourage middle managers to speak out and challenge decisions made at the top.

Michelin's Personnel Management

Philosophy

Michelin's personnel department, which employed 1,400 people worldwide, was independent of the other management structures, and the chain of command was not as straightforward as in many other multinational companies, not to mention Chinese companies. The department's main mission was to:

- Build individual professional advancement in line with personal aspirations and proven skills and performance.
- Satisfy the personnel requirements of the group's entities, in both the short term and the long term.

To achieve this mission, the personnel function focused on five activities: (1) individual career management; (2) training and development; (3) management of current and future staffing levels and competency development; (4) management of labor relations; and (5) development of tools to assist in personnel management. Jugier commented:

> Everybody is unique and has his own quality or characteristics. The personnel function is to find the special quality of individuals and enable them to flourish within the company for the benefit of the company. In Michelin, the personnel is not simply a support or service, it plays a strategic role.
>
> The personnel function is a mix of personnel professionals and people from other functions such as manufacturing and marketing, which can help better understand jobs and individual qualities to find the best fit between individuals and the company.

The boundaries between the personnel department and other business units were blurred, and personnel managers would have to work closely with their partners in various business units. To play the role of such a strategic partner required soft management skills. This was one of the major challenges facing Michelin's personnel specialists in China, since they did not have a formal place in the hierarchy.

Recruitment

The interview procedure at Michelin was a two-way process that allowed the applicant and the company to get to know each other better. In addition to competencies, background, and education, Michelin gave priority to candidates' character. After an exploratory interview, candidates would be invited for in-depth one-on-one interview sessions with several company representatives, including the manager of the relevant department and a manager from personnel. Interviews covered both technical and behavioral aspects, evaluating communication, leadership, teamwork, vision, planning skills, sensitivity, motivation, and adaptability. Alan Duke, international career manager at Michelin, explained:

> In Michelin, recruiters make hiring decisions independently. Most recruiters come from operations, have sensitivity to others and know the company well. Selection is very rigorous and humanistic; we do not use tests but rely on the dialogue with individuals. Recruiters make their final decision based on the assessment of the candidate's fit with Michelin's culture and values. We rarely recruit for jobs. We look for human values, not skills. We choose a person first and develop his potential to achieve the highest level. When people join Miche-

lin, no matter what their nationalities are, they must share a common vision for the company.

Integration

At the headquarters in France, all new professional recruits had at least a three-month probation, or "integration," period designed to help them better understand the company and to explore their personal career aspirations and talent.

During the integration period, new professional hires came together for a systematic introduction to the company. During this time, they could make appointments with any company executive to seek answers to their questions and concerns. They were also given brief assignments so that they could experience firsthand what it was like to work in the company. Throughout this period, career coaches (i.e., senior managers with years of experience working at Michelin) were available to answer new employees' questions and guide them in their professional aspirations for the future. Each career coach was responsible for 8 to 10 new hires and, at the end of the three-month integration phase, made a recommendation regarding the first job assignment, having assessed the employee's ambitions and talents in the light of company needs. Elizabeth Grimaldi, integration manager, commented:

> It is Michelin policy to put new people—whether they are hired for a senior management position or as a management trainee—in a production plant to work as a production worker for three weeks. Sometimes the environment is far from where they used to operate. During this period they live and work like a worker. They need to have a very good understanding about our production processes and Michelin culture at the front line. Then, they are asked to write a memo about their experience. We will have some vague ideas about the job assignment after the first month, form a better view at the end of the second month, and make a proposal to the new hire at the end of the third month. If the desire of the person doesn't fit with the company's needs, he/she has to leave.

Career Management

Individual career plans and personal progression were an integral part of Michelin philosophy. Every professional employee mapped out long-term career directions and interests, received ongoing feedback and evaluation, and was engaged in discussions about career interests.

Career development was a shared responsibility between an employee, his or her manager, and a career manager. A career manager "followed" all employees, regardless of level, throughout their career with Michelin, meeting with them every two years to assess their needs and opinions. According to the performance and responsibility charter:

> We manage careers on a long-term basis; they are generally developed over periods of around 20 years. We are very selective about people we recruit and we continue to assist them in order to give them the opportunities for real career development.

Michelin required career managers to be trustworthy and transparent and to have credibility in previous jobs, the right attitude, the capacity to listen and a strong interest in people. They usually came from all parts of the company. (Refer to Exhibit 5 for the career management procedure.) On average, a Michelin manger changed jobs every three to four years.

Exhibit 5   Career Management Procedure

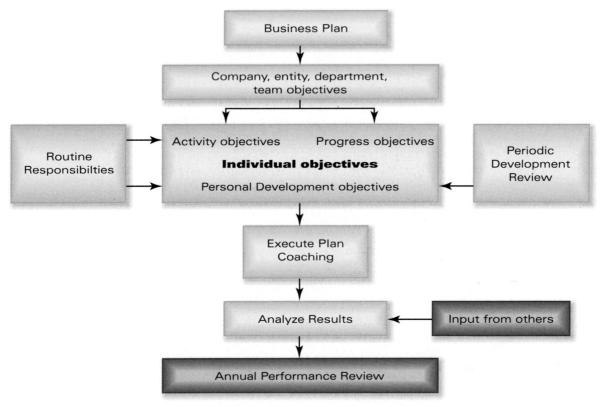

Source: Company information.

Performance Appraisal and Development Process

Michelin's appraisal process consisted of two parts: an annual performance review (APR) and a periodic development process (PDR). The line manager and career manager worked together to conduct the appraisal, which particularly emphasized providing direction and recognition, developing individuals and teams, listening and coaching. In APR, individual objectives were based on company, department, and team objectives to ensure consistency. Individuals also gave feedback to managers who were responsible for following up, coaching, providing resources, removing obstacles and modifying objectives if necessary. At the end of every year, manager and employee would meet for an appraisal interview and send the completed APR form to the personnel department.

PDR was considered an important part of career management. It was not tied to APR and could be done at any time, but at least once every two years. During the PDR meeting, manager and employee would try to come to an agreement on the "orientation envisioned by manager," "strengths," "improvement areas," and "proposals for additional training/experience." According to Michelin policy, employees' compensation was linked with the performance of each entity. The purpose of this was to increase employees' identification with the entity to enhance cultural cohesion within the group.

Cultural and Managerial Issues Facing Michelin in China

Respect for Hierarchy and Seniority

The traditional Chinese culture was one of power distance and humility, where people had great respect for fixed hierarchical relationships. Conventional business structures reflected this, with the leader having natural authority. The top-down tradition made subordinates less proactive.

Promotions at work were in many cases based on age rather than ability. This was especially typical of SOEs, where the pay structure also rewarded seniority rather than merit. The "iron rice bowl mentality" symbolized guaranteed lifetime employment, leading to minimal pay differentials and no accountability.

Implementing the career management system was one of the main challenges in terms of hierarchy. Traditionally, the Chinese viewed functional departments as more important than supporting functions such as IT and personnel. Thus, some functional managers insisted, "I have the say about where my people go," and it was difficult for them to listen to a third party—the career manager—who was not their direct boss. Jugier commented:

> Chinese employees respect functional managers a lot. They think that personnel people are closer to the general manager and feel that the career manager is another guy watching them.

Jugier hoped that employees would be happy to find someone other than their direct boss to discuss their career options with. However, Chinese employees did not quite see it in this light.

Finding qualified career managers in China was another challenge, according to Jugier:

> Career managers must have the necessary character and competence to do the job. They have to discuss with managers and convince them. That's why most career managers are from business functions. We should do the same in China. We have to develop competent career managers and recruiters here. We are here to develop people and enable them to take more important positions and make more contributions. It is one of my tasks. We have many positions to fill in China and we need people from other countries. We are in the starting stage.

The Importance of Face

The Chinese placed much significance on the concept of face. They went to great lengths to avoid calling attention to errors, indiscretions, or emotions that would cause themselves or others to lose face, particularly in front of other people. Good relationships were maintained by conflict avoidance and helping each other to save face. Causing other people to lose face could be seen as a challenge to their position in the hierarchy, which could threaten group harmony and the social order.

In keeping with the value of face, Chinese businesspeople tended not to be confrontational. They would not point out a mistake for fear of causing loss of face. It was also considered disrespectful for a junior person to interrupt or correct a senior. A testing engineer in Michelin reported that some of his colleagues were not happy with the management style of an expatriate manager who provided them with the direct and instantaneous feedback, causing many people to lose face, without the expatriate even realizing it.

Guanxi

There is no exact translation for the Chinese concept of *guanxi*—a mutually beneficial relationship providing an ongoing link between individuals—which was the foundation on which most things were built in China. One person would do a favor for another, with the expectation that the person being helped would provide some type of unspecified future assistance in return. Such relationships might exist between neighbors, with the clerk in a local store, with government officials or with business associates. Expatriate managers often spent less time cultivating personal relationships, and from the Chinese point of view, such "inadequate attention" to managing personal relationships undermined managerial effectiveness.

Jugier explained:

> We had to make employees learn the way we approach our business and understand Michelin. Chinese people emphasized *guanxi* rather than teamwork. We had to teach them how to work together in an organization. Many employees could not even understand why it was necessary to sign a new labor contract with SMW.

Communication and Decision Styles

The Chinese had a high-context and nonverbal style of communication. It was high-context in the sense that certain knowledge was already assumed, as opposed to a low-context culture, where more information was exchanged during each communication. Nonverbal communication included implied meanings, nonverbal cues, indirect statements, and symbolic language. In addition, the Chinese were comfortable with silences or pauses in conversation.

The indirect nature of Chinese communication came from a long history of close families and interpersonal relations. It assumed a shared understanding between communicants. For instance, Chinese businesspeople would rarely say "no" directly in response to a suggestion. Instead they would often propose that the matter be studied further. Similarly, open-ended questions were common, avoiding the possibility of forcing someone into a corner by requiring a "yes" or "no" answer. Rather than valuing directness, the Chinese were more likely to be polite but vague.

Michelin's management placed more emphasis on processes and structures, allowing people to delegate more. Chinese managers were concerned that the rigid structure was an obstacle to speed in the decision-making process. Michelin required them to follow procedures to solve problems in a step-by-step manner as opposed to finding short cuts and quick fixes to solve problems.

Personal Development

In China, being technically solid was a prerequisite in order to become a manager. Without sound technical knowledge and skills, it was difficult to earn respect from staff. Interpersonal skills in the managerial selection process played a secondary role in China.

Expatriates at Michelin noticed that the individual qualities of some of the Chinese staff were excellent. However, they often lacked the expected teamwork capability and responsibility in the decision-making process. The Chinese education system placed far greater emphasis on testing individual technical skills than on leadership and teamwork.

Because of the fast growth in foreign direct investment in China, companies were competing for talents, and talent retention and development were major issues. The lack of management talent in China was often referred as "famine in the midst of abundance." People who had managed to acquire good management skills were in short supply, which led to salary escalation, high staff turnover, and less commitment from the company to invest in training and development. Chinese managers at Michelin were frequently approached by headhunters or other companies. Retention of experienced local managers was always a key challenge for multinational companies in China, and Michelin was no exception.

Summary

These cultural differences created the need to strike a balance between seemingly opposing values. To Jugier it seemed a daunting task. Indeed, cultural differences could significantly affect the common set of Michelin's values worldwide. With some 125,000 employees around the world, the company had always tried to ensure consistent understanding of its management principles, and these common principles had to be shared by its employees in China.

Endnotes

[1]Radial tires, invented by Michelin more than 50 years ago, use more advanced technology and are safer than bias tires, which are still mass produced in China.

[2]In 1996 STRC acquired a bankrupt factory for $9 million in Hainan province, but the factory continued to lose money. In 1998 STRC acquired Xuzhou Tire Group. When STRC tried to lay off workers, the Xuzhou government balked, and the company lost $1.45 million in 2000. Later in 1998 STRC bought 60 percent of a tractor maker in Luoyang, but it turned out to be another failure.

[3]In China tire producers were once considered of strategic importance to the state and the industry was highly protected to the extent that foreign investors were prohibited from controlling it.

[4]Honesty, objectivity, a shared vision of reality, and a love of truth.

[5]Michelin Web site.

Suggested Reading

Articles

Bassolino, Francis, and Joseph Tse. "Leveraging Technology in the PRC." *China Business Review* 26, no. 1 (January/February 1999).

China Global Insight, China Country Monitor, July 2003.

Davis, Bruce. "Tire Makers' Expansion Plans Exceed $1 Billion." *Rubber & Plastics News* 32, no. 3 (September 2002).

Raleigh, Patrick. "Michelin and Shanghai Tire Ink JV Deal." *European Rubber Journal* 183, no. 5 (May 2001).

"Re-inventing the Wheel." *Business China* 23, no. 4 (February 17, 1997).

Tierney, Christine; Ann Therese Palmer; Chester Dawson; and Joann Muller. "Michelin Rolls." *Business Week,* September 30, 2002.

Walters, Peter G. P. "Executive Insights: Marketing Strategy in Emerging Markets: The Case of China." *Journal of International Marketing* 11, no. 1 (2003).

Wang, Yong. "China's Domestic WTO Debate." *China Business Review* 27, no. 1 (January/February 2000).

Xing, Wayne W. J. "Automakers in the Fast Lane." *China Business Review* 29, no. 4 (July/August 2002).

Yang, John Z.; John Farley; and Scott Hoenig. "When MNCs Come to China, Who Changes Whom?" *China Business Review* 26, no. 2 (March/April 1999).

Books

Dahlman, Carl J., and Jean-Eric Aubert. *China and the Knowledge Economy: Seizing the 21st Century.* World Bank, October 2001.

Lardy, Nicholas R. *Integrating China into the Global Economy.* The Brookings Institution, 2002.

OECD. *China in the World Economy: The Domestic Policy Challenges.* Paris 2002.

Singapore Airlines 2004
Managing Organizational Change in a Turbulent Environment

Wee Beng Geok
Nanyang Business School

Shirley Koh
Nanyang Business School

On 7 April, 2004, SIA's CEO Chew Choon Seng announced that the company was confident it would meet its profit target of S$600 million for the fiscal year ending March 31. As promised to SIA staff earlier in the financial year, SIA would make a one-off payment to employees to compensate for wage cuts made earlier in the fiscal year 2002–2003. This was in addition to a 15 percent one-off bonus to be granted to all employees. At the same press conference, Chew also asserted that the company might have to cut costs by up to 20 percent or S$1.6 billion a year in order to remain economically viable in the long term. He saw the cut as necessary in order to meet the airline's target of eight percent return on capital employed (ROCE). However, in the best-case scenario, the cut could be 10 percent or S$800 million per year. He added that failure to meet this ROCE target did not imply that SIA was making losses, as the target was simply a measure of whether the airline provided an adequate ROCE compared with other alternative investments.[1]

For many years, Singapore Airline (SIA) was a regular recipient of accolades such as "best airline," "preferred airline," "most admired company," "best frequent flyer program," "best cabin outfit," "best catering," "best crew on board," "best staff on ground," and "best in-flight entertainment." In 2003 alone, the airline topped the lists in various surveys conducted in 18 travel or business magazines. That year, it was ranked top in the airline category in *Fortune* (USA) magazine's "The World's Most Admired Companies Survey."

THE ASIAN
BUSINESS CASE CENTRE

The case is based on public sources. As the case is not intended to illustrate either effective or ineffective practices or policies, the information presented reflects the authors' interpretation of events and serves merely to provide opportunities for classroom discussions.

Exhibit 1 PROFITABILITY OF SINGAPORE AIRLINES, 1989–2003
(in millions of Singapore $)

Financial Year	Profit after Tax
1989–90	1,176.8
1990–91	886.8
1991–92	920.7
1992–93	741.1
1993–94	722.6
1994–95	939.0
1995–96	875.9
1996–97	901.8
1997–98	919.5
1998–99	813.7
1999–00	1,267.1
2000–01	1,422.2
2001–02	567.2
2002–03	618.0

Source: SIA annual reports.

Exhibit 2 SINGAPORE AIRLINES' OPERATING STATISTICS, 1998–2003

	Financial Year				
	2002–03	2001–02	2000–01	1999–2000	1998–99
Passenger load factor (%)	74.5%	74.0%	76.8%	74.9%	72.5%
Cargo load factor (%)	69.6	67.5	69.5	70.1	67.9
Overall load factor (%)	71.1	69.6	72.0	71.2	68.8
Overall breakeven load factor (%)	67.7	68.4	66.9	66.2	66.9

Source: SIA annual report, 2002–03.

SIA remained profitable in the face of major world events such as the Gulf War (1991), Asian economic crisis (1997–1999), and September 11 terrorist attacks (2001). (Exhibit 1 tracks the profitability of SIA over the years while Exhibit 2 provides statistics on SIA's load factors.)

SIA's Continuous Search for Excellent Service

SIA consistently worked at differentiating its products and services. It was the first airline to provide a choice of meals, complimentary drinks, and free headsets in economy class.[2] Although this service was considered radical in the early 1970s, by 2000, it was a standard feature of many international airlines. Other industry firsts from SIA included a video-on-demand in-flight entertainment system, a first-class check-in lounge[3] and the world's first global in-flight e-mail system. Exhibit 3 is a summary of some of SIA's recent product innovations.

**Exhibit 3   SINGAPORE AIRLINES' RECORD OF PRODUCT AND SERVICE INNOVATIONS,
1998–2004**

1998

- Installed four auto check-in kiosks at Singapore Changi Airport for passengers holding automated ticket and boarding pass tickets and without check-in luggage.
- Introduced the World Gourmet Cuisine for all classes. A panel of world-renowned chefs and food experts who advised SIA on the latest culinary trends created over 40 signature dishes. First- and raffles-class travelers departing from selected cities could pre-order a wide range of signature dishes.
- First-class travelers were provided with a flexi-meal service, allowing them to dine whenever they wanted during the flight.

1999

- Introduced the Dolby Headphone Surround Sound technology in in-flight entertainment systems.
- Introduced the Wisemen audiovideo-on-demand entertainment for first- and raffles-class travelers.
- Extended telephone check-in service to economy-class travelers, allowing them to check in from 48 hours down to 2 hours before flight departure.
- SIA Service Centre opened in Orchard Road city center with automated check-in facilities.
- From the SIA Web site, first- and raffles-class passengers could view a real-time seating plan and book their preferred seats online.
- All SIA aircraft equipped with automatic external defibrillators for reviving passengers with cardiac arrest.

2000

- Launched the Telemedical Service on its flights, allowing cabin crew to consult medical staff on the ground in the event of illnesses.
- Introduced Mobile Services, which allowed customers to access up-to-the-minute flight information anywhere and at any time of the day using wireless application protocol (WAP) phones.
- The new Silver Kris Lounge opened at Singapore Changi Airport.
- Launched a co-brand credit card with American Express in four Asian markets (Singapore, Hong Kong, Malaysia, and Taiwan) that allowed customers to earn KrisFlyer miles from everyday purchases.

2001

- Launched the world's first global in-flight e-mail system and a new-generation entertainment system. The e-mail system used a satellite-based communications network and was available to customers in all three classes.
- Became the first airline to offer global air flight alerts via the short message service (SMS).
- Unveiled the new U.S.$100 million SpaceBed, the biggest business-class bed on planes.

2002

- Launched new Internet check-in service, which allowed passengers to choose their desired seats up to two days before departure.
- SIA and Visa International launched the Singapore Airlines Splendour Card, offering customer discounts at more than 300 outlets and attractions in Singapore.
- Progressively installed SpaceBed after further refinements, including modifications to reduce the weight of the seat.
- New Silver Kris lounge opened in Terminal 2 of Chiang Kai Shek International Airport in Taipei. The new lounge was three times the size of the one it replaced in Terminal 1. Features included business workstations, first-class slumberette rooms, and shower facilities.
- Revamped menu options in the Book the Cook service.
- Offered free mobile phone rental to first- and raffles-class passengers, and discounted rental to economy-class passengers traveling to Japan, Korea, and the United States.

2004

- Launch of first 18-hour nonstop flight from Singapore to Los Angeles providing business-class passengers an extra 15 cm to stretch out. Economy-class passengers had extra 12.5 cm legroom and an extra 5 cm for leaning back. Also featured: a snack bar available to all passengers.

2006 (planned)

- SIA will be the first airline to fly the world's largest plane, the double-deck Airbus A380. A380 will be divided into different sections serving business travelers and families.

Sources: SIA annual reports; "Premium Service on SIA's LA-Direct Flights," *Straits Times (Singapore)*, January 2, 2004; and "Travellers Have Say in Design of SIA's New Plane," *Straits Times (Singapore)*, September 1, 2002.

The airline not only benchmarked its customer services against other airlines but also took into account similar services offered by other industries such as car rental companies, hotels, and restaurants:

> We need to give our customers a great experience and good value. It is important to realize that they are not just comparing SIA with other airlines. They are comparing us against many industries, and on many factors. . . Our customers, albeit subconsciously, will benchmark us against the best in almost everything. The new ball game for SIA is not just to be the best of the best in the airline industry, but to work at being the best service company. So we serve the best champagne, and even when we serve local dishes such as chicken rice, it has to be the best when compared to the local market.

> Yap Kim Wah
> Senior Vice President
> Product and Service, SIA[4]

To achieve the same consistency in quality service, the cabin crew followed procedures which had been fine-tuned by research and trials. There was a keen awareness among senior managers of the high demands that customers placed on the company and the challenges this posed of being the best in whatever they did.[5] The service challenge for SIA was that of staying ahead:

> Therefore, in SIA, it's about coming up with new things all the time. We want to be a little better all the time in everything we do. It is the new things that create the "wow." There is a whole realm of things that customers don't know they want [yet] . . .
>
> It is the totality that counts. This also means that it does not need to be too expensive. If you want to provide the best food, you might as well serve lobster on short-haul flights. However, you might go bankrupt.
>
> We just have to do better than our competitors in everything we do . . . This allows us to make a small profit from the flight to enable us to innovate without pricing ourselves out of the market. This makes it much harder for our competitors.

> Yap Kim Wah
> Senior Vice President[6]

To forge ahead, SIA identified the next service challenge as one of transforming customer service, and in May 1999 the company launched the Transforming Customer Service (TCS) initiative, which focused on integrating people, processes, and products. As an ongoing process (instead of a one-off campaign), TCS required SIA staff to constantly explore creative and innovative ways to transform service. As expectations of customers changed, TCS would evolve.

The first phase—"I Can, I Will"—was concerned with "embedding" the TCS mindset (the "whats" and "whys" of TCS) among staff in five key operational areas—cabin crew, engineering, ground services, flight operations, and sales support.[7] The second phase—"I Can, I Will. Higher. Further"—addressed the "how to" of TCS by seeking to equip staff with new skill sets and tools to achieve the objectives of the 30/30/40 formula:

We focus 40 percent of resources [for this initiative] on training and invigorating people, 30 percent on the review of processes and procedures, and 30 percent on creating new products and service ideas.

> Lam Seet Mui
> Senior Manager
> Human Resource Development[8]

A major component of TCS was service process redesign—seeking ways to simplify procedures and processes, and removing those that hindered good and consistent service delivery. In seeking solutions to customers' problems, staff were encouraged to think out of the box and steer away from the rule book and normal procedures. Process redesign would be embarked on by empowered teams of front-liners under the supervision of a team leader.[9]

TCS was a manifestation of the airline's two core values—"Customer First" ("Our customers are foremost in our minds all the time. We go the extra mile to exceed their expectations") and "Pursuit of Excellence" ("We strive for the highest professional standards in our work and aim to be the best in everything we do").

Dr. Cheong Koong Kong, former CEO of SIA, explained that the TCS initiative was launched to widen the gap between SIA and its rival airlines. While competitors could catch up with SIA by copying its hardware, imitating its in-flight services and ordering the same in-flight entertainment systems, the airline was determined to "make it next to impossible" to duplicate its human resource.[10]

Continuous Improvement—Investment in Employee Training

The company saw training as central to its goal of continuous improvement. There were two types of training—functional training and general management training. The aim of functional training was to equip staff with skills so that they would be technically competent and confident in their jobs. Training in each of the core functional areas—cabin crew, flight operations, commercial training, IT, security, airport services training, and engineering—was conducted by seven training schools in the SIA Group. The SIA Management Development Centre provided general management training, emphasizing the acquisition of "soft" skills. This came under the purview of the Human Resources Division. Each year, more than 9,000 staff from the different functional areas attended the training programs offered by SIA's training group.[11]

Because of its reputation for excellent service, SIA's front-line staff had to meet the high standards that passengers had come to expect from the airline:

> So the staff are really under a lot of pressure. We have a motto, "If SIA can't do it for you, no other airline can." So we encourage staff to try to sort things out, to do as much as they can for the customer . . . We need to help them deal with the emotional turmoil of having to handle their customers well and, at the same time, feel that they're not being taken advantage of. The challenge is to help our staff deal with the difficult situations and take the brickbats. This will be the next thrust of our training.

> Yap Kim Wah
> Senior Vice President[12]

Focus on Costs and Profits

Cost consciousness was drilled into all managers from the first day of employment. Management was consistently reminded of the airline's key goal to be the most profitable airline in the world. Meeting profitability goals determined managers' bonuses as well as the bonuses of other employees.

SIA managers were rotated between departments every few years. The goal was to develop managers who could see the big picture. However, managers were also expected to have a fine eye for detail and hence be able to operate efficiently at both the macro and micro level.

The company assessed employee productivity regularly through measures such as value added per employee as well as revenue generated per employee. (Exhibit 4 provides information on these measures from 1993 to 2003.) The underlying policy was that wage increases should lag behind productivity growth to ensure that costs did not outstrip productivity.[13]

Fleet Renewal

SIA maintained one of the most modern and youngest fleets in the world, with the average aircraft age at 5 years and 11 months as at March 31, 2003. In contrast, the average aircraft age of the industry was approximately twice that of SIA.[14] SIA's fleet renewal program was described by Dr. Michael Fam, a former chairman of the board, as "one of its hallmarks and has contributed much to the success of the airline over the past two decades."[15]

Between September 2000 and February 2001, SIA announced plans to purchase up to 60 aircraft worth U.S.$13.9 billion. Although the fleet renewal program involved heavy capital outlays, there were savings on fuel costs by operating a newer fleet, particularly as such costs accounted for 20 percent of operating costs.[16] Besides lower fuel consumption, newer aircraft traveled faster, had less downtime, required lower maintenance, and were viewed as safer by passengers.

Investments in New Products and Services

SIA passengers were the first to enjoy a video-on-demand in-flight entertainment system, and global in-flight e-mail. SIA also invested heavily in operational systems and processes, particularly information technology (IT). The airline's fully automated catering center produced an average of 34,000 meals a day.[17] In 1998, a system of electronic transmission of airway bill data and bar-code labeling of shipments was implemented in the airline's cargo operations.[18] This improved shipment tracking by customers using the Internet. In 2002, SIA began to implement KrisMax II, a new revenue management system, which avoided situations where customers in one market segment were waitlisted for seats while other market segments had unsold seats.[19]

Marketing the SIA Brand

The "Singapore Girl" had been the centerpiece of SIA's marketing campaigns since 1973. According to a survey conducted by the International Research Association, SIA's advertising recall was then 21 percent.[20] This figure rose to 50 percent six years later in 1979. In 1993, the "Singapore Girl" marketing icon became the first commercial wax figure to be displayed in wax at Madam Tussaud's Museum in London. The smiling and graceful wax image of the idealized air stewardess symbolized the central features of

Exhibit 4   SINGAPORE AIRLINES' PRODUCTIVITY AND EMPLOYEE DATA, 1993-2003

	Financial Year									
	2002-03	2001-02	2000-01	1999-2000	1998-99	1997-98	1996-97	1995-96	1994-95	1993-94
Average number of employees	14,418	14,205	14,254	13,720	13,690	13,506	13,258	12,966	12,557	12,363
Revenue per employee (S$)	558,122	541,690	647,516	607,966	526,859	524,012	500,649	490,591	481,365	457,462
Value added per employee (S$)	191,566	189,806	284,369	291,494	228,254	236,828	221,044	210,319	215,091	195,276

Note: SIA Cargo was corporatised on July 1, 2001. Statistics for 2000-01 and prior years show the combined results of both passenger and cargo operations.
Source: SIA annual report, 2002-03.

Exhibit 5 SHARE PRICE AND DIVIDENDS, SINGAPORE AIRLINES, 1994–2003

	Financial Year								
	1994–95	1995–96	1996–97	1997–98		1999–2000	2000–01	2001–02	2002–03
Share price									
High (S$)	15.10	15.70	15.00	13.90	13.60	20.80	19.20	14.90	14.40
Low (S$)	11.00	11.80	11.40	9.20	6.40	12.40	12.90	7.00	8.55
Closing (S$)	14.10	14.60	11.60	11.50	12.50	16.00	13.60	14.40	8.75
Dividends									
Gross dividends (cents per share in Singapore currency)	22.50	22.50	30.00	22.50	25.00	30.00	35.00	15.00	15.00

Note: SIA local shares and SIA foreign shares were merged on 11 September 1999. For comparison, share prices for 1998–99 and prior years were that of SIA foreign shares.

Source: SIA annual reports.

SIA's service—care and attentiveness. In practice, these traits were carefully inculcated in the cabin crew through rigorous training and continuous monitoring.[21]

SIA Shareholders and Value Creation

In a review of the performance of Singapore's listed companies between 1998 and 2003, Singapore-based financial reporter Teh Hooi Ling identified SIA as leading the pack in terms of the absolute amount of shareholder value created during this period.[22] According to Teh, SIA paid out S$1.2 billion in dividends and returned S$1.7 billion of capital to shareholders either via share buybacks or capital reduction between 1998 and 2003. Teh argued that during this period, SIA generated more than S$6 billion in shareholder value, which "translated into a respectable return of 12 percent a year over the last six years."[23] (See Exhibit 5 for the price and dividend payout of SIA shares over the years.)

Teamwork SIA

Employee Share Option Plans

In 2000, following the approval of shareholders, SIA implemented a broad-based share option scheme, the Employee Share Option Plan, for all employees. SIA believed that the Employee Share Option Plan would "help promote group cohesiveness and team spirit through a sense of ownership," as well as "attract, retain and motivate senior executives whose participation in policy and decision-making can influence performance and returns to shareholders."[24]

SIA was actually reinstating an old scheme which ended with the public listing of the airline in 1985.[25] Under the new scheme, which would last 10 years, SIA could issue up to a maximum of 13 percent of its existing shares as options to eligible employees. However, these option shares could only be sold after a vesting period, as the objective of the scheme was to retain and motivate staff. To qualify for the scheme, a senior executive of SIA must have rendered at least two years of full-time service for the company while junior staff must have at least eight years of full-time service.[26] More than 50 percent of SIA staff qualified for the scheme. The chief executive was eligible for a maximum of 240,000 share options a year, while other senior executives were limited to between 2,400 and 200,000 shares.[27] In June 2003, the airline announced that it was seeking to remove the cap on the number of share options it could issue to senior executives.

Company Spirit

In 2001, in the wake of the dramatic fall in air travel in Asia after the September 11 terrorist attacks in the United States, SIA employees agreed to five months of voluntary pay cuts. Despite the difficult business conditions that followed, the company registered an after-tax profit of S$631 million for the financial year 2001–02.

SIA Cabin Crew

SIA's management regarded the creation of esprit de corps among the cabin crew as important. To create camaraderie, the airline divided the 6,600 cabin crew employees into teams of 13, and as far as possible, the team members would fly together. The leader of each cabin crew team was both mentor and counselor to team members. At the next level, a group of "check trainers" supervised 12 or 13 cabin crew teams each. Their role was to monitor team performances and facilitate team development. Through this system of supervision, the airline maintained meticulous and detailed records of each cabin crew's performance and was able to quickly identify members who needed retraining as well as earmark cabin crew members for promotion.[28]

Being a "Singapore Girl" had its attractions. The airline received thousands of applications for these positions, and it was not uncommon for a flight attendant to be selected after repeated attempts. Besides the lure of glamour and the romance of travel, an SIA flight attendant received almost S$3,400 in monthly salary and allowances.[29] In comparison, a new O or A Level school-leaver in Singapore typically earned less than S$2,000, while the median salary of a new university graduate was less than S$3,000.

Well-trained and experienced SIA cabin crew members were regarded as a good source of talent by firms in the service industry such as hotels, banks, and real estate, which often regarded them as possessing the right mix of skills and competencies they required in their front-line personnel. Over the years, there had been many accounts of ex–flight attendants who made a successful transition into marketing and sales jobs in other industries.

SIA and the Pilots

Since 1981, there had been 24 disputes between the pilots' union, Air Line Pilots Association—Singapore (Alpha-S) and SIA management. Nineteen of them were brought either to the Ministry of Labour or the Industrial Arbitration Court for arbitration.[30]

A feature of the airline industry was that pilots had greater leverage compared to other airline workers. As the professional training for pilots was costly (between S$500,000 to S$700,000), some airlines regarded the poaching of pilots from rivals as a cheaper alternative to training fresh recruits.

According to the Alpha-S, in 2003, the basic monthly pay of a SIA captain flying a B-747 was between S$10,000 and S$19,500.[31] Cathay Pacific pilots were paid S$21,000 to S$34,000 while Qantas pilots received between S$16,000 to S$25,500. The starting tax-free salary of an Emirates captain was S$11,234.

Since the expiration of a collective agreement between the company and the pilots in 1998, negotiations for a new agreement had dragged on with no sign of a conclusion. In February 2001, after 26 months of negotiations, the talks between the company and the pilots' union broke down. The dispute was brought to the attention of the Industrial Arbitration Court.[32] The terms for the new collective agreement were only settled shortly after the court ordered both parties to continue negotiations after hearing submissions from both sides.

Barely a year later, in February 2002, a dispute arose between the company and the pilots' union regarding the use of economy rather than business class seats for pilots taking their in-flight breaks. The catalyst for this dispute was the introduction of new SpaceBed seats in the business-class section. As the new seats could be converted into beds and hence used up more space, there were fewer seats available for sale. Consequently, SIA told the pilots that they had to take their meal breaks and midflight rests in economy-class seats.[33] While the pilots argued that this new arrangement violated the collective agreement concluded only a year earlier, SIA management maintained that this was not the case.[34] By August, with no agreement in sight, at an extraordinary meeting of the union, members of Alpha-S voted in favor of a resolution to hold a secret ballot on whether to take industrial action against the company by a majority of 86 percent.[35] Industrial action could take the form of work-to-rule action. This was likely to result in costly delays and flight cancellations. A week later, following the intervention of the Ministry of Manpower (formerly known as the Ministry of Labour), and after 10 hours of intense negotiations, a compromise was reached between the company and Alpha-S. The compromise reached was for one business class seat to be set aside for pilots and S$200 compensation for pilots who had to sit in economy class. However, pilots would be given priority to upgrade to business class ahead of passengers and other staff.

Between 2001 and 2002, the company went on an aggressive recruitment drive for overseas-based foreign pilots, on terms that excluded expatriate pilots' relocation costs to Singapore. Further, these pilots were not represented by Alpha-S.[36]

Another thorny issue was the problem of a huge backlog of annual leave owed to the pilots. In a letter to Senior Minister Lee Kuan Yew, Alpha-S wrote that "there have been countless times when, at [SIA's] request, dispensations to work beyond the flight and duty time limits of the collective agreement were granted by the association, so as to minimize flight delays and disruptions, thereby promoting the good public image of SIA, reducing costs, and optimizing operational efficiency."[37] The association also revealed that its pilots had never turned down SIA's requests to defer their annual leave. This resulted in 15,000 outstanding leave days owed to the pilots at the end of 2002.

Developments in 2003

In early 2003, a flu-like epidemic, identified as the severe acute respiratory syndrome (SARS), swept through many parts of East Asia. In Singapore, SARS infected more than 200 people and killed 32. However, by the end of May that year, the epidemic was brought under control in Singapore and the World Health Organization took Singapore off the list of SARS-infected countries on May 31.

As fear of the epidemic gripped the world, tourists and other air travelers stayed away from Asia, causing the region's travel industry to be badly hit. For the first quarter (April–June 2003) of its financial year 2003–04 ending June 30, SIA recorded its first ever net loss of S$312 million.

When SIA posted losses of S$204 million in April 2003 and S$166 million in May 2003, SIA's management took wage cuts of 27.5 percent and imposed compulsory no-pay leave for its cabin crew. Passenger capacity was cut by more than 30 percent in April and airfares were slashed by 50 to 75 percent.[38] Despite the negative business conditions, SIA announced that it planned to launch a new fleet of long-range planes (Airbus A340-500) services in 2004.[39]

In June 2003, the company announced its first layoff since the 1980s. Some 414 employees based in Singapore, comprising office staff, airport workers, and engineering personnel and representing 1.5 percent of the SIA Group's workforce, were made redundant. To the company, the redundancy exercise was the "last step in response to the current operating environment, following earlier moves to stringently manage costs."[40]

In the following month, 26 pilots and 156 cabin crew were laid off. There were then 1,800 pilots and 6,600 cabin crew in the company.[41]

At about the same time, the company began making offers of early retirement to some long-service administrative officers, managers, and cabin crew. The compensation offered included one month's pay for every year of service and the usual SIA retirement benefits, including annual free flights. However, cabin crew received higher packages of up to 35 months' pay, as they were entitled to a gratuity on retirement, and this was added to the lump sum payment. Some 165 employees took up the offer.[42]

With wages at almost a fifth of its total cost,[43] employees were asked to take compulsory no-pay leave and to accept wage cuts of between 5 and 16.5 percent to further reduce operating cost.[44] The monthly salaries of the pilots were cut by 16.5 percent, while the first officers' salaries were cut by 11 percent.[45] Cabin crew and general staff took a 7 percent pay cut while for employees earning $1,500 or less per month, the cut was 5 percent.[46] To soften the blow, SIA's management reached an agreement with the unions that the company would return 50 percent of the total amount of the wage cut to employees if net profit for the financial year 2003–04 exceeded S$300 million. Compensation would be 75 percent if the net profit exceeded S$400 million and 100 percent of the wage cut would be restored if the net profit exceeded S$500 million.[47]

Employee Sentiments

With the cost-cutting measures and the post-SARS recovery, the company recorded a net profit of S$306 million for the second quarter of its financial year 2003–04.

Incidentally, in 2001, after the September 11 terrorist attacks, SIA employees, in the wake of poor business conditions, took voluntary pay cuts. Although the company made an after-tax profit of S$631 million for that financial year, there was no reimbursement of the voluntary pay cuts.

This time, even as the turnaround brought cheer, it also brought to the surface sentiments in some quarters that the unprecedented large-scale lay-offs had been too hasty. One union spokesman called the redundancy exercise a "knee-jerk reaction."[48] In November 2003, the airline announced that it was recruiting pilots and cabin crew again, and that former cabin crew trainees would be the first to receive job offers.[49] However, former SIA employees would "receive no preferential treatment nor be guaranteed a position in the selection process." During the year, SIA had lost more than 20 pilots to other airlines. In the second half of the year, it hired more than 20 cadet pilots.

In November 2003, Alpha-S's existing council was voted out by 55 percent of the association's 1,600 members. Some members were said to be unhappy with the union leadership's deal with the SIA management over the wage cuts earlier in the year.

Concerns in government circles grew over the escalating conflict between the company and Alpha-S, and at the end of the year, the Singapore government, as the major shareholder of SIA, stepped in to resolve the dispute.

Senior Minister (SM) Lee Kuan Yew warned that the government would not allow the pilots to "hold the airline to ransom by taking a confrontational stance."[50] The concern was that the ouster was a signal of a more aggressive stance on the part of the pilots' union with a new collective agreement due for negotiation.

In January 2004, SM Lee called on SIA to close the books on its troubled relations with the pilots and start afresh:

> I'm not here to defend the human relations side of SIA. I think if it were well done, we wouldn't have had this problem . . . For positive relations, you need trust. The employee must know that the employer has his interests at heart. He's not just out to squeeze him and show profits and be done with it and he gets big bonuses. In other words, there must be confidence.[51]

The newly elected Alpha-S president expressed the union's desire to improve relations with SIA's management and to end the forthcoming new collective agreement on a positive note.[52] Alpha-S also aired its grievances with SIA in a letter to the SM.

Shortly following this, the leaders of three other SIA unions—Singapore Airlines Staff Union, Singapore Airport Terminal Services Workers' Union, and SIA Engineering Company Engineers and Executive Union—sent a joint note to Lim Boon Heng, the secretary-general of the National Trade Union Congress (NTUC), the union federation of which these unions were members. The letter gave their views on the recent spate of problems with the SIA management.[53] These included:

1. A growing "culture of fear," which had emerged over the last three to four years, was replacing the "family spirit" that had characterized employer–employee relations in the group. The unionists felt that workers were worried about making mistakes as they were often threatened with being fired. This, they felt, was bringing down employee morale and affecting the sense of pride employees had in their work.

2. The unions were unhappy as they felt the management adopted a bullying attitude in negotiations. The impression given to the unions was that the management had the board's and the government's backing. There was little information-sharing between the unions and SIA's management, and as a result, union leaders sometimes learned of company matters from the mass media and the NTUC, instead of the company.

3. The middle management was perceived to be the cause of some unhappiness among workers. The unionists felt that the middle managers should take more responsibility in explaining decisions and policies to employees, but felt that these managers tended to assign the reasons for decisions implemented as "instructions from the top."

4. The management was perceived as quick to act when it favored itself, but slow to act on employees' concerns. For example when the Unions proposed that new staff be included in profit-sharing entitlements, it was turned down. However, when a new group of managers joined the company, the qualifying criterion was changed to benefit these new managers.

In response, SIA's chief executive officer, Chew Choon Seng, promised that SIA would "take pains to get staff to understand the unprecedented layoffs."[54] He also affirmed that SIA's management would hold regular meetings with unions and he encouraged staff to e-mail their feedback "without fearing retribution."[55]

A New Competitive Environment

The year 2003 was a turning point for Asia's air travel and tourist industry. Low-fare carriers were expanding across Asia, and these budget airlines seemed set for take-off:

> Asia, geographically challenged and hobbled by poor road and rail infrastructure, is about to be linked by a fast efficient air network accessible to the masses. Think telecoms in the 1990s: Much of the region, lacking the millions of kilometres of cable needed for adequate fixed-line services, instead made a quantum leap to cheap and widely available mobile networks.[56]

Changes in the mindset of governments were emerging, from one of protecting national air carriers to the realization of the benefits of open skies for the tourism industry, and hence the GDP of the country.

By April 2004, five ventures to operate budget airlines out of Singapore had been announced. This included Australia's Qantas Airways' plans to set up a low-fare carrier with Singapore's government-owned Temasek Holdings and two businessmen's bids to operate a budget airline based in Singapore.[57]

New Challenges

In early April 2004, at a forum with management and unions of the SIA Group, as well as airport and tourism officials, SM Lee warned that the SIA Group was headed for major organizational restructuring. In his view, SIA's business model was increasingly challenged by tough market conditions and the airline group was entering an era where it would not be able to significantly charge higher premium fares without redefining the concept of "premier service." Hence, cost management was critical if SIA was to remain profitable. He added that profit-sharing formulas should reflect greater emphasis on company and individual performances and not just group performance.[58] His message to SIA staff was that they should be prepared for wrenching changes to protect their jobs.[59] He added:

> What I am asking you to understand is that we have not embarked on this [restructuring] lightly. We could wait for another two, three or four years, until the pressure builds up, but then we would have lost the chance to become the hub for low-cost carriers, which we cannot afford.[60]

At the forum, Singapore's Ministry of Transport officials also shared their perspective on the future prospects of Changi Airport as a premier aviation hub. Long-haul planes, made possible by new aircraft technology, could lead airlines to bypass Singapore. On the other hand, this same technology, as well as that of larger planes, could present an opportunity for Singapore and SIA to consolidate passengers from the other countries in the region to fly to the rest of the world. However, there was growing and intense competition from regional airlines as well as regional airports all seeking to be the aviation hub for the region. Similarly, new growth markets in China and India would also create more competition as well as new business opportunities for Singapore's airport maintenance, repairs and overhaul, and airport development sectors.[61]

Faced with these challenges, especially that of the emergence of no-frills budget airlines, in early 2004, SIA set about reexamining its cost components again. To reduce wage cost, Chew hoped to increase the flexible component in wages (which was pegged to company performance) from 20 to 30 percent for general staff, from 30 to 40 percent for executives, and from 20 to 50 percent for senior managers.[62] SIA unions also reported that besides salary restructuring, SIA management wanted caps on re-dundancy benefits, a revamp of the airline's medical benefits, a review of the annual salary increments, as well as a new profit-sharing agreement.[63]

However, SM Lee felt that SIA's cost-cutting efforts should not focus only on wages.[64] There was the need to examine other means of cost-cutting such as outsourc-ing some operations to low-cost countries like India, as well as improving operational efficiencies through exercises such as the reorganization of the roster systems of pilots and cabin crew.

In April 2004, just months into his role as the new man at the helm, CEO Chew had a tough balancing act to play. He had to fight the turbulent forces in SIA's com-petitive environment as well as manage the demands of the internal organization—the people, organizational structures, systems, and processes that had made SIA the best airline for many years.

A few months earlier, Singapore's Transport Minister Yeo Cheow Tong had called on "the SIA management to focus on the business challenges ahead and for the entire company to work harmoniously. . . rather than wasting time fighting among them-selves."[65]

Endnotes

[1]"SIA Must Cut Costs by Up to $1.6 b: CEO," *Straits Times (Singapore)*, April 8, 2004.
[2]SIA annual report, 1998/99, p. 25.
[3]"Flying High, Going Global, Doing Good," *Straits Times (Singapore)*, October 7, 2000.
[4]J. Wirtz and R. Johnston, "Singapore Airlines: What It Takes to Sustain Service Excellence—A Senior Man-agement Perspective," *Managing Service Quality* 13, no. 1 (2003), pp. 10–19.
[5]Ibid.
[6]Ibid.
[7]Singapore Airlines, *Outlook*, August 2001, p. 9.
[8]Wirtz and Johnston, "Singapore Airlines."
[9]Singapore Airlines, *Outlook*, p. 9.
[10]Ibid, p. 1.
[11]Wirtz and Johnston, "Singapore Airlines."
[12]Ibid.
[13]"Labour Chief: How to Get It Right," *Straits Times (Singapore)*, February 25, 2004.
[14]SIA annual report, 1997/98, p. 72.
[15]SIA annual report, 2000/01, p. 6.
[16]"Analysts Still Calling SIA a Buy Despite War Fears," *Business Times (Singapore)*, February 21, 2003.
[17]"Fine Dining on the Fly," *Business Times (Singapore)*, October 11, 2003.
[18]SIA annual report, 1998/99, p. 28.
[19]SIA annual report, 2001/02, p. 14.
[20]Singapore Airlines, *Media*, June 27, 2003.
[21]Wirtz and Johnston, "Singapore Airlines."
[22]"Sad Truth about Singapore Firms," *Business Times (Singapore)*, December 20, 2003.
[23]Ibid.
[24]"Over Half of SIA Staff to Be Offered Options," *Business Times (Singapore)*, February 12, 2000.
[25]Ibid.
[26]"SIA to Offer All Employees Share Options," *Straits Times (Singapore)*, February 12, 2000.
[27]"SIA Seeks to Remove Cap on Share Options," *Straits Times (Singapore)*, June 27, 2003.
[28]Wirtz and Johnston, "Singapore Airlines."
[29]"A S$4,200 Singapore Girl," *Straits Times (Singapore)*, July 13, 1997.
[30]In 1980, SIA pilots' union was de-listed after SM Lee, then prime minister, intervened to resolve disputes be-tween Alpha-S' predecessor and SIA management.
[31]"SIA Silent on How It Will Try to Improve," *Straits Times (Singapore)*, December 2, 2003.
[32]"SIA, Pilots to Take Dispute to Court," *Business Times (Singapore)*, February 23, 2001.
[33]"Govt May Intervene in Pilots' Dispute," *Straits Times (Singapore)*, August 15, 2002.
[34]"SIA Tried to Reach Out to Pilots," *Straits Times (Singapore)*, August 16, 2002.
[35]"SIA and Pilots in Talks over Seat Dispute," *Straits Times (Singapore)*, August 18, 2002.
[36]"Overseas-Based Pilots Are a 'Thorn in the Flesh,'" *Straits Times (Singapore)*, February 28, 2004.
[37]"Pilots to SM: We Will Cooperate," *Straits Times (Singapore)*, February 24, 2004.
[38]"Singapore Airlines to Lay Off 414 Workers to Trim Cost," Kyoda News Service, June 19, 2003.
[39]"SIA to Retire Airbus Fleet Five Months Early," *Straits Times (Singapore)*, April 23, 2003.
[40]"Singapore Airlines to Lay Off 414 Workers to Trim Cost."
[41]"Singapore Airlines Retrenches 26 Pilots and 156 Cabin Crew," Agence France Press, July 21, 2003.

[42]"Early Retirement for 165 SIA Staff," *Business Times (Singapore),* July 3, 2003.

[43]"SIA Can't Carry On Like Before: SM," *Straits Times (Singapore),* January 6, 2004.

[44]"SIA Hires Agency to Help Improve Operations," *Straits Times (Singapore),* August 20, 2003.

[45]"Singapore Airlines Retrenches 26 Pilots and 156 Cabin Crew."

[46]"SIA Strikes 5 Percent–11 Percent Pay Cut Deal," *Straits Times (Singapore),* July 4, 2003.

[47]"SIA Profit Sparks Union Hopes of Restored Pay," *Straits Times (Singapore),* October 31, 2003.

[48]Ibid.

[49]"SIA Starts Recruiting Pilots, Crew Again," *Straits Times (Singapore),* November 6, 2003.

[50]"SIA Can't Carry On Like Before: SM."

[51]"On SIA Management: Start Afresh and Earn Staff's Trust," *Straits Times (Singapore),* January 6, 2004.

[52]"Mok Clinches Presidency of SIA Pilots' Union by Wide Margin," *Business Times (Singapore),* December 20, 2003.

[53]"SIA Unions: What Went Wrong," *Straits Times (Singapore),* February 25, 2004.

[54]"Turbulent Times with Pilots' Union," *Straits Times (Singapore),* December 24, 2003.

[55]Ibid.

[56]"Budget Airlines: Asia Takes to Cheaper Skies," *Far East Economic Review,* February 26, 2004.

[57]"Qantas Joins S'pore Fray," *Streats (Singapore),* April 7, 2004.

[58]"SIA Headed for Major Revamp, Outsourcing of Some Services," *Business Times (Singapore),* April 6, 2004.

[59]"SM Lee to SIA Staff: Prepare for Wrenching Changes to Protect Jobs," *Business Times (Singapore),* April 6, 2004.

[60]"Will Workers Get the Message?" *Straits Times (Singapore),* April 7, 2004.

[61]"The Remaking of Changi Airport," *Business Times (Singapore),* April 7, 2004.

[62]"SIA Seeks to Peg 50 Percent of Top Exec Pay to Company Performance," *Business Times (Singapore),* December 20, 2003.

[63]"Ties with Other Unions on the Mend," *Straits Times (Singapore),* February 28, 2004.

[64]"SIA Can't Carry On Like Before: SM."

[65]"Turbulent Times with Pilots' Union."

Best Buy
Staying at the Top

Balaji Chakravarthy
International Institute for Management Development

Henri Bourgeois
International Institute for Management Development

> *Best Buy's competitive advantage is fading vis-à-vis Wal-Mart, Dell and others. We have to shift our focus from products to customers and redefine our value proposition.*
> —Brad Anderson, CEO of Best Buy

It was a pleasant day in March. Spring was in the air. As the sun set on Best Buy's brand new corporate campus, Brad Anderson, the company's CEO, was particularly pleased by the events of the day. Best Buy, America's largest consumer electronics retail chain, had stunned the financial community by reporting a 51% surge in fiscal fourth-quarter profit, well above what the analysts had estimated. Results for the entire fiscal year 2004 were also spectacular. Wall Street was quick to acknowledge the good news, lifting the company's stock by 7% at the closing bell.

While the stock was heading in the right direction, it had some catching up to do. Anderson recalled the 22% slump in Best Buy's stock price in November 2003. He had made customer centricity a key strategic pillar, soon after taking over as the company's CEO in July 2002. The new customer-centric strategy was launched in May 2003 and was being tested in 32 of the company's stores, but so far no concrete results on their performance had been reported to investors. They were concerned.

Anderson knew he was walking a tightrope. On the one hand, he had to reassure the investment community that the experiment was a success. On the other hand, his team needed time to analyze the data from the test stores (called lab stores) and prepare the organization for what he saw as a revolutionary change. Best Buy not only would be pursuing a daring new strategy, but also would be changing its structure and processes radically. When would he know enough to call this initiative a success? How fast should he roll it out to the remaining stores? These were some of the questions that Anderson pondered as he gathered his papers to leave for the day.

Research Associate Henri Bourgeois prepared this case under the supervision of Professor Balaji Chakravarthy as a basis for class discussion rather than to illustrate either effective or ineffective handling of a business situation.

This case is a sequel to the Harvard Business School and University of Minnesota's case study (No 9-598-016), authored by Professors Balaji Chakravarthy, V. Kasturi Rangan, and Research Associate Susan McEvily.

IMD Research Associates Els Van Weering and Deepak Khandpur also helped with the research for this sequel.

Professor Kamran Kashani's comments on an earlier draft of the case are gratefully acknowledged.

A Leader in Its Industry

Based in Richfield, Minnesota, Best Buy was the largest consumer electronics (CE) retailer in North America. Sales were $24.5 billion for the fiscal year ending February 28, 2004, and the earnings per share was a record $2.15, or $2.44 from continuing operations, the company's best result in five years (refer to Exhibit 1 for a financial summary). The company had grown its U.S. sales at a 17% compound annual growth rate (CAGR) since 1996, far outpacing the industry, which grew only at a 4.9% over the same period. Despite a recent drop, the company's share price had more than doubled in 2003. In its January 12, 2004, issue, *Forbes* magazine declared Best Buy as the Company of the Year.[1]

In addition to the consumer electronics category that made up 37% of its sales, Best Buy's product mix also included home office (34%), entertainment software (23%), and appliances (6%). Best Buy outpaced other consumer electronics retailers in all these categories. Moreover, with market share gains coming mainly from high-margin products (digital TV and recording, wireless handsets, mobile video, and others), the company's margins were also improving.

The company operated 608 consumer Best Buy stores across the United States and 19 more in Canada. It also operated an additional 22 stores under the name Magnolia Audio Video on the West Coast of the United States and 108 stores in Canada under the name Future Shop. The traditional U.S. stores had an average footprint of 43,800 square feet and generated annual sales of around $31 million each. The Canadian stores (and some of the newer U.S. units) were smaller, with a footprint in the range of 20,000 to 25,000 square feet.[2] Together, these North American stores gave Best Buy the number one spot, with a 16% share of the $130 billion market for retailing electronics and packaged media. While the square footage growth would appear to be slowing down, this was because of the company's increased emphasis on smaller stores (refer to Figure 1). However, the revenues per store square foot were actually growing.

The company's traditional rival, Circuit City (the industry leader until 1996), was slipping in comparison (refer to Exhibit 2 for a head-to-head comparison). It was easy for Best Buy to get complacent. However, Circuit City had started to imitate many elements of Best Buy's successful strategy, notably improving the lighting in their stores, deploying a non-commissioned sales force, and displaying available merchandise in the store itself and getting rid of back room storage. Besides the ever-present threat of imitation, Best Buy's top management was also worried that profitable opportunities for the company may be limited to 1,000 stores in the United States. The company already had 606 stores and was opening an additional 75 each year. Growth through new store openings did not look promising. Studies had also shown that the EVA (Economic Value Added) by a store peaked at about six to eight years from its opening. A changing mix toward older stores was also projected to hurt Best Buy's future profitability.

Anderson reasoned that the real threat to the company would come not from other specialty retailers, but from mass-market retailers like Wal-Mart and electronic retailers like Dell, Amazon.com, and eBay. The digital revolution had blurred the distinctions between consumer electronics and computers; data, voice, and moving images. Mike Keskey, President of Best Buy Retail (U.S. Stores), offered this sobering reminder:

The retail graveyard is filled with retailers who used to dominate a particular niche. They thought they had made it good and stopped investing in innovation.

Exhibit 1   BEST BUY'S FINANCIAL PERFORMANCE, 1998–2000 ($ in millions except per share data)

Annual Income Statement (fiscal year ending March)	1998	1999	2000	2001	2002	2003	2004
Statement of earnings data							
Revenues	$8,358	$10,078	$12,494	$15,327	$18,506	$20,946	$24,547
Cost of goods sold	7,026	8,250	10,100	12,267	13,895	15,710	18,350
Selling, general, and admin expenses	1,145	1,463	1,854	2,454	3,704	4,225	4,893
Operating income	187	364	593	604	903	1,010	1,304
Net income	95	224	346	396	564	99*	705
EPS	$0.31	$0.72	$1.09	$1.24	$1.75	$0.30	$2.18
Year-to-year change							
Sales	7.5%	21%	24%	23%	21%	13%	17%
Net income	1,466%	138%	54%	14%	43%	(81)%	612%
EPS	1,600%	129%	51%	13%	40%	(82)%	626%
Comparable store sales	2%	13.5%	11.1%	4.9%	1.9%	2.4%	7.1%
Margin analysis							
Gross margin	15.7%	18.0%	19.2%	19.8%	21.3%	25.0%	25.2%
SG&A	13.7%	14.5%	14.8%	15.8%	16.2%	20.2%	19.9%
Net margin	1.2%	2.2%	2.7%	2.6%	3.0%	0.05%	2.8%
Year-end data							
Cash and cash equivalents	$ 785	$ 750	$ 757	$1,855	$1,861	$1,914	$2,600
Working capital	666	662	453	214	895	1,074	1,223
Total assets	2,070	2,532	2,995	4,840	7,367	7,694	8,652
Merchandise inventories	1,046	1,184	1,767	2,256	1,875	2,077	2,607
Long-term debt, including current portion	225	61	31	296	820	834	850
Shareholders' equity	536	1,034	1,096	1,822	2,521	2,730	3,422
Number of stores	284	311	357	432	576	679	757

*Includes a $441 million loss for discontinued operations.
Source: Company reports, Bank of America Securities.

C-557

Figure 1   Best Buy's U.S. Stores: Square Footage Growth and Mix by Store Size

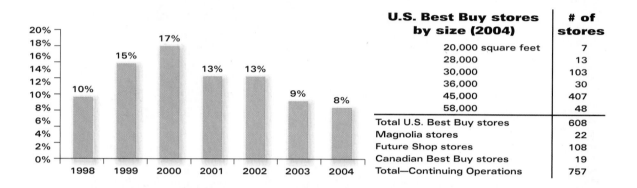

U.S. Best Buy stores by size (2004)	# of stores
20,000 square feet	7
28,000	13
30,000	103
36,000	30
45,000	407
58,000	48
Total U.S. Best Buy stores	608
Magnolia stores	22
Future Shop stores	108
Canadian Best Buy stores	19
Total—Continuing Operations	757

Exhibit 2   BEST BUY VERSUS CIRCUIT CITY, 2003 ($ in millions except for EPS)

	Best Buy		Circuit City	
	2003	Change from Prior Year	2003	Change from Prior Year
Number of stores	679	41%	626	0%
Average sales per store	$30.8	2.5	$15.9	4
Total sales	$20,946	13	$9,953	5
Gross margin	25.0%	19	23.6%	(4)
SG&A ratio	20.2%	24	22.9%	2.5
Operating margin	4.8%	(6)	0.7%	(68)
Net income	$621*	9	$41	(68)
EPS	$1.91*	8	$0.20	(68)
Cash and cash equivalents	$1,914	3	$884	(29)
Working capital	1,074	20	1,823	(1)
Merchandise inventories	2,077	10	1,409	14
Total assets	7,694	4	3,799	(16)
Long-term debt including current portion	834	2	13	(66)
Shareholders' equity	2,730	8	2,341	(14)

*Loss of $441 million from discontinued operations not included.
Source: CIBC World Markets Corp. estimates and company data.

Then came another retailer with the next best thing. At Best Buy, we are at the top of our game. History tells us that this success will be short-lived. We have to be paranoid and reinvent ourselves before we are made obsolete by competition.

Best Buy had successfully transformed itself five times over the past four decades (refer to Exhibit 3 for a summary), and Anderson felt that it was time to renew the company once again if it were to remain at the top.

Exhibit 3 OVERVIEW OF BEST BUY STORE CONCEPTS, 1983–2003

Concept	Description	Target audience	Characteristics
Sound of Music 1966–1983 **Concept I: 1983–1988** Driver: Commoditization of the audio market	Audio store, 5,000 sq. ft. Superstore, 25,000 sq. ft.	Males 18–25 Educated middle-class male and female	■ Customized service for audio equipment ■ More floor space ■ Large selection including video appliances ■ Promotional prices ■ Commissioned sales staff ■ Fun place to shop
Concept II: 1989–1994 Driver: Increased competition and drop in profitability, need for growth and purchasing power	Warehouse, 28,000 sq. ft.	Well-educated and knowledgeable shoppers	■ No-pressure, non-commissioned sales force ■ Everyday low price ■ Answer centers ■ More selling space, no backroom ■ Expanded assortment: PCs & Entertainment software
Concept III: 1995–1998 Driver: Need to increase margins	Hybrid: Boutiques in the warehouse; 45,000–58,000 sq. ft.	One-stop shop for the family	■ Upgraded and enlarged product mix to include more "high touch" products that needed the advice of salespeople. ■ Interactive selling (information kiosks and touch screen answer centers) ■ Persisted with non-commissioned sales force but began emphasizing extended warranties more (Called Performance Service Plans or PSPs, these were still designed to offer more value for money than competing extended warranties) ■ Streamlined the inventory management process and in-store logistics to serve both "high touch" and commodity products
Concept IV: 1999–2000 Driver: The digital revolution, need to educate the consumer	■ Introduction of "high touch" areas. ■ Introduction of BestBuy.com	Differentiation to technology savvy customers (male, 15–39, above average income) in addition to the family	■ Changed the product mix to include more high margin products ■ Created digital imaging sections in the stores, with a focus on cross selling computer related and entertainment products as bundled solutions ■ Revised selling process with more team incentives, but still sticking to no commissions for the sales force
Concept V: 2001–2003 Driver: Increasingly complex transactions and expanded product offering	■ The modular store, 45,000–58,000 sq. ft. ■ Small market stores ■ Inner city stores	Technology savvy customers (15–39, above average income) and the family	■ Modularity in the store (rapid reconfiguration was now possible) ■ Provided consulting on complicated transactions ■ Bigger emphasis on service

Source: Company information.

A History of Continuous Renewal

In 1966, at the age of 25, Richard (Dick) Schulze, the company's founder, opened a small audio components store in St. Paul, Minnesota, called Sound of Music. Specializing in high-end audio equipment targeted at young males, the company grew steadily to 11 stores in Minneapolis/St. Paul by the early 1980s. But the company was up against fierce new competitive pressures. Then, in 1981 a tornado tore the roof off Sound of Music's largest and most profitable store located in Roseville, Minnesota. Lacking business interruption insurance, family members and employees retrieved stereos and TVs from surrounding parking lots and fields and ran a Sound of Music Tornado Sale. The event was a spectacular success. Schulze saw in it the outlines of a new strategy. He would later refer to this as Concept I—focusing more on inventory turns than unit margins and making discount shopping a fun experience. The first Best Buy Concept I superstore opened in 1983 in Burnsville, Minnesota.

Best Buy had grown to 100 stores by 1988. That year, a regional rival, Highland Superstores, initiated a price war. Even though Best Buy had joined a buyers' cooperative to improve its own power over vendors, it could not match the aggressive pricing policies of the much larger Highland. The company faced bankruptcy. Schulze and his team decided to survey Best Buy's customers on what appealed to them the most. The results were sobering. The average customer, especially women, disliked the shopping experience in a Best Buy Concept I store. She felt intimidated by the commissioned salespersons in the store and was often forced to buy higher ticket items under the pretext that the product originally asked for was not in stock. Stung by the findings of its survey, Best Buy introduced its Concept II stores in 1989—an everyday low-price consumer electronics warehouse.

The main features of a Concept II store were:

- An even larger store footprint: 28,000 square feet.

- 50% more selling space. All available merchandise was on display in the store. The backroom was eliminated.

- A self-service, discount-style format, everyday low price.

- No commissioned sales force: salespeople were on straight salary and were there in the store only to help/advise customers when approached.

- An expanded assortment that included PCs and entertainment software.

During the period 1989–94, sales exploded from $500,000 to nearly $5 billion. The number of stores grew to 151. Suppliers who had shunned Best Buy when it switched to Concept II were now eager to do business with it. The company had also successfully trimmed its SG&A expense ratio from 20.8% of sales in 1989 to 11.2% in 1995. The company had grown rapidly, but its margins had evaporated. Schulze felt it was time to reinvent the company yet again. Concept III (1995–98) and Concept IV (1998–2000) helped improve the company's profitability while sustaining its impressive growth trajectory.

Concept V, introduced in 2001, was aimed at keeping up with the rapid technological innovations in the consumer electronics and computer industries, while helping customers tie old and new products together. Some of its key features were:

- In-store consultants who handled complicated transactions and sold packages (product, services, warranty). For example, a customer who recently walked in to buy a digital camera ($999) and a camcorder ($499) bought additional complementary products worth $2,198, accessories worth $607, extended warranties worth $250, and in-home installation and service worth $350, making a total purchase of more than three times what the customer first came in to buy.[3]

■ Increased cross-selling by displaying complementary products and accessories together in the store rather than in their respective product departments.

■ Making the stores more modular. Store layouts could be reconfigured overnight, when necessary. This flexibility was deemed necessary both for adapting to the changing needs of the customer and for matching the latest retailing innovations offered by competitors.

The company continued to grow strongly and operated 679 stores in 2003. Gross margins climbed from 13.5% in 1997 to 25% in 2003. That year, the company's founder, Schulze, handed over the CEO's job to Anderson and stepped back to the less active role of chairman. Schulze had worked long and hard to take the company that he had founded to a leadership position in its industry. He now wanted to spend more time with his family. Schulze was only 62.

Anderson's Early Strategy Moves

Hired by Schulze as a stereo salesman in 1973, Anderson had worked closely with the founder on all of the major strategic moves that Best Buy had made in the past. Even though the company could claim five successful transformations, both Anderson and Schulze considered the transformation from Concept I to II to be the only revolutionary one among these. Anderson was indeed concerned by the looming market saturation for Best Buy's core store format, the 45,000-square-foot superstore. To maintain its growth momentum, Anderson started investigating other sources of revenues including acquisitions, new store formats, and development of the online business.

Best Buy spent $1.2 billion acquiring three electronics and music retailers with the dual objective of broadening its product offering and geographic footprint. The purchase of Magnolia Hi-Fi, a West Coast consumer electronics chain, gave Best Buy access to the high-end segment of the industry. In parallel, Best Buy expanded internationally by purchasing Future Shop, the leading Canadian electronics merchant with a 16% market share and the number one retail Web store in Canada. Future Shop was positioned toward a more upscale market segment and shared less than 55% of its product assortment with Best Buy. The company also acquired Musicland, which operated as Sam Goody, Media Play, and Suncoast stores. Best Buy had purchased this 1,300-store chain in January 2001 to reach new customer segments—teenagers and women, who tended to shop at malls. But the post–September 11 (2001) drop in mall traffic and the steep decline in CD sales due to music piracy hurt this initiative. Anderson finally got rid of the money-losing chain in June 2003. The various write-offs cost the company $441 million.

In addition to opening its first stores in urban areas like New York City, the company began testing its smaller 20,000-square-foot stores in select markets. These smaller stores constituted half of Best Buy's new stores openings in fiscal year 2004. Investors worried that the lower sales and anticipated higher operating costs would reduce the profitability of these stores. However, Best Buy hoped to generate a healthy return given the lower capital investment and higher sales per square foot in these stores.

BestBuy.com™, Best Buy's foray into electronic retailing, showed promise. It was ranked second among click-and-mortar retailers during the 2002 holiday season.[4] The

Figure 2   Consumer Electronics Market by Channel, 2000–2002[5]

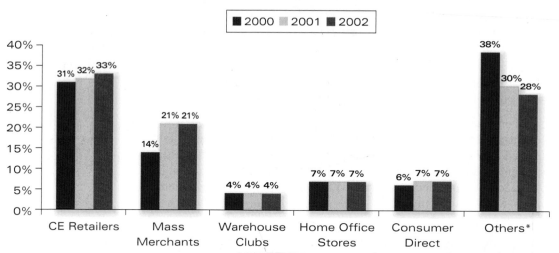

*Data include 15% of sales that are not easily classified by channel.

company planned to further improve its Web site by offering a broader assortment than that available in a typical Best Buy store, and providing new innovative financing options and a more powerful search engine. The success of BestBuy.com was relatively modest, however, when compared to Internet giants like Amazon, Yahoo, and eBay. In fact, the exponential growth of online retail was one of the major industry trends that worried Anderson.

Stiffer and Broader Competition

Electronics-only retailers, such as Best Buy and Circuit City, enjoyed only a third of the consumer electronics market in 2003 (refer to Figure 2).

Mass discounters led by Wal-Mart and Target had increased their share from 14% in 2000 to 21% in 2002, driven by two forces: their faster square-footage growth and the accelerating commoditization of new consumer electronics products such as DVD players and analog TVs. Wal-Mart's Everyday Low Price strategy enabled the retail giant to grab an increasing share of the commodity end of the electronics market. As Anderson put it, "If we do nothing, Wal-Mart will surpass us due to the simple fact that they add more stores each year than we do." Traditional national retailers like Sears, Staples, CompUSA, and Office Depot were also looking to grow their consumer electronics sales (refer to Exhibit 4).

Consumer direct or Internet competitors were also getting stronger in most consumer electronics categories. Dell was already ranked the no. 4 retailer of consumer electronics in dollar terms. With its direct model (make to order, just in time manufacturing, online sales), Dell was bypassing distribution retailers and offering customers the opportunity to order a computer tailored to their needs at a very competitive price. Dell's key strengths were its leading share of the PC market (18%), superb execution (total operating expenses stable at 9.6% of total revenue), and strong growth in the non-PC segment and international sales. Total revenues had increased 14% to $35 billion in 2002, and Dell enjoyed a 5.2% share of the consumer electronics market. In

Exhibit 4   STATISTICS FOR U.S. CONSUMER ELECTRONICS RETAILERS IN 2001–2002

Store	Estimated U.S. Consumer Electronics Sales ($ million)			Estimated Market Share			Sales/ Square Foot ($)
	2001	2002	% Change	2001	2002	Change	2002
1 Best Buy	$14,629	$16,730	14.4%	15.3%	16.5%	1.18%	$753
2 Wal-Mart	12,522	14,141	12.9	13.1	13.9	0.83	563
3 Circuit City	9,520	9,960	4.6	10.0	9.8	−0.15	485
4 Dell	4,485	5,300	18.2	4.7	5.2	0.53	n.a.
5 Target	4,236	4,799	13.3	4.4	4.7	0.30	269
6 Radio Shack	4,775	4,577	−4.1	5.0	4.5	−0.49	382
7 CompUSA	3,953	4,155	−5.1	4.1	4.1	−0.04	692
8 Staples	3,632	3,863	6.4	3.8	3.8	0.01	178
9 Sears	3,250	2,750	−15.4	3.4	2.7	−0.69	181
10 Office Depot	2,688	2,670	−0.7	2.8	2.6	−0.18	103
11 Sam's Club	2,351	2,536	7.9	2.5	2.5	0.04	—
12 Kmart	2,603	2,215	−14.9	2.7	2.2	−0.54	—
13 Gateway	3,033	2,125	−29.9	3.2	2.1	−1.08	—
14 Costco	1,374	1,584	15.3	1.4	1.6	0.12	—
15 OfficeMax	1,530	1,580	3.3	1.6	1.6	−0.04	—
16 Fry's	1,465	1,543	5.3	1.5	1.5	−0.01	—
17 Game Stop	1,121	1,353	20.7	1.2	1.3	0.16	—
18 Toys "R" Us	1,216	1,204	−1.0	1.3	1.2	−0.09	—

Source: Morgan Stanley, TWICE Market Research. Sales only include CE-related products, including computers.

2003 Dell announced it would further expand in the consumer electronics market by launching a line of printers (through a partnership with Lexmark) and a Digital Juke-box music player (Dell DJ). Dell started competing directly with Best Buy in the most promising digital market, LCD-based TV, offering three models of LCD TVs (17, 23, and 30 inches). This segment was expected to grow from $260 million to $809 million by 2007.[6]

Auction sites, led by eBay, increased consumer access to used consumer electronics products and to competitive bidding by suppliers for new products. This was another emerging competitive threat to Best Buy.[7] Finally, the recent boom of music digital downloading was another potential threat to an already ailing category at Best Buy, entertainment software. While this category was not as profitable as others, it was a prominent traffic driver for other categories (more than half of customer transactions included an entertainment-related purchase). This could change, however, with the development of online music purchase offered by Apple (iTunes), Musicmatch, Napster, Sony, and even Wal-Mart!

Exhibit 5 presents a quick comparison of the different business models that Best Buy had to compete against.

Taken together, these competitive trends made Best Buy's future very uncertain. Anderson believed it was time for change. The need was for a revolutionary Concept VII. Concept VI was intentionally skipped to send a signal to the organization.

Exhibit 5   A FINANCIAL SNAPSHOT OF BEST BUY AND FOUR COMPETITORS, 2003
($ million)

	Best Buy	Wal-Mart	eBay	Dell	Amazon.com
Revenues	20,946	256,329	2,165	35,404	5,263
Gross margin	25%	22%	81%	18%	17%
SG&A	20%	18%	52%	9%	18%
Net margin	0.05%	6%	21%	6%	1%
Cash	1,914	5,200	1,381	4,317	1,102
Working capital	1,074	−2,997	1,499	−263	568
Inventory	2,077	26,612	—	327	293
Inventory turn	10×	9.7×	—	108×	17×
ROIC	15.7%	14.8%	9%	31%	NA
Debt ratio	11%	16%	2%	3%	90%

Phil Schoonover, executive VP, recalled an incident that took place soon after Anderson became CEO that may have had some influence in shaping Concept VII:

> I invited Brad (Anderson) to visit one of our Musicland stores with me. It was in the afternoon. The Mall Rats, our pseudonym for an important segment—young males—were in our store. They enjoy very specific kinds of music: heavy metal, rap, etc; and we were playing Garth Brooks! We then walked into a competing store called Hot Topic. It was just right for the Mall Rat, down to the body jewelry of the store employees. It was obvious that we had to move away from the standard big box retailing, where we merely pushed products that the vendor preferred, to a more tailored approach where we offered products that our customers needed and sold them in a way that they would appreciate.

Anderson was convinced that Best Buy could not stay at the top by merely pushing products on to customers. He elaborated:

> In the 80s and 90s, we relied mostly on new products to foster growth. This strategy is fading. Also, Best Buy's historical competitive advantage has been in its operational efficiency. But that was when we were competing with other consumer electronics retailers. Today our competitors are Wal-Mart and Dell. We cannot play the old game and win against these efficiency experts. However, we control "the last 10 feet" to the customer better than our competitors. This has to be our competitive advantage going forward. Our main challenge now is to come up with a unique value generating proposition that will connect us back with our customers and serve as a solid foundation for the company's future growth.

Concept VII: Customer Centricity

Concept VII consisted of four interconnected strategic initiatives: "customer centricity," "efficient enterprise," "win the home with service," and "win entertainment." However, customer centricity was the real centerpiece. The other three initiatives were designed to support it.

Exhibit 6 BEST BUY'S FIVE TARGET CUSTOMER SEGMENTS

The Affluent Professional—Barry

- Wants the best technology and entertainment
- Demands excellent service
- Potential market size $12.5 billion
- Best Buy's market share: 11%

The Focused, Active, Younger Male Customer—Buzz

- Wants the latest technology and entertainment
- Potential market size $16.5 billion
- Best Buy's market share: 10%

The Small Business Customer—BBfB

- Use Best Buy's product solutions and services to enhance the profitability of his or her business
- Potential market size $58.7 billion
- Best Buy's market share: 4.5%

The Family Man—Ray

- Wants technology that improves life
- Practical adopter of technology
- Potential market size $21 billion
- Best Buy's market share: 15%

The Suburban Soccer Mom—Jill

- Wants to enrich her children's life with technology and entertainment
- Potential market size $9.2 billion
- Best Buy's market share: 13%

Source: Company information.

The Basic Approach

The approach[8] that Anderson chose required Best Buy to quantify the profitability of each of its customers. Best Buy's marketing team then tried to understand why some customers were profitable and others not, and using the insights from this analysis came up with five potentially profitable segments for the company (refer to Exhibit 6). The new segments were defined more in terms of consumer needs and behavior and not demographic characteristics as in the past, such as males 19–35 years of age. Under the new approach, a 19–35-year-old male could belong to four of the five new segments. He could be a family man, an active youngster, an affluent professional, or a small business owner. Each segment was further divided into three subsegments based on similarity of customer needs. For example, the family man could have a stay-at-home spouse, or a working spouse, or be an empty nester.

The next challenge was to find ways to reengineer the customer experience and address the specific needs within each segment and its subsegments. New value propositions were put forward to enhance customer satisfaction (and thus profitability). Best Buy estimated that such a customer-centric approach would translate to a higher share of existing customers' wallets, up from 23% of their home expenditures to a target of 30% to 35%. Each value proposition had a well-thought-out store strategy as well. This meant tailoring product assortments, reviewing the 25,000 SKUs to determine whether they were appropriate to a particular store, and adjusting the merchandise according to the income level and buying habits of local shoppers. A store-operating model was then defined to help implement the selected strategy. The three broad steps in Best Buy's approach are summarized below:

1. Customer Segmentation
   - Profitability as an important criterion.
   - Demographics/behaviors as other criteria.
   - Create value propositions to enhance customer satisfaction in each of the chosen segments/subsegments.

2. Store Strategy
   - Who lives near each store?
   - Who shops at Best Buy?
   - Who are the local competitors?
   - What is the appropriate store strategy? Which segments should it emphasize?

3. Store Operating Model
   - Define the operating model to deliver the chosen store strategy.
   - Create an owner/operator mentality—reward entrepreneurial efforts that are linked to customer centricity.
   - Build skills/competency to deliver against the new strategy.

Implementing Customer Centricity

The new concept was first tested in 32 laboratory (lab) stores. Best Buy's marketing team came up with a precise value proposition for each segment and translated that into preferred store layout, product assortment, and tailored services (financing, geek squad, reward zone, etc.). Each value proposition was then tested in select lab stores whose demographics best fit one or more of the five chosen customer segments. In addition, each lab also had to determine the extent to which each value proposition

Figure 3   Segment Representation in Customer Centricity Rollout

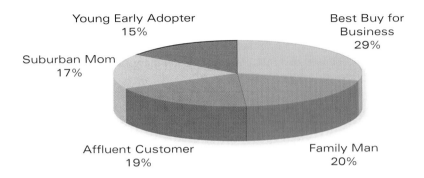

Young Early Adopter
15%

Best Buy for
Business
29%

Suburban Mom
17%

Affluent Customer
19%

Family Man
20%

appealed to or detracted from other customer segments, and whether or not the value proposition was consistent with Best Buy's overall brand strategy.

Keskey, who temporarily stepped down from his position as the president of Best Buy Retail stores, was the manager of this project. A small team of people were hand-picked and trained for these lab stores. From an original count of 16, the team rapidly grew to 6,600 people—200 in each of 32 lab stores spread across three key markets and 400 people in the corporate office. The chosen markets were all far enough from New York City to be protected from Wall Street's curiosity.

The performance of the lab stores was monitored with classic metrics such as return on invested capital (ROIC), conversion rate, unit sales/customer, net operating profit after tax (NOPAT), and customer loyalty. These metrics were slated to become the new "bumpers" used to determine when to roll out customer centricity to the remaining stores. Best Buy planned to convert approximately 70 stores to the new format in 2004 and the rest over the coming years. An approximate mix of customer segments represented in the initial rollout is shown in Figure 3.

Analysts estimated that the rollout would cost Best Buy around $300,000 per store. The major cost components were the additional personnel required in each store and increased inventories. An additional $200,000 to $300,000 per store in capital expenditure would also be required, mostly related to store remodeling, a new customer support center and changes in signage. Offsetting these costs were the expected growth in both sales and margins. Early results from the lab stores showed an average of 12% increase in sales. In some stores the improvement was as high as 25%. For example, a California lab store found that it could serve real estate agents better by bundling products like notebooks, cameras, and software. It also learned that there were three subsegments of realtors: a newcomer to the business, the established realtor, and the manager of an office, each with a need for a different bundle of products and services. By serving these distinct needs, the store increased its sales to this segment by 400%.

The net impact of the customer centricity effort on the company's EPS (earnings per share) was seen as a wash early in the implementation process but projected to improve subsequently. Daren Jackson, executive VP Finance and the company's CFO, felt confident that the investors would see the long-term benefit of the new approach. He offered two arguments in support of this:

First, the highest point in the value chain for any business, especially retail, is the customer. How can anyone argue with a company focused on moving higher up the value chain?

Second, the street does not like hiccups in operating performance while a company is engaged in the promised strategic change. Best Buy has credibility in this regard, based on its past record of renewing itself from Concepts I–V. We have shown that we are implementing the current change thoughtfully, through our lab stores. We are focused on growing revenues and margins in these stores and we will share our results with investors.

Supporting Strategies

The customer centricity drive was supported by three complementary initiatives. "The efficient enterprise" initiative focused on controlling costs and investment spending. This included reducing administrative expenses, streamlining decision making, eradicating bureaucracy, and empowering employees to flatten the organization. The savings were to be used to fund customer centricity projects. Corporate headcount was already down by 8% in fiscal 2003. Best Buy also began using online auctions to lower its supply costs and had opened an office in China to source commodity products directly.

"Win the home with service" referred to Best Buy's plans to offer content, connections, applications, accessories, and services in addition to its core products. For example, customers who bought home theater equipment would be offered the opportunity, for a fee, to have specialists help them design the home system and supervise the installation. Such a bundling was expected to raise the average ticket by $230 and pump up gross margins, especially on digital equipment, from 30% to 35% to 40%.[9] Best Buy was also seeking to broaden its computer repair offer. The Geek Squad, a service company acquired in early 2003, would be Best Buy's new service arm. It offered complete PC services everywhere, 24 hours a day.

"Win entertainment" meant beating competition in the entertainment category that included music, movies, video game hardware and software, and other related products. Anderson regarded this category as a key traffic driver for Best Buy stores. However, the development and delivery of these products had undergone significant changes, as exemplified by the steep decline of prerecorded music sales. To counter this trend and establish Best Buy as a market maker for entertainment services, Best Buy sought to partner with vendors in developing new entertainment related services. Examples included access to digitally downloaded entertainment (partnerships with Rhapsody and Napster), exclusive concert clubs for members, and other exclusive promotions and pre-orders on BestBuy.com™.[10]

A Radical Change

Customer centricity was, however, not just a strategic change. It had a profound impact on the company's structure, internal processes, and employees.

Impact on the Organization

Senior executives in Anderson's top management clearly saw the rationale for the new approach. Ron Boire was Best Buy's executive VP and general merchandising manager.

He had previously been president of Sony Electronics Consumer Sales Inc. He was a supporter and had the following perspective on the proposed change:

> If you really understand the customer and operate against that, it scales you into the $6 trillion marketplace, not the $130 billion marketplace that we are in today. Consumer electronics is self-limiting; Wal-Mart has not allowed itself to get bogged down like that. They have taken their core competency, which is in logistics and information management and applied it against a wide range of new opportunities. They grow by a Best Buy every year. I think customer centricity can do the same for our growth.

Bob Willett, executive VP of Operations, another newcomer and a supporter, offered an interesting imagery in describing the new organization:

> Our sales people have become modern-day butlers. They will have to anticipate the needs of their customers and be ready to serve them whenever a demand is made.

But there were major organizational issues to deal with. In the lab stores, where customer centricity was being tested, there was a noticeable shift of power from the corporate office to the retail stores. For example, product assortment in the stores was historically modified five times a year. The merchant and the general merchandise teams would meet, decide what they wanted, and communicate their decisions to the field for implementation. Local stores did not have a say in the process. Now they did, and on a much more regular basis.

Newcomers to Best Buy's executive team had mixed reactions to this change. Some had been brought in specifically to strengthen corporate functions. For example, under the customer-centric approach, lab stores were given control over their advertising budget. A direct consequence of the lab stores' autonomy was a sudden inflow of new ideas, not all of them brilliantly thought through. Mike Linton, the chief marketing officer, confessed that his team, which had been trying to strengthen the marketing discipline within the company, took a while to adapt to the new reality:

> The lab stores were coming up with a lot of new initiatives, some in clear violation of the positioning of our brand in their marketing communications materials. We had to come down hard in those instances, but we also had to allow challenges to our marketing guidelines. It is a thin line that we have learned to walk.

The resistance was higher among old-timers. Keskey acknowledged candidly:

> Without Brad, we wouldn't be doing it because it is so hard. In order to make the customer the king or queen, whoever is closest to the customer has to be the new royalty. Just think of the implications, changes in the locus of power within the organization, people and systems implications, customer implications, and above all investor implications. I'll be very honest. Initially I was fighting it. But I'm glad that Brad persisted. It took me probably four months to see the merits of the customer centric approach. Today, I am one of its champions.

Brian Dunn, EVP of Best Buy Retail (U.S. Stores), concurred:

> We were on a burning platform, but most of us could not feel the heat. That is why Brad had to lead the change. It has been a forced march; the senior team has gone through fear and anxiety. Now we understand why we had to change.

Imagine fighting like hell in the bar room just to stay alive and then scrambling at the last minute to catch the stagecoach that is leaving. It is only when you get on that you realize that the win in the bar room had merely let you into a bigger arena where giants like Wal-Mart and Dell were waiting to bruise you.

There is no silver bullet here; no magic flute. The customer segments that we target will change; new segments will emerge. Customers will vote again on who is best prepared to serve them. Companies that stop reinventing themselves will be left behind. And by the way, I don't think it takes twenty years or ten years to get left behind anymore. I think it's just a couple of years.

With only 32 lab stores, there were already stresses in the organization. As Tina Decker, senior VP human capital strategy, described:

This is a nice, midwestern company. . . so we are nice, really nice. And it is pretty consensus-driven around here. So people go to have their conversations where they think they can have an influence. But if you offer a counter-opinion to what is going on then you can be seen as a resister, then that has pretty significant ramifications for your career. . . at least that is the perception. So I think people have been a bit more measured of late.

But Dunn felt that these tensions were easing:

With the magnitude of change that we are faced with, it is natural for some to question: Is this the place I want to be? Am I appreciated here? There are stresses on the operating model, relationships—and where there are hidden fractures, they soon grow and become huge and visible. The way we deal with this is to say if there's an elephant in the room; let's get it on the table and talk about it. . . We've got much better at that. The conversations are more candid and constructive.

Managing these tensions skillfully was another of Anderson's challenges. He noted:

When you are as successful as we have been recently, there is a tendency for the organization to be bogged down in the status quo. The CEO has the responsibility to shake the organization out of its complacency. I am dispassionate, like to study things and get a broader view before I am ready to announce a change. But once I am convinced, I have learned an important skill from our founder, Schulze. I will go through the wall, if necessary. That is what I am doing now.

He knew he had to shift the power pendulum away from corporate executives more toward mid-level managers in the field and in the stores. Anderson began giving these managers more of a voice in key corporate decisions. He was gratified to see that this broader consultative process seemed to have worked. Some of the initial resistance to the change agenda in his senior executive team had eased. Allowing them to voice their concerns openly seemed to have helped. There was broad-based support now for customer centricity.

Impact on Business Processes

Another challenge was to balance two competing financial objectives: the economic opportunity that customer centricity represented and the scale efficiency and standardization that product centricity offered. The primary value proposition of Best Buy had always been its ability to procure, ship, and sell volume merchandise at competitive prices. As Anderson noted:

Under the new strategy we still have to buy millions of computers, but for much more differentiated purposes.

Best Buy had to build complete transparency in its value chain and get good at "anticipatory demand forecasting." In the lab stores, inventories per square foot had already risen by 10% to improve stocks in high-demand categories. Vendor inventories also could rise. Some components had a very long lead-time. Boire's global merchandise team was ready to buy these directly from suppliers and deliver them to the vendors. But his team needed to strengthen its skills in hedging against price fluctuations on these core components. It also would have to consider supplying a store brand, if it could not get the total cooperation of vendors. Collecting slotting fees from vendors when their sales were not guaranteed was a tricky matter to tackle. To succeed in this new game, Best Buy had to educate its suppliers too. Boire summarized the likely impact of customer centricity on Best Buy's supply chain:

> Our suppliers have to create transparent systems that we can plug into. They will have to trust us in ways they never have before and we will provide them transactional data, virtual real time!

Building these new processes would be an ongoing effort. Suppliers like Microsoft seemed to be already on board. Others were beginning to see the win–win opportunities in the customer centricity idea.

Employee Engagement

Anderson also believed that there was a strong correlation between employee engagement and customer centricity. Recent employee satisfaction surveys seemed to support this belief. If the company average was a 3.33 on a 5-point scale, employee satisfaction had climbed to 4.06 in the lab stores. In a customer-centric store the employees had to feel empowered in order to drive decisions. Anderson commented:

> 60% of our expenses are on employees. If they are engaged they will be more productive, and that helps our profitability too. I am a strong believer in the strength-based system. We have to invite each of our store employees to recognize their strengths and find the space to contribute. Unleashing the power of our people is key to our success.

He went on to emphasize that the core values of Best Buy were all people centric:

- Have fun while being the best.
- Learn from challenge and change.
- Treat others with respect, humility and integrity.
- Unleash the power of our people.

John Walden, EVP of human resources, elaborated on this new approach to employee engagement:

> Strength base is a philosophy that we have for selecting talent for a particular role. We try to ascertain what our employees are great at, as opposed to what they are not good at. Then we make sure that they have the opportunity to work on a task that they are great at, that they enjoy and get energy from. So one of the things that we have done, rather boldly, is to eliminate our competency model. The competency model focused on the desired skills that an employee

must have depending on his/her job category. In a strength-based model, it is more about performance. All we look for is results.

Decker continued:

So I would say to you, as a supervisor here is your scorecard; here are the results that you have to deliver. If you are good at leading others and taking initiatives but weak in planning surround yourself with team members who are good at planning. We have realigned our performance management system, our rewards system, and our conversations around development, in a way to support the strength-based philosophy. Salary bands were broadened so that people could stay in a job they liked and still envision a motivating career.

Succeeding at the New Game

Best Buy had built one of the best operating models in the retail industry. Anderson did not wish to sacrifice everything at the altar of customer centricity. He observed:

The key tension will be to balance the importance of a customer segment with our global financial objectives. It will be a very sophisticated game, one that has not been tried before. I have always believed the social system is the most significant competitive advantage that a company can have. Social system and culture are crucial for delivering a new strategy. Our bet is that our social system will trump that of our competitors.

Anderson wondered how he could strengthen Best Buy's ability to play this new game.

Endnotes

[1]Tatge, Mark, "Company of the Year," *Forbes* magazine, December 1, 2003.
[2]Best Buy Company, Inc., SunTrust Robinson Humphrey, January 16, 2004.
[3]Copeland, M. V., "Best Buy's Selling Machine," *Business 2.0,* July 2004, p. 100.
[4]According to Comscore Media Metrix, Best Buy annual report, fiscal 2003.
[5]"Wal-Mart," Morgan Stanley analyst report, February 12, 2004.
[6]Stamford Resources estimates.
[7]Rowen M., eBay, Inc., Prudential Equity Group, LLC, May 7, 2004.
[8]This was the one advocated by Larry Seldon, a consultant. See Seldon, Larry, and Geoffrey Colvin, *Angel Customers & Demon Customers,* New York: Portfolio, 2003, for details of this approach.
[9]Tatge, Mark, "Company of the Year," *Forbes* magazine, December 1, 2004.
[10]Best Buy annual report, fiscal 2003.

Deloitte & Touche
Integrating Arthur Andersen

Ken Marks
The University of Western Ontario

Gerard Seijts
The University of Western Ontario

Introduction

It was a rainy September morning. Terry Noble, the Toronto Group Managing Partner for Deloitte & Touche (Deloitte), stretched his back and contemplated the results of the most recent "Pulse Survey" that were just presented to him.

Noble co-chaired the national integration team that was faced with a huge challenge: to develop a company-wide plan to create support materials to aid the Deloitte people in integrating more than 1,000 Arthur Andersen (Andersen) people into their 5,600-person-strong organization. Noble's team monitored the integration process through a monthly Pulse Survey, which would allow the team to benchmark unit to unit over time, and to take remedial action if, at specific stages, the integration goals were not attained.

The data that Noble just had seen did not come as a total surprise. In fact, he and the Deloitte senior management team were feeling a certain degree of backlash from a number of people in their own organization. Some Deloitte employees, it seemed, feared that Deloitte management, in its haste to consummate this new deal and welcome Andersen, was forgetting about its own employees. There was an attitude among some employees within Deloitte, the larger organization, that people coming from Andersen were "damaged goods" and that these people should be grateful that they had found a good home. Comments such as "Damn the torpedoes and let's get on with business" and "It's our way or the highway . . . after all, we acquired the Andersen business" began to surface. The cultural issues were showing up in day-to-day behavior. Noble mulled over how he might best address this issue. Should he address it at all? For example, he did not yet know whether the opinions voiced came from a few vocal employees, or if others in the Deloitte organization shared their sentiment. The integration issues were rather complicated because, at the outset, the integration message was interpreted by some as "a merger of two equals."

The Integration

On June 3, 2002, across Canada, approximately 1,000 Andersen people (700 professional staff, 200 support staff, and 70 partners) would join Deloitte, effectively creating the country's largest professional services organization. The large majority of these people would be located in Toronto. Noble estimated that the value of Andersen annual billings brought to Deloitte was between Cdn$100 million and Cdn$180 million. If the integration were somehow mismanaged, annual billings would be around Cdn$90 million or even less. However, if the integration were successful, the number would be closer to the Cdn$180 million mark. The combined entity would employ 6,600 people in total, representing annual billings of approximately Cdn$1.1 billion.

A welcome breakfast involving 1,300 people was planned to kick off the integration at the Metro Toronto Convention Centre, followed by a series of introductory speeches. Colin Taylor, Deloitte's chief executive and managing partner stated:

> Now we're integrating the Andersen people and clients into Deloitte with the same energy, enthusiasm and speed that we brought to closing the transaction. We have a lot of work ahead of us and our goal is to make this transition absolutely seamless for our clients and as smooth as possible for our people.

At Deloitte, "Making a Difference Together" was the vision for the integrated organization that expressed the combined company's commitment to its clients and each other. It also expressed the belief that the integration with Andersen would strengthen existing capabilities. Deloitte included these words in a new logo created to highlight all integration communications. The logo symbolized Deloitte's conviction that, as the number one professional services firm in Canada, it will be even stronger and more successful in the marketplace (see Exhibit 1).

Deloitte & Touche

Deloitte in Canada was part of a worldwide group named Deloitte Touche Tohmatsu. Deloitte Touche Tohmatsu was a Swiss Verein, an association, and each of its national practices was a separate and independent legal entity.

In Canada, Deloitte had 2001 revenues of Cdn$895 million and 5,600 people (including 515 partners). Its main services were four-fold. Assurance and Advisory services provided attest services (financial audits of organizations, rendering an independent opinion). Financial Advisory services included investigative services directed at solving business crime and reorganization services to allow managers to regain control amid organizational crisis—essentially crisis management services. In addition, this group facilitated public offerings of stock or debt, mergers and acquisitions, and performed due diligence work for clients. Consulting-type services were offered to help clients develop and enhance their business strategies. Tax services supported personal and corporate filings as well as advised clients on how to achieve tax savings. Deloitte had offices in all major cities across Canada. The four services listed above were offered in each of these offices.

Exhibit 1   **Deloitte's New Logo for the Integrated Organization**

MAKING A DIFFERENCE

TOGETHER

Source: Company files.

Andersen

Andersen Worldwide SC, a Swiss Societe Cooperative, was a coordinating entity for its autonomous member firms that had agreed to cooperate in the market with a common brand, philosophy, and technologies and practice methods. Thus, each Andersen Worldwide member firm, including Andersen in the United States and Andersen in Canada, had its own governance and capital structure. There were Andersen consultants serving clients in 390 locations around the world.

In 1960, Andersen established its Canadian practice with 26 people. Prior to 2002, it was considered the smallest of the five largest accounting firms in Canada with 1,300 people. At the time of the integration in 2002, Andersen had sized itself down to approximately 970 employees. The firm serviced clients across the country from seven offices located in Vancouver, Calgary, Winnipeg, Mississauga, Toronto, Ottawa, and Montreal. It offered services that were very similar to those offered by Deloitte.

Noble was impressed with the Andersen organization in Canada, stating:

> We knew that Andersen had the best litigation record of any professional services firm in Canada. We admired and envied Andersen. At Deloitte, we would often hold Andersen practices up as the industry benchmark, including their tools, skills, marketing, and knowledge management capabilities. Their link to a global network of consultants with expertise in a multitude of areas, and which could be accessed at any given time, was unparalleled.

The Events That Led Up to the Integration

In 1999, Enron had been the seventh largest U.S. company (based on reported revenues). For the last 10 years, it had evolved from a regional natural gas provider to, among other things, a trader of natural gas, electricity, and other commodities, with retail operations in energy and other products. In 1998, Enron was number 73 on *Fortune*'s annual list of "100 Best Companies to Work For."

Andersen U.S. provided Enron with internal audit services as well as serving as Enron's external auditor. Although Andersen's international branches were legally separate from Andersen U.S., the Andersen name became a huge liability as a result of the Enron scandal. Andersen U.S. faced a felony charge of obstruction of justice, accused of trying to block a Securities and Exchange Commission (SEC) investigation into Enron's financial disclosures by destroying documents related to the accounting firm's audits.

In statements released to the media, Andersen stated that the action taken against its firm by the U.S. Department of Justice was "both factually and legally baseless." Nevertheless, the damage had been done and the company faced a crisis from which it would not recover.

Enron's collapse and allegations of illegal activity by Andersen created debate around auditor independence and scope of services. Criminal indictment of Andersen U.S. created a negative impact on the accounting profession. One of the questions that persisted in the public arena was whether an accounting firm could objectively perform an audit when it also made millions of dollars providing other services to the same client. Audit firms refuted that an audit could be enhanced by the extra knowledge the firm gained through its consulting arm.

The collapse of Enron and the court of public opinion effectively destroyed the Andersen brand in a few months. In accepting Andersen professionals, some Deloitte managers were concerned that the Enron fallout might carry over to the Deloitte brand.

The Integration Talks

Although it was thought that rival accounting firms—either KPMG or Ernst & Young—already had a deal to acquire Andersen, Deloitte's senior management team was pleasantly surprised when it found out that Andersen's U.S. tax practice had urged Andersen Canada to talk to Deloitte. In the United States, Andersen's tax practice had aligned with its Deloitte counterpart. In the first week of April 2002, Andersen Canada contacted Deloitte to begin integration talks.

On Friday, April 12, 2002, Deloitte completed a memorandum of agreement with Andersen Canada to integrate its practice with Deloitte. This transaction was subject to a due diligence review, partner approvals by both firms and regulatory approval. Because of its size, the transaction was subject to regulatory review by the Competition Bureau under Canada's Competition Act. Noble stated:

> The run-up to the integration has been a disaster for Andersen. Despite their Canadian client base and staff remaining loyal, their phones were not ringing. Even when they were the frontrunner for new business, potential clients would almost always shy away from them. The day-to-day press surrounding Andersen was very negative.

Andersen had been negotiating with KPMG and the media was speculating that a deal was imminent. Deloitte took a less public profile, avoiding speculation. Because both sides moved rapidly, the transaction was completed in six weeks. Closing the transaction quickly was critical because a lengthy process increased the risk that a major client and a significant number of talented professionals would be lost.

Alan Booth, director of National Human Resources with Deloitte, explained that the detailed negotiations on people and other critical integration issues proved very challenging due to various reasons, including:

1. Strict limitations on contact between Deloitte and Andersen to permit regulatory review;

2. Imminent systems loss at Andersen set to occur when it would withdraw from Andersen worldwide;

3. Numerous rumors that fed anxiety among people in both organizations; and

4. Coordination of messages to people from Deloitte and Andersen was greatly affected by the necessary contact limitations.

On Friday, May 31, 2002, at 5:00 PM Pacific Daylight Time, Andersen Canada "went dark." All its systems including phones, e-mail, and personal computers (PCs) were disconnected from the worldwide Andersen network. This signaled the beginning of the actual integration of the former Andersen people into the Deloitte organization.

The National Integration Team

A national integration team consisting of 12 individuals was formed to lead the integration. The team was co-chaired by Terry Noble, who had trained as a chartered accountant with Andersen in Canada, and Russ Robertson, Andersen's managing partner. Colin Taylor, Deloitte's chief executive, knew that both men had been classmates at the Western Business School undergraduate program at the University of Western Ontario, London, Canada, in the 1960s, and thus knew each other. Equal numbers of Deloitte and Andersen personnel were represented on the team. An effort was made to ensure that key people from both sides were involved, in order to guide the integration challenge. For example, heads of functions, integrating officers from the five Deloitte offices, and several "thought leaders" were part of the team.

The main goals of the integration team were to put together a company-wide plan for integration and to create support materials (e.g., "A Primer on Organizational Grieving") to aid the Deloitte people in integrating their new colleagues into their organization. Geographic and functional leaders were to execute the plan with support from national functions such as human resources (HR), information technology (IT), and finance. For example, HR was, to a large extent, responsible for communicating the Deloitte policies, as well as explaining administrative items, such as compensation, the incentive plan, pensions and benefits, and promotion policies. The IT department was responsible for issues such as a seamless transition of e-mail, telephone systems and computer applications. There were significant differences in the IT systems between the two companies. However, by the end of Monday, June 3, 2002, almost all new Deloitte people had their PCs reconfigured to the Deloitte systems, a new phone number, a connection to the network and new business cards to give to their clients.

The national integration team would monitor the integration process through an Internet-based Pulse Survey, which would allow the team to benchmark unit to unit

Exhibit 2   PULSE SURVEY QUESTIONS

No.	Questions
1.	Overall, the integration is going well.
2.	The firm is committed to making the integration as smooth as possible for our people.
3.	I am being kept informed about how the integration will affect me.
4.	I am being treated fairly during the integration.
5.	My ability to do my job effectively has been maintained or improved as a result of the integration.
6.	I am confident dealing with client questions about the integration.
7.	Client service levels have been maintained or improved as a result of the integration.
8.	My clients are feeling positive about the integration.
9.	I intend to be with D&T one year from now.
	Overall score.

over time, and to take immediate remedial action if in the various stages the integration goals were not attained. The Pulse Survey was conducted every month with a random sample of people from both organizations. For example, among other things, people were asked:

1. How they felt the integration was proceeding overall;
2. If they were kept informed about the personal impact integration would have on them;
3. Whether they perceived fair treatment;
4. Whether their ability to do their jobs was maintained or increased;
5. If they felt that client service levels were being maintained or improved; and
6. If they intended to remain with Deloitte one year into the future.

Participants in the survey were also given the opportunity to provide open comments on how they felt the integration was progressing, or any other message they wanted to communicate in confidence. All offices received detailed feedback on all of the questions that were incorporated in the survey. The questions that were part of the Pulse Survey are listed in Exhibit 2.

Once every two weeks, the managing partners of each of the five Deloitte offices would convene for a conference call to share updates and ideas, some of which resulted from the Pulse Survey. Best practices were identified, and integrating officers were encouraged to implement these practices across offices. Last, the integration team would present status updates to Deloitte's executive committee and board of directors.

Commenting on the Deloitte and Andersen integration, in November of 2002, Noble stated:

> Integration is easier said than done. It takes at least three to five years. There is often a strong tendency on the part of those leading the change efforts to declare victory too soon. Early on we need to outline the present and future state of our organization. Cultures do not change that quickly. We do not want a situation where the integration unravels and turns into a bad business deal because we did not manage the process, people, systems, and business fundamentals in a proper fashion.

One thousand Andersen professionals are joining us and not one of them had chosen to be part of our organization. The integration is like an arranged marriage and we have to find common ground. The Andersen people probably have a fear that they will be taken over and their identity and sense of value will be lost. I'm sure that they are not prepared to let that happen.

There are workplace productivity issues that we will have to manage. At first, the Andersen people will be busy getting used to their new titles, new surroundings, and new colleagues. Many people will be concerned with "me" issues: my office, my promotion, my salary, my computer, my role and responsibilities, and so forth. While they have all that to sort through, our job is to figure out how to mitigate the productivity drop. A significant drop in our productivity could tie up the organization for years.

Of course, we want to be able to retain all of our clients—particularly those that are brought in by Andersen. We want our new clients to be proud of their association with Deloitte and confident in the ability of the combined entity to deliver quality and excellent service. Our combined client base needs to be convinced that Deloitte will not be affected by the aftershocks of the Andersen events in the U.S. We cannot afford to slip on our client service delivery. Otherwise there would not be enough work for our people.

Risks Identified by the Integration Team

As Noble saw it, the real challenge for the Deloitte and Andersen organizations was to move beyond the integrated HR and IT systems toward a unified, market-leading organization. The actual successes achieved in the marketplace would hold the combined entities together. For example, financial success served as glue and, as Noble observed, would all but ensure that partners felt they had shared in the success of the transaction. Essential to the long-term success of the integration, therefore, was that individuals would see (or feel in their pocket) that investing significant resources in the transaction, time and money, was indeed worth it. Noble believed that the Andersen people would be blamed if the combined organization missed the financial targets that it intended to achieve. Such scapegoating would detract from the integration efforts.

Noble identified the top three risk factors that threatened to derail the success of the integration: cultural misalignment and subsequent conflict, insufficient integration, and lack of organizational synergies. Exhibits 3 and 4 describe the method and results of the cultural assessment that was conducted in July 2002 to determine the differences between the Deloitte and Andersen cultures.

The results of the assessment revealed how each organization viewed itself, the "other" organization and the challenges of the integration. The cultural gaps between members of the two organizations identified critical organizational issues that required special attention from the national integration team. It was quite clear that people from Deloitte and Andersen were different from an organizational culture point of view.

Noble elaborated:

The Andersen organization is being told that they will join a new organization. They would not have volunteered to integrate with us if not for the crisis that occurred in the U.S. Will they be enthusiastic about the integration? Some of them may be. However, others may not completely understand why we do

Exhibit 3   Methodology Used to Test Cultural Alignment between Deloitte and Andersen

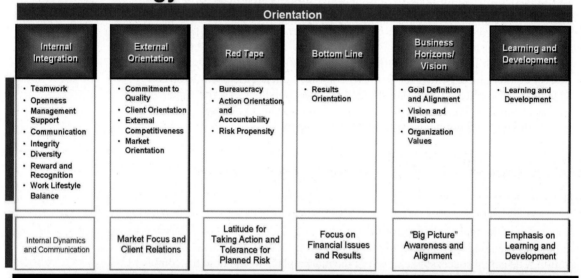

Deloitte
& Touche

Methodology/Framework

Orientation					
Internal Integration	**External Orientation**	**Red Tape**	**Bottom Line**	**Business Horizons/ Vision**	**Learning and Development**
• Teamwork • Openness • Management Support • Communication • Integrity • Diversity • Reward and Recognition • Work Lifestyle Balance	• Commitment to Quality • Client Orientation • External Competitiveness • Market Orientation	• Bureaucracy • Action Orientation and Accountability • Risk Propensity	• Results Orientation	• Goal Definition and Alignment • Vision and Mission • Organization Values	• Learning and Development
Internal Dynamics and Communication	Market Focus and Client Relations	Latitude for Taking Action and Tolerance for Planned Risk	Focus on Financial Issues and Results	"Big Picture" Awareness and Alignment	Emphasis on Learning and Development

Findings from the focus groups, interviews, questionnaires, and documentation review were grouped based on 6 key cultural orientations, which are characterized by a series of measurement dimensions outlined above.

Making a Difference Together   **DRAFT CONFIDENTIAL—NOT FOR DISTRIBUTION**

Source: Company files.

things in a certain way here at Deloitte. Addressing the differences between the two cultures was essential to successfully guiding the integration.

The great payoff will be, that if we do this right, and utilize the talent of Andersen employees, we will not only become the best professional services firm, but also the largest in the country.

Ultimately, this is a talent play for us. We've got the best 1,000 people coming into our organization fully trained. We have to figure out how we can get their commitment to us and to serve our clients. We want the Andersen people to be proud of their new organization.

We will lose people, but we want to lose them for the right reasons. People may have goals or values that are different from the ones espoused at Deloitte. However, we don't want to lose people because of poor interpersonal treatment.

Exhibit 4   Results of Cultural Assessment

Deloitte & Touche

Overall Assessment

CULTURAL SYNERGIES		CULTURAL GAPS	
Dimension	**Degree of Alignment**	**Dimension**	**Degree of Alignment**
Commitment to Quality	⬤	Bureaucracy	◔
Client Orientation	⬤	Market Orientation	◔
Teamwork	◕	Diversity	◔
Communication	◕	Action Orientation and Accountability	◑
Openness	◕	Learning and Development	◑
Integrity	◕	Reward and Recognition	◑
External Competitiveness	◕	Organizational Values	◑
Results Orientation	◕	Work Lifestyle Balance	◑
Risk Propensity	◑	Management Support	◑
Vision and Mission	◕	Goal Definition and Alignment	◑

Legend: Degree of Cultural Alignment

Low ◷ ◑ ◕ ⬤ High

Ten areas were identified as having either a moderate or low degree of cultural alignment. The remaining ten areas revealed a relatively high degree of cultural alignment.

Source: Company files.

The September Meeting

The data from the Pulse Survey (the third since June of 2002) that Noble had received earlier in the morning confirmed, at least to some extent, what he had been hearing through the grapevine. The data suggested that a number of Deloitte employees feared that Deloitte management, in its haste to consummate the deal with Andersen and welcome the new employees, was forgetting about its own people. Some elements within the Deloitte organization did not understand the amount of attention given to the Andersen people, whom they viewed as "damaged goods." Comments indicating that it was time for all people involved in the integration to "get on with business and focus on the market" began to surface.

However, Noble was not certain of the number of individuals that shared such views. Were these the concerns of a few vocal people? Or did these individuals voice what many others in the Deloitte organization were thinking? Clearly, this was not the kind of feedback he was hoping for. The results from the Pulse Survey led Noble to contemplate how he and his colleagues from the integration team could best deal with the cultural differences in the short term. In his words:

> There is the naive view that a new culture will be formed with relative ease. I doubt it. Cultures involve deep-seated beliefs. For example, at Andersen, there had always been a strong drive to focus on the clients' needs above everything else. In contrast, at Deloitte, while acknowledging the importance of commitment to quality and the client's needs, there was also a focus on employee issues.
>
> A Frenchman and an Englishman will always retain their culture. But they can learn to work together to achieve a common goal. Or can they really?
>
> It takes a lot of effort and patience to help new behaviors and practices grow deep roots.

In Noble's mind, this was a complex issue to manage. Furthermore, there were a number of situational constraints on actions that could be undertaken to address the issue. For example, Noble and his integration team had to contend with the fact that people were constantly on-site at the client's business. How then should managers work to resolve tensions that might arise between the two cultures? Moreover, taking the people from the two organizations to an off-site location to deal with the issue of cultural differences would certainly affect billable hours. Were we prepared to do that? On the other hand, addressing these and other issues in a timely and proper fashion could make the difference between being a good organization versus being great organization. True integration would be hard to achieve without the knowledge, skill and, above all, the commitment of the Deloitte people. It was 10:29 AM, and Noble got up to go to the meeting with the integration team.

Smithfield Foods' Vertical Integration Strategy

Harmful to the Environment?

LaRue T. Hosmer
The University of Michigan

In 2004 Smithfield Foods was the largest hog producer and pork processor in the world. The company raised 14 million hogs domestically (a 14 percent U.S. share) and processed 27 million hogs annually (a 27 percent U.S. share). Smithfield marketed chops, roasts, ribs, loins, ground pork, bacon, hams, sausages, and sliced deli meats under such brands as Smithfield, Smithfield Lean Generation, John Morrell, Gwaltney, Patrick Cudahy, Stefano's, Farmland, Quick-n-Easy, and Jean Caby (France), plus it had the two best-known meat brands in Poland—Krakus and Morliny. Smithfield specialized in producing exceptionally lean hogs; the company had exclusive U.S. franchise rights to a proprietary breed of SPG sows that accounted for about 55 percent of its herd and provided live hogs for its best-selling Smithfield Lean Generation Pork products. In 2004 Smithfield operated 40 pork processing plants and 4 beef processing plants. A new state-of-the-art ham processing plant opened in 2004.

Since 1981, the company had made some 25 acquisitions to expand geographically, diversify into new product segments, and vertically integrate its pork business. Smithfield's acquisitions of Moyer Packing Company and Packerland Holdings in 2002 made it the fifth largest beef producer in the United States. In 1998, Smithfield began expanding into foreign markets, making acquisitions in Canada, France, and Poland and establishing joint ventures in Mexico, Spain, and China. Two meat processors in Poland and Romania were acquired in 2004, along with a Romanian hog farming operation with 15,000 sows producing 200,000 market hogs annually. Management believed its acquisitions and joint ventures gave the company strong market positions, high-quality manufacturing facilities, and excellent growth and exporting potential to serve regions that already had high pork consumption levels and that were emerging as major meat consumers. Executives were particularly excited about the company's opportunities in the European Union.

In pork, Smithfield had pursued a vertical integration strategy, establishing operations in hog farming, feed mills, meat packing plants, and distribution. Smithfield's hog processing group, the chief subsidiary of which was Murphy-Brown LLC, owned and operated hog farms with close to 960,000 sows in North Carolina, South Carolina, Virginia, Utah, Colorado, Texas, Oklahoma, Kansas, South Dakota, Minnesota, Missouri, Illinois, Mexico, Brazil, and Poland.

Smithfield Foods was headquartered in Smithfield, Virginia, where it operated two large hog processing plants. But large parts of the company's operations were in North

Exhibit 1   FINANCIAL AND OPERATING SUMMARY, SMITHFIELD FOODS, 1995–2004
(in millions, except per share amounts)

	2004	2003	2001	1999	1995
Operations					
Sales revenues	$9,267.0	$7,135.4	$5,123.7	$3,550.0	$1,526.5
Gross profit	938.9	602.2	762.3	448.6	126.9
Selling, general, and administrative expenses	570.8	497.9	416.2	280.4	62.4
Depreciation expense	167.5	$151.5	114.5	59.3	19.7
Interest expenses	121.3	87.8	81.5	38.4	14.1
Income from continuing operations	162.7	11.9	214.3	89.6	31.9
Net income	227.1	26.3	223.5	94.9	27.8
Earnings per share	$2.03	$0.24	$2.03	$1.16	$0.40
Financial position					
Working capital	$1,056.6	$833.0	$635.4	$ 215.9	$ 60.9
Total assets	4,813.7	4,410.6	3,250.9	1,771.6	550.2
Total debt	1,801.5	1,642.3	1,188.7	610.3	234.7
Shareholders' equity	1,617.2	1,299.2	1,053.1	542.2	184.0
Current ratio	2.09	2.02	2.01	1.46	1.35
Total debt to total capitalization	52.7%	55.8%	53.0%	53.0%	58.4%
Other statistics					
Capital expenditures	$151.4	$172.0	$113.3	$92.0	$90.6
Number of employees	46,400	44,100	34,000	33,000	9,000

Source: 2004 annual report.

Carolina—Smithfield's biggest pork processing plant was in Bladen County, North Carolina, and the company's Murphy-Brown hog production subsidiary had a very sizable hog farming operation in eastern North Carolina. Smithfield opened a new state-of-the-art ham processing plant in Kinston, North Carolina, in 2005 that employed 206 workers; the Kinston plant was expected to be the most efficient premier-cooked-ham plant in the United States, employing the newest technologies available and meeting the highest food standards in the industry. Smithfield's large southern base provided low wages and relatively low operating costs across much of its integrated operations, factors that helped pave the way for Smithfield's competitive prices and strong growth.

The company's longtime chairman and CEO, Joseph W. Luter III, continually emphasized the need to drive down costs and push up sales. Top executives at Smithfield Foods wanted to continue the company's rapid and profitable expansion and were constantly on the lookout for opportunities to grow the company's business. Going into 2005, Smithfield had annualized sales of close to $10 billion, up from $1.5 billion in 1995; revenues had grown at a compound average rate of close to 24 percent during the past decade. Exhibit 1 provides historical financial data.

Opposition to Smithfield's Expansion

Over the last decade, Smithfield Foods had met with mounting opposition to expansion of its business, particularly in hog farming. The chief pockets of opposition to Smithfield's hog farming activities came from rural residents in eastern North Carolina, where there were some 8,000 hog farms. Neighboring residents complained that commercial hog farming had essentially been imposed on them and that it entailed substantial adverse impacts in the form of low wages and environmental discharges.

Eastern North Carolina and Smithfield's Hog Farming Operations

Eastern North Carolina, essentially the area extending about 150 miles from Raleigh (the state capital) to the Atlantic coast, is a region of flat land, sandy soil, and ample rainfall. At one time it was a relatively prosperous region, with thousands of small family farms, each of which had a tobacco allotment. During the 1930s far more tobacco had been grown than was needed, and the price plummeted. One of the government initiatives of the Depression era was a restriction on the total amount of tobacco that could be grown, and this total amount was divided up among the existing growers by restricting each to a set percentage of the amount of their land that had been devoted to the crop during a given base year. These restrictions on growth first stabilized and latter increased the price, and the possession of an allotment almost guaranteed the financial prosperity of the farm.

The typical family farm would have 150 to 200 acres. Perhaps 15 acres would be devoted to tobacco, and the balance would be sown in corn, wheat, rye, or soybeans, or left as pasture for cattle or—more frequently—hogs. The grains grown locally would be trucked to the nearest town within the region to be milled into feed and then returned to the farm for the livestock. The cattle and hogs produced locally would be trucked to the nearest town to be sold at auction, and then slaughtered and processed at a nearby packing plant. These towns were also relatively prosperous, as the farmers and their families purchased clothing and household goods at local stores and automobiles and farm machinery at local dealers.

This prosperity started downhill in the 1970s as the national campaigns against smoking led to continual reductions in the size, and consequently the profitability, of the tobacco allotments, which eventually came almost to an end. Local prosperity continued to decline in the 1980s as very large feed lots in Nebraska, Iowa, and Kansas developed a much less costly means of raising hogs prior to slaughter; the piglets spent only the first 12 to 15 months of their lives on the farms where they were bred before being brought to fenced open-air corrals where they were closely confined but fed continuously to gain weight. Farmers in eastern North Carolina had to compete against this new and far more efficient production process. Prices for the hogs raised in eastern North Carolina declined sharply, and many of the local packing plants went out of business.

Local prosperity stabilized to some extent in the 1990s, though with a greatly changed distribution of income, as Smithfield Foods introduced the concept of the factory farm. Large metal sheds with concrete floors were built, each designed to hold up to 1,000 hogs. Feeding was by means of a mechanized conveyor that carried food alongside both walls. Waste was removed by hosing it off the floors to a central trough that carried it to a storage lagoon. Temperature was controlled by huge fans at each end of each shed. Every effort was made to reduce costs. Feed grains were no longer grown, purchased, and milled locally; instead most grains were grown, purchased, and milled in the Midwest and transported to eastern North Carolina by unit feed trains, which were strings of covered hopper cars that moved as a unit, without switching, from the feed mill in Nebraska or Iowa directly to one of the company's distribution centers in North Carolina. Some feed grains were grown and purchased even more cheaply abroad, primarily in Australia and Argentina, and then carried by ship to a company-leased milling facility and distribution center in Wilmington (a port in southeastern North Carolina, near the South Carolina border).

Limited farm machinery was needed for this new method of raising hogs, given that few feed grains were grown locally, but the little that was needed was purchased by the Smithfield headquarters office directly from the manufacturer. Many farm equipment dealers within the region were forced to close. Even diesel fuel, needed for the trucks that transported the feed grains to the farms and the mature hogs to the packing plants, was purchased from the refinery, transported by railway tank cars to large storage tanks at the distribution centers, and pumped directly into the trucks. Local fuel dealers got little or none of this business. All truck purchases were arranged by bid from national dealers located in Detroit (auto companies had refused to sell outside their dealer chains, but they allegedly gave favored prices to very large dealers near their corporate headquarters) at very low prices, and all subsequent truck repairs were done at company-owned repair shops located at the company-owned distribution centers. Some truck dealers in the region were forced to close.

Executives at Smithfield Foods did not apologize for the business model that they had created. Their attitude could be summed up as follows: "This is the way the world is going and this is what the market demands. All we have done is to create a competitive system that works. Moreover, we have saved farms and brought jobs to the eastern North Carolina region through this system, and we have provided better (leaner) pork products at lower prices to our customers." Smithfield's development of a "competitive system that works" had won Joseph Luter an award as Master Entrepreneur of the Year in 2002; a Smithfield news release dated December 21, 2002, said:

> Joseph W. Luter III has been named the Ernst & Young 2002 Virginia Master Entrepreneur of the Year. The Ernst & Young program recognizes entrepreneurs who have demonstrated excellence and extraordinary success in such areas as innovation, financial performance and personal commitment to their businesses and communities . . .
>
> Since becoming chairman and chief executive officer of Smithfield Foods, Inc. in 1975, Mr. Luter transformed the company from a small, regional meat packer with sales of $125 million and net worth of $1 million to an international concern with annual sales of $8 billion and a net worth of $1.4 billion.

Smithfield Foods did not own the farms that raised the hogs. Instead, company representatives would select a reasonably large farm, one that had been successful in the past and therefore was financially solvent now, and negotiate a contract with the owning family to raise hogs at a set price per animal. The farm family would frequently using a loan provided through the Smithfield Corporation and a contractor licensed by the Smithfield Corporation, build the metal barns with concrete floors, feed conveyors, ventilation fans, and waste systems; connect the waste systems to storage lagoons (five to eight acres in size); construct feed bins and loading ramps; and be ready for business. Smithfield Corporation would then deliver the hogs at piglet stage, provide a constant supply of feed grains mixed with antibiotics (to prevent disease in the crowded conditions of the metal barns), and offer free veterinarian service. The responsibility of the farm family was to raise those hogs to marketable weight as quickly and as efficiently as possible. This was termed *contract farming;* it was described in the following terms in a five-part investigative series that ran February 19–26, 1995, in the *Raleigh News and Observer:*

Greg Stephens is the 1995 version of the North Carolina hog farmer. He owns no hogs. Stephens carries a mortgage on four new confinement barns that cost him $300,000 to build. The 4,000 hogs inside belong to a company called Prestage Farms, Inc. (one of the larger suppliers of Smithfield Foods). Prestage simply pays Stephens a fee to raise them . . .

This arrangement is called contract farming, and it's hardly risk-free. But for anyone wanting to break into the swine business these days, it's the only game in town. "Without a contract, there's no way I'd be raising hogs," says Stephens, "and even if I had somehow gotten in, my pockets aren't nearly deep enough to let me stay in."

Welcome to corporate livestock production, the force behind the swine industry's explosive growth in North Carolina. The backbone of the new system is a network of hundreds of contractors like Stephens, the franchise owners in a system that more closely resembles a fast-food chain than traditional agriculture.

Nowhere in the nation has this change been as dramatic, or as officially embraced, as in North Carolina. As a result, the hog population has more than doubled in four years, and nearly all of that growth has occurred on farms controlled by the big companies. Meanwhile, independent farmers have left the business by the thousands.

In 1998 Smithfield Foods reportedly had a two-year waiting list of farmers wishing to obtain hog farming contracts. Industry observers, however, worried about the practice of saddling hundreds of small farmers with thousands of dollars of debt. As one elected state representative said, "Why invest your capital when you can get a farmer to take the risk? Why own the farm when you can own the farmer?"[1]

The problem foreseen by industry observers was the possibility that a company could cancel its contract with only 30 days' notice, leaving the farmer with the debt and no income to repay it, or could threaten to cancel and then renew the contract only with a sharply lower price per animal. Both sudden cancellations and lower prices were said to have happened frequently in the poultry industry:

> The changes that are sweeping the swine industry today were pioneered by chicken and turkey growers in the 1960s and '70s. Total confinement housing, vertical integration, and contract farming are all standard practices in the feather world. As a result, you need only look at chickens to see where pork is headed.
>
> The poultry industry today is fully integrated—meaning a handful of companies control all phases of production—and the labor is performed by an army of contract growers, some of them decidedly unhappy. "It's sharecropping, that's what it is," said Larry Holder, a chicken farmer and president of the Contract Poultry Growers Association.

The *Raleigh News and Observer* interviewed a number of farmers with hog-growing contracts in North Carolina. One farmer with 10 years of experience growing for Carroll Farms (another large supplier of Smithfield Foods), said, "They've been nothing but good to me."[2] Greg Stephens, the farmer quoted earlier, told the *News and Observer* that in his case the biggest selling point had been his freedom from market risk: "If hog prices go south, as they did two months ago, the contract farmer is barely affected. The company that owns the pigs takes on more risk than you do."[3]

The survival of over 1,000 family farms as contract hog growers is cited as one of the major benefits of the industrialization of agriculture in eastern North Carolina. Another is the creation of new agricultural jobs. Each of the contract farms averages 7,500 animals. The owning families cannot care for all those animals, even though the hogs are closely confined and automatically fed and watered. The typical farm will employ five people from the community at wages of $7 to $8 an hour; working conditions are hard and unpleasant. Most of the people filling such jobs are untrained and poorly educated area residents.

Smithfield's three newest slaughterhouses in North Carolina employed about 3,200 people. Many of the jobs at these plants were regarded as hard and unpleasant; some involved killing and disemboweling the hogs. The killing was said to be painless, and much of the early processing (scraping the carcass to remove the hair, and dealing with the internal organs) was automated. One of the more labor-intensive tasks involved preparing cuts of meat for packaged sale at grocery chains. Most grocery chains, to reduce their internal costs, had eliminated the position of store butchers, opting instead to buy their fresh meats cut, wrapped, packaged, and ready for sale. The cutting at meatpacking facilities was done on a high-speed assembly line, using very sharp laser-guided knives; workers were under continual pressure to perform and were exposed to dangers of injury. Workers who became skilled at this cutting and were able to endure the stress earned $10 to $12 an hour; turnover was relatively high because of the strenuous job demands. Many of the workers at the high-volume packing plants in eastern North Carolina were immigrants from Central or South America. The jobs were described in the following terms by an undercover reporter for the *New York Times* who worked at one of the Smithfield packing plants for three weeks on what was termed the picnic line:

> One o'clock means it is getting near the end of the workday [for the first shift]. Quota has to be met, and the workload doubles. The conveyor belt always overflows with meat around 1 o'clock. So the workers redouble their pace, hacking pork from shoulder bones with a driven single-mindedness. They stare blankly, like mules in wooden blinders, as the butchered slabs pass by.
>
> It is called the picnic line: 18 workers lined up on both sides of a belt, carving meat from bone. Up to 16 million shoulders a year come down that line here at Smithfield Packing Co., the largest pork production plant in the world. That works out to about 32,000 per shift, 63 a minute, one every 17 seconds for each worker for eight and a half hours a day. The first time you stare down at that belt you know your body is going to give in way before the machine ever will.[4]

Smithfield's vertical integration strategy, which had resulted in very limited purchasing of feed, machinery, and fuel from local sources; the debt-laden nature of the farm contracts, which fueled concerns about the possibility of future contract cancellations or price reductions; and the low-pay/low-quality nature of the jobs that had been created at both the farms and the packing plants had combined to create strong, often vocal, opposition on the part of many local residents to any planned expansion of Smithfield Foods within eastern North Carolina.

A much bigger and far more intense issue, however, was the alleged impact of hog farming on the environment:

> Imagine a city as big as New York suddenly grafted onto North Carolina's Coastal Plain. Double it. Now imagine that this city has no sewage treatment plants. All the wastes from 15 million inhabitants are simply flushed into open pits and sprayed onto fields.
>
> Turn those humans into hogs, and you don't have to imagine at all. It's already here. A vast city of swine has risen practically overnight in the counties east of Interstate 95. It's a megalopolis of 7 million animals that live in metal

confinement barns and produce two to four times as much waste, per hog, as the average human.

All that manure—about 9.5 million tons a year—is stored in thousands of earthen pits called lagoons, where it is decomposed and sprayed or spread on crop lands. The lagoon system is the source of most hog farm odor, but industry officials say it's a proven and effective way to keep harmful chemicals and bacteria out of water supplies. New evidence says otherwise:

- The *News and Observer* has obtained new scientific studies showing that contaminants from hog lagoons are getting into groundwater. One N.C. State University report estimates that as many as half of existing lagoons—perhaps hundreds—are leaking badly enough to contaminate groundwater.

- The industry also is running out of places to spread or spray the waste from lagoons. On paper, the state's biggest swine counties already are producing more phosphorous-rich manure than available land can absorb, state Agriculture Department records show.

- Scientists are discovering that hog farms emit large amounts of ammonia gas, which returns to earth in rain. The ammonia is believed to be contributing to an explosion of algae growth that's choking many of the state's rivers and estuaries.[5]

Raising hogs is admitted even by farm families to be a messy and smelly business. Hogs eat more than other farm animals, and they excrete more. And those excretions smell far, far worse. Having 50 to 100 hogs running free in a fenced pasture is one thing. The odor is clearly noticeable, but that sharp and pungent smell is felt to be part of rural living. Having 5,000 to 10,000 hogs closely confined in metal barns, with large ventilation fans moving the air continually from each barn, and the wastes from those hogs collected in huge open-air lagoons is something else. People who live near one of the large hog farms say that, unless you've experienced it, you just can't know what it is like:

At 11 o'clock sharp on a Sunday morning the choir marched into the sanctuary of New Brown's Chapel Baptist Church. And the stench of 4,800 hogs rolled right in with them.

The odor hung oppressively in the vestibule, clinging to church robes, winter coats and fancy hats. It sent stragglers scurrying indoors from the parking lot, some holding their noses. Sherry Leveston, 4, pulled her fancy white sweater over her face as she ran. "It stinks," she cried.

It was another Sunday morning in Brownsville, a Greene County North Carolina hamlet that's home to 200 people and one hog farm. Like many of its counterparts throughout the eastern portion of the state, the town hasn't been the same since the hogs moved in a couple of years ago.

To some, each new gust from the south [the direction of the farm] is a reminder of serious wrongs committed for which there has been no redress. "We've basically given up," said the Rev. Charles White, pastor at New Brown's Chapel.

In scores of rural neighborhoods down east [the eastern portion of North Carolina] the talk is the same. There's something new in the air, and people are furious about it.

Hog odor is by far the most emotional issue facing the pork industry—and the most divisive. Growers assert their right to earn a living; neighbors say they have a right to odor-free air. Hog company officials, meanwhile, accuse activists of exaggerating the problem to stir up opposition . . .

For other residents [of Brownsville, close to New Brown's Chapel] hog odor has simply become an inescapable part of their daily routine. It's usually heaviest about 5 A.M., when Lisa Hines leaves the house for her factory job. It seeps into her car and follows her on her commute to work. It clings to her hair and clothes during the day. And it awaits her when she returns home in the afternoon.

"It makes me so mad," she said. "The owner lives miles away from here, and he can go home and smell apples and cinnamon if he wants to. But we have no choice."[6]

The 7 million hogs in eastern North Carolina currently generated about 9.5 million tons of manure each year. This waste was stored in large earthen pits called lagoons. These pits were open so that sunlight would decompose the wastes and kill the harmful bacteria; the manure was then spread on farm fields as organic fertilizer. This had been the accepted means for disposing of animal wastes on small family farms for centuries. It was a method fully protected by federal, state, and local laws; a hog farmer—whether a small family or large contract farm—could not be sued for any inconveniences brought about by the hogs, unless those inconveniences were the result of clear negligence in caring for the hogs.

The difference now, of course, comes from the huge expansion of scale. Again, the wastes of 50 to 100 animals were easily accommodated. There was a noticeable effect on air quality, but that was felt to be a natural consequence of living in the country, and the smell came from your own farm, or that of your neighbor, or that of a person who had been there for years. There was a probable effect on water quality, but farm wells were always located uphill and a substantial distance from manure piles, and it was thought that neighbors would be protected by natural filtration through the clay subsoils of the region. No one worried very much about possible public health effects of small numbers of farm animals.

The wastes from 5,000 to 10,000 animals could not be so easily accommodated, and people did worry about the possible public health effects of very large numbers of farm animals. Debilitating asthma had become a much more frequent condition among young children who lived near large hog farms, and there was concern that waste was leaking from the lagoons and contaminating the groundwater. The conventional wisdom about the lagoons was that the heavier sludge was supposed to settle on the bottom and form a seal that would prevent the escape of harmful bacteria or destructive chemicals:

> As recently as two years ago, the U.S. Division of Environmental Management told state lawmakers in a briefing that lagoons effectively self-seal within months with "little or no groundwater contamination." Wendell H. Murphy, a former state senator who was also [in partnership with Smithfield Corporation] the nation's largest producer of hogs, said in an interview this month that "lagoons will seal themselves" and that "there is not one shred, not one piece of evidence anywhere in this nation that any groundwater is being contaminated by any hog lagoon."
>
> What Murphy didn't know was that a series of brand-new studies, conducted among Eastern North Carolina hog farms, showed that large numbers of lagoons are leaking, some of them severely.[7]

The *Raleigh News and Observer* had reported that researchers at North Carolina State University had dug test wells near 11 lagoons that were at least seven years old. They found that more than half of the lagoons were leaking moderately to severely; even those lagoons that were described as leaking only moderately still produced groundwater nitrate levels up to three times the allowable limit. The researchers also found that lagoons were not the only source of groundwater contamination. They dug test wells and examined water quality in fields where hog waste had been sprayed as fertilizer, and found evidence of widespread bacterial and chemical contamination. It was felt that fully as much water contamination came from the practice of attempting to dispose of the decomposed waste through spraying on crops as from the earlier storage of decomposing waste in the lagoons. According to the *Raleigh News and Observer* reporter, too much waste was being sprayed on too few fields, even though almost all farmers in the region now accepted this natural fertilizer in lieu of buying commercial products.

The researchers from North Carolina State University, however, did not urge rural residents to rush out to buy bottled water. In most of the cases they concluded that the contaminants appeared to be migrating laterally toward the nearest ditch or stream, and they found no evidence that a private well had been contaminated. But they did find evidence that numerous streams had been contaminated, partially from leakage but primarily from spills and overflows:

> Frequently major spills are cleaned up quickly so that the public never hears about them. That's what happened in May 1995 when a 10-acre lagoon ruptured on Murphy's Farms' 8,000-hog facility in Magnolia, North Carolina. A limestone layer beneath the lagoon collapsed, sending tons of waste cascading into nearby Millers Creek in an accident that was never reported to state water-quality officials.
>
> An employee of the town's water department discovered the problem when he saw corn kernels and hog waste floating by in the creek that runs through the center of town. He alerted the company, and within hours a task force had been assembled to plug the leak.
>
> It took four days to find the source and fix the problem. But neither Magnolia town officials nor Murphy Farms executives ever notified the state about the spill.
>
> "In retrospect, maybe we should have," Wendell Murphy said, "but I would also say that to my knowledge no harm has ever come of it."
>
> Former employees of hog companies, however, told *News and Observer* reporters that spills were a common occurrence. "Hardly a week goes by," said a former manager for one of the largest hog farms in the state, "that there isn't some sort of leak or overflow. Almost any heavy rain will bring an overflow. When that happens, workers do the best they can to clean it up. After that it's just pray no one notices and keep your mouth shut," he explained.[8]

The waste lagoons could not be covered with a roof to prevent overflows associated with heavy rains, or enclosed with a building to prevent the escape of odors; They were simply too large—five to eight acres—and it was necessary to have direct sunlight to create the natural conditions that would break down the toxic chemicals and kill the harmful bacteria in the wastes. Company officials seemed to believe that there was no possible solution to the problem of the extremely bad odors; essentially they said it would just be necessary for people to learn to live with the smell, which extends up to two miles from the open lagoons and the sprayed fields. According to the *Raleigh News and Observer,*

> Wendell Murphy, chairman of Murphy Family Farms [part of the Murphy Brown hog farming subsidiary of Smithfield Foods] said that while the hog industry is extremely sensitive to the odor problem, he thinks the industry's economic importance should be considered in the equation. "Should we expect the odor to never drift off the site to a neighbor's house? If so, then we're out of

business. We all have to have some inconvenience once in a while for the benefits that come with it."[9]

As the *Raleigh News and Observer* reported, feelings ran high among eastern North Carolina residents in opposing further expansion of hog farming in the region:

Three weeks ago, the tiny town of Faison held a referendum of sorts on whether its residents wanted a new industrial plant, with 1,500 new jobs, built in their community. The jobs lost.

Because the industry in question was a hog-processing plant, people packed the local fire station an hour early to blast the idea. They jeered and hissed every time the county's industrial recruiter mentioned pigs or the plant. "I want to know two things," thundered one burly speaker thrusting a finger at that much smaller industrial recruiter, Woody Brinson. "How can we stop this thing, and how can we get you fired?"

The town council's eventual 3–0 vote against the proposed IBP [a subsidiary of Smithfield Foods] hog slaughterhouse may have little effect on whether the plant is built. [Zoning within rural North Carolina is controlled by the county, not the municipality, and agriculturally related zoning has always been very loosely applied, to benefit local farmers.] What was striking about this meeting, and this vote, was that both occurred in the heart of Duplin County, an economic showcase for the hog industry.

With a pigs-per-person ratio of 32-to-1, Duplin has seen big payoffs from eastern North Carolina's hog revolution in the past decade. The county's revenues from sales and property taxes have soared, and Duplin's per capita income has risen from the lowest 25 percent statewide to about the middle.

Pork production also has spawned jobs in support businesses in Duplin and neighboring counties. People in the hog business say farm odor—"the smell of money"—is a small price to pay for a big benefit. "These hog farms are putting money in people's pockets," says Woody Brinston [the county's director of industrial development]. "Duplin County is booming."

But even here, some bitterly resent the way the industry has transformed the way the countryside looks and smells. Some say that their property has gone down in value. Others note the contrasts in the economic picture. In Duplin County, just 70 miles east of the booming Research Triangle [an area located between Raleigh, Durham, and Chapel Hill with a large number of advanced electronic and biotechnology firms], the population hasn't grown in 10 years. Farm jobs are dwindling despite the rise in hog production.

Daryl Walker, a newly elected Duplin County commissioner, says he hears these arguments all the time. "If this is prosperity," he says, "many of my constituents would just as soon do without it. They are scared to death that there are just going to be more and more hogs, and more and more of the problems that come with those hogs.[10]

A subsequent letter to the editor of the *Raleigh News and Observer* said:

Last Sunday, returning from a weekend at Wrightsville Beach, we stopped at an Interstate 40 rest area near Clinton. When we stepped from our car the stench brought tears to our eyes. So add to the ever-mounting environment damage the poor image our state now leaves with tourists heading towards our beautiful coast. We'll never know how many big tourism bucks are now and soon will be going elsewhere.[11]

Smithfield's Efforts to Address Concerns about the Environmental Impact of Its Vertical Integration Strategy

Smithfield management was endeavoring to combat opposition to its operations in eastern North Carolina and elsewhere and to respond to the environmental challenges that its pork business presented. Exhibit 2 describes examples of Smithfield's environmental improvement projects during 2000–2004. Exhibit 3 presents Smithfield Foods'

Exhibit 2   EXAMPLES OF SMITHFIELD FOODS' ENVIRONMENTAL PROJECTS, 2000–2004

- In 2000, Smithfield signed an agreement with the Office of the North Carolina Attorney General to contribute $2 million per year for 25 years to a fund used for such environmental enhancement projects as constructing and maintaining wetlands, preserving environmentally sensitive lands, and promoting similar projects. In 2003, the attorney general used Smithfield's contributions for grants to five recipients: the Cape Fear River Assembly, Save Our State, the Green Trust Alliance, the North Carolina Coastal Land Trust, and the North Carolina Foundation for Soil and Water Conservation Districts.

- Smithfield had funded a $15 million research project at North Carolina State University to investigate 18 different technologies to modify or replace current methods of swine waste removal at hog farms. A major goal of the project was to achieve cleaner air by finding ways to reduce methane and ammonia emissions of the swine waste lagoons. Smithfield had agreed to implement the recommended technologies, if they were commercially feasible, at all of its hog farms.

- In 2001, all of Murphy-Brown's company-owned swine production farms in North Carolina, South Carolina, and Virginia implemented "environmental management systems" (EMSs) to identify and manage parts of Smithfield's activities that have, or could have, an impact on the environment—the objective was to monitor environmental performance, pinpoint problem areas, and implement any needed preventive and corrective action. These farms then went an extra step and achieved ISO 14001 certification, making Murphy-Brown the first livestock operation in the world to do so—ISO 14001 certification was considered the gold standard for environmental excellence in implementing methods to monitor and measure the environmental impact of production operations and pinpoint problem areas. Since that time, Murphy-Brown has completed EMS implementation and achieved ISO 14001 certification for all company-owned farms in the United States.

- Smithfield was investing up to $20 million in a majority-owned subsidiary, BEST BioFuels, to build a waste collection system and a central treatment facility in southwestern Utah that used proprietary technology to convert livestock waste (which contained methane, a greenhouse gas) into biomethanol. Biomethanol could be processed with a variety of vegetable- or animal-based oils to create biodiesel, an environmentally friendly alternative to petroleum diesel. The waste-to-biomethanol treatment facility in Utah, which began operations in 2004, was connected by an underground sewage network to 23 area farms and received waste from approximately 257,000 hogs over the course of a year. The Utah plant shipped its much of its 2.7 million gallons of biomethanol to a newly constructed BEST Biofuels plant in Texas, where it was processed with used cooking oil, rendered animal fat, or other oil feedstock to create biodiesel, an environmentally friendly alternative to petroleum diesel that emitted nearly 50 percent less carbon monoxide and hazardous particulate matter than regular petroleum diesel. Fuel distributors then blended biodiesel with conventional petroleum diesel in a 20/80 ratio to create a cleaner diesel fuel.

- Cooling towers were installed at four of Smithfield's company processing plants to recirculate water needed in operating the plants; these water conservation measures reduced use of groundwater and relieved stresses on local water tables.

- Smithfield had partnered with its primary corrugated packaging suppliers to pursue cardboard recycling in its operations. Since 2002, close to 50,000 tons of cardboard had been recycled rather than being sent to landfills.

- Several Smithfield plants had modified their facilities to allow biogas—a fuel source derived from plant wastewater—to be used as an energy source. Most all Smithfield plants were pursuing projects to conserve on the use of electric energy.

Source: Information contained in Smithfield's 2003 Stewardship Report and information posted at www.smithfieldfoods.com, accessed December 26, 2002, and November 23, 2004.

Exhibit 3   SMITHFIELD FOODS' ENVIRONMENTAL POLICY STATEMENT, 2004

- It is the corporate policy of Smithfield Foods, Inc., and its subsidiaries to conduct business in a manner consistent with continual improvement in regard to protecting the environment.
- Smithfield Foods, Inc., is committed to protecting the environment through pollution prevention and continual improvement of our environmental practices.
- Smithfield Foods, Inc., seeks to demonstrate its responsible corporate citizenship by complying with relevant environmental legislation and regulations, and with other requirements to which we subscribe. We will create, implement, and periodically review appropriate environmental objectives and targets.
- Protection of the environment is the responsibility of all Smithfield Foods, Inc., employees.

Source: www.smithfieldfoods.com, accessed November 23, 2004.

Exhibit 4   STATEMENT OF SMITHFIELD FOODS' MANAGEMENT REGARDING THE COMPANY'S STRATEGY FOR RESPONSIBLE GROWTH

Over the past few years, our company has set the foundations for continuous improvement in our stewardship responsibilities, which include our environmental, employee safety and animal welfare–related performance. We have firmly established the necessary policies, organizations, management systems, programs, funding, and expertise.

This foundation is now in place within the majority of our U.S. operations. We continue to move forward guided by the principles of accountability, transparency, and sustainability, and by our primary objectives:

- Achieve 100 percent regulatory compliance, 100 percent of the time.
- Move well beyond compliance in stewardship responsibilities.
- Reduce the frequency and severity of injuries to employees.
- Enhance communications and transparency with external stakeholders.
- Continue to expand community involvement.

We also have a more ambitious vision, and that is to be recognized as the industry leader for stewardship. To do this, we will continue to explore approaches to the issues that are unique to our industry. We will continue to find ways to participate productively in key industry and multi-stakeholder groups where we can help facilitate win–win solutions. We will share our experiences and best practices with our peers and other interested parties. We will also work toward policy changes that promote industry innovation and enable our company to better deliver financial, environmental, and social value.

In 2003, Smithfield embarked on a major project, committing to invest $20 million to implement technology beneficial to the environment and that will also play a key role in the solution for our global energy needs. We are using the untapped energy stored in livestock waste to create a fully renewable motor fuel—biodiesel. Our renewable fuel project at Circle Four Farms in Utah will produce in excess of 7,000 gallons of biomethanol per day. Blended with rendered fats, this biomethanol is converted to biodiesel that would meet the daily fuel requirements for about 300 over-the-road trucks, offsetting the need to import crude oil to produce that quantity of traditional diesel fuel. The project is highlighted in more detail in other sections of this report and is expected to be in full operation in late spring 2004.

We are very encouraged by the results we have seen over the past few years. Moving forward, Smithfield's strategy for responsible growth can be summed up as follows: more of the same. And by that we mean more management systems, more measurement and target setting, more innovative thinking and partnering, further support of environmentally superior waste management technologies, more communication, transparency and relationship building, more improvement—and more listening. This is what Smithfield will strive to accomplish.

Source: Smithfield Foods, *2003 Stewardship Report*, pp. 11–12.

environmental policy statement. Exhibit 4 presents senior management's statement regarding the company's "Strategy for Responsible Growth." Exhibit 5 presents excerpts from the company's Code of Business Conduct.

During the spring of 2003, the highest seasonal rainfall in North Carolina's recorded history caused elevated lagoon levels at many eastern North Carolina hog

Exhibit 5   EXCERPTS FROM SMITHFIELD FOODS' CODE OF BUSINESS CONDUCT, 2004

Smithfield is committed to compliance with the laws, rules, and regulations applicable to the conduct of our business wherever we operate. Our ultimate goal is 100% compliance, 100% of the time. Employees must avoid activities that could involve or lead to involvement of Smithfield or its personnel in any unlawful practice.

Employee awareness of Smithfield operating practices must include knowledge of the environmental laws and Smithfield policies governing their operations. Employees must immediately control and report all spills and releases as required by applicable regulations and facility rules.

The nature of Smithfield's business requires it to conduct various monitoring, inspecting, and testing to ensure compliance with applicable laws and regulations. Such monitoring, inspecting, and testing must be performed, and accurate records thereof made and retained, in compliance with all applicable legal requirements. Employees who have questions about legal requirements applicable to such areas should consult their supervisor or a member of the Smithfield Law Department.

Smithfield employees are expected to comply with all federal, state, local, and foreign environmental laws and all Smithfield policies related to environmental affairs. We expect 100% compliance 100% of the time. It is each employee's responsibility to know and understand the legal, policy, and operating practice requirements applicable to his or her job and to notify management when the employee believes that a violation of law or Smithfield policies has occurred. Any employee who has concerns regarding compliance in this area should immediately consult with the environmental contact for his or her facility or subsidiary, a senior environmental officer, or the Smithfield Law Department. The Smithfield Foods, Inc. Employee Hotline (1-877-237-5270) is available for reporting employee concerns anonymously.

Compliance with environmental laws and all Smithfield policies is the single highest priority for the company's environmental program. Our employees' job performance is important to us, and is evaluated not only on business results achieved, but also on whether our employees, and particularly our management team, operate within our expectations for environmental performance. We hold all of our employees to a high standard of conduct and accountability for environmental performance.

Compliance with the Smithfield Foods, Inc., Code of Business Conduct and Ethics is a condition of employment. Failure to comply may result in a range of disciplinary actions, including termination. Failure by any Smithfield employee to disclose violations of these standards and practices by other Smithfield employees or contract workers is also grounds for disciplinary action.

Source: Smithfield Foods' Code of Business Conduct, accessed at www.smithfieldfoods.com November 23, 2004.

farms. Farmers reported the levels to the state agency, as was the standard practice, but officials at North Carolina's Department of Environment and Natural Resources nonetheless sent out hundreds of notices of violations (NOVs), 55 of which were to farms operated by Smithfield's Murphy-Brown subsidiary. While elevated lagoon levels did not compromise the structural integrity of the lagoons, they did decrease the reserve designated for storage of rainfall accumulated over a 24-hour period from intense storms. Many farmers and legislative leaders protested the number of NOVs issued, prompting the Department of Environment and Natural Resources to reconsider their having issued so many NOVs; a substantial number were subsequently reclassified as notices of deficiency (NODs). Following the severe weather, Smithfield moved swiftly to get its lagoon levels back to compliance levels and no further regulatory actions were taken. All told, Smithfield received 77 notices of violations or noncompliance in 2003, resulting in fines of $124,204. The biggest fine ($77,000) was for a wastewater incident at its Moyer beef processing plant in Pennsylvania, and a $17,875 fine was imposed for an ammonia release at a Georgia plant.

Endnotes

[1]Quoted in the five-part series by Joby Warrick and Pat Stith, "Boss Hog: North Carolina's Pork Revolution—Hog Waste Is Polluting the Ground Water," *Raleigh News and Observer,* February 19, 1995. This series, based on a seven-month investigation and run in the *News and Observer,* February 19–26, 1995, was awarded the Pulitzer Prize for Public Service Journalism in 1996.

[2]Ibid.

[3]Ibid.

[4]Charlie LeDuff, "At a Slaughterhouse, Some Things Never Die," *New York Times,* June 16, 2000, p. A1.

[5]*Raleigh News and Observer,* February 19, 1995.

[6]Joby Warrick and Pat Stith, "Boss Hog: North Carolina's Pork Revolution—Money Talks," *Raleigh News and Observer,* February 24, 1995, p. A9.

[7]Ibid.

[8]Ibid.

[9]Ibid.

[10]Joby Warrick and Pat Stith, "Boss Hog: North Carolina's Pork Revolution—Pork Barrels," *Raleigh News and Observer,* February 26, 1995.

[11]*Raleigh News and Observer,* March 4, 1995, p. A10.

Merck and the Recall of Vioxx

Arthur A. Thompson
The University of Alabama

On September 30, 2004, officials at Merck & Company, Inc., the sixth largest pharmaceutical firm in the United States and a respected blue-chip company, announced that Merck was withdrawing its pain reliever Vioxx from the market because a new study indicated that the drug doubled the risks of heart attacks and strokes in patients taking it longer than 18 months. Merck's stock immediately plunged 27 percent and continued to fall further in upcoming weeks, in response to the $2.5 billion annual revenue loss from Merck's second best-selling drug and a rapidly mounting potential for costly lawsuits. An estimated 20 million Americans and another 60 million people in 80 foreign countries had taken Vioxx, primarily for relief of arthritis and acute pain, since it had been introduced in May 1999. Merck estimated that 105 million U.S. prescriptions were written for Vioxx from May 1999 through August 2004. An estimated 2 million people in the United States were taking Vioxx at the time of the recall.

As early as 2000, there had been warning signs of problems with Vioxx. Prior to the recall, roughly 30 lawsuits alleging that Vioxx was unsafe and had caused patients to suffer heart attacks and strokes, some resulting in death, had been filed in state and federal courts. In the weeks following the recall, the number of lawsuits multiplied quickly, reaching close to 700 by some counts. Some of these were class-action suits filed by high-profile trial lawyers on behalf of all potential claimants. Wall Street analysts estimated that Merck's legal costs associated with the Vioxx claims could range as high as $18 billion over the next decade.

As of 2004, the largest drug-product liability case on record involved Wyeth's recall of weight-loss remedies Redux and Pondimin in 1997, which contained a compound known as fen-phen and were estimated to cause heart-valve damage in as many as 30 percent of the people who took the pills. Some 6 million Americans had taken Redux or Pondimin; Wyeth's payouts to date had exceeded $13 billion of the $16.6 billion in reserves that the company had set aside to cover settlement costs.

Five weeks after the Vioxx recall, Standard & Poor's (S&P), which had placed a triple-A rating on Merck's debt since 1975, announced that it had put Merck's ratings on its watch list. Merck was one of only seven companies outside the financial services industry that had a triple-A S&P debt rating. The week following S&P's credit watch announcement, Moody's Investors Service lowered the rating of Merck's long-term debt two notches, to Aa2 from Aaa (its highest rating), and said it was keeping Merck's rating under review for a possible further downgrade. Moody's cited the loss in revenues and Merck's Vioxx litigation exposure as reasons for the downgrade. The Moody's downgrade and the threat of an S&P downgrade had little immediate impact on Merck—the company had $7 billion in cash and short-term investments and $10 billion in current assets to apply against its current liabilities of $2.2 billion and long-term debt of only $4.4 billion at the time of the recall, putting it in a position of strong liquidity. Nonetheless, the actions of the two credit rating agencies signaled concerns about the extent to which legal settlements would sap the company's financial resources down the road.

Moreover, the company's reputation as the gold standard of the pharmaceutical industry and one of the bluest of the blue-chip companies took a huge hit as the circumstances surrounding the recall came to light over the next several months. Internal e-mails, training aids sent to Merck salespeople, and pressures that Merck put on outside medical experts suggested that Merck personnel knew of or at least suspected Vioxx's dangers well before the recall. A front-page *Wall Street Journal* story on November 1, 2004, was headlined "E-Mails Suggest Merck Knew Vioxx's Dangers at Early Stage."

Merck's Situation in 2004

In 2004, Merck & Company, Inc., was a global research-driven company with annual sales of $22.5 billion; profits of $6.8 billion; 59,000 employees; 12 major drug research centers in the United States, Canada, Europe, and Japan; 32 manufacturing facilities; and a broad range of human and animal heath care products marketed in 150 countries. Exhibit 1 shows the company's mission and core values.

Merck's Strategy

For the past 10 years or so, Merck's strategy had been to concentrate its considerable scientific and research expertise on developing blockbuster new drugs. The research-grounded strategy had three core elements:

■ Develop a core competence in drug research by supporting the efforts of the best and brightest scientists and medical researchers Merck could assemble.

■ Do very thorough clinical studies of promising drugs discovered in Merck's research labs to determine their effectiveness on patients and to explore the nature and extent of side effects.

■ Seek to gain speedy regulatory approval of newly discovered medicines by using the results of the previously done research and clinical studies to thoroughly document the benefits and safety of the drugs submitted for approval. Rapid approval to market new drugs could produce a significant competitive edge by not only allowing Merck to get its drug discoveries into the marketplace ahead of rivals but also giving it more time to sell the drug before patent expirations.

Merck's resource strengths in executing this strategy over the years had been a major factor in the company's success and in developing and fortifying what had come to be a storied reputation for first-rate scientific research and for having the best research personnel and research capabilities in the business. During the past two decades,

Exhibit 1   MERCK'S MISSION AND CORE VALUES, 2004

OUR MISSION

The mission of **Merck** is to provide society with superior products and services by developing innovations and solutions that improve the quality of life and satisfy customer needs, and to provide employees with meaningful work and advancement opportunities, and investors with a superior rate of return.

OUR VALUES

1. **Our business is preserving and improving human life.** All of our actions must be measured by our success in achieving this goal. We value, above all, our ability to serve everyone who can benefit from the appropriate use of our products and services, thereby providing lasting consumer satisfaction.

2. **We are committed to the highest standards of ethics and integrity.** We are responsible to our customers, to Merck employees and their families, to the environments we inhabit, and to the societies we serve worldwide. In discharging our responsibilities, we do not take professional or ethical shortcuts. Our interactions with all segments of society must reflect the high standards we profess.

3. **We are dedicated to the highest level of scientific excellence and commit our <u>research</u> to improving human and animal health and the quality of life.** We strive to identify the most critical needs of consumers and customers, and we devote our resources to meeting those needs.

4. **We expect profits, but only from work that satisfies customer needs and benefits humanity.** Our ability to meet our responsibilities depends on maintaining a financial position that invites investment in leading-edge research and that makes possible effective delivery of research results.

5. **We recognize that the ability to excel—to most competitively meet society's and customers' needs—depends on the integrity, knowledge, imagination, skill, diversity and teamwork of our employees, and we value these qualities most highly.** To this end, we strive to create an environment of mutual respect, encouragement and teamwork—an environment that rewards commitment and performance and is responsive to the needs of our employees and their families.

Source: www.merck.com (accessed November 29, 2004).

Merck personnel had published more scientific papers than personnel at any other drug company, and Merck had patented more compounds than any of its competitors.[1] And the company's track record in getting new drugs approved expeditiously was excellent in comparison to other pharmaceutical manufacturers.

The central figure in executing Merck's research-based drug discovery strategy was Edward M. Scolnick, a graduate of Harvard Medical School who had published roughly 200 scientific papers and risen through the ranks at Merck to become its chief of research. Scolnick was reputed to have a superior intellect, and his persistent drive for research excellence permeated Merck's research activities. According to a former Merck cancer researcher, "You never went before him unprepared. He would begin probing very directly and very quickly. He would often identify some controlled experiment that should have been done and wasn't."[2] For at least a decade before he retired in 2003, Scolnick was considered the de facto number two person at Merck (after CEO Raymond V. Gilmartin).[3] Scolnick was appointed to Merck's board of directors in 1997; he was the only inside executive on Merck's board besides the CEO. Merck's newest research lab, dedicated in October 2004—a multimillion-dollar building in Boston not far from Harvard Medical School—was named for Scolnick.

Under Scolnick's drug research leadership, Merck had racked up dazzling successes. Zocor, a cholesterol-reducing drug introduced in the early 1990s, soon became

Exhibit 2   MERCK'S SALES BY DRUG CATEGORY, 2001–2003
(in millions)

Drug Category	2003	2002	2001
Atherosclerosis	$ 5,077.9	$ 5,552.1	$ 5,433.3
Hypertension/heart failure	3,421.6	3,477.8	3,584.3
Anti-inflammatory/analgesics (includes Vioxx)	2,677.3	2,587.2	2,391.1
Osteoporosis	2,676.6	2,243.1	1,629.7
Respiratory	2,009.4	1,489.8	1,260.3
Vaccines/biologicals	1,056.1	1,028.3	1,022.5
Antibacterial/antifungal	1,028.5	821.0	750.4
Ophthalmologicals	675.1	621.5	644.5
Urology	605.5	547.3	545.4
Human immunodeficiency virus (HIV)	290.6	294.3	380.8
Other	2,967.3	2,783.4	3,556.7
Total	$22,485.9	$21,445.8	$21,199.0

Source: Merck, 2003 10K report.

the market-leading prescription for lowering cholesterol and Merck's best-selling drug. Zocor had annual sales in 2003 of $5 billion. During the 1995–2001 period, Merck won approval from the U.S. Federal Drug Administration (FDA) for 15 new drugs, many of which became big market successes—Singulair (asthma), Fosamax (osteoporosis), Cozarr and Hyzarr (hypertension), Procepia (baldness), Vioxx (arthritis and pain relief), and Crixivan (HIV). These successful new drug introductions helped drive Merck's stock price to an all-time high of $95 per share in the fall of 2000. A breakdown of Merck's drug sales by category is shown in Exhibit 2.

But just as important to Merck's strategic success as a research-based drug-discovery organization was Scolnick's oversight of the process of gaining regulatory approval to introduce new drugs and the resulting competitive edge that accrued to Merck. The research-and-approval process for new drugs was known for being risky and tedious, both because of the need to conduct lengthy and convincing studies of drug effectiveness and safety (a high proportion of chemical compounds under investigation never survived this step) and because regulatory approval was rife with bureaucracy and sometimes contentious review procedures that could take several years. Scolnick's approach to dealing with the regulatory approval process was for Merck to submit fastidious supporting documentation for the new drugs it asked the FDA to approve, an approach that had worked well for Merck.

During the 1995–2001 period, Merck's vaunted scientific reputation, high-caliber clinical studies, and solid supporting documentation allowed the company to gain approval for all 13 new drugs it submitted to the FDA, with an average review time of 11 months. Vioxx won approval following a six-month review.[4] At Pfizer, the world's largest pharmaceutical firm in 2004, the new drug submissions during the same period had an average review time of two years. Analysts at Merrill Lynch estimated that Merck's drug research documentation capabilities and short approval times allowed the company to achieve extra sales of $3.3 billion during 1995–2001.[5]

Merck's Record of Corporate Social Responsibility and Good Citizenship

Merck was strongly committed to being a solid corporate citizen and conducting its business in an ethical manner. This commitment had long been guided by the vision of the company's modern-day founder, George W. Merck, who said in 1950:

> We try never to forget that medicine is for the people. It is not for the profits. The profits follow, and if we have remembered that, they have never failed to appear.
>
> We cannot step aside and say that we have achieved our goal by inventing a new drug or a new way by which to treat presently incurable diseases, a new way to help those who suffer from malnutrition, or the creation of ideal balanced diets on a worldwide scale. We cannot rest till the way has been found, with our help, to bring our finest achievement to everyone.[6]

The two chief components of Merck's social responsibility strategy were charitable contributions and its actions to further the cause of public health by making its drugs more widely available. In 2003, Merck's philanthropic contributions totaled $843 million, consisting of cash contributions ($54 million), its patient assistance program ($393 million), and product donations ($396 million). Exhibit 3 shows Merck's recent record of charitable contributions.

Exhibit 3   Merck's Corporate Philanthropy Contributions, 1998–2003

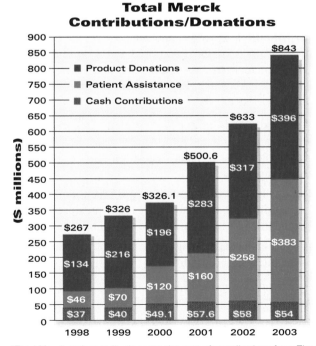

*Total Merck cash contributions are the sum of contributions from The Merck Company Foundation, Merck & Co., Inc., and Merck Genome Research Institute.

Source: www.merck.com, accessed November 30, 2004.

Merck's efforts to live up to its commitment to make its drugs available to everyone are demonstrated in the following four examples of actions that the company had recently taken:[7]

1. Merck announced in February 2004 that the company would provide its medicines free for low-income Medicare beneficiaries who exhaust their $600 transitional assistance allowance in Medicare-endorsed drug discount cards. This action was consistent with Merck's long-standing Patient Assistance Program, which provided free medicine to patients who lacked drug coverage and could not afford Merck's drugs.

2. Since 1987, Merck had donated more than 300 million doses of its Mectizan drug to treat people in developing and third world countries who were suffering from onchocerciasis, a ravaging disease more commonly known as river blindness. Mectizan was a highly effective medicine that not only controlled and prevented river blindness but also helped limit the agonizing and disfiguring skin infections caused by the disease. The Mectizan Donation Program, a public/private partnership regarded as one of the world's most successful global health care collaborations, and funded in part by Merck, had long worked to improve the lives and prevent blindness for millions of people in Africa, Latin America, and Yemen. In 2004, doses of Mectizan reached more than 40 million people in 34 countries.

3. In poor African countries that had been hard hit by the AIDS epidemic, Merck had arranged to provide two of its HIV-fighting drugs, Stocrin and Crixivan, at prices at which it made no profit. Merck had also granted a royalty-free license to a South African pharmaceutical company to manufacture and sell a generic version of its HIV/AIDS drug Efavirenz.

4. In 2003, Merck launched the Merck Vaccine Network–Africa, an initiative designed to contribute to improving the immunization infrastructure in Africa. Merck's initiative involved funding the establishment of a network of vaccination training centers at academic institutions in Kenya and Mali to provide a sustainable source of skilled health care workers in those countries and across the region. Africa had the highest per capita incidence of vaccine-preventable diseases in the world, with only half of all children in sub-Saharan Africa getting basic life-saving vaccinations during their first year of life.

In 1999 Merck developed a lengthy code of conduct entitled "Our Values and Standards: The Basis of Our Success" and distributed it to Merck employees. The company's Web site postings, in elaborating on the company's core values (see Exhibit 1) and the conduct expected of Merck employees, said:

■ Every Merck employee is responsible for adhering to business practices that are in accordance with the letter and spirit of the applicable laws and with ethical principles that reflect the highest standards of corporate and individual behavior.

■ Improper behavior cannot be rationalized as being in the company's interest. No act of impropriety advances the interest of the Company.

In May 2004, *Business Ethics* magazine named Merck one of its "100 Best Corporate Citizens" for the fifth consecutive year. Merck, ranked 48, was the only pharmaceutical company to gain a spot on the list in each of the five years that *Business Ethics* had published it and was also one of only two pharmaceutical companies to make the list.

Merck's Troubles in 2004 Prior to the Vioxx Recall

Since 2001, Merck had been struggling to maintain its earlier momentum of growing sales via a stream of new product introductions. None of its recently introduced drugs had generated annual sales of $1 billion or more. During the 1999–2001 period, Merck had lost its patent protection on five of its best-selling drugs—Vasotec (hypertension), Pepcid (ulcers), Mevacor (cholesterol), Prilosec (ulcers), and Prinivil (hypertension). The company's market-leading treatment for high cholesterol, Zocor, which generated annual sales revenues of about $5 billion, was coming off patent in 2006 and, like most other drugs without patent protection, was expected to experience sharp sales erosion when lower-priced generic imitations came onto the market. In 2003, Merck had to cancel work on four major new drugs, which were in big, costly Phase III trials. All four were thought to have real promise and had been touted by management as having major revenue potential. One of the four drugs, for depression, failed a pivotal clinical trial, and a second, for diabetes, was found in animal studies to pose a risk of cancer.

As a consequence, Merck's sales had flattened (Exhibit 2) and its net profits had eroded from the all-time peak of $7.3 billion and earnings per share (EPS) of $3.14 in 2001 to $6.8 billion and an EPS of $3.03 in 2003. Investors were fully aware of Merck's struggling condition—the company's stock price, after having risen 475 percent from 1994 to its all-time high of $95 per share in the fall of 2000, had trended downward and was trading at around $45 per share in the weeks prior to the Vioxx recall. Shareholders were restless, having suffered a loss in market capitalization of over $130 billion during the past four years. While Merck still had a number of new products in the pipeline that it expected to be able to release in upcoming years—treatments for diabetes, shingles, and assorted viruses—most analysts did not believe the new drugs had the sales potential to overcome the anticipated falloff of Zocor's sales in 2006–2007.

However, Merck was not alone in its struggle to discover and introduce new blockbuster drugs; virtually the whole pharmaceutical industry worldwide was finding the discovery of new drugs with big sales potential tough sledding. New drugs in the pipeline at a number of major pharmaceutical companies were disturbingly low from the standpoint of boosting future revenue growth and profitability—a condition that had already prompted several large mergers and acquisitions (to try to gain better scale economies in research), as well as strategy changes. New strategy elements already in place at Merck involved cost reduction, partnering with small innovative companies on new drug discovery, and licensing promising compounds.

Events at Merck Leading Up to the Introduction of Vioxx

Vioxx was the last of Merck's multibillion-dollar drugs under Scolnick's leadership. Discovered in laboratory experiments by Merck researchers in 1994, the drug was one of a new class of painkillers, called Cox-2 inhibitors, that reduced pain and inflammation without such side effects as ulcers and gastrointestinal bleeding. Some people had experienced such side effects while taking daily doses of aspirin, ibuprofen (the painkiller in Advil and Motrin), and naproxen (the painkiller in Aleve) for chronic pain relief. Pain relievers containing aspirin, ibuprofen, and naproxen were designated nonsteroidal anti-inflammatory drugs (NSAIDs). By some estimates, intestinal bleeding associated with long-term use of NSAIDs was responsible for the deaths of 10,000 Americans annually.

Internal e-mails at Merck indicated that the company was well aware that Vioxx had limited market potential unless it could gain acceptance in the mass market for painkillers and be preferred to cheap over-the-counter NSAIDs. A November 1996 memo by a Merck official indicated that company personnel were wrestling with this marketing dilemma.[8] There was discussion of conducting a trial to demonstrate that Vioxx was gentler on the stomach than over-the-counter painkillers. To show the difference, takers of Vioxx could not take any aspirin, which some arthritis patients took because of its blood-thinning and cardio-protective benefits. But the necessity of excluding aspirin raised concerns at Merck. The author of the memo noted that "there is a substantial chance that significantly higher rates" of cardiovascular problems would occur in the group taking only Vioxx. A February 1997 e-mail by another Merck official said that unless patients in the Vioxx group also took aspirin "you will get more thrombotic events and kill the drug."[9] In response, a Merck vice president for clinical research indicated the company was in a "no-win situation" because giving study subjects both Vioxx and aspirin could result in gastrointestinal problems and not giving them aspirin raised "the possibility of increased CV [cardiovascular] events."[10]

It is not clear what came out of the discussion Merck officials had about the study in 1996–1997.[11] But in early 1999, around the time that Merck won FDA approval to market Vioxx, Merck began an 8,000-person clinical trial that compared people taking a high dose of Vioxx against those taking naproxen. The patients taking Vioxx were not allowed to take aspirin.

In 1998 medical researchers at the University of Pennsylvania reported findings that Cox-2 inhibitors *might* interfere with enzymes thought to play key roles in warding off cardiovascular disease; the findings were communicated to the companies developing Cox-2 inhibitors and were also published.[12] In Merck's first round of clinical trials, patients taking Vioxx had about the same rate of heart attacks and strokes as did patients who took NSAIDs or a sugar placebo. An unpublished 1998 Merck clinical trial called "Study 090," which involved 978 patients, showed that serious cardiovascular events, including heart attack and stroke, occurred about six times more often in patients taking Vioxx than in patients taking another arthritis drug or a placebo.[13] Merck said that study was too small and the results were not statistically significant enough to allow the company to draw any conclusions.

Merck's application to the FDA for Vioxx approval in November 1998 included data on approximately 5,400 osteoarthritis patients who participated in eight studies. In these studies, there were similar rates of thrombotic cardiovascular adverse events with Vioxx, placebos, and three NSAIDs (ibuprofen, diclofenac, and nabumetone). After a six-month review, Vioxx gained FDA approval on May 21, 1999, despite apparent reservations on the part of some reviewers about its possible blood vessel effects.

But the studies of Vioxx reportedly did not establish that it was a more effective painkiller than NSAIDs. The real selling proposition for Vioxx—and the main basis for its approval by the FDA—was simply a lower incidence of stomach bleeding and gastrointestinal problems, as compared to conventional pain relievers like aspirin, Tylenol, Aleve, Advil, and other over-the-counter remedies (which cost about five cents a pill versus several dollars a pill for Vioxx).[14] Thus, the chief basis for Vioxx's approval by the FDA rested mainly on its relevance for the estimated 15 percent of arthritis sufferers who could not take over-the-counter pain relievers on a sustained basis because of the resulting gastrointestinal side effects.[15]

Merck's Direct-to-Consumer Marketing Campaign for Vioxx

When Vioxx won FDA approval in 1999, Merck's marketing strategy included sales pitches to doctors about the drug's benefits (along with the usual free samples they could try out on patients) and an aggressive direct-to-consumer advertising campaign. The cover of Merck's 1999 annual report headlined that Vioxx was the company's "biggest, fastest, and best launch ever." In the five or so years that arthritis pain reliever Vioxx was on the market, Merck spent roughly $100 million annually for television, newspaper, and magazine ads touting Vioxx's benefits and appealing to pain suffers to ask their doctor about Vioxx.[16] Sales of Vioxx climbed steadily from 1999 to 2004, and the drug became a $2.5 billion annual revenue source for Merck. It was the second best-selling Cox-2 inhibitor when it was pulled from the market, trailing only Celebrex, which had $3 billion in annual sales. Pfizer had become the marketer of Celebrex when it acquired rival drugmaker Pharmacia in 2003.

Vioxx was one among many blockbuster drugs that had benefited from direct-to-consumer advertising opportunities that opened up in 1997 when, during the Clinton administration, the FDA loosened regulations on how pharmaceutical companies could advertise to a general audience. Since then, drugs that were originally meant to treat specific medical problems had become used in far broader populations—partly because doctors had been willing to prescribe them when requested by patients (who presumably were intrigued by the newly allowed ads for prescription drugs) and partly because the costs of such prescriptions were paid for by patients' health insurance programs. A study by Bruce Stuart at the University of Maryland showed that the biggest determinant of whether a patient took a prescription Cox-2 inhibitor or a far cheaper over-the-counter pain reliever like Aleve, Motrin, or Advil was whether the patient had health insurance that would cover much of the prescription costs.[17]

Warning Signs of Trouble Prior to the Recall

In March 2000, Merck found surprising results from an 8,000-person clinical trial it had initiated in early 1999 to see if Vioxx posed fewer gastrointestinal risks than NSAIDs. The trial showed that arthritis patients taking Vioxx had more than two times as many serious cardiovascular events as those on naproxen, an NSAID sold under the Aleve brand, among other brand names (see Exhibit 4). A total of 45 serious cardiovascular

Exhibit 4   SUMMARY RESULTS OF VIOXX–NAPROXEN STUDY IN 2000

	People Taking Vioxx	People Taking Naproxen
Total number of people in clinical trial	4,047	4,029
Number of adverse cardiovascular events	101	46
Number of digestive system adverse events	48	97

Source: FDA's analysis of the clinical trial results, as reported in Anna Wilde Mathews and Barbara Martinez, "E-Mails Suggest Merck Knew Vioxx's Dangers at Early Stage," *Wall Street Journal*, November 1, 2004, p. A10.

thrombotic events occurred among the 4,047 patients taking Vioxx, whereas only 19 had occurred among the 4,029 patients taking naproxen. According to Merck, the higher number was largely due to a difference in the incidence of *nonfatal* heart attacks: 18 for Vioxx and 4 for naproxen. The number of *fatal* cardiovascular thrombotic events was similar in patients treated with Vioxx ($n = 7$) compared to naproxen ($n = 6$). Deeper analysis, however, showed that the heart-attack rate in the Vioxx group appeared to be four times as high as the naproxen group. Something akin to these results had been seemingly anticipated in the 1996–1997 memos and e-mails.

In a March 9, 2000, e-mail with the subject line "Vigor"—the name Merck gave to the Vioxx–naproxen clinical trial—Merck's chief of research, Ed Scolnick, wrote that the results showed that the cardiovascular events "are clearly there. It is a shame but it is a low incidence and it is mechanism based as we worried it was." He compared Vioxx to other drugs with known side effects, writing, "There is always a hazard."[18] Scolnick went on to say that he wanted other data available before the Vioxx–naproxen results were made public, so that it would be "clear to the world" that hazard was a characteristic of all Cox-2 inhibitors, not just Vioxx.[19]

Medical experts outside Merck who were familiar with the Vioxx–naproxen study hypothesized that the results raised valid concerns that Vioxx could indeed be causing cardiac problems. Merck took the position that the differential risks could be attributable to the added side benefits of taking naproxen rather than to problems with Vioxx. Merck personnel reportedly believed that known properties of naproxen were responsible for the differential. Nonetheless, Merck immediately put out a press release describing the Vioxx–naproxen results and informed the FDA.

But, for unknown reasons, it was not until February 8, 2001, that the FDA Arthritis Advisory Committee met to discuss concerns about the potential cardiovascular risks associated with Vioxx. On May 22, 2001, a little over three months after the FDA advisory committee meeting, Merck issued a press release entitled "Merck Reconfirms Favorable Cardiovascular Safety of Vioxx"; this effort to address doubts about Vioxx was complemented by numerous papers in peer-reviewed medical literature by Merck employees and their consultants.[20] The company sponsored continuing medical "education" symposiums at national meetings in an effort to temper concerns about the adverse cardiovascular effects of Vioxx.[21] The essence of Merck's message was that Vioxx had no cardiovascular toxicity but, rather, naproxen was cardio-protective. (The FDA, however, has said there is no conclusive evidence that naproxen protects the heart.)[22] In response to Merck's pro-Vioxx campaign, the FDA sent an eight-page warning letter to the company in September 2001 saying that sales representatives "have engaged in false or misleading promotional activities," and that the company's promotional campaign "minimizes the potentially serious cardiovascular findings" about Vioxx and "discounts the fact [that] patients on Vioxx were observed to have a four to five-fold increase" in heart attacks, compared with patients on naproxen.[23]

But it was not until two years later, in April 2002, that the FDA instructed Merck to include certain precautions about cardiovascular risks in its package insert. At about the same time, the FDA also decided to go a step further and do its own follow-up study of Vioxx safety, opting to sponsor a study of the medical records of 1.4 million patients insured by Kaiser Permanente, the nation's largest nonprofit health maintenance organization (HMO), serving 8.2 million members in nine states and the District of Columbia.

In November 2000, the results of the Vioxx–naproxen study were published in the *New England Journal of Medicine;* the article was co-authored by Merck employees and by academics who had received consulting contracts or research grants from Merck. But the Vioxx–naproxen trial also spurred Merck to do further clinical studies on the possible links between Vioxx and heart trouble. Shortly after learning of the Vioxx–naproxen cardiovascular differential, Merck embarked on a long-term study called APPROVe to see whether Vioxx would lead to a reduction of colon polyps (which if shown to be the case would give doctors another reason to prescribe Vioxx). APPROVe, which involved 2,600 patients, was a true controlled trial that compared Vioxx with a placebo instead of another drug, thereby providing a more definitive test of whether Vioxx increased blood vessel risk.

Merck's "Dodge Ball Vioxx" Training Document

To help its sales personnel deal with questions doctors were asking about Vioxx's safety, Merck developed a sales aid entitled "Dodge Ball Vioxx." The 16-page document, addressed to "all field personnel" was intended as an "obstacle handling guide"; each of the first 12 pages listed one "obstacle" or concern that doctors might have about Vioxx, such as "I am concerned about the cardiovascular effects of Vioxx" and "The competition has been in my office telling me the incidence of heart attacks is greater with Vioxx than Celebrex."[24] Suggested responses for each obstacle were provided. The final four pages each contained a single word in capital letters: DODGE.[25] A former Merck sales representative told *60 Minutes* that when a doctor expressed concerns about the cardiovascular effects of Vioxx, "We were supposed to tell the physician that Vioxx did not cause cardiovascular events, that instead, in the studies, naproxen has aspirin-like characteristics which made naproxen a heart-protecting type of drug where Vioxx did not have that heart-protecting side."[26]

Merck's Offensive to Combat the Concerns of Academic Researchers about Vioxx's Safety

In 2000–2001, Merck took actions to combat the concerns of several academic researchers who were openly questioning the safety of Vioxx. A Stanford University professor who regularly gave prescription drug-related lectures sponsored by Merck and other drug companies pressed Merck for additional data about Vioxx.[27] When Merck failed to provide it, the professor added a slide to his lectures showing a man (representing the missing data) hiding under a blanket. Merck then canceled its sponsorship of several lectures by the professor, and a Merck official called Stanford Medical School, complaining that the professor's presentations were "irresponsibly anti-Merck and specifically anti-Vioxx." The Merck official suggested that if the lectures continued, the professor would "flame out" and there would be consequences for Stanford (presumably in the form of fewer Merck-sponsored research grants).

A professor at the University of Minnesota who had given Merck-sponsored lectures also got a call from Merck complaining about what was being said about Vioxx, as did a rheumatologist at Beth Israel Deaconess Medical Center in Boston who had worked on research with rival Celebrex but who had also worked with Merck on occasion. In the summer of 2002, a professor at the Catalan Institute of Pharmacology in Barcelona, Spain, edited a publication that repeated criticisms of Merck's handling of

Vioxx that had been published in *The Lancet,* a respected British medical journal.[28] Merck approached the professor on three occasions to print a Merck-authored rebuttal. When the professor refused, Merck sued the professor and the Catalan Institute under a Spanish law that allowed plaintiffs to demand a public correction of inaccurate published information. In January 2004, the judge ruled in favor of the defendants and ordered Merck to pay the court costs. In March 2004, the professor was asked to give a featured presentation to a conference of 1,000 Spanish family physicians—a conference that Merck had helped sponsor for eight straight years. When Merck learned of the invitation, it called the conference organizer and indicated that it "preferred" that the professor not be on the program. When the organizer refused to delete the professor's presentation, Merck withdrew its $140,000 funding for the conference.[29]

Other External Warning Signs of Trouble with Vioxx

While Merck's multiyear APPROVe study was under way, several developments outside Merck further signaled there might be cardiovascular problems with Vioxx:

- An article by three medical researchers, published in the *Journal of the American Medical Association* on August 22, 2001, reviewed four studies with a total of about 18,000 patients and concluded that "the available data raise a cautionary flag about the risk of cardiovascular events with Cox-2 inhibitors."[30] One of the researchers communicated the results of the study to Merck's CEO, Ray Gilmartin, offering to visit Merck and present their findings. Neither Gilmartin nor anyone else at Merck responded to the researcher's phone calls. Merck reportedly asked the *New England Journal of Medicine* to run a Merck-authored rebuttal, but the journal editors refused.[31]

- *The Wall Street Journal* ran a front-page story on the heart risks of Vioxx and other Cox-2 inhibitor drugs on August 22, 2001, citing the concerns of several medical researchers and the Vioxx–naproxen results.

- The National Trial Lawyers Guild formed a "Cox-2 litigation group" in early 2002 and at their national convention in 2003 devoted a session to Vioxx.

- Before the Vioxx recall, more than 400 lawsuits had been filed on behalf of Vioxx patients.[32]

- A Merck-sponsored analysis, conducted by researchers at Harvard and Merck, found that Vioxx was "associated with an elevated relative risk" of heart attacks compared to the use of Pfizer's painkiller Celebrex or no similar painkiller. When Merck asked the researchers to tone down the conclusion about the no-painkiller group and the Harvard researcher refused, Merck removed the name of the Merck researcher prior to the article's publication in *Circulation* in May 2004.[33]

- A book published in the summer of 2004 by John Abramson, a family doctor and clinical instructor at Harvard Medical School, concluded that even people who did not have a history of heart problems doubled their risk of developing a cardiovascular problem by taking Vioxx instead of naproxen.[34]

All of these developments served to switch the debate on Vioxx from whether it lacked some of the cardiac-related benefits of NSAIDs to whether it was inherently risky from a cardiac-stroke perspective.

Meanwhile, in the summer of 2004, the earlier study of the medical records of 1.4 million people insured by Kaiser Permanente was producing important findings. The study, financed by the FDA and conducted by David J. Graham, associate director for science and medicine in the FDA's Office of Drug Safety, compared the outcomes of 40,405 patients who took Celebrex and 26,748 patients who took Vioxx. The results, which were reported at a conference in France on August 25, 2004, showed two significant facts:

- Patients taking the typical starting dose of Vioxx had a 50 percent greater chance of heart attacks and sudden cardiac death than patients taking Celebrex.

- Patients taking the highest recommended daily dosage of Vioxx had nearly 2.7 times the risk of heart attack and sudden cardiac death as patients taking Celebrex.

Merck issued a press release saying it strongly disagreed with the FDA study's conclusions.[35]

The Recall Decision

On Thursday afternoon, September 23, 2004, almost four and a half years after the AP-PROVe study began, Peter Kim, who had taken over as Merck's chief of research when Scolnick retired, met with Ray Gilmartin to inform him that the results of the AP-PROVe study were showing that patients on Vioxx longer than 18 months had begun experiencing heart attacks and strokes at about double the rate of the control group taking placebos. Results for the first 18 months of the study did not show an increased risk of cardiovascular problems with Vioxx; these results were similar to those of two prior placebo-controlled studies described in the current U.S. labeling for Vioxx. The decision to recall Vioxx came seven days later. Exhibit 5 presents a time line of Vioxx-related actions and events at Merck up to the recall.

The Fallout Following Merck's Voluntary Withdrawal of Vioxx

A torrent of criticism was directed at Merck in the days and weeks following the withdrawal of Vioxx from the market. Some outsiders objected strongly to the company's hyped-up marketing tactics. With Merck's share price dropping from about $45 to the $27–$29 range, equal to a $42 billion loss in market capitalization, shareholders expressed concerns about management's handling of Vioxx, arguing that a better option to the recall was to (1) immediately inform doctors writing Vioxx prescriptions for patients of the above-average risks of heart attacks and strokes, and (2) seek FDA approval to amend the warning label on Vioxx to state that patients with heart-attack and stroke risk should not take Vioxx for longer than 18 months. Indeed, the majority of the outside clinicians Merck consulted between September 23 and September 30, 2004, advised Merck to go to the FDA and other regulatory authorities and have the prescribing information for Vioxx updated with the new findings of increased cardiovascular risk, especially since millions of people were benefiting from use of Vioxx.

Medical experts opined that Merck should have done more studies when doubts about Vioxx first surfaced. William Castelli, former director of the Framingham Heart Study, which investigated cardiac risk factors, told *Fortune* that since Cox-2 inhibitors

Exhibit 5   TIMELINE OF INFORMATION ABOUT VIOXX, AS COMPILED BY MERCK

1998	April: Results of FitzGerald study first presented. Among the results of the study were indications that Cox-2 inhibitors may increase the risk of cardiovascular events.
	April: Trial of Vioxx versus placebo in the prevention of Alzheimer's in patients with mild cognitive impairment (MCI) begins.
1999	January: Vioxx–naproxen trial initiated; patients taking aspirin for cardiac protection were excluded from the study.
	February: First trial of Vioxx versus placebo for the treatment of Alzheimer's disease begins.
	April: Public meeting of FDA Arthritis Advisory Committee on Vioxx's approval.
	May: Vioxx approved by the FDA.
	October: Terms of APPROVe trial finalized, with enrollment of 2,600 patients, ages 40–96, beginning in February 2000. Purpose was to determine ability of Vioxx to reduce colon polyps over a period of three years, with cardiovascular events to be closely monitored. Patients were allowed to take aspirin.
2000	March: Preliminary results from Vioxx–naproxen study become available to Merck. News release on preliminary results of Vioxx–naproxen results issued by Merck; preliminary Vioxx–naproxen results submitted to the FDA. Two ongoing Alzheimer's studies—one for prevention and one for treatment—show no difference in cardiovascular event rates between Vioxx and placebo.
	April: Second trial of Vioxx versus placebo for the treatment of Alzheimer's begins.
	May: Article discussing preliminary Vioxx–naproxen data submitted to the *New England Journal of Medicine* for review and publication. Vioxx–naproxen preliminary results presented at Digestive Disease Week.
	June: Final Vioxx–naproxen study data submitted to FDA in a supplemental new drug application, which included a draft prescribing new disclosure information regarding uses and possible side effects.
	November: Vioxx–naproxen findings published in the *New England Journal of Medicine.* First Vioxx versus placebo trial in the treatment of Alzheimer's disease ends; second interim analysis of safety data from Alzheimer's prevention and treatment trials shows no difference in cardiovascular event rates between Vioxx and placebo.
2001	February: Public meeting of FDA Arthritis Advisory Committee on Vioxx–naproxen results.
	May: Second trial of Vioxx versus placebo for treatment of Alzheimer's disease stopped.
	September: Merck and Oxford University sign letter of intent to conduct a randomized, double-blind, placebo-controlled, international, multicenter study of Vioxx in 7,000 colorectal cancer patients following potentially curative therapy (designated as the VICTOR trial). The primary hypothesis to be tested in the study was that Vioxx administered for two years would result in greater overall survival compared with placebo. Cardiovascular events were to be monitored.
	October: Pooled analysis of cardiovascular data from Phase II/III studies published in *Circulation,* the journal of the American Heart Association. Analysis demonstrated that Vioxx was not associated with excess cardiovascular thrombotic events compared with either placebo or non-naproxen NSAIDs.
	November: APPROVe enrollment completed.
2002	April: U.S. prescribing information for Vioxx updated as a consequence of the Vioxx–naproxen study information and data from two placebo-controlled studies. First patient is enrolled in VICTOR trial.
	June: Pooled analysis of placebo-controlled studies in patients with Alzheimer's and MCI presented to European League Against Rheumatism. The incidence of serious cardiovascular adverse events in this population was similar for both Vioxx and placebo.
2003	March: Design of a study to test ability of Vioxx to reduce incidence of prostate cancer in 15,000 patients (named Vioxx in Prostate Cancer, or ViP, trial) finalized; adverse cardiovascular events were to be monitored.
	April: Trial of Vioxx versus placebo in MCI ends.
	June: ViP trial enrollment begins. Updated pooled analysis of Alzheimer's treatment and MCI data presented to European League Against Rheumatism. The cardiovascular event rate in patients taking 25-milligram doses of Vioxx continued to be similar to the rate in patients taking a placebo; mean duration of treatment was 1.2 years in Vioxx group and 1.3 years in placebo group.
	October: Updated pooled analysis published in the *American Heart Journal* demonstrated that Vioxx was not associated with excess cardiovascular thrombotic events compared with either placebo or non-naproxen NSAIDs.
2004	September: APPROVe External Data Safety Monitoring Board notifies Merck of its recommendation to end APPROVe trial due to high Vioxx incidence of cardiovascular problems. APPROVe, ViP, and VICTOR trials also terminated early. Merck voluntarily withdraws Vioxx from the market.

Source: Information posted at www.merck.com, accessed December 4, 2004.

reduce inflammation (one of the risk factors for cardiac disease), a red flag should have immediately gone up when some studies suggested that Vioxx raised the risk of heart attacks instead of reducing them.[36]

Eric J. Topol, chairman of cardiology at the Cleveland Clinic and a vocal Merck critic, said in a commentary concerning Merck's withdrawal of Vioxx that was published in the October 21, 2004, issue of the *New England Journal of Medicine,* "Had the company not valued sales over safety, a suitable trial could have been initiated rapidly at a fraction of the cost of Merck's direct-to-consumer advertising campaign." Topol believed that the early estimates of 28,000 heart attacks that might be attributable to Vioxx were low and estimated that the number of people injured by Vioxx could be as high as 160,000 (a number Merck believed was far too high). But it was pretty clear that every person who took Vioxx during 1999–2004 and subsequently had a heart attack or stoke was a potential litigant.

A month after the Vioxx recall, on November 2, 2004, the FDA announced that David J. Graham's study of the Kaiser Permanente data indicated that Vioxx may have contributed to an additional 27,785 heart attacks, strokes, or deaths that might have been avoided if patients had taken Celebrex instead. Three days later, in a study published online by *The Lancet,* Swiss researchers at the University of Berne publicly reported their conclusions that Vioxx should have been "withdrawn several years earlier."[37] Their study, funded by the Swiss National Science Foundation, analyzed 18 randomized controlled Vioxx trials and 11 related observational studies; much of the information for the study was based on prior data and study results obtained primarily from the FDA. Merck posted a strongly worded rebuttal of the *Lancet* article on its Web site, citing a variety of problems with the analysis done by the Swiss researchers.

Reaction and Response in Regulatory Circles

European prescription drug regulators launched investigations of other Cox-2 inhibitor drugs, such as Pfizer's Celebrex and Bextra. On November 30, 2004, Swiss pharmaceutical manufacturer Novartis announced that it was temporarily withdrawing its application for European Union approval of its new Cox-2 painkiller Prexige in order to gather more detailed data—Prexige had already been approved in Britain and 20 other countries. Novartis was also working with the FDA on what documentation was needed to win approval to market Prexige in the United States. It was unclear to what extent Merck's next big drug, Arcoxia, would be delayed at the FDA following the FDA's request for further safety and benefit data in October 2004.

Members of Congress, as well as prominent doctors, had recently called for an investigation of the FDA, its drug approval procedures, and whether the relationship between the pharmaceutical firms and FDA officials was too cozy to produce independent oversight and adequately protect the public interest. In a congressional hearing on November 18, 2004, the FDA's David J. Graham testified that the agency downplayed mounting negative data on Vioxx and that it "seriously undervalues, disregards and disrespects drug safety" in general. Graham listed five other potentially dangerous medications currently on the market—Accutane, Bextra, Crestor, Meridia, and Serevent. Exhibit 6 lists drugs that *Forbes* magazine identified as targets for litigation. In early 2005, concerns about the safety of Celebrex began to multiply.

Exhibit 6   OTHER DRUGS THAT COULD BE THE TARGET OF LITIGATION

Drug	Manufacturer	Global Sales	Possible Problems
Zyprexa	Eli Lilly	$4.3 billion	A group convened by the American Diabetes Association says that this drug, used to treat schizophrenia, raises diabetes risk relative to other drugs—75 lawsuits have been filed.
Paxil	GlaxoSmithKline	$3.1 billion	This antidepressant (and others) may be linked to suicidal thoughts in children.
Neurontin	Pfizer	$2.7 billion	In May 2004, a Pfizer subsidiary paid $430 million to promote this epilepsy drug for unapproved uses; a class-action lawsuit has been filed.
Prempro	Wyeth	$1.3 billion	Almost 2,000 lawsuits involving 3,136 women who took estrogen replacement drugs Premarin or Prempro have been filed following medical trials showing that both drugs raise the risk of heart attack and that Prempro raises the risk of breast cancer. Wyeth says the increased risk of breast cancer was disclosed.
Bextra	Pfizer	$990 million	Bextra, like Vioxx, was a Cox-2 inhibitor and was being scrutinized by trial lawyers because of two studies showing it raised risks in heart surgery patients. However, Bextra was not an approved drug for heart surgery patients.
Accutane	Roche	$410 million	This acne drug has been linked to causing birth defects and has alleged links to suicide. Roche says birth defect links were prominently disclosed.
Crestor	AstraZeneca	$130 million	Public Citizen, an advocacy group, is claiming possible liver and muscle side effects; one lawsuit is pending in Mississippi.

Source: "Merck's Mess," *Forbes*, November 1, 2004, p. 51.

In response to its critics, the FDA announced that it was moving to modify its system for evaluating the safety of drugs, particularly those already on the market and those applications where there was disagreement among FDA scientists reviewing new drug applications. Under the proposed new system, when FDA reviewers failed to reach consensus, an ad hoc panel would be convened, with the panel consisting of scientists who were not involved in the original decision-making process, including some from outside the agency. The panel would have 30 days to make a recommendation to the director of FDA's Center for Drug Evaluation & Research. However, Senate Finance Committee chair Charles E. Grassley (R-Iowa) and other knowledgeable FDA observers believed that more far-reaching changes were needed to prevent another Vioxx debacle. At the close of the November 18 hearing, Grassley said he would be pushing for an autonomous board at the FDA to track the safety of drugs after they go on the market. The board would have the power to make label changes and to withdraw drugs from the market. Advocates of an independent board argued that it was unreasonable to expect that the same agency responsible for approval of drug licensing and labeling also be committed to the task of actively seeking evidence that might indicate its decisions to approve the drug or its warning label were wrong.[38]

Since adoption of the 1992 Prescription Drug User Fee Act, the FDA had received approximately $825 million in "user fees" from drug and biologic manufacturers from fiscal years 1993 through 2001 to augment its budget and help pay for the costs of streamlining its new drug-review-and-approval process.[39] During that time, median approval times for standard, or nonpriority, drugs decreased from 27 months in 1993 to 14 months in 2001. However, drug recalls following approval increased from 1.56 percent during 1993–1996 to 5.35 percent during 1997–2001. In addition, an investigation of 18 FDA expert advisory panels revealed that more than half of the members of these panels had direct financial interests in the drug or topic they were evaluating and for which they were making recommendations.[40]

The Specter of Litigation and Merck's Exposure

As of December 2004, trial lawyers in the United States and elsewhere were still taking calls from potential clients daily in regard to Vioxx. Several prominent law firms with expertise in product liability were in the process of (1) soliciting and interviewing potential clients who believed they had been harmed by taking Vioxx, (2) preparing and/or filing lawsuits of one kind or another, and (3) identifying and working with medical experts who might be called to testify about Vioxx's causal connections to clients' health problems. While every person who took Vioxx and subsequently suffered a heart attack or stroke could be a potential litigant, the science seemed to indicate that the cardiovascular risks of Vioxx began after 18 months of usage (which could significantly limit the number of legitimate plaintiffs and Merck's litigation exposure). Moreover, a successful plaintiff would have to prove that it was Vioxx and not any of a myriad of other reasons—smoking, poor eating habits, excess weight, lack of exercise—that *caused* the health problem.

On the other hand, lawyers for the plaintiffs believed they could introduce documents and testimony showing that Merck swept adverse evidence about Vioxx's safety under the rug. In litigation in New Jersey and Alabama, where over 150 Vioxx cases were pending, plaintiffs' lawyers had successfully gotten discovery rights from the courts and obtained some 3 million Merck documents and e-mails relating to Vioxx.[41] In the New Jersey cases, plaintiffs' lawyers were also expected to claim that Merck's direct-to-consumer advertising campaign had induced patients to ask their doctors for Vioxx—in New Jersey (and other jurisdictions), a drugmaker that employed direct-to-consumer marketing lost the protection of a legal rule that says it need only provide safety warnings sufficient to alert doctors (not patients) to a drug's risks.

Some of the plaintiffs' lawyers were seeking to have their pending cases consolidated and transferred to jurisdictions where jury awards for damages were quite generous. Merck was trying to get many of the federal cases transferred to courts in Maryland, where it believed the judicial climate was more favorable to its position.[42]

Merck's Position on Its Decision to Withdraw Vioxx from the Market

When Merck pulled Vioxx from the market on September 30, 2004, CEO Raymond Gilmartin said that the new study findings prompting Merck's decision were "unexpected" and that Merck's voluntary withdrawal was "really putting patient safety first"—needy patients could readily switch to other Cox-2 inhibitors such as Celebrex or NSAIDs.

Merck's position right up until it withdrew Vioxx was that the evidence about Vioxx's cardiovascular effects was inconclusive. For example, in the first round of clinical trials, patients who took Vioxx had about the same rate of heart attacks and strokes as patients who took NSAIDs or a sugar-pill placebo.[43] Merck said that it had conducted a number of studies before and after FDA approval that did not show the heart risk seen in the Vioxx–naproxen study.[44]

And management believed it had done the right things, pointing out that:[45]

- It had extensively studied Vioxx before seeking regulatory approval to market it.

- After it saw the results of the Vioxx–naproxen trial, it immediately put out a press release.

- It added warning language to its Vioxx label and prescription usage information.

- When questions arose, it took additional steps, including conducting further studies to gain more clinical information. For example, it voluntarily and ethically initiated the APPROVe study, which ultimately identified the increased cardiovascular risks of long-term use of Vioxx.

- When information from the additional clinical trials became available, Merck had put patient safety first and promptly recalled Vioxx rather than amend the prescription warnings.

According to Merck general counsel Kenneth Frazier:

> We communicated appropriately about the product, we monitored it appropriately, we studied it appropriately, and in the end we took the actions that benefited patients.[46]

Endnotes

[1]John Simons and David Stipp, "Will Merck Survive Vioxx?" *Fortune,* November 1, 2004, p. 96.
[2]Ibid.
[3]Ibid., p. 94.
[4]Ibid., p. 96.
[5]As cited in ibid., pp. 96–97.
[6]Quotes posted at www.merck.com (accessed November 30, 2004).
[7]These examples are based on information in company press releases posted at www.merck.com (accessed November 30, 2004).
[8]Anna Wilde Mathews and Barbara Martinez, "E-Mails Suggest Merck Knew Vioxx's Dangers at Early Stage," *The Wall Street Journal,* November 1, 2004, p. A10.
[9]Ibid.
[10]Ibid.
[11]Ibid.
[12]Simons and Stipp, "Will Merck Survive Vioxx?" p. 102.
[13]"Prescription for Trouble," a *60 Minutes* documentary posted at www.cbsnews.com, November 14, 2004 (accessed December 4, 2004).
[14]Holman W. Jenkins Jr., "Was Withdrawing Vioxx the Right Thing to Do?" *Wall Street Journal,* November 10, 2004, p. A17.
[15]Ibid.
[16]Amy Isao, "Drug Ads—Without Harmful Side Effects," *Business Week Online,* posted November 8, 2004.
[17]Jenkins, "Was Withdrawing Vioxx the Right Thing to Do?" p. A17.
[18]Mathews and Martinez, "E-Mails Suggest Merck Knew," p. A10.
[19]Ibid.
[20]Eric J. Topol, "Failing the Public Health—Rofecoxib, Merck, and the FDA," *New England Journal of Medicine* 351, no. 17 (October 21, 2004), p. 1707.
[21]Ibid.
[22]"Prescription for Trouble."
[23]Ibid.
[24]Mathews and Martinez, "E-Mails Suggest Merck Knew," p. A10, and "Prescription for Trouble."
[25]Mathews and Martinez, "E-Mails Suggest Merck Knew," p. A10.
[26]"Prescription for Trouble."
[27]Mathews and Martinez, "E-Mails Suggest Merck Knew," p. A10.
[28]Ibid.
[29]Ibid., p. A11.
[30]Debabrata Mukherjee, Steven E. Nissen, and Eric J. Topol, "Risk of Cardiovascular Events Associated with Selected Cox-2 Inhibitors," *Journal of the American Medical Association* 286, no. 8 (August 22, 2001), pp. 954–59.
[31]Mathews and Martinez, "E-Mails Suggest Merck Knew," p. A10.

[32]According to LexisNexis "Mealey Reports," and cited in "Merck's Mess," *Forbes,* November 1, 2004, p. 51.

[33]Mathews and Martinez, "E-Mails Suggest Merck Knew," p. A11.

[34]John Abramson, *Overdosed America: The Broken Promise of American Medicine* (New York: HarperCollins, 2004); and Mathews and Martinez, "E-Mails Suggest Merck Knew," p. A10.

[35]Mathews and Martinez, "E-Mails Suggest Merck Knew," p. A11.

[36]Simon and Stipp, "Will Merck Survive Vioxx?" p. 104.

[37]Peter Jüni, Linda Nartey, Stephan Reichenbach, Rebekka Sterchi, Paul A Dieppe, and Matthias Egger, "Risk of Cardiovascular Events and Rofecoxib: Cumulative Meta-Analysis," *The Lancet* 364, no. 9450 (November 5, 2004), pp. 2021ff.

[38]Phil B. Fontanarosa, Drummond Rennie, and Catherine D. DeAngelis, "Postmarketing Surveillance—Lack of Vigilance, Lack of Trust," *Journal of the American Medical Association* 292, no. 21 (December 1, 2004), p. 2649.

[39]Ibid., p. 2647.

[40]Ibid., p. 2647.

[41]Roger Perloff, "How Bad Will the Lawsuits Get?" *Fortune,* November 1, 2004, p. 97.

[42]Barbara Martinez, "Preparing for Vioxx Suits, Both Sides Seek Friendly Venues," *The Wall Street Journal,* November 17, 2004, p. B1.

[43]Simon and Stipp, "Will Merck Survive Vioxx?" p. 102.

[44]"Prescription for Trouble."

[45]"An Open Letter from Merck," appearing in many newspapers, November 12, 2004.

[46]As quoted in Perloff, "How Bad Will the Lawsuits Get?" p. 96.

Photo Credits

Endnotes

Chapter 1

[1]For a discussion of the different ways that companies can position themselves in the marketplace, see Michael E. Porter, "What Is Strategy?" *Harvard Business Review* 74, no. 6 (November-December 1996), pp. 65–67.

[2]W. Chan Kim and Renée Mauborgne, "Blue Ocean Strategy," *Harvard Business Review* 82, no. 10 (October 2004), pp. 76–84.

[3]See Henry Mintzberg and Joseph Lampel, "Reflecting on the Strategy Process," *Sloan Management Review* 40, no. 3 (Spring 1999), pp. 21–30; Henry Mintzberg and J. A. Waters, "Of Strategies, Deliberate and Emergent," *Strategic Management Journal* 6 (1985), pp. 257–272; Costas Markides, "Strategy as Balance: From 'Either-Or' to 'And,'" *Business Strategy Review* 12, no. 3 (September 2001), pp. 1–10; Henry Mintzberg, Bruce Ahlstrand, and Joseph Lampel, *Strategy Safari: A Guided Tour through the Wilds of Strategic Management* (New York: Free Press, 1998), chaps. 2, 5, and 7; and C. K. Prahalad and Gary Hamel, "The Core Competence of the Corporation," *Harvard Business Review* 70, no. 3 (May-June 1990), pp. 79–93.

[4]For an excellent treatment of the strategic challenges posed by high-velocity changes, see Shona L. Brown and Kathleen M. Eisenhardt, *Competing on the Edge: Strategy as Structured Chaos* (Boston: Harvard Business School Press, 1998), chap. 1.

[5]Joseph L. Badaracco, "The Discipline of Building Character," *Harvard Business Review* 76, no. 2 (March-April 1998), pp. 115–124.

[6]Joan Magretta, "Why Business Models Matter," *Harvard Business Review* 80, no. 5 (May 2002), p. 87.

[7]For a more in-depth discussion of the challenges of developing a well-conceived vision, as well as some good examples, see Hugh Davidson, *The Committed Enterprise: How to Make Vision and Values Work* (Oxford: Butterworth Heinemann, 2002), chap. 2; W. Chan Kim and Renée Mauborgne, "Charting Your Company's Future," *Harvard Business Review* 80, no. 6 (June 2002), pp. 77–83; James C. Collins and Jerry I. Porras, "Building Your Company's Vision," *Harvard Business Review* 74, no. 5 (September-October 1996), pp. 65–77; and Michel Robert, *Strategy Pure and Simple II* (New York: McGraw-Hill, 1998), chap. 2, 3, and 6.

[8]Davidson, *The Committed Enterprise,* pp. 20, 54.

[9]Ibid., pp. 36, 54.

[10]As quoted in Charles H. House and Raymond L. Price, "The Return Map: Tracking Product Teams," *Harvard Business Review* 60, no. 1 (January-February 1991), p. 93.

[11]The concept of strategic intent is described in more detail in Gary Hamel and C. K. Pralahad, "Strategic Intent," *Harvard Business Review* 89, no. 3 (May-June 1989), pp. 63–76; this section draws on their pioneering discussion. See also Michael A. Hitt, Beverly B. Tyler, Camilla Hardee, and Daewoo Park, "Understanding Strategic Intent in the Global Marketplace," *Academy of Management Executive* 9, no. 2 (May 1995), pp. 12–19.

[12]For a fuller discussion of strategy as an entrepreneurial process, see Mintzberg, Ahlstrand, and Lampel, *Strategy Safari,* chap. 5. Also see Bruce Barringer and Allen C. Bluedorn, "The Relationship between Corporate Entrepreneurship and Strategic Management," *Strategic Management Journal* 20 (1999), pp. 421–444, and Jeffrey G. Covin and Morgan P. Miles, "Corporate Entrepreneurship and the Pursuit of Competitive Advantage," *Entrepreneurship: Theory and Practice* 23, no. 3 (Spring 1999), pp. 47–63.

[13]The strategy-making, strategy-implementing roles of middle managers are thoroughly discussed and documented in Steven W. Floyd and Bill Wooldridge, *The Strategic Middle Manager* (San Francisco: Jossey-Bass, 1996), chaps. 2 and 3.

[14]For more discussion of this point, see Orit Gadiesh and James L. Gilbert, "Transforming Corner-Office Strategy into Frontline Action," *Harvard Business Review* 79, no. 5 (May 2001), pp. 72–79, and Kathleen M. Eisenhardt and Donald N. Sull, "Strategy as Simple Rules," *Harvard Business Review* 79, no. 1 (January 2001), pp. 106–116.

[15]For an excellent discussion of why a strategic plan needs to be more than a list of bullet points and should in fact tell an engaging, insightful, stage-setting story that lays out the industry and competitive situation as well as the vision, objectives, and strategy, see Gordon Shaw, Robert Brown, and Philip Bromiley, "Strategic Stories: How 3M Is Rewriting Business Planning," *Harvard Business Review* 76, no. 3 (May-June 1998), pp. 41–50.

[16]For a discussion of what it takes for the corporate governance system to function properly, see David A. Nadler, "Building Better Boards," *Harvard Business Review* 82, no. 5 (May 2004), pp. 102–105. See also Cynthia A. Montgomery and Rhonda Kaufman, "The Board's Missing Link," *Harvard Business Review* 81, no. 3 (March 2003), pp. 86–93; John Carver, "What Continues to Be Wrong with Corporate Governance and How to Fix It," *Ivey Business Journal* 68, no. 1 (September-October 2003), pp. 1–5; and Gordon Donaldson, "A New Tool for Boards: The Strategic Audit," *Harvard Business Review* 73, no. 4 (July-August 1995), pp. 99–107.

Chapter 2

[1]A large number of studies have examined the size of the cost reductions associated with experience; the median cost reduction associated with a doubling of cumulative production volume is approximately 15 percent, but there

is a wide variation from industry to industry. In semiconductors, strong *learning and experience* effects in manufacturing cause unit costs to decline about 20 percent each time *cumulative* production volume doubles. In other words, if the first 1 million chips cost $100 each to produce, by a production volume of 2 million chips costs would drop to $80 each (80 percent of $100), by a production volume of 4 million each chip would cost $64 to produce (80 percent of $80), and so on.

[2]The five-forces model of competition is the creation of Professor Michael Porter of the Harvard Business School. For his original presentation of the model, see Michael E. Porter, "How Competitive Forces Shape Strategy," *Harvard Business Review* 57, no. 2 (March-April 1979), pp. 137–145. A more thorough discussion can be found in Michael E. Porter, *Competitive Strategy: Techniques for Analyzing Industries and Competitors* (New York: Free Press, 1980), chap. 1.

[3]Adapted with permission of the Free Press, a division of Simon & Schuster Adult Publishing Group, from *Competitive Advantage: Creating and Sustaining Superior Performance,* by Michael Porter, Copyright © 1995, 1998 by Michael E. Porter. All rights reserved.

[4]Ibid., pp. 7–17.

[5]When profits are sufficiently attractive, entry barriers are unlikely to be an effective entry deterrent. At most, they limit the pool of candidate entrants to enterprises with the requisite competencies and resources and with the creativity to fashion a strategy for competing with incumbent firms. For a good discussion of this point, see George S. Yip, "Gateways to Entry," *Harvard Business Review* 60, no. 5 (September-October 1982), pp. 85–93.

[6]Porter, "How Competitive Forces Shape Strategy," p. 140, and Porter, *Competitive Strategy,* pp. 14–15.

[7]Porter, "How Competitive Forces Shape Strategy," p. 142, and Porter, *Competitive Strategy,* pp. 22–24.

[8]Porter, *Competitive Strategy,* p. 10.

[9]Ibid., pp. 27–28.

[10]Ibid., pp. 24–27.

[11]For a more extended discussion of the problems with the life-cycle hypothesis, see Porter, *Competitive Strategy,* pp. 157–162.

[12]Porter, *Competitive Strategy,* p. 162.

[13]Ibid., pp. 164–183.

[14]For an excellent discussion of the different patterns of change in industries, see Anita M. McGahan, "How Industries Change," *Harvard Business Review* 82, no. 10 (October 2004), pp. 87–94.

[15]Porter, *Competitive Strategy,* chap. 7.

[16]Ibid., pp. 129–130.

[17]For an excellent discussion of how to identify the factors that define strategic groups, see Mary Ellen Gordon and George R. Milne, "Selecting the Dimensions That Define Strategic Groups: A Novel Market-Driven Approach," *Journal of Managerial Issues* 11, no. 2 (Summer 1999), pp. 213–233.

[18]Porter, *Competitive Strategy,* pp. 152–154.

[19]Ibid., pp. 130, 132–138, 154–155.

[20]Strategic groups act as good reference points for predicting the evolution of an industry's competitive structure. See Avi Fiegenbaum and Howard Thomas, "Strategic Groups as Reference Groups: Theory, Modeling and Empirical Examination of Industry and Competitive Strategy," *Strategic Management Journal* 16 (1995), pp. 461–476. For a study of how strategic group analysis helps identify the variables that lead to sustainable competitive advantage, see S. Ade Olusoga, Michael P. Mokwa, and Charles H. Noble, "Strategic Groups, Mobility Barriers, and Competitive Advantage," *Journal of Business Research* 33 (1995), pp. 153–164.

[21]For a discussion of legal ways of gathering competitive intelligence on rival companies, see Larry Kahaner, *Competitive Intelligence* (New York: Simon & Schuster, 1996).

[22]Kahaner, *Competitive Intelligence,* pp. 84–85.

[23]Some experts dispute the strategy-making value of key success factors. Professor Ghemawat has claimed that

the "whole idea of identifying a success factor and then chasing it seems to have something in common with the ill-considered medieval hunt for the *philosopher's stone,* a substance which would transmute everything it touched into gold." Pankaj Ghemawat, *Commitment: The Dynamic of Strategy* (New York: Free Press, 1991), p. 11.

Chapter 3

[1]Many business organizations are coming to view cutting-edge knowledge and intellectual resources as valuable competitive assets and have concluded that explicitly managing these assets is an essential part of their strategy. See Michael H. Zack, "Developing a Knowledge Strategy," *California Management Review* 41, no. 3 (Spring 1999), pp. 125–145 and Shaker A. Zahra, Anders P. Nielsen, and William C. Bogner, "Corporate Entrepreneurship, Knowledge, and Competence Development," *Entrepreneurship Theory and Practice,* Spring 1999, pp. 169–189.

[2]In the past decade, there's been considerable research into the role a company's resources and competitive capabilities play in crafting strategy and in determining company profitability. The findings and conclusions have coalesced into what is called the *resource-based view* of the firm. Among the most insightful articles are Birger Wernerfelt, "A Resource-Based View of the Firm," *Strategic Management Journal,* September-October 1984, pp. 171–180; Jay Barney, "Firm Resources and Sustained Competitive Advantage," *Journal of Management* 17, no. 1 (1991), pp. 99–120; Margaret A. Peteraf, "The Cornerstones of Competitive Advantage: A Resource-Based View," *Strategic Management Journal,* March 1993, pp. 179–191; Birger Wernerfelt, "The Resource-Based View of the Firm: Ten Years After," *Strategic Management Journal* 16 (1995), pp. 171–174; Jay B. Barney, "Looking Inside for Competitive Advantage," *Academy of Management Executive* 9, no. 4 (November 1995), pp. 49–61; Christopher A. Bartlett and Sumantra Ghoshal, "Building Competitive Advantage through

People," *MIT Sloan Management Review* 43, no. 2 (Winter 2002), pp. 34–41; and Danny Miller, Russell Eisenstat, and Nathaniel Foote, "Strategy from the Inside Out: Building Capability-Creating Organizations," *California Management Review* 44, no. 3 (Spring 2002), pp. 37–54.

[3]George Stalk, Jr., and Rob Lachenauer, "Hard Ball: Five Killer Strategies for Trouncing the Competition," *Harvard Business Review* 82, no. 4 (April 2004), p. 65.

[4]For a more extensive discussion of how to identify and evaluate the competitive power of a company's capabilities, see David W. Birchall and George Tovstiga, "The Strategic Potential of a Firm's Knowledge Portfolio," *Journal of General Management* 25, no. 1 (Autumn 1999), pp. 1–16, and Nick Bontis, Nicola C. Dragonetti, Kristine Jacobsen, and Goran Roos, "The Knowledge Toolbox: A Review of the Tools Available to Measure and Manage Intangible Resources," *European Management Journal* 17, no. 4 (August 1999), pp. 391–401. Also see David Teece, "Capturing Value from Knowledge Assets: The New Economy, Markets for Know-How, and Intangible Assets," *California Management Review* 40, no. 3 (Spring 1998), pp. 55–79.

[5]See David J. Collis and Cynthia A. Montgomery, "Competing on Resources: Strategy in the 1990s," *Harvard Business Review* 73, no. 4 (July-August 1995), pp. 120–123.

[6]See Jack W. Duncan, Peter Ginter, and Linda E. Swayne, "Competitive Advantage and Internal Organizational Assessment," *Academy of Management Executive* 12, no. 3 (August 1998), pp. 6–16.

[7]Value chains and strategic cost analysis are described at greater length in Michael E. Porter, *Competitive Advantage* (New York: Free Press, 1985), chaps. 2 and 3; Robin Cooper and Robert S. Kaplan, "Measure Costs Right: Make the Right Decisions," *Harvard Business Review* 66, no. 5 (September-October, 1988), pp. 96–103; and John K. Shank and Vijay Govindarajan, *Strategic Cost Manage-ment* (New York: Free Press, 1993), especially chaps. 2–6 and 10.

[8]Porter, *Competitive Advantage*, p. 36.

[9]Ibid., p. 34.

[10]The strategic importance of effective supply chain management is discussed in Hau L. Lee, "The Triple-A Supply Chain," *Harvard Business Review* 82, no. 10 (October 2004), pp. 102–112.

[11]M. Hegert and D. Morris, "Accounting Data for Value Chain Analysis," *Strategic Management Journal* 10 (1989), p. 180.

[12]For more on how and why the clustering of suppliers and other support organizations matters to a company's costs and competitiveness, see Michael E. Porter, "Clusters and the New Economics of Competition," *Harvard Business Review* 76, no. 6 (November-December 1998), pp. 77–90.

[13]For discussions of the accounting challenges in calculating the costs of value chain activities, see Shank and Govindarajan, *Strategic Cost Management*, pp. 62–72 and chap. 5, and Hegert and Morris, "Accounting Data for Value Chain Analysis," pp. 175–188.

[14]Porter, *Competitive Advantage*, p. 45.

[15]For a discussion of activity-based cost accounting, see Cooper and Kaplan, "Measure Costs Right"; Shank and Govindarajan, *Strategic Cost Management*, chap. 11; and Joseph A. Ness and Thomas G. Cucuzza, "Tapping the Full Potential of ABC," *Harvard Business Review* 73, no. 4 (July-August 1995), pp. 130–138.

[16]Shank and Govindarajan, *Strategic Cost Management*, p. 62.

[17]For more details, see Gregory H. Watson, *Strategic Benchmarking: How to Rate Your Company's Performance against the World's Best* (New York: Wiley, 1993); Robert C. Camp, *Benchmarking: The Search for Industry Best Practices That Lead to Superior Performance* (Milwaukee: ASQC Quality Press, 1989); Christopher E. Bogan and Michael J. English, *Benchmarking for Best Practices: Winning through Innovative Adaptation* (New York: McGraw-Hill, 1994); and Dawn Iacobucci and Christie Nordhielm, "Creative Benchmarking," *Harvard Business Review* 78, no. 6 (November-December 2000), pp. 24–25.

[18]Jeremy Main, "How to Steal the Best Ideas Around," *Fortune,* October 19, 1992, pp. 102–103.

[19]Shank and Govindarajan, *Strategic Cost Management,* p. 50.

[20]Porter, *Competitive Advantage,* chap. 3.

[21]An example of how Whirlpool Corporation transformed its supply chain from a competitive liability to a competitive asset is discussed in Reuben E. Stone, "Leading a Supply Chain Turnaround," *Harvard Business Review* 82, no. 10 (October 2004), pp. 114–121.

[22]James Brian Quinn, *Intelligent Enterprise* (New York: Free Press, 1993), p. 54.

[23]Ibid., p. 34.

Chapter 4

[1]This classification scheme is an adaption of one presented in Michael E. Porter, *Competitive Strategy: Techniques for Analyzing Industries and Competitors* (New York: Free Press, 1980), chap. 2, especially pp. 35–40 and 44–46. For a discussion of the different ways that companies can position themselves in the marketplace, see Michael E. Porter, "What Is Strategy?" *Harvard Business Review* 74, no. 6 (November-December 1996), pp. 65–67.

[2]Porter, *Competitive Advantage,* p. 97.

[3]The items and explanations in this listing are condensed from ibid., pp. 70–107.

[4]Ibid., pp. 135–138.

[5]For a more detailed discussion, see George Stalk, Philip Evans, and Lawrence E. Schulman, "Competing on Capabilities: The New Rules of Corporate Strategy," *Harvard Business Review* 70, no. 2 (March-April 1992), pp. 57–69.

[6]Porter, *Competitive Advantage,* pp. 160–162.

[7]Gary Hamel, "Strategy as Revolution," *Harvard Business Review* 74, no. 4 (July-August 1996), p. 72. For an interesting and entertaining presentation

of Trader Joe's mission, strategy, and operating practices, see the information the company has posted at www.traderjoes.com.

[8]Yves L. Doz and Gary Hamel, *Alliance Advantage: The Art of Creating Value through Partnering* (Boston: Harvard Business School Press, 1998), pp. xiii, xiv.

[9]Jason Wakeam, "The Five Factors of a Strategic Alliance," *Ivey Business Journal* 68, no 3 (May-June 2003), pp. 1–4.

[10]Jeffrey H. Dyer, Prashant Kale, and Harbir Singh, "When to Ally and When to Acquire," *Harvard Business Review* 82, no. 7/8 (July-August 2004), p. 109.

[11]Salvatore Parise and Lisa Sasson, "Leveraging Knowledge Management across Strategic Alliances," *Ivey Business Journal* 67, no. 2 (March-April 2002), p. 42.

[12]Michael E. Porter, *The Competitive Advantage of Nations* (New York: Free Press, 1990), p. 66. For a discussion of how to realize the advantages of strategic partnerships, see Nancy J. Kaplan and Jonathan Hurd, "Realizing the Promise of Partnerships," *Journal of Business Strategy* 23, no. 3 (May-June 2002), pp. 38–42.

[13]Doz and Hamel, *Alliance Advantage,* pp. 16–18.

[14]Dyer, Kale, and Singh, "When to Ally and When to Acquire," p. 109.

[15]For an excellent discussion of the pros and cons of alliances versus acquisitions, see Dyer, Kale, and Singh, "When to Ally and When to Acquire," pp. 109–115.

[16]For an excellent review of the strategic objectives of various types of mergers and acquisitions and the managerial challenges that different kinds of mergers and acquisitions present, see Joseph L. Bower, "Not All M&As Are Alike-And That Matters," *Harvard Business Review* 79, no. 3 (March 2001), pp. 93–101.

[17]For a more expansive discussion, see Dyer, Kale, and Singh, "When to Ally and When to Acquire," pp. 109–110.

[18]Kathryn R. Harrigan, "Matching Integration Strategies to Com-
petitive Conditions," *Strategic Management Journal* 7, no. 6 (November-December 1986), pp. 535–556. For a more extensive discussion of the advantages and disadvantages of vertical integration, see John Stuckey and David White, "When and When Not to Vertically Integrate," *Sloan Management Review,* Spring 1993, pp. 71–83.

[19]The resilience of vertical integration strategies despite the disadvantages is discussed in Thomas Osegowitsch and Anoop Madhok, "Vertical Integration Is Dead or Is It?" *Business Horizons* 46, no. 2 (March-April 2003), pp. 25–35.

[20]For more details, see James Brian Quinn, "Strategic Outsourcing: Leveraging Knowledge Capabilities," *Sloan Management Review* 40, no. 4 (Summer 1999), pp. 9–21.

[21]Dean Foust, "Big Brown's New Bag," *BusinessWeek,* July 19, 2004, pp. 54–55.

[22]"The Internet Age," *BusinessWeek,* October 4, 1999, p. 104.

[23]For a good discussion of the problems that can arise from outsourcing, see Jérôme Barthélemy, "The Seven Deadly Sins of Outsourcing," *Academy of Management Executive* 17, no. 2 (May 2003), pp. 87–100.

[24]For an excellent discussion of aggressive offensive strategies, see George Stalk, Jr., and Rob Lachenauer, "Hardball: Five Killer Strategies for Trouncing the Competition," *Harvard Business Review* 82, no. 4 (April 2004), pp. 62–71. A discussion of offensive strategies particularly suitable for industry leaders is presented in Richard D'Aveni, "The Empire Strikes Back: Counterrevolutionary Strategies for Industry Leaders," *Harvard Business Review* 80, no. 11 (November 2002), pp. 66–74.

[25]Ian C. MacMillan, "How Long Can You Sustain a Competitive Advantage?" in *The Strategic Planning Management Reader,* ed. Liam Fahey (Englewood Cliffs, NJ: Prentice Hall, 1989), pp. 23–24.

[26]Ian C. MacMillan, Alexander B. van Putten, and Rita Gunther McGrath, "Global Gamesmanship," *Harvard*
Business Review 81, no. 5 (May 2003), pp. 66–67; also see Askay R. Rao, Mark E. Bergen, and Scott Davis, "How to Fight a Price War," *Harvard Business Review* 78, no. 2 (March-April, 2000), pp. 107–116.

[27]Stalk and Lachenauer, "Hardball," p. 64.

[28]Ibid., p. 67.

[29]A good example of the use of this type of strategic offensive in the battle between Netscape and Microsoft over Internet browsers is presented in David B. Yoffie and Michael A. Cusumano, "Judo Strategy: The Competitive Dynamics of Internet Time," *Harvard Business Review* 77, no. 1 (January-February 1999), pp. 70–81.

[30]For an interesting study of how small firms can successfully employ guerrilla-style tactics, see Ming-Jer Chen and Donald C. Hambrick, "Speed, Stealth, and Selective Attack: How Small Firms Differ from Large Firms in Competitive Behavior," *Academy of Management Journal* 38, no. 2 (April 1995), pp. 453–482. Other discussions of guerrilla offensives can be found in Ian MacMillan, "How Business Strategists Can Use Guerrilla Warfare Tactics," *Journal of Business Strategy* 1, no. 2 (Fall 1980), pp. 63–65; William E. Rothschild, "Surprise and the Competitive Advantage," *Journal of Business Strategy* 4, no. 3 (Winter 1984), pp. 10–18; Kathryn R. Harrigan, *Strategic Flexibility* (Lexington, MA: Lexington Books, 1985), pp. 30–45; and Liam Fahey, "Guerrilla Strategy: The Hit-and-Run Attack," in *The Strategic Management Planning Reader,* ed. Liam Fahey (Englewood Cliffs, NJ: Prentice Hall, 1989), pp. 194–197.

[31]The use of preemptive strike offensives is treated comprehensively in Ian MacMillan, "Preemptive Strategies," *Journal of Business Strategy* 14, no. 2 (Fall 1983), pp. 16–26.

[32]For an excellent discussion of how to wage offensives against strong rivals, see David B. Yoffie and Mary Kwak, "Mastering Balance: How to Meet and Beat a Stronger Opponent," *California Management Review* 44, no. 2 (Winter 2002), pp. 8–24.

[33]Porter, *Competitive Advantage,* pp. 489–494.

[34]Ibid., pp. 495–497. The list here is selective; Porter offers a greater number of options.

[35]For a more extensive discussion of how the Internet impacts strategy, see Michael E. Porter, "Strategy and the Internet," *Harvard Business Review* 79, no. 3 (March 2001), pp. 63–78.

[36]Porter, *Competitive Advantage,* pp. 232–233.

[37]For research evidence on the effects of pioneering versus following, see Jeffrey G. Covin, Dennis P. Slevin, and Michael B. Heeley, "Pioneers and Followers: Competitive Tactics, Environment, and Growth," *Journal of Business Venturing* 15, no. 2 (March 1999), pp. 175–210, and Christopher A. Bartlett and Sumantra Ghoshal, "Going Global: Lessons from Late-Movers," *Harvard Business Review* 78, no. 2 (March-April 2000), pp. 132–145.

[38]Gary Hamel, "Smart Mover, Dumb Mover," *Fortune,* September 3, 2001, p. 195.

[39]Ibid., p. 192.

Chapter 5

[1]For an insightful discussion of how much significance these kinds of demographic and market differences have, see C. K. Prahalad and Kenneth Lieberthal, "The End of Corporate Imperialism," *Harvard Business Review* 76, no. 4 (July-August 1999), pp. 68–79.

[2]Michael E. Porter, *The Competitive Advantage of Nations* (New York: Free Press, 1990), pp. 53–54.

[3]Ibid., p. 61.

[4]For more details on the merits of and opportunities for cross-border transfer of successful strategy experiments, see C. A. Bartlett and S. Ghoshal, *Managing across Borders: The Transnational Solution,* 2d ed. (Boston: Harvard Business School Press, 1998), pp. 79–80 and chap. 9.

[5]H. Kurt Christensen, "Corporate Strategy: Managing a Set of Businesses," in *The Portable MBA in Strategy,* ed.

Liam Fahey and Robert M. Randall (New York: Wiley, 2001), p. 42.

[6]Porter, *The Competitive Advantage of Nations,* pp. 53–55.

[7]Ibid., pp. 55–58.

[8]C. K. Prahalad and Yves L. Doz, *The Multinational Mission* (New York: Free Press, 1987), p. 60.

[9]Porter, *The Competitive Advantage of Nations,* p. 57.

[10]Ibid., pp. 58–60.

[11]Ian C. MacMillan, Alexander B. van Putten, and Rita Gunther McGrath, "Global Gamesmanship," *Harvard Business Review* 81, no. 5 (May 2003), pp. 63–68.

[12]Porter, *The Competitive Advantage of Nations,* p. 66; see also Yves L. Doz and Gary Hamel, *Alliance Advantage* (Boston: Harvard Business School Press, 1998), especially chaps. 2–4.

[13]Christensen, "Corporate Strategy," p. 43.

[14]For an excellent discussion of company experiences with alliances and partnerships, see Doz and Hamel, *Alliance Advantage,* chaps. 2–7, and Rosabeth Moss Kanter, "Collaborative Advantage: The Art of the Alliance," *Harvard Business Review* 72, no. 4 (July-August 1994), pp. 96–108.

[15]Jeremy Main, "Making Global Alliances Work," *Fortune,* December 19, 1990, p. 125.

[16]Details of the disagreements are reported in Shawn Tully, "The Alliance from Hell," *Fortune,* June 24, 1996, pp. 64–72.

[17]Doz and Hamel, *Alliance Advantage,* chaps. 4–8.

[18]Much of this section is based on Prahalad and Lieberthal, "The End of Corporate Imperialism," pp. 68–79, and David J. Arnold and John A. Quelch, "New Strategies in Emerging Markets," *Sloan Management Review* 40, no. 1 (Fall 1998), pp. 7–20. For a more extensive discussion of strategy in emerging markets, see C. K. Prahalad, *The Fortune at the Bottom of the Pyramid: Eradicating Poverty through Profits* (Upper Saddle River, NJ: Wharton, 2005), especially chaps. 1–3.

[19]Brenda Cherry, "What China Eats (and Drinks and . . .)" *Fortune,* October 4, 2004, pp. 152–153.

[20]Prahalad and Lieberthal, "The End of Corporate Imperialism," pp. 72–73.

[21]Niroj Dawar and Tony Frost, "Competing with Giants: Survival Strategies for Local Companies in Emerging Markets," *Harvard Business Review* 77, no. 1 (January-February 1999), p. 122; see also Guitz Ger, "Localizing in the Global Village: Local Firms Competing in Global Markets," *California Management Review* 41, no. 4 (Summer 1999), pp. 64–84.

[22]Dawar and Frost, "Competing with Giants," p. 124.

[23]Ibid., p. 125.

[24]Steve Hamm, "Tech's Future," *BusinessWeek,* September 27, 2004, p. 88.

[25]Dawar and Frost, "Competing with Giants," p. 126.

[26]Hamm, "Tech's Future," p. 89.

Chapter 6

[1]For a further discussion of when diversification makes good strategic sense, see Constantinos C. Markides, "To Diversify or Not to Diversify," *Harvard Business Review* 75, no. 6 (November-December 1997), pp. 93–99.

[2]Michael E. Porter, "From Competitive Advantage to Corporate Strategy," *Harvard Business Review* 45, no. 3 (May-June 1987), pp. 46–49.

[3]Michael E. Porter, *Competitive Strategy: Techniques for Analyzing Industries and Competitors* (New York: Free Press, 1980), pp. 354–355.

[4]Ibid., pp. 344–345.

[5]Yves L. Doz and Gary Hamel, *Alliance Advantage: The Art of Creating Value through Partnering* (Boston: Harvard Business School Press, 1998), chaps. 1 and 2.

[6]Michael E. Porter, *Competitive Advantage* (New York: Free Press, 1985), pp. 318–319, 337–353, and Porter, "From Competitive Advantage to Corporate Strategy," pp. 53–57. For an empirical study confirming that strategic fits are capable of enhancing performance

(provided the resulting resource strengths are competitively valuable and difficult to duplicate by rivals), see Constantinos C. Markides and Peter J. Williamson, "Corporate Diversification and Organization Structure: A Resource-Based View," *Academy of Management Journal* 39, no. 2 (April 1996), pp. 340–367.

[7]For a discussion of the strategic significance of cross-business coordination of value chain activities and insight into how the process works, see Jeanne M. Liedtka, "Collaboration across Lines of Business for Competitive Advantage," *Academy of Management Executive* 10, no. 2 (May 1996), pp. 20–34.

[8]"Beyond Knowledge Management: How Companies Mobilize Experience," *The Financial Times,* February 8, 1999, p. 5.

[9]For a discussion of what is involved in actually capturing strategic-fit benefits, see Kathleen M. Eisenhardt and D. Charles Galunic, "Coevolving: At Last, a Way to Make Synergies Work," *Harvard Business Review* 78, no. 1 (January-February 2000), pp. 91–101. Adeptness at capturing cross-business strategic fits positively impacts performance; see Constantinos C. Markides and Peter J. Williamson, "Related Diversification, Core Competences and Corporate Performance," *Strategic Management Journal* 15 (Summer 1994), pp. 149–165.

[10]Peter Drucker, *Management: Tasks, Responsibilities, Practices* (New York: Harper & Row, 1974), pp. 692–693.

[11]While arguments that unrelated diversification is a superior way to diversify financial risk have logical appeal, there is research showing that related diversification is less risky from a financial perspective than is unrelated diversification; see Michael Lubatkin and Sayan Chatterjee, "Extending Modern Portfolio Theory into the Domain of Corporate Diversification: Does It Apply?" *Academy of Management Journal* 37, no. 1 (February 1994), pp. 109–136.

[12]For a review of the experiences of companies that have pursued unrelated diversification successfully, see Patricia L. Anslinger and Thomas E. Copeland, "Growth through Acquisitions: A Fresh Look," *Harvard Business Review* 74, no. 1 (January-February 1996), pp. 126–135.

[13]Of course, management may be willing to assume the risk that trouble will not strike before it has had time to learn the business well enough to bail it out of almost any difficulty. But there is research that shows this is very risky from a financial perspective; see, for example, Lubatkin and Chatterjee, "Extending Modern Portfolio Theory," pp. 132–133.

[14]For research evidence of the failure of broad diversification and the trend of companies to focus their diversification efforts more narrowly, see Lawrence G. Franko, "The Death of Diversification? The Focusing of the World's Industrial Firms, 1980–2000," *Business Horizons* 47, no. 4 (July-August 2004), pp. 41–50.

[15]For an excellent discussion of what to look for in assessing these fits, see Andrew Campbell, Michael Gould, and Marcus Alexander, "Corporate Strategy: The Quest for Parenting Advantage," *Harvard Business Review* 73, no. 2 (March-April 1995), pp. 120–132.

[16]Ibid., p. 128.

[17]Ibid., p. 123.

[18]A good discussion of the importance of having adequate resources, and also the importance of upgrading corporate resources and capabilities, can be found in David J. Collis and Cynthia A. Montgomery, "Competing on Resources: Strategy in the 90s," *Harvard Business Review* 73, no. 4 (July-August 1995), pp. 118–128.

[19]Ibid., pp. 121–122.

[20]Drucker, *Management: Tasks, Responsibilities, Practices,* p. 709.

[21]See, for, example, Constantinos C. Markides, "Diversification, Restructuring, and Economic Performance," *Strategic Management Journal* 16 (February 1995), pp. 101–118.

[22]For a discussion of why divestiture needs to be a standard part of any company diversification strategy, see Lee Dranikoff, Tim Koller, and Antoon Schneider, "Divestiture: Strategy's Missing Link," *Harvard Business Review* 80, no. 5 (May 2002), pp. 74–83.

[23]Drucker, *Management: Tasks, Responsibilities, Practices,* p. 94.

[24]See David J. Collis and Cynthia A. Montgomery, "Creating Corporate Advantage," *Harvard Business Review* 76, no. 3 (May-June 1998), pp. 72–80.

[25]Drucker, *Management: Tasks, Responsibilities, Practices,* p. 719.

[26]Evidence that restructuring strategies tend to result in higher levels of performance is contained in Markides, "Diversification, Restructuring, and Economic Performance," pp. 101–118.

[27]Dranikoff, Koller, and Schneider, "Divestiture: Strategy's Missing Link," p. 76.

[28]C. K. Pralahad and Yves L. Doz, *The Multinational Mission* (New York: Free Press, 1987), p. 2.

[29]Ibid., p. 15.

[30]Ibid., pp. 62–63.

[31]For a fascinating discussion of the chess match in strategy that can unfold when two DMNCs go head-to-head in a global marketplace, see Ian C. MacMillan, Alexander B. van Putten, and Rita Gunther McGrath, "Global Gamesmanship," *Harvard Business Review* 81, no. 5 (May 2003), pp. 62–71.

Chapter 7

[1]James E. Post, Anne T. Lawrence, and James Weber, *Business and Society: Corporate Strategy, Public Policy, Ethics,* 10th ed. (Burr Ridge, IL: McGraw-Hill Irwin, 2002), p. 103.

[2]See, for instance, Mark. S. Schwartz, "A Code of Ethics for Corporate Codes of Ethics," *Journal of Business Ethics* 41, nos. 1–2 (November-December 2002), pp. 27–43.

[3]For more discussion of this point, see ibid., pp. 29–30.

[4]T. L. Beauchamp and N. E. Bowie, *Ethical Theory and Business* (Upper Saddle River, NJ: Prentice-Hall, 2001), p. 8.

[5]Based on information in U.S. Department of Labor, "The Department of Labor's 2002 Findings on the Worst Forms

of Child Labor," 2003, accessible at www.dol.gov/ILAB/media/reports.

[6]ILO-IPEC (SIMPOC), "Every Child Counts: New Global Estimates on Child Labour," Geneva, April 2002, available from www.ilo.org/public/english/standards/ipec/simpoc/others globalest.pdf. The estimate of the number of working children is based on the definition of the "economically active population," which restricts the labor force activity of children to "paid" or "unpaid" employment, military personnel, and the unemployed. The definition does not include children in informal work settings, noneconomic activities, "hidden" forms of work, or work that is defined by ILO Convention 182 as the worst forms of child labor.

[7]W. M. Greenfield, "In the Name of Corporate Social Responsibility," *Business Horizons* 47, no. 1 (January-February 2004), p. 22.

[8]Thomas Donaldson and Thomas W. Dunfee, "When Ethics Travel: The Promise and Peril of Global Business Ethics," *California Management Review* 41, no. 4 (Summer 1999), p. 53.

[9]John Reed and Erik Portanger, "Bribery, Corruption Are Rampant in Eastern Europe, Survey Finds," *The Wall Street Journal,* November 9, 1999, p. A21.

[10]Transparency International, *2004 Global Corruption Report,* www.globalcorruptionreport.org, accessed at November 2, 2004; in particular, see pp. 277–294 and secs. 8 and 9.

[11]Donaldson and Dunfee, "When Ethics Travel," p. 59.

[12]George A. Steiner and John F. Steiner, Business, Government, and Society: *A Managerial Perspective* (Burr Ridge, IL: McGraw-Hill/Irwin, 2003), p. 213.

[13]See John. J. Hannifin, "Morality and the Market in China: Some Contemporary Views," *Business Ethics Quarterly* 12, no. 1 (January 2002), pp. 6–9.

[14]Stephen J. Carroll and Martin J. Gannon, *Ethical Dimensions of International Management* (Thousand Oaks, CA: Sage Publications, 1997), p. 9.

[15]For more documentation of cross-country differences in what is considered ethical, see Robert D. Hirsch, Branko Bucar, and Sevgi Oztark, "A Cross-Cultural Comparison of Business Ethics: Cases of Russia, Slovenia, Turkey, and United States," *Cross Cultural Management* 10, no. 1 (2003), pp. 3–28; P. Maria Joseph Christie, Ik-Whan G. Kwan, Philipp A. Stoeberl, and Raymond Baumhart, "A Cross-Cultural Comparison of Ethical Attitudes of Business Managers: India, Korea, and the United States," *Journal of Business Ethics* 46, no. 3 (September 2003), pp. 263–287; and Turgut Guvenli and Rajib Sanyal, "Ethical Concerns in International Business: Are Some Issues More Important than Others?" *Business and Society Review* 107, no. 2 (June 2002), pp. 195–206.

[16]Thomas Donaldson and Thomas W. Dunfee, *Ties That Bind: A Social Contracts Approach to Business Ethics* (Boston: Harvard Business School Press, 1999), pp. 35, 83.

[17]Based on a report in M. J. Satchell, "Deadly Trade in Toxics," *U.S. News and World Report,* March 7, 1994, p. 64, and cited in Donaldson and Dunfee, "When Ethics Travel," p. 46.

[18]Two of the definitive treatments of integrated social contracts theory as applied to ethics are Thomas Donaldson and Thomas W. Dunfee, "Towards a Unified Conception of Business Ethics: Integrative Social Contracts Theory," *Academy of Management Review* 19, no. 2 (April 1994), pp. 252–284, and Donaldson and Dunfee, *Ties That Bind,* especially chaps. 3, 4, and 6. See also Andrew Spicer, Thomas W. Dunfee, and Wendy J. Bailey, "Does National Context Matter in Ethical Decision Making? An Empirical Test of Integrative Social Contracts Theory," *Academy of Management Journal* 47, no. 4 (August 2004), p. 610.

[19]P. M. Nichols, "Outlawing Transnational Bribery through the World Trade Organization," *Law and Policy in International Business* 28, no. 2 (1997), pp. 321–322.

[20]Donaldson and Dunfee, "When Ethics Travel," pp. 55–56.

[21]Archie B. Carroll, "Models of Management Morality for the New Millennium," *Business Ethics Quarterly* 11, no. 2 (April 2001), pp. 367–369.

[22]Ibid., pp. 369–370.

[23]For survey data on what managers say about why they sometimes behave unethically, see John F. Veiga, Timothy D. Golden, and Kathleen Dechant, "Why Managers Bend Company Rules," *Academy of Management Executive* 18, no. 2 (May 2004), pp. 84–89.

[24]For more details, see Ronald R. Sims and Johannes Brinkmann, "Enron Ethics (Or: Culture Matters More than Codes)," *Journal of Business Ethics* 45, no. 3 (July 2003), pp. 244–246.

[25]As reported in Gardiner Harris, "At Bristol-Myers, Ex-Executives Tell of Numbers Games," *The Wall Street Journal,* December 12, 2002, pp. A1, A13.

[26]Ibid., p. A13.

[27]Veiga, Golden, and Dechant, "Why Managers Bend Company Rules," p. 36.

[28]The following account is based largely on the discussion and analysis in Sims and Brinkmann, "Enron Ethics," pp. 245–252.

[29]Chip Cummins and Almar Latour, "How Shell's Move to Revamp Culture Ended in Scandal," *The Wall Street Journal,* November 2, 2004, p. A14.

[30]Gedeon J. Rossouw and Leon J. van Vuuren, "Modes of Managing Morality: A Descriptive Model of Strategies for Managing Ethics," *Journal of Business Ethics* 46, no. 4 (September 2003), pp. 389–400.

[31]Empirical evidence that an ethical culture approach produces better results than the compliance approach is presented in Terry Thomas, John R. Schermerhorn, and John W. Dienhart, "Strategic Leadership of Ethical Behavior," *Academy of Management Executive* 18, no. 2 (May 2004), p. 64.

[32]Anna Wilde Mathews and Barbara Martinez, "E-Mails Suggest Merck Knew Vioxx's Dangers at Early Stage," *The Wall Street Journal,* November 1, 2004, pp. A1, A10.

[33]Archie B. Carroll, "The Four Faces of Corporate Citizenship," *Business*

and Society Review 100–101 (September 1998), p. 6.

34Business Roundtable, "Statement of Corporate Responsibility," New York, October 1981, p. 9.

35Sarah Roberts, Justin Keeble, and David Brown, "The Business Case for Corporate Citizenship," a study for the World Economic Forum, accessed at www.weforum.org/corporatecitizenship, October 14, 2003, p. 3.

36N. Craig Smith, "Corporate Responsibility: Whether and How," *California Management Review* 45, no. 4 (Summer 2003), p. 63.

37Jeffrey Hollender, "What Matters Most: Corporate Values and Social Responsibility," *California Management Review* 46, no. 4 (Summer 2004), p. 112.

38World Business Council for Sustainable Development, "Corporate Social Responsibility: Making Good Business Sense," January 2000, p. 7, accessed at www.wbscd.ch, October 10, 2003. For a discussion on how companies are connecting social initiatives to their core values, see David Hess, Nikolai Rogovsky, and Thomas W. Dunfee, "The Next Wave of Corporate Community Involvement: Corporate Social Initiatives," *California Management Review* 44, no. 2 (Winter 2002), pp. 110–125. See also Susan Ariel Aaronson, "Corporate Responsibility in the Global Village: The British Role Model and the American Laggard," *Business and Society Review* 108, no. 3 (September 2003), p. 323.

39www.chick-fil-a.com, accessed October 16, 2003.

40Smith, "Corporate Responsibility," p. 63; see also World Economic Forum, "Findings of a Survey on Global Corporate Leadership," accessed at www.weforum.org/corporatecitizenship, October 11, 2003.

41Roberts, Keeble, and Brown, "The Business Case for Corporate Citizenship," p. 6.

42Ibid., p.3.

43Wallace N. Davidson, Abuzar El-Jelly, and Dan L. Worrell, "Influencing Managers to Change Unpopular Corporate Behavior through Boycotts and Divestitures: A Stock Market Test," *Business and Society* 34, no. 2 (1995), pp. 171–196.

44Tom McCawley, "Racing to Improve Its Reputation: Nike Has Fought to Shed Its Image as an Exploiter of Third-World Labor yet It Is Still a Target of Activists," *Financial Times,* December 2000, p. 14, and Smith, "Corporate Social Responsibility," p. 61.

45Based on data in Amy Aronson, "Corporate Diversity, Integration, and Market Penetration," *BusinessWeek,* October 20, 2003, pp. 138ff.

46Smith, "Corporate Social Responsibility," p. 62.

47See Social Investment Forum, 2001 Report on Socially Responsible Investing Trends in the United States (Washington, DC: Social Investment Forum, 2001).

48Smith, "Corporate Social Responsibility," p. 63.

49See James C. Collins and Jerry I. Porras, *Built to Last: Successful Habits of Visionary Companies,* 3d ed. (London: HarperBusiness, 2002); Roberts, Keeble, and Brown, "The Business Case for Corporate Citizenship," p. 4; and Smith, "Corporate Social Responsibility," p. 63.

50Roberts, Keeble, and Brown, "The Business Case for Corporate Citizenship," p. 4.

51Smith, "Corporate Social Responsibility," p. 65; Lee E. Preston and Douglas P. O'Bannon, "The Corporate Social-Financial Performance Relationship," *Business and Society* 36, no. 4 (December 1997), pp. 419–429; Ronald M. Roman, Sefa Hayibor, and Bradley R. Agle, "The Relationship between Social and Financial Performance: Repainting a Portrait," *Business and Society* 38, no. 1 (March 1999), pp. 109–125; and Joshua D. Margolis and James P. Walsh, *People and Profits* (Mahwah, NJ: Lawrence Erlbaum, 2001).

52Smith, "Corporate Social Responsibility," p. 70.

Chapter 8

1As quoted in Steven W. Floyd and Bill Wooldridge, "Managing Strategic Consensus: The Foundation of Effective Implementation," *Academy of Management Executive* 6, no. 4 (November 1992), p. 27.

2For an excellent and very pragmatic discussion of this point, see Larry Bossidy and Ram Charan, *Execution: The Discipline of Getting Things Done* (New York: Crown Business, 2002), chap. 1.

3For an insightful discussion of how important staffing an organization with the right people is, see Christopher A. Bartlett and Sumantra Ghoshal, "Building Competitive Advantage through People," *MIT Sloan Management Review* 43, no. 2 (Winter 2002), pp. 34–41.

4See Bossidy and Charan, *Execution: The Discipline of Getting Things Done,* chap. 1.

5John Byrne, "The Search for the Young and Gifted," *Business Week,* October 4, 1999, p. 108.

6James Brian Quinn, *Intelligent Enterprise* (New York: Free Press, 1992), pp. 52–53, 55, 73–74, 76. Also see Christine Soo, Timothy Devinney, David Midgley, and Anne Deering, "Knowledge Management: Philosophy, Processes, and Pitfalls," *California Management Review* 44, no. 4 (Summer 2002), pp. 129–151, and Julian Birkinshaw, "Why Is Knowledge Management So Difficult?" *Business Strategy Review* 12, no. 1 (March 2001), pp. 11–18. Adapted with permission of the Free Press, a division of Simon & Schuster Adult Publishing Group, from *Intelligent Enterprise,* by James Brian Quinn, Copyright © 1992, 1992 by James Brian Quinn, All rights reserved.

7Robert H. Hayes, Gary P. Pisano, and David M. Upton, *Strategic Operations: Competing through Capabilities* (New York: Free Press, 1996), pp. 503–507. Also see Jonas Ridderstråle, "Cashing In on Corporate Competencies," *Business Strategy Review* 14, no. 1 (Spring 2003), pp. 27–38, and Danny Miller, Russell Eisenstat, and Nathaniel Foote,

"Strategy from the Inside Out: Building Capability-Creating Organizations," *California Management Review* 44, no. 3 (Spring 2002), pp. 37–55.

[8]Quinn, *Intelligent Enterprise*, p. 43.

[9]Quinn, *Intelligent Enterprise*, pp. 33, 89; James Brian Quinn and Frederick G. Hilmer, "Strategic Outsourcing," *Sloan Management Review* 35, no. 4 (Summer 1994), pp. 43–55; and James Brian Quinn, "Strategic Outsourcing: Leveraging Knowledge Capabilities," *Sloan Management Review* 40, no. 4 (Summer 1999), pp. 9–22. See also Jussi Heikkilä and Carlos Cordon, "Outsourcing: A Core or Non-Core Strategic Management Decision," *Strategic Change* 11, no. 3 (June-July 2002), pp. 183–193. For a discussion of why outsourcing initiatives fall short of expectations, see Jérôme Barthélemy, "The Seven Deadly Sins of Outsourcing," *Academy of Management Executive* 17, no. 2 (May 2003), pp. 87–98.

[10]Quinn, "Strategic Outsourcing: Leveraging Knowledge Capabilities," p. 17.

[11]For a more extensive discussion of the reasons for building cooperative, collaborative alliances and partnerships with other companies, see James F. Moore, *The Death of Competition* (New York: HarperBusiness, 1996), especially chap. 3; Quinn and Hilmer, "Strategic Outsourcing"; and Quinn, "Strategic Outsourcing: Leveraging Knowledge Capabilities," pp. 9–22.

[12]Quinn, *Intelligent Enterprise*, pp. 39–40; also see Barthélemy, "The Seven Deadly Sins of Outsourcing."

[13]The importance of matching organizational design and structure to the particular needs of strategy was first brought to the forefront in a landmark study of 70 large corporations conducted by Professor Alfred Chandler of Harvard University. Chandler's research revealed that changes in an organization's strategy bring about new administrative problems that, in turn, require a new or refashioned structure for the new strategy to be successfully implemented. He found that structure tends to follow the growth strategy of the firm—but often not until inefficiency and internal operating problems provoke a structural adjustment. The experiences of these firms followed a consistent sequential pattern: new strategy creation, emergence of new administrative problems, a decline in profitability and performance, a shift to a more appropriate organizational structure, and then recovery to more profitable levels and improved strategy execution. See Alfred Chandler, *Strategy and Structure* (Cambridge, MA: MIT Press, 1962).

[14]The importance of empowering workers in executing strategy and the value of creating a great working environment are discussed in Stanley E. Fawcett, Gary K. Rhoads, and Phillip Burnah, "People as the Bridge to Competitiveness: Benchmarking the 'ABCs' of an Empowered Workforce," *Benchmarking: An International Journal* 11, no. 4 (2004), pp. 346–360.

[15]Iain Somerville and John Edward Mroz, "New Competencies for a New World," in *The Organization of the Future*, ed. Frances Hesselbein, Marshall Goldsmith, and Richard Beckard (San Francisco: Jossey-Bass, 1997), p. 70.

[16]Exercising adequate control over empowered employees is a serious issue. For example, a prominent Wall Street securities firm lost $350 million when a trader allegedly booked fictitious profits; Sears took a $60 million write-off after admitting that employees in its automobile service departments recommended unnecessary repairs to customers. For a discussion of the problems and possible solutions, see Robert Simons, "Control in an Age of Empowerment," *Harvard Business Review* 73 (March-April 1995), pp. 80–88.

[17]For a discussion of the importance of cross-business coordination, see Jeanne M. Liedtka, "Collaboration across Lines of Business for Competitive Advantage," *Academy of Management Executive* 10, no. 2 (May 1996), pp. 20–34.

[18]Rosabeth Moss Kanter, "Collaborative Advantage: The Art of the Alliance," *Harvard Business Review* 72, no. 4 (July-August 1994), pp. 105–106.

[19]For an excellent review of ways to effectively manage the relationship between alliance partners, see ibid., pp. 96–108.

[20]John P. Kotter and James L. Heskett, *Corporate Culture and Performance* (New York: Free Press, 1992), p. 7. See also Robert Goffee and Gareth Jones, *The Character of a Corporation* (New York: HarperCollins, 1998).

[21]Kotter and Heskett, *Corporate Culture and Performance*, pp. 7–8.

[22]Ibid., p. 5.

[23]John Alexander and Meena S. Wilson, "Leading across Cultures: Five Vital Capabilities," in *The Organization of the Future*, ed. Frances Hesselbein, Marshall Goldsmith, and Richard Beckard (San Francisco: Jossey-Bass, 1997), pp. 291–292.

[24]Kotter and Heskett, *Corporate Culture and Performance*, p. 5.

[25]Avan R. Jassawalla and Hemant C. Sashittal, "Cultures That Support Product-Innovation Processes," *Academy of Management Executive* 16, no. 3 (August 2002), pp. 42–54.

[26]Kotter and Heskett, *Corporate Culture and Performance*, pp. 15–16. Also see Jennifer A. Chatham and Sandra E. Cha, "Leading by Leveraging Culture," *California Management Review* 45, no. 4 (Summer 2003), pp. 20–34.

[27]Terrence E. Deal and Allen A. Kennedy, *Corporate Cultures* (Reading, MA: Addison-Wesley, 1982), p. 22. See also Terrence E. Deal and Allen A. Kennedy, *The New Corporate Cultures: Revitalizing the Workplace after Downsizing, Mergers, and Reengineering* (Cambridge, MA: Perseus, 1999).

[28]Vijay Sathe, *Culture and Related Corporate Realities* (Homewood, IL: Irwin, 1985).

[29]Kotter and Heskett, *Corporate Culture and Performance*, chap. 6.

[30]Ibid., p. 68.

[31]This section draws heavily on the discussion in ibid., chap. 4.

[32]There's no inherent reason why new strategic initiatives should conflict with core values and business principles.

While conflict is always possible, most strategy makers lean toward choosing strategic initiatives that are compatible with the company's character and culture and that don't go against ingrained values and beliefs. After all, the company's culture is usually something that strategy makers have had a hand in building and perpetuating, so they are not often anxious to undermine core values and business principles without serious soul-searching and compelling business reasons.

[33]Kotter and Heskett, *Corporate Culture and Performance,* p. 52. Adapted with permission of the Free Press, a division of Simon & Schuster Adult Publishing Group, from *Corporate Culture and Performance,* by John P. Kotter and James L. Heskett, Copyright © 1992, 1992 by James Brian Quinn, All rights reserved.

[34]Ibid., pp. 84, 144, 148.

[35]Judy D. Olian and Sara L. Rynes, "Making Total Quality Work: Aligning Organizational Processes, Performance Measures, and Stakeholders," *Human Resource Management* 30, no. 3 (Fall 1991), p. 324.

[36]For several perspectives on the role and importance of core values and ethical behavior, see Joseph L. Badaracco, *Defining Moments: When Managers Must Choose between Right and Wrong* (Boston: Harvard Business School Press, 1997); Joe Badaracco and Allen P. Webb. "Business Ethics: A View from the Trenches," *California Management Review* 37, no. 2 (Winter 1995), pp. 8–28; Patrick E. Murphy, "Corporate Ethics Statements: Current Status and Future Prospects," *Journal of Business Ethics* 14 (1995), pp. 727–740; and Lynn Sharp Paine, "Managing for Organizational Integrity," *Harvard Business Review* 72, no. 2 (March-April 1994), pp. 106–117.

[37]See Mark S. Schwartz, "A Code of Ethics for Corporate Codes of Ethics," *Journal of Business Ethics* 41, nos. 1–2 (November-December 2002), p. 27.

[38]For a study of the status of formal codes of ethics in large corporations, see Emily F. Carasco and Jang B. Singh, "The Content and Focus of the Codes of Ethics of the World's Largest Transnational Corporations," *Business and Society Review* 108, no. 1 (January 2003), pp. 71–94, and Patrick E. Murphy, "Corporate Ethics Statements: Current Status and Future Prospects," *Journal of Business Ethics* 14 (1995), pp. 727–740. For a discussion of the strategic benefits of formal statements of corporate values, see John Humble, David Jackson, and Alan Thomson, "The Strategic Power of Corporate Values," *Long Range Planning* 27, no. 6 (December 1994), pp. 28–42. An excellent discussion of whether one should assume that company codes of ethics are always ethical is presented in Schwartz, "A Code of Ethics for Corporate Codes of Ethics," pp. 27–43.

[39]www.dardenrestaurants.com, accessed October 2004, and Robert C. Ford, "Darden Restaurants CEO Joe Lee on the Importance of Core Values: Integrity and Fairness," *Academy of Management Executive* 16, no. 1 (February 2002), pp. 31–36.

[40]For some cautions on implementing ethics compliance, see Robert J. Rafalko, "A Caution about Trends in Ethics Compliance Programs," *Business and Society Review* 108, no. 1 (January 2003), pp. 115–126. A good discussion of the failures of ethics compliance programs can be found in Megan Barry, "Why Ethics and Compliance Programs Can Fail," *Journal of Business Strategy* 26, no. 6 (November-December 2002), pp. 37–40.

[41]For documentation of cross-country differences in what is considered ethical, see Robert D. Hirsch, Branko Bucar, and Sevgi Oztark, "A Cross-Cultural Comparison of Business Ethics: Cases of Russia, Slovenia, Turkey, and United States," *Cross Cultural Management* 10, no. 1 (2003), pp. 3–28, and P. Maria Joseph Christie, Ik-Whan G. Kwan, Philipp A. Stoeberl, and Raymond Baumhart, "A Cross-Cultural Comparison of Ethical Attitudes of Business Managers: India, Korea, and the United States," *Journal of Business Ethics* 46, no. 3 (September 2003), pp. 263–287.

[42]Ford, "Darden Restaurants CEO Joe Lee on the Importance of Core Values."

Chapter 9

[1]Jim Collins, "Turning Goals into Results: The Power of Catalytic Mechanisms," *Harvard Business Review* 77, no. 4 (July-August 1999), pp. 72–73; Robert Levering and Milton Moskowitz, "The 100 Best Companies to Work For," *Fortune,* February 4, 2004, p. 73; and Robert Levering and Milton Moskowitz, "The 100 Best Companies to Work For," *Fortune,* January 12, 2004, p. 78.

[2]For a discussion of the value of benchmarking in implementing strategy, see Christopher E. Bogan and Michael J. English, *Benchmarking for Best Practices: Winning through Innovative Adaptation* (New York: McGraw-Hill, 1994), chaps. 2 and 6; Mustafa Ungan, "Factors Affecting the Adoption of Manufacturing Best Practices," *Benchmarking: An International Journal* 11, no. 5 (2004), pp. 504–520; Paul Hyland and Ron Beckett, "Learning to Compete: The Value of Internal Benchmarking," *Benchmarking: An International Journal* 9, no. 3 (2002), pp. 293–304; and Yoshinobu Ohinata, "Benchmarking: The Japanese Experience," *Long-Range Planning* 27, no. 4 (August 1994), pp. 48–53.

[3]Michael Hammer and James Champy, *Reengineering the Corporation* (New York: HarperBusiness, 1993), pp. 26–27.

[4]Ibid.

[5]Gene Hall, Jim Rosenthal, and Judy Wade, "How to Make Reengineering Really Work," *Harvard Business Review* 71, no. 6 (November-December 1993), pp. 119–131.

[6]For more information on business process reengineering and how well it has worked in various companies, see James Brian Quinn, *Intelligent Enterprise* (New York: Free Press, 1992), p. 162; Ann Majchrzak and Qianwei Wang, "Breaking the Functional Mind-Set in Process Organizations," *Harvard Business Review* 74, no. 5 (September-October 1996), pp. 93–99; Stephen L. Walston, Lawton R. Burns, and John R. Kimberly, "Does Reengineering Really Work? An Examination of the Context and Outcomes of Hospital Reengineer-

ing Initiatives," *Health Services Research* 34, no. 6 (February 2000), pp. 1363–1388; and Allessio Ascari, Melinda Rock, and Soumitra Dutta, "Reengineering and Organizational Change: Lessons from a Comparative Analysis of Company Experiences," *European Management Journal* 13, no. 1 (March 1995), pp. 1–13. For a review of why some company personnel embrace process reengineering and some don't, see Ronald J. Burke, "Process Reengineering: Who Embraces It and Why?" *TQM Magazine* 16, no. 2 (2004), pp. 114–119.

[7]For some of the seminal discussions of what TQM is and how it works written by ardent enthusiasts of the technique, see M. Walton, *The Deming Management Method* (New York: Pedigree, 1986); J. Juran, *Juran on Quality by Design* (New York: Free Press, 1992); Philip Crosby, *Quality Is Free: The Act of Making Quality Certain* (New York: McGraw-Hill, 1979); and S. George, *The Baldrige Quality System* (New York: Wiley, 1992). For a critique of TQM, see Mark J. Zbaracki, "The Rhetoric and Reality of Total Quality Management," *Administrative Science Quarterly* 43, no 3 (September 1998), pp. 602–636.

[8]For a discussion of the shift in work environment and culture that TQM entails, see Robert T. Amsden, Thomas W. Ferratt, and Davida M. Amsden, "TQM: Core Paradigm Changes," *Business Horizons* 39, no. 6 (November-December 1996), pp. 6–14.

[9]For easy-to-understand overviews of what six sigma is all about, see Peter S. Pande and Larry Holpp, *What Is Six Sigma?* (New York: McGraw-Hill, 2002); Jiju Antony, "Some Pros and Cons of Six Sigma: An Academic Perspective," *TQM Magazine* 16, no. 4 (2004), pp. 303–306; Peter S. Pande, Robert P. Neuman, and Roland R. Cavanagh, *The Six Sigma Way: How GE, Motorola and Other Top Companies Are Honing Their Performance* (New York: McGraw-Hill, 2000); and Joseph Gordon and M. Joseph Gordon, Jr., *Six Sigma Quality for Business and Manufacture* (New York: Elsevier, 2002). For how six sigma can be used in

smaller companies, see Godecke Wessel and Peter Burcher, "Six Sigma for Small and Medium-Sized Enterprises," *TQM Magazine* 16, no. 4 (2004), pp. 264–272.

[10]Based on information posted at www.isixsigma.com, November 4, 2002.

[11]Kennedy Smith, "Six Sigma for the Service Sector," *Quality Digest Magazine,* May 2003, posted at www.qualitydigest.com, accessed September 28, 2003.

[12]Del Jones, "Taking the Six Sigma Approach," *USA Today,* October 31, 2002, p. 5B.

[13]Smith, "Six Sigma for the Service Sector."

[14]Pande, Neuman, and Cavanagh, *The Six Sigma Way,* pp. 5–6.

[15]Jones, "Taking the Six Sigma Approach."

[16]Terry Nels Lee, Stanley E. Fawcett, and Jason Briscoe, "Benchmarking the Challenge to Quality Program Implementation," *Benchmarking: An International Journal* 9, no. 4 (2002), pp. 374–387.

[17]For a recent study documenting the imperatives of establishing a supportive culture, see Milan Ambrož, "Total Quality System as a Product of the Empowered Corporate Culture," *TQM Magazine* 16, no. 2 (2004), pp. 93–104. Research confirming the factors that are important in making TQM programs successful in both Europe and the U.S. is presented in Nick A. Dayton, "The Demise of Total Quality Management," *TQM Magazine* 15, no. 6 (2003), pp. 391–396.

[18]Judy D. Olian and Sara L. Rynes, "Making Total Quality Work: Aligning Organizational Processes, Performance Measures, and Stakeholders," *Human Resource Management* 30, no. 3 (Fall 1991), pp. 310–311, and Paul S. Goodman and Eric D. Darr, "Exchanging Best Practices Information through Computer-Aided Systems," *Academy of Management Executive* 10, no. 2 (May 1996), p. 7.

[19]Thomas C. Powell, "Total Quality Management as Competitive Advan-

tage," *Strategic Management Journal* 16 (1995), pp. 15–37. See also Richard M. Hodgetts, "Quality Lessons from America's Baldrige Winners," *Business Horizons* 37, no. 4 (July-August 1994), pp. 74–79, and Richard Reed, David J. Lemak, and Joseph C. Montgomery, "Beyond Process: TQM Content and Firm Performance," *Academy of Management Review* 21, no. 1 (January 1996), pp. 173–202.

[20]Based on information at www.otiselevator.com, accessed October 14, 2004.

[21]Stephan H. Haeckel and Richard L. Nolan, "Managing by Wire," *Harvard Business Review* 75, no. 5 (September-October 1993), p. 129.

[22]Quinn, *Intelligent Enterprise,* p. 181.

[23]Fred Vogelstein, "Winning the Amazon Way," *Fortune,* May 26, 2003, pp. 70, 74.

[24]Such systems speed organizational learning by providing fast, efficient communication, creating an organizational memory for collecting and retaining best-practice information, and permitting people all across the organization to exchange information and updated solutions. See Goodman and Darr, "Exchanging Best Practices Information through Computer-Aided Systems," pp. 7–17.

[25]Vogelstein, "Winning the Amazon Way," p. 64.

[26]For a discussion of the need for putting appropriate boundaries on the actions of empowered employees and possible control and monitoring systems that can be used, see Robert Simons, "Control in an Age of Empowerment," *Harvard Business Review* 73 (March-April 1995), pp. 80–88.

[27]Ibid. See also David C. Band and Gerald Scanlan, "Strategic Control through Core Competencies," *Long Range Planning* 28, no. 2 (April 1995), pp. 102–114.

[28]The importance of motivating and empowering workers so as to create a working environment that is highly conducive to good strategy execution is discussed in Stanley E. Fawcett,

Gary K. Rhoads, and Phillip Burnah, "People as the Bridge to Competitiveness: Benchmarking the 'ABCs' of an Empowered Workforce," *Benchmarking: An International Journal* 11, no. 4 (2004), pp. 346–360.

[29]Jeffrey Pfeffer and John F. Veiga, "Putting People First for Organizational Success," *Academy of Management Executive* 13, no. 2 (May 1999), pp. 37–45; Linda K. Stroh and Paula M. Caliguiri, "Increasing Global Competitiveness through Effective People Management," *Journal of World Business* 33, no. 1 (Spring 1998), pp. 1–16; and articles in *Fortune* on the 100 best companies to work for (1998, 1999, 2000, and 2001).

[30]As quoted in John P. Kotter and James L. Heskett, *Corporate Culture and Performance* (New York: Free Press, 1992), p. 91.

[31]For a provocative discussion of why incentives and rewards are actually counterproductive, see Alfie Kohn, "Why Incentive Plans Cannot Work," *Harvard Business Review* 71, no. 6 (September-October 1993), pp. 54–63.

[32]See Steven Kerr, "On the Folly of Rewarding A While Hoping for B," *Academy of Management Executive* 9, no. 1 (February 1995), pp. 7–14; Steven Kerr, "Risky Business: The New Pay Game," *Fortune,* July 22, 1996, pp. 93–96; and Doran Twer, "Linking Pay to Business Objectives," *Journal of Business Strategy* 15, no. 4 (July-August 1994), pp. 15–18.

[33]Kerr, "Risky Business." p. 96.

[34]For excellent discussions of the problems and pitfalls in leading the transition to a new strategy and to fundamentally new ways of doing business, see Larry Bossidy and Ram Charan, *Confronting Reality: Doing What Matters to Get Things Right* (New York: Crown Business, 2004); Larry Bossidy and Ram Charan, *Execution: The Discipline of Getting Things Done* (New York: Crown Business, 2002), especially chaps. 3 and 5; John P. Kotter, "Leading Change: Why Transformation Efforts Fail," *Harvard Business Review* 73, no. 2 (March-April 1995), pp. 59–67; Thomas M. Hout and John C. Carter, "Getting It Done: New Roles for Senior Executives," *Harvard Business Review* 73, no. 6 (November-December 1995), pp. 133–145; and Sumantra Ghoshal and Christopher A. Bartlett, "Changing the Role of Top Management: Beyond Structure to Processes," *Harvard Business Review* 73, no. 1 (January-February 1995), pp. 86–96.

[35]For a pragmatic, cut-to-the-chase treatment of why some leaders succeed and others fail in executing strategy, especially in a period of rapid market change or organizational crisis, see Bossidy and Charan, *Confronting Reality.*

[36]Vogelstein, "Winning the Amazon Way," p. 64.

[37]For a more in-depth discussion of the leader's role in creating a results-oriented culture that nurtures success, see Benjamin Schneider, Sarah K. Gunnarson, and Kathryn Niles-Jolly, "Creating the Climate and Culture of Success," *Organizational Dynamics,* Summer 1994, pp. 17–29.

[38]Jeffrey Pfeffer, "Producing Sustainable Competitive Advantage through the Effective Management of People," *Academy of Management Executive* 9, no. 1 (February 1995), pp. 55–69.

[39]James Brian Quinn, *Strategies for Change: Logical Incrementalism* (Homewood, IL: Irwin, 1980), pp. 20–22.

[40]Ibid., p. 146.

[41]For a good discussion of the challenges, see Daniel Goleman, "What Makes a Leader," *Harvard Business Review* 76, no. 6 (November-December 1998), pp. 92–102; Ronald A. Heifetz and Donald L. Laurie, "The Work of Leadership," *Harvard Business Review* 75, no. 1 (January-February 1997), pp. 124–134; and Charles M. Farkas and Suzy Wetlaufer, "The Ways Chief Executive Officers Lead," *Harvard Business Review* 74, no. 3 (May-June 1996), pp. 110–122. See also Michael E. Porter, Jay W. Lorsch, and Nitin Nohria, "Seven Surprises for New CEOs," *Harvard Business Review* 82, no. 10 (October 2004), pp. 62–72.

Name Index

Organization Index

Subject Index